The Business and Law of Fashion and Retail

The Business and Law of Fashion and Retail

Barbara Kolsun
Director, The FAME Center for Fashion, Arts, Media and Entertainment Law,
Cardozo School of Law, Yeshiva University
Professor of Practice, Cardozo School of Law, Yeshiva University

Douglas Hand
Partner, Hand, Baldachin & Associates LLP
Adjunct Professor of Fashion Law,
NYU School of Law,
Cardozo School of Law, Yeshiva University

Carolina Academic Press
Durham, North Carolina

LCCN: 2020939115
ISBN: 978-1-5310-1619-7
eISBN: 978-1-5310-1620-3

Carolina Academic Press
700 Kent Street
Durham, North Carolina 27701
Telephone (919) 489-7486
Fax (919) 493-5668
www.cap-press.com

Printed in the United States of America

The co-editors would like to express special gratitude to
Simone A. Dvoskin and Nabeela M. Hanif
for their enormous contributions in making this casebook a success.

• • •

The co-editors would like to thank the following contributors
for their work and research on the casebook:
Anna Antonova
Julianne Bagley
Lauren Bass
Anabela Bello
Nikki Breeland
Andrea W. Dorado
Emily Faro
Katherine Joseph
Rebecca Kravitz
Daphne Lazar
Jessica Mauceri
Maya Rand
Katie Riley
Jolie Schenerman
George C. Sciarrino
Filippa Olsson Skalin
Kristina Stanković
Mona Zeitoun

Contents

About the Editors

Barbara Kolsun is a Professor of Practice at Cardozo School of Law, Yeshiva University, and is also the Director of The FAME Center for Fashion, Arts, Media and Entertainment Law at Cardozo School of Law, the first law school program providing training and development opportunities relating to the representation of businesses driven by the creative process. She has been a leading fashion industry attorney for 35 years, and was also co-editor of the first handbook on Fashion Law, *Fashion Law: A Guide for Designers, Fashion Executives and Attorneys* (Bloomsbury, 2010, 2014), and the first casebook on Fashion Law, *Fashion Law: Cases and Materials* (Carolina Academic Press, 2016). She developed the first joint JD/MBA course in Fashion Law and Business at New York University and has also taught at Fordham Law School and guest lectured at dozens of law schools and fashion schools. She started the legal departments at three "startups"—Kate Spade, Seven for All Mankind and Stuart Weitzman and was the first General Counsel at all three companies. She was Assistant GC at Calvin Klein Jeans and Westpoint Stevens and has probably been through more mergers than most lawyers in the fashion business. While in private practice, her clients included Tommy Hilfiger and Ralph Lauren, and currently she continues to consult with fashion companies on various issues. She has chaired and been a regular speaker at the Luxury Law Summit in New York and London for several years. She has been honored with lifetime achievement awards in 2015 by the Luxury Summit and the World Trademark Forum, and another lifetime achievement award from the Women in Law Empowerment Forum. She has also served as Chairman of the Board of the International Anticounterfeiting Coalition and has spoken and published widely on fashion law around the world.

Douglas Hand is a Partner at Hand, Baldachin & Associates, LLP in New York and an Adjunct Professor at NYU Law School (where he also sits on the Fashion & Luxury Council) and Cardozo School of Law, Yeshiva University (where he also sits on the Board of Advisors for The FAME Center for Fashion, Arts, Media and Entertainment Law). He is also the Secretary and Board Member of the Fashion Institute of Technology (FIT) Foundation and a member of the CFDA Fashion Awards Guild. Douglas' experience in the fashion and retail world has led him to counsel global brands such as Everlane, Rag & Bone, Stella McCartney and Zadig & Voltaire. His book, *The Laws of Style,* was published by the American Bar Association in 2018 and he hosts a podcast of the same name.

About the Authors

Catherine Adam is a Partner at K&L Gates in London where she specializes in commercial contracts, advising fashion clients from start-ups to global brands as well as having a particular specialism in logistics for e-commerce. She was recently named a "Next Generation Partner" for Commercial Contracts by the Legal 500. Catherine studied Law & Business Studies at the University of Edinburgh and has worked in London, Milan, New York and Luxembourg and brings this international outlook and experience to her clients for whom she provides complex yet user friendly commercially driven advice.

Arthur Artinian is a Partner at K&L Gates in London and head of the IP and Technology Group. He is an internationally recognized intellectual property lawyer, representing numerous iconic brands, including leading fashion, luxury and retail brands, in complex cross-border IP counselling, litigation, enforcement and transactional matters. His work has been recognized in a number of publications including Chambers, Legal 500, World Trademark Review, World IP Review Leaders, Who's Who, and Client Choice. He holds bar registrations in the UK, Ireland, Belgium, and Australia and has worked in London, New York, Tokyo, and Sydney.

Robertson D. Beckerlegge is a Partner in the New York office of Baker & Hostetler LLP focusing on litigation, brand protection, and anticounterfeiting. Whether online or brick and mortar, he works with numerous brands to help protect their invaluable IP.

Christopher Buccafusco is Professor of Law and Director of the Intellectual Property and Information Law Program at Cardozo School of Law, Yeshiva University.

Nancy S. Cleveland, now retired, was a private practice lawyer for many years before she co-founded Sustrana LLC, a sustainability management software and consulting company in 2009. Nancy became an accredited FSA II (SASB) and LEED® AP and was trained in GRI reporting and as a TSC Service Provider to better support her career in sustainability management. For several years, she co-chaired the Governance and Sustainability sub-committee of the American Bar Association's Business Law Section.

Barry Lewin is a Partner at Gottlieb, Rackman & Reisman, P.C., an Intellectual Property boutique in New York. He is a licensed patent attorney and has been practicing patent law and advising domestic and foreign fashion and technology clients for over a decade.

Miriam Farhi is a Partner in the Technology Transactions & Privacy practice at Perkins Coie LLP. She represents brands, retailers, and online marketplaces on issues relating to privacy, data security, ecommerce, social media, advertising, consumer protection, and the adoption of new technologies that transform the retail experience.

Frances P. Hadfield is a Counsel in Crowell & Moring's International Trade Group in the firm's New York office. Her practice focuses on customs litigation and regulatory compliance and she regularly advises corporations on matters involving customs compliance, audits, forced labor, customs enforcement, as well as import penalties.

Meredith Halama is a Partner in Perkins Coie's Privacy and Data Security group and co-chairs the firm's Ad Tech and Data Management group. She counsels ad technology companies, publishers, and retailers on privacy matters, including self-regulatory obligations and compliance with federal and state laws governing the collection and use of data.

Sherry L. Jetter is considered to be a pioneer in the establishment of the field of fashion law. She has practiced law in the fashion and retail industries for over 30 years, founded and held leadership positions in legal departments of the foremost luxury brands, and is currently an Adjunct Professor at Cardozo School of Law, Yeshiva University and in private practice specializing in intellectual property, global licensing and commercial transactions.

Ted Max is a Partner at Sheppard Mullin Richter & Hampton in New York who leads its Fashion Apparel and Beauty Industry Group and has counseled clients in the fashion and retail industries and has written and lectured extensively. He combines his skill and experience as a trial attorney with his knowledge of intellectual property and commercial law in assisting emerging designers and leading fashion and retail companies.

Tiffani McDonough Solomon is the Director, Senior Counsel, Employment & Litigation for Louis Vuitton with sole responsibility for managing labor and employment matters and litigation for all corporate offices, workshops and retail locations throughout the United States, Canada, Mexico, Central America, the Caribbean, and South America. In addition, she oversees the Louis Vuitton legal externship program and serves as the Senior Employment Counsel for Berluti LLC.

Olivera Medenica is a Partner at Dunnington Bartholow & Miller LLP and chairs its Fashion and Trademark Law Practice Groups. She has almost two decades of experience advising domestic and foreign businesses in fashion, retail, media and entertainment on transactional, litigation and arbitration matters.

Marc Reiner is the Head of the Intellectual Property Group at Hand Baldachin & Associates LLP where he represents a broad variety of fashion and retail clients. He has practiced trademark law for over two decades, including trademark prosecution, licensing, litigation, anti-counterfeiting, and managing international trademark portfolios.

Amanda Simpson is an international trade attorney who predominantly focuses on matters relating to customs and import compliance. She is passionate about helping her clients find practical solutions to complex issues from an import perspective, as well as identifying and implementing duty savings strategies.

Lee S. Sporn is Of Counsel at Olshan, Frome & Wolosky, having served as SVP Business Affairs & General Counsel at Michael Kors for 13 years, and in various capacities at Ralph Lauren for 11 years, after his career in private practice at Proskauer. With co-editor Barbara Kolsun and Dean Melanie Leslie, he was instrumental in the creation of the The FAME Center for Fashion, Arts, Media and Entertainment Law at Cardozo School of Law, Yeshiva University and continues to serve on its advisory board, and currently teaches Fashion Law at Penn and Villanova law schools. Lee is a contributor to *Fashion Law: A Guide for Designers, Fashion Executives & Attorneys* (Fairchild Books, 2014), was the co-editor of the seminal treatise *Trademark Counterfeiting* (Aspen Law & Business, 1999) and in May of 2016 he received the Lifetime Achievement Award at the Luxury Law Awards in London.

Julie Zerbo is the Founder and Editor-in-Chief of The Fashion Law (*www.thefashionlaw.com*), a modern media company that provides unique insight on and unparalleled access to the legal and business aspects of the rapidly evolving fashion and retail industries.

The Business and Law of Fashion and Retail

Introduction to Fashion Law

Barbara Kolsun and Douglas Hand

"Know, first, who you are, and then adorn yourself accordingly."

—Epictetus

A. Defining the Scope of and Need for Fashion Law

Fashion law is the business law specialty that deals with the everyday problems and legal issues of fashion and lifestyle companies, including their retail operations. The fashion and lifestyle industry is a multi-trillion-dollar global industry and a driving force in the world economy. This industry covers not only apparel, accessories and footwear, but also beauty, perfume, eyewear, textiles, and the retailers that sell them to consumers. Viewed from a different angle, the fashion industry consists of four levels: (1) the production of textiles, fibers, skins, and other raw materials; (2) the production of fashion items by designers, manufacturers, and contractors; (3) retail sales of those products; and (4) various forms of advertising, promoting and marketing those products and the brands they represent. This casebook addresses the principal legal issues and commercial challenges facing this industry in both the United States and globally, and how these issues inform the practice of law at fashion and lifestyle companies.

We, the co-editors of this casebook, have established careers in fashion law representing some of the leading fashion brands in the industry. We have built our practice understanding not only the law, but the business behind these brands. Our vision for this casebook is for law students to grasp the business principles tied integrally with the law as we have come to learn from our careers.

Barbara Kolsun is the Director of the The FAME Center for Fashion, Arts, Media and Entertainment Law and Professor of Practice at Cardozo School of Law, Yeshiva University. Barbara began her legal career clerking in the U.S. Court of Appeals for the Second Circuit and transitioned into life at a law firm where she developed a practice working on all aspects of trademark, copyright, licensing, IP litigation, anticounterfeiting, and business issues representing such brands as Ralph Lauren and Tommy Hilfiger. Barbara then stepped into her first in-house counsel role as the Assistant General Counsel of Calvin Klein Jeanswear Company followed by WestPoint Stevens, Inc. Through untiring perseverance and love for the law and retail business, Barbara then went on to serve as the first in-house lawyer and General Counsel for Kate Spade, Seven For All Mankind, and Stuart Weitzman. Barbara has taught fashion law courses at NYU School of Law, NYU Stern School of Business, Fordham Law School, and Cardozo School of Law, where she has mentored and continues to mentor countless law students.

Douglas Hand is a partner at Hand Baldachin & Associates LLP in New York City. Douglas began his legal career as an attorney at Shearman and Sterling in their New York and Paris offices, focusing on mergers and acquisitions. Douglas is a member of the Business Advisory Committee of the Council of Fashion Designers of America (CFDA), on the Advisory Board of the CFDA's Incubator, and a member of the CFDA Fashion Awards Guild. He is also an adjunct professor of Fashion Law at both NYU School of Law (where he sits on the Fashion & Luxury Council) and Cardozo School of Law, Yeshiva University (where he sits on the Board of Advisors for The FAME Center for Fashion, Arts, Media and Entertainment Law) and is on the Fashion Institute of Technology (FIT) Foundation Board of Directors. It is no surprise, then, that fashion and the law are part of Douglas's repertoire. He has been featured and profiled in numerous media publications, including *The New York Times, The Wall Street Journal, Vanity Fair,* the *American Bar Association Journal, Women's Wear Daily, The Business of Fashion*, and hosts a podcast called *The Laws of Style.*

Fashion law is taught with a focus on real-world issues confronting companies and their in-house counsel in many different contexts and for which answers are found in a broad range of substantive laws, and the learning outcomes and associated performance criteria are similarly broad, but include:

Ethics and standards of professionalism. Ethical issues confronting in-house counsel of a fashion business, with special emphasis on the no-contact rule, present particular challenges and potential conflicts, as well as competency considerations for counsel responsible for legal work in many domestic and international jurisdictions.

Knowledge and understanding of substantive and procedural law. The casebook covers a broad range of substantive law impacting the fashion industry, with special emphasis on intellectual property, licensing, counterfeiting, employment, data protection, privacy, advertising, and trade. The fashion lawyer works with legal sources, analyzes problems, and provides contextualized advice. Properly understanding legal/risk analysis based on industry realities and providing sound advice to fashion business professionals and creatives is a primary goal of the casebook.

Financial concepts. One full chapter is devoted to fashion finance, focusing on the relative benefits and disadvantages of equity versus debt, particularly at different stages of a company's growth. It also deals specifically with the primary issues in revolving credit agreements and factoring agreements, as well as providing an overview of issues relating to mergers and acquisitions and an initial public offering ("IPO"). In addition, all examples of conflicts that arise throughout the casebook are considered from the potential financial impact (positive or negative) on the business involved.

Environmental impact and sustainability. The impact of the fashion industry on the planet and its inhabitants has become a topic too massive to ignore. This casebook dedicates a chapter to exploring not only these issues, but also the current regulatory and international frameworks that attempt to address them.

B. Fashion Lawyers Must Wear Many Hats

Fashion has achieved the status of a truly global industry, and the rapid growth of fashion law is now catching up to the challenges facing mass-market fashion brands. Yet law school graduates, even from the finest law schools, come into the workplace with little experience in counseling clients. Throughout our careers counseling leading fashion businesses, including Kate Spade, Calvin Klein Jeans, Stuart Weitzman, Donna Karan, Stella McCartney, Everlane, Rag & Bone, and Seven for All Mankind, we have had to apply the law to the fashion industry. Just as designers must cultivate their unique sense of style, fashion lawyers need a special set of sharp skills to get the right cut.

Big law firms train the best and brightest associates by slotting them into specialty areas in their first year of practice (e.g., project finance, compensation and benefits, anti-trust, real estate, etc.). Meanwhile, clinics related to criminal law practice and other disciplines have become the norm in law schools across the country. But when it comes to fashion and other highly creative industries, the focus on the training of lawyers needs a new design.

It's Not Just IP Anymore

Most lawyers in creative businesses are expected early on to wear more than one hat. While intellectual property is often most associated with fashion design, early on in our careers we had to learn the mechanics of the fashion business from multiple legal perspectives in order to provide effective counsel. Working with creative entrepreneurs on tight deadlines creates a need for unique legal expertise. There are many practice areas related to the fashion business that require specialized legal know-how in order to deal with digital sales, distribution, and advertising, as well as a host of new technological advances. That's because in fashion, as in other creative fields, lawyers are now routinely acting as solo in-house lawyers. This is especially true for startups, which have complicated legal issues. But many larger companies now see the need for in-house legal teams that can understand business decisions and assess risk while still allowing for growth.

Certainly fashion companies seek protection of intellectual property, especially brand names, logos, and other trademarks. Fashion is an unusually imitative industry. IP law allows a measure of protection, though it is a highly limited protection. Furthermore, the internet and ecommerce have flooded the market with counterfeits, and the old rules for enforcing trademark rights against flea markets and retail stores selling fakes are no longer enough. The *Tiffany v. eBay* and *Gucci v. Alibaba* lawsuits have defined, and are defining, the law as it relates to third-party liability. While many law students think that fashion law is synonymous with IP law, in fact, "fashion lawyers" advise on many issues.

Understanding the Business of Fashion

There are a myriad of issues beyond IP that fashion lawyers must understand. For example, they must deal with employment issues (retail employees as well as corporate employees, independent sales representatives, consultants who may act as the company's major designers, and international and state laws related to where these employees and others who act as employees live or work). Employment law is a creature of federal, state, and even local law. Once a company opens stores in London, Paris, and elsewhere there are international laws to consider, which are very different from U.S. law. Training is another matter—and since sales employees come and go, it must be ongoing. Employees must be trained in law-related issues dealing with discrimination, privacy, wage-and-hour issues, truth in advertising, and product safety.

Lawyers for fashion companies have the added job of reviewing dress codes. Fashion companies are allowed to establish how their retail employees dress, as a reflection of the brand. These dress codes, however, must not discriminate. A recent Supreme Court case involving a prospective employee at Abercrombie & Fitch outlines the complicated nature of that balance.

Fashion lawyers touch every part of the business. They negotiate and advise on leases, product and store licenses, import and export and trade issues, product safety, human rights compliance, mergers and acquisitions, advertising and marketing, social media, and tax issues. In addition, they negotiate endless agreements such as for advertising campaigns with influencers, photographers, models, videographers, and shoot location sites.

The CEO and the Legal Counsel

The relationship between a chief executive officer and the general counsel of any company is necessarily complex. The challenge is to fully integrate the legal function into an entrepreneurial-driven global business environment. Law students need to understand that fashion is an industry where counsel functions as guardian of the company, and yet must be fully integrated into the business to support its goals while ensuring compliance and minimizing potential liability. A few years ago, we hosted an event with John Idol, CEO of Michael Kors, at Cardozo Law School for students in our FAME Center to understand this key relationship. In growing his company, Idol told the students, a good general counsel must operate as a business partner and not simply as a person who knows the law. It is key to work together to create a tone from the top down that is focused on compliance and puts processes in place that fully consider all business actions from multiple perspectives.

That is no small task, and the relationship between CEO and GC is vital. Lawyers must understand that the CEO's mission is to innovate, drive business, and expand into new products and territories, and that is tempered by constantly evolving legal rights and obligations. When the business is both public and global in nature, things get even more complex.

Miscalculations Are Costly

Miscalculations in any of these areas can make or break an emerging fashion company. Some common mistakes young lawyers make include: not documenting promises made to employees and consultants regarding equity or promotions or ownership of IP; not warning a designer who uses her name as the name of the company that she is effectively giving away her name for all future commercial ventures; not thinking globally and protecting the brand's trademarks in future markets; and not staffing up appropriately to make sure all contracts are enforced and all potential liabilities and deadlines are managed.

Timing Is Crucial

Fashion companies must get their product into the marketplace on a short timeline, which means lawyers will have little time to spend on dense and complex legal documents. Advertising campaigns may involve 20 agreements, each with a 24-hour turnaround. Fashion law practitioners need to focus on the big picture—what are the vulnerabilities they must spot to protect the company from risk. They must understand the business, and the timing of all the agreements that need to be in place to get product in stores for the holiday or back-to-school seasons, for example. This vastly complicates contract completion.

It's a Matter of Tone

Throughout our careers, we have learned that drafting of written communications is key—and tone can be everything. For example, a high-end fashion brand that has fought hard to locate a store within a particular shopping mall may have a landlord conflict requiring a letter. This is not the time for a typical "cease and desist" letter, which a lot of younger lawyers might jump to write. Such an approach could damage a relationship that may have taken considerable time and effort to develop. Understanding the business requires developing an ear for how to draft such a letter.

Another example occurs when luxury fashion companies, in order to elevate their brand, strategically decide to restrict points of sale to ensure that product is sold at specific stores only—reflecting the high-end aspiration of the company. Such "selective distribution" is legal, and counsel must require that product licenses reflect those business goals.

Overlap of Fashion and Entertainment

Another important, distinct aspect of fashion is the role that a celebrity plays in the industry. One of the structural characteristics of the fashion industry is a reliance for many brands on licensing, and that means entering into transactions in which the owner of intellectual property allows another party to manufacture branded fashion items pursuant to the licensor's quality and design standards.

Add to those issues the tremendous growth in the value of fashion trademarks and the serious business problems of global trademark counterfeiting, which represents a threat to corporate identity as well as an increasing drain on the corporate treasury—not to mention the support of consumers.

The legal profession needs to engage professionals from these various industries with a more unified and systematic approach. The goal is to combine deep instruction in IP, corporate, real estate, employment, international trade, commercial, and contract courses with specialized courses taught by lawyers with experience in each of these special disciplines. And these young lawyers need to be ready to say "yes" to growth and to understand risk as part of the fabric of creative industries.

Fashion lawyers need to understand the entrepreneurial mindset and story creation of this very competitive business. They need to adjust their analysis so that they can help balance risk with spirited inspiration and the bold business strategy necessary to stay ahead in a live-or-die global competition. When the legal counsel can see eye-to-eye with both the Creative Director and the CEO of a brand, trust in the boardroom can translate into runway success and a successful business.

C. Cases and Materials

1. The Fashion Industry and Legal Scholarship

Fashion permeates society and, as we discover further in this casebook, impacts the entire planet. Several notable legal scholars have written about the legal, economic, and social impact of the fashion industry. The following paper by Professors C. Scott Hemphill and Jeannie Suk argues that while "influence" and "imitation" are critical components of trend-creation, copying discourages innovation and can be harmful. Here we offer excerpts from the paper, which also provides a useful outline for understanding the fashion process.

*The Law, Culture, and Economics of Fashion**

C. Scott Hemphill & Jeannie Suk

61 Stanford Law Review 1147 (2009)

Introduction

Fashion is one of the world's most important creative industries. It is the major output of a global business with annual U.S. sales of more than $200 billion—larger than those of books, movies, and music combined. Everyone wears clothing and inevitably participates in fashion to some degree. Fashion is also a subject of periodically rediscovered fascination in virtually all the social sciences and the humanities. It has provided economic thought with a canonical example in theorizing about consumption and conformity. Social thinkers have long treated fashion as a window upon social class and social change. Cultural theorists have focused on fashion to reflect on symbolic meaning and social ideals. Fashion has also been seen to embody representative characteristics of modernity, and even of culture itself.

Indeed, it is hard to imagine a locus of social life—whether in the arts, the sciences, politics, academia, entertainment, business, or even law or morality—that does not exhibit fashion in some way. People flock to ideas, styles, methods, and practices that seem new and exciting, and then eventually the intensity of that collective fascination subsides, when the newer and hence more exciting emerge on the scene. Participants of social practices that value innovation are driven to partake of what is "original," "cutting edge," "fresh," "leading," or "hot." But with time, those qualities are attributed to others, and another trend takes shape. This is fashion. The desire to be "in fashion"—most visibly manifested in the practice of dress—captures a significant aspect of social life, characterized by both the pull of continuity with others and the push of innovation toward the new.

... At this moment, fashion itself has the attention of federal policymakers, as Congress considers whether to provide copyright protection for fashion design, a debate that is sure to continue in the face of fashion designers' many complaints of harm by design copyists. Despite being the core of fashion and legally protected in Europe, fashion design lacks protection against copying under U.S. intellectual property law. Thus, it has seemed sensible to posit that fashion design is relevantly different from literature, music, and art, where legal protection from copying is thought to be necessary to provide producers an incentive to create. Indeed, some commentators even suggest that perhaps fashion design is so different from other arts that its vitality, or even survival, paradoxically depends on the existence of the opposite kind of regime—a culture of tolerated rampant copying ...

* * *

2. What Is Fashion?

Fashions change. Styles emerge, become fashionable, and are eventually replaced by new fashionable styles. What is obvious is that the demand for new fashions is not reducible simply to material or physical needs. Though one may need a replacement pair of jeans when an old pair gets holes from wear, or a warmer coat when the weather gets cold, for most people across the socio-economic spectrum, the purchase of clothing is far from limited to these kinds of situations. Nearly all of us inevitably participate in fashion, even if we do not try to follow it.

a. Status

The most influential and widely held theory posits fashion as a site of struggle over social status. This is a view most concretely articulated in terms of social class at the turn of the century by Georg Simmel, the German sociologist, who was in turn influenced by Thorstein Veblen's classic work, *The Theory of the Leisure Class*.

According to this view, fashion is adopted by social elites for the purpose of demarcating themselves as a group from the lower classes. The lower classes inevitably admire and emulate the upper classes. Thereupon, the upper classes flee in favor of a new fashion in a new attempt to set themselves apart collectively. This trickle-down process, moving from the highest to the lowest class, is characterized by the desire for group distinction on the part of the higher classes, and the attempt to efface external class markers through imitation on the part of the lower classes. Change in fashion is thus endlessly propelled by the drive to social stratification on the one hand and to social mobility on the other.

When the magazine *Vogue* was founded in 1892, its first published pages presented the editorial goal as the representation of the lifestyle of New York high society, "the establishment of a dignified authentic journal of society, fashion and the ceremonial side of life." According to a recent history of the magazine, at the turn of the century, the social context of *Vogue*'s origin was one in which the most privileged families of New York "felt invaded by parvenus who, with little lineage but plenty of money, attempted to join in its aristocratic activities." From the beginning, *Vogue*'s representations of the fashions of the upper class were accompanied by those of the homes and parties of prominent families, as well as articles on social etiquette . . . The drive of the ordinary consumer to emulate those who can afford the most expensive fashion is assumed and indeed promoted in the popular discourse of fashion.

b. Zeitgeist

The other major theory of fashion sometimes goes by the term "collective selection," associated with the sociologist Herbert Blumer. On this theory, fashion emerges from a collective process wherein many people, through their individual choices among many competing styles, come to form collective tastes that are expressed in fashion trends. The process of trend formation begins vaguely and then sharpens until a particular fashion is established. The themes of the trend reflect the spirit of the times in which we are living.

This theory arises as a direct critique of the trickle-down theory. The driver of fashion is not necessarily imitation of high-status people per se. Rather, people follow fashion because they desire to be in fashion. That is, people want to associate themselves with things that are new, innovative, and state of the art. They want to keep pace with change. If a particular fashion starts in a certain group, then other people join, not simply out of desire to emulate that group, but because being in fashion is desirable.

As a means of signaling and communicating about oneself, and of perceiving messages about others, dress has a symbolic function and is even considered by some social theorists to be a code or a language that provides visual cues and signifiers of identity, personality, values, or other social meanings . . .

Fashion features the tension between the desire to be distinct as an individual and the desire to connect with a collectivity. Another way of saying this is that the fashion process imposes social constraints and parameters within which individual choices of communication and expression are shaped and directed. Fashion is then driven forward as a combination of individual differentiation and collective identification, and of the personal and the social impulses. Without necessarily denying the importance of status or imitation in the explanation of fashion trends, what we are calling the zeitgeist theory is in effect a critique of a status account in which fashion trends essentially consist of imitation of high-status people . . .

c. Copies Versus Trends

In each of these theories, consumers desire, and producers provide, articles that are on trend. Some observers assume that the trendy articles are copies: either the exact same article purchased from the same producer, or else a close copy of most elements of the original's design. But such copies play only a limited role in the rise and fall of trends. Participation in a trend—by a consumer or a designer—does not necessarily or usually entail copying.

First, one individual may seek to imitate another—as the status theory suggests—but without necessarily copying her dress. One can imitate another's style by consciously or unconsciously being influenced to wear clothes in that style. Copying is a more literal and direct process in which one targets the original for replication. For example, a consumer can imitate the length of a skirt without necessarily purchasing a copy of that skirt. Copying, in other words, is only a subset of a wide range of imitative practices.

Second, consumers may join trends without an imitative motive . . . People can want to be in fashion without necessarily having as their object the emulation of the lifestyle, values, or status associated with a particular group that first sported the style. They may instead—or also—seek to join a collective moment. Such convergence does not require a copy of what others are wearing.

Third, designers may furnish on-trend articles without closely copying one another. Instead, they may engage in interpretation, or "referencing." They may quote, comment upon, and refer to prior work. Unlike much close copying, such interpretation does not pass off the work as the work that is being copied. Instead, it marks awareness of the difference between the two works as it looks to the prior work as a source of influence, or even a precursor . . . For example, the look of a Chanel knit jacket has been interpreted repeatedly in other designers' styles, so that it has become a classic style drawing on the spirit of the look without purporting to be a Chanel product. Another Chanel classic, the quilted handbag, has been similarly reinterpreted.

This practice, by which designers draw freely upon ideas, themes, and styles available in the general culture, and refer back to others' prior designs, has led to the widespread but incorrect view that there is no real originality in fashion design. This view is no more correct than the analogous complaint about music: that homage and pastiche somehow deny any claim of originality to new works. The important point is that interpretations are different from copies in their goals and effects. Close copies can substitute for and reduce the value of the original, thereby reducing the incentive to create, to a greater extent. Rather than being substitutes, interpretations may even be complements for other on-trend articles.

A status theory of fashion might lend to the view that trend-joining is essentially copying. Accordingly, the fashion trend rises as a form of emulation, and then declines when elites or early adopters feel the need to distinguish themselves from the copying masses and adopt a new style as a means to do so. If one thus equates trend-joining with copying, then one might reasonably conclude that fashion is driven by copying.

But it is important to see that status does not exhaust the motivations for fashion. Under a zeitgeist theory, fashion is not just imitation of elites or early adopters, and is not reducible to copying . . . Copies may play a role in fashion change, but they are not the engine without which innovation in fashion would slow and stagnate.

d. Why Promote Innovation in Fashion?

Before further developing and applying these distinctions between copying and trends, we first pause with readers who may wonder whether fashion is worth promoting . . . Everyone inevitably expresses themselves through the clothes they wear (even if to communicate that they are too serious to care about fashion). But some may consider fashion frivolous or wasteful. They may believe that we would be better off if fashion did not exist and if clothing were used only for the literal purpose of covering the body or keeping warm.

This set of intuitions lies behind the Anglo-American and European history of sumptuary laws, which, until the eighteenth century, purported to limit the expenditures people could make on clothing, to protect against the vice of wasteful spending for personal appearance and ostentatious display, including for purposes of following fashions. Moral disapproval of expenditure on fashion is traditional. Normative regulation of fashion goes back to the Greeks and the Bible. The moral stance found, albeit incompletely enforced, in many religious traditions from Christianity to Buddhism, rejects luxury spending on garments and promotes plain garb.

Another reason for looking askance at fashion may be concern about visible markers of status hierarchy. Many historical sumptuary laws actually imposed hierarchical dress codes, granting privileges to wear certain garments to the upper class or prohibiting the lower class from wearing certain garments. Perhaps fashion is normatively undesirable because it is a way in which class and wealth disparities can easily be shown. Chairman Mao, in the pursuit of egalitarianism and Marxist rejection of surplus value, dictated that a billion people should wear an identical unadorned outfit, and for some decades they did so, notwithstanding China's rich history of fashion and its contemporary unabashed re-embrace of consumer capitalism.

With respect to the morality of expenditures or the issue of wastefulness, for the purposes of this Article, we treat fashion consumption the same way we would ordinarily treat the consumption of other non-harmful goods that have creative and expressive components, such as books, music, films, and art . . . It is difficult to see how the argument about wastefulness or immorality of spending on a coveted suit or dress would be different in kind from paying a sum for a work by a highly regarded painter. We assume that if consumers are prepared to pay for fashion in its various forms, regulation ought to be set to promote innovation and allow consumers a variety of options.

Some readers may resist this set of assumptions in various ways. First, the idea that the measure of the value of fashion is akin to the measure of the value of books, music, and art may strike some as absurd. Even though fashion is not widely regarded as one of the "fine arts," it is undeniably a creative good that has expressive features. It is no more logical to denigrate the value fashion choices confer upon consumers than to denigrate the value of the best-selling thriller many are reading or the hit song many are listening to. We may of course engage in value judgments about, say, the artistic value of Grisham relative to Proust, of pop music relative to Bach—and of fashion relative to literature and music. But that kind of hierarchical value distinction among cultural products is not to be confused with the notion of value on which we rely here. The choice to purchase these goods is, on our welfare account, evidence of value, and that is unrelated to the quality or merits of particular cultural products or genres of cultural production. Indeed it is the only evidence that can be measured, short of a separate normative assessment of whether people are wise to desire the things they do. Here we assume the desirability of investments in creative goods and in fashion as a creative good . . .

For the purposes of this Article, we assume that, especially when it comes to economic choices that are not necessary for human survival, adults' decisions may be construed as voluntary and therefore as a desirable pursuit of their life plans.

Finally, there may be concerns about negative positional externalities of fashion. These concerns pertain to status signals generated by fashion as a means of displaying wealth or other markers of status. For example, if fashion serves to distinguish some from others, the satisfaction some people receive from signaling their high status through fashion may be offset by the disutility of others. On this view, participation in fashion trends is spending to reduce that disutility. This expenditure is wasteful. It would be better if nobody spent in this way. Accordingly, if fashion were eliminated (à la Mao, or school uniforms), social welfare would improve; increasing fashion innovation cannot be seen as a gain in welfare.

This is a plausible view of negative externalities that corresponds to a theory of fashion as driven by status. But if the centrality of such status seeking is displaced with what we have been calling the zeitgeist theory, the status signal is not the dominant aspect of fashion. As we have explained above, the desire to be "in fashion" involves more than signals about status. It is a means of individual expression through which people partake in collective movement and the spirit of the times. Fashion enables this expressive process, and as such has benefits much like those associated with other consumptive goods that are also expressive. Signals of status are undeniably present in all these goods (just think of the high-end art market, high-brow literary fiction, or opera performance), but so too—and more importantly—are means of expression. Our view that innovation in fashion is socially desirable rests on assumptions *1164 that are shared with the assumption that in general the creation of new novels and new songs is socially desirable.

* * *

D. Differentiation and Flocking

Through fashion, people communicate and express themselves. Fashionable individuals' personal style is often described as "unique" or "inimitable." If consumers use fashion to express themselves as distinctive individuals, then it is valuable to have available a large range of different identifiers. Fashion goods provide a vocabulary. What consumers might value in fashion then is the availability of a variety of goods to choose from, a proliferation of the number of meanings that can be made. The availability of a variety of different goods enlarges the vocabulary and the meanings that can be communicated.

If consumers have a taste for differentiation of identity through fashion, then individual differentiation becomes an identifiable desired feature, for the purpose of intellectual property regulation of fashion. We posit that "differentiation" is a key feature of the consumption and production of fashion.

But fashion would not be fashion were it not for its basically collective character. Even as individuals strive to differentiate themselves through fashion choices, fashion is a means of participating in group movement. We call this "flocking."

Consumers tend to engage in flocking in buying new clothes, not because they need them, but because their existing clothes seem outdated. They want to be "in fashion." Flocking among consumers is again not necessarily a function of imitation or copying of any particular groups or individuals, though it may be. It can be a manifestation of a desire to partake of the collective moment, to be in step with society, or to be in touch with the present. It may be pleasurable for people to move in a collective direction, joined by others in expressive endeavor. There may be pleasure in a convergence, in participation in similar themes and ideas that reflect the times that all are experiencing.

Fashion is simultaneously characterized by differentiation and flocking—two phenomena that might appear to be in tension . . . The idea is well captured by Anna Wintour, editor of *Vogue*, who noted that what is laudable in fashionable people is at once "looking on-trend and beyond trend and totally themselves."

. . . People want to engage in flocking in a way that allows individual differentiation within it. They want to be part of a trend, but not be a replica of others who also join the trend. It would not be fashion if only flocking behavior were present. A world in which exactly one design of suit exists, due to demand or fiat, could be said to have apparel but not fashion. Nor would it be fashion if only individual differentiation were present. A world in which no collective patterns could be discerned could not be said to have fashion either. Fashion consists of both human desires, to flock and to differentiate, in relation to each other.

... Notice that the relation between flocking and differentiation maps on to the relation between copying and innovation. Just as direct reproduction of an existing novel is not innovation, if fashion were all about producing exact copies of existing articles, it would not be a practice of innovation. The impulse to flock in fashion is expressed in the aspects of fashion that draw on and sometimes copy existing works, but what makes the field a creative endeavor is the drive to differentiate—to reinterpret, change, remix, and transform, and as such, resist the sheer replication of existing works even while incorporating them. That is the creative impulse. In other words, differentiation constitutes innovation in fashion ...

1. Trend Adoption

The process of trend adoption reflects differentiation and flocking. Think of a fashion item as having two kinds of attributes, a trend feature (around which consumers flock) and various differentiating features. The trend feature is some shared, recognizable design element such as a wrap dress, a fitted fringed jacket, a driving shoe, or a floral print. The differentiating features are all design elements other than the trend feature that make the items within the trend nevertheless different from each other. Consumers are able to identify a trend feature, factoring it out from the other features. Their recognition process may be simple—seeing many items with the trend feature in stores or on the street—or it may be enhanced by advertising or magazine articles that identify the trend feature.

Many consumers prefer new items that are part of a trend. A consumer does not care solely about the presence of a trend, however. In addition, the consumer has a taste for differentiation in the article's other features, and preferences that vary according to body shape, aesthetics, or personal style. Fashion-conscious people generally do not seek to wear precisely the same outfit as someone else. Rather the consumer seeks goods that contain the trend feature but are differentiated.

How does a trend catch on? Suppose designers in one season produce, say, an unusually large number of designs with floral prints. Consumers recognize the floral print as the feature that is part of the potential trend, by seeing the prints in stores and on other consumers ... To take off, the trend must offer something sufficiently new. After all, new clothing is not an essential good in this context, and the new trend is competing with a closet full of existing clothes ... If multiple vendors offer the same new trend element at the same time, together with the differentiating details also necessary to satisfy consumer demand for differentiation, this is more likely to produce a successful new trend ...

2. Trend Production

Designers, too, engage in a process of differentiation and flocking. In any given season, they flock to similar hemlines, dress shapes, and tailoring. They converge on similar or related styles and themes. Yet the precise result reached by each producer is different ...

Flocking results, in part, from shared influences. If images of war fill the news, military-inspired styles may enter multiple collections ... Forecasting services furnish a common input to some designers, particularly the followers . . . Common pressures in the real world—women's entry into the professional workplace in unprecedented numbers, for example—can lead to a "convergent evolution" of independently derived, parallel innovation. New technological possibilities, such as a novel fabric, can produce commonalities in collections as well.

Flocking also results from mutual influences and inspiration among designers. They and their assistants attend fabric and other trade shows, where they learn from suppliers what other designers have planned—sometimes with the suppliers' active encouragement. Stylists, magazine editors, and buyers travel from designer to designer, cross-pollinating as they move. The shows are not quite simultaneous, extending across several weeks and cities, and last-minute tinkering can incorporate the influence of designers who have had earlier shows.

These shared influences promote convergence around a trend, but not identical articles. For one thing, the shared influences are usually too general to produce identical articles. Moreover, each producer has substantial incentives to produce a differentiated product . . .

The differentiation-flocking model of production, like that of consumption, has limits. It may not apply to "it" handbags, for example. Where consumers are uninterested in differentiation—where they do not even have idiosyncratic physical needs (due to body shape or coloration), but simply want the status signaled by the item—the model may not apply. There may be apparel items that are like "it" handbags. But for most apparel, there are idiosyncratic preferences, and a taste for differentiation, that make the differentiation-flocking model applicable.

Another academic perspective focuses on a more nefarious aspect of fashion which is its ability to categorize and label according to social class. The following paper by Professor Barton Beebe posits that current intellectual property laws function as a de facto sumptuary code, relegating consumers who cannot afford certain high-fashion items to a less-desirable "unfashionable" social standing.

*Intellectual Property Law and the Sumptuary Code**

Barton Beebe

123 Harvard Law Review 809 (2010)

The Roman *leges sumptuariae* sought to regulate luxury expenditure and enforce social hierarchy in republican and imperial Rome. Since these early Roman precursors, the history of sumptuary law has been a bizarre one. Consider the Japanese decree of 1668 that provided that "puppet costumes must not be sumptuous. Gold and silver leaf must not be used on anything. But puppet generals only may wear gold and silver hats." Or consider a sumptuary ordinance of seventeenth-century

* Reprinted with permission of Barton Beebe.

Nuremberg that lamented that "it is unfortunately an established fact that both men- and womenfolk have, in utterly irresponsible manner, driven extravagance in dress and new styles to such shameful and wanton extremes that the different classes are barely to be known apart." Most remarkable, perhaps, is the behavior of the Venetian Senate. In 1472, it called for the appointment of *Provveditori sopra le Pompe*, supervisors of luxury, to enforce the state's sumptuary laws, and in 1511, it issued, not for the last time, a decree to the effect that "all new fashions are banned. . . . [H]ence-forth no new fashion that may be imagined or told shall be suffered." The next year, as the powerful League of Cambrai prepared to attack, the Senate found itself debating sleeve widths and shoe designs. But it is not just the content of such laws that may strike the reader as strange. For all of the "enormous sumptuary productivity" of early modern Europe or the "ferocity of detail" of Tokugawa sumptuary law, these laws were almost invariably ignored, circumvented, or openly defied—so that an eighteenth-century London stage character would declare: "I don't care for it, now it is not prohibited." Indeed, the history of sumptuary law is filled with the likes of one Hannah Lyman, who, in 1676, chose to appear before a court in Northampton, Massachusetts, in the very dress that she was proscribed from and there being tried for wearing.

Though historians have advanced many competing theories to explain the pervasiveness and persistence of sumptuary regulation in human social history, one general proposition appears to be well accepted: societies impose sumptuary laws in an effort to regulate and enforce their sumptuary codes. A society's sumptuary code is its system of consumption practices, akin to a language (or at least "a set of dialects"), by which individuals in the society signal through their consumption their differences from and similarities to others. . . . Historically, laws seeking to govern a society's system of consumption-based distinction have most commonly taken the form of direct controls on consumption—an example, by no means atypical, is the 1463 English ordinance limiting to two inches the extent to which the shoes of persons of rank could extend beyond their toes. Societies have regularly imposed such controls when their governing classes come to believe that too much of their society's wealth is being wasted on conspicuous or decadent forms of consumption or that their society's system of relative consumption no longer operates reliably to differentiate and distinguish—if not to discipline—the various members of the society. This latter problem—the breakdown of a society's consumption-based system of social distinction—has typically occurred when formerly rare commodities or their equivalents suddenly become abundant or when lower-status social groups gain the economic power to consume goods that formerly only upper-status social groups consumed. It has also occurred with urbanization, which tends to complicate the signaling and recognition of social position . . .

. . . I argue that we have recently undertaken a new round of sumptuary lawmaking, not just in the United States, but globally, and for reasons comparable to those that drove previous sumptuary turns. Sumptuary law did not disappear with industrialization and democratization, as is generally believed. Rather, it has taken on a new—though still quite eccentric—form: intellectual property law. To be sure, the express purpose and primary effect of intellectual property law remains the prevention of misappropriation and the promotion of technological and cultural progress. But for various reasons, we are increasingly investing intellectual property law with, and forcing the law to adapt to, a new purpose. This purpose is to preserve and stabilize our modern sumptuary code in the face of emerging social and technological conditions that threaten its viability and that intellectual property law is uniquely well-suited to address. We are thus increasingly relying on intellectual property law not so much to enforce social hierarchy as simply to conserve—or in Pierre Bourdieu's terminology, to "reproduce"—our system of consumption-based social distinction and the social structures and norms based upon it. The result is that intellectual property law now consists of two conflicting sides: the familiar progressive side of the law, which works, in the terms of the U.S. Constitution, "To promote the Progress of Science and useful Arts," and the unappreciated sumptuary side of the law, which is not progressive but rather socially and technologically reactionary.

... While intellectual property law will not directly control which class of consumers may consume which distinctive goods, as did previous forms of sumptuary law, it does provide us with the means to govern the modern sumptuary code indirectly, by facilitating the private control of the production of such goods through the prevention of the unauthorized copying of them. This alone may explain why so much of our sumptuary code is now based on distinctive intellectual properties (such as trademarks) and why so much of our intellectual property enforcement is devoted to protecting such properties from unauthorized copying.

... [S]umptuary intellectual property law cannot succeed in stabilizing the modern sumptuary code, but ... this outcome is normatively desirable. In its sumptuary aspect, intellectual property law aggressively protects existing intangible forms of distinction from unauthorized copying and dilution, but in its progressive aspect, intellectual property law also strongly encourages the development of new such forms of distinction. The result is a dangerously open-ended form of sumptuary law that will only destabilize our sumptuary order all the more. Yet this promises to be a fortunate failure. In advanced post-industrial economies if not elsewhere, intellectual property law has been embraced as a last redoubt for a social system so much of whose received social and cultural norms are based on conditions of scarcity and rarity and so much of whose technology is increasingly able to overcome those conditions. In its sumptuary aspect, intellectual property law is an effect of, at the same time that it has become a cause of, social "inertia." By contrast, the phenomena of dilution and inauthenticity attest to the socially progressive, even liberatory potential of our mimetic technologies to render obsolete, by flooding it with copies, our system of consumption-based social differentiation. We have enlisted intellectual property law in a last-ditch and ultimately futile effort to suppress this socially revolutionary potential of our copying technology. Our doing so is inconsistent with the progressive project of intellectual property law specifically and of modernity more generally.

We will explore the issue of a brand's products being "knocked off" and the legal implications of this reality in Chapter 7. In a nimble and thoughtful twist, law professors Kal Raustiala and Christopher Sprigman have become well-known for their argument that knockoffs are good for the fashion industry because they stimulate the fashion cycle of continued consumption.

*The Piracy Paradox Revisited**

Kal Raustiala & Christopher Sprigman
61 Stanford Law Review 1201 (2009)

For over two centuries the United States has used copyright and patent to stimulate the production of many forms of creativity. Over time these rights have grown more economically significant; today intellectual property (IP) law is rightly seen not as a fringe topic, but as part of the core of contemporary economic and cultural policy debates. Increasingly, both lawyerly and lay discussions about creativity in the arts and sciences touch upon issues of ownership, control, and incentives, which together comprise the foundational questions of IP law. Some forms of creative work, however, have never been protected by American law. These forms of creativity exist in IP's "negative space"—by which we mean the territory where IP law might regulate, but (perhaps for accidental or nonessential reasons) does not. The study of these unprotected forms of creativity ought to be of great interest. If we see these creative endeavors languishing as a result of uncontrolled copying, we might decide to extend IP law in order to curtail appropriation and induce investment and innovation. On the other hand, if an unprotected area of creative work thrives in the absence of legal rules against copying, we would do well to know how. We might also ask whether other currently protected forms of creativity could also flourish without expensive and potentially inefficient monopoly protections.

Nonetheless, IP's negative space has rarely been explored in any depth. Earlier analyses of unprotected creativity tended simply to note the absence of IP protections, assume a market failure in the absence of protection, and move reflexively to a proposal to beef up the law.[1] This tendency has started to change in recent years

---

1. *See, e.g.*, Anne Theodore Briggs, *Hung Out to Dry: Clothing Design Protection Pitfalls in United States Law*, 24 Hastings Comm. & Ent. L.J. 169, 194, 213 (2002); Samantha L. Hetherington, *Fashion Runways Are No Longer the Public Domain: Applying the Common Law Right of Publicity to Haute Couture Fashion Design*, 24 Hastings Comm. & Ent. L.J. 43, 71 (2001); Laura C. Marshall, *Catwalk Copycats: Why Congress Should Adopt a Modified Version of the Design Piracy Prohibition Act*, 14 J. Intell. Prop. L. 305 (2007); Shelley C. Sackel, *Art is in the Eye of the Beholder: A Recommendation for Tailoring Design Piracy Legislation to Protect Fashion Design and the Public Domain*, 35 AIPLA Q.J. 473 (2007); S. Priya Bharathi, Comment, *There Is More than One Way to Skin a Copycat: The Emergence of Trade Dress to Combat Design Piracy of Fashion Works*, 27 Tex. Tech L. Rev. 1667, 1669–72 (1996); Leslie J. Hagin, Note, *A Comparative Analysis of Copyright Laws Applied to Fashion Works: Renewing the Proposal for Folding Fashion Works into the United States Copyright Regime*,

as studies of the fashion industry, stand-up comedians, magicians, typefaces, academic scientists, "jam bands," chefs, and perfumers have begun to appear in the nation's law reviews and economics journals. Much of this recent work has been thoughtful and balanced regarding the implications of the lack of IP protections in these areas.[2]

Fashion has emerged as a central focus of this new exploration of IP's negative space. Fashion is a large and vibrant global industry, yet the core of the creative enterprise in fashion—the design—is not, and never has been, protected by U.S. copyright law. For this reason fashion presents a fascinating puzzle for orthodox theories of IP. How does the industry maintain high levels of investment in new designs without protection against copying? Every season thousands of new designs are produced by the large number of firms competing in a market approaching $200 billion in U.S. sales annually. And a significant portion of this output involves copying. The major policy question is whether to continue to permit such copying, or to reverse the current low-IP regime in favor of some kind of system of copyright protection.

We are not disinterested bystanders in this debate. In a previous article, *The Piracy Paradox: Innovation and Intellectual Property in Fashion Design*,[3] and two

---

26 Tex. Int'l L.J. 341, 364–66 (1991); Karina K. Terakura, Comment, *Insufficiency of Trade Dress Protection: Lack of Guidance for Trade Dress Infringement Litigation in the Fashion Design Industry*, 22 U. Haw. L. Rev. 569 (2000); Jennifer Mencken, *A Design for the Copyright of Fashion*, 1997 B.C. Intell. Prop. & Tech. F. 121201, http://www.bc.edu/bc_org/avp/law/st_org/iptf/articles/content/1997121201.html.

2. *See, e.g.*, Michele Boldrin & David Levine, *The Case Against Intellectual Property*, 92 Am. Econ. Rev. 209, 212 (2002); Christopher J. Buccafusco, *On the Legal Consequences of Sauces: Should Thomas Keller's Recipes Be* Per Se *Copyrightable?*, 24 Cardozo Arts & Ent. L.J. 1121 (2007); Emmanuelle Fauchart & Eric von Hippel, *Norms-Based Intellectual Property Systems: The Case of French Chefs*, 19 Org. Sci. 187 (2008); Jacob Loshin, *Secrets Revealed: How Magicians Protect Intellectual Property Without Law*, *in* Law and Magic: A Collection of Essays (Christine A. Corcos ed., 2008), *available at* http://ssrn.com/abstract=1005564; Dotan Oliar & Christopher Sprigman, *There's No Free Laugh (Anymore): The Emergence of Intellectual Property Norms and the Transformation of Stand-Up Comedy*, 94 Va. L. Rev. 1787 (2008); Mark F. Schultz, *Fear and Norms and Rock & Roll: What Jambands Can Teach Us About Persuading People to Obey Copyright Law*, 21 Berkeley Tech. L.J. 651 (2006); Katherine J. Strandburg, *Curiosity-Driven Research and University Technology Transfer*, *in* 16 Advances in the Study of Entrepreneurship, Innovation and Economic Growth 97 (2005); Jacqueline D. Lipton, *To © or Not to ©? Copyright and Innovation in the Digital Typeface Industry* (Case Research Paper Series in Legal Studies, Working Paper No. 09-1, 2009), *available at* http://ssrn.com/ abstract=1311402; Fiona Murray et al., *Of Mice and Academics: Examining the Effect of Openness on Innovation* (Nov. 5, 2008) (unnumbered working paper, MIT Sloan School of Management), *available at* http://fmurray.scripts.mit.edu/docs/MADKS_Draft_11.05.2008. pdf; Charles Cronin, *Genius in a Bottle: Perfume, Copyright, and Human Perception* (unnumbered working paper, presented at UCLA Law School, Feb. 9, 2009). An early and exemplary recognition of the anomalous nature of fashion (and food) within IP is Jessica Litman, *The Exclusive Right to Read*, 13 Cardozo Arts & Ent. L.J. 29, 44–45 (1994).

3. Kal Raustiala & Christopher Sprigman, *The Piracy Paradox: Innovation and Intellectual Property in Fashion Design*, 92 Va. L. Rev. 1687 (2006).

shorter follow-up pieces,[4] we sought to answer the question at the heart of the fashion industry—why does that industry prosper when copying of new designs is perfectly lawful? We made two major claims. First, we argued that design copying contributes to a process of *induced obsolescence*—that is, copying helps to diffuse designs into the mainstream, where they lose their appeal for fashion cognoscenti. The desire for new designs is "induced" by this process. Second, we argued that copying helps *anchor* trends. Fashion-conscious consumers seek to follow trends; copying helps the industry create trends and communicates to consumers what these new trends are, thereby allowing consumers to follow them.

These two arguments explain what we characterized as the "piracy paradox": piracy is paradoxically beneficial to the fashion industry. This paradox helped in turn to explain the political economy question that drove our initial analysis: why, with regard to copyright, is fashion so unlike other creative industries? Why has Congress not afforded the high levels of IP protection we see elsewhere?

In recent years other scholars have begun to publish analyses of innovation in the fashion industry as well.[5] Yet there is still much we do not know about how law, norms, markets, and creativity interact in the apparel business. For these reasons, Scott Hemphill and Jeannie Suk's Article, *The Law, Culture, and Economics of Fashion*,[6] in this issue of the *Stanford Law Review* is very welcome. Their treatment of the fashion-IP nexus is stimulating and unique in its marriage of economic and cultural analysis. In this brief essay we look closely at their arguments and offer some critiques and suggestions for future research. Because they devote significant attention to our earlier work, we consider at some length the areas of tangency and tension between our respective analyses.

On the whole, we find much to agree with in *The Law, Culture, and Economics of Fashion*. Indeed, we believe the article has usefully employed, extended, and in some cases refined several of our original insights. We do inevitably part company in several places, and we will detail three primary disagreements here. First, we see the issue of design copying somewhat differently than do Hemphill and Suk.

4. Kal Raustiala & Christopher Sprigman, *Where IP Isn't* (UCLA Sch. of Law Pub. Law & Legal Theory Research Paper Series, No. 07-05, 2007), *available at* http://papers.ssrn.com/sol3/papers.cfm?abstract_id=962736; Kal Raustiala & Christopher Sprigman, *How Copyright Could Kill the Fashion Industry*, New Republic Online, Aug. 14, 2007, http://www.law.ucla.edu/home/News/Detail.aspx?recordid=1188 [hereinafter Raustiala & Sprigman, *How Copyright Could*]; *see also* Kal Raustiala, *Fashion Victims*, New Republic Online, Mar. 15, 2005, http://www.law.ucla.edu/raustiala/publications/ tnr/fasion_victims.pdf.

5. *See, e.g.*, Jonathan M. Barnett, *Shopping for Gucci on Canal Street: Reflections on Status Consumption, Intellectual Property, and the Incentive Thesis*, 91 Va. L. Rev. 1381 (2005); Susan Scafidi, *F.I.T.: Fashion as Information Technology*, 59 Syracuse L. Rev. 69 (2008); Jonathan M. Barnett et al., *The Fashion Lottery: Cooperative Innovation in Stochastic Markets* (USC Legal Studies, Research Paper No. 08-21, 2008), *available at* http://law.usc.edu/academics/centers/cleo/working-papers/cleo/2008.cfm.

6. C. Scott Hemphill & Jeannie Suk, *The Law, Culture, and Economics of Fashion*, 61 Stan. L. Rev. 1147 (2009).

In particular, we define and analyze fashion copying consistent with the understanding of "copying" embedded in U.S. copyright law, and this leads us to different conclusions. Second, we believe that Hemphill and Suk understate the diversity of consumer interests at stake in the consumption of fashion goods, and that a proper understanding of these interests makes the Hemphill/Suk model fit our views as well as, if not better than, theirs. Third, we hold a different, and we think more accurate, view of the political economy of IP law. As a result, we are far less sanguine about the legislative fix proposed in *The Law, Culture, and Economics of Fashion*. In fact, we think this policy prescription is both misguided, and—perhaps more importantly—likely to mutate into something more malignant than its authors intend.

The issue of appropriate policy is of great contemporary interest. Just prior to the publication of *The Piracy Paradox*, a group of elite designers, operating through the New York-based Council for Fashion Designers of America, convinced a Republican congressman from rural Virginia to introduce a bill that would for the first time extend copyright protection to fashion design.[7] This bill has failed in two successive Congresses, but there is every reason to believe that we will soon see debate joined again over the merits of extending American IP law to fashion design.

Our differences over the proper regulatory regime for fashion design should not obscure the larger areas of agreement. Hemphill and Suk agree with us on a fundamental point: that the fashion industry operates best in an environment of comparatively weak IP rules. They, like us, think that fashion design should not be "normalized" within copyright law. We also share a basic interest in the phenomenon of creativity without copyright. Remarkably little is known about either the contours of IP's negative space or the mechanisms by which creativity persists, and even blossoms, within that space.

In the next Part of this Article we summarize our original approach in *The Piracy Paradox* and compare and contrast it to Hemphill and Suk's analysis. We identify some of the difficulties we see in their model, take on some of their specific claims about copying in the fashion world, and discuss several areas where we believe *The Law, Culture, and Economics of Fashion* either misfires or raises more questions than it answers.

I. The Copying Conundrum in Fashion

The Law, Culture, and Economics of Fashion advances an analysis of the interrelationships among law, apparel, social norms, and preferences. First, the Article distinguishes between two forms of appropriation: (1) line-by-line copying, and (2) the creation of derivative works. "Derivative" in this context means a work that appropriates certain design elements of a model design, but is nonetheless

---

7. *See* Design Privacy Prohibition Act, S. 1957, 110th Cong. (2007); Kal Raustiala & Christopher Sprigman, *Response: The Piracy Paradox Revisited*, 61 Stan. L. Rev. 1201, 1205; Prohibition Act, H.R. 2033, 110th Cong. (2007); H.R. 5055, 109th Cong. (2006).

visually distinguishable to the average observer. Second, it offers a theory of consumer preferences for new apparel designs. Demand arises from consumers' desire simultaneously to differentiate themselves from others, and also to "flock" together with others, via their clothing choices. Hemphill and Suk summarize their theory of demand concisely: "[I]n fashion we observe the interaction of the tastes for differentiation and for flocking, or more precisely, differentiation within flocking."[8]

Based on these postulates, Hemphill and Suk acknowledge that derivative reworking of original designs is beneficial to the fashion industry. The existence of derivative reworking contributes to consumers' opportunities to flock, because the derivatives partake of a common design element and thus provide a shared design vocabulary. These derivatives do not, they contend, impair consumers' ability to differentiate because they are visually distinguishable.

On the other hand, Hemphill and Suk argue that line-by-line or "close" copies, while they serve consumers' flocking interest, harm their differentiation interest (because the garments are visually indistinguishable except at very close range). Because consumers desire both to flock and to differentiate, the article concludes that close copies are harmful and should be made unlawful.[9] A showing of "substantial difference," however, would serve as a valid defense to infringement.[10] Quoting Tim Gunn of *Project Runway* (and of the Parsons School of Design)—"I draw a line at something that, if you squint your eyes, you really can't discern it from the original"—Hemphill and Suk offer the "squint test" for infringement.[11] If one can discern a difference in the two garments even when squinting, that difference is likely to be substantial enough to negate an infringement claim. In short, they propose a sui generis legal standard to regulate design piracy in fashion.[12]

---

8. Hemphill & Suk, *supra* note 6, at 1165.

9. To the extent that Hemphill and Suk argue that copyright should apply in order to protect *consumers'* interest in differentiation, that is an idiosyncratic reading of copyright law and policy. *See* Hemphill & Suk, *supra* note 6, at 1179 ("Fashion has the potential to afford a broad vocabulary for the expression of a vast range of possible messages. Conscious or not, people's fashion choices signify and communicate, with meaningful individual and collective valences. We have identified this dynamic between differentiation and flocking as the key to the experience of fashion in social life. People use fashion to signal individual differences while also partaking in common movement with the collectivity. This model has informed our analysis of the formation and function of fashion trends among producers and consumers."). Unlike trademark, copyright is not designed to protect consumers against confusion or to protect the integrity of consumer purchasing decisions. Copyright is designed to provide authors exclusivity as needed for an incentive to create original works. Within copyright's producer-focused incentives framework, close copies are harmful only to extent that they impair sales or reasonable licensing of the original, not because consumers might be less satisfied with what they have purchased per se.

10. *Id.* at 1188.

11. *Id.*

12. The possibility of a standard of this sort, limited to proscription of close copies, was originally raised at a congressional hearing on H.R. 5055. *See A Bill to Provide Protection for Fashion Design, House of Representatives: Hearing on H.R. 5055 Before the Subcomm. on Courts, the Internet, and Intellectual Property of the H. Comm. on the Judiciary*, 109th Cong. 7 (2006) [hereinafter

While Hemphill and Suk understandably seek to distinguish their analysis from the one we presented in *The Piracy Paradox*, we believe they overstate the differences. We will leave the details of our argument for a full reading of our original article, but in the interests of clarity will provide a quick summary of our main points. In *The Piracy Paradox* we advanced an explanation for fashion's unusual low-IP regime—unusual both in its political stability and its ability to generate substantial innovation in the face of widespread copying—that rests on two features: induced obsolescence and anchoring. Both reflect the status-conferring power of fashion, and both suggest that copying, rather than impeding fashion-industry innovation and investment, promotes them.

First, what do we mean by induced obsolescence? Fashion is a status conferring, or "positional," good. In affluent societies, apparel purchases are motivated to a large degree by status seeking, rather than a desire to cover nakedness or stay warm. And fashion goods are subject to an unusual form of "two-sided" positionality. As an attractive design begins to spread, its positional or status-conferring value grows as fashion-forward consumers consume it. But as the design diffuses beyond the fashionable to the ordinary consumer, its positional value declines, and fashion-conscious early adopters are primed for the next new thing. Obligingly, the fashion industry has a new round of design innovations ready for them to consume. The cycle of innovation and diffusion starts again.

This is the fashion cycle, which is familiar stuff to anyone who has thought about the industry or even paged through an issue of *Vogue*.[13] Less well appreciated is the fashion cycle's connection with fashion's low-IP regime. The industry's practice of copying and reworking attractive new designs—a practice made possible by the low-IP rule—speeds up the fashion cycle by diffusing designs more quickly, and then driving them toward exhaustion. Copying and derivative reworking produce a faster creative cycle and more consumption of fashion due to the quicker deterioration of apparel's status conferring value. And as we will discuss below, both line-by-line copying and the more limited appropriation involved in derivative reworking feed this process.

In *The Piracy Paradox* we also described a second dynamic—anchoring—that works along with induced obsolescence in stabilizing fashion's low-IP equilibrium. The basic thrust of the anchoring dynamic is simple: The consumption cycle, if it is

---

Hearings] (Rep. Bob Goodlatte asking whether language in bill should be tightened "to make it clear that it only protects against copies that are significantly similar and not those merely inspired by other designs"). We understand, based on private conversations with various industry participants, that in later negotiations between the CFDA and a number of important apparel industry firms, the possibility of a liability standard limited to "near exact" copies was raised by firms opposed to a broad "substantial similarity" liability standard, but was rejected by the CFDA as insufficient.

13. We are grateful to Hemphill and Suk for uncovering an insightful analysis of the fashion cycle from the 1930s. Helen Everett Meiklejohn, *Dresses—The Impact of Fashion on a Business*, *in* Price and Price Policies 299, 338–39 (Walton Hamilton ed., 1938).

to work well, must quickly exhaust the status-conferring value of our clothing and induce us (the consumer) to chase the new thing.[14] For a new trend to drive consumption, the industry must somehow communicate to us what the new thing is (or what the set of new things are). It does that by turning out a large number of copies and derivative reworkings of a limited number of designs each season. In other words, the industry "anchors" its seasonal output to a discrete set of designs—trends—that characterize what is, at least for the moment, in fashion. In this way, copying and derivative reworking create trends—and trends are the basis of much fashion consumption.[15] In turn, trends send signals that reduce the information costs that all of us face in getting dressed—namely, what are we to wear? These signals about trends are useless to some, but for many they are significant. Put in trademark language, trends reduce the search costs of style.

Together, anchoring and induced obsolescence help explain the otherwise puzzling persistence of continuous fashion creativity in the face of extensive copying. Certain designers and firms suffer from the appropriation of designs so common in the industry. But in the aggregate, over time, copying is helpful, not harmful. And this, in turn, helps explain why fashion design has never been subject to copyright protection under U.S. law. The existing regime has served many interests, and thus a political coalition powerful enough to overturn the legal status quo has never appeared. Over the years various scattered efforts to enact copyright protection have ensued; none has yet proved successful.

In writing *The Piracy Paradox* we sought not only to explain the unusual stability of fashion's low-IP regime. We also aimed to open up a new frontier in IP theory. Many creative industries live in what we have called IP's "negative space." This space encompasses those creative arenas that in theory could be regulated by some aspect

14. Hemphill and Suk do not directly address our "anchoring" arguments, and they offer no argument countering our model of how copies lower information costs and facilitate fashion purchases. This is an elision in the Hemphill and Suk article, and one which weakens the foundation of their policy proposal. This is especially true because there is no reason to think that line-by-line copies are less effective than looser derivative works in reducing the information costs of apparel purchases. As a consequence, it is not enough simply to assert that line-by-line copies cause harm to innovation incentives—a claim that in any event we think incorrect. We also must consider whether eliminating line-by-line copies might harm the industry's ability to lower transaction costs and induce fashion purchases via the anchoring dynamic.

15. Hemphill and Suk note that "[g]oods that are part of the same trend are not necessarily close copies or substitutes." They later suggest, inaccurately, that we equate "trend-joining with copying." Hemphill & Suk, *supra* note 6, at 1153, 1161. We in fact agree that goods that are part of the same trend are not necessarily close copies or substitutes, and we do not equate (and never have equated) trend-joining with copying—although much trend-joining does in fact involve copying. In practice, trends vary widely but most incorporate a mix of what they would call close copies and a set of looser derivative works and, perhaps, even independent but similar creations. It is even theoretically possible for trends to develop without any copying: for many firms to alight on the same design by chance (or by tapping into an ineffable but powerful zeitgeist) and thereby create a trend. But much more common, we believe, is a trend that develops through some mix of copying, remixing, and derivative works.

of IP law, but, like fashion design, are not. The concept of IP's negative space points toward two important challenges for legal theory. One is to explain why some creative acts fall in the negative space and some in the positive space. Why are fashion designs, fennel-crusted pork chops, and football plays unprotected, but painting, poetry, and pharmaceuticals protected? The other challenge is to account for how creativity thrives in the negative space despite the lack of legal protection. This latter issue, with its clear policy implications, has begun to attract some attention and deserves more. Understanding how innovation persists absent legal protection is, given the great costs of IP rights, an extremely important task. We intend to address both of these issues at length in future work, but our early article flagged them as important and relatively unexplored areas of IP theory.

The Law, Culture, and Economics of Fashion has a narrower ambit; it is concerned primarily with making the case for a legislative change that would tweak current copyright doctrine to render a small subset of design copies unlawful. There are nonetheless important areas of connection between our article and Hemphill and Suk's; primarily in the explication of the dynamics of fashion and IP and, closely related, in the policy questions raised by these dynamics. And on these foundational points we agree much more than we disagree. Most importantly, Hemphill and Suk conclude, as do we, that the production of derivative designs helps to drive the fashion cycle—i.e., that the low-IP legal regime, which permits the creation of fashion design derivatives, is symbiotic with design change. Indeed, the low-IP regime acts as an accelerant of innovation.

Again, the important point here is not that there is a fashion cycle. It is instead the role that law plays in driving that cycle. Hemphill and Suk, like us, see copying as an essential part of the creative ecology of fashion. Fashion piracy may be parasitic on original designs, but it is a parasite that does not kill its host: though it may weaken individual designers it also, paradoxically, strengthens the industry and drives its evolution.[16] In an industry that cannot look to continuous improvements in quality to drive demand, piracy substitutes for functional innovation. This is a very important point: piracy is the fashion industry's equivalent of the new feature on a cell phone. It is a force that encourages a consumer to discard a perfectly serviceable garment and purchase the new, new thing.

For these reasons, we have argued that ordinary rules of copyright ought not to govern the fashion world, and Hemphill and Suk apparently agree. This view, which cuts against nearly all prior legal writing on the topic, is one reason we perceive

16. The "parasitism" of fashion piracy plays out in ways that are analogous at a general level to the function of parasites in the natural world: parasites can harm individual organisms, but they also drive evolution and indeed have served as one of the primary forces inducing biological diversity. *See* Carl Zimmer, Parasite Rex: Inside the Bizarre World of Nature's Most Dangerous Creatures (2000).

substantial common ground between our analyses.[17] Below we explore what we believe are the chief remaining areas of disagreement.

A. Differentiation, Flocking, and the "D/F Ratio"

An important area of disagreement between the analysis in *The Law, Culture, and Economics of Fashion* and ours is over the proper treatment of nearly exact, or line-by-line, copies. Whereas Hemphill and Suk wish to ban line-by-line copies, we find no reason to treat them differently from the copying done to create derivative fashion designs. The significance of the distinction between line-by-line and derivative works rests partly on the claim that line-by-line copies are particularly harmful. In support of this claim, *The Law, Culture, and Economics of Fashion* develops a model of consumer preferences about fashion which distinguishes between individuals' desire to flock together and to differentiate themselves from others. This is a useful distinction. But the analysis misfires, in our view, when it treats differentiation and flocking as desires fixed together in the psyches of individual consumers.

We think it is far more useful and accurate to view an individual consumer's desire to flock and differentiate as located somewhere on a continuum. Conceptualizing this way, one can talk of a "D/F ratio," which represents where along the continuum between pure differentiation and pure flocking an individual's preferences fall.[18] Some consumers (though a very small group) are oriented strongly toward differentiation—think of Bjork and her famous swan dress.[19] These consumers have a relatively high D/F ratio. Others, perhaps the vast majority, are dedicated flockers, who seek to stand out as little as possible. These consumers have a relatively low D/F ratio. In between are many varied middle positions—positions that probably change over time even for a single person, according to that individual's age, wealth, marital status, and a host of other social circumstances.

Once differentiation and flocking are seen in terms of a ratio that varies among individuals and even within the life of particular persons, the Hemphill and Suk model may actually support our analysis better than it does theirs. To see this, let us restate our model from *The Piracy Paradox* in the argot of *The Law, Culture, and Economics of Fashion*. In our model, the early adopters are those who manifest a much higher D/F ratio than the ordinary apparel consumer.[20] Early adopters sample many new (and sometimes outlandish) designs, most of which will never be adopted

---

17. We also agree with Hemphill and Suk that normative claims that fashion is a wasteful or harmful status-reinforcing pursuit—the sort of considerations that undergird traditional sumptuary laws—are not very persuasive. We have taken a broadly liberal view about fashion design, in which more design choice—i.e., more innovation—is better because it gives consumers more options.

18. Hemphill and Suk note that differentiation and flocking ratios can vary, but they do not explore the implications of these observations for their model.

19. *See* Bjork.com images, http://www.bjork.com/db/images/103-lg-sfw.jpg (last visited Feb. 18, 2009).

20. Those with high D/F ratios are not necessarily runway fashion followers, however. Some are idiosyncratic stylists who only wear vintage clothes from the 1920s or favor unusual signature

widely. Eventually, the purchases of some early adopters catch on—in a process both we and Hemphill and Suk treat as exogenous—and signify a trend. Derivative works based on the model design, as well as some line-by-line copies, begin to flood the market as those with lower D/F ratios (i.e., ordinary consumers) join the trend. As many ordinary consumers adopt the design, the early adopters begin to flee it. Soon they move on to the next new design, and the cycle begins again.

Copying, in other words, signals a trend, solidifies it, and then exhausts it. Why does it exhaust the trend? Because the early adopters' relatively powerful desire for differentiation is retriggered soon after the ordinary consumer's relatively powerful flocking inclination leads to wider adoption of the previously vanguard design.[21]

---

garments. But for many high D/F individuals, the ever-changing offerings of the high fashion industry serve as the primary palette for their sartorial self-expression.

21. Hemphill and Suk use Dr. Seuss's story *The Sneetches* as a parable to illustrate a separate criticism of our model in *The Piracy Paradox*. Hemphill & Suk, *supra* note 6, at 1182. In the story, an enterprising and amoral salesman named Sylvester McMonkey McBean encounters a group of bird-like beach dwellers, the Sneetches. Some Sneetches have stars on their bellies, and the star-bellies disdain their plain-bellied counterparts. The plain-bellies resent the social snubs they receive from the star-bellies; they are both treated and view themselves as a subordinate group. McBean, sensing an opportunity to play on the Sneetches' star-consciousness, deploys a machine that, for a fee, stamps stars on the plain-bellies. This anger and confuses the over-Sneetches, who find that their stars no longer distinguish them from the formerly plain-bellied. McBean responds by offering the original star-bellies admission—again for a fee—to a star-removal machine. Racial separation is thereby restored, but only for as long as it takes McBean to convince the under-Sneetches that plain bellies are now preferable, and that they must pay for removal of the stars he recently applied. The cycle of applying and removing stars continues until the Sneetches are out of money. And in the frenzy of star application and removal everything becomes jumbled—no one can tell who was originally starred and who wasn't. At the end of the story, the Sneetches drop their star-based discrimination and kumbaya reigns. In all, a hopeful ending—the Sneetches are suckers, but even suckers can learn. DR. SEUSS, THE SNEETCHES AND OTHER STORIES (Random House 1961) (1953). *The Sneetches* is obviously a parable about race. But the moral that Hemphill and Suk draw from *The Sneetches* is about microeconomics. The problem with the Sneetches, Hemphill and Suk say, is that they are bad at lifecycle pricing—i.e., they fail to understand that neither the star-based distinctiveness nor sameness they seek is fated to last for long. If only the Sneetches understood this, Hemphill and Suk suggest, they would not have paid McBean in the first place. Yet unlike the Sneetches, Hemphill and Suk assert, fashion consumers *are* competent lifecycle pricers. And as a result, they claim, the fashion industry does not profit in the aggregate from copying. Consumers will understand that a faster cycle means that the differentiation or flocking that they seek will be less durable, and therefore less valuable. As a result, copying might drive consumers to buy clothing more often, but it would also cause them to pay less for each purchase. We are very skeptical of this argument. First, Hemphill and Suk have raised empirical questions—do fashion consumers lifecycle price? do they do so effectively?—but they offer no evidence in favor of their claims. And even at a theoretical level the role of lifecycle pricing in fashion consumption is complex. From the perspective of the early-adopters, the ferreting out of an up-and-coming design may well be one of the pleasures of being a fashionista. So too is the experience of watching the masses tag along behind you: the fashion-forward may not want to dress like the fashion-follower, but the opportunity to watch everyone else try to catch up can be an important part of the return to investment in trend-spotting. So for an important class of fashion consumer, rapid style change is arguably not a cost, but a benefit, as it provides more opportunity both to engage in connoisseurship and to observe the followers emulating one's good taste. Whether or not fashion buyers lifecycle price is

The market for new designs is driven by the high D/F ratio consumers, who tend to discard their old clothes and buy new designs when too many ordinary consumers buy the copies, thereby impairing the originality and status of the previously new design. So in a sense the market for new designs is driven by the "harm" caused to one set of consumers by purchases of copies by another, generally larger, set of consumers. This is part of the paradox that underlies our decision to title our article *The Piracy Paradox*. Importantly, given this dynamic and in the absence of empirical evidence to the contrary, there is no compelling reason to distinguish between line-by-line copies and derivative reworkings for the purposes of differentiation and flocking. Both forms of design copying fuel the fashion industry's cycle of induced obsolescence.

Perhaps what Hemphill and Suk mean to argue is that some consumers are content with the minor differentiation permitted by derivative works; in other words, they want some differentiation, but don't need much—a few minor details are enough. If true, that suggests that the D/F ratio of these consumers is not very high. More dedicated differentiators will not be content to merely be distinguished from the crowd by minor details: they will want more. As this suggests, without knowing much more about consumer preferences, and how they are manifested in actual purchases, we are ill-equipped to move from simple models to the development of actual legal proposals.

This skepticism fits well with the thrust of *The Piracy Paradox*, which offers arguments that are essentially conservative. The American legal system has gone some two centuries without formal design protection for fashion, and the industry itself has lacked any effective self-help against design copying since the government terminated, via an antitrust lawsuit, the Fashion Originators Guild cartel that operated between 1933 and 1941. In the decades since the toppling of the Guild, the fashion industry has grown despite (or, in our view, partly *because of*) its low-IP regime. Indeed, there is no compelling evidence that copying, whether close or not, has produced systematic harm for the industry.[22]

Historically minded opponents of this view sometimes point to the example of the Fashion Originators Guild itself. Hemphill and Suk, for example, contend that the Guild episode is "[s]trong real-world evidence" for the utility of design protection.[23] We disagree for two reasons. First, whether or not the Guild "reduced copying greatly," as they suggest it did, is largely beside the point.[24] The Constitution

---

an empirical question the answer to which no one yet knows. But the foregoing suggests it may well be just as likely that if fashionistas lifecycle price, they do so in reverse—less durable trends are preferred. It is therefore also not clear that the fashion originator would benefit from longer trend cycles—the originator cannot charge more for something a consumer does not especially value.

22. We are not suggesting that no one is harmed by copying; we recognize that often substantial harm accrues to individual firms and designers. But in the aggregate we are skeptical that there is meaningful harm, and indeed we think in the aggregate copying is beneficial.

23. Hemphill & Suk, *supra* note 6, at 1193.

24. *Id.*

makes plain that copyright exists to "promote the Progress of Science and Useful Arts." At the most fundamental level it is enhanced creativity and innovation, not reduced copying, that is the goal of copyright law. Whether a regime of relatively free appropriation promotes or inhibits innovation in any particular creative field is an empirical question, and we believe the answer with regard to apparel is clear, if admittedly counterintuitive: over time and across the industry as a whole, copying does not inhibit fashion innovation. So the success of the Guild in reducing copying is not tantamount to an argument that the Guild was good for innovation. Second, even if the Guild system led some firms to shift from copying to originating, as Hemphill and Suk claim, that does not mean that there was more innovation overall. Like all anticompetitive cartels, the Guild was set up to restrict—and succeeded in restricting—supply. The key policy question therefore is whether *aggregate innovation* was higher, not whether incumbents changed their market strategy. On that question the jury is decidedly out.

What is unassailable is that in the decades since the fall of the Guild the American fashion industry has not only survived absent design copyright; it has thrived. For this reason alone we believe the burden of persuasion rests heavily on those who seek to overturn the legal status quo. In our view, advocates for copyright protection for fashion designs have not yet met that burden. Moreover, because what is proposed is a wholesale alteration of the regulatory environment, the case for change requires systematic evidence. In an industry as big, dynamic, and competitive as fashion, there are always winners and losers. The proponents of copyright protection for fashion often tell stories about designers who suffered harm from copying; they rarely tell stories about designers who benefited by joining an emerging trend, or by originating a design that became popular and widely consumed via trend-driven copying.[25] The broader question is whether innovation and competition are better served under a form of regulation more restrictive than what we have now. Persuasive evidence for this proposition is lacking. Until we see such evidence, Congress should let well enough alone.

B. Some Difficulties with Differentiation

Again, none of this criticism gainsays the fact that we believe that the concepts of differentiation and flocking are helpful, and that these concepts better orient the analysis of copying in the fashion world. But there remain many unanswered questions about consumers' desire simultaneously to flock and differentiate. Here are a few we believe deserve more attention in future work.

1. Why is the desire for differentiation better served in an environment in which there are lots of derivatives but no line-by-line copies?

Hemphill and Suk assume that consumers' desire for differentiation can be sated so long as we preserve the uniqueness of small details in a design. That has to be their view, or their "squint test" recommendation (i.e., that appropriation should not

25. *See, e.g.*, *Hearings*, *supra* note 12.

be actionable so long as it results in a design that is minimally visually distinguishable) makes no sense. But how do we know that the wide production of derivatives—i.e., garments that recognizably appropriate the appealing trend element of the model design—does not erode consumers' ability to differentiate? Put differently, what if consumers' differentiation desire focuses on *styles* rather than small details? In that case, the production of derivatives of the same general style would interfere with differentiation as surely as line-by-line copies. We do not know if this is true. But for the differentiation concept to have more purchase as a normative construct, we need to know at what level consumers differentiate. *The Law, Culture, and Economics of Fashion* does not offer much evidence about this issue (nor have we seen evidence presented elsewhere). This would not be a problem if Hemphill and Suk had confined themselves to offering a general model. But without a more complete understanding of differentiation, their policy prescriptions are premature.

2. Is differentiation only a matter of design?

The idea that line-by-line copies interfere with consumers' ability to differentiate themselves lends support to a ban on such copies. But of course possession of a desirable and unusual design is not the only way to differentiate. For example, it is possible that the desire for differentiation could be satisfied via quality differences in a garment that cannot be reproduced by a cheaper copy. Expensive originals are generally of markedly superior quality in terms of fabric, craftsmanship, and tailoring.[26] Sometimes these quality differences are readily apparent to others, at least to the careful observer. Sometimes they produce pleasure only for the wearer. Perhaps quality differences can serve as differentiators too.

Much the same can be said of distinctive trademarks. Trademarks are widely used in the apparel industry, central to the value of many famous brands, and vigorously protected against infringement. Distinctive brands feed the desire for differentiation and arguably provoke it as well. For some consumers it is probably enough to know that inside their jacket is a label that reads "Marc Jacobs." Yet there are many subtle (and not so subtle) ways that apparel companies display trademarks aside from relatively hidden interior labels; buttons often feature brand names, for example, and some companies put small but visible external labels or insignia on garments. Some have even trademarked colors and patterns, as in Burberry's famous tan plaid.

---

26. Not all copies are cheap, and not all originals are expensive. L'affaire Nicholas Ghesquiere is a good example. In 2002, Ghesquiere, young designer for the fabled house of Balenciaga, was lambasted for passing off a patchwork vest originally designed in 1973 by Kaisik Wong, a virtually unknown designer from San Francisco, as his own. *See* Booth Moore, *Still Dazzling*, L.A. TIMES, Dec. 16, 2002, at 11. Borrowing from a lesser-known designer is not unusual, nor is borrowing from the street (as in the frequent raiding of Japanese teen styles from Tokyo neighborhoods such as Harajuku). But the more common pattern, at least according to the major designers, is that their designs are appropriated and tweaked by lesser, or less successful, lights.

In *The Piracy Paradox* we did not focus on trademarks per se, but they played an important subsidiary role in our analysis. Labels and marks are essential to many apparel buyers, and not only in relation to the paradigmatic consumer search cost and producer reputation concerns that undergird the economics of trademark.[27] Some consumers appear to treat labels as almost an end in themselves, and are eager to get whatever Gucci or Prada put out. And many apparel companies differentiate within a single family of brands by using submarks. So-called bridge or diffusion lines are a common example; Giorgio Armani uses some five different submarks (Emporio Armani, Armani Exchange, Armani "black label," etc.) to differentiate his garments into multiple brands operating at different price points.[28]

The central point is that while fashion design operates in a low-IP regime, it does not operate in a no-IP regime. Rather, while copyright protection for fashion designs is almost entirely absent, the apparel industry is strongly protected by, and invested in, trademark law. The existence of powerful brands is an important aspect of the economics of fashion. Once a trend becomes widely adopted, its days are usually numbered. But in the interim, as the trend is building, buyers face a plethora of similar designs. To a large degree consumers choose among these based on price, quality, and the like. But they also choose based on labels. The fact that major fashion houses aggressively protect their trademarks provides a potent contrast to their behavior with regard to design, notwithstanding the recent efforts by the CFDA and its supporters. To understand the role of differentiation and flocking, we need to better understand the degree to which brand-based differentiation can substitute for, or complement, design-based differentiation.[29]

---

27. William M. Landes & Richard A. Posner, The Economic Structure of Intellectual Property Law 166–209 (2003).

28. *See generally* Jonathan M. Barnett, *Shopping for Gucci on Canal Street: Reflections on Status Consumption, Intellectual Property, and the Incentive Thesis*, 91 Va. L. Rev. 1381 (2005). Consumers are also differentiated by time. High-valuing consumers get exclusivity and status for new designs for a short period of time—and this is a function not so much of the lack of copies (indeed, copies and derivative reworkings often appear very quickly) but the length of time it takes for low-valuing consumers to understand the trend and decide to join it. As low-valuing consumers enter the market, high-valuing consumers increasingly move on to the next new designs and so on. The premium charged to high-valuing consumers provides fashion designers with return on investment, while the masses enjoy new fashions that can be copied and sold to them more cheaply.

29. Hemphill and Suk equivocate about whether they think the law ought to discriminate among consumption patterns. At some points in the article they eschew normative judgments about the value of fashion, such as those underlying traditional sumptuary laws. But later they decry the "distorting" nature of trademark protection, arguing that the resulting "logoification" is somehow problematic. While as an aesthetic matter we share some of this concern, as an analytic matter we think "distortion" is inherent in the creation of monopolies and we think normative judgments in favor of one or another type of innovation should largely remain outside our policy analysis unless truly compelling reasons exist. To name just one aspect of the "distortion" argument that strikes us as problematic, Hemphill and Suk assert that a focus on differentiation via trademarks constrains the ways in which apparel can aid individuals in constructing identity and communicating messages. *See* Hemphill & Suk, *supra* note 6, at 1179. There is a substantial literature describing the ways in which both trademark owners and consumers use marks to do precisely

There are other potential forms of differentiation as well. Fabric designs, or patterns, have long been covered by copyright law, and they obviously provide an important source of differentiation even when the shape or cut of two garments is identical.[30] The shopping experience itself is another potential form of differentiation, though not one intrinsic to and attached to the garment. There are surely others. The important point is that, absent a careful consideration of these varied forms of differentiation, policy recommendations to alter copyright law to include apparel design.

3. You can't always get the differentiation you want (but you might get the differentiation you need)

Hemphill and Suk write that "[f]ashion-conscious people generally do not seek to wear precisely the same outfit as someone else."[31] Though not a major element in their article, this claim seems to miss a basic point about the logic of differentiation. Even if there were absolutely no copying of a given design, there could still be large numbers of the same dress produced by its originator. Except for the highest-end custom couture, apparel is not a one-off product. The fear of "the same dress" they identify is only partly the result of design copying. We point this out because it illustrates a difficulty that attends their analysis throughout: any system in which some appropriation is allowed will always interfere with the ability of those with high differentiation desires to achieve stable differentiation. But that is in fact precisely the dynamic that drives the industry. It is important that sufficient differentiation opportunities exist such that early adopters receive a reward for their investment in differentiation. And it is also important that this reward be evanescent—the loss of differentiation is the fuel for the next round of innovation and consumption. Whether inadvertently or by design, the industry's current low-IP environment appears to us to strike this balance remarkably well.

C. Line-By-Line vs. Derivative Copying

In *The Law, Culture, and Economics of Fashion,* Hemphill and Suk assert that in our original article on fashion and copyright we failed to disaggregate different forms of copying. We plead guilty. Our goal in writing *The Piracy Paradox* was not primarily normative or focused on policy recommendations. Rather, as the first major article in the field we sought to address what we thought to be the fundamental questions: why the low-IP equilibrium in the fashion industry had been stable for many decades, and why firms continue to make significant investments in the

---

these things. The argument against trademarks here seems to us to devolve into an argument not in favor of increased communication and identity-construction, but against *a particular form* of these activities. Thus the argument is heavily value-laden and contestable, and, for that reason alone, requires much more development and justification before it can be used as a reason to extend copyright protection to fashion design.

30. Indeed, several of the examples used in Hemphill & Suk, *supra* note 6, are really examples of fabric pattern copying, rather than design copying.

31. Hemphill & Suk, *supra* note 6, at 1166.

production and distribution of new fashion designs that others are perfectly free to copy. To answer these questions, we had no need of distinctions—mostly irrelevant as a legal matter—between line-by-line copying and the creation of derivative works. Both involve copying. Both would be unlawful if the normal rules of copyright applied. Because copyright law does not apply, both are engaged in freely.

In later writing,[32] and in testimony before Congress,[33] we took a more strongly normative stance. We did so in response to the legislative proposals then pending to extend copyright to fashion designs. These proposals did not distinguish between line-by-line copying and derivatives, but instead extended the standard copyright liability test of "substantial similarity" to fashion design. We thought then, and think now, that this is an exceptionally bad idea. The substantial similarity liability standard "presents one of the most difficult questions in copyright law, and one that is least susceptible of helpful generalizations."[34] But the standard, as it has been worked out by the courts over a large number of cases, is apt to condemn as infringement any not in substantial taking of protected material if the material taken is qualitatively significant.[35] The appealing element of a fashion design trend would be,

---

32. *See* Raustiala & Sprigman, *How Copyright Could*, *supra* note 4.

33. *See A Bill to Provide Protection for Fashion Design: Hearing on H.R. 5055 Before the Subcomm. on Courts, the Internet, and Intellectual Property of the H. Comm. on the Judiciary*, 109th Cong. 87–89 (2006) [hereinafter *Hearings on H.R. 5055*] (statement of Christopher Sprigman, Associate Professor, University of Virginia School of Law).

34. 4 Nimmer on Copyright § 13.03[A] (2008).

35. *See, e.g.*, Cavalier v. Random House, Inc., 297 F.3d 815 (9th Cir. 2002) (finding drawing in children's book that included arrangement of stars and clouds similar to plaintiff's drawing substantially similar, despite significant overall differences in the drawings); Castle Rock Entm't, Inc. v. Carol Publ'g Group, Inc., 150 F.3d 132 (2d Cir. 1998) (finding trivia book questions quizzing readers about their knowledge of plot incidents from "Seinfeld" television series substantially similar to television show); United States v. Hux, 940 F.2d 314 (8th Cir. 1991) (sustaining criminal copyright conviction in a case involving computer programs, despite evidence that only 205 bytes of defendant's program were similar to copyright claimant's 16,384 bytes), *overruled by* United States v. Davis, 978 F.2d 415 (8th Cir. 1992); Baxter v. MCA, Inc., 812 F.2d 421 (9th Cir. 1987) (use of six-note sequence creates substantial similarity); Whelan Assocs., Inc. v. Jaslow Dental Lab., Inc., 797 F.2d 1222 (3d Cir. 1986) (finding substantial similarity based on appropriation of computer program's structure and organization, despite parties' agreement that there was no literal copying of program code); Horgan v. MacMillan, Inc., 789 F.2d 157 (2d Cir. 1986) (finding three black and white photographs of ballet performance infringe copyright in choreography of lengthy ballet); Grand Upright Music Ltd. v. Warner Bros. Records, Inc., 780 F. Supp. 182 (S.D.N.Y. 1991) (finding use of three words and short musical phrase creates substantial similarity); Kisch v. Ammirati & Puris, Inc., 657 F. Supp. 380 (S.D.N.Y. 1986) (finding substantial similarity based on similar "underlying tone or mood" of photographs, despite significant differences in subject, pose, lighting, and other elements); Bright Tunes Music Corp. v. Harrisongs Music Ltd., 420 F. Supp. 177 (S.D.N.Y. 1976) (finding substantial similarity in unconscious copying of three-note and five-note phrase from musical composition); Robertson v. Batten, Barton, Durstine & Osborne, Inc., 146 F. Supp. 795 (S.D. Cal. 1956) (finding copying two bars of musical composition creates substantial similarity); *see also* Universal Pictures Co. v. Harold Lloyd Corp., 162 F.2d 354, 360 (9th Cir. 1947) ("[A]n infringement is not confined to literal and exact repetition or reproduction; it includes also the various modes in which the matter of any work may be adopted, imitated, transferred or reproduced, with more or less colorable alterations to disguise the piracy."); Davis v. E.I. du Pont

almost by definition, a qualitatively substantial taking. And that fact points toward very wide copyright liability under the substantial similarity standard. This is especially true in light of an *aperçu* from Judge Learned Hand's opinion in *Sheldon v. Metro-Goldwyn Pictures Corp.*, an early motion picture copyright case, which has become a commonplace in courts' judgments of substantial similarity: "no plagiarist can excuse the wrong by showing how much of his work he did not pirate."[36]

Our primary concern, in weighing in on these policy questions, was to show that this particular approach was apt to interfere substantially with the industry's ability to develop and sustain trends via design copying. Placed in the fashion context, the substantial similarity standard would sweep a lot into its net. On that basis (and our concern over the economic impact of extensive and uncertain litigation) we thought the harms that would flow from this extension of this standard were likely to substantially outweigh the benefits. Again, in this branch of the debate neither we nor, apparently, anyone else, had need of fine distinctions between line-by-line copying and copying to create derivative works. Indeed, when the possibility of such a distinction was raised early in the consideration of the House bill,[37] it was, to our understanding, rejected immediately by the representatives of Council for Fashion Designers of America (CFDA) and has never surfaced again, at least in the form of any proposal for changes to legislative language.

For these reasons, the assertion that we failed to separate line-by-line copying from the creation of trends misses the mark. Our point was that a broad freedom to copy is vital, because copying drives the trend cycles that in turn drive consumption of fashion. Yet the creation of fashion design derivatives involves "copying" just as surely as the creation of exact copies does, at least as the copyright law understands the meaning of the term.

At this later point in the debate, Hemphill and Suk want to shift the ground away from the substantial similarity standard and its wholesale condemnation of both line-by-line and derivative copying. We think they are right to do so. But Hemphill and Suk err when they characterize themselves as occupying a middle position between us and the high-protectionists who wish to impose standard copyright rules on the industry.[38] They do not occupy the middle, but rather a position very close to our own. Their "squint test" standard is a far cry from the sweeping understanding of substantial similarity that undergirds contemporary copyright doctrine.

---

de Nemours & Co., 240 F. Supp. 612, 621 (S.D.N.Y. 1965) ("[P]araphrasing is tantamount to copying in copyright law."); *cf.* Bridgeport Music, Inc. v. Dimension Films, 410 F.3d 792, 798 (6th Cir. 2005) (finding two-second sample of guitar solo infringing, noting "no substantial similarity or de minimis inquiry should be undertaken at all when the defendant has not disputed that it digitally sampled a copyrighted sound recording").

36. 81 F.2d 49, 56 (2d Cir. 1936).

37. *See Hearings on H.R. 5055*, *supra* note 33, at 7 (Rep. Bob Goodlatte asking whether language in bill should be tightened "to make it clear that it only protects against copies that are significantly similar and not those merely inspired by other designs.").

38. Hemphill & Suk, *supra* note 6, at 1153.

We also have an important prudential concern. As an empirical matter, Hemphill and Suk's distinction between line-by-line copies and derivative works is unobjectionable—although, for reasons we detailed above, they make rather more of this distinction than we think it merits. It is crucially important, however, to underscore that U.S. copyright law does *not* distinguish between the two types of copying in the way that Hemphill and Suk do. Indeed, in defending the superiority of their distinction, Hemphill and Suk argue that our usage of "copy" in the *Piracy Paradox* is "contrary to ordinary and fashion-industry usage." They contend that "copy" suggests a close copy, not a reworking.[39]

Again, we are guilty as charged, and deliberately so. They are correct that there is not a single meaning for the word "copy" in ordinary language. One may differentiate colloquially between many types of copies—close, exact, partial, and so forth. But U.S. copyright law is different, and it does not follow the usage of fashion insiders or the general public.[40] Instead there is a well-developed set of doctrines, internal to the copyright law and the judicial opinions interpreting it, that controls what constitutes a "copy" for purposes of infringement. As applied to fashion design, these doctrines make clear that both line-by-line copying and the more limited appropriation required to create a derivative design would be unlawful.[41] In short, for analytic purposes we believe the relevant meaning of "copy" is that of a judge interpreting copyright law, not a fashion designer operating within her very different world.

This point is not only doctrinal. If the past is any guide, any copyright standard that is enacted for fashion design—even one initially narrower than the generally applicable substantial similarity standard—will tend to become increasingly expansive and prohibitory over time.[42] This is the clear trend in copyright law as a whole. Copyright started as a very limited right to control "printing, reprinting, publishing, and vending" of maps, charts, and books for fourteen years, renewable once if the author survived the initial term.[43] Even this limited right was extended only to authors who complied with a demanding set of formalities, including registration, deposit, marking of published copies, and renewal.[44] Today, copyright extends a very broad range of rights that afford rightsholders powerful control over the use of a much wider range of creative works. Copyright law today defines as

39. *See id.* at 1181–82.

40. Fashion insiders, moreover, often traffic in apocryphal rules about permissible copying, such as the common belief that copying more than twenty percent of a garment will result in infringement. Interview with Ilse Metchek, President, California Fashion Association (Mar. 25, 2009).

41. *See* 17 U.S.C. § 106(1) (2006) (reproduction right); 17 U.S.C. § 106(2) (2006) (derivative work right).

42. *See* Neil Netanel, *Why Has Copyright Expanded?: Analysis and Critique* (UCLA Sch. of Law Pub. Law & Legal Theory Research Paper Series, No. 07-34, 2007), *available at* http://papers.ssrn.com/sol3/papers.cfm?abstract_id=1066241.

43. Act of May 31, 1790, ch. 15, 1 Stat. 124 (1790).

44. Christopher Sprigman, *Reform(aliz)ing Copyright*, 57 STAN. L. REV. 485, 492 (2004).

infringing conduct any not insubstantial use of material protected by copyright, and it employs this inaptly named "substantial similarity" standard to judge the legality of copies, derivative works, public performances, and public displays. These broad rights are granted for terms that average nearly a century and are no longer conditioned on compliance with any mandatory copyright formality. The result has been a tremendous expansion both in the amount of creative work subject to copyright law and the types of conduct that are treated as infringing.

The law's expansion has been accompanied and in some ways induced by an ideological shift. The exclusive rights granted by copyright law were, at copyright's inception into U.S. federal law, treated as a limited and wholly instrumental departure from the norm of free competition in creative works.[45] Over time, copyright's ideology shifted toward a conception that treats exclusive rights as the baseline, and competition as the threat to creative incentives. Copyright's exclusive rights are, moreover, no longer viewed wholly or even mostly in utilitarian or instrumental terms, but as reflecting basic fairness toward creators. These developments have laid IP policymaking (and judicial decision making) wide open to inapt analogies between real and intellectual property.[46] IP rights ought to be crafted to ensure proper incentives for innovation and creativity, while also facilitating wide public access to knowledge. But they are increasingly talked about and treated as if they are absolute property rights that need vigilant defense against any and all trespasses by "pirates." Too often the result is that initially limited IP rights are either extended beyond reason by Congress or interpreted ever more stringently by the courts.

A full exploration of this shift is far beyond the scope of this essay. But Hemphill and Suk's "squint test," based as it is in an instrumentalist model of fashion consumption, will likely be caught up in the powerful noninstrumentalist current that is sweeping the whole of copyright law toward complete propertization. For these reasons, even a narrow expansion of copyright law to cover fashion design would likely soon grow into something much more encompassing—and possibly harmful to the fashion industry.[47]

---

45. *See, e.g.*, James Boyle, The Public Domain: Enclosing the Commons of the Mind (2008).

46. *See generally id.*; William W. Fisher III, Promises to Keep: Technology, Law, and the Future of Entertainment (2004); Lawrence Lessig, Remix (2008); Mark Lemley, *Property, Intellectual Property, and Free Riding*, 83 Tex. L. Rev. 1031 (2005).

47. There is yet another problem with the proposal for a limited copyright for fashion design: how to determine what is the "original" and what is the "copy." The Senate version of the Design Piracy Prohibition Act, S. 1957, for example, proposed addressing this through a registry system. The administrative burden of this system would of course be great. As the head of the California Fashion Association has noted, in spring '09 alone some 300 runway shows took place in Milan, each featuring dozens of items. To create the capacity for registering 10,000 or more garments per season is likely well beyond the current capacity of the Copyright Office. Interview with Ilse Metchek, *supra* note 40.

D. Who Benefits from Stronger Design Protection?

Let us set these problems aside and take the squint test exactly as Hemphill and Suk present it. One immediate question is, who is doing the squinting? It appears that it is the ultimate fact finder (the jury, or the judge in a bench trial) who must determine (1) that the defendant copied, and (2) that the copying is so close that it meets the squint standard. A fashion copyright case based on a squint test that involves any contested issues of fact—Did the defendant copy? Would an ordinary person perceive a difference between the two garments?—is poorly suited for summary disposition. And a form of litigation that must in most circumstances proceed to a trial on the merits disfavors resource-poor parties even more than expensive federal court litigation typically does.

This observation is important in part because Hemphill and Suk assert that fashion's current low-IP equilibrium disfavors less-well-known and new designers. In our view, the converse is more likely true. First, the assertion that fashion's low-IP regime harms small designers lacks empirical support. Even a cursory look at the fashion industry will reveal thousands of new and young designers competing for their place in the industry, seemingly undeterred by the prevalence of fashion copying—and, often, engaging in it. But more importantly, extending copyright is likely to harm, not help, new or small designers. Relatively unknown and poorly funded entrants are at a disadvantage, relative to a rich and well-known incumbent, in most any market. However, fashion's low-IP equilibrium does at least deprive large fashion firms of one anticompetitive tool that big firms operating in high-IP markets often use to grind down upstarts: lawyers.

Given this baseline, it is unlikely that introducing lawyers into the mix will make things better for the weak at the expense of the strong. We should not forget that in a system of fashion copyright new entrants may be defendants as well as plaintiffs, and that the threat of lawsuits, the creative and even frivolous use of cease-and-desist letters, and the potentially massive statutory damages and other powerful remedies available under current law[48] (remedies which the proponents of fashion copyrights have attempted to further increase), will oblige small-fry and large incumbents alike to spend time and resources "clearing" designs and contesting claims. These costs—and the residual risk of litigation even when efforts are made to avoid liability—are more easily borne by large firms. (Indeed, the support for a new legal regime shown by many leading fashion designers, as discussed in the next section, is consistent with this view—they are the relative beneficiaries).[49] The

48. *See* 17 U.S.C. § 504 (2006) (specifying measures of actual and statutory damages available to prevailing copyright plaintiffs); 17 U.S.C. § 505 (2006) (authorizing courts to award costs and attorney fees to prevailing copyright plaintiffs).

49. The role of litigation threat is of course hard to discern. Hemphill and Suk focus on existing litigation trends to suggest that design protection is desirable. While we welcome their efforts to look empirically at the question of fashion litigation, what they offer is a mélange of different types of cases, including trademark and fabric print cases (both covered by existing IP law). *See* Hemphill & Suk, *supra* note 6, at 1174 tbl.1. Given that the design protection they espouse does not apply

effect of a fashion copyright regime may be precisely the opposite of what Hemphill and Suk intend.

E. What Does the Fashion Industry Want?

Finally, some might argue that the proper legal regime in a given economic domain ought to reflect the stated preferences of the regulated industry. We disagree with this producerist perspective in general: it ignores consumer interests and therefore cannot fairly assess policy in terms of overall social welfare. Aside from this general objection, we think there is substantial reason to be particularly wary of enacting the preferences of the regulated parties in the context of IP policy. Collective action problems are especially intense in the context of IP policymaking, and they distort policy in favor of producer interests. In IP-producing industries such as recorded music, motion pictures, and commercial software and book publishing, a few large producers control a significant share of output. In contrast, consumers of these IP goods are many and dispersed. Producers are therefore in a much better position to overcome the costs of organizing to seek favorable changes to the law. Large producers internalize significant benefits from favorable legal changes, whereas individual consumers benefit only marginally.[50] The result is policy skewed toward producer interests, at the expense of consumers and overall social welfare.

A version of this same story applies in the fashion industry. Elite designers—the people who run the CFDA—are few and probably would be positioned to benefit from the legal change that they have proposed. But there is certainly little reason to believe that their interests align with those of nonelite designers, or of manufacturers, distributors, retailers, consumers, or, indeed, overall welfare. That said, even if we are skeptical that the designers' preferences are likely to coincide with social welfare, it may nonetheless be helpful to know what industry preferences are.

We think there is substantial evidence against the view, espoused by Hemphill and Suk, that the American fashion industry is strongly opposed to design copying.[51]

---

to either category, and given that current law already does, it is hard to know what inferences ought to be drawn from these cases.

50. *See generally* Boyle, *supra* note 45; Lessig, *supra* note 46; Mancur Olson, The Logic of Collective Action (1965); George J. Stigler, *The Theory of Economic Regulation*, 2 Bell J. Econ. & Mgmt. Sci. 3 (1971). Aside from the policy distortions arising from collective action asymmetries, the content industries have a substantial record of misjudging which intellectual property and technology policies will serve their long-term interests. The motion picture industry was deeply opposed to the VCR and fought it in the courts; that they lost is probably one of the best things that ever happened to the industry, which went on to earn billions from the sale of videos and DVDs. *See* Sony Corp. v. Universal City Studios, Inc., 464 U.S. 417 (1984). A similar and more recent example is the early resistance of the recorded music industry to online music selling. The industry's failure to get behind a consumer-friendly online market contributed first to an explosion of illegal music file-swapping over peer-to-peer networks, and then the rise to market dominance of Apple's iTunes service—which now threatens to displace the record labels as the major player in the distribution of recorded music. *See* Christopher Sprigman, *The 99¢ Question*, 5 J. Telecomm. & High Tech. L. 87 (2006).

51. Hemphill & Suk, *supra* note 6, at 1183–84.

The CFDA in reality only represents a small number of elite and often very successful designers. (Members include such luminaries as Tom Ford, Calvin Klein, Ralph Lauren, and Diane von Furstenberg.)[52] CFDA designers tend to dominate the press on the issue of design piracy in fashion, in part because they are famous names and sometimes colorful figures. But they cannot be said to represent the industry as a whole. A large number of apparel firms, particularly those in the California Fashion Association (fashion is the largest manufacturing industry in Los Angeles, the second largest city in the nation), have made clear that they are opposed to legal protection for fashion designs.[53] And the member firms of the American Association of Footwear and Apparel (AAFA), the major national trade association representing apparel companies, held a vote and found that opinion was too divided to allow it to support the proposed design protection legislation.

If this was not evidence enough of the substantial disagreements within the fashion industry over expanding copyright protection, one need only look at the long-term stability of the current low-IP regime. Despite scattered and generally feeble efforts over the last few decades to amend the law, fashion design has remained outside the scope of American copyright.[54] In a world in which content providers have, in recent years, successfully lobbied Congress for an amazing array of new protections, it bears repeating that the persistence of the current legal regime for apparel is remarkable. We think the most compelling explanation for this doctrinal persistence is the simplest: the industry's preferences have been too heterogeneous, and too many players have perceived ample benefit and little downside from the freedom to copy and draw inspiration.

Conclusion

To many, the IP dimensions of the fashion industry probably seem trivial. Fashion has never received the scholarly attention granted to other creative industries, such as music, film, or even fine art. Yet the apparel industry is both economically significant and highly creative. Most significantly, fashion operates under an unusual legal regime, in which design appropriation is a pervasive aspect of the business. That the industry remains viable, and even vibrant, in the face of widespread copying is both interesting and important.

---

52. For the membership roll, see Council of Fashion Designers of America, http://www.cfda.com (follow the "Members" hyperlink) (last visited Feb. 18, 2009).

53. One of us (Raustiala) has consulted with the California Fashion Association regarding its efforts to meet with California Senators and Congressmen and women in order to express opposition to the proposed design copyright legislation.

54. Hemphill and Suk claim that the reason we do not see copyright protection for fashion design—the central question in our original paper—is that the designers "are not sufficiently powerful" and were opposed by retailers and manufacturers. Hemphill & Suk, *supra* note 6, at 1184. We addressed this hypothesis at length in *The Piracy Paradox* and rejected it. While the question is hardly closed, nothing in *The Law, Economics, and Culture of Fashion* changes our view on this point.

The Law, Culture, and Economics of Fashion is a welcome contribution to the growing literature on the IP of fashion. We certainly disagree with Hemphill and Suk on the particulars of legal reform in the area, and we have deeper theoretical disagreements as well. But we are nonetheless pleased that they have tackled the issue in a serious manner, and have offered a novel synthesis of cultural and economic analysis.

Like other recent work on fashion, cuisine, magic, and the like, *The Law, Culture, and Economics of Fashion* also helps us to better understand IP's negative space. It is understandable why lawyers and legal scholars would largely focus on what IP law protects, rather than what it ignores. But we believe that understanding why some forms of creativity are in IP's domain while others are out is an urgent and important task. The larger lessons that can be drawn from fields like fashion and food are not yet clear. But to some degree this is a function only of our long-standing inattention and resultant (albeit remediable) ignorance, and for this reason we are glad that more scholars now see fit to explore these unusual fields.

Moreover, a better understanding of the dynamics of creativity in fashion and other fields where intellectual production takes place without, or with little, IP law will shed new and important light on the ongoing debates over the proper scope of IP rights. As many scholars before us have argued, IP rights are costly monopoly grants that ought to be created only when necessary to foster innovation. If, indeed, substantial innovation occurs absent legal protection, we ought to know why and when. The fashion industry, which survives and even thrives without substantial IP protections for its designs, provides an excellent window on this question.

D. Conclusion

Fashion is dynamic, ephemeral, global, and thought provoking. Moreover, we can all relate to it. We all get dressed and we all make choices about what we wear and what those choices mean more broadly—to people we interact with and to ourselves. This casebook addresses the principal legal issues and commercial challenges facing this industry in both the United States and internationally, and how these issues inform the practice of law and the way we think about the law. As *Vogue* editor and fashion legend Anna Wintour once famously said, "You either know fashion or you don't." Our sincere goal with this casebook is that you definitively get to "know fashion" as it intersects with the law. So let's get to it!

Chapter 1

Formation, Fashion Finance, and Mergers and Acquisitions

Douglas Hand

A. Forming the Company

1. Introduction

First there is an idea: Perhaps it's a single garment; Maybe it's an entire line of lifestyle products for women, men, and children; It could be a retail concept centered on beauty products and wellness. Whatever it is, this idea and a person's willingness to pursue it as a business drives the choices that follow. At the outset of a fashion brand or retail concept, founders consider many of the same criteria as other company founders when it comes time to formalize their business and turn their fashion concepts and creations into profit.

The number of founders, for example, will help determine whether the business should be structured as a sole proprietorship, a partnership, a limited liability company ("LLC"), or a corporation. In addition to the number of players involved, the founder's comfort level with risk and the necessity for outside capital can also guide the ultimate entity structure. Most founders want to limit their risk and exposure to the value of their initial investment. As this chapter will lay out, limiting liability is a primary factor that points toward formal entity formation, as opposed to pursuing more common law arrangements, which do not insulate the business owner from personal liability. In addition to reducing risk, formal entity structures like corporations and limited liability companies make it easier for companies to raise outside capital. Investors are more comfortable going into business with founders when they clearly understand the legal structure in place. Aside from assessing risk and fundraising, founders should carefully consider the primary location of the business and the tax implications inherent in each entity form.

The most commonly formed entity types are sole proprietorships, partnerships, corporations, and LLCs. Each of these entities has different ways of dealing with governance and the competing factors of risk and reward that are inherent in growing fashion companies.

2. Sole Proprietorship

A sole proprietorship is the most basic company form. This model is classified as an individual engaging in a business without forming a separate legal entity. A sole proprietor keeps all of the profits of their business, but also assumes all of the risks of their venture. If the sole proprietorship becomes insolvent, holders of outstanding accounts can look to the proprietor's personal assets to satisfy obligations.

Though this model does not require the formation of a distinct legal entity, individuals engaging in a sole proprietorship should adhere to certain best practices. For ease of accounting and tax management down the line of the company's lifespan, a sole proprietor should open a bank account separate from their personal account. In order to provide evidence of their business name to banks upon opening an account, sole proprietors should file a "doing business as" or "DBA" certificate in the applicable county clerk's office. In addition to satisfying certain banking requirements, the filing of a DBA certificate puts both the government and the public in the jurisdiction where filed on notice that the proprietor is doing business under a pseudonym. The filing fee for DBA certificates varies across state lines but is generally modest. New York's DBA filing fee, for example, is $25.[1] Sole proprietors should also obtain an employment identification number, or EIN, prior to hiring employees. Having an EIN in place before building out a staff helps the company comply with federal tax requirements. A sole proprietor can file for an EIN by completing the SS-4 form found on the Federal Internal Revenue Service's website. State law, like that in place in New York and California, may also require additional tax identification numbers.

3. Partnership

A partnership is a company model pursued by two or more individuals. Unlike a sole proprietorship, partnerships may exist informally, as a common law partnership, or formally, through the codification of their business unit in a partnership agreement. A partnership agreement is a contract by and between the partners to set the terms of their relationship to each other and to their business. These sorts of agreements specify the partners' ownership percentages, the method for distributing profits and allocating losses among the partners, the length of the partnership, and the process to withdraw from or join in the partnership. Partnership agreements, therefore, can reduce uncertainty and manage the expectations of the initial players. Common law partnerships do not afford this sort of protection but have the advantage of being more flexible.

Partnerships, like sole proprietorships, should have their own bank account, file for a DBA certificate, and apply for an EIN. In a general partnership, the owners

1. For a profile of New York filing fees, see generally *Certificate of Assumed Name*, N.Y. St. Dep't St., Division of Corps., St. Recs. & UCC, www.dos.ny.gov/corps/assdnmins.html (last visited June 2, 2020).

of the business share in all of the profits and losses of the enterprise. Limited partnerships, however, allow certain partners to limit their liability to the value of the funds they have contributed to the business. Limited partners are not allowed to become involved in the day-to-day management of the business, and a heavy hand can ruin their status and open them up to the same liability as the other partners. Private equity firms often invest through limited partners to protect the assets of the firm. Partnerships, whether limited or general, are also known for their "pass-through" tax treatment. The partnership itself is not taxed; income and deductions are instead reported on the partners' personal tax returns.

4. Corporations

Other legal entity models, such as the corporation, are not defined by the number of initial owners and are far more prevalent among fashion brands and retail companies. Corporations are formed under state law and can have one or many owners. The owners of a corporation are called shareholders and their ownership interests are represented by shares of capital stock. Because these entities have more owners than just the initial founders, it is common for founders to restrict and control the actions of company shareholders with stockholder agreements.

Corporations are created by a formal filing process. Interested founders should file a certificate of incorporation, also known as a charter, with the Secretary of State or the Department of Corporations. The individual filing office varies state-by-state, but all charters should clearly establish the corporation's name, purpose, and registered agent. The purpose set forth in the charter can be as vague as "to engage in anything not prohibited by state law" but, for a fashion brand or retail company, more often articulates a very broad ability to engage in any and all business enterprises related to fashion and retail (so as not to require a charter amendment if and when a new product category—e.g., a brand expanding from selling apparel to also including accessories—is added). Corporate charters must also specify the type and number of authorized shares of company equity (or stock), along with the rights and preferences associated with each class of shares. Because of this, the charter is a living document and must be amended when the company changes its corporate capital structure. These sorts of changes occur when the company goes through a financing or adopts a stock and reserves certain common shares for issuance thereunder.

Like all other entities, a corporate bank account should be opened in connection with the business. The corporate bank account should be established at the first meeting so that the company can deposit the proceeds from initial stockholders. In addition to a charter, corporations need to have bylaws, a board of directors, officers, annual meetings, and minute books. Corporate bylaws are the primary documents for corporations and direct the operations of these types of companies in greater detail than charters. The leaders of the corporation include the board of directors, who are elected by the shareholders, and the officers, who are appointed by the board of directors after the formation of the company. The directors are charged with corporate governance at the highest level, whereas the officers are responsible for the day-to-day operation of the business. Common required initial officer positions, which vary state by state, include: a president, a treasurer, and a corporate secretary. Required annual meetings must be held for both the directors and for all of the shareholders of the company. These meetings are recorded in the minute books along with other corporate resolutions for actions taken by the board and the shareholders. Examples of these actions include amending the charter, implementing a stock pool, granting stock options, and issuing company debt over a certain threshold. The requirement to follow these formalities is sometimes why start-ups are reluctant to form as a corporation. However, in order to go public in an initial public offering ("IPO") and trade on an exchange like the New York Stock Exchange or NASDAQ, a company must be a corporation. Examples of fashion companies that have successfully completed IPOs include household mega-brands like Ralph Lauren and Michael Kors.

5. C-Corporations and S-Corporations—Tax Considerations

Unlike "pass-through" entities such as partnerships, corporations are taxed on profits at corporate tax rates, and this most common type of corporation is called a C-corporation. If a corporation elects, however, the company may be treated as an S-corporation under Subchapter S of the Internal Revenue Code. S-corporations are treated as partnerships for tax purposes. As a result, corporate profits in S-corporations pass through the company to the stockholders. The stockholders are taxed on the profits and losses as part of their individual tax obligations.

In order to qualify as an S-corporation, the company may only have one class of stock and cannot have more than 100 stockholders. Moreover, S-corporations cannot have institutional or international shareholders—this makes it virtually impossible for S-corporations to be financed by venture capital firms or private equity firms and retain their pass-through tax status. The investors, if any, and founders need to be domestic individuals, estates, tax-exempt organizations, or qualifying trusts. This domestic individual qualification can also make the S-corporation status unattainable by many companies as many investors and the talent with which fashion brands may be founded upon are found outside of the United States.

S-corporations must re-elect to be treated as such each year. If an S-corporation fails to qualify at any time, it will be treated as a C-corporation and taxed under the default rule.

6. B-Corporations

Another subclassification of corporations is a B-corporation. A B-corporation is a company that meets predetermined standards for social and environmental performance, public transparency, and legal accountability. The standards for

B-corporations are set by B Lab, a global nonprofit organization.[2] In addition to meeting the criteria set forth by B Lab, B-corporations must pay an annual fee ranging from $500 to $50,000. The exact annual fee depends on the company's annual sales and companies must re-qualify every three years. B Lab was motivated by the idea that companies should answer to more than just their shareholders. B-corporations must consider the impact of their activities beyond shareholder returns, answering to employee, community, and environmental interests. Prominent fashion brands that are certified B-corporations include Toms, Athleta, Allbirds, and Eileen Fisher. Some of these companies, like Toms, go as far as committing to deliver free merchandise to those in need for each retail product sold.

7. LLCs

A limited liability company, or LLC, is an entity form with fewer formalities than a corporation, but more formalities than a sole proprietorship or partnership. Like corporations, LLCs are formed under state law. LLCs have multiple classes of membership interests in the company and those owners are referred to as members.

To form a limited liability company, founders must prepare and file articles of organization with the Secretary of State or the Department of Corporations. Like a corporation's charter, the cost and location for filing the articles of organization depends on the company's jurisdiction. The articles of organization state the name of the LLC, the registered agent of the LLC, whether the LLC is managed by members or managers, the effective date of the LLC, the duration of the LLC (often perpetual), and the names and signatures of the organizers of the LLC. The primary document of limited liability companies, however, is the operating agreement, not the articles of organization. The operating agreement goes further than the articles of organization with respect to setting the terms of the entity's governance. As such, the operating agreement specifies things like the methods for distributing profits and allocating losses, the methods for adding new members, and the rules with respect to interest transfers.

LLCs are often a good starting point for companies because they provide greater flexibility with respect to structuring the enterprise. Moreover, it is typically easier (as well as more common) to convert a limited liability company into a corporation than it is to convert a corporation into a limited liability company. In certain jurisdictions, limited liability companies are more expensive to establish than corporations. The primary cost driving factor is the amount of time that goes into preparing and negotiating the operating agreement, which needs to account for the specific needs of the business, but there can be other costs. Founders should be aware that some states have an expensive publication requirement for newly established LLCs. The cost to publish in New York County, New York, for example, can be as high as $1,500.

---

2. For a profile of B-Corporations and the non-profit organization, B-Lab, see *About B Corps*, Certified B Corp., https://bcorporation.net/about-b-corps (last visited June 2, 2020).

Many emerging brands were founded and still exist as limited liability companies, like Tory Burch and Rag & Bone. If these brands elect to go public in an IPO in the future, they can do so by converting to a corporation. Until then, they may function without the requirements of the corporate form.

8. Conclusion

Deciding what business type to pursue as a founder of a fashion retail brand can be intimidating. Though sole proprietorships and partnerships are associated with smaller start-up costs, these entities do not insulate their owners from liability, which may lead to tension as the company grows and the founders seek outside investment. Corporations and limited liability companies not only provide for continuity of the business through changes in ownership and management, but also provide clear paths for outsiders to fund the company through the issuance of shares and membership interests. The administrative hurdles that come with establishing the more formal corporate model, however, may guide founders to delay them until later in the company's lifecycle.

Notes

1. Why do you think founders might prefer the lack of formality that a sole proprietorship, partnership, or LLC offers to the more formal requirements of a corporation? Why don't we see more examples of sole proprietorships or partnerships among established fashion brands or retailers?

2. Why might a fashion brand that espouses environmental sustainability or fair labor practices prefer to be a B Lab-certified B-corporation? Do you think that the brand's customers notice it?

3. What states do you think most legal entities for fashion brands are formed in?

4. Do you think there are any reasons a fashion brand would form more than one legal entity for the same business? If so, how many and for what purposes?

B. Financing the Company

1. Introduction

After their founding, newly minted fashion companies will require some form of financing to provide for their basic platform. Established fashion companies will also often require financing for growth. This is due to the fact that the cash flows from operating often are not sufficient to exploit growth opportunities. Particularly in fashion, global recognition can come rapidly, which makes expansion to capitalize on increased access to customers and revenues important. If the founders cannot provide the capital necessary on their own, it is common practice to look outside to third parties.

Two financing options available to companies are the issuance of debt and equity. In addition to selling company equity and borrowing through debt, fashion companies can also use factoring and, if they are lucky, an IPO to support their business. Outside financing is not a decision to be taken lightly and the founders should make sure they are comfortable with the arrangements in place. Financing often means inviting another individual to have a stake, rights, or claim on your business idea. Founders should consider their desired amount of company control, the extent of a direct relationship that they want to retain with their customers, and the proposed reach and maintenance of their brand. Founders/designers can be quite particular regarding the type of people or organizations they allow to invest in their brands—for good reason.

2. Debt and Equity Financing

Most companies obtain capital through traditional debt and equity financing. Debt financing is when a lender, usually a bank, provides money to the company and the company, in turn, promises to repay the borrowed amount with interest. Equity financing is when an investor provides capital in exchange for a direct ownership interest in the company. The investor's ownership interest can take the form of membership interests (which can be stated as a percentage of the LLC or a number of units) for an LLC or shares for a corporation. Debt and equity financing involve varied risk from the perspective of the company and the third-party investors. Debt financing is safer for investors when it comes to potential returns. This is because loans contractually obligate the borrower to repay the lender at a specific time. Loans also provide lenders with higher priority than equity in the context of distribution waterfalls and liquidation. Equity financing is riskier for the owners of the company with respect to the founders' control over company operations and rights to distributions if the company is eventually sold. Diminished authority or voting power for the founders can even lead to a diluted brand reputation if the decisions made by investors run contrary to the expectations of customers.

a. Debt Financing

When a company raises capital through debt, they promise to repay the lender the borrowed amount (the principal) at an agreed upon time (the maturity date). Loans often require interest to be paid on the principal at an interest rate, such as two percent per year. The interest rate varies with respect to the creditworthiness of the borrower. The less creditworthy the borrower, the higher the interest rate. In arrangements with high rates, the lender is worried that the borrower may not repay on time and incentivizes them accordingly by raising the total amount owed. The interest paid on loans is generally tax deductible.

Debt financing, however, is not without its disadvantages. If a company finances through debt too much, there is an increased risk that the company will not be able to satisfy the obligations to all its lenders. Interest payments can become crippling, a hurdle to paying back principal on the debt. The storied brand and retailer, J. Crew, encountered issues with debt repayment in 2018–2019 when its revenues (while still quite solid) faltered slightly and put it on a course where repayment of interest obligations became difficult. J. Crew declared bankruptcy in 2020. Other companies, like Barney's and Neiman Marcus, have fallen prey to a similar fate and had to declare bankruptcy.

Future lenders will be hesitant to issue loans to companies with a significant amount of debt. Moreover, because debt enjoys a higher status when it comes to repayment in a liquidation, companies saddled with massive debt will likely also have trouble raising money through equity financing. This is due to the fact that all debt must be repaid before any equity investor is paid any portion of their investment.

All debt is not created equal. Debt can be issued as a term loan or a revolving loan and may be secured or unsecured. A term loan is a loan for a specified amount of money for a specified amount of time. A revolving loan, however, is a loan that can be drawn upon, repaid, and then redrawn upon again until the maturity date. In this way, revolving loans act like personal credit cards where a consumer agrees to a certain credit ceiling, to be drawn against and repaid monthly. Revolving loans, therefore, provide borrowers with the ability to limit their interest payments to the amount of money they need at any given time.

Secured debt differs from unsecured debt because it provides lenders with an additional remedy in the case of default. Because unsecured loans are not supported by company assets, the only remedy for a lender with an unpaid unsecured loan is to sue the borrower. Secured loans, however, are backed by company assets. This is called a security interest and it may be filed under the Uniform Commercial Code ("UCC"), which has the effect of perfecting it. This puts all other creditors on notice and allows the lender to take possession of the assets they have a security interest in. Because there is a lower credit risk associated with secured debt, these sorts of loans have lower interest rates than unsecured debt. As a result, secured debt is useful for borrowers with poor credit profiles because the lenders consider the value of the underlying asset when evaluating risk, not the value of the company overall.

Asset-based lending is a type of secured debt. For these loans, the funds available to the borrower are tied to the value and quality of the specified assets. The specified assets are also known as the borrowing base. The borrowing base for a fashion brand often comes in the form of the company's accounts receivable[3] and its inventory, but the borrowing base can also include intellectual property and other assets. These sorts of loans allow fashion companies to weather the working capital gaps that are likely to occur in their standard business cycles. Asset-based loans

3. Accounts receivable represent the right for the company to receive payment for goods that are already sold.

with an accounts receivable borrowing base often have a larger loan advance rate than asset-based loans with an inventory or intellectual property borrowing base, because accounts receivable are more liquid—meaning they are easier to convert into cash. There are not many financial institutions that want to be in the retail business selling a fashion brand's inventory, let alone having to monetize a brand's intellectual property. Converting a brand's accounts receivable to cash is typically far easier. However, there are circumstances where even accounts receivable are not so liquid—for instance, where the retailer that issued the accounts receivable to the borrower is itself in financial distress.

Asset-based lenders come in the form of non-bank commercial companies and banks. Bank lenders tend to be more lenient with respect to their required control over the borrowing base assets. Non-bank commercial lenders require detailed asset reports at regular intervals and direct control of accounts receivable collection. Some non-bank commercial lenders go to the lengths of creating a lockbox, which is a bank account exclusively for the benefit of the lender. Lenders with a lockbox will direct the company's customers to deposit their payments to the lender directly. It is not uncommon for these sorts of lenders to require physical access agreements in order to be able to seize control of inventory and equipment held in leased properties. A benefit of asset-based loans compared to other secured loans, despite the level of control required, is the absence of burdensome financial covenants. The maximum leverage ratio, for example, is a term included in most secured loans that limits the total amount of debt that the borrower can take on as compared to the company balance sheet. These sorts of financial covenants can indirectly limit other investment opportunities.

b. Equity Financing

In an equity financing, investors provide capital to a company in exchange for an ownership interest in the business. The value of this ownership is often dependent upon the valuation of the company prior to the investment. Equity ownership interests ("equity") are represented by shares of stock (in a corporation) or membership interests (in an LLC). Equity typically comes in two different class types, common and preferred. Common equity is indicative of company ownership with voting rights and provides the owners with an entitlement to share in company profits. Founders enjoy the benefits of common equity ownership. Preferred equity comes in many different forms, subject to what the investors in this class negotiate for (and therefore, to a large extent, are based upon the relative leverage they have at the time of the investment.) Holders of preferred equity are usually provided with several forms of protection in connection with their investment, in addition to voting. But with respect to voting, the preferred equity holders may have a specific list of items they are entitled to vote on but that they, as a class, must approve in order for the company action to take place. These are commonly referred to as preferred "veto rights" and usually cover major company actions that would:

- dilute the preferred equity holder's rights (e.g., additional issuances of preferred stock of an equal or higher class);
- reduce the preferred equity holder's priority to distributions of cash (e.g., taking on more debt);
- spend a large amount of cash (e.g., expenditures over a certain amount outside the ordinary course of business); or
- fundamentally change the business (e.g., a sale of the company or a change in the line of business from fashion or retail).

While many of these fundamental business decisions are quite appropriate for the preferred equity holders to have a veto right on, other areas of company decisions, notably creative decisions, design direction, marketing decisions, and even channels of distribution are areas that founder designers will seek to retain for themselves.

Outside of the veto rights, some of the other protections associated with preferred equity are the liquidation preference, the right to be paid a dividend, the option of conversion, the inclusion of antidilution adjustments, and the right to redeem their investment. Liquidation preferences give holders of preferred equity a priority over common equity holders by guaranteeing to pay them a certain amount before the holders of common equity receive any proceeds. Holders of preferred equity with dividend rates are entitled to a return on their investment if the company has enough surplus capital or profit. Preferred equity is also often convertible into common equity, allowing the holders to participate in the growth of the company's value and share with other common stockholders if there is a liquidity event like an IPO.

As a company issues more equity to more investors, the percentage ownership that preexisting investors have in the company is diminished. In order to combat this, holders of preferred equity with a conversion feature will often have an antidilution protection provision. If a company finances with equity at a lower valuation than the one whereby the preexisting preferred holders received their equity, these preexisting preferred investors get to have their equity repriced.

There are two main types of antidilution provisions: full ratchet and weighted average. A full ratchet antidilution adjustment reprices the cost per share to the price at which the new shares are issued in subsequent financing rounds. A weighted average antidilution adjustment sets the new conversion price as a function of the old conversion price, multiplied by the quotient of: (i) the sum of the number of outstanding shares before the new issuance of equity and the total consideration received by the company for the new issuance of equity to (ii) the sum of the number of outstanding shares or membership interests before the new issuance of equity and the number of new shares or membership interests to be issued. Some types of preferred equity also come with optional or mandatory redemption rights. Through the exercise of these rights, the investor can receive an immediate return on a fixed date.

Founders that primarily finance their company through the issuance of equity must be able to get their hands around a broad ownership base. In order to help manage and limit the cohort of investors to be dealt with at any given moment, companies often enter into agreements with their investors that restrict and/or direct equity transfers. Right of first offer and right of first refusal give investors the opportunity to purchase the equity of other investors before they can be sold to third parties. Tag-along rights require an investor wishing to sell their equity to a third party to notify the other investors and offer them an opportunity to participate in the sale. Similarly, drag-along rights allow for an investor, or group of investors, to compel other investors to participate in a sale of shares if the number of shares proposed for sale is above a certain agreed-upon threshold. Not all of these rights, however, are purely beneficial from a company standpoint. Preemptive rights, for example, clearly benefit existing investors at the expense of the company by requiring the company to offer stock to them before selling stock to new investors.

The company and its investors may look forward to the time when their company will go public in the hopes that it will provide for a substantial return on their investment. Investors holding private equity will need to have their equity registered with the U.S. Securities and Exchange Commission ("SEC") before they can offer them to be sold to the public. As a result, investors and companies often cooperate in the registration process. A demand right allows the investor to request that the company register their equity, whereas piggy-back rights allow investors to take part in the registered offering that the company undergoes for itself in connection with an IPO.

c. Initial Public Offering

A company can raise a substantial amount of capital by selling stock to the public through an IPO. An IPO allows a company to raise more funds with fewer restrictions on use. Because common stock is offered to the public at-large, IPOs can help with brand awareness and notoriety in a way that private stock sales cannot.

IPOs are costly undertakings with high accounting and legal fees. Because IPOs increase the number of stakeholders in the company who are not directly involved in its business, there is increased pressure on management to perform and provide returns. Management personnel often lament that public investors are too focused on short-term returns rather than long-term performance. Depending on where the company lists, management will also have to wrestle with certain securities laws. U.S. federal securities laws, for example, allow a purchaser in an IPO to recover damages on losses of their investment if the offering materials they relied upon to invest had an untrue statement of a material fact or omitted a material fact.[4] This opens the issuer of the IPO, the directors and corporate officers of the company, and the underwriters of the IPO to potential liability. Moreover, the SEC frequently conducts investigations and enforcement actions with respect to the company's accounting practices—potentially creating a burden on corporate officers.

4. Securities Act of 1933, 15 U.S.C. § 77a.

An IPO involves the coordination of multiple players, including company insiders and company outsiders. Underwriters, often investment banks with enough capital, commit to purchase all the shares being sold by the company and then hold them out for sale to the public. Underwriters and the company agree that the underwriter will purchase their shares at a fixed price pursuant to an underwriting agreement. To assist with the financial statements that are provided in connection with an IPO, companies engage an independent auditor. These independent auditors must be registered with the Public Company Accounting Oversight Board. Given the significant responsibility and potential liability inherent in public offerings, both the underwriters and the company engage separate legal counsel. The company's legal counsel works with management and key employees on almost all aspects of the offering, while the underwriter's counsel primarily coordinates due diligence for the underwriters.

Publicity restrictions should be put in place before the offering so that no public statements are made about the transaction that would improperly stimulate interest. This may be hard for fashion companies with large public followings, but such restrictions should remain in place from the time the company reaches an understanding with the managing underwriter until the later of the completion of the distribution of the securities or the expiration of the prospectus delivery period.[5]

In the United States, the first step in the IPO process is for the company and the underwriters to file a registration statement and prospectus with the SEC. The SEC Division of Corporation Finance then reviews and comments on the materials provided. The issuer can respond to the SEC's comments through subsequent amendments to the registration statement. After the registration statement is satisfactory in the eyes of the SEC, the company and the underwriters meet with prospective investors to convince them to invest. These meetings span multiple months and are commonly referred to as a roadshow. At the end of the roadshow, the company and the underwriters formally request that the SEC declare the registration statement to be effective. Once deemed effective, actual sales on the market can begin. Because underwriters want to avoid oversupplying the market to prevent an artificially low price, lock-up agreements are often signed with preexisting investors. Lock-up agreements require pre-IPO stockholders to hold on to their stock for up to 180 days following the IPO, unless otherwise agreed to by the underwriters.

The prospectus and registration statement must meet the specifications set forth by the SEC. These two documents allow the investors to evaluate the company prior to deciding to invest and are updated periodically to keep public stockholders in the loop regarding the company vitals. The prospectus and registration statement are supported by required financials, like audited balance sheets at the end of the company's two most recent fiscal years, income and financial statements for the company's three most recent fiscal years, and select financial data for up to a total of five years. These requirements are slightly less burdensome for companies

5. Latham & Watkins, LLP, *US IPO Guide 2019 Edition* (Dec. 3, 2019), https://www.lw.com/thoughtLeadership/lw-us-ipo-guide.

that qualify under the Jumpstart Our Business Startups Act enacted on April 5, 2012.[6] In addition to financial data, companies must provide a narrative on the status of the company's operations and a key description of the business. This narrative allows investors to view the company through the eyes of management. The description of the business must include detailed information on principal products, markets, suppliers, raw materials, key customers, back-log orders, and competitive advantages in the industry. When the financial success of a company is based on something as ephemeral as a brand and the loyalty of fashion customers, these sections can sometimes prove to be a challenging disclosure. Companies must also provide biographical information on principal management and directors, executive compensation information, and certifications evidencing CEO and CFO compliance with the SEC financial reporting and disclosure control requirements.

In addition to the financial and business information provided by the company to help investors decide whether to invest, the prospectus must explicitly state the risk factors that potential buyers of stock should be aware of prior to making their decision. These risk factors can range from the general to the specific. An example of a general risk factor included in most prospectuses is, "our industry is highly competitive and if we do not compete effectively, our operating results could be adversely affected." An example of a risk factor specific to fashion companies is, "if we are unable to anticipate and respond to changing customer preferences and shifts in fashion and industry trends in a timely manner, our business, financial condition and operating results could be harmed."[7] For eponymous brands with a living designer, another obvious risk factor is the human risk associated with the loss (or ignominy) of the designer (as we'll learn about further in the *Women's Wear Daily* article below).

With respect to deciding where to list, a company can register on the New York Stock Exchange, the NASDAQ, or an international exchange. These markets do not vary as significantly as they did in the past, taking some of the pressure off the choice of jurisdiction. Companies, however, should still steer clear of regions with particularly onerous regulatory regimes, like Hong Kong. In the end, most fashion companies list their shares to be sold in the region where they are headquartered and the place where their products sell.

d. The Challenge for Eponymous Brands

What's in a Name? The Challenge of M&A for Eponymous Brands

> "What's in a name? That which we call a rose by any other name would smell as sweet."
>
> *Romeo and Juliet (II, ii, 1–2)*

---

6. *See generally, Jumpstart Our Business Startups Act Frequently Asked Questions: Generally Applicable Questions on Title I of the JOBS Act*, SEC, https://www.sec.gov/divisions/corpfin/guidance/cfjjobsactfaq-title-i-general.htm (last visited June 2, 2020).

7. *See* Revolve Group, Inc., Registration Statement Under The Securities Act of 1933, SEC (Sept. 28, 2018), https://www.sec.gov/Archives/edgar/data/1746618/000156459018023704/ck0001746618-s1.htm.

In one of Shakespeare's most famous lines, Juliet maintains that a name is an artificial construct; a meaningless convention. I suppose Juliet, then, would have no problem selling her name to the highest bidder. For the vast majority of fashion designers, however, this prospect is met with trepidation and anxiety. Moreover, in my experience, investors often have their own particular concerns when it comes to acquiring eponymous fashion and lifestyle brands. In the context of M&A transactions, this can present a challenge for lawyers and bankers.

For some pretty obvious reasons, a namesake brand is difficult for a founder to part with. Examples of designers who have lost control of eponymous brands are far from uncommon in fashion, Joseph Abboud, Jimmy Choo, Emanuel Ungaro, Hervé Léger, Helmut Lang, Simon Spurr, Doori Chung and, of course, Jil Sander. When the very brand and trademark being sold are tied inexorably to the individual selling it, there is a fear over loss of control not just of a company, but of personal image management. The brand's story, the experience of it and its overall narrative—most of which have been based on a designer's own life—are now in the hands of an acquirer. When the founder is a fashion designer, used to tight control over the dissemination of this personal brand message (as most strong designers are), there is a profound reluctance to acquiesce.

In my experience representing brands both large and small, for the owner of an eponymous brand, the prospect of selling one's legacy, selling the family name, is a difficult choice. Add to that reluctance the fact that the business bearing the brand often amounts to a designer life's work, and it can be a difficult sell. To many strong-willed designers it may feel like a Faustian pact. As Simon Spurr aptly put it when ruminating on his dealings with his company's investors in a recent *Esquire* article: "It is like I gave birth to a beautiful baby . . . and then it was ripped from me."

From the investors' perspective as well, a namesake brand presents challenges. Consider that the investor is faced with the risk that the designer, through their designs, tastes, age, words, or actions, may go seriously off-brand. The investor cannot control the designer. In fact, the investor cannot demand that the designer continue to work for their namesake brand (even non-lawyers will recognize that forced servitude is not legal). Jil Sander walked away (the first of three times) from her brand a mere four months after it was acquired by Patrizio Bertelli, CEO of Prada. I'm quite certain that was not in Mr. Bertelli's business plan at the time of the acquisition.

By way of a recent, concrete example, juxtapose the negligible damage John Galliano's recorded anti-Jewish tirade was able to do to the house of Christian Dior (where he was creative director at the time of the incident) with what has happened to the John Galliano brand (which LVMH, to its undoubted consternation, still owns). In June, the Galliano brand announced it will overhaul its gothic logo to coincide with its transition into a "premium-contemporary" line following a licensee deal with Modalis. Right—good luck with that.

Even for a more compliant designer, the evolving (and most commercially viable) view of the brand message may be difficult to keep up with. Seeking additional revenue in geographic expansion, product extensions and ever-faster marketing and social media campaigns can take its toll. The designer may not be able to live up to the sexy, youthful, or glamorous hallmarks the brand is supposed to symbolize 24/7. Most investors have an expectation that the designer will continue to epitomize the brand, "be" the brand, but eventually (some would say inevitably) the designer may just age out. You can only take an eponymous brand with a living figurehead so far. Take the example of Donna Karan, who recently stepped down from her namesake brand. In April, Pierre-Yves Roussel, chairman of the LVMH Fashion Group, said that LVMH "knows for a fact that most people who buy DKNY did not even know it was by Donna Karan."

As Vanessa Friedman of the *New York Times* recently put it: "When designers leave, by choice or not, the value proposition becomes broken. No one needs a new bag, or a fancy dress; they desire them because of what they represent . . . Without that—the seduction and the sentiment, the promise of transformation—it's just stuff."

So how do you quantify all of these risks in a way that an investor can appropriately (read—mathematically) evaluate or that an investing public (if an IPO is the endgame) understands? Actuarial tables aside, it's very, very difficult. Hence, valuations can reflect not just in financial fundamentals, but inherently vague intangibles related to the designer and their emotional stability, family situation, internal drive, and (in a contradiction of desired personality traits) compliance.

Advisors who practice in the fashion industry with regularity are able to take these diverse elements into consideration not only when considering eponymous brand valuation, but also throughout the process of structuring and negotiating M&A transactions. Elements such as a right of first offer on the brand's trademarks (giving the designer an ability to reacquire their name if it is proposed to be sold to a third party); practical employment and noncompete provisions; and deadlock mechanisms to deal sensibly with disagreements—are all potentially on the table in a well-negotiated market deal.

The most important component of any successful M&A transaction for an eponymous brand is the fit and trust between investor and designer. That is hopefully established well before any negotiation begins and can aid in its process and successful conclusion. But the other practical alternative for a designer of a fashion and lifestyle brand upon conception and launch is to think long and hard about using their own name. If the design style and the provenance of the brand message are associated with the product, by any other name it will sell as well.

e. Factoring

Factoring is a type of financing available to companies before and after an IPO. Factoring allows fashion companies to get a percentage of their accounts receivable before they are paid, providing day-to-day cash flow that would otherwise be unavailable. When fashion companies sell their products to retailers and boutiques, they issue the buyers an invoice for the goods sold. Invoices are often payable on net-30 terms, which means that the buyer has 30 days to pay for the order. It is not uncommon, however, for buyers to take longer than the terms provide to pay, and fashion companies are rightfully hesitant to sue their retailers in the event of default. Without factoring, fashion companies must wait for the invoices to be satisfied to receive payment. Whether or not the invoices are paid on time, the fee structure creates a cash flow problem for fashion companies and makes it harder for them to satisfy future orders. Factoring solves this problem.

The third-party financier, also known as the factor, takes on all of the rights and obligations of the fashion company's accounts receivable by purchasing the outstanding invoices for an agreed upon value. The factor then notifies the company customers of their interest in the invoice and instructs them to pay the factor directly. While this arrangement can reduce the administrative and collection costs for the fashion company, it can also erode the company's relationship with its customers and retailers if the factor pursues aggressive collection techniques. In most cases, if a receivable is not paid for a reason other than the account debtor's inability to satisfy the invoice, the fashion company is charged back for the outstanding amount. This, however, is not the case for non recourse factoring, where the factor takes on the credit risk in addition to the collection costs. Because non-recourse factoring provides the company with more protection, it is often a more expensive arrangement.

Factoring relationships can also contain a debt component. In advance factoring, for example, the factor provides the business with a loan before making payment for the purchase of receivables. Advance factoring comes with the benefit of off-balance sheet financing for the business because the loans from the factor do not appear on the balance sheet.

Fashion companies are partial to factoring because it allows them to deal with fluctuations that are common in the industry, like seasonal market changes and spikes in profitability from new product lines. As with asset-based lending, factoring depends on the value of the accounts receivable, not the company credit profile, and may be available when other forms of financing are not. Fashion companies, however, should be wary to rely exclusively on factoring as a form of financing. The 2009 U.S. financial crisis highlighted this problem when a major factor faced bankruptcy and the possibility of leaving upward of 50 percent of the United States apparel and footwear companies without financing.

Notes

1. Why do you think founders might prefer debt financing to equity financing?

2. What are some of the arguments a designer/founder's counsel can make to reject proposed veto rights that touch on creative decisions, design direction, marketing

decisions, and channels of distribution? Why are those areas inappropriate for a financial investor to have control of?

3. What issues must an investor consider when investing in an eponymous brand? Why do you think, despite those risks, many investors still invest in fashion brands?

4. Do you think fashion brands do better or worse (financially) as public companies? How about in terms of their design credibility and product quality?

C. Mergers and Acquisitions

Another type of liquidity event for founders and investors is an outright sale of the company. The market for mergers and acquisitions (M&A) in fashion is an oft-reported-on subject.

M&A and Fashion: If the Deal Fits—Buy It![8]

Douglas Hand

Over the course of the last three decades, the fashion industry has undergone enormous change. Formerly, the industry was characterized by high fragmentation and smaller, family-owned enterprises. Companies sold to wholesalers rather than directly to consumers. More recently, increased consolidation and growth have led to the creation of massive international luxury corporations. The e-commerce revolution has freed many brands from reliance on wholesalers. As a result of these factors, today fashion and apparel is one of the largest sectors of the global economy.[9]

Increased globalization and advances in technology, manufacturing and distribution have changed nearly every aspect of the industry, especially the attitudes and appetites of consumers themselves.[10] Indeed, while today's Americans spend nearly the same amount (adjusted for inflation) on apparel as they did in 1965, they buy nearly twice as many articles of clothing.[11] Amidst all of this transformation, many

---

8. The following is an altered and updated version of a two-part article published in the New York University Annual Survey of American Law, reprinted courtesy of New York University School of Law.

9. *See* FASHION LAW: A GUIDE FOR DESIGNERS, FASHION EXECUTIVES, AND ATTORNEYS (Guillermo C. Jimenez & Barbara Kolsun eds., 2009); *see also* Scott C. Hemphill & Jeannie Suk, *The Law, Culture, and Economics of Fashion*, 61 STAN. L. REV. 1147, 1148 (2009).

10. *See generally* Vertica Bhardawaj & Ann Fairhurst, *Fast Fashion: Response to Changes in the Fashion Industry*, 20 THE INT'L. REV. OF RETAIL, DISTRIBUTION AND CONSUMER RES., 165, 173 (2010).

11. FASHION LAW, *supra* note 9, at 6.

fashion companies[12] have undertaken strategic mergers and acquisitions ("M&A") to consolidate risk and capitalize on opportunities.[13]

M&A has historically proven enormously successful for the world's leading fashion companies,[14] which, by most critical accounts, have been able to successfully exploit their size without diminishing the value of their brands.[15] Smaller companies have also turned to M&A to improve brand awareness and gain market share.[16] Companies seeking to grow through M&A have "chosen vertical integrations in order to strengthen their positions inside the pipeline; others have implemented horizontal growth by acquiring competitors or companies with related product lines."[17] Private equity funds and entrepreneurs have also been involved in acquiring fashion companies, with mixed levels of success.[18]

---

12. In this Article, I use the term "fashion companies" generically to refer to fashion and apparel businesses, which may take on any number of legal entity forms.

13. Vicki M. Young, *Study Predicts More Megadeals; Rebound in Valuations Ahead*, Women's Wear Daily (May 22, 2017), http://wwd.com/business-news/mergers-acquisitions/study-predicts-more-mega-deals-rebound-valuations-ahead-a-t-kearney-retail-consumer-mergers-acquisitions-10891405/; Kali Hays, *Mergers Could Be the New Trend in Luxury*, Women's Wear Daily (Apr. 3, 2017), http://wwd.com/business-news/mergers-acquisitions/mergers-could-be-the-new-trend-in-luxury-fashion-10855930/; *See, e.g.*, Luisa Zargani, *Global M&A Activity Up 30% in 2016*, Women's Wear Daily (Mar. 10, 2017), http://wwd.com/business-news/mergers-acquisitions/global-ma-activity-up-30-in-10841891/.

14. Jennifer Hirshlag, *Marriages Made to Profit*, Women's Wear Daily (Sept. 11, 2006), http://www.wwd.com/beauty-industry-news/financial/marriages-made-to-profit-524616; *see also* Fashion Law *supra* note 9, at 7.

15. *See* Barbara Rovetta, *Growth Through Acquisitions: The Case of Fashion Industry* (SDA Bocconi, Research Div. Working Paper No. 01-60, 2001), http://papers.ssrn.com/sol3/papers.cfm?abstract_id=292580. Some companies have had greater challenges implementing a multi-brand strategy. *Id.* at 13–16.

16. *Id.* at 12. *See also* Lisa Lockwood, *Analysis: Sell Or Go It Alone*, Women's Wear Daily (July 6, 2011), http://www.wwd.com/markets-news/ready-to-wear-sportswear/staying-independent-vs-selling-out-3701351.

17. Rovetta, *supra* note 15, at 18. *See, e.g.*, Elizabeth Paton & Chad Bray, *Michael Kors to Buy Jimmy Choo in $1.2 Billion Deal*, N.Y. Times (July 25, 2017), https://www.nytimes.com/2017/07/25/business/dealbook/jimmy-choo-michael-kors.html.

18. Vicki M. Young, *True Religion Bankruptcy: A Harbinger for Fashion Brands?*, Women's Wear Daily (July 6, 2017), http://wwd.com/business-news/financial/true-religion-bankruptcy-raises-questions-fashion-brands-restructuring-leveraged-balance-sheet-private-equity-nine-west-vince-nydj-10940002/ (discussing how several private equity-backed retailers face bankruptcy); William Louch & Paul Hodkinson, *3i lost £45 million on Agent Provocateur*, Financial News (Mar. 3, 2017), https://www.fnlondon.com/articles/3i-lost-45-million-on-agent-provocateur-20170303 (discussing how London-based private equity firm 3i Group lost £45 million on its investment in Agent Provocateur); Andrew Roberts & Anne-Sylvanie Chassany, *Can Private Equity and Fashion Look Good Together?*, Bloomberg Businessweek (Apr. 22, 2010), http://www.businessweek.com/magazine/content/10_18/b4176061970665.htm (describing how Apax Partners sold Tommy Hilfiger for $3 billion, quintupling its investment in the American design house); *Luxury Fashion a la Mode for Private Equity Buyers*, Made In Italy Fund (Nov. 2, 2018), https://www.madeinitalyfund.com/luxury-fashion-a-la-mode-for-private-equity-buyers/ (noting that "Carlyle's luxury coat brand Moncler listed on the Italian stock exchange in a €1bn IPO in 2013—one of the biggest ever flotations in the European luxury sector—and Permira made a 2.3x return on

1. Strategic Development — The Process Before the Process

a. Synergies

Regardless of the industry category or structure, most mergers and acquisitions share a common objective: the combining of two companies worth more together than separately — or in M&A parlance, achieving synergies.[19] While in theory achieving synergies is reasonably simple, historical trends show that roughly two-thirds of mergers will fail to achieve the anticipated financial success projected by principals and investment bankers.[20] As one senior financial professional stated, "failure starts right at the beginning," as acquirers get excited about an opportunity and cast any notion of strategy to the side.[21] For an acquirer in the fashion industry in particular, formulating and implementing the right M&A strategy and sticking to it can mean the difference between a successful investment or acquisition and a financial failure.

The evaluation of strategic development for a fashion company needs to be viewed with an eye toward maximizing revenues (which itself is a project largely dependent on an ever-evolving, entitled, and fickle customer base), and/or minimizing costs while simultaneously managing and incentivizing the eponymous or lead designer and existing management team, as applicable.

The strategic development process begins as a highly introspective one, given that finding the right fit requires the fashion company to first determine its own strengths and weaknesses. Potential acquirers should ask themselves: (1) what do we lack that can be supplied by an acquisition? and (2) what strengths or assets,

---

its Valentino and Hugo Boss investments in 2015" and reflecting that "[t]he influx of private equity investors into fashion has tangibly grown, and the industry has seen several large deals backed by private equity in recent years"); *See, e.g.*, Evan Clark & David Moin, *Retail's Private Equity Legacy: Big Debt, Big Problems*, WOMEN'S WEAR DAILY (May 10, 2017), http://wwd.com/business-news/financial/retail-private-equity-legacy-big-debt-big-problems-bankruptcy-chapter-stores-malls-10884150/ (describing how several private equity-backed retailers have recently faced liquidation and restructuring (such as The Limited and Gymboree) and/or heavily leveraged (such as Neiman Marcus)); *But see, e.g.*, Scott Deveau & Alex Barinka, *Canada Goose Soars in Debut After IPO Puts It Atop Luxury Peers*, BLOOMBERG (Mar. 16, 2017), https://www.bloomberg.com/news/articles/2017-03-16/canada-goose-soars-in-trading-debut-with-peak-luxury-valuation (describing how Bain Capital acquired a majority 70% stake in Canada Goose in 2013 at a valuation of $250 million and successfully closed the brand's $3.4 billion initial public offering in March 2017).

19. STANLEY FOSTER REED & ALEXANDRA REED LAJOUX, THE ART OF M&A: A MERGER ACQUISITION BUYOUT GUIDE 26 (2nd ed. 1995) (defining synergy as the value of the combined companies is greater than the sum of their parts — one plus one equaling three).

20. PAUL A. PAUTLER, THE EFFECTS OF MERGERS AND POST-MERGER INTEGRATION: A REVIEW OF BUSINESS CONSULTING LITERATURE 5 n.6 (2003), http://www.ftc.gov/be/rt/businesreviewpaper.pdf.

21. *See* Robert J. Aiello & Michael D. Watkinds, *The Fine Art of Friendly Acquisition*, HARV. BUS. REV. (2000), http://www.manyworlds.com/logContent.aspx?to=coViewURLLink&coid=CO1113001225669.

human and physical, do we have that are transferable to the merger or acquisition?[22] The sources of revenues for fashion companies typically come from one of three fairly distinct sources:

- wholesale sales to retail stores and online e-commerce retailers;[23]
- direct retail sales (via directly owned retail stores or e-commerce sites);[24] and
- ancillary royalty and/or design services revenue from licensing, franchising, or collaborations.[25]

The sources of costs typically associated with fashion companies are:

- raw materials (fabric, leather, finishings);
- production costs;
- shipping and associated costs;
- marketing, public relations, and advertising;
- sales; and
- retail store and/or e-commerce operations.

A company looking to make an acquisition needs to determine which of these resources it is seeking to gain, and which it can provide.

This philosophy also applies to private equity and other financial acquirers—buying companies that fit within the acquirer's scope of expertise is preferable, both for the acquirer and the target. The success of Apax Partners, a private equity firm with

---

22. At any point during this process of introspection, the parties may discover that the potential sale or acquisition is simply not worth pursuing. For example, following a lengthy period of negotiation and due diligence, Aldo Group and Camuto Group halted plans for the sale of Camuto Group's footwear and accessories business to Aldo Group. The parties acknowledged their complementary strengths and expressed that they look forward to exploring other opportunities with one another in the future. Vicki M. Young, *Aldo and Camuto Put the Brakes on Acquisition Plan*, Women's Wear Daily (Oct. 19, 2017), http://wwd.com/business-news/mergers-acquisitions/aldo-group-camuto-group-stop-acquisition-11-31789; *see* Chantal Fernandez, *Aldo Group Calls Off Camuto Group Acquisition*, Bus. of Fashion (Oct. 20, 2017), https://www.businessoffashion.com/articles/news-analysis/aldo-group-calls-off-camuto-group-acquisition.

23. This is the traditional business of fashion houses from Acne Studios to Zadig + Voltaire.

24. Traditionally, direct retail sales are the purview of large fashion companies, such as The Gap and J.Crew, and a growing segment for smaller fashion companies, such as Steven Alan and Theory. It is worth noting that a direct-to-consumer trend has emerged in recent years with smaller fashion companies seeking to eliminate intermediaries and offer consumers higher quality products at a lower price point. Popular direct-to-consumer fashion companies include, for example, Warby Parker, Reformation, Cuyana, The Arrivals, Everlane, Leonard and Church, Tamara Mellon and Away.

25. As the economic climate in retail continues to evolve, shorter term collaborations are growing increasingly popular in lieu of longer-term licensing and franchising arrangements. Collaborations allow fashion companies to negotiate one-off or limited capsule collections with other retailers or manufacturers, among others, and avoid the multi-year and otherwise more rigid obligations inherent in a traditional licensing or franchising agreement. Vera Wang, Calvin Klein, and Kenneth Cole, to name a few, have all effectively implemented collaborations in recent years.

a consumer retail focus, which exited from its Tommy Hilfiger investment in 2010 (quintupling its investment in four years), is a good example of industry knowledge leading to desired results.[26] Other examples of recent private equity acquisitions abound and include, among others, Apax Partners' September 2017 acquisition of British luxury e-commerce group matchesfashion.com for approximately £800 million, the Carlyle Group's February 2017 acquisition of Italian luxury sneaker company Golden Goose Deluxe Brand for an undisclosed amount,[27] Crescent Capital Partners' February 2017 acquisition of Australian swimwear company Tigerlily for $46 million[28] and Palamon Capital Partners January 2017 acquisition of Swedish sock design company Happy Socks for $81.2 million.[29] Similarly, in 2017, the Carlyle Group, purchased a 50 percent stake in Supreme, which is currently one of the fastest-growing streetwear brands in the fashion industry.[30] International investment firms have also taken an interest in the fashion industry. For example, in 2018, China's conglomerate investment firm Fosun purchased a majority stake in *France's* oldest surviving couture house, Lanvin,[31] and bought a majority stake in Austrian lingerie brand, Wolford, in a €55 million transaction.[32]

---

26. *See* Roberts & Chassany, *supra* note 18.

27. *See* Luisa Zargani, *The Carlyle Group to Acquire Golden Goose Deluxe Brand*, Women's Wear Daily (Feb. 2, 2017), http://wwd.com/business-news/mergers-acquisitions/carlyle-group-to-acquire-golden-goose-deluxe-brand-10775256.

28. *See* Patty Huntington, *Billabong Sheds Tigerlily in $46 Million Deal*, (Feb. 22, 2017), Women's Wear Daily, http://wwd.com/business-news/mergers-acquisitions/billabong-sheds-tiger-lily-46-million-dollar-deal-10815307/

29. *See* Vicki M. Young, *Happy Socks Acquired by Palamon Capital Partners for $81.2M*, Women's Wear Daily (Jan. 16, 2017), http://wwd.com/business-news/mergers-acquisitions/happy-socks-acquired-palamon-capital-partners-81-2m-mergers-acquisitions-accessories-hosiery-10751755.

30. *See* Evan Clark, *Supreme Finances, the Hot Brand Looks for CFO,* Women's wear daily (Dec. 20 2017) https://wwd.com/business-news/financial/supreme-finances-cfo-skate-carlyle-goode-11078735/; *see also* Evan Clark and Aria Hughes, *A Supreme Deal: 1B Valuation From Carlyle* Women's wear daily (Oct. 9 2017), https://wwd.com/business-news/financial/supreme-deal-carlyle-1b-valuation-skate-private-equity-james-jebbia-11022869/ ("[Supreme] sold a 50 percent stake in its business to private equity giant Carlyle for $500 million . . .").

31. Robert Williams, *China Giant Buys France's Oldest Fashion House*, Bloomberg (Feb. 22, 2018), https://www.bloomberg.com/news/articles/2018-02-22/fosun-international-acquires-oldest-french-fashion-house-lanvin (noting that "Fosun International Ltd. has acquired a majority stake in French fashion house Lanvin for an undisclosed sum as Chinese conglomerates build up their luxury-goods holdings"); *See China's Fosun Buys Majority Stake in French Fashion House Lanvin*, Reuters (Feb. 22, 2018, 4:21 AM), https://www.reuters.com/article/lanvin-ma-fosun-intl/chinas-fosun-buys-majority-stake-in-french-fashion-house-lanvin-idUSFWN1QC0JG.

32. Prachi Singh, *Fosun Completes Acquisition of Majority Stake in Wolford*, Fashion United (May 7, 2018), https://fashionunited.com/executive/management/fosun-completes-acquisition-of-majority-stake-in-wolford/2018050721021 (noting that "[f]ollowing the acquisition of 50.87 percent of the shares from the previous majority shareholders, Fosun Industrial Holdings Limited, a group controlled by Chinese billionaire Guo Guangchang is now the new main shareholder of Wolford, maker of luxury hosiery, bras, and bodywear"); *see* Kirsti Knolle, *China's Fosun to Take Control of Austrian Lingerie Maker Wolford*, Reuters (Mar. 1, 2018, 6:04 AM), https://www.reuters.com/article/us-wolford-m-a-fosun-intl/chinas-fosun-to-take-control-of-austrian-lingerie-maker-wolford-idUSKCN1GD4PW.

b. Cautionary Tales

Being actively involved in the business of fashion has often been a necessary key to success. Even a disciplined institutional investor with only slight knowledge of the fashion industry may find the intangible assets of a fashion company difficult to value; misjudge the lasting appeal of the brand; make poor judgments in operating (or choosing who operates) the brand; or choose the wrong design talent. Recent cautionary tales abound:

- Men's Wearhouse acquired competitor Jos A. Bank for $1.8 billion in 2014, creating one of the largest men's apparel chains in the United States under the new holding company name "Tailored Brands, Inc." ("TBI").[33] As part of its post-acquisition strategy, TBI eliminated Jos A. Bank's well-known "buy one suit, get three" deals in 2015. The company has experienced severe losses ever since. While there was significant improvement in TBI's financial results in its most recent quarter,[34] it remains to be seen whether the acquisition is finally paying off, or whether the uptick is a final fleeting sign of life pre-death.
- London-based private equity firm 3i Group acquired luxury lingerie brand Agent Provocateur for approximately £40 million in 2007.[35] Although 3i Group injected additional investments into the brand and even implemented a debt restructuring to save its initial investments, the brand entered bankruptcy protection and was sold off in early 2017.[36] 3i Group attributed the loss to a mix of declines in Russian consumer spending, the inconsistent execution of its recent store expansion program, and the discovery of accounting issues.[37]
- LVMH Moët Hennessy Louis Vuitton ("LVMH") had struggled with Donna Karan International ("DKI") since acquiring the brand in 2001.[38] In 2015, Ms. Karan exited as lead designer of her eponymous brand, pointing to her strained relationship with LVMH and telling *The New York Times* that "Vuitton ha[d] given [her] the cold shoulder."[39] The next year, LVMH sold DKI to G-III Apparel Group for a disclosed enterprise value of $650 million, essentially breaking

---

33. Austen Hufford, *Men's Wearhouse Continues to Be Hurt by Jos. A. Bank*, Wall St. J. (Feb. 16, 2016), https://www.wsj.com/articles/jos-a-banks-same-store-sales-drop-32-1455627723; *See* Phil Wahba, *Buying Jos. A Bank Has Been a Catastrophe for Men's Wearhouse*, Fortune (Dec. 10, 2015), http://fortune.com/2015/12/10/jos-a-bank-mens-wearhouse-results/.

34. Press Release, Tailored Brands, Inc., Tailored Brands, Inc. Reports Fiscal 2017 Second Quarter Results (Sept. 7, 2017), https://ir.tailoredbrands.com/press-releases/detail/1822.

35. Louch & Hodkinson, *supra* note 18.

36. Samantha Conti, *Four Holdings Buys Ailing Agent Provocateur*, Women's Wear Daily (Mar. 2, 2017), http://wwd.com/business-news/mergers-acquisitions/four-holdings-buys-ailing-agent-provocateur-10828884/.

37. Louch & Hodkinson, *supra*, note 18. *See* Vicki M. Young, *supra* note 18 (describing how private equity firms over-leverage retailers, putting them on a slippery slope to bankruptcy).

38. *See* Vanessa Friedman, *Ivanka Trump's Manufacturer Just Bought Donna Karan Label From LVMH*, N.Y. Times (July 25, 2016), https://www.nytimes.com/2016/07/26/business/dealbook/lvmh-sells-donna-karan.html.

39. *Id.*

even in what was perceived to be a "rare admission of failure on the part of LVMH."[40]

c. Growth Strategies

One potential strategy for growth is market intensification or, as it is sometimes called, horizontal integration. Market intensification is accomplished by buying out companies that are in direct competition and share the same product lines and markets. Adidas' acquisition of Reebok in 2005 is a classic example of such a transaction,[41] with more recent examples being Luxottica Group's January 2017 $49 billion merger with Essilor of France,[42] Net-a-Porter Group's 2015 £936 million merger with yoox.com,[43] and L'Occitane's roughly $900 million purchase of luxury skincare brand, Elemis.[44] Similarly, in June 2018, Authentic Brands Group LLC (ABG) closed on its $340 million acquisition of Nine West and Bandolino, expanding ABG's reach and rendering it a dominant leader in the footwear industry.[45] Market intensification transactions can allow a company to gain market share and may have additional synergistic benefits. Often this strategy is about infusing a tired brand with that ephemeral but critical component of "cool." For example, accessible luxury retailer Michael Kors Holdings ("Michael Kors") acquired U.K.-based luxury footwear company Jimmy Choo in July 2017 for £896 million as part of its larger strategy to update Michael Kors with a more international, "upmarket aura" following an extended period of languishing profits.[46] Continuing its efforts to

---

40. *Id.*

41. *See The Adidas-Reebok Merger*, CASESTUDYINC.COM (Jan. 8, 2010), http://www.casestudyinc.com/Case-Study-Adidas-Reebok-Merger.

42. *See* Chad Bray & Elizabeth Paton, *Luxottica, Owner of Ray-Ban, in $49 Billion Merger With Essilor*, N.Y. TIMES (Jan. 16, 2017), https://www.nytimes.com/2017/01/16/business/dealbook/luxottica-essilor-merger.html.

43. Chad Bray & Vanessa Friedman, *Yoox to Merge With Net-a-Porter in All-Share Deal*, N.Y. TIMES (Mar. 31, 2015), https://www.nytimes.com/2015/04/01/business/dealbook/yoox-group-agrees-to-merge-with-net-a-porter-in-all-share-deal.html.

44. *See* Press Release, Groupe L'Occitane, The L'Occitane Group Acquires Premium Skincare Brand ELEMIS (Jan. 1, 2019), https://group.loccitane.com/group/news/loccitane-group-acquires-premium-skincare-brand-elemis; *see also* Daphne Howland, *L'Occitane Buys British Skincare Brand Elemis for $900M*, RETAIL DIVE (Jan. 16, 2019), https://www.retaildive.com/news/loccitane-buys-british-skincare-brand-elemis-for-900m/546183/; *see also* Zaneta Cheng, *L'Occitane Profits Surges 21.8 Percent*, WWD (June 17, 2019), https://wwd.com/beauty-industry-news/skin-care/loccitane-profits-surges-21-8-percent-1203181866/ (discussing that "the increase in profits can be attributed to targeted investments and acquisitions made to strengthen the brand's position in the skincare market").

45. Vicki M. Young, *Nine West, Bandolino Brands Sold to ABG for $340 Million*, WWD (June 11, 2018), https://wwd.com/fashion-news/fashion-scoops/nine-west-bandolino-brands-sold-to-abg-authentic-brands-group-bankruptcy-340m-1202702786/; *see* Press Release, Authentic Brands Group, ABG Completes the Acquisition of Nine West and Bandolino (July 3, 2018), https://www.authenticbrandsgroup.com/news/2018/7/9/abg-completes-the-acquisition-of-nine-west-and-bandolino.

46. Paton & Brady, *supra* note 15.

expand within the luxury goods market, in 2018, Michael Kors purchased the iconic Italian brand Versace for $2.1 billion.[47] That said, having two former competitors exist under one roof can be fraught with challenges—like having two peacocks in the same pen. Managers run the risk of undermining the "core values on which the brand(s) have built their identity."[48] Thus, anticipating the challenges unique to each acquisition and having a post-acquisition integration plan in place is critical.

Another potential strategy is a product extension acquisition. Such a transaction involves the acquirer purchasing another company that sells different-but-related products in the same market. Think swimwear and underwear; luggage and accessories; or fragrance and cosmetics. This allows the acquirer to add a product to a company's existing line of products "that can be sold in [its] present geographic area [or] to its present customers."[49] A product extension acquisition or merger can be of particular value to companies that have seasonal business as well as to companies that are entrenched in a particular market.[50] Also, to the extent the acquirer plans on extending into the related product line under its own label, acquiring a brand already in that product line speeds up that extension (and potentially permits the acquired company to extend into the acquirer's product core competency under the guidance of the acquirer). For example, Coach Inc., traditionally a leather goods company, acquired designer footwear company Stuart Weitzman for up to $574 million in January 2015, and rival handbag and apparel maker Kate Spade Inc. for $2.4 billion in May 2017.[51] Coach Inc. changed its holding company name to the more wide-ranging "Tapestry Inc." in the process, with [then-] chief executive officer Victor Luis explaining the desire to not be limited to any specific product category.[52] On a smaller scale, in October 2017 Lacoste Group acquired an 80 [percent] stake in Tecnifibre, a French company specializing in tennis and squash equipment. Thierry Guibert, chief executive officer of Lacoste Group, stated that the acquisition

---

47. Michael J. de la Merced & Elizabeth Paton, *Michael Kors to Buy Versace for $2.1 Billion in Bid to Expand*, N.Y. Times (Sept. 25, 2018), https://www.nytimes.com/2018/09/25/business/dealbook/michael-kors-versace.html; *see* Nicole Phelps, *Michael Kors Acquires Versace for More Than $2.12 Billion*, Vogue (Sept. 25, 2018), https://www.vogue.com/article/michael-kors-acquires-versace?verso=true; Lauren Hirsch, *Michael Kors to Buy Versace for $2.1 Billion and Change Its Name to Capri Holdings*, CNBC (Sept. 25, 2018, 7:01 AM), https://www.cnbc.com/2018/09/25/michael-kors-to-buy-versace-laying-claim-to-european-luxury-market.html.

48. *See* Rovetta, *supra* note 15, at 16.

49. *Id.*; *see, e.g.*, Kathryn Hopkins, *Delta Galil to Acquire Intimates Company Bogart*, Women's Wear Daily (June 10, 2019), https://wwd.com/business-news/financial/deltagalil-acquires-intimates-company-bogart-1203163724/ (discussing Delta Galil's, a group that "already owns Seven For All Mankind and Splendid/Ella Moss," planned acquisition of Bogart, which allows the group to "tak[e] a bigger slice of the intimate market" by "turn[ing] its attention to Asia").

50. *See, e.g.*, Rovetta, *supra* note 7 at 27–28.

51. Vanessa Friedman, *Coach Inc. Is Dead. Long Live Tapestry*, N.Y. Times (Oct. 11, 2017), https://www.nytimes.com/2017/10/11/fashion/coach-inc-rebrands-tapestry-american-fashion-group.html.

52. *Id.*

would facilitate the development of technical equipment by the Lacoste brand.[53] Most recently, Milliken & Company, a textile manufacturer, acquired Polartec, LLC, a brand that is famous for its outdoor and military apparel. Halsey Cook, president and CEO of Milliken & Company, noted that "[t]he strategic acquisition broadens our textile capabilities with a product offering to now include fleece and soft-shell outerwear . . . allowing us to grow in new and exciting spaces."[54] Similarly, Canada Goose Holdings Inc., a brand best-known for its winter coats, acquired Baffin, Inc., a company that manufactures performance outdoor and industrial footwear, for C$32.5 million.[55]

Market extension is another strategy that fashion companies consider. In a market extension, a company extends its geographical reach by acquiring a company that sells the same products in different markets.[56] Market extensions can increase efficiency by reducing operational costs. Recent examples of market extension transactions include Canadian retailer Hudson's Bay Co.'s ("HBC") $2.9 billion acquisition of Saks Inc. in 2013 and $250 million acquisition of Gilt Groupe in 2016, each of which gave HBC greater access to the U.S. market.[57] Any company considering a market extension needs to analyze the intended growth markets based on what matters to those consumers, versus its existing customers. Brands don't necessarily translate in all markets.[58]

---

53. *See* Jennifer Weil, *Lacoste Acquires Sporting Equipment Maker Tecnifibre*, Women's Wear Daily (Aug. 31, 2017), http://wwd.com/business-news/mergers-acquisitions/lacoste-acquires-sporting-equipment-maker-tecnifibre-10968953/.

54. *See Milliken & Company to Acquire Polartec from Versa Capital Management*, Business Wire (June 11, 2019, 12:13 PM), https://www.businesswire.com/news/home/20190611005819/en/Milliken-Company-Acquire-Polartec-Versa-Capital-Management (noting that "[t]he addition of the Polartec brand—particularly its outdoor and fleece textiles—rounds out Milliken's comprehensive portfolio, allowing the company to deliver unprecedented access to a range of performance textiles for consumers, industrial workers and military personnel around the world"); *see also* Jean E. Palmieri, *Milliken to Acquire Polartec From Versa Capital*, WWD (June 11, 2019), https://wwd.com/business-news/mergers-acquisitions/milliken-to-acquire-polartec-from-versa-capital-1203165975/.

55. *See* Vicki M. Young, *Canada Goose Acquires Baffin Inc.*, WWD (Nov. 1, 2018), https://wwd.com/fashion-news/fashion-scoops/canada-goose-holdings-acquires-baffin-inc-footwear-acquisitions-1202896769/ (noting that "Dani Reiss, president and chief executive officer of Canada Goose, said, 'For decades, our products have lived side-by-side in the coldest places on Earth. The Arctic heritage and best-in-class functionality of Baffin boots are synonymous with what Canada Goose stands for'").

56. Reed & Lajoux, *supra* note 19, at 21.

57. Vicki M. Young, *Hudson's Bay Is No Stranger to Making Acquisitions*, WWD (Mar. 15, 2017), http://wwd.com/business-news/mergers-acquisitions/hudsons-bay-no-stranger-to-making-acquisitions-timeline-nrdc-gilt-galeria-kaufhof-10844011/. A similar example is the February 2017 acquisition of L.A.-based, young fashion brand Nasty Gal by British online retailer Boohoo Group for $20 million, which is expected to give Boohoo Group greater access to the U.S. market. Shan Li, *Nasty Gal, Once a Fashion World Darling, Is Now Bankrupt. What Went Wrong?*, L.A. Times (Feb. 24, 2017), http://www.latimes.com/business/la-fi-nasty-gal-20170224-story.html.

58. *See* David A. Aaker & Erich Joachimsthaler, *The Lure of Global Branding*, Harv. Bus. Rev. (1999), http://hbr.org/1999/11/the-lure-of-global-branding/ar/pr ("Honda means quality and

Vertical integration, whereby a company purchases a customer or a supplier, is a strategy employed by many companies looking to "achieve economies in purchasing, sales and distribution."[59] One means of vertical integration is a vertical backward integration in which a company is buying a "current or potential supplier."[60] A vertical integration can mean increased sales for the acquired supplier entity, as well as increased profits for the company, which will be able to purchase raw materials at a more competitive price. In particular, it is common for large luxury fashion companies to acquire their suppliers. Chanel alone has purchased multiple silk companies and invested in feather providers, glove-makers, milliners, cashmere producers and tulle and lace suppliers.[61] Other examples include LVMH's purchase of a tannery, Hermès's watch division's purchase of a supplier,[62] and the Japanese distributor, Look Holdings Inc.'s acquisition of Italian leather goods company, Il Bisonte.[63] Alternatively, vertical forward integration involves "buying a current or potential customer."[64] Examples of this can be seen in Li & Fung's past acquisition

---

reliability in the United States, but in Japan, where quality is a given for most cars, Honda represents speed, youth and energy."). *Compare* Steve Dennis, *Macy's Acquires Story: Game Changer Or Much Ado About Nothing?*, Forbes (May 3, 2018), https://www.forbes.com/sites/stevendennis/2018/05/03/macys-acquires-story-game-changer-or-much-ado-about-nothing/#50b96d395813 ("There is no question that Story is cool and innovative. There is no question that Story has punched way above its weight when it comes to generating industry and media attention. And the notion of 'store as media' is an intriguing one that is appropriately starting to change the way brands must think about their brick & mortar experience.") Sometimes brands engage in a market extension that does not entail international growth, but rather an expansion in the kinds of markets their goods are sold. For example, Macy's recent acquisition of Story, a New York City concept store, constituted a novel extension of Macy's traditional domain in an effort to appeal to a new market of consumers.

59. Reed & Lajoux, *supra* note 19, at 22.

60. *Id.*

61. Astrid Wendlandt, *Chanel Snaps Up Four Companies to Secure High-End Silk Supplies*, Reuters (July 22, 2016), https://www.reuters.com/article/us-fashion-chanel/chanel-snaps-up-four-companies-to-secure-high-end-silk-supplies-idUSKCN10222T; *see also* Joelle Diderich, *Chanel Invests in Green Chemistry Firm Evolved by Nature*, WWD (June 11, 2019), https://wwd.com/business-news/mergers-acquisitions/chanel-invests-in-green-chemistry-firm-evolved-by-nature-1203165153/ (noting that Chanel "acquired a minority stake in green chemistry company Evolved by Nature," which makes Activated Silk, "as part of its strategy of developing sustainable materials").

62. *See* Joelle Diderich, *Hermes Watch Divisions Acquires 32.5% in Supplier*, Women's Wear Daily (Sept. 29, 2011), http://www.wwd.com/business-news/mergers-acquisitions/herms-watch-division-acquires-325-percent-in-supplier-5236804; Miles Socha, *LVMH Invests in Crocodile Tannery*, Women's Wear Daily (Oct. 9, 2011), http://www.wwd.com/business-news/mergers-acquisitions/lvmh-invests-in-crocodile-tannery-5274560.

63. *See* Sandra Salibian, *Il Bisonte Gets New Owner*, WWD (June 12, 2019), https://wwd.com/business-news/mergers-acquisitions/il-bisonte-gets-new-owner-1203171238/; *see also* Press Release, Il Bisonte, Il Bisonte: 100% Acquired by Look Holdings Inc., Eminent Japanese Distributor and Licensee of the Iconic Leather Goods Brand (June 12, 2019), https://stories.ilbisonte.com/journal/news/il-bisonte-100-acquired-by-look-holdings-inc-eminent-japanese-distributor-and-licensee-of-the-iconic-leather-goods-brand/.

64. Reed & Lajoux, *supra* note 19, at 22.

of and investments in smaller fashion houses.[65] More recently, in July 2017 eyewear manufacturer Luxottica Group acquired Brazilian optical retail chain Oticas Carol for €110 million, allowing Luxottica Group to significantly expand its control over its retail presence in Brazil.[66] Whether a company is buying up or down the supply line, there are many advantages to vertical transactions, including greater quality control, inventory control and distribution.

d. Culture and Other Considerations

While the decision to acquire or merge with a company is often centered on increasing the bottom line, other equally important considerations, such as cultural differences, are often ignored.[67] Accordingly, another key component to the strategic development process is planning for ways to preempt and manage culture and personnel issues, particularly in light of ever-increasing globalization.[68]

One concern is whether the transaction will cause top management to be spread too thin, and how this will affect the rest of the management structure and the existing core business. Personnel issues are not always easily overcome, and in the fashion industry, where human capital plays an integral role in the company's success or failure, anticipating potential issues and strategizing in advance as to how they will be managed and overcome is crucial. For fashion companies, losing an eponymous designer can be catastrophic.[69] In addition to the exit of Ms. Karan from her eponymous brand discussed earlier, Jil Sander famously exited from her eponymous brand (the first of three times) a mere four months after it was acquired by the Prada Group in 1999. The brand suffered significant financial setbacks as a result.[70] If the designer is going to remain with the company, there must also be a plan to manage the company's relationship with the designer.[71] If the designer had previously enjoyed an enormous amount of autonomy, a shift in the management

---

65. Li & Fung acquired Fishman & Tobin and Crimzon Rose and invested in the Hang Ten brand. All were theretofore customers of Li & Fung's massive production capabilities in Southeast Asia. *See* Kate O'Keeffe & Nisha Gopalan, *Li & Fung Company Makes $340.7 Million Offer for Hang Ten*, Wall St. J. (Dec. 20, 2011, 12:23 pm); Michael Wei & Frank Longid, *Li & Fung Goes on an Acquisition Spree*, Businessweek (Aug. 25, 2011, 4:45 pm), http://www.businessweek.com/magazine/li-amp-fung-goes-on-an-acquisition-spree-08252011.html.

66. *See* Alessandra Turra, *Luxottica Group Acquires Brazilian Oticas Carol*, Women's Wear Daily (July 6, 2017), http://wwd.com/accessories-news/eyewear/luxottica-group-acquires-brazilian-oticas-carol-10940880/.

67. "Many mergers and acquisitions have gone awry because the buyer ventured into an unknown industry, paid too high a price, forecasted too bullishly, or did not recognize the importance of the target's people." *Id.* at 67.

68. Rovetta, *supra* note 15, at 16.

69. Rovetta, *supra* note 15, at 16–17.

70. *See* Douglas Hand, *Think Tank: Douglas Hand on the Challenge of M&A for Namesake Brands*, Women's Wear Daily (Jan. 23, 2016), http://wwd.com/business-news/mergers-acquisitions/douglas-hand-challenges-mergers-namesake-brands-10320585/.

71. *See infra* Section 2 b (ii).

structure can lead to friction.[72] If the target's management and/or design team does not share the same ideas as the acquirer with respect to how to grow the business, this can undermine the success of the post-acquisition process and in turn have a detrimental effect on the bottom line.[73]

2. Valuing the Deal

Emmanuel Chirico, the chairman and chief executive officer of PVH Corp. ("PVH"), once stated: ". . . great brands are expensive. It's OK to pay huge premiums for a great brand, but make sure you're actually buying a great brand."[74] The buyer and seller in any M&A deal will have opposing goals regarding the valuation of the target. In order to determine whether a potential transaction is worthwhile, companies and investors must determine how much the company being acquired is worth *to them*. Several established valuation methods are analyzed below.

a. Overview of Valuation Methods

The replacement value method asks the question: "What will it cost the buyer to duplicate the target right now?"[75] Such an evaluation includes adding together the cash costs of all hard assets, such as machinery (if any) and inventory, and soft assets, such as intellectual property ("IP"). In the fashion industry, where the brand itself constitutes a key asset, there are many drawbacks to the replacement value method. As a consequence, it is rarely used with any degree of persuasiveness. For example, the replacement value method may not take into consideration the length of time it may take to develop a popular brand or assemble good design and management teams that work together. While the replacement value method does include the soft assets of the company, it still can inaccurately portray the company's worth.

Another valuation method is comparative ratios. In a comparative ratio valuation, the company in question is compared to similar companies that are currently trading in the market but not involved in a merger or acquisition.[76] Certain financial information of the comparable company, such as its earnings or sales, forms a ratio with its market price; once the ratio of a comparable company is determined,

---

72. Amy M. Spindler, *Editor's Notebook; Is There a Designer In the House?*, N.Y. Times, Nov. 5, 2000 ("Designers, who once owned their own companies along with a business partner, are now answering to such higher powers."); *see also* Roberts & Chassany, *supra* note 18, "Perhaps the biggest obstacle to successful deals is the fact that many family-run businesses are unwilling to cede control to financial investors."

73. *See infra* Section 2 b (ii).

74. *See* Vicki M. Young, *Men's Wear CEO Summit: The Power and Pitfalls of the Acquisition Game*, WWD (Apr. 7, 2011), http://www.wwd.com/menswear-news/retail-business/mens-wear-ceo-summit-the-power-and-pitfalls-of-the-acquisition-game-3576392?full=true.

75. Reed & Lajoux, *supra* note 19, at 132.

76. Rutherford B. Campbell Jr., *The Impact of Modern Finance Theory in Acquisition Cases*, 53 Syracuse L. Rev. 1, 16 (2003).

the company in question is valued according to that multiplier.[77] This method is not always used in fashion transactions as one may get different multiplier values depending on which financial data is used for comparison, and in the fashion industry there are many different metrics to consider (e.g., direct to consumer sales, wholesale account sales, licensing royalty revenue, franchise sales, etc.). Therefore, when evaluating the company, weighting or prioritization is necessary, and this judgment call makes the method less objective and precise.[78]

The discounted cash flow ("DCF") method is a frequently used approach to the valuation of a company. In a DCF analysis, a company is worth its estimated cash flows, or the revenue it is expected to earn for a certain period of time into the future, less the appropriate discount rate.[79] Two important factors comprise the discount rate: the time value of money and risk. The first takes into account that by investing in a company, an investor gives up "the use of her or his money for a period of time, [and] . . . must defer consumption or forego a return on the invested sum [until] . . . the investment is repaid."[80] The discount rate also indicates the risk that may accompany a particular investment or the "volatility or variability of possible outcomes" inherent in that company.[81]

One drawback to the DCF method is that in a constantly changing and evolving economy, where new products and ideas for engaging fashion consumers emerge daily, it can be difficult to estimate future cash flows.[82] Few industries undergo such constant and drastic changes as the fashion industry. As Coco Chanel once remarked, "Fashion should slip out of your hands. The very idea of protecting the seasonal arts is childish. One should not bother to protect that which dies the minute it is born."[83] These changes can have a drastic impact on the value of a company, particularly ones that are narrowly focused in producing particular goods. For example, private equity firm TowerBrook Capital Partners acquired True Religion in 2013 for $835 million. The premium denim company filed for bankruptcy

---

77. "For example, if the present trading price of [X company] is two times its total revenues, then under this methodology one might claim that the fair value of [a similar company, Y, also] should be two times [its] total revenues." *Id.* at 15.

78. *Id.*

79. *Id.* at 7.

80. *Id.* at 9.

81. *Id.* at 10.

82. A glance at the risk factor and forward-looking statement disclosure of any public fashion company highlights the challenges of any evaluation method that estimates future earnings. For example, in their 2016 annual report on Form 10-K, Michael Kors notes that any forward-looking statements are qualified by risk factors as varied as global market and competition uncertainties, macroeconomic conditions, consumer traffic, changing fashion and retail trends, dependence on distributors and suppliers, cyber security risks, the continued employment of Michael Kors and executive management, etc. Michael Kors Holdings Ltd., Annual Report (Form 10-K) (May 31, 2017), https://www.sec.gov/Archives/edgar/data/1530721/000153072117000022/kors0401201710-k.htm#sCD21C047E2D191E85CD643C39398C89A.

83. Clare Coulson & Justine Picardie, *Is Fashion Too Fickle*?, Telegraph (London) (Oct. 5, 2005), http://fashion.telegraph.co.uk/news-features/TMG3345633/Is-fashion-too-fickle.html.

reorganization in July 2017, with critics citing that the brand failed to adapt as its "signature large stitching and flashy logos plastered on t-shirts [fell] woefully out of style [with] many younger shoppers."[84]

b. Due Diligence Process

It is only through targeted due diligence that an acquirer can obtain the data points necessary to make an informed projection of the target's post-acquisition financial performance. As the valuation of a target is dependent upon such projections,[85] due diligence is an extremely important aspect of any M&A transaction. Much more than merely "kicking the tires," successful acquirers approach the due diligence process cautiously, with a plan that includes a variety of actors from inside and outside the company to assess the value of the target.[86]

Due diligence is accomplished by inquiring into all aspects of the past, present, and, to the extent predictable, future of the business to be purchased. However, the due diligence process is not uniform across all companies. Rather, it must be, ahem, tailored to the particular transaction, and may vary based on the characteristics of both the acquiring and target companies, including size, maturity, jurisdiction, and whether the target is public or private. In addition, due diligence can be adjusted based on the companies' needs and desires.[87] If the parties are eager to deal, they may substitute extensive representations and warranties in the purchase agreement in place of more comprehensive due diligence.[88]

The parameters for due diligence are usually agreed upon by the buyer and seller during the initial stages of the deal. While some parties will begin to negotiate the definitive transaction agreements governing the merger or acquisition concurrently with the due diligence review, other parties will prefer to wait until the review is completed, or at least well under way, before spending the time and money drafting and negotiating long form agreements.

To ensure a smooth due diligence process, the acquirer usually will expect a covenant from the seller permitting the buyer adequate time and access to complete due diligence.[89] Such a covenant is often found in the term sheet or letter of intent ("LOI"), if such a document is executed in connection with a transaction, and, in any case, in the definitive transaction documents. In the event that significant due diligence has been performed by the acquirer prior to the execution of the transaction agreements, the parties will negotiate the inclusion of a closing condition that the

---

84. Greg Petro, *True Religion Lost Its Focus On the Consumer*, Forbes (July 26, 2017), https://www.forbes.com/sites/gregpetro/2017/07/26/true-religion-lost-its-focus-on-the-consumer/#1f15bd85cbfb.

85. Reed & Lajoux, *supra* note 19, at 375.

86. Aiello & Watkinds, *supra* note 21.

87. Reed & Lajoux, *supra* note 19, at 378.

88. *Id.* at 379.

89. *Id.*

acquirer's post-signing due diligence has been completed to its satisfaction. The target does not want the acquirer to have the right to walk away from a deal based upon an arguably insignificant due diligence finding.[90] The acquirer wants the comfort of a due diligence "catch-all" that enables it to terminate the definitive agreements in the event that facts are uncovered that are detrimental to the target's value.[91]

Important first steps in any due diligence review are to ensure that the target was legally formed, is in good standing and has the necessary power and authority to enter into the definitive agreements. The acquirer must also be satisfied that the target is not in violation or breach or in default under any existing agreement or law to which the target is bound. Additionally, careful due diligence needs to be performed to determine the target's capitalization (including reviewing the target's stock ledger, and in the case of a stock deal, locating and taking possession of all share certificates). The acquirer needs to be certain that the number of shares whose favorable vote is required for any aspect of a transaction can be correctly calculated and, in the case of a stock deal, that all of the outstanding shares of stock are being transferred.

An acquirer also typically performs a lien and litigation docket search of public records in order to determine if any of the target's assets are subject to a security interest or the target is subject to any pending litigation. Any such liens or litigation can greatly affect the valuation of the deal.

Acquirers should review the target's commercial and other material contracts. The rationale for and structure of the deal will dictate which contracts (and particular provisions of such contracts) are crucial to its success. For example, backward vertical integration and market intensification transactions will have different objectives, and, consequently, will require a focus on different documents in the diligence process.

In addition to representations and warranties about many aspects of a target's business, including active litigations (and even potential future litigations), potential defaults under existing contracts, IP rights, products liability, environmental liabilities, unpaid taxes, etc., a target is generally expected to make a representation and warranty that there are no undisclosed liabilities not reflected on the target's balance sheet. The acquirer will require an indemnity from the target for any breaches of such representations and warranties. This protection notwithstanding, the acquirer should also review the due diligence materials to confirm, to the extent possible, that the seller's representations are true. It is far preferable for the acquirer to know about a latent liability and factor it into a reduced purchase price, if not into the decision to undertake the acquisition at all, than to bring an indemnity claim against the seller post-closing.[92]

90. *Id.* at 395.

91. *Id.* at 380, 393, 395.

92. *Id.* at 461–62.

The due diligence process is typically organized by way of a due diligence request list that would usually include, among other things, the following list of areas and documents to be reviewed:

- All financial statements reflecting past operating and financial performance
- Market studies/reports on company's product and relative profitability of the company's various classes of products and business segments compared to companies of similar size in the industry
- Key intellectual property (design patents, trademarks, trade names and copyrights)
- Leases, title documents to real estate and personal property
- License and collaborative agreements
- Supply and sales agreements
- Employment and consulting agreements, as well as any design services or independent contractor agreements, agreements with labor, pension, profit-sharing plans, and insurance policies
- Ownership of company's securities—trace title of present owners of corporation
- Product backlogs, purchasing, inventory and pricing policies
- Market and product studies (contact major customers to determine their level of satisfaction)

i. IP Due Diligence

A comprehensive and accurate IP review is particularly critical in the case of fashion industry transactions. IP is usually the seller's most valuable asset.[93] Due diligence review in a fashion transaction should investigate all trademark, copyright, and design patent registrations, domestic and foreign, to verify ownership and to ensure there is no potential litigation that may arise over the use of the brand name or the designs. This should happen both where such IP is currently being used and in potential expansion markets. Needless to say, the costs associated with legal review in multiple jurisdictions can skyrocket.[94]

The IP review must also cover common law IP rights to the extent registration is not permitted or was simply not undertaken by the target. In the case of unregistered trademarks (which are usually limited to names used for particular products rather than the brand name itself) or trade dress or other IP that is not registered, date of first use, evidence of that use, and proof of secondary meaning should be obtained and reviewed for accuracy.[95]

---

93. *See* Fashion Law, *supra* note 9, at 25–26.

94. *See* Mona Pearl, *Going Global: Improving Your Chances of Success in International M&A*, QFinance, at 2, http://www.qfinance.com/mergers-and-acquisitions-best-practice/going-global-improving-your-chances-of-success-in-international-m-and-a.

95. Reed & Lajoux, *supra* note 19.

ii. Designer Diligence

As mentioned previously, an integral consideration for an acquirer of a fashion company, and a component that differentiates the fashion M&A due diligence process, is the need to determine what role the eponymous or lead designer/design team will play in the future of the company after the transaction is consummated.[96] A head designer, particularly in a smaller fashion house, but in many cases in larger ones as well, not only designs the merchandise, but may also have decision making authority as to licensing; what markets the merchandise is sold in (i.e., couture, ready-to-wear ("RTW"), contemporary etc.); what types of raw materials are sourced; and where merchandise is sold (e.g., some designers may want to sell only to the highest end retailers, which may result in significant negotiation between the parties).[97] Whether an eponymous or lead designer stays or leaves after the transaction is consummated thus plays an integral role in the future of the brand, both from a design perspective and an image perspective.[98] Accordingly, when applicable, the acquirer will almost always meet several times with the eponymous or lead designer/design team and discuss the future of the to-be-acquired company as part of the due diligence process.[99]

Losing an eponymous or lead designer can diminish the value of the brand and, as a result, cause a potential acquirer to pay less for the brand than it would have paid if the designer remained.[100] For example, LVMH would likely have been able to command a higher price for DKNY in its 2016 sale to G-III Apparel Group had Ms. Karan not exited the brand in the prior year. The importance attached to an eponymous or lead designer may also depend on the level of control such designer actually possesses over the day-to-day operations of the company, both in terms of design and in terms of management and operations. Some designers may be the creative force but delegate extensively to a highly effective design team that understands the look and feel of the brand and could therefore replicate the brand's aesthetic going forward.[101] Some designers may also delegate management and operations functions to a trained team, which could similarly ease the transition of the business to the

---

96. *See* Rovetta, *supra* note 15, at 9, 11.

97. *See, e.g.*, Gina Bellafante, *Front Row; Jil Sander Is Divorcing Prada. After Next Month's Fall Women's Collection in Milan, She Plans to Leave Her Signature Company*, N.Y. Times (Jan. 25, 2000), http://www.nytimes.com/2000/01/25/style/front-row-jil-sander-divorcing-prada-after-next-month-s-fall-women-s-collection.html; Wilson, *supra* note 61.

98. *See generally* Amy M. Spindler, *Editor's Notebook; Is There a Designer In the House?*, N.Y. Times (Nov. 5, 2000), http://www.nytimes.com/2000/11/05/magazine/editor-s-notebook-is-there-a-designer-in-the-house.html?pagewanted=all&src=pm.

99. *See, e.g.*, Michael J. De La Merced & Liz Alderman, *For Bulgari, LVMH Deal Paves Way to Growth*, N.Y. Times Deal Book (Mar. 7, 2011), http://dealbook.nytimes.com/2011/03/07/for-bulgari-lvmh-deal-paves-way-to-growth/.

100. *See, e.g.*, Wilson, *supra* note 60 (noting the diminished value of the Helmut Lang brand after the designer left, and the possibility for the Prada Group to sell).

101. *See, e.g.*, Wilson, *supra* note 61.

acquirer.[102] Accordingly, losing an eponymous or lead designer who wears all of the hats in the company will likely have a far more deleterious impact on the company and the brand than losing a designer who has delegated effectively and serves as a more general creative influence.[103] Stuart Weitzman's near-term retirement was contemplated by both parties during the sale of his eponymous label to Coach Inc. in 2015.[104] As a result, when Mr. Weitzman stepped down as lead designer the following year, he remained actively involved in the selection of the newly appointed creative designer and design team and there was no deleterious effect to the brand as a result of the transition.[105]

Discussing the future direction of the company with the eponymous or lead designer is another critical step for acquirers. While this is considerably more important in the event that the designer is expected to remain with the company, it may also be relevant in situations where the designer is expected to exit. An eponymous designer may, for example, seek to limit the use of their name to certain categories of merchandise or dictate the channels of distribution, regardless of whether they remain or exit.[106] Because licensing/franchising and brand extension have become such potent profit-raising strategies for fashion companies, such potential limitations should be discussed with the designer as part of the due diligence process.[107] If, for example, part of the acquirer's growth strategy is to turn a company that sells only RTW into a lifestyle brand, an eponymous designer must be willing to license their name to many categories of goods. Alternatively, if the acquirer wants to take a couture brand and create an RTW and contemporary line, they must ensure the designer is in agreement.[108] Eponymous designers may consider their brand an extension of themselves, and, as a result, may be less willing to execute these potentially highly lucrative strategies due to a perceived negative impact on their reputation.

---

102. *See, e.g.*, *Jones Apparel to Acquire Majority Stake in Stuart Weitzman* (June 9, 2010), https://apparelmag.com/jones-apparel-acquire-majority-stake-stuart-weitzman APPAREL MAGAZINE (Stuart Weitzman explaining how the running of the business fits with the operation, accounting, etc. systems already in place at Jones Apparel Group).

103. *Compare* Bellafante, *supra* note 97 (Jil Sander leaving after the Prada Group acquired a 75 percent stake), *with* De La Merced & Alderman, *supra* note 99 (Bulgari recognizing its need for stronger management).

104. *See* Neil Weilheimer, *Exclusive: Stuart Weitzman Talks to FN About Calling It Quits After 50 Years*, FOOTWEAR NEWS (Mar. 20, 2017), http://footwearnews.com/2017/business/designers/stuart-weitzman-celebrity-red-carpet-shoes-retirement-328770/.

105. *Id.*

106. William Lozito, *Tommy Hilfiger's $3.38 Billion Acquisition Biggest Deal Ever in Apparel Naming and Branding*, NAME WIRE (Mar. 16, 2011) http://www.namedevelopment.com/blog/archives/2010/03/tommy_hilfigers.html/."[W]hat is really interesting is that PVH is trying to ensure that control of Tommy Hilfiger himself rests with them. PVH is seeking 'ironclad' ability to control the name, and not just the trademarks. Hilfiger is staying on as 'Principal Designer and Visionary' for the Tommy Hilfiger brand but he has been quietly acquiring smaller brands, leading to the worry on the part of PVH that Hilfiger may have plans to create a breakout, competitive brand name." (emphasis omitted).

107. *See* REED & LAJOUX, *supra* note 19, at 397.

108. *See generally* FASHION LAW, *supra* note 9, at 83–86.

Another important due diligence consideration is how the company will be managed, and who will maintain control over strategy.[109] An eponymous or lead designer may demand a certain amount of control over the business in order to remain with the company. Such a demand might not suit an acquirer with a definite strategic vision for the brand that would be subject to the designer's influence.[110] Furthermore, even if the designer relinquishes control of certain aspects of the company, care must be taken to ensure that the designer will work well within the new management structure.

3. Structuring Considerations

a. Overview of Traditional Structures

A transaction to acquire a fashion business or merge with another fashion company can take many different forms, and often determining what form it will take can be the most challenging aspect of any deal. Generally speaking, there are three primary forms used for the acquisition of a business: (i) a purchase of all or substantially all of the assets of the business or an "asset acquisition"; (ii) a purchase of a controlling interest in the stock (or other form of equity) of the company (or companies) that houses the business or a "stock acquisition"; and (iii) a merger of the acquirer (or an affiliate) with the target.[111] No particular form, or combination thereof, predominates M&A transactions in the fashion industry.

Less frequently invoked structural alternatives to traditional M&A in the fashion industry include IP licenses and joint ventures.

i. Asset Acquisition

In an asset acquisition, the target transfers to the acquirer (or a subsidiary, generally newly formed, of the acquirer) its "hard" assets, including equipment and inventory, as well as "soft" or intangible assets such as IP or contract rights. An asset acquisition, however, does not require the sale of all the company's assets, and in fact the decision to do an asset transaction over a stock deal or merger may be dictated by the fact that the sale only involves part of the selling company's business. For example, a company may sell its accessories or footwear business and keep its

---

109. *See, e.g.*, Lauren Thomas, *Macy's Acquires New York Concept Shop Story*, CNBC (May 2, 2018, 9:25 AM), https://www.cnbc.com/2018/05/02/macys-acquires-ny-based-concept-store-story.html (discussing Macy's acquisition of NYC concept store, Story, noting that upon acquiring Story, Macy's "named the business' founder as 'brand experience officer' for the department store chain. In that capacity, Rachel Shechtman's responsibilities will include partnering with brands and creating better in store experiences," demonstrating that sometimes strategic acquisitions hinge on the ideas and innovations conceived of by key target company personnel).

110. *See, e.g.*, Wilson, *supra* note 60 (noting how Helmut Lang's stubbornness in working with seemingly inferior fabrics, despite lower costs, contradicted the Prada Group's desire to bring the brand into profitability).

111. *See* Reed & Lajoux, *supra* note 19.

RTW business or, if the company has several different product lines, it could sell off one line and keep the others. Similarly, a company could sell its retail operations but maintain its wholesale business. While, in my experience, this does not happen often, it is worth noting. To effectuate an asset acquisition, the target will execute specific documents needed to transfer each of the purchased assets, such as bills of sale and assignments.

In addition to providing the opportunity to buy or sell only certain assets of a company, asset transactions offer two other advantages, which generally drive this choice of acquisition form for acquirers. The first advantage is that, as a legal matter, the acquirer can cherry-pick the target's liabilities that it is prepared to assume. The second advantage is that an asset acquisition can generate significant tax savings by increasing the asset basis to the purchase price where the tax basis of the target's assets is lower than the selling price.

There are, however, drawbacks to an asset acquisition. Primarily, the tax cost to the seller is higher.[112] If the seller is a C-corporation, the sale proceeds will be subject to double taxation at corporate rates and again at dividend rates. If the seller is a pass-through entity like an S-corporation or a limited liability company, it will not be subject to double taxation, but it still may be taxed at a higher rate than necessary.[113]

In my experience, an asset transaction generally takes longer to complete and is more expensive because of legal and regulatory technicalities. Certain contractual assets are not assignable without the consent of third parties—particularly retail leases. Even assuming the third party is willing to consent to the assignment of the contract, their consent may be contingent on additional considerations. Some fashion companies may also need to obtain new licenses or permits upon new ownership. It should also be noted that the bulk sales law may govern an asset transaction.[114]

ii. Stock Acquisition

In a stock acquisition, the seller transfers its shares in the target to the acquirer. Unlike an asset transaction, where sometimes only certain assets of the target are acquired, in a stock acquisition the entire company and all of its liabilities are being acquired. A stock deal may be necessary in the event of difficult or expensive third-party consents, or where the size of the company makes an asset deal too unwieldy.

---

112. *Id.* at 285.

113. *Id.* at 317.

114. *Id.* The bulk sales law, subject to variations among states, requires the purchaser of a major part of the material, supplies, merchandise, or other inventory of a seller whose principal business is bulk sales—the sale of merchandise from inventory to give at least 10 days' advance notice of the sale to each creditor of the seller. The notice must identify the seller and the acquirer and state whether or not the debts of the seller will be paid as they fall due. If orderly payment will not be made, further information must be disclosed. In addition, many states require the acquirer to ensure that the seller uses proceeds from the sale to satisfy existing debts, and to hold in escrow an amount sufficient to pay any disputed debts. *Id.* at 286–87.

Sellers will frequently prefer a stock deal because they are usually selling off all of their liabilities.[115]

There are several disadvantages to a stock acquisition. First, the acquirer may have to obtain the target's shares from disparate sources if there are many shareholders. Like a small tear in a stocking can unravel it entirely, one holdout stockholder can scuttle an entire transaction in certain circumstances. The stock transaction may also result in post-acquisition tax disadvantages.[116]

iii. Mergers

A merger takes place when one corporation absorbs another. The entire transfer of ownership rights and responsibilities occurs by filing a certificate of merger with the state. Generally, there are two primary types of mergers: forward and reverse. There are three types of consideration that can be paid in each: cash, stock, or a combination of cash and stock.

In a reverse merger, the acquirer (or a newly formed subsidiary of the acquirer) is absorbed by the target and the shareholders of the acquirer acquire stock in the target while the shareholders of the target receive consideration. In a reverse merger, the shareholders of the acquirer will own the target and the shareholders of the target are bought out, unless they receive stock in the acquirer as consideration. It should be noted that for federal tax purposes, a reverse merger is often treated like a stock acquisition.[117]

By contrast, in a forward merger, the target will merge with and into the acquirer (or a newly formed subsidiary of the acquirer), and the target's shareholders will exchange their stock for an agreed-upon purchase price. As a consequence of a forward merger, the acquirer will succeed to all of the assets and liabilities of the target. Such a transaction is treated as a liquidation distribution for federal tax purposes, as if the target sold its assets and liquidated and distributed the proceeds of the sale to the target's shareholders.[118] Because in a forward merger the assets of the target will end up in another entity, such a transaction is more susceptible to violate transfer restrictions or other change of control provisions in the target's retail store leases and commercial contracts like distribution agreements or licenses and collaboration agreements.

The merger process for two corporations generally requires that the board of directors of each participating corporation adopt a resolution approving an agreement of merger.[119] Depending on each constituent company's charter and the laws of the jurisdiction of incorporation, shareholders owning a majority of the stock

---

115. *Id.* at 288. Typically, the battle over what liabilities are excluded and what are included is a pitched one between acquirer and seller.

116. *Id.*

117. *Id.*

118. *Id.*

119. *Id.* at 290.

(or in some cases an even greater percentage of shareholders) of such constituent corporation must also approve the transaction. After these approvals (and any other conditions to closing that may be in the merger agreement), the merger becomes effective by operation of law upon the filing of a certificate of merger.[120] It should be noted that the agreement of merger has essentially the same provisions as the transaction agreement in either a stock or asset deal, with an exception being that the assets and liabilities are transferred by operation of law without the need for specific contractual language (as well as, in some cases, consents and actions) to make such transfer effective.

The merger method shares many of the advantages of a stock deal in that it is generally simple and avoids some of the headaches of an asset transaction. Unlike a stock deal, however, a merger agreement is executed only with the target and, although it generally must be approved by a majority of the stockholders, it has the benefit of not being dependent upon reaching an agreement with each individual stockholder.[121] Instead, the dissenting stockholders are required, as a matter of law ("subject to certain statutory protections for minority investors, or 'dissenters' rights'") to go along with the deal.[122] Furthermore, mergers are seen from the viewpoint of secured lenders in a leveraged buyout as the preferred format because the lender "lends to the surviving corporation (either directly or to a holding company that owns it) and [in return] obtains a security interest in the assets of that corporation" with the loan proceeds "used to satisfy the obligation to pay off the stockholders of the target."[123]

b. Licensing and Joint Ventures as M&A

For fashion companies looking to increase their revenues and expand their global presence, deploying a licensing strategy or entering into a joint venture presents an alternative to being involved in a typical M&A transaction.[124] On an outward-facing basis to customers, an exclusive license to use a target's trademarks (and, in most cases, designs) is tantamount to a merger or an acquisition of the target's brand for a period of time. Licensing transactions can also involve joint ventures, where the traditional licensor and licensee jointly own the entity that exploits the license. In any event, both of these transactions share hallmarks with traditional mergers or deals involving the issuance of acquirer stock, where the seller may still maintain a stake in the acquirer and a change of control may not necessarily occur.

---

120. *Id.* ("Under Delaware law the approval of the surviving corporation's shareholders is necessary only if its certificate of incorporation will be amended by the merger and if the shares of the survivor issued to the sellers comprise less than 20 percent of the outstanding shares of the survivor.").

121. *Id.*

122. *Id.*

123. *Id.* at 290.

124. *See* Fashion Law, *supra* note 9, at 299–303 (discussing the pros and cons of different international expansion strategies).

i. Licensing

As discussed more fully in Chapter 8, Licensing enables a brand with an established trademark to leverage the value of that trademark by expanding geographic territories and product lines to cover regions and increase product offerings. The Licensing Industry Merchandizer's Association estimated that fashion licensing generated $32.1 billion in 2017.[125] In the past, many major brands, such as Calvin Klein, Tommy Hilfiger and Ralph Lauren, expanded globally and/or to new product categories through geographic licensing.[126] When the licensee is up to the task, and the licensor is committed to the project, the business around the new product or territory can be established more quickly and at a lower overall cost than the licensor would have been able to achieve by entering into the product category or region directly.[127]

PVH is a not only a major conglomerate (owning Calvin Klein and Tommy Hilfiger, among other brands), but it also holds licenses for DKNY, Michael Kors, Sean John and others.[128] Certainly on an outward/customer-facing basis, these brands are either "owned" by PVH or, at the very least, have in some sense "merged" their business, even if it is for a limited time or over a limited geographic area. Similarly, the licensing division of Perry Ellis International maintains an exclusive licensing agreement with 1928 Jewelry Company to manufacture, design and distribute fashion jewelry products under the Laundry by Shelli Segal brand name.[129] Who owns what in such an arrangement? As one fashion reporter put it:

> "This agreement is like those Russian dolls where you pull it apart and you find another doll inside. A designer develops a brand that buys another brand and then licenses *that* brand to someone to make something completely different, but cool in the same way the brand is cool.
>
> And that's how you got those earrings you're wearing."[130]

---

125. *Types of Licensing*, LIMA (last visited July 25, 2018) http://www.licensing.org/education/introduction-to-licensing/types-of-licensing/ (showing estimated revenues of different forms of licensing).

126. "Licensing is a common means for companies to extend their product lines; manufacturers paid $5.9 billion in licensing royalties in the US in 2005 . . . up 1.8% from 2004, according to the International Licensing Industry Merchandisers' Association. . . . Licensing is a key element of an integrated brand marketing program, enabling a company to extend its brand into new categories. For instance, in March 2003, Liz Claiborne licensed certain women's dresses and suits under its Liz Claiborne, Liz Claiborne Woman, and Liz Claiborne Petites labels to apparel manufacturer Kellwood Co. More recently, bookmaker Timberland Co. in February 2006 licensed its brand name to Phillips Van-Heusen to make Timberland apparel in North America." Marie Driscoll & Esther Kwon, Standard & Poor's, Industry Surveys Apparel & Footwear 19 (Nov. 29, 2007), *available at* http://homepage.smc.edu/thomas_phillip/rpt/Apparelandfootware.pdf.

127. *See* Fashion Law, *supra* note 9, at 82–84 (discussing the advantages of licensing).

128. PVH Corp., Annual Report (Form 10-K) (Mar. 24, 2017), https://www.sec.gov/Archives/edgar/data/78239/000007823917000009/pvh10k2016.htm.

129. Macala Wright, *Mid-Tier to Luxury Fashion Brands Open Their Doors to Licensing*, Macala Wright (Oct. 16, 2011), http://maca.la/2011/10/fashion-licensing-deals/.

130. *Id.*

Not unlike the strategy employed in a fashion M&A deal, the typical license for a fashion industry company involves an extension into complementary products or a geographic region.[131] For clothing manufacturers, product extension generally involves "accessories, jewelry, eyewear, and fragrance, with possible later extensions into other product lines, such as cosmetics, linens, tabletop decor, and furniture."[132] "Kenneth Cole, Vera Wang, and Martha Stewart are good examples of companies that have actually produced few categories of products but have had a significant brand presence across product categories through licensing."[133] In lieu of deploying a market extension strategy, companies can use a representative geographic license to expand "into another territory, such as Southeast Asia, or country, such as China, where the licensee typically has an established production and distribution network."[134]

If the term of a particular license is lengthy and includes renewal rights in favor of the licensee, the license very much replicates an acquisition of the IP assets of the licensor and so is not unlike an asset deal.[135] Except in this case, the deal is like a lease (i.e., it is ultimately limited in time) rather than a legal acquisition and transfer of ownership.[136] The justification for a lengthy license term and renewals is that more time than the initial term is needed to fully recoup the investment to start the brand in a new category or region.[137] It also may be the case that the licensee's wherewithal is so great (e.g., in the recent past, PVH, Li & Fung, Luxottica Group) that they simply have the leverage (i.e., can offer the financial returns) to demand a lengthy term.[138]

ii. Joint Ventures

Joint ventures typically involve the formation of a special purpose vehicle ("JV"), jointly owned by the licensor and the joint venture partner, which would have been the licensee in a traditional licensing context.[139] Here, the JV is the licensee.[140]

---

131. Douglas Hand, *When Licensing and Branding Meet,* in Navigating Fashion Law: Leading Lawyers on Exploring the Trends, Cases, and Strategies of Fashion Law *1 (Jan. 2012), *available at* Westlaw 2012 WL 167356.

132. *Id.*

133. *Id.*

134. *Id.*

135. *Compare* Fashion Law, *supra* note 9, at 82–84 (discussing licensing and its effects on IP rights), and Hand, *supra* note 131, at *2 (providing background information on common renewal schemes for licensing), *with* Reed & Lajoux, *supra* note 19, at, 283–87 (explaining basic asset transactions).

136. Black's Law Dictionary 889 (6th ed. 1990) (defining a lease as an "[a]greement under which owner gives up possession and use of his property for valuable consideration and for definite term and at end of term owner has absolute right to retake, control and use property").

137. Hand, *supra* note 131, at *2.

138. *See generally* Fashion Law, *supra* note 9 at 91–92.

139. *See* Reed & Lajoux, *supra* note 19, at 15.

140. *See* Nigel Parker, *Intellectual Property Issues in Joint Ventures and Collaborations,* 11 J. Intell. Prop. L. & Prac. 729, 733 (2007).

The partner and the licensor split the JV's profits after covering the costs of its operations.[141] There may be little or no royalty payment made to the licensor.[142]

This arrangement reduces the downside risk of the party that would have been the licensee in a traditional licensing context in that its cost outlay may be paid back before any payments are made to the licensor.[143] In fact, the licensor, as an owner of the special purpose vehicle, may be required to partially fund its operations.[144] The upside for the licensor is sharing a greater amount of the revenues than would be garnered in the mix of royalties, design fee and marketing spend in a traditional license.[145]

Collaborations or co-branding joint ventures involve two brands putting their respective trademarks on a product within one or both of their respective product categories.[146] Structurally, the holder of trademark X and the holder of trademark Y each license their respective trademarks to the JV, which manufactures and markets the XY brand. The two separate licenses can make the arrangement more of a pure 50/50 joint venture and therefore easier to negotiate. In either case, it is important that the scope of a collaboration agreement is narrowly defined so the parties do not take the co-brand into product categories that would create confusion with the existing product offering.[147] To achieve this, the JV's licenses can set forth the physical placement of the two trademarks in conjunction with one another on the product itself as well as on marketing and PR materials.[148]

141. *See* Gordon V. Smith & Russel L. Parr, Intellectual Property: Licensing and Joint Venture Profit Strategies 290 (3d ed. 2004).

142. *See* Parker, *supra* note 140, at 735.

143. *See generally* Smith, *supra* note 141, at 290 (discussing benefits of JV vehicle).

144. *See* Parker, *supra* note 140, at 732 (discussing the structural formation of a JV and the allocation of funding responsibilities).

145. *See generally* Smith, *supra* note 141, at 290 (discussing benefits of JV vehicle).

146. Ann Hurwitz, *A Symposium On Franchise Law: Article: Co-Branding: Managing Franchise Brand Associations*, 20 Okla. City U.L. Rev. 373, 374 (1995).

147. *See generally* Parker, *supra* note 140, at 738 (discussing that special considerations are needed when trademarks are used in a JV).

148. For example, G-III Apparel Group Ltd. entered into a joint venture with Karl Lagerfeld's parent company "in an effort to help develop the designer's brand in the North American market." *See* Associated Press, *G-III in Joint Venture with Karl Lagerfeld's Parent Company*, Bus. of Fashion (June 8, 2015, 1:12 PM), https://www.businessoffashion.com/articles/news-analysis/g-iii-in-joint-venture-with-karl-lagerfelds-parent-company (noting that "[t]he joint venture will have access to the Karl Lagerfeld brand for consumer products and clothing in the U.S. and Canada" and "G-III, which has a 49 percent stake in the joint venture, [] received a five-year license for women's clothing, women's handbags and men's outwear"). Another example of a joint venture is presented by H&M and Alexander Wang's successful collaboration in 2014. *See, e.g.*, Nicola Fumo, *The Alexander Wang X H&M Hype Machine: A Case Study*, Racked (Nov. 18, 2014), https://www.racked.com/2014/11/18/7568609/alexander-wang-hm-collaboration-collection-strategy.

c. Some Tax Considerations

For any M&A deal there will be important tax considerations that will play a role in structuring the transaction. Acquirers and sellers will approach these considerations from different viewpoints. For acquirers, the primary goal of tax planning is to, on a present value basis, minimize the total tax costs of not only acquiring the target but also operating and even re-selling the target or certain of its assets.[149] By contrast, the seller's main goal with regard to tax planning is to, on a present value basis, maximize the after-tax proceeds from the sale.[150] To accomplish this, the seller will, in anticipation of the acquisition, attempt to develop means to offer tax benefits to a potential acquirer (with little tax cost to the seller) and prepare for the receipt of tax-deferred consideration from the acquirers.[151] That said, usually, the most beneficial tax plan for the acquirer will conversely be the least advantageous plan from the seller's point of view.[152] Because the immediate and prospective tax costs of a transaction are likely to affect the price, the parties should seek to structure the transaction to minimize the aggregate tax costs of the seller and acquirer and allocate the tax burden between them through an adjustment in price.[153]

While the specific tax considerations for a transaction will depend upon the particular facts and circumstances of that specific deal, there are certain tax issues that are far more common in the context of a fashion industry transaction than in others, given that:

- the preponderance of the value of a fashion company is usually in its intangible assets and goodwill and;
- in many M&A transactions in the fashion industry, a portion of the overall consideration may be paid to the company's head/eponymous designer.[154]

Therefore, preliminary structural considerations are often: (i) whether the transfer will be affected as a stock acquisition or as an asset acquisition; (ii) whether the operating entity will be a C-corporation, an S-corporation or a general or limited partnership; and (iii) what the financing agreement will be, including the debt/equity distinction and the effect of the original issue discount rules.[155] In addition, the target's head/eponymous designer may be invited to purchase stock or granted

149. *See* Reed & Lajoux, *supra* note 19, at 294.

150. *Id.*

151. *Id.*

152. *See id.* For example, the tax benefit of a high basis in the assets of the target corporation may be available to the purchaser only at a significant tax cost to the seller. But acquirers rarely if ever pursue tax benefits at the seller's expense.

153. *See id.*

154. *See generally id.*, at 294–95 ("There is no definitive checklist of tax issues that may arise in every acquisition or divestiture.").

155. *See id.* at 294.

stock options, stock appreciation rights, bonuses or some other form of incentive compensation, each of which can have different tax results.[156]

The tax effects that the proposed structure will have on the post-acquisition operations of the target should also be considered. For example, net operating loss, credit carrybacks and carryforwards, amortization of goodwill, the alternative minimum tax, planned asset dispositions, elections of taxable year and accounting methods, integration of the target's accounting methods into the acquirer's existing operations, foreign tax credits, and the interrelationships among the differing tax systems of the countries in which the acquirer and target do business should all be reviewed by tax advisors.

4. Negotiation, Documentation and Closing

The actual negotiation of the transaction is, perhaps, the most critical aspect for the legal practitioner involved in any M&A. Accordingly, it is important to understand the constituent agreements in an M&A context and, for a fashion company transaction in particular, to understand how these documents distinctively treat the most important assets—IP and talent.

a. Nondisclosure Agreement/Letter of Intent

For the acquirer, the point at which any M&A deal becomes less theoretical is when a confidentiality or nondisclosure agreement ("NDA") between the parties is signed.[157] Particularly in the case of a fashion company, this initial step is important as it will work to protect both parties' confidential information (including, for example, designs and lists of suppliers), and will also work to maintain the confidentiality of the deal. In addition to protecting their IP, maintaining the confidentiality of the deal is particularly important as both acquirers and targets will want to be able to control messaging to the public in order to protect their share price (if they are a publicly traded company) and consumer confidence in their respective products.[158] Having the NDA in place allows for the exchange of information that is required in the valuation and due diligence processes described above. An M&A deal often starts in earnest with the signing of an LOI.[159] An LOI is a pre-contractual written instrument that describes and may to some degree crystalize the basic terms of the deal, which up to that point have only been the subject of oral negotiations. In most cases, an LOI is not intended to be binding and to that end most letters of intent will specifically state that they do not create a binding obligation to close the

156. *See id.* (discussing the possibility of providing different incentive compensation).

157. *See id.*, *supra* note 2, at 42.

158. For example, if a high-end line is about to be purchased by a company that owns more mainstream brands, consumers may fear that the brand is going to be tarnished and may not want to invest in it with a big purchase.

159. *See id.* at 453–55.

transaction. Importantly, an LOI usually creates binding obligations with respect to the confidentiality provisions and "no-shop"[160] provisions that will offer the parties similar protection to an NDA. In my experience, an LOI will typically include the proposed structure of the transaction, the price, and other general features of the deal. While commonly used, term sheets or LOIs are by no means mandatory and experienced deal makers may choose to forego an LOI and move straight to negotiating definitive M&A agreements.

b. Negotiation Considerations

Even though it is not binding, the terms of the LOI will usually set the boundaries of all future deal negotiations and will serve to discourage attempts to re-trade on the principal terms. This is particularly true in many fashion M&A contexts because personality and human capital play such a crucial role in a successful fashion deal. Therefore, potential acquirers should be diplomatic and sensitive in their negotiation tactics. Because fashion houses sometimes begin as family businesses, eponymous designers may take aggressive negotiations personally and refuse to make deals if they think they are being treated unfairly or that the acquirer has "re-traded" on points.[161]

c. Transaction Agreement

In most M&A transactions, once the merger or acquisition agreement is executed, such agreement alone will govern the parties' pre-closing and post-closing behavior, as well as their respective rights, obligations, and remedies. Based on many drafts I've seen governing deals large, small, and in-between, the transaction agreement will in essence:

(i) define the structure and terms of the deal;

(ii) make representations and warranties about all of the important legal and financial aspects of the target, as well as relevant information about the acquirer (particularly in the case of a merger or a deal where stock is being used as consideration);

(iii) obligate both parties to use their best efforts and good faith to consummate the transaction and obligate the target to ensure there are no material changes between the time the transaction agreement is signed and the date

---

160. A provision requiring the seller to refrain from negotiating with other parties for a specified period of time in order to give the acquirer a proper chance to negotiate a deal. *Id.* at 456–57.

161. Andrew Roberts, *Hermes Reports 44% Profit Jump, Says Not Interested in LVMH Collaboration*, Bloomberg News (Mar. 4, 2011), http://www.bloomberg.com/news/2011-03-04/hermes-profit-trails-estimates-says-it-will-maintain-control.html (quoting Hermes CEO Patrick Thomas' statement: "If you want to seduce a beautiful woman, you don't start by raping her from behind."); *See, e.g.*, Michael J. De La Merced & Chris V. Nicholson, *LVMH to Take Control of Italy's Bulgari*, N.Y. Times (Mar. 6, 2010), http://dealbook.nytimes.com/2011/03/06/lvmh-to-take-control-of-italys-bulgari (detailing Bulgari's decision to sell to LVMH).

the deal closes (if there is a gap between these two events because of closing conditions that have to be satisfied);

(iv) set forth any closing conditions and govern the rights of the parties in the event of any pre-closing issue, if for example either party discovers problems that should have been disclosed either in the agreement or before the closing that were not properly disclosed; and

(v) contain any ongoing covenants agreed to by the parties as to how the business will be operated or rights the seller/designer may have in certain circumstances.

Unlike the LOI, the transaction agreement is legally binding under the governing law applied[162] and allocates the legal and financial risk associated with doing the deal.

i. Risk Allocation — Representations and Warranties

The acquirer and target have opposing goals with respect to risk allocation. The acquirer will want to make sure that after it has paid the seller a fair price that it will be appropriately compensated for any loss that results from undisclosed problems, including flaws of which even the target was not aware.[163] These respective concerns of the acquirer and seller are reflected in the representations and warranties section of the transaction agreement. The acquirer will seek the broadest possible representations and warranties from the seller, while the seller will strive to narrow them as much as possible. This is the case irrespective of the industry the transaction occurs in. The fewer and narrower the representations, warranties, and covenants of the target, the lower the risk will be that a closing condition will not be satisfied or that the seller will be exposed to post-closing indemnity liabilities. Conversely, with broad representation and warranties, there is a greater likelihood of a breach that will allow the acquirer to "walk" and a greater degree of protection afforded to the acquirer by the indemnity provision.

One particular challenge in fashion M&A is determining the risks associated with the intangible assets before attempting to allocate such risks. A fashion company target cannot reasonably be expected to represent that there are no trademark liabilities, known or unknown, with respect to its brand anywhere on the globe. Doing so would allocate an entire unknown risk (that is, for all practical purposes, unknowable) to the sellers, which would amount to a very valuable insurance policy. This is rarely done, but in some cases the acquirer may fairly argue that they are buying a global brand and, therefore, the acquirer should be indemnified if the trademarks cannot be used in *certain* jurisdictions.

162. Typically, Delaware or New York.

163. Reed & Lajoux, *supra* note 19, at 466.

ii. Ongoing Covenants

The transaction document may also contain ongoing covenants related to the operation of the business that, in the context of a fashion company, usually relate to the use of the trademark—especially in the case of a sale by an eponymous designer. When the brand and designer are associated with a particular market segment, this provision would prohibit the licensing of the trademark for certain products. Moreover, this restriction may even preclude product extension into certain product categories without designer approval. The seller may negotiate for a covenant restricting the channels through which products may be sold without designer consent to ensure that products are only sold in a manner befitting the brand. These types of covenants are rare and only present, in my experience, where the designer maintains an equity stake in the acquirer or combined company, as they present an artificial restriction on the short-term profitability of the business in the name of preserving brand integrity. To accept this type of covenant, the acquirer must be convinced that the trade-off regarding short-term profits and long-term brand integrity favors the preservation of brand equity.

d. Employment Agreements in M&A

When fashion companies change hands, the manner in which key personnel are retained by the newly merged or acquired company is critical.[164] Accordingly, the employment agreement—which sets forth how and on what terms key personnel will be retained—is very important.

i. Eponymous or Lead Designer's Employment Commitment

As will be discussed further in Chapter 10, from the acquirer's perspective the most important component of the employment agreement may be to ensure that the eponymous or lead designer will be committed to the company for as long as possible.[165] This is important in a practical sense and also from a public relations

164. *See* William J. Gole & Paul J. Hilger, Corporate Divestitures: A Mergers and Acquisitions Best Practices Guide 74 (John Wiley and Sons 2008), *available at* http://books.google.com/books?id=Ce6-nRCuIJYC&pg=PA61&dq=mergers+and+Acquisition+importance+of+identifying+and+retaining+key+personnel+employment+agreement&hl=en&sa=X&ei=__83T83_L6Xv0gH6g5jZAg&ved=0CD4Q6AEwAQ#v=onepage&q&f=false ("It is important that all key individuals are identified as early as possible in the process and that a plan is formulated to reward them, for staying with the property being sold, for at least as long as it take to execute a transaction.").

165. *See* Randall Schuler & Susan Jackson, *HR Issues and Activities in Mergers and Acquisitions*, 19 Eur. Mgmt. J. 239, 247 (2001), *available at* http://www.strategies-for-managing-change.com/support-files/mergerhrissues.pdf ("Retention of key employees is crucial to achieving performance goals through the transition period and the long-term competitive advantage associated with specialized knowledge . . . Employees who get financial incentives may be asked to sign written agreements indicating they will remain with the new entity for a specific time span.").

standpoint.[166] Practically speaking, it can be time-consuming and potentially detrimental to the brand to have to replace key design and management personnel.[167] In fact, it may be impossible to find a replacement who can mimic the design aesthetic of a particular brand and maintain the company's customer base.[168] Such was the fate of one the most famous American designers of all time—Bill Blass.[169] Blass was ill at the time of the acquisition of his company and there was no question that he would not be staying.[170] Not only did the acquirers not have a successor lined up, but to complicate matters further, Blass warned his long-time assistants and top designers that they would "not [...] like the people who bought the company."[171] Two of his top assistants left the company, leaving no heir apparent to continue the Blass design legacy and ultimately unraveling the Blass empire.[172]

A related provision important to an acquirer is that the employment obligations are transferable in the event that the company is further sold or merged.[173] If an acquirer does not bargain for this type of right, they may find that they give the designer hold-up value for any subsequent sale of the company and reduce the transferability of the company (and hence their own liquidity).[174] The designer, however, may strongly resist this type of transferability arguing, with some conviction, that they are agreeing to be sold or merged with *this* acquirer but not necessarily any acquirer. Practically

---

166. *See, e.g.*, Jacqueline Lewis, *Executives Talk M&A at AAFA Forum*, Footwear News (Oct. 11, 2011)("[Wesley] Card noted the strategy behind successful acquisitions like [Nine West Group, Inc. and Barneys New York Inc.] included building relationships with key players at soon-to-be acquired companies. 'You'll have a much easier relationship and the ability to make changes,' he said."); Michael Kors Holdings Ltd. (Form F-1) (Dec. 2, 2011) (12).

167. Steven M. Bragg, Mergers & Acquisitions: A Condensed Practitioner's Guide, (John Wiley and Sons 2008), *available at* http://books.google.com/books?id=DfHH2B543xEC&pg=PT157&dq=Mergers+and+acquisitions+issues+retain++key+personnel+benefits+problems&hl=en&sa=X&ei=Ukc5T7vyCYfV0QG5xZWxAg&sqi=2&ved=0CEUQ6AEwAA#v=onepage&q=Mergers%20and%20acquisitions%20issues%20retain%20%20key%20personnel%20benefits%20problems&f=false ("In any acquisition, the acquiree will have a key cluster of employees who are subject matter experts or rain makers who are responsible for the bulk of all sales. These employees are likely at the core of the acquiree's central value proposition, and so are extremely valuable.... If they leave, there may be a devastating decline in organizational knowledge and morale, along with a very high replacement cost.").

168. *See, e.g.*, Eric Wilson, *Question for Prada: Now What?*, N.Y. Times, Jan. 25, 2005 ("'I always think it's a challenge when the creative force of a company leaves his own brand,' said Ron Frasch, the chief merchant of Saks Fifth Avenue.... 'Commercially, I don't know how valid Helmut Lang is without Helmut,' said Sue Patneaude, the executive vice president of designer apparel at Nordstrom, which dropped the collection two years ago.").

169. Eric Wilson, *The Long Fall of the House of Blass*, N.Y. Times (Dec. 25, 2008), http://www.nytimes.com/2008/12/25/fashion/25BLASS.html.

170. *Id.*

171. *Id.*

172. *Id.*

173. Fashion Law, *supra* note 9.

174. *See* Douglas Hand, *Think Tank: Douglas Hand on the Challenge of M&A for Namesake Brands*, WWD (Jan. 23, 2016), http://wwd.com/business-news/mergers-acquisitions/douglas-hand-challenges-mergers-namesake-brands-10320585/.

speaking, the designer effectively has this right (even if not necessarily as a contractual right) since as long as the designer remains highly valued, they can in most cases effectively dictate to whom the company is sold and with whom they work going forward. An acquirer will rarely want to pay full value for a business with a designer who has expressed a desire not to work under their ownership. In other words, potential acquirers with whom the designer has expressed a willingness to work will likely value the business more (and hence can afford to pay more).

Given these factors, it is not surprising that prior to the announcement of the Michael Kors initial public offering back in 2011, the company's owners had already locked down a lifetime employment contract with Mr. Kors[175] and a multi-year agreement with the company's Chairman and Chief Executive Officer, John Idol.[176]

ii. Creative Control

From the designer's point of view, particularly in the case of an eponymous designer, the designer will want to ensure that he or she retains a certain level of control over creative aspects like the design of the products bearing the designer's name, as well as how those products, and the designer herself, are promoted and marketed.[177] As part of Michael Kors' agreement to remain with the company for life, he was given creative and aesthetic control of the products produced and sold under or bearing the Michael Kors and related trademarks, including exclusive control of the design of such products.[178] In many instances, these types of creative control provisions will be fine with the acquirer. In many respects, the creative spark is exactly what the acquirer is purchasing and will clear the designer's path to ensure it survives. The only areas where creative control may be limited is where the design is effectively determining price points or, in some cases, where product material choices dictate price points. However, management has a meaningful check on such issues through the control of the budgetary process.

A failure to deal with these issues contractually can lead to the types of problems encountered with the Prada Group's acquisition of Jil Sander.[179] According to industry accounts, Jil Sander left the company shortly after its acquisition of her namesake brand due to a strained relationship with the company's chief executive,

---

175. *See* Michael Kors Holdings Ltd. (Form F-1) (Dec. 2, 2011) (76–77). Kors signed his deal several months prior to the filing for the initial public offering and stipulated that he will be employed by the firm until his death, disability, or dismissal for cause. *Id.*

176. *See* Michael Kors Holdings Ltd. (Form F-1) (Dec. 2, 2011) (76–77).

177. *See* Hand, *supra* note 174.

178. *See* Michael Kors Holdings Ltd. (Form F-1), *supra* note 67. *See also* Ella Alexander, *In Demand*, Vogue U.K. (Dec. 16, 2011), http://www.vogue.co.uk/news/2011/12/05/michael-kors-ipo---36-billion-dollars-initial-public-offering.

179. Gina Bellafante, *Front Row; Jil Sander is Divorcing Prada*, N.Y. Times (Jan. 25, 2000), *available at* http://www.nytimes.com/2000/01/25/style/front-row-jil-sander-divorcing-prada-after-next-month-s-fall-women-s-collection.html. After next month's fall women's collection in Milan, she plans to leave her signature company.

Patrizio Bertelli, which developed over disagreements as to what direction the brand should take.[180]

iii. Noncompetes

A final critical aspect of any designer's employment agreement is a noncompete, a guarantee from the designer that in the event they leave the company, they will not compete with it.[181] Agreements not to compete typically will prohibit an employee from: (i) competing with the employer by participating in a competing business or aiding a competitor, (ii) using confidential information and proprietary designs or (iii) owning equity in a competitor (other than insubstantial interests-less than 5 to 10 percent of publicly held companies).[182] Importantly, the courts in certain jurisdictions (California in particular[183]) are hesitant to enforce noncompete clauses that are for an extensive period or that cover a large territory,[184] therefore, the clause must be carefully worded and the agreement must provide for independent consideration for the noncompete beyond the general terms of the employment agreement. In my experience, the noncompete obligation is placed both in the employment agreement *and* in the transaction agreement to increase the consideration being provided to support the noncompete obligation.

The concept of a noncompete is also extended in the fashion industry to the use of an eponymous designer's name after they have sold their namesake company.[185] Indeed, a designer may even negotiate for the right to compete in the industry in exchange for relinquishing their ability to use their name in association therewith.[186] A failure to clearly identify the boundaries of such a scenario, however, can lead to costly litigation—as was the case with both Paolo Gucci and Joseph Abboud. In the case of Paolo Gucci, Paolo wished to continue in the fashion industry after a falling-out with his family's famous apparel company, which resulted in him being sued by the family

---

180. *Id.*; *see also* Christina Passariello, *Prada Sells Jil Sander to Private-Equity Fund*, Wall St. J. (Feb. 24, 2006), http://www.changecapitalpartners.com/news/read/491c47bdadefaf816a9fb14c7a58d6a0.

181. Reed & Lajoux, *supra* note 2, at 502–3, 592; *see, e.g., Tommy Hilfiger's $3.38 Billion Acquisition: Biggest Deal Ever in Apparel Naming and Branding*, Name Wire (March 16, 2010) ("Following Phillips Van Heusen Corporation's (PVH) acquisition of Tommy Hilfiger, PVH then sought ability to control name, out of fear that Hilfiger was acquiring smaller brands himself in order to create a breakout, competitive brand.").

182. Reed & Lajoux, *supra* note 19, at 502–3.

183. Bob Egelko, *State Supreme Court Rejects Noncompete Clauses*, S.F. Chron. (Aug. 8, 2008), *available at* http://www.sfgate.com/cgi-bin/article.cgi?f=/c/a/2008/08/07/BAUH12716R.DTL&tsp=1.

184. *Id.* at 503.

185. Fashion Law, *supra* note 9.

186. For example, designers Kate Spade and Robert Mouret. *See Kate Spade Turns Kate Valentine, Demonstrates the Risks of the Personal Brand Name*, The Fashion Law (June 5, 2018), http://www.thefashionlaw.com/home/kate-spade-turns-kate-valentine-demonstrates-the-risks-of-the-personal-brand-name; Dolly Jones, *Roland Mouret Returns*, Vogue (Sept. 9, 2010), https://www.vogue.co.uk/article/roland-mouret-buys-back-his-name-and-prepares-a-standalone-boutique.

company.[187] The court held that Paolo could make limited use of his proper name in connection with clothing, including identifying himself as the designer of products sold under a separate trademark, but Paolo was enjoined from using the name Gucci or Paolo Gucci as a trademark or trade name.[188] The Second Circuit created a similar limitation for designer Joseph Abboud, who, after selling his trademark to JA Apparel Corp. began marketing a new line under the name "jaz," which name was often accompanied by a tag line including the name "Joseph Abboud."[189] JA Apparel Group sued and the result was a limited injunction whereby Abboud could use his name only in promotional or advertising materials, only in connection with the trademark "jaz" and only if a statement accompanied such use disclaiming any association with products sold under the trade name Joseph Abboud.[190]

e. The Closing

To consummate any M&A deal, several different items will have to carefully synchronize in order to produce a harmonious closing. The closing of the transaction is an actual event through which the parties complete the transaction by executing and delivering certain documents and, if applicable, transferring funds. The closing process may last for a few hours, or days or weeks depending on how much negotiation of the satisfaction of certain closing conditions is left for the final moments and upon the ability of the parties to satisfy the conditions precedent to closing in a timely manner.[191] In the context of a fashion deal, in my experience, there are three key aspects to a closing that must be borne in mind: (i) the transfer of IP; (ii) the execution of key employment agreements; and, if the brand has retail stores, (iii) the transfer of retail leases.

Given the relative importance that IP plays in the overall deal, ensuring: (i) that there is no litigation respecting the ownership of the IP, and (ii) that the IP will be properly transferred to the acquirer are usually conditions that must be met in order for the transaction to close.[192]

As already discussed, one of the critical elements of a fashion M&A deal is negotiating the employment agreement with the head designer.[193] The acquirer will, to

---

187. Fashion Law, *supra* at note 15. *See also* Robert McG. Thomas, Jr., *Paolo Gucci, 64, Prestigious, if Litigious, Designer,* N.Y. Times (Oct. 14, 1995), *available at* http://www.nytimes.com/1995/10/14/nyregion/paolo-gucci-64-prestigious-if-litigious-designer.html.

188. Fashion Law, *supra* at note 9; Gucci v. Gucci Shops, Inc., 688 F. Supp. 916, 928 (S.D.N.Y. 1988).

189. Fashion Law, *supra* at note 9; JA Apparel Corp. v. Abboud, 682 F. Supp. 2d 294, 322 (S.D.N.Y. 2010).

190. JA Apparel Corp., 682 F. Supp. 2d 294, 322 (S. D. N. Y. 2010).

191. Reed & Lajoux, *supra* note 19, at 601.

192. *See* Lanning G. Bryer & Scott J. Lebson, *Intellectual Property in Mergers and Acquisitions,* WIPO, 2, http://www.wipo.int/sme/en/documents/pdf/mergers.pdf (last visited Feb. 15, 2011).

193. *See, e.g.,* Annette L. Ranft & Michael D. Lord, *Acquiring New Knowledge: The Role of Retaining Human Capital in Acquisitions of High-Tech Firms,* 11 J. High Tech. Mgmt. Res. 295, 299 (2000) (discussing the irreplaceable value that top executives contribute to an enterprise).

the extent feasible, negotiate the principal terms of this agreement (price, duration, noncompete) in advance and make its execution a condition to closing.[194] This will reduce the risk that the designer holds up the closing of the deal by trying to renegotiate the terms at the closing table.

Retail leases may also be involved in the closing process as the transfer of a retail lease, directly through an asset transfer, or sometimes indirectly through a stock transfer, typically involving the landlord.[195] Retail leases commonly contain a restriction on the assignment of the lease without the landlord's consent, and in some cases may trigger a landlord's right to terminate the lease.[196] In either event, this gives the landlord the right to renegotiate the lease terms before providing consent.[197]

5. Post-Closing Integration

As discussed in Section 1, regardless of the category or structure, all mergers and acquisitions share a common objective—achieving synergies.[198] Its achievement is highly dependent upon the successful post-acquisition integration of the combined entity.[199] With knowledge of such a fundamental requirement for success almost certainly in the hands of all parties responsible for the post-transaction integration process, why is it that so many mergers fail to live up to expectations?[200]

The answer lies in one of three places—the perceived rationales for doing the deal were illusory, the integration plan was flawed, or the implementation of the integration plan was ineffective. As we cannot speak to the contents of any specific integration plan—no grounds exist for such information to become public—we will not be able to distinguish integrations that failed due to poor integration planning from those that failed because of poor integration. Therefore, we will necessarily make the assumption that the integration plans for the less successful transactions on which there is any significant valuable commentary failed due

---

194. *See* Reed & Lajoux, *supra* note 19, at 502–04.

195. *See* Alan A. Sachs, *Lease Assignment Issues in Retail Business Acquisitions*, 49 Prac. Law. 57, 5, 2003 at 57–58.

196. *Id.*

197. *Id.*

198. *See* Rovetta, *supra*, note ("[T]he fact that the key success factor of an acquisition is the creation of synergies among companies is taken for granted.").

199. *See Merger Success Hinges on Effective Integration*, Deloitte & Touche LLP, http://www.deloitte.com/view/en_CA/ca/insights/insights-and-issues/d0da33d0303fb110VgnVCM100000ba42f00aRCRD.htm (last visited Feb. 15, 2011) [hereinafter *Merger Success*] ("Many M&A transactions fail to realize the synergies that are often highlighted when a transaction is first announced. After a company has developed its M&A strategy and executed the deal, the bottom line comes down to successful integration.").

200. *Merger Integration: Delivering on the Promise*, Booz-Allen & Hamilton Inc. (2001), http://www.boozallen.com/media/file/76776.pdf [hereinafter *Merger Integration*] ("A study of deals that closed in 1997 and 1998 discovered that 53 percent of the deals had failed to deliver their expected results.").

to poor post-transaction implementation of integration and not poor integration planning, and that the successful transactions benefited from the strength of the implementation of a sound integration plan.

a. Elements of an Effective Integration Plan

Before discussing the specifics of sound integration planning, it is worthwhile to note two challenges inherent in post-transaction integration that are magnified in the case of M&A activity in the fashion industry. Successful integration must navigate corporate culture issues and address potential rifts between the creative team and the management team in cases where such roles are filled by distinct organizations. "It is clear that such a strategic acquisition doesn't create value unless the purchase is followed by a concrete sharing of values, experiences and management practice."[201]

In the case of horizontal transactional activity, the ability to achieve anticipated synergies might depend largely on how the cultures of the various brands can mesh for the common good of the enterprise, while maintaining the core distinguishing attributes of the individual brands. Benefits should not be limited to the immediate impact on sales or market share, but should include the long-term exploitation of advantages in production and distribution activities, and above all, better exploitation of common competencies and know-how.[202]

However, cross-brand cultural integration risks "homogenization as well as the loss of the distinctive identities of the single brands."[203] The risk is particularly acute in the case of fashion companies—whose success is indelibly linked to the symbolic aspects of their products.[204] The differentiation of such brands from their competitors is exclusively based on the stylistic features of the product and on its consistency with the brand image.[205] For that reason, managing different brands through a single parent company is very risky and could undermine the entire system of core values on which the brand and the company have built their identity.[206]

As previously discussed, management considerations are a sensitive subject with significant potential for bottom-line implications. However, it is usually the case that many responsibilities for the non-creative management of the target brand will be taken away from the target's creative leadership.[207] This practice allows the creative team to focus on its core competencies, while delegating the non-creative

---

201. Rovetta, *supra* note 15, at 15.

202. *Id.* at 13.

203. *Id.* at 15–16.

204. *Id.*

205. *See* Stefania Saviolo, *Brand and Identity Management in Fashion Companies*, 10–11, http://www.fashionnetworks.com/images/article_pdf/wp66_WXJYXKZLUARZ7FH8GE01T01192111699.pdf ("In industries based on fashion and style the stylistic identity is the focal point of the product and brand system. . . .").

206. *See* Rovetta, *supra* note 15, at 15–16.

207. *Id.* at 15.

business requirements to the acquirer's established managerial functions.[208] Even if the designer is willing to relinquish control of certain aspects of the company, care must be taken to ensure that the designer will work well with the new management structure. There is a risk that the creative team will lose all sight of the economics of brand success or passion for the brand's design aesthetic amidst the cultural changes going on.[209] Incentive compensation can often bring employees' incentives into alignment, but certain creative leaders (particularly eponymous designers) may be less willing to execute certain profitable strategies that they view as detrimental to their reputation regardless of the compensation for such perceived diminution in reputation.[210]

Keeping the foregoing in mind, the following are likely to be elements of any successful integration plan:

i. Assign a Dedicated Team, Backed by Executive Support, to Manage the Integration Program[211]

Transition teams must be solely focused on the integration process and granted sufficient authority to mandate changes at the operating level to effectively manage the integration process.[212] It is of course critical that the right personnel be assigned to the integration team. Certain roles will be critical in virtually all integrations, including information technology and systems, human resources, and communications.[213] Other members of the integration team might vary by the transactional strategy and the nature of the synergies to be exploited.[214]

In the case of market intensification, where the transaction involves direct head-to-head competitors, maintaining the core values on which each formerly competitive brand has built its identity will be a fundamental challenge. For example, in the case of the Adidas and Reebok merger, it was important that Adidas maintain its image as a technology leader, while Reebok not lose its ability to recognize and respond to shifting trends.[215] But, it can also be synergistic for each brand's core competencies to rub off on its former competitor. Pre-integration decisions will need to be made regarding the best reporting structure for managing such issues—if there is to be a single person ultimately responsible for the marketing of both brands, then she would likely be on the integration team; whereas, if the brand identities are going to be managed by coequals, then both should likely participate. Such decisions can

208. *See id.*

209. *See id.*

210. *See, e.g.*, Ranft, *supra* note 193, at 302 (explaining how financial incentives are used to retain key employees after acquiring a high-tech business).

211. *See generally Merger Success*, *supra* note 199.

212. *Id.*

213. *See Merger Integration*, *supra* note 200, at 12–13.

214. *Id.*

215. Linda Balboul, *Adidas-Reebok Merger*, Article Base (Mar. 13, 2010), http://www.articlesbase.com/marketing-articles/adidasreebok-merger-1983240.html.

impact the direction the integration ultimately takes. For example, how best to implement executive management's directive to permit Adidas to leverage Reebok's comparatively advantaged apparel business?[216]

If the strategy behind the transaction was a product extension the acquirer will strive to add the target's products to the company's existing line of products. An example of such a transaction was the acquisition of the Persol brand of eyewear by the Luxottica Group.[217] Persol's distribution was expanded from purveyors of luxury eyewear to being offered at Sunglass Hut, and their price points dropped significantly. It is clear that the integration team was charged with the executive decision to take the Persol brand down market. There can be little doubt that the Luxottica Group marketing leadership dominated the marketing function on the integration team. It is also likely that much of Persol's sales staff, accustomed to calling on luxury boutique sales staff, was consolidated and that the remaining sales force needed to become facile with all of the other brands and products sold by Luxottica Group. In this case, a senior member of the Luxottica Group sales team would be a likely participant on the integration team in order to ensure that the potential synergies are exploited fully.

The synergistic keys to success in a vertical integration are achieving economies in purchasing, sales and distribution.[218] In a backward vertical integration it is important to be able to enable the acquirer to purchase raw materials at a more competitive price.[219] There exists the possibility for a complete revamping of the supply chain, as certain materials formerly purchased by the acquirer are now sourced internally and the raw materials previously required by the target are now raw materials required to be purchased by the combined entity. Thus, the purchasing function will need to play a fundamental role on the transition team. In the case of a forward vertical integration, where a supplier buys a current or potential customer, each of the acquired brands will, for the first time, have full cycle design, manufacturing, and sales functions in-house.[220] Therefore, integration of such brands will require that virtually all functions have a seat at the integration table.

ii. Plan for Workforce Integration and Create a Retention Strategy for Key Personnel

Successful integration of the organizational capabilities of the participants is key to the success of a brand acquisition. Management should establish clear internal organizational expectations and guidelines for the interaction of employees, resources, and brands to ensure that all activities smooth the transition.

---

216. *Id.*

217. *Persol*, Luxottica (last visited July 25, 2018), http://www.luxottica.com/en/eyewear-brands/persol.

218. Reed & Lajoux, *supra* note 19, at 22–23.

219. *See, e.g.*, Diedrich, *supra* note 55; Socha *supra* note 55.

220. Reed & Lajoux, *supra* note 19, at 23.

Almost all M&A activity results in redundancies, but missteps regarding personnel issues are not always easily overcome in the fashion industry, where human capital plays an integral part in the company's success or failure. It is absolutely essential that the functional leaders work with human resources to shape the functionality of the post-rationalization entity as closely as possible to executive management's vision for the post-integration entity.

If an eponymous designer is associated with the target brand, there must be a plan as to whether and under what terms they will remain with the company because post-transaction disputes between an eponymous designer and the entity owning the brand bearing her name can be disastrous.[221]

iii. Address Perceived Impact on Customer Base

After the transaction, the combined entity must manage its outward-facing image and the individual brands. For this reason, properly incentivized and highly functional brand management is the key to the success of any brand acquisition.

However, the combined company might be so overwhelmed with the mechanics of integration that the work of implementing the planned-for synergies is subjugated. Managers at each of the pre-transaction entities are likely to be desperate for any indication of their future value to the combined entity (and scrambling for alternatives if their value looks to be diminished). It is up to the executives of the combined entity to ensure that managers deliver the expected level of service and productivity during the transition so that no decline in quality or service is permitted. Any adverse impact on customer loyalty and perception, even if the cause for such impact is temporary, could have potentially devastating consequences to the long-term success of the combined entity.[222]

b. Success or Failure?

After consummating an M&A transaction and developing a coherent integration plan, are combined entities not home free? Unfortunately, far from it. The most difficult task lies ahead—implementing integrations.[223]

So, how successful have fashion companies been in implementing integrations? The ultimate answer in the success or failure of M&A transactions is whether the combined entity delivers value over time to shareholders in excess of the value that would have been created had the M&A transaction not taken place. There is scant

---

221. *See, e.g.*, note 97 *supra* ("After next month's fall women's collection in Milan, she plans to leave her signature company"); Passariello, *supra* note 180.

222. Hand, *supra* note 174.

223. *Merger Integration*, *supra* note 200 ("Integrating Companies is a massive undertaking. The tactical issues are tremendous. Indeed, when companies explained why they had not met expectations, more than two-thirds cited execution related reasons . . . Only 32 percent attributed their failure to meet expectations to more strategic concerns such as poor fit or overly ambitious vision").

evidence on whether fashion M&A has been more or less successful than M&A in other industries.[224]

While anecdotal results indicate that M&A activity can be a sound growth strategy for fashion companies, it is certain that positive results depend on the acquirer running a successful process from start to finish—locating appropriate targets available at properly conceived valuations, performing thorough due diligence on chosen targets to validate the applicable valuation, choosing the most appropriate transaction structure (from both value-enhancement and potential liability perspectives), negotiating and documenting the final terms of the acquisition in a manner that best protects the acquirer's interests, putting in place an effective integration plan and executing the integration. Fashion companies would be wise to keep M&A in their arsenal of growth strategies, but in my opinion (and as an M&A lawyer I speak, perhaps against my own financial interest) given all of the potential for error in the M&A process, M&A should not be pursued at the expense of considering the many means available for organic internal growth.

Notes

1. Among the three methods for valuing a deal, is there one you see as preferable? Are there ones that are better suited to different kinds of acquirers or acquisition strategies? What would motivate you to choose one above the other?

2. Regarding asset acquisition, why might a company sell only part of its business or product but not all of it?

---

224. Rovetta, *supra* note 15, at 4–5 ("Although the strategic arguments the analysis is based on can be verified even in a short time span (at least because the reference sample is broader as it includes all the companies in the sector, listed and unlisted), it is definitely harder to develop the due mathematical and statistical analysis that the subject requires. . . . Furthermore, the small number of companies listed so far is a concrete limit for the cases sample this analysis can work with. Although a very big number of acquisitions have been carried out, only a few of them involved listed companies.").

Chapter 2

Sustainability and the Fashion Industry

Nancy S. Cleveland
With contributions from Kimberly Quick

> *"We believe that the world needs to urgently work towards creating a sustainable future—one where everyone thrives on a healthy planet and a level-playing field. We are committed to innovating our way into that future, both within Nike and in partnership with others."*
>
> —Mark Parker, CEO, Nike

Fashion brands have experienced mounting pressure to demonstrate socially and environmentally responsible practices. High-profile disasters like the 2012 Tazreen factory fire and the 2013 Rana Plaza garment factory collapse have called the world's attention to dangerous working conditions in less developed countries and elevated the problem in the minds of consumers. Social media campaigns like #fashionrevolution and #slowfashion encourage consumers to demand more ethical manufacturing and transparency about how their clothes are made. As a result, many shoppers—particularly millennials and younger generations—have become more sustainability conscious. When new controversies related to negative environmental or social impacts or other unethical behaviors emerge, companies can face significant legal and reputational risks.[1]

On the opportunity side, investing in environmentally and socially responsible practices can help prepare the fashion industry for a prosperous future. Lawyers should become knowledgeable about the significant sustainability issues facing the fashion industry so they can meet the evolving expectations and needs of clients seeking to futureproof their business and stay ahead of regulation. In these times of growing volatility in global markets and shifts in consumer preferences, only brands that are able to demonstrate sustainability best practices will keep pace with fast-changing conditions and thrive.

1. *See, e.g.*, Chavie Lieber, *Why Fashion Brands Destroy Billions' Worth of Their Own Merchandise Every Year*, Vox (Sep. 17, 2018, 08:00 AM), https://www.vox.com/the-goods/2018/9/17/17852294/fashion-brands-burning-merchandise-burberry-nike-h-and-m [https://perma.cc/H5V5-PA7H]; Elizabeth Paton, *Burberry to Stop Burning Clothing and Other Goods It Can't Sell*, N.Y. Times (Sep. 6, 2018), https://www.nytimes.com/2018/09/06/business/burberry-burning-unsold-stock.html [https://perma.cc/KY3P-4EM2].

A. Sustainability Basics

In general terms, sustainability is defined as the capacity to thrive into the future; the ability to make a profit without doing harm. Capacity building requires balancing short-term realities with long-term objectives to manage risks and opportunities wherever they arise. More specifically, corporate sustainability means using management practices that create a more prosperous and responsible future by looking at the impact a business has on people, the environment, and the economy through the governance decisions the business makes on how to allocate capital resources.

1. Systems Thinking

Systems thinking is an essential framework for sustainability-based governance, operations, and goal setting.[2] A systems approach highlights the extended relationships and connections a company has with regard to the three core areas of sustainability's focus: environment, society, and economy.

The global interconnections among people, the planet, and prosperity form a complex web. To build sustainability capacity, systems thinking is a useful and critical way of analyzing complex problems that may pose risks for a company and solutions that mitigate risk or present new opportunities. Systems thinking clarifies and reveals:

- the general nature and function of the larger systems within which businesses operate, like the Earth's ecosystems and climate;
- how a business interacts with those systems and contributes to problems, directly and indirectly;
- what a business can do, on its own or in concert with others, to be part of the solution.

To be effective, managing a business through the lens of sustainability requires a holistic understanding of how things work together. A systems approach helps those engaged in this work understand the complexity of the world around them. It encourages thinking about relationships, connectedness, cycles, and feedback loops.

2. Company Valuation and the Six Capitals

In the last half-century, the value of a business has been transitioning from being largely physical and financial assets to predominantly intangible assets (e.g., brand, human capital, and intellectual property). This transition has come about because of a variety of factors, such as improvements in transportation and communications

2. *See* Learning For Sustainability, https://learningforsustainability.net/systems-thinking/ [https://perma.cc/9GQX-N6GH].

that have made outsourcing and globalization feasible. Just as financial tools developed after the Great Depression to measure and disclose the financial condition of a business, today new tools for measuring and reporting on so-called nonfinancial, intangible assets are being developed. At the same time, global risks and drivers such as climate change, population growth, urbanization, and resource depletion are causing a profound shift in how stakeholders view value creation.

Today there are several types of capital that make up a company's overall value. Traditional financial value metrics such as net income, return on investment ("ROI"), and cash flow are based on standards issued by regulatory bodies such as the Financial Accounting Standard Board ("FASB"), and the International Accounting Standards Board ("IASB"). Mature accounting standards and practices provide a robust framework for managing, valuing, and reporting on tangible assets such as:

- **Financial Capital**—including all available funds, whether debt or equity; and
- **Manufactured Capital**—including material goods and infrastructure that are owned, leased, or controlled by the company.

Financial statements and market valuation have not historically taken social and environmental externalities into account. They do not provide a good mechanism for measuring these intangibles. As a result, the full picture of a company's value and level of risk is incomplete. Managing, valuing, and reporting on the following common capitals is becoming an increasingly important aspect of both business strategy and investing:

- **Intellectual Capital**—including brand, reputation, research and development, the means of creating competitive advantage, and business processes;
- **Human Capital**—including the direct and indirect workforce, made up of individual capabilities and skills to complete tasks and create intellectual property essential to business success, along with a willingness to continue using that ability for the benefit of the company;
- **Social/Relationship Capital**—including stakeholders and business networks, the ability to conform to social norms and build trust and license to operate, with or without regulation; and
- **Natural Capital**—including direct and indirect access to and use of environmental resources and ecosystem services such as food and nutrient cycles that include things like pollination and soil regeneration, raw materials for medicines and industry, clean air, and clean water.

Effectively managing and reporting on all forms of capital are critical aspects of capturing the full value of a company and understanding risks and opportunities that may impact that value. Optimal use and balancing of these six types of capital help an organization to be more successful and prosper over the long-term. These concepts extend beyond the important baseline of making sure that an organization is profitable. They incorporate and recognize the influence of a wider array of stakeholders than just shareholders. With the adoption of the B-corporate form, many states are acknowledging the importance of other stakeholders and interests rather than just shareholders and profit maximization.[3] The so-called non-financial capitals require a business to take into account environmental and social concerns about business activities. Sustainability management practices provide the best tools available today for doing that.

When companies strategically incorporate sustainability as a management practice, it means they are taking social, environmental, and economic risks and opportunities into account in business planning and decision making. Embedding sustainability thinking as part of corporate governance and culture is gaining traction in the world's largest companies and slowly rippling through global economies. It is increasingly evident that there is financial value to be gained by addressing sustainability.[4] Sustainability management can reduce expenses and grow revenue by enabling companies to better manage risks and capitalize on opportunities that might otherwise be overlooked.

3. The Role of Legal Counsel

Because sustainability provides a lens to help fashion industry clients understand current and emerging risks and opportunities, to effectively advise fashion clients, lawyers must be conversant with relevant sustainability issues for the fashion business and how changing conditions are putting pressure on the industry to demonstrate responsible practices. Lawyers can contribute their expertise to help fashion clients integrate sustainability into their businesses.

Sustainability issues touch many key organizational activities that fall within the purview of corporate counsel, including regulatory compliance, supply chain management, access to capital, mergers and acquisitions, human capital management, project financing, and reporting disclosures. Lawyers can and should advise clients on sustainability issues, including insights into current and emerging stakeholder priorities, regulatory requirements or roadblocks, and corporate disclosure requirements on environmental, social, and governance ("ESG") issues.[5] By understanding

3. *See* Chapter 1, *supra*.

4. Mozaffar N. Khan, George Serafeim & Aaron Yoon, *Corporate Sustainability: First Evidence on Materiality*, Harvard Business School Working Paper, No. 15-073 (Mar. 2015), http://nrs.harvard.edu/urn-3:HUL.InstRepos:14369106 [https://perma.cc/4WVR-WP7C]; *see also* Virginia Harper Ho, *From Public Policy to Materiality: Non-Financial Reporting, Shareholder Engagement, and Rule 14a-8's Ordinary Business Exception*, 76 Wash. & Lee. L. Rev. 3 (2019), https://scholarlycommons.law.wlu.edu/wlulr/vol76/iss3/5[https://perma.cc/S9K4-UFHM].

5. For public company sustainability disclosure analysis, *see* Nancy S. Cleveland, David M. Lynn & Stephen A. Pike, *Sustainability Reporting: The Lawyer's Response*, Bus. L. Today (Jan. 2015); *see also* Ho, *supra* note 4; Virginia Harper Ho, *Disclosure Overload? Lessons for Risk Disclosure & ESG Reporting Reform from the Regulation S-K Concept Release*, 65 Vill. L. Rev. 1 (2020).

industry sustainability issues, particularly with respect to reputation and ESG disclosures, lawyers will be better equipped to manage the business' social license to operate as well as litigation risks.

Lawyers can also help clients evaluate how a commitment to, and meaningful actions toward achieving, sustainability can support strategic business goals. For example, lawyers are well-equipped to advise boards, executives, and senior management on the opportunities associated with making sustainability commitments on global platforms, such as a company website or public filings, having considered the pros and cons of voluntary versus required disclosures or differences in operating circumstances in various jurisdictions in which a company operates.

B. Key Sustainability Issues for the Fashion Industry

The major sustainability issues for the fashion industry fall into several categories: managing the supply chain, working conditions, and the efficient use of water, energy, and chemicals. These issues are multifaceted and interconnected. Environmental impacts can influence social impacts, and vice versa. For example, environmental pollution may affect the welfare of workers and the surrounding community.

1. Managing the Supply Chain

The fashion industry is a highly globalized industry, with products typically designed in one country, manufactured in one or more others, and distributed worldwide. This is done through complex supply chains that are often difficult to understand and track. Because factories in producing countries may manufacture for many different brands and retailers, brands may not be able to promote sustainable practices without "coopetition," where competitors cooperate and work with each other to effect change. Coopetition is often used to break through a market barrier when no one competitor can do so alone. Once the barrier is removed, competition resumes in the newly created, more sustainable market.

Although this model of production may maximize efficiency or cost, it also creates pervasive supply chain challenges. Many companies are unaware of social and environmental issues beyond the first tier of their suppliers. As materials move downstream and across borders, it becomes increasingly difficult to track the origins of finished products. Companies often are unaware that their suppliers are outsourcing production. Subcontracted companies could also be outsourcing to other manufacturing facilities.

A lack of transparency in the supply chain exposes companies in the fashion industry to risks on a wide array of significant social and environmental impacts. Negative impacts associated with production—whether pollution, child or forced labor, dangerous working conditions or unfair compensation—often occur before

Tier 1 suppliers, but the complexity of the industry's supply chains makes the impact difficult to track, monitor, and change.

These types of supply chain risks became clear after a series of high-profile accidents resulting from unsafe working conditions. In September 2012, 254 people died in a fire at the Ali Enterprises Garment Factory in Pakistan. Another fire occurred two months later at a garment factory in Bangladesh, where at least 111 people died. In 2013, the deadliest accident occurred at Rana Plaza. This building housed five garment factories that manufactured products for European and American apparel brands. When the building collapsed due to structural issues, 1,137 people lost their lives.

These accidents highlight systemic issues within the fashion industry and a lack of supply chain transparency. The industry's complex supply chains conceal hazardous health and safety issues for workers. Fashion retailers face increased demand for inexpensive clothing, which leads to tighter production deadlines for suppliers. In particular, "fast fashion," which seeks to capitalize on new fashion trends through rapid turnarounds from runway to store, demands extremely cheap and fast labor. As a result, the rise of fast fashion and relatively tight margins in the industry as a whole have incentivized many factories in producing countries to seek the lowest possible labor costs so that they can attract trade. The fast fashion customers' demands have resulted in significant human rights violations, cut corners at every turn, overlooked building safety, and imposed abusive work schedules deep into the supply chain.

Companies unaware of issues within their supply chains face considerable risks. For example, Wal-Mart was unaware that some of its garments had been produced at Rana Plaza. After the accident, the company faced considerable public backlash.[6]

While many smaller brands lack the capacity to effectively monitor and enforce best practices in their supply chains, advocating and putting contractual requirements in place should be a minimum point of departure for all. As larger companies become more transparent about the sustainability of their supply chains, smaller companies will gain supply chain insights from this information and likely will benefit from increased market pressures for adherence to best practices.[7]

Cooperation among companies is needed to address pervasive and systemic challenges within the industry's supply chain practice. Chain-of-custody and other accountability systems can help improve knowledge about where materials are sourced and produced. Blockchain technology is an example of how digital advances might be used to improve transparency. Blockchain's distributed ledger

---

6. *Three Years After Tazreen Factory Fire Walmart Still Refuses to Pay*, CLEAN CLOTHES CAMPAIGN (Nov. 18, 2015), https://cleanclothes.org/news/2015/11/18/three-years-after-tazreen-factory-fire-walmart-still-refuses-to-pay [https://perma.cc/7PC7-29UF].

7. Morten Lehmann et al., *Pulse of Fashion Industry*, GLOBAL FASHION AGENDA, at 34 (2018), *available at* https://www.globalfashionagenda.com/publications/#pulseofthefashionindustry [https://perma.cc/U9U5-S536].

systems enable end-to-end value chain traceability and faster trade transactions by creating digital histories of inventory items. The Lenzing Group, in cooperation with TextileGenesis, is one of the first companies to offer the digital traceability of textile products. Their technology also allows consumers to verify apparel composition and the underlying textile supply chain at the point of sale, by scanning the barcode with a mobile device.[8]

2. Working Conditions and Human Rights

The protection of workers and human rights in the global fashion supply chain is of growing concern among consumers, regulators, NGOs, and leading brands. Primary aspects of this issue include compensation, working hours, employee health and safety, preventing harassment and abuse, freedom of association, child labor, and forced labor.

The industry relies on a complex multitiered system of suppliers, licensees, subcontractors, agents, and recruitment firms that make it challenging for brands to monitor and manage labor conditions across the supply chain. The majority of garment manufacturing is carried out by low-wage workers in emerging markets where labor regulations are limited. Workers in the fashion value supply chains are frequently exposed to occupational hazards, including dangerous working conditions; and environmental hazards, such as improper management of toxic substances.

National minimum wage requirements in most producing countries are below the poverty level. In many areas, garment workers earn less than $2 US per day. Low wages and strict production deadlines can result in the equivalent of slave labor, when workers are required to complete excessive overtime shifts to keep their jobs. Apparel workers rarely have access to employee benefits such as healthcare.

In more developed countries, companies that lack the proper workforce health and safety measures are at risk of fines and litigation for compliance violations. Similarly, strikes and other labor-related work stoppages or slow-downs related to workplace conditions cause production disruptions and potential downstream reputational risks.

Virtually all major fashion companies have committed to avoiding labor abuses in the supply chain. Legal counsel for brands can play an important role in drafting contracts as well as policy and code of conduct documents that require the facilities and agents the brand works with to maintain respectful and secure working

8. Stefan Doboczky, *Ending the Era of Dirty Textiles*, World Econ. F. (Sept. 17, 2019), https://www.weforum.org/agenda/2019/09/ending-the-era-of-dirty-textiles/ [https://perma.cc/79RJ-XBUX].

conditions. To prevent human rights abuses and protect company value, leading brands work with suppliers to monitor labor conditions and ensure compliance.[9]

3. Efficient Use of Energy, Water, and Chemicals

For fashion companies, the biggest environmental impacts are embedded in the materials used to create their products. Whether made of natural or synthetic materials, or a combination of both, material selection is an important factor in determining the environmental and social footprint of a product. Driving factors include quality, performance, cost, and style.

Resources such as energy, water, and chemicals are used at all stages of production and consumption across the fashion value chain, from raw material sourcing to consumer use. The industry predominantly relies on nonrenewable resources including: fertilizers to grow cotton; oils to produce synthetic fibers; chemicals for dyeing and finishing; and fossil fuels for transporting products. Air pollution stems from the industry's energy use, while water pollution results from the discharge of chemicals during dyeing and tanning processes. Activities with the largest impact on pollution are typically found in the product manufacturing stage. Figure 2.1 illustrates the inputs and outputs at each stage of the apparel lifecycle for a cotton t-shirt.

Figure 2.1. Life Cycle Inputs and Outputs of a Cotton T-Shirt

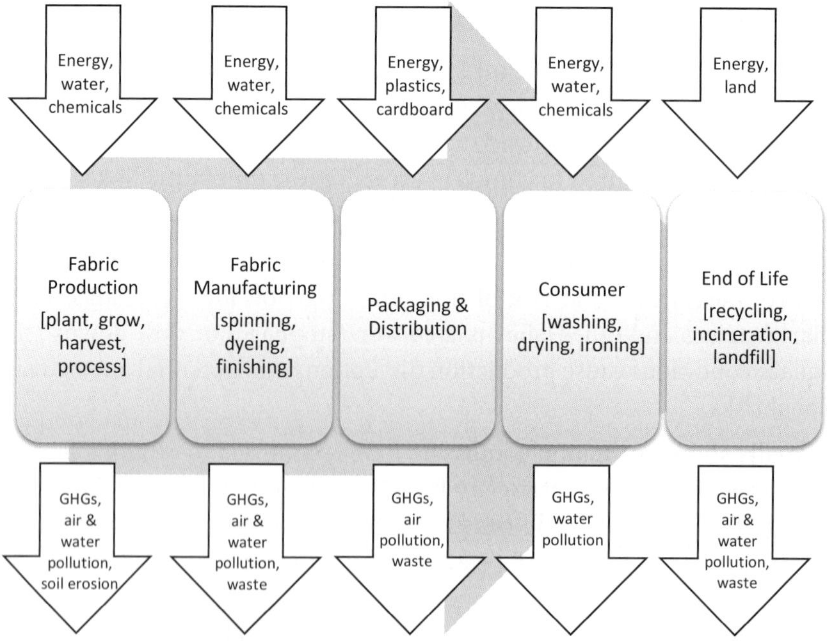

9. Jennifer Anderson, Nancy Cleveland & Amanda Stevens, *Building Sustainable Supply Chains: Approaches to Engagement by Leading Companies*, Sustrana (2017), https://www.sustrana.com/wp-content/uploads/2018/08/Sustrana_Building_Sustainable_Supply_Chains_Research_Paper.pdf [https://perma.cc/L88Z-PHUA].

Although the fashion industry is not thought of as an energy-intensive industry, a significant amount of energy is consumed in the fabrication and processing of textile materials. The apparel and footwear industry combined account for eight percent of global carbon emissions.[10] Textile manufacturing emits 1.2 billion tons of greenhouse gases annually—more than all international flights and maritime shipping combined.[11]

The fashion industry, in particular during textile wet processing, is one of the largest consumers of water in manufacturing and also one of the main producers of industrial wastewater. Textiles production, including cotton farming, represents approximately four percent of global freshwater withdrawals annually. Many key cotton-producing countries are in high water-stressed or water-scarce regions, including China, India, Pakistan, Turkey, and the United States.[12] There are many competing interests among stakeholders when it comes to water access and availability. Water-related challenges can undermine business viability and success. Improper management and poor planning for water resources create negative public perception of a company's commitment to water stewardship and its ability to anticipate and adjust to water conditions, which can ultimately impact a company's ability to operate in a particular location.

Chemicals are used in many different textile processes like pretreatment, dyeing, printing, and finishing. Without active chemical management throughout the supply chain, textile wastewater often contains many hazardous chemicals. If wastewater is not properly treated before discharge, it can cause serious environmental damage and risks to public health. Discharging harmful effluents from production facilities can increase legal and reputational risks and attract scrutiny on the part of consumers and other stakeholders. Reducing the use and release of hazardous chemicals reduces pollution and improves the health of workers and surrounding communities.

Issues such as climate change, water shortage, and resource scarcity are already adversely affecting the fashion industry. If environmental degradation continues

10. Quantis, *Measuring Fashion: Environmental Impact of the Global Apparel and Footwear Industries Study*, at 18 (2018), https://quantis-intl.com/wp-content/uploads/2018/03/measuringfashion_globalimpactstudy_full-report_quantis_cwf_2018a.pdf [https://perma.cc/C7Q9-ZH6D] (see a similar graphic illustration of industry impacts at 10).

11. Ellen McArthur Foundation, *A New Textiles Economy: Redesigning Fashion's Future*, at 3 (Nov. 28, 2017), https://www.ellenmacarthurfoundation.org/publications/a-new-textiles-economy-redesigning-fashions-future [https://perma.cc/492F-28XJ]; *see also* Megan Cerullo, *Fashion Industry's Carbon Impact Bigger than Airline Industry's*, CBS News (Apr. 19, 2019, 12:42 PM), https://www.cbsnews.com/news/earth-day-2019-fashion-industrys-carbon-impact-is-bigger-than-airline-industrys/ [https://perma.cc/2P2E-RSZP]; *see also* United Nations Framework Convention on Climate Change, *Fashion Industry, UN Pursue Climate Action for Sustainable Development* (Jan. 22, 2018), https://unfccc.int/news/fashion-industry-un-pursue-climate-action-for-sustainable-development [https://perma.cc/TEZ9-4CW4].

12. Ellen McArthur Foundation, *supra* note 11.

unabated, this will have disruptive effects on fashion industry supply chains. Companies can help abate negative impacts on people and the environment by working with supplier operations to build capacity for the efficient and considered use of energy, water, and chemicals. The first step involves measuring and establishing baselines. From there, the focus should be on pollution reduction through efficiency and conservation programs and investing in innovative technologies. It is estimated that textile processing mills on average can cut water use by 11 percent and energy use by seven percent, with a return on investment within nine months.[13] In many instances, a lack of know-how is a key obstacle; in others, the will to innovate is key.

Leading brands looking to maintain their competitiveness and protect their supply chains have already started investing in innovative and sustainable solutions to reduce their exposure to price volatility and supply chain disruptions in the future. In the early 2000s, Levi Strauss and Co.'s designers set out to create an entirely new approach for using less water during production. Levi's Water<Less®[14] products reduce the use of water in the finishing process by up to 96 percent for some styles.[15] The company has set a goal for 80 percent of Levi's products to be produced using Water<Less® techniques by 2020. Their ultimate vision is to use only as much water as replenishes naturally, everywhere they operate. The company's Water Action Strategy takes a localized approach to water conservation that is dependent on the needs of the surrounding community in sourcing locations.[16] This contextual approach focuses water reduction efforts where they are most needed and helps protect Levi's social license to operate, particularly in regions of the supply chain facing high water stress.

By taking a proactive approach to the responsible use of resources, companies can minimize risks, reduce costs, enhance the brand, and develop new market opportunities.

---

13. Lehmann, *supra* note 7.

14. Levi Strauss & Co., *How We Make Jeans with Less Water* (Mar. 22, 2018), https://www.levi.com/US/en_US/blog/article/how-we-make-jeans-with-less-water/ [https://perma.cc/G5BJ-NVMX].

15. Levi Strauss & Co. (last visited Nov. 4, 2019), https://www.levi.com/US/en_US/features/sustainability [https://perma.cc/6SNF-9FVF].

16. Levi Strauss & Co., *2025 Water Action Strategy* (Aug. 2019), https://www.levistrauss.com/wp-content/uploads/2019/08/2019_LSCO_WATER_STRATEGY_REPORT.pdf [https://perma.cc/H6JL-6F39].

C. Growing Stakeholder Pressure

Over the years, there has been increasing pressure on fashion brands to demonstrate their commitment to sustainability.[17] Examples of market and stakeholder pressures include:

- Shifting consumer preferences
- Proliferation of disruptive innovators advancing in sustainability and capturing market share
- Reduction in access to capital fueled by the investment community's expanding focus on sustainability factors in determining credit risk

Growing awareness of the environmental and social degradation that sustainability best practices address is prompting internal and external company stakeholders to take a closer look at the fashion industry. This is increasing pressure on companies to improve and disclose information about their sustainability performance. Many companies now report on sustainability issues, whether required by law or voluntarily via annual sustainability reports, websites, social media, or other communication methods.

Sustainability marketing and messaging can prove both beneficial and challenging for brands. Apps like Good On You[18] and Done Good[19] provide brand ratings based on the brand's environmental and social impact. Heightened awareness makes it even more important for brands to get it right with sustainability messaging. Some companies are reluctant to communicate about their progress and challenges because they fear accusations of inauthenticity, "green washing," or skepticism of their efforts. With increasing demands for transparency, brands must walk a fine line with sustainability disclosures. A communications omission or misstep can result in backlash and boycotts, fueled by the rapid spread of information through social media.

Legal counsel will need to balance legal requirements and stakeholder pressures when providing advice on disclosure matters. These will differ based on entity form as well, with certified B-Corps and benefit corporations that have stated pro environmental and social missions, having the highest level of disclosure required. Despite the risks, stakeholders will likely be more forgiving of brands that are able to demonstrate progress while being open and transparent about the challenges they face.

---

17. Lehmann, *supra* note 7; *see also* Global Fashion Agenda, Boston Consulting Group & Sustainable Apparel Coalition, *The Pulse of the Fashion Industry 2019 Update*, at 16-18 (May 2019), https://www.globalfashionagenda.com/pulse-2019-update/ [https://perma.cc/J7DZ-8GTH].

18. Good on You, https://goodonyou.eco/ [https://perma.cc/4EZB-7JLD].

19. Done Good, https://donegood.co/ [https://perma.cc/YB4K-DY5M].

1. Shifting Consumer Preferences

When choosing a product, consumers consider many factors including cost, quality, and style. "Fast fashion" has enabled shoppers to expand and refresh their wardrobes at low costs. Many consumers treat low-priced garments as virtually disposable, discarding them often after only a few wears. Research shows that the average person today buys 60 percent more items of clothing than they did 15 years ago but keeps that clothing only half as long.[20] At the same time, consumer concerns about sustainability and the impact of their purchasing choices on the environment and people continue to grow. This presents a significant conundrum for the fashion industry.

But consumers are becoming increasingly aware of and concerned about social and environmental responsibility in the fashion industry, as research by Boston Consulting Group shows:[21]

- 75 percent of consumers surveyed view sustainability as extremely or very important.
- Mentions of sustainability in social media increased one-third faster than overall social media growth between 2015 and 2018.
- Consumers mostly acquire information about sustainability issues through online search (35 percent), social media (31 percent), and non-digital print media (29 percent).
- The strongest triggers for conscious behavior concerning sustainability are climate change efforts (50 percent) and natural disasters (49 percent)
- More than one-third of consumers report they have already switched from their preferred brand to another because it credibly stands for positive environmental and/or social practices.
- More than 50 percent of consumers plan to switch brands in the future if another brand acts more environmentally and socially friendly than their preferred one.

2. Disruptive Innovators

Shifts in consumer preferences away from traditional ownership of apparel have spurred new business models that challenge the "fast fashion" model. Disruptive

20. Nathalie Remy, Eveline Speelman & Steven Swartz, *Style That's Sustainable: A New Fast-Fashion Formula*, McKinsey & Co. (Oct. 2016), https://www.mckinsey.com/business-functions/sustainability/our-insights/style-thats-sustainable-a-new-fast-fashion-formula [https://perma.cc/AK2M-EB5J].

21. Global Fashion Agenda, Boston Consulting Group & Sustainable Apparel Coalition, *supra* note 17, at 2.

innovators like Rent the Runway[22] and The RealReal[23] have capitalized on these shifting consumer preferences by creating online subscription clothing services and consignment resale operations. These companies enable shoppers to have it both ways—they can stay in style and have variety while also supporting more sustainable practices. The goal of these disruptors is to reduce and offset fashion's adverse impact on the environment, while also appealing to consumer desire for variety in their attire.

The emergence of social media advertising has dramatically leveled the playing field by enabling challenger brands to disrupt the marketplace. Direct-to-consumer brand Reformation[24] uses a methodology, called RefScale, that tracks the company's environmental footprint in terms of water, carbon dioxide, and waste. It covers everything: growing raw materials, dyeing, manufacturing, packaging, shipping, and consumer care. Reformation has seen strong growth in profitability since opening in 2009 and has more than one million followers on Instagram.

Established brands know they must innovate and keep abreast of new fashion trends if they are to remain competitive and relevant among young consumers. Many have embraced disruption by launching accelerators and incubators to test new concepts and approaches in a less risky environment. One example is Kering's collaboration with Plug and Play and Fashion for Good to create an accelerator aimed at fast-tracking sustainable innovations within the fashion industry.[25] Start-ups selected for the accelerator participate in a program to help them scale-up their innovations through mentoring, training, networking opportunities, and other valuable resources.[26]

According to the Business of Fashion's 2019 *State of Fashion* report, the clothing resale market is expected to outpace fast fashion within 10 years. Established brands like Stella McCartney[27], Patagonia,[28] and Eileen Fisher have ventured into rental,

---

22. Rent the Runway, https://www.renttherunway.com/sustainable-fashion[https://perma.cc/WU7A-AUGA].

23. The Real Real, https://www.therealreal.com/sustainability [https://perma.cc/LJ3E-59TV].

24. Reformation, https://www.thereformation.com/pages/sustainability-report-q3 [https://perma.cc/M6X2-NRP2].

25. Plug and Play, https://www.plugandplaytechcenter.com/about/ [https://perma.cc/P87C-9XGN]; Fashion for Good, https://fashionforgood.com/about-us/?gclid=EAIaIQobChMIybD9u-yh5gIVy8DICh2gbQlUEAAYASAEEgKeZ_D_BwE [https://perma.cc/9N9D-HDPK].

26. Kering, *Plug and Play, Fashion for Good and Kering Announce 12 Start-Ups to Be Supported by Innovation Accelerator* (Apr. 13, 2017), https://www.kering.com/en/news/plug-play-fashion-good-announce-12-start-ups-be-supported-by-innovation-accelerator [https://perma.cc/K66A-CMQN].

27. Stella McCartney, https://www.stellamccartney.com/experience/en/sustainability/ [https://perma.cc/AVS3-WUEG].

28. Patagonia, https://www.patagonia.com/responsible-company.html [https://perma.cc/LG8S-TVGD].

refurbishment, reuse, and resale models of doing business.[29] Many of these brands have take-back programs of their own clothing in exchange for store credit. For example, Eileen Fisher has taken back more than one million gently worn pieces of used clothing since 2009 through its RENEW program. Whenever possible, the garments are repaired, cleaned, and returned to the shop floor for resale. The resulting revenue has been donated to more than 100 charity organizations.[30] Returned items that are beyond repair are transformed by Eileen Fisher designers into one-of-a-kind pillows, artwork, and wall hangings using a custom felting method.[31] Efforts such as these aim to reduce waste sent to landfills by "closing the loop" on the clothing life cycle.

3. Investor Pressure and Access to Capital

Investors play an important role in influencing the behavior of their portfolio companies by encouraging the incorporation of ESG factors into investment decision making. In 2018, more than 360 investors with more than $34 trillion in assets under management joined the Climate Action 100+ initiative[32] to advocate for increased governance, oversight, and disclosure of climate-related risks at the companies in which they invest. Additionally, many of the world's largest investment fund managers have signed the UN's Principles for Responsible Investment,[33] which commits them to incorporating ESG criteria into investment and ownership decisions.

The world of sustainable investment is developing and growing at a healthy pace. According to the US SIF Foundation, sustainable and responsible investing in the United States grew from $8.7 trillion in 2016 to $12.0 trillion in 2018—a 38 percent increase.[34] This represents 26 percent (1 in 4 dollars) of the total U.S. assets under professional management.

---

29. Allison Engel & Margaret Engel, *Eileen Fisher Wants Those Clothes Back When You're Done*, Wash. Post (Aug. 31, 2018), https://www.washingtonpost.com/business/economy/eileen-fisher-wants-those-clothes-back-when-youre-done/2018/08/31/cd873aea-ac58-11e8-b1da-ff7faa680710_story.html [https://perma.cc/369S-E2GS].

30. Lehmann, *supra* note 7.

31. Eileen Fisher, *Waste No More*, https://www.eileenfisher.com/waste-no-more?country=US&currency=USD [https://perma.cc/FWT4-9W32].

32. Climate Action 100+, *Global Investors Driving Business Transition*, http://www.climateaction100.org/ [https://perma.cc/Q5FK-MMUF].

33. United Nations, Principles for Responsible Investments, https://www.unpri.org/ [https://perma.cc/PU74-GH5M].

34. The US SFI Foundation, *2018 Report on US Sustainable, Responsible and Impact Investing Trends* (2018), https://www.ussif.org/files/Trends/Trends%202018%20executive%20summary%20FINAL.pdf [https://perma.cc/TRF5-3Q8F].

Figure 2.2[35]

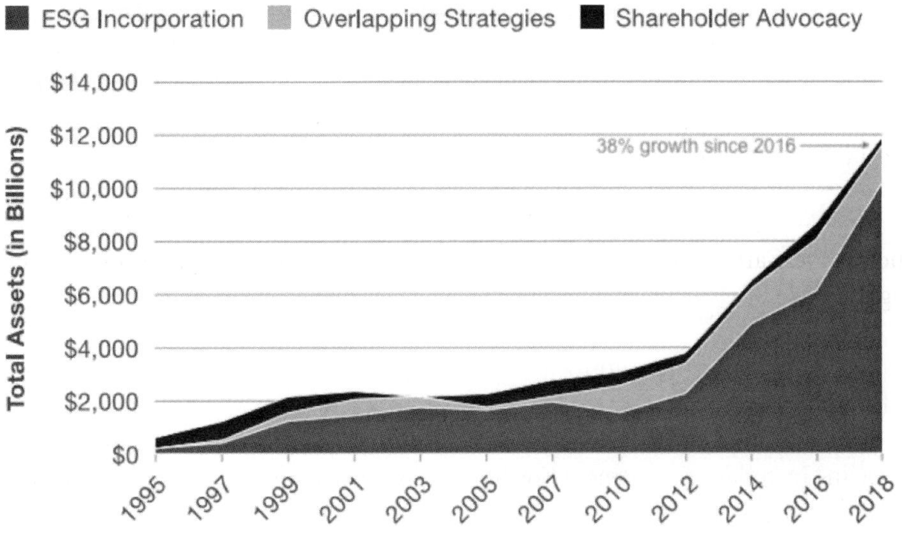

SOURCE: US SIF Foundation.

One key reason the investment community is taking such an interest in ESG components is that market valuation is increasingly based on intangible assets. Investors have realized that companies that embrace and incorporate sustainability practices into business management and culture are better at protecting and creating corporate value. Institutional investors, portfolio managers, and financial services companies are working to improve, standardize, and refine their ESG analysis and screening. As sustainable investment and ESG criteria and metrics evolve, they will hone the factors that provide the most decision-useful information for an investment decision.

A growing number of stakeholders are pressuring companies in the fashion industry to report their sustainability performance to investors. In the United States, advocacy has increased for regulation to ensure more decision-useful sustainability reporting.[36] To further promote such reporting, the Sustainability Accounting Standards Board ("SASB") has developed sustainability accounting standards as guidelines for disclosure decision-making processes for U.S. public companies. SASB standards include a list of material sustainability topics for the apparel, accessories, and footwear industry that provide public companies and their investors with metrics to evaluate disclosure requirements related to key industry sustainability issues. The SASB industry standards are intended to help companies communicate more effectively to investors about sustainability performance on the most significant issues a company is working to manage and improve on.

35. © 2018 The US SIF Foundation. Reprinted with permission.

36. *See* Ho, *supra* note 5.

In 2018 and again in 2019, Larry Fink, founder and CEO of BlackRock, one of the world's largest asset managers, sent a letter to business leaders calling on them to make positive contributions to society or risk losing funding. Founded in 1988, BlackRock has a significant market in the U.S. with approximately $6 trillion in investments through 401(k) plans, exchange-traded funds, and mutual funds. Mr. Fink wrote:

> To prosper over time, every company must not only deliver financial performance, but also show how it makes a positive contribution to society. Companies must benefit all of their stakeholders, including shareholders, employees, customers, and the communities in which they operate.[37]

BlackRock and other significant asset managers like Vanguard and State Street believe companies risk losing their license to operate from key stakeholders if they do not learn to act responsibly and engage with the communities they serve and work in. In today's investment world, having a strong sense of social purpose is being inextricably linked to a company's ability to maintain its profits over the long term.

As the number of investors looking for opportunities to invest in sustainability-focused companies grows, fashion companies that can demonstrate progress with socially and environmentally responsible practices will not only enjoy better access to capital but could benefit from discounts based on the perceived ability to better address and mitigate market risks.

4. Putting Sustainability on the Corporate Agenda

Fashion brands are coming around to the idea that sustainability is more than a passing trend. The industry knows it needs to take action to minimize impacts and address critical environmental, social, and ethical challenges. In recent years, sustainability has risen on the corporate agenda of major apparel brands as more and more companies work to improve sustainability performance. In November 2018, for the first time in the State of Fashion Report, published by McKinsey & Company, sustainability landed in the top four of respondents' list of the "single biggest challenge for the fashion industry next year," following behind global market volatility, online competition, and the speed of changing consumer preferences.[38]

While some progress is being made to improve sustainability in the fashion industry, growth in the industry is outpacing sustainability efforts to counterbalance its

37. BlackRock, *Larry Fink's 2017 Letter to CEOs* (Jan. 23, 2017), https://www.blackrock.com/corporate/investor-relations/2017-larry-fink-ceo-letter [https://perma.cc/S2DP-SCY3].

38. Imran Amed et al., *The State of Fashion 2019*, Bus. of Fashion & McKinsey & Co., at 14 (Nov. 2018), https://www.mckinsey.com/~/media/McKinsey/Industries/Retail/Our%20Insights/The%20State%20of%20Fashion%202019%20A%20year%20of%20awakening/The-State-of-Fashion-2019-final.ashx [https://perma.cc/UJ6B-LP8H].

negative environmental and social impacts, particularly as consumerism, population growth, and a growing middle class exert an unprecedented strain on planetary resources. Increasing demand in Asia-Pacific and developing countries has led to an annual growth rate of approximately five percent.[39] By 2030, it is projected that the fashion industry will manufacture 102 million tons of clothes and shoes annually.[40] Rising demand from a growing middle class across the globe means that the fashion industry's ecological footprint could expand to catastrophic proportions if business as usual continues.

Fashion brands have an opportunity to maintain and ensure profitability in the future by taking action now to improve sustainability performance and reduce negative impacts. If no action is taken, companies will be exposed to risks such as increasing labor costs and resource scarcity. Wages may rise faster than in other industries as fashion brands draw more public attention for harsh working conditions and low compliance with paying a living wage. Energy prices may increase, particularly if strife in the Middle East expands or governments institute carbon taxes to mitigate climate change.

Examples of other risks that could threaten the future profitability of fashion companies include, but are not limited to:

- **Financial Risks**—Companies with poor working conditions in their supply chain may experience a loss of productivity. This often results in decreased financial performance.
- **Regulatory Risks**—When a company's suppliers are violating labor rights, it may incur penalties for noncompliance. This is also true for suppliers that are polluting the environment with chemical waste.
- **Operational Risks**—Droughts and other water shortages may slow vital production processes such as dyeing and finishing.
- **Reputational Risks**—Companies who ignore their social and environmental impacts may face negative backlash from consumers and NGOs.
- **Market Risks**—Many consumers are demanding sustainable alternatives to traditional apparel. Failing to capitalize on this new market may decrease market share.

Addressing these and other risks should be a core component of sustainability management for companies in the fashion industry.

---

39. Global Fashion Agenda, Boston Consulting Group, & Sustainable Apparel Coalition, *supra* note 17.

40. Elizabeth Segran, *Bad News: The Fashion Industry Is Actually Slowing Down on Sustainability*, Fast Company (May 13, 2019), https://www.fastcompany.com/90347710/bad-news-the-fashion-industry-is-actually-slowing-down-on-sustainability [https://perma.cc/SBQ3-5K2V].

D. Frameworks for Addressing Sustainability[41]

Companies typically go through stages when implementing sustainable practices—from *Compliance* to *Beyond Compliance* to *Transformation*.[42] These stages overlap to some extent and not all companies follow a linear path. While some are able to "leapfrog" to more advanced stages by purposefully embedding sustainability into management processes from the start, the vast majority of companies today are still in the initial stages of sustainability integration. Many will progress from one stage to the next over a multiyear period and exhibit a range of attributes that span several stages.

At early stages of maturity, most companies do not yet have enough knowledge and experience with sustainability management to fully understand the universe of risks and opportunities. Over time, sustainability typically evolves from a risk management function to a reputation enhancement and process improvement function to an innovation function. Even in the best cases, achieving a culture of sustainability is an arduous process. By making gradual progress and engaging employees along the way, companies can advance through continuous improvement.

A solid understanding of the different phases of the sustainability journey can help lawyers evaluate where an organization falls along the continuum and how best to enable the journey. What follows is a high-level explanation of each stage and examples from the fashion industry.

1. Three Stages of Corporate Sustainability

There are three primary stages of maturity in a company's journey to use sustainability management to protect and create value:

Stage 1: Compliance—"Doing only what we have to do."

In this stage, a company is focused on mitigating risks and liabilities by obeying all applicable laws and regulations in the jurisdictions where they operate. It seeks to avoid fines, shutdowns, lawsuits, and public condemnation for unethical or unsustainable practices clearly proscribed in the jurisdiction. Environmental and

---

41. The content in this section has been adapted from Sustrana, *Three Steps for Public Companies to De-Risk ESG Shareholder Resolutions* (2018), *available at* https://www.sustrana.com/blog/white_papers/three-steps-for-public-companies-to-de-risk-esg-shareholder-resolutions/ [https://perma.cc/YMF2-JYGN].

42. This sustainability maturity analysis is based on broad experience and is supported by others in the field of sustainability management, though some break it down into more granular categories. *See also* Darcy Hitchcock, *Three Phases of Sustainability: Where Is Your Organization?* Triple Pundit (Aug, 10, 2015), https://www.triplepundit.com/story/2015/three-phases-sustainability-where-your-organization/3271 [https://perma.cc/XX34-8WQM]; Bob Willard, *The 5-Stage Sustainability Journey*, The Sustainability Advantage (Jul. 27, 2010), https://sustainabilityadvantage.com/2010/07/27/the-5-stage-sustainability-journey/ [https://perma.cc/TK5A-QK6F].

social actions are taken from a defensive or reactive stance and only to comply with what is legally required. Environmental and social actions are treated as costs of doing business with little or no direct financial benefit.

An example for fashion brands whose products are sold in the United States would be to conduct a thorough review of chemicals used in their products to ensure they are in compliance with the Lautenberg Chemical Safety Act. This legislation, passed in 2016, amends the 1979 Toxic Substance Control Act ("TSCA"), the nation's primary chemicals management law. The new law included a number of notable expansions to the TSCA, such as:[43]

- Mandatory requirement for EPA to evaluate existing chemicals with clear and enforceable deadlines;
- Risk-based chemical assessments;
- Increased public transparency for chemical information; and
- Consistent source of funding for EPA to carry out the responsibilities under the new law.

If a company learns that a banned chemical is being used in its products, it will need to develop a plan to eliminate the use of that chemical. A helpful resource is the American Apparel and Footwear Association's Restricted Substances List ("RSL").[44] This resource provides apparel and footwear companies with information about laws and regulations that ban certain chemicals in textile, apparel, and footwear products around the world.

Stage 2: Beyond Compliance—"Meeting stakeholder expectations and driving long-term value."

Once a company ensures it is in compliance with applicable laws and regulations, sustainability dictates moving beyond compliance to anticipate, prepare for, and respond to emerging risks and stakeholder expectations. Many regulated industries have been particularly vulnerable to legal changes in recent years. As new data and information become available, laws and regulations evolve. From a sustainability perspective, it is better to prepare early through self-regulation than to wait until changes occur. An organization can stay one step ahead of the compliance and regulation curve by accounting for environmental, social, and economic impacts and risks. For example, a company that anticipates the impacts of expected carbon regulation can start self-regulating. It can come out ahead of the competition by devising its own ways of diminishing carbon in its business operations and supply chain

43. U.S. Environmental Protection Agency, The Frank R. Lautenberg Chemical Safety for the 21st Century Act (Aug. 14, 2019), https://www.epa.gov/assessing-and-managing-chemicals-under-tsca/frank-r-lautenberg-chemical-safety-21st-century-act [https://perma.cc/D333-U9NQ].

44. American Apparel & Footwear Association, *Restricted Substance List*, https://www.aafaglobal.org/AAFA/Solutions_Pages/Restricted_Substance_List.aspx [https://perma.cc/LX9F-ERQ3].

on a longer compliance timetable, thereby optimizing its change process. Taking these proactive measures transitions a company from stage 1 to stage 2.

Many early stage 2 initiatives are tactical, ad hoc, and may or may not have the support of company executives and top management. Common activities include identifying sustainability-related risks and reducing costs through eco-efficiencies by producing goods and services with less energy and water and with more sustainable materials.

Efforts at this stage often focus on cleaning up messes. A relevant example from the fashion industry comes from athletic giant Nike, whose interest in sustainability came after a number of high-profile scandals revealed labor abuses in the supply chain. In the mid-1990s, news outlets like CBS and ESPN began broadcasting footage from inside sweatshops where Nike products were manufactured.[45] A leaked Ernst & Young report showed that 77 percent of workers had respiratory problems and were being exposed to carcinogens 177 times above the legal limit. Nike initially took a defensive approach by insisting that it had no control over third-party supplier activities. As the scandals mounted, it became increasingly clear that the company had a serious public image problem that was taking a toll on company revenues. In 1998, Nike hired its first sustainability coordinator to focus on improving the company's environmental and social performance. At the beginning of its journey, the first step for Nike was to secure adequate worker conditions in its global supply chain.

At more advanced levels of stage 2, companies take a strategic approach and work to fully integrate sustainability into core business strategies and culture. Governance systems are realigned with sustainability principles. At this stage, the company recognizes that sustainability can help it gain a competitive advantage and help contribute to the long-term success of the organization. Many will begin engaging with suppliers to improve working conditions and capture eco-efficiencies within their suppliers' operations and processes. Those that work with suppliers to monitor, audit, and impose standards are better positioned to protect business value over the long term.

Today, Nike's sustainability strategy spans the entire organization across board level, design, sourcing and production teams, and third-party factories. Teams are accountable for corporate responsibility as part of their business key performance indicators. Thousands of materials in Nike's production chain have an environmental rating; the company's water footprint is tracked across major vendors; an internal tool monitors contract factories on wages, health, safety, and environmental criteria; and product designs are rated based on sustainability criteria.[46] While the company's sustainability initiatives were originally launched in response to

45. Kate Abnett, *Just Fix It: How Nike Learned to Embrace Sustainability*, Bus. of Fashion (Nov. 1, 2016, 05:30 AM), https://www.businessoffashion.com/articles/people/just-fix-it-hannah-jones-nike [https://perma.cc/ZGB9-GQ83].

46. *Id.*

stakeholder criticism and pressure, they have now become a tool for protecting and enhancing company value.

Stage 3: Transformation—"Doing what society needs."

The *transformation* level of sustainability maturity involves a company changing the fundamentals of their business model to become fully sustainable. Stage 3 companies are driven by a sense of purpose and a commitment to build a better world because it is the right thing to do. They are characterized by a commitment from C-suite executives and managers to integrate sustainability into the company's DNA. Forward-looking stage 3 players develop innovative technologies and approaches to create solutions for the industry's deepest challenges. In doing so, in many cases, they are better able to attract new customers and employees, enhance brand loyalty, and improve access to capital.

Very few companies have reached the stage 3 level of maturity along the sustainability continuum. One exception is Eileen Fisher—a company that exemplifies this transformational approach to sustainability in the fashion industry. Eileen Fisher promotes the vision of "an industry where human rights and sustainability are not the effects of a particular initiative but the cause of a business well run."[47] The company measures its sustainability performance in the following impact areas: materials, chemicals, carbon, waste, supply chain practices, product life cycle, workplace inclusivity, benefits and wellness, business for good, and helping to change an industry.

An important goal for sustainability in the fashion industry is the creation of a circular economy in which all materials are either infinitely recyclable or biodegradable along the entire product value chain. In contrast to the traditional take-make-waste extractive industrial model of consumption, the circular economy model reduces dependence on natural resources by shifting to a regenerative borrow-use-return approach. According to the leading NGO proponent of a circular economy, the Ellen MacArthur Foundation, a circular economy is based on the following principles:[48]

1. Design out waste and pollution
2. Keep products and materials in use
3. Regenerate natural systems

The circular economy seeks to redefine growth by focusing on positive society-wide benefits. The focus is to go beyond reducing harm and aim to create tangible benefits to people and the environment along the entire product life cycle.

The Global Fashion Agenda's 2020 Circular Fashion System Commitment asks companies to pledge to take specific actions that will help move the fashion

---

47. Eileen Fisher, *Vision 2020*, https://www.eileenfisher.com/vision-2020?country=US&currency=USD [https://perma.cc/3J43-W29N].

48. Ellen McArthur Foundation, *supra* note 11.

industry from a linear take-make-waste model toward a circular one. As a signatory, for example, Eileen Fisher's 2020 Circular Fashion System Commitment Targets include:[49]

- Increase the number of garments that have been remanufactured through the circular program, EILEEN FISHER RENEW, by 50 percent.
- Increase the number of garments collected through the RENEW program by 20 percent.
- Increase the resale of used garments by 25 percent.
- Implement circular design principles to create a closed-loop product offering.
- Increase the volume of used garments recycled into textile fibers.

An industry leader in ethical and sustainable fashion, Eileen Fisher is an exemplar working toward a world where the clothes people wear today become the raw materials of tomorrow's fashion.

2. Industry Leadership and Collaboration

As members of one of the largest, most dynamic, and influential industries in the world, the fashion industry has a unique and important role to play in the transition to a sustainable future. The sustainability challenge offers the industry an opportunity to do what it does best—be creative. Many of the world's most pressing issues call for new approaches, new business models, and new partnerships. Lawyers are well-positioned to guide and enable this transition.

Fashion brands can only achieve so much in isolation. Individual companies cannot create systemic change on their own. To drive and scale impact through shared best practices and promising innovations, a strong network of collaboration is needed. Companies, governments, non-governmental organizations, academia, communities, and individuals on a global scale have formed coalitions and are committing to common goals and systems by which to measure sustainability and tackle environmental and social challenges together.

The United Nations' Sustainable Development Goals ("SDGs") are a collection of 17 bold and transformative global goals set to be achieved by 2030. They cover a broad range of interrelated sustainable development issues, setting far-reaching, comprehensive, and people-centered goals to shift the world to a sustainable and resilient pathway for the future. The SDGs recognize that furthering economic prosperity must go hand-in-hand with strategies that address a range of social needs including education, health, social protection, and job opportunities, while tackling climate change and environmental protection. SDG 12, Responsible Consumption and Production, is particularly relevant for the fashion industry.

---

49. Global Fashion Agenda, *Eileen Fisher*, https://www.globalfashionagenda.com/logo/eileen-fisher/ [https://perma.cc/MSA3-62V3].

The Global Fashion Agenda ("GFA") is a leadership forum for industry collaboration on sustainability in fashion. The GFA engages decision makers in the industry across various stakeholder groups to enhance collaboration and facilitate the sharing of best practices and solutions. In their CEO Agenda, the GFA details a useful framework by identifying eight crucial priorities and providing guidance on how fashion companies can focus their efforts. The framework comprises four core priorities for immediate implementation and four transformational priorities for fundamental change in the long term.[50]

Core Priorities:

- Supply Chain Traceability
- Respectful and Secure Work Environments
- Efficient Use of Water, Energy, and Chemicals
- Combating Climate Change[51]

Transformational Priorities:

- Sustainable Material Mix
- Circular Fashion System
- Promotion of Better Wage Systems
- Fourth Industrial Revolution

A leading framework for self-assessment and reporting in the fashion industry is the Higg Index, which was created by the Sustainable Apparel Coalition ("SAC") and is operated by a public benefit technology company, Higg Co. LLC.[52] The Higg Index is a comprehensive set of sustainability performance self-assessment and benchmarking tools for fashion companies. It measures sustainability impacts throughout the product life cycle (including sourcing, production, and product disposal) and creates valuable content for sustainability reporting. The framework provides a detailed industry perspective on the core sustainability issues where change is most actively being sought.

Higg Index scores are not required to be publicly reported, but companies can use the information generated from completing the Higg Index as the foundation for a sustainability report. A Higg Index score also makes it possible to compare a company's sustainability performance to others in the industry.

---

50. Global Fashion Agenda, *CEO Agenda*, https://www.globalfashionagenda.com/ceo-agenda-2019/# [https://perma.cc/6C46-VCFV].

51. Another example of industry collaboration on combating climate change is the United Nations Framework Convention on Climate Change, *Fashion Industry Charter* (Dec. 2018), https://unfccc.int/sites/default/files/resource/Industry%20Charter%20%20Fashion%20and%20Climate%20Action%20-%2022102018.pdf [https://perma.cc/6W2L-QHSD].

52. The Sustainable Apparel Coalition, *The Higg Index*, https://apparelcoalition.org/the-higg-index/ [https://perma.cc/8H2G-KQXV].

By regularly tracking progress, fashion companies contribute to and influence evolving and emerging industry best practices. There are many ways to address management problems, and every company that contributes to the database helps to advance the growth of sustainable practices in the industry. In this way, the Higg Index helps define industry-wide best practices for sustainability performance.

E. Conclusion

As a major employer and driver of economic prosperity in many less developed countries, the fashion industry is well positioned to make a positive impact and improve social conditions for millions. The apparel industry alone employs more than 300 million people along the global value chain.[53] According to the McKinsey Global Fashion Index, in 2017, the fashion industry was worth approximately $2.5 trillion, which would make it the world's seventh-largest economy if ranked along individual countries' GDPs.[54] Given the global reach of the industry, coordinated action is needed to overcome challenges and inspire solutions. This will require unprecedented levels of collaboration and innovation to bring about system-level change for a fully sustainable fashion industry. Lawyers will play an essential role in making it possible for fashion companies to achieve sustainability and keep them on that path.

---

53. Ellen McArthur Foundation, *supra* note 11.

54. Imran Amed, Achim Berg, Leonie Brantberg & Saskia Hedrich, *The State of Fashion 2017*, Bus. of Fashion & McKinsey & Co., at 6 (Dec. 2016), https://www.mckinsey.com/~/media/McKinsey/Industries/Retail/Our%20Insights/The%20state%20of%20fashion/The-state-of-fashion-2017-McK-BoF-report.ashx [https://perma.cc/4WNH-Z84L].

Chapter 3

International Trade

Frances P. Hadfield and Amanda Simpson

A. History

1. U.S. Customs Service—History

The United States was burdened with significant debt as a result of the Revolutionary War and increasing government operating expenses. The Tariff Act of 1789 was the first source of revenue for the newly formed United States.[1] On July 31, 1789, just four months following the ratification of the United States Constitution and at the recommendations of President George Washington, Alexander Hamilton, and the First Congress, the U.S. Customs Service ("Customs Service") was created. Congress originally allowed the individual shipping ports of entry to appoint a "reputable merchant" to appraise value and determine duties on goods being unloaded. This changed in 1818 with the establishment of a formal "customs appraiser" as a profession based on experience and expertise. These appraisers would examine goods that came into a port and collect the tariffs (or duties) when the goods were unloaded.

Up until the implementation of the income tax in 1913, the revenue collected through import tariffs by customs appraisers represented the majority of funds used to support the federal government. An import tariff is a tax on goods from a foreign nation. The revenue from these import taxes was used to build such things as Washington, D.C., and the Transcontinental Railroad. It was also used to purchase approximately 1.5 million square miles of territory through deals such as the Louisiana Purchase and other critical national infrastructure projects, many of which are still in use. Additionally, the passage and maintenance of protective tariffs, which involved increasing the duties on certain imports to protect domestic industries from foreign producers, grew in conjunction with the United States' industrial revolution. Accordingly, a protectionist tariff philosophy prevailed in the post-Civil War period and continued on through the first third of the twentieth century.[2] Such tariffs are reemerging in the twenty-first century as the United States has imposed significant tariffs on goods from China.

1. 1 Stat. 24 (July 4, 1789).

2. *See generally* John M. Dobson, Two Centuries of Tariffs (1976), available at https://www.usitc.gov/publications/332/pub0000.pdf.

The majority of fashion goods sold in the United States are manufactured abroad. The Smoot-Hawley Tariff Act of 1930 ("Tariff Act") governs importation into the United States and is enforced by "Customs," an overarching term used in this Chapter to describe the Customs Service and its successor, CBP, as defined in Section A.2.[3] Merchandise imported into a country is "classified" under a tariff system for such purposes as tariff (or duty) assessment and import restrictions, among other concerns. The modern U.S. tariff system is called the Harmonized Tariff Schedule of the United States ("HTSUS").

Historically, the customs appraisers and then the Customs Service determined the amount owed by persons or companies importing goods into the United States. However, on December 8, 1993, the Customs Modernization Act, P.L. 103-182, 107 Stat. 2057 ("Mod Act") became effective. Its provisions altered the relationship between importers and the Customs Service by shifting to the importer the legal responsibility for declaring the value of imported goods, their correct tariff classification, and the rate of duty applicable to the entered merchandise.

The Mod Act addressed two important concepts that are referred to as "informed compliance" and "shared responsibility," which are intended to promote voluntary compliance with the customs laws and regulations by informing the trade community of its legal obligations. The concept of "informed compliance" imposes an obligation on Customs to provide the public information concerning the trade community's rights and responsibilities under its regulations and laws. To this end, Customs hosts an online database of Customs Rulings.[4] The concept of "shared responsibility" places the responsibility for carrying out these requirements on both Customs and the trade community. Many of these are set forth in the Informed Compliance Publications ("ICPs") that are published on Customs' website.[5]

2. U.S. Customs and Border Protection—The Agency Today

The Customs Service, which was stationed along the U.S. border, took on many roles historically, including enforcement of importation, immigration, and other laws regulating border traffic. It was part of the Department of the Treasury. But prior to September 11, 2001, the major responsibility of the Customs Service was to administer the tariff and import laws.

---

3. As a consequence of the passage of the Tariff Act of 1930, many countries retaliated against the United States with their own increased tariffs on goods exported from the United States. *See* Samsung Electronics Co. v. United States, 873 F.2d 1427, 1431 (Fed. Cir. 1989) (stating "Customs law has ceased to be a matter of domestic interest only, as Congress so disastrously treated it in 1930, with the odious Smoot-Hawley Tariff Act of that year. It is a matter of international concern.").

4. The customs ruling database is available at *Customs Rulings Online Search System*, U.S. Customs & Border Prot., https://rulings.cbp.gov/home (last visited June 3, 2020).

5. *See Informed Compliance Publications*, U.S. Customs & Border Prot., https://www.cbp.gov/trade/rulings/informed-compliance-publications (last visited June 3, 2020).

On March 1, 2003, the Customs Service merged with other enforcement agencies to become Customs and Border Protection ("CBP"). Today it is an agency of the Department of Homeland Security ("DHS"). The newly organized agency merged the functions of the former U.S. Customs Service, Immigration and Naturalization Service, Border Patrol, and Animal and Plant Health Inspection Service. Today, the responsibilities of CBP include examination of people and goods entering the United States to ensure adherence to import, immigration, intellectual property, environmental, and consumer protection laws.

3. The Role of the Department of Commerce—International Trade Administration

In 1980, the Department of Commerce founded the International Trade Administration ("ITA"). This agency was designed to promote fair trade and competition globally. By ensuring global compliance with trade laws and agreements, the ITA works to strengthen the competitiveness of the U.S. industry through various protectionist measures, such as additional tariffs on certain imports to protect the domestic industry from foreign competition.

While the ITA is the agency that may issue such measures, it is CBP (formerly the Customs Service) that acts as the enforcement arm to ensure compliance at the border. By way of example, in *Rhone Poulenc v. United States*, the court addressed an order issued by the ITA to collect additional duties on certain imports as a form of protectionist measure. A French producer imported ASM, a chemical found in detergents, waste paper de-inking, and clay processing, which was subject to this order and the additional duties.[6] The dispute between the importer and the government mainly centered around the information required from the importer to the ITA for purposes of determining the amount of duties owed at the time of import under the order.[7] However, the key takeaway from this case is that, while the ITA may administer protective measures in the form of duties to reduce "unfair" trading, Customs is clearly tasked with enforcing the collection of those duties.

4. The Role of U.S. International Trade Commission in Trade and Fashion

The U.S. International Trade Commission ("USITC") affects three areas of U.S. international trade: (1) adjudication; (2) research and analysis; and (3) maintaining the HTSUS. More specifically, the USITC investigates and makes determinations in proceedings involving imports claimed to injure a domestic industry or violate U.S. intellectual property rights; provides independent analysis and information on

6. Rhone Poulenc, Inc. v. United States, 13 C.I.T. 218, 710 F. Supp. 341 (Ct. Int'l Trade 1989).

7. Rhone Poulenc, Inc. v. United States, 899 F.2d 1185 (Fed. Cir. 1990).

tariffs and trade and competitiveness. The USITC is headed by six Commissioners. They are nominated by the President and confirmed by the U.S. Senate.

Investigations under 19 U.S.C. § 337 ("Section 337") are often conducted by the USITC and frequently involve claims regarding intellectual property rights, including allegations of patent infringement and trademark infringement by imported goods. Both utility and design patents, as well as registered and common law trademarks, may be asserted in these investigations. However, other forms of unfair competition involving imported products, such as infringement of registered copyrights, misappropriation of trade secrets or trade dress, passing off, and false advertising, may also be asserted. Additionally, antitrust claims relating to imported goods may be asserted.

The primary remedy available in § 337 investigations is an exclusion order that directs CBP to stop infringing imports from entering the United States. In addition, the Commission may issue cease-and-desist orders against named importers and other persons engaged in unfair acts that violate this Section. Expedited relief in the form of temporary exclusion orders and temporary cease-and-desist orders may also be available in certain exceptional circumstances.

5. The Role of the U.S. Trade Representative in Trade and Fashion

The U.S. Trade Representative ("USTR") is responsible for developing and coordinating U.S. international trade, commodity, and direct investment policy, and overseeing negotiations with other countries. The USTR coordinates trade policy, resolves disagreements, and frames issues for presidential decision.

a. Section 301

Sections 301 and related provisions of the Trade Act of 1974 ("Section 301") are one of the principal statutory means by which the United States enforces its rights under trade agreements and addresses what it considers to be "unfair" foreign barriers to U.S. exports.[8] Once the USTR begins a Section 301 investigation, it seeks a negotiated settlement with the foreign country concerned (either through compensation or an elimination of the particular barrier or practice) for cases involving trade agreements, such as those under the Uruguay Round trade agreements in the World Trade Organization ("WTO"). The USTR is required to use the formal dispute proceedings specified by the agreements.

On August 18, 2017, the USTR initiated a § 301 investigation to determine whether acts, policies, and practices of the government of the People's Republic of China ("PRC") related to technology transfer, intellectual property, and innovation were

8. 19 U.S.C. §§ 2411–2417.

actionable under the Trade Act of 1974.[9] This Section sets out three categories of acts, policies, or practices of a foreign country that are potentially actionable: (i) trade agreement violations; (ii) acts, policies or practices that are unjustifiable (defined as those that are inconsistent with U.S. international legal rights) and that burden or restrict U.S. Commerce; and (iii) acts, policies, or practices that are unreasonable or discriminatory and that burden or restrict U.S. Commerce.[10] Section 301 defines "discriminatory" to "include, when appropriate, any act, policy, and practice which denies national or most-favored nation treatment to United States goods, service, or investment."[11]

For Section 301 cases (except those involving a trade agreement or an IPR issue) the USTR has 12 to 18 months to seek a negotiated resolution. If one is not obtained, the USTR then determines whether to retaliate (which usually takes the form of increased tariffs on selected imports) at a level equivalent to the estimated economic losses incurred by U.S. firms from the foreign barrier or practice. A large portion of imported footwear, apparel, and textile articles were subject to the additional duties at a 15 percent rate, effective September 1, 2019.

b. How Section 301 Tariffs Can Affect Fashion— The United States-China Trade War

President Donald Trump's use of Section 301 rather than the WTO dispute settlement process to address the issues of concern is a departure from past practice. On March 22, 2018, President Trump signed a Memorandum on Actions by the United States related to the Section 301 investigation on the PRC.[12] The memorandum identified four broad policies that justified U.S. action against China under this statutory provision. As a consequence of what is described as China's "economic aggression" against the United States, four lists of products that were subject to additional tariffs were launched against Chinese imports. The fourth list included a significant list of apparel and other fashion imports.

B. Importing Goods into the United States

As mentioned previously, the Tariff Act still governs importation into the United States and is today enforced by CBP. The North American Free Trade Agreement Implementation Act, commonly referred to as the Mod Act, also governs trade and has updated portions of the Tariff Act.

---

9. 19 U.S.C. §§ 2411–2417

10. Trade Act of 1974, 19 U.S.C. § 2411(a)–(b).

11. 19 U.S.C. § 2411(d)(5).

12. *See* Memorandum on Actions by the United States Related to the Section 301 Investigation of China's Laws, Policies, Practices, or Actions Related to Technology Transfer, Intellectual Property, and Innovation, 2018 Daily Comp. Pres. Doc. 180 (Mar. 22, 2018), https://www.govinfo.gov/content/pkg/DCPD-201800180/pdf/.

1. Importer of Record

"Importer of Record" ("Importer") is a term used in customs law to refer to an entity or individual who is responsible for ensuring that goods are imported in accordance with the regulations and laws.[13] The Importer may be either the owner or purchaser of the merchandise, which is defined by CBP as any party with a financial interest in the transaction, including, but not limited to, the actual owner of the goods, the actual purchaser of the goods, a buying or selling agent, or a person or firm who imports on consignment.[14]

A nonresident individual or entity may be an Importer. The requirements and procedures permitting a nonresident to act as an Importer are, for the most part, the same as those that apply to U.S. individuals or entities. The requirements applicable to both resident and nonresident individuals or entities. Importers are discussed in more detail below.

2. Reasonable Care

By law, even before the apparel arrives at the U.S. border, the Importer must provide formalized information to the U.S. government about the fashion articles it intends to import, which allows CBP to assess proper duties, determine product admissibility (neither illegal nor prohibited), import restrictions, other partner government agency requirements, and tariff preference program eligibility.[15] The process of providing this information to the U.S. government is called entry.[16]

Under the Tariff Act, the Importer is responsible for using reasonable care to enter imported goods.[17] This means that the Importer is responsible for declaring the proper data elements, discussed in more detail below, that relate to its merchandise at the time of entry. CBP will finalize the data elements, either by accepting the declaration, requesting additional information from the Importer, or making the required changes. There are a number of sources available to Importers for import guidance, including, but not limited to, case law under the United States Court of International Trade and CBP administrative rulings, which are CBP's determinations on an Importer's specific products as requested by the Importer.

An Importer's failure to exercise reasonable care could delay release of the merchandise and, in some cases, could result in the imposition of penalties or criminal enforcement.[18]

13. 19 C.F.R. § 101.1.
14. CBP Directive 3530-002A, Section 5.3.1.
15. *See* 19 U.S.C. §§ 1481, 1484–85 (2013); 19 C.F.R. Part 141 (2013).
16. 19 U.S.C. § 1484 (2013).
17. *Id.*
18. 19 U.S.C. § 1592.

3. Customs Brokers

Although not required by law, an Importer may hire a licensed customs broker and freight forwarder to assist with international logistics and customs clearance.

Only Importers have the right to make entry of merchandise; however, an Importer may appoint a licensed customs broker to do so on his or her behalf.[19] Customs brokers are licensed by CBP to prepare and file the necessary entries to affect the release of the imported goods. In order for the customs broker to file documentation with CBP in the name of the Importer, the Importer must sign a power of attorney.[20] While an Importer may file entries on its own, most companies use a customs broker because of the complex electronic filing requirements for entry documentation.

In *National Customs Brokers & Forwarders Association of America. v. United States*, customs brokers challenged interim regulations issued by CBP that allowed a party other than the Importer and customs broker, specifically a consignee of the merchandise, to enter merchandise valued at $200.00 or less.[21] Since an Importer isn't always necessarily the buyer of the imported merchandise, consignees are typically the party in the United States to whom the overseas shipper sold the imported merchandise.[22] Pursuant to 19 U.S.C. § 1484(a)(2)(B), generally only an Importer or a licensed customs broker, as an agent of the Importer, may make entry.[23] Consignees are not expressly authorized to act as the Importer; however, 19 U.S.C. § 1498(a) and 19 U.S.C. § 1321 authorize the Secretary of the Treasury to prescribe regulations for the entry of merchandise valued at $2,500.00 or less.[24] Here, the Secretary prescribed interim regulations that allowed consignees to act as Importer for shipments valued at $200.00 or less.[25] It was held by the court that CBP's decision to allow consignees to make entry for goods valued at $200.00 or less was, while an exception to the general rule, permissible under the aforementioned statutes and CBP was acting within its authority.[26]

Conversely, a freight forwarder is typically responsible for addressing concerns such as hiring common carriers or issues about packing the goods for shipment. A freight forwarder may not file entries on behalf of an Importer.

19. *Right to Make Entry*, Customs Directive No. 3530-002A (June 2003); 19 U.S.C. § 1484(a)(2)(B).

20. 19 C.F.R. § 141.46.

21. Nat'l Customs Brokers & Forwarders Ass'n of Am. v. United States, 59 F.3d 1219 (Fed. Cir. 1995).

22. *Ultimate Consignee at Time of Entry or Release*, Customs Directive No. 3550-079A (June 2003).

23. *Nat'l Customs Brokers*, at 1220.

24. *Id.*

25. *Id.* at 1221.

26. *Id.* at 1224.

4. Classification of Imported Goods

The HTSUS is a commodity identification system that has been adopted throughout most countries around the world. The movement of merchandise in international trade would be slow and expensive if the merchandise had to be classified under differing countries' tariff systems. Therefore, in the late 1960s, the major trading countries of the world decided that an internationally recognized product or tariff classification system was needed in order to facilitate the international trade of merchandise and this work continued until the current system was enacted in the United States in 1989.[27]

Today, all goods entering the commerce of the United States are assigned a 10-digit numerical code under the HTSUS, the first six of which are universal across the globe. This code is referred to as the tariff classification of imported goods. The first four digits represent the broader category of products. For example, Heading 6104, HTSUS, provides for "women's or girls' suits, ensembles, suit-type jackets, blazers, dresses, skirts, divided skirts, trousers, bib and brace overalls, breeches and shorts (other than swimwear), knitted or crocheted." Every subsequent set of two digits narrows the broader category into specific products. Using the same example, Subheading 6104.59, HTSUS, provides for "women's or girls' suits, ensembles, suit-type jackets, blazers, dresses, skirts, divided skirts, trousers, bib and brace overalls, breeches and shorts (other than swimwear), knitted or crocheted: *skirts and divided skirts.*" Subheading 6104.59.1005, HTSUS, is further narrowed to "skirts and divided skirts: *of other textile materials: of artificial fibers: containing 23 percent or more by weight of wool or fine animal hair.*" An image of the current HTSUS applicable to this subheading is set forth in Figure 3.1:

27. *See* U.S. Customs & Border Prot., What Every Member of the Trade Community Should Know About: Tariff Classification (2004), https://www.cbp.gov/sites/default/files/documents/icp017r2_3.pdf.

Figure 3.1

Harmonized Tariff Schedule of the United States (2019) Revision 12

Annotated for Statistical Reporting Purposes

XI
61-30

Heading/ Subheading	Stat. Suf-fix	Article Description	Unit of Quantity	Rates of Duty 1 General	Rates of Duty 1 Special	Rates of Duty 2
6104 (con.)		Women's or girls' suits, ensembles, suit-type jackets, blazers, dresses, skirts, divided skirts, trousers, bib and brace overalls, breeches and shorts (other than swimwear), knitted or crocheted: (con.)				
		Skirts and divided skirts: (con.)				
6104.59		Of other textile materials:				
6104.59.10		Of artificial fibers		8%	Free (AU, BH, CA, CL, CO, IL, JO, KR, MA, MX, OM, P, PA, PE, SG)	72%
	05	Containing 23 percent or more by weight of wool or fine animal hair (442)	doz. kg			
		Other:				
	30	Women's (642)	doz. kg			
	60	Girls' (642)	doz. kg			
6104.59.40	00	Containing 70 percent or more by weight of silk or silk waste (742)	doz. kg	0.9%	Free (AU, BH, CA, CL, CO, E, IL, JO, KR, MA, MX, OM, P, PA, PE, SG)	45%
6104.59.80		Other		5.6%	Free (AU, BH, CA, CL, CO, E*, IL, JO, KR, MA, MX, OM, P, PA, PE, SG)	45%
	10	Subject to cotton restraints (342)	doz. kg			
	20	Subject to wool restraints (442)	doz. kg			
	30	Subject to man-made fiber restraints (642)	doz. kg			
	90	Other (842)	doz. kg			

It is this 10-digit code that signifies to CBP the following: the specific product being imported (e.g., a women or girls' skirt composed of artificial fibers and containing 23 percent or more by weight of wool or fine animal hair); the associated duty rate (e.g., eight percent of the value of the imported skirt); any import restrictions, such as quota; preferential treatment (e.g., North America Free Trade Agreement ("NAFTA") or the currently pending United States-Mexico-Canada ("USMCA") eligibility resulting in zero or reduced duties, etc.) eligibility; and partner government agency requirements.

In determining the proper tariff classification, CBP would have to determine what was the product being examined in its condition as imported. This is important because, for example, a container of unstrung pearls might have a different import tariff then strung pearls (i.e., jewelry). For example, in *United States v. Citroen*, an Importer entered 37 pearls, unset and unstrung.[28] At the time of this case, unset or unstrung pearls were considered pearls in their natural state and subject to only a 10 percent duty rate.[29] Conversely, set or strung pearls were considered jewelry and subject to a 60 percent duty rate.[30] Here, the Court held that "the fact that [the subject pearls] were reported to have been previously strung abroad" has no consequence on the tariff classification of the unset and unstrung pearls upon importation.[31] Accordingly, the pearls were classified in their condition as imported and subject to the lower rate.[32] Since tariff classification is an issue of statutory interpretation, it is often litigated by Importers. For example, in *Victoria's Secret Direct, LLC v. United States*, the Importer argued that shelf-bra tank tops were properly classified as brassieres under Heading 6212 at a 6.6 percent duty rate, and not camisoles under Heading 6109 at a 16.5 percent duty rate.[33] In its argument, the Importer claimed that the subject merchandise, despite being worn as outerwear, provided support akin to the articles classified as brassieres.[34] The court disagreed with the Importer, stating that while the shelf-bra tank tops were similar in construction and purpose as brassieres, it could not conclude that the subject merchandise "on the whole" was similar to brassieres.[35] The court did agree, however, that classification of the shelf-bra tank tops as camisoles under Heading 6212 was inaccurate as it would "enlarge the scope" of the heading to include garments that provide support impermissibly and would be contrary to legislative intent.[36] The court ultimately determined that the subject tops were classifiable in a catch-all provision at a

---

28. United States v. Citroen, 223 U.S. 407, 413 (1912).
29. *Id.* at 417.
30. *Id.* at 424.
31. *Id.* at 420.
32. *Id.*
33. Victoria's Secret Direct, LLC v. United States, 908 F. Supp. 2d 1332 (Ct. Int'l Trade 2013), *aff'd*, 759 F.3d 1102 (Fed. Cir. 2014).
34. *Id.* at 1357.
35. *Id.* at 1355.
36. *Id.* at 1352–1353.

10.8 percent duty rate for "other [knit] garments," mainly because the merchandise was not more specifically described elsewhere in the HTSUS.[37]

Clearly, the proper tariff classification of imported merchandise can be a complicated analysis. CBP often questions the tariff classification of imports, largely due to the direct impact on duties owed.

5. Valuation of Imported Goods

All merchandise imported into the United States is subject to appraisement by CBP.[38] CBP's preferred method of appraisement is the "Transaction Value" method, which under 19 U.S.C. § 1401a(b) is the "price actually paid or payable for the merchandise when sold for exportation to the United States."[39] In order for imported merchandise to be appraised under the transaction value method, it must be a *bona fide* sale between a buyer and seller and clearly destined for exportation to the United States.[40] In the event that merchandise cannot be appraised on the basis of transaction value, the following methods may be utilized in the following order: (1) transaction value of identical merchandise, (2) transaction value of similar merchandise, (3) deductive value, (4) computed value, and (5) values if other values cannot be determined.[41]

There is a rebuttable presumption that all payments made by a buyer to a seller, or a party related to a seller, are part of the transaction value.[42]

Costs associated with the following activities, if not already included in the "price actually paid or payable," must be included in the transaction value (or other certain methods of appraisement) at the time of entry: (a) packing costs incurred by the buyer; (b) selling commissions; (c) assists; (d) royalties or license fees that the Importer is required to pay related to the imported merchandise; and (e) proceeds of any subsequent resale that accrue either directly or indirectly to the seller of the merchandise.[43] Depending on the terms of the transactions, certain costs may be excluded from the transaction value. This includes international freight charges and certain post-importation charges.[44]

A common valuation error is the failure to include in the transaction value assist costs. Under 19 U.S.C. § 1401a(h)(1), "assists" are defined as the following articles "supplied directly or indirectly, and free of charge or at reduced cost, by the buyer

37. *Id.* at 1358–1359.
38. *Customs Value*, CBP, Informed Compliance Publication, 7 (July 2006).
39. 19 U.S.C. § 1401a(b).
40. HQ H286286 (June 9, 2018).
41. § 1401a(a).
42. HQ 545663 (July 14, 1995).
43. *Id.*
44. 19 C.F.R. § 152.103(a)(5).

of imported merchandise for use in connection with the production or the sale for export to the United States of the merchandise:

(i) Materials, components, parts, and similar items incorporated in the imported merchandise.

(ii) Tools, dies, molds, and similar items used in the production of the imported merchandise.

(iii) Merchandise consumed in the production of the imported merchandise.

(iv) Engineering, development, artwork, design work, and plans and sketches that are undertaken elsewhere than in the United States and are necessary for the production of the imported merchandise."[45]

In *Texas Apparel Co. v. United States*, the Court of International Trade reviewed a scenario wherein CBP claimed that the costs for sewing equipment that were provided free of charge to a foreign manufacturer and seller of the imported merchandise should have been added to the transaction value as an assist.[46] The Importer argued that the sewing equipment did not fall within the meaning of "tools, dies, molds, and similar items used in the production of imported merchandise" as defined under the statute, because equipment that falls under this category should be specialized to the particular merchandise only.[47] Here, the equipment used was capable of diverse functions on other products.[48] CBP argued that the equipment used was an integral component of the manufacturing process and, thus, a required addition to the customs value.[49] The court held that the sewing equipment was essential to the fabrication of the apparel and that to include that cost of production in the customs value would reflect the fair and accurate value of the merchandise.[50] Accordingly, the sewing equipment was an assist within the meaning of the statute.[51]

As evidenced above, identifying the accurate customs value can be a complicated, yet necessary, task. Like tariff classification, CBP is often focused on customs valuation issues, because of the direct impact on duties owed.

6. Import Duties

Duties are typically assessed on an *ad valorem* basis, which is a percentage of the imported products' value.[52] Most apparel imports, whether knit or woven, range

45. *See also* 19 C.F.R. § 152.102.

46. Tex. Apparel Co. v. United States, 12 C.I.T. 1002, 698 F. Supp. 932 (Ct. Int'l Trade 1988), *aff'd*, 883 F.2d 66 (Fed. Cir. 1989), *cert. denied*, 110 S. Ct. 728 (1990).

47. *Id.* at 1002.

48. *Id.* at 1004.

49. *Id.*

50. *Id.* at 1006.

51. *Id.*

52. *See* CBP, *Importing into the United States: A Guide for Commercial Importers*, CBP Pub. 0000-0504 at 40 (Dec. 5, 2006), *available at* https://www.cbp.gov/sites/default/files/documents/Importing%20into%20the%20U.S.pdf (last accessed May 10, 2013).

from 5 to 24.5 percent and average at 16 percent. Using the above example, an Importer that brings in 1,000 units of a women's skirt valued at $100.00 per unit and classifiable under Subheading 6104.59.1005, HTSUS (8%) would be required to pay $8,000.00 at the time of entry. Most footwear imports, however, are subject to a 37.5 percent duty rate. Therefore, if 1,000 pairs of shoes were imported and valued at $100.00 per unit, under most tariff classifications under the HTSUS, an Importer would be required to pay $37,500.00 in import duties.

7. Valueless or Damaged Goods

No duties are assessed on goods that CBP or the Importer discover to be so damaged as to be entirely without commercial value at the time of importation into the United States. CBP considers an incident of this type to be a "nonimportation."[53]

One of the more difficult issues for a fashion Importer is how to receive a refund from CBP on defective, but not commercially valueless, merchandise. There are three elements that are necessary to proving a defective merchandise case. The Importer must: (1) prove to CBP that it contracted for defect-free merchandise; (2) be able to link the defective merchandise to specific entries; and (3) prove the amount of the allowance for each entry. The third element is often the most difficult to prove for fashion Importers.[54]

8. Country of Origin of Imported Merchandise

The analysis to ascertain the proper country of origin varies depending on whether the assessment pertains to: (1) import declarations made at entry, (2) preferential treatment under a free trade agreement or some other duty preference program, and (3) marking and labeling of imported products. All three analyses are described in more detail below.

a. Import Declarations

At the time of entry, an Importer must declare to CBP the proper country of origin of its imported merchandise. The regulations define the "country of origin" as "the country of manufacture, production, or growth of any article of foreign origin entering the United States."[55] Where an article is fully produced in a given country, the country of origin is that country for import declaration purposes. Take, for example, a men's cotton tee shirt from Peru. To the extent that the cotton fibers

53. 19 C.F.R. § 158.11 (2019).

54. HQ Ruling 543106 (July 29, 1983) provides that "[t]he concerned Customs officer should, of course, be mindful of his [sic] primary mission to protect the revenue, but nonetheless should avoid imposing overly rigid evidentiary requirements on the Importer and should grant relief when the Importer's evidence affords a valid legal reason for doing so."

55. 19 C.F.R. § 134.1(b).

were picked from a cotton field in Peru, the cotton fibers were spun into yarn in Peru, the yarn was knit into fabric in Peru, and knit fabric was cut and sewn into a men's tee shirt in Peru, the article would be considered a good wholly manufactured in Peru. Thus, the country of origin would clearly Peru.

If, however, the manufacturing operations occur in more than one country, or the manufacturing of a fashion article includes components from various countries, the determination as to country of origin is more complicated. To that end, the regulations go on to state that "[f]urther work or material added to an article in another country must effect a substantial transformation in order to render such other country the 'country of origin . . .'" Accordingly, the test is whether a "substantial transformation" has occurred. A substantial transformation of an article occurs when it is used in manufacture that results in an article having a name, character, or use differing from that of the article before the processing.[56] However, if the manufacturing or combining process is merely a minor one that leaves the identity of the article intact, a substantial transformation has not occurred.[57] This analysis takes into account the following data points for all countries wherein operations of an imported article occur: processing operations, complexity of the labor involved, costs, number of components, and more. Clearly then, the country of origin of an article isn't necessarily the last country where manufacturing operations occurred.

In Ruling HQ H187035 (Jan. 3, 2012), CBP reviewed the country of origin of footwear uppers. In that ruling, U.S.-origin cowhide was shipped to Mexico to be tanned. The cowhide was manufactured into footwear uppers either in Mexico or the Dominican Republic by the sewing and/or gluing together of components such as eyelets, linings, fittings, and thread from either Mexico or the Dominican Republic. The uppers were then shipped to the United States to be incorporated into finished footwear. Here, CBP held that a substantial transformation occurred when the tanned cowhide was formed into an upper in the Dominican Republic or Mexico. In other words, the tanned cowhide, once formed into a footwear upper, took on a new name, character, and use. Further, an additional substantial transformation occurred when the uppers were assembled in the United States into finished footwear due to the further shaping of the uppers and, thereafter, assembly along with insoles, midsoles, and shanks in the United States.

It is worth noting that the country of origin of merchandise on import declarations can affect product admissibility into the United States; import restrictions such as quota, which generally no longer applies to fashion goods; and other government agency requirements.

---

56. Uniroyal, Inc. v. United States, 3 C.I.T. 220, 542 F. Supp. 1026, 1029 (Ct. Int'l Trade 1982), *aff'd*, 702 F.2d 1022 (Fed. Cir. 1983).

57. *Id.*

b. Preferential Treatment

Certain bilateral and multilateral free trade agreements, and other preferential treatment programs, provide for a reduction or elimination of duties upon importation, provided the rules of origin of the relevant agreements are met. While the requirements for eligibility under each free trade agreement vary, most agreements necessitate, among other requirements, one or a combination of the following:

> A regional value content (meaning the import is composed of materials, and/or has processing costs, associated with the territory of the agreement) of a certain percentage or more (e.g., 35 percent or more of the costs of a women's dress, which may consist of the value of the material and/or labor costs, are attributable to a country within the territory of an agreement). The remaining percentage can relate to material and labor costs that pertain to countries not within the agreement.
>
> A change in tariff classification. In other words, materials that are sourced from countries outside of the agreement are imported into a country within the territory of the agreement, which are then manufactured into another article (e.g., foreign components classifiable as knit fabric imported into a country within the territory of an agreement, wherein the knit fabric is then manufactured into and classified as a finished women's dress upon import into the United States).

Most origin rules relating to fashion merchandise under free trade agreements are based on a change in tariff classification. For example, in Ruling NY N300466, (Oct. 4, 2018), CBP reviewed the eligibility of gloves from Honduras under the Dominican Republic-Central America-United States Free Trade Agreement ("DR-CAFTA"). In this ruling, the following operations occurred: in the United States or Honduras, yarns from China and the United States underwent a gimping process; the gloves were knit to shape in Honduras using the gimped yarn, in addition to two yarns of U.S. origin; and after knitting, the gloves were dipped in polyurethane or other latex product originating from outside the territory of the agreement. Because the gloves were composed of yarns originating outside of the territory of the agreement, CBP had to review the facts in the context of the rule of origin specific to this particular product. The tariff classification of the finished gloves upon importation into the United States was Subheading 6116.10.5520, HTSUS, which provides for "gloves . . . impregnated, coated or covered with plastics or rubber . . . containing 50 percent or more by weight of cotton, man-made fibers or other textile fibers, or any combination thereof." Under DR-CAFTA, the relevant rule of origin was a tariff shift rule, which for goods classifiable under Subheading 6116.10.5520, was as follows:

> A change to headings 6114 through 6116 from any other chapter, except from headings 5111 through 5113, 5204 through 5212, 5310 through 5311, chapter 54, headings 5508 through 5516 or 6001 through 6006, provided that the good is cut or knit to shape, or both, and sewn or otherwise assembled in the territory of one or more of the parties.

Since the non-originating materials, that being the gimped yarn from China and polyurethane also from outside of the territory of the agreement, were classifiable under provisions that met the tariff shift rule specific to the type of gloves at issue, the merchandise was eligible for preferential treatment under DR-CAFTA.

In making these determinations, an Importer would need to identify either the costs of all non-originating components, the tariff classification of all non-originating components when imported into the territory for further processing, or a combination of the two.

c. Marking and Labeling

In the United States, the marking statute[58] requires that, unless excepted, every article of foreign origin (or its container) imported into the United States shall be marked with its country of origin in a conspicuous place as legibly, indelibly, and permanently as the nature of the article (or its container) will permit, in such a manner as to indicate to the ultimate purchaser in the United States the English name of the country of origin of the article. Therefore, CBP generally requires that a country of origin label be permanent sewn, or imprinted via stamp, into each imported fashion article.

Country of origin marking on products involving claims of U.S. origin, such as "Made in the United States" or "Assembled in the United States" are governed by the Federal Trade Commission ("FTC") and, in some instances, state law. All claims of foreign origin are, however, governed by CBP. The FTC also has additional labeling requirements for fashion articles sold in the United States.

An Importer's violation of the Textile, Wool, and Fur Acts is considered an unfair method of competition and an unfair and deceptive act or practice under the Federal Trade Commission Act.[59] If an Importer violates these acts, it may be subject to monetary civil penalties of up to $11,000.00 for each violation. Each instance of mislabeling under the Textile, Wool, and Fur Acts is considered a separate violation. Furthermore, improperly labeled imported items can be held by CBP, and the Importer may be subject to damages.[60]

9. Supply Chain Considerations and Forced Labor

The Trade Facilitation and Trade Enforcement Act of 2015 ("TFTEA") changed forced labor enforcement by CBP. Specifically, the TFTEA law repealed the "consumptive demand" exception in 19 U.S.C. § 1307. This exception had allowed importation of certain forced labor-produced goods if the goods were not produced

58. Section 304, Tariff Act of 1930, as amended (19 U.S.C. § 1304).
59. 19 U.S.C. §§ 70a, 70e, 68a, 68d, 69a, and 69f (2013).
60. 19 U.S.C. §§ 70a(d)(5)(2013); 16 C.F.R. § 303.31(2013).

"in such quantities in the United States as to meet the "consumptive demands" of the United States."

Section 307 of the Tariff Act ("Section 307") now prohibits the importation of merchandise mined, produced, or manufactured, wholly or in part, in any foreign country by forced or indentured child labor—including forced child labor with no exceptions.[61] Such merchandise is subject to exclusion and/or seizure, and may lead to criminal investigation of the Importer. This means if any button, piece of trim, or part of a good or an apparel article is fabricated using forced labor, it is prohibited from entering the commerce of the United States.

Importing into the United States is a privilege and not a right.[62] Accordingly, when information reasonably but not conclusively indicates that merchandise within the purview of this provision is being imported, the Commissioner of CBP ("Commissioner") may issue orders withholding release of such goods pursuant to 19 C.F.R. § 12.42(e). If the Commissioner is provided with information sufficient to make a determination that the goods in question are subject to the provisions of Section 307, the Commissioner will publish a formal finding to that effect in the Customs Bulletin and in the Federal Register pursuant to 19 C.F.R. § 12.42(f).

International standards on child labor and forced labor were developed by the International Labor Organization ("ILO"), a specialized United Nations agency that brings together governments, employers', and workers' representatives of 187 member states to set international labor standards, develop policies, and devise programs to promote rights at work and decent work for all persons. The internationally recognized definition of forced or compulsory labor is found in ILO Convention 29. According to this Convention, forced or compulsory labor is "all work or service which is exacted from any person under the menace of any penalty and for which the said person has not offered himself voluntarily." There are four key elements to this definition, and indicators related to each element. The combination of indicators for each situation must be analyzed in order to determine whether the situation is one of forced labor or not.

- *All work or service*: This includes all types of work, service, and employment, regardless of the industry, sector, or occupation within which it is found, and encompasses legal and formal employment as well as illegal and informal work.
- *Any person*: This refers to adults and children.
- *Menace of any penalty*: This refers to a worker believing he or she will face a penalty if they refuse to work. "Menace" means the penalty need not be exacted, but rather, that threats of penalty may be sufficient, if the employee believes the employer will exact the penalty. A wide variety of penalties,

61. 19 U.S.C. § 1307.

62. "As a result of the complete power of Congress over foreign commerce, it necessarily follows that no individual has a vested right to trade with foreign nations. . . ." Buttfield v. Stranahan, 192 U.S. 470, 493 (1904).

such as confinement to the workplace, violence against workers or family members, retention of identity documents, dismissal from employment, and non-payment of wages, denunciation to authorities, or other loss of rights or privileges, may be sufficient to fulfill this element of the test for forced labor.

- *Voluntary:* This refers to workers' consent to enter into employment and their freedom to leave the employment at any time, with reasonable notice in accordance with national law or collective agreements. In essence, persons are in a forced labor situation if they enter work or service against their free choice, and cannot leave it without penalty or the threat of penalty. Involuntariness does not have to result from physical punishment or constraint; it can also stem from other forms of retaliation, such as the loss of rights or privileges or non-payment of wages owed. Note that a worker can be considered to be in forced labor even if his or her consent was given, if that consent was obtained through the use of force, abduction, fraud, deception or the abuse of power or a position of vulnerability, or if the consent has been revoked.

ILO Convention 105, another convention on forced labor, specifies that forced labor should never be used for the purpose of economic development or as a means of political coercion, discrimination, labor discipline, or punishment for having participated in labor strikes.

The U.S. Department of Labor ("DOL") and CBP use these definitions when determining whether imported goods were manufactured using forced labor. The DOL also utilizes two websites/apps: Comply Chain[63] and Sweat and Toil.[64] These are helpful in determining when a company is importing so that it may determine whether it has purchased suspect products from an "at risk" location.

C. Other Government Agency Laws and Regulations

CBP is responsible for not only enforcing its own rules and regulations surrounding import compliance, but also rules of partner government agencies for purposes of determining product admissibility and other requirements necessary. The list of partner government agencies includes the following:

U.S. Department of Agriculture
U.S. Department of Commerce
U.S. Department of Health and Human Services
U.S. Department of Interior
U.S. Department of Treasury

---

63. *See Comply Chain*, Dep't of Labor, https://www.dol.gov/ilab/complychain/ (last visited June 3, 2020).

64. *See Sweat & Toil: Child Labor, Forced Labor, and Human Trafficking Around the World*, Dep't of Labor, https://www.dol.gov/general/apps/ilab (last visited June 3, 2020).

U.S. Department of Transportation
U.S. Environmental Protection Agency
Consumer Product Safety Commission
Federal Communications Commission

Fashion imports are largely impacted by rules and requirements issued by the U.S. Fish and Wildlife Department, which is an agency that sits under the Department of Interior and regulates certain imports composed of animal components (e.g., apparel and other fashion items composed of fur, feathers, animal skins, etc.). At times, these imports are either fully prohibited under international, country, or state laws. For example, *Crocodylus siamensis* (Siamese crocodile) skins, and all articles made of such skins, are prohibited from importation. In other instances, they are restricted in that certain licenses or permits are required for importation.

Also of relevance to the fashion industry is the Food and Drug Administration, which sits under the Department of Health and Human Services and regulates beauty products and cosmetics pursuant to the Federal Food, Drug and Cosmetic Act. Here, again, Importers are often required to obtain registrations or meet certain requirements to import certain beauty products. For example, cosmetics must meet certain labeling requirements, which includes ingredient labeling, warning statements, name of place of business, etc.

D. Administrative Penalties

Title 19 U.S.C. § 1592 is the statutory provision typically used for the enforcement of customs laws. A violation of this section occurs when Importers make material misstatements or omissions that occur as a result of fraud, gross negligence, or negligence in connection with their entries (or attempted entry) of merchandise into the United States. If found in violation, CBP may issue penalties as high as the full domestic value of the imported merchandise. Criminal action or seizure or forfeiture of goods are other potential penalties.

Importers are responsible for any statements made by their vendors or any other party to the importing transaction, for instance, a foreign agent, as it is the Importer's responsibility to exercise reasonable care as discussed in prior sections.[65] Accordingly, in the fashion industry, errors made by a vendor in stating such items as component material in chief weight or country of origin of the fabric or representations regarding the proper classification or valuation of imported merchandise can result in penalty liability even though the Importer was not the one who made the misstatement.[66]

65. 19 U.S.C. § 1484 (2013).

66. *See* In re Cliquot's Champagne, 70 U.S. 114 (1865) (holding that the act of the agent or consignee is attributable to the guilty principal); *but see* Timken Co. v. United States, 25 C.I.T. 939, 964, 166 F. Supp. 2d 608, 634 (Ct. Int'l Trade 2001) (holding that *Cliquot's Champagne* could not serve as precedent to create a connection between a freight forwarder and a manufacturer).

To avoid such penalties, 19 U.S.C. § 1592 provides a safe harbor for reduced or eliminated penalties to an Importer that notifies CBP of a violation of customs laws and regulations prior to, and without knowledge of, the commencement of a formal investigation by CBP. However, disputes surrounding the scope of a formal investigation may not always be so apparent. In *United States v. Ford Motor, Co.*, CBP notified the top three automakers, including the Importer, of an investigation to identify undeclared assists and indirect payments relating to imports of vehicles and vehicle components.[67] The Importer and CBP thereafter met to discuss the scope of "indirect payments" under the investigation.[68] Though the court here found that the Importer "knew or should have known" that the investigation included all payments following the meeting with CBP, the question turned on whether "the scope of an investigation which, by its terms, is limited to 'assists and indirect payments,' may be broadened by such informal communications to include direct payments."[69] Under 19 C.F.R. § 162.74(e), an investigation is commenced when a CBP official makes an inquiry of the Importer concerning "the type of circumstances of additional violations." It was held that at the time of the meeting, when CBP had inquired as to the direct payments, the scope of the investigation was expanded to include such payments and, thus, any violations disclosed by the Importer following that date did not constitute a prior disclosure.[70]

Since, CBP's assessment of civil penalties *may* amount to as much as the full domestic value of the imported merchandise, as well as a criminal action or a seizure or forfeiture action for imported goods, it is often in an Importer's best interests to disclose import violations immediately.

E. Litigation

Disputes regarding the nature of imported goods (or other associated value issues) sometimes cannot be resolved through the administrative process. In these instances, an Importer may file a lawsuit in the U.S. Court of International Trade ("CIT"). The CIT is an Article III court[71] headquartered in New York City with jurisdiction over all import cases throughout the United States,[72] including any civil action that arises out of an import transaction. The United States Court of Appeals for the Federal Circuit has nationwide appellate jurisdiction over a number of subjects, including importation sand international trade cases. Appeals to this

67. United States v. Ford Motor Co., 463 F.3d 1267, 1272 (Fed. Cir. 2006).

68. *Id.*

69. *Id.* at 1280.

70. *Id.*

71. Article III courts were established by Congress and are so called because they were defined by Article III of the U.S. Constitution. These courts include the Supreme Court of the United States as well as lower federal courts.

72. The CIT is also authorized to hold hearings in foreign countries.

court come from federal district courts throughout the United States, the United States Court of Federal Claims, the CIT, and the United States Court of Appeals for Veterans' Claims.

Before seeking to recover in court, the Importer must go through the appropriate administrative protest process, which is essentially contesting a final determination made by CBP.[73] Where CBP disagrees with an Importer's declarations at the time of entry (e.g., as to classification, valuation, origin, free trade agreement eligibility, etc.), CBP will deny a protest. Once denied, an Importer has 180 days to file a summons in court.[74] It is in an Importer's best interest to identify all entries wherein protest was denied. For example, in *Pollak Import-Export Corp. v. United States*, the Federal Circuit court confirmed that a denial of administrative protest decisions requires only that a suit be initiated by the filing of a summons within 180 days after a government's denial of a protest.[75] Additionally, while the court stated that the failure to identify all entries protested within the summons was not a jurisdictional bar, the proper ground for dismissal would have been failure to state a claim on which relief could be granted.[76]

Since fashion articles have an average duty rate of 16 percent, and footwear imports are predominantly at a 37.5 percent rate, both of which are high, the tariff classification of such goods is often litigated in court.

F. Conclusion

Fashion brands manufacture the majority of their apparel, footwear, and other related articles outside of the United States. As exemplified in this chapter, import compliance can be complex and challenging. Importers of such goods must ensure compliance with all of the laws of the multitude of agencies that regulate their products. Failure to do so could result in significant disruptions to the business in the form of shipment delays or seizures, in addition to direct impact to a company's bottom line due to the issuance of penalties.

---

73. 19 C.F.R. § 174.12.
74. 28 U.S.C. §§ 1581, 2636(a), 2632(b).
75. 52 F.3d 303, 308 (Fed. Cir. 1995).
76. *Id.*

Chapter 4

Copyright Law

Christopher Buccafusco

Copyright law is one of the principal forms of intellectual property law in the United States, and it grants rights to a wide range of creators, from painters and musicians to architects and computer programmers. But the creative efforts of fashion designers have typically not been covered by copyright law in the United States. A recent decision by the Supreme Court—the 2017 opinion in *Star Athletica v. Varsity Brands*—may indicate, however, that the situation is changing.

This chapter will introduce you to the basic rules of U.S. copyright law that pertain to fashion design. It will describe the doctrinal requirements that designs must meet to obtain copyright protection as well as the major doctrinal hurdle to that protection—the useful articles doctrine. Finally, it will explore the ways in which copyright protection can be used to prevent others from selling similar goods.

A. A Bit of Copyright Theory

Before considering the specific legal rules that govern copyright law, it is essential to understand why governments provide copyright protection for certain kinds of activities in the first place. In the United States, copyright law is based in the federal Constitution. Article I, section 8, clause 8 gives Congress the power to "promote the progress of science and useful arts, by securing for limited times to authors and inventors the exclusive right to their respective writings and discoveries." Historically, courts and scholars have understood the prefatory reference to "promoting the Progress of Science and useful Arts" as grounding copyright law in a utilitarian effort to make the world a better place. Under this theory, copyright law is valuable to the extent that granting exclusive rights to certain works is good for society. If and when copyrights make society better off, the government should create them, but if copyrights are not needed, then government need not (and should not) give them out.

The American understanding of copyright law stands in stark contrast to the foundational assumptions of other legal systems. Throughout Europe, for example, authors receive copyrights in their works not because doing so achieves some social good but because they *deserve* them. Copyright protection in these "moral rights" jurisdictions is about what is fair or just rather than what makes the world a better place. This theoretical difference can have substantial implications for the copyright doctrines that jurisdictions adopt.

So, if copyright law in the United States is based on utilitarian goals of improving society, how might it do that? Copyright law exists to solve a particular problem known as the public goods problem of information. It works like this: information, like a new song or the design of a necklace, is often expensive to produce but cheap to copy. Consider a songwriter named Taylor. She may spend hours, days, or weeks of her time composing a song—time that she could have spent doing something else remunerative (like becoming a lawyer). So when Taylor decides to sell copies of the song, she will want to recoup the investment in her creativity. But once she releases the song to the world, if copyright law doesn't exist, others can copy it and distribute it. Because the copyists did not invest any time creating the song, they can charge a lower price than Taylor can. Before she even writes the song, Taylor can see how this will play out, and instead of wasting her time and energy composing lyrics, she chooses to attend law school. And now the world is left without her creativity.

This is where copyright may help. Copyright protection gives the author the exclusive right to sell her work for a period of years (currently the life of the author plus 70 years postmortem). During this time, as the only seller of her work, she can charge elevated prices for access to it. When you paid for this book, you didn't just pay a price that reflects the cost of producing a single copy. That would only be about $8. The much higher price that you paid reflects the fact that the publisher is effectively a monopolist for the content of the book. This monopoly-like price is supposed to give creators an opportunity to recoup the costs of their investments. The opportunity to charge supracompetitive prices is intended to give authors an incentive to invest in creativity.

But note, this incentive is incredibly costly. All consumers of a copyrighted work pay more for access to it than they would if it were not protected by copyright. That's money that *they* could be spending elsewhere. Perhaps more importantly, many would-be consumers simply won't be able to afford to access the work at its copyright price. Although many people might have been willing to pay $8 for a copy of this book, far fewer of them will be able and willing to pay the copyright price for it. This is another cost of copyright law. Finally, giving copyright protection to one creator limits the opportunities of future creators. Future creators will be prevented from creating substantially similar works for a century or more, or they will have to pay for licenses from the copyright holders. This hinders future creators' opportunities, and it dramatically reduces the options that consumers may choose from. Instead of being able to purchase multiple versions of a work from numerous producers at different price points, consumers will only be able to select from the products the copyright owner offers and at the copyright owner's price.

Seen in its full perspective, copyright law is a tax on consumers and future creators for the benefit of past and current creators. As with all taxes that redistribute income from one group to another, copyright law is only worth it if its benefits exceed its costs. Policymakers must determine whether society gets more and better creativity with copyright or without, and, if the answer is with copyright, the particular form of copyright law should seek to minimize its costs and maximize its benefits.

Turning to fashion, we should ask whether giving designers copyrights would result in a world with more or better fashion than a world without copyright protection. This is, of course, a difficult (if not impossible) empirical question. We might, instead, begin by asking what "progress" in fashion design even means. While everyone would agree that innovations in pharmaceuticals, surgical techniques, and electronics have made considerable progress in the last half-century, what would they say about progress in fashion design? Are today's designs "better" in some meaningful way than the designs of the 1990s or 1950s? As Kal Raustiala and Christopher Sprigman put it, "[f]ashion never stops but it never goes anywhere either." KAL RAUSTIALA & CHRISTOPHER SPRIGMAN, THE KNOCKOFF ECONOMY 41 (2012).

The empirical evidence that exists with respect to copyright and fashion creativity doesn't suggest that copyright law is especially needed to encourage more creativity. According to Raustiala and Sprigman's data, despite the widespread lack of copyright protection for fashion design, the prices for high-end women's fashion have been increasing steadily since 1998. Controlling for inflation, the price of a high-fashion women's dress almost doubled between 1998 and 2012. *Id* at 46. That's at least some evidence that the most creative fashion designers are not suffering too much from the lack of copyright protection. In fact, Raustiala and Sprigman argue that the *lack* of copyright protection is making fashion design more creative. They suggest the ability of designers to copy one another leads to the formation of trends as the most fashionable people flock to a particular style. As copying increases, however, the style spreads to less elite members of society. Eventually, the copied style is devalued in the eyes of the most elite folks, and they look for a new style. Raustiala and Sprigman call this phenomenon "induced obsolescence," and they suggest that it tends to speed up design innovation relative to a world in which copyright law blocked copying. *Id.* at 44. *But see* C. Scott Hemphill & Jeannie Suk, *The Law, Culture, and Economics of Fashion*, STAN. L. REV. 1147 (2009).

B. What Copyright Law Protects

In the United States, copyright law has generally provided little protection to most fashion designers. Although jewelry designers and fabric designers have been able to take advantage of copyright protection, garment designers largely have not. This section will explain the doctrines that have produced these results and why they may be changing.

1. Criteria of Copyrightability: Fixation and Originality

In the United States, copyright law is virtually entirely a product of federal law. Since 1790, the United States has given the creators of certain sorts of objects copyrights. In copyright law, we refer to creators as "authors" and their creations as "writings" or "works." So, in copyright parlance, a painter is just as much an author of a writing as a novelist. The current copyright statute is the Copyright Act of 1976 in Title 17 of the United States Code. Section 102(a) of the Act provides:

> (a) Copyright protection subsists, in accordance with this title, in original works of authorship fixed in any tangible medium of expression, now known or later developed, from which they can be perceived, reproduced, or otherwise communicated, either directly or with the aid of a machine or device. Works of authorship include the following categories:
>
> (1) literary works;
>
> (2) musical works, including any accompanying words;
>
> (3) dramatic works, including any accompanying music;
>
> (4) pantomimes and choreographic works;
>
> (5) pictorial, graphic, and sculptural works;
>
> (6) motion pictures and other audiovisual works;
>
> (7) sound recordings; and
>
> (8) architectural works.

17 U.S.C. § 102(a) (2012).

Here, we are concerned with category 5—pictorial, graphic, and sculptural (PGS) works. The opening paragraph explains the two fundamental requirements for copyrightability: fixation and originality. The first is an incredibly simple concept, but the latter is more complex.

In order to receive copyright protection, a work must be fixed in a tangible medium of expression for a period of more than transitory duration. 17 U.S.C. § 101 (2012). For fashion designs, this simply means that the work must be drawn, sculpted, or otherwise visibly rendered in some more or less permanent medium. A work cannot be protected before it has been fixed. Importantly, however, copyright protection begins *as soon as a work is fixed* if the work meets the other statutory requirements. This means that copyright protection begins (if it does) the moment the designer sets her pen to the page or her finger to the keyboard. Registration is not necessary. (Although we will see later that registration is important for a number of reasons.)

More significantly, in order to be copyrightable a work must be "original." But the term original, in copyright law, doesn't necessarily mean what it means in ordinary speech. It does not mean novel, unique, or never-seen-before. And it doesn't imply any degree of aesthetic value. Rather, as the U.S. Supreme Court explained:

> Original, as the term is used in copyright, means only that the work was independently created by the author (as opposed to copied from other works), and that it possesses some minimal degree of creativity. To be sure, the requisite level of creativity is extremely low; even a slight amount will suffice. The vast majority of works make the grade quite easily, as they possess some creative spark, "no matter how crude, humble or obvious" it might be.

Feist Publ'ns, Inc. v. Rural Tel. Serv. Co., 499 U. S. 340, 345 (1991) (internal citation omitted).

Thus, the concept of originality can be decomposed into two separate criteria: (1) the work (or some aspect of it) must be original to the author rather than copied from another source, and (2) the work must demonstrate some more-than-trivial creative spark. In order to analyze these requirements, courts will consider the *expressive choices* that authors make about *how* they create their works. Courts will ask whether those choices, taken as a whole, were original to the author and demonstrate some spark of creativity or cleverness. Consider the following examples:

(1) The plaintiff published a white pages telephone book with names and phone numbers that were arranged alphabetically by last name. The plaintiff selected the names to include based on a required geographic criterion. The Court ruled that these choices about the "selection, coordination, and arrangement" of names and phone numbers were neither original to the author (because they had been copied from other phonebooks) nor minimally creative (because they were "garden variety" and "entirely typical"). *Feist*, 499 U.S. at 362.

(2) An artist created the following logo for a preppy fashion designer with the initials T.H. by borrowing the red and white fields from the Nautical Flag Alphabet for the letters "T" and "H":

The Copyright Office declined to register the logo, because it lacked even the low level of authorship necessary for protection. The Office found that the design was a simple combination of basic shapes derived from existing public domain material.

https://www.copyright.gov/rulings-filings/review-board/docs/tommy-hilfiger-flag.pdf

Which of the following logos do you think would pass the originality threshold?

If you answered No—Yes—Yes then your judgment corresponds with the Copyright Office's. *See* https://www.copyright.gov/rulings-filings/review-board/docs/d-with-ball-design.pdf.

Would these logos receive protection under trademark law? If so, why would the companies also seek copyright registrations?

2. Limitations on Copyrightability: Idea/Expression and Useful Articles

Although copyright law will generally protect fixed and original works of authorship, there are important limits on that protection. Two copyright doctrines—the idea/expression distinction and, more importantly, the useful articles doctrine—are the reasons why many fashion designs will not receive copyrights.

a. Ideas versus Expressions

One of the foundational principles of copyright law is that a copyright only extends to an author's expression and not the underlying ideas that she expresses. A screenwriter who creates a script for a boxing movie cannot receive a copyright on the "idea" of boxing movies or even on the idea of an underdog boxer who makes good or a female boxer fighting for recognition in a male-dominated world. The screenwriter will only obtain a copyright for his particular expression of that idea.

The same issue can arise in design. Imagine that a designer produces a jeweled pin in the shape of a bumblebee, like the one below:

If she obtains a copyright in her design, she will not be able to use that copyright to prevent others from making their own jeweled bee pins, because copyright does not protect the idea of "jeweled bee pin." If anything, she will only receive protection for her version of a jeweled bee pin, so the following pin probably would not infringe her copyright:

Moreover, in some cases, the number of possible ways of expressing an idea will be extremely narrow. There may be a tightly circumscribed range of potential creative expressions of an idea. In those cases, a court may say that the idea *merges* with its expressions, and the expressions themselves are uncopyrightable. Going back to our initial discussion, this is because granting a copyright in such a case would impose too much cost on the public and other creators. When there are only a few ways to express an idea, the few people who got copyrights on those expressions would effectively monopolize the idea itself. *Herbert Rosenthal Jewelry Corp. v. Kalpakian*, 446 F.2d 738 (9th Cir. 1971)

b. The Useful Articles Doctrine

By far the larger hurdle to obtaining copyrights in fashion designs is the useful articles doctrine. Recall from above that fashion designs, whether for garments, shoes, or jewelry, fall into the category of "pictorial, graphic, and sculptural works" (PGS). When Congress passed the 1976 Act, it imposed a special set of requirements on some PGS works—those that it classified as "useful articles." In order to receive copyrights, useful articles must meet additional criteria beyond fixation and originality. They must contain expression that is "separable" from their utilitarian aspects. Traditionally, most fashion designs have failed to meet this requirement and have been excluded from copyright automatically.

Before examining the doctrine, it is essential to understand the goal Congress was trying to achieve with it. As we've seen, copyright law protects an author's expression. It is not, however, supposed to protect how objects function. Functionality is the domain of utility patent law. Unlike copyrights, which are easy to obtain, require limited creativity, and last for a very long time, patents require examination by the Patent and Trademark Office, must meet a high standard of creativity that involves both novelty and nonobviousness, and only last for 20 years. Congress was concerned that, in some cases, creators might take advantage of copyright's lenient standards to obtain protection for functionality without having to subject themselves to the rigors of patent law. Unless copyright law screens out certain kinds of works, people might be able to obtain "backdoor patents." Christopher Buccafusco & Mark A. Lemley, *Functionality Screens*, 103 Va. L. Rev. 1293, 1304–05 (2017).

Now let's look at how copyright law tries to do this. Copyright law subjects certain kinds of PGS works—those classified as useful articles—to an additional hurdle for copyrightability. First, then, we must figure out what counts as a useful article. The Copyright Act defines a useful article as:

> an article having an intrinsic utilitarian function that is not merely to portray the appearance of the article or to convey information.

17 U.S.C. § 101 (2012).

Of course, all works have *some* utilitarian function. A Picasso painting can be burned for heat if necessary. And many works have *some* aesthetic expression. A stapler may have some appealing shape to it. But the definition asks whether the work has an *intrinsic* utilitarian function. One way of thinking about what this means to ask what the work is *for.* A stapler is for stapling. That is a utilitarian function. A painting is for looking at. And as the definition explains, when the value of the work is in portraying appearances or conveying information, those values are not to be treated as functional. Thus, a stapler is a useful article, while a painting is not. This means that the painting is copyrightable if it is original, while the stapler has to meet the additional criteria.

Before we continue to those criteria, stop to consider what sorts of fashion designs may or may not count as useful articles. Courts have uniformly held that garments are useful articles. Their intrinsic value is for covering the body and providing warmth and modesty. But what about a Halloween costume? Or a mask? Or the jeweled bumblebee pin we discussed above? What is a bracelet or a necklace for?

If a PGS work is a useful article, the Copyright Act imposes an additional hurdle for copyrightability. The Act explains:

> the design of a useful article, as defined in this section, shall be considered a pictorial, graphic, or sculptural work only if, and only to the extent that, such design incorporates pictorial, graphic, or sculptural features that can be identified separately from, and are capable of existing independently of, the utilitarian aspects of the article.

Id.

Copyright lawyers refer to this requirement as "separability." Before we get too deeply into the doctrine, it is again helpful to understand why Congress added this section. The legislative history explains that Congress:

> is seeking to draw as clear a line as possible between copyrightable works of applied art and uncopyrightable works of industrial design. A

> two-dimensional painting, drawing, or graphic work is still capable of being identified as such when it is printed on or applied to utilitarian articles such as textile fabrics, wallpaper, containers, and the like. . . . On the other hand, although the shape of an industrial product may be aesthetically satisfying and valuable, the Committee's intention is not to offer it copyright protection under the bill. Unless the shape of an automobile, airplane, ladies' dress, food processor, television set, or any other industrial product contains some element that, physically or conceptually, can be identified as separable from the utilitarian aspects of the article, the design would not be copyrighted under the bill.

H.R. Rep. No. 94-1476, at 55 (1976), *reprinted in* 1976 U.S.C.C.A.N. 5659. Congress was saying that, although many products of industrial design are aesthetically appealing and contain expressive elements, those products are not protectable unless they have some separate and distinct PGS features such as "a carving on the back of a chair or a floral relief design on silver flatware." *Id.*

In its simplest formulation the useful articles doctrine asks whether the design has PGS features that can be identified separately from, and are capable of existing independently of, the utilitarian aspects of the article. This seems to require a court to identify the PGS features of the work, identify the utilitarian aspects of work, and then ask whether the former can be identified separately from and exist independently of the latter. While this task may seem straightforward, it has proven enormously challenging for courts and commentators to apply. After the passage of the 1976 Act, courts struggled to interpret and apply the separability criteria. Various tests emerged that focused on whether the design was primarily ornamental or primarily useful, whether the design stimulates in the mind of the beholder the concept of a work of art, and whether there were design elements that reflected the creator's artistic judgment independently from utilitarian concerns.

In virtually all of these cases that dealt with garment designs, the court rejected the designer's copyright. *See, e.g., Jovani Fashion, Ltd. v. Fiesta Fashions*, 500 F. App'x 42 (2d Cir. 2012). Although the lines of the garment, the shape of its sleeves, or its ruching at the waist might be aesthetically pleasing, they were also utilitarian aspects of the designs and, thus, inseparable. If the designer was only claiming a two-dimensional fabric pattern, however, that design could be protectable because it was not functional and could be separated from the underlying garments to which it might be applied.

A recent case challenged the distinction between these two lines of cases. In *Star Athletica v. Varsity Brands*, the plaintiff asserted a copyright in the design of various cheerleading uniforms. The plaintiff, Varsity Brands, is the largest manufacturer of cheerleading uniforms in the world, with as much as 90 percent of the market. Star Athletica is a new competitor in the market.

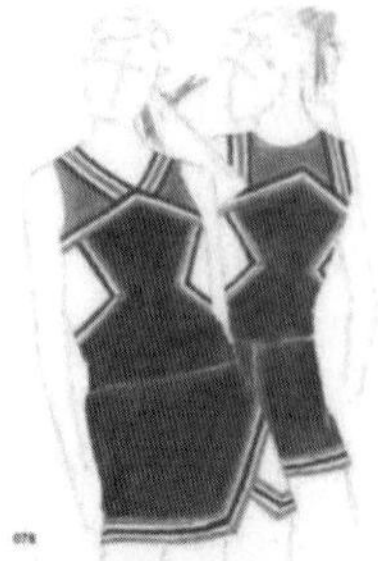

Design 078
Registration No. VA 1-417-427

Design 0815
Registration No. VA 1-675-905

Design 299B
Registration No. VA 1-319-226

Design 299A
Registration No. VA 1-319-228

The trial court rejected Varsity's copyright infringement action, because it deemed the designs inseparable aspects of the underlying useful article. According to the trial court, the stripes, chevrons, and color blocking on the uniforms evoked the concept of cheerleading uniforms and were necessary for the utilitarian function of identifying the wearers as cheerleaders. Varsity appealed the decision to the Sixth Circuit Court of Appeals, and that court reversed the trial court, finding the designs separable. The Sixth Circuit opinion went like this:

(1) The plaintiff's design is for a PGS work.

(2) The design is a useful article because uniforms have intrinsic utilitarian functions.

(3) The design has certain utilitarian aspects, including sweat wicking, allowing movement, and covering the body. But "decorative" or "identifying" aspects of the designs were not functional aspects.

(4) The PGS features—stripes, chevrons, and color blocking—could be identified separately from those utilitarian aspects and exist independently of them.

Star Athletica appealed to the U.S. Supreme Court, and the Court agreed to hear the case. The Court's opinion, written by Justice Thomas, the concurring opinion written by Justice Ginsburg, and the dissenting opinion, written by Justice Breyer, are reproduced below.

Star Athletica, LLC v. Varsity Brands, Inc.

137 S. Ct. 1002 (2017)

Justice THOMAS delivered the opinion of the Court.

Congress has provided copyright protection for original works of art, but not for industrial designs. The line between art and industrial design, however, is often difficult to draw. This is particularly true when an industrial design incorporates artistic elements. Congress has afforded limited protection for these artistic elements by providing that "pictorial, graphic, or sculptural features" of the "design of a useful article" are eligible for copyright protection as artistic works if those features "can be identified separately from, and are capable of existing independently of, the utilitarian aspects of the article." *17 U. S. C. § 101.*

We granted certiorari to resolve widespread disagreement over the proper test for implementing *§ 101*'s separate identification and independent-existence requirements. *578 U. S. ___, 136 S. Ct. 1823, 194 L. Ed. 2d 829 (2016).* We hold that a feature incorporated into the design of a useful article is eligible for copyright protection only if the feature (1) can be perceived as a two- or three-dimensional work of art separate from the useful article and (2) would qualify as a protectable pictorial, graphic, or sculptural work—either on its own or fixed in some other tangible medium of expression—if it were imagined separately from the useful article into which it is incorporated. Because that test is satisfied in this case, we affirm.

I

Respondents Varsity Brands, Inc., Varsity Spirit Corporation, and Varsity Spirit Fashions & Supplies, Inc., design, make, and sell cheerleading uniforms. Respondents have obtained or acquired more than 200 U. S. copyright registrations for two-dimensional designs appearing on the surface of their uniforms and other garments. These designs are primarily "combinations, positionings, and arrangements of elements" that include "chevrons . . . , lines, curves, stripes, angles, diagonals, inverted [chevrons], coloring, and shapes." App. 237. At issue in this case are Designs 299A, 299B, 074, 078, and 0815. See Appendix, *infra.*

Petitioner Star Athletica, L. L. C., also markets and sells cheerleading uniforms. Respondents sued petitioner for infringing their copyrights in the five designs. The District Court entered summary judgment for petitioner on respondents' copyright claims on the ground that the designs did not qualify as protectable pictorial, graphic, or sculptural works. It reasoned that the designs served the useful, or "utilitarian," function of identifying the garments as "cheerleading uniforms" and therefore could not be "physically or conceptually" separated under *§ 101* "from the utilitarian function" of the uniform. *2014 U.S. Dist. LEXIS 26279, 2014 WL 819422, *8-*9 (WD Tenn., Mar. 1, 2014).*

The Court of Appeals for the Sixth Circuit reversed. *799 F. 3d 468, 471 (2015).* In its view, the "graphic designs" were "separately identifiable" because the designs "and a blank cheerleading uniform can appear 'side by side'—one as a graphic design, and one as a cheerleading uniform." *Id., at 491* (quoting Compendium of U. S. Copyright Office Practices §924.2(B) (3d ed. 2014) (Compendium)). And it determined that the designs were "'capable of existing independently'" because they could be incorporated onto the surface of different types of garments, or hung on the wall and framed as art. *799 F. 3d, at 491, 492.*

Judge McKeague dissented. He would have held that, because "identifying the wearer as a cheerleader" is a utilitarian function of a cheerleading uniform and the surface designs were "integral to" achieving that function, the designs were inseparable from the uniforms. *Id., at 495-496.*

II

The first element of a copyright-infringement claim is "ownership of a valid copyright." *Feist Publications, Inc. v. Rural Telephone Service Co.,* 499 U. S. 340, 361, 111 S. Ct. 1282, 113 L. Ed. 2d 358 (1991). A valid copyright extends only to copyrightable subject matter. See 4 M. Nimmer & D. Nimmer, *Copyright* § 13.01[A] (2010) (Nimmer). The Copyright Act of 1976 defines copyrightable subject matter as "original works of authorship fixed in any tangible medium of expression." *17 U. S. C. § 102(a).*

"Works of authorship" include "pictorial, graphic, and sculptural works," *§ 102(a)(5),* which the statute defines to include "two-dimensional and three-dimensional works of fine, graphic, and applied art, photographs, prints and art reproductions, maps, globes, charts, diagrams, models, and technical drawings, including architectural plans," *§ 101.* And a work of authorship is "'fixed' in a tangible medium of expression when it [is] embodi[ed] in a" "material objec[t] . . . from which the work can be perceived, reproduced, or otherwise communicated." *Ibid.* (definitions of "fixed" and "copies").

The Copyright Act also establishes a special rule for copyrighting a pictorial, graphic, or sculptural work incorporated into a "useful article," which is defined as "an article having an intrinsic utilitarian function that is not merely to portray the appearance of the article or to convey information." *Ibid.* The statute does not protect useful articles as such. Rather, "the design of a useful article" is "considered a pictorial, graphical, or sculptural work only if, and only to the extent that, such design incorporates pictorial, graphic, or sculptural features that can be identified separately from, and are capable of existing independently of, the utilitarian aspects of the article." *Ibid.*

Courts, the Copyright Office, and commentators have described the analysis undertaken to determine whether a feature can be separately identified from, and exist independently of, a useful article as "separability." In this case, our task is to determine whether the arrangements of lines, chevrons, and colorful shapes appearing on the surface of respondents' cheerleading uniforms are eligible for copyright protection as separable features of the design of those cheerleading uniforms.

A

As an initial matter, we must address whether separability analysis is necessary in this case.

1

Respondents argue that "[s]eparability is only implicated when a [pictorial, graphic, or sculptural] work is the 'design of a useful article.'" Brief for Respondents 25. They contend that the surface decorations in this case are "two-dimensional graphic designs that appear *on* useful articles," but are not themselves designs *of* useful articles. *Id.*, at 52. Consequently, the surface decorations are protected two-dimensional works of graphic art without regard to any separability analysis under *§101. Ibid.*; see 2 W. Patry, Copyright §3:151, p. 3–485 (2016) (Patry) ("Courts looking at two-dimensional design claims should not apply the separability analysis regardless of the three-dimensional form that design is embodied in"). Under this theory, two-dimensional artistic features on the surface of useful articles are "inherently separable." Brief for Respondents 26.

This argument is inconsistent with the text of *§101.* The statute requires separability analysis for any "pictorial, graphic, or sculptural features" incorporated into the "design of a useful article." "Design" refers here to "the combination" of "details" or "features" that "go to make up" the useful article. 3 Oxford English Dictionary 244 (def. 7, first listing) (1933) (OED). Furthermore, the words "pictorial" and "graphic" include, in this context, two-dimensional features such as pictures, paintings, or drawings. See 4 *id., at 359, 111 S. Ct. 1282, 113 L. Ed. 2d 358* (defining "[g]raphic" to mean "[o]f or pertaining to drawing or painting"); 7 *id.*, at 830 (defining "[p]ictorial" to mean "of or pertaining to painting or drawing"). And the statute expressly defines "[p]ictorial, graphical, and sculptural works" to include "two-dimensional . . . works of . . . art." *§101.* The statute thus provides that the "design of a useful article" can include two-dimensional "pictorial" and "graphic" features, and separability analysis applies to those features just as it does to three-dimensional "sculptural" features.

B

We must now decide when a feature incorporated into a useful article "can be identified separately from" and is "capable of existing independently of" "the utilitarian aspects" of the article. This is not a free-ranging search for the best copyright policy, but rather "depends solely on statutory interpretation." *Mazer v. Stein*, 347 U. S. 201, 214, 74 S. Ct. 460, 98 L. Ed. 630, 1954 *Dec. Comm'r Pat.* 308 (1954). "The controlling principle in this case is the basic and unexceptional rule that courts must give effect to the clear meaning of statutes as written." *Estate of Cowart v. Nicklos Drilling Co.*, 505 U. S. 469, 476, 112 S. Ct. 2589, 120 L. Ed. 2d 379 (1992). We thus begin and end our inquiry with the text, giving each word its "ordinary, contemporary, common meaning." . . . We do not, however, limit this inquiry to the text of § 101 in isolation. "[I]nterpretation of a phrase of uncertain reach is not confined to a single sentence when the text of the whole statute gives instruction as to its meaning." . . . We thus "look to the provisions of the whole law" to determine *§ 101*'s meaning.

1

The statute provides that a "pictorial, graphic, or sculptural featur[e]" incorporated into the "design of a useful article" is eligible for copyright protection if it (1) "can be identified separately from," and (2) is "capable of existing independently of, the utilitarian aspects of the article." *§ 101.* The first requirement—separate identification—is not onerous. The decisionmaker need only be able to look at the useful article and spot some two- or three-dimensional element that appears to have pictorial, graphic, or sculptural qualities. See 2 Patry § 3:146, at 3-474 to 3-475.

The independent-existence requirement is ordinarily more difficult to satisfy. The decisionmaker must determine that the separately identified feature has the capacity to exist apart from the utilitarian aspects of the article. See 2 OED 88 (def. 5) (defining "[c]apable" of as "[h]aving the needful capacity, power, or fitness for"). In other words, the feature must be able to exist as its own pictorial, graphic, or sculptural work as defined in § 101 once it is imagined apart from the useful article. If the feature is not capable of existing as a pictorial, graphic, or sculptural work once separated from the useful article, then it was not a pictorial, graphic, or sculptural feature of that article, but rather one of its utilitarian aspects.

Of course, to qualify as a pictorial, graphic, or sculptural work on its own, the feature cannot itself be a useful article or "[a]n article that is normally a part of a useful article" (which is itself considered a useful article). § 101. Nor could someone claim a copyright in a useful article merely by creating a replica of that article in some other medium—for example, a cardboard model of a car. Although the replica could itself be copyrightable, it would not give rise to any rights in the useful article that inspired it.

2

The statute as a whole confirms our interpretation. The Copyright Act provides "the owner of [a] copyright" with the "exclusive righ[t] . . . to reproduce the copyrighted work in copies." § 106(1). The statute clarifies that this right "includes the right to reproduce the [copyrighted] work in or on any kind of article, whether useful or otherwise." § 113(a). Section 101 is, in essence, the mirror image of § 113(a). Whereas § 113(a) protects a work of authorship first fixed in some tangible medium other than a useful article and subsequently applied to a useful article, § 101 protects art first fixed in the medium of a useful article. The two provisions make clear that copyright protection extends to pictorial, graphic, and sculptural works regardless of whether they were created as freestanding art or as features of useful articles. The ultimate separability question, then, is whether the feature for which copyright protection is claimed would have been eligible for copyright protection as a pictorial, graphic, or sculptural work had it originally been fixed in some tangible medium other than a useful article before being applied to a useful article.

3

This interpretation is also consistent with the history of the Copyright Act. In *Mazer*, a case decided under the 1909 Copyright Act, the respondents copyrighted a statuette depicting a dancer. The statuette was intended for use as a lamp base, "with electric wiring, sockets and lamp shades attached." *347 U. S., at 202, 74 S. Ct. 460, 98 L. Ed. 630*. Copies of the statuette were sold both as lamp bases and separately as statuettes. *Id., at 203, 74 S. Ct. 460, 98 L. Ed. 630*. The petitioners copied the statuette and sold lamps with the statuette as the base. They defended against the respondents' infringement suit by arguing that the respondents did not have a copyright in a statuette intended for use as a lamp base. *Id., at 204-205, 74 S. Ct. 460, 98 L. Ed. 630*.

Two of *Mazer*'s holdings are relevant here. First, the Court held that the respondents owned a copyright in the statuette even though it was intended for use as a lamp base. See *id., at 214, 74 S. Ct. 460, 98 L. Ed. 630*. In doing so, the Court approved the Copyright Office's regulation extending copyright protection to works of art that might also serve a useful purpose. See *ibid.* (approving 37 CFR § 202.8(a) (1949) (protecting "works of artistic craftsmanship, in so far as their form but not their mechanical or utilitarian aspects are concerned")).

Second, the Court held that it was irrelevant to the copyright inquiry whether the statuette was initially created as a freestanding sculpture or as a lamp base. *347 U. S., at 218-219, 74 S. Ct. 460, 98 L. Ed. 630* ("Nor do we think the subsequent registration of a work of art published as an element in a manufactured article, is a misuse of copyright. This is not different from the registration of a statuette and its later embodiment in an industrial article"). *Mazer* thus interpreted the 1909 Act consistently with the rule discussed above: If a design would have been copyrightable as a standalone pictorial, graphic, or sculptural work, it is copyrightable if created first as part of a useful article.

Shortly thereafter, the Copyright Office enacted a regulation implementing the holdings of *Mazer*. See 1 *Nimmer* § 2A.08[B][1][b] (2016). As amended, the regulation introduced the modern separability test to copyright law:

> "If the sole intrinsic function of an article is its utility, the fact that the article is unique and attractively shaped will not qualify it as a work of art. However, if the shape of a utilitarian article incorporates features, such as artistic sculpture, carving, or pictorial representation, which can be identified separately and are capable of existing independently as a work of art, such features will be eligible for registration." *37 CFR § 202.10(c) (1960)* (punctuation altered).

Congress essentially lifted the language governing protection for the design of a useful article directly from the post-*Mazer* regulations and placed it into *§ 101* of the 1976 Act. Consistent with *Mazer*, the approach we outline today interprets *§§ 101* and *113* in a way that would afford copyright protection to the statuette in *Mazer* regardless of whether it was first created as a standalone sculptural work or as the base of the lamp. See *347 U. S., at 218-219, 74 S. Ct. 460, 98 L. Ed. 630*.

C

In sum, a feature of the design of a useful article is eligible for copyright if, when identified and imagined apart from the useful article, it would qualify as a pictorial, graphic, or sculptural work either on its own or when fixed in some other tangible medium.

Applying this test to the surface decorations on the cheerleading uniforms is straightforward. First, one can identify the decorations as features having pictorial, graphic, or sculptural qualities. Second, if the arrangement of colors, shapes, stripes, and chevrons on the surface of the cheerleading uniforms were separated from the uniform and applied in another medium—for example, on a painter's canvas—they would qualify as "two-dimensional . . . works of . . . art," *§ 101*. And imaginatively removing the surface decorations from the uniforms and applying them in another medium would not replicate the uniform itself. Indeed, respondents have applied the designs in this case to other media of expression—different types of clothing—without replicating the uniform. See App. 273–279. The decorations are therefore separable from the uniforms and eligible for copyright protection.[1]

The dissent argues that the designs are not separable because imaginatively removing them from the uniforms and placing them in some other medium of expression—a canvas, for example—would create "pictures of cheerleader uniforms." *Post,* at 10 (opinion of Breyer, J.). Petitioner similarly argues that the decorations cannot be copyrighted because, even when extracted from the useful article, they retain the outline of a cheerleading uniform. Brief for Petitioner 48-49.

This is not a bar to copyright. Just as two-dimensional fine art corresponds to the shape of the canvas on which it is painted, two-dimensional applied art correlates to the contours of the article on which it is applied. A fresco painted on a wall, ceiling panel, or dome would not lose copyright protection, for example, simply because it was designed to track the dimensions of the surface on which it was painted. Or consider, for example, a design etched or painted on the surface of a guitar. If that entire design is imaginatively removed from the guitar's surface and placed on an album cover, it would still resemble the shape of a guitar. But the image on the cover does not "replicate" the guitar as a useful article. Rather, the design is a two-dimensional work of art that corresponds to the shape of the useful article to which it was applied. The statute protects that work of art whether it is first drawn on the album cover and then applied to the guitar's surface, or vice versa. Failing to protect that art would create an anomaly: It would extend protection to two-dimensional designs that cover a part of a useful article but would not protect the same design if it covered the entire article. The statute does not support that distinction, nor can

---

1. We do not today hold that the surface decorations are copyrightable. We express no opinion on whether these works are sufficiently original to qualify for copyright protection, see *Feist Publications, Inc. v. Rural Telephone Service Co.*, 499 U. S. 340, 358-359, 111 S. Ct. 1282, 113 L. Ed. 2d 358 (1991), or on whether any other prerequisite of a valid copyright has been satisfied.

it be reconciled with the dissent's recognition that "artwork printed on a t-shirt" could be protected. *Post,* at 4 (internal quotation marks omitted).

To be clear, the only feature of the cheerleading uniform eligible for a copyright in this case is the two-dimensional work of art fixed in the tangible medium of the uniform fabric. Even if respondents ultimately succeed in establishing a valid copyright in the surface decorations at issue here, respondents have no right to prohibit any person from manufacturing a cheerleading uniform of identical shape, cut, and dimensions to the ones on which the decorations in this case appear. They may prohibit only the reproduction of the surface designs in any tangible medium of expression—a uniform or otherwise.[2]

D

Petitioner and the Government raise several objections to the approach we announce today. None is meritorious.

1

Petitioner first argues that our reading of the statute is missing an important step. It contends that a feature may exist independently only if it can stand alone as a copyrightable work *and* if the useful article from which it was extracted would remain equally useful. In other words, copyright extends only to "solely artistic" features of useful articles. Brief for Petitioner 33. According to petitioner, if a feature of a useful article "advance[s] the utility of the article," *id.,* at 38, then it is categorically beyond the scope of copyright, *id.,* at 33. The designs here are not protected, it argues, because they are necessary to two of the uniforms' "inherent, essential, or natural functions"—identifying the wearer as a cheerleader and enhancing the wearer's physical appearance. *Id.,* at 38, 48; Reply Brief 2, 16. Because the uniforms would not be equally useful without the designs, petitioner contends that the designs are inseparable from the "utilitarian aspects" of the uniform. Brief for Petitioner 50.

The Government raises a similar argument, although it reaches a different result. It suggests that the appropriate test is whether the useful article with the artistic feature removed would "remai[n] *similarly* useful." Brief for United States as *Amicus Curiae* 29 (emphasis added). In the view of the United States, however, a plain white cheerleading uniform is "similarly useful" to uniforms with respondents' designs. *Id.,* at 27-28.

The debate over the relative utility of a plain white cheerleading uniform is unnecessary. The focus of the separability inquiry is on the extracted feature and

2. The dissent suggests that our test would lead to the copyrighting of shovels. *Post,* at 7; Appendix to opinion of Breyer, J., fig. 4, *post.* But a shovel, like a cheerleading uniform, even if displayed in an art gallery, is "an article having an intrinsic utilitarian function that is not merely to portray the appearance of the article or to convey information." 17 U.S.C. § 101. It therefore cannot be copyrighted. A drawing of a shovel could, of course, be copyrighted. And, if the shovel included any artistic features that could be perceived as art apart from the shovel, and which would qualify as protectable pictorial, graphic, or sculptural works on their own or in another medium, they too could be copyrighted. But a shovel as a shovel cannot.

not on any aspects of the useful article that remain after the imaginary extraction. The statute does not require the decisionmaker to imagine a fully functioning useful article without the artistic feature. Instead, it requires that the separated feature qualify as a nonuseful pictorial, graphic, or sculptural work on its own.

Of course, because the removed feature may not be a useful article—as it would then not qualify as a pictorial, graphic, or sculptural work—there necessarily would be some aspects of the original useful article "left behind" if the feature were conceptually removed. But the statute does not require the imagined remainder to be a fully functioning useful article at all, much less an equally useful one. Indeed, such a requirement would deprive the *Mazer* statuette of protection had it been created first as a lamp base rather than as a statuette. Without the base, the "lamp" would be just a shade, bulb, and wires. The statute does not require that we imagine a nonartistic replacement for the removed feature to determine whether that *feature* is capable of an independent existence.

Petitioner's argument follows from its flawed view that the statute protects only "solely artistic" features that have no effect whatsoever on a useful article's utilitarian function. This view is inconsistent with the statutory text. The statute expressly protects two- and three-dimensional "applied art." *§ 101*. "Applied art" is art "employed in the decoration, design, or execution of useful objects," Webster's Third New International Dictionary 105 (1976) (emphasis added), or "those arts or crafts that have a *primarily utilitarian function*, or . . . the designs and decorations used in these arts," Random House Dictionary 73 (1966) (emphasis added); see also 1 OED 576 (2d ed. 1989) (defining "applied" as "[p]ut to practical use"). An artistic feature that would be eligible for copyright protection on its own cannot lose that protection simply because it was first created as a feature of the design of a useful article, even if it makes that article more useful.

Indeed, this has been the rule since *Mazer*. In holding that the statuette was protected, the Court emphasized that the 1909 Act abandoned any "distinctions between purely aesthetic articles and useful works of art." *347 U. S., at 211, 74 S. Ct. 460, 98 L. Ed. 630*. Congress did not enact such a distinction in the 1976 Act. Were we to accept petitioner's argument that the only protectable features are those that play absolutely no role in an article's function, we would effectively abrogate the rule of *Mazer* and read "applied art" out of the statute.

Because we reject the view that a useful article must remain after the artistic feature has been imaginatively separated from the article, we necessarily abandon the distinction between "physical" and "conceptual" separability, which some courts and commentators have adopted based on the *Copyright Act's* legislative history. See H. R. Rep. No. 94-1476, p. 55 (1976). According to this view, a feature is *physically* separable from the underlying useful article if it can "be physically separated from the article by ordinary means while leaving the utilitarian aspects of the article completely intact." Compendium § 924.2(A); see also *Chosun Int'l, Inc. v. Chrisha Creations, Ltd.*, 413 F. 3d 324, 329 (CA2 2005). *Conceptual* separability applies if the feature physically could not be removed from the useful article by ordinary means.

See Compendium § 924.2(B); but see 1 P. Goldstein, Copyright § 2.5.3, p. 2:77 (3d ed. 2016) (explaining that the lower courts have been unable to agree on a single conceptual separability test); 2 Patry §§ 3:140-3:144.40 (surveying the various approaches in the lower courts).

The statutory text indicates that separability is a conceptual undertaking. Because separability does not require the underlying useful article to remain, the physical-conceptual distinction is unnecessary.

2

Petitioner next argues that we should incorporate two "objective" components, Reply Brief 9, into our test to provide guidance to the lower courts: (1) "whether the design elements can be identified as reflecting the designer's artistic judgment exercised independently of functional influence," Brief for Petitioner 34 (emphasis deleted and internal quotation marks omitted), and (2) whether "there is [a] substantial likelihood that the pictorial, graphic, or sculptural feature would still be marketable to some significant segment of the community without its utilitarian function," *id.*, at 35 (emphasis deleted and internal quotation marks omitted).

We reject this argument because neither consideration is grounded in the text of the statute. The first would require the decisionmaker to consider evidence of the creator's design methods, purposes, and reasons. *Id.*, at 48. The statute's text makes clear, however, that our inquiry is limited to how the article and feature are perceived, not how or why they were designed. See *Brandir Int'l, Inc. v. Cascade Pacific Lumber Co.*, 834 F. 2d 1142, 1152 (CA2 1987) (Winter, J., concurring in part and dissenting in part) (The statute "expressly states that the legal test is how the final article is perceived, not how it was developed through various stages").

The same is true of marketability. Nothing in the statute suggests that copyrightability depends on market surveys. Moreover, asking whether some segment of the market would be interested in a given work threatens to prize popular art over other forms, or to substitute judicial aesthetic preferences for the policy choices embodied in the *Copyright Act*. See *Bleistein v. Donaldson Lithographing Co.*, 188 U. S. 239, 251, 23 S. Ct. 298, 47 L. Ed. 460, 1903 *Dec. Comm'r Pat.* 650 (1903) ("It would be a dangerous undertaking for persons trained only to the law to constitute themselves final judges of the worth of pictorial illustrations, outside of the narrowest and most obvious limits").

3

Finally, petitioner argues that allowing the surface decorations to qualify as a "work of authorship" is inconsistent with Congress' intent to entirely exclude industrial design from copyright. Petitioner notes that Congress refused to pass a provision that would have provided limited copyright protection for industrial designs, including clothing, when it enacted the 1976 Act, see *id.*, at 9-11 (citing S. 22, Tit. II, 94th Cong., 2d Sess., 122 Cong. Rec. 3856–3859 (1976)), and that it has enacted laws protecting designs for specific useful articles—semiconductor chips and boat hulls, see *17 U. S. C. §§ 901-914, 1301–1332*—while declining to enact other industrial design statutes, Brief for Petitioner 29, 43. From this history of failed legislation petitioner reasons that Congress intends to channel intellectual property claims for industrial design into design patents. It therefore urges us to approach this question with a presumption against copyrightability. *Id.*, at 27.

We do not share petitioner's concern. As an initial matter, "[c]ongressional inaction lacks persuasive significance" in most circumstances. *Pension Benefit Guaranty Corporation v. LTV Corp.*, 496 U. S. 633, 650, 110 S. Ct. 2668, 110 L. Ed. 2d 579 (1990) (internal quotation marks omitted). Moreover, we have long held that design patent and copyright are not mutually exclusive. See *Mazer*, 347 U. S., at 217, 74 S. Ct. 460, 98 L. Ed. 630. Congress has provided for limited copyright protection for certain features of industrial design, and approaching the statute with presumptive hostility toward protection for industrial design would undermine Congress' choice. In any event, as explained above, our test does not render the shape, cut, and physical dimensions of the cheerleading uniforms eligible for copyright protection.

III

We hold that an artistic feature of the design of a useful article is eligible for copyright protection if the feature (1) can be perceived as a two- or three-dimensional work of art separate from the useful article and (2) would qualify as a protectable pictorial, graphic, or sculptural work either on its own or in some other medium if imagined separately from the useful article. Because the designs on the surface of respondents' cheerleading uniforms in this case satisfy these requirements, the judgment of the Court of Appeals is affirmed.

It is so ordered.

Justice Ginsburg, concurring in the judgment.

I concur in the Court's judgment but not in its opinion. Unlike the majority, I would not take up in this case the separability test appropriate under *17 U. S. C. § 101*. Consideration of that test is unwarranted because the designs at issue are not designs *of* useful articles. Instead, the designs are themselves copyrightable pictorial or graphic works *reproduced on* useful articles.[2]

A pictorial, graphic, or sculptural work (PGS work) is copyrightable. *§ 102(a)(5)*. PGS works include "two-dimensional and three-dimensional works of fine, graphic, and applied art." *§ 101*. Key to this case, a copyright in a standalone PGS work "includes the right to reproduce the work in or on any kind of article, whether useful

2. Like the Court, I express no opinion on whether the designs otherwise meet the requirements for copyrightable subject matter. See *ante*, at 11, n. 1; 17 U. S. C. § 102(a) ("Copyright protection subsists, in accordance with this title, in original works of authorship fixed in any tangible medium of expression, now known or later developed, from which they can be perceived, reproduced, or otherwise communicated."). In view of the dissent's assertion that Varsity's designs are "plainly unoriginal," *post*, at 11, however, I note this Court's recognition that "the requisite level of creativity [for copyrightability] is extremely low; even a slight amount will suffice," *Feist Publications, Inc. v. Rural Telephone Service Co.*, 499 U. S. 340, 345, 111 S. Ct. 1282, 113 L. Ed. 2d 358 (1991); *see Atari Games Corp. v. Oman*, 979 F. 2d 242, 298 U.S. App. D.C. 303 (CADC 1992).

or otherwise." § *113(a)*. Because the owner of a copyright in a pre-existing PGS work may exclude a would-be infringer from reproducing that work on a useful article, there is no need to engage in any separability inquiry to resolve the instant petition.

The designs here in controversy are standalone pictorial and graphic works that respondents Varsity Brands, Inc., et al. (Varsity) reproduce on cheerleading uniforms. Varsity's designs first appeared as pictorial and graphic works that Varsity's design team sketched on paper. App. 281. Varsity then sought copyright protection for those two-dimensional designs, not for cheerleading costumes; its registration statements claimed "2-Dimensional artwork" and "fabric design (artwork)." Appendix, *infra*, at 4-7, 9-10, 12-14. Varsity next reproduced its two-dimensional graphic designs on cheerleading uniforms, also on other garments, including T-shirts and jackets. See, *e.g.*, App. 274, 276.[3]

In short, Varsity's designs are not themselves useful articles meet for separability determination under § *101*; they are standalone PGS works that may gain copyright protection as such, including the exclusive right to reproduce the designs on useful articles.[4]

Justice Breyer, with whom Justice Kennedy joins, dissenting.

I agree with much in the Court's opinion. But I do not agree that the designs that Varsity Brands, Inc., submitted to the Copyright Office are eligible for copyright protection. Even applying the majority's test, the designs *cannot* "be perceived as ... two- or three-dimensional work[s] of art separate from the useful article." *Ante*, at 1.

Look at the designs that Varsity submitted to the Copyright Office. You will see only pictures of cheerleader uniforms. And cheerleader uniforms are useful articles. A picture of the relevant design features, whether separately "perceived" on paper or in the imagination, is a picture of, and thereby "replicate[s]," the underlying useful

---

3. That Varsity's designs can be placed on jackets or T-shirts without replicating a cheerleader's uniform supports their qualification as fabric designs. The dissent acknowledges that fabric designs are copyrightable, but maintains that Varsity's designs do not count because Varsity's submissions depict clothing, not fabric designs. *Post*, at 10-11. But registrants claiming copyrightable designs may submit drawings or photos of those designs as they appear on useful articles. See Compendium of U. S. Copyright Office Practices § 1506 (3d ed. 2014) ("To register a copyrightable design that has been applied to the back of a useful article, such as a chair, the applicant may submit drawings of the design as it appears on the chair[.]"), online at https://www.copyright.gov/comp3/docs/compendium.pdf (as last visited Mar. 8, 2017). And, as noted in text, Varsity's registration statements claimed "2-Dimensional artwork" and "fabric design (artwork)." Appendix, *infra*, at 4-7, 9-10, 12-14.
The dissent also acknowledges that artwork printed on a T-shirt is copyrightable. *Post*, at 4. Varsity's colored shapes and patterns can be, and indeed are, printed on T-shirts. See, *e.g.*, App. 274. Assuming Varsity's designs meet the other requirements for copyrightable subject matter, they would fit comfortably within the Copyright Office guidance featured by the dissent. See *post*, at 4 (citing Compendium of U. S. Copyright Office Practices, *supra*, § 924.2(B).

4. The majority declines to address this route to decision because, it says, Varsity has not advanced it. *Ante*, at 5-6. I read Varsity's brief differently. See Brief for Respondents 25 (explaining that the Copyright Act "expressly provides that PGS designs do not lose their protection when they appear 'in or on' a useful article," quoting § 113(a)); id., at 52 (disclaiming the need for separability analysis because the designs are themselves PGS works).

article of which they are a part. *Ante,* at 1, 10. Hence the design features that Varsity seeks to protect are not "capable of existing independently o[f] the utilitarian aspects of the article." *17 U. S. C. § 101.*

I

The relevant statutory provision says that the "design of a useful article" is copyrightable "only if, and only to the extent that, such design incorporates pictorial, graphic, or sculptural features that can be identified separately from, and are capable of existing independently of, the utilitarian aspects of the article." *Ibid.* But what, we must ask, do the words "identified separately" mean? Just when is a design separate from the "utilitarian aspect of the [useful] article?" The most direct, helpful aspect of the Court's opinion answers this question by stating:

> "Nor could someone claim a copyright in a useful article merely by creating a replica of that article in some other medium — for example, a cardboard model of a car. Although the replica could itself be copyrightable, it would not give rise to any rights in the useful article that inspired it." *Ante,* at 7-8.

Exactly so. These words help explain the Court's statement that a copyrightable work of art must be "perceived as a two- or three-dimensional work of art separate from the useful article." *Ante,* at 1, 17. They help clarify the concept of separateness. Cf. 1 M. Nimmer & D. Nimmer, *Nimmer on Copyright § 2A.08[A][1]* (2016) (Nimmer) (describing courts' difficulty in applying that concept). They are consistent with Congress' own expressed intent. *17 U. S. C. § 101*; H. R. Rep. No. 94-1476, pp. 55, 105 (1976) (H. R. Rep.). And they reflect long held views of the Copyright Office. See Compendium of U. S. Copyright Office Practices § 924.2(B) (3d ed. 2014), online at *http://www.copyright.gov/comp3/docs/compendium.pdf* (as last visited Mar. 7, 2017) (Compendium).

Consider, for example, the explanation that the House Report for the *Copyright Act of 1976* provides. It says:

> "Unless the shape of an automobile, airplane, ladies' dress, food processor, television set, or any other industrial product contains some element that, *physically or conceptually,* can be identified as separable from the utilitarian aspects of that article, the design would not be copyrighted. . . ." H. R. Rep., at 55 (emphasis added).

These words suggest two exercises, one physical, one mental. Can the design features (the picture, the graphic, the sculpture) be physically removed from the article (and considered separately), all the while leaving the fully functioning utilitarian object in place? If not, can one nonetheless conceive of the design features separately without replicating a picture of the utilitarian object? If the answer to either of these questions is "yes," then the design is eligible for copyright protection. Otherwise, it is not. The abstract nature of these questions makes them sound difficult to apply. But with the Court's words in mind, the difficulty tends to disappear.

An example will help. Imagine a lamp with a circular marble base, a vertical 10-inch tall brass rod (containing wires) inserted off center on the base, a light bulb fixture emerging from the top of the brass rod, and a lampshade sitting on top. In front of the brass rod a porcelain Siamese cat sits on the base facing outward. Obviously, the Siamese cat is *physically separate* from the lamp, as it could be easily removed while leaving both cat and lamp intact. And, assuming it otherwise qualifies, the designed cat is eligible for copyright protection.

Now suppose there is no long brass rod; instead the cat sits in the middle of the base and the wires run up through the cat to the bulbs. The cat is not physically separate from the lamp, as the reality of the lamp's construction is such that an effort to physically separate the cat and lamp will destroy both cat and lamp. The two are integrated into a single functional object, like the similar configuration of the ballet dancer statuettes that formed the lamp bases at issue in *Mazer v. Stein*, 347 U. S. 201, 74 S. Ct. 460, 98 L. Ed. 630, 1954 *Dec. Comm'r Pat.* 308 (1954). But we can easily imagine the cat on its own, as did Congress when conceptualizing the ballet dancer. See H. R. Rep., at 55 (the statuette in *Mazer* was "incorporated into a product without losing its ability to exist independently as a work of art"). In doing so, we do not create a mental picture of a lamp (or, in the Court's words, a "replica" of the lamp), which is a useful article. We simply perceive the cat separately, as a small cat figurine that could be a copyrightable design work standing alone that does not replicate the lamp. Hence the cat is *conceptually separate* from the utilitarian article that is the lamp. The pair of lamps pictured at Figures 1 and 2 in the Appendix to this opinion illustrate this principle.

Case law, particularly case law that Congress and the Copyright Office have considered, reflects the same approach. Congress cited examples of copyrightable design works, including "a carving on the back of a chair" and "a floral relief design on silver flatware." H. R. Rep., at 55. Copyright Office guidance on copyrightable designs in useful articles include "an engraving on a vase," "[a]rtwork printed on a t-shirt," "[a] colorful pattern decorating the surface of a shopping bag," "[a] drawing on the surface of wallpaper," and "[a] floral relief decorating the handle of a spoon." Compendium § 924.2(B). Courts have found copyrightable matter in a plaster ballet dancer statuette encasing the lamp's electric cords and forming its base, see *Mazer, supra*, as well as carvings engraved onto furniture, see *Universal Furniture Int'l, Inc. v. Collezione Europa USA, Inc.*, 618 F. 3d 417, 431-435 (CA4 2010) (per curiam), and designs on laminated floor tiles, see *Home Legend, LLC v. Mannington Mills, Inc.*, 784 F. 3d 1404, 1412–1413 (CA11 2015). See generally Brief for Intellectual Property Professors as *Amici Curiae*.

By way of contrast, Van Gogh's painting of a pair of old shoes, though beautifully executed and copyrightable as a painting, would not qualify for a shoe design copyright. See Appendix, fig. 3, *infra*; 17 U. S. C. §§ 113(a)-(b). Courts have similarly denied copyright protection to objects that begin as three-dimensional designs, such as measuring spoons shaped like heart-tipped arrows, *Bonazoli v. R. S. V. P. Int'l, Inc.*, 353 F. Supp. 2d 218, 226-227 (RI 2005); candleholders shaped like sailboats, *Design Ideas, Ltd. v. Yankee Candle Co.*, 889 F. Supp. 2d 1119, 1128 (CD Ill. 2012); and wire spokes on a wheel cover, *Norris Industries, Inc. v. International Tel. & Tel. Corp.*, 696 F.

2d 918, 922-924 (CA11 1983). None of these designs could qualify for copyright protection that would prevent others from selling spoons, candleholders, or wheel covers with the same design. Why not? Because in each case the design is not separable from the utilitarian aspects of the object to which it relates. The designs cannot be physically separated because they themselves make up the shape of the spoon, candleholders, or wheel covers of which they are a part. And spoons, candleholders, and wheel covers are useful objects, as are the old shoes depicted in Van Gogh's painting. More importantly, one cannot easily imagine or otherwise conceptualize the design of the spoons or the candleholders or the shoes *without that picture, or image, or replica being a picture of spoons, or candleholders, or wheel covers, or shoes.* The designs necessarily bring along the underlying utilitarian object. Hence each design is not conceptually separable from the physical useful object.

The upshot is that one could copyright the floral design on a soupspoon, but one could not copyright the shape of the spoon itself, no matter how beautiful, artistic, or esthetically pleasing that shape might be: A picture of the shape of the spoon is also a picture of a spoon; the picture of a floral design is not. See Compendium § 924.2(B).

To repeat: A separable design feature must be "capable of existing independently" of the useful article as a separate artistic work that is not itself the useful article. If the claimed feature could be extracted without replicating the useful article of which it is a part, and the result would be a copyrightable artistic work standing alone, then there is a separable design. But if extracting the claimed features would necessarily bring along the underlying useful article, the design is not separable from the useful article. In many or most cases, to decide whether a design or artistic feature of a useful article is conceptually separate from the article itself, it is enough to imagine the feature on its own and ask, "Have I created a picture of a (useful part of a) useful article?" If so, the design is not separable from the useful article. If not, it is.

In referring to imagined pictures and the like, I am not speaking technically. I am simply trying to explain an intuitive idea of what separation is about, as well as how I understand the majority's opinion. So understood, the opinion puts design copyrights in their rightful place. The law has long recognized that drawings or photographs of real world objects are copyrightable as drawings or photographs, but the copyright does not give protection against others making the underlying useful objects. See, *e.g., Burrow-Giles Lithographic Co. v. Sarony,* 111 U. S. 53, 4 S. Ct. 279, 28 L. Ed. 349, 1884 *Dec. Comm'r Pat.* 186 (1884). That is why a copyright on Van Gogh's painting would prevent others from reproducing that painting, but it would not prevent others from reproducing and selling the comfortable old shoes that the painting depicts. Indeed, the purpose of § 113(b)was to ensure that "'copyright in a pictorial, graphic, or sculptural work, portraying a useful article as such, does not extend to the manufacture of the useful article itself.'" H. R. Rep., at 105.

II

To ask this kind of simple question—does the design picture the useful article?—will not provide an answer in every case, for there will be cases where it is difficult to say whether a picture of the design is, or is not, also a picture of the useful article. But the question will avoid courts focusing primarily upon what I believe is an unhelpful feature of the inquiry, namely, whether the design can be imagined as a "two- or three-dimensional work of art." *Ante,* at 1, 17. That is because virtually any industrial design can be thought of separately as a "work of art": Just imagine a frame surrounding the design, or its being placed in a gallery. Consider Marcel Duchamp's "readymades" series, the functional mass-produced objects he designated as art. See Appendix, fig. 4, *infra*. What is there in the world that, viewed through an esthetic lens, cannot be seen as a good, bad, or indifferent work of art? What design features could not be imaginatively reproduced on a painter's canvas? Indeed, great industrial design may well include design that is inseparable from the useful article—where, as Frank Lloyd Wright put it, "form and function are one." F. Wright, An Autobiography 146 (1943) (reprint 2005). Where they are one, the designer may be able to obtain 15 years of protection through a design patent. 35 U. S. C. §§ 171, 173; see also McKenna & Strandburg, Progress and Competition in Design, 17 Stan. Tech. L. Rev. 1, 48–51 (2013). But, if they are one, Congress did not intend a century or more of copyright protection.

III

The conceptual approach that I have described reflects Congress' answer to a problem that is primarily practical and economic. Years ago Lord Macaulay drew attention to the problem when he described copyright in books as a "tax on readers for the purpose of giving a bounty to writers." 56 Parl. Deb. (3d Ser.) (1841) 341, 350. He called attention to the main benefit of copyright protection, which is to provide an incentive to produce copyrightable works and thereby "promote the Progress of Science and useful Arts." *U. S. Const., Art. I, § 8, cl. 8.* But Macaulay also made clear that copyright protection imposes costs. Those costs include the higher prices that can accompany the grant of a copyright monopoly. They also can include (for those wishing to display, sell, or perform a design, film, work of art, or piece of music, for example) the costs of discovering whether there are previous copyrights, of contacting copyright holders, and of securing permission to copy. *Eldred v. Ashcroft,* 537 U. S. 186, 248-252, 123 S. Ct. 769, 154 L. Ed. 2d 683 (2003) (Breyer, J., dissenting). Sometimes, as Thomas Jefferson wrote to James Madison, costs can outweigh "the benefit even of limited monopolies." Letter from Thomas Jefferson to James Madison (July 31, 1788), in 13 Papers of Thomas Jefferson 443 (J. Boyd ed. 1956) (Jefferson Letter). And that is particularly true in light of the fact that Congress has extended the "limited Times" of protection, *U. S. Const., Art. I, § 8, cl. 8*, from the "14 years" of Jefferson's day to potentially more than a century today. Jefferson Letter 443; see also *Eldred, supra,* at 246-252, 123 S. Ct. 769, 154 L. Ed. 2d 683 (opinion of BREYER, J.).

The Constitution grants Congress primary responsibility for assessing comparative costs and benefits and drawing copyright's statutory lines. Courts must respect those lines and not grant copyright protection where Congress has decided not to do so. And it is clear that Congress has not extended broad copyright protection to the fashion design industry. See, *e.g.*, 1 *Nimmer* § 2A.08[H][3][c] (describing how

Congress rejected proposals for fashion design protection within the 1976 Act and has rejected every proposed bill to this effect since then); *Esquire, Inc. v. Ringer,* 591 F. 2d 796, 800, n. 12, 192 U.S. App. D.C. 187 (CADC 1978) (observing that at the time of the 1976 *Copyright Act,* Congress had rejected every one of the approximately 70 design protection bills that had been introduced since 1914); *e.g.,* H. R. 5055, 109th Cong., 2d Sess.: "To Amend title 17, United States Code, to provide protection for fashion design" (introduced Mar. 30, 2006; unenacted). Congress has left "statutory . . . protection . . . largely unavailable for dress designs." 1 *Nimmer* § 2A.08[H][3][a]; Raustiala & Sprigman, The Piracy Paradox: Innovation and Intellectual Property in Fashion Design, 92 Va. L. Rev. 1687, 1698–1705 (2006).

Congress' decision not to grant full copyright protection to the fashion industry has not left the industry without protection. Patent design protection is available. 35 U. S. C. §§ 171, 173. A maker of clothing can obtain trademark protection under the *Lanham Act* for signature features of the clothing. *15 U. S. C. § 1051 et seq.* And a designer who creates an original textile design can receive copyright protection for that pattern as placed, for example, on a bolt of cloth, or anything made with that cloth. *E.g.,* Compendium § 924.3(A)(1). "[T]his [type of] claim . . . is generally made by the fabric producer rather than the garment or costume designer," and is "ordinarily made when the two-dimensional design is applied to the textile fabric and before the garment is cut from the fabric." 56 Fed. Reg. 56531 (1991).

The fashion industry has thrived against this backdrop, and designers have contributed immeasurably to artistic and personal self-expression through clothing. But a decision by this Court to grant protection to the design of a garment would grant the designer protection that Congress refused to provide. It would risk increased prices and unforeseeable disruption in the clothing industry, which in the United States alone encompasses nearly $370 billion in annual spending and 1.8 million jobs. Brief for Council of Fashion Designers of America, Inc., as *Amicus Curiae* 3-4 (citing U. S. Congress, Joint Economic Committee, The New Economy of Fashion 1 (2016)). That is why I believe it important to emphasize those parts of the Court's opinion that limit the scope of its interpretation. That language, as I have said, makes clear that one may not "claim a copyright in a useful article merely by creating a replica of that article in some other medium," which "would not give rise to any rights in the useful article that inspired it." *Ante,* at 7-8.

IV

If we ask the "separateness" question correctly, the answer here is not difficult to find. The majority's opinion, in its appendix, depicts the cheerleader dress designs that Varsity submitted to the Copyright Office. Can the design features in Varsity's pictures exist separately from the utilitarian aspects of a dress? Can we extract those features as copyrightable design works standing alone, without bringing along, via picture or design, the dresses of which they constitute a part?

Consider designs 074, 078, and 0815. They certainly look like cheerleader uniforms. That is to say, they look like pictures of cheerleader uniforms, just like Van

Gogh's old shoes look like shoes. I do not see how one could see them otherwise. Designs 299A and 2999B present slightly closer questions. They omit some of the dresslike context that the other designs possess. But the necklines, the sleeves, and the cut of the skirt suggest that they too are pictures of dresses. Looking at all five of Varsity's pictures, I do not see how one could conceptualize the design features in a way that does not picture, not just artistic designs, but dresses as well.

Were I to accept the majority's invitation to "imaginatively remov[e]" the chevrons and stripes *as they are arranged* on the neckline, waistline, sleeves, and skirt of each uniform, and apply them on a "painter's canvas," *ante,* at 10, that painting would be of a cheerleader's dress. The esthetic elements on which Varsity seeks protection exist only as part of the uniform design—there is nothing to separate out but for dress-shaped lines that replicate the cut and style of the uniforms. Hence, each design is not physically separate, nor is it conceptually separate, from the useful article it depicts, namely, a cheerleader's dress. They cannot be copyrighted.

Varsity, of course, could have sought a design patent for its designs. Or, it could have sought a copyright on a textile design, even one with a similar theme of chevrons and lines.

But that is not the nature of Varsity's copyright claim. It has instead claimed ownership of the particular "'treatment and arrangement'" of the chevrons and lines of the design as they appear at the neckline, waist, skirt, sleeves, and overall cut of each uniform. Brief for Respondents 50. The majority imagines that Varsity submitted something different—that is, only the surface decorations of chevrons and stripes, as in a textile design. As the majority sees it, Varsity's copyright claim would be the same had it submitted a plain rectangular space depicting chevrons and stripes, like swaths from a bolt of fabric. But considered on their own, the simple stripes are plainly unoriginal. Varsity, then, seeks to do indirectly what it cannot do directly: bring along the design and cut of the dresses by seeking to protect surface decorations whose "treatment and arrangement" are *coextensive with that design and cut.* As Varsity would have it, it would prevent its competitors from making useful three-dimensional cheerleader uniforms by submitting plainly unoriginal chevrons and stripes as cut and arranged on a useful article. But with that cut and arrangement, the resulting pictures on which Varsity seeks protection do not simply depict designs. They depict clothing. They depict the useful articles of which the designs are inextricable parts. And Varsity cannot obtain copyright protection that would give them the power to prevent others from making those useful uniforms, any more than Van Gogh can copyright comfortable old shoes by painting their likeness.

I fear that, in looking past the three-dimensional design inherent in Varsity's claim by treating it as if it were no more than a design for a bolt of cloth, the majority has lost sight of its own important limiting principle. One may not "claim a copyright in a useful article merely by creating a replica of that article in some other medium," such as in a picture. *Ante,* at 7. That is to say, one cannot obtain a copyright that would give its holder "any rights in the useful article that inspired it." *Ante,* at 8.

With respect, I dissent.

Notes

1. Can you restate Justice Thomas's test for separability? Notice that the opinion states "respondents have no right to prohibit any person from manufacturing a cheerleading uniform of identical shape, cut, and dimensions to the ones on which the decorations in this case appear." But why not? What about Justice Thomas's test would prevent a designer from claiming the shape of a dress?

2. Justice Thomas seems concerned that the initial medium in which a work is fixed should not affect its copyrightability if it is ultimately fixed in a different medium. So, because these designs could have been fixed on paper, they should not be deemed uncopyrightable because they were first fixed on uniforms.

But Justice Breyer's dissenting opinion uses the example of a painting of a pair of boots to emphasize that the medium of fixation *does* matter. While a pair of boots fixed on a painter's canvas is nonfunctional, that same pair of boots fixed in leather and rubber is functional. What about the designs of the stripes, chevron, and color blocking in this case?

In an amicus brief to the Court and in a separate article, Professors Christopher Buccafusco and Jeanne Fromer argued that designs in this case should be treated as functional when affixed to clothing because they do not "merely portray the appearance of the article." 17 U.S.C. § 101 (2012). Rather, the designs also affect the way in which the wearer's body appears. The designs take advantage of optical illusions to influence how the wearer's body appears. For example, the chevrons are a version of a famous optical illusion about the length of various lines.

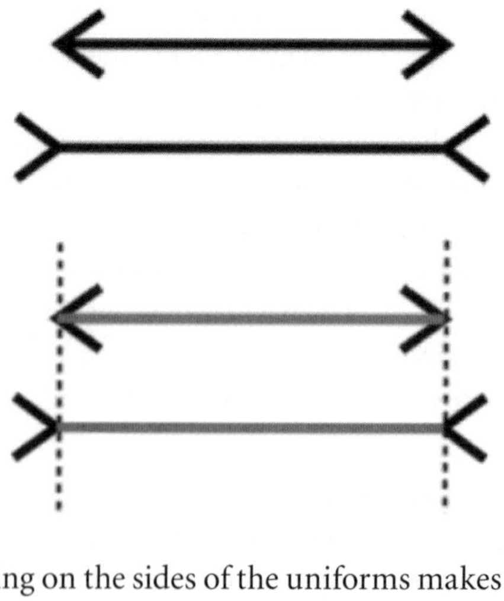

And the color blocking on the sides of the uniforms makes the wearer's body look slimmer. Compare the Varsity uniforms to this dress by Stella McCartney:

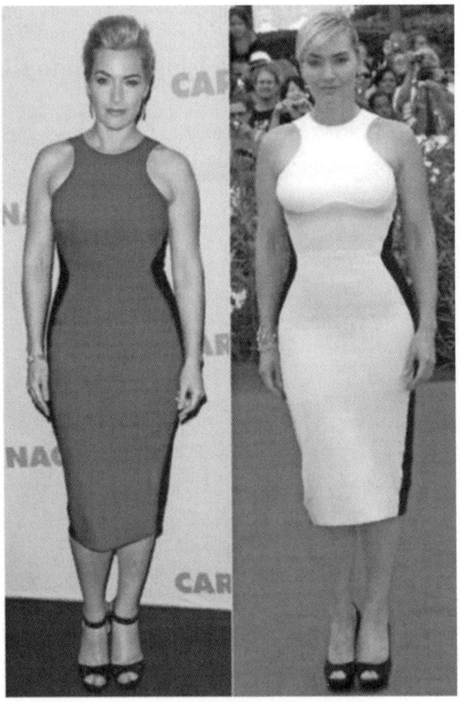

Should these aspects of the designs have altered the outcome of the case? Will future designers be able to assert copyright protection for other two-dimensional features that produce three-dimensional effects? If so, does such protection inappropriately limit the abilities of competitor designers to achieve the same effects? Is there a role for the merger doctrine, discussed above, in these contexts?

3. To many commentators, the most significant part of Justice Thomas's opinion is Part II.D.1, where he explains that after the PGS features have been "imagined away" from the useful article, the conceptually remaining article does not have to be as useful at it once was. What this means is that the imagined PGS features can contain some degree of functionality—that's why the remaining article is less useful. This marked a major shift in how the doctrine had been interpreted. In most prior cases, the only PGS features that were to be imagined away were those that were exclusively aesthetic and nonfunctional. All functional aspects and all aspects of an article that are *simultaneously aesthetic and functional* were supposed to be left behind. Justice Thomas's opinion, then, allows designers to claim copyrights in aspects of their designs that are partially functional. *See* Christopher Buccafusco & Mark A. Lemley, *Functionality Screens*, 103 VA. L. REV. 1293 (2017).

4. Notice that none of the opinions decide whether the designs at issue here were sufficiently original to be protectable. Do you think they were? The case settled after the Supreme Court opinion, so we will never have an official ruling on the matter.

Examples

Review the opinions in *Star Athletica* and apply them to the following examples:

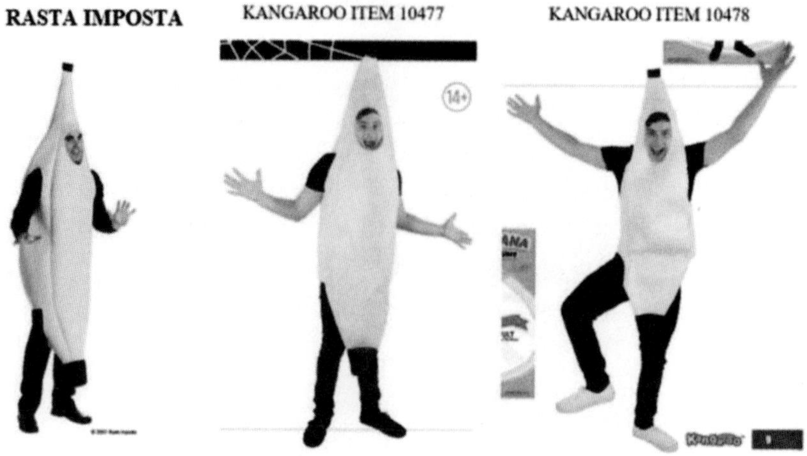

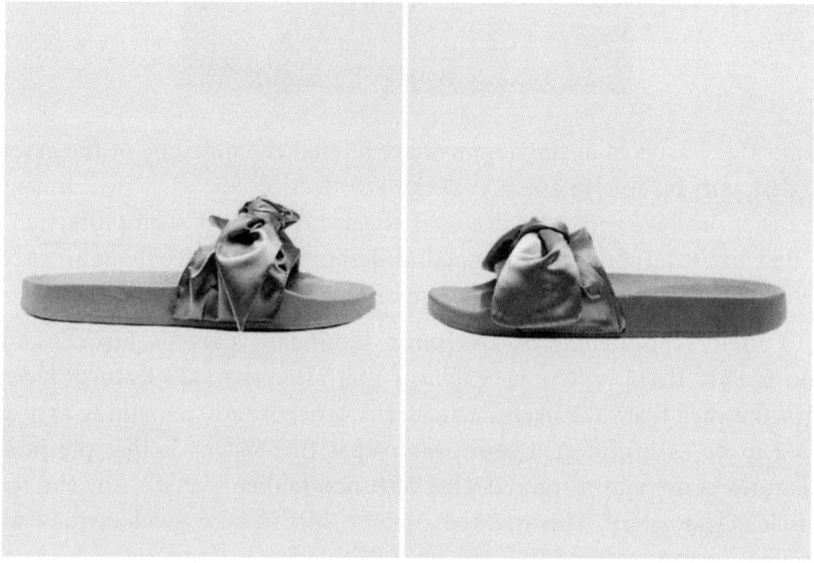

C. Congratulations! You've Cleared the Threshold. What's Next?

1. Copyright Ownership and Duration

If a design meets the fixation and originality criteria and it satisfies the useful articles test, it is copyrighted. (Note, all of these rules apply to works created after 1978. Works created before that date must meet different rules.) A work obtains a copyright the moment that it is fixed in a tangible medium of expression. The author does not need to register the work with the Copyright Office, although it is wise to do so. Authors must register their works before they file an infringement lawsuit, and registering a work before it is infringed can substantially increase the damages that the owner may obtain. Registration is cheap and fairly easy, so it's generally a good idea.

Ownership of a copyright vests in the work's author or authors—those people who originated the work's expression—unless the work is "made for hire." Works made for hire are generally works created by employees within the scope of their employment. Copyright law typically follows the common law of agency in order to determine who counts as an employee and what the scope of her employment is. *Community for Creative Non-Violence v. Reid*, 490 U.S. 730 (1989).

The duration of a copyright depends on who created it. If the work is created by a natural person, the copyright lasts for the life of the author plus an additional 70 years postmortem. If the work is jointly authored by two or more people, it lasts for 70 years after the death of the longest surviving author. If a work is produced as a work made for hire, then the initial owner of the work is the company, and the copyright lasts for 95 years from the date of publication or 125 years from the date of creation, whichever is shorter. At the expiration of a copyright, the work enters the public domain and is free for others to use.

2. Infringement

Ownership of a copyright entails a series of exclusive rights listed in Section 106 of the Copyright Act. For purposes of fashion design, the two most important are the right to reproduce the work in copies and the right to prepare derivative works. The reproduction and derivative works rights overlap considerably. In essence, they prevent other creators from copying the protected design. This section will describe the prima facie case for copyright infringement of these rights, paying particular attention to how the scope of the plaintiff's copyright is determined. That is to say, how similar does the defendant's work have to be to the plaintiff's in order to infringe the copyright?

In order to bring a copyright infringement action, the plaintiff must be the owner of a registered copyrighted work. The prima facie case for infringement involves two separate elements: (1) copying-in-fact and (2) unlawful appropriation.

a. Copying-In-Fact

One of copyright's fundamental premises is that the independent creation of a work is never copyright infringement. That means that even if a defendant produces a work that is identical in all details to the plaintiff's work, the defendant will not be liable for copyright infringement unless she *actually copied* the plaintiff's work. If two creators hit on the same expression independently of one another, neither one is an infringer, and both of them own separate copyrights in their works.

Thus, in order to recover, a plaintiff must prove that the defendant, in fact, copied from the plaintiff. How might she do this? Sometimes, there will be direct evidence of copying. Perhaps the defendant will admit to copying from the plaintiff, perhaps because the defendant was trying to design around the plaintiff's rights. In many cases, however, the plaintiff will have to resort to indirect or circumstantial evidence of copying. In order to do this, the plaintiff will typically need to prove that copying was possible, by showing that the defendant had access to her work, and that copying was likely, by showing that the two works demonstrate similarities that are not likely to have arisen from independent creation. In the following case, Judge Richard Posner explains how a plaintiff can prove copying via circumstantial evidence.

Ty, Inc. v. GMA Accessories, Inc.

132 F.3d 1167 (7th Cir. 1997)

POSNER, Chief Judge.

Ty, the manufacturer of the popular "Beanie Babies" line of stuffed animals, has obtained a preliminary injunction under the Copyright Act against the sale by GMA (and also a retailer, but we can disregard that aspect of the injunction) of "Preston the Pig" and "Louie the Cow." These are bean-bag animals manufactured by GMA that Ty contends are copies of its copyrighted pig ("Squealer") and cow ("Daisy"). Ty began selling the "Beanie Babies" line, including Squealer, in 1993, and it was the popularity of the line that induced GMA to bring out its own line of bean-bag stuffed animals three years later. GMA does not contest the part of the injunction that enjoins the sale of Louie, but asks us on a variety of grounds to vacate the other part, the part that enjoins it from selling Preston.

We have appended to our opinion five pictures found in the appellate record. The first shows Squealer (the darker pig, actually pink) and Preston (white). The second is a picture of two real pigs. The third and fourth are different views of the design for Preston that Janet Salmon submitted to GMA several months before Preston went into production. The fifth is a picture of the two bean-bag cows; they are nearly identical. A glance at the first picture shows a striking similarity between the two bean-bag pigs as well. The photograph was supplied by GMA and actually understates the similarity (the animals themselves are part of the record). The "real" Preston is the same length as Squealer and has a virtually identical snout. The difference in the lengths of the two animals in the picture is a trick of the camera. The difference in snouts results from the fact that the pictured Preston was a manufacturing botch. And GMA put a ribbon around the neck of the Preston in the picture, but the Preston that it sells doesn't have a ribbon.

The two pigs are so nearly identical that if the second is a copy of the first, the second clearly infringes Ty's copyright. But identity is not infringement. The Copyright Act forbids only copying; if independent creation results in an identical work, the creator of that work is free to sell it. *Selle v. Gibb*, 741 F.2d 896, 901 (7th Cir. 1984). The practical basis for this rule is that unlike the case of patents and trademarks, the creator of an expressive work—an author or sculptor or composer—cannot canvass the entire universe of copyrighted works to discover whether his poem or song or, as in this case, "soft sculpture" is identical to some work in which copyright subsists, especially since unpublished, unregistered works are copyrightable. The more a work is both like an already copyrighted work and—for this is equally important—unlike anything that is in the public domain, the less likely it is to be an independent creation. As is generally true in the law, circumstantial evidence—evidence merely probabilistic rather than certain—can confer sufficient confidence on an inference, here of copying, to warrant a legal finding.

The issue of copying can be broken down into two subissues. The first is whether the alleged copier had access to the work that he is claimed to have copied; the second is whether, if so, he used his access to copy. It might seem that access could not be an issue where, as in this case, the allegedly copied work is a mass-produced consumer product purchasable for $ 5. But we shall see that GMA has attempted to make an issue of access.

Obviously, access does not entail copying. An eyewitness might have seen the defendant buy the copyrighted work; this would be proof of access, but not of copying. But copying entails access. If, therefore, two works are so similar as to make it highly probable that the later one is a copy of the earlier one, the issue of access need not be addressed separately, since if the later work was a copy its creator must have had access to the original. Of course the inference of access, and hence of copying, could be rebutted by proof that the creator of the later work could not have seen the earlier one or (an alternative mode of access) a copy of the earlier one. But unlike the court in *Towler v. Sayles*, 76 F.3d 579, 584-85 (4th Cir. 1996), and the authors of 4 *Nimmer on Copyright* § 13.02[B], pp. 13–24 to 13–25 (1997), we do not read our decision in *Selle* to hold or imply, in conflict with the *Gaste* decision, that no matter how closely the works resemble each other, the plaintiff must produce some (other) evidence of access. He must produce evidence of access, all right—but, as we have just said, and as is explicit in *Selle* itself, see 741 F.2d at 901, a similarity that is so close as to be highly unlikely to have been an accident of independent creation is evidence of access.

What troubled us in *Selle* but is not a factor here is that two works may be strikingly similar—may in fact be identical—not because one is copied from the other but because both are copies of the same thing in the public domain. In such a case—imagine two people photographing Niagara Falls from the same place at the same time of the day and year and in identical weather—there is no inference of access to anything but the public domain, and, equally, no inference of copying from a copyrighted work. A similarity may be striking without being suspicious.

But here it is both. GMA's pig is strikingly similar to Ty's pig but not to anything in the public domain—a real pig, for example, which is why we have included in our appendix a photograph of real pigs. The parties' bean-bag pigs bear little resemblance to real pigs even if we overlook the striking anatomical anomaly of Preston—he has three toes, whereas real pigs have cloven hooves. We can imagine an argument that the technology of manufacturing bean-bag animals somehow prevents the manufacturer from imitating a real pig. But anyone even slightly familiar with stuffed animals knows that there are many lifelike stuffed pigs on the market, and whether they are stuffed with beans or other materials does not significantly affect their verisimilitude—though here we must emphasize that any factual assertions in this opinion should be treated as tentative, since the case is before us on an appeal from the abbreviated record of a preliminary-injunction proceeding and a full trial may cast the facts in a different light.

Real pigs are not the only pigs in the public domain. But GMA has not pointed to any fictional pig in the public domain that Preston resembles. Preston resembles only Squealer, and resembles him so closely as to warrant an inference that GMA copied Squealer. In rebuttal all that GMA presented was the affidavit of the designer, Salmon, who swears, we must assume truthfully, that she never looked at a Squealer before submitting her design. But it is not her design drawing that is alleged to infringe the copyright on Squealer; it is the manufactured Preston, the soft sculpture itself, which, as a comparison of the first with the third and fourth pictures in the appendix reveals, is much more like Squealer than Salmon's drawing is. And remember that the manufactured Preston *in the photograph* is a sport, with its stubby snout and its ribbon. Interestingly, these are features of Salmon's drawing but not of the production-model Preston, suggesting design intervention between Salmon's submission and actual production.

It is true that only a few months elapsed between Salmon's submission of the drawing to GMA and the production of Preston. But the record is silent on how long it would have taken to modify her design to make it more like Squealer. For all we know, it might have been done in hours—by someone who had bought a Squealer. The Beanie Babies are immensely popular. They are also, it is true, sometimes hard to find (though not this Christmas, in Chicago at any rate). Ty's practice, apparently, is to create a shortage (that is, to price its bean-bag animals below the market-clearing price) in order to excite the market. But it is unbelievable that a substantial company like GMA which is in the same line of business as Ty could not have located and purchased a Squealer if it wanted to copy it. A glance at the last picture in the appendix shows an identity between Louie the Cow and Ty's Daisy that is so complete (and also not explainable by reference to resemblance to a real cow or other public domain figure) as to compel an inference of copying. If GMA thus must have had access to Louie, it is probable, quite apart from any inference from the evidence of similarity, that it had access to Squealer as well.

Access (and copying) may be inferred when two works are so similar to each other and not to anything in the public domain that it is likely that the creator of the second work copied the first, but the inference can be rebutted by disproving access or otherwise showing independent creation—and in this connection GMA complains that the district judge refused to conduct an evidentiary hearing at which it might have presented evidence of independent creation.

AFFIRMED.

Notes

1. Judge Posner wants to make sure that the similarities that exist between the plaintiff's toys and the defendant's toys are the result of copying rather than independent creation. This is why he contrasts the defendant's toys with other toys or other pigs in the public domain. In considering the similarities between the plaintiff's and defendant's works, he is looking for similarities that are "suspicious"—those that make the fact finder think that the defendant copied. Notice the kinds of similarities that might *not* count as suspicious, including those determined by the manufacturing process. To the extent that plaintiff's and defendant's toys were similar because of limitations in making stuffed toys, those similarities wouldn't tell us anything about whether the defendant copied or not. The same would be true of similarities that arise from standard and traditional ways of creating designs.

Note, however, that suspicious or probative similarities do not have to arise from protected expression in the plaintiff's work. In the *Feist* telephone book case, the plaintiff could tell that the defendant copied from it, because the defendant reproduced several fake listings that had been added to detect copying. And in another case, the defendant's reproduction of a mistaken double hairline on a mannequin proved that it had copied from the plaintiff, because there was no other reason why the mistake would show up in both places. *Pivot Point International, Inc. v. Charlene Products, Inc.*, 372 F.3d 913 (7th Cir. 2004)

2. Copyright is a species of civil litigation, so the plaintiff is only responsible for proving that copying-in-fact was more likely than not.

3. Courts typically require the plaintiff to show that the defendant did have or reasonably could have had access to its work. Access means an opportunity to view or experience the work. Yet proof of access is only proof that copying was possible. And more access to a work doesn't necessarily mean that copying was more possible. Although Alexander Wang had access to Diane von Furstenberg's famous wrap dress when he designed Kate Middleton's wedding dress, there is no reason to think that he copied it. Why? Because the two dresses don't look anything alike. Access makes copying possible, but similarities make copying probable.

b. Unlawful Appropriation

Copying by competitors is not always bad, and it is not always unlawful. Copying can expand variety and lower prices for consumers, and it can lead to new breakthroughs by competitors. Accordingly, copyright law does not impose liability on all copying. The law's goal is to single out as unlawful copying that is likely to significantly harm the plaintiff's incentive to create. Only those appropriations are deemed unlawful.

The ultimate question here is how similar the defendant's work has to be to the plaintiff's in order to trigger liability. The answer usually depends on the nature of the plaintiff's work and the amount of creativity that it demonstrates. The more creative the plaintiff's work—and the more room for other parties to create their own works—the broader the plaintiff's copyright will be. But when the plaintiff's work is not very creative, or when the opportunities for other creativity are limited, the plaintiff's copyright will be thin. Again, the reasons for this doctrine reflect copyright law's underlying normative commitments—to provide sufficient incentives to authors without excessively burdening consumers and future creators. In the next three cases, consider how the courts attempt to strike this balance.

Tufenkian Import/Export Ventures, Inc. v. Einstein Moomjy, Inc.

338 F.3d 127 (2d Cir. 2003)

CALABRESI, Circuit Judge.

This copyright infringement case involves two textile designs, each of which combines, with modifications, the "primary border" and the "half field" of two unrelated public domain carpets, one a classical Indian Agra and the other a Persian antique. Viewed uncritically, the two designs at issue are substantially similar. For the defendant's rug to infringe upon the plaintiff's design, however, the defendant's composition must be substantially similar to that which is original in the plaintiff's expression. The district court (S.D.N.Y., Pauley, J.) found no infringement, concluding as a matter of law that whatever substantial similarity there may be emerges from unprotected public domain materials in the allegedly infringed design. See Tufenkian Imp./Exp. Ventures, Inc. v. Einstein Moomjy, Inc., 237 F.Supp.2d 376 (S.D.N.Y.2002). We disagree.

Background

In March 1995, James Tufenkian, a designer and manufacturer of Tibetan style carpets, filed a copyright registration for the "Floral Heriz" ("Heriz") carpet design that is the subject of this lawsuit. He had composed the Heriz two years earlier by scanning into his computer two public domain images, one of the "Battilossi" carpet (a Persian antique), the other of the "Blau" carpet (an Indian Agra, designed by Dorris Blau). The field of the Battilossi rug is a dense, bilateral symmetrical design of stylized branching-vine, leaf and flower motifs. Tufenkian selected roughly the central third of the upper[1] half of this Battilossi field. From this dense pattern, he culled out a number of motifs. He then stretched the field slightly in one direction and used the thus modified design as the entire field of the Heriz. In the process, Tufenkian created an asymmetrical pattern, for he used only an off-center portion of what had been a symmetrical design. From the Blau, he took the principal border, which, with modifications, became the major border of the Heriz. Finally, he added two minor borders of his own creation. One of these consists of stick-figure animals, the other of even simpler, castle-like figures.

Tufenkian describes his principal creative contributions as: (1) combining two unrelated rug styles; (2) designing and adding the minor borders; (3) selectively removing entire design motifs from the Battilossi so as to create a more 'open' aesthetic from those remaining; (4) converting the symmetrical Battilossi image into a design "with no central focus" (by copying from only half of the Battilossi field); and (5) elongating the Battilossi pattern.

Sometime in 1995, Appellee Bashian retained Appellee Nichols-Marcy, who had worked for Tufenkian, to oversee the designing of the "Bromley 514" ("Bromley"). Nichols-Marcy and his Nepalese contractors began work on the Bromley in early 1996, two years after the Heriz was first marketed. These designers were familiar with the Heriz, and the appellees do not challenge the district court's determination that some copying of the Heriz actually occurred.

Nonetheless, the appellees contend that the Heriz's extensive use of designs taken from the public domain combined with the Bromley's distinctiveness precludes a finding of infringement. In the latter regard, they point to the following as instances of their own creative work that distinguishes the Bromley from the Heriz: (1) addition of a second "beetle" (or "flower") element to the field, placed in a roughly symmetrical position to an existing "beetle" shape so as to give the Bromley a more balanced feel than the Heriz; (2) retention of a "leaf shape" from the Battilossi that

1. Or of the lower half, since the two are identical.

Tufenkian did not include in the Heriz; (3) removal of a vine-like line segment from the Battilossi that Tufenkian had retained; and (4) greater modification of the Blau border design, with "different shapes at different angles."

In November 1999, Tufenkian initiated this lawsuit, claiming copyright infringement and seeking various injunctive and monetary remedies. Both parties moved for summary judgment on the issue of copyright infringement. The district court concluded that "Tufenkian infused [the Heriz] with sufficient originality to support copyright protection," Tufenkian, 237 F.Supp.2d at 384; that Bashian actually copied the Heriz, id. at 385–86; but that the Bromley 514 was not substantially similar to protected expression in the Heriz, id. at 386–88. The court therefore awarded summary judgment to Bashian.

Discussion

I.

* * *

B. The Test for Copyright Infringement

"Copyright infringement is established when the owner of a valid copyright demonstrates unauthorized copying." To demonstrate unauthorized copying, the plaintiff must first "show that his work was actually copied"; second, he must establish "substantial similarity" or that "the copying amounts to an improper or unlawful appropriation," i.e., (i) that it was protected expression in the earlier work that was copied and (ii) that the amount that was copied is "more than de minimis."

C. The Scope of Copyright Protection: Original Expression

"[O]riginality is 'the sine qua non of copyright.'" It is universally true, however, that even works which express enough originality to be protected also contain material that is not original, and hence that may be freely used by other designers. This is not simply an artifact of some rather lenient caselaw on the originality requirement. The principle is more fundamental: all creative works draw on the common wellspring that is the public domain.

In this pool are not only elemental "raw materials," like colors, letters, descriptive facts, and the catalogue of standard geometric forms, but also earlier works of art that, due to the passage of time or for other reasons, are no longer copyright protected. Thus the public domain includes, for example, both the generic shape of the letter "L" and all of the elaborately more specific "L's" from the hundreds of years of font designs that have fallen into the public domain.

D. Conundrums of Infringement by Inexact Copies

It has long been settled that "no plagiarist can excuse the wrong by showing how much of his work he did not pirate," Sheldon v. Metro-Goldwyn Pictures Corp., 81 F.2d 49, 56 (2d Cir.1936) (Hand, J.), and this aphorism applies equally to exact reproduction of visual works. As a result, a would-be appropriator who wishes to test the limits of copyright law gains nothing from "adding on" to what she has precisely reproduced. But she might prevail insofar as her work transforms the copied expression into a design that in some respects resembles the original, yet does not actually excerpt ("cut and paste") a more-than-de-minimis protected portion of the original. Such designs may be termed "inexact copies," in recognition of the fact that they alter the prior image yet mimic its structure in some fashion. Jurists have long been vexed by the task of precisely identifying that which separates inexact copies that infringe from those that do not.[2]

In recent years we have often found it productive to assess claims of inexact-copy infringement by comparing the contested design's "total concept and overall feel" with that of the allegedly infringed work.

Some commentators have worried that the "total concept and feel" standard may "invite[ ] an abdication of analysis," because "feel" can seem a "wholly amorphous referent." Melville B. Nimmer & David Nimmer, 4 Nimmer on Copyright § 13.03[A][1][c] (2003). Likewise, one may wonder whether a copyright doctrine whose aspiration is to protect a work's "concept" could end up erroneously protecting "ideas." But our caselaw is not so incautious. Where we have described possible infringement in terms of whether two designs have or do not have a substantially similar "total concept and feel," we generally have taken care to identify precisely the particular aesthetic decisions—original to the plaintiff and copied by the defendant—that might be thought to make the designs similar in the aggregate.

II.

The appellant charges that, in comparing the two designs' total concept and feel, the district court improperly factored out public domain elements from the Heriz and the Bromley. As the above discussion of doctrine indicates, however, the court was surely correct to factor such elements out. For copying is not unlawful if what was copied from the allegedly infringed work was not protected, for example, if the copied material had itself been taken from the public domain. This principle applies, moreover, whether the copied, unprotected expression at issue is a selection, coordination, or arrangement of elements, or whether it is the exact design itself.

But in its comparison of the two rugs, the district court failed to consider—apart from total concept and feel—whether material portions of the Bromley infringed on corresponding parts of the Heriz. Here the court erred.

What makes this case perplexing is that, to the judicial observer who has a passing familiarity with carpet design, many of the plaintiff's expressive choices may seem to be rather mechanical or conventional acts, which might be deemed to be either non-original or else so weakly original that their copying would appropriate

2. *Cf.* Nichols v. Universal Pictures Corp., 45 F.2d 119, 121 (2d Cir.1930) (Hand, J.) ("Upon any work . . . a great number of patterns of increasing generality will fit equally well, as more and more of the incident is left out. The last may perhaps be no more than the most general statement of what the [work] is about . . . but there is a point in the series of abstractions where they are no longer protected. . . .").

no more than a de minimis amount of protected expression. Consider, for example, the cropping and elongating of the Battilossi half-field so as to create a typical "longer than wide" field for the Heriz; the use of one primary and two minor borders; the proportions between borders and field; and the design of the outer minor border. On the other hand, the record contains little evidence of what is conventional (and hence, by analogy to "scenes a faire," unprotected) in these respects.

Even the Heriz's pairing of the Battilossi half-field with the Blau-derived border was, arguably, a fairly simple exercise. One might contend that the pairing is too minor to surmount even the low threshold for copyright protection, or else conclude that it is protected only against very close copies.[3] The question of infringement thus might be thought to turn on subtle differences in the Heriz and Bromley adaptations of the Blau border.

Whether the Bromley infringes on the Heriz, however, need not depend on variation between the primary borders, or on a determination of the extent to which various features of the Heriz design are conventions. There is one substantial respect in which the creator of the Heriz made distinctly idiosyncratic and particular design decisions—decisions whose effect permeates the entire field of the Heriz—and in this respect the Bromley is a virtually exact copy of the Heriz. The plaintiff not only cropped and elongated the Battillossi half-field, he also selectively eliminated numerous design motifs, creating a more open, less busy aesthetic.

Of course, mere simplification of an ornate public domain carpet into a mass market knock-off may not be protectible. But the plaintiff's half-field modification was not a uniform or homogeneous simplification akin to removing all serifs from a font, blurring the petals on all flowers, or eliminating every third leaf on a stem. Rather, the plaintiff seems to have engaged in a selective and particularized culling of a leaf here, a complex of leaves and flowers there, and so forth. And close visual inspection of the two rugs confirms that the Bromley precisely mimics the Heriz in nearly all of these choices.

This non-mechanical adaptation of individually unprotectible elements from the public domain is precisely the type of "original selection" that the Supreme Court indicated was protectible expression in Feist.

We conclude that this is one of those relatively unusual cases in which the infringing work has copied the original and "particular" or "same" selections embodied in the allegedly infringed upon work. The number of motifs present (or absent) in the Bromley field which mirror those the Heriz selected (or deleted) in an original way

---

3. In suggesting these possibilities, we note only that they are arguable, and we express no opinion as to whether the arguments, if made, would prove correct. We do believe, however, that the district court probably erred in categorically dismissing as an unprotected "idea" the plaintiff's combination of the Battilossi half-field and Blau-ish border. The plaintiff's particular combination of these two rugs is an expression, albeit one protected by a thin copyright. *Cf.* Beaudin v. Ben & Jerry's Homemade, Inc., 95 F.3d 1, 2 (2d Cir.1996) ("Where the quantum of originality is slight and the resulting copyright is 'thin,' infringement will be established only by very close copying. . . .").

from the Battilossi is overwhelming. And the structural layout of these elements is essentially the same in both designs.

It should be noted that while the Bromley field is based on a near-exact copy of the Heriz's original selections from the Battilossi, the Bromley does depart from the Heriz in one salient respect. Specifically, the Bromley field has a second, anchoring "beetle" or "flower" element, which conveys a sense of balance that is absent in the Heriz. This addition, and the resulting faux symmetry, was important to the district court's determination that the "total concept and feel" of the Bromley was not substantially similar to that of the Heriz. *See* Tufenkian, 237 F.Supp.2d at 387–88. Whatever the possible relevance of the Bromley's second beetle element to a comparison of the two rugs' "overall feel"—an issue we need not decide today—this addition does not alter the fact that the rest of the Bromley field is a near-exact copy of the Heriz field, and therefore infringing. To hold otherwise would be rather like holding that one who closely copies a long poem can do so without prima facie infringement if she replaces one (admittedly significant) stanza with verse of her own invention and thereby alters the poem's "feel."

III.

For the forgoing reasons, we hold that the Bromley is substantially similar to the Heriz. We therefore VACATE the judgment of the district court and REMAND for further proceedings. On remand the district court may consider the defense of fraud on the copyright office. If that defense proves unavailing, and if other defenses are waived or do not prove meritorious, the court should enter judgment for the plaintiff and proceed to determine the appropriate remedies.

Nola Spice Designs, LLC v. Haydel Enterprises

783 F.3d 527 (5th Cir. 2015)

HIGGINSON, Circuit Judge.

This case concerns the intersection between intellectual property rights and a Mardi Gras tradition. Haydel Enterprises appeals the district court's grant of summary judgment to Nola Spice Designs and Raquel Duarte on claims of trademark infringement, unfair competition, trademark dilution, copyright infringement, and unfair trade practices. We affirm.

Facts and Proceedings

During Mardi Gras parades in New Orleans, parade "krewes" throw strands of plastic beads to onlookers, who, in turn, have created "bead dogs" by twisting these strands into the shape of a dog. Haydel Enterprises ("Haydel") owns Haydel's Bakery in New Orleans, which makes and sells pastries and cakes, including its popular king cake sold during the Mardi Gras season. In 2008, Haydel commissioned an artist to design a mascot, which was named "Mardi Gras Bead Dog." On October 13, 2009, and December 1, 2009, the United States Patent and Trademark Office ("PTO") issued two trademark registrations to Haydel for, respectively, the phrase

"MARDI GRAS BEAD DOG" and its bead dog design. The design consists of a "stylized dog wearing a beaded necklace, with the dog being formed by a series of spheres designed to look like Mardi Gras style beads. The dog has two eyes and a nose, all formed by smaller beads." Both registrations cover king cake pastries, jewelry, and clothing (shirts, hats, and baby jumpsuits). Haydel sells these items in its New Orleans store, online, and through its licensee Fleurty Girl, a New Orleans retailer. In September 2012, Haydel obtained a certificate of copyright registration for its work titled "Bead Dog" in "photograph(s), jewelry design, 2-D artwork, sculpture." Haydel has acknowledged that its mascot "brings to mind the traditional bead dog" made of Mardi Gras beads. Nevertheless, Haydel asserts that its mascot and its use of the phrase "Mardi Gras Bead Dog" differ from the Mardi Gras tradition in key respects, which we will discuss.

In May 2012, Raquel Duarte formed Nola Spice Designs, which sells jewelry and accessories, including necklaces and earrings featuring bead dog trinkets. Duarte twists each bead dog by hand from beads and wire, following the same general method that she used to make bead dogs as a child during Mardi Gras. By contrast, the bead dogs in Haydel's jewelry are made of sterling silver. Duarte sells her jewelry on the Internet under titles that include the phrase "bead dog," but not "Mardi Gras bead dog." The appendix to this opinion contains images of Haydel's bead dog sculpture, jewelry, and trademarked design, as well as images of Nola Spice's jewelry and of a traditional bead dog trinket.

* * *

On August 28, 2013, the district court granted in part and denied in part the motion for summary judgment filed by Nola Spice Designs and Duarte (collectively, "Nola Spice") and denied Haydel's motion for summary judgment. Specifically, the district court granted summary judgment to Nola Spice on its claim for a declaratory judgment that it was not infringing Haydel's trademarks, and the court cancelled those trademarks as unprotectable, but it denied Nola Spice's motion for summary judgment on its LUTPA claims. The district court also granted summary judgment to Nola Spice on Haydel's claims of trademark infringement, unfair competition, trademark dilution, copyright infringement, and unfair trade practices. Haydel timely appealed the district court's August 28 order. Nola Spice did not appeal the district court's dismissal with prejudice of its LUTPA claim.

Discussion

* * *

V. Copyright Infringement

"To prove copyright infringement, a plaintiff must establish (1) ownership of a valid copyright; (2) factual copying; and (3) substantial similarity." As to the first element, Haydel obtained a certificate of a copyright registration for its work titled "Bead Dog," in the form of "photograph(s), jewelry design, 2-D artwork, [and] sculpture." The Copyright Act provides that a certificate of copyright registration "made before or within five years after first publication of the work shall constitute prima facie evidence of the validity of the copyright." 17 U.S.C. § 410(c). Although the presumption of validity may be rebutted, Nola Spice does not develop any argument that Haydel's work as a whole is unprotectable. We therefore do not assess the validity of Haydel's copyright. Nola Spice also does not argue against a finding of factual copying, the second element required for a copyright infringement claim. Rather, Nola Spice argues that the third element is absent because its works are not substantially similar to Haydel's bead dog design.

The district court relied on the merger doctrine in granting summary judgment to Nola Spice on Haydel's copyright infringement claim. The merger doctrine is based on the statutory prohibition against copyright protection for ideas. *See* 17 U.S.C. § 102(b). "If an idea is susceptible to only one form of expression, the merger doctrine applies and § 102(b) excludes the expression from the Copyright Act." Veeck v. S. Bldg. Code Cong. Int'l, Inc., 293 F.3d 791, 801 (5th Cir.2002). However, examples of bead dogs in the record make clear that the idea of a bead dog may be expressed in various ways. The merger doctrine therefore does not alone preclude a finding of copyright infringement. Still, "we may affirm the district court's decision on any ground supported by the record, even if it was not the basis for the judgment." We find that the grant of summary judgment was appropriate based on the absence of substantial similarity between Haydel's and Nola Spice's bead dogs.

While the question of substantial similarity "typically should be left to the factfinder, summary judgment may be appropriate if the court can conclude, after viewing the evidence and drawing inferences in a manner most favorable to the nonmoving party, that no reasonable juror could find substantial similarity." To assess substantial similarity, we have often cited the following test: "[A] side-by-side comparison must be made between the original and the copy to determine whether a layman would view the two works as 'substantially similar.'" However, where the copyrighted work contains unprotectable elements, the first step is to distinguish between protectable and unprotectable elements of the copyrighted work. The next inquiry is whether the allegedly infringing work bears a substantial similarity to the protectable aspects of the original work. This determination should be based on the perspective of a "layman" or "ordinary observer." Our precedents also support consideration of the importance of the copied protectable elements to the copyrighted work as a whole.

Applying these principles to Haydel's claim, we first identify the unprotectable elements in Haydel's bead dog design, which is manifested most clearly in sculpture form. Haydel concedes that its bead dog design is a "derivative" work, meaning that it is "based upon one or more preexisting works." 17 U.S.C. § 101. "The copyright in a . . . derivative work extends only to the material contributed by the author of such work, as distinguished from the preexisting material employed in the work, and does not imply any exclusive right in the preexisting material." Id. § 103(b); *see also* Yurman Design, Inc. v. PAJ, Inc., 262 F.3d 101, 109–110 (2d Cir.2001). Haydel concedes that the body of its bead dog design is unprotectable as preexisting material because it mimics the body of a traditional bead dog. Haydel nevertheless contends that its "original contributions include, among other things, the selection and arrangement of a necklace, nose, eyes, and a tail, all made of smaller beads." However, anatomical features on replicas of animals are ideas not entitled to copyright protection. As for the "necklace" in Haydel's design, the ring of spheres around the neck of Haydel's bead dog may be characterized as a collar. Collars on dogs, like anatomical features, are common ideas that belong to the public domain. Still, while the idea of eyes, a nose, a tail, and a collar are not protectable, the manner in which Haydel expresses these features may be protectable, as long as that expression is original and not dictated by the underlying idea.

We now compare Nola Spice's bead dog to the protectable elements of Haydel's bead dog, assuming the perspective of an ordinary observer and considering the significance of the protectable elements to Haydel's work as a whole. Haydel argues that only some of Nola Spice's bead dogs are infringing and identifies examples in the record. Focusing on the protectable elements of Haydel's design, the similarity between Nola Spice's and Haydel's bead dogs is the expression of the collar as a ring of small spheres. As for the differences, the torso of Haydel's bead dog has three spheres, while the torso of Nola Spice's bead dog has one sphere. The spheres that make up Haydel's bead dog are pressed together, whereas visible wire connects the spheres that make up Nola Spice's bead dogs. Whereas the tail of Haydel's bead dog consists of two spheres and no wire, the tails of Nola Spice's bead dogs include a curled wire, either alone or atop one or two spheres. Likewise, the noses of Nola Spice's bead dogs include a curled wire, either alone or atop a single sphere, while the nose of Haydel's bead dog is a single sphere. Unlike Haydel's bead dog, Nola Spice's bead dogs do not have eyes. No reasonable juror could conclude that Nola Spice's bead dogs bear a substantial similarity to the way in which the eyes, nose, and tail are expressed in Haydel's bead dog. Indeed, Haydel focuses its argument on the collar, conceding that its "copyright infringement claim is narrow. Only to the extent that Nola Spice copied Haydel's original expression by, at least adding a necklace made of smaller beads to what would otherwise look like a dog trinket made of larger beads, has Nola Spice infringed Haydel's copyrighted expression." We must therefore decide whether the collar on Nola Spice's bead dogs could suffice to support a finding of substantial similarity in the mind of a reasonable juror.

Because the idea of a collar is unprotectable, only its expression as a string of spheres is relevant to the analysis of substantial similarity. As a threshold matter, we question whether using bead-shaped spheres for a bead dog's collar is sufficiently original to merit copyright protection. Although the requirement of originality demands only a "creative spark, no matter how crude, humble or obvious," the level of creativity must be more than "trivial." Even if a bead-shaped collar possesses the requisite creative spark, its minimal originality counsels against a finding of substantial similarity. In addition, the collar is both qualitatively and quantitatively insignificant in relation to Haydel's work as a whole, which is designed to represent a traditional bead dog trinket and is dominated by unprotectable elements. In light of these considerations, no reasonable jury could find substantial similarity based solely on Haydel's expression of a collar.

Haydel argues that the "best evidence" of substantial similarity consists of statements by the Haydel family that its customers were confused about the relationship between Nola Spice's bead dogs and Haydel's mascot. Haydel points to a sworn statement by David Haydel, Sr. that he "personally heard several customers of Haydel's Bakery asking whether Nola Spice Designs sells Haydel's MARDI GRAS BEAD DOG jewelry and telling our staff that they (the customers) believed that Nola Spice Designs sold Haydel's MARDI GRAS BEAD DOG jewelry." This vague allegation of consumer confusion by a self-interested party possesses little probative value. More important, any confusion by Haydel's customers would have stemmed from a comparison of the two bead dog designs in their entirety, and would therefore have been based largely on unprotectable elements. Given that the substantial similarity analysis requires a focus on protectable elements, Haydel's evidence of confusion does not raise a genuine issue for trial. Because no reasonable jury could conclude that Nola Spice's and Haydel's bead dogs are substantially similar in protectable expression, the district court properly granted summary judgment to Nola Spice on Haydel's copyright infringement claim.

Bill Diodato Photography, LLC v. Kate Spade, LLC

388 F. Supp. 2d 382 (S.D.N.Y. 2005)

CHIN, District Judge.

In 2001, Bill Diodato took a photograph, shown here, of the bottom of a bathroom stall.

Through the opening underneath the door, one can see a woman's feet, astride a toilet, in stylish, colorful shoes, her underwear hanging above her ankles, and a handbag resting on the floor. Diodato submitted the photograph to defendant Kate Spade LLC ("Kate Spade") in January 2003. Although representatives of Kate Spade deny they saw the photograph, Kate Spade's November 2003 advertising campaign included a photograph, shown below, of a woman's feet, astride a toilet, in stylish, colorful shoes, with a handbag on the floor. Diodato's company, plaintiff Bill Diodato Photography, LLC ("BDP"), sued for copyright infringement and unfair competition.

Before the Court is Kate Spade's motion for summary judgment and BDP's motion for additional discovery pursuant to Fed. R. Civ. P. 56(f). As discussed more fully below, although the idea of using a woman sitting on a toilet to showcase stylish shoes and other fashion accessories is a clever one, it is an idea that has been used often in popular culture. Hence, Diodato's photograph contains elements that are not protected by the copyright laws. Even assuming there was copying here, Kate Spade's motion for summary judgment must be granted and the complaint dismissed. In addition, for the reasons set forth below, BDP's Rule 56(f) motion is denied.

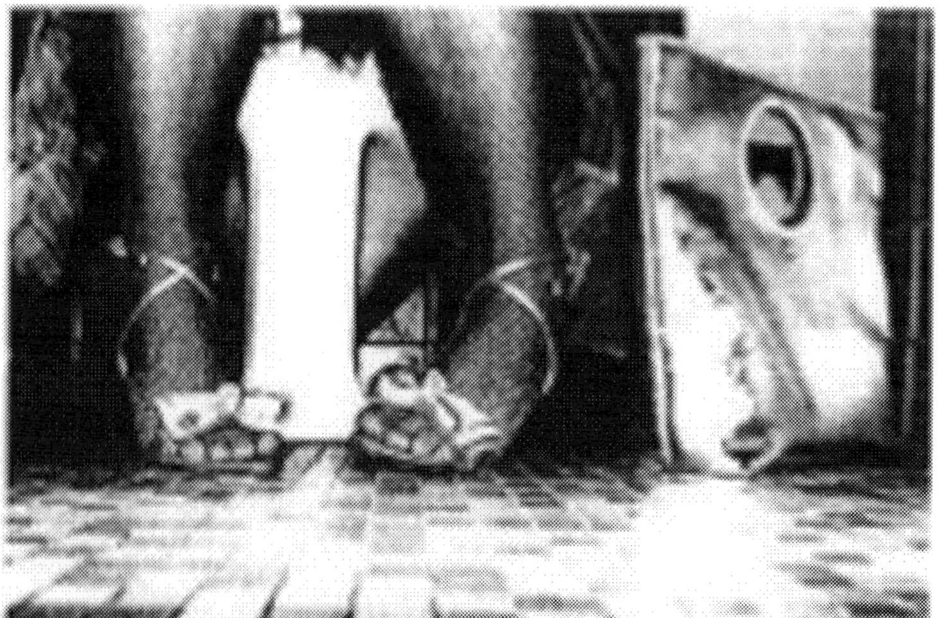

Background

A. Facts

The following facts are drawn from the pleadings and the parties' motion papers and supporting materials. All conflicts in the evidence have been resolved in favor of BDP, the party opposing summary judgment.

1. The BDP Photograph

Diodato is a fashion accessory photographer and the principal of BDP. In late 2001, BDP was hired by the magazine Angeleno to shoot a series of photographs featuring fashion accessories with New York City as a central theme. Diodato chose to illustrate that "highly fashionable women can be somewhat tacky," and on December 14, 2001 he photographed models in a Burger King restaurant, on streets in New York City, and in a taxi cab. The photograph at issue here (the "BDP Photograph") was among the photographs in the series.

The BDP Photograph was taken from the floor outside a bathroom stall. It depicts the bottom portion of the stall and a woman's feet in pink shoes decorated with green, yellow, and purple leaves, with thin pink straps criss-crossing up her legs. The woman's lime green underpants are taut just above her ankles. A light brown handbag rests on the floor next to the woman's left foot, and a white toilet is visible in the background. The woman's feet are on the floor, her heels raised at a stiff angle by the heels of her shoes. The woman's ankles are turned in, with her toes painted red.

The BDP Photograph is taken from a distance, with the bathroom stall and door separating the subject and the camera. Almost the entire bottom half of the photograph consists of the light grey lines of the floor tiles, with virtually all of the floor out-of-focus. The floor comes into focus halfway up the photograph, where the woman's feet touch the ground and the handbag sits. The photograph is framed at the top and on the left by the darker grey of the bathroom stall and door. A light seems to shine on the legs, toilet, and handbag, in contrast to the shadows in the foreground and background. The overall tone of the photograph is whimsical, fun, and bright.

Angeleno did not run the BDP Photograph as part of the series, and the BDP Photograph has not been published commercially. It has been a part of BDP's fashion accessory portfolio (the "Portfolio") from late 2002 to the present and is, in one form or another, on the BDP website.

2. Interactions Between BDP and Kate Spade

Since at least late 2002, BDP has been represented by a photography agency, Marge Casey & Associates ("MCA"). On January 13, 2003, MCA received a call from Kate Spade requesting the Portfolio, among other portfolios. According to Margaret Casey, an owner of MCA, the request was made by Julia Leach, Kate Spade's executive vice president of brand strategy/creative services, or someone on Leach's behalf. Notes taken by an MCA employee on an "MCA Photo Request Form" dated

January 13, 2003 and referring to BDP portfolios include "Julia Leach" written next to "Contact" and "Kate Spade" written next to "Agency."

On January 15, 2003, the Portfolio was sent by messenger to Kate Spade. It was returned to MCA on January 22, 2003, after a Kate Spade employee told MCA that Kate Spade liked the Portfolio and wanted to see it again in three or four weeks when Kate Spade planned to create concepts and shoot photographs for an advertising campaign.

The Portfolio was sent again to Kate Spade on February 13, 2003. While Kate Spade had the Portfolio, Casey called to inquire whether Kate Spade was interested in using BDP as a photographer. Casey was told by a Kate Spade "assistant" that Kate Spade only worked with important or well-known photographers. The Portfolio was returned to MCA on February 24, 2003. Kate Spade did not contact MCA or BDP further about the advertising campaign.

3. The Kate Spade Photograph

Photographer Jessica Craig Martin was contacted by Kate Spade in March 2003 about the company's fall 2003 advertising campaign. Craig Martin met with principals of Kate Spade in April or May 2003, at which time Craig Martin's portfolio was reviewed and ideas for the advertising campaign were discussed. It was agreed that Kate Spade would throw a party to celebrate its tenth anniversary and that Craig Martin would take candid, paparazzi-style photographs at the party. According to Kate Spade, ideas for potential images were discussed at the meeting, and Kate Spade officials referenced photographs in Craig Martin's portfolio as exemplifying what they wanted. Among those photographs was one taken by Craig Martin in 2000 from the floor of a bathroom, featuring a side view of the feet and gold shoes of two women in bathroom stalls (the "2000 Craig Martin Photograph"). In that photograph, one of the women is wearing fishnet stockings and bright light reflects from the women's shoes and the floor. The 2000 Craig Martin Photograph has been exhibited publicly and distributed as a postcard, and copies of the photograph have been sold.

Kate Spade eventually hired Craig Martin to conceptualize and shoot photographs for the advertising campaign. In early June 2003, Craig Martin took photographs at Kate Spade's anniversary party at the Explorers' Club in New York City, as planned. Among those was the allegedly infringing photograph, taken in the bathroom of the Explorers' Club (the "Kate Spade Photograph"). It was among the thirty to fifty images that Kate Spade ordered from Craig Martin after the shoot, and it ultimately was one of the approximately fourteen photographs used in Kate Spade's fall 2003 advertising campaign.

The Kate Spade Photograph is taken from the tiled floor in front of a toilet. A woman's legs are visible from just below the knees; she wears purple-tinted fishnet stockings and satin pink shoes with straps criss-crossing once around her ankle, and her light tulle petticoats fall to the side of the toilet. A shiny, silver square handbag sits next to her left foot. The Kate Spade Photograph is cropped close to the woman, the toilet between her legs, and the handbag, so that little of the surrounding area is visible, aside from square tiles on the wall. The bottom portion of the Kate Spade Photograph consists of smaller floor tiles, mottled in color and texture.

With the exception of the extreme foreground, the floor and other images are in focus, grounding the photograph. In addition, there seems to be a spotlight shining on the center of the frame, creating sharp contrasts in light.[5] The entire photograph is detail-rich and textured. The purse has a metallic shine and creases; light reflects off the bows on the satin shoes; and the distinct patterns of the wide-net stockings and the tile floor add energy to the photograph. The woman's feet are pointed toward each other, her left foot is slightly raised and leaning on its side. The image seems to be of an evening event, as the woman is dressed in party attire and the shadows are dark.

According to Kate Spade, Craig Martin created all the photographs for the advertising campaign without direction or instruction from Kate Spade, except that Kate Spade provided direction as to which Kate Spade products were to appear in the campaign. Likewise, Leach testified that Kate Spade did not provide photographs, sketches, or preparatory materials for the shoot to Craig Martin and that Kate Spade does not have copies of the Portfolio in its offices.

4. Other Uses of the Concept

The idea of a woman's feet at the base of a toilet to showcase shoes and other fashion accessories has been used often in popular culture. Kate Spade attaches to its papers copies of photographs of this type, culled from image banks of stock photography agencies. These include photographs of: (1) a woman on a toilet with animal-patterned underwear around her ankles, her knees together and her feet pointed inward; (2) a woman's ankles and feet in hot pink sandals with flowers on the straps, toenails painted, and toes pointed inward, tile floor and toilet bowl cleaner visible; (3) the view under two toilet stall doors of two models (it is unclear whether they are male or female) in heels, with one model's toes pointed inward; (4) a side view of two stalls that seem to be in a bathroom, a woman in black heels visible in one stall and a woman in heeled loafers with a briefcase in the other; (5) a side view of a woman on a toilet seat, hot pink underwear near her ankles, her feet awkwardly angled in her high heels and toes seemingly pointed inward; and (6) a woman in a cut-off jeans skirt on a toilet seat, blue and white g-string underwear around her calves, her heels raised and toes pointed inward.

The record does not indicate when these photographs were taken, but these are stock photographs readily available from photography agencies. Some appear to be

---

5. Craig Martin testified that the "signature element of all of [her] work ... is the very strong artificial light and flash that [she] always use[s]." (Craig Martin Aff. P20). Her camera is "configured in a paparazzi-style setup" and she "never take[s] photographs at a polite distance." (*Id.*).

taken many years ago. Nor are the photographs limited to women; one is a photograph of the bottoms of two bathroom stalls, showing the feet of two men in boots, their blue jeans down around their legs and feet.

Finally, as noted above, Craig Martin had previously photographed the feet of two women, in shiny gold shoes and side-by-side bathroom stalls, in a photograph that was widely circulated. In the 2000 Craig Martin Photograph, the viewer sees only the feet, shoes, floor, and a small portion of a low bathroom stall divider.

Discussion

A. Copyright Infringement

1. Applicable Law

To prevail on a claim of copyright infringement, a plaintiff must prove two elements: (1) ownership of a valid copyright, and (2) copying of constituent elements of the work that are original. As BDP provided the Court with a copy of the certificate of copyright registration for the BDP Photograph, and Kate Spade does not contest the validity of the copyright, I assume BDP owns a valid copyright in the BDP Photograph. The second element, copying, is comprised of two requirements: actual copying and improper appropriation.

a. Actual Copying

Actual copying may be established by either (1) direct evidence of copying or (2) circumstantial proof of copying, consisting of evidence that the alleged infringer had access to the protected work and "that there are similarities between the two works that are probative of copying." "Access may be . . . inferred from the fact that a work was widely disseminated or that a party had a reasonable possibility of viewing the prior work." "A reasonable possibility" is not simply a "bare possibility"; "access cannot be based on mere speculation or conjecture." The copyright owner must offer "significant, affirmative and probative evidence" to support a claim of access. The existence of similarities supports the inference of copying, and a probative similarity "requires only the fact that the infringing work copies something from the copyrighted work."

b. Improper Appropriation

Once actual copying has been established, the copyright owner must then satisfy the "improper appropriation" requirement by demonstrating that "substantial similarities" as to the protected elements of the work would cause an average lay observer to "recognize the alleged copy as having been appropriated from the copyrighted work." "For [this] prong it is essential that the similarity relate to copyrightable material." When similar works resemble each other only in unprotected aspects—for example, when similarities inhere in ideas, which are by definition unprotected, or in expression that is not proprietary to plaintiff—defendant prevails.

Careful scrutiny is necessary when the protected work contains unprotectible elements.

Critical to the issue of improper appropriation is whether the copied elements of the work are original and nontrivial. For purposes of copyright law, "original" means that "the work was independently created by the author (as opposed to copied from other works), and that it possesses at least some minimal degree of creativity." Notwithstanding proof that copying occurred, copying that is so trivial as to fall below the quantitative threshold of substantial similarity will be considered *de minimis* and, thus, not actionable.

A central tenet of copyright law is that only a copyright owner's particular expression of his or her idea is protected, not the idea itself.

2. Application

a. Actual Copying

Genuine issues of material fact exist as to whether Kate Spade actually copied the BDP Photograph. First, issues of fact exist as to whether Leach, a creative director at Kate Spade, or one of her assistants had access to and viewed the BDP Photograph. Leach is the Kate Spade employee who seems to have been most involved in the 2003 advertising campaign. She testified that she did not solicit, receive, or review the Portfolio, but she does not deny that Kate Spade received the Portfolio. Messenger logs demonstrate that some BDP portfolios went to Kate Spade prior to Kate Spade's hiring of Craig Martin. In addition, the recollection of Diodato's agent, Marge Casey, supports BDP's assertion that Leach or someone who worked with Leach requested and had access to the Portfolio and, consequently, the BDP Photograph. Accordingly, an issue of fact exists as to whether Kate Spade employees involved in the advertising campaign had access to the BDP Photograph.

Significantly, the alleged access, if proven at trial, was more than "bare corporate receipt" of the BDP Photograph. "Bare corporate receipt of [copyrighted] work, without any allegation of a nexus between the recipients and the alleged infringers, is insufficient to raise a triable issue of access." Here, it is not disputed that Leach met with the photographer of the allegedly infringing photograph and discussed ideas for the photography shoot that resulted in the Kate Spade Photograph. A relationship existed between Craig Martin and Kate Spade employees in control of the advertising campaign and, allegedly, those same employees had access to the BDP Photograph. Although Craig Martin and Leach both deny that anyone at Kate Spade instructed Craig Martin on the taking of the Kate Spade Photograph, those relationships create an issue of fact as to the reasonable possibility of access. A plaintiff "is not required to establish *actual* access." "It is enough to prove that the infringer (or his intermediary) had the mere opportunity to see the work."

Second, the BDP Photograph and the Kate Spade Photograph have similarities probative of copying. Both photographs depict a woman's feet, toes pointed slightly inward, as she sits on a toilet seat, and they both showcase the fashionable shoes worn by the women and the handbags at their side.

Kate Spade argues that there is undisputed evidence that Craig Martin created the Kate Spade Photograph independently. Kate Spade relies on *Silberstein v. Fox Entm't Group, Inc.* in arguing that "evidence of independent creation is an established ground for granting summary judgment." In *Silberstein,* however, the defendants produced "copious undisputed testimonial and documentary evidence that the [allegedly infringing cartoon character] evolved organically out of the research and creative and narrative developmental work performed by the film's creators." Here, Craig Martin's testimony must be weighed against BDP's evidence of access and copying, a task more appropriate for a factfinder.

In sum, material issues of fact exist as to the actual copying aspect of the second element. A reasonable jury could find both access and probative similarity.

b. Improper Appropriation

Assuming for purposes of this motion that Kate Spade actually copied the BDP Photograph, the analysis turns to whether the appropriation was improper and, therefore, whether actionable infringement occurred. Even assuming the two photographs share substantial similarities, there is no infringement unless protectible elements were copied. Hence, it is necessary to distinguish between the protectible and unprotectible elements of the BDP Photograph.

To the extent that aspects of the BDP Photograph are derived from the idea of the photograph, or naturally flow from that idea, they are not protectible. As a result, the vast majority of elements in the BDP Photograph that are similar to those in the Kate Spade Photograph are not protectible.

The idea in the BDP Photograph is the depiction of a woman's feet as she sits on the toilet, used as a striking device to highlight fashion accessories. Accordingly, the following elements are not protectible: the dominant shapes of the woman's legs and the toilet base in the BDP Photograph; the inclusion of fashionable shoes and underwear; and the bathroom walls in the background. The bathroom as a setting is also not protectible. These elements are common to the other fashion photographs identified above that feature feet and shoes in a bathroom stall or a person sitting on a toilet.

Relatedly, aspects of the BDP Photograph that necessarily flow from its idea are not protectible. Under the doctrine of *scenes a faire,* elements of an image that flow naturally and necessarily from the choice of a given concept cannot be claimed as original. Accordingly, that the legs and handbags are framed by the floor and the bathroom walls is not protectible; to shoot a photograph of the bottom part of a woman's legs in a bathroom stall or on a toilet, it is necessary that the floor and the surrounding bathroom walls are in the frame.

Likewise, it is standard for the photographer to take such a photograph from or near the floor, and it follows that a portion of the floor closest to the camera might be out of focus. A natural consequence of that positioning is also, often, a head-on view of the toilet. In addition, a photographer of such a scene would generally want the fashion and model to be in sharp focus.

Other elements that are commonly included in images of this type clearly are not original to BDP, and therefore not protectible. The positioning of the model's feet in the BDP Photograph may seem unique; yet, numerous images in popular culture with similar premises pose women on toilets, usually in high heels, their toes pointed slightly inward. While seemingly unnatural, the positioning is clearly not original. Moreover, such a pose cannot be copyrighted. "In cases involving photographs, a 'plaintiff's copyrights cannot monopolize the various poses used,' and 'can protect only plaintiff's particular photographic expression of these poses and not the underlying ideas therefor.'"

A photographer's use of this pose makes sense. In fashion photographs, photographers generally want the shoes, accessories, or other fashion to be highly visible and the depiction to be in some way interesting, attractive, or eye-catching. If the model's feet are positioned straight toward the camera, less of the shoes are visible and the image is more staid; if the model's feet are turned outward, the image is less attractive. With toes pointed inward toward the center of the frame, the viewers eyes are drawn into the photograph, a portion of the shoes sides are visible, and character is added to the image. The pose is common and predictable in such a photograph, and thus not protectible.

The use and placement of the handbag in the BDP Photograph is a closer question, but this also cannot be protected. The handbags in both photographs are to the left of the model's left foot, angled toward the center of the photograph. In a fashion photograph set in a toilet stall, it is natural to include a handbag. Even if it is not standard, assuming that Kate Spade—a company known for its handbags—copied the idea of the BDP Photograph, it would naturally include a handbag. If one is to be included, there are few places that it can be strategically positioned so as not to conceal the model's shoes or fade into the background. To make the handbag most visible, it must be placed at an angle. To the extent that the placement of the bag is not standard in a photograph of this type—and thus original to the BDP Photograph and not protectible—I find its use in the Kate Spade Photograph *de minimis.* The scene created by Diodato as a whole was not original, even if the technical choices he made in rendering the photograph were, and Kate Spade's alleged copying of the placement of the handbag is incidental in this context.

Indeed, although the protectibility and nonprotectibility of individual components of the copyrighted photograph must be considered by the Court, ultimately originality may be determined by the "'total concept and feel'" of the photograph. Each photograph of this type—women's feet astride a toilet, fashion accessories highlighted—is rendered in a distinct way, but the BDP Photograph is, ultimately, one of many. Diodato's idea, and elements that naturally flow from it, cannot be protected.

The elements that are unique to Diodato's expression of the idea—and thus protectible—in fact distinguish it from the allegedly infringing photograph. For example, Diodato uses an abundance of negative grey space; the BDP Photograph is brightly lit; and the selected accessories give the photograph an airy and provocative feel. The model and her accessories are highlighted by their color and seem almost planted into the backdrop of a toilet stall. In the Kate Spade Photograph, the mood, colors, lighting, and depth of objects are distinct, and the view is tightly cropped.

Judge Kaplan recently discussed the "difficulty of distinguishing between idea and expression" in copyright infringement cases, finding that "in the context of photography, the idea/expression distinction is not useful or relevant." He ultimately determined that, despite contradictions in the case law, "the cases agree that the relevant comparison is between the protectible elements in the [two photographs], but that those elements are not to be viewed in isolation." In *Mannion,* there was no serious issue as to the originality of the plaintiff's photograph. Judge Kaplan held that it was an issue of fact whether the images at issue were substantially similar and he therefore denied summary judgment, but he found that the rendition of plaintiff's photograph and the "creation of the subject" were original.

Here, in contrast, the creation of the subject was not original to Diodato. The BDP Photograph was certainly rendered in an original way—the technical aspects of the photograph were Diodato's own—but the scene depicted in the BDP Photograph is a concept that has appeared often in popular culture. The elements that are arguably copied in the Kate Spade Photograph are non-original, unprotectible elements. The elements that Diodato adds to the concept—his "take" on the idea—are elements that make the BDP Photograph distinct from the Kate Spade Photograph, as the latter is original in its rendition as well.

c. Summary Judgment

A party seeking summary judgment on a claim of non-infringement of copyright must establish that at least one element of the alleged infringement cannot be proven as a matter of law. Summary judgment may be granted when the similarity between the works relate only to non-copyrightable elements or when no reasonable jury could find the two works substantially similar.

A jury could find that Kate Spade actually copied the BDP Photograph and that the two photographs are substantially similar, but a jury could not reasonably find that any substantial similarities between the photographs relate to protected elements of the copyrighted work. Because I hold that significant elements of the BDP Photograph that are similar to the Kate Spade Photograph are not protectible—and that elements that are protectible are not similar to the Kate Spade Photograph or are *de minimis*—summary judgment is granted in favor of Kate Spade dismissing the copyright claim.

Notes

1. Consider how each of the cases that you read attempted to separate protectable original expression from unprotectable facts, ideas, or public domain material. This is typically the most important legal component of a copyright infringement lawsuit.

2. Copyright infringement is a question of fact to be determined by the factfinder, often a jury. How well do you think lay jurors can do at recognizing public domain elements or understanding which features of a work are protectable? What role do you think expert witnesses should play in determining copyright infringement?

3. As these cases indicate, most copyright lawsuits are not based on exact duplication of the plaintiff's work by the defendant. Instead, the defendant's work is similar to the plaintiff's work. Accordingly, the court must determine how similar the defendant's work has to be in order to infringe the plaintiff's copyright. Typically, the standard is "substantial similarity." *See Nola Spice, supra*. But courts may narrow the scope the of the plaintiff's copyright in some circumstances. Where there are few opportunities for creative expression, courts typically hold that the plaintiff only receives "thin" copyright protection that protects only against "virtually identical" copying. *Satava v. Lowry*, 323 F.3d 805 (9th Cir. 2003).

4. As you saw in *Nola Spice*, the plaintiff was asserting trademark and unfair competition rights in addition to a copyright. Why might plaintiffs want to do this? Based on your understanding of trademark law from Chapter 5, how do the standards for validity and infringement differ between trademark law and copyright law? And how is trade dress law's functionality doctrine different from copyright's useful articles doctrine?

D. Limitations on Copyrights—The First Sale Doctrine and Fair Use

Although copyright law reserves to owners certain exclusive rights in their works, the law also ensures that other activities are not restrained. The two most important limitations on copyright for fashion lawyers to understand are the "first sale" doctrine and fair use.

1. The First Sale Doctrine

Copyright law gives the owner of a copyright the exclusive right to distribute copies of the work. 17 U.S.C. § 106(3). But the distribution right has historically been limited to the "first sale" of the work. *Bobbs-Merrill Co. v. Strauss*, 210 U.S. 339 (1908). That means that after a copyright owner sells a copy of a work to a purchaser, the purchaser can freely sell the work to others without the copyright owner's consent. 17 U.S.C. § 109(a). Thus, if you purchase a piece of jewelry that is covered by a copyright, you may resell the piece to another person without having to seek the copyright holder's permission.

Consider how this doctrine might apply in the fashion context. If the owner of a patch or graphic applies it to jacket, this activity is protected by the first sale doctrine. *See Lee v. A.RT. Co.*, 125 F.3d 580 (7th Cir. 1997). But the person may not reproduce copies of the patch or graphic or otherwise print multiple copies on a piece of clothing. This would violate the reproduction right.

2. Fair Use

Perhaps the most important limitation on copyright owners' exclusive rights is the fair use doctrine, which exempts from liability certain otherwise infringing behaviors. Congress included the fair use doctrine in § 107 of the Copyright Act. It reads:

> Notwithstanding the provisions of sections 106 and 106A, the fair use of a copyrighted work, including such use by reproduction in copies or phonorecords or by any other means specified by that section, for purposes such as criticism, comment, news reporting, teaching (including multiple copies for classroom use), scholarship, or research, is not an infringement of copyright. In determining whether the use made of a work in any particular case is a fair use the factors to be considered shall include—
>
> (1) the purpose and character of the use, including whether such use is of a commercial nature or is for nonprofit educational purposes;
>
> (2) the nature of the copyrighted work;
>
> (3) the amount and substantiality of the portion used in relation to the copyrighted work as a whole; and
>
> (4) the effect of the use upon the potential market for or value of the copyrighted work.
>
> The fact that a work is unpublished shall not itself bar a finding of fair use if such finding is made upon consideration of all the above factors.

Fair use can be a complicated legal standard, and we cannot explore its many details here. It is worth noting, however, that since the Supreme Court's opinion in *Campbell v. Acuff-Rose Music, Inc.*, 510 U.S. 569 (1994), the most important determinant of fair use has been whether, under the first factor, the defendant's work was "transformative" of the plaintiff's work. The question is "whether the new work merely supersedes the objects of the original creation, or instead adds something new, with a further purpose or different character, altering the first with new expression, meaning, or message." Id. at 579. If the defendant's use is transformative of the plaintiff's work, the rest of the factors will tend to tip in favor of a finding of fair use. Consider the following case.

Louis Vuitton Malletier S.A. v. Haute Diggity Dog, LLC

464 F. Supp. 2d 495 (E.D. Va. 2006)

Memorandum Opinion

CACHERIS, District Judge.

This matter comes before the Court on Plaintiff's and Defendants' cross-motions for summary judgment. This "dog of a case" gave the Court a great amount of facts to chew upon and applicable law to sniff out. Nonetheless, having thoroughly gnawed through the record, this Court finds that no material dispute of fact remains, and summary judgment is appropriate on all counts. For the following reasons, the Court will deny Plaintiff's motion and grant Defendants' motion.

I. Background

Plaintiff, Louis Vuitton Malletier S.A., ("LVM") is a manufacturer of luxury consumer goods, including luggage and handbags. In 1896, LVM created a Monogram Canvas Pattern Design mark and trade dress, which includes, inter alia, an entwined L and V monogram with three motifs and a four pointed star, and is used to identify its products. In 2002, Vuitton introduced a new signature design in collaboration with Japanese designer Takashi Murakami. LVM manufactures a limited number of high-end pet products, such as leashes and collars that range in price from $250 to $1600.

Plaintiff filed this action on March 24, 2006 against Defendants Haute Diggity Dog, LLC ("HDD"), Victoria Dauernheim, and Woofies, LLC d/b/a Woofie's Pet Boutique. HDD is a company that markets plush stuffed toys and beds for dogs under names that parody the products of other companies. HDD sells products such as Chewnel # 5, Dog Perignon, Chewy Vuiton, and Sniffany & Co. in pet stores, alongside other dog toys, bones, beds, and food, and most are priced around $10. Plaintiff's complaint specifically refers to HDD's use of the mark "Chewy Vuiton" and alleges that this mark, as well as other marks and designs that imitate Plaintiff's trademarks and copyrights, violate Plaintiff's trademark, trade dress, and copyright rights. Plaintiff and Defendants have filed cross-motions for summary judgment. These motions are currently before the Court.

[The court dismissed plaintiff's trademark and trade dress claims.]

Count IV: Copyright Violation

* * *

B. Defendants' Fair Use Defense

Defendants next argue that, even if a valid and enforceable copyright is owned by LVM, Defendants' use of the LVM design is a non-infringing, fair use of the copyrighted material for the purpose of parodying the LVM design. The Supreme

Court has developed a test to determine fair use, by which courts are to consider by a totality of the circumstances:

> (1) purpose and character of the use, including whether such use is of a commercial nature or is for nonprofit educational uses; (2) nature of the copyrighted work; (3) amount and substantiality of the portion used in relation to the copyrighted work as a whole; (4) the effect of the use upon potential market for or value of the copyrighted work.

Campbell v. Acuff-Rose Music, Inc., 510 U.S. 569, 577, 114 S.Ct. 1164, 127 L.Ed.2d 500 (1994). Fair use is an affirmative defense with the burden of proof on the defendant. *Id.* at 590, 114 S.Ct. 1164.

This Court must first consider the purpose and character of the use. Commercial use is one factor to be considered in determining fairness, and is not by itself presumptively unfair. *Id.* at 591, 114 S.Ct. 1164. Parody, even when done for the purpose of commercial gain, can be a fair use, as the Supreme Court has stated specifically that it is more likely that "the new work [a parody] will not affect the market for the original in a way cognizable under this factor, that is, by acting as a substitute for it." *Id.* at 591, 114 S.Ct. 1164. In this case, the use of similar marks and name in a line of dog chew toys and beds parodies the high-end fashion status of LVM's products in a market that LVM does not participate—the market for pet toys and beds. This Court finds that the use of similar markings and colors to those copyrighted by LVM for Chewy Vuiton products is a parody.

The next element, nature of the copyrighted work (creative) is a less-important factor for a parody case and "not much help" in separating infringers from parodies. *Id.* at 586, 114 S.Ct. 1164. Therefore, this Court will not address nature of the copyrighted work, other than to acknowledge that it is a creative design.

This Court will finally consider the amount and substantiality of the portion used in relation to the copyrighted work as a whole. The Supreme Court held that in a parody case, the parody itself

> necessarily springs from recognizable allusion to its object through distorted imitation. Its art lies in the tension between a known original and its parodic twin. When parody takes aim at a particular original work, the parody must be able to "conjure up" at least enough of that original to make the object of its critical wit recognizable.

Id. at 588, 114 S.Ct. 1164.

In this case, the name "Chewy Vuiton" is an obvious wordplay on the name Louis Vuitton, and the superimposed C and V on the logo are intended to "conjure up" enough of the Louis Vuitton logo in order to make the object of its wit—a humorous play on Louis Vuitton's high-end image in the form of dog toys—recognizable. The parody is not possible unless the logo and name are similar to those of Plaintiff, and therefore such parody constitutes a fair use in this respect.

Finally, this Court considers interference with the potential market for plaintiff's original and derivative works caused by Defendants' actions. First, the market overlap between Plaintiff and Defendants is tenuous. Louis Vuitton's primary market is for high-end women's apparel, not pet toys. As explained supra, Plaintiff does sell some pet items, but not toys or beds, and only in a limited, high-end market. Second, Plaintiff has offered no evidence of interference with potential markets or control of its copyrights. Defendants, on the other hand, have presented deposition testimony and an expert declaration indicating that there has been no effect on LVM's potential markets or control of its copyrights. (Def.'s Mot. Summ. J. Ex. E–F). For the foregoing reasons, summary judgment should be granted for the Defendants.

Notes

1. Notice how, although the defendant used a substantial amount of the plaintiff's work, the court still found the use to be fair because the defendant's parody was transformative. Courts have also noted that when considering Factor 4, the impact on the market for plaintiff's work, the law will not consider the possibility of a market for parodies or the negative effects created by a scathing parody.

2. Consider whether the following would qualify as fair use:

Chapter 5

Trademark

Marc Reiner and Ted Max

A. The Importance of Trademarks in Fashion

One of the most important assets owned by a fashion company is its brand name. A company's brand is a signifier of its quality, its flair, and its exclusivity. Although fashions often change from year to year, the strength of a company's core brands can continue to grow steadily if the company protects those brands. Unlike copyrights or patents, trademark rights stem from use in commerce and do not expire so long as they continue to be used and recognized by the public as identifying a single source of goods. Trademarks allow brands to invest in the quality of their goods along with advertising such quality without worry that a newcomer will steal the goodwill the brand has accumulated by attempting to use the same trademark. One of the reasons luxury brands may price their pieces so high is because the public ascribes a certain value to the worth of the good due to the trademark.

Trademark rights are based on the ability of a trademark to be associated with a singular source in the minds of a segment of the public. As a result, trademarks are not limited to particular words or logos. Anything that identifies a singular company or source of goods can be a protectable trademark. For example, the distinctive shade of blue used by Tiffany & Co. on its packaging is the subject of a trademark registration, as is the red color used on the soles of heels sold by Christian Louboutin. Burberry's distinctive plaid is claimed as a trademark by the company, as are the green-red-green stripes used by Gucci. Levi Strauss claims the exclusive right to use a red tag on the back pocket of jeans and Adidas asserts that virtually any three-stripe design on apparel or footwear infringes its trademark rights.

Trademark protection is available for unregistered trademarks, but that protection is limited in geographical scope to only the areas where the goods in question are sold. In contrast, a federal trademark registration on the Principal Register of the U.S. Patent and Trademark Office ("PTO") gives the owner of the registration a nationwide right of priority and is prima facie evidence of the validity of the registered mark. 15 U.S.C. § 1057. It is therefore advisable to seek a registration at the earliest possible opportunity.

Most fashion brands do not have only one trademark that they use. Typically, there is an overarching trademark that applies to all the company's goods and a series of trademarks that are associated with the style names or categories beneath that larger trademark. Each of these trademarks is eligible for registration, but companies often do not apply for registrations for trademarks of styles that are only temporarily being sold by the company. Best practices include regular meetings between branding professionals and trademark counsel to ensure the style names that are used in upcoming seasons do not conflict with the trademark rights of others. In addition, these discussions should include whether any current style names should be registered.

B. Choosing and Registering a Trademark

Considering the importance of a company's trademark, the selection of that mark is crucial and must be done carefully and dispassionately. Companies cannot select generic or merely descriptive names for their trademarks because to grant only one company the exclusive use of these words would harm competition. Generic and merely descriptive words are necessary for all competitors to describe and market their goods fairly. This legal principle often leads to an initial conflict between a company's marketing professionals and its legal advisors. Marketing experts often prefer an informative brand name that describes the nature of the goods in order to reduce the costs to inform the public about the quality of the goods. Attorneys will generally push back and advise that such a descriptive trademark would be less likely to register and to defend against infringers.

As described in the case below, trademarks fall along a spectrum from "strong" to "weak," with generic and merely descriptive trademarks being weak or even unprotectable. The more mental leaps between a mark and the good or service that it identifies, the stronger the mark will be. An arbitrary (no connection) or fanciful (made up) mark will be inherently distinctive, whereas a generic mark will not be distinctive at all and will garner no protection. Secondary meaning is when a company can prove that their mark identifies their good or service in the eyes of the public and it can be used to provide trademark protection to a descriptive mark. Do you agree with the Court's categorization of the mark at issue in the following case?

20th Century Wear, Inc. v. Sanmark-Stardust Inc.

747 F.2d 81 (2d Cir. 1984)

OAKES, Circuit Judge.

This appeal involves a registered trademark—"Cozy Warm ENERGY-SAVERS"—in connection with the sale of flannel pajamas and nightgowns. The United States District Court for the Southern District of New York, Robert L. Carter, *Judge,* found "Cozy Warm ENERGY-SAVERS" to be a "suggestive" term entitled to trademark protection; and it subsequently found defendant liable for trademark infringement under section 32(1) of the Lanham Trade-Mark Act, 15 U.S.C. § 1114(1) (1982). In addition, the court noted that the infringer's practices also violated state unfair competition law. The judgment awarded a permanent injunction and $252,982.52 in damages (including $81,718.67 paid in commissions by the infringer to its selling agent), plus prejudgment interest at 9% from October 9, 1981, and $25,000 in attorneys' fees. We reverse and remand for further findings with respect to the protection of the trademark and to defendant's liability under New York state unfair competition law.

Background

In the shadow of the energy crisis of 1973, the OPEC oil price increases, and the resultant impairment of the United States economy and individual standards of living, the United States government, aided by private industries, editorial opinion and numerous other sources, made a tremendous effort to impress the importance of energy saving and conservation on the American public. This campaign took many forms, from the publication of Department of Energy "tips" to Department of Agriculture Energy Management Checklists. There was a National Energy Plan, a Federal Energy Administration—later the Department of Energy—and an enormous effort at all levels of government to promote energy efficiency. Examples of the public and private interest in energy efficiency include the federal imposition of the 55-mile per hour speed limit, the introduction of smaller and lighter automobiles, and public acceptance of hundreds of other new or neglected products and measures designed to conserve electricity, home heating oil, gas, and all other forms of energy—housing insulation, heating insulation, window shades, lamp adaptors and dimmers, storm windows and doors, shower heads, caulking strips, wood stoves, fewer window openings to the north, greater use of solar energy, to mention just a few examples.

Not surprisingly, this national movement was partially focused on the use in winter of warm clothing to permit the lowering of temperatures in homes, office buildings, factories, government buildings, and so on—as perhaps epitomized by the President's appearing on national television in his cardigan sweater. Clothing makers, as well as purveyors of household items such as sheets, blankets, comforters, blanket throws and drapes, took to advertising their products as "saving energy," "energy saving," and the like. Department stores and clothing stores did likewise in reference to, among other things, sweaters, underwear, robes, gowns, nightshirts, children's sleepers, boots and so-called body warmers or wraparounds, which doubled as comforters. For example, the "Bundle-Up" was advertised as an "all purpose energy saver . . . to keep warm," providing "superior insulation . . . and cozy warmth." The consumer was urged to "turn your thermostat down, conserve energy and still be comfortable."

* * *

The Facts in this Case

20th Century Wear, Inc. (20th Century), is a New York corporation in the wholesale business of importing and selling women's pajamas and nightgowns to retailers, mail order and discount houses and other merchandisers. Sanmark-Stardust, Inc. (Sanmark), is a New York corporation—incidentally situated in the building next to 20th Century's—that deals in many other forms of clothing in addition to women's pajamas and nightgowns.

20th Century markets its pajamas in the customary form of a transparent plastic bag containing the garment and various tags. Sewn onto the collar of the garment is a tag bearing the name "20th Century" in blue, and below that the phrases "guaranteed washable" in red and "100% cotton" in blue. Three hang tags accompany the product. One of them includes a picture of a woman with her hands on her hips modeling the packaged garment, a printed description of the garment, and the slogan "for the style of your life" printed in red. The second tag contains the cotton producers' well-known "Cotton Boll" logo, the phrases "A Natural Fiber" and "As Seen on the Today Show," and the 20th Century name. The third insert has a red background and white border with bold print "Cozy Warm ENERGY-SAVERS" in white with the trademark notice. The writing appears diagonally across the rectangular tag. A bold line appears under the last two letters of "ENERGY" and the first five letters of "SAVERS."

The United States Patent & Trademark Office accepted the mark "Cozy Warm ENERGY-SAVERS" for registration on March 17, 1981, for use with pajamas, nightgowns, dusters (three-quarter length cotton robes), and loungewear. It required, however, that 20th Century disclaim exclusive use of the words "cozy" and "warm" apart from the mark as registered. *See* Registration No. 1,148,448 (Int'l Class 25, 37 C.F.R. § 6.1(25) (1984)) ("No claim is made to exclusive use of 'cozy' and 'warm' apart from the mark as shown.").

Beginning in July, 1981, and continuing until October 19, 1981, Sanmark sold women's pajamas and nightgowns under the "Sheila Anne" label and used a tag bearing the words "Cozy Warm CONSERVES-ENERGY" in connection therewith. Like many other pajama wholesalers, Sanmark's products are also packaged in transparent cellophane wrapping. The collar tag lists the name "Sheila Anne" in blue print lettering, and underneath, in smaller lettering, "pre-shrunk," "guaranteed machine washable," and "100% cotton," with the size indicated in red. The Sanmark transparent plastic bag also contains three hang tags. One describes the garment and depicts a woman with her hands on her hips modeling the garment. The second insert, in white and blue, contains the cotton producers' logo and the phrase "Made of A Natural Fiber." The third insert has a white border and blue background with the phrase "Cozy Warm" in red under which, in white, is the phrase "CONSERVES-ENERGY" underscored with a red line. The writing appears diagonally across the rectangular tag in type that is virtually the same size, style, and format as the type used by 20th Century. Even the hyphen, which is grammatically unnecessary, simulates the distinctive type style of the hyphen in 20th Century's mark. A bold line, similar to that used by 20th Century, appears under the last three letters of "CONSERVES" and the first four letters of "ENERGY."

The district court held Sanmark liable for trademark infringement. The court began by noting that the opposing parties sell to many of the same customers, generally shops, stores, and clothing chains, and that 20th Century's sales fell off when Sanmark began selling its Sheila Anne pajamas and nightgowns. Turning to trademark law, the court stated that the registered trademark "does not bring women's pajamas and nightgowns to mind, and requires 'imaginative [*sic*] thought and perception,' *Stix Products, Inc. v. United Merchants & Manufacturers, Inc.*, 295 F. Supp. 479, 488 (S.D.N.Y.1968), to relate the mark to women's sleepwear." Accordingly, purporting to follow *Abercrombie & Fitch Co. v. Hunting World, Inc.*, 537 F.2d 4, 11 (2d Cir. 1976), the district court held that the mark was suggestive, not descriptive, and entitled to protection without regard to whether the mark had acquired a secondary meaning.

The court also concluded that there was a likelihood of confusion between Sanmark's trade dress and mark and those used by 20th Century. The court, by visual examination of the packaged products, found that an appreciable number of ordinary, prudent purchasers were likely to be confused or misled into believing that Sanmark's garments were 20th Century's. According to the court, Sanmark's "Cozy Warm CONSERVES-ENERGY" is confusingly similar to 20th Century's registered trademark, and "the imitative trade dress compounds the confusion." But while the court found a violation under section 32(1) of the Lanham Trade-Mark Act, 15 U.S.C. § 1114(1), it did not find a federal false designation of origin violation under section 43(a) of the Act, 15 U.S.C. § 1125(a). In the court's view, a claim of false designation of origin could not stand, because Sanmark had clearly marked its products as a Sheila Anne design. The court then stated that "while it is clear that" Sanmark and its selling agent, Domino Industries, "are guilty of unfair competition under New York law, . . . since [20th Century was given] complete relief under federal statutes, the violation of New York law adds nothing to [20th Century's] entitlement to recovery."

Discussion

1. Trademark Infringement

Section 32(1)(a) of the Lanham Trade-Mark Act, 15 U.S.C. § 1114(1)(a), provides a federal cause of action for trademark infringement when a "colorable imitation of a registered mark . . . is likely to cause confusion." Success depends on "whether there is any likelihood that an appreciable number of ordinarily prudent purchasers are likely to be misled, or indeed simply confused, as to the source of the goods in question." *Mushroom Makers, Inc. v. R.G. Barry Corp.*, 580 F.2d 44, 47 (2d Cir. 1978). This court has repeatedly held that a finding of infringement turns on an assessment of several factors including the strength of the senior user's mark, the similarity of the marks, the similarity of the products and the trade dress, actual confusion, the junior user's good faith, and the sophistication of the buyers. *See, e.g., Spring Mills, Inc. v. Ultracashmere House, Ltd.*, 689 F.2d 1127, 1129 (2d Cir. 1982); *Polaroid Corp. v. Polarad Electronics Corp.*, 287 F.2d 492, 495 (2d Cir. 1961); *see also Toys 'R' Us, Inc. v. Canarsie Kiddie Shop, Inc.*, 559 F. Supp. 1189, 1195 (E.D.N.Y. 1983). In this case, we address the strength of the mark "Cozy Warm ENERGY-SAVERS," and remand for further findings on whether the mark has acquired secondary meaning.

As Judge Friendly's opinion in *Abercrombie & Fitch*, 537 F.2d at 9, points out, there are four different levels of trademark protection: (1) generic (not entitled to protection even with proof of secondary meaning), (2) descriptive (entitled to protection with proof of secondary meaning), (3) suggestive (entitled to protection without proof of secondary meaning), and (4) arbitrary or fanciful (enjoying "the rights accorded to suggestive terms as marks—without the need of debating whether the term is 'merely descriptive,'" *id.* at 11). The difficulty, of course, lies in determining what level of protection a particular mark deserves. This determination in turn depends upon the particular context of the mark's use, the context of its time of use, and the context of its group of users. *See Abercrombie & Fitch*, 537 F.2d at 9; *see also McGregor-Doniger, Inc. v. Drizzle, Inc.*, 599 F.2d 1126, 1131 (2d Cir. 1979). Making such a determination—pigeonholing or labeling—has always been a slippery business, as Cardozo reminded us so many times. *See, e.g., Henneford v. Silas Mason Co.*, 300 U.S. 577, 586, 57 S. Ct. 524, 528, 81 L. Ed. 814 (1937); *Techt v. Hughes*, 229 N.Y. 222, 246, 128 N.E. 185, 193 (1920); Cardozo, *Mr. Justice Holmes*, 44 Harv. L. Rev. 682, 689 (1931), *reprinted in Selected Writings of Benjamin N. Cardozo* 83 (1947).

This case involves the distinction between suggestive and descriptive terms, a distinction, Judge Friendly noted, "that the courts have had great difficulty in defining." *Abercrombie & Fitch*, 537 F.2d at 10. A useful standard, however, can be stated:

> A term is suggestive if it requires imagination, thought and perception to reach a conclusion as to the nature of goods. A term is descriptive if it forthwith conveys an immediate idea of the ingredients, qualities or characteristics of the goods.

Stix Products, Inc. v. United Merchants & Manufacturers, Inc., 295 F. Supp. 479, 488 (S.D.N.Y. 1968), *quoted in Abercrombie & Fitch*, 573 F.2d at 11.

We hold that "Cozy Warm ENERGY-SAVERS" is a descriptive term. The district court mischaracterized the mark because it failed to consider how the meaning of the words "Cozy Warm ENERGY-SAVERS" had changed over time. The court assumed that a step of the imagination is needed to connect the concept of energy saving to women's pajamas and concluded that the mark is "suggestive" rather than "descriptive." And it may be true that such a step would have been needed, say, in 1973 or 1975. But by 1981, the connection between "Cozy Warm ENERGY-SAVERS" and the warming quality of plaintiff's pajama no longer required imagination, since many people were using this kind of language to describe clothing.

As one of the leading commentators reminds us, a term can be descriptive in two ways. It can literally describe the product, or it can describe the purpose or utility of the product. Under the first branch, "if qualities, ingredients, effects or other features of the product are indicated naturally and in ordinary language, so that the consumer understands its significance without any exercise of the imagination, the words are descriptive." 3 R. Callmann, *supra* note 6, § 18.05, at 17. Under the second brand, Callmann distinguishes among three subcategories of marks that describe the product's purpose or utility: (1) marks describing the problem or condition that the trademarked product is designed to remedy or otherwise deal with; (2) marks that describe the use to which the product or service is put; and (3) marks that describe the effect that the product or service is supposed to produce after it is used. *Id.* at 27. He notes that courts generally hold that marks in the first two subcategories are descriptive, but that some courts have improperly tended to hold that marks in the third subcategory are not descriptive of goods or services. *Id.* at 17, 27–29.

Had this suit been brought before the energy crisis, we might well have concluded that the mark was suggestive. But by the time of the alleged infringement, "Cozy Warm ENERGY-SAVERS" fell on the descriptive rather than the suggestive side of a shifting line and as such was not entitled to protection absent proof of secondary meaning. "Cozy Warm ENERGY-SAVERS" defies Callmann's subcategorization. It does describe the quality of warming that wearing the flannel pajamas or nightwear involves, and hence the effect of such wearing, since the use of flannel pajamas presumably permits one to turn down the heat somewhat lower at night. It also describes the problem or condition—energy waste—with which the product deals, however indirectly. Numerous clothing businesses and hundreds, if not thousands, of other businesses as a result of the energy crisis began using "energy saving" and "cozy warm" to describe or extol the virtues of their products. In the wake of this common usage, the public was so well educated to the concept of something "cozy warm" as an "energy saver" that consumers did not have to engage in any sort of multistage reasoning process to link the term to the virtues of any number of products, including but not limited to flannel pajamas and nightgowns. *See id.* § 18.09, at 55 ("[c]onsumer reaction to the mark, at the time in question, is the test"); Restatement (Second) of Torts § 721, at 85 (Tent.Draft No. 8 1963) ("The test [for descriptiveness] is the meaning attached to the designation by prospective purchasers. . . .").

This usage is seen more readily perhaps by noting that the class of products for which 20th Century was given a registered mark included dusters and loungewear, not merely pajamas and nightgowns. Any clothing made for warmth—bathrobes, gowns, "body warmers" or the like—thus falls within the scope of the registered trademark. As we have said, makers of all kinds of warm clothing had sought to capitalize on the connection in the public's mind between wearing warm clothing and saving energy. Comforters, blankets, sheets, bathrobes and numerous other products associated with the human way of sleeping are and have been advertised as energy saving because they are "warm," "cozy," "snuggy," "trapping body heat," "thermal," "snuggle soft" and "snuggle warm," "warm as a bunny hug from top to toe," "toasty to your toes."

* * *

This analysis is also supported by the rationale for distinguishing between suggestive and descriptive terms and the purpose behind the protection of trademarks. Trademarks identify the source of a product and hence protect the source's good will. *See United Drug Co. v. Theodore Rectanus Co.,* 248 U.S. 90, 97, 39 S. Ct. 48, 50,

63 L. Ed. 141 (1918); *Field Enterprises Educational Corp. v. Cove Industries*, 297 F. Supp. 989, 994 (E.D.N.Y. 1969); 3 R. Callmann, *supra* note 6, § 18.03, at 7. Descriptive terms deserve less protection than suggestive terms both because descriptive terms normally do not distinguish among similar products and because such terms "should not be monopolized by a single use." *Id.* The common usage of "cozy warm" and "energy savers" suggests that the terms cannot be used to distinguish 20th Century's clothing. In addition, exclusive use of the term might unfairly "monopolize" common speech.

All the foregoing assumes, of course, that the phrase "Cozy Warm ENERGY-SAVERS" in connection with women's flannel pajamas has not acquired secondary meaning. As noted above, the mark still deserves protection if plaintiffs can show "that the primary significance of the term in the minds of the consuming public is not the product but the producer." *Kellogg Co. v. National Biscuit Co.*, 305 U.S. 111, 118, 59 S. Ct. 109, 113, 83 L. Ed. 73 (1938). The record shows that 20th Century entered proof of secondary meaning at trial. Thus, appellant argues that even if we hold that the mark is descriptive we should find that the mark deserves protection because it has acquired secondary meaning. We remand, however, for an assessment of the evidence of secondary meaning by the district court. We note first that "proof of secondary meaning entails vigorous evidentiary requirements," *Ralston Purina Co. v. Thomas J. Lipton, Inc.*, 341 F. Supp. 129, 134 (S.D.N.Y. 1972), and that 20th Century has the burden of showing that the term had acquired secondary meaning in the summer of 1981 when Sanmark first began using its phrase on hang tags, *see Saratoga Vichy Spring Co., Inc. v. Lehman*, 625 F.2d 1037, 1043 (2d Cir. 1980); *Le Sportsac, Inc. v. Dockside Research, Inc.*, 478 F. Supp. 602, 608 (S.D.N.Y. 1979). In assessing whether 20th Century has satisfied this heavy burden, there are many forms of evidence that help show secondary meaning, including how long the mark has been used, *see Saratoga Vichy Spring Co. v. Lehman*, 491 F. Supp. 141, 150 (N.D.N.Y. 1979), *aff'd*, 625 F.2d 1037 (2d Cir. 1980), whether consumer studies, *see Grotrian, Helfferich, Shultz, TH. Steinweg Nachf. v. Steinway and Sons*, 523 F.2d 1331, 1340–41 (2d Cir. 1975), or successful advertising, *see McGregor-Doniger Inc. v. Drizzle, Inc.*, 599 F.2d at 1132, 1133 n. 4, show that the purchasing public associated the phrase with 20th Century's goods; or even whether Sanmark intentionally copied the term, *see Mastercrafters Clock & Radio Co. v. Vacheron & Constantin-Le Coultre Watches, Inc.*, 221 F.2d 464, 467 (2d Cir. 1955); 3 R. Callmann, *supra* note 6, § 19.27, at 93. *See also RJR Foods v. White Rock Corp.*, 603 F.2d 1058, 1060 (2d Cir. 1979).

In sum, "Cozy Warm ENERGY-SAVERS" does not deserve the protection accorded to suggestive marks. Nevertheless, if the district court finds that the term has acquired secondary meaning, the court can, of course, go on to find likelihood of confusion as to source, and thus trademark infringement.

* * *

Judgment reversed and remanded for further proceedings in accordance with this opinion.

Notes

1. This opinion spends considerable "energy" on whether 20th Century's trademark should be classified as descriptive or as suggestive. The implication of that determination is whether the trademark owner needs to meet the heavy burden of proving secondary meaning, for a descriptive trademark, or whether the trademark is suggestive and therefore may be protected without such a showing. Most battles about trademark classification are fought over whether trademarks are descriptive or suggestive. Do you believe that descriptive and suggestive trademarks are so distinct from one another as to justify such a disparate treatment under the law?

2. One noteworthy feature of this opinion is the court's acknowledgement that the ENERGY-SAVERS trademark would have been considered suggestive before the energy crisis of the mid- to late- 1970s, though after those events the trademark was descriptive for warm apparel. Is it possible that apparel manufacturers such as 20th Century could have led to trademarks such as ENERGY-SAVERS becoming descriptive rather than suggestive? That is, the prevalence of apparel in that category could have made a distinctive trademark a common one. What can a trademark holder do to keep this phenomenon from happening?

3. Arbitrary and fanciful trademarks are among the most conceptually distinctive of trademarks. Fanciful trademarks are generally those that are invented solely for their use as trademarks, such as Xerox or Exxon. Arbitrary trademarks are common or preexisting words that are applied in an unfamiliar way, such as Apple computers, Delta airlines, or Starbucks coffee. These two classes of trademarks are generally treated as having the same conceptual strength. But should they be? Preexisting words already have an association of some sort in the minds of consumers, perhaps even with another brand such as Apple music or Delta faucets. Although these trademarks are not descriptive and therefore need not be used by competitors, the association between the trademark and the particular company may be greatly weakened by the other associations that accompany the trademark.

1. Trademark Searches and Willful Infringement

When selecting a trademark, marketing objectives can routinely conflict with legal objectives. Marketing professionals often look to select a trademark that eases their job of communicating the essential qualities of the product. Trademark counsel, in contrast, is concerned with whether the proposed trademark is available and protectable. The more descriptive and informative that a trademark is, the less likely that it will be exclusive to the brand. As discussed in the case below, one company is not allowed to monopolize a term that is used to describe an essential quality of a product. The strongest and most protectable trademarks are the ones that have no meaning other than as a source indicator for a brand.

A common error for fashion startups, and even some established brands, is failure to retain trademark counsel at the outset of a brand's lifecycle. This omission is understandable because counsel can be expensive for a brand that is seeking to save money, but failure to conduct a search and seek trademark protection can be far more expensive down the line. For example, a fashion startup might seek funding based on a trademark, create labels, prepare marketing materials, secure a domain name and prepare a website, and only then think to have counsel determine if the trademark is available. As would be expected, it is extremely disruptive and expensive at this point to change the company's chosen trademark. The only thing more expensive is to be sued and incur significant legal bills later on.

Counsel from experienced trademark attorneys can avoid this type of problem and should be sought at the earliest possible instance. The goal of a trademark search is to ensure that the chosen trademark is sufficiently distinctive and that there is not an undue risk of conflict with an existing trademark owner. There are two types of searches. The PTO provides online search options through its "TESS" website that laypeople can use; this may be called a knockout search. But for important decisions such as a fashion company's signature brand, it is best to rely upon the professional opinion of counsel as to the risks involved and the likelihood of conflict with other trademark owners. Even when a search has been conducted, the results are often mixed. For example, someone may have registered a similar trademark for somewhat different products. The identification of potential conflicts in advance can help a fashion company avoid expensive litigation or the changing of a brand well into production. In addition, the failure to conduct a full search can be evidence of "willful" trademark infringement in a subsequent lawsuit, as can the adoption of a trademark in the face of adverse search results, as seen in the following case. The following case is an appeal of the district court's holding that monetary relief was not available because of its finding that there was no "willfulness" by the defendant. The Supreme Court has since held that willfulness is not a prerequisite for a monetary award under the Lanham Act. *See Romag Fasteners, Inc. v. Fossil Group, Inc.*, No. 18-1233 (U.S. Apr. 23, 2020). The Court further held, however, that willfulness is "a highly important consideration in determining whether an award of profits is appropriate" (*id.*), therefore the interplay between trademark searches and willfulness remains highly relevant.

International Star Class Yacht Racing Ass'n v. Tommy Hilfiger, U.S.A., Inc.

80 F.3d 749 (2d Cir. 1996)

OAKES, Senior Circuit Judge.

This appeal involves the availability of monetary relief and attorney fees in a trademark infringement action brought under § 43(a) of the Lanham Act, 15 U.S.C. § 1125(a) (1994). The International Star Class Yacht Racing Association ("ISCYRA") appeals from a portion of the judgment of the United States District Court for the Southern District of New York (Robert P. Patterson, Jr., Judge), entered on May 19, 1995. The district court, after a bench trial, granted ISCYRA's application for a permanent injunction against use of its "STAR CLASS" mark by the appellee Tommy Hilfiger U.S.A., Inc. ("Hilfiger") but denied injunctive relief as to ISCYRA's insignia, a solid five-pointed star. The district court also denied ISCYRA an accounting of Hilfiger's profits, actual damages, and attorney fees.

ISCYRA contends that the district court's denial of an accounting and fees was based on its erroneous finding that Hilfiger showed no bad faith in the use of ISCYRA's unregistered mark. ISCYRA also argues that there was sufficient consumer confusion generated by Hilfiger's products to justify the award of actual damages. Finally, ISCYRA contests the district court's conclusion that it is entitled to no trademark protection for its five-pointed star insignia. Because we find that the district court made erroneous and incomplete factual findings on the issue of Hilfiger's bad faith, we vacate its denial of an accounting of profits and attorney fees and remand for reconsideration of the bad faith issue. On the other two points, we affirm.

Background

ISCYRA is a non-profit corporation founded in 1922 for the purpose of governing and promoting the sport of Star Class yacht racing. Star Class sailboats are sophisticated one-design racing craft sailed in high-profile regattas and championship series around the world, including the Summer Olympics. ISCYRA owns the rights to the design of Star Class boats and closely monitors the construction, certification, and registration of each boat in the class. One requirement of a genuine Star Class boat is that its main sail bear the solid red five-pointed star which serves as ISCYRA's insignia or a star of green, blue, silver or gold awarded at ISCYRA championship races. The red star is also used, along with the words "STAR CLASS," on the yachting hats, clothing, flags, decals and pins sold by ISCYRA. ISCYRA permits yacht clubs hosting regattas to use the insignia and "STAR CLASS" on promotional items, and has collected royalties for their use in jewelry and posters.

Hilfiger is a successful designer and marketer of men's clothing with sales of over $227 million in 1993. Its 1994 Spring Collection included garments bearing the words "STAR CLASS" with a solid red five-pointed star. These garments were marketed as "classic nautical sportswear" with "authentic details taken from the sport of competitive sailing" and "elements and patterns taken directly from actual racing sails." Hilfiger's name and flag trademarks also appeared prominently on all the garments, which were marketed in the United States and abroad.

While designing the 1994 Spring Collection, Hilfiger requested a trademark screening search for the words "STAR CLASS" from its attorneys. Hilfiger did not specify that it planned to use the words on "nautical" clothing with details from "competitive sailing," and the search was limited to federal trademarks in class 25, a clothing classification. The screening search did not reveal any identical registered or applied-for federal trademarks, but Hilfiger's attorneys advised it to conduct a "full trademark search" before using the words "STAR CLASS." Hilfiger did not conduct such a search until after it was sued by ISCYRA, at which point it learned that "STAR CLASS" was indeed a mark in the yachting context.

In April 1994, ISCYRA initiated this action against Hilfiger for false designation of origin under §43(a) of the Lanham Act, 15 U.S.C. §1125(a) (1994), common law trademark infringement and unfair competition, and injury to business reputation and trademark dilution under New York state law. Despite notice of ISCYRA's suit and the results of the full trademark search, Hilfiger did not recall its allegedly infringing merchandise from retailers and had sold over $3 million worth of garments bearing the "STAR CLASS" mark by the time the case came to trial in January 1995. No one from Hilfiger took the witness stand during the two-day bench trial.

The district court granted ISCYRA's application for a permanent injunction under the Lanham Act against use of its "STAR CLASS" mark by Hilfiger, but denied injunctive relief as to ISCYRA's insignia, a solid five-pointed star. The district court also denied ISCYRA's request for accounting of profits, actual damages, and attorney fees, and dismissed ISCYRA's state law and unfair competition claims.

On appeal, ISCYRA argues that the district court erred in denying an accounting and attorney fees based on its conclusion that Hilfiger did not act in bad faith in using the "STAR CLASS" mark. ISCYRA maintains that (1) Hilfiger's failure to conduct a comprehensive trademark search; (2) Hilfiger's failure to recall garments bearing "STAR CLASS" from its inventory and its continued sales of these garments after ISCYRA's lawsuit put it on notice of ISCYRA's common law trademark; and (3) the evidence of Hilfiger's intentional copying of ISCYRA's mark were sufficient to establish bad faith and warrant both an accounting of Hilfiger's profits and the award of attorney fees. ISCYRA further argues that the district court clearly erred both in denying actual damages because no actual confusion was caused by Hilfiger's merchandise and in finding that ISCYRA had no protectable trademark rights in its five-pointed star insignia. We agree with ISCYRA that the district court's bad faith finding is based on incomplete findings of fact and erroneous conclusions. We therefore vacate the denial of an accounting of profits and attorney fees, which rested on the finding of an absence of bad faith, and remand the case to the district court for reconsideration of Hilfiger's bad faith. We affirm the remainder of the district court's decision.

Discussion

I. The Standards for Monetary Relief and Attorney Fees

Section 35(a) of the Lanham Act governs claims for monetary relief and attorney fees made by plaintiffs who have successfully established a trademark violation. It provides:

> the plaintiff shall be entitled, . . . subject to the principles of equity, to recover (1) defendant's profits, (2) any damages sustained by the plaintiff, and (3) the costs of the action. . . . The court in exceptional cases may award reasonable attorney fees to the prevailing party.

15 U.S.C. § 1117(a) (1994). Applying Section 35(a), the district court found that ISCYRA could not recover an accounting of Hilfiger's profits, actual damages, or attorney fees. We review the district court's decision for abuse of discretion. *George Basch Co., Inc. v. Blue Coral, Inc.*, 968 F.2d 1532, 1537 (2d Cir.), *cert. denied*, 506 U.S.

991, 113 S. Ct. 510, 121 L. Ed. 2d 445 (1992); *Goodheart Clothing Co., Inc. v. Laura Goodman Enterprises, Inc.*, 962 F.2d 268, 272 (2d Cir. 1992).

Proof of actual confusion is ordinarily required for recovery of damages for pecuniary loss sustained by the plaintiff. *Restatement (Third) of Unfair Competition* § 36 cmt. i (1995). Such damages may include compensation for (1) lost sales or revenue; (2) sales at lower prices; (3) harm to market reputation; or (4) expenditures to prevent, correct, or mitigate consumer confusion. *Id.* at § 36(2). Because ISCYRA offered no evidence of actual confusion caused by Hilfiger's infringing use of the "STAR CLASS" mark and indeed presented no evidence of pecuniary loss, remedy for these actual damages is not available.

The unavailability of actual damages as a remedy, however, does not preclude ISCYRA from recovering an accounting of Hilfiger's profits or attorney fees. In order to recover an accounting of an infringer's profits, a plaintiff must prove that the infringer acted in bad faith. *Restatement (Third), supra,* § 37 cmt. e; *George Basch Co.*, 968 F.2d at 1540; *see also Resource Developers, Inc. v. Statue of Liberty-Ellis Island Foundation, Inc.*, 926 F.2d 134, 139–40 (2d Cir. 1991); *W.E. Bassett Co. v. Revlon, Inc.*, 435 F.2d 656, 664 (2d Cir. 1970). Similarly, an award of attorney fees may be justified when bad faith infringement has been shown. *Goodheart Clothing*, 962 F.2d at 272; *Quaker State Oil Refining Corp. v. Kooltone, Inc.*, 649 F.2d 94, 95 (2d Cir. 1981) (per curiam). In order to determine whether the district court abused its discretion in denying an accounting of Hilfiger's profits and an award of attorney fees, we therefore must turn to its finding that Hilfiger did not act in bad faith when it infringed on ISCYRA's mark.

II. The District Court's Bad Faith Finding

The district court's conclusion that Hilfiger did not act in bad faith or willfully infringe in its use of the "STAR CLASS" mark was based on several factual findings which we review for clear error. *Bambu Sales, Inc. v. Ozak Trading Inc.*, 58 F.3d 849, 854 (2d Cir. 1995); *Nikon, Inc. v. Ikon Corp.*, 987 F.2d 91, 94 (2d Cir. 1993). For the following reasons, we hold these findings to be clearly erroneous and incomplete, necessitating a remand to the district court for further consideration of the issue.

Initially, we note a factual error in the district court's opinion which goes directly to the question of the willfulness of Hilfiger's infringement. The district court stated that the trademark search conducted by Hilfiger prior to its use of ISCYRA's "STAR CLASS" mark was of federal and state marks. In fact, the search was limited solely to registered or applied-for *federal* trademarks; despite its attorneys' advice that a wider search be conducted, Hilfiger did not do one until after ISCYRA filed its suit.

The district court relied on Hilfiger's limited first search as proof that Hilfiger did not "engage in a deceptive commercial practice" or otherwise act in bad faith in using ISCYRA's mark. We are not convinced, however, that such a limited search should exonerate Hilfiger, particularly when Hilfiger ignored the specific advice of its attorneys to search more thoroughly.

The district court also found that although Hilfiger intentionally copied ISCYRA's "STAR CLASS" mark, it did not intend to copy a trademark owned by another. The court recognized that Hilfiger's failure to offer a "credible innocent explanation" for its use of ISCYRA's mark could support an inference of bad faith under *Centaur Communications, Ltd. v. A/S/M Communications,* 830 F.2d 1217, 1228 (2d Cir. 1987). The court nevertheless concluded that Hilfiger had not willfully infringed on ISCYRA's mark, citing as evidence the limited trademark search discussed above.

In light of Hilfiger's minimal efforts to ascertain whether "STAR CLASS" was, in fact, a trademark, we agree with ISCYRA that the district court clearly erred in finding Hilfiger guilty only of simple copying and not of intent to copy a mark. Given Hilfiger's awareness that it was copying "authentic details . . . from the sport of competitive sailing," it should have shown greater concern for the possibility that it was infringing on another's mark. Hilfiger's choice not to perform a full search under these circumstances reminds us of two of the famous trio of monkeys who, by covering their eyes and ears, neither saw nor heard any evil. Such willful ignorance should not provide a means by which Hilfiger can evade its obligations under trademark law.

In addition to the district court's two clearly erroneous findings, we believe that its analysis of Hilfiger's bad faith was incomplete. First, the district court did not address the fact that Hilfiger failed to conduct a full trademark search on "STAR CLASS" before using the mark in direct contravention of the advice of its attorneys. Other courts have found that an infringer who "acts in reasonable reliance on the advice of counsel" generally cannot be said to have acted in bad faith. *See, e.g., Sands, Taylor & Wood Co. v. Quaker Oats Co.,* 978 F.2d 947, 962 (7th Cir. 1992), *cert. denied,* 507 U.S. 1042, 113 S. Ct. 1879, 123 L. Ed. 2d 497 (1993); *Cuisinarts, Inc. v. Robot-Coupe Int'l Corp.,* 580 F. Supp. 634, 637–39 (S.D.N.Y. 1984). Conversely, the *failure* to follow the advice of counsel given before the infringement must factor into an assessment of an infringer's bad faith.

Second, the district court gave no consideration to Hilfiger's conduct after ISCYRA brought suit for trademark infringement. The suit gave Hilfiger notice of its potential trademark violation, and the full trademark search that it conducted soon thereafter confirmed the existence of ISCYRA's mark. Hilfiger nonetheless continued to sell its merchandise with the infringing mark, racking up over $3 million in sales, without regard for the rights of ISCYRA. As counsel for Hilfiger admitted during oral argument, Hilfiger was betting on the fact that ISCYRA would not prevail in its suit. Hilfiger lost that bet, and should not escape the consequences of its conduct. *See Stuart v. Collins,* 489 F. Supp. 827, 832 (S.D.N.Y. 1980) (finding willful infringement when defendant continued to use plaintiff's mark after plaintiff's attorney demanded that it cease, thereby giving "short shrift to plaintiff's claim out of arrogance and confidence that he would not mount any significant legal attack"); *see also Polo Fashions, Inc. v. Dick Bruhn, Inc.,* 793 F.2d 1132, 1135 (9th Cir. 1986) (courts should remove economic incentive to engage in infringing activity); *W.E. Bassett Co.*, 435 F.2d at 664 (an accounting of profits serves to deter willful infringers).

As recognized by the Restatement, an accounting of profits should be limited to cases of fraudulent infringement, i.e. "to acts intended to create confusion or deceive prospective purchasers," *Restatement (Third), supra,* § 37 cmt. e, and not be awarded in cases where a defendant "deliberately but in good faith used a mark." *Id.* We note that, under this standard, Hilfiger cannot lay claim to a "good faith" belief that it was not infringing on ISCYRA's mark because it neither fully explored others' rights to "STAR CLASS" nor ceased its infringing behavior when it was sued. *See Nalpac, Ltd. v. Corning Glass Works,* 784 F.2d 752, 755–56 (6th Cir. 1986) (exploitation of another's mark after knowledge of its existence suggests bad faith).

We conclude that the district court, in determining whether Hilfiger acted in bad faith, relied on two clearly erroneous factual findings and did not consider all the evidence pertaining to the willfulness of Hilfiger's infringement. We therefore remand the issue of Hilfiger's bad faith for reconsideration in light of our analysis above. As a result, we cannot review the district court's denial of an accounting of profits and attorney fees, but instead must vacate the denial and remand.

III. Protectability of ISCYRA's Five-Pointed Star Mark

ISCYRA contends that the district court "appears" to hold that ISCYRA enjoys no trademark protection at all in its five-pointed star insignia, and that the court clearly erred to the extent that its opinion so holds. ISCYRA maintains that it has limited trademark protection of the insignia when it is used in relation to yachts or professional sailing.

We agree with the district court that Hilfiger cannot be enjoined from the use of a five-pointed star symbol on its garments and affirm the district court's denial of injunctive relief to ISCYRA as to this mark. We do not read the court's opinion to reach beyond Hilfiger's use of the insignia on clothing in the manner presented by the facts of this case. The issue of the insignia's protectibility in a case involving yachting or professional sailing, therefore, was not decided by the district court and is not addressed by our affirmance.

Conclusion

For the foregoing reasons, we vacate the denial of an accounting of profits and attorney fees, and remand the question whether Hilfiger acted in bad faith by using ISCYRA's "STAR CLASS" mark to the district court for reconsideration. In all other respects, we affirm.

Notes

1. The Second Circuit appeared to be particularly moved by the fact that the advice of trademark counsel to order a full search of trademarks, and not just federal trademarks, was not heeded. The advice of counsel would normally be privileged. Why do you suppose that privilege was waived or otherwise not honored in

this case? Did Hilfiger rely upon the advice in order to show good faith, only to have the advice be the subject of a finding of bad faith?

2. The Second Circuit held that it was bad faith for Hilfiger to continue selling products after it commissioned a full search after the lawsuit had begun. Should accused defendants always stop alleged infringing activities until they can be resolved at court?

2. Priority Disputes Between Commercial Use and Registration

Trademark attorneys frequently insist on reviewing "full" search reports commissioned by outside vendors when advising clients who are preparing to invest considerable resources in developing a new brand. One of the reasons for this insistence is because those reports do not just analyze trademarks that are the subject of registrations or applications. Instead, they review a wide number of publicly available sources to see if other companies are making commercial use of the brand in question that might create a conflict moving forward. To review, trademark rights stem from use in commerce. Therefore, disputes sometimes develop over which mark was used in commerce first. If there is a potential conflict, a trademark attorney might seek confirmation from the senior trademark owner that there will be no legal problems. This approach is not without risk, however, as the senior trademark owner might seek to profit from this uncertainty. One solution to concurrent trademark use is a coexistence agreement where two potential users agree not to bring litigation against each other for the use of the same mark in differing categories of goods or services. The following case provides examples of good and not-so-good ways to deal with these types of uncertainties, in addition to how a court conceptualizes the use in commerce that gives rise to trademark rights.

Zazú Designs v. L'Oréal, S.A.

979 F.2d 499 (7th Cir. 1992)

EASTERBROOK, Circuit Judge.

In 1985 Cosmair, Inc., concluded that young women craved pink and blue hair. To meet the anticipated demand, Cosmair developed a line of "hair cosmetics"—hair coloring that is easily washed out. These inexpensive products, under the name ZAZU, were sold in the cosmetic sections of mass merchandise stores. Apparently the teenagers of the late 1980s had better taste than Cosmair's marketing staff thought. The product flopped, but its name gave rise to this trademark suit. Cosmair is the United States licensee of L'Oréal, S.A., a French firm specializing in perfumes, beauty aids, and related products. Cosmair placed L'Oréal's marks on the bottles and ads. For reasons the parties have not explained, L'Oréal rather than Cosmair is the defendant even though the events that led to the litigation were orchestrated in New York rather than Paris. L'Oréal does not protest, so for simplicity we refer to Cosmair and L'Oréal collectively as "L'Oréal."

L'Oréal hired Wordmark, a consulting firm, to help it find a name for the new line of hair cosmetics. After checking the United States Trademark Register for conflicts, Wordmark suggested 250 names. L'Oréal narrowed this field to three, including ZAZU, and investigated their availability. This investigation turned up one federal registration of ZAZU as a mark for clothing and two state service mark registrations including that word. One of these is Zazú Hair Designs; the other was defunct.

Zazú Hair Designs is a hair salon in Hinsdale, Illinois, a suburb of Chicago. We call it "ZHD" to avoid confusion with the ZAZÚ mark. (ZHD employs an acute accent and L'Oréal did not; no one makes anything of the difference.) The salon is a partnership between Raymond R. Koubek and Salvatore J. Segretto, hairstylists who joined forces in 1979. ZHD registered ZAZÚ with Illinois in 1980 as a trade name for its salon. L'Oréal called the salon to find out if ZHD was selling its own products. The employee who answered reported that the salon was not but added, "we're working on it". L'Oréal called again; this time it was told that ZHD had no products available under the name ZAZÚ.

L'Oréal took the sole federal registration, held by Riviera Slacks, Inc., as a serious obstacle. Some apparel makers have migrated to cosmetics, and if Riviera were about to follow Ralph Lauren (which makes perfumes in addition to shirts and skirts) it might have a legitimate complaint against a competing use of the mark. *Sands, Taylor & Wood Co. v. Quaker Oats Co.*, 24 U.S.P.Q.2d 1001, 1011 (7th Cir. 1992). Riviera charged L'Oréal $125,000 for a covenant not to sue if L'Oréal used the ZAZU mark on cosmetics. In April 1986, covenant in hand and satisfied that ZHD'S state trade name did not prevent the introduction of a national product, L'Oréal made a small interstate shipment of hair cosmetics under the ZAZU name. It used this shipment as the basis of an application for federal registration, filed on June 12, 1986. By August L'Oréal had advertised and sold its products nationally.

Unknown to L'Oréal, Koubek and Segretto had for some time aspired to emulate Vidal Sassoon by marketing shampoos and conditioners under their salon's trade name. In 1985 Koubek began meeting with chemists to develop ZHD'S products. Early efforts were unsuccessful; no one offered a product that satisfied ZHD. Eventually ZHD received acceptable samples from Gift Cosmetics, some of which Segretto sold to customers of the salon in plain bottles to which he taped the salon's business card. Between November 1985 and February 1986 ZHD made a few other sales. Koubek shipped two bottles to a friend in Texas, who paid $13. He also made two shipments to a hair stylist friend in Florida—40 bottles of shampoo for $78.58. These were designed to interest the Floridian in the future marketing of the product line. These bottles could not have been sold to the public, because they lacked labels listing the ingredients and weight. See 21 U.S.C. § 362(b); 15 U.S.C. §§ 1452, 1453(a); 21 C.F.R. §§ 701.3, 701.13(a). After L'Oréal's national marketing was under way, its representatives thrice visited ZHD and found that the salon still had no products for sale under the ZAZÚ name. Which is not to say that ZHD was supine. Late in 1985 ZHD had ordered 25,000 bottles silkscreened with the name ZAZÚ. Later it ordered stick-on labels listing the ingredients of its products. In September 1986 ZHD began to sell small quantities of shampoo in bottles filled (and labeled) by hand in the salon. After the turn of the year ZHD directed the supplier of the shampoo and conditioner to fill some bottles; the record does not reveal how many.

After a bench trial the district court held that ZHD'S sales gave it an exclusive right to use the ZAZÚ name nationally for hair products. 9 U.S.P.Q.2d 1972 (N.D.Ill. 1988). The court enjoined L'Oréal from using the mark (a gesture, since the product had bombed and L'Oréal disclaimed any interest in using ZAZU again). It also awarded ZHD $100,000 in damages on account of lost profits and $1 million more to pay for corrective advertising to restore luster to the ZAZÚ mark. Finding that L'Oréal had infringed ZHD'S mark intentionally and used "oppressive and deceitful" tactics in the litigation, the court awarded an additional $1 million in punitive damages, topped off with $76,000 to cover ZHD'S legal expenses. (L'Oréal has changed law firms for the appeal; its current counsel did not participate in the events that the district judge found to be unethical.)

Between the filing of the opinion and the entry of judgment, L'Oréal made a motion under Fed. R. Civ. P. 52(b) for an additional hearing. It wanted to present evidence that it believed would show the judge that he misunderstood the actions and motives of its lawyers. The court denied this motion without comment and entered judgment. Not dissuaded, L'Oréal served an all-but-identical motion within ten days of the judgment. Two years later the court granted this motion. After taking additional evidence the court modified some of its findings, but not its judgment. ZHD won an additional $92,000 in legal fees to compensate for the cost of the new hearing. L'Oréal at last appealed, and the parties have ignored a potential problem: a second post-trial motion does not extend the time for appeal. *Charles v. Daley,* 799 F.2d 343 (7th Cir. 1986). But because only one of these motions was filed after the judgment, it suspended the judgment's finality and makes the appeal timely, even though the denial of the first motion shows that the duplicate was unlikely to succeed. *United States v. Ibarra,*502 U.S. 1, 112 S. Ct. 4, 116 L. Ed. 2d 1 (1991).

I

Federal law permits the registration of trademarks and the enforcement of registered marks. Through § 43(a) of the Lanham Act, 15 U.S.C. § 1125(a), a provision addressed to deceit, it also indirectly allows the enforcement of unregistered marks. But until 1988 federal law did not specify how one acquired the rights that could be registered or enforced without registration. That subject fell into the domain of state law, plus federal common law elaborating on the word "use" in § 43(a). *Two Pesos, Inc. v. Taco Cabana, Inc.,* 505 U.S. 763,——, 112 S. Ct. 2753, 2757, 120 L. Ed. 2d 615 (1992); *id.* 505 U.S. at——, 112 S. Ct. at 2766–67 (Thomas, J., concurring). See also 15 U.S.C. § 1127 ("'trademark' includes any word . . . used by a person"). At common law, "use" meant sales to the public of a product with the mark attached. *Trade-Mark Cases,* 100 U.S. 82, 94–95, 25 L.Ed. 550 (1879); *Menendez v. Holt,* 128 U.S. 514, 520–21, 9 S. Ct. 143, 143–44, 32 L.Ed. 526 (1888). See also *Hanover Star Milling Co. v. Metcalf,* 240 U.S. 403, 414, 36 S. Ct. 357, 360, 60 L.Ed. 713 (1916);

United Drug Co. v. Theodore Rectanus Co., 248 U.S. 90, 97, 39 S. Ct. 48, 50, 63 L.Ed. 141 (1918).

"Use" is neither a glitch in the Lanham Act nor a historical relic. By insisting that firms use marks to obtain rights in them, the law prevents entrepreneurs from reserving brand names in order to make their rivals' marketing more costly. Public sales let others know that they should not invest resources to develop a mark similar to one already used in the trade. *Blue Bell, Inc. v. Farah Manufacturing Co.,* 508 F.2d 1260, 1264–65 (5th Cir. 1975); see also William M. Landes and Richard A. Posner, *Trademark Law: An Economic Perspective,* 30 J.L. & Econ. 265, 281–84 (1987). Only active use allows consumers to associate a mark with particular goods and notifies other firms that the mark is so associated.

Under the common law, one must win the race to the marketplace to establish the exclusive right to a mark. *Blue Bell v. Farah; La Societe Anonyme des Parfums LeGalion v. Jean Patou, Inc.,* 495 F.2d 1265, 1271–74 (2d Cir. 1974). Registration modifies this system slightly, allowing slight sales plus notice in the register to substitute for substantial sales without notice. 15 U.S.C. § 1051(a). (The legislation in 1988 modifies the use requirement further, but we disregard this.) ZHD'S sales of its product are insufficient use to establish priority over L'Oréal. A few bottles sold over the counter in Hinsdale, and a few more mailed to friends in Texas and Florida, neither link the ZAZÚ mark with ZHD's product in the minds of consumers nor put other producers on notice. As a practical matter ZHD had no product, period, until months after L'Oréal had embarked on its doomed campaign.

In finding that ZHD'S few sales secured rights against the world, the district court relied on cases such as *Department of Justice v. Calspan Corp.,* 578 F.2d 295 (C.C.P.A. 1978), which hold that a single sale, combined with proof of intent to go on selling, permit the vendor to register the mark. See also *Axton-Fisher Tobacco Co. v. Fortune Tobacco Co.,* 82 F.2d 295 (C.C.P.A. 1936); *Maternally Yours, Inc. v. Your Maternity Shop, Inc.,* 234 F.2d 538, 542 (2d Cir. 1956); *Community of Roquefort v. Santo,* 443 F.2d 1196 (C.C.P.A. 1971). But use sufficient to register a mark that soon is widely distributed is not necessarily enough to acquire rights in the absence of registration. The Lanham Act allows only trademarks "used in commerce" to be registered. 15 U.S.C. § 1051(a). Courts have read "used" in a way that allows firms to seek protection for a mark before investing substantial sums in promotion. See *Fort Howard Paper Co. v. Kimberly-Clark Corp.,* 390 F.2d 1015 (C.C.P.A. 1968); cf. *Jim Dandy Co. v. Martha White Foods, Inc.,* 458 F.2d 1397, 1399 (C.C.P.A. 1972) (party may rely on advertising to show superior registration rights); but see *Weight Watchers International, Inc. v. I. Rokeach & Sons, Inc.,* 211 U.S.P.Q. 700, 709 (T.M.T.A.B. 1981) (more than minimal use is required to register because the statute allows only "owner[s]" to register, and ownership of a mark depends on commercial use). Liberality in registering marks is not problematic, because the registration gives notice to latecomers, which token use alone does not. Firms need only search the register before embarking on development. Had ZHD registered ZAZÚ, the parties could have negotiated before L'Oréal committed large sums to marketing.

ZHD applied for registration of ZAZÚ after L'Oréal not only had applied to register the mark but also had put its product on the market nationwide. Efforts to register came too late. At oral argument ZHD suggested that L'Oréal's knowledge of ZHD'S plan to enter the hair care market using ZAZÚ establishes ZHD'S superior right to the name. Such an argument is unavailing. Intent to use a mark, like a naked registration, establishes no rights at all. *Hydro-Dynamics, Inc. v. George Putnam & Co.,* 811 F.2d 1470, 1472 (Fed.Cir. 1987). Even under the 1988 amendments, which allow registration in advance of contemplated use, an unregistered *plan* to use a mark creates no rights. Just as an intent to buy a choice parcel of land does not prevent a rival from closing the deal first, so an intent to use a mark creates no rights a competitor is bound to respect. A statute granting no rights in bare registrations cannot plausibly be understood to grant rights in "intents" divorced from either sales or registrations. Registration itself establishes only a rebuttable presumption of use as of the filing date. *Rolley, Inc. v. Younghusband,* 204 F.2d 209, 211 (9th Cir. 1953). ZHD made first use of ZAZÚ in connection with hair *services* in Illinois, but this does not translate to a protectable right to market hair *products* nationally. The district court construed L'Oréal's knowledge of ZHD'S use of ZAZÚ for salon services as knowledge "of [ZHD'S] superior rights in the mark." 9 U.S.P.Q.2d at 1978. ZHD did not, however, have superior rights in the mark as applied to hair products, because it neither marketed such nor registered the mark before L'Oréal's use. Because the mark was not registered for use in conjunction with hair products, any knowledge L'Oréal may have had of ZHD'S plans is irrelevant. *Cf. Weiner King, Inc. v. Wiener King Corp.,* 615 F.2d 512 (C.C.P.A. 1980).

Imagine the consequences of ZHD'S approach. Businesses that knew of an intended use would not be entitled to the mark even if they made the first significant use of it. Businesses with their heads in the sand, however, could stand on the actual date they introduced their products, and so would have priority over firms that intended to use a mark but had not done so. Ignorance would be rewarded—and knowledgeable firms might back off even though the rivals' "plans" or "intent" were unlikely to come to fruition. Yet investigations of the sort L'Oréal undertook prevent costly duplication in the development of trademarks and protect consumers from the confusion resulting from two products being sold under the same mark. See *Natural Footwear Ltd. v. Hart, Shaffner & Marx,* 760 F.2d 1383, 1395 (3d Cir. 1985).

L'Oréal should not be worse off because it made inquiries and found that, although no one had yet used the mark for hair products, ZHD intended to do so. Nor should a potential user have to bide its time until it learns whether other firms are serious about marketing a product. The use requirement rewards those who act quickly in getting new products in the hands of consumers. Had L'Oréal discovered that ZHD had a product on the market under the ZAZÚ mark or that ZHD had registered ZAZÚ for hair products, L'Oréal could have chosen another mark before committing extensive marketing resources. Knowledge that ZHD planned to use the ZAZÚ mark in the future does not present an obstacle to L'Oréal's adopting it today. *Selfway, Inc. v. Travelers Petroleum, Inc.,* 579 F.2d 75, 79 (C.C.P.A. 1978).

Occasionally courts suggest that "bad faith" adoption of a mark defeats a claim to priority. *See California Cedar Products Co. v. Pine Mountain Corp.*, 724 F.2d 827, 830 (9th Cir. 1984); *Stern Electronics, Inc. v. Kaufman*, 669 F.2d 852, 857 (2d Cir. 1982); *Blue Bell v. Farah*, 508 F.2d at 1267. Although ZHD equates L'Oréal's knowledge of its impending use with "bad faith," the cases use the term differently. In each instance the court applied the label "bad faith" to transactions designed merely to reserve a mark, not to link the name to a product ready to be sold to the public. In *California Cedar Products*, for example, two firms sprinted to acquire the abandoned DURAFLAME mark. One shipped some of its goods in the abandoning company's wrapper with a new name pasted over it. Two days later the other commenced bona fide sales under the DURAFLAME mark. The court disregarded the first shipment, calling it "both premature and in bad faith", 724 F.2d at 830, and held that the first firm to make bona fide sales to customers was the prior user. "Bad faith" was no more than an epithet stapled to the basic conclusion: that reserving a mark is forbidden, so that the first producer to make genuine sales gets the rights. If these cases find a parallel in our dispute, ZHD occupies the place of the firm trying to reserve a mark for "intended" exploitation. ZHD doled out a few samples in bottles lacking labeling necessary for sale to the public. Such transactions are the sort of pre-marketing maneuvers that these cases hold insufficient to establish rights in a trademark.

The district court erred in equating a use sufficient to support registration with a use sufficient to generate nationwide rights in the absence of registration. Although whether ZHD's use is sufficient to grant it rights in the ZAZÚ mark is a question of fact on which appellate review is deferential, *California Cedar Products*, 724 F.2d at 830; *cf. Scandia Down Corp. v. Euroquilt, Inc.*,772 F.2d 1423, 1428–29 (7th Cir. 1985), the extent to which ZHD used the mark is not disputed. ZHD'S sales of hair care products were insufficient as a matter of law to establish national trademark rights at the time L'Oréal put its electric hair colors on the market.

* * *

REVERSED AND REMANDED.

CUDAHY, Circuit Judge, dissenting.

On the important issue of good faith, L'Oréal's conduct here merits a very hard look. In the case of Riviera, a *men's* clothing retailer, L'Oréal was careful to pay $125,000 for an agreement not to sue. Yet men's clothing and hair cosmetics marketed to women hardly seem related at all. On the other hand, a women's hair salon developing a line of hair care products is a purveyor of goods and services that seem closely related to hair cosmetics. Therefore, L'Oréal's knowledge of ZHD's use defeats any claim L'Oréal may have to priority.

One of the keys here seems to be the use of ZAZU as a service mark connected with the provision of salon services by ZHD. A service mark can be infringed by its use on a closely related product. *See, e.g., Re Hyper Shoppes (Ohio), Inc.*, 837 F.2d 463 (Fed.Cir. 1988) (affirming refusal to register two "closely related" marks: one for furniture and the other for general merchandise services that included the sale of furniture); *Steelcase, Inc. v. Steelcare, Inc.*, 219 U.S.P.Q. 433 (TMTAB 1983) (mark used for furniture refinishing service likely to be confused with mark used for office furniture); *see also* 2 J. Thomas McCarthy, *Trademark and Unfair Competition* § 24:6, at 71 (2d ed. 1984 & Supp.1991) (stating that "[w]here the services consist of retail sales services, likelihood of confusion is found when another mark is used on goods which are commonly sold through such a retail outlet"). A service and a product are related if buyers are likely to assume a common source or sponsorship. *Tisch Hotels, Inc. v. Americana Inn, Inc.*, 350 F.2d 609, 612 (7th Cir. 1965); 2 McCarthy, *supra*, § 24:6 at 183 ("The 'related goods' test is merely a facet of the ultimate and final test of 'likelihood of confusion.'"). The salon services and hair products at issue in this case, which are nearly as kindred as a service and product can be, offer the paradigmatic illustration of things that are closely related. Thus the majority's disregard for ZHD's substantial use of ZAZU in connection with salon services is unfounded.

As the majority correctly notes, the standard for granting federal registration is somewhat less exacting than that for establishing common law trademark rights. *See La Societe Anonyme des Parfums le Galion v. Jean Patou, Inc.*, 495 F.2d 1265 (2d Cir. 1974). But that distinction is so slight as to be inconsequential here. While any bona fide transaction that is more than a "mere sham" will, when combined with intent to continue use, suffice to support federal registration, *Avakoff v. Southern Pacific Co.*, 765 F.2d 1097, 1098 (Fed.Cir. 1985); 1 McCarthy, *supra*, § 19:37 at 967, any use greater than de minimis will still warrant trademark protection in the absence of registration. *See SweeTarts v. Sunline, Inc.*, 380 F.2d 923, 929 (8th Cir. 1967) (market penetration "need not be large" but must be "significant enough to pose the real likelihood of confusion"); 1 McCarthy, *supra*, § 16:2(B) at 723; § 16.2(C) at 726. Thus, bona fide test marketing or small experimental sales—indeed, any use that is not nominal or token—can satisfy the test. *E.I. du Pont de Nemours & Co. v. G.C. Murphy Co.*, 199 U.S.P.Q. 807, 812 (TMTAB 1978); 1 McCarthy, *supra*, § 16:2(B) at 723.

In this case, ZHD's use of the ZAZU mark, both in its highly successful salon service business, which drew some out-of-state clients, and in its local and interstate product sales to customers and to a potential marketer, surely is more than de minimis. The extensive evidence of ZHD's intent to step up hair product sales—such as its order for 25,000 ZAZU-emblazoned bottles and its inquiry about advertising rates in a national magazine—bolsters this assessment. Even if ZHD did fail to demonstrate more than a de minimis market penetration nationally, at the very least it successfully established exclusive rights within its primary area of operation. The salon's substantial advertising, increasing revenue and staff and preliminary product sales indicate sufficient market penetration to afford trademark protection in that region. *See Natural Footwear Ltd. v. Hart, Schaffner & Marx*, 760 F.2d 1383 (3d Cir. 1985) (senior user can establish common law rights in geographic areas where it achieved market penetration); *SweeTarts*, 380 F.2d at 928 (plaintiff's prior use of trademark within a given market area entitles it to exclusive use of that mark within that area); *V & V Food Products, Inc. v. Cacique Cheese Co.*, 683 F. Supp. 662 (N.D.Ill. 1988).

L'Oréal concedes that ZHD has exclusive rights to use ZAZU for salon services in the Hinsdale area. Those exclusive rights also preclude L'Oréal from using the mark on hair products in the local area because of the likelihood of confusion between those products and ZHD's salon services, even apart from any confusion between the two parties' *products.* Given the deferential standard of review on the factual question of use, therefore, I think it clear that ZHD has achieved market penetration and exclusive rights to the ZAZU mark at the very least in the Chicago area.

ZHD's contention that its rights in the ZAZU mark extend beyond the local area is enhanced by evidence that L'Oréal did not, as we have noted, act in good faith. The majority's consideration of the good faith issue minimizes the important role good faith plays in trademark disputes, particularly disputes involving unregistered marks. *See* 2 McCarthy, *supra,* § 26:4 at 292 (noting that good faith has "significant, if not independent, importance" in disputes involving unregistered marks). Bad faith can defeat claims to priority. *See, e.g., A.J. Canfield Co. v. Honickman,* 808 F.2d 291 (3rd Cir. 1986) (stating the doctrine that a senior user "has enforceable rights against any junior user who adopted the mark with knowledge of its senior use"); *Johanna Farms, Inc. v. Citrus Bowl, Inc.,* 468 F. Supp. 866, 876 (E.D.N.Y. 1978) (stating that junior users who do not adopt the mark in good faith "will not be accorded the right to exploit the mark, even in areas previously untouched by the senior user"); 2 McCarthy, *supra,* § 26:3 at 289; § 26:4 at 292. Contrary to the majority's narrow characterization of bad faith as a concept employed solely to deter attempts to reserve marks prior to genuine sales, courts have examined junior users' good faith in a variety of contexts. In fact, this court has held that a good faith junior user is simply one that begins using a mark without knowledge that another party already is using it. *The Money Store v. Harriscorp Finance, Inc.,* 689 F.2d 666, 674 (7th Cir. 1982); *see* 2 McCarthy, *supra,* § 26:4 at 292 (equating good faith to "the junior user's lack of knowledge"). And while such knowledge may not automatically negate good faith, only the most unusual situations encompass both knowledge and good faith. *See GTE Corp. v. Williams,* 904 F.2d 536, 541 (10th Cir. 1990).

In sum, I believe ZHD's sale of ZAZU services and products constituted sufficient use to establish exclusive trademark rights in the Chicago area, if not nationally. In any event, L'Oréal's pursuit of its line of hair cosmetics in spite of its knowledge of ZHD's use defeats L'Oréal's position. Therefore, I respectfully dissent.

Notes

1. Do you agree with the majority's holding that Cosmair's search and review process was sufficient? Cosmair evidently did not know about any sales consummated by Zazú Hair Designs ("ZHD"). Would a more thorough search have uncovered them? Had L'Oréal known about ZHD's prior sales, what would or should it have done differently?

2. Do you agree with the dissent that, regardless of any sales of products, the beauty services offered by ZHD were sufficient to give it priority with respect to closely related goods?

3. Assuming that the majority opinion was correct, and no damages of any consequence were suffered by ZHD and L'Oréal had no intention of ever using the ZAZU brand name again, why did ZHD go to the trouble and expense of bringing this lawsuit?

C. Eponymous Brands

In all product categories, it is relatively common for brands to be based on the name of a product's designer. In the fashion category, however, the use of personal names as brand names is much more common; brand names are almost expected to be the personal name of the brand's designer and/or owner. There are a variety of reasons for fashion's unique practice in this regard. It may be because fashion designers, even more than creators of other goods, are driven by the pride and satisfaction of seeing their name stitched onto their creations. Instead, this phenomenon may be driven by customer demand. Customers may appreciate the "personal touch" and personal story that the use of a designer's personal name may suggest. Perhaps this phenomenon results from both reasons or neither of them. But the use of personal names as trademarks so frequently in the fashion world has led to a series of legal and practical problems that we will discuss below. Designers choosing their brands and companies acquiring brands based on personal names should be aware of these issues and consider their effects. The leading article on eponymous brands in fashion and the particular challenges they present appears at the end of this section.

1. Registration Issues

An initial issue with using a personal name is the potential difficulty in clearing and registering that name as a trademark. There are millions of registered trademarks and, as noted above, it is common in the fashion industry for brands to use personal names. It is therefore very likely that at least one, if not both, the designer's first name and surname are already the subject of a registration. In short, trademark registrations are issued at a faster rate than parents are coining new names. Furthermore, even if the designer's full name is registrable, she could be restricted from using a shorter version of that name that has greater marketing appeal. For example, the supermodel Gigi Hadid participated in a co-branding with Tommy Hilfiger and was threatened by the owner of the trademark GIGI. Although issues with respect to United States law are discussed below, similar issues are just as likely to arise on a worldwide level in other trademark jurisdictions.

Another difficulty in registering personal names as trademarks is the Lanham Act's prohibition on registering a trademark that is "primarily merely a surname" without proof of secondary meaning. 15 U.S.C. § 1052(e). Determining whether a trademark is considered "primarily a surname" requires the Examining Attorney to look at: (1) whether the surname is rare; (2) whether the term is the surname of anyone connected with the applicant; (3) whether the term has a meaning other than as a surname; (4) whether it has the "structure and pronunciation" of a surname; and (5) whether the stylization of lettering is distinctive enough to create a separate commercial impression. PTO Trademark Manual of Examining Procedure ("TMEP") § 1211.01. The Patent and Trademark Office very commonly issues "surname" objections for any trademark application that even slightly resembles a surname. Applicants can avoid such objections in a variety of ways. First, they can ensure that the trademark also consists of a first name or initials. Alternatively, they can demonstrate secondary meaning by showing that the surname is well-known and the subject of considerable sales and promotion. Such a showing is difficult if not impossible for new brands, however, which is when trademark registration is most advisable. If neither of these options is desired or advisable, the applicant can register a surname trademark on the Supplemental Register, where it enjoys most, but not all, of the benefits of trademark protection. While on the Supplemental Register, the applicant can develop the secondary meaning necessary to later apply for registration on the Principal Register.

Trademark registration issues may also arise for later acquirers of eponymous brands. If a trademark identifies a living person, the applicant must provide the written and signed consent from that person as part of the application. This requirement is not onerous when an eponymous brand's designer is affiliated with the trademark applicant. But it can be more difficult when the individual no longer cooperates with the brand bearing her name. Although the applicant may rely upon prior consent filed with the trademark office, such consent only applies to the "same goods and/or services, or such goods and/or services as would encompass those in the subsequent application." TMEP § 1206.04(c). It is therefore incumbent upon acquiring companies to ensure the ongoing cooperation of eponymous brand owners as part of the deal.

2. Use of a Name Similar to a Famous Trademark

Through hard work, and more than a modicum of luck, fashion designers can achieve the rare accomplishment of converting their given or adopted name to a broadly famous trademark. However, it is possible that many other people may share that name and it may be considered unfair to block those individuals from also using their name commercially. As seen in the following case regarding a family dispute, courts must resolve difficult disputes where more than one party has a valid interest in the use of a particular name.

Gucci v. Gucci Shops, Inc.

688 F. Supp. 916 (S.D.N.Y. 1988)

CONNER, District Judge.

Since the time of Cain and Abel, family disputes have been marked by the irrational and impulsive decisions of those involved, the fierce battles which ensue, and the senseless destruction they cause. This case is but a skirmish in one of the most publicized family disputes of our time, among the heirs of Guccio Gucci, who founded the business empire which bears his name. It is recognized internationally as a manufacturer and retailer of high-quality leather goods and other fashion accessories and gift items. The Gucci family feud, which has raised legal issues currently being litigated before judges and arbitration panels throughout the world, at enormous cost to members of the family and the businesses they control, is also the focus of a recent best-selling book written by Gerald McKnight entitled *Gucci: A House Divided.*

In this action for declaratory judgment, plaintiff Paolo Gucci seeks the Court's declaration that: (1) he has the right to use his name Paolo Gucci in the United States in his business of designing and developing products; (2) he may authorize third parties to use his name Paolo Gucci in connection with products designed by him or under his supervision; and (3) that such use of his personal name does not infringe the trademark or other proprietary rights of defendant Gucci Shops or otherwise compete unfairly with Gucci Shops. In addition, plaintiff has asserted causes of action for unfair competition and tortious interference with his business and contractual relations based on threats and allegedly unsupported claims by defendant which have effectively prevented plaintiff from proceeding with his business ventures.

Defendant Gucci Shops has counterclaimed against plaintiff for trademark infringement and dilution, unfair competition, breach of a 1972 Shareholders Agreement, false designation of origin and abuse of process.

Background

Plaintiff Paolo Gucci is a citizen of Haiti and maintains an office and residence in New York City and a residence in England. Defendant Gucci Shops, Inc. (now Gucci America, Inc.) is a New York corporation having its principal place of business on Fifth Avenue in New York City. Defendant maintains a retail store on Fifth Avenue and additional retail stores throughout the United States. While the Gucci name is a well-known trademark throughout the world, Gucci Shops operates only in the United States.

Plaintiff was born in Florence, Italy on March 29, 1931. The name given to him at birth was Paolo Gucci and he has been known by that name throughout his life. Paolo Gucci's grandfather, Guccio Gucci, started a leather goods business under the name Gucci in Florence, Italy in the early 1900's. Guccio Gucci had three sons—Aldo, who is plaintiff's father, and Rodolfo and Vasco. Over the years, Aldo, Rodolfo and Vasco have been involved in the Gucci family business. Rodolfo and Vasco are deceased. Aldo Gucci has three sons—Paolo, Roberto and Giorgio. Rodolfo Gucci had one son, Maurizio Gucci. Vasco Gucci had no offspring relevant to this case.

The first Gucci store was located in Florence, Italy. In 1939, a Gucci store was opened in Rome and plaintiff's family moved to Rome and lived in a house in the back of the store. Aldo Gucci was responsible for operating the store. Plaintiff became formally employed at the Gucci store in Rome in 1952 as an assistant salesman. After approximately two years in Rome, plaintiff was married and moved back to Florence. After the move, plaintiff divided his time between the Gucci store in Florence and the Gucci factory in Florence.

Defendant Gucci Shops was organized in 1953 by members of the Gucci family in New York. Today, Gucci Shops is the owner in the United States of the trademark "GUCCI" and of the other Gucci trademarks it employs, and it sells "Gucci" products made in Italy and in Miami, Florida.

Gucci Shops has grown considerably over the past thirty years, and today it owns and operates 21 retail stores throughout the United States. An additional 13 retail stores and boutiques are operated in the United States by persons who have been granted franchises by Gucci Shops. In addition to the sales of "Gucci" merchandise at Gucci stores owned or franchised by Gucci Shops, "Gucci" merchandise is sold in hundreds of better department stores, jewelry stores and other retail outlets throughout the United States.

In 1953, plaintiff's grandfather Guccio Gucci died and the Gucci business was carried on by his sons Aldo, Vasco and Rodolfo. In 1983, Rodolfo Gucci died. Plaintiff's cousin Maurizio Gucci now controls 50% of the shares of Gucci Shops, which he received upon the death of his father Rodolfo. The remaining 50% is divided among plaintiff's father, Aldo, plaintiff's brothers Roberto and Giorgio, and a third party to whom plaintiff sold his shares. Plaintiff no longer holds any interest in any Gucci companies.

Plaintiff was employed by Guccio Gucci S.r.l. in various positions from approximately 1952 through September 1978. Despite vigorous attempts by defendant to refute plaintiff's contention that he was a designer and stylist of "Gucci" products, all of the credible evidence at trial, including defendant's own documents, established conclusively that Paolo Gucci was a designer and stylist of many Gucci products. Two former employees of Guccio Gucci who worked with Paolo Gucci, Sergio Cocchi and Massimo Filo Guarnieri, both testified that Paolo Gucci was the designer and stylist for Gucci. Indeed, according to their testimony, after Paolo Gucci left his position, the company promoted and hired a series of stylists who were intended to replace him but who were unable to maintain the unique Gucci image. This testimony merely confirmed what was evident from many of defendant's own internal documents—that Paolo Gucci was Gucci's chief designer and stylist.

In addition to his involvement in the design of "Gucci" products, Paolo Gucci has, at various times, been an officer director and employee of Gucci Shops, Guccio Gucci S.r.l. and Gucci Parfum Company. He was also a shareholder of either Guccio Gucci S.r.l. or Guccio Gucci S.p.A. continuously from February 24, 1972 to at least February 3, 1986.

The removal of Paolo Gucci from various positions he held at Gucci entities stemmed from friction which developed between Paolo and other family members. In the 1970's, Aldo Gucci managed the American Gucci Shops operation while Rodolfo Gucci was in charge of the Italian operation. Plaintiff's uncle, Vasco Gucci, was in charge of the Gucci factory in Florence. When Vasco Gucci died in 1974, plaintiff became head of the Florence factory while remaining chief designer for the company. By the mid-1970's, according to Paolo, Rodolfo's interference with Paolo's work as head of the factory and chief designer strained their relationship to the breaking point. On one occasion, when Rodolfo tried his hand at designing a handbag and then showed his work to Paolo, Paolo disgustedly threw it out the window. Shortly thereafter, during Paolo's presentation of the new Gucci collection to buyers, he was publicly upbraided causing him to stalk out, abandoning the presentation. This, according to defendant, led to Paolo's suspension.

In 1978, plaintiff's father Aldo invited plaintiff to come work with him at Gucci Shops in the United States. Plaintiff accepted this offer and moved to New York in early 1978 where he became Vice President of marketing for Gucci Shops.

Thereafter, plaintiff sought confirmation from Rodolfo in Italy that he retained his employment status with Guccio Gucci, S.r.l. to protect his employment benefits under Italian law. According to Paolo, litigation which he commenced to collect his severance pay led to the termination of his employment by the Italian Gucci company in 1978. Gucci Shops contends that Paolo was discharged for the additional reason of his alleged organization and participation in several companies in Haiti making handbags allegedly in competition with Gucci. Paolo maintains that this production was undertaken merely to assure a supply of high-quality merchandise for Gucci Shops.

After losing his job, plaintiff attempted to earn a living by exploiting his skill and experience as a designer. Having been denied his family's approval for his new venture, plaintiff commenced an action for declaratory judgment in federal court in the Southern District of New York seeking a declaration of his right to use his personal name as a trademark and also to identify himself as a designer. The Court dismissed that action for lack of a justiciable controversy because the record did not establish that any goods had yet been offered for sale under plaintiff's name.

Following the dismissal of the lawsuit and various attempts at reconciliation, in June 1982 plaintiff was fired by the Italian Gucci Parfum company, and the following month was terminated from employment by the remaining Gucci companies at which he was employed. He was removed as a director of Gucci S.p.a. in 1983. Plaintiff has received no compensation or other form of remuneration from any Gucci entities since July 1982.

Following Paolo's unsuccessful attempts at reconciliation with members of his family, Paolo once again attempted to revive his career as a designer. Plaintiff designed handbags and other leather goods for an Italian company called Italia Italia and licensed that company to use his full name Paolo Gucci in connection with such products. Italia Italia shipped samples of the "Paolo Gucci" handbags to a United States company called Saffron which placed the bags on display in its showroom. Plaintiff also placed an advertisement in the New York Times for the "Paolo Gucci" bags which were to be distributed by Saffron. After seeing the advertisement, defendant's counsel wrote to Saffron advising Saffron that Gucci Shops owns the exclusive rights to the trademark "Gucci" in the United States and demanding that Saffron refrain from any use of the "Gucci" name that violated the rights of Gucci Shops. This letter caused Saffron to terminate its arrangement with Paolo Gucci.

Shortly thereafter, in June 1983 plaintiff commenced the present action requesting a declaration that he has the right to use the name Paolo Gucci on products of the same type as those sold by Gucci Shops, and requesting injunctive relief to prevent Gucci Shops from claiming that plaintiff's use of the Paolo Gucci name infringes upon Gucci Shops' rights in the trademark "Gucci". Initially, defendant sought to have this action dismissed for lack of a justiciable controversy. At approximately the same time, plaintiff licensed a company called Pacific Jewelry (Panache) to use his full name Paolo Gucci in connection with items of costume jewelry to be designed by or in collaboration with plaintiff. He also licensed Kimball, a furniture manufacturer, to use his name Paolo Gucci in connection with office furniture and pianos to be designed in collaboration with plaintiff. After receiving letters from defendant's attorneys, however, those companies terminated their dealings with Paolo Gucci.

In a final attempt at reconciliation, in mid-1984 Maurizio Gucci and Paolo Gucci entered into an agreement in which Paolo agreed to sell his shareholder's interest in the various Gucci Companies to Maurizio, and consented to the appointment of Maurizio as President and Chairman of the Board of Directors of the various Gucci companies. Maurizio Gucci was also to receive a commitment from Paolo that he would not use his name commercially. As part of the arrangement, Paolo was to be appointed President of a Gucci licensing company which would license the Gucci name throughout the world. Paolo received a 10% down payment from Maurizio for his Gucci shares and voted to place Maurizio in charge of the Gucci companies. Pursuant to the agreement, plaintiff entered into a consent preliminary injunction in this action and also dropped his pending trademark applications. The deal between Paolo and Maurizio, which was to become effective at the end of 1984, was never consummated. An arbitration panel in Geneva, Switzerland is now adjudicating the dispute in which both parties seek rescission of the agreement as well as damages.

Plaintiff is currently designing lamps, sunglasses, furniture, sleep wear, bedding accessories and fabrics, wall coverings, ladies underwear, lingerie, plates and flatware. In this action, plaintiff seeks a declaration from this Court describing in what manner, if any, he may use his name on the products he designs. Defendant maintains that plaintiff may not use his name in any manner on products he designs for two reasons: (1) plaintiff is prohibited by the terms of a Guccio Gucci Shareholders Agreement which he signed in 1972 from using his personal name in any commercial endeavor; and (2) any use by Paolo Gucci of his personal name on products he designs will create confusion in the minds of the purchasing public with products marketed under defendant's "Gucci" trademark. Plaintiff, on the other hand, asserts that (1) he is not bound by the 1972 Shareholders Agreement; and (2) the use of his personal name, Paolo Gucci, on products which he designs will not cause members of the public to believe that they are purchasing defendant's "Gucci" products.

Discussion

The 1972 Shareholders Agreement

Clause 1 of the Shareholders Agreement of 1972 provides that Messrs. Aldo, Rodolfo, Giorgio, Paolo, Roberto and Vasco Gucci "all have an interest as shareholders" in the capital stock of Guccio Gucci and of another company, and that the "Gucci" family name not be used for business purposes, except in connection with the company's operations. The agreement continues as follows:

> On the basis of the foregoing statement, which shall be considered an integral and substantial part of this instrument for all legal purposes, in order to clarify the provisions of Article 7 of the bylaws of "GUCCIO GUCCI s.r.l." and the charter of BOUTIQUE GUCCI s.r.l.,", the following is agreed and stipulated.... 1) These Messrs. Gucci jointly and severally promise one another on behalf of themselves, their heirs and successors, to refrain, and they do from this time forward refrain, from the use of the family name of "GUCCI" for the exercise of any further industrial, commercial or artisan activity, even if additions or changes were to be made to said name with a view to avoiding confusion with the name of the companies ... for the entire duration of the respective company charter, now extending to December 31, 2075.

This clause from the 1972 Shareholders Agreement reflects, almost literally, the provision set out in Article 7 of the Articles of Guccio Gucci S.r.l. which provides that "the status of quota-holder entails an absolute prohibition to use the 'Gucci' family name in connection with the exercise of any other future industrial, commercial and artisan activity even if additions or changes were made to such name for the purpose of avoiding confusion with the Company's denomination ... [S]uch prohibition shall continue throughout the life of the company, i.e. until 31st December 2075 or until such later date which may be agreed upon at a future time and shall apply also to a quota-holder who may have lost such status for whatsoever reason."

According to defendant, the 1972 Shareholders Agreement is unambiguous and under Italian law clearly prevents Paolo Gucci from using his name, in any manner, even to identify himself as the designer of a specific product. Plaintiff, on the other hand, maintains that under Italian law the 1972 Shareholders Agreement is no longer binding on Paolo Gucci for several reasons discussed below. After a careful review of the testimony of the Italian legal experts, and all other relevant materials, as well as a review of the conduct of the parties since the transformation of Guccio Gucci from an S.r.l. to an S.p.A., the Court concludes that the 1972 Shareholders Agreement is no longer binding on Paolo Gucci.

In sum, although the 1972 Shareholders Agreement is somewhat ambiguous, when viewed in light of subsequently executed corporate documents and in light of the conduct of the parties following the transformation of Guccio Gucci from and S.r.l. to an S.p.a., it is clear the 1972 Agreement is binding currently only on shareholders of Guccio Gucci. Having concluded that the Shareholders Agreement is no longer binding on Paolo Gucci, the Court must now turn to the issue of the likelihood of customer confusion of the name Paolo Gucci with the Gucci trademark if Paolo Gucci were to use his name as either a trademark or to identify himself as the designer of a product.

Likelihood of Confusion

Defendant Gucci Shops has for many years used the trademark "Gucci" on a wide range of products including leather goods, accessories, scarves, footwear and apparel. In addition, Gucci Shops owns 19 United States Trademark Registrations for the mark "Gucci", covering such diverse products as leather goods, clothing, ties, scarves, shoes, belts, keyrings, automobiles, cigarettes, bathrobes, perfume, linens, china and eyeglasses. Gucci Shops has also used, and owns four United States Trademark Registrations for a repeating pattern of diamond-shaped figures, with the linked letters "GG" at the corners of each diamond.

In determining whether plaintiff committed federal trademark infringement under 15 U.S.C. § 1114(a), false designation of origin under 15 U.S.C. § 1125(a) or common law trademark infringement, "the crucial issue is whether there is any likelihood that an appreciable number of ordinarily prudent purchasers are likely to be misled, or indeed simply confused as to the source of goods in question." Resolution of this issue "depends upon a consideration of the facts and circumstances in each case."

In *Polaroid Corp. v. Polarad Electronics Corp.*, 287 F.2d 492 (2d Cir.), the Court of Appeals for the Second Circuit listed the following factors which a court should consider in determining the likelihood of confusion: (1) the strength of the senior user's mark; (2) the degree of similarity between the two marks; (3) the proximity of the products; (4) the likelihood that the senior user will bridge the gap; (5) actual confusion; (6) the junior user's good faith; (7) the quality of the junior user's product; and (8) the sophistication of the buyers.

The great strength of the "Gucci" mark, the very close similarity between the mark "Gucci" and the name "Paolo Gucci" and the near identity of the nature of the primary products bearing those names creates a likelihood that an appreciable number of ordinarily prudent purchasers will be misled or confused as to the source or sponsorship of goods which bear plaintiff's name as a trademark or trade name. The evidence at trial of actual confusion, the testimony of individuals experienced in the field, as well as the Crossland Survey which, although somewhat flawed, provided credible evidence of a likelihood of confusion if plaintiff were to use his name as a trademark or trade name, further support this conclusion. There was no persuasive evidence presented at trial, however, that customers are likely to be confused if Paolo Gucci is permitted to identify himself as the designer of products sold under a separate trademark and/or trade name. Nor is there any reason to believe that the generally sophisticated customer, of the type who purchases Gucci merchandise, would be misled into thinking that a set of Samsonite luggage that carried a label indicating that it was designed by Paolo Gucci, would likely cause the customer to believe he was purchasing a Gucci Shops product.

It was undisputed at trial that the "Gucci" mark is a well-known mark internationally and is, therefore, entitled to "strong protection." *Scarves By Vera, Inc. v. Todo Imports Ltd.*, 544 F.2d 1167, 1170–73 (2d Cir. 1976). Similarly, the Gucci repeating diamond "GG" design is a distinctive mark that is associated in the minds of the public with "Gucci" products.

Plaintiff's "Paolo Gucci" mark incorporates the entirety of Gucci Shops' famous "Gucci" trademark. The two marks are distinguished only by plaintiff's addition of the forename "Paolo" to the surname "Gucci." At trial, plaintiff introduced evidence indicating that he has typically displayed a photograph of himself on the items bearing his name as well as a disclaimer indicating that he is no longer associated with the original Gucci line of products. Plaintiff maintains that this photograph and disclaimer are sufficient to dispel any confusion which may result from the similarity between his trade name Paolo Gucci and the Gucci trademark. Based on the testimony and survey evidence presented at trial, however, the Court cannot agree.

While actual confusion is not a prerequisite to a finding of infringement, "there can be no more positive proof of likelihood of confusion than evidence of actual confusion." *Lawn Tennis Association v. British Tennis Agency*, 1 U.S.P.Q.2d 1283, 1288 (S.D.N.Y. 1986). The testimony at trial indicated that although only a small number of plaintiff's products have been sold in the United States, some of them have been brought to Gucci Shops' stores for repair. *See Gemveto Jewelry Co. v. Jeff Cooper, Inc.*, 613 F. Supp. 1052, 1063 (S.D.N.Y. 1985)(erroneous returns evidence of confusion as to source of products).

In addition to this evidence of actual confusion between Paolo Gucci and Gucci products, defendant also retained the firm of Crossley Surveys, Inc. to conduct a survey to assess the likelihood of customer confusion between "Gucci" products and "Paolo Gucci" products. The survey, which was administered by trained interviewers who intercepted shoppers at three separate shopping malls, involved showing the interviewees six cards each of which bore the name of a well-known designer, a seventh card which bore the name Paolo Gucci, and an eighth card which bore the name Cavaluzzo—a fictitious name added to weed out those respondents who were guessing. After being shown each card, the interviewees were asked a series of questions. The survey results indicated that when consumers were shown a card bearing the name Paolo Gucci, eighty-seven percent of them claimed that they had heard of Paolo Gucci handbags even though only a limited number of such bags have been sold in the United States. When asked where these handbags could be purchased, a large majority of these respondents indicated that Paolo Gucci handbags could be bought at locations at which Gucci Shops are located or at stores at which Gucci but not Paolo Gucci handbags are sold. Clearly, these consumers were confused by Paolo Gucci's name and believed that it referred to products which are manufactured by defendant and available at stores owned or licensed by it.

While it is true, as plaintiff contends, that the survey was somewhat flawed in that it used cards bearing the designers' names instead of actual products—such as handbags, and it did not include a card bearing the name "Gucci," these imperfections in the survey do not unduly taint its reliability in assessing customer confusion. The Crossley Survey was conducted properly and is entitled to significant weight. It canvassed a significant segment of the relevant population, was formulated and supervised by qualified experts, contained appropriate questions, and permitted interviewees to frame answers in their own terms. Finally, although plaintiff launched a full-scale attack on the methods employed in defendant's survey in an effort to discredit it, plaintiff chose not to sponsor an independent survey of his own.

In addition to the evidence of actual confusion as well as the survey evidence on likelihood of confusion discussed above, on three separate occasions the United States Patent & Trademark Office has refused to register marks consisting of or including the name "Paolo Gucci" based on a likelihood of confusion with the "Gucci" mark. Most recently, the PTO has initially refused to register the expression "Paolo Gucci Designs for Riviera," finding that "Gucci is a dominant feature of the mark" and would thus create confusion with products bearing the "Gucci" mark. The Court of Appeals in this circuit has previously noted that these refusals are entitled to substantial weight. *W.E. Bassett Co. v. Revlon, Inc.*, 435 F.2d 656, 662 (2d Cir. 1970).

On the basis of the evidence outlined above, the Court finds that there is a likelihood of appreciable customer confusion if Paolo Gucci were to continue to use his name as a trade name or trademark. The Court must now address the possibility of customer confusion if Paolo Gucci were to identify himself as the designer of products sold under a different trademark which did not include the name "Gucci." Courts have long recognized that to prohibit an individual from using his true family surname is to take away his identity: without it he cannot make known who he is to those who may wish to deal with him; and that is so grievous an injury that courts will avoid imposing it, if they possibly can. This is especially so where the second comer has spent his entire mature life working in the relevant business and, as a result, possesses extraordinary experience, skill and a desire to work in his field. Under those circumstances it cannot be said that the individual is entering the particular field for no apparent reason other than to use a conveniently confusing surname to his advantage.

Balanced against the interests of the individual in using his name in connection with products he designs, is the very strong need of avoiding confusion with the goods of the initial user. "The ultimate aim is to frame an injunction that will avoid confusion in the marketplace, protect a prior company's property interest in its name, and permit an individual to exploit his own identity and reputation in a legitimate manner." *Joseph Scott Co. v. Scott Swimming Pools, Inc.*, 764 F.2d 62 (2d Cir. 1985). In balancing these interests, courts have often noted their concern that injunctions in cases such as this be drawn as narrowly as possible. *Id. See also Waterman Co. v. Modern Pen Co.*, 235 U.S. 88, 35 S. Ct. 91, 59 L. Ed. 142 (1914).

With these principles in mind, it is evident that Paolo Gucci is entitled to identify himself as the designer of products so long as he does so in a manner which will not lead an appreciable number of consumers to believe that his products are "Gucci" products. There was no credible evidence presented at trial indicating that customers would be confused if Paolo were to identify himself as the designer of products sold under a different trademark and/or trade name. Further, common sense dictates that if a consumer is purchasing a suitcase, sold under the trademark of "American Tourister," bearing a label stating that it was designed by Paolo Gucci, there is little if any chance that the consumer will be believe he is purchasing a "Gucci" product manufactured by defendant. Moreover, there was overwhelming evidence at trial that Paolo Gucci spent many years cultivating his talent while serving as Gucci's chief designer. Accordingly, it cannot be argued that Paolo Gucci wishes to enter the field of design simply to capitalize on his name, and therefore any decree which would prohibit him from using his name in a manner not likely to lead to customer confusion would be unjustified.

Finally, plaintiff's other claims and defendant's counterclaims are all dismissed. There was no credible evidence at trial that either plaintiff or defendant acted in bad faith at any time.

Conclusion

In sum, it is clear based on the evidence adduced at trial that if Paolo Gucci were to continue to use his name as a trademark or trade name, an appreciable number of consumers would confuse his goods with those of the defendant. Therefore, in order to protect the interests of defendant in the "Gucci" name, Paolo is enjoined from using "Paolo Gucci" as a trademark or trade name. To enable Paolo to exploit his own talents and identity, however, he is entitled to use his name to identify himself as the designer of products sold under a separate trademark which does not include the name "Gucci." To avoid confusion, the name Paolo Gucci must always appear after the trademark in advertisements and on labels, and must be no more prominent than the trademark. Moreover, plaintiff must use a disclaimer, similar to the one he now employs, which notifies consumers that he is no longer affiliated with any of the Gucci entities.

Notes

1. Paolo Gucci appears to have been acting under the assumption that he had a right to use his name as a brand for goods that he produced. The court described it not as a right, but as an "interest" in using his name that way. Should individuals have a right to use their name or surname as a brand? How powerful a showing would need to be made in order to overcome such a right? Would it be more than a likelihood of confusion?

2. How important to this decision was the fame and relative uncommon nature of the Gucci surname? Would the decision be different if Ralph Lauren was attempting to stop someone with the first name Lauren from using her name to sell apparel?

3. The court enjoined the use of the Paolo Gucci name as a brand and also prohibited the use of his name to identify himself as a designer if it was done in a way that would lead to consumer confusion. Should designers avoid using their names or surnames as brands for fear of limiting the freedom for themselves or relatives to use their own names when not associated with the eponymous company? This issue is discussed more fully in the following section.

3. Losing the Right to Use One's Name

The previous subsection discussed the potential bars to being able to develop one's own name as a trademark and brand. Perhaps more painful is the situation where a designer achieves fame and renown that is intertwined with her eponymous brand and then, as the result of the sale of that brand, she is no longer allowed to use her name and likeness in the field in which she achieved such great success. Notwithstanding the legal counsel they undoubtedly receive, designers may not completely grasp that they no longer will be able to use their names in connection with their new fashion ventures after selling their names for handsome sums.

Although designers who have sold their names may not use those names as a trademark—i.e., as a brand that identifies the source of the goods—they may still use their own names to identify themselves as the designer of a new brand so long as the brand itself does not incorporate the name itself or otherwise appear to be trademark use. For example, the designer's name can be used in press releases or on promotional materials such as websites. Even these uses might be the subject of the original purchasing agreement, however, and the designer should negotiate such rights if she anticipates needing them. These issues arose prominently in the case of the designer Joseph Abboud.

JA Apparel Corp. v. Abboud

682 F. Supp. 2d 294 (S.D.N.Y. 2010)

KATZ, Magistrate Judge.

In this action, Plaintiff JA Apparel Corp. ("Plaintiff" or "JA Apparel") sues Defendants Joseph Abboud ("Abboud"), Houndstooth Corp. ("Houndstooth"), and Herringbone Creative Services, Inc. ("Herringbone") (at times, collectively "Abboud") for (1) breach of contract, (2) trademark infringement, false designation of origin, unfair competition, trademark dilution, false and deceptive trade practices, and (3) a declaratory judgment regarding the nature of its rights, stemming from a June 16, 2000 Purchase and Sale Agreement (the "Agreement"), and a related July 13, 2000 Side Letter Agreement (the "Side Letter"), between, on the one hand, JA Apparel, and on the other, Abboud and Houndstooth.

* * *

Factual Background

The facts underlying this action are set out in more complete detail in the Court's initial Opinion. *See JA Apparel Corp. v. Abboud*, 591 F. Supp. 2d 306, 311–15 (S.D.N.Y. 2008) (*Abboud I*), *vac'd*, 568 F.3d 390 (2d Cir. 2009). The Court assumes the reader's familiarity with those facts, and, in this Opinion, includes only relevant background information, procedural history, and facts relating to any extrinsic evidence of the parties' intent and Abboud's proposed use of his name in promoting his new clothing line.*

I. The Purchase and Sale Agreement

At the heart of this litigation is the interpretation of the Purchase and Sale Agreement, executed on June 16, 2000, by and between JA Apparel, Abboud and Houndstooth. In exchange for a payment of $65.5 million, which was to be "allocated 100% to Abboud," Abboud agreed to "sell, convey, transfer, assign and deliver" to JA Apparel "all of [his] right, title and interest in and to" the following:

(A) The names, trademarks, trade names, service marks, logos, insignias and designations identified on Schedule 1.1(a)(A), and all trademark registrations and applications therefor, and the goodwill related thereto (collectively, the "Trademarks") . . . and all other Intellectual Property (as hereinafter defined).

(B) All licenses to use the Trademarks granted by Houndstooth or Abboud . . . (collectively, the "License Agreements").

(C) All rights to use and apply for the registration of new trade names, trademarks, service marks, logos, insignias and designations containing the words "Joseph Abboud," "designed by Joseph Abboud," "by Joseph Abboud," "JOE" or "JA," or anything similar to or derivative thereof, either alone or in conjunction with other words or symbols (collectively, the "New Trademarks"), for any and all products and services.

(D) All books, financial records, invoices, and other documents, records and data files relating primarily to the Trademarks or the License Agreements.

(E) The goodwill of or pertaining to the Trademarks. (The items referred to in clauses (A) through (E) of this Section 1.1(a) are collectively referred to as the "Assets").

(PX-1 ¶ 1.1(a)(A)-(E).) The Schedule attached as an exhibit to the Agreement is labeled "Trademark Report by Mark," and contains the name Joseph Abboud.

* * *

---

* As noted by the Court in *Abboud I*, the parties have limited their arguments to "whether Abboud can use his name in advertising or marketing materials to promote his 'jaz' line" of clothing. *Abboud I*, 591 F. Supp. 2d at 316 n. 4. Abboud is "not seeking to use the Joseph Abboud name on clothes, labels, or hang-tags for the 'jaz' line;" nor is Plaintiff "seeking to prevent Abboud from being in business and competing, or personally presenting his new 'jaz' line to prospective purchasers." *Id.*

II. The Side Letter

On July 13, 2000, the same parties entered into the Side Letter, pursuant to which Abboud agreed to serve as "Chairman Emeritus" of JA Apparel, and, for a period of five years, provide JA Apparel with, among other things, consulting services relating to fashion design and brand promotion of products sold under the Abboud marks. The Side Agreement, therefore, was to expire on July 13, 2005, but the terms provided that upon expiration, Abboud would not compete with JA Apparel for a period of two years—until July 13, 2007 (the "Restricted Period").

III. The Underlying Dispute

Not long after the execution of the Agreement and the Side Letter, the parties' relationship soured. They fought over Abboud's role in the creative process at JA Apparel, and Abboud filed and later dismissed a lawsuit against JA Apparel. The parties temporarily resolved their differences in the summer of 2004 by way of a June 29, 2004 Letter Agreement, pursuant to which Abboud was given new responsibilities at JA Apparel. The following year, in the spring of 2005, Abboud informed JA Apparel that he would no longer continue in his position with JA Apparel. The Personal Services period terminated on July 13, 2005, thereby triggering the Restricted Period that was to run until July 13, 2007.

In early 2007, Abboud began plans to start his new "jaz" clothing line, which would compete in certain respects with the clothing and accessories sold by JA Apparel under the Joseph Abboud trademark. But it was not until August 2007 that JA Apparel first learned of Abboud's intentions to use his name in connection with the new venture through an article published in DNR, a leading magazine of the men's fashion industry. (*See* PX-8.) The DNR article initially stated that "Abboud, the person, is prohibited from using the Joseph Abboud name on any product or marketing materials." (PX-8.) The article's author, however, notified JA Apparel that Defendants had requested a correction (*see* PX-9), and DNR later ran a "Clarification," which stated that Abboud is "allowed to use his name on marketing and advertising materials for Jaz." (PX-10.) In August 2007, the *Wall Street Journal* ran a similar article announcing the new "jaz" line, and which reported that Abboud "plans to promote his new label with the tagline 'a new composition by designer Joseph Abboud.'" (PX-11.)

Subsequently, Abboud created several "mock-ups" of proposed ads for the new "jaz" clothing line. (*See, e.g.*, PX-42, PX-43, DX-187, and DX-188.) Each of these ads includes the words "Joseph Abboud" in addition to Abboud's new trademark, "jaz." While the ads are similar in many respects, the font, size, and placement of the words differ in each of the ads, and are discussed in greater detail in this Opinion's fair use analysis.

JA Apparel maintains that while Abboud is free to compete in the menswear market, he sold all rights to use his name in connection with goods and services, and that his proposed uses of his name in connection with the "jaz" line would violate the Agreement, infringe JA Apparel's trademarks, and constitute unfair competition.

Defendants, conversely, maintain that Abboud merely sold the use of his name as a trademark and did not sell the exclusive right to use his name for all commercial purposes. Thus, they argue, the proposed use of his name in advertising constitutes trademark fair use. In furtherance of that position, Defendants assert Counterclaims against JA Apparel and Staff for using the Joseph Abboud name in ways that they claim deceive consumers, trade on Abboud's personal reputation, and constitute unfair competition.

* * *

Discussion

On remand from the Court of Appeals, this Court must first decide two narrow questions: (1) based on the Agreement's language and any extrinsic evidence of the parties' intent, did Abboud agree to sell his name, other than as a trademark or related intellectual property, to JA Apparel?; and (2) if Abboud sold his name only as a trademark or related intellectual property, do his proposed ads qualify as fair use under the Lanham Act? Answering the first question in the affirmative disposes of the need to address the second, as well as the parties' other remaining claims and counterclaims.

I. Contract Interpretation

* * *

Although the parties previously maintained that the Agreement is unambiguous, and this Court agreed, we are nonetheless bound by the Second Circuit's conclusion that the Agreement is, in fact, ambiguous. Thus, the Court must consider both the plain language of the Agreement and any extrinsic evidence of intent in order to decide whether Abboud sold the exclusive right to use his name commercially to JA Apparel. Upon a careful review of the Agreement and all attendant circumstances to its execution, the Court concludes that he did not.

On November 11, 1999, after preliminary discussions regarding the transaction that would ultimately result in the Agreement and the Side Letter, Abboud sent a "letter of understanding" to Mr. Roberto Jorio Fili, CEO of JA Apparel's then-owner, GFT. (*See* DX-161.) Specifically, Abboud noted as one of three "Points of Agreement," the sale of "all Joseph Abboud trademarks." (*Id.*) The letter made no mention of the sale of Abboud's personal name for commercial use, but concluded with Abboud's self-proclaimed ultimate goal: "to build the Joseph Abboud name into the successful global brand I know it can be." (*Id.*) On December 3, 1999, Mr. Paolo Vigitello of GFT, responded to Abboud, noting that "it must be defined that the acquisition target is represented by all Joseph Abboud trademarks personally owned by Mr. Abboud." (DX-2.)

On February 2, 2000, the parties met in Milan, Italy to discuss further details of the sale. In minutes from this meeting, Fili "stresses that GFT wants to buy only the trademarks and not the two companies currently owned by J[oseph] Abboud." (DX-162.) A letter outlining the "key points" from the verbal agreement reached at this meeting makes clear that the "[o]bject of the operation" is the "acquisition of trademarks." (DX-3.)

Two days later, on February 4, 2000, Vigitello sent a letter to Abboud confirming that the "[t]arget of the deal" is the "purchase of all the trademarks existing and worldwide registered plus exclusive and perpetual right to the buyer to use and apply for registration of whatever new denomination in association with the name 'Joseph Abboud' and/or using 'designed by Joseph Abboud' or simply 'by Joseph Abboud' linked to automotive industries products, to clothing, casualwear, sportswear and furnishing products and/or accessories in the most wide meaning . . . and home products." (DX-4.) Vigitello continued, "[If JA Apparel intends to use] the name 'Joseph Abboud' in association with products different from the ones above mentioned[, it] must obtain the previous written consent [of Abboud] . . . , which consent cannot be unreasonably withheld." (*Id.*)

The following week, on February 10, 2000, the parties entered into a letter of intent, specifying the "[a]ssets to be [p]urchased" as all "right, title and interest in and to all trade names, trademarks and service marks existing as of the Closing (as defined below) and registered or used in any country in the world (collectively, the 'Trademarks'), together with all registrations and applications therefor, the goodwill related thereto and any and all claims for past infringement." (DX-5.) The letter of intent also denoted that JA Apparel was purchasing "all licenses to use the Trademarks" and "all of the right, title and interest . . . to use and apply for the registration of new trade names, trademarks and service marks containing the words 'Joseph Abboud,' 'designed by Joseph Abboud,' 'by Joseph Abboud,' 'JOE' or 'JA,' or anything similar thereto or derivative thereof, either alone or in conjunction with other words or symbols (collectively, the 'New Trademarks')." (*Id.*) The letter of intent did not include the sale of "names."

As discussions continued, the agreement not to compete became a point of contention for Abboud. In a February 23, 2000 letter, Abboud's counsel, Mr. Theodore Dinsmoor, wrote to JA Apparel's counsel, Mr. Jeffrey LaGueux, alerting him that:

> [Abboud] wants to have the opportunity to pursue his trade as a designer of apparel [after the expiration of the five-year Personal Services period.] In this regard, Mr. Abboud understands that any effort on his part to pursue his trade as a designer of apparel could not include his use of the name "Joseph Abboud" or any of the other trademarks conveyed to JA Apparel.

(PX-347.)

Concerned that the tension between the parties might derail the deal, Fili wrote directly to Abboud on February 25, 2000, and reiterated that "[r]ight from the initial steps of our negotiation I have always declared that our objective was and still is the acquisition of the trade marks." (DX-8.) In response, Abboud wrote to Fili:

> If, for whatever reasons, the corporation does not want to continue with my services after five years, I want the option to practice my skills should

> I choose to continue working in the future. It goes without saying that at *no time* will I have any rights to any of the Joseph Abboud trademarks. Here is where you must separate Joseph Abboud personally from the Joseph Abboud trademarks.

(DX-9.) In conclusion, Abboud wrote that his decision is "emotional, because I am relinquishing my name (albeit for a large sum) which I have worked toward building since I entered this industry full time in 1972, 28 years ago." (*Id.*)

On March 17, 2000, the parties entered into a letter agreement, whose language mirrored that of the February 10, 2000 letter of intent. (DX-165.) Again, the letter agreement made no mention of the sale of "names."

JA Apparel, as agreed upon by the parties, prepared the first draft of the Agreement.7 The draft Agreement, sent from LaGueux to Dinsmoor on May 3, 2000, described certain of the assets to be purchased as "[t]he *names,* trademarks, trade names, service marks, logos, insignias and designations identified on Schedule 1.1(a)(i)(A)." (PX-318 (emphasis added).) This was the first time the word "names," standing alone as an asset to be purchased, appeared in any of the parties' correspondence. Dinsmoor wrote to LaGueux on May 19, 2000, proposing various changes to the draft Agreement, but did not comment on the newly inserted term, "names." (DX-163.) As discussed by the parties, Dinsmoor compiled a listing of all trademarks owned by Abboud that was to be used as Schedule 1.1(a)(A), and sent it to LaGueux on May 23, 2000. (DX-185.) The parties exchanged a second draft of the Agreement in June (*see* DX-166), which continued to include the word "names," but Dinsmoor again did not address its inclusion or meaning. (*See* DX-167.)

On June 16, 2000, the parties prepared a draft press release to accompany the acquisition. (*See* DX-178.) The release noted that "[o]n the basis of the signed contract, GFT Net will acquire the trademarks and licensing agreements registered in the name of Joseph Abboud." (*Id.*) A subsequent revised release contained similar language, referencing the purchase of "all existing trademarks and licensing agreements and all future trademarks bearing the Joseph Abboud name." (DX-14.) Neither version of the release indicated that the "name" Joseph Abboud, as anything other than a trademark, would be sold.

At the closing of the sale, Abboud assigned "all rights, title and interest in and to the Marks and registrations or applications associated with them, together with the goodwill of the business symbolized by and associated with the Marks and their respective registrations or applications." (DX-180.) Abboud did not assign any rights to his name, other than for use as a trademark.

The final Agreement, as did the drafts, included the sale of "names," in addition to "trade names, trademarks, service marks, logos, insignias and designations identified on Schedule 1.1(a) (A)," but there is no evidence of any negotiations or discussions of the sale of Abboud's name as an asset distinct from the trademarks and related intellectual property. (PX-1.)

Despite the "fairly extensive extrinsic evidence" submitted at trial, *see Abboud I*, 591 F. Supp. 2d at 318, this evidence sheds little, if any, light on the parties' intended meaning of the term "names." That said, the parties' communications indicated that from the outset of their negotiations they intended to buy or sell only trademarks and related intellectual property. (*See, e.g.*, DX-161 ("letter of understanding" from Abboud to Fili denoting a "Point of Agreement" as the sale of "all Joseph Abboud trademarks"); DX-2 (letter from Vigitello to Abboud, noting that "the acquisition target is represented by all Joseph Abboud trademarks"); DX-162 (meeting minutes indicating that GFT "wants to buy only the trademarks"); DX-4 (letter from Vigitello to Abboud identifying the "[t]arget of the deal" as the "purchase of all the trademarks"); DX-5 (letter of intent specifying the "[a]ssets to be [p]urchased" as all "trade names, trademarks and service marks"); DX-8 (letter from Fili to Abboud reiterating that "our objective was and still is the acquisition of the trade marks").) It was only at the drafting stage that the word "names" entered the picture as a term of the Agreement. (*See* PX-318 (May 3, 2000 draft of the Agreement including, for the first time, the word "names").) In fact, the word "names" as an asset to be sold is included only in the drafts and final version of the Agreement, and in no other correspondence relating to the transaction. Indeed, neither party has been able to point the Court to any extrinsic evidence that evinces the reason for this word's inclusion or meaning in the Agreement.

JA Apparel focuses primarily on Abboud's failure to object to the term "names" in the draft Agreement to support its proposed interpretation. The Court does not find such silence to constitute sufficient evidence of an intent to buy or sell an additional and distinct asset never discussed by the parties.

JA Apparel does, however, emphasize two letters that it claims illustrate that "Abboud did not retain the right to use his name under the terms of the Agreement." (*See* Pl.'s Post-Remand Mem. at 16.) The first is a letter written several months before the Agreement was executed, from Abboud's attorney to JA Apparel's attorney. (*See* PX-347.) In the letter, Dinsmoor writes, "Mr. Abboud understands that any effort on his part to pursue his trade as a designer of apparel *could not include the use of the name Joseph Abboud* or any of the other trademarks conveyed to JA Apparel." (*Id.* (emphasis added).) Although at first glance this sentence appears to preclude "use of the name Joseph Abboud," it is followed by the phrase "or any of the other trademarks." (*Id.*) The inclusion of the word "other" to qualify "trademarks" demonstrates that "Joseph Abboud" was also referenced as a trademark. But the Court need not rely on this academic exercise of sentence deconstruction, because in the same letter, Dinsmoor writes, "technically JA Apparel is only acquiring Mr. Abboud's trademarks." (*Id.*)

JA Apparel also relies heavily on a letter from Abboud to Fili in March of 2000, in which he characterizes his decision to consummate the sale as "emotional, because I am relinquishing my name (albeit for a large sum) which I have worked toward building since I entered this industry full time in 1972, 28 years ago." (DX-9.) JA Apparel argues that Abboud could not be referring to only trademarks in this sentence, because "Joseph Abboud" was not used as a trademark until 1987. (*See* Pl.'s Post-Remand Mem. at 16–17.) At first blush, this document does lend some support to JA Apparel's position. Nevertheless, in the same letter, Abboud writes, "It goes without saying that at *no time* will I have any rights to any of the Joseph Abboud trademarks." (DX-9.) And then, in a sentence that perhaps underscores the essence of this entire dispute, Abboud writes, "Here is where you must separate Joseph Abboud personally from the Joseph Abboud trademarks." (*Id.*)

Although JA Apparel has offered both a reasonable and persuasive interpretation of the Agreement—and one that the Court previously adopted—Abboud has offered a competing interpretation that the Second Circuit has concluded is equally reasonable. *See JA Apparel Corp.*, 568 F.3d at 398–99. This fact, coupled with the extrinsic evidence that explicitly discusses the sale of trademarks and related intellectual property, and the absence of any extrinsic evidence that addresses Abboud's sale of his personal name for all other commercial purposes, compels the Court to conclude that section 1.1(a)(A) did not convey to JA Apparel the exclusive right to use Abboud's name for commercial purposes other than as a trademark, service mark, trade name, or brand name.

The Court, however, is mindful that such an interpretation might be construed as rendering the word "names" mere surplusage. *See God's Battalion of Prayer Pentecostal Church, Inc. v. Miele Assocs., LLP*, 6 N.Y.3d 371, 374, 812 N.Y.S.2d 435, 437, 845 N.E.2d 1265 (2006) ("A contract 'should be read to give effect to all its provisions.'") (quoting *Mastrobuono v. Shearson Lehman Hutton, Inc.*, 514 U.S. 52, 63, 115 S. Ct. 1212, 1219, 131 L. Ed. 2d 76 (1995)); *see also Two Guys from Harrison--N.Y., Inc. v. S.F.R. Realty Assocs.*, 63 N.Y.2d 396, 403, 482 N.Y.S.2d 465, 468, 472 N.E.2d 315 (1984) ("[O]ne of a court's goals is to avoid an interpretation that would leave contractual clauses meaningless."). Nevertheless, as Judge Sack noted in his concurring opinion in the Court of Appeals' remand decision:

> [T]he rule [against surplusage] should nonetheless be applied with a grain or two of salt when examining a list of words having similar or even overlapping meaning in a commercial agreement. Such an itemization of terms may reflect an intent to occupy a field of meaning, not to separate it into differentiated parts. Indeed, this is a common—perhaps all-too-familiar—technique used in drafting agreements, commercial and otherwise. With this technique, words are used more like the brush strokes of a house painter than of those of a portrait painter—each intended principally to ensure that the surface is covered, not to convey a separate piece of information.

JA Apparel Corp., 568 F.3d at 407 n. 4 (Sack, J., concurring).

In memorializing their intent, the parties included what amounted to a laundry list of words that fell under the more general penumbra of "trademarks" and related intellectual property (which can include, e.g., brand names or commercial names). That the word "names" could bear a broader meaning, including one's personal name, cannot overcome the dearth of extrinsic evidence in support of JA Apparel's interpretation of the Agreement. Thus, it is more reasonable to conclude that the word names was intended to mean something similar to the other assets sold in section 1.1(a)(A) of the Agreement—such as "brand names" or "commercial names"—and not the exclusive right to all commercial use of Abboud's personal name. This is consistent with the language of section 1.1(a)(C), in which Abboud sold to JA Apparel the right to use and apply for new marks containing Abboud's personal name.

Because the Court concludes that Abboud did not sell the exclusive right to use his personal name commercially, the Court must continue with an analysis of JA Apparel's trademark claims.

II. Trademark Infringement

Based upon Abboud's proposed use of his name in advertising the "jaz" line of clothing, JA Apparel also asserts claims for trademark infringement under Section 32 of the Lanham Act, 15 U.S.C. § 1114(1), and New York common law. In response, Abboud relies on the defense of "fair use" pursuant to Section 33(b)(4) of the Lanham Act, 15 U.S.C. § 1115(b)(4). In addition, Abboud argues that his "proposed use is protected commercial speech under the First Amendment to the United States Constitution, and that JA Apparel is not entitled to equitable relief on its infringement claims because of its own unclean hands." *Abboud I,* 591 F. Supp. 2d at 327.

Before addressing the merits of the trademark claims and defenses, it bears noting the inherent relationship between the trademark and contract claims. Despite the Court's conclusion that Abboud did not sell the exclusive right to commercially use his name, there is no question that Abboud sold his trademarks to JA Apparel, which include the mark "Joseph Abboud." Thus, if JA Apparel prevails on its trademark claims, Abboud is not only liable for infringement, but also for breach of contract.

A. Legal Standard for Trademark Infringement

In order to prevail on a claim for trademark infringement under Section 32(1) of the Lanham Act, 15 U.S.C. § 1114(1), a plaintiff is required to show that its marks are valid and entitled to protection and that a defendant's use of those marks is likely to cause consumer confusion as to the origin or sponsorship of the defendant's goods. *See, e.g., Virgin Enters. Ltd. v. Nawab,* 335 F.3d 141, 146 (2d Cir. 2003); Time, *Inc. v. Petersen Publ'g Co.,* 173 F.3d 113, 117 (2d Cir. 1999).

In evaluating the likelihood of confusion, courts in this Circuit regularly apply what have become known as the *Polaroid* factors: (1) strength of plaintiff's mark; (2) degree of similarity between the two marks; (3) proximity of the parties' products or services; (4) likelihood that the prior owner will bridge the gap between the parties' products or services; (5) actual confusion; (6) defendant's bad faith in adopting its mark; (7) quality of defendant's products or services; and (8) sophistication of the relevant consumers. *Polaroid Corp. v. Polarad Elecs. Corp.,*

287 F.2d 492, 495 (2d Cir. 1961); *see also Natural Organics, Inc. v. Nutraceutical Corp.*, 426 F.3d 576, 578 (2d Cir. 2005).

B. Application

As determined by the Court in *Abboud I:*

> Plaintiff put on competent evidence at trial demonstrating, among other things: (a) the strength of the Abboud marks (*see* TT at 30–41, 246, 257, 540–41); (b) the close proximity of the goods and services at issue (*see id.* at 72–73, 76, 87–88, 95–96, 610–614; PX 8, 11, 38); and (c) at least some instances of actual confusion within the industry (*see id.*, at 128–29, 276–280, 293–94, 300–03; PX 13, 187, 189), despite the fact that the "jaz" products have not even hit the market. Based on this evidence, the Court has no difficulty concluding that there exists a substantial likelihood of confusion between Abboud's proposed uses and Plaintiff's trademarks.

Abboud I, 591 F. Supp. 2d at 328. Similarly, the Second Circuit concluded that, on appeal, "defendants effectively conceded that JA owned valid 'Joseph Abboud' trademarks and that it had made a *prima facie* showing under the *Polaroid* test, [and] that [Abboud's] use of his name as a trademark would likely cause confusion." *JA Apparel Corp.*, 568 F.3d at 400 (internal citations omitted). Despite Abboud's attempt to relitigate the likelihood of confusion on remand (*see* Defs.' Post-Remand Mem. I at 80–81), the Court sees no reason to revisit this issue. Accordingly, the Court need only address Abboud's fair use defense, and, if necessary, his First Amendment and unclean hands defenses.

C. Legal Standard for Statutory Fair Use

The fair use defense, which allows for some level of confusion, is an absolute defense to claims of trademark infringement, trademark dilution, and false designation of origin. To successfully assert the fair use defense, an alleged infringer must demonstrate that:

> [T]he use of the name, term, or device charged to be an infringement is a use, otherwise than as a mark, . . . of a term or device which is descriptive of and used fairly and in good faith only to describe the goods or services of such party, or their geographic origin.

15 U.S.C. § 1115(b)(4). Thus, in order to determine whether the use of a term is "fair" under this defense, courts endeavor to assess whether the term is used (1) descriptively, (2) other than as a mark, and (3) in good faith. *See, e.g., Car-Freshner Corp. v. S.C. Johnson & Son, Inc.*, 70 F.3d 267, 269 (2d Cir. 1995).

Abboud argues that he is not seeking to use his name as a trademark. By the use of such phrases as "by the award-winning designer Joseph Abboud" and "a new composition by designer Joseph Abboud," Abboud argues that he is merely seeking to use his name descriptively to convey information to the public about the products sold under his "jaz" trademark.

A use of a mark is descriptive where "the name or term is used 'to describe the goods.'" *Cosmetically Sealed Indus., Inc. v. Chesebrough-Pond's USA Co.*, 125 F.3d 28, 30 (2d Cir. 1997) (quoting 15 U.S.C. § 1115(b)(4)). The Second Circuit has not limited the phrase "to describe the goods" to the description of a characteristic of the goods, but rather, allows for the use of words or images "in their 'descriptive sense.'" *See id.* (quoting *Car-Freshner Corp.*, 70 F.3d at 269). "Descriptive use is evident in such situations '[w]here a mark incorporates a term that is the only reasonably available means of describing a characteristic of another's goods.'" *Dessert Beauty, Inc. v. Fox*, 568 F. Supp. 2d 416, 426 (S.D.N.Y. 2008) (quoting *EMI Catalogue P'ship v. Hill, Holliday, Connors, Cosmopulos, Inc.*, 228 F.3d 56, 65 (2d Cir. 2000)). Confusion that may result from a defendant's descriptive use of a plaintiff's mark is often viewed as "a risk entailed in the [plaintiff's] selection of a mark with descriptive attributes." *Car-Freshner Corp.*, 70 F.3d at 270; *accord Cosmetically Sealed Indus.*, 125 F.3d at 30.

To determine if a defendant is using the challenged term or phrase "as a trademark," courts examine whether a defendant's use is designed to "indicate [] the source or origin of consumer products." *Dessert Beauty*, 568 F. Supp. 2d at 424 (citing *Tommy Hilfiger Licensing, Inc. v. Nature Labs, LLC*, 221 F. Supp. 2d 410, 414 (S.D.N.Y. 2002)). Put another way, "the use of [a] term as a symbol to attract public attention" is generally considered "use . . . as a mark." *Safeway Stores, Inc. v. Safeway Properties, Inc.*,307 F.2d 495, 499 (2d Cir. 1962). When use of the challenged words or phrase is accompanied by a defendant's own, conspicuously visible mark, this generally does not constitute trademark use. *See Cosmetically Sealed Indus.*, 125 F.3d at 30-31 (concluding that non-trademark use is "evidenced by the fact that the source of the defendants' product is clearly identified by the prominent display of the defendants' own trademarks"); *see also Car-Freshner Corp.*, 70 F.3d at 270 (finding defendant's use did not constitute "use as a mark" when product was sold "in boxes prominently bearing [defendant's] trademark [and] corporate logo"); *but see E. Gluck Corp. v. Rothenhaus*, 585 F. Supp. 2d 505, 513 (S.D.N.Y. 2008) (stating that "multiple marks may be used together"); *Quiksilver Inc. v. Kymsta Corp.*, 466 F.3d 749, 757 (9th Cir. 2006) ("A product mark like 'ROXY,' even if always displayed with a house mark like 'QUIKSILVER,' may acquire independent trademark significance."). Courts should also consider the "'physical nature of the use in terms of size, location, and other characteristics in comparison with the appearance of other descriptive matter or other trademarks,' as well as the 'presence or absence of precautionary measures such as labeling or other devices designed to minimize the risk that the term will be understood in its trademark sense.'" *See JA Apparel Corp.*, 568 F.3d at 401 (quoting *Restatement (Third) of Unfair Competition* § 28 cmt. c).

With respect to the third factor, bad faith is often evinced by an "intent to confuse." *See id.* A defendant who "inten[ds] to trade on the good will of the trademark holder by creating confusion as to source or sponsorship" cannot claim that his use is employed in good faith. *See EMI Catalogue P'ship*,228 F.3d at 66. This analysis is similar to the sixth *Polaroid* factor, which examines whether a defendant "intended to capitalize on plaintiff's good will." *See id.; see also Fun-Damental Too, Ltd. v. Gemmy Indus.*, 111 F.3d 993, 1005 (2d Cir. 1997); *Sports Auth., Inc. v. Prime Hospitality Corp.*, 89 F.3d 955, 964 (2d Cir. 1996). In this step, a court may also consider any likelihood of confusion. *See KP Permanent Make-Up, Inc. v. Lasting Impression I, Inc.*, 543 U.S. 111, 123, 125 S. Ct. 542, 550, 160 L. Ed. 2d 440 (2004) (noting that the fair use defense "does not foreclose the relevance of the extent of any likely consumer confusion"); *Madrigal Audio Labs., Inc. v. Cello, Ltd.*, 799 F.2d 814, 823 (2d Cir. 1986) (permitting defendant to advertise with his surname, provided he does so "in a not overly intrusive manner"); *see also* 2 McCarthy § 11:47 ("I think it clear that traditional evidence of likely confusion is indeed admissible and relevant on the issue of classic fair use.").

The fact that a defendant uses another's mark with knowledge of a plaintiff's federal registration or without consulting counsel does not preclude the fair use defense. *See Car-Freshner Corp.*, 70 F.3d at 270. Nevertheless, some courts have found that an inference of a lack of good faith may be drawn from a defendant's breach of an agreement not to use the disputed trademark. *See Inst. for Scientific Info. v. Gordon & Breach, Sci. Publishers, Inc.*, 931 F.2d 1002, 1009 (3d Cir. 1991).

In the context of surnames, additional circumstances may warrant consideration. While a surname may acquire secondary meaning and become a trademark, it will generally "continue[ ] to serve the important function to its bearer of acting as a symbol of that individual's personality, reputation and accomplishments as distinguished from that of the business, corporation or otherwise, with which he has been associated." *Madrigal Audio Labs.*, 799 F.2d at 822. Historically, courts believed that "[e]very man has the absolute right to use his own name in his own business, even though he may interfere with or injure the business of another person bearing the same name." *Meneely v. Meneely*, 62 N.Y. 427, 427 (1875). The more modern view, however, is that the "so-called 'sacred right' theory that every man may employ his own name in his business is not unlimited." *David B. Findlay v. Findlay*, 18 N.Y.2d 12, 19, 271 N.Y.S.2d 652, 655, 218 N.E.2d 531 (1966).

If an individual has previously sold "use of his name and its goodwill, to the plaintiff, . . . courts will be especially alert to foreclose attempts by the seller to 'keep for himself the essential thing he sold, and also keep the price he got for it.'" *Levitt Corp. v. Levitt*, 593 F.2d 463, 468 (2d Cir. 1979) (quoting *Guth v. Guth Chocolate Co.*, 224 F. 932, 934 (4th Cir. 1915)); *see also Equibrand Corp. v. Reinsman Equestrian Prods., Inc.*, No. 03-cv-0536, 2007 WL 1461393, at *13 (N.D.Tex. May 17, 2007) (finding that if an individual sells the right to use his name in connection with certain products, a subsequent attempt to use his name with different products "is not a 'fair use' . . . even if it is an accurate description of the products"). If a court determines that an individual sold only the right to use his name as a trademark, as opposed to the exclusive right to use his name commercially, the seller may advertise his affiliation with a new company, but must do so "in a not overly intrusive manner." *Madrigal Audio Labs.*, 799 F.2d at 823. Finally, in addressing whether use of a surname is in bad faith, there is certainly a distinction to be made between a defendant who happens to have the same surname as the plaintiff's trademark, and a defendant who has previously sold his surname-trademark to the plaintiff. *See* 2 McCarthy § 13:15 ("If a person whose surname has been legally adopted by a senior user, then severs his ties with that company and goes into business for himself, he has no unqualified right to use his own name, if the result is likelihood of confusion.").

D. Application

Throughout the trial, Abboud waffled as to the precise manner in which he believes he can use his name under the Agreement. At the outset of the trial, JA Apparel introduced as evidence several "mock-ups" of proposed ads created by Abboud. (*See, e.g.*, PX-42, PX-43.) Abboud, however, testified that these were only "potential layouts for a concept for advertising," and he had not yet "decided what he was going to do" with them. (*See* TT 575–78, 596–601.) Although Abboud is reluctant to commit to these earlier proposed ads, the Court will consider them as relevant to Abboud's intentions and potential uses of the Joseph Abboud name in advertising. Towards the end of the trial, Abboud submitted two additional proposed ads that he believes will not infringe on JA Apparel's trademark rights, and to which he was willing to commit for purposes of this Court's fair use analysis. (*See* DX-187, DX-188.) The Court has included as exhibits to this Opinion one of the ads contained in Plaintiff's Exhibit 42, Plaintiff's Exhibit 43, and Defendants' Exhibit 187.

1. Descriptive, Non-Trademark Use

In the Court's view, the two proposed ads that Abboud believes qualify under the fair use defense, Defendants' Exhibits 187 and 188, do not use Abboud's name as a trademark. A viewer of these ads is immediately drawn to the large, white scripted font, approximately four inches wide by two inches high, in which Abboud's duly owned trademark, "jaz," is displayed. The words "Joseph Abboud" in these two exhibits appear in the context of a complete sentence, "JAZ IS A NEW LUXURY COLLECTION CREATED BY THE AWARD-WINNING DESIGNER JOSEPH ABBOUD." This sentence is in a significantly smaller font than "jaz," roughly 3/16 of an inch high, and placed in the lower left-hand corner of the ad. The ad also includes the words "FALL 2008" in the upper left-hand corner, and "NEW YORK" and "MONTREAL," each followed by a telephone number, in the lower right-hand corner. All of these words are in the same font, color, and size as the tagline that includes Abboud's name. As a result, Abboud's name is no more the focal point of the ads than the company's telephone number. Nor is it positioned in such a way as to attract significant public attention.

Turning to the next factor in the fair use test, Abboud uses his name, at least in Defendants' Exhibits 187 and 188, in its descriptive sense. The phrase "JAZ IS A NEW LUXURY COLLECTION CREATED BY THE AWARD-WINNING DESIGNER JOSEPH ABBOUD" alerts viewers that Abboud, the individual, is the designer behind the new "jaz" clothing line. And indeed, Abboud is an award-winning designer who has created "jaz." Furthermore, Abboud's use of his name is the only "reasonably available means" by which he can inform his potential customers that he is the designer of the "jaz" line. *See Dessert Beauty*, 568 F. Supp. 2d at 426. Thus, the Court concludes that Abboud's proposed use of his name in Defendants' Exhibits 187 and 188 is a descriptive, non-trademark use.

Certain of Abboud's other proposed uses, however, may not be so easily characterized as descriptive, non-trademark uses. For example, in several of the mock-ups to which Abboud refused to commit, "Joseph Abboud" is displayed in block letters, either just below or to the side of the only slightly larger trademark, "jaz." (*See, e.g.*, PX-42.) Although Abboud's name is always preceded by the phrase "a new composition by," oftentimes that phrase is much smaller and/or in a different font than the words "Joseph Abboud." In addition, the words "Joseph Abboud," in some of these ads, are written in what appears to be the identical font as one of JA Apparel's federal trademark registrations. (*See* Pl.'s Post-Trial Mem. at 16 (Registration No. 2690336).) And while Abboud's trademark, "jaz," certainly grabs the viewer's attention, the words "Joseph Abboud," in at least some of the mock-ups, are similarly eye-catching. In the Court's view, such a use takes Abboud's name outside of the realm of descriptive, non-trademark use, because, while perhaps technically describing the authorship of the "jaz" line, the name is used more as an attention-grabbing symbol. *See Safeway Stores*, 307 F.2d at 499.

On the other hand, Plaintiff's Exhibit 43 is clearly a descriptive, non-trademark use. In that ad, Abboud's trademark, "jaz," is prominently displayed, in the same large, white scripted font used in Defendants' Exhibit 187. Abboud's name is used only within a block of very small text in the lower right-hand corner of the ad next to Abboud's photo. It is practically a strain on the eyes to read the miniscule text (approximately 1/16 of an inch high), which simply identifies Abboud as the model in the ad's photo and indicates he is the designer behind the "jaz" line: "DESIGNER JOSEPH ABBOUD IN A 2 BUTTON SUPER 120 S CHARCOAL CHALKSTRIPE FROM HIS FALL 2008 JAZ COLLECTION." (*Id.*) Further, those words are followed by a disclaimer that "DESIGNER JOSEPH ABBOUD IS NO LONGER ASSOCIATED OR AFFILIATED WITH JA APPAREL CORP., THE OWNER OF THE TRADEMARK 'JOSEPH ABBOUD.'™" (*Id.*) The disclaimer certainly assists in eliminating any confusion that might result. In fact, JA Apparel all but admits that this ad would be a permissible use by Abboud. (*See* Pl.'s Post-Remand Mem. at 22–23.)

2. Good Faith Use

The more difficult question posed by Abboud's fair use defense, however, is whether Abboud intends to use his name in good faith. Abboud argues primarily that his use is in good faith due to the fact that he has refrained from running any ads, sought guidance from counsel, and requested declaratory relief from the Court on the permissible fair use of his personal name. (*See* Defs.' Post-Remand Mem. I at 69–72.) While the Court appreciates Abboud's deference to the legal process, this reasoning is misplaced. Because the Court is asked to consider Abboud's *proposed* uses, the analysis must look to whether, *if* the ad ran, Abboud is using his name with an intent to confuse. *See JA Apparel Corp.*, 568 F.3d at 401. If the Court concludes that Abboud, in fact, "inten [ds] to trade on the good will of [JA Apparel] by creating confusion as to source or sponsorship," he cannot meet the third factor of the fair use test. *See EMI Catalogue P'ship,* 228 F.3d at 66. Any likelihood of confusion that results—even unintentionally—is also relevant. *See KP Permanent Make-Up,* 543 U.S. at 123, 125 S. Ct. at 551 ("[W]e do not rule out the pertinence of the degree of consumer confusion under the fair use defense.").

The Court is troubled by several of Abboud's admissions with respect to his intent to use his name in advertising. First, Abboud testified that he intends to use "the *slogan* or *tagline* 'a new composition by designer Joseph Abboud.'" (TT 579 (emphasis added).) Use of a "slogan" or "tagline" certainly suggests an intent to create an affiliation between "jaz" products and "Joseph Abboud." And, although Abboud's subjective intent might be "to inform the public that [Abboud the individual is] the creator of the product," (*id.*) as opposed to JA Apparel, absent a disclaimer, this seems likely to create significant confusion in certain of the proposed ads.

Further, Abboud testified that he wants his name to "[c]ertainly [be] large enough" for consumers to see and read. (TT 569.) This statement again suggests that Abboud, in effect, wants to promote his "jaz" line by using "Joseph Abboud" as a symbol to attract public attention. *See Safeway Stores,* 307 F.2d at 499.

Perhaps most telling, is Abboud's admission that he wants to inform the public that he is the "source" of the new "jaz" line. (*See* TT 580.) Trademarks are designed to identify the "source" of goods and services. *See TCPIP Holding Inc. v. Haar Commc'ns, Inc.,* 244 F.3d 88, 95 (2d Cir. 2001) (noting that "trademarks functions [sic] as source-identifiers"). While Abboud admittedly used the term "source" as a layman (*see* Defs.' Post-Remand Reply Mem. at 7 n. 9), the Court cannot ignore the significance of this statement when coupled with the other evidence regarding Abboud's intentions.

Abboud's counsel has argued on remand that "Abboud's identification by *personal* name enables consumers to assess his talent, skill, artistic ability and reputation and thereby discern the quality, proficiency, suitability and safety of his 'jaz' collection." (Defs.' Post-Remand Mem. I at 73.) This is, again, precisely what trademarks are designed to protect. *See TCPIP Holding Co.,* 244 F.3d at 95 (noting that trademark law "'helps assure a producer that it will reap the financial, reputation-related rewards associated with a desirable product'") (quoting *Qualitex Co. v. Jacobson Prods., Co.,* 514 U.S. 159, 164, 115 S. Ct. 1300, 1303, 131 L. Ed. 2d 248 (1995)); *see also Levitt Corp.,* 593 F.2d at 468 ("When a business purchases trademarks and goodwill, the essence of what it pays for is the right to inform the public that it is in possession of the special experience and skill symbolized by the name of the original concern, and the sole authority to market its products."); 1 McCarthy § 3:1 (stating that trademarks "identify" and "distinguish" goods, alerting consumers that they come from a single "source" and are of a particular "quality").

As Abboud sold the goodwill of the Joseph Abboud trademark to JA Apparel—for $65.5 million—he cannot now claim fair use based on his desire to capitalize on that reputation. (*See* PX-1 ¶ 1.1(a)(A) (selling the trademarks "and the goodwill related thereto").) *See also In re The Leslie Fay Cos., Inc. ("Nipon"),* 216 B.R. 117, 124 (Bankr. S.D.N.Y. 1997) ("The sale of a trademark includes the sale of the mark along with the goodwill and tangible business assets that go along with the trademark."). Although it may seem unfair to Abboud, because he "worked toward building [his name] since . . . enter[ing] th[e] clothing industry full time in 1972" (*see* DX-9), New York law is clear that the seller cannot "attempt[ ] to arrogate to himself the trade reputation for which he received valuable consideration." *Levitt Corp.,*593 F.2d at 468.

In sum, Abboud may alert consumers that he is the designer behind the new "jaz" line, but he cannot do so in an "overly intrusive manner," *Madrigal Audio Labs.,* 799 F.2d at 823; nor can he do so in a way that is utterly confusing. *See KP Permanent Make-Up,* 543 U.S. at 123, 125 S. Ct. at 550. The Court is mindful that "[t]his is not a case where a first comer seeks to save himself a place in a new market he has not yet entered by denying to a man the use of his own name in exploiting that market." *Taylor Wine Co., Inc. v. Bully Hill Vineyards,* 569 F.2d 731, 733 (2d Cir. 1978). Rather, this is a case in which an individual elected to use his name for many years as a trademark, building up substantial goodwill; he then sold the same, but intends to continue to commercially exploit his name by designing clothes in competition with the purchaser of the trademark. This case therefore presents an inherently difficult scenario, because Abboud's use of his name in the sale of clothing will inevitably lead to consumer confusion.

Defendants' Exhibits 187 and 188—while a close call—satisfy all of the elements of the fair use defense, provided that Abboud includes a disclaimer as discussed below. Abboud has used his name in its descriptive sense, embedded in a complete sentence that identifies Abboud the individual as the designer of the "jaz" line. Further, Abboud's name is accompanied by the more prominently displayed "jaz" trademark.

Nevertheless, in view of the fact that the average consumer would have great difficulty discerning a difference in sources between clothes marketed under the Joseph Abboud mark and clothes designed by Joseph Abboud the person, Abboud's use of his name is not unlimited, and must yield to such consumer confusion. *See Levitt Corp.,* 593 F.2d at 469-70 (upholding injunction of individual's use of his name in advertising "to prevent confusion and to protect the value of plaintiff's goodwill"). Thus, Abboud may not use his name in Defendants' Exhibits 187 and 188 or anything similar absent a disclaimer of his affiliation with JA Apparel and products sold under the Joseph Abboud trademarks. *See Joseph Scott Co. v. Scott Swimming Pools. Inc.,* 764 F.2d 62, 69 (2d Cir. 1985) (permitting defendant's use of his surname, provided he "make perfectly clear that his firm is no longer associated with, and is not a successor to, [plaintiff]"); *Taylor Wine Co.,* 569 F.2d at 736 (requiring similar disclaimer); *but see Soltex Polymer Corp. v. Fortex Indus., Inc.*, 832 F.2d 1325, 1330 (2d Cir. 1987) (noting that disclaimers "may not always provide an effective remedy against an infringing use"). Any disclaimer must be no smaller than the accompanying text in which Abboud uses his name.

The decision of the Court would be easier if Abboud were to embrace the mock-up proposed in Plaintiff's Exhibit 43. In that ad, Abboud's use of his name unquestionably qualifies under the fair use defense. In fact, the placement, size, and usage of Abboud's name in Plaintiff's Exhibit 43, together with the disclaimer, arguably removes the likelihood of any confusion, and abrogates the need to even discuss the affirmative defense of fair use.

The Court cannot conclude, however, that the ads in Plaintiff's Exhibit 42 constitute fair use. As noted above, the size and font of "Joseph Abboud"—virtually identical to the Joseph Abboud trademark—remove it from the realm of descriptive, non-trademark use. And by doing so, Abboud creates utterly confusing ads that cannot withstand scrutiny under the fair use test, even if a disclaimer were included. Although the "jaz" trademark is also displayed in each of these ads, consumers might be led to believe that "jaz" is simply a sub-line of clothing created by the rightful owner of the "Joseph Abboud" trademark—JA Apparel. This is particularly so given the prominence of the name "Joseph Abboud" in each of these ads. Together with Abboud's admissions noted *supra*, the Court concludes that these ads (PX-42) evince an intent to confuse and do not constitute fair use.

* * *

IV. Permanent Injunctive Relief

On appeal, the Second Circuit did not address the injunctive relief awarded by this Court "except to note that an injunction of scope similar to that originally entered would seem to be inappropriately broad if based solely on trademark infringement rather than on breach of contract." *JA Apparel Corp.*, 568 F.3d at 403. Because the Court on remand has determined that Abboud did not sell the exclusive right to commercially use his name, the original injunction must be modified to address only those proposed uses that would constitute trademark infringement, not otherwise protected by the fair use defense, and, thus, breach the Agreement. The Court will not go through the redundant exercise of fully explaining the standard for injunctive relief. The standard remains the same as that set forth in *Abboud I*. *See Abboud I*, 591 F. Supp. 2d at 334–37. Several points, however, are worthy of note.

First, as a general matter, injunctions in trademark cases involving use of an individual's personal name should be narrowly tailored. *See, e.g., Joseph Scott Co.*, 764 F.2d at 67; *see also Taylor Wine Co.*, 569 F.2d at 735 ("[w]hen the defendant demonstrates a genuine desire to build a business under his own name, courts have generally been reluctant to proscribe all surname use"). Notwithstanding the general rule, "[w]here, as here . . . the infringing party has previously sold his business, including use of his name and its goodwill, to the plaintiff, sweeping injunctive relief is more tolerable." *Levitt Corp.*, 593 F.2d at 468. In framing an injunction, the Court must seek to "avoid confusion in the marketplace, protect a prior company's property interest in its name, and permit an individual to exploit his own identity and reputation in a legitimate manner." *Gucci v. Gucci Shops, Inc.*, 688 F. Supp. 916, 927 (S.D.N.Y. 1988) (quoting *Joseph Scott Co.*, 764 F.2d at 67).

In line with these principles, the Court concludes that Plaintiff JA Apparel is entitled to a permanent injunction prohibiting Abboud—personally, through Houndstooth, or through any other entity with which he is affiliated—from using his name as a trademark, service mark, trade name, or brand name. Abboud may not use his name in any manner on "jaz" clothes, labels, hang-tags, or product packaging. Should Abboud choose to use his name in promotional and advertising materials, he must do so in a way that is not inconsistent with this Court's fair use analysis. Abboud's name must be used descriptively, in the context of a complete sentence or descriptive phrase, and must be no larger or more distinct than the surrounding words in that sentence or phrase. Abboud is to prominently display his trademark "jaz" (or any other trademark) elsewhere in the advertisement, both to alert consumers that "jaz" is the source—in the trademark sense—of the new clothing line, and to minimize any resulting confusion. Finally, should Abboud use his name as proposed in Defendants' Exhibit 187 and 188 or anything similar, he must include a disclaimer of any affiliation with JA Apparel and products sold under the Joseph Abboud trademarks. The disclaimer must be displayed in a font that is no smaller than the accompanying text in which Abboud uses his name.

* * *

Conclusion

For all of the foregoing reasons, the Court concludes:

1) In the June 16, 2000 Purchase and Sale Agreement, Abboud did not sell, and JA Apparel did not purchase, the exclusive right to use the "Joseph Abboud" name commercially. Rather, Abboud sold, and JA Apparel purchased, the "Joseph Abboud" name as a trademark and related intellectual property (which can include brand names or commercial names);

2) Abboud's proposed uses of his name in connection with his new "jaz" line, as shown in Defendants' Exhibits 187 and 188, and Plaintiff's Exhibit 43, would qualify as fair use under Section 33(b)(4) of the Lanham Act, 15 U.S.C. § 1115(b)(4), provided Abboud includes a disclaimer of any affiliation with JA Apparel and products sold under the Joseph Abboud trademarks on Defendants' Exhibits 187 and 188 or any similar ads. Such disclaimer shall be no smaller than the accompanying text in which Abboud uses his name;

3) Abboud's proposed uses of his name in connection with his new "jaz" line, as shown in Plaintiff's Exhibit 42, would constitute trademark infringement under Section 32(1) of the Lanham Act, 15 U.S.C. § 1114(1), not otherwise insulated by

the fair use defense, and thus, a breach of the June 16, 2000 Purchase and Sale Agreement;

* * *It is hereby ORDERED that Abboud is permanently enjoined from the following conduct:

1) Abboud may not use his name—either personally, through Houndstooth, or through any other entity with which he is affiliated—as a trademark, service mark, trade name or brand name;

2) Abboud may not use his name in any manner on "jaz" clothes, labels, hang-tags, or product packaging;

3) Abboud may not use his name in promotional and advertising materials, unless his name is used descriptively, in the context of a complete sentence or descriptive phrase, and it must be no larger or more distinct than the surrounding words in that sentence or phrase;

4) Abboud must prominently display his trademark "jaz" (or any other trademark) on any ad containing his personal name as discussed above; and

5) Should Abboud use his name as proposed in Defendants' Exhibit 187 and 188 or anything similar, he must include a disclaimer of any affiliation with JA Apparel and products sold under the Joseph Abboud trademarks. Such disclaimer shall be no smaller than the accompanying text in which Abboud uses his name.

The Clerk of Court shall enter Judgment consistent with the terms of this Memorandum Opinion and Order.

PLAINTIFF'S EXHIBIT 42

PLAINTIFF'S EXHIBIT 43

DEFENDANT'S EXHIBIT 187

Notes

1. The district court's central holding with respect to the agreement was that "Abboud did not sell, and JA Apparel did not purchase, the exclusive right to use the 'Joseph Abboud' name commercially. Rather, Abboud sold, and JA Apparel purchased, the 'Joseph Abboud' name as a trademark." If the parties intended that the transaction covered the exclusive right to use the name, what language should the agreement have used? Must an agreement expressly limit the selling party from using his or her personal name in a commercial context?

2. The district court granted Abboud the right to use his name "in the context of a complete sentence or descriptive phrase" so long as the name is "no larger or more distinct than the surrounding words in that sentence or phrase." Do you agree with this permission? Is a proper noun, such as Joseph Abboud, always distinct compared to the rest of a sentence or phrase? Does the fame of the Joseph Abboud name make that name stand out of any sentence that contains it?

3. The district court required Abboud to include a disclaimer of affiliation with JA Apparel and its related products. Would a buyer such as JA Apparel be happy with a statement that it is not affiliated with Joseph Abboud? Would such a statement be likely to allow Abboud to enjoy some of the goodwill that he sold to JA Apparel?

4. How would domain names and social media accounts be treated under the court's ruling? Is the use of the Joseph Abboud name in either of those ways a "trademark use" that would be owned by JA Apparel? What would be the best way for the purchasing agreement to resolve this issue?

The Designer Formerly Known As . . . : Intellectual Property Issues Arising From Personal Names as Fashion Brands

George C. Sciarrino & Matthew D. Asbell
107 Trademark Reporter 1150*

I. Introduction

Christian Lacroix, Kate Spade, Paul Frank, Joseph Abboud, David J. Pliner, Catherine Malandrino, and Karen Millen—aside from being well-known designers, all have something else in common: they no longer own the right to use their personal names as their brands. In the fashion industry, designers often use their personal names to refer to their clothing designs and related products. However, this practice raises concerns that designers should consider when starting an eponymous brand and that companies purchasing the brands of those designers should consider when acquiring such brands.[1]

---

* Adapted by the authors from George C. Sciarrino & Matthew D. Asbell, *The Designer Formerly Known as . . . Intellectual Property Issues Arising from Personal Names as Fashion Brands.* Originally published in The Trademark Reporter (TMR), a publication of the International Trademark Association (INTA), 107 TMR 1150 (2017). Reprinted by permission.

1. *See* Marc P. Misthal, *Trademarks and Trade Dress" in* Fashion Law: A Guide for Designers, Fashion Executives, and Attorneys 28 (Guillermo C. Jimenez & Barbara Kolsun eds., 2014).

Before deciding to use their personal names as fashion brands, designers should be aware that there are a number of risks that they could encounter at the outset. Initially, they may encounter hurdles when clearing and attempting to register their personal names as trademarks in the United States and worldwide. If they eventually decide to sell their companies, they could lose rights to use their personal names in future fashion ventures or as trademarks for similar products.[2] When this predicament is discovered after a purchase agreement has been made, it can result in onerous and expensive disputes that do not benefit either party. With an international fashion brand, these disputes can arise on multiple fronts around the world.

In spite of these concerns, designers still may prefer to use their personal names as their brands for several reasons. From a marketing perspective, shoppers may be more likely to purchase products from a brand that has a relatable story and personal identity, and the use of a designer's own name and persona may contribute to sales and the overall value of the brand.[3] Ultimately, for an emerging designer, achieving fame and widespread name recognition may outweigh any potential risks. The later sale of the company often comes with a large price tag, as acquiring entities are willing to pay sizable sums for successful fashion brands, making any potential future name problem seem relatively inconsequential at the time of sale.

Both the designer and the purchasing company should perform due diligence when developing or contracting for the sale of an eponymous brand. To avoid pitfalls and future disputes, it is imperative for both parties to consider the various ways designers may wish to (or even be required to) use their names in connection with future ventures, such as in press releases, on third-party websites, in keyword advertising, on social media pages and posts, in domain names, and in connection with other intellectual property documents, including, for example, listings as inventors on design patent applications. Designers also should strategically manage their intellectual property portfolios, planning for the day when they may ultimately sell their assets. After selling their brands, designers may need to rebrand themselves by taking on a new name and utilizing legally permissible ways to identify themselves and their products to consumers, in some cases by becoming "the designer formerly known as. . . ."

This article reviews the various issues relating to eponymous fashion brands from initial clearance to disputes after sale of the company; outlines how designers have addressed post-sale references to their former brands, with and without objection from the brand acquirers; and provides examples of brands that manage to avoid the possible issue altogether while still maintaining a "personal" approach to branding.

---

2. *Id.*

3. *See* Maria Bobila, *Should Fashion Designers Name Labels After Themselves*, FASHIONISTA (Dec. 3, 2015) (available at https://fashionista.com/2015/12/designer-namesake-label (last visited Nov. 19, 2017)).

II. Clearing and Registering Personal Names as Trademarks

For designers, it may be difficult to clear and register a personal name as a trademark. First, the marketplace and applicable trademark registers may be already crowded with marks that include the designer's given name.[4] Such existing given name marks may pose obstacles to registration and use, even though the designer may initially plan to use his or her given name only in combination with other elements such as his or her surname. Initial plans can change over time and result in disputes over the given name when used alone, as happened, for example, with the CALVIN KLEIN brand's eventual use of CALVIN by itself.[5] Depending on the markets in which they manufacture, sell, or plan to sell their products, designers must also consider early on whether to clear and register versions of their names in non-Latin characters in certain jurisdictions, including for example, China.

In the United States, a mark can be refused registration for its surname significance; under the Lanham Act, a mark that is deemed "primarily merely a surname" cannot be registered on the Principal Register without proof of secondary meaning, which requires a showing that in the minds of relevant consumers, the surname indicates the source of the goods or services.[6] Whether a trademark is deemed "primarily merely a surname" depends on the discretion of the Examining Attorney and a number of different factors, including: (1) whether the term is a rare surname; (2) whether the term is the surname of anyone connected with the applicant; (3) whether the term has any recognized meaning apart from being a surname; (4) whether the term has the "look and feel" of a surname; and (5) whether the mark has a unique text stylization or other graphic element that creates a distinct commercial impression.[7] This evolving case-by-case test looks at the probable reaction of consumers in the marketplace.[8] Before preparing an application for a mark composed of a surname by itself or even in combination with additional elements, such as preceding initials, it is important to formulate ways to build and demonstrate secondary meaning to increase the likelihood of the mark being registered

---

4. Consider, for example, the recent dispute over the mark KYLIE between Kylie Minogue and Kylie Jenner. *See, e.g.*, KDB Pty Ltd. v. Kylie Jenner, Inc., Opposition No. 91228567, filed in the U.S. Patent and Trademark Office Trademark Trial and Appeal Board in 2016. The opposition was withdrawn by the opposer, after a reported settlement.

5. Calvin Klein Trademark Trust v. Calvin Clothing Co., Cancellation No. 92041543 (filed Dec. 26, 2002) (available at http://ttabvue.uspto.gov/ttabvue/v?pno=92041543&pty=CAN&eno=1 (last accessed Nov. 20, 2017)).

6. *See* 15 U.S.C. § 1052(e).

7. *See* TMEP § 1211.01.

8. *See* In re Weiss Watch Co., Inc., Serial No. 86782562 (June 13, 2017) (TTAB affirmed surname refusal of the mark WEISS WATCH COMPANY, finding that the inclusion of generic words "watch company" did not overcome the mark's surname significance); *see also* In re Aulback Lizenz AG, Serial No. 79156860 (Nov. 7, 2016) (TTAB affirmed surname refusal of the mark HECHTER for leather goods and clothing, despite rareness of surname); Dana Justus, *What's In a Name?: Overview of TTAB's Recent Surname Decisions*, The National Law Review (Feb. 1, 2017) (available at https://www.natlawreview.com/article/what-s-name-overview-ttab-s-recent-surname-decisions (last accessed Dec. 14, 2017)).

or to be prepared for lesser protection. Fortunately, in the United States, surname refusals typically only occur when the applied-for mark consists of little more than a surname. Designers who adopt the combination of their surname with their given name or multiple initials are unlikely to face such a refusal.[9]

If, at the time of the application in the United States, the designer's surname is already well-known and substantial resources have been allocated to promoting the mark, the designer may consider making a claim of acquired distinctiveness to show that the mark has established a secondary meaning.[10] Otherwise, the designer may register the surname mark on the Supplemental Register, where it may enjoy some limited trademark protection while distinctiveness is acquired in the marketplace. After using the mark in commerce for at least five continuous years, the designer may file a new application seeking registration on the Principle Register with a claim of acquired distinctiveness.[11]

Another issue arising in the context of seeking registration of a personal name as a fashion brand is the requirement for written consent. Under the Lanham Act, if the mark identifies a living person and the applicant is not that person, the applicant must provide written consent from that person.[12] For a designer registering his or her own name in the name of his or her company, this may be achieved rather simply by submitting a statement of consent with the trademark application. However, purchasing companies may encounter issues relying on past statements of consent when seeking to register the designer's name in new applications. Disputes may arise between designers and purchasing companies over the scope and duration of consent previously granted, which is typically silent on these issues.

For example, the U.S. Patent and Trademark Office Trademark Trial and Appeal Board (TTAB) recently dismissed an opposition filed by haute couture and ready-to-wear designer Christian Lacroix against the registration of the mark CHRISTIAN LACROIX by the company Christian Lacroix, Snc.[13] The TTAB found that opposer Lacroix had assigned to the applicant all of his trademark rights in his name and held that a reasonable reading of the trademark purchasing agreement implied

9. *See* In re P.J. Fitzpatrick, Inc., 95 U.S.P.Q.2d 1412 (T.T.A.B. 2010) (precedential) (TTAB reversed surname refusal of mark P.J. FITZPATRICK INC., stating "'if a mark consists of two initials (or more) coupled with a surname, it typically will convey a commercial impression of a personal name, and thus generally will not be primarily a surname."); *see also* In re Reebok Int'l Ltd., Serial No. 78271326 (Oct. 26, 2005) (TTAB reversed surname refusal of the mark J.W. FOSTER for footwear, headwear, and clothing).

10. *See* TMEP § 1211.

11. *See* Matthew Asbell, *Inherent and Acquired Distinctiveness and the Principal and Supplemental Registers for U.S. Trademarks* (May 22, 2014) (available at http://ladas.com/education-center/inherent-acquired-distinctiveness-principal-supplemental-registers-u-s-trademarks/ (last accessed Nov. 20, 2017)).

12. *See* 15 U.S.C. § 1052(c); *see also* TMEP § 813.01(a).

13. Christian Lacroix v. Christian Lacroix, Snc., T.T.A.B. Opposition Nos. 91201563 and 91202642 (Mar. 10, 2017).

that he had consented to the use and registration of the CHRISTIAN LACROIX trademark by the applicant.

In addition, according to the U.S. Patent and Trademark Office's Trademark Manual of Examining Procedure (TMEP), a consent in a prior registration may satisfy the consent requirement in a subsequent application.[14] TMEP Section 1206.4 states that new consent is not required if consent is of record in a valid registration owned by applicant: "An applicant does not have to submit a new consent if a consent to register is already part of the record in the file of a valid registration for a mark comprised in whole or in part of the same name, portrait, or signature for the same goods and/or services, or such goods and/or services as would encompass those in the subsequent application."[15] Therefore, when attempting to register a personal name as a trademark, designers and purchasing companies should contemplate the potentially long-lasting effects of any consent provided, as well as the potential need for new consents for future applications covering new goods and services.

When considering possible rights outside the United States, designers who wish to own and use their names as trademarks should also evaluate whether they will use or need to prevent others from using a phonetically equivalent version of their name in the local language. Former basketball star Michael Jordan learned this the hard way when he spent nearly five years fighting in Chinese courts to finally get the rights to a Chinese character version of his surname, 乔丹(Qiaodan), from Qiaodan Sports Co., Ltd., which previously registered the mark and continues to operate nearly 3,000 retail locations in China (and recently sued Jordan—so the dispute is still not entirely resolved).[16] As Jordan's ultimate success in court with respect to at least one of the marks at issue was principally a result of his worldwide fame, designers who are less well-known (despite their aspirations or destinies) are wise to consider applying to register the most likely to be used versions of their names in non-Latin characters in relevant jurisdictions as early as possible rather than discover later that another party has adopted and registered the local version of their name before them.[17] Local contacts and counsel should be consulted to pick, clear, and proactively register at least one reasonable translation or transliteration of the name.

---

14. *See* TMEP §§ 813, 1206.04(c).

15. TMEP § 1206.04(c), *citing* In re McKee Baking Co., 218 U.S.P.Q. 287, 288 (T.T.A.B. 1983).

16. *See* Yixian Chen, *CHINA: SPC Rules on Michael Jordan's Chinese Name Rights: Decision and Applications*, INTA Bulletin (Mar. 15, 2017) (available at http://www.inta.org/INTABulletin/Pages/China_7205.aspx (last accessed Nov. 20, 2017)); *see also* Zhang Rui, *Chinese Sports Brand Qiaodan Sues Michael Jordan*, China.org.cn, July 21, 2017 (reporting on "infringement of reputation" action brought by the Chinese company against Michael Jordan and his lawyers, asserting that Jordan and his counsel mischaracterized the Supreme Court decision in communications with sports authorities in an attempt to stop them from working with Qiaodan Sports) (available at http://www.china.org.cn/sports/2017-07/21/content_41257321.htm (last accessed Nov. 20, 2017)).

17. Chen, *supra* note 16.

An additional consideration applies if a designer files an intent-to-use application for his or her eponymous mark: there are limitations on the ability to transfer the pending application. With the primary purpose of ensuring assignment only along with some business or goodwill and to prevent trafficking in trademarks, U.S. trademark law provides that a U.S. trademark applicant "cannot assign the application [based on intent to use] before the applicant files an allegation of use (i.e., either an amendment to allege use under 15 U.S.C. § 1051(c) or a statement of use under 15 U.S.C. § 1051(d)), *except to a successor to the applicant's business, or portion of the business to which the mark pertains, if that business is ongoing and existing.*"[18] Where the assignee of an intent-to-use application, prior to the filing an allegation of use, is not the successor to the applicant's business or portion of the business to which the mark pertains, the improper assignment renders the application void, and any resulting registration may ultimately be cancelled.[19] Accordingly, depending on the terms and structure of the acquisition by a successor entity, a fashion designer who has not yet used one or more of his or her particular applied-for marks and who intends to continue operating in the business in one manner or another may not be able to presently assign some of the marks. This issue can be addressed through an agreement requiring the mark to be assigned at some future date, after use has commenced, and for the assignor to cooperate in executing the assignment at that time, or by ensuring that the present assignment includes language confirming the transfer of the business.[20]

When entering into a purchase agreement, both the designer and purchasing company should consider how to define the assignment of any intent-to-use applications, as well as the scope and duration of consent to use a personal name and any potential limitations of the designer's use of his or her given name, in order to avoid later disputes that may impact both parties globally.

III. Global Disputes Over Personal Names

When managing a global fashion brand based on the designer's name, disputes may arise contemporaneously in multiple jurisdictions. This happened in a legal

---

18. *See* 15 U.S.C. § 1060 (emphasis added); *see also* TMEP § 501.01(a).

19. *See* TMEP § 501.01(a); *see also* Cent. Garden & Pet Co. v. Doskocil Mfg. Co., 108 U.S.P.Q.2d 1134, 1146 (T.T.A.B. 2013) (TTAB cancelled registration due to improper assignment of the originating intent-to-use application, in which applicant continued operating business under the assignee, parent company).

20. One commentator suggests the following contract language: "Assignor does hereby assign to Assignee the mark in U.S. Trademark Application No. __________, together with the goodwill of the business symbolized by the trademark. This application is being assigned as part of the entire business or portion thereof to which the mark pertains, as required by Section 10 of the Trademark Act, 15 U.S.C. § 1060." Miriam D. Trudell, *Issues to Consider in Assignments of U.S. Trademark Applications and Registrations*, INTA BULLETIN, Nov. 15, 2014 (available at https://www.inta.org/INTABulletin/Pages/IssuestoConsiderinAssignmentsofUSTradema (last accessed Dec. 15. 2017)).

battle involving London-based international fashion brand Karen Millen Fashions Limited (KMFL) and designer Karen Millen over the right to use her name.[21]

By way of background, in 2004, Karen Millen sold her company, along with the rights to use her name on future competing ventures, to KMFL's predecessor-in-interest, the Icelandic group Baugur, by way of a purchase agreement. Litigation ensued in 2011 in the United Kingdom when Millen announced an intent to return to the fashion business using the name KAREN.[22] In 2015, Millen reached a settlement with regard to use of her name in the United Kingdom and European Union, which generally prevented her from using her name on fashion or lifestyle products in these jurisdictions but did not address the U.S. or Chinese markets.[23] Millen then attempted to register a number of trademarks in the United States that included her name.[24] The conflict escalated, and Millen filed cancellation actions in the United States against several KMFL marks that included her name. KMFL initiated litigation in the Eastern District of Virginia, claiming, inter alia, breach of contract.[25] The district court dismissed the case following Millen's motion, which was based on claims that the court lacked personal jurisdiction over U.K. resident Millen and subject matter jurisdiction over the U.K. contract; that the doctrine of *forum non conveniens* made the Virginia court an inconvenient forum; and that principles of international comity required the Virginia court to decline to hear the case, while also noting that the U.K. contract's forum selection clause designated U.K. courts.[26] KMFL then appealed to the Fourth Circuit but ultimately moved to voluntarily dismiss the appeal on October 11, 2016.[27]

Relying on a forum selection clause in the purchase agreement that allegedly required contractual disputes to be litigated in the United Kingdom, Millen brought an action in the High Court of England and Wales that included a claim for declaration that she could use the marks KAREN and KAREN MILLEN in the United States.[28] In the High Court decision, Judge Meade ruled that the designer Karen Millen no longer had the right in the United States to use KAREN MILLEN as a trademark for home wares and lifestyle ventures or KAREN for any goods and services.[29] The court noted

---

21. *See Karen Millen Loses Right To Trade under Her Name*, WIPR (Aug. 18, 2016) (available at http://www.worldipreview.com/news/karen-millen-loses-right-to-trade-under-her-name-12052 (last accessed Nov. 20, 2017)).

22. *See facts recited in* Millen v. Karen Millen Fashions Ltd. & Anor, EWHC 2104 (Ch) (2016) (available at http://www.bailii.org/ew/cases/EWHC/Ch/2016/2104.html (last accessed Nov. 20, 2017)).

23. *Id.*

24. *Id.*

25. Karen Millen Fashion Limited v. Karen Millen, Civil Action No. 1:14-cv-00720-CMHTCB (E.D. Va. 2014).

26. *Id.*

27. *Id.*

28. *See decision at* Millen v. Karen Millen Fashions Ltd. & Anor, EWHC 2104 (Ch) (2016) (available at http://www.bailii.org/ew/cases/EWHC/Ch/2016/2104.html (last accessed Nov. 20, 2017)).

29. *Id.*

that it would have been inclined to allow the mark KAREN to be used if the designer had claimed limited rights with respect to the geographic scope and description of goods and services that did not conflict with KMFL's rights. Instead, as the Judge explained:

> Were the Claimant to have sought a decision that the use of the KAREN solus marks was not a breach, in circumstances where there was no possibility of any association with the name MILLEN, and if the declarations had defined her intended use more closely in terms of geographic positioning and the like, then I think this aspect of her claim might have succeeded. Mainly because of the weak and possibly non-existent distinctiveness of the first name alone, along with the other KAREN brands in the fashion industry, I think it is possible to conceive of uses, perhaps many uses, which would not cause confusion and would not be a breach of clause 5.1.7.
>
> However, I have accepted the Defendants' submissions that the breadth of the declarations sought is very great. It extends to the use of KAREN marks on clothes in close physical proximity to the Defendants' stores, along with simultaneous use by the Claimant on other goods of KAREN MILLEN, and (potentially, although again I do not regard it as decisive) in connection with the Claimant attempting to explain and indeed exploit her past connections to the KAREN MILLEN business, which may or may not succeed in avoiding a trade mark type of association. If these factors were to be combined, which I think is a situation within the scope of the declarations, favourable to the Defendants but not artificially or ridiculously so, then I consider there would be confusion. The declarations therefore include acts which would be a breach of clause 5.1.7.[30]

Millen was further ordered to consent to additional registrations by KMFL that include her name.[31]

Since the High Court decision, Millen abandoned the United States trademark applications and registrations for marks that include her full name.[32] A pending application filed by Millen for HOME BY KAREN proceeded to publication and was opposed by KMFL.[33] The opposition was suspended pending the disposition of the High Court decision; however the application was later expressly abandoned by the applicant's trustee in bankruptcy on October 5, 2017, and the opposition was

---

30. *Id.* at ¶¶ 309-310.

31. *Id.*

32. *See, e.g.*, Notice of Abandonment, U.S. App. No. 86246014 for KAREN BY KAREN MILLEN (Sept. 9, 2016); *see also, e.g.*, Notice of Abandonment, U.S. App. No. 86246046 for KAREN MILLEN (Sept. 9, 2016); *see also, e.g.*, Notice of Abandonment, U.S. App. No. 86246059 for HOME BY KAREN MILLEN (Sept. 9, 2016).

33. *See* U.S. App. No. 86246065 for HOME BY KAREN; *see also* T.T.A.B. Opposition No. 91230754.

thereafter withdrawn.[34] Having not appealed the High Court's decision, Millen will most likely need to redevelop her new brand under a different name.

IV. Possible Ways Around Losing One's Own Name and Likeness

After selling their brands, designers may not fully realize that they can no longer use their names in connection with their new fashion ventures. In some cases, they still can identify themselves as the designer of a new brand without using their name to identify the brand itself. The distinction often made in these scenarios is between the trademark, which identifies the source of goods or services, and the designer's use of his or her name and likeness independent of the products he or she designs.

In most U.S. states, a person's right to control the use of his or her name and likeness commercially falls under the category of the right of publicity, which was derived from the right of privacy. The nature of the right, the term used to describe it, and the term and assignability of the right, will be different depending upon the state or country where the designer resides. The right exists independently of the product with which the name or likeness may be associated, and thus falls outside the ambit of trademark, patent and copyright laws in the United States. In some jurisdictions, like France and other European countries, the connection between the designer and his or her work may be considered inalienable as a matter of moral rights in copyright law. In such countries, copyright law may recognize a fashion designer's moral rights over his or her design at the moment the original work is created. Moral rights normally include the right of attribution (the right to be identified as the author); the right of integrity (the right to prohibit modification or destruction of the work); the right of disclosure (the right of control over publicizing of the work); and the right of withdrawal (the right to take back the work from the public after it has been released).[35] In jurisdictions that recognize moral rights, the law typically does not allow assignment of the right of attribution, because it is inherent in the author. Therefore, after selling their eponymous brands, designers may retain the moral right to attribute themselves as the creator of their past and future designs, at least those protected by copyright.

When moral rights do not exist or do not apply to fashion works, as in the United States, a designer who can no longer use his or her name or likeness should consider any available alternative ways of identifying himself or herself as the designer of his or her new brand that comply with the terms of the purchase agreement. The designer should explore when and how the name or likeness can be used in press

---

34. *See* http://ttabvue.uspto.gov/ttabvue/v?pno=91230754&pty=OPP&eno=10 (Oct. 10, 2017); *see also* http://ttabvue.uspto.gov/ttabvue/v?pno=91230754&pty=OPP&eno=11 (Oct. 18, 2017).

35. *See* Francesca Montalvo Witzburg, *Protecting Fashion: A Comparative Analysis of Fashion Design Copyright Protection in the U.S. and Europe*, Cardozo Arts & Ent. L.J. Blog (Sept. 19, 2014) (available at http://www.cardozoaelj.com/2014/09/19/protecting-fashion-a-comparative-analysis-of-fashion-design-copyright-protection-in-the-u-s-and-europe/ (last accessed Nov. 20, 2017)).

releases, on third-party websites, in keyword advertising, on social media posts, in domain names, and even in design or utility patents. For example, although there is not currently a generic top level domain such as .person, .individual, or .designer, a designer might be able to negotiate to allow registration of his or her name on the top level domains .name, .me,[36] or .ren (which is Chinese for "person"), on the grounds that a consumer looking for the branded fashion products would not likely be confused by the designer's name as a personal domain. Furthermore, to the extent possible, the designer should negotiate the purchase agreement in a manner that allows for the desired uses, and the purchasing entity should anticipate how it wants to handle such issues when negotiating with the designer. These and similar issues arose in disputes involving the names of Joseph Abboud, Paulo Gucci, Paul Frank Sunich, David Pliner, and Catherine Malandrino.

A. The Joseph Abboud Case

As menswear designer Joseph Abboud stated, "The consumer has a right to know the creator of a work."[37] After selling his trademarks to JA Apparel Corp. for $65.5 million in 2000, Abboud sought to create a new line called "Jaz" and to use the tagline "a new composition by designer Joseph Abboud." JA Apparel sued in the Southern District of New York for breach of contract.[38] In a passage that highlights the importance of the language in the purchase agreement, the court held that "Abboud did not sell, and JA Apparel did not purchase, the exclusive right to use the 'Joseph Abboud' name commercially. Rather, Abboud sold, and JA Apparel purchased, the 'Joseph Abboud' name as a trademark."[39] The court went on to grant Abboud certain qualified rights, like the ability to use his name "in the context of a complete sentence or descriptive phrase," as long as it be "no larger or more distinct than the surrounding words in that sentence or phrase."[40] However, he would have to display the term "Jaz" prominently in advertisements to make the source clear and include a disclaimer of any affiliation with JA Apparel and its related products. Thus, while Abboud effectively could no longer freely use his name in any manner on any "Jaz" labels, packaging, or hang-tags, Abboud had various other options available to him to communicate to the public that he was the designer behind the "Jaz" label.[41] In this case, the contract was ambiguous because it contained a sale of Abboud's "name" in relation to his trademark rights, but it did not expressly limit Abboud from using his personal name commercially, a distinction that was recognized by the court.

---

36. ME is the country-code level domain for Montenegro. *See* https://domain.me/about-me/.

37. *See* Susanne Kapner, *When Is Kate Spade Not Kate Spade? When She's Frances Valentine*, Wall St. J. (Aug. 23, 2016) (available at https://www.wsj.com/articles/when-is-kate-spade-not-kate-spade-when-shes-frances-valentine-1471971817 (last accessed Nov. 20, 2017)).

38. *See* JA Apparel Corp. v. Abboud, 682 F. Supp. 2d 294 (S.D.N.Y. 2010).

39. *Id.* at 307.

40. *See* 15 U.S.C. § 1115(b)(4).

41. *See supra* note 37.

B. The Paulo Gucci Case

In another case resulting in restrictions on the use of a personal name while permitting some use, also in the Southern District of New York, the court ruled that Paulo Gucci, former chief designer of Gucci and grandson of the founder, could not use the name "Gucci" as a trademark.[42] However, he could continue to use his personal name to identify himself as the designer of products sold under a different brand name, as long as his name "always appear[ed] after the trademark in advertisements and on labels" and was less prominent than the trademark. He was also required to disclaim any affiliation with the Gucci entities in connection with the use of his name on his designs.[43] Unlike the Abboud case, Paulo Gucci did not enter into a purchase agreement, and the court had to balance his right to accurately identify himself with the established trademark rights of an existing entity.

C. The Paul Frank Sunich Case

The designer Paul Frank Sunich also found himself in a legal battle with the owners of his former company Paul Frank Industries, Inc. over his use of his full name on T-shirts.[44] A court in the Central District of California ruled that Sunich could not use his name on T-shirts, which the public had come to associate with his former company, but that he could identify himself as the designer of his newly developed products (e.g., on business cards or on his website), so long as he disclaimed affiliation with his former company when doing so.[45] In this case, Sunich left his former company after a falling out with the other co-founders. Designers should be aware that when they part ways with their companies, they may inevitably leave behind the trademark rights to their names.

D. The Donald J. Pliner Case

While Abboud, Gucci, and Frank were able to use their own names in some way in connection with their new brands, some designers find themselves not as free to do so. For instance, after Donald J. Pliner and his wife Lisa Pliner sold their footwear and accessories fashion brand, DONALD J PLINER, to DJP Holdings, LLC (DJP) in 2011 for "millions of dollars" (as stated in DJP's complaint) along with their trademark rights to their names and personality rights, they developed a new footwear brand and allegedly "put their names on the packaging for their new footwear."[46] In 2016, the purchasing company filed suit in the U.S. District Court for the District of Delaware against the former owners alleging, in part, trademark infringement and breach of contract. In their complaint, DJP alleged that Mr. Pliner was using a silhouetted image, shown below, on his business cards and that the image closely resembled the image of Mr. Pliner that DJP was using on its website.[47] The two sides

42. *See* Gucci v. Gucci Shops, Inc., 688 F. Supp. 916 (S.D.N.Y. 1988).
43. *Id.*
44. *See* Paul Frank Indus., Inc. v. Paul Sunich, 502 F. Supp. 2d 1094 (C.D. Cal. 2007).
45. *Id.*
46. DJP Holdings, LLC v. Pliner, Civil Action No. 1:16CV00661-LPS (D. Del. Aug. 1, 2016).
47. *Id.*

ultimately reached a settlement, and Mr. Pliner now designs under the label Right Bank Shoe Co.[48] The website for the new company attempts to exploit the inability of Mr. Pliner to use his name and likeness as a marketing technique by including the term "INCOGNITO" in large bold red font, with the definition of the term given as "(of a person) having one's true identity concealed."[49] The publicity generated by the dispute is such that members of the public searching for information about Mr. Pliner may be able to decipher the connection between him and his new brand even without direct statements from Mr. Pliner.

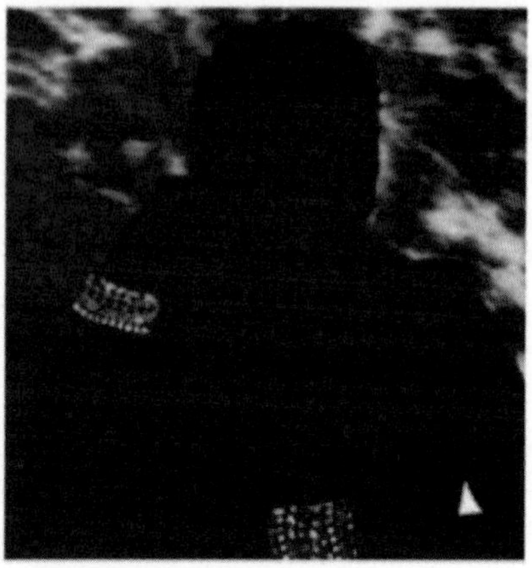

Excerpt from DJP's complaint showing comparison of Mr. Pliner's image from DJP's website (left) and a silhouetted image allegedly used on Mr. Pliner's business cards (right)

E. The Catherine Malandrino Case

After a legal battle with and separation from her business partners at CM Brand Holdings LLC,[50] Catherine Malandrino tried to continue using her name in connection with a new brand for the Home Shopping Network (HSN).[51] However, it appears she was not able to do so in connection with the new brand. The owners of the trademarks containing Malandrino's name apparently claimed the right to control Malandrino's "likeness, being and persona." Malandrino's attorney was quoted as saying that would "make her an indentured servant."[52]

---

48. *See* Right Bank Shoe Co. homepage (available at http://www.rightbankshoeco.com/ (last accessed Nov. 20, 2017)); *see also* Sheena Butler-Young, *Designer Donald J. Pliner & Wife Launch New Shoe Line After Settling with Former Label*, FootwearNews.com (Jan. 30, 2017) (available at http://footwearnews.com/2017/business/retail/designer-donald-j-pliner-wife-lisa-pliner-launch-shoe-line-djp-holdings-settlement-304493/ (last accessed Nov. 20, 2017)).

49. *See* http://www.rightbankshoeco.com/ (last accessed Nov. 20, 2017).

50. *See* http://www.rightbankshoeco.com/ (last accessed Nov. 20, 2017).

51. *See supra* note 37.

52. *Id.*

When Malandrino launched her new collection at a much lower price point, HSN sent out promotional emails labeling the brand as French Rendez Vous by Catherine Malandrino.[53] HSN later reportedly stopped using Malandrino's name in connection with the line, possibly in response to a demand letter, and there is now no use of Malandrino's name on the HSN webpage for that product line.[54]

Nevertheless, the connection between the new brand and the designer has been noted and recognized without HSN's use of her name directly. A number of articles in major fashion publications, including Vogue,[55] InStyle,[56] and WWD,[57] have connected Malandrino with the new HSN fashion line. While Malandrino may be restricted from using her name and likeness in connection with new ventures, she appears to still be able to influence the media to use her name to draw the connection for her. In addition, search engine queries for Malandrino's name also include references to her new collection on the HSN website (even though the website itself does not use her name).

In fact, there are a variety of search engine optimization ("SEO") strategies that designers may use to disseminate the news and draw the link between their new brands and their personal names. For example, a website factually describing the designer's history and including links to other websites related to the designer may rank higher in organic search results than the site might otherwise rank. Additionally, when a designer purchases keywords from a search engine operator that include his or her name, the triggered ads can make a connection without necessarily using the designer name in the ad itself or otherwise causing consumer confusion.[58]

To avoid disputes, both designers and purchasing companies should consider ways designers may wish to (or even be required to) use their names in connection with future ventures, such as in press releases, on third-party websites, in keyword advertising, on social media pages and posts, in domain names, and in connection

---

53. *Id.*

54. *See* http://www.hsn.com/search?query=catherine+malandrino (Mar. 22, 2017) (showing no results in a search for Catherine Malandrino (last accessed Nov. 20, 2017)).

55. *See* Emily Farra, *Catherine Malandrino Is Back With a See-Now-Buy-Now Collection*, Vogue (July 20, 2016) (available at http://www.vogue.com/article/catherine-malandrino-new-see-now-buy-now-hsn-collection (last accessed Nov. 20, 2017)).

56. *See* Eric Wilson, *Catherine Malandrino's French Collection for HSN Is as Crave-Inducing as a Baguette*, InStyle (June 24, 2016) (available at http://www.instyle.com/fashion/preview-catherine-malandrino-hsn-collection (last accessed Nov. 20, 2017)).

57. *See* Lisa Lockwood, *Catherine Malandrino's Rendez Vous With HSN*, WWD (June 14, 2016) (available at http://wwd.com/business-news/retail/catherine-malandrinos-rendez-vous-hsn-10454729/ (last accessed Nov. 20, 2017)).

58. *See, e.g.*, 1-800 Contacts, Inc. v. Lens.com, Inc., 722 F.3d 1229, 1242 (10th Cir. 2013) (holding mere purchase of a competitor's trademark as a keyword to trigger sponsored links that did not show their trademarks is unlikely to constitute infringement); *see also, e.g.*, Network Automation, Inc. v. Advanced Sys. Concepts, Inc., 638 F.3d 1137, 1145 (9th Cir. 2011) (purchase of keyword advertisement using competitor's trademark did not constitute infringement).

with other intellectual property documents, including, for example, listings as inventors on design patent applications.

F. Patent Applications

Designers also must use their personal names in connection with certain legal documents, including, for example, patents they pursue for their new companies. When filing a patent for an ornamental design of an article of manufacture, as is often done to protect new fashion designs in the United States, applicants must designate the legal name(s) of the actual inventor(s), which often will be the individual designer(s), rather than a juristic entity, although the patent may be assigned to an entity. For example, the "individual" designer Kate Spade signed a U.S. patent application in 2005 for an ornamental design of a bag clasp, depicted below, listing herself as the inventor and the company Kate Spade LLC as the assignee.[59] After selling the right to use his or her name, a designer cannot be precluded from listing his or her name as the inventor in a patent application or in other documents requiring his or her legal name.[60] As designers seek to redefine themselves and their work, filing and publicizing design patent applications listing themselves as inventors may provide permissible nexuses between their new brands and their personal names, even in cases where the designers are otherwise precluded from using their names.

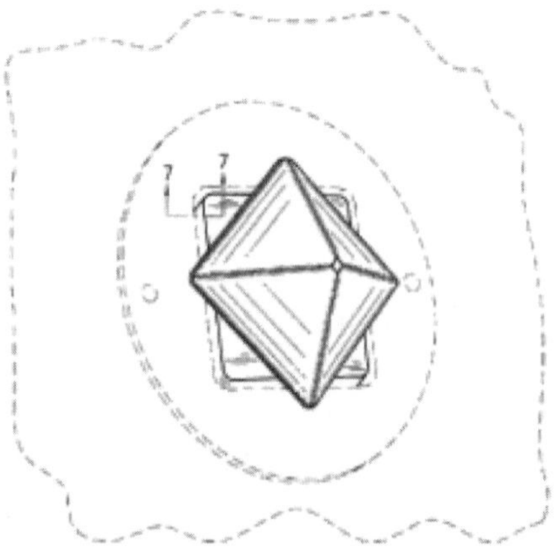

Excerpt from U.S. Patent No. D533,719
for bag clasp invented by Kate Spade

G. Domain Names and Social Media Accounts

Other often overlooked assets associated with intellectual property rights that must be considered in relation to the sale of an eponymous brand are domain names

59. *See* U.S. Patent No. D533,719.

60. *See* MPEP § 602; 35 U.S.C. 115 ("The inventor, or each individual who is a joint inventor of a claimed invention, in an application for patent must execute an oath or declaration directed to the application," which must include the inventor or joint inventor's legal name.).

and social media accounts that incorporate the designer's name. Upon the sale of their rights, designers may be required to transfer domains comprising their names. A subsequent effort by the designer to register and use a version of his or her name that was clearly sold may be considered "bad faith" and could support the assignee's efforts to transfer, suspend, or cancel the domain by way of a Uniform Domain Name Dispute Resolution Proceeding (UDRP),[61] Uniform Rapid Suspension System (URS), or other proceeding. With regard to the designer's social media accounts, the purchasing company should contemplate acquiring any login information or administrative privileges at the time of closing. The social network provider may not be willing to release such information or facilitate a transfer of ownership as doing so may violate the site's terms of use or policies. Before reaching an agreement, the designer and purchasing company should come to a mutual understanding as to which, if any, domain names and social media accounts will be transferred and which may be retained and used, and as to whether the designer will be able to include his or her name in any manner in future domain names and social media accounts. Before closing a deal, the designer should consider securing a mutually acceptable domain name and/or social media username and account.

V. Developing a Non-Personal Namesake Brand that is Personal to Customers

While purchasers may gravitate toward brands with identifiable stories, naming a fashion line after the designer is not the only way to develop a brand that evokes a personal connection. As designers and intellectual property attorneys become more aware of the potential problems surrounding personal names as brands, a growing trend for fashion lines is to take on entirely original names that still relate to an "origin story" for the brand without referencing the founding designer's name. Doing so still allows consumers to identify with the fashion line in a personal way.[62]

For example, the high-end women's line, DRAPER JAMES, launched by actress Reese Witherspoon in 2015 has a rather unique origin story that relates to the founder herself without using her name. The company name was created in honor of Witherspoon's Southern heritage and in particular as a tribute to her grandparents, Dorothea Draper and William James Witherspoon.[63] In a statement on the

---

61. *See* ICANN Uniform Domain Name Dispute Resolution Policy (Oct. 24, 1999) (available at https://www.icann.org/resources/pages/policy-2012-02-25-en (last accessed Dec. 4, 2017)); *see also* Roberta Horton and Michael Kientzle, *A Better UDRP Standard for Personal Names: Part 1*, Law 360 (May 16, 2017) (available at https://www.apks.com/en/perspectives/publications/2017/05/a-better-udrp-standard-for-personal-names-part-1 (last accessed Dec. 4, 2017)).

62. It is also possible to closely align and leverage a persona with the promotion of a brand under an entirely separate trademark, such as GOOP founded by Gwyneth Paltrow, which includes her personal initials. *See* GOOP "WHAT'S GOOP?" page on brand's website (available at https://goop.com/whats-goop/ (last accessed Dec. 4, 2017)).

63. *See* Draper James' "About Us" page on the brand's website (available at https://www.draperjames.com/about-us/ (last accessed Nov. 20, 2017)).

company website that includes the signature "Reese" at the bottom of the webpage, Witherspoon states, "When I returned to Nashville with my own family, I wanted to recapture and celebrate all that I love and remember about my grandparents and the South. That is why I created Draper James." While the brand itself has a personal flair and origin story, the trademark does not specifically refer to a living individual's name, allowing the company to avoid some of the issues with clearing and registering the trademark and potential contentious battles over the right to use a celebrity's personal name that is already well-recognized and valuable on its own.

Ms. Witherspoon is not the only apparel company founder following this formula. The designer formerly known as Kate Spade was actually born Katherine Noel Brosnahan.[64] Shortly after starting their "Kate Spade Handbags" business, she married her boyfriend and business partner Andy Spade, and adopted the name Kate Spade. Since then, the name Kate Spade not only became synonymous with high-end handbags and shoes, it also became the well-known identifier of the designer herself.[65]

In 2006, Brosnahan sold her company, along with the right to use "Kate Spade" as the brand, to Liz Claiborne Inc., which rebranded the company as Kate Spade & Co.[66] She then began using her full birth name Katherine Noel Frances Valentine Brosnahan and now designs under the label Frances Valentine.[67]

There are several U.S. federal registrations and pending applications for the mark FRANCES VALENTINE in the name of Quince New York Shoes, LLC, covering, inter alia, sunglasses, handbags, clothing, and shoes. Before one of the registrations issued, Reg. No. 4965459, the Examining Attorney inquired whether the mark identifies a living person.[68] As previously discussed, the Lanham Act requires that marks that identify a living person must have written consent.[69] The applicant for the mark FRANCES VALENTINE responded that the name portrayed in the mark "does not identify a particular living individual."[70] This appears to be contrary to media reports that the mark is a reference to the designer's personal name. In any event, as a result of this statement, Brosnahan was not required to provide her written consent, and the mark proceeded to registration.

64. *See supra* note 37.

65. *Id.*

66. In 2017, the KATE SPADE brand was sold to Coach, Inc. (now Tapestry, Inc.).

67. *Id.*

68. *See* USPTO Office Action, Reg. No. 4965459 FRANCES VALENTINE (Feb. 1, 2015) (available at http://tsdr.uspto.gov/documentviewer?caseId=sn86421476&docId=OOA20150201200019#docIndex=21&page=1 (last accessed Nov. 20, 2017)).

69. *See supra* note 37.

70. *See* Response to Office Action, Reg. No. 4965459 FRANCES VALENTINE (Feb. 3, 2015) (available at http://tsdr.uspto.gov/documentviewer?caseId=sn86421476&docId=ROA20150204173616#docIndex=19&page=1 (last accessed Nov. 20, 2017)).

While the claim of a personal connection was not made in the U.S. trademark prosecution history for the new brand, retail partners of Frances Valentine are able to connect the brand with the designer and her history by using clever language in promotional materials. In April 2016, Nordstrom Inc. hosted a reception for the designer in Boca Raton, Florida, and the invitations reportedly described her as the "former designer and founder of [the] Kate Spade brand."[71] Carefully drafted language like this was likely vetted by an attorney in order to introduce Brosnahan's new brand in connection with her former brand without infringing the trademark rights of the new owner of the KATE SPADE brand. In a video interview, described as "Watch Kate Spade explain her 3 names," the designer herself states that "Kate Spade is me and it is also the name of my former company that my husband and I founded with two other partners."[72]

Screenshot of interview referencing Brosnahan's name as "KATE VALENTINE" and her title as "Kate Spade, Frances Valentine fashion designer"

According to the Wall Street Journal, the former CEO of Kate Spade & Co., Craig Leavitt, stated that his only concern is that the new brand offered by the designer not be "confusing to our customers or infringing on our trademarks."[73] Brosnahan's name change and ability to carry on with at least some "former designer of" language is something of a game changer for designers who have sold their eponymous brands, as it shows how designers can start new ventures under different personal names while apprising consumers of a factually accurate, historical connection between the designer's former brand and new name.

71. *See supra* note 37.

72. Rob Stafford Hagwood, *Designer Kate Spade launches new Frances Valentine line in Boca*, SouthFlorida.com (Apr. 12, 2016) (available at http://www.southflorida.com/video/sf-boca-fashion-kate-spade-20160412-story.html (last accessed Nov. 20, 2017)).

73. *See supra* note 37.

VI. Summary of Considerations When Using or Acquiring a Personal Name as a Brand

Before designers use their personal names as their brands, they should consider whether they can accept the possibility of eventually having to forfeit the right to use their names on future ventures in exchange for financial gains that may be achieved if they decide to sell their trademarks and related rights. If a designer is not prepared to face these potential limitations, the designer who wants a "personal brand" should consider branding alternatives that still evoke a personal story or connection. When considering the sale of a namesake brand, it is important to have a carefully drafted, clear purchasing agreement, preferably with exhaustive consideration of the various types of name uses that may be made by the designer going forward. When designers sell the rights to their personal names, they should consider alternative ways to identify themselves in connection with their new brands, including whether to take on a different personal name and use the introduction "the designer formerly known as. . . ."

Points to Consider When Contracting for the Sale of a Namesake Brand

Acquirer

- ❑ Are all trademark registrations under the same name? If not, who will be responsible for updating chains of title?
- ❑ Does the sale include social media accounts accessible only to the person who created the accounts? If so, should administrative access be provided at closing?
- ❑ Does the contract transfer or license rights of publicity in the designer's persona, likeness, and name, apart from the designer's trademarks?
- ❑ Should the designer retain a minority ownership interest in the company or other employment or consulting relationship that would incentivize the designer to maintain their own image in support of the brand?
- ❑ Are there any pending trademark applications that were filed on an intent-to-use basis for which an allegation of use has not yet been filed and that the acquirer expects to own? If so, consider including language in the contract deferring the assignment until use has commenced or confirming that the business or relevant portion thereof has been assigned with the mark.
- ❑ Should the contract include a consent from the designer or a requirement that the designer reasonably cooperate in later providing said consent to allow registration of the name for goods/services beyond those previously registered?

Designer

- ❑ Will there be any limitations on how the designer uses his or her first and last name, initials, nicknames, legal aliases, or other variations of the name? For example, are autographs or autobiographical publications permitted?
- ❑ Will there be any limitations on how the designer is able to use his or her likeness, persona, and image in connection with future ventures or as a private citizen?

- ❑ Are there one or more domain names that the designer should be allowed to use and/or register after the sale?
- ❑ Will family members be restricted from using the designer's surname as part of their own trademarks for similar or related goods?
- ❑ Will the designer be able to use the introduction "the designer formerly known as _____"?

D. Product Design and Trade Dress Trademarks

1. Apparel Design as Trade Dress

As stated above, the Lanham Act defines trademarks as not just words and logos but any "device" that indicates the source of the product or service. The protection of ornamental and visual representation of goods, either product packaging or design, is also known as trade dress and can be a valid trademark. To what extent may the design of a product itself serve as a trademark? The Supreme Court addressed this question in the following case.

Wal-Mart Stores, Inc. v. Samara Bros., Inc.

529 U.S. 205 (2000)

Justice SCALIA delivered the opinion of the Court.

In this case, we decide under what circumstances a product's design is distinctive, and therefore protectible, in an action for infringement of unregistered trade dress under § 43(a) of the Trademark Act of 1946 (Lanham Act).

I

Respondent Samara Brothers, Inc., designs and manufactures children's clothing. Its primary product is a line of spring/summer one-piece seersucker outfits decorated with appliques of hearts, flowers, fruits, and the like. A number of chain stores, including JC Penney, sell this line of clothing under contract with Samara.

Petitioner Wal-Mart Stores, Inc., is one of the Nation's best known retailers, selling among other things children's clothing. In 1995, Wal-Mart contracted with one of its suppliers, Judy-Philippine, Inc., to manufacture a line of children's outfits for sale in the 1996 spring/summer season. Wal-Mart sent Judy-Philippine photographs of a number of garments from Samara's line, on which Judy-Philippine's garments were to be based; Judy-Philippine duly copied, with only minor modifications, 16 of Samara's garments, many of which contained copyrighted elements. In 1996, Wal-Mart briskly sold the so-called knockoffs, generating more than $1.15 million in gross profits.

In June 1996, a buyer for JC Penney called a representative at Samara to complain that she had seen Samara garments on sale at Wal-Mart for a lower price than JCPenney was allowed to charge under its contract with Samara. The Samara representative told the buyer that Samara did not supply its clothing to Wal-Mart. Their suspicions aroused, however, Samara officials launched an investigation, which disclosed that Wal-Mart and several other major retailers—Kmart, Caldor, Hills, and Goody's—were selling the knockoffs of Samara's outfits produced by Judy-Philippine.

After sending cease-and-desist letters, Samara brought this action in the United States District Court for the Southern District of New York against Wal-Mart, Judy-Philippine, Kmart, Caldor, Hills, and Goody's for copyright infringement under federal law, consumer fraud and unfair competition under New York law, and—most relevant for our purposes—infringement of unregistered trade dress under §43(a) of the Lanham Act. All of the defendants except Wal-Mart settled before trial.

After a weeklong trial, the jury found in favor of Samara on all of its claims. Wal-Mart then renewed a motion for judgment as a matter of law, claiming, inter alia, that there was insufficient evidence to support a conclusion that Samara's clothing designs could be legally protected as distinctive trade dress. The District Court denied the motion and awarded Samara damages, interest, costs, and fees totaling almost $1.6 million, together with injunctive relief. The Second Circuit affirmed the denial of the motion for judgment as a matter of law, and we granted certiorari.

II

The Lanham Act provides for the registration of trademarks, which it defines in to include any word, name, symbol, or device, or any combination thereof used or intended to be used to identify and distinguish a producer's goods from those manufactured or sold by others and to indicate the source of the goods. In addition to protecting registered marks, the Lanham Act gives a producer a cause of action for the use by any person of "any word, term, name, symbol, or device, or any combination thereof . . . which . . . is likely to cause confusion . . . as to the origin, sponsorship, or approval of his or her goods. . . ." 15 U.S.C. § 1125(a). It is the latter provision that is at issue in this case.

The breadth of the definition of marks registrable under § 2, and of the confusion-producing elements recited as actionable by §43(a), has been held to embrace not just word marks, such as "Nike," and symbol marks, such as Nike's "swoosh" symbol, but also "trade dress"—a category that originally included only the packaging, or "dressing," of a product, but in recent years has been expanded by many Courts of Appeals to encompass the design of a product. *See, e.g., Ashley Furniture Industries, Inc. v. Sangiacomo N. A., Ltd.*, 187 F.3d 363 (C.A.4 1999) (bedroom furniture); *Knitwaves, Inc. v. Lollytogs, Ltd.*, 71 F.3d 996 (C.A.2 1995) (sweaters).

These courts have assumed, often without discussion, that trade dress constitutes a "symbol" or "device" for purposes of the relevant sections, and we conclude likewise. Since human beings might use as a symbol or device almost anything at all that is capable of carrying meaning, this language, read literally, is not restrictive.

The text of §43(a) provides little guidance as to the circumstances under which unregistered trade dress may be protected. It does require that a producer show that the allegedly infringing feature is not "functional," and is likely to cause confusion with the product for which protection is sought. Nothing explicitly requires a producer to show that its trade dress is distinctive, but courts have universally imposed that requirement. Distinctiveness is, moreover, an explicit prerequisite for registration of trade dress. *Two Pesos, Inc. v. Taco Cabana, Inc.*, 112 S. Ct. 2753(1992).

In evaluating distinctiveness courts have held that a mark can be distinctive in one of two ways. First, a mark is inherently distinctive if its intrinsic nature serves to identify a particular source. In the context of word marks, courts have applied the now-classic test originally formulated by Judge Friendly, in which word marks that are "arbitrary" ("Camel" cigarettes), "fanciful" ("Kodak" film), or "suggestive" ("Tide" laundry detergent) are held to be inherently distinctive. *See Abercrombie & Fitch Co. v. Hunting World, Inc.*, 537 F.2d 4, 10–11 (C.A.2 1976). Second, a mark has acquired distinctiveness, even if it is not inherently distinctive, if it has developed secondary meaning, which occurs when, "in the minds of the public, the primary significance of a [mark] is to identify the source of the product rather than the product itself." *Inwood Laboratories, Inc. v. Ives Laboratories, Inc.*, 102 S. Ct. 2182 (1982).

The judicial differentiation between marks that are inherently distinctive and those that have developed secondary meaning has solid foundation in the statute itself. Section 2 requires that registration be granted to any trademark "by which the goods of the applicant may be distinguished from the goods of others"—subject to various limited exceptions. 15 U.S.C. §1052. It also provides, again with limited exceptions, that "nothing in this chapter shall prevent the registration of a mark used by the applicant which has become distinctive of the applicant's goods in commerce"—that is, which is not inherently distinctive but has become so only through secondary meaning. Nothing demands the conclusion that every category of mark necessarily includes some marks "by which the goods of the applicant may be distinguished from the goods of others" without secondary meaning—that in every category some marks are inherently distinctive.

Indeed, with respect to at least one category of mark—colors—we have held that no mark can ever be inherently distinctive. *See Qualitex*, 115 S. Ct. 1300. In *Qualitex*, petitioner manufactured and sold green-gold dry-cleaning press pads. After respondent began selling pads of a similar color, petitioner brought suit under §43(a), then added a claim after obtaining registration for the color of its pads. We held that a color could be protected as a trademark, but only upon a showing of secondary meaning. Reasoning by analogy to the Abercrombie & Fitch test developed for word marks, we noted that a product's color is unlike a "fanciful," "arbitrary," or "suggestive" mark, since it does not almost automatically tell a customer that it refer[s] to a brand, and does not immediately signal a brand or a product source. However, we noted that, over time, customers may come to treat a particular color on a product or its packaging as signifying a brand. Because a color, like a "descriptive" word mark, could eventually "come to indicate a product's origin," we concluded that it could be protected upon a showing of secondary meaning.

It seems to us that design, like color, is not inherently distinctive. The attribution of inherent distinctiveness to certain categories of word marks and product packaging derives from the fact that the very purpose of attaching a particular word to a product, or encasing it in a distinctive packaging, is most often to identify the source of the product. Although the words and packaging can serve subsidiary functions—a suggestive word mark (such as "Tide" for laundry detergent), for instance, may invoke positive connotations in the consumer's mind, and a garish form of packaging (such as Tide's squat, brightly decorated plastic bottles for its liquid laundry detergent) may attract an otherwise indifferent consumer's attention on a crowded store shelf—their predominant function remains source identification. Consumers are therefore predisposed to regard those symbols as indication of the producer, which is why such symbols "almost automatically tell a customer that they refer to a brand," *id.* 115 S. Ct. 1300, and "immediately . . . signal a brand or a product 'source'". And where it is not reasonable to assume consumer predisposition to take an affixed word or packaging as indication of source—where, for example, the affixed word is descriptive of the product ("Tasty" bread) or of a geographic origin ("Georgia" peaches)—inherent distinctiveness will not be found. That is why the statute generally excludes, from those word marks that can be registered as inherently distinctive, words that are "merely descriptive" of the goods, or "primarily geographically descriptive of them". In the case of product design, as in the case of color, we think consumer predisposition to equate the feature with the source does not exist. Consumers are aware of the reality that, almost invariably, even the most unusual of product designs—such as a cocktail shaker shaped like a penguin—is intended not to identify the source, but to render the product itself more useful or more appealing.

The fact that product design almost invariably serves purposes other than source identification not only renders inherent distinctiveness problematic; it also renders application of an inherent—distinctiveness principle more harmful to other consumer interests. Consumers should not be deprived of the benefits of competition with regard to the utilitarian and esthetic purposes that product design ordinarily serves by a rule of law that facilitates plausible threats of suit against new entrants based upon alleged inherent distinctiveness. How easy it is to mount a plausible suit depends, of course, upon the clarity of the test for inherent distinctiveness, and where product design is concerned we have little confidence that a reasonably clear test can be devised.

Respondent and the United States as amicus curiae urge us to adopt for product design relevant portions of the test formulated by the Court of Customs and Patent Appeals for product packaging in *Seabrook Foods, Inc. v. Bar-Well Foods*, Ltd., 568 F.2d 1342 (1977). That opinion, in determining the inherent distinctiveness of a product's packaging, considered, among other things, whether it was a 'common' basic shape or design, whether it was unique or unusual in a particular field, and whether it was a mere refinement of a commonly-adopted and well-known form of ornamentation for a particular class of goods viewed by the public as a dress or ornamentation for the goods. Such a test would rarely provide the basis for summary disposition of an anticompetitive strike suit. Indeed, at oral argument, counsel for the United States quite understandably would not give a definitive answer as to whether the test was met in this very case, saying only that "[t]his is a very difficult case for that purpose." Tr. of Oral Arg. 19.

It is true, of course, that the person seeking to exclude new entrants would have to establish the nonfunctionality of the design feature—a showing that may involve consideration of its esthetic appeal. Competition is deterred, however, not merely by successful suit but by the plausible threat of successful suit, and given the unlikelihood of inherently source-identifying design, the game of allowing suit based upon alleged inherent distinctiveness seems to us not worth the candle. That is especially so since the producer can ordinarily obtain protection for a design that is inherently source identifying (if any such exists), but that does not yet have secondary meaning, by securing a design patent or a copyright for the design—as, indeed, respondent did for certain elements of the designs in this case. The availability of these other protections greatly reduces any harm to the producer that might ensue from our conclusion that a product design cannot be protected under §43(a) without a showing of secondary meaning.

Respondent contends that our decision in *Two Pesos* forecloses a conclusion that product-design trade dress can never be inherently distinctive. In that case, we held that the trade dress of a chain of Mexican restaurants, which the plaintiff described as "a festive eating atmosphere having interior dining and patio areas decorated with artifacts, bright colors, paintings and murals," 505 U.S., at 765, could be protected without a showing of secondary meaning. *Two Pesos* unquestionably establishes the legal principle that trade dress can be inherently distinctive, but it does not establish that product-design trade dress can be. Two Pesos is inapposite to our holding here because the trade dress at issue, the decor of a restaurant, seems to us not to constitute product design. It was either product packaging—which, as we have discussed, normally is taken by the consumer to indicate origin—or else some *tertium quid* that is akin to product packaging and has no bearing on the present case.

Respondent replies that this manner of distinguishing *Two Pesos* will force courts to draw difficult lines between product-design and product-packaging trade dress. There will indeed be some hard cases at the margin: a classic glass Coca-Cola bottle, for instance, may constitute packaging for those consumers who drink the Coke and then discard the bottle, but may constitute the product itself for those consumers who are bottle collectors, or part of the product itself for those consumers who buy Coke in the classic glass bottle, rather than a can, because they think it more stylish to drink from the former. We believe, however, that the frequency and the difficulty of having to distinguish between product design and product packaging will be much less than the frequency and the difficulty of having to decide when a product design is inherently distinctive. To the extent there are close cases, we believe that courts should err on the side of caution and classify ambiguous trade dress as product design, thereby requiring secondary meaning. The very closeness will suggest the existence of relatively small utility in adopting an inherent-distinctiveness principle, and relatively great consumer benefit in requiring a demonstration of secondary meaning.

We hold that, in an action for infringement of unregistered trade dress under §43(a) of the Lanham Act, a product's design is distinctive, and therefore protectible, only upon a showing of secondary meaning. The judgment of the Second Circuit is reversed, and the case is remanded for further proceedings consistent with this opinion.

Notes

1. The central holding of this decision is Justice Scalia's statement that product design, like color, cannot be inherently distinctive and can only be protected upon a showing of secondary meaning. Is product design equivalent to color in this context? Color trademarks require a finding of secondary meaning in part due to the finite options on a color wheel. Are there similar limitations for the number of styles of dresses that may be created, for example? Are there no dresses, suits, shirts, etc., that are so unusual or even arbitrary that they would be fairly described as inherently distinctive? Did Justice Scalia reach this opinion based on the belief, correct or not, that because all clothes share certain elements—e.g., openings for the head and limbs and basic covering of the body—that they cannot truly be distinctive?

2. What is the basis for Justice Scalia's holding that "it seems to us that product design . . . is never inherently distinctive"? As the central holding of the case, it is surprising that the Court gives no explanation for its reasoning. What are some products that you can think of that would be inherently distinctive, even though they also serve a function?

3. Fashion designers may be particularly harmed by this ruling. The required secondary meaning can take years and considerable sales and promotion to establish. Even more than other industries, a successful fashion design will be copied through "fast fashion" not long after the release of that design. Fashion designers would not have trade dress rights to assert against these instantaneous copiers. By the time that secondary meaning could ordinarily be shown—after several years—it will therefore be difficult to show a singular identification with one source because of the prevalence of knockoffs that the original designer was powerless to prevent.

2. Functionality

Trade dress protection does not extend to functional elements of products. The burden of showing functionality or nonfunctionality depends upon whether the trade dress at issue is registered with the PTO. If the trade dress is registered, it is the defendant's burden to show functionality as a defense. *See* 15 U.S.C. § 1125(a)(3). If the trade dress is not registered, it is the burden of the proponent of the trade dress to prove that it is nonfunctional. *Id.* Even though several elements of a given trade dress may be individually functional, if the trade dress as a whole is nonfunctional the trade dress will be protectable, as seen in the following case.

Adidas-Salomon AG v. Target Corp.

228 F. Supp. 2d 1192 (D. Or. 2002)

REDDEN, District Judge.

This is an action by adidas-Salomon AG and adidas America, Inc., alleging that defendants have offered for sale and sold shoes with features that bear confusingly similar imitations of adidas' trademark diagonal three stripes and the trade dress of adidas' Original Superstar shoe. Plaintiffs assert claims for violation of federal copyright law and the Lanham Act, 15 U.S.C. §§ 1051-1127, and state laws governing trademark dilution, injury to business reputation, unfair competition, and deceptive trade practices. The defendants filed a motion to dismiss, which the court converted to a motion for summary judgment. On July 31, 2002, Magistrate Judge Stewart filed Findings and Recommendations that the defendants' motion be denied.

The matter is now before me pursuant to 28 U.S.C. § 636(b)(1) and Rule 72(b) of the Federal Rules of Civil Procedure. Section (b)(1)(A) authorizes a magistrate to hear and determine any pretrial matter pending before the court except certain specified "dispositive" motions. *United States v. Raddatz,* 447 U.S. 667, 673, 100 S. Ct. 2406, 65 L. Ed. 2d 424 (1980). Review by the district court of the magistrate's determination of dispositive motions excepted under § 636(b)(1)(A) is *de novo.* Fed.R.Civ.P. 72(b); *Bhan v. NME Hospitals, Inc.,* 929 F.2d 1404, 1414 (9th Cir. 1991).

Defendants have filed timely objections to Magistrate Judge Stewart's Findings and Recommendation. I have given the Findings and Recommendation *de novo* review.

Defendants' first objection to the Findings and Recommendation is that Judge Stewart's Findings and Recommendation permits adidas to bring an anti-competitive strike suit in the guise of product design trade dress claims. This, say the defendants, flies in the face of the encouragement of copying product designs not protected by copyright or patent law.

A product's "trade dress" is its total image and overall appearance; it includes "features such as size, shape, color, color combinations, texture, or graphics." *Vision Sports, Inc. v. Melville Corp.,* 888 F.2d 609, 613 (9th Cir. 1989) (internal quotations and citation omitted). To sustain a claim for trade dress infringement, the plaintiff must prove that its claimed dress is nonfunctional, serves a source-identifying role either because it is inherently distinctive or has acquired secondary meaning, and that the defendant's product creates a likelihood of consumer confusion. *Clicks Billiards, Inc. v. Sixshooters, Inc.,* 251 F.3d 1252, 1257 (9th Cir. 2001).

adidas asserts that the trade dress of its original Superstar shoe is based on four elements: the trademarked three stripes on the side of the shoe, a flat sole, a rubber toe with a shell design ("shell toe,") and a "heel patch" including a trefoil design.

Defendants' first objection is based on the functionality doctrine. Under the functionality doctrine, the law distinguishes between trademark and trade dress features "which constitute the actual benefit that the consumer wishes to purchase, which do not engender trademark protection," and "an assurance that a particular entity made, sponsored, or endorsed a product, which, if incorporated into the product's design by virtue of arbitrary embellishment, does have trademark significance." *Tie Tech, Inc. v. Kinedyne Corp.*, 296 F.3d 778, 785 (9th Cir. 2002) (internal citations and quotations omitted). Under the functionality doctrine, competitors can replicate important non-reputation-related product features. *Qualitex Co. v. Jacobson Prods. Co., Inc.*, 514 U.S. 159, 169, 115 S. Ct. 1300, 131 L. Ed. 2d 248 (1995). However, the copying of "arbitrary embellishments" that have acquired distinctiveness or secondary meaning is prohibited. *Tie Tech,* 296 F.3d at 785.

Thus, trade dress protection extends only to design features that are nonfunctional. *Clicks Billiards,* 251 F.3d at 1258. A product feature is functional if the feature is essential to the use or purpose of the article or if it affects the cost or quality of the article. *Qualitex,* 514 U.S. at 165, 115 S. Ct. 1300; *TrafFix Devices, Inc. v. Marketing Displays, Inc.*, 532 U.S. 23, 121 S. Ct. 1255, 1259, 149 L. Ed. 2d 164 (2001). In determining whether trade dress is nonfunctional, the whole collection of features must be taken together. *See International Jensen, Inc. v. Metrosound U.S.A., Inc.*, 4 F.3d 819, 822–23 (9th Cir. 1993)

The fact that individual elements of the trade dress may be functional does not necessarily mean that the trade dress as a whole is functional; rather, functional elements that are separately unprotectable can be protected together as part of a trade dress. *Clicks Billiards,* 251 F.3d at 1259. Trade dress is "the composite tapestry of visual effects." *Id.*

Judge Stewart concluded that when all of the elements of the Original Superstar shoe's trade dress were taken together, they were nonfunctional and therefore protectable. Defendants have conceded that two elements of the Original Superstar's trade dress, the three-stripe mark and the heel patch, are nonfunctional. However, they assert that the flat sole and the rubber shell toe are widely used in the shoe industry and therefore are functional elements which render the Original Superstar's trade dress also functional.

adidas has proffered evidence that the flat sole of the Original Superstar was considered optimal for a performance basketball shoe in 1969, when adidas introduced the Original Superstar, but that it is considered optimal no longer. adidas has also introduced evidence that the rubber toe of the Original Superstar shoe adds neither durability nor performance to the shoes, but is purely ornamental and actually increases the production cost, Judge Stewart concluded from this evidence that adidas had established the nonfunctionality of the Original Superstar trade dress. I agree with that conclusion. Defendants' first objection is rejected.

Defendants' second objection is that adidas failed to show that its claimed Original Superstar trade dress has acquired distinctiveness or secondary meaning. They also argue that Judge Stewart erroneously inferred that the B.U.M. shoe had been copied from the Original Superstar shoe, and that such copying conferred secondary meaning on the Original Superstar shoe. They also contend that the evidence proffered by adidas on the existence of acquired distinctiveness of the Original Superstar trade dress was merely circumstantial and therefore not probative. This objection is also without merit.

In evaluating the sufficiency of evidence of secondary meaning, the court looks to a number of factors, including 1) whether actual purchasers of the product bearing the claimed trade dress associate the trademark with the producer, 2) the degree and manner of advertising under the claimed trade dress, 3) the length and manner of use of the claimed trade dress, and 4) whether use has been exclusive. See *Committee for Idaho's High Desert, Inc. v. Yost*, 92 F.3d 814, 822 (9th Cir. 1996); *Japan Telecom, Inc. v. Japan Telecom America, Inc.*, 287 F.3d 866, 873 (9th Cir. 2002). Secondary meaning requires a showing that there is a "mental recognition in buyers' and potential buyers' minds that products connected with the mark are associated with the same source." *Japan Telecom*, 287 F.3d at 873 (internal quotations and citations omitted).

adidas has submitted evidence showing that since 1986, when the rap group "Run DMC" performed the song "My adidas" while wearing the Original Superstar shoes, several rap and hip-hop musical artists have written and performed songs whose lyrics refer to the adidas "shell toe." adidas has also proffered evidence showing unsolicited media references identifying the Original Superstar's trade dress, particularly the shell toe, with adidas.

In determining whether a plaintiff's advertising is enough to establish secondary meaning, the court looks at the advertising's "amount, nature and geographical scope" with an "eye toward how likely the advertising is to expose a large number of the relevant consuming public to the use of the symbol . . ." *Japan Telecom*, 287 F.3d at 875. adidas' evidence shows extensive and diverse advertising of both the three-stripe mark and the Original Superstar shoe itself. This includes print advertising and placement of the Original Superstar shoe on famous athletes. In addition, adidas has shown that the Original Superstar shoe has been marketed continuously since 1969. The evidence is sufficient to create a triable issue of fact on secondary meaning.

Defendants claim that adidas has not proffered sufficient evidence to constitute a triable issue of fact on whether the "retro look" of the B.U.M. shoe is likely to cause consumer confusion with the adidas Original Superstar. The likelihood of confusion is "the central element of trademark infringement." *GoTo.com. Inc. v. Walt Disney Co.*, 202 F.3d 1199, 1205 (9th Cir. 2000). Likelihood of confusion involves consideration of the "total effect of the defendant's product and package on the eye and mind of an ordinary purchaser." *First Brands Corp. v. Fred Meyer, Inc.,* 809 F.2d 1378, 1383-84 (9th Cir. 1987). The existence of customer confusion is determined by application of the so-called *Sleekcraft* factors, announced in *AMF, Inc. v. Sleekcraft Boats,* 599 F.2d 341, 348 (9th Cir. 1979). These factors include 1) strength of the mark; 2) proximity of the goods; 3) similarity of the marks; 4) evidence of actual confusion; 5) marketing channels used; 6) type of goods and the degree of care likely to be exercised by the purchaser; 7) defendant's intent in selecting the mark, and 8) likelihood of expansion of the product lines. Magistrate Stewart concluded that adidas had demonstrated the existence of triable issues of fact on the *Sleekcraft* factors.

Similarity is always a crucial question in a *Sleekcraft* analysis. *GoTo.com* 202 F.3d at 1205. The greater the similarity, the greater the likelihood of confusion. *Id.* at 1205-06. Two of the axioms which guide this comparison are first that the marks must be considered in their entirety and as they appear in the marketplace, and second that similarities are weighed more heavily than differences. *Id.* at 1206; see also *Entrepreneur Media, Inc. v. Smith,* 279 F.3d 1135, 1144 (9th Cir. 2002).

The Original Superstar (plaintiffs' Exhibit 3) and the B.U.M. "Jonah" shoe (defendants' Exhibit 2) are strikingly similar. The B.U.M. "Jonah" shoe design consists of a flat sole nearly identical to that of the Original Superstar, a shell toe with the same number of decorative ridges (six) as the Original Superstar shell toe (although with a different pattern between the ridges), stitching around the eyelet holes that is essentially indistinguishable from that of the Original Superstar, diagonal stripes with serrated edges on the side of the shoe (the Original Superstar has three stripes with perforations between them, the B.U.M. shoe has four stripes without perforations, but the size, angle, location and color of the stripes is nearly identical), and a heel patch of the same color and similar shape to the heel patch on the Original Superstar, but without the trefoil and three stripes design and the word "adidas." Both the B.U.M. and the adidas shoes have a wide seam centered beneath the heel patch.

adidas has also submitted evidence showing the strength of the mark and the proximity of the goods (i.e., that the products are sold to the same class of purchasers and are similar in function). And finally, through the evidence of the double-blind survey, adidas has demonstrated a triable issue of fact on the issue of post-sale confusion, which occurs when consumers other than the purchaser see the item after it has been purchased. Defendants' objection is rejected.

Defendants next object that adidas has not proffered evidence of the fame of the Original Superstar trade dress sufficient to raise a triable issue of fact on trade dress dilution. The court found sufficient adidas' evidence that 1) shoes bearing Original Superstar trade dress have been manufactured and sold since the late 1960s; 2) they were worn by a number of famous basketball players in the 1970s and thereby achieved sufficient fame; 3) adidas has sold large numbers of shoes bearing the Original Superstar trade dress, particularly during the last five years; and 4) adidas has spent substantial sums to promote the Original Superstar trade dress over a wide geographical area. The Judge also noted the absence of any evidence that third parties have used designs incorporating all four elements of the Original Superstar trade dress.

I agree with Magistrate Stewart that this evidence is sufficient to withstand defendants' motion for summary judgment.

Accordingly, I ADOPT Magistrate Judge Stewart's Findings and Recommendation filed July 31, 2002 (doc. # 131). The defendants' motion (doc. # 22) is DENIED. Defendants' motion for leave to file a reply memorandum in support of its amended objections to the Findings and Recommendation (doc. # 146) is DENIED.

IT IS SO ORDERED.

Note

Adidas successfully argued that the flat sole of its Superstar shoe may have been functional when the shoe was introduced in 1969, but it is no longer "considered optimal." Under the applicable test for functionality, does a feature need to be "optimal" for it to be considered functional? If a feature provided a functional benefit at a point in the past, how would it no longer provide that benefit going forward?

3. Color Trademarks and Aesthetic Functionality

The Court in *Wal-Mart Stores, Inc. v. Samara Brothers, Inc.* referred to its prior opinion in *Qualitex v. Jacobson,* which held that color may be protectable as a trademark if it has acquired secondary meaning. Like all other trademarks, however, color trademarks must not be functional if they are to be protectable. The correct intellectual property regime for protection of a functional item is patent law, in which functional inventions are protected for a limited number of years. Trademark law grew out of unfair competition law, thus, granting a trademark, which is protected so long as it is in use, for a functional item would be detrimental to competition. For three-dimensional trademarks, functionality applies to elements that affect the performance or cost of the product, such as a particularly useful means of buttons or zippers for apparel. For color trademarks, however, the functionality doctrine at issue is more likely to be aesthetic functionality, as discussed in the case below.

Christian Louboutin S.A. v. Yves Saint Laurent America Holding, Inc.

696 F.3d 206 (2d Cir. 2012)

CABRANES, Circuit Judge.

The question presented is whether a single color may serve as a legally protected trademark in the fashion industry and, in particular, as the mark for a particular style of high fashion women's footwear. Christian Louboutin, a designer of high-fashion women's footwear and accessories, has since 1992 painted the "outsoles" of his women's high-heeled shoes with a high-gloss red lacquer. In 2008, he registered the red lacquered outsole as a trademark with the United States Patent and Trade Office ("PTO"). We are asked to decide whether that mark is protectable under federal trademark law.

Christian Louboutin S.A. ("Louboutin"), bring this interlocutory appeal from an August 10, 2011 order of the United States District Court for the Southern District of New York (Victor Marrero, Judge) denying a motion for a preliminary injunction against alleged trademark infringement by Yves Saint Laurent America Holding, Inc., Yves Saint Laurent S.A.S., and Yves Saint Laurent America, Inc. (jointly, "YSL"). The District Court, in addressing a difficult and novel issue of trademark law, held that, because a single color can never be protected by trademark in the fashion industry, Louboutin's trademark was likely not enforceable. It therefore declined to enter a preliminary injunction to restrain YSL's alleged use of the mark.

Background

This appeal arises out of an action for injunctive relief and enforcement of a trademark brought by Louboutin, together with the corporate entities that constitute his eponymous French fashion house, against YSL, a venerable French fashion institution. Louboutin is best known for his emphasis upon the otherwise-largely-ignored outsole of the shoe. Since their development in 1992, Louboutin's shoes have been characterized by their most striking feature: a bright, lacquered red outsole, which nearly always contrasts sharply with the color of the rest of the shoe.

Christian Louboutin introduced his signature footwear to the fashion market in 1992. Since then, his shoes have grown in popularity, appearing regularly on various celebrities and fashion icons. The District Court concluded, and YSL does not dispute, that Louboutin had invested substantial amounts of capital building a reputation and good will, as well as promoting and protecting Louboutin's claim to exclusive ownership of the mark as its signature in women's high fashion footwear. The District Court further found that Louboutin had succeeded in promoting his shoes to the point where, in the high-stakes commercial markets and social circles in which these things matter a great deal, the red outsole became closely associated with Louboutin. As a result of Louboutin's marketing efforts, the District Court found, the "flash of a red sole" is today "instantly" recognizable, to "those in the know," as Louboutin's handiwork.

On the strength of the fashion world's asserted recognition of the red sole, Louboutin filed an application with the PTO to protect his mark (the "Red Sole Mark" or the "Mark"). The trademark was granted in January 2008, and stated: "The color(s) red is/are claimed as a feature of the mark. The mark consists of a lacquered red sole on footwear." The written description was accompanied by a diagram indicating the placement of the color:

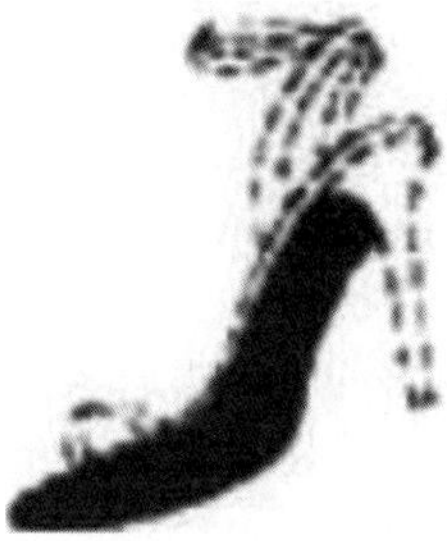

In 2011, YSL prepared to market a line of "monochrome" shoes in purple, green, yellow, and red. YSL shoes in the monochrome style feature the same color on the entire shoe, so that the red version is all red, including a red insole, heel, upper, and outsole. This was not the first time that YSL had designed a monochrome footwear line, or even a line of footwear with red soles; indeed, YSL maintains that since the 1970s it had sold such shoes in red and other colors.

In January 2011, Louboutin avers, his fashion house learned that YSL was marketing and selling a monochrome red shoe with a red sole. Louboutin requested the removal of the allegedly infringing shoes from the market, and Louboutin and YSL briefly entered into negotiations in order to avert litigation.

The negotiations having failed, Louboutin filed this action on April 7, 2011, asserting claims under the Lanham Act for (1) trademark infringement and counterfeiting, (2) false designation of origin and unfair competition, and (3) trademark dilution, as well as state law claims for (4) trademark infringement, (5) trademark dilution, (6) unfair competition, and (7) unlawful deceptive acts and practices. Louboutin also sought a preliminary injunction preventing YSL from marketing, during the pendency of the action, any shoes, including red monochrome shoes, bearing outsoles in a shade of red identical to the Red Sole Mark, or in any shade which so resembles the Red Sole Mark as to cause confusion among consumers.

In response, YSL asserted two counterclaims: (1) seeking cancellation of the Red Sole Mark on the grounds that (a) it is not "distinctive," but instead merely "ornamental," (b) it is "functional," and (c) it was secured by fraud on the PTO; and (2) seeking damages for (a) tortious interference with business relations and (b) unfair competition. On July 22, 2011, after a limited and expedited discovery process, the parties argued the preliminary injunction motion.

On August 10, 2011, the District Court issued a Decision and Order denying the injunction and holding that the Louboutin fashion house had not shown a likelihood of success on the merits of its claims. As the District Court saw it, the "narrow question" presented by the case was "whether the Lanham Act extends protection to a trademark composed of a single color used as an expressive and defining quality of an article of wear produced in the fashion industry"—that is, "whether there is something unique about the fashion world that militates against extending trademark protection to a single color." *Louboutin*, 778 F. Supp. 2d at 451.

Interpreting the Supreme Court's holding in *Qualitex*, the District Court explained that color is protectable as a trademark only if it "'acts as a symbol that distinguishes a firm's goods and identifies their source, without serving any other significant function.'" Id. at 450 (quoting *Qualitex*, 514 U.S. at 166, 115 S. Ct. 1300). The District Court further observed, albeit without citation to authority, that "whatever commercial purposes may support extending trademark protection to a single color for industrial goods do not easily fit the unique characteristics and needs—the creativity, aesthetics, taste, and seasonal change—that define production of articles of fashion." *Id.* at 451. For that reason, the District Court held that, in the fashion industry, single-color marks are inherently "functional" and that any such registered trademark would likely be held invalid. *Id.* at 457. The Court therefore held that Louboutin was unlikely to be able to prove that the Red Sole Mark was eligible for trademark protection, and denied Louboutin's motion for a preliminary injunction. This appeal followed.

On appeal, Louboutin argues that the District Court erred in (1) holding, based on the doctrine of "aesthetic functionality," that the Red Sole Mark was not entitled to legal protection; (2) applying the doctrine of aesthetic functionality to hold that a single color on a fashion item could not act as a trademark; (3) failing to give weight to the statutory presumption of validity deriving from the Red Sole Mark's registration; (4) applying an improper analysis of trademark infringement and dilution; (5) ignoring allegedly undisputed proof of likelihood of confusion and irreparable harm; and (6) announcing a per se rule of functionality in a manner that violated Federal Rule of Civil Procedure 52.7

Discussion

I. Standard of Review

The District Court may grant a preliminary injunction if the moving party establishes "(a) irreparable harm and (b) either (1) likelihood of success on the merits or (2) sufficiently serious questions going to the merits to make them a fair ground for litigation and a balance of hardships tipping decidedly toward the party requesting the preliminary relief."

We address the District Court's order in three parts. We first consider whether a single color is protectable as a trademark, both generally and in the specific context of the fashion industry. We then address the doctrine of "aesthetic functionality" and consider whether, as the District Court held, a single-color mark is necessarily "functional" in the context of the fashion industry—with the result that no such mark could ever be trademarked in that industry. Finally, we determine whether the Red Sole Mark is a valid trademark entitled to the protection of the Lanham Act.

II. Trademark Protection of Single-Color Marks

The principal purpose of federal trademark law is to secure the public's interest in protection against deceit as to the sources of its purchases, and the businessman's right to enjoy business earned through investment in the good will and reputation attached to a trade name.

Trademark law, by preventing others from copying a source-identifying mark, reduces the customer's costs of shopping and making purchasing decisions, for it quickly and easily assures a potential customer that this item—the item with this mark—is made by the same producer as other similarly marked items that he or she liked (or disliked) in the past. At the same time, the law helps assure a producer that it (and not an imitating competitor) will reap the financial, reputation-related rewards associated with a desirable product.

Nevertheless, trademark law is not intended to protect innovation by giving the innovator a monopoly over a useful product feature. *Fabrication Enters.*, Inc., 64 F.3d at 59 n. 4. Such a monopoly is the realm of patent law or copyright law, which seek to encourage innovation, and not of trademark law, which seeks to preserve a vigorously competitive market for the benefit of consumers.

A. The Analytical Framework

We analyze trademark infringement claims in two stages.

First, we look to see whether plaintiff's mark merits protection. In order for a trademark to be protectable, the mark must be "distinctive" and not "generic." A mark is said to be "inherently" distinctive if "[its] intrinsic nature serves to identify a particular source." *Two Pesos, Inc. v. Taco Cabana, Inc.*, 505 U.S. 763, 768 (1992). Even a mark that is not inherently distinctive may nonetheless "acquire" distinctiveness by developing "secondary meaning" in the public mind. A mark has acquired "secondary meaning" when, in the minds of the public, the primary significance of a product feature is to identify the source of the product rather than the product itself.

Second, if the plaintiff's trademark is "distinctive" within the meaning of trademark law and is therefore valid and protectable, we must then determine whether the defendant's use of a similar mark is likely to cause consumer confusion. In this second stage, if a markholder has successfully demonstrated that its mark is valid and that the competitor's mark is likely to cause confusion, the competitor can nevertheless prevail by showing that the [mark] is functional—a traditional defense to the enforcement of a trademark.

B. A Brief History of Single-Color Marks

Prior to the adoption of our modern statutory trademark scheme in the Lanham Act, the status of single-color trademarks rested on uncertain ground. After the Lanham Act codified in the broadest of terms the "universe" of things eligible for trademark protection, courts gradually rejected the dictum of earlier cases to the effect that color alone is not subject to trademark protection, and owners of color-related marks began to enjoy a degree of enforcement success. Nevertheless, the issue of single-color mark registration lay largely dormant until 1985, when the United States Court of Appeals for the Federal Circuit decided *Owens-Corning*.

Faced with the question of whether a fiberglass manufacturer could trademark the pink color of its residential insulation material, the Federal Circuit observed that "Owens-Corning's use of the color 'pink' performs no non-trademark function, and is consistent with the commercial and public purposes of trademarks." *Id.* at 1123.

C. Single-Color Marks Today

The question of whether a color can be protected as a trademark or trade dress was finally resolved in 1995 by the Supreme Court's decision in *Qualitex*, which involved a claim for trade dress protection of the green-gold color of a dry cleaning press pad. The Court concluded that "color alone, at least sometimes, can meet the basic legal requirements for use as a trademark. It can act as a symbol that distinguishes a firm's goods and identifies their source, without serving any other significant function." *Id.* at 166, 115 S. Ct. 1300.

III. The "Functionality" Defense

As the Supreme Court observed in Qualitex, aspects of a product that are "functional" generally "cannot serve as a trademark." *Id.* at 165. This is so because functional features can be protected only through the patent system, which grants a limited monopoly over such features until they are released into general use (typically after either 14 or 20 years, depending on the type of patent). As noted above, two forms of the functionality doctrine are relevant to us today: "traditional" or "utilitarian" functionality, and "aesthetic" functionality. Both forms serve as an affirmative defense to a trademark infringement claim.

A. "Traditional" or "Utilitarian" Functionality

According to our traditional understanding of functionality, a product feature is considered to be "functional" in a utilitarian sense if it is (1) essential to the use or purpose of the article, or if it (2) affects the cost or quality of the article. A finding that a product feature is functional will ordinarily render the feature ineligible for trademark protection.

B. "Aesthetic Functionality"

When the aesthetic design of a product is itself the mark for which protection is sought, we may also deem the mark functional if giving the markholder the right to use it exclusively "would put competitors at a significant non-reputation-related disadvantage," *Qualitex*, 514 U.S. at 165.

As set forth below, the test for aesthetic functionality is threefold: At the start, we address the two prongs of the *Inwood* test, asking whether the design feature is either "essential to the use or purpose" or "affects the cost or quality" of the product at issue. Next, if necessary, we turn to a third prong, which is the competition inquiry set forth in *Qualitex*. In other words, if a design feature would, from a traditional utilitarian perspective, be considered "essential to the use or purpose" of the article, or to affect its cost or quality, then the design feature is functional under *Inwood* and our inquiry ends. But if the design feature is not "functional" from a traditional perspective, it must still pass the fact-intensive *Qualitex* test and be shown not to have a significant effect on competition in order to receive trademark protection.

i. The Development of the Aesthetic Functionality Doctrine

Although the theory of aesthetic functionality was proposed as early as 1938, the first court to adopt the theory as the basis for denial of protection of a design was the United States Court of Appeals for the Ninth Circuit in *Pagliero v. Wallace China Co.*, 198 F.2d 339 (9th Cir. 1952). In Pagliero, the Court of Appeals determined that the Wallace China Company was not entitled to the exclusive use of a particular floral design on hotel china, despite its "creation of a substantial market for its products bearing these designs by virtue of extensive advertising." *Id.* at 340. The design, the Court held, was "functional" because it satisfied "a demand for the aesthetic as well as for the utilitarian." *Id.* at 343–44.

Despite its apparent counter-intuitiveness (how can the purely aesthetic be deemed functional, one might ask?), our Court has long accepted the doctrine of aesthetic functionality. Accordingly, we have held that the doctrine of aesthetic functionality bars protection of a mark that is necessary to compete in the relevant market

ii. A Modern Formulation of the Aesthetic Functionality Doctrine

In 1995, the Supreme Court in *Qualitex* gave its imprimatur to the aesthetic functionality doctrine, holding that "[t]he ultimate test of aesthetic functionality . . . is whether the recognition of trademark rights [in an aesthetic design feature] would significantly hinder competition." *Qualitex*, 514 U.S. at 170(1993). Six years later, reiterating its Qualitex analysis, the Supreme Court in *TrafFix* declared that where "[a]esthetic functionality [is] the central question," courts must "inquire" as to whether recognizing the trademark "would put competitors at a significant non-reputation-related disadvantage." *TrafFix*, 532 U.S. at 32–33.

In short, a mark is aesthetically functional, and therefore ineligible for protection under the Lanham Act, where protection of the mark significantly undermines competitors' ability to compete in the relevant market. In making this determination, courts must carefully weigh "the competitive benefits of protecting the source-identifying aspects" of a mark against the "competitive costs of precluding competitors from using the feature."

Finally, we note that a product feature's successful source indication can sometimes be difficult to distinguish from the feature's aesthetic function, if any. Because aesthetic function and branding success can sometimes be difficult to distinguish, the aesthetic functionality analysis is highly fact-specific. In conducting this inquiry, courts must consider both the markholder's right to enjoy the benefits of its effort to distinguish its product and the public's right to the "vigorously competitive market protected by the Lanham Act," which an overly broad trademark might hinder.

iii. Aesthetic Functionality in the Fashion Industry

We now turn to the per se rule of functionality for color marks in the fashion industry adopted by the District Court—a rule that would effectively deny trademark protection to any deployment of a single color in an item of apparel. As noted above, the *Qualitex* Court expressly forbade the implementation of a per se rule that would deny protection for the use of a single color as a trademark in a particular industrial context. *Qualitex* requires an individualized, fact-based inquiry into the nature of the trademark, and cannot be read to sanction an industry-based per se rule. The District Court created just such a rule, on the theory that "there is something unique about the fashion world that militates against extending trademark protection to a single color." *Louboutin*, 778 F. Supp. 2d at 451.

Even if *Qualitex* could be read to permit an industry-specific per se rule of functionality (a reading we think doubtful), such a rule would be neither necessary nor appropriate here. We readily acknowledge that the fashion industry, like other industries, has special concerns in the operation of trademark law; it has been argued forcefully that United States law does not protect fashion design adequately. Indeed, the case on appeal is particularly difficult precisely because, as the District Court well noted, in the fashion industry, color can serve as a tool in the palette of a designer, rather than as mere ornamentation.

Nevertheless, the functionality defense does not guarantee a competitor the greatest range for his creative outlet, but only the ability to fairly compete within a given market. In short, "by focusing upon hindrances to legitimate competition, the aesthetic functionality test, carefully applied, can accommodate consumers' somewhat conflicting interests in being assured enough product differentiation to avoid confusion as to source and in being afforded the benefits of competition among producers." *Stormy Clime*, 809 F.2d at 978–79.

IV. The Red Sole Mark

Having determined that no per se rule governs the protection of single-color marks in the fashion industry, any more than it can do so in any other industry, we turn our attention to the Red Sole Mark. As we have explained, we analyze a trademark infringement claim in two stages, asking first whether the mark "merits protection" and, second, whether the allegedly infringing use of the mark (or a similar mark) is "likely to cause consumer confusion."

As the District Court correctly noted, Louboutin's certificate of registration of the Red Sole Mark gives rise to a statutory presumption that the mark is valid. But the District Court found, in effect, that YSL had rebutted that presumption by showing that the Red Sole Mark is ineligible for protection because a single color can never achieve trademark protection in the fashion industry. As explained above, that holding was error.

Although, as set forth below, we determine that the Mark as it currently stands is ineligible for protection insofar as it would preclude competitors' use of red outsoles in all situations, including the monochromatic use now before us, we conclude that the Mark has acquired secondary meaning—and thus the requisite "distinctness" to merit protection—when used as a red outsole contrasting with the remainder of the shoe. Because in this case we determine that the Red Sole Mark merits protection only as modified, and because YSL's use of a red outsole on monochromatic red shoes does not infringe on the Mark as modified, we need not, and do not, reach the issues of customer confusion and functionality at the second stage of the trademark infringement analysis described above.

A. Distinctiveness

We first address whether the Red Sole Mark "merits protection" as a distinctive mark. For the reasons that follow, we hold that the Red Sole Mark has acquired limited secondary meaning as a distinctive symbol that identifies the Louboutin brand, and that it is therefore a valid and protectable mark as modified below.

Although a single color, standing alone, can almost never be inherently distinctive because it does not "almost automatically tell a customer that it refers to a brand," *Qualitex*, 514 U.S. at 162–63, a color as used here is certainly capable of acquiring secondary meaning. As the *Qualitex* Court put it,

> over time, customers may come to treat a particular color on a product or its packaging (say, a color that in context seems unusual, such as pink on a firm's insulating material or red on the head of a large industrial bolt) as signifying a brand. And, if so, that color would have come to identify and distinguish the goods—i.e., "to indicate" their "source"—much in the way that descriptive words on a product . . . can come to indicate a product's origin. *Id.* at 163, 115 S. Ct. 1300 (emphasis added).

In the case of a single-color mark, therefore, distinctiveness must generally be proved by demonstrating that the mark has acquired secondary meaning.

We see no reason why a single-color mark in the specific context of the fashion industry could not acquire secondary meaning—and therefore serve as a brand or source identifier—if it is used so consistently and prominently by a particular designer that it becomes a symbol, the primary significance of which is to identify the source of the product rather than the product itself.

The crucial question in a case involving secondary meaning always is whether the public is moved in any degree to buy an article because of its source. Factors that are relevant in determining secondary meaning include (1) advertising expenditures, (2) consumer studies linking the mark to a source, (3) unsolicited media coverage of the product, (4) sales success, (5) attempts to plagiarize the mark and (6) length and exclusivity of the mark's use. Where, as here, the record contains sufficient undisputed facts to resolve the question of distinctiveness—not to speak of facts found by the District Court that are based upon evidence of record and not clearly erroneous—we may do so as a matter of law.

The record before the District Court included extensive evidence of Louboutin's advertising expenditures, media coverage, and sales success, demonstrating both that Louboutin has created a "symbol" within the meaning of *Qualitex*, and that the symbol has gained secondary meaning that causes it to be "uniquely" associated with the Louboutin brand. There is no dispute that Louboutin originated this particular commercial use of the lacquered red color over twenty years ago. As the District Court determined, Louboutin invested substantial amounts of capital building a reputation and good will, as well as promoting and protecting Louboutin's claim to exclusive ownership of the mark as its signature in women's high fashion footwear. Indeed, the Chief Executive Officer of YSL's parent corporation, François-Henri Pinault, himself acknowledged that, "in the fashion or luxury world, it is absolutely clear that we recognize the notoriety of the distinctive signature constituted by the red sole of LOUBOUTIN models in contrast with the general presentation of the model, particularly its upper, and so for all shades of red."

In light of the evidence in the record, including extensive consumer surveys submitted by both parties during the preliminary injunction proceedings, and of the factual findings of the District Court, we think it plain that Louboutin's marketing efforts have created a brand with worldwide recognition.

We further hold that the record fails to demonstrate that the secondary meaning of the Red Sole Mark extends to uses in which the sole does not contrast with the upper—in other words, when a red sole is used on a monochromatic red shoe. As the District Court observed, "[w]hen Hollywood starlets cross red carpets and high fashion models strut down runways, and heads turn and eyes drop to the celebrities' feet, lacquered red outsoles on high-heeled, black shoes flaunt a glamorous statement that pops out at once." *Louboutin*, 778 F. Supp. 2d at 448. As clearly suggested by the District Court, it is the contrast between the sole and the upper that causes the sole to "pop," and to distinguish its creator.

The evidentiary record further demonstrates that the Louboutin mark is closely associated with contrast. For example, Pinault, the chief executive of YSL's parent company, wrote that the "distinctive signature" of the Mark is in its "contrast with the general presentation of the [shoe], particularly its upper." Of the hundreds of pictures of Louboutin shoes submitted to the District Court, only four were monochrome red. And Louboutin's own consumer surveys show that when consumers were shown the YSL monochrome red shoe, of those consumers who misidentified the pictured shoes as Louboutin-made, nearly every one cited the red sole of the shoe, rather than its general red color. We conclude, based upon the record before us, that Louboutin has not established secondary meaning in an application of a red sole to a red shoe, but only where the red sole contrasts with the "upper" of the shoe.

Because we conclude that the secondary meaning of the mark held by Louboutin extends only to the use of a lacquered red outsole that contrasts with the adjoining portion of the shoe, we modify the Red Sole Mark insofar as it is sought to be applied to any shoe bearing the same color "upper" as the outsole. We therefore instruct the Director of the Patent and Trade Office to limit the registration of the Red Sole Mark to only those situations in which the red lacquered outsole contrasts in color with the adjoining "upper" of the shoe. We therefore affirm the denial of the preliminary injunction insofar as Louboutin could not have shown a likelihood of success on the merits in the absence of an infringing use of the Red Sole Mark by YSL.

Having limited the Red Sole Mark as described above, and having established that the red sole used by YSL is not a use of the Red Sole Mark, it is axiomatic that we need not—and should not—address either the likelihood of consumer confusion or whether the modified Mark is functional.

Notes

1. In this case, both the district court and the circuit court seemed to believe that the monochromatic Yves Saint Laurent shoe was not infringing and each court took exceptional steps to make such a holding. The district court clearly found that Christian Louboutin had secondary meaning with respect to the "flash of a red sole" on shoes, finding that it was "instantly" recognizable. To avoid finding that the YSL shoe was infringing, however, the district court went so far as to find, without citing evidence, that color trademarks are uniquely unavailable in the fashion industry, notwithstanding the ruling in *Qualitex*. The circuit court recognized that such a per se rule is without basis and unwarranted. In order to avoid a finding of infringement, however, the circuit court rewrote Christian Louboutin's trademark rights: instead of a red sole applied to women's shoes, the trademark was held to be a red sole applied to women's shoes of a contrasting color. Whether such a rewriting is within the court's authority on appeal, the evidence underlying it was thin at best. The circuit court pointed out that most, though not all, of Christian Louboutin's styles involved contrasting uppers. But the court also noted that survey respondents shown YSL's monochrome shoes would cite the red sole as the basis for their belief that the shoes originated from Christian Louboutin. Do you believe that the court reached the right result here? In the correct way?

2. As the court noted here, the term "aesthetic functionality" seems to almost be a contradiction in terms. The court held that aesthetic functionality did not apply in this case. Can you think of some examples where the aesthetic appearance of a product is necessary for the sake of competition?

3. This case had tremendous stakes for Christian Louboutin. The district court held that its valuable red-sole trademark was likely invalid and if that determination stood it would have been difficult, if not impossible, for the company's future enforcement of its trademark. Anytime a company brings a litigation for enforcement of its trademarks it risks a determination that its trademark rights are weak or even invalid. Based on what you read in this case, do you believe that it was wise for Christian Louboutin to take that risk in this case?

E. Determining Trademark Infringement

To prevail on a case for trademark infringement, a plaintiff must show: (1) valid trademark rights and (2) a likelihood of confusion among purchasers of the junior user's goods. The issue of valid trademark rights has been addressed above. Determining the existence of a likelihood of confusion is traditionally analyzed through a multi-factor test that was originally assembled in the early 1960s. In the Second Circuit, which has a robust intellectual property jurisprudence, these factors are known as the "*Polaroid* factors," but each circuit has its own test, generally with the same, or nearly the same, factors. The following case demonstrates the application of such a test and the difficulties that can be associated with that application.

1. Multi-Factor Analysis: The *Polaroid* Factors

Lois Sportswear, U.S.A., Inc. v. Levi Strauss & Co.

799 F.2d 867 (2d Cir. 1986)

TIMBERS, Circuit Judge.

Lois Sportswear, U.S.A., Inc. and Textiles Y Confecciones Europeas, S.A. (collectively "appellants") appeal from a summary judgment entered September 30, 1985 in the Southern District of New York, Robert W. Sweet, District Judge, enjoining appellants from using a back pocket stitching pattern similar to the trademark jean back pocket stitching pattern of Levi Strauss & Company ("appellee") on appellants' jeans. The question presented by this appeal is whether summary judgment for the trademark owner is appropriate on claims of trademark infringement and unfair competition when the trademark owner has shown that a rival jeans manufacturer is using the trademark owner's registered back pocket stitching pattern trademark on its competing jeans, and the undisputed evidence shows that the trademark is intimately associated with the trademark owner's products in the minds of jeans consumers.

I.

We summarize only those facts believed necessary to an understanding of the issues raised on appeal. Appellee is a world famous clothing manufacturer. One of its most popular products is a line of casual pants known as Levi Jeans. Appellee began manufacturing its denim jeans in the 1850s. Each pair of jeans contains numerous identifying features. One such feature is a distinct back pocket stitching pattern. This pattern consists of two intersecting arcs which roughly bisect both pockets of appellee's jeans. Appellee has an incontestable federal trademark in this stitching pattern. Appellee has used this pattern on all its jeans continuously since 1873. In many ways the back pocket stitching pattern has become the embodiment of Levi Jeans in the minds of jeans buyers. The record is replete with undisputed examples of the intimate association between the stitching pattern and appellee's products in the buying public's mind. Not only has appellee spent considerable sums on promoting the stitching pattern, but various competitors have run nation-wide advertisement campaigns touting the advantages of their jeans' back pockets over appellee's. In addition, one of the largest chains of jeans retailers, the Gap Stores, has run numerous advertisements featuring pictures of appellee's back pocket stitching pattern as the entire visual portion of the ad. The record also contains numerous examples of the public's phenomenal reaction to the stitching pattern and the jeans it epitomizes. These examples range from national magazine cover stories to high school yearbook dedications.

Appellant Lois Sportswear, U.S.A., Inc. ("Lois") imports into the United States jeans manufactured in Spain by Textiles Y Confecciones Europeas, S.A. ("Textiles"). The instant litigation was commenced because appellants' jeans bear a back pocket stitching pattern substantially similar to appellee's trademark stitching pattern. On appeal appellants do not challenge the district court's conclusion that the two stitching patterns are substantially similar. Nor could they; the two patterns are virtually identical when viewed from any appreciable distance. In fact, the results from a survey based on showing consumers videotapes of the back pockets of various jeans, including appellants', indicate that 44% of those interviewed mistook appellants' jeans for appellee's jeans. Appellants instead rely on their use of various labels, some permanent and some temporary, to distinguish their jeans and defeat appellee's trademark infringement and unfair competition claims.

The parties have clashed over appellants' use of a back pocket stitching pattern similar to appellee's trademark stitching pattern continuously since 1979. In that year appellee lodged a protest with the United States Customs Bureau concerning Lois' importation of Textiles' jeans. Appellee claimed that appellants' use of a back pocket stitching pattern similar to its trademark stitching pattern violated its trademark rights and was grounds for barring further importation. The Customs Service agreed and banned the continued importation of appellants' jeans in early 1980. On June 4, 1981, however, the Customs Service reversed itself and permitted renewed importation of appellants' jeans. This reprieve was short lived because on June 30, 1982 the Customs Service again reversed itself and once again banned the importation of appellants' jeans. On December 14, 1982 appellants, apparently tiring of the Customs Service's fickle attitude, commenced an action in the Court of International Trade against the Commissioner of Customs. This action sought an order enjoining the Customs Service from interfering with the importation of appellants' jeans. On May 3, 1983 the court issued a preliminary injunction enjoining the Customs Service from banning the importation of appellants' jeans. The court held that the Customs Service had violated its own procedures in banning the importation of appellants' jeans.

Lois, leaving no stone unturned, also commenced the instant action in the district court on December 14, 1982. Lois sought a declaratory judgment that its use of the stitching pattern did not violate appellee's trademark rights. Appellee counterclaimed for injunctive and monetary relief, alleging that appellants' use of the stitching pattern constituted trademark infringement and unfair competition in violation of the Lanham Act. Finally, appellee commenced a separate action against Textiles in the district court. Appellee's complaint tracked its counterclaim in the earlier declaratory judgment action. Textiles' answer and counterclaim tracked Lois' declaratory judgment complaint. The two actions were consolidated in the district court.

After extensive discovery, both sides moved for summary judgment. On July 12, 1985 the court held a hearing on the motions at which depositions, exhibits and memoranda were received. Most of the evidence sought to show that appellee's back pocket stitching pattern had achieved a strong secondary meaning, *i.e.*, that jeans consumers associated the pattern with appellee's products. This evidence is undisputed for the most part. The remainder of the evidence is focused on the respective quality of the two products at issue and the likelihood that consumers somehow would confuse the source of appellants' jeans.

The evidence is undisputed that appellants and appellee manufacture and sell a similar product. While stratifying the jeans market with various styles and grades seems to be the current rage, there can be no dispute that the parties before us compete to sell their jeans to the public. The record does indicate that appellants have attempted to target their "designer" jeans at a decidedly upscale market segment. There also was evidence, however, that appellants' jeans were selling at deep discount in cut-rate clothing outlets. Moreover, there was substantial evidence which indicated that appellee's jeans, although originally marketed as work pants, had achieved a certain elan among the fashion conscious. The evidence suggests that appellee's jeans have achieved fad popularity in all sectors of the jeans market. Finally, appellee produced affidavits stating that it was planning to enter the designer jeans market.

In short, the uncontested facts show that appellants' jeans exhibit a back pocket stitching pattern substantially similar to appellee's incontestable registered trademark back pocket stitching pattern. The record also makes plain that the stitching pattern is closely associated with appellee's jeans, and that appellants' use of the stitching pattern on arguably competing jeans at least presents the possibility that consumers will be confused as to the source of appellants' jeans or the relationship between appellants and appellee.

The district court granted appellee's motion for summary judgment. The court held that, while appellants' labeling and trade dress prevented most possible consumer confusion as to source at the point of sale, appellants' use of a stitching pattern substantially similar to appellee's trademark stitching pattern was likely to cause confusion as to source when the jeans were observed in the post-sale context. The court also held that there was a likelihood that consumers mistakenly might assume that there was some sort of connection between appellee and appellants due to the similar stitching patterns. The court enjoined appellants from selling jeans bearing the similar stitching pattern.

With these facts in mind, we turn to the relevant law of trademark infringement and unfair competition in our Court.

II.

Appellants' arguments focus only on the likelihood that consumers will buy appellants' jeans thinking they are appellee's jeans due to the similar stitching patterns. Appellants point to their labeling as conclusive proof that no such confusion is likely. We agree with the district court, however, that the two principle areas of confusion raised by appellants' use of appellee's stitching pattern are: (1)

the likelihood that jeans consumers will be confused as to the relationship between appellants and appellee; and (2) the likelihood that consumers will be confused as to the source of appellants' jeans when the jeans are observed in the post-sale context.

As a threshold matter, in the past we have found it useful to decide how much protection a particular trademark is to be given by first determining what type of trademark is at issue. In *Abercrombie & Fitch Co. v. Hunting World, Inc.*, 537 F.2d 4, 9 (2nd Cir. 1976), Judge Friendly set forth what has become the governing law of trademark classification:

> Arrayed in an ascending order which roughly reflects their eligibility to trademark status and the degree of protection accorded, these classes are (1) generic, (2) descriptive, (3) suggestive, and (4) arbitrary or fanciful.

Superimposed on this framework is the rule that registered trademarks are presumed to be distinctive and should be afforded the utmost protection. *Vibrant Sales, Inc. v. New Body Boutique*, Inc., 652 F.2d 299, 304 (2nd Cir. 1981).

It is clear under this framework that appellee's back pocket stitching pattern deserves the highest degree of protection. First, the mark is registered and incontestable. This, of course, entitles the mark to significant protection. Second, the mark, being a fanciful pattern of interconnected arcs, is within Judge Friendly's fourth category and is entitled to the most protection the Lanham Act can provide. In deciding the likelihood of confusion issues, therefore, appellee's mark is entitled to a liberal application of the law.

Turning to the principal issues under the Lanham Act, in either a claim of trademark infringement or a claim of unfair competition, a prima facie case is made out by showing the use of one's trademark by another in a way that is likely to confuse consumers as to the source of the product.

In deciding the issue of likelihood of confusion in the instant case, the district court relied on the multifactor balancing test set forth by Judge Friendly in *Polaroid Corp. v. Polarad Electronics Corp.*, 287 F.2d 492, 495 (2nd Cir. 1961). We agree wholeheartedly that Judge Friendly characteristically has provided the controlling law. Appellants argue that the court's opinion indicates that only two of the eight Polaroid factors weigh in favor of appellee and therefore, if anything, summary judgment was only appropriate in appellants' favor. This argument not only mischaracterizes the district court opinion but also misapplies the *Polaroid* test. A more flexible application of the *Polaroid* test indicates that the district court was correct in enjoining appellants' use of appellee's back pocket stitching pattern.

At the outset, it must be remembered just what the *Polaroid* factors are designed to test. The factors are designed to help grapple with the "vexing" problem of resolving the likelihood of confusion issue. *Polaroid, supra*, 287 F.2d at 495. Therefore, each factor must be evaluated in the context of how it bears on the ultimate question of likelihood of confusion as to the source of the product. *Spring Mills, Inc. v. Ultracashmere House, Ltd.*, 689 F.2d 1127, 1134 (2nd Cir. 1982). It also must be emphasized that the ultimate conclusion as to whether a likelihood of confusion exists is not to be determined in accordance with some rigid formula. The *Polaroid* factors serve as a useful guide through a difficult quagmire. Each case, however, presents its own peculiar circumstances. In the instant case it also is critical first to determine just what type of actionable confusion as to source is presented. Appellants place great reliance on their labeling as a means of preventing any confusion. While such labeling may prevent appellants' use of appellee's stitching pattern from confusing consumers at the point of sale into believing that appellee manufactured and marketed appellants' jeans, the labeling does nothing to alleviate other forms of likely confusion that are equally actionable.

First, a distinct possibility raised by appellants' use of appellee's immediately identifiable stitching pattern is that consumers will be confused into believing that appellee either somehow is associated with appellants or has consented to appellants' use of its trademark. Therefore, the Polaroid factors must be applied in the instant case with an eye to how they bear on the likelihood that appellants' use of appellee's trademark stitching pattern will confuse consumers into thinking that appellee is somehow associated with appellants or has consented to their use of the stitching pattern regardless of labeling.

Second, it is equally clear that post-sale confusion as to source is actionable under the Lanham Act. In the instant case, this post-sale confusion would involve consumers seeing appellant's jeans outside of the retail store, perhaps being worn by a passer-by. The confusion the Act seeks to prevent in this context is that a consumer seeing the familiar stitching pattern will associate the jeans with appellee and that association will influence his buying decisions. Clearly, in this post-sale context appellants' labels, most of which having been long since discarded, will be of no help. The Ninth Circuit case of *Levi Strauss & Co. v. Blue Bell, Inc.*, 632 F.2d 817 (9th Cir. 1980), is very persuasive on this point. In Blue Bell, the court upheld an injunction preventing the manufacturer of Wrangler jeans from using a back pocket name tag similar to the one used on Levi's jeans. The court held that Wrangler's extensive labeling, including its own name on the very tag at issue, was not sufficient to avoid confusion as to source in the post-sale context. The court held that "Wrangler's use of its projecting label is likely to cause confusion among prospective purchasers who carry even an imperfect recollection of Strauss's mark and who observe Wrangler's projecting label after the point of sale." Precisely the same considerations apply in the instant case. The Polaroid factors therefore must be applied with an eye toward post-sale confusion also.

Turning to an application of the Polaroid test, we must stress at the outset that the district court's detailed findings on each of the Polaroid factors are entitled to considerable deference.

The first factor—the strength of the mark—weighs heavily in appellee's favor. We have defined the strength of a mark as "its tendency to identify the goods sold under the mark as emanating from a particular source". As discussed above, appellee's back pocket stitching pattern is a fanciful registered trademark with a very strong secondary meaning. Virtually all jeans consumers associate the stitching pattern with appellee's products. We agree with the district court that the evidence indicates as a matter of law that appellee's stitching pattern is a very strong mark. This factor is crucial to the likelihood of confusion analysis since appellee's intimate association with the trademark makes it much more likely that consumers will assume wrongly that appellee is somehow associated with appellants' jeans or has authorized the use of its mark, or, in the post-sale context, that appellee has manufactured the jeans.

The second factor—the degree of similarity of the marks—also weighs in favor of appellee. As the district court correctly observed, the two stitching patterns are "essentially identical." Both patterns consist of two intersecting arcs placed in the exact same position on the back pockets of the jeans. The only difference—the fact that appellants' arcs extend 3/4 inch further down the pocket at their intersection—is imperceptible at any significant distance. In light of the fact that the stitching pattern is in no way dictated by function and an infinite number of patterns are possible, the similarity of the two patterns is striking. When this striking similarity is factored into the likelihood of confusion analysis, its great importance becomes clear. In view of the trademark's strength, this nearly identical reproduction of the stitching pattern no doubt is likely to cause consumers to believe that appellee somehow is associated with appellants or at least has consented to the use of its trademark. In the post-sale context, this striking similarity no doubt will cause consumers to transfer the goodwill they feel for appellee to appellants, at least initially. This misuse of goodwill is at the heart of unfair competition. Appellants' reliance on the effect of their labeling with respect to this factor underscores their misguided focus on only the most obvious form of consumer confusion. Appellants' labeling in no way dispels the likelihood that consumers will conclude that appellants' jeans are somehow connected to appellee by virtue of the nearly identical stitching patterns.

The third factor—the proximity of the products—also weighs in favor of appellee. Both products are jeans. Although appellants argue that their jeans are designer jeans and are sold to a different market segment than appellee's jeans, there is significant evidence in the record of an overlap of market segments. Moreover, even if the two jeans are in different segments of the jeans market, such a finding would not switch this factor to appellants' side of the scale. We are trying to determine if it is likely that consumers mistakenly will assume either that appellants' jeans somehow are associated with appellee or are made by appellee. The fact that appellants' jeans arguably are in a different market segment makes this type of confusion more likely. Certainly a consumer observing appellee's striking stitching pattern on appellants' designer jeans might assume that appellee had chosen to enter that market segment using a subsidiary corporation, or that appellee had allowed appellants' designers to use appellee's trademark as a means of reaping some profits from the designer jeans fad without a full commitment to that market segment. Likewise, in the post-sale context a consumer seeing appellants' jeans on a passer-by might think that the jeans were appellee's long-awaited entry into the designer jeans market segment. Motivated by this mistaken notion—appellee's goodwill—the consumer might then buy appellants' jeans even after discovering his error. After all, the way the jeans look is a primary consideration to most designer jeans buyers. As Judge Learned Hand wrote almost sixty years ago, "unless the borrower's use is so foreign to the owner's as to insure against any identification of the two, it is unlawful." *Yale Electric Corp. v. Robertson*, 26 F.2d 972, 974 (2nd Cir. 1928). Appellants' use of appellee's stitching pattern is anything but foreign.

The fourth factor—bridging the gap—is closely related to the proximity of the products and does not aid appellants' case. Under this factor, if the owner of a trademark can show that it intends to enter the market of the alleged infringer, that showing helps to establish a future likelihood of confusion as to source. We have held that the trademark laws are designed in part to protect "the senior user's interest in being able to enter a related field at some future time". *Scarves By Vera, Inc. v. Todo Imports Ltd.*, 544 F.2d 1167, 1172 (2nd Cir. 1976). In the instant case, the district court rejected as irrelevant appellee's affidavits which stated that appellee was planning to enter the designer jeans market, since the affidavits did not assert that appellee's designer jeans entry would utilize the stitching pattern. We do not believe, however, that the form appellee's entry into the market segment might take is especially relevant to the likelihood of confusion issue. Appellee's entry into the market, regardless of the form it might take, would increase the chances of consumer confusion as to the source of appellants' jeans because of likely consumer expectations that appellee's designer jeans would bear its famous stitching pattern. If one knew only that appellee had entered the designer jeans market and then saw appellants' jeans in a post-sale context, it is very likely that one could confuse them for appellee's entry. Also, appellee has an interest in preserving its trademark should it ever wish to produce designer jeans with the stitching pattern. The Lanham Act is meant to protect this interest. *Scarves by Vera, Inc.*, supra, 544 F.2d at 1174 (scarf designer has right to prevent use of her tradename on cosmetics even without proof that she presently intends to enter cosmetic market).

The fifth factor—actual confusion—while not helping appellee, does not really hurt its case. Appellee's only evidence of actual confusion was a consumer survey which the district court discounted due to methodological defects in simulating the post-sale environment. Of course, it is black letter law that actual confusion need not be shown to prevail under the Lanham Act, since actual confusion is very difficult to prove and the Act requires only a likelihood of confusion as to source. *E.g., W. E. Bassett Co. v. Revlon, Inc.*, 435 F.2d 656, 662 (2nd Cir. 1970). While the complete absence of actual confusion evidence after a significant period of competition may weigh in a defendant's favor, such an inference is unjustified in the instant case in view of the survey evidence, even with its methodological defects. While these defects go to the weight of the survey, it is still somewhat probative of actual confusion in the post-sale context. In any event, the record indicates that sales of appellants' jeans have been minimal in the United States thus far and there has been little chance for actual confusion as yet. It would be unfair to penalize appellee for acting to protect its trademark rights before serious damage has occurred.

The sixth factor—the junior user's good faith in adopting the mark—weighs in favor of appellants. The evidence before the district court, when viewed in a light favorable to appellants, indicates that appellants happened on the stitching pattern serendipitously. It must be remembered, however, that intentional copying is not a requirement under the Lanham Act. Also, intent is largely irrelevant in determining if consumers likely will be confused as to source. The history of advertising suggests that consumer reactions usually are unrelated to manufacturer intentions.

The seventh factor—the quality of the respective goods—does add some weight to appellants' position. Appellee has conceded that appellants' jeans are not of an inferior quality, arguably reducing appellee's interest in protecting its reputation from debasement. It must be noted, however, that under the circumstances of this case the good quality of appellants' product actually may increase the likelihood of confusion as to source. Particularly in the post-sale context, consumers easily could assume that quality jeans bearing what is perceived as appellee's trademark stitching pattern to be a Levi's product. The fact that appellants have produced a quality copy suggests that the possibility of their profiting from appellee's goodwill is still likely.

The eighth and final factor—the sophistication of relevant buyers—does not, under the circumstances of this case, favor appellants. The district court found, and the parties do not dispute, that the typical buyer of "designer" jeans is sophisticated with respect to jeans buying. Appellants argue that this sophistication prevents these consumers from becoming confused by nearly identical back pocket stitching patterns. On the contrary, we believe that it is a sophisticated jeans consumer who is most likely to assume that the presence of appellee's trademark stitching pattern on appellants' jeans indicates some sort of association between the two manufacturers. Presumably it is these sophisticated jeans buyers who pay the most attention to back pocket stitching patterns and their "meanings". Likewise, in the post-sale context, the sophisticated buyer is more likely to be affected by the sight of appellee's stitching pattern on appellants' jeans and, consequently, to transfer goodwill. Finally, to the extent the sophisticated buyer is attracted to appellee's jeans because of the exclusiveness of its stitching pattern, appellee's sales will be affected adversely by these buyers' ultimate realization that the pattern is no longer exclusive.

Our review of the district court's application of the Polaroid factors convinces us that the court correctly concluded that consumers are likely to mistakenly associate appellants' jeans with appellee or will confuse the source of appellants' jeans when the jeans are observed in the post-sale context. This result is eminently reasonable in view of the undisputed evidence of the use by one jeans manufacturer of the trademark back pocket stitching pattern of another jeans manufacturer, coupled with the fact that the trademark stitching pattern is instantly associated with its owner and is important to consumers. There is simply too great a risk that appellants will profit from appellee's hard-earned goodwill to permit the use.

* * *

IV.

To summarize:

We affirm the district court's grant of summary judgment in favor of appellee. When the Polaroid factors are applied to the undisputed facts in the instant case within the context of the proper likelihood of confusion possibilities, it is clear that the district court was correct in enjoining appellants' use of appellee's trademark back pocket stitching pattern. While appellants' trade dress may dispel some point of sale confusion engendered by appellants' use of appellee's distinctive trademark, the labeling does nothing to prevent consumers from mistakenly assuming that appellee is somehow associated with appellants or has consented to the mark's use. Also, the record shows the distinct likelihood of post-sale confusion. In light of the undisputed evidence which compels these legal conclusions, summary judgment in favor of appellee was appropriate. In short, we hold that the Lanham Act forecloses one jeans manufacturer from using another jeans manufacturer's distinctive back pocket stitching pattern trademark when the evidence is undisputed that the trademark stitching pattern is intimately associated with its owner and the infringing use likely will cause confusion as to the source of the jeans and an unfair shift of goodwill.

Affirmed.

MINER, Circuit Judge, dissenting:

In arriving at the conclusion that the Lois arcuate is likely to cause confusion among potential consumers, the district court resolved various issues of material fact presented by the cross-motions for summary judgment. When a party moves for summary judgment, however, the judge's function is not himself to weigh the evidence and determine the truth of the matter but to determine whether there is a genuine issue for trial. Because I am of the opinion that the district judge improperly undertook to decide disputed factual matters and that summary judgment in favor of Levi therefore was unwarranted, I respectfully dissent.

Based upon factual findings as to each of the eight Polaroid factors, the district court concluded that only two of the factors favored Levi—strength of the mark and the degree of similarity between the two marks. With respect to strength of the mark, Lois produced evidence of extensive third-party use of the Levi arcuate. The widespread use of virtually identical marks makes it difficult to identify goods as emanating from a particular source. To be considered strong, the mark must be associated in the public mind with the goods in question or their maker. So far, there is no credible evidence in the record that consumers focus their attention on back-pocket stitching when purchasing jeans. Indeed, the evidence is that Levi employs several trademarks other than the arcuate to focus public attention on its jeans. These include a red or orange fabric tag with the word "Levi" in white letters attached to the right rear pocket, a leather waistband patch bearing the "Two Horse Brand" trademark, and a copper button bearing the Levi trade name. In addition, Levi's jeans are sold with other distinctive features, including sewn-in labels, buttons and temporary cardboard labels. In view of the foregoing, the strength of the mark question should have been left for the trier of fact and not decided on the conflicting evidentiary submissions made at the summary judgment stage.

In determining the degree of similarity between the two marks, the district court again undertook the task of weighing the evidence. Consideration of the similarity factor invokes not only a comparison of the two marks, but also an examination of the entire context in which the two marks are presented. In a number of cases, we have held that the prominent display of a manufacturer's brand name and identifying symbols on its product may effectively mitigate any likelihood of confusion arising from similarity between competing marks.

Although the Lois arcuate generally resembles the letter "Y" and the Levi arcuate is more similar to the letter "V," the marks are substantially identical. However, the evidence is clear that Lois employs a variety of temporary and permanent labels distinguishing its jeans from those of Levi. For instance, Lois jeans are sold with "hang tags" displaying the Lois brand name and the trade symbol of a bull. There are two stitched-on cardboard tags, one measuring approximately five inches by three inches and the other measuring approximately one inch by three inches. Both tags display the Lois brand name and bull symbol as well as the legend "imported from Europe" in conspicuous print. Affixed permanently to Lois jeans are various identifying features: a two inch by one inch leather tag attached to the left rear pocket bearing the brand name and bull symbol; a sizing and care tag stitched to the inner waist seam bearing the Lois brand name and indicating that both the fabric and product are made in Spain; a brass button on the waistband bearing the Lois brand name; and a quarter circle leather on fabric patch, stitched to the right front pocket, bearing the bull symbol. Such features have been found sufficient to dispel any possibility that substantially similar arcuates would deceive an "unwary purchaser" into confusing jeans made by Levi with jeans of another manufacturer. *Levi Strauss & Co. v. Longley*, 272 F.2d 820, 821 (6th Cir. 1959) (per curiam). At the very least, then, there is a genuine factual dispute as to the similarity factor, and the district judge should not have decided it before trial.

Recognizing the "small" likelihood that a consumer would purchase Lois jeans thinking they were made by Levi, the district court nevertheless concluded that "there is a substantial likelihood of confusion among prospective purchasers viewing the marks in a post-sale context," 631 F. Supp. 735, 748. The only evidentiary support for that conclusion was a consumer survey conducted by the market research firm of Bruno & Ridgeway at the behest of Levi. The survey was commissioned for the purpose of determining whether or not the Lois arcuate design was likely to be associated erroneously with Levi when Lois jeans were worn in public and seen by others. The survey consisted of interviewing shopping mall customers before and after showing them a videotape portraying, from a rear perspective, a male model alternately wearing jeans manufactured by Lois, Levi, Wrangler and J.C. Penney. The district court noted that serious methodological flaws in the study substantially undercut its evidentiary value in the point-of-sale context, but apparently relied on it to some extent in concluding that there was a likelihood of confusion in the post-sale context.

There can be no doubt that the study was seriously flawed. For example, no criteria were used for selecting the six locations where the testing took place or to determine what jeans were available in those areas. While it is likely that Levi jeans were available in all of the test locations, the same cannot be said for Lois jeans. Besides failing to depict accurately a point-of-sale situation, the videotape also failed to faithfully reflect realistic post-sale conditions—all identifying marks other than the rear pocket stitching were either removed from the jeans or imperceptible in the videotape, the camera focused on the back pockets, and the tape concluded with close-up shots of the various stitching designs being surveyed. The survey therefore was deficient in both the point-of-sale and post-sale contexts and cannot be relied upon as evidence of likelihood of confusion.

While stressing that "considerable deference" is due the findings of the district court as to each of the Polaroid factors, the majority completely revises several of those findings in reaching the ultimate conclusion that there is a likelihood of confusion as to the source of Lois jeans and as to the relationship between Lois and Levi. Where the district court found a "limited 'competitive distance'" between the products, 631 F. Supp. at 743, the majority finds that the proximity of products factor weighs in favor of Levi. Where the district court found that Levi "has failed to establish with any certainty that it is likely to bridge any gap between the products," the majority affords weight to Levi's expressed intention to enter the designer jeans market. The district court determined that Lois jeans are not qualitatively inferior to Levi jeans and that the qualitative advantage of the Lois product "may serve to differentiate the products with consumers"; the majority finds that the good quality of the Lois product may increase the likelihood of confusion as to source. Although the district court found "a relatively high degree of sophistication" on the part of the Lois jeans purchasers, a finding that ordinarily would be considered favorable to Lois, the majority says that the sophisticated buyer is more likely to be confused by similar stitching patterns.

While a district court's decision respecting likelihood of confusion, based on the relative weight given to each of the findings, represents a conclusion of law reviewable on appeal, "the district court's determination of each of the Polaroid factors is a finding of fact to which the clearly erroneous standard is applicable." *Plus Products v. Plus Discount Foods, Inc.*, 722 F.2d 999, 1004 (2d Cir. 1983). However, neither the district court nor this court is empowered to engage in fact-finding at the summary judgment stage in the face of such conflicting evidence as has been presented here.

"The likelihood of confusion is factually the most complex issue encountered in trademark infringement and false designation of origin litigation." Burton, Summary Judgments in Trademark Cases, 75 Trade-Mark Rep. 497, 520. For that reason, "disputes between parties as to trade-mark validity and infringement can rarely be determined satisfactorily on a motion for summary judgment." Traditionally, we have applied a "stringent standard" for summary judgment in trademark infringement cases. Levi's failure to meet that standard compels my dissent.

Notes

1. Before the court discussed the famous *Polaroid* factors, it addressed Lois' argument that its own trademarks placed on hangtags and otherwise on its products prevented any confusion as to whether the products came from Levi. The court dismissed this argument, holding that consumers may believe that the products were "associated" with Levi even if they did not originate from Levi. What do you think of this holding? Are collaborations more common in the fashion or apparel industry such that consumers would believe that products would be associated with a trademark holder even if they plainly came from another company? Could you envision the use of a house mark that would eliminate a likelihood of confusion?

2. The court also held that the use of hangtags would not prevent "post-sale confusion" because those labels would not be visible after the sale took place. Should trademark law be used to prevent confusion that does not take place at the point of sale? What are the benefits, if any, of preventing post-sale confusion?

3. The *Polaroid* factors were coined in 1961, before the widespread use of color television, much less the means of commerce widely used today. Which *Polaroid* factors do you believe are most important in determining the likelihood of confusion? Which, if any, do you believe are not relevant to that issue? Are there any factors that you believe are important to determining likelihood of confusion that are not included among the *Polaroid* factors?

4. Courts often consider survey evidence as part of the actual confusion factor. This placement has always been awkward because a survey is an artificial construction and is not the actual confusion of actual consumers in an actual marketplace. In addition, a survey measuring likelihood of confusion goes to the ultimate issue in the case and should not be confined to merely one factor in a multi-factor *Polaroid* analysis.

5. As the court held in this case, a likelihood of confusion does not depend upon the intent of the defendant. Innocently creating a likelihood of confusion, as was the case here, is just as actionable. Is the "good faith" *Polaroid* factor still relevant? The rationale behind the factor is that a defendant who intends to deceive consumers is likely to succeed in doing so. Is this true?

6. The "quality of goods" factor is also one that may no longer be highly relevant to a likelihood of confusion. This factor originally did not measure confusion, but rather spoke to the potential harm that would be done to the trademark owner if its mark was associated with products of poor quality. The factor has evolved, however, such that *similar* quality goods are more likely to create a likelihood that consumers will not be able to differentiate the products and will be confused. Query whether this factor has therefore become duplicative of the "similarity of products" factor.

7. The "sophistication of consumers" factor is often misapplied by courts. This factor is often shorthand for the cost of the products, under the assumption that buyers of expensive products treat their purchase with great care and are less likely to be confused. Do you agree with this assumption? An alternative, and perhaps preferable, approach is that purchasers of expensive items have considerable disposable income and are therefore *less* attentive in purchasing decisions. That is, someone who can afford only a $50 purse spends as much time thinking about the decision as someone who can afford a $1,500 purse.

8. Do you agree with the dissenting judge that there was a disputed issue of fact regarding the likelihood of confusion? The dissenting judge stated that the district court found that only two of the *Polaroid* factors favored Levi—strength of Levi's trademark and similarity of the trademarks. Although those are only two of the eight *Polaroid* factors, they are clearly two of the very strongest. The dissenting opinion highlights a problem with multi-factor tests in that they become an exercise in checking boxes where all factors are mistakenly granted the same weight.

2. Trade Dress Infringement

As discussed above, trademark protection is afforded not only to names and logos, but also the distinctive and ornamental visual presentation of a party's goods, otherwise known as "trade dress." Trade dress can incorporate the shape of a product or the packaging of the product. As held in *Wal-Mart v. Samara Brothers*, product design trade dress may not be inherently distinctive and may only be protectable upon the showing of secondary meaning. Due to the limited protections afforded by copyright and design patent law, fashion designers often turn to trade dress law to try to protect their valuable designs, as seen in the case below.

Coach Leatherware Co. v. AnnTaylor, Inc.

933 F.2d 162 (2d Cir. 1991)

KAUFMAN, Circuit Judge.

Copying women's designer handbags appears to be a convenient device for those seeking to ride fashion's often unpredictable waves. Abundant support for this observation is provided on Manhattan's Fifth Avenue where within close proximity of the flagship stores of Louis Vuitton, Gucci and Chanel, street vendors peddle imitations of these familiar designs. More confusing, and thus more troublesome, is the sale of copies by respected retailers. At the heart of this case is just such a circumstance—the sale of imitation Coach Leatherware Company, Inc. ("Coach") handbags by the AnnTaylor, Inc. ("AnnTaylor") chain of retail stores. At issue is the potential for consumer confusion caused by this situation.

In an effort to maintain its market share and its preferred status among customers, Coach instituted this action against appellants AnnTaylor, Laura Leather Goods, Inc. ("Laura") and A & R Handbag, Inc. ("A & R") for trademark infringement pursuant to section 43(a) of the Lanham Act and for unfair competition under New York State common law. Coach alleged that appellants had produced imitations of its distinctive leather handbags in a manner likely to cause confusion in the marketplace. Following Coach's motion for a preliminary injunction and appellants' cross-motion for summary judgment, Judge Duffy, sua sponte, granted summary judgment in favor of the nonmoving party, Coach.

I. Background

We need discuss only those facts and prior proceedings relevant to the disposition of this appeal. Some contextual detail, however, is unavoidable because of the complex nature of trademark infringement claims.

Coach, a New York corporation, has been engaged in the design, manufacture, marketing, distribution and sale of high quality, leather fashion products for approximately fifty years. Coach products are sold exclusively under its own label and are marketed in about fifty Coach-owned stores, in clearly designated Coach displays situated in expensive department stores and through Coach mail order catalogues.

AnnTaylor, a prominent retailer of quality women's apparel, is a wholly-owned subsidiary of AnnTaylor Holding, Inc., which in turn is owned by Merrill Lynch Co., Inc. AnnTaylor, like Coach, considers its market to consist of the stereotypical successful career women. Presently, the more than 160 AnnTaylor stores are located primarily in upscale malls, exclusive thoroughfares, and specialty retail centers. Laura, and its affiliate, A & R (collectively "Laura"), are also New York corporations engaged in the business of designing, manufacturing and selling handbags.

The instant litigation was initiated after Coach learned that some of its "classic" handbag designs, which have been part of its product line for the past fifteen years, were being copied and sold at AnnTaylor. AnnTaylor and Laura had allegedly replicated for sale three handbag styles made prominent by Coach: the "Dinky Bag"—a small handbag with a narrow profile, a flap that extends to cover the entire face of the bag and a shoulder length strap; the "Duffle Sac"—a large handbag with a circular bottom, tapered sides and a leather strap affixed to its top by solid brass hardware; and the "Convertible Clutch"—a larger version of the Dinky Bag. Though dissimilar in several significant respects, each Coach bag shares several features: all are produced from full-grain cowhide, contain exterior binding at external seams and incorporate brass hardware components. In addition, the inside of each bag contains a Coach registration number and various informational paraphernalia unique to Coach marketing tactics.

Over the years, Coach has attached to all of its handbags distinctive lozenge-shaped leather tags embossed with the name "Coach Leatherware." The tags, suspended from beaded brass chains, have become distinctive and valuable through Coach's promotional efforts and by virtue of its upscale reputation—Coach store managers report that the tags alone are often subject to theft. Though Coach bags are not themselves registered, the Coach tag is registered on the Principal Register of the United States Patent and Trademark Office. Apparently seeking to capitalize on the popularity of the Coach "look", the AnnTaylor handbags, in the Coach style, carry a similar leather tag embossed, however, with AnnTaylor's name and distinctive typeface.

II. Proceedings Below

Coach filed a complaint alleging that Laura and AnnTaylor manufactured and sold handbags which mimic design features made famous by Coach. Subsequently, the parties engaged in extensive discovery: both sides retained experts, took depositions, secured affidavits and exchanged documents. Coach went so far as to conduct a survey to determine whether consumers would confuse the AnnTaylor bags with Coach bags, even when the products were clearly labelled. AnnTaylor, though it has not elicited its own evidence to challenge the survey data, contends it should be given no weight since serious methodological flaws, including result-oriented questions, biased the results.

Coach moved preliminarily to enjoin appellants from replicating the Dinky Bag, the Duffle Sac, and the Convertible Clutch. Coach argued that it was likely to succeed on its trademark infringement and unfair competition claims, and contended that failure to issue an injunction immediately would result in irreparable loss of profits and goodwill.

In response, appellants cross-moved for summary judgment, alleging that Coach had not established a prima facie case of infringement. AnnTaylor averred that its clear labelling of the merchandise, its dissimilar trade name and logo, and its failure to parody Coach's unique product packaging, eliminated any likelihood that customers were confused as to the source of the product.

Judge Duffy determined appellants' handbags were confusingly similar to those manufactured by Coach. Accordingly, he denied appellants' summary judgment motion and instead granted summary judgment in favor of Coach, finding AnnTaylor and Laura liable, as a matter of law, for trade dress infringement and common law unfair competition.

The judgment permanently enjoined appellants from replicating any of Coach's approximately fifty handbag styles.

Because we believe the district court's action prevented AnnTaylor and Laura from raising a genuine issue of material fact, we reverse the summary judgment insofar as it determines appellants' copying of the bags violates the Lanham Act and the New York common law of unfair competition. We affirm, however, the grant of summary judgment with regard to the copying of the registered Coach tags.

* * *

Unregistered Trademark Infringement

Coach's federal claim is based on section 43(a) of the Lanham Act, which provides a civil action in favor of those who believe they have been damaged, or are likely to be damaged, by the use of a "false designation of origin" on a good or service. Though enacted as part of the Trademark Act, this provision functions as a federal law of unfair competition for unregistered goods. Section 43(a) extends protection to a product's "trade dress"—the total image of a good as defined by its overall composition and design, including size, shape, color, texture, and graphics.

To prevail on a trade dress claim, the plaintiff must demonstrate that the product's appearance has acquired "secondary meaning"—the consuming public immediately identifies the product with its maker—and that purchasers are likely to confuse the imitating goods with the originals. Even if the plaintiff establishes these elements, the defendant may still avoid liability by demonstrating that the imitated features are "functional"—essential to the basic purpose the article is meant to serve.

A. Secondary Meaning

The trade dress of a product attains secondary meaning when the purchasing public "associates" its design with a single producer or source rather than simply with the product itself. The plaintiff is not required to establish that all consumers relate the product to its producer; it need only show that a substantial segment of the relevant consumer group makes this connection.

Coach contends that compelling circumstantial and direct evidence confirms that consumers associate the Dinky Bag, the Duffle Sac, and the Convertible Clutch with Coach alone. Appellee claims its product awareness survey establishes customer recognition since a majority of respondents associated the AnnTaylor bags with Coach. It concludes that similarities in the aesthetic configuration of the products indicate purposeful replication and thus secondary meaning.

AnnTaylor and Laura respond that Coach has failed to establish, as a matter of law, that the consuming public identifies Coach as the sole source of the handbag designs at issue. They concede Coach handbags are widely recognized, but assert that the designs have become so commonplace that customers do not reflexively assume Coach produced them. Support for this proposition, appellants contend, can be found in Coach's advertising slogan—"It's Not a Coach Bag Without the Coach Tag"—which encourages consumers to distinguish its goods from those of its many imitators. If permitted to conduct additional discovery, they argue that at a minimum they would be able to raise a genuine factual dispute on this issue for trial. We agree.

Our cases make clear that proof of secondary meaning entails vigorous evidentiary requirements. When attempting to resolve this essentially factual determination, we have assessed advertising expenditures, consumer studies, unsolicited media coverage of the product, sales success, attempts to plagiarize the mark, and length and exclusivity of use. The careful weighing of evidence necessary to determining secondary meaning renders it an unlikely candidate for summary judgment. The case against summary judgment is even stronger where the opposing party has not been afforded an adequate opportunity to seek potentially favorable information.

With these principles in mind, we find Coach has failed to establish that a reasonable jury must conclude the overall design of its handbags have acquired secondary meaning. Though intentional copying constitutes persuasive evidence of consumer recognition, conscious replication alone does not establish secondary meaning. Moreover, production of the Coach consumer awareness survey does not satisfy the requisite evidentiary burden. Though we have found such surveys probative when granting summary judgment for a registered trademark owner, see *Lois Sportswear, U.S.A., Inc. v. Levi Strauss & Company*, 799 F.2d 867, 869 & n.1 (2d Cir. 1986), we are especially reluctant to rely upon them when considering whether a product's unregistered trade dress has been infringed as a matter of law.

Though the failure to establish secondary meaning renders resolution of the section 43(a) claim premature, this does not conclude our inquiry. In particular, a showing of secondary meaning is not necessary to prove unfair competition under New York State common law, one of the grounds upon which the district court based its judgment. See *Perfect Fit Indus., Inc. v. Acme Quilting Co.*, 618 F.2d 950 (2d Cir. 1980), cert. denied, 459 U.S. 832(1982). To prevail on the state law claim, Coach need only demonstrate a likelihood of confusion.

B. Likelihood of Confusion

AnnTaylor maintains that differences in packaging and in the size, shape, logo and name on the hang tag ensure that a consumer looking to purchase a Coach product is unlikely to be confused as to its source. Design variations in the imitation wares, including the spacing of the eyelets and the length of shoulder straps, the thickness in the hasp in the buckle and the overall width of the bags, are said to eliminate the consuming public's doubts as to maker. Appellants argue that the sophisticated consumers likely to purchase Coach products are informed enough to realize that handbags lacking a Coach registration number and the Coach name are not Coach products.

Coach responds that the district court's visual inspection was highly probative and largely conclusive of customer confusion. It argues the virtual identity in overall appearance, combined with other significant evidence, including the inability of Laura's President to distinguish across a conference table the differences between Coach and AnnTaylor submissions, would necessarily lead a rational trier of fact to conclude these products were likely to confuse consumers as to manufacturer.

We conclude that Coach has not presented sufficient convincing evidence to prevail on summary judgment. Similarity in overall appearance alone cannot establish source confusion as a matter of law. Nor is the addition of the anecdotal evidence and the consumer awareness survey dispositive. After drawing all reasonable inferences in favor of appellants, we are unable to conclude Coach has established that AnnTaylor and Laura engaged in unfair competition under New York state law.

Registered Trademark Infringement

Despite Coach's failure to prove unfair competition liability on summary judgment, we find it has established infringement of its registered hang tags. Though

Coach has not expressly pleaded a cause of action under section 32 of the Lanham Act, it seeks in its complaint a permanent injunction preventing "the use of any . . . symbol, representation, description or designation which is likely to create the erroneous impression that defendants' goods emanate from Coach . . . or are otherwise authorized by Coach." We read this broad request for relief to include protection of its tags.

When assessing the protectable nature of a registered trademark, we first consider its strength. The four basic classifications, arranged from least to greatest degree of protection accorded, are: (1) generic, (2) descriptive, (3) suggestive, and (4) arbitrary or fanciful. The inherently distinctive shape and composition of the Coach hang tag leads us to conclude the mark is a fanciful one. This determination, which is supported by registration on the federal Principal Register, eliminates the trademark owner's need to prove secondary meaning. Accordingly, to prevail on its section 32 claim, Coach need only establish a likelihood of confusion as to its registered mark.

Presumptions of differing weight govern determination of the likelihood of confusion issue with regard to registered trademarks as opposed to unregistered trade dress. When engaging in this inquiry, registered marks are entitled to a liberal application of the law. And, unlike unregistered trade dress claims, disposition by summary judgment is often appropriate where the protection of a registered trademark is at issue. Therefore, our conclusion that Coach has not proven a likelihood of confusion among the handbags does not pre-determine resolution of the claim regarding its hang tags.

We agree with Judge Duffy that AnnTaylor's tag, although it contains AnnTaylor's name, is nonetheless confusingly similar to that of Coach's tag in look and feel. This observation, coupled with the fact that the tags are affixed to almost identical products marketed towards the same consumer group establishes likelihood of confusion under section 32.

Recognition of Coach's sophisticated customer base does not necessarily bolster AnnTaylor's claim that confusion is unlikely. When rejecting a similar argument raised by a designer jeans manufacturer who had incorporated a pocket stitching pattern nearly identical to the one made famous by Levi Strauss & Co., we concluded that it is the sophisticated consumer who is most likely to assume that the presence of appellee's trademark stitching pattern on appellants' jeans indicates some sort of association between the two manufacturers. Presumably it is these sophisticated jeans buyers who pay the most attention to back pocket stitching patterns. *Lois Sportswear*, 799 F.2d at 875. Finally, Coach's failure to document significant evidence of actual confusion does not undermine the propriety of summary judgment. To warrant injunctive relief, plaintiffs were not required to establish unquestioned confusion but a mere likelihood of it; proof of real and precise confusion is necessary only for the recovery of monetary damages. As we have indicated, this determination awaits resolution of the proceedings now pending before Magistrate Judge Buchwald.

The Functionality Defense to Section 43(a)

Trade dress protection does not extend to a product's functionality—those characteristics of the product which are essential to its purpose or use.

Judge Duffy, however, held as a matter of law that appellants' functionality defense was meritless, since the three Coach handbags are distinctive in their overall design and composition. He determined that many of the component parts, such as the distinctive lozenge-shaped leather tag, are purely ornamental and serve primarily to signify origin. Moreover, he found it possible to produce acceptable variations of the Coach styles. Based on these conclusions, the court proceeded to issue expansive relief, enjoining appellants from copying any Coach handbag.

Though Judge Duffy is undoubtedly correct that there are several ways to produce the handbag styles at issue without creating so great a likelihood of confusion for consumers, there is more to the functionality defense. Lanham Act protection does not extend to configurations of ornamental features which would significantly limit the range of competitive designs available. *Wallace Int'l*, 916 F.2d at 81. We are concerned that the grant of such broad relief chills competition excessively.

Coach produces from fifty to sixty different styles of handbags in various shapes and sizes. Though the scope of the injunction may reflect the court's desire to conserve judicial resources and stem re-litigation of substantially similar infringement claims, we are skeptical that Coach could produce evidence sufficient to support such sweeping protection for its entire line of handbags. An extensive injunction prohibiting emulation of all types of Coach bags could have the unacceptable effect of removing non-infringing design innovations from the market. Similar concerns are raised by an injunction preventing replication of such elemental features as the size, shape, color and materials of Coach bags.

Conclusion

Regretfully, the body of law relating to the Lanham Act has developed into a tangled morass. Courts struggling to move mountains often find they have only affected minuscule changes in trademark jurisprudence and occasionally have created their own likelihood of confusion. Be that as it may, our review of the record leads us to conclude that though Judge Duffy prematurely determined AnnTaylor and Laura have infringed upon Coach's unregistered trade dress in its handbags, permanent injunctive relief was properly extended to the registered Coach tag.

We affirm in part the grant of summary judgment, finding appellants' replication of the Coach tag violated Coach's trademark under section 32 of the Lanham Act. That part of the judgment finding appellants have infringed on Coach's trade dress under section 43(a) of the Lanham Act and the New York common law of unfair competition is reversed and remanded for further proceedings consistent with this opinion.

Dissent

WINTER, Circuit Judge, concurring in part and dissenting in part:

I agree with my colleagues that we must reverse the sweeping relief ordered by the district judge in his *sua sponte* grant of summary judgment for the plaintiff. However, I respectfully dissent from the affirmance on entirely new grounds of a portion of that judgment. My disagreement is based on procedural as well as substantive concerns.

If procedural regularity is to be accorded even minimal observance, an appellate court should be extraordinarily cautious about issuing a sua sponte grant of summary judgment against a defendant on a fact-specific claim that the plaintiff did not make in its complaint or on appeal. On the merits, I agree with my colleagues that the overall similarity in appearance of the bags with hang tags does not, as a matter of law, create a likelihood of confusion as to source. Precisely because I agree on the trade dress issue, however, I do not agree that there is an infringement of a registered trademark as a matter of law. Ann Taylor's hang tags are different from Coach's registered tag, and, as Judge Kaufman notes, have a potential for creating confusion as to source only when attached to handbags that are substantially identical in appearance. The bags, however, are not part of the registered mark. Because it is the substantially identical handbags that create the confusion, if any, the issue is one of trade dress rather than trademark infringement—as Coach has insisted throughout.

* * *

II

Turning to the merits, I of course agree with my colleagues that the extraordinarily broad order of the district court is plain error. I also agree that summary judgment was inappropriate on the issues of secondary meaning and likelihood of confusion as to source resulting from similar trade dress. Ann Taylor's bags were on the market for months, but Coach has been unable to offer any substantial evidence of actual confusion as to source. That is to say, Coach has not shown that consumers who buy Ann Taylor bags believe they are buying bags produced by Coach rather than imitations of Coach bags produced by Ann Taylor. To be sure, the bags are remarkably—and not accidentally—similar in design, and each has a "lozenge" shaped (but different) hang tag. However, even identical appearances are insufficient by themselves to show confusion as to source as a matter of law, the indispensable element of a trademark claim. Unlike a design patent or copyright owner, a trademark claimant does not have an exclusive right to a design; its right is solely in protecting its identity as the source of its product. Ann Taylor thus has every right to copy Coach's bags so long as consumers know they are buying Ann Taylor bags. Whether confusion exists should be resolved at a trial.

My disagreement with the majority on the merits relates to its making and then adopting the claim of registered trademark infringement. It is correct that a failure to show likelihood of confusion under Section 43(a)—a trade dress claim—does not preclude assertion of a registered trademark claim. For example, if the tag used by Ann Taylor were identical to Coach's, including the use of the name "Coach," the fact that it was attached to shoes rather than handbags would not legitimate that use. However, Ann Taylor's hang tag is different. Ann Taylor's tag is oval-shaped whereas Coach's tag is rectangular. Their respective sizes are different. Moreover, each has a very different name and logo style embossed on it. I cannot, therefore, agree with my colleagues that the Ann Taylor tag infringes the Coach tag, because no reasonable trier of fact could find infringement if the two tags were hung on handbags with different appearances.

My colleagues seem to agree with this analysis, because they qualify their holding by noting that only when the hang tags are put on identical handbags—which are not part of the registered trademark—does a likelihood of confusion exist. By limiting their holding to circumstances involving items that are not part of the registered mark, however, they abandon the infringement theory only to embrace the very trade dress claim that is held in the immediately preceding section of Judge Kaufman's opinion not to have been established as a matter of law.

By converting a rejected trade dress claim into a registered trademark claim and then granting relief on the registered trademark claim on a trade dress rationale, the majority opinion completely blurs the distinction between these two legal theories. The closest precedent relied upon by the majority is *Lois Sportswear, U.S.A., Inc. v. Levi Strauss & Company*, 799 F.2d 867 (2d Cir. 1986). In that case—in which a registered trademark claim was made—we held that use of a back pocket stitching pattern that was part of a registered mark and had secondary meaning violated the Lanham Act where the products—ordinary jeans and designer jeans—were not identical and were sold in overlapping but different markets. The fact that the products were different was regarded as making confusion "more likely." 799 F.2d at 874. The present decision turns *Lois Sportswear* on its head. Secondary meaning has not been established as a matter of law for either the tags or the bags, and it is the identity of the products, which are not part of the registered mark, that supplies the critical element causing the supposed confusion. I believe, therefore, that the present decision will be the source of much future mischief.

Notes

1. The court found that AnnTaylor's use of similar tags—with the AnnTaylor name prominently stamped in the middle of those tags—constituted infringement of Coach's trade dress rights in its own tags. Putting aside the differences between the tags as described in the dissenting opinion, is this a case where the prominent use of the defendant's own brand makes clear the origin of the products bearing the tag? Would consumers believe that AnnTaylor's bags either originated from that company or that competitors such as Coach and AnnTaylor collaborated on a bag?

While reading the next case, think about the importance of protecting a mark from similar or confusing uses. Why might luxury retailers be especially zealous about bringing infringement actions against those who use marks that might look similar?

Gucci America, Inc. v. Guess?, Inc.

868 F. Supp. 2d 207 (S.D.N.Y. 2012)

SCHEINDLIN, District Judge.

I. Introduction

This is a trademark infringement case between two global fashion companies. Gucci claims that Defendants have infringed or counterfeited four of its trademarks, and one trade dress on over one thousand stock keeping units ("SKUs") in an attempt to "Gucci-fy" their product line:

1) the Green-Red-Green Stripe mark ("GRG Stripe");

2) the Repeating GG Pattern,

3) the Diamond Motif Trade Dress, which is the Repeating GG Pattern with a pair of inverted Gs in each corner rendered in a brown/beige color combination,

4) the Stylized G Design mark ("Stylized G"), and

5) the Script Gucci Design mark ("Script Gucci").

Gucci also seeks cancellation of Guess's "4G Square Repeating Logo" trademark on the basis of abandonment.

Defendants answered the Second Amended Complaint, denying all of Gucci's claims, while also raising more than a dozen affirmative defenses as well as a counterclaim.

I held a bench trial from March 28, 2012 to April 19, 2012.

II. Findings of Fact

A. Parties

Gucci is organized under the laws of New York.

Guess is organized under the laws of Delaware.

MFF is organized under the laws of Delaware.

Max Leather/Cipriani is organized under the laws of New York.

Signal is organized under the laws of California.

Swank is organized under the laws of Delaware.

B. History of the Brands

Guess

Guess was founded in 1981 by the Brothers Marciano—Georges, Maurice, Paul, and Armand. Over the next three decades, it grew into an internationally recognized brand. Guess sells branded apparel and accessories, both on its own and with select licensees. It operates hundreds of its own retail stores, and places its products in more than one thousand department stores nationwide.

Guess has developed a distinctive and unique brand image over the past thirty years. It has established itself as a mid-market lifestyle brand, somewhere below the "haute couture" fashion houses, but nonetheless above low-end retail discounters like Target or Wal-Mart. The ideal Guess customer is the "Guess Girl," a brand-conscious young woman between the ages of fifteen and thirty who identifies with the sexy, trendy, flashy image of the Guess brand. She is willing to pay a premium above unbranded products to display that image through Guess-branded products.

Between 2008 and 2010 alone, Defendants spent more than ninety million dollars advertising the Guess brand in various media channels, including magazines such as Vogue, Vanity Fair, In Style, Allure, Elle, and People, as well as billboards and buses.

The Guess style makes frequent use of "loud" colors, exaggerated fabric details, and embellishments such as rhinestones. These act as indicators that Guess is the source of the product. Based on the results of surveys conducted by Women's Wear Daily identifying the thirty most well-known brands, consumers understand that the Guess brand and style is not the same as Gucci's. The Guess brand has come to be identified with such celebrity "Guess Girls" as Anna Nicole Smith and Claudia Scheiffer.

Gucci

Guccio Gucci established his eponymous brand in Florence, Italy in 1921. In the decades that followed, Gucci became famous for its fine leather goods, and then built on its reputation to become one of the largest luxury goods, fashion and accessory brands in the world.

Gucci opened its pioneering New York City store in 1953, introducing Americans to Italian fashion. Since then it has expanded its presence into twenty-two states and now operates more than ninety U.S. stores. Over the years it has sold under the Gucci brand name everything from watches to cars.

Gucci considers the designs at issue in this case to be among its "icons," and places them on products to enable its customers to communicate that they are members of the "exclusive club" that the Gucci brand signifies. Over the past twenty years, seventy-five percent of the products have borne at least one of these designs. Sales data show that they are tremendously successful, with approximately $1.3 billion worth of product sold between 2004 and 2009 alone.

In addition to "lifestyle" consumers—wealthy individuals who wear Gucci products regularly—Gucci also targets "aspirational" consumers, who are younger and less wealthy, but nonetheless aspire to the exclusivity that the Gucci brand represents. Because these consumers are less well-off than the "lifestyle" consumer, they tend to purchase Gucci's more popularly priced articles, such as canvas products bearing the Diamond Motif Trade Dress and/or the Repeating GG Pattern.

Gucci spends millions of dollars on advertising each year, including more than twenty million dollars in the period from 2001 to 2009 on the marks at issue. It advertises in fashion magazines such as Vogue, Vanity Fair, and Elle, as well as "lifestyle" magazines like Town & Country, and even teen-oriented magazines such as Lucky or Teen Vogue, all in an effort to reach a broad range of consumers.

In addition to magazine and newspaper ads, Gucci advertises on billboards, on buses, in malls, and in a variety of online media. It also receives unpaid editorial coverage in the fashion press, which a third-party service assessed at a value of approximately twenty-five million dollars per year for the period from 2006 to 2009. Additional media exposure comes from celebrities ranging from Charlize Theron to Nicole "Snooki" Polizzi, who are often photographed wearing Gucci products.

As a result of its advertising and commercial success, Gucci is consistently recognized as one of the top luxury brands in the world by a variety of publications. It has also been recognized as one of the top global brands, irrespective of "luxury" status.

C. The Marks at Issue

As noted above, this case involves five Gucci designs: the GRG Stripe, the Repeating GG Pattern (along with the Diamond Motif Trade Dress), the Stylized G, and the Script Gucci. Gucci imposes strict quality standards on all of its products, including those bearing these marks. Over the years, it has vigorously enforced its trademark rights, with a particular focus on the problem of counterfeiting.

The GRG Stripe

Gucci has used the GRG Stripe since the 1960s. It consists of outside green stripes flanking a center stripe rendered in red. The GRG Stripe has appeared on approximately twenty percent of all Gucci accessories in the past two decades. From 2005 to 2009, sales of such products totaled approximately $250 million. At trial and during depositions, Defendants acknowledged that the GRG Stipe is a key identifier of Gucci. Based on its extensive nationwide sales and publicity, its recognition as an identifier of Gucci, and the fact that it was first registered more than thirty years ago, I find that the GRG Stripe is a famous mark within the meaning of the Trademark Dilution Revision Act ("TDRA") of 2006.

The Repeating GG Pattern and the Diamond Motif Trade Dress

Gucci has used the Repeating GG Pattern—a pair of inward facing, inverted G's set at the corners of a repeating, diamond-shaped pattern connected by two dots forming straight diagonal lines—since 1966. Gucci has sold billions of dollars worth of products bearing the Repeating GG Pattern/Diamond Motif Trade Dress. To support sales of products with these marks, Gucci spent more than thirteen million dollars on advertising in the U.S. between 2001 and 2009.

At trial and during depositions, Defendants acknowledged that the Repeating GG Pattern is a key identifier of Gucci that transmits the brand's characteristic qualities of heritage, quality, and exclusivity.

I find that the Repeating GG Pattern is a famous mark within the meaning of the TDRA.

The Stylized G

Gucci began using the Stylized G in 1994. From 2004 through 2009, Gucci sold approximately fifteen million dollars worth of products bearing the Stylized G, combined wholesale and retail. Over the period from 2001 to 2009, it spent approximately $1.3 million advertising such products in the U.S.

Gucci increased its use of the Stylized G in 1995 and 1996, and the mark became the focus of an entire ready-to-wear collection in 1998. However, after a controversial, pornographic advertisement created by Tom Ford featuring the Stylized G ran in Spring 2003, Gucci scaled back on its use.

As discussed below, Guess designed its own Square G at some time during 1995, and first used it in commerce in 1996, if not earlier. At that time, Gucci had not yet registered the Stylized G in the U.S., and it had only sold and advertised it for a few years at most. Furthermore, Gucci has not shown that consumers actually recognized the Stylized G as an indicator of Gucci. Accordingly, even if the Stylized G did eventually become famous, I find that it was not famous when Guess commenced use of its Square G in 1996.

The Script Gucci

The Script Gucci mark was developed from the signature of Guccio Gucci, the brand's founder. Gucci began using the mark in 1967 and has used it ever since. Approximately five percent of all Gucci products sold in the last two decades have borne the Script Gucci Mark. Gucci sold fifty-eight million dollars worth of products bearing this mark at retail between 2004 and 2009. For the period from 2005 to 2009, it sold $195 million at wholesale.

I do not reach the question of whether the Script Gucci mark is famous because I find that, even if it were famous, the Script Guess mark does not dilute it, either by tarnishment or by blurring.

D. Defendants' Design Processes

Guess uses various licensees to produce its accessory products. In anticipation of each selling "season," Guess's in-house design team researches trends in the fashion industry, and creates apparel designs consistent with the carefully cultivated Guess brand. Guess's in-house counsel checks these designs for compliance with intellectual property laws.

Guess provides its licensees with "trend inspiration" via semi-annual trend design meetings. At these meetings, Guess distributes "trend design books" that include cuttings from magazines, trend watch services, and the results of shopping trips, amongst other things, all in an attempt to create a cohesive look and feel across all Guess-branded products. Guess's reliance on these materials shows that it is a trend follower, not a trend leader.

The accessory licensees use the trend design materials as a starting point for their own design process, which culminates in products that Guess reviews and approves for aesthetics and brand cohesion. Guess's licensing department monitors the licensees' products and works with them to achieve a consistent and coherent style for each season. This department is also responsible for monitoring the licensees' use and modification of Guess's intellectual property, including its trademarks and signature logos.

After designs are approved, the licensees produce sample products for physical review, resulting in approval, rejection, or requests for modification. These "line reviews" are typically attended by Mr. Paul Marciano and at least one member of the Guess licensing department.

Due to the volume of products involved, Guess does not individually clear each approved product for intellectual property conflicts. Instead, the licensees are obligated to do so by the terms of their licensing agreements. Nonetheless, Guess's licensing department will raise issues with Guess's legal department if it thinks any of the products come too close to the intellectual property of another brand. By way of example, approximately fifty designs were brought to the attention of the legal department in 2011, approximately twenty percent of which were disapproved on intellectual property grounds.

Despite these efforts, Guess does not have an unblemished record when it comes to complying with intellectual property laws. During the last decade, Guess has received approximately one dozen trademark complaints from other fashion companies complaining about Guess products that allegedly infringed on the trademark rights of the senior user. In each instance, Guess either immediately stopped using the mark or amicably resolved the matter with the competitor.

Guess has also frequently received complaints about footwear products developed by MFF. From October 2007 to August 2008, either Guess or MFF received four cease-and-desist letters from national brands including Jimmy Choo, Coach, Adidas, and Yves Saint Laurent. Guess warned MFF that this was unacceptable and claims to have sent a license agreement violation letter, but was unable to produce it during discovery or trial. Guess also did nothing to follow up on its demand that MFF put an effective intellectual property clearance procedure into place.

Like Gucci, Guess actively protects its intellectual property rights, using more than one hundred law firms to do so. By way of example, Guess has enforced its registered Quattro G Pattern against such companies as Aldo and Wal-Mart. Guess also works with U.S. Customs and Border Protection to prevent counterfeits from entering the country.

E. Development of the Allegedly Infringing Guess Marks

Gucci asserts that Guess and its Licensees knowingly and slavishly replicated Gucci's world famous design elements and designations [in order to] take advantage of the markets and demand Gucci has created for such designs without having to incur the developmental, promotional and advertising expenses that Gucci has incurred. In order to determine whether Gucci has proved this allegation, I must examine each mark in turn.

Defendants' Use of the GRG Stripe

Seven men's shoe models designed and manufactured by MFF in 2008 bore a GRG Stripe. Ample evidence shows that the GRG Stripe on these shoes was intentionally copied from Gucci. In a November e-mail discussing the Melrose 2 men's shoe, Jury

Artola—assistant to the head designer of men's footwear Paul Vando—instructed MFF's manufacturer that the striping detail should be "Green/Red/Green like the GUCCI." On May 2, 2008, Vando instructed his factory to "please reference the GUCCI sneaker" for the stripe color of one shoe, and that the "webbing whould [sic] be Green/Red/Green as on [the Gucci] sample." The very next day, when discussing the Deacon men's shoe, Vando instructed his sample manufacturer to "follow the Gucci colorway" for the GRG Stripe, and even offered to follow up by sending a Gucci shoe as an example.

Nonetheless, a Gucci investigator was able to purchase a Guess shoe bearing the GRG Stripe on November 29, 2008, more than a week after McManus's recall instructions went out. Indeed, on December 8, 2008—more than two weeks after the recall was ordered, MFF's CFO told McManus that MFF intended to continue production and sale of GRG Stripe shoes at wholesale. The next day, MFF instructed its factory to make a "running change" to a brown-red-brown stripe on the advice of McManus.

Despite its apparent agreement to stop using the GRG Stripe on shoes, MFF continued to ship such shoes until February or March 2009. Mark Parsley—Vice President of Sales for MFF's men's division—testified that MFF did so because it had not yet received shoes with the modified stripe from its factory, and in order to preserve delicate customer relationships in a highly competitive marketplace.

The evidence also shows that third-party retailers were still selling shoes bearing the GRG Stripe in April 2009. McManus was unable to explain why this was so, and testified that Guess left the task of third-party recalls to MFF.

I find that MFF intentionally copied the GRG Stripe from Gucci, and that Guess's licensing department approved of its use on men's shoes designed by MFF despite recognizing the GRG Stripe as an identifier of Gucci. Nonetheless, I find that Guess's recall of products bearing the GRG Stripe design—imperfect as it may have been—when they came to the attention of its legal department is indicative of its good faith. Because MFF made the conscious decision to continue shipping and selling shoes after it was directed to stop doing so, I find that it acted in bad faith.

I further find that a brown/red/brown stripe is visually dissimilar from the GRG Stripe and will not cause confusion, even in the post-sale context. Gucci has produced no evidence of actual confusion or association stemming from Guess's use of a brown/red/brown stripe, either through anecdotal consumer complaints or survey evidence.

Guess's Use of the Quattro G Pattern

The use of all-over logo patterns is common in the fashion industry, especially on handbags. Such logos are often based on initials of the brand. Examples include Fendi, Michael Kors, Givenchy, Coach, and Louis Vuitton.

Guess had used several different logos by the early-to mid-2000's, when the logo trend began to pick up steam. In 2003, in order to capitalize on the logo trend, a designer at Guess began experimenting with multiple G logos, eventually coming up with the standalone Quattro G. There is no evidence that he referenced or copied Gucci or any other company in doing so. Marciano liked the design and personally approved it.

Later that year, Guess engaged outside counsel—the Los Angeles firm of Christie, Parker, and Hale—to register the standalone Quattro G design as a trademark in a vertical orientation. Gucci did not oppose or object to Guess's application for the standalone Quattro G trademark, and Gucci does not contend that the standalone Quattro G infringes any Gucci mark.

In late 2003, the same designer used the standalone Quattro G to develop various patterns. Eventually, Guess selected a pattern with the Quattro G rotated 45 degrees clockwise and surrounded by a stitched diamond-shaped border without G's in the corners. Guess sought a registration for this mark in 2004. However, the accompanying artwork depicted the design in a square shape rather than a diamond, and did not mention that it would be a repeating pattern.

Prior to applying for registration, McManus—who had recently graduated from law school—conducted a trademark search, through which she determined that Gucci's Repeating GG Pattern was registered only for use on jewelry. Other registrations for use on handbags, belts, and footwear had expired as of 2003.

Several Guess witnesses testified that they had never seen the Quattro G Pattern used in a square orientation without Gs in the corners, and that Guess never intended that use. Nonetheless, after having seen the Gucci Repeating GG Pattern registration, McManus registered the Quattro G Pattern, which consisted of the standalone mark "bordered by a square composed of a dashed line." At trial, she gave conflicting reasons for why she did so. First, she testified that the vertical/square orientation was selected in order to achieve maximum protection against infringers. Later, she testified that the orientation of the mark and the orientation of the border was "irrelevant" to the scope of protection afforded by the registration.

The evidence shows that the PTO Examiner did not limit his comparative search to repeating square patterns. Instead, as explained by Guess's expert Gary Krugman, and as indicated by the Examiner's notes on file at the PTO, he performed a comparative search for registered trademarks bearing a "G" or "GG." However, the entry in the Official Gazette did not mention Gs in the corner or a diamond-shaped pattern, making it less likely that the application would come to Gucci's attention.

The history of the application in the PTO is also somewhat suspect. Originally, the Examiner rejected the application based on the finding that the Quattro G Pattern was merely ornamental. Months later, Guess argued that the pattern was either inherently distinctive, or that it had acquired distinctiveness through secondary meaning. The Examiner rejected this argument and noted that the pattern as described "does not appear on any of applicant's evidence." Three weeks later, however, the Examiner reversed himself and accepted the mark for registration. At trial,

Krugman said that he was told by Guess's counsel the day before his testimony that this reversal was a result of a phone call to the Examiner by Guess's counsel.

I find that Guess described the Quattro G Pattern as a square in order to avoid having the Repeating GG Pattern cited against its application, and in order to prevent Gucci from taking notice of the application when it was published for opposition.

Guess first provided the Quattro G Pattern fabric to Signal in 2004. As can be seen in the "Quatro G" handbag group from 2005, the Quattro G Pattern did not originally feature a two-tone weave or use shading inside the G's. In order to achieve a two-tone woven canvas look and a brown-beige color scheme, Becker sent clippings of Gucci fabrics to Claser, its Italian fabric agent.

Ringwood, who spearheaded the effort to create the two-tone weave, and who prepared dozens of detailed specifications for women's shoes using the Quattro G Pattern, testified that she never noticed the shading in the Gs until the legal proceedings began. Likewise, Marc Fisher, who has ultimate responsible for the design of women's shoes at his namesake company, testified that he never focused on the shading. The testimony of these witnesses on this subject is not credible.

The evidence shows that Guess and its licensees attempted to replicate other features of the Gucci fabric. For example, in September 2006, Ringwood asked Claser to replicate a Gucci embossing technique, and Joy Kramer of Guess's licensing department asked for a swatch of the resulting fabric to share with the licensees. E-mail records show that Signal was attempting to copy the Gucci brown/beige color scheme, of which Jason Rimokh—CEO of Signal—testified that he was enamored. MFF tried to replicate other Gucci colors on several occasions in 2008, while both Signal and MFF attempted to mimic coatings used on Gucci fabrics.

On several occasions, individuals associated with Guess and its licensees noted that the Quattro G Pattern looked similar to Gucci. For example, Kramer of Guess's licensing department stated in a June 2006 e-mail noted that a Guess shoe with the Quattro G Pattern with shading "looks so similar to Gucci but it is nice. . . ." Richard Danderline, the former CFO of MFF, wrote to another MFF executive in June 2008 that "the 'quattro G' pattern is pretty close to the Gucci pattern."

On the basis of the foregoing and other evidence in the record, I find that Guess intended to copy the upscale look of the Repeating GG Pattern and the Diamond Motif Trade Dress. This was intended to make the customer happy by giving him or her "the feeling of having something 'designer-ish' without it being the actual one, just similar."

Guess's Use of a Square G

Guess first sold products bearing the Square G in 1996. Guess sold more than 4.2 million units of products bearing allegedly-infringing variants of the Square G. Between 1999 and 2001 alone, the mark appeared on approximately fifty handbag style groups offered for sale. According to Guess witnesses, this means that handbags with Square G designs would have been available in nearly every one of Guess's 1400 then-existing distribution points in the United States.

Gucci asserts that a wide variety of square- or rectangle-shaped Gs used by Defendants infringe on the registered Stylized G. After exhaustively reviewing the photos and exemplars of accused products submitted post-trial, I find that Guess did not act in bad faith in the development or sale of products bearing any Square G design.

Guess's Use of the Script Guess Mark

It is undisputed that Guess has announced its brand name in a script-font on products since the early 1980s. It is also undisputed that Guess has used a "loop" in the letter "G" at the beginning of the Guess name and/or an underline under the Guess name since the same time. Gucci concedes that the complained-of Script Guess mark is the only allegedly infringing mark, and that it was not used until 2008. Gucci admits that without the "iconic underlining," the Script Guess would not infringe its trademark Script Gucci.

I find that the two marks are decidedly dissimilar, and that they do not create the same overall commercial impression, that Guess did not copy Script Gucci—intentionally or otherwise—and that Guess did not intend to deceive consumers as to the source of products bearing the Script Guess. I also note that Gucci introduced no evidence of confusion, either via survey or in any other way.

F. Gucci's Knowledge of Guess's Use of the Allegedly Infringing Marks

Guess introduced overwhelming evidence of its open, pervasive, and continuous promotion, sale, and advertising of its branded products, including millions of products bearing one or more of the marks at issue in this case. Indeed, from 2003 to 2010, Guess sold nearly seven million units of accused products, for an average of nearly one million accused products per year.

Many of Guess's stores are located near Gucci stores; in some instances, they are even in the same mall. Guess prominently displayed its products—including allegedly infringing products—at these stores. Allegedly infringing products were also openly for sale through Guess's website, and the websites of third-party retailers.

Gucci and Guess both have large advertising budgets, and the evidence shows that they often advertise in the same magazines. For example, Gucci and Guess both ran advertisements in Elle in August 2005, in Interview in December 2005/January 2006, and Allure in April 2007. Daniella Vitale—Gucci's former CEO—insisted that she was unaware of any issue regarding the Guess products at issue in this case until 2008. This testimony is not credible.

When pressed at trial, Vitale could not offer any explanation as to why not a single Gucci employee had ever notified any Gucci executive or attorney with concerns about the allegedly infringing Guess products. Jonathan Moss—former Legal Counsel for Gucci—similarly testified that he did not recall knowing anything about Guess's use of the allegedly infringing marks until 2006, although he has a remarkably clear memory of the events surrounding Guess's use of the word "twirl" to describe a watch. His testimony on these matters is not credible.

When asked at trial why Gucci allowed Guess to sell so many products Gucci claimed were harming its brand, Moss responded that the reason was "budgetary," and that the majority of Gucci's legal budget was taken up by combating counterfeiters. This was corroborated by Milton Springut (outside IP counsel for Gucci from 1984 to 2007), who testified that he never provided legal advice concerning possible infringement by Guess because such issues never arose, despite employing a team of investigators nationwide, including in cities where Guess had stores.

Gucci's behavior with respect to Guess is not consistent with its conduct towards other brands. Over the years, Gucci has sent out hundreds of cease and desists letters to entities ranging from national companies such as Bebe, Juicy Couture, and Williams-Sonoma, all the way to small-time infringers, such as a counterfeiter working out of her Los Angeles apartment and a rabbi in New York, who they suspected might sell counterfeit Gucci products to benefit his synagogue.

In addition to the incident involving the Guess "twirl" watch noted above, the evidence also shows that Moss discussed products that Gucci has put at issue in this case. Despite his clear memory of the "twirl" incident, Moss testified that he could not recall these e-mails or the surrounding circumstances at trial. This testimony is not credible.

In light of the foregoing, and all the other evidence admitted at trial, I find that Gucci knew or should have known about Guess's use of the Quattro G Pattern by 2006 at the very latest.

As a result of Gucci's delay in bringing suit or otherwise contacting Guess about its infringement concerns, I find that Guess has suffered evidentiary prejudice in the following ways:

1) It has no sales records before 2004, either for its own sales or for Gucci's.

2) It has lost evidence to corroborate the earliest uses of the Square G recalled by its witnesses.

3) It has lost details about the early development of the Quattro G Pattern.

4) It has been unable to interview witnesses due to their death or departure from the companies.

However, I find that Guess will not be prejudiced if it is prevented from using any of the allegedly infringing marks.

G. Expert Testimony

Plaintiff and Defendants both called expert witnesses on various topics. Guess called Gabrielle Goldaper to testify about the design process in the fashion industry, while MFF called Bonnie Smith on the design processes specific to footwear. On confusion, Gucci called George Mantis as a survey expert, while Guess called Dr. Shari Diamond and Dr. Carol Scott. On dilution, Gucci called Dr. Michael Mazis as a survey expert to explain association, and Dr. Michel Pham to discuss blurring and tarnishment, while Guess called Professor Mark McKenna to rebut Dr. Pham. Finally, Gucci called Basil Imburgia as a damages expert, while Guess called Dr. Alan

Goedde and MFF called Ronald Vollmar. Although some of these experts have been mentioned above, I make specific findings as to each group in detail below.

Design Process Experts

Smith and Goldaper testified that copying the designs of other companies is accepted practice in the fashion world. Both also testified as to the importance of following trends. While the law allows emulation of successful product features in order to spur competition and benefit consumers, it prohibits emulation from crossing over into copying that causes consumer confusion. Accordingly, Goldaper and Smith, if anything, add support to the finding that I have already made above, namely, that Guess and its licensees crossed the line and intentionally copied certain Gucci designs. However, the fact that Guess and its licensees acted according to accepted industry practices does not mean that they acted in good faith, or that their actions are permissible under New York or Federal trademark laws.

Confusion Experts

In support of its trade dress infringement claim, Gucci submitted the Mantis survey, which tested a Guess men's cross-body bag using the Quattro G Pattern executed in a brown/beige colorway. The survey claims to find a net confusion level of 15.6%. The Mantis Survey—when viewed in light of the testimony of all the confusion experts at trial—is not entitled to significant weight, and therefore provides only weak evidence in support of Gucci's trade dress claims.

Dilution Experts

In support of its dilution claim, Gucci submitted a survey by Dr. Mazis that claims to show a twelve percent level of a likelihood of association between Guess's Quattro G Pattern on a beige background and Gucci. I find that Dr. Mazis's survey—while somewhat flawed because it used questions that primed respondents to answer with brands and products—provides valid, relevant evidence as to the likelihood that consumers will associate the Quattro G Pattern with Gucci when rendered in a brown/beige colorway.

Dr. Pham testified as to the potential blurring or tarnishment that Guess's use of the accused marks would cause to Gucci. He did so on a brand-wide basis instead of doing a mark-by-mark analysis.

Dr. Pham's analysis is based solely on general propositions derived from marketing research literature, rather than specific studies of consumer attitudes regarding the Gucci marks and Diamond Motif Trade Dress. Dr. Pham's opinions do not rely on any real-world evidence of any purported blurring or tarnishment of the Gucci marks or the Gucci brand. Accordingly I find that Dr. Pham's testimony is insufficient to establish that the Gucci marks have experienced or are likely to experience any blurring or tarnishment.

Damages Experts—Profits from Accused SKUs

All three damages experts agree that profits are properly determined by deducting costs incurred and attributable to the design, manufacture, and sale of the accused products. The experts disagree, however, about which costs have a nexus sufficient to justify such deductions from profits.

Profits for All Defendants Except MFF

Based on information obtained from Defendants, Imburgia determined that Defendants sold over $204 million worth of products bearing the accused designs, resulting in profits of approximately eighty million dollars.

After deducting "store occupancy" costs from Imburgia's analysis, I find that Guess sold $79,822,325 of accused products, and earned a net profit of $41,978,543; it also received a total of $10,807,966 from all of its non-footwear licensees combined. Swank sold $193,894 for a profit of $66,459. Max Leather/Cipriani sold $4,016,682 for a profit of $1,361,904, while Signal sold $94,787,324 for a profit of $22,431,158.

However, for the reasons discussed in the Conclusions of Law below, I find that Gucci is not entitled to profits from every allegedly infringing SKU. Instead, I find that it is entitled to profits only to those SKUs listed in Appendix A to this opinion.

Based on the method of calculation I just described, I calculate Guess's retail profits from sales of those handbags to be $1,018,591.

Profits for MFF

I find that Gucci is not entitled to MFF's profits for every SKU it put in issue. Instead, only those listed in Appendix B to this opinion are infringing, for the reasons explained in the Conclusions of Law below.

Damages Experts—Reasonable Royalty as Actual Damages

Imburgia proposed a hypothetical royalty as a measure of Gucci's actual damages in lieu of making any showing of lost sales or profits.

Matteo Mascazinni, Gucci's Chief Operation Officer, stated that a royalty agreement would "never be advantageous" to Gucci. Guess's current licensees testified that it would not make economic sense for them either.

Imburgia assumed, without factual support, that Guess's current licensees would to sell the exact same products at a premium, even if they only licensed the Gucci design marks and not the Gucci name. He did not take into account the possibility that Guess's current licensees could easily avoid paying the royalty by making minor changes to their designs.

In view of the foregoing and all the other evidence in the record, I find that Imburgia's hypothetical royalty analysis is highly speculative, and entitled to no weight.

III. Applicable Law

Trademark Infringement

In order to succeed on its claim of trade dress infringement, Gucci must demonstrate (i) that the Diamond Motif Trade Dress has acquired distinctiveness through secondary meaning; (ii) that there is a likelihood of confusion between Defendants' trade dress and Gucci's; and (iii) that the trade dress is non-functional.

In this case, Gucci's infringement claims are premised solely on post-sale confusion. As with point-of-sale confusion, a post-sale confusion plaintiff must still establish a likelihood of confusion among an appreciable number of post-sale observers, taking into account all the vagaries involved with post-sale observation. Indeed, the fact that post-sale observers are removed from purchasing decisions makes post-sale trademark cases inherently difficult to prove, speculative, and subject to increased scrutiny.

Courts in the Second Circuit look to all of the traditional Polaroid factors in analyzing claims of post-sale confusion.

* * *

IV. Affirmative Defenses

Defendants raised the following affirmative defenses: (1) laches, (2) equitable estoppel, (3) acquiescence, (4) abandonment, (5) unclean hands, (6) trademark misuse, (7) prior use, (8) innocent use, (9) aesthetic functionality, and (10) statute of limitations. MFF does not join in the defenses of abandonment, trademark misuse, prior use, innocent use, or statute of limitations.

V. Discussion of Infringement Claims

A. The Registered Gucci Marks Are Valid and Entitled to Protection

As noted above, all four of the Gucci trademarks at issue have been registered since 2006 at the latest. Accordingly, they are all incontestible as to validity. Indeed, other courts have found that the GRG Stripe and the Repeating GG Pattern are strong, famous marks entitled to the strictest protection the law affords.

The Diamond Motif Trade Dress is Entitled to Protection

In light of Gucci's evidence of (1) extensive advertising expenditures; (2) unsolicited media coverage; (3) sales success; and (4) exclusive use of the Diamond Motif Trade Dress for over fifty years, I conclude that the Diamond Motif Trade Dress possesses strong secondary meaning, both with consumers and within the trade. The evidence that Defendants meticulously copied the Diamond Motif Trade Dress further supports this conclusion.

The evidence also establishes that the combination of elements comprising the Diamond Motif Trade Dress is not essential to the use or purpose of products on which such elements appear. Accordingly, I conclude that it is not functional.

C. The Polaroid Factors Generally

Several of the Polaroid factors are the same with respect to each mark:

(a) Bridging the Gap: The evidence shows that Gucci and Guess do not, as a general proposition, target the same markets. However, part of Gucci's overall marketing strategy is to target the "aspirational" customer who may be saving up in order to buy his or her first product as an entry ticket into Gucci's "exclusive club." Accordingly, I conclude that this factor does not weigh in favor of either party.

(b) Quality of Defendants' Products: Having examined exemplars of products bearing each of the accused designs—side by side and serially, from a distance and from up close, for varying periods of time, and by handling them physically—I conclude that they are of sufficiently high quality that Gucci's reputation in the eyes of the casual observer in the post-sale setting would not be harmed. Therefore, I conclude that this factor weighs in Defendants' favor.

(c) Sophistication of Consumers: Neither party has presented evidence of the sophistication of the casual observer in the post-sale setting. This factor therefore favors Guess, as Gucci bears the burden of proof.

With these factors in mind, I proceed to a mark-by-mark analysis of the Polaroid factors.

D. There Is a Likelihood of Confusion Between Certain Uses of Guess's Quattro G Pattern and the Repeating GG Pattern/Diamond Motif Trade Dress

Strength of Plaintiff's Mark: The record evidence of sales, advertising, and the importance of the Repeating GG Pattern and Diamond Motif Trade Dress to Gucci is clear.

Similarity of Both Marks: The Quattro G Pattern is visually dissimilar from the Repeating GG Pattern in at least two ways. First, the diamonds are "anchored" by the standalone Quattro G in the former, whereas they are empty in the latter. Second, the former has single Gs (sometimes inverted, sometimes right side up), whereas the latter has a pair of inward facing inverted Gs at each corner

On balance, I conclude that the Quattro G Pattern is visually similar to the Repeating GG pattern, although this factor does not weigh very heavily in Gucci's favor.

When rendered in brown/beige colorways on a two-tone canvas background, and with shading inside the G's the Quattro G Pattern is more similar to the Diamond Motif Trade Dress than to the Repeating GG Pattern. I conclude that when these circumstances coincide, this factor weighs strongly in Gucci's favor.

Competitive Proximity: As noted above, when the first two factors favor the plaintiff, this one does as well.

Guess argues that the difference between its target market and that of Gucci—mid-market versus high-end—pushes this factor in its favor. However, in the post-sale context, the target selling market is of decreased importance, as the confusion that exists in the general viewing public is what matters.

Gucci has no plans to move into the mid-market with a "diffusion line." Nonetheless, the idea of such a line is common enough in the fashion industry that consumers unaware of Gucci's strong position against making one may well believe that the Quattro G Pattern represents such an effort.

Actual Confusion: Gucci has no evidence of actual confusion between the Repeating GG Pattern and the Quattro G Pattern.

Guess intentionally copied the Repeating GG Pattern and the Diamond Motif Trade Dress in developing the Quattro G Pattern. Accordingly, Gucci is entitled to a presumption of actual confusion with respect to both.

Defendant's Intent/Bad Faith: The evidence strongly supports the inference that Guess acted in bad faith in copying the Repeating GG Pattern and the Diamond Motif Trade Dress. Additionally, Guess has received numerous cease-and-desist letters in the past, which provides additional evidence to find that this factor favors Gucci.

Weighing the Factors: After considering all of the Polaroid factors, I conclude that there is a likelihood of confusion between the Diamond Motif Trade Dress and the Quattro G Pattern, when it is rendered in brown/beige colorways. To be clear, by "brown/beige colorway," I refer to colorways that give the impression of a dark brown design on a lighter beige background, as depicted in paragraph 42 of the Conclusions of Law. Accordingly, Gucci has succeeded on its Lanham Act claims for infringement and false designation of origin, as well as its infringement claim under New York common law. These conclusions apply only to the SKU/color combinations listed in Appendix A.

Despite the presumption of confusion that arises from Guess's intentional copying of the Repeating GG Design and its bad faith, I find that the overall commercial impression transmitted by products bearing the Quattro G Pattern in non-brown/beige colorways is substantially different from Gucci. These products frequently feature bright and/or neon colors, garish or "bling-y" hardware, and generally succeed in communicating the "Guess Girl" image that defendants have been careful to cultivate over the years. Accordingly, the SKUs not listed in Appendix A are unlikely to cause confusion with the Diamond Motif Trade Dress or the Repeating GG pattern, and therefore do not infringe either of those designs.

E. Defendants' Use of a GRG Stripe Causes a Likelihood of Confusion with Gucci's GRG Stripe

Gucci has submitted evidence that MFF knowingly and in bad faith copied Gucci's GRG Stripe. This conduct was so egregious that a full Polaroid analysis is not necessary to conclude that there is a likelihood of confusion with Gucci's GRG Stripe. Accordingly, I conclude that Gucci has succeeded on its infringement claims under the Lanham Act and New York common law, as well as its false designation of origin claim, as those claims relate to this mark. Nonetheless, a few additional conclusions are required.

Stripe patterns are "basics" that every brand must be able to use freely in order to compete—excepting, of course, those instances where a particular configuration has come to be identified with a particular brand. The GRG Stripe is one such configuration, and should be given strong protection. However, that protection must be limited to a narrow range. For example, it covers all reds and all greens, but does not cover a central stripe that is yellow instead of red, or outer stripes that are brown instead of green.

I conclude as a matter of law that the defendants' use of stripes causes a likelihood of confusion with respect to only those SKUs in Appendix B. The findings of intentional copying and bad faith also apply only to these SKUs.

F. Guess's Use of Certain Block G Designs Causes a Likelihood of Confusion With Gucci's Stylized G

Strength of Plaintiff's Mark: I have already concluded that the distinctiveness of the Stylized G is incontestible. The conclusion that a mark is distinctive, however, does not ineluctably lead to the conclusion that it is "strong." Instead, with "basic" marks like letters and geometrical shapes, the protection must be narrow and specific, so as to preserve the ability of various brands to compete in the marketplace and thereby benefit the customer.

Of all of the marks at issue, the Stylized G accounts for the fewest sales dollars, and has been the subject of the least amount of advertising. Furthermore, the primary use of the mark in the post-Tom Ford era—on the lining of Gucci handbags—is only minimally relevant to post-sale confusion, if relevant at all. Gucci has failed to conduct a survey to test for consumer recognition of the Stylized G. In light of these considerations and the findings of fact above, I conclude that the Stylized G is a weak mark.

Similarity of the Marks: I have already found that, except for the belt with SKU 913019, the "Misty" shoe, and the "Scraps" shoe, Guess's Square Gs are not similar to Gucci's Stylized G. Accordingly, this factor weighs in Guess's favor.

Competitive Proximity: Because the Stylized G is a weak mark, and since Guess's Square Gs are generally dissimilar to it, this factor weighs in Guess's favor.

Actual Confusion: Gucci produced no evidence of actual confusion, whether anecdotal or in survey form.

Defendant's Intent/Bad Faith: I have already found that Guess did not intentionally copy Gucci, or act in bad faith in adopting the Square G. Accordingly, this factor favors Guess.

Weighing the Factors: Based on all the foregoing, I conclude that Guess's use of the Square G on the products listed in paragraph 79 of the Findings of Fact is likely to cause post-sale confusion. Gucci has successfully proven its Lanham Act infringement and false designation claims, as well as its common law infringement claim related the Square G only as to these products.

G. Guess's Use of the Script Guess Does Not Cause a Likelihood of Confusion

Strength of Plaintiff's Mark: In light of the fact that the use of script fonts is extremely common in the fashion industry, the only source-identifying properties of the Script Gucci mark stem from the fact that it spells out the word "Gucci." Additionally, Gucci concedes that the complained-of Script Guess without the underline would not be infringing. This demonstrates the "thinness" of the mark, and shows that this factor decidedly favors Guess.

Similarity of the Marks: I have already found that the Script Guess is not similar to the Script Gucci mark, and that it creates a distinct commercial impression in line with the "Guess Girl" aesthetic. Accordingly, I conclude that this factor favors Guess.

Competitive Proximity: For the same reasons as noted in my discussion of the Stylized G, this factor favors Guess.

Actual Confusion: Gucci has produced no evidence of any kind that any casual observer in the post-sale setting has ever confused the Script Guess mark for the Script Gucci mark.

Defendant's Intent/Bad Faith: I have already found that Guess did not act in bad faith in creating or using the Script Guess.

Weighing the Factors: Considering all the Polaroid factors and all the record evidence, I find that the Script Guess causes no likelihood of confusion whatsoever. Accordingly, Gucci's claims for infringement and false designation of origin under the Lanham Act and common law fail.

* * *

VIII. Discussion of Remedies

A. Gucci Is Not Entitled to Actual Damages in the Form of a Reasonable Royalty

Gucci has no evidence of, and hence can only speculate about, actual damages in the form of lost sales or harm to brand value. Accordingly, the only possible basis for recovery of actual damages is a reasonable royalty.

Imburgia's calculations are the only evidence that Gucci presented in support of a reasonable royalty. Because his analysis is highly speculative, I conclude that Gucci has not met its burden of proof on this issue. Accordingly, Gucci is not entitled to actual damages as measured by a reasonable royalty.

B. Gucci Is Entitled to an Accounting of Profits for Defendants' Use of the Quattro G Pattern in Brown/Beige Colorways and the GRG Stripe

I conclude that Defendants intentionally and willfully copied the Quattro G Pattern executed in brown/beige colorways from the Diamond Motif Trade Dress, and that Gucci is thereby entitled to an accounting of profits that Defendants made on the infringing SKUs. As noted in the Findings of Fact, excluding Guess's profits from its retail sales of handbags, defendants realized a total profit of $2,886,479 on the infringing SKUs.

I conclude that Guess's profits from retail sales of handbags to be $1,018,591.

* * *

In weighing all of the equities—including the need to deter future willful infringement—I find that the total amount that Gucci is entitled to receive is $4,613,478.

C. Gucci Is Entitled to a Permanent Injunction Barring Guess from Using the Quattro G Pattern, the GRG Stripe, and Certain Square G Marks

The conclusions of infringement and dilution made above give rise to a presumption that Gucci has suffered irreparable harm in that it has lost goodwill towards its unique brand as well as the ability to control its reputation in the marketplace. Because these injuries cannot be quantified or fully remedied by a monetary award, I conclude that Gucci lacks an adequate remedy at law.

Defendants have been successful with a wide variety of different designs, and it has not been difficult for them or harmful to their brand to stop using certain of the designs at issue during the pendency of this litigation. While they might like to resume use of the other successful designs, the equities favor Gucci, which should not have to suffer another brand's use of marks confusingly similar to its own. Finally, the public interest would be well-served by an injunction that eliminates the use of confusingly similar marks, thereby enabling both brands to clearly communicate their core characteristics to the public.

Courts in this circuit have long held that a permanent injunction should issue in trademark cases where a defendant asserts that its pre-lawsuit use was lawful, and that pre-lawsuit behavior may serve as a basis for a permanent injunction, as it may indicate that defendant's intentions are in doubt. Both of these rationales apply here. Accordingly, an injunction shall issue against Guess and its licensees.

IX. Discussion of Affirmative Defenses

A. Defendants Are Not Entitled to Any of Their Equitable Defenses

Defendants have asserted three classic, closely related equitable defense—laches, acquiescence, and equitable estoppel. These defenses are rejected for two reasons. First, equity will not give relief to an intentional infringer. Here, Defendants intentionally infringed on the Diamond Motif Trade Dress by using the Quattro G Pattern in brown colorways, while MFF intentionally infringed on the GRG Stripe. Second, equity requires that the prejudice be substantial before these defenses can prevail. While Defendants have suffered substantial evidentiary prejudice with respect to some of the allegedly infringing marks, the evidence shows that it will not be difficult for them to stop using any of them. Accordingly, while I will consider the equities of Gucci's delay in calculating Gucci's entitlement to a monetary award of Defendants' profits, I conclude that Defendants have not carried their burden of proof on these defenses, and/or are not entitled to them.

* * *

X. Conclusion

Over the past three years, the parties have put in countless hours and spent untold sums of money, all in the service of fashion—what Oscar Wilde aptly called "a form of ugliness so intolerable that we have to alter it every six months." With the instant disputes now resolved, and with Gucci's entitlement to the relief noted above, it is my hope that this ugliness will be limited to the runway and shopping floor, rather than spilling over into the courts.

Notes

1. The district court held that the fact that Guess had received approximately 12 claims for trademark infringement was evidence of bad faith copying of Gucci's styles. In response to each of those claims, Guess either stopped selling the product or otherwise reached an agreement with the claimant. Is the district court considering those settlements to be evidence of copying? Is the district court therefore penalizing Guess for settling claims rather than going to trial on all of them? This would seem to be bad policy for courts, which generally try to encourage settlement.

2. The evidence demonstrated that Gucci had long been aware, or should have been aware, of the Guess products at issue in this case. Gucci explained away its inaction by stating that it had been focusing on counterfeiters and did not have the resources to take on Guess. Considering the size of Gucci and Guess, as well as the scope of the activities at issue, do you find this explanation to be adequate? Should Gucci's delay have played a larger role in the district court's decision?

3. Trademark Dilution and Fashion Brands. The world's most famous brands occupy a unique emotional space in the minds of the world's consumers. In that regard, they may become familiar and consumers engage with them on a more personal basis. These famous marks may be used in ways that do not cause likelihood of confusion but do, however, expose the user to liability. Trademark "dilution" is an assertion that the alternate use of a mark by another party diminishes the strength or value of the trademark owner's mark by either "blurring" the mark's distinctiveness or "tarnishing" the mark's image by connecting it to something distasteful or objectionable. Congress passed the Federal Trademark Dilution Act in 1995 ("FTDA") as an amendment to Section 43 of the Lanham Act, the federal law governing trademarks. See 15 U.S.C. § 1125(c). The FTDA provided a right of action by the "owner of a famous mark" for injunctive relief against "another person's commercial use in commerce of a mark or trade name, if such use begins after the mark has become famous and causes dilution of the distinctive quality of the mark." *Id.* "Dilution" is defined as "the lessening of the capacity of a famous mark to identify and distinguish goods or services, regardless of the presence or absence of" likelihood of confusion or competition between the marks. 15 U.S.C. § 1127. When do such imitations go too far? The following cases explore the limits of protection available against dilution actions.

Louis Vuitton Malletier SA v. Haute Diggity Dog, LLC

507 F.3d 252 (4th Cir. 2007)

NIEMEYER, Circuit Judge.

Louis Vuitton Malletier S.A., a French corporation located in Paris, that manufactures luxury luggage, handbags, and accessories, commenced this action against Haute Diggity Dog, LLC, a Nevada corporation that manufactures and sells pet products nationally, alleging trademark infringement, trademark dilution, copyright infringement, and related statutory and common law violations. Haute

Diggity Dog manufactures, among other things, plush toys on which dogs can chew, which, it claims, parody famous trademarks on luxury products, including those of Louis Vuitton Malletier. The particular Haute Diggity Dog chew toys in question here are small imitations of handbags that are labeled "Chewy Vuiton" and that mimic Louis Vuitton Malletier's LOUIS VUITTON handbags.

On cross-motions for summary judgment, the district court concluded that Haute Diggity Dog's "Chewy Vuiton" dog toys were successful parodies of Louis Vuitton Malletier's trademarks, designs, and products, and on that basis, entered judgment in favor of Haute Diggity Dog on all of Louis Vuitton Malletier's claims.

I

Louis Vuitton Malletier S.A. ("LVM") is a well-known manufacturer of luxury luggage, leather goods, handbags, and accessories, which it markets and sells worldwide. LVM has adopted trademarks and trade dress that are well recognized and have become famous and distinct. Indeed, in 2006, BusinessWeek ranked LOUIS VUITTON as the 17th "best brand" of all corporations in the world and the first "best brand" for any fashion business.

LVM has registered trademarks for "LOUIS VUITTON," in connection with luggage and ladies' handbags (the "LOUIS VUITTON mark"); for a stylized monogram of "LV," in connection with traveling bags and other goods (the "LV mark"); and for a monogram canvas design consisting of a canvas with repetitions of the LV mark along with four-pointed stars, four-pointed stars inset in curved diamonds, and four-pointed flowers inset in circles, in connection with traveling bags and other products (the "Monogram Canvas mark"). In 2002, LVM adopted a brightly-colored version of the Monogram Canvas mark in which the LV mark and the designs were of various colors and the background was white (the "Multicolor design"), created in collaboration with Japanese artist Takashi Murakami. For the Multicolor design, LVM obtained a copyright in 2004. In 2005, LVM adopted another design consisting of a canvas with repetitions of the LV mark and smiling cherries on a brown background (the "Cherry design").

As LVM points out, the Multicolor design and the Cherry design attracted immediate and extraordinary media attention and publicity in magazines such as Vogue, W, Elle, Harper's Bazaar, Us Weekly, Life and Style, Travel & Leisure, People, In Style, and Jane. The press published photographs showing celebrities carrying these handbags, including Jennifer Lopez, Madonna, Eve, Elizabeth Hurley, Carmen Electra, and Anna Kournikova, among others. When the Multicolor design first appeared in 2003, the magazines typically reported, "The Murakami designs for Louis Vuitton, which were the hit of the summer, came with hefty price tags and a long waiting list." People Magazine said, "the wait list is in the thousands." The handbags retailed in the range of $995 for a medium handbag to $4500 for a large travel bag. The medium size handbag that appears to be the model for the "Chewy Vuiton" dog toy retailed for $1190. The Cherry design appeared in 2005, and the handbags including that design were priced similarly—in the range of $995 to $2740. LVM does not currently market products using the Cherry design. The original LOUIS VUITTON, LV, and Monogram Canvas marks, however, have been used as identifiers of LVM products continuously since 1896.

During the period 2003–2005, LVM spent more than $48 million advertising products using its marks and designs, including more than $4 million for the Multicolor design. It sells its products exclusively in LVM stores and in its own in-store boutiques that are contained within department stores such as Saks Fifth Avenue, Bloomingdale's, Neiman Marcus, and Macy's. LVM also advertises its products on the Internet through the specific websites www.louisvuitton.com and www.eluxury.com.

Although better known for its handbags and luggage, LVM also markets a limited selection of luxury pet accessories—collars, leashes, and dog carriers—which bear the Monogram Canvas mark and the Multicolor design. These items range in price from approximately $200 to $1600. LVM does not make dog toys.

Haute Diggity Dog, LLC, which is a relatively small and relatively new business located in Nevada, manufactures and sells nationally—primarily through pet stores—a line of pet chew toys and beds whose names parody elegant high-end brands of products such as perfume, cars, shoes, sparkling wine, and handbags. These include—in addition to Chewy Vuiton (LOUIS VUITTON)—Chewnel No. 5 (Chanel No. 5), Furcedes (Mercedes), Jimmy Chew (Jimmy Choo), Dog Perignonn (Dom Perignon), Sniffany & Co. (Tiffany & Co.), and Dogior (Dior). The chew toys and pet beds are plush, made of polyester, and have a shape and design that loosely imitate the signature product of the targeted brand. They are mostly distributed and sold through pet stores, although one or two Macy's stores carries Haute Diggity Dog's products. The dog toys are generally sold for less than $20, although larger versions of some of Haute Diggity Dog's plush dog beds sell for more than $100.

Haute Diggity Dog's "Chewy Vuiton" dog toys, in particular, loosely resemble miniature handbags and undisputedly evoke LVM handbags of similar shape, design, and color. In lieu of the LOUIS VUITTON mark, the dog toy uses "Chewy Vuiton"; in lieu of the LV mark, it uses "CV"; and the other symbols and colors employed are imitations, but not exact ones, of those used in the LVM Multicolor and Cherry designs.

In 2002, LVM commenced this action, naming as defendants Haute Diggity Dog; Victoria D.N. Dauernheim, the principal owner of Haute Diggity Dog; and Woofies, LLC, a retailer of Haute Diggity Dog's products, located in Asburn, Virginia, for trademark, trade dress, and copyright infringement. Its complaint includes counts for trademark counterfeiting; trademark infringement; trade dress infringement; unfair competition; trademark dilution; trademark infringement, under Virginia common law; trade dress infringement, under Virginia common law; unfair competition, under Virginia common law; copyright infringement of the Multicolor design; and violation of the Virginia Consumer Protection Act.

On cross-motions for summary judgment, the district court granted Haute Diggity Dog's motion and denied LVM's motion, entering judgment in favor of Haute Diggity Dog on all of the claims. It rested its analysis on each count principally on the conclusion that Haute Diggity Dog's products amounted to a successful parody of LVM's marks, trade dress, and copyright.

LVM appealed and now challenges, as a matter of law, virtually every ruling made by the district court.

II

LVM contends first that Haute Diggity Dog's marketing and sale of its "Chewy Vuiton" dog toys infringe its trademarks because the advertising and sale of the "Chewy Vuiton" dog toys is likely to cause confusion.

LVM argues: The defendants in this case are using almost an exact imitation of the house mark VUITTON, and they painstakingly copied Vuitton's Monogram design mark, right down to the exact arrangement and sequence of geometric symbols. They also used the same design marks, trade dress, and color combinations embodied in Vuitton's Monogram Multicolor and Monogram Cerises handbag collections. Moreover, HDD did not add any language to distinguish its products from Vuitton's, and its products are not widely recognized.

Haute Diggity Dog contends that there is no evidence of confusion, nor could a reasonable fact-finder conclude that there is a likelihood of confusion, because it successfully markets its products as parodies of famous marks such as those of LVM. It asserts that precisely because of the famous mark's fame and popularity confusion is avoided, and it is this lack of confusion that a parodist depends upon to achieve the parody.

Thus, responding to LVM's claims of trademark infringement, Haute Diggity Dog argues: The marks are undeniably similar in certain respects. There are visual and phonetic similarities. Haute Diggity Dog admits that the product name and design mimics LVM's and is based on the LVM marks. It is necessary for the pet products to conjure up the original designer mark for there to be a parody at all. However, a parody also relies on equally obvious dissimilarities between the marks to produce its desired effect.

Concluding that Haute Diggity Dog did not create any likelihood of confusion as a matter of law, the district court granted summary judgment to Haute Diggity Dog. We review its order de novo.

To prove trademark infringement, LVM must show (1) that it owns a valid and protectable mark; (2) that Haute Diggity Dog uses a "re-production, counterfeit, copy, or colorable imitation" of that mark in commerce and without LVM's consent; and (3) that Haute Diggity Dog's use is likely to cause confusion.

The validity and protectability of LVM's marks are not at issue in this case, nor is the fact that Haute Diggity Dog uses a colorable imitation of LVM's mark. Therefore, we give the first two elements no further attention. To determine whether the

"Chewy Vuiton" product line creates a likelihood of confusion, we have identified several nonexclusive factors to consider: (1) the strength or distinctiveness of the plaintiff's mark; (2) the similarity of the two marks; (3) the similarity of the goods or services the marks identify; (4) the similarity of the facilities the two parties use in their businesses; (5) the similarity of the advertising used by the two parties; (6) the defendant's intent; and (7) actual confusion. See *Pizzeria Uno Corp. v. Temple*, 747 F.2d 1522, 1527 (4th Cir.1984). These *Pizzeria Uno* factors are not always weighted equally, and not all factors are relevant in every case. See CareFirst, 434 F.3d at 268.

Because Haute Diggity Dog's arguments with respect to the *Pizzeria Uno* factors depend to a great extent on whether its products and marks are successful parodies, we consider first whether Haute Diggity Dog's products, marks, and trade dress are indeed successful parodies of LVM's marks and trade dress.

For trademark purposes, a parody is defined as a simple form of entertainment conveyed by juxtaposing the irreverent representation of the trademark with the idealized image created by the mark's owner. A parody must convey two simultaneous—and contradictory—messages: that it is the original, but also that it is not the original and is instead a parody. This second message must not only differentiate the alleged parody from the original but must also communicate some articulable element of satire, ridicule, joking, or amusement. Thus, "a parody relies upon a difference from the original mark, presumably a humorous difference, in order to produce its desired effect." *Jordache Enterprises, Inc. v. Hogg Wyld, Ltd.*, 828 F.2d 1482, 1486 (10th Cir.1987) (finding the use of "Lardashe" jeans for larger women to be a successful and permissible parody of "Jordache" jeans).

When applying the PETA criteria to the facts of this case, we agree with the district court that the "Chewy Vuiton" dog toys are successful parodies of LVM handbags and the LVM marks and trade dress used in connection with the marketing and sale of those handbags. First, the pet chew toy is obviously an irreverent, and indeed intentional, representation of an LVM handbag, albeit much smaller and coarser. The dog toy is shaped roughly like a handbag; its name "Chewy Vuiton" sounds like and rhymes with LOUIS VUITTON; its monogram CV mimics LVM's LV mark; the repetitious design clearly imitates the design on the LVM handbag; and the coloring is similar. In short, the dog toy is a small, plush imitation of an LVM handbag carried by women, which invokes the marks and design of the handbag, albeit irreverently and incompletely. No one can doubt that LVM handbags are the target of the imitation by Haute Diggity Dog's "Chewy Vuiton" dog toys.

At the same time, no one can doubt also that the "Chewy Vuiton" dog toy is not the "idealized image" of the mark created by LVM. The differences are immediate, beginning with the fact that the "Chewy Vuiton" product is a dog toy, not an expensive, luxury LOUIS VUITTON handbag. The toy is smaller, it is plush, and virtually all of its designs differ. Thus, "Chewy Vuiton" is not LOUIS VUITTON ("Chewy" is not "LOUIS" and "Vuiton" is not "VUITTON," with its two Ts); CV is not LV;

the designs on the dog toy are simplified and crude, not detailed and distinguished. The toys are inexpensive; the handbags are expensive and marketed to be expensive. And, of course, as a dog toy, one must buy it with pet supplies and cannot buy it at an exclusive LVM store or boutique within a department store. In short, the Haute Diggity Dog "Chewy Vuiton" dog toy undoubtedly and deliberately conjures up the famous LVM marks and trade dress, but at the same time, it communicates that it is not the LVM product.

Finally, the juxtaposition of the similar and dissimilar—the irreverent representation and the idealized image of an LVM handbag—immediately conveys a joking and amusing parody. The furry little "Chewy Vuiton" imitation, as something to be chewed by a dog, pokes fun at the elegance and expensiveness of a LOUIS VUITTON handbag, which must not be chewed by a dog. The LVM handbag is provided for the most elegant and well-to-do celebrity, to proudly display to the public and the press, whereas the imitation "Chewy Vuiton" "handbag" is designed to mock the celebrity and be used by a dog. The dog toy irreverently presents haute couture as an object for casual canine destruction. The satire is unmistakable. The dog toy is a comment on the rich and famous, on the LOUIS VUITTON name and related marks, and on conspicuous consumption in general. This parody is enhanced by the fact that "Chewy Vuiton" dog toys are sold with similar parodies of other famous and expensive brands—"Chewnel No. 5" targeting "Chanel No. 5"; "Dog Perignonn" targeting "Dom Perignon"; and "Sniffany & Co." targeting "Tiffany & Co."

Finding that Haute Diggity Dog's parody is successful, however, does not end the inquiry into whether Haute Diggity Dog's "Chewy Vuiton" products create a likelihood of confusion. There are confusing parodies and non-confusing parodies. All they have in common is an attempt at humor through the use of someone else's trademark. The finding of a successful parody only influences the way in which the *Pizzeria Uno* factors are applied. Indeed, it becomes apparent that an effective parody will actually diminish the likelihood of confusion, while an ineffective parody does not. We now turn to the Pizzeria Uno factors.

A

As to the first Pizzeria Uno factor, the parties agree that LVM's marks are strong and widely recognized. They do not agree, however, as to the consequences of this fact. LVM maintains that a strong, famous mark is entitled, as a matter of law, to broad protection. While it is true that finding a mark to be strong and famous usually favors the plaintiff in a trademark infringement case, the opposite may be true when a legitimate claim of parody is involved. As the district court observed, "In cases of parody, a strong mark's fame and popularity is precisely the mechanism by which likelihood of confusion is avoided." Louis Vuitton Malletier, 464 F.Supp.2d at 499. An intent to parody is not an intent to confuse the public.

We agree. It is a matter of common sense that the strength of a famous mark allows consumers immediately to perceive the target of the parody, while simultaneously allowing them to recognize the changes to the mark that make the parody funny or biting. See *Tommy Hilfiger Licensing, Inc. v. Nature Labs*, LLC, 221 F.Supp.2d 410, 416 (S.D.N.Y.2002) (noting that the strength of the "TOMMY HILFIGER" fashion mark did not favor the mark's owner in an infringement case against "TIMMY HOLE-DIGGER" novelty pet perfume). In this case, precisely because LOUIS VUITTON is so strong a mark and so well recognized as a luxury handbag brand from LVM, consumers readily recognize that when they see a "Chewy Vuiton" pet toy, they see a parody. Thus, the strength of LVM's marks in this case does not help LVM establish a likelihood of confusion.

B

With respect to the second Pizzeria Uno factor, the similarities between the marks, the usage by Haute Diggity Dog again converts what might be a problem for Haute Diggity Dog into a disfavored conclusion for LVM.

Haute Diggity Dog concedes that its marks are and were designed to be somewhat similar to LVM's marks. But that is the essence of a parody—the invocation of a famous mark in the consumer's mind, so long as the distinction between the marks is also readily recognized. While a trademark parody necessarily copies enough of the original design to bring it to mind as a target, a successful parody also distinguishes itself and, because of the implicit message communicated by the parody, allows the consumer to appreciate it.

In concluding that Haute Diggity Dog has a successful parody, we have impliedly concluded that Haute Diggity Dog appropriately mimicked a part of the LVM marks, but at the same time sufficiently distinguished its own product to communicate the satire. The differences are sufficiently obvious and the parody sufficiently blatant that a consumer encountering a "Chewy Vuiton" dog toy would not mistake its source or sponsorship on the basis of mark similarity.

This conclusion is reinforced when we consider how the parties actually use their marks in the marketplace. The record amply supports Haute Diggity Dog's contention that its "Chewy Vuiton" toys for dogs are generally sold alongside other pet products, as well as toys that parody other luxury brands, whereas LVM markets its handbags as a top-end luxury item to be purchased only in its own stores or in its own boutiques within department stores. These marketing channels further emphasize that "Chewy Vuiton" dog toys are not, in fact, LOUIS VUITTON products.

C

Nor does LVM find support from the third *Pizzeria Uno* factor, the similarity of the products themselves. It is obvious that a "Chewy Vuiton" plush imitation handbag, which does not open and is manufactured as a dog toy, is not a LOUIS VUITTON handbag sold by LVM. Even LVM's most proximate products—dog collars, leashes, and pet carriers—are fashion accessories, not dog toys. As Haute Diggity Dog points out, LVM does not make pet chew toys and likely does not intend to do so in the future.

D

The fourth and fifth Pizzeria Uno factors, relating to the similarity of facilities and advertising channels, have already been mentioned. LVM products are sold exclusively through its own stores or its own boutiques within department stores. It also sells its products on the Internet through an LVM-authorized website. In contrast, "Chewy Vuiton" products are sold primarily through traditional and Internet pet stores, although they might also be sold in some department stores.

Likewise with respect to advertising, there is little or no overlap. LVM markets LOUIS VUITTON handbags through high-end fashion magazines, while "Chewy Vuiton" products are advertised primarily through pet-supply channels.

The overlap in facilities and advertising demonstrated by the record is so minimal as to be practically nonexistent.

E

The sixth factor, relating to Haute Diggity Dog's intent, again is neutralized by the fact that Haute Diggity Dog markets a parody of LVM products. As other courts have recognized, "An intent to parody is not an intent to confuse the public." Jordache, 828 F.2d at 1486.

F

On the actual confusion factor, it is well established that no actual confusion is required to prove a case of trademark infringement, although the presence of actual confusion can be persuasive evidence relating to a likelihood of confusion.

While LVM conceded in the district court that there was no evidence of actual confusion, on appeal it points to incidents where retailers misspelled "Chewy Vuiton" on invoices or order forms, using two Ts instead of one. Many of these invoices also reflect simultaneous orders for multiple types of Haute Diggity Dog parody products, which belies the notion that any actual confusion existed as to the source of "Chewy Vuiton" plush toys. The misspellings pointed out by LVM are far more likely in this context to indicate confusion over how to spell the product name than any confusion over the source or sponsorship of the "Chewy Vuiton" dog toys. We conclude that this factor favors Haute Diggity Dog.

In sum, the likelihood-of-confusion factors substantially favor Haute Diggity Dog. But consideration of these factors is only a proxy for the ultimate statutory test of whether Haute Diggity Dog's marketing, sale, and distribution of "Chewy Vuiton" dog toys is likely to cause confusion. Recognizing that "Chewy Vuiton" is an obvious parody and applying the Pizzeria Uno factors, we conclude that LVM has failed to demonstrate any likelihood of confusion. Accordingly, we affirm the district court's grant of summary judgment in favor of Haute Diggity Dog on the issue of trademark infringement.

III

LVM also contends that Haute Diggity Dog's advertising, sale, and distribution of the "Chewy Vuiton" dog toys dilutes its LOUIS VUITTON, LV, and Monogram

Canvas marks, which are famous and distinctive, in violation of the Trademark Dilution Revision Act of 2006 ("TDRA"), 15 U.S.C.A. § 1125(c). It argues, "Before the district court's decision, Vuitton's famous marks were unblurred by any third party trademark use." "Allowing defendants to become the first to use similar marks will obviously blur and dilute the Vuitton Marks." It also contends that "Chewy Vuiton" dog toys are likely to tarnish LVM's marks because they "pose a choking hazard for some dogs."

Haute Diggity Dog urges that, in applying the TDRA to the circumstances before us, we reject LVM's suggestion that a parody "automatically" gives rise to "actionable dilution." Haute Diggity Dog contends that only marks that are "identical or substantially similar" can give rise to actionable dilution, and its "Chewy Vuiton" marks are not identical or sufficiently similar to LVM's marks.

Claims for trademark dilution are authorized by the TDRA, which provides in relevant part:

> Subject to the principles of equity, the owner of a famous mark ... shall be entitled to an injunction against another person who ... commences use of a mark or trade name in commerce that is likely to cause dilution by blurring or dilution by tarnishment of the famous mark, regardless of the presence or absence of actual or likely confusion, of competition, or of actual economic injury.15 U.S.C.A. § 1125(c)(1).

The TDRA defines "dilution by blurring" as the "association arising from the similarity between a mark or trade name and a famous mark that impairs the distinctiveness of the famous mark." It defines "dilution by tarnishment" as the "association arising from the similarity between a mark or trade name and a famous mark that harms the reputation of the famous mark."

Thus, to state a dilution claim under the TDRA, a plaintiff must show:

> (1) that the plaintiff owns a famous mark that is distinctive;
>
> (2) that the defendant has commenced using a mark in commerce that allegedly is diluting the famous mark;
>
> (3) that a similarity between the defendant's mark and the famous mark gives rise to an association between the marks; and
>
> (4) that the association is likely to impair the distinctiveness of the famous mark or likely to harm the reputation of the famous mark.

In the context of blurring, distinctiveness refers to the ability of the famous mark uniquely to identify a single source and thus maintain its selling power. In proving a dilution claim under the TDRA, the plaintiff need not show actual or likely confusion, the presence of competition, or actual economic injury.

The TDRA creates three defenses based on the defendant's (1) "fair use" (with exceptions); (2) "news reporting and news commentary"; and (3) "noncommercial use." Id. § 1125(c)(3).

A

We address first LVM's claim for dilution by blurring.

The first three elements of a trademark dilution claim are not at issue in this case. LVM owns famous marks that are distinctive; Haute Diggity Dog has commenced using "Chewy Vuiton," "CV," and designs and colors that are allegedly diluting LVM's marks; and the similarity between Haute Diggity Dog's marks and LVM's marks gives rise to an association between the marks, albeit a parody. The issue for resolution is whether the association between Haute Diggity Dog's marks and LVM's marks is likely to impair the distinctiveness of LVM's famous marks.

In deciding this issue, the district court correctly outlined the six factors to be considered in determining whether dilution by blurring has been shown. But in evaluating the facts of the case, the court did not directly apply those factors it enumerated. It held simply:

> The famous mark's strength is not likely to be blurred by a parody dog toy product. Instead of blurring Plaintiff's mark, the success of the parodic use depends upon the continued association with LOUIS VUITTON. Louis Vuitton Malletier, 464 F.Supp.2d at 505.

The amicus supporting LVM's position in this case contends that the district court, by not applying the statutory factors, misapplied the TDRA to conclude that simply because Haute Diggity Dog's product was a parody meant that "there can be no association with the famous mark as a matter of law." Moreover, the amicus points out correctly that to rule in favor of Haute Diggity Dog, the district court was required to find that the "association" did not impair the distinctiveness of LVM's famous mark.

LVM goes further in its own brief, however, and contends that when a defendant uses an imitation of a famous mark in connection with related goods, a claim of parody cannot preclude liability for dilution. In short, LVM suggests that any use by a third person of an imitation of its famous marks dilutes the famous marks as a matter of law. This contention misconstrues the TDRA. The TDRA prohibits a person from using a junior mark that is likely to dilute (by blurring) the famous mark, and blurring is defined to be an impairment to the famous mark's distinctiveness. "Distinctiveness" in turn refers to the public's recognition that the famous mark identifies a single source of the product using the famous mark.

To determine whether a junior mark is likely to dilute a famous mark through blurring, the TDRA directs the court to consider all factors relevant to the issue, including six factors that are enumerated in the statute:

> (i) The degree of similarity between the mark or trade name and the famous mark.
>
> (ii) The degree of inherent or acquired distinctiveness of the famous mark.
>
> (iii) The extent to which the owner of the famous mark is engaging in substantially exclusive use of the mark.

> (iv) The degree of recognition of the famous mark.
>
> (v) Whether the user of the mark or trade name intended to create an association with the famous mark.
>
> (vi) Any actual association between the mark or trade name and the famous mark.

15 U.S.C.A. § 1125(c)(2)(B).

Not every factor will be relevant in every case, and not every blurring claim will require extensive discussion of the factors. But a trial court must offer a sufficient indication of which factors it has found persuasive and explain why they are persuasive so that the court's decision can be reviewed. The district court did not do this adequately in this case. Nonetheless, after we apply the factors as a matter of law, we reach the same conclusion reached by the district court.

We begin by noting that parody is not automatically a complete defense to a claim of dilution by blurring where the defendant uses the parody as its own designation of source, i.e., as a trademark. Although the TDRA does provide that fair use is a complete defense and allows that a parody can be considered fair use, it does not extend the fair use defense to parodies used as a trademark. As the statute provides:

> The following shall not be actionable as dilution by blurring or dilution by tarnishment under this subsection:
>
> > (A) Any fair use . . . other than as a designation of source for the person's own goods or services, including use in connection with . . . parodying. . . . 15 U.S.C.A. § 1125(c)(3)(A)(ii).

Under the statute's plain language, parodying a famous mark is protected by the fair use defense only if the parody is not "a designation of source for the person's own goods or services."

Thus, it would appear that a defendant's use of a mark as a parody is relevant to the overall question of whether the defendant's use is likely to impair the famous mark's distinctiveness. While a parody intentionally creates an association with the famous mark in order to be a parody, it also intentionally communicates, if it is successful, that it is not the famous mark, but rather a satire of the famous mark. That the defendant is using its mark as a parody is therefore relevant in the consideration of these statutory factors.

Similarly, the degree of similarity between the two marks, the degree of distinctiveness of the famous mark, and its recognizability—are directly implicated by consideration of the fact that the defendant's mark is a successful parody. Indeed, by making the famous mark an object of the parody, a successful parody might actually enhance the famous mark's distinctiveness by making it an icon. The brunt of the joke becomes yet more famous.

In sum, while a defendant's use of a parody as a mark does not support a "fair use" defense, it may be considered in determining whether the plaintiff-owner of a famous mark has proved its claim that the defendant's use of a parody mark is likely to impair the distinctiveness of the famous mark.

In the case before us, it is readily apparent that LVM's marks are distinctive, famous, and strong. It may not be too strong to refer to these famous marks as icons of high fashion.

While the establishment of these facts satisfies essential elements of LVM's dilution claim, the facts impose on LVM an increased burden to demonstrate that the distinctiveness of its famous marks is likely to be impaired by a successful parody. Even as Haute Diggity Dog's parody mimics the famous mark, it communicates simultaneously that it is not the famous mark, but is only satirizing it. And because the famous mark is particularly strong and distinctive, it becomes more likely that a parody will not impair the distinctiveness of the mark. In short, as Haute Diggity Dog's "Chewy Vuiton" marks are a successful parody, we conclude that they will not blur the distinctiveness of the famous mark as a unique identifier of its source.

It is important to note, however, that this might not be true if the parody is so similar to the famous mark that it likely could be construed as actual use of the famous mark itself. If Haute Diggity Dog used the actual marks of LVM (as a parody or otherwise), it could dilute LVM's marks by blurring, regardless of whether Haute Diggity Dog's use was confusingly similar, whether it was in competition with LVM, or whether LVM sustained actual injury. Thus, "the use of DUPONT shoes, BUICK aspirin, and KODAK pianos would be actionable" under the TDRA because the unauthorized use of the famous marks themselves on unrelated goods might diminish the capacity of these trademarks to distinctively identify a single source. Moseley, 537 U.S. at 431, 123 S.Ct. 1115 (quoting H.R.Rep. No. 104–374, at 3 (1995)). This is true even though a consumer would be unlikely to confuse the manufacturer of KODAK film with the hypothetical producer of KODAK pianos.

But in this case, Haute Diggity Dog mimicked the famous marks; it did not come so close to them as to destroy the success of its parody and, more importantly, to diminish the LVM marks' capacity to identify a single source. Haute Diggity Dog designed a pet chew toy to imitate and suggest, but not use, the marks of a high-fashion LOUIS VUITTON handbag. It used "Chewy Vuiton" to mimic "LOUIS VUITTON"; it used "CV" to mimic "LV"; and it adopted imperfectly the items of LVM's designs. We conclude that these uses by Haute Diggity Dog were not so similar as to be likely to impair the distinctiveness of LVM's famous marks.

Haute Diggity Dog intentionally associated its marks, but only partially and certainly imperfectly, so as to convey the simultaneous message that it was not in fact a source of LVM products. Rather, as a parody, it separated itself from the LVM marks in order to make fun of them.

In sum, when considering the relevant factors to determine whether blurring is likely to occur in this case, we readily come to the conclusion, as did the district court, that LVM has failed to make out a case of trademark dilution by blurring by failing to establish that the distinctiveness of its marks was likely to be impaired by Haute Diggity Dog's marketing and sale of its "Chewy Vuiton" products.

B

LVM's claim for dilution by tarnishment does not require an extended discussion. To establish its claim for dilution by tarnishment, LVM must show, in lieu of blurring, that Haute Diggity Dog's use of the "Chewy Vuiton" mark on dog toys harms the reputation of the LOUIS VUITTON mark and LVM's other marks. LVM argues that the possibility that a dog could choke on a "Chewy Vuiton" toy causes this harm. LVM has, however, provided no record support for its assertion. It relies only on speculation about whether a dog could choke on the chew toys and a logical concession that a $10 dog toy made in China was of "inferior quality" to the $1190 LOUIS VUITTON handbag. The speculation begins with LVM's assertion in its brief that "defendant Woofie's admitted that 'Chewy Vuiton' products pose a choking hazard for some dogs. Having prejudged the defendant's mark to be a parody, the district court made light of this admission in its opinion, and utterly failed to give it the weight it deserved," citing to a page in the district court's opinion where the court states:

> At oral argument, plaintiff provided only a flimsy theory that a pet may someday choke on a Chewy Vuiton squeak toy and incite the wrath of a confused consumer against LOUIS VUITTON. Louis Vuitton Malletier, 464 F.Supp.2d at 505.

The court was referring to counsel's statement during oral argument that the owner of Woofie's stated that "she would not sell this product to certain types of dogs because there is a danger they would tear it open and choke on it." There is no record support, however, that any dog has choked on a pet chew toy, such as a "Chewy Vuiton" toy, or that there is any basis from which to conclude that a dog would likely choke on such a toy.

LVM failed to demonstrate a claim for dilution by tarnishment.

* * *

The judgment of the district court is

AFFIRMED.

Notes

1. Is the concept of trademark tarnishment more readily understood than dilution by blurring? Does the question of dilution depend upon the context of the infringement? Consider *Polo Ralph Lauren L.P. v. Schuman*, 46 U.S.P.Q.2d 1046, 1048 (S.D. Tex. 1998); *Mattel, Inc. v. Internet Dimensions Inc.*, 55 U.S.P.Q.2d 1620,

1627 (S.D.N.Y. 2000); *Dallas Cowboys Cheerleaders, Inc. v. Pussycat Cinema, Ltd.*, 467 F. Supp. 366, 377 (S.D.N.Y. 1979) with *Nike, Inc. v. Peter Maher and Patricia Hoyt Maher*, 100 U.S.P.Q.2d 1018 (TTAB 2011), the preceding case and the following case.

2. Should the commercial or noncommercial nature of the particular use impact the dilution by blurring inquiry and, if so, how?

Consider how a style name may play into the analysis of fair use.

Hard Candy, LLC v. Anastasia Beverly Hills, Inc.

921 F.3d 1343 (11th Cir. 2019)

MARCUS, Circuit Judge.

* * *

I.

Hard Candy, LLC, is a cosmetics company headquartered in Hollywood, Florida. The company's predecessor first filed a trademark application for the HARD CANDY mark in 1995. Since then, Hard Candy has continuously used the HARD CANDY mark in connection with the sale of cosmetics.[1] Hard Candy does not produce cosmetics itself; it licenses the mark to a third-party cosmetics producer, NuWorld Corporation, which makes nail polish, eye shadow, lip gloss, and various facial beauty products that are sold under the Hard Candy name. These items are sold exclusively at Wal-Mart stores and on Wal-Mart's website, and have generated sales in excess of $36 million each year since 2011.

Anastasia Beverly Hills, Inc., a California-based corporation, is also in the cosmetics business. In December 2015, Anastasia announced the release of a new edition in its line of "Glow Kits," which are flip-open makeup palettes containing four different shades of facial highlighter. The Gleam Glow Kit included the words "hard candy" in capital letters on the back and inside of the package to designate a peach-pink shade of makeup. Anastasia says that it chose this name because the product had a "shimmer" that reminded the developer of candies that her grandmother gave her when she was young. The developer testified that she was aware of Hard Candy, LLC, as a seller of nail polish in the 1990s, but she was not aware of the company's continued existence when she came up with the name.

The following pictures show the front, back, and inside of the kit offered by Anastasia:

1. Hard Candy owns at least fourteen federally registered trademarks. See Registration Nos. 1,987,262; 2,343,732; 2,552,029; 2,666,792; 3,695,602; 2,362,340; 2,567,186; 2,150,397; 2,666,793; 4,218,371; 4,735,879; 4,818,389; 2,059,480; and 4,713,229.

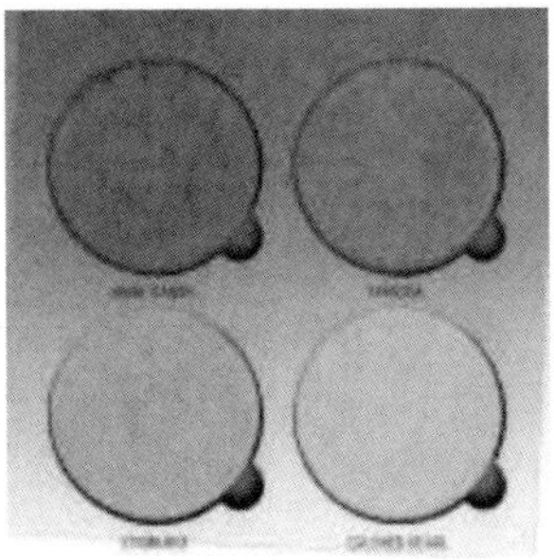

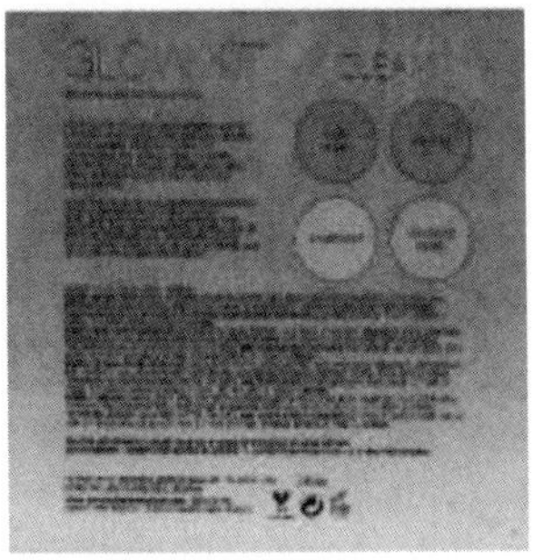

The day after Anastasia announced the release of the Gleam Glow Kit, Hard Candy sent Anastasia a cease and desist letter asserting that it had infringed on its trademark. Anastasia's owner, Anastasia Soare, attempted to call the CEO of Hard Candy but she was unable to make contact; Anastasia's and Hard Candy's attorneys also exchanged emails without resolving the issue before discussions broke off. Anastasia went on to sell the kit—with the "hard candy" shade—online and in various retail stores, including Macy's, Ulta, and Sephora. The words "hard candy" appeared in Anastasia's marketing materials and social media posts, as well as on the product itself. In documents provided to retailers, the company described the shade as a "mood-changing golden peach with a pink pearl reflective finish." The Gleam Glow Kit was on the market from December 2015 until August 2016, consistent with Anastasia's initial plan to make it a limited-edition product.

Hard Candy filed a complaint in the United States District Court for the Southern District of Florida against Anastasia, claiming trademark infringement under § 32(a) of the Lanham Act, 15 U.S.C. § 1114(1); unfair competition under § 43(a) of the Lanham Act, 15 U.S.C. § 1125(a); common law trademark infringement; and common law unfair competition. Hard Candy sought an accounting and the disgorgement of Anastasia's profits, statutory damages, a permanent injunction barring Anastasia's use of its mark, declaratory relief, and fees and costs. The complaint included a request for actual damages, but, notably, Hard Candy dropped this application before trial. The district court then struck Hard Candy's jury trial demand because all of the remaining remedies were equitable in nature.

To prevail on each of its claims, Hard Candy had to establish that Anastasia's use of the words "hard candy" created a likelihood of confusion. *See Tally-Ho, Inc. v.*

Coast Cmty. Coll. Dist., 889 F.2d 1018, 1026 & n.14 (11th Cir. 1989) (noting that the elements of trademark infringement under common law and the Lanham Act "are the same," and that "an unfair competition claim based only upon alleged trademark infringement is practically identical to an infringement claim"). Applying our seven-factor likelihood of confusion test, the district court determined that Hard Candy had not met its burden. The court also concluded that even if Hard Candy could establish infringement, Anastasia had made out a fair use defense because it used the term "hard candy" in good faith as a description of the product, not as a mark.

DC holding

This appeal followed.

* * *

III.

Hard Candy also challenges the district court's resolution of its claims on the merits. "After a bench trial, we review the district court's conclusions of law *de novo* and the district court's factual findings for clear error." *Proudfoot Consulting Co. v. Gordon*, 576 F.3d 1223, 1230 (11th Cir. 2009). Findings as to whether a plaintiff has ultimately shown a likelihood of confusion, as to each of the factors, and as to the elements of the fair use defense are subject only to clear error review. *N. Am. Med. Corp. v. Axiom Worldwide, Inc.*, 522 F.3d 1211, 1220 (11th Cir. 2008) (likelihood of confusion); *Sands, Taylor & Wood Co. v. Quaker Oats Co.*, 978 F.2d 947, 952 (7th Cir. 1992) (fair use).

A.

We begin with the likelihood of confusion. The district court applied our seven-factor test and concluded that Hard Candy had not shown a likelihood of confusion. On review, "[t]he real question is whether the court's ultimate determination about the 'likelihood of confusion' was correct." *Univ. of Ga. Athletic Ass'n v. Laite*, 756 F.2d 1535, 1543 (11th Cir. 1985); *see also Safeway Stores, Inc. v. Safeway Disc. Drugs, Inc.*, 675 F.2d 1160, 1164 n.3 (11th Cir. 1982) ("Our review . . . is governed by the clearly erroneous test even though the court's analysis of the factors relevant to a finding of likelihood of confusion was incomplete."). Accordingly, "we may affirm an ultimate finding on the issue of confusion that is not clearly erroneous, even when the district court fails to consider all seven factors" of the test or errs in its analysis of any one. *See Wesco Mfg., Inc.*, 833 F.2d at 1489.

Our precedent sets out a seven-factor test to determine whether a purportedly infringing product creates a likelihood of consumer confusion. We look to the:

> (1) type of mark, (2) similarity of mark, (3) similarity of the products the marks represent, (4) similarity of the parties' retail outlets and customers, (5) similarity of advertising media used, (6) defendant's intent and (7) actual confusion.

Test

Lone Star Steakhouse & Saloon, Inc. v. Longhorn Steaks, Inc., 122 F.3d 1379, 1382 (11th Cir. 1997). On summary judgment, the court determined that three of them—similarity of products, similarity of trade channels and customers, and similarity of advertising—favored Hard Candy. There was no dispute that both companies sell cosmetics products online and in retail stores, their customers are primarily women between the ages of 18 and 35, and both advertise their products through trade shows, social media, and traditional print media. The court rejected Anastasia's proposed distinction between the "high-end" and "low-end" segments of the cosmetics market.

The district court then held a three-day bench trial. Afterwards, the court determined that the mark was "arbitrary" since it bears no relationship to the products, which meant that the mark was "strong" and that the type-of-mark factor weighed in Hard Candy's favor; that the similarity-of-mark factor favored Anastasia, because it was not using "hard candy" as a mark; that Anastasia did not intentionally infringe on the mark; and that there was no evidence of actual confusion. Viewing the evidence as a whole, the trial court determined that Hard Candy had not established a likelihood of confusion and issued a decision to that effect from the bench. The record indicates that there was ample factual evidence to support the trial court's findings and, indeed, that the court weighed each of the factors with great care.

Hard Candy responds with three legal arguments; none of them are persuasive. For starters, Hard Candy asserts that the district court erred by finding that the "similarity of mark" factor favored Anastasia. The district court concluded that "Anastasia's use of 'Hard Candy' does not create a likelihood of confusion on this factor [because] while Anastasia uses the same words, all in capital letters, the Court must consider the overall impression created by the use of the mark as a whole, rather than comparing the individual features, and . . . the use creates a different overall impression." Hard Candy, in essence, claims that the trial court should have stopped at the point that it recognized that Anastasia's use of the term "hard candy" was formally identical to the company's mark—HARD CANDY, in capital letters—and concluded that the factor weighed in its favor.

But the trial court must "compare[] the marks and consider[] the overall impressions that the marks create, including the sound, appearance, and *manner in which they are used.*" *Frehling Enters., Inc. v. Int'l Select Grp., Inc.*, 192 F.3d 1330, 1337 (11th Cir. 1999) (emphasis added); *John H. Harland Co. v. Clarke Checks, Inc.*, 711 F.2d 966, 975 (11th Cir. 1983) ("This consideration includes a comparison of the appearance, sound and meaning of the marks, as well as the manner in which the marks are used."). The district court looked to the overall impression created by the Gleam Glow Kit—the words "HARD CANDY" appeared only on the back and inside of the kit, "nam[ing] one shade of a product that is otherwise clearly and prominently featured as an Anastasia Beverly Hills mark." In this way, the district court concluded that Anastasia was using the words merely "to describe a shade," and for that reason it found that this factor favored Anastasia.

The district court's analysis is fully consistent with our precedent. In *John H. Harland Co.*, we considered as part of this analysis things like the placement of the mark, the mark's usage to label a specific part of the product, and the size of the print. 711 F.2d at 975-76. Hard Candy has provided no case law holding that the similarity-of-mark factor bars consideration of whether the alleged infringer was using the words as a mark. The point of the similarity-of-mark analysis "is that the closer the marks are, the more likely reasonable consumers will mistake the source of the product that each mark represents." *Frehling Enters., Inc.*, 192 F.3d at 1337. For that reason, "[t]he probability of this potential confusion is the touchstone." Id. Thus, although Anastasia used words that are identical to Hard Candy's mark, it was reasonable for the district court to determine that Anastasia was not using the words in a "manner" likely to cause confusion as to the source of the goods.

Second, Hard Candy claims that the district court erred by giving "substantial and overwhelming weight to Anastasia's lack of intent to infringe." Br. for Plaintiff-Appellants at 49. Hard Candy argues that we should follow courts outside this Circuit that have said that "[i]ntent . . . is an issue whose resolution may benefit only the cause of a [plaintiff], not of an alleged infringer." *Daddy's Junky Music Stores, Inc. v. Big Daddy's Family Music Ctr.*, 109 F.3d 275, 287 (6th Cir. 1997); *see also Beacon Mut. Ins. Co. v. OneBeacon Ins. Grp.*, 376 F.3d 8, 19 (1st Cir. 2004). The problem with the argument is that the factual predicate is not reflected in the record. The district court never said that it was giving any affirmative (let alone overwhelming) weight to its finding that Anastasia lacked intent to infringe. The court concluded its discussion this way: "And for all of these reasons, and the cases I've cited, I find that Anastasia did not intend to infringe on the mark and was not intentionally blind after receiving the cease and desist." It did not say that this factor weighed in Anastasia's favor. Hard Candy seems to assume that the district court gave it too much weight merely because the issue took up more space in the ruling, but there is no indication in the record that Anastasia's intent received undue consideration.

Finally, Hard Candy argues that the district court placed too much weight on the lack of a showing of actual confusion. We have said that evidence of actual confusion "is not necessary to a finding of likelihood of confusion." *John H. Harland Co.*, 711 F.2d at 978. Hard Candy says that the district court erred by giving the lack of actual confusion evidence "substantial weight," since this evidence is often difficult to produce and the product was on the market for only eight months.

Our cases have often recognized actual confusion as one of the most important factors. *Fla. Int'l Univ. Bd. of Trs. v. Fla. Nat'l Univ., Inc.*, 830 F.3d 1242, 1264 (11th Cir. 2016) ("the best evidence of a likelihood of confusion"); *Caliber Auto. Liquidators, Inc. v. Premier Chrysler, Jeep, Dodge, LLC*, 605 F.3d 931, 936 (11th Cir. 2010) ("the most weighty consideration"); *Lone Star Steakhouse & Saloon, Inc.*, 122 F.3d at 1382 (one of "the two most important factors"); *John H. Harland Co.*, 711 F.2d at 978 ("the best evidence of likelihood of confusion"). "The presence or absence of actual confusion can be highly effective in showing a high, or a low, likelihood of confusion if there has been ample opportunity for consumer confusion." *Nabisco, Inc. v. PF Brands, Inc.*, 191 F.3d 208, 228 (2d Cir. 1999) (emphasis omitted). "If consumers have been exposed to two allegedly similar trademarks in the marketplace for an adequate period of time and no actual confusion is detected either by survey or in actual reported instances of confusion, that can be powerful indication that the junior trademark does not cause a meaningful likelihood of confusion." *Id.*

In this case, there was enough opportunity for confusion to make the absence of any evidence significant. Uncontroverted testimony at trial established that Anastasia sold 248,075 Gleam Glow Kits, totaling over $5 million in revenue. The product was posted on Anastasia's corporate social media accounts, which have millions of followers. And still, Hard Candy did not produce any evidence that a customer was ever actually confused about the source of the Gleam Glow Kit. A reasonable person could conclude that the lack of evidence is at least probative of the conclusion that there was no likelihood of confusion—hundreds of thousands of cosmetics consumers purchased the allegedly infringing kit, several times more likely saw it on store shelves or online, and still there is no evidence that anyone, anywhere, was ever confused about whether Anastasia or Hard Candy was responsible for the product. Hard Candy hasn't established clear error here either.

In sum, the record does not suggest that the district court committed clear error as to any of its findings, and it does not show clear error as to the court's ultimate conclusion that Hard Candy had not shown a likelihood of confusion. Even if we were to accept one or two of Hard Candy's arguments—and on this record, we don't—that would not compel reversal. "[A] district court's error in its analysis of one of the subsidiary factors in the likelihood of confusion test is not enough to allow us to overturn the district court's decision." *Fla. Int'l Univ. Bd. of Trs.*, 830 F.3d at 1255 (internal quotation marks omitted). Our review of the record, taken as a whole, does not leave us "with the definite and firm conviction that a mistake has been committed" about the district court's basic finding that there was no likelihood of confusion. *See United States v. United States Gypsum Co.*, 333 U.S. 364, 395, 68 S. Ct. 525, 92 L. Ed. 746 (1948).

B.

Hard Candy also challenges the district court's conclusion that Anastasia made out a fair use defense to infringement. A defendant is entitled to the fair use defense if it establishes that it used the allegedly infringing term "(1) other than as a mark, (2) in a descriptive sense, and (3) in good faith." *Int'l Stamp Art, Inc. v. U.S. Postal Serv.*, 456 F.3d 1270, 1274 (11th Cir. 2006) (internal quotation marks omitted). Hard Candy challenges the district court's finding as to the second element, arguing that the district court erred "by completely disregarding the central requirement that whether a trademark is being used in a 'descriptive sense' starts and ends with consumer perception." Br. for Plaintiff-Appellants at 41.

"The 'fair-use' defense, in essence, forbids a trademark registrant to appropriate a descriptive term for [its] exclusive use and so prevent others from accurately describing a characteristic of their goods." *Int'l Stamp Art, Inc.*, 456 F.3d at 1274 (quoting *Soweco, Inc. v. Shell Oil Co.*, 617 F.2d 1178, 1185 (5th Cir. 1980)). This Court has not elaborated on what it means to use a mark "in a descriptive sense."

We have, however, explained that a descriptive mark "identifies a characteristic or quality of an article or service as, for example, its color, odor, function, dimensions, or ingredients." *Soweco, Inc.*, 617 F.2d at 1183 (citation and quotations omitted). The Seventh Circuit has interpreted the fair use element of use "in a descriptive sense" in a roughly similar way, explaining that "it is not necessary that a descriptive term depict the [product] itself, but only that the term refer to a characteristic of the [product]." *Sands, Taylor & Wood Co.*, 978 F.2d at 952.

To the extent that Hard Candy argues that the district court erred by not considering how a hypothetical consumer would perceive the use of the mark, we think it has ignored what the district court said in its ruling. The court looked to "the overall context; the lettering, the type, the style, the size, [and] the visual placement" of the words on the product. It accepted the argument that "hard candy" was used in a descriptive sense because "it was used to describe the sheen" of the makeup shade that the term labeled. Anastasia introduced evidence that cosmetics companies regularly describe shades with words that are not literal color descriptions, like the other three shades in the kit named "Starburst," "Mimosa," and "Crushed Pearl." The district court was attempting to discern how a reasonable consumer of cosmetics would perceive Anastasia's use of the mark, not relying purely on Anastasia's subjective intent, contrary to Hard Candy's assertion. And to the extent Hard Candy argues that the district court should have required Anastasia to introduce evidence of actual consumer perception, that proposition has no support in the law. *See, e.g., Sorensen v. WD-40 Co.*, 792 F.3d 712, 725 (7th Cir. 2015) (upholding fair use defense without any such evidence); *Cosmetically Sealed Indus., Inc. v. Chesebrough-Pond's USA Co.*, 125 F.3d 28, 30 (2d Cir. 1997) (same). We are hard-pressed to find clear error of any kind.

IV.

The long and the short of it is that Hard Candy has failed to convince us that the district court erred in its resolution of this case. The historical evidence reveals that the particular remedy sought by Hard Candy—an accounting and disgorgement of Anastasia's profits as an alleged infringer—is a creature of equity. For that reason the Seventh Amendment's guarantee of a jury trial does not apply. On the merits, we can discern no error in the district court's resolution of Hard Candy's claims, and, accordingly, affirm.

AFFIRMED.

Notes

1. Are you convinced by the way the Court categorizes Anastasia's use of the mark as descriptive?

2. At what point does a style name or color cross over into the realm of becoming a trademark for the brand?

3. Do you think that this opinion will complicate or clarify style name clearances for brands?

Legislative history becomes increasingly important as appeals span different laws. Consider the next case, which depends on whether a legal standard survived Congress' enactment of the Trademark Dilution Revision Act of 2006 ("TDRA").

Levi Strauss & Co. v. Abercrombie & Fitch Trading Co.

633 F.3d 1158 (9th Cir. 2011)

RIPPLE, Senior Circuit Judge.

Levi Strauss & Co. ("Levi Strauss") seeks review of a district court judgment that Abercrombie & Fitch Trading Co. ("Abercrombie") did not dilute Levi Strauss's trademarked "Arcuate" design in violation of the Trademark Dilution Revision Act of 2006 ("TDRA"), 15 U.S.C. § 1125(c). Levi Strauss maintains that the district court applied an incorrect legal standard in evaluating its dilution claim, namely that the junior mark be "identical or nearly identical" to the senior one. We agree with Levi Strauss that the "identical or nearly identical" standard did not survive Congress's enactment of the TDRA and that the district court's use of the incorrect standard was not harmless error. Accordingly, we reverse the judgment of the district court and remand the case for further proceedings consistent with this opinion.

Background

A. The Stitched Designs

Levi Strauss created, and began selling, blue jeans in the 1870s. Since 1873, the company has stitched the back pocket of its jeans with two connecting arches that meet in the center of the pocket; Levi Strauss holds a federally registered trademark on this "Arcuate" design. Sales of garments bearing the Arcuate mark have accounted for more than ninety-five percent of Levi Strauss's revenue over the past thirty years, totaling roughly fifty billion dollars. Levi Strauss actively monitors use of competing stitching designs and enforces its trademark rights against perceived infringers.

In 2006, Abercrombie began using a stitching design on the back pockets of its jeans that, according to Levi Strauss, "incorporates the distinctive arcing elements of the Arcuate trademark." Appellant's Br. 4. Abercrombie's "Ruehl" design consists of two less-pronounced arches that are connected by a "dipsy doodle," which resembles the mathematical sign for infinity. The design on the Abercrombie jeans sits lower on the pocket than Levi Strauss's Arcuate design.

B. District Court Proceedings

In 2007, Levi Strauss brought an action against Abercrombie for trademark infringement, unfair competition and trademark dilution under both federal and California state law. Before trial, Levi Strauss dropped its state-law trademark dilution claim, and it withdrew its claim for monetary relief on its federal dilution claim. Consequently, Levi Strauss's federal trademark dilution claim, for which it sought only injunctive relief, was tried before *1160 the court with advisory rulings from the jury.

During trial, Levi Strauss presented the testimony of Dr. Sanjay Sood. Dr. Sood conducted a survey to evaluate whether women associated Abercrombie's Ruehl design with Levi Strauss. Dr. Sood's "Confusion Survey" revealed that "[a]pproximately 30% of all respondents identified the Ruehl jeans as made, sponsored or endorsed by the same company that made the LEVI'S® jeans, as compared to lower percentages for the 'control' jeans." *Levi Strauss & Co. v. Abercrombie & Fitch Trading Co.,* No. C 07-03752 JSW, 2009 WL 1082175, at 4 (N.D.Cal. Apr. 22, 2009). Dr. Sood testified that "the Ruehl design would erode the distinctiveness of the Arcuate mark, in light of what he opined was a significant level of confusion between the Ruehl jeans and the [Levi Strauss] jeans." *Id.* Dr. Sood also testified concerning a "Recognition Survey" that he had conducted. According to Dr. Sood, the survey revealed that "approximately 32% to 35% of the respondents actually associated the Arcuate mark with [Levi Strauss]." *Id.* at 5.

For its part, Abercrombie presented the testimony of Dr. Gerald Ford, who had been engaged in commercial marketing research for more than three decades and had offered expert testimony in over 50 trademark cases. Dr. Ford testified that Dr. Sood's confusion survey was not conducted according to generally accepted and standard practices; as a result, the survey was "'so flawed that it render[ed] the survey results' and Dr. Sood's conclusions 'meaningless.'" *Id.* (internal citations omitted). Nevertheless, Dr. Ford acknowledged that, "[i]f a likelihood of confusion survey is conducted in a valid and reliable manner, a finding that ten percent or more of the population is confused is problematic to a trademark owner." *Id.* Dr. Ford opined that Dr. Sood's recognition survey was problematic; specifically, it "was flawed[ ] because it did not control for spurious recognition, used ambiguous questions, lacked an appropriate control cell, and suffered from order bias." *Id.*

As part of its deliberations, the district court requested that the jury provide advisory rulings on factual issues related to Levi Strauss's federal dilution claims. With respect to the elements of the dilution claim, the court asked the jury to answer the following question: "Is Abercrombie's Ruehl design identical or nearly identical to the Arcuate trademark?" ER 67. Although the jury later determined that the Arcuate trademark was famous and distinctive, it found that the marks were not identical or nearly identical and also determined that the Arcuate trademark was not likely to be diluted by the Ruehl design.

C. Findings of Fact and Conclusions of Law

On April 22, 2009, the district court entered judgment in favor of Abercrombie on Levi Strauss's federal dilution claim. In its findings of fact, the district court noted that, "[w]ith the exception of visual depictions of the two designs, Dr. Sood's testimony regarding the results of the Confusion Survey was [Levi Strauss]'s only evidence that the Ruehl design was *identical or nearly identical* to the Arcuate mark." *Levi Strauss & Co.,* 2009 WL 1082175, at 5 (emphasis added). Although the district court acknowledged that Dr. Sood's survey suggested confusion among thirty percent of the participants, the court determined that Dr. Ford's critique of

Dr. Sood's methodology was persuasive and that his testimony was more reliable than that offered by Dr. Sood.

Turning to its conclusions of law, the court first reviewed the elements of a claim under the TDRA, 15 U.S.C. § 1125(c). The court stated:

> To prevail on its dilution claim, [Levi Strauss] has the burden of proving by a preponderance of evidence the following elements: (a) that [Levi Strauss] is the owner of a trademark that is famous; (b) that the famous mark is distinctive, either inherently or through acquired distinctiveness; (c) that [Abercrombie] is making or has made use in commerce of an *identical or nearly identical* trademark, in this case the Ruehl design; (d) that [Abercrombie]'s use of its Ruehl design began after [Levi Strauss]'s Arcuate mark became famous; and (e) that [Abercrombie]'s use of its Ruehl design is likely to cause dilution by blurring of [Levi Strauss]'s Arcuate mark. 15 U.S.C. § 1125(c); *Jada Toys, Inc. v. Mattel, Inc.*, 518 F.3d 628, 634 (9th Cir. 200[8]).

Levi Strauss & Co., 2009 WL 1082175, at 7 (emphasis added). The district court noted that the advisory jury had not found that the Ruehl design and the Arcuate mark were "*identical or nearly identical*," a standard that required that "the two marks . . . be similar enough that a significant segment of the target group of customers sees the two marks as *essentially the same*." *Id.* (emphasis added).

After setting forth this standard for similarity, a standard which "'is more stringent than in the infringement context,'" *id.* at 8 (quoting *adidas-America, Inc. v. Payless Shoesource, Inc.*, 546 F.Supp.2d. 1029, 1060 (D.Ore.2008)), the court observed that, although the evidence showed that Levi Strauss had "expended significant amounts of money advertising the Arcuate mark," this was not "a case where the two marks at issue involve only minor differences," *id.* The district court then reviewed aspects of the Arcuate mark and the Ruehl design and observed that "[t]his evidence demonstrates that a significant segment of the target group of customers would not view the marks as *essentially the same*." *Id.* (emphasis added). It concluded that, consistent with the advisory jury's finding, Levi Strauss "has not established that [Abercrombie] is making commercial use of a mark that *is identical or nearly identical* to the Arcuate mark." *Id.* at 9 (emphasis added). The court then concluded:

> As noted, the test for similarity of the marks is more stringent in the dilution context than for likelihood of confusion purposes, and the two marks must be "*essentially the same mark*." For the reasons set forth above, the Court finds that the Ruehl design and the Arcuate mark are not visually similar. Furthermore, as set forth above, the Court does not find the results of Dr. Sood's survey to be entitled to any great weight. Thus, [Levi Strauss] has not put forth persuasive evidence of actual association between the Arcuate mark and the Ruehl design. Therefore, these factors weigh in [Abercrombie]'s favor and against a finding of likelihood of dilution.
>
> * * *
>
> Having considered all of the evidence, even if the degree of inherent or acquired distinctiveness of the Arcuate mark and the degree of recognition of the mark

DC test

new holding

> weigh in [Levi Strauss]'s favor, the Court finds that those factors do not outweigh the factors that weigh in [Abercrombie]'s favor. Accordingly, the Court concludes, consistent with the advisory jury's finding, that [Levi Strauss] has not met its burden to establish by a preponderance of the evidence that the Ruehl design is likely to cause dilution by blurring of the Arcuate mark.

Id. (quoting *Thane Int'l, Inc. v. Trek Bicycle Corp.*, 305 F.3d 894, 907 (9th Cir.2002); footnote omitted; emphasis added). The district court therefore entered judgment in favor of Abercrombie.

Discussion

Levi Strauss submits that the district court erred in requiring it to establish that its mark was identical or nearly identical to the Ruehl design. Levi Strauss looks to the plain language of 15 U.S.C. § 1125(c) and notes that the terms "identical or nearly identical" appear nowhere in the language of the statute. The statute, it maintains, does not require a prima facie showing of substantial similarity before a district court balances the dilution factors listed in § 1125(c)(2)(B). Instead, "degree of similarity" is one of several factors that a district court must balance in order to determine whether dilution has occurred and whether, therefore, a plaintiff is entitled to injunctive relief.

Abercrombie, by contrast, bases its argument not on the language of the statute but, instead, on the case law of this court. It argues that, even after the passage of the TDRA, this court thrice has determined that a junior mark must be "identical or nearly identical" to that of the senior user in order for a trademark-dilution plaintiff to be entitled to relief. *See Perfumebay.com Inc. v. eBay, Inc.*, 506 F.3d 1165 (9th Cir.2007); *Jada Toys, Inc. v. Mattel, Inc.*, 518 F.3d 628 (9th Cir.2008); *Visa Int'l Serv. Ass'n v. JSL Corp.*, 610 F.3d 1088 (9th Cir.2010).

To properly evaluate the parties' contentions, we must look at the origins of the "identical or nearly identical" standard, how it has been employed and whether it remains viable after the enactment of the TDRA.

A. Origin of the "Identical or Nearly Identical" Standard

The "identical or nearly identical" requirement traces its roots in this circuit to *Playboy Enterprises, Inc. v. Welles*, 279 F.3d 796 (9th Cir.2002). In that case, a former "Playmate of the Year," Terri Welles, had used this descriptive on a website devoted to the sale of her pictures and to the promotion of her services as a spokeswoman. Playboy sued Welles on various theories, including a federal trademark dilution claim under the prior statute. We determined that most of Welles's use of "Playmate of the Year" were nominative uses and, therefore, excepted from coverage. However, Welles's use of the abbreviation "PMOY" on the wallpaper of her site was not nominative, and, therefore was "not excepted from the anti-dilution provisions." *Playboy Enters.*, 279 F.3d at 806. As a result, we reversed the judgment in favor of Welles on the dilution issue and gave the following instructions to the district court:

> We note that if the district court determines that "PMOY" is not entitled to trademark protection, PEI's claim for dilution must fail. The trademarked term, "Playmate

> of the Year" is not *identical or nearly identical* to the term "PMOY." Therefore, *use of the term "PMOY" cannot, as a matter of law, dilute the trademark "Playmate of the Year."*

Id. (emphasis added; footnote omitted).

Our authority for the "identical or nearly identical" language employed in *Playboy Enterprises* was *Luigino's, Inc. v. Stouffer Corp.,* 170 F.3d 827, 832 (8th Cir.1999), and J. Thomas McCarthy, McCarthy on Trademarks and Unfair Competition § 24:90.2 (4th ed.2001). *See Playboy Enters.,* 279 F.3d at 806 n. 41. In *Luigino's,* the Eighth Circuit held that, "[t]o support an action for dilution by blurring, 'the marks must at least be similar enough that a significant segment of the two target groups of customers sees the two marks as essentially the same.'" 170 F.3d at 832 (quoting J. Thomas McCarthy, McCarthy on Trademarks and Unfair Competition § 24:90.1, at 24-145 (4th ed.1998)). In support of this proposition, the Eighth Circuit not only relied on McCarthy on Trademarks and Unfair Competition, but also *Mead Data Central, Inc. v. Toyota Motor Sales, U.S.A., Inc.,* 875 F.2d 1026, 1029 (2d Cir.1989).

Tracing the ancestry of the standard a step further, *Mead Data Central* involved a trademark dilution claim brought under a New York state statute. According to the Second Circuit, the legislative history of that act stated "the purpose of the statute as preventing 'the whittling away of an established trade-mark's selling power and value through *its* unauthorized use by others upon dissimilar products.'" *Mead Data Cent.,* 875 F.2d at 1028 (quoting 1954 N.Y. Legis. Ann. 49; emphasis added by the Second Circuit). The court continued:

> If we were to interpret literally the italicized word "its", we would limit statutory violations to the unauthorized use of the identical established mark. . . . However, since the use of obvious simulations or markedly similar marks might have the same diluting effect as would an appropriation of the original mark, the concept of exact identity has been broadened to that of substantial similarity. Nevertheless, in keeping with the original intent of the statute, the similarity must be substantial before the doctrine of dilution may be applied.

Id. at 1028-29 (internal citations omitted). The court stopped short of requiring that "the marks in question . . . be sufficiently similar that confusion may be created as between the marks themselves." *Id.* at 1029. Instead, it held that "the marks must be 'very' or 'substantially' similar and that, absent such similarity, there can be no viable claim of dilution." *Id.*

Thus, the requirement of identity, or substantial similarity, pre-dates the adoption of the FTDA in 1996 and has its origins in state dilution law, specifically that of the State of New York.

B. Case Law Employing the "Identical or Nearly Identical" Standard

After *Playboy Enterprises,* we again employed the "identical or nearly identical" formulation in *Thane International, Inc. v. Trek Bicycle Corp.,* 305 F.3d 894 (9th Cir.2002). In *Thane,* we grappled with the issue whether Thane's use of "OrbiTrek" diluted Trek's trademarked name. In considering the "Identity of the

Marks," the court gave a more thorough explanation for its adoption of the "identical or nearly identical" standard:

> We begin from the recently-established requirement that for a dilution claim to succeed, the mark used by the alleged diluter must be identical, or nearly identical, to the protected mark. *Playboy Enterprises,* 279 F.3d at 805. Such a requirement comports with *the statutory language, the four-part dilution test derived from that language* outlined in *Panavision Int'l L.P. v. Toeppen,* 141 F.3d 1316, 1324 (9th Cir.1998) and *Avery Dennison* [*Corp. v. Sumpton,* 189 F.3d 868, 874 (9th Cir.1999)],[] and *with the statute's legislative history and purposes.*
>
> The statute establishes that the junior user, to be liable for dilution, must use "a mark or trade name . . . after *the* mark has become famous." § 1125(c)(1) (emphasis added). As articulated in *Panavision* and *Avery Dennison,* the test for dilution similarly provides that to make out an antidilution cause of action, a plaintiff must show that "*its* mark is famous" and "the defendant is making commercial use of *the* mark in commerce." *Avery Dennison,* 189 F.3d at 874 (emphasis added); *see Panavision,* 141 F.3d at 1324; *see also Mattel, Inc. v. MCA Records, Inc.,* 296 F.3d 894, 903 (9th Cir.2002) ("'Dilution' refers to the 'whittling away of the value of a trademark' when *it's* used to identify different products.") (emphasis added) (citation omitted). These locutions indicate that the defendant must use essentially the *same* mark, not just a similar one.

Id. at 905 (emphasis in first paragraph added). Thus, *Thane* tied the requirement for identity or near identity to the language of the then-governing FTDA and to the tests that we had developed in interpreting the FTDA.

In adopting this standard, we also were persuaded by the legislative history of the FTDA and by the McCarthy treatise's explanation of the nature of a dilution claim. The legislative history, although "not definitive on the issue," "suggest[ed] that the marks must be identical or close thereto." *Id.* Specifically, the Senate Report had given the following examples of dilution: Kodak being used for pianos and Buick being used for aspirin. *Id.* at 906 (citing S. Rep. No. 100-515, at 7 (1988), *as reprinted in* 1988 U.S.C.C.A.N. 5577, 5583). Furthermore, referencing the McCarthy treatise, we observed that "a dilution claim alleges a form of appropriation." *Id.* We continued:

> Appropriation implies the adoption of the mark itself, not the use of a similar mark. As discussed previously, infringement is designed to protect against consumer confusion about the source of a product that may arise, *inter alia,* because a company uses a similar mark. Dilution, on the other hand, protects the distinctiveness of a particular mark whether or not the products compete or consumer confusion exists. § 1127. Because dilution and likelihood of confusion tests are directed at different actions, it does not make sense to import the relatively subjective similarity of the marks test from the likelihood of confusion context into the dilution context. *See* 4 J. McCarthy, *Trademarks and Unfair Competition,* § 24:90.2 (4th ed.2001).

Id.

Finally, we observed, other courts similarly had adopted an "identical or nearly identical" requirement. Indeed, *Playboy Enterprises* had borrowed this standard from the Eighth Circuit's decision in *Luigino's*, and other circuits had employed equally stringent standards for similarity.

Thus, although the identical or nearly identical standard had its roots in pre-FTDA state dilution law, we determined in *Thane* that our adoption of the standard was rooted in the language of the FTDA, the legislative history and purpose of that statute, our prior interpretations of the FTDA, and the policies we believed were embodied in that statute.

C. The *Moseley* Decision and Adoption of the TDRA

After our decision in *Thane*, the Supreme Court handed down a decision that greatly impacted many courts of appeals' interpretations of the FTDA. In *Moseley v. V Secret Catalogue, Inc.*, 537 U.S. 418, 123 S. Ct. 1115, 155 L. Ed. 2d 1 (2003), the Court held, contrary to the approach that had been taken by this court, as well as the courts of appeals for the Second and Sixth Circuits, that the text of the FTDA "unambiguously requires a showing of *actual* dilution, rather than a *likelihood* of dilution." *Id.* at 433, 123 S. Ct. 1115 (emphasis added).

However, this requirement of actual dilution was not long-lived. In 2006, largely in response to the *Moseley* decision, Congress enacted the TDRA. In doing so, Congress did not simply alter the language on which the Court in *Moseley* had relied; instead, Congress replaced the FTDA with a more detailed statute. The TDRA did provide relief for "likely," as opposed to actual, dilution. 15 U.S.C. § 1125(c)(1). However, it also explicitly provided relief for dilution "by blurring" or by "tarnishment," *id.*, and defined both types of dilution, *id.* § 1125(c)(2). Section 1125(c)(1) of Title 15 now states in relevant part:

> Subject to the principles of equity, the owner of a famous mark that is distinctive, inherently or through acquired distinctiveness, shall be entitled to an injunction against another person who, at any time after the owner's mark has become famous, commences use of a mark or trade name in commerce that is likely to cause dilution by blurring or dilution by tarnishment of the famous mark, regardless of the presence or absence of actual or likely confusion, of competition, or of actual economic injury.

15 U.S.C. § 1125(c)(1). Subsection (c)(2) defines "dilution by blurring" accordingly:

> (B) For purposes of paragraph (1), "dilution by blurring" is association arising from the similarity between a mark or trade name and a famous mark that impairs the distinctiveness of the famous mark. In determining whether a mark or trade name is likely to cause dilution by blurring, the court may consider all relevant factors, including the following:
>
> (i) The degree of similarity between the mark or trade name and the famous mark.
>
> (ii) The degree of inherent or acquired distinctiveness of the famous mark.

(iii) The extent to which the owner of the famous mark is engaging in substantially exclusive use of the mark.

(iv) The degree of recognition of the famous mark.

(v) Whether the user of the mark or trade name intended to create an association with the famous mark.

(vi) Any actual association between the mark or trade name and the famous mark.

15 U.S.C. § 1125(c)(2)(B).

Several aspects of the TDRA are worth noting. The first, as mentioned previously, is that Congress did not merely make surgical linguistic changes to the FTDA in response to *Moseley.* Instead, Congress created a new, more comprehensive federal dilution act. Furthermore, any reference to the standards commonly employed by the courts of appeals—"identical," "nearly identical," or "substantially similar"—are absent from the statute. The TDRA defines "dilution by blurring" as the "association arising from the *similarity* between a mark or a trade name and a famous mark that impairs the distinctiveness of the famous mark." *Id.* § 1125(c)(2)(B)(emphasis added). Moreover, in the non-exhaustive list of dilution factors that Congress set forth, the first is "[t]he degree of similarity between the mark or trade name and the famous mark." *Id.* § 1125(c)(2)(B)(i). Thus, the text of the TDRA articulates a different standard for dilution from that which we utilized under the FTDA.

* * *

E. Interpretation of the TDRA

1.

Our method of statutory interpretation is well established:

Statutory interpretation begins with the language of the statute. *See United States v. Ron Enters., Inc.,* 489 U.S. 235, 241, 109 S. Ct. 1026, 103 L. Ed. 2d 290 (1989). When the plain meaning of a statutory provision is unambiguous, that meaning is controlling. *Id.* at 242, 109 S. Ct. 1026. To determine the plain meaning of a statutory provision, we examine not only the specific provision at issue, but also the structure of the statute as a whole, including its object and policy. *See Green v. Commissioner,* 707 F.2d 404, 405 (9th Cir.1983). If ambiguity exists, we may use legislative history as an aid to interpretation. *See id.; Mt. Graham Red Squirrel v. Madigan,* 954 F.2d 1441, 1453 (9th Cir.1992).

Children's Hosp. & Health Ctr. v. Belshe, 188 F.3d 1090, 1096 (9th Cir.1999) (parallel citations omitted). Here, moreover, the language of the new statute, when compared to the language of the former statute, provides a firm basis for decision.

Beginning with subsection (c)(1) of 15 U.S.C. § 1125, Congress provided that "the owner of a famous mark . . . shall be entitled to an injunction against another person who . . . commences use of *a* mark or trade name in commerce that is likely to cause dilution." 15 U.S.C. § 1125(c) (emphasis added). When referring to the junior mark, Congress did not authorize an injunction against another person who commences use of "the" mark; use of the definite article "the" clearly would have signaled that the junior mark had to be the same as the senior. Instead, Congress employed the indefinite article "a," which indicates that any number of unspecified, junior marks may be likely to dilute the senior mark.

Turning to the language of subsection (c)(2)(B), the TDRA defines "dilution by blurring" as the "association arising from the *similarity* between a mark and a trade name and a famous mark that impairs the distinctiveness of the famous mark." *Id.* § 1125(c)(2)(B) (emphasis added). Congress did not require an association arising from the "substantial" similarity, "identity" or "near identity" of the two marks. The word chosen by Congress, "similarity," sets forth a less demanding standard than that employed by many courts under the FTDA.

This analysis of the language of the statute, and our comparison of this language with the now-repealed statute, are further supported by Congress's decision to employ, in subsection (c)(2)(B), a non-exhaustive list of relevant factors to determine when dilution has occurred. Congress's implementation of such a methodology is simply not compatible with a determination that identity, near identity or substantial similarity are necessary to constitute a threshold showing for relief under § 1125(c). Indeed, Congress chose instead to make the "degree of *similarity* between the mark or trade name and the famous mark," *id.* § 1125(c)(2)(B)(i) (emphasis added), to be the first of the six (or more) relevant factors to be considered.

No doubt, similarity has a special role to play in the implementation of the new statute's multifactor approach. After all, dilution by blurring is defined by the statute as an "association arising from the similarity between a mark . . . and a famous mark." *Id.* § 1125(c)(1)(B). It is also the *first* factor listed in the multifactor approach. Nevertheless, Congress's decision to make "degree of similarity" one consideration in a multifactor list strongly suggests that it did not want "degree of similarity" to be the necessarily controlling factor.

Finally, we believe that it is significant that, in adopting the TDRA, Congress decided to re-write 15 U.S.C. § 1125(c), as opposed to altering discrete wording or subsections. This action suggests that Congress did not wish to be tied to the language or interpretation of prior law, but instead crafted a new approach to our consideration of dilution-by-blurring claims.

Thus, the plain language of 15 U.S.C. § 1125(c) does not require that a plaintiff establish that the junior mark is identical, nearly identical or substantially similar to the senior mark in order to obtain injunctive relief. Rather, a plaintiff must show, based on the factors set forth in § 1125(c)(2)(B), including the degree of similarity, that a junior mark is likely to impair the distinctiveness of the famous mark.

Our interpretation of the TDRA is compatible with the case law of the only other court of appeals to have addressed squarely the question whether the requirement of identity or substantial similarity survives the TDRA. In *Starbucks,* the company brought a federal dilution claim against Wolfe's based on its use of the term "Charbucks" in connection with one of its coffee blends. The district court found that "the marks were not substantially similar" and "that '[t]his dissimilarity alone is sufficient to defeat [Starbucks's] blurring claim.'" *Starbucks,* 588 F.3d at 107. The Second Circuit disagreed. It acknowledged that, pre-TDRA, it had required plaintiffs to show that the marks were "'very' or 'substantially similar'" before they could prevail on a federal dilution claim. *Id.* (quoting *Playtex Prods., Inc. v. Georgia-Pacific Corp.,* 390 F.3d 158, 167 (2d Cir.2004)). This was no longer the case under the TDRA, the court explained:

> The post-TDRA federal dilution statute, however, provides us with a compelling reason to discard the "substantially similar" requirement for federal trademark dilution actions. The current federal statute defines dilution by blurring as an "association arising from the similarity between a mark . . . and a famous mark that impairs the distinctiveness of the famous mark," and the statute lists six non-exhaustive factors for determining the existence of an actionable claim for blurring. 15 U.S.C. § 1125(c)(2)(B). Although "similarity" is an integral element in the definition of "blurring," we find it significant that the federal dilution statute does not use the words "very" or "substantial" in connection with the similarity factor to be considered in examining a federal dilution claim.

Id. at 108. Furthermore, the court continued, in addition to leaving out any modifier for "similarity," Congress also employed specific language that cannot be reconciled with a requirement of substantial similarity; the court stated:

> [O]ne of the six statutory factors informing the inquiry as to whether the allegedly diluting mark "impairs the distinctiveness of the famous mark" is "[t]he *degree* of similarity between the mark or trade name and the famous mark." 15 U.S.C. § 1125(c)(2)(B)(i) (emphasis added). Consideration of a "degree" of similarity as a factor in determining the likelihood of dilution does not lend itself to a requirement that the similarity between the subject marks must be "substantial" for a dilution claim to succeed.

Id. (internal citations omitted); *see also Tiffany (NJ) Inc. v. eBay, Inc.,* 600 F.3d 93, 111 n. 18 (2d Cir.2010) ("We have recently explained that under the [TDRA] the similarity between the famous mark and the allegedly blurring mark need not be 'substantial' in order for the dilution by blurring claim to succeed.").

Although we did not speak directly to the issue in *Visa International,* we believe that our decision in that case is consonant with the interpretation of the TDRA that we adopt here. In *Visa International,* we reviewed the district court's grant of summary judgment in favor of Visa on its trademark dilution claim. We noted that "likelihood of dilution" is a factual inquiry "generally not appropriate for decision on summary judgment." *Visa Int'l,* 610 F.3d 1088, 1089. We pointed out that Congress had "enumerated factors courts may use to analyze the likelihood of dilution, including the similarity between the two marks and the distinctiveness and recognition of the plaintiff's mark." *Id.* (citing 15 U.S.C. § 1125(c)(2)(B)(i), (ii), (iv)). Evaluating these factors, we determined that "[t]he district court was quite right in granting summary judgment to Visa." *Id.* at 1092. In essence, we considered the evidence in light of the factors set forth in § 1125(c)(2)(B). We identified "similarity" as one of the factors a court should consider and, notably, did not mention a requirement that the marks be "identical or nearly identical." Most importantly, we took the degree of similarity into account along with the other § 1125(c)(2)(B) factors in determining whether dilution was likely to occur. In short, although not addressing the issue now before us head-on in *Visa International,* we applied the methodology that we have described here and made no reference to a requirement of "identity or near identity" of the marks.

F. The District Court's Error Was Not Harmless

Abercrombie also submits that, even if the district court erred in applying the "identical or nearly identical" requirement, the judgment nonetheless should be affirmed because any error was harmless. According to Abercrombie, the district court determined the Arcuate mark and the Ruehl design were not visually similar. Because "similarity" is the correct standard under the TDRA, Levi Strauss suffered no prejudice as a result of the district court's application of the incorrect standard. Abercrombie also notes that, in assessing the likelihood of dilution, the district court not only considered whether the marks were identical, but also took into account the other five factors set forth in § 1125(c)(2)(B). Abercrombie maintains that, because the court engaged in a weighing of all of the factors, the "similarity" requirement played only an insignificant role in its determination.

Abercrombie presents a very strained view of the district court's opinion. In its order entering judgment for Abercrombie, the court noted that "[t]he advisory jury found that the Ruehl design and the Arcuate mark were not identical or nearly identical." *Levi Strauss & Co.,* 2009 WL 1082175, at 7. It also observed that the test for similarity in a dilution context "is more stringent than in the infringement context." *Id.* (internal quotation marks omitted). After evaluating the visual depictions of the designs, the court concluded that "[t]his evidence demonstrates that a significant segment of the target group of customers would not view the marks as *essentially the same.*" *Id.* at 8 (emphasis added). The court then reviewed Dr. Sood's testimony and concluded that, given the survey shortcomings, there was insufficient evidence that target customers would "see the Ruehl design and the Arcuate mark as *essentially the same.*" *Id.* (emphasis added). In summary, the court stated: "[T]he Court concludes, consistent with the advisory jury's finding, that [Levi Strauss] has not established that [Abercrombie] is making commercial use of a mark that is identical or nearly identical to the Arcuate mark." *Id.* at 9. Use of the "identical or nearly identical" standard permeated the court's analysis and provided the basis upon which the court evaluated the evidence.

This standard also played a pivotal role in the court's determination that the Ruehl design was not likely to dilute the Arcuate mark. With respect to the similarity of the marks, the court observed that the two marks must be essentially the same and that, "[f]or the reasons set forth above, the Court finds that the Ruehl design and the Arcuate mark are not visually similar." *Id.* In other words, the court equated similarity with sameness and employed the latter, more stringent definition when entering its findings of fact.

Finally, our review of the district court's balancing of the relevant factors convinces us that application of the incorrect standard affected its dilution determination. According to the district court, degree of similarity was only one of three factors that weighed in Abercrombie's favor. The district court assumed, without deciding, that Levi Strauss also had two factors—acquired distinctiveness and degree of recognition—that weighed in its favor. Thus, application of the correct, less-demanding standard could have tipped the balance in favor of Levi Strauss. The degree of similarity between the Ruehl and Arcuate marks may be insufficient to support a likelihood of dilution, but that conclusion can come only after consideration of the degree of similarity in light of all other relevant factors and cannot be determined conclusively by application of an "essentially the same" threshold.

Given the relative balance of the parties' positions, we cannot say, with any confidence, that the district court would have reached the same result absent the legal error. *See Galdamez v. Potter,* 415 F.3d 1015, 1025 (9th Cir.2005) ("presum[ing] prejudice where civil trial error is concerned" and shifting the burden to the defendant "to demonstrate that 'it is more probable than not that the jury would have reached the same verdict' had it been properly instructed" (quoting *Obrey v. Johnson,* 400 F.3d 691, 701 (9th Cir. 2005))). We therefore must reverse the judgment of the district court with respect to Levi Strauss's claim under the TDRA.

REVERSED and REMANDED.

Note

If a fashion company uses a famous trademark as part of its fashion collection, would this be considered a fair use? Consider the case of Moschino and McDonalds:

F. The Defense of Parody in Fashion Law Cases

Parodies of trademarks may be permissible if the trademark use in question is not too directly tied to commercial use. For example, the First Amendment to the U.S. Constitution protects artistic and editorial parodies of trademarks that serve a valuable critical function. Federal courts have adopted different ways of balancing and protecting First Amendment interests with the Lanham Act likelihood of confusion and likelihood of dilution analysis. Certain courts have applied the general "likelihood of confusion" analysis, using the First Amendment element as one factor in the analysis, while other courts have expressly balanced First Amendment considerations against the degree of likely confusion. Still other courts have held that the First Amendment effectively trumps trademark law under certain factual circumstances. As a general rule, the less commercial the parody, the more sympathetic courts may be to the parody of the trademark. The more the parody is used in the context of the commercial use of the mark, the less sympathetic the court may be.

For example, parodies in print and film media demonstrating an exercise of First Amendment rights were held to be non-infringing parodies, including a risqué magazine parody of an L.L. Bean magazine advertisement in *L.L. Bean, Inc. v. Drake Publishers, Inc.*, 811 F.2d 26, 28 (1st Cir. 1987); and the use of a character named "Spa'am" in a Muppet movie in *Hormel Foods Corp. v. Jim Henson Prods.*, 73 F.3d 497 (2d Cir. 1996) (use of "Spa'am" did not infringe "Spam" trademark). On the other hand, "Gucchie Goo" diaper bags were held to be infringing and not protected under the parody defense. *Gucci Shops, Inc. v. R.H. Macy & Co.*, 446 F. Supp. 838 (S.D.N.Y. 1977). Similarly, posters bearing the logo "Enjoy Cocaine" in Cyrillic print similar to the well-known slogan "Enjoy Coca-Cola" were found to violate Coca-Cola's rights. *Coca-Cola Co. v. Gemini Rising, Inc.*, 346 F. Supp. 1183 (E.D.N.Y. 1972).

Coca-Cola Co. v. Gemini Rising, Inc.

346 F. Supp. 1183 (E.D.N.Y. 1972)

NEAHER, District Judge.

The Coca-Cola Company brings this action to enjoin defendant from printing, distributing and selling commercially a poster which consists of an exact blown-up reproduction of plaintiff's familiar "Coca-Cola" trademark and distinctive format except for the substitution of the script letters "ine" for "-Cola", so that the poster reads "Enjoy Cocaine." Jurisdiction is based on 28 U.S.C. §§ 1338 and 1332.

Plaintiff has moved, pursuant to Rule 65(a), F.R.Civ.P., for a preliminary injunction restraining defendant from further sale of the poster pending trial on the merits. Defendant opposes the motion asserting that the court is without jurisdiction of the subject matter on any cognizable ground and contending that, in any event, there is no trademark infringement, no proof of any damage to plaintiff and no basis in statutory or common law for injunctive relief. Additionally, defendant contends that its copyright on the poster precludes issuance of an injunction; that such relief would raise serious First Amendment questions; and that plaintiff has been guilty of laches in delaying suit for some 15 months. Initially defendant raised an objection to venue but withdrew it after plaintiff adduced sworn testimony that the poster is currently being sold in this district.

From the pleadings, affidavits and other papers submitted by the parties, the following facts appear to be incapable of substantial dispute. Plaintiff is a Delaware corporation with its principal place of business in Atlanta, Georgia. Since prior to 1893 it has manufactured and sold a soft drink beverage under the trademark "Coca-Cola" and has continuously and extensively employed the trademark in connection with its business to the present time. Three federal trademark registrations pertaining to "Coca-Cola" have been obtained by plaintiff No. 22,406 issued January 31, 1893, No. 47,189 issued October 31, 1905, and No. 238,145 issued January 31, 1928. Each registration statement specifies either "beverages" or "beverages and syrups" as the class of merchandise to which the trademark is appropriated. The registrations have been renewed from time to time and are currently in full force and effect. Two of them, Nos. 47,189 and 238,145, have become incontestable pursuant to the Lanham Act, 15 U.S.C. § 1051 et seq. The trademark is also registered in the State of New York.

Since the original registration in 1893 plaintiff has displayed the trademark "Coca-Cola" in distinctive stylized script lettering with the lower portion of the "C" in "Coca" extending under the remaining letters in the form of a curved dash. In the traditional print format, the word "Enjoy" appears above "Coca-Cola" and below it, the word "Trademark" followed by "R" in a circle. In more recent years a sweeping white curved band has been added below "Coca-Cola". The trademark as so described has been widely presented to the public in white lettering against a bright red background in advertising of all kinds, *e.g.*, magazines, newspapers, billboards, display materials, television, truck panels and the like.

Defendant is a New York corporation with its principal office and place of business in New York County. It is engaged in the business of creating, printing, distributing and selling commercially posters of various kinds. In November 1970 defendant "created" and began the sale of the poster which reproduces plaintiff's distinctive trademark and format as previously described. The poster is approximately two feet by three feet in size and printed in the same white lettering on a bright red background as plaintiff employs.

Defendant admits it has sold over 100,000 copies of the "Enjoy Cocaine" poster throughout the United States since November 1970. A purchase of the poster was recently made in this district at a retail price of $2.00. It is a fair inference, therefore, that defendant is deriving substantial revenue from their sale.

Defendant filed the poster and a notice in the United States Copyright Office on May 4, 1971, and, following a copyright application, obtained a "Registration of Copyright" numbered K 94714 dated July 15, 1971. On February 8, 1972, upon learning of plaintiff's intention to bring this suit, defendant filed a changed copy of the poster with the United States Copyright Office. Defendant concedes that the new poster is in all respects the same as the former poster with one exception, *i. e.*, "Trade-Mark" has been changed to "Raid-Mark".

Defendant does not and could not seriously deny that it is deliberately imitating plaintiff's trademark in its "Enjoy Cocaine" poster. Although it contends that the word "Coca-Cola" as such does not appear anywhere on the poster one would have to be a visitor from another planet not to recognize immediately the familiar "Coca" in its stylized script and accompanying words, colors and design. Indeed, defendant's assertion that "the poster was intended to be a spoof, satirical, funny, and to have a meaning exactly the opposite of the word content" would be meaningless except in the context of an immediately recognizable association with the "Coca-Cola" trademark. This is buttressed by the only change made in the new poster, *i. e.,* "Raid-Mark" in place of "Trade-Mark" a clear indication of defendant's predatory intent, however humorous defendant considers it. But whether such an unauthorized use of plaintiff's trademark warrants injunctive relief in these novel circumstances is another matter, to which we now turn.

To obtain injunctive relief pendente lite in a trademark case a plaintiff must show a reasonable probability of success at trial or at least raise "questions going to the merits so serious, substantial, difficult and doubtful, as to make them a fair ground for litigation and thus for more deliberate investigation" with a tipping of "the balance of hardships . . . decidedly toward plaintiff" even though a strong likelihood of success is not demonstrated. *Omega Importing Corp. v. Petri-Kine Camera Company,* 451 F.2d 1190, 1193 (2d Cir. 1971), quoting from *Hamilton Watch Co. v. Benrus Watch Co.,* 206 F.2d 738, 740 (2d Cir. 1953). A district court, moreover, is instructed not to determine serious issues with respect to trademarks "on an incomplete showing by way of affidavits . . . in the absence of clear proof of necessity for interlocutory injunctive relief." 451 F.2d at 1194, n. 5, quoting from *Cerruti, Inc. v. McCrory Corp.,* 438 F.2d 281, 284 (2d Cir. 1971).

Although no evidentiary hearing has been held, the court is satisfied from the affidavits and exhibits submitted by both parties that plaintiff has made a sufficiently clear showing of need for immediate protection of its trademark and business reputation to warrant preliminary injunctive relief. While, to borrow Chief Judge Friendly's apt phrasing, "[t]he case bristles with difficult questions of trademark law," *Cerruti, supra,* at 283, unlike *Cerruti,* the source of plaintiff's claimed irreparable injury has not been removed but is increasing by every "Enjoy Cocaine" poster which rolls off the press.

The record before the court, as already indicated, establishes beyond dispute plaintiff's ownership and registration of its widely known trademark, which is also the dominant element of its corporate trade name. There can be no question that the mark is valid and worthy of protection. "The mere fact of registration . . . creates a strong presumption of validity, a presumption which in this case stands unrebutted by any of the evidence presented on behalf of defendant." *Miss Universe, Inc. v. Patricelli,* 271 F. Supp. 104, 108 (D. Conn. 1967), *aff'd per curiam* 386 F.2d 997 (2 Cir. 1967); *see also* 408 F.2d 506 (2 Cir. 1969).

Defendant does not really challenge this. Its position is simply "that the protection of the trademark law does not extend to this particular situation, since there is no attempt by the defendant to sell merchandise similar to the plaintiff's; nor is there any reasonable likelihood, considering the nature of the poster, that anyone could or would be confused as to the origin of the poster; *i.e.*, that it was either published or authorized by the plaintiff." Although defendant also urges 17 affirmative defenses as barring relief to plaintiff, which are dealt with below, the main thrust of its argument is that defendant is entirely free to deliberately imitate and exploit plaintiff's trademark and format for its own business purposes so long as it is not done in connection with any goods or services which might be confused with those of plaintiff.

Admittedly the parties are not in competition in the ordinary sense. "But recognition . . . that [defendant is] not making infringing sales of a kind of goods that plaintiff sells under a trade mark, does not end the matter." *Hobart Manufacturing Company v. Kitchen Aid Service, Inc.*, 260 F. Supp. 559, 561 (E.D.N.Y.1966). Here there is no question that both are seeking to attract public attention and patronage for their respective products by the graphic display of a distinctive and widely known trademark. That trademark belongs to and is uniquely identified with plaintiff and its products. Plaintiff's property right in its mark clearly extends to its reproduction and publication in advertising and for other promotional uses regarding its products. In this case defendant's products simulated bill poster is itself one of the common forms of advertising utilized by plaintiff. Hence it is not surprising that plaintiff has received "numerous communications from all over the country" concerning defendant's poster a clear indication of public identification of the poster with plaintiff and strong confirmation of the public confusion which defendant contends does not exist.

Moreover, defendant's argument that no trespass infringing plaintiff's rights has been committed, because the protected words "Coca-Cola" do not appear in its poster, is disingenuous to say the least. Although "Cola" is missing, "Coca" is recognizably visible, albeit changed into "Cocaine". It is precisely this change plaintiff claims as the source of its grievance and likelihood of injury. Judicial notice may be taken that cocaine is a narcotic drug possession of which for nonmedical purposes is a felonious criminal offense against the laws of the United States punishable by substantial prison terms and fines. *See* 21 U.S.C. §§ 812, 841. The stringency of those laws reflects the national concern that cocaine far from being "enjoyable" is part of the tragic drug problem currently afflicting this nation, and particularly its youth. To associate such a noxious substance as cocaine with plaintiff's wholesome beverage as symbolized by its "Coca-Cola" trademark and format would clearly have a tendency to impugn that product and injure plaintiff's business reputation, as plaintiff contends. In other words, to paraphrase Judge Dooling in *Hobart, supra,* while the argument "that [defendant has] not used plaintiff's trademark precisely . . . might have force in other and innocent circumstances, on the facts it is altogether clear that [defendant] here exactly and successfully trespassed on just that area of unmistaken identifications of the word ["Coca-Cola"] with plaintiff that did exist." 260 F. Supp. at 561.

Defendant nonetheless scoffs at the suggestion that the poster "would confuse any person of average intelligence, or even below average intelligence)" and that its "very nature . . precludes anyone from believing that it originates with the plaintiff." That is simply defendant's self-serving *ipse dixit.* The appearance of defendant's name in relatively small lettering on the poster does not meet plaintiff's factual proof that some persons of apparently average intelligence did attribute *sponsorship* to plaintiff and discontinued their use of Coca-Cola as an expression of resentment Not only does visual comparison of defendant's poster with specimen advertising of plaintiff indicate the likelihood of such a mistaken attribution but recent so-called "pop art" novelty advertising utilized by plaintiff may have served to further the impression that defendant's poster was just another effort of that kind by plaintiff to publicize its product.

At all events, in assessing the probability of confusion "[t]he standard to be employed is the ordinary purchaser, not the expert." *Omega, supra,* 451 F.2d at 1195. And the ordinary purchaser consists of a "vast multitude which includes the ignorant, the unthinking and the credulous, who, in making purchases, do not stop to analyze, but are governed by appearances and general impressions." *Florence Mfg. Co. v. J. C. Dowd & Co.*, 178 F. 73, 75 (2 Cir. 1910). Judged by that standard, plaintiff has made a sufficiently clear showing of a high probability of confusion resulting from defendant's use of the "Coca-Cola" trademark format in an advertising context.

Given that showing, "injury irreparable in the sense that it may not be fully compensable in damages almost inevitably follows." *Omega, supra,* 451 F.2d at 1195. That is the likely situation here. Except for the protesting patrons and others referred to in plaintiff's affidavits, it would obviously be difficult, if not impossible, to quantify the effect of defendant's poster upon plaintiff's sales. As plaintiff points out, it expends large sums to induce people to order Coca-Cola without hesitation or concern in preference to other products. The continued success of plaintiff's business depends upon millions of purchase decisions made daily. The soft drink industry is highly competitive. Many substitute products are available, so that even the slightest negative connotation concerning a particular beverage may well affect a consumer's decision. In this day of growing consumer resistance to advertising gimmicks, a strong probability exists that some patrons of Coca-Cola will be "turned off" rather than "turned on" by defendant's so-called "spoof", with resulting immeasurable loss to plaintiff. In such circumstances injunctive relief is the only adequate remedy if the right to it exists.

Plaintiff asserts the right to protect its mark by injunction on a variety of grounds: defendant's poster unfairly disparages plaintiff's product by falsely associating it with cocaine (first count); defendant's imitation of plaintiff's registered mark is likely to cause confusion or mistake as to the source or sponsorship of the poster and constitutes trademark infringement under the Lanham Act, 15 U.S.C. § 1114 (second count); the poster creates a strong likelihood of injury to plaintiff's business reputation within the meaning of New York's General Business Law, McKinney's Consol. Laws, c. 20, § 368-d (third count); and is per se a libel in its implicit representation that plaintiff is marketing a product containing a dangerous drug (fourth count). Little purpose would be served at this juncture by discussing the cases plaintiff cites in support of these several legal theories. They underscore the wisdom of Judge Feinberg's recent comment that "[u]nder what circumstances the owner of a trademark can protect it against use on products other than those to which he has applied the mark is a familiar problem . . . [which] 'does not become easier of solution with the years'." *King Research, Inc. v. Shulton, Inc.*, 454 F.2d 66 (2d Cir. 1972).

Viewing this unusual case on its own facts, the real thrust of plaintiff's claim is that unless defendant's unauthorized use of the "Coca-Cola" trademark and format is enjoined, plaintiff's good will and business reputation are likely to suffer in the eyes of those who, believing it responsible for defendant's poster, will refuse to deal with a company which would seek commercial advantage by treating a dangerous drug in such jocular fashion. Certainly that claim finds support in the reaction of some members of the public as set forth in plaintiff's affidavits, *supra* n. 9. And it points up the special feature of this case already noted; *i.e.,* that defendant's "product," if it can be considered such, impinges directly upon plaintiff's own advertising use of its mark in a manner which creates confusion and is likely to cause injury to plaintiff even though that may not be defendant's intent.

Defendant's intent, however, is immaterial. Where, as here, plaintiff's trademark "has acquired a secondary meaning, it is of no consequence that the defendant did not intend an association with the wares of the plaintiff[s] if that association does in fact occur" (citations omitted). *Cue Publishing Co. v. Kirshenberg*, 22 Misc.2d 188, 190, 198 N.Y.S.2d 993, 997 (Sup.Ct., N.Y.Co.1960). Nor is it any defense that defendant has appropriated only a portion of plaintiff's mark. The Supreme Court long ago made this clear in *American Steel Foundries v. Robertson*, 269 U.S. 372, 46 S. Ct. 160, 70 L. Ed. 317 (1925), declaring at 381, 46 S. Ct. at 162:

The general doctrine is that equity not only will enjoin the appropriation and use of a trade-mark or trade name where it is completely identical with the name of the corporation, but will enjoin such appropriation and use where the resemblance is so close as to be likely to produce confusion as to such identity to the injury of the corporation to which the name belongs.

Here, as already noted, the resemblance between defendant's poster and plaintiff's trademark format as used in advertising is not only so close as to be virtually identical but obviously deliberately so. "The right of the trademark owner in his mark is the right to be protected with respect to its three functions," one of the three being its use "as a medium of advertisement." 3 Callman, Unfair Competition, Trademarks and Monopolies § 66.3 (3d ed. 1969). Even though in this case there is no confusion of goods or passing off in the strict trademark sense, there is a sufficiently clear showing of the impairment of plaintiff's mark as a selling device because of defendant's use. See Callman, *supra,* § 84.2. The effect of that use as a dilution of plaintiff's trademark rights is certainly a serious question calling for more deliberate investigation.

A further apparently unanswered serious question relates to the applicability of § 368-d of the New York General Business Law, upon which plaintiff relies. That statute by its terms extends injunctive relief to cases of "[l]ikelihood of injury to business reputation or of dilution of the distinctive quality of a mark or trade name" without regard to the absence of competition or confusion. Defendant contends that in a case akin to this, *Girl Scouts of United States of America v. Personality Posters Mfg. Co.*, 304 F. Supp. 1228 (S.D.N.Y.1969), which discussed New York authorities, the statute was held to afford no relief against a poster regarded as defamatory of the plaintiff. That case, however, is quite different from this. The Girl Scouts are not engaged in trade and their uniform, insignia and slogan are in no sense trademarks. Judge Lasker, moreover, found no evidence of any confusion, which is clearly not the case here, and all the more so if defendant's poster may be regarded as a "product" for that purpose another of the unusual questions in this case. Finally, there are numerous New York cases granting injunctive relief to protect one's trade name or mark from another's imitation "in the absence of a threat of confusion as to the source or sponsorship of the goods or services." *Sullivan v. Ed Sullivan Radio & T. V.*, 1 A.D.2d 609, 152 N.Y.S.2d 227 (1st Dept. 1956), and cases cited therein; *Tiffany and Company v. L'Argene Products Co.*, 67 Misc.2d 384, 324 N.Y.S.2d 326 (Sup. Ct., N.Y.Co.1971).

There remains the question of whether any of defendant's 17 affirmative defenses bar relief at this stage. Most of them relate to the court's jurisdiction and are now moot by reason of defendant's acceptance of venue. The defense asserting a violation of the antitrust laws because plaintiff brought this action to enjoin defendant's poster is patently frivolous.

* * *

Finally, defendant contends that its poster is but an instance of free expression secured by the First Amendment, which constitutes fair comment and cannot be defamatory without a claim of malice. Defendant again relies on *Girl Scouts, supra,* in which it was stated that in the absence of special circumstances "a court of equity will not enjoin or restrain literary or spoken material," 304 F. Supp. at 1234, quoting a passage from *Konigsberg v. Time, Inc.*, 288 F. Supp. 989 (S.D.N.Y. 1968). While plaintiff does assert a claim that the association of cocaine with its trademark is defamatory, the thrust of its claim is against defendant's imitative use of that trademark in a manner injurious to the mark and to plaintiff's business reputation and good will. The special circumstances mentioned in *Girl Scouts, supra,* are here present, for if they were not then any unauthorized reproduction of a trade name or mark would be without remedy. The Lanham Act itself, 15 U.S.C. § 1114(2) (a) and (b), recognizes that even newspapers, magazines and periodicals, as well as printers, may be enjoined from *innocent* infringement of another's mark as to future publication. Nothing in *Paulsen v. Personality Posters, Inc.*, 59 Misc.2d 444, 299 N.Y.S.2d 501 (Sup. Ct. 1968), cited by defendant, would bar such an injunction under New York law.

In the court's opinion plaintiff has sufficiently demonstrated its right to injunctive relief under either federal or state law relating to the protection of trade names and marks from defendant's unauthorized use of the "Coca-Cola" format in its poster. Apposite here is Judge Lasker's comment in *Estee Lauder, Inc. v. Watsky*, 323 F. Supp. 1064 (S.D.N.Y.1970) at 1068):

> It is true that the granting of an injunction may impose hardship on the defendants, but the failure to grant relief would impose a greater hardship on the plaintiff. To the defendants the product involved is one of a large number in which each of them deals; it is a small part of their business. To the plaintiff its name is at stake, and continued injury to its reputation and good will would be a far more serious blow to it than the curtailment of the sale by the defendants would be to them.

Here also the balance of hardships tips decidedly toward the plaintiff, since the temporary discontinuance of one poster *pendente lite* is hardly likely to put defendant out of business. Plaintiff has already posted security in the form of a bond for $25,000 in connection with a temporary restraining order. Similar security will assure recovery of any loss by defendant occasioned by the preliminary injunction should it eventually prove to be unwarranted.

Plaintiff's motion for a preliminary injunction is granted on condition that it furnish security for any costs or damages of defendant in the amount of $25,000. The foregoing constitutes the court's findings of fact and conclusions of law for purposes of Rule 52, F.R.Civ.P.

Settle order on notice.

Note

Would the case have been different if the use involved "Enjoy Cocaine" on tee shirts? What about the use of "Enjoy Cocaine" on a beach hat or bowling shirt?

Gucci Shops, Inc. v. R. H. Macy & Co.

446 F. Supp. 838 (S.D.N.Y. 1977)

MOTLEY, District Judge.

Plaintiff Gucci Shops, Inc. (Gucci Shops), alleges in its complaint four separate claims for relief arising under federal and state law relating to trademark infringement and unfair competition. The gravamen of plaintiff's suit is to prohibit Fashioncraft Products, Incorporated (Fashioncraft) from manufacturing a "diaper bag" with a diagonal stripe on both side panels consisting of green, red and green bands. Above the stripe, the manufacturer has silk screened the word "GUCCHI," and below the stripe, the word "GOO." Jurisdiction is based on 28 U.S.C. § 1338.

Plaintiff moved pursuant to Rule 65, Fed. R.Civ.P., for a preliminary injunction restraining defendants Fashioncraft and Gimbel Brothers, Inc. (Gimbels) from manufacturing, distributing, selling, or otherwise acting in a manner which would infringe any of plaintiff's trademarks.

At the hearing on the motion brought on by plaintiff, counsel for Fashioncraft appeared and argued in opposition. Prior to the hearing, defendant R. H. Macy & Co., Inc., voluntarily removed the offending product from its shelves. Counsel for Gimbels did not appear and the court was advised by counsel for plaintiff that Gimbels would not oppose plaintiff's application for preliminary injunction.

Though plaintiff alleges numerous claims for relief, the standard to determine whether a preliminary injunction shall issue is the same. Gucci Shops bears the burden of establishing either "probable success on the merits and possible irreparable injury, *or*—sufficiently serious questions going to the merits to make them a fair ground for litigation *and* a balance of hardships tipping decidedly toward the party requesting the preliminary relief." *Sonesta International Hotels Corp. v. Wellington Associates*, 483 F.2d 247, 250 (2d Cir. 1973); *Triebwasser & Katz v. American Telephone & Telegraph Co.*, 535 F.2d 1356, 1358 (2d Cir. 1976).

I.

Probability of Success on the Merits

Plaintiff, in its affidavits, states that it is engaged in the sale and distribution of quality merchandise, which has an international and national reputation for superb craftsmanship and design. Indeed the name "Gucci" has become synonymous with that which is chic or elegant.

To enhance the uniqueness of its goods, Gucci Shops developed a number of "signatures." Two of these trademarks are the subject of this proceeding. The first, the name "GUCCI", has been used in the United States since 1953 and was registered in 1969 for use on such classes of articles as pocketbooks, travel and duffel bags, attaché and toilet cases. The other, the Gucci stripe consisting of the red band bounded by a green band on each side, has been placed on numerous items sold by the plaintiff in the United States since 1963. These two marks, when used in conjunction with each other, clearly identify the product with the plaintiff. In fact, the marks were selected to associate particular merchandise with the plaintiff's founders. The trademark "GUCCI" is the name of the family that founded plaintiff, and the stripe is taken from the family flag.

The statutory test of infringement on a registered trademark is whether use of the imitating mark "is likely to cause confusion, or to cause mistake, or to deceive." 15 U.S.C. § 1114(1).

As to the *registered* trademark "GUCCI," except for the addition of the letter "H," defendant's mark is identical. More importantly, defendant's mark is placed on a similar item. Though Fashioncraft carefully stresses that it manufactures a "diaper bag," the article closely resembles an ordinary travel or tote bag, one of the items upon which plaintiff places the trademark "GUCCI" in conjunction with the Gucci stripe. It is not inconceivable that at a glance, the "GUCCHI" mark on what appears to be a tote bag could mislead members of the public into believing that the plaintiff has allowed its mark to be copied or that plaintiff is somehow associated with the manufacture, promotion, and sale of the "diaper bag."

Additionally, the words "GUCCI" and "GUCCHI" are identical when pronounced. Phonetic similarity is another factor to be considered in determining the likelihood of confusion. *Grotrian, Helfferich, Schultz, Th. Steinweg Nachf. v. Steinway & Sons*, 523 F.2d 1331, 1340 (2d Cir. 1975).

Even if, as defendant Fashioncraft argues, no one could possibly confuse the diaper bag with the Gucci tote or travel bag, the use of the mark "GUCCHI" with the mark "GOO" on an item similar to a tote bag indicates an intent to "poke fun at" or ridicule plaintiff. The fact that the offending product was intended only as a joke is of no consequence. A well-known registered trademark such as "GUCCI" may still be protected from such ridicule by a preliminary injunction. *Coca-Cola Co. v. Gemini Rising, Inc.*, 346 F. Supp. 1183 (E.D.N.Y. 1972).

Plaintiff also seeks to protect its unregistered trademark, the Gucci stripe. On this point, defendant Fashioncraft alleges that *Ventura Travelware, Inc. v. Baltimore Luggage Co.*, 66 Misc.2d 646, 322 N.Y.S.2d 93 (Sup.Ct., N.Y. County 1971), is clearly applicable. However, the *Ventura* opinion was concerned with trademarks that consisted of stripes. In this matter, Fashioncraft has used *both* the "GUCCHI" mark and a red and green stripe. Therefore, in determining whether Fashioncraft used "any false description or representation" on its goods in commerce, the entire packaging or appearance of the product must be examined. *Sutton Cosmetics (P.R.), Inc. v. Lander Co.*, 455 F.2d 285, 287-88 (2d Cir. 1972). It is not unreasonable to assume that defendant's use of the "GUCCHI" mark *and* the stripe on the "diaper bag" would mislead members of the public into believing that plaintiff is somehow connected with the "diaper bag."

This court concludes that defendant Fashioncraft's trademarks have come sufficiently close to those used by the plaintiff that it is very probable that plaintiff will succeed on the merits.

II.

Irreparable Injury

The Savarine affidavit states that plaintiff has spent over $1 million in the past five years alone to promote its merchandise and exploit the identification value of the "GUCCI" name and the Gucci stripe trademarks. To allow Fashioncraft to continue in the manufacture of an inexpensive "diaper bag," which either misleads the public into mistakenly associating plaintiff's quality products with defendant's or ridicules plaintiff's marks, damages plaintiff's reputation and the value of plaintiff's marks. Damage to the business reputation is not compensable with money damages and may be irreparable. Therefore, the granting of the preliminary injunction against Fashioncraft is warranted. *Coca-Cola Co. v. Gemini Rising, Inc.*, 346 F. Supp. 1183, 1189 (E.D. N.Y.1972); *Cutler-Hammer, Inc. v. Universal Relay Corp.*, 285 F. Supp. 636, 639 (S.D. N.Y.1968).

Submit order on notice.

Notes

1. The Court noted: "Even if, as defendant Fashioncraft argues, no one could possibly confuse the diaper bag with the Gucci tote or travel bag, the use of the mark

"GUCCHI" with the mark "GOO" on an item similar to a tote bag indicates an intent to 'poke fun at' or ridicule plaintiff. The fact that the offending product was intended only as a joke is of no consequence." Does the decision of the Tenth Circuit Court of Appeals in the next case comport with this principle?

2. The court also noted that: "[E]ven if the 'diaper bag' is not in competition with the Gucci tote bag and there is no possibility of confusion between plaintiff's goods and those of defendant, Fashioncraft's imitation of the 'GUCCI' trademark and the Gucci stripe on an inexpensive 'diaper bag' dilutes the distinctive quality of plaintiff's trademarks." How is this case different from the Fourth Circuit Court of Appeals decision in *Louis Vuitton Malletier SA v. Haute Diggity Dog, LLC*?

Please note the lengthy discussion of tarnishment in the next case. Another aspect of note is that both companies deal in blue jeans.

Jordache Enterprises, Inc. v. Hogg Wyld, Ltd.

828 F.2d 1482 (10th Cir. 1987)

TACHA, Circuit Judge.

This case, a trademark infringement action brought against a manufacturer that identifies its blue jeans for larger women with a smiling pig and the word "Lardashe" on the seat of the pants, reminds us that "you can't make a silk purse out of a sow's ear." Appellant Jordache Enterprises, Inc., alleges error in a district court decision finding no likelihood of confusion between the Jordache and Lardashe trademarks and finding no violation of New Mexico's antidilution statute. We affirm.

Appellant, a New York corporation formed by three immigrant brothers in 1978, is the fourth largest blue jeans manufacturer in the United States. It produces and markets all types of apparel for men, women, and children, the principal product being designer blue jeans. Most items are identified by one of appellant's several registered trademarks, including the word "Jordache" printed in block letters, the word "Jordache" printed in block letters and superimposed over a drawing of a horse's head, and a drawing of a horse's head alone. Some products are identified by the word "Jordache" written in script lettering, a mark which has not been registered.

An intensive advertising campaign has created great customer awareness of Jordache products. In 1984, for example, appellant spent about thirty million dollars annually on television, radio, newspaper, and magazine advertisements and other promotional efforts. The message of this advertising has been that Jordache jeans convey "the look of the good life." Jordache jeans are now sold in retail outlets throughout the world.

Appellant has licensed Shaker Sport to manufacture and market Jordache jeans for larger women. Shaker Sport has expended substantial resources in advertising these jeans, and it had sold between 33,000 and 60,000 pairs by 1985.

In 1984, appellees Marsha Stafford and Susan Duran formed Hogg Wyld, Ltd., now Oink, Inc., for the purpose of marketing designer blue jeans for larger women.

In an operation conducted out of their homes in New Mexico, the two women designed a product, selected a manufacturer, and ultimately sold over 1,000 pairs of jeans. Sales were limited to specialty shops in several southwestern states and to acquaintances or others who heard of the product. The women have not directly advertised their jeans, although several retailers have done so.

The name of the Oink, Inc. blue jeans gave rise to this suit. Names suggested at one time or another for the jeans by Stafford, Duran, or others, included "Thunder Thighs," "Buffalo Buns," "Seambusters," "Rino Asirus," "Hippo Hoggers," "Vidal Sowsoon," and "Calvin Swine." Other names and marks were suggested as a take-off on Stafford's childhood nickname, "lardass." This nickname inspired ideas such as "Wiseashe" with a picture of an owl, "Dumbashe" with a picture of a donkey, "Horsesashe" with a picture of a horse, and "Helium Ash" with a picture of a balloon. The women decided to name their jeans "Lardashe."

Appellant first became aware of Lardashe jeans after an Albuquerque TV station broadcast a news segment, which was also broadcast nationally by NBC, highlighting the new product. Jordache brought suit against Stafford, Duran, and their corporation, alleging trademark infringement in violation of the Lanham Trade-Mark Act, 15 U.S.C. §§ 1051-1127, the New Mexico Trademark Act, N.M.Stat.Ann. §§ 57-3-1 to -14 (1987), and common law. The district court, after a three-day bench trial, held that no trademark infringement had occurred on any of the alternative claims. *Jordache Enters. v. Hogg Wyld, Ltd.*, 625 F.Supp. 48 (D. N.M.1985). Jordache now appeals to this court.

I.

The Lanham Act prohibits the unauthorized use of a reproduction, copy, or imitation of a registered trademark in a way that "is likely to cause confusion" with the registered mark. 15 U.S.C. § 1114(1)(a); *see also* 15 U.S.C. § 1125(a) (similar test for infringement of an unregistered trademark by a junior user). "Confusion occurs when consumers make an incorrect mental association between the involved commercial products or their producers." *San Francisco Arts & Athletics, Inc. v. United States Olympic Comm.*, ___ U.S. ___, 107 S.Ct. 2971, 2995, 97 L.Ed.2d 427 (1987) (Brennan, J., dissenting). This court has identified several factors, originally set forth in Restatement of Torts § 729 (1938), that are relevant to whether there is a likelihood of confusion between two marks:

> (a) the degree of similarity between the designation and the trade-mark or trade name in
>
> (i) appearance;
>
> (ii) pronunciation of the words used;
>
> (iii) verbal translation of the pictures or designs involved;
>
> (iv) suggestion;
>
> (b) the intent of the actor in adopting the designation;

(c) the relation in use and manner of marketing between the goods or services marketed by the actor and those marketed by the other;

(d) the degree of care likely to be exercised by purchasers.

Beer Nuts, Inc. v. Clover Club Foods Co. (Beer Nuts II), 805 F.2d 920, 925 (10th Cir.1986) (quoting *Beer Nuts, Inc. v. Clover Club Foods Co. (Beer Nuts I),* 711 F.2d 934, 940 (10th Cir.1983)). This list is not exhaustive. All of the factors are interrelated, and no one factor is dispositive. *Id.* The party alleging infringement has the burden of proving likelihood of confusion. *Lindy Pen Co. v. Bic Pen Corp.,* 725 F.2d 1240, 1243 (9th Cir.1984), *cert. denied,* 469 U.S. 1188, 105 S.Ct. 955, 83 L.Ed.2d 962 (1985).

The district court examined these factors and concluded that there is no likelihood of confusion between the Jordache trademark and the Lardashe trademark. 625 F. Supp. at 53-54. Likelihood of confusion is a question of fact that we review under the clearly erroneous standard. *Amoco Oil Co. v. Rainbow Snow, Inc.,* 809 F.2d 656, 661 (10th Cir.1987); *see also Beer Nuts II,* 805 F.2d at 923 n. 2. Appellant contends that the district court erred as a matter of law in its consideration of several of the factors and that, in any event, the court's findings are clearly erroneous.

A.

The similarity between the marks in appearance, pronunciation of the words used, translation of the designs used, and suggestion or meaning is the first factor to consider in determining whether there is a likelihood of confusion. The district court found that the Jordache mark and the Lardashe mark are not confusingly similar. Appellant argues that the court employed an improper legal construction of "suggestion" or "meaning" in reaching this result. Even if we were to reject this argument, appellant would have us hold the finding of no similarity to be clearly erroneous.

Trademarks may be confusingly similar if they suggest the same idea or meaning. For example, this court has held that a trademark consisting of an overflowing stein with the words "Brew Nuts" conveys the same meaning as a trademark consisting of the words "Beer Nuts." *Beer Nuts II,* 805 F.2d at 926. The district court in the present case found that "the two marks suggest dissimilar images or concepts." 625 F. Supp. at 53. Appellant alleges that the district court erred as a matter of law in its application of this factor by attributing a meaning of "class" or "style" to the Jordache mark. According to appellant, since the word "Jordache" has no inherent meaning, the district court necessarily must have relied upon a legally incorrect understanding of "suggestion" or "meaning" in order to find no similarity between the marks.

This argument mischaracterizes the findings of the district court. The court found the *words* "Jordache" and "Lardashe" similar, but not the horse and pig *designs.* The court did not find the word "Jordache" has an inherent meaning. Rather the "meaning" described by the court referred to the "relatively subtle and refined" horse design that is employed in the Jordache trademarks. The district court did not attach an improper "meaning" to the Jordache marks.

Appellant further argues that the district court erred in finding the trademarks are not confusingly similar. Similarities between trademarks are to be given more weight than differences. *Beer Nuts II,* 805 F.2d at 925. The district court found that "[t]he overall differences between the two marks greatly overcomes the similarity in spelling and pronunciation of the names Jordache and Lardashe." 625 F. Supp. at 53.

Our review of the evidence shows that the marks, and their suggested images, are obviously different. Many of the Jordache jeans are identified by a small brown patch with the word "Jordache" written in white in block letters with a gold horse's head superimposed over the lettering. In other instances, the patch is white with blue block lettering and no horse. Sometimes "Jordache" is written in script or only the horse's head is used. In contrast, the Lardashe jeans have a large, brightly colored pig head and two hooves, giving the appearance that a pig is peering over the back pocket. The word "Lardashe" is written in script beneath the pig's head, below which is an upside down embroidered heart. *See* appendix. We agree with the district court that the "striking, brightly colored, and far from subtle" pig design is "humorous, or 'cute,' or facetious." 625 F. Supp. at 53. Thus, while the similarity of the words used in the mark would support an inference of likelihood of confusion, we agree with the district court's finding that the striking dissimilarities in the designs used in the marks greatly outweigh any similarities.

B.

The intent of a party in selecting a trademark is another factor in determining whether there is a likelihood of confusion. The district court found the appellees' "intent was to employ a name that, to some extent, parodied or played upon the established trademark Jordache"; appellees "did not intend to 'palm off' their jeans as Jordache jeans; that is, to confuse the public into believing it was buying a Jordache product." *Id.* at 52. Appellants contend the court erred in its analysis of intent and the relevance of parody.

The "deliberate adoption of a similar mark may lead to an inference of intent to pass off goods as those of another which in turn supports a finding of likelihood of confusion." *Beer Nuts II,* 805 F.2d at 927. "The proper focus is whether defendant had the intent to derive benefit from the reputation or goodwill of plaintiff." *Sicilia Di R. Biebow & Co. v. Cox,* 732 F.2d 417, 431 (5th Cir.1984); *accord* Restatement of Torts §729 comment f at 594-95 (1938). A conscious choice of a mark similar to a mark already established in the marketplace usually supports a finding of a likelihood of confusion "because the court presumes that [the alleged infringer] 'can accomplish his purpose: that is, that the public will be deceived.'" *Beer Nuts I,* 711 F.2d at 941 (quoting *AMF Inc. v. Sleekcraft Boats,* 599 F.2d 341, 354 (9th Cir.1979)).

Given the unlimited number of possible names and symbols that could serve as a trademark, it is understandable that a court generally presumes one who chooses a mark similar to an existing mark intends to confuse the public. However, where a party chooses a mark as a parody of an existing mark, the intent is not necessarily to confuse the public but rather to amuse. *See* Note, *Trademark Parody: A Fair Use and First Amendment Analysis,* 72 Va.L.Rev. 1079, 1079-80 n. 4 (1986) [hereinafter Note, *Trademark Parody*] (the purpose of a parody is "to create a comic or satiric contrast to a serious work").

In one sense, a parody is an attempt "to derive benefit from the reputation" of the owner of the mark, *Sicilia,* 732 F.2d at 431, if only because no parody could be made without the initial mark. The benefit to the one making the parody, however, arises from the humorous association, not from public confusion as to the source of the marks. A parody relies upon a difference from the original mark, presumably a humorous difference, in order to produce its desired effect.

"Now everything is funny as long as it is happening to somebody Else, but when it happens to you, why it seems to lose some of its Humor, and if it keeps on happening, why the entire laughter kinder Fades out of it." W. Rogers, *Warning to Jokers: Lay Off the Prince,* in *The Illiterate Digest,* I-3 *The Writings of Will Rogers* 75 (1974). The same is true in trademark law. As McCarthy writes, "No one likes to be the butt of a joke, not even a trademark. But the requirement of trademark law is that a likely confusion of source, sponsorship or affiliation must be proven, which is not the same thing as a 'right' not to be made fun of." 2 J. McCarthy, *Trademarks and Unfair Competition* § 31:38 at 670 (2d ed. 1984).

Of course, a parody of an existing trademark can cause a likelihood of confusion. For example, where two marks are confusingly similar, or where there is evidence of actual confusion, a likelihood of confusion can exist despite the intent to create a parody. Our single concern here, however, is whether an intent to parody an existing trademark supports an inference of a likelihood of confusion under the reasoning that one who chooses a mark similar to an existing mark intends to confuse the public. *See Beer Nuts II,* 805 F.2d at 927. We hold that it does not. An intent to parody is not an intent to confuse the public.

The district court found the appellee's explanation for their adoption of the Lardashe mark not credible. The court found that their real intent was to parody Jordache. 625 F. Supp. at 52. After examining the record, we hold the district court's findings are not clearly erroneous. We therefore reject appellant's challenge to the district court's refusal to infer a wrongful intent.

C.

Another factor to be considered in determining whether there is a likelihood of confusion is "the degree of care likely to be exercised by purchasers." *Beer Nuts II,* 805 F.2d at 925. The district court found that customers are likely to exercise a high degree of care in purchasing clothing that costs between fifteen and sixty dollars. 625 F. Supp. at 53. Appellant says that "[o]ne can just as easily surmise" that a lesser degree of care will be used in selecting a pair of blue jeans. Brief of Appellant at 27. Appellant has offered only a guess, not any evidence of the degree of care that would satisfy its burden of proof. The district court's finding of a high degree of care is not clearly erroneous.

D.

Obviously, the best evidence of a likelihood of confusion in the marketplace is actual confusion. *Standard Oil Co. v. Standard Oil Co.,* 252 F.2d 65, 74 (10th Cir.1958). Appellant offered evidence that it believed showed actual confusion, but the district court did not find this evidence compelling. Appellant challenges the court's findings.

Paul Ornstein, Executive Vice President of Shaker Sports, testified that he was called by associates who asked whether Lardashe jeans were affiliated with Jordache. The district court ruled that this testimony was hearsay and that even if it was admissible, it was not evidence of actual confusion by consumers in the marketplace. 625 F. Supp. at 54. We hold that Ornstein's testimony was admissible because it was offered to show the then existing state of mind of Ornstein's associates. *See* Fed.R.Evid. 803(3).

Although Ornstein's testimony was admissible, the district court correctly gave it little weight. McCarthy advises, "The better view would seem to be that while [customer] enquiry evidence is admissible and relevant, standing alone with no other evidence it is insufficient proof of actual confusion." 2 J. McCarthy, *Trademarks and Unfair Competition* § 23:2(B) at 54 (2d ed. 1984). We hold that even when combined with other evidence inquiries to the plaintiff about the source of a product are of comparatively little value.

Appellant also offered a survey of seventy people contacted in the Student Union building on the University of New Mexico campus as evidence of actual confusion. The district court afforded little weight to this survey. 625 F. Supp. at 54. We have acknowledged that public recognition surveys can be used to show actual confusion. *Standard Oil Co.,* 252 F.2d at 75. However, the evidentiary value of such surveys depends on the relevance of the questions asked and the technical adequacy of the survey procedures. *See id.*

In *Beer Nuts I,* this court observed:

> In evaluating similarity, "[i]t is axiomatic in trademark law that 'side-by-side' comparison is not the test." *Levi Strauss & Co. v. Blue Bell, Inc.,* 632 F.2d 817, 822 (9th Cir.1980); *American Home Products Corp. v. Johnson Chemical* 1488*1488 *Co.,* 589 F.2d 103, 107 (2d Cir.1978); *James Burrough Ltd. v. Sign of Beefeater, Inc.,* 540 F.2d 266, 275 (7th Cir.1976); *Fotomat Corp.* [*v. Cochran*], 437 F. Supp. [1231] at 1244 [D. Kan. 1977]. The marks "must be compared in the light of what occurs in the marketplace, not in the courtroom." *James Burrough Ltd.,* 540 F.2d at 275. "A prospective purchaser does not ordinarily carry a sample or specimen of the article he knows well enough to call by its trade name, he necessarily depends upon the mental picture of that which symbolizes origin and ownership of the thing desired." *Avrick v. Rockmont Envelope Co.,* 155 F.2d 568, 573 (10th Cir.1946). Therefore, the court must determine whether the alleged infringing mark will be confusing to the public when singly presented. *Id.* at 572-73; *American Home Products,*

> 589 F.2d at 107; *James Burrough Ltd.*, 540 F.2d at 275; *Union Carbide* [*Corp. v. Ever-Ready, Inc.*], 531 F.2d [366] at 382 [(7th Cir.), *cert. denied*, 429 U.S. 830 [97 S.Ct. 91, 50 L.Ed.2d 94] (1976)].

711 F.2d at 941.

Jordache's survey relied upon a "side-by-side" comparison. After the survey participants were asked several preliminary questions, they were handed a pair of Lardashe jeans and a pair of Jordache jeans and told to examine them. The participants were then asked if they thought the jeans were produced by the same manufacturer. This type of "side-by-side" comparison bears little resemblance to the actual workings of the marketplace. The district court did not err in giving little weight to the survey results.

E.

Appellant argues that the allegedly inferior quality of Lardashe jeans compared to Jordache jeans supports a finding of likelihood of confusion, and that the district court erred in not considering the quality of the jeans. If there is a difference in quality between the jeans, the public is less likely to be confused. A showing that products are of dissimilar quality affords no support for a finding of a likelihood of confusion

F.

The district court weighed all of the factors and concluded there is no likelihood of confusion between the Lardashe mark and the Jordache marks. We have examined the record, including the testimony of Becky Ingram concerning industry confusion and all of the other evidence appellant contends the district court overlooked. We hold the district court's finding of no likelihood of confusion is not clearly erroneous.

II.

Jordache also raises a claim under New Mexico's antidilution statute which provides:

> Likelihood of injury to business reputation or of dilution of the distinctive quality of a trademark or trade name . . . is a ground for injunctive relief notwithstanding the absence of competition between the parties or the absence of confusion as to the source of goods or services.

N.M.Stat.Ann. § 57-3-10 (1987). No state court in New Mexico has interpreted this 1489*1489 statute. We are thus presented with a question of law regarding what interpretation the New Mexico courts would adopt for this statute.

It has been widely observed that many courts have been hostile to state antidilution statutes. *See* 2 J. McCarthy *Trademarks and Unfair Competition* § 24:13(B) at 215-18 (2d ed. 1984 & Supp. 1986); 1 J. Gilson, *Trademark Protection and Practice* § 5.05(9) at 5-40 to -46 (1987 ed.); Denicola, *Trademarks as Speech: Constitutional Implications of the Emerging Rationales for the Protection of Trade Symbols,* 1982 Wis.L.Rev. 158, 183-84 (1982) [hereinafter *Trademarks as Speech*]. The decisions holding that antidilution statutes do not apply to competitive products are an indication of this hostility. *See, e.g., EZ Loader Boat Trailers, Inc. v. Cox Trailers, Inc.*, 746 F.2d 375, 380-81 (7th Cir.1984) (citing *Filter Dynamics Int'l, Inc. v. Astron Battery, Inc.*, 19 Ill.App.3d 299, 314-15, 311 N.E.2d 386, 398-99 (1974)); *Smithkline Beckman Corp. v. Proctor & Gamble Co.*, 591 F.Supp. 1229, 1246-47 (N.D.N.Y.1984), *aff'd*, 755 F.2d 914 (2d Cir.1985). As the district court noted, "The paradigmatic dilution case involves the situation where the same or very similar marks are being used on vastly different products. Examples might include BEEFEATER used for a restaurant; DIOR used for a cleaning establishment; BACARDI used for jewelry; PLAYBOY used for auto repair." 625 F. Supp. at 56 (citation omitted). Indeed, the first exposition of the dilution doctrine stated the real injury in dilution cases "is the gradual whittling away or dispersion of the identity and hold upon the public mind of the mark or name by its use upon *non-competing* goods." Schechter, *The Rational Basis of Trademark Protection*, 40 Harv.L.Rev. 813, 825 (1927) (emphasis added).

The district court in this case recognized that other courts have limited antidilution statutes to cases involving noncompeting products, but the district court did not so limit the New Mexico statute. Given the plain language of the statute that relief is available "notwithstanding the absence of competition between the parties," we agree the statute cannot be limited to cases involving noncompeting products. "Had the [legislature] intended to make the absence of competition a prerequisite to . . . relief, it could easily have done so." *LeSportsac, Inc. v. K Mart Corp.*, 617 F. Supp. 316, 319 (E.D.N.Y.1985). We will not ignore the clear words of the New Mexico legislature.

There are three grounds under which an owner of a distinctive trademark may obtain relief under an antidilution statute. Relief may be granted if:

> [T]here is a likelihood of dilution due to (1) injury to the value of the mark caused by actual or potential confusion, (2) diminution in the uniqueness and individuality of the mark, or (3) injury resulting from use of the mark in a manner that tarnishes or appropriates the goodwill and reputation associated with plaintiff's mark.

L.L. Bean, Inc. v. Drake Publishers, Inc., 811 F.2d 26, 30 (1st Cir.), *cert. denied*, ___ U.S. ___, 107 S.Ct. 3254, 97 L.Ed.2d 753 (1987). Dilution, like likelihood of confusion, is a question of fact that we review under the clearly erroneous standard.

The first ground merely repeats the likelihood of confusion test for relief under the Lanham Act. We have held there is no likelihood of confusion between the Lardashe and the Jordache trademarks. Therefore, there is no dilution of Jordache's marks in this sense.

Dilution of a trademark can also occur if the challenged mark blurs the mental image conveyed by the original mark. The statutorily protected distinctive quality of a trademark is diluted as the mark's propensity to bring to mind a particular product or source is weakened. *Stop the Olympic Prison v. United States Olympic Comm.*, 489 F. Supp. 1112, 1123 (S.D.N.Y. 1980). As the distinctive quality disappears, the trademark becomes generic and loses its legal protection. *Cf. Beer Nuts I*, 711 F.2d at 939.

In the present case, the district court found that "[b]ecause of the parody aspect of Lardashe, it is not likely that public identification of JORDACHE with the plaintiff will be eroded; indeed, parody tends to increase public identification of a plaintiff's mark with the plaintiff." 625 F. Supp. at 57. The court further found that "[u]nder all the circumstances, the continued existence of LARDASHE jeans simply will not cause JORDACHE to lose its distinctiveness as a strong trademark for jeans and other apparel." *Id.* We hold these findings are not clearly erroneous.

The third element of dilution law is tarnishment. A mark can be tarnished if it is used in an unwholesome context. Precisely what suffices as an unwholesome context is not immediately evident. *Compare Toho Co. v. Sears, Roebuck & Co.*, 645 F.2d 788, 793 (9th Cir.1981) (use of "Bagzilla" mark on garbage bags not "unsavory or degrading"); *Tetley, Inc. v. Topps Chewing Gum, Inc.*, 556 F. Supp. 785, 794 (E.D.N.Y. 1983) ("Petley Flea Bags" does not tarnish "Tetley Tea Bags"); *Girl Scouts of United States v. Personality Posters Mfg.*, 304 F. Supp. 1228, 1233-34 (S.D.N.Y.1969) (use of "Be Prepared" slogan on poster portraying a pregnant girl in a Girl Scout uniform does not injure the Girl Scouts), *with Dallas Cowboys Cheerleaders, Inc. v. Pussycat Cinema, Ltd.*, 604 F.2d 200, 205 (2d Cir.1979) (use of Dallas Cowboys Cheerleaders uniforms in "sexually depraved" movie improperly injures plaintiff's business reputation); *Original Appalachian Artworks, Inc. v. Topps Chewing Gum, Inc.*, 642 F. Supp. 1031, 1039-40 (N.D.Ga.1986) (use of "Garbage Pail Kids" on various products sufficient evidence of tarnishment to support a preliminary injunction); *Coca-Cola Co. v. Gemini Rising, Inc.*, 346 F. Supp. 1183, 1189 (E.D.N.Y. 1972) (use of Coca-Cola design in "Enjoy Cocaine" poster improper tarnishment). The district court found that while LARDASHE "might be considered to be in poor taste by some consumers . . . it is not likely to create in the mind of consumers a particularly unwholesome, unsavory, or degrading association with plaintiff's name and marks." 625 F. Supp. at 57. We have examined the record, including the marks in question, and we conclude that the district court's finding is not clearly erroneous.

Appellant contends that tarnishment can also occur in another manner that was not discussed by the district court. A few cases have held a trademark was tarnished by "use in a context which, while not inherently 'unwholesome', is out-of-keeping with plaintiff's high-quality image." 2 J. McCarthy, *Trademark and Unfair Competition Law* § 24:13(E) at 222 and cases cited therein (2d ed. 1984). *See also* 1 J. Gilson, *Trademark Protection and Practice* § 5.05(2)(a) at 5-29 to -31 (1987). According to appellant, these cases require a finding of tarnishment here because of the alleged disparity in quality between Lardashe jeans and Jordache jeans.

This argument presumes that the public will associate the manufacturer of Lardashe jeans with the manufacturer of Jordache jeans, thereby causing damage to the high quality image of Jordache. Because we find that the Lardashe mark was an intentional parody of the Jordache mark, we assume that the public will to some extent associate the two marks. To be actionable, however, the association of 1491*1491 the two marks must tarnish or appropriate the good will and reputation of the owner of the mark. If the public associates the two marks for parody purposes only and does not associate the two sources of the products, appellant suffers no actionable injury. Indeed, a manufacturer of a high quality product will typically benefit if its competitors are marketing a poor quality product at similar prices—*unless* the public associates the manufacturer of the poor quality product with the manufacturer of the high quality product. *See id.* at 5-31 ("A trademark owner should not be made to tolerate an unknown quality level for products, whether similar or not, *if they would likely be associated with his business.*") (emphasis added). Thus, the actionable association of marks is limited to an association of the source of the marks. Association of marks for parody purposes without corresponding association of manufacturers does not tarnish or appropriate the good will of the manufacturer of the high quality similar product.

The New Mexico statute plainly states that an actionable dilution of a trademark can occur despite the absence of competition between the parties and despite the absence of confusion as to the source of the products. But the statute also provides that relief is available only if there is some likelihood of injury to business reputation or of dilution of the distinctive quality of the trademark. There can be no likelihood of either injury if the public does not associate a product bearing one trademark with the manufacturer of a product bearing a different trademark.

The cases finding a trademark had been tarnished even though there was no unwholesome context all involve the use of identical, or almost identical, trade names on different products. *See Steinway & Sons v. Robert Demars & Friends,* 210 U.S.P.Q. 954 (C.D.Cal.1981) (Steinway pianos and Stein-Way clip-on beverage can handles); *Cartier, Inc. v. Three Sheaves Co., Inc.,* 465 F. Supp. 123 (S.D.N.Y.1979) (Cartier jewelry, china, and silver and Cattier cosmetics and toiletries); *Carling Brewing Co. v. Philip Morris Inc.,* 297 F. Supp. 1330 (N.D.Ga.1968) (Black Label beer and Black Label cigarettes); *Tiffany & Co. v. Boston Club, Inc.,* 231 F. Supp. 836 (D.Mass.1964) (Tiffany jewelry, china, silverware, and glassware and Tiffany's Restaurant and Lounge); *see also Yale Elec. Corp. v. Robertson,* 26 F.2d 972, 974 (2d Cir.1928) (Hand, L., J.) (Yale locks and Yale flashlights). In each of these cases the public could readily associate one product with the manufacturer of the other product on the assumption that the manufacturer is in the business of producing two separate and distinct products. This is not the case here. It is unlikely that the public would assume that the same manufacturer would use quite different marks on substantially the same product. While we do not hold that this type of tarnishment is established only where the Lanham Act likelihood of confusion test has been satisfied, the antidilution statute does require some showing that the public will associate both products with the same manufacturer. Our review of the record convinces us that the public will not associate Lardashe jeans with the appellant or, if they do, they will only make the association because of the parody and not because they believe Jordache Enterprises, Inc. manufactures Lardashe jeans. Therefore, there is no likelihood of an injury to appellant, and its dilution claim must fail.

III.

"'If it had grown up,' she said to herself, 'it would have been a dreadfully ugly child; but it makes rather a handsome pig, I think.'" L. Carroll, *Alice's Adventures in Wonderland* 78-79 (1892).

The judgment of the district court is affirmed.

Note

Does it make a difference to the analysis whether the parody is funny to the general public or not?

Tommy Hilfiger Licensing, Inc. v. Nature Labs, LLC

221 F. Supp. 2d 410 (S.D.N.Y. 2002)

MUKASEY, District Judge.

Defendant Nature Labs, LLC manufactures, markets and sells a line of pet perfumes whose names parody elegant brands sold for human consumption Timmy Holedigger (Tommy Hilfiger), CK-9 (Calvin Klein's cK-1), Pucci (Gucci), Bono Sports (Ralph Lauren's Polo Sports), Miss Claybone (Liz Claiborne), and White Dalmations (Elizabeth Taylor's White Diamonds). Most of the companies that purvey these expensive human fragrances have chosen either to accept the implied compliment in this parody that the mere association of their high-end brand names with a product for animals is enough to raise a smile or, if they have taken offense, to suffer in silence. Not so [for] plaintiff Tommy Hilfiger Licensing, Inc., which sues for trademark infringement, trademark dilution, false designation of origin, false advertising, and related claims under New York statutory and common law. Defendant moves for summary judgment. For the reasons stated below, defendant's motion is granted.

I.

The following facts are not in dispute. Tommy Hilfiger Licensing, Inc. ("Hilfiger") is the owner of the world-famous TOMMY HILFIGER and flag design trademarks used in connection with the sale of numerous high-end products, including fragrances. (Compl.§ 9) The flag design mark is comprised of a combination of red, white, and blue geometric shapes. (*Id.* § 8) These marks are federally registered, and several of those registrations have achieved incontestable status pursuant to 15 U.S.C. § 1065. (*Id.* § 10)

In 1995, Nature Labs began developing its line of parody perfume products for use on pets. (Harris Dep. at 14; Pl. 56.1 § 1; Def. 56.1 § 1) Nature Labs' initial spoof of Hilfiger was called Tommy Holedigger and had a flag-shaped label with side-by-side *413 red and white squares bordered on top and bottom by a blue stripe with white letters. Hilfiger complained that this use infringed its marks. Nature Labs then changed the name to Timmy Holedigger and changed the label to its present form: inverted side-by-side yellow and red triangles bordered on top and bottom by a blue stripe with white letters. Beneath the new logo design, the following phrase appears: "If You Like Tommy Hilfiger Your Pet Will Love Timmy Holedigger." Although neither party claims to have performed a disciplined olfactory comparison or chemical analysis, John Harris, the general partner of Nature Labs, testified at his deposition that the two scents are similar, based on his recollection of Hilfiger cologne. An asterisk following the words "Tommy Hilfiger" references a disclaimer in red type on the back label, which states, "This imitation fragrance is not related to Tommy Hilfiger Licensing, Inc." (Pl. 56.1 §7; Def. 56.1 §7; Lessem Decl. Ex. B; Harris Dep. at 56, 105-06) Another current version of the product, a two-ounce bottle being marketed primarily to PetCo, changes the flag-shape label to a bone with red and yellow triangles and a thick blue border. (Harris Dep. at 74; Lessem Decl. Ex. E) Hilfiger persists that these uses constitute unlawful use of its trademarks.

As noted, Nature Labs' line of animal perfume includes parodies of several designer fragrances. (Pl. 56.1 §2; Def. 56.1 §2) All the parody pet colognes are packaged in the same type of bottle, and Nature Labs' resellers stock at least three and often more of the pet colognes, displaying them next to one another. (*Id.* §3) The displays Nature Labs provides to its retailers are labeled "famous pet cologne"; some also include the slogan "Strong enough for a man, but made for a chihuahua." (Lessem Decl. Exs. D, E) Nature Labs sells its products primarily to pet stores and gift shops, where they retail at approximately $10.00 per four-ounce bottle. (Harris. Dep. at 41, 44). No company other than Tommy Hilfiger has complained to Nature Labs that Nature Labs is inappropriately using its marks. (Pl. 56.1 §4; Def. 56.1 §4)

II.

Plaintiff's complaint sets forth six categories of claims: (1) trademark infringement under section 32 of the Lanham Act, 15 U.S.C. §1114, and New York common law; (2) false designation of origin under section 43(a) of the Lanham Act, 15 U.S.C. §1125(a); (3) unfair competition under New York common law; (4) trademark dilution under section 43(c) of the Lanham Act, 15 U.S.C. §1125(c), and New York General Business Law §360-*l*; (5) false advertising under section 43(a) of the Lanham Act, 15 U.S.C. §1125(a); and (6) deceptive business practices under New York General Business Law §349.

A. Trademark Infringement, False Designation of Origin, and Unfair Competition

The central issue in an action for trademark infringement or false designation of origin under the Lanham Act is whether the unauthorized use of the mark is "likely to cause confusion." 15 U.S.C. §1114(1); 15 U.S.C. §1125(a) (1) (A). Confusion exists where there is a "likelihood that an appreciable number of ordinary prudent purchasers" will be misled or confused as to the source of the goods in question, *Mushroom Makers, Inc. v. R.G. Barry Corp.*, 580 F.2d 44, 47 (2d Cir. 1978), or where consumers are likely to believe that the mark's owner sponsored, endorsed, or otherwise approved of the defendant's use of the mark, *Dallas Cowboys Cheerleaders, Inc. v. Pussycat Cinema, Ltd.*, 604 F.2d 200, 204-05 (2d Cir.1979). The court's conclusion as to whether there is a likelihood of confusion also determines plaintiff's common-law trademark infringement and unfair competition claims. *See Pirone v. MacMillan, Inc.,* 894 F.2d 579, 581, 584-85 (2d Cir.1990).

Hilfiger contends that defendant's use of the Tommy/Timmy Holedigger name and flag design is likely to cause confusion in the marketplace. Nature Labs appears to defend on two grounds: First, it asserts that there is no likelihood of confusion because the use constitutes an obvious parody. Second, it argues that even if there were some confusion, trademark parodies are a protected form of expression under the First Amendment.

Turning first to the second defense upon which Nature Labs principally relies the Second Circuit has recognized that where the unauthorized use of a trademark is part of an expressive work, such as a parody, the Lanham Act must be construed narrowly. *Harley-Davidson, Inc. v. Grottanelli,* 164 F.3d 806, 813 n. 14 (2d Cir.1999) (quoting Restatement (Third) of Unfair Competition § 25 cmt. i (1995)). Specifically, it has held that the public interest in avoiding consumer confusion must be balanced against the public interest in free speech. *Cliffs Notes, Inc. v. Bantam Doubleday Dell Publ'g,* 886 F.2d 490, 494 (2d Cir.1989). Cases finding that First Amendment interests prevail involve nontrademark uses of mark that is, where the trademark is not being used to indicate the source or origin of consumer products, but rather is being used only to comment upon and, in the case of parody, to ridicule, the trademark owner. *See, e.g., id.; Charles Atlas, Ltd., v. DC Comics, Inc.,* 112 F. Supp. 2d 330 (S.D.N.Y. 2000); *Yankee Publ'g Inc. v. News Am. Publ'g Inc.,* 809 F. Supp. 267 (S.D.N.Y. 1992). In such cases, the parodist is not trading on the good will of the trademark owner to market its own goods; rather, the parodist's sole purpose for using the mark is the parody itself, and precisely for that reason, the risk of consumer confusion is at its lowest. *See id.*

The balancing test adopted by the Second Circuit thus takes into account the purpose behind trademark law, and "allows greater latitude for works such as parodies, in which expression, and not commercial exploitation of another's trademark, is the primary intent, and in which there is a need to evoke the original work *415 being parodied." *Cliffs Notes,* 886 F.2d at 495.

Hilfiger argues that Nature Labs is not entitled to any consideration under the First Amendment because, first, its product admittedly makes no comment about Hilfiger, and second, the use of the mark as a source identifier on the pet perfume is a trademark use of the mark. Hilfiger points out that when asked at his deposition whether his product was intended to make any comment about Hilfiger, Hilfiger products, or Hilfiger customers, John Harris, the general partner of Nature Labs, said no. (Harris Dep. at 36-37) Harris did, however, testify that he was intending to create a "parody . . . target[ing] . . . Tommy Hilfiger," "a fun play on words," or "spoof . . . [t]o create enjoyment, a lighter side." (*Id.* at 30-31, 36) Although Harris had difficulty expressing the parodic content of his communicative message, courts have explained that:

> Trademark parodies . . . do convey a message. The message may be simply that business and product images need not always be taken too seriously;

> a trademark parody reminds us that we are free to laugh at the images and associations linked with the mark. The message also may be a simple form of entertainment conveyed by juxtaposing the irreverent representation of the trademark with the idealized image created by the mark's owner.

See L.L. Bean, Inc. v. Drake Publishers, Inc., 811 F.2d 26, 34 (1st Cir.1987); *see also Anheuser-Busch, Inc. v. L & L Wings, Inc.,* 962 F.2d 316, 321 (4th Cir.1992) (quoting *id.*). One can readily see why high-end fashion brands would be ripe targets for such mockery, and why pet perfume is a clever vehicle for it. Even if not technically a parody, Nature Labs' use is at least a pun or comical expression ideas also held to be entitled to First Amendment protection. *See Yankee Publ'g,* 809 F. Supp. 267, 279 n. 11; *Charles Atlas,* 112 F. Supp. 2d at 337-38 & n. 11.

Hilfiger's second contention, however, merits more attention, for it is clear that when another's mark is used for source identification in a way likely to cause consumer confusion, it is actionable under the Lanham Act. *See, e.g., Harley-Davidson,* 164 F.3d at 812. The First Amendment affords no protection because trademark law permissibly regulates misleading commercial speech. *See Yankee Publ'g,* 809 F. Supp. at 276. *See generally* Robert C. Denicola, *Trademarks as Speech,* 1982 Wisc. L.Rev. 158; Note, *Trademark Parody,* 72 Va. L.Rev. 1079 (1986). In this case, Nature Labs arguably uses an adaptation of the Hilfiger mark for the dual purpose of making an expressive comment and selling a noncompeting product, an area where it has been noted that line-drawing becomes rather difficult. *See Deere & Co. v. MTD Products, Inc.,* 41 F.3d 39, 45 (2d Cir. 1994); *N.Y. Stock Exch. v. New York, New York Hotel, LLC,* 69 F. Supp. 2d 479, 493-94 (S.D.N.Y.1999), *aff'd in part and rev'd in part,* 293 F.3d 550 (2d Cir.2002). However, because the mark is being used at least in part to promote a somewhat nonexpressive, commercial product, the First *416 Amendment does not extend to such use, or to the extent that it does, the balance tips in favor of allowing trademark recovery, if in fact consumers are likely to be confused. *See Harley-Davidson,* 164 F.3d at 812-13; *United We Stand Am., Inc., v. United We Stand, Am. N.Y., Inc.,* 128 F.3d 86, 93 (2d Cir.1997); *Schieffelin & Co. v. Jack Co. of Boca,* 850 F. Supp. 232, 249 n. 9 (S.D.N.Y.1994). When a parodist makes trademark use of another's mark, it should be entitled to less indulgence, even if this results in some residual effect on the free speech rights of commercial actors.

Nevertheless, even without recourse to the First Amendment, Nature Labs' comical adaptation is still relevant to the extent that the joke is clear enough to result in no confusion under the statutory likelihood of confusion analysis. In such cases, "parody is not really a separate 'defense' as such, but merely a way of phrasing the traditional response that customers are not likely to be confused as to source, sponsorship or approval." *Schieffelin,* 725 F. Supp. at 1323. In determining whether there is a likelihood of confusion, courts in this Circuit are guided by the eight-factor test articulated by Judge Friendly in *Polaroid Corp. v. Polarad Electronics Corp.,* 287 F.2d 492, 495 (2d Cir.1961). These factors are: (1) the strength of the plaintiff's mark; (2) the degree of similarity between the two marks; (3) the proximity of the products; (4) the likelihood that the prior owner will bridge the gap between the products; (5) actual confusion; (6) the defendant's bad faith in adopting plaintiff's mark; (7) the quality of defendant's product; and (8) the sophistication of the buyers. Although these factors plainly involve factual inquiries, the application of these factors to the ultimate question of likelihood of confusion is a question of law. *See Hormel Foods Corp. v. Jim Henson Prods.*, 73 F.3d 497, 502 (2d Cir.1996); *Cliffs Notes*, 886 F.2d at 495. Thus, where the relevant facts are undisputed, or fall one way as a matter of law, summary judgment is appropriate. *See Universal City Studios, Inc. v. Nintendo Co.*, 746 F.2d 112, 116 (2d Cir.1984).

1. Strength of Plaintiffs Mark

It is undisputed that plaintiff's mark is widely recognized. (Harris Dep. at 51-52) In the usual trademark case, a strong mark is a factor pointing toward a likelihood of confusion. However, "[w]here the plaintiff's mark is being used as part of a jest . . . the opposite can be true." *Yankee Publ'g*, 809 F. Supp. at 273; *see also N.Y. Stock Exch.*, 69 F. Supp. 2d at 484 (citing *Hormel Foods*, 73 F.3d at 502-03). "The strength and recognizability of the mark may make it easier for the audience to realize that the use is a parody and a joke on the qualities embodied in trademarked word or image." *McCarthy on Trademarks and Unfair Competition* § 31:153 (4th ed.2001) [hereinafter "*McCarthy*"]. That is, it is precisely because of the mark's fame and popularity that confusion is avoided, and it is this lack of confusion that a parodist depends upon to achieve the parody. *See Hormel Foods*, 73 F.3d at 503; *Schieffelin*, 850 F. Supp. at 248. ("Certainly it is unremarkable that [defendant] selected as the target of parody a readily recognizable product; indeed, one would hardly make a spoof of an obscure or unknown product!"). In the present case, Nature Labs' adaptation of Hilfiger's famous mark likely allows consumers both immediately to recognize the target of the joke and to appreciate the obvious changes to the marks that constitute the joke. A distinctive mark will not favor plaintiff in these circumstances.

2. Similarity of the Marks

The marks are undeniably similar in certain respects. There are visual and phonetic similarities between the words "Tommy Hilfiger" and "Tommy Holedigger" or even "Timmy Holedigger." Nature Labs admits that its logo deliberately mimics Hilfiger's and is based upon the Hilfiger mark. (Harris Dep. at 52) It is necessary for the pet perfume to conjure up the original designer fragrance for there to be a parody at all. However, a parody also relies on "equally obvious dissimilarit[ies] between the marks" to produce its desired effect. *Tetley, Inc. v. Topps Chewing Gum, Inc.*, 556 F. Supp. 785, 790 (E.D.N.Y. 1983). "If the difference in wording or appearance of the designation together with the context and overall setting is such to convey to the ordinary viewer that this is a joke, not the real thing, then confusion as to source, sponsorship, affiliation, or connection is unlikely." *McCarthy* § 31:155. Here, "the very broadness of the joke is a measure of the difference" between Hilfiger's marks and Nature Labs' pet perfume. *Tetley*, 556 F. Supp. at 790. The whimsical substitution of the dog-related pun, "Holedigger," on dog perfume, and in some versions, the use of the bone-shaped logo, clearly convey a joking variation on the original. In addition to these changes, there are further alterations to the Hilfiger trademarks on both the early and current pet perfume label designs. In the original "Tommy Holedigger" label, the red and white square are reversed and a different font is used. In the current version, "Tommy" is changed to "Timmy," and the colors and shapes are revised: the red and white squares are changed to red and yellow triangles. These changes reinforce the imitative, yet comedic scheme inherent in a humorous takeoff.

"Moreover, an inquiry into the degree of similarity between the two marks does not end with a comparison of the marks themselves." *Hormel Foods,* 73 F.3d at 503 (citation omitted). One must also look to context, because "the setting in which a designation is used affects its appearance and colors the impression conveyed by it." *Id.* As noted, the marks in this case appear on pet perfume, a product which itself underscores the parody or pun captured in the label. Further, the packaging of the product bears headings or slogans that highlight the intended silliness. These include: "famous pet perfume"; "Strong enough for a man, but made for a chihuahua"; "T. Holedigger keeps your best friend smelling fresh and clean"; "If You Like Tommy Hilfiger, Your Pet Will Love Timmy Holedigger." (Lessem Decl. Exs. C, D, & E) As another Court put it, "such broad satirical adaptation draws a heavy line between itself and the object of satire." *Tetley,* 556 F. Supp. at 785. The last of the above-listed slogans also references a statement in red print on the back of the product that explicitly disclaims any relation between defendant and Tommy Hilfiger. Finally, the Tommy/Timmy Holedigger product is always presented to the consumer along with a variety of other parody pet colognes, such as CK-9 and Pucci, each appearing in an identically shaped bottle. As Nature Labs argues, this context immediately reinforces the message that the perfumes are a parody, and that they come from a single source rather than the multiple sources of the parodied marks.

Taken as a whole and in context, as it should be for a fair evaluation, Nature Labs' presentation accomplishes what the Second Circuit has said it must: "A parody must convey two simultaneous and contradictory messages that it is the original but also that it is not the original and is instead a parody." *Cliffs Notes,* 886 F.2d at 494. Because the parody is sufficiently strong, the similarities between the marks are outweighed by the differences, and do not contribute to a likelihood of confusion.

3. Proximity of the Products

Although an action for trademark recovery is not limited to cases involving competing products, courts are most vigilant to guard against a likelihood of confusion when the plaintiff and defendant use their marks on directly competing products. *See, e.g., Polaroid,* 287 F.2d at 495-498. This is true both generally and in particular as to parodies. Thus, even where the use is humorous, courts have shown little tolerance where the mark is used on a competing product. *See, e.g., Harley-Davidson,* 164 F.3d at 812-13 ("We have accorded considerable leeway to parodists whose expressive works aim their parodic commentary at a trademark or trademarked product, but have not hesitated to prevent a manufacturer from using an alleged parody of a competitor's mark to sell a competing product."); *Gucci Shops, Inc. v. R.H. Macy & Co.,* 446 F. Supp. 838, 839-40 (S.D.N.Y.1977) (GUCCHI

GOO diaper bag found to infringe GUCCI tote bags); *Nabisco Brands, Inc. v. Kaye*, 760 F. Supp. 25 (D.Conn.1991) (A2 steak sauce held to infringe A1 steak sauce); *cf. N.Y. Stock Exch.*, 69 F. Supp. 2d at 493 (distinguishing other cases on the basis that this case "involves some degree of satiric expression by a non-competitor"); *Deere*, 41 F.3d at 44 (noting that joking uses of trademarks are deserving of less protection when the object of the joke is the mark of a directly competing product).

Hilfiger urges that its own cologne and the pet cologne fall within the same general class fragrances and thus are in competitive proximity. Hilfiger further cites testimony that the Holedigger product was created to smell like Hilfiger's fragrances, and is marketed by comparative advertising, to support a professed concern that the pet perfume may serve as a market substitute for its own product. This argument simply does not withstand scrutiny. The products in fact do not compete, and they occupy distinct, non-over-lapping markets. Because pet perfume is for use on pets, not humans, the products "differ in essential character." *Recot Inc. v. Becton*, 2000 WL 1367190, 56 U.S.P.Q.2d 1859, 1861 (2000). Moreover, pet perfume, in its very conception, is a novelty item, a parody of an actual product, for which there is no market independent of the parody. As one Court has noted, "[c]ases involving novelty items are the best examples of parody precluding any possibility for consumer confusion." *Schieffelin*, 725 F. Supp. at 1324. Even if there is a connection between fragrances for pets and humans, or even if a dense and humorless consumer could mistakenly conclude that plaintiff itself sponsored the humorous line of fragrances, plaintiff's and defendant's products are sold in different kinds of stores the former in department or designer stores, the latter in pet stores or gift shops at markedly different prices. *See Tetley*, 556 F. Supp. at 790-91. It is thus plain that the products do not have the market proximity to one another that could create a likelihood of confusion.

4. Likelihood Plaintiff Will Bridge the Gap

Plaintiff has presented no evidence that it is likely to bridge the gap and offer a pet perfume like defendant's, and the evidence does not suggest that the purchasing public would attribute such an enterprise to plaintiff. "In view of [plaintiff's] concern that [defendant's] use of [plaintiff's] marks may tarnish them, it would be surprising if [plaintiff] had such plans." *N.Y. Stock Exch.*, 69 F. Supp. 2d at 485. This factor cannot favor Hilfiger.

5. Actual Confusion

Nor is there evidence of actual confusion in this case. This is not surprising, as a review of the factors thus far shows that the character and context of Nature Labs' products quickly dispels any confusion. Although actual confusion need not be shown for a plaintiff to prevail, "[i]f consumers have been exposed to two allegedly similar trademarks in the marketplace for an adequate period of time and no actual confusion is detected either by survey or in actual reported instances of confusion, that can be powerful indication that the junior trademark does not cause a meaningful likelihood of confusion." *Id.* (quoting *Nabisco, Inc. v. PF Brands,*

Inc., 191 F.3d 208, 228 (2d Cir.1999)). Where, as here, a product has been on the market for several years, the absence of evidence on this point is considered "a very significant deficiency." *Yankee Publ'g,* 809 F. Supp. at 274. Here, it is also significant that Nature Labs now parodies at least 13 other designer brands, not one of which has complained about consumer confusion. *See Tetley,* 556 F. Supp. at 790. That loud silence gives rise to only one inference: consumers have not been confused.

6. Defendant's Bad Faith

Plaintiff cites Nature Labs' intentional copying of Hilfiger's marks as evidence that defendant acted in bad faith. That evidence, however, does not show that defendant acted with the intent relevant in trademark cases that is, an intent to capitalize on consumer deception or hitch a free ride on plaintiff's good will. *See N.Y. Stock Exch.*, 293 F.3d 550, 556 n. 1; *Yankee Publ'g,* 809 F. Supp. at 275. Although it is true that the deliberate adoption of a similar mark may give rise, in the usual case, to a presumption that the copier intended to confuse consumers, in the case of parody, "the intent is not necessarily to confuse the public but rather to amuse":

> In one sense, a parody is an attempt to derive benefit from the reputation of the owner of the mark, if only because no parody could be made without the initial mark. The benefit to the one making the parody, however, arises from the humorous association, not from public confusion as to the source of the marks.

Jordache Enters., Inc. v. Hogg Wyld, Ltd., 828 F.2d 1482, 1486 (10th Cir.1987) (holding that LARDASHE mark on jeans for oversized women was an intentional parody of JORDACHE, but finding no intent to confuse); *accord Anheuser-Busch,* 962 F.2d at 321-22. The commercial success of a parodist's product is attributable to consumers who purchased because "they were amused by the cleverness of its design," and not because they believed it to *420 be the original. *Anheuser-Busch,* 962 F.2d at 322. Of course, confusion can exist despite the intent to create a parody. "[The] single concern here, however, is whether an intent to parody an existing trademark supports an inference of a likelihood of confusion. . . . [I]t does not. An intent to parody is not an intent to confuse the public." *Jordache,* 828 F.2d at 1486.

7. Quality of Defendant's Product

The next factor in the Polaroid analysis can cut either way, depending on the product involved. "An inferior product may cause injury to the plaintiff trademark owner because people may think that the senior and junior user came from the same source; or . . . products of equal quality may tend to create confusion as to source because of this very similarity." *Hormel Foods,* 73 F.3d at 505. In any event, there is no evidence in this case regarding the quality of defendant's product.

8. Sophistication of Consumers

The final factor to be considered is the sophistication of the consumers and the degree of care likely to exercised in purchasing the product. This factor also fails to assist plaintiff. Although the record does not disclose the exact price of Hilfiger's product, both sides agree that it is a "high-end" designer fragrance. The substantial price associated with such goods "requires buyers to exercise care before they part with their money, and such sophistication generally militates against a finding of confusion." *Charles of the Ritz,* 832 F.2d at 1323. It is also counterintuitive that buyers of any sophistication will "impulse buy" a bottle of pet perfume priced at $10.00 a bottle. "To the extent that a shopper might make such a purchase, it would likely be after viewing the bottle carefully, grasping the joke, and seeking to share it with others." *Schieffelin,* 850 F. Supp. at 250; *see also id.* ("This case is not one where unsophisticated customers may fall prey to similar marks of inexpensive products that are in competitive proximity with each other.") Because defendant's "theme and pun on the [Hilfiger] marks are obvious, even a minimally prudent customer would not be confused by the source or affiliation of [defendant's products]. The purchasing public must be credited with at least a modicum of intelligence." *N.Y. Stock Exch.,* 69 F. Supp. 2d at 487.

An analysis of the foregoing factors yields the conclusion that there is no triable issue of fact on the likelihood of confusion. Rather, defendant's use of the mark is an obvious parody or pun, readily so perceived, and unlikely to cause confusion among consumers. *Compare N.Y. Stock Exch.,* 293 F.3d 550 (granting defendant summary judgment on infringement claims because a Las Vegas casino's use of "New York Slot Exchange" on a replica of the Stock Exchange was an "obvious pun and would not cause any confusion among consumers"), *Hormel Foods,* 73 F.3d 497 (holding that the Muppet puppet "Spa'am" was an obvious parody of the luncheon meat SPAM and thus not likely to cause confusion), *Tetley,* 556 F. Supp. 785 (concluding that "Wacky Pack" sticker featuring "Petley Flea Bags" was a heavy-handed parody of TETLEY tea bags unlikely to cause confusion), *with Schieffelin,* 850 F. Supp. 232 (finding DOM POPIGNON popcorn was not a sufficiently strong parody of DOM PERIGNON champagne to avoid confusion, and explaining "[t]his conclusion is compelled in large measure by the evidence of actual confusion").

Hilfiger fails to see the humor in all of this. In support of its dour position on the subject, it cites two opinions in which dog treats parodying human food items were found to infringe on the owner's marks. *See Recot,* 2000 WL 1367190, 56 U.S.P.Q.2d 1859 (refusing to register the *421 mark FIDO-LAY for dog treats because of the likelihood of confusion with FRITO-LAY (but "confess[ing] that [they] have at least some doubt about [their] conclusion")); *Grey v. Campbell Soup Co.,* 650 F. Supp. 1166 (C.D.Cal.1986) (DOGIVA dog biscuits held to infringe GODIVA chocolates), *aff'd,* 830 F.2d 197 (9th Cir.1987) (unpublished table decision). I find these cases distinguishable on at least three relevant grounds: first, the dog and human products in those cases were both offered for sale in the same retail establishments; second, unlike *Grey,* there is no evidence of actual confusion in this case; and third, dog treats are not inherently a parody item as pet perfume is. To the extent these cases are on point, I respectfully disagree with them.

Hilfiger, and perhaps some others, would do well to read *McCarthy* on the subject: "No one likes to be the butt of joke, not even a trademark. But the requirement of trademark law is that a likely confusion of source, sponsorship, or affiliation must be proven, which is not the same thing as a 'right' not to be made fun of." *McCarthy* § 31:155; *see also Anheuser-Busch,* 962 F.2d at 322 ("The purpose of the Lanham Act is to eliminate consumer confusion, not to banish all attempts at poking fun or eliciting amusement . . . [or] deprive the commercial world of all humor and levity."). Although Hilfiger is unamused, it has not offered evidence on the issue of confusion that would justify denying Nature Labs' motion for summary judgment. That motion therefore is granted.

B. Trademark Dilution

Plaintiff's claims of trademark dilution under section 43(c) of the Lanham Act, 15 U.S.C. § 1125(c), and New York General Business Law § 360-1, are also dismissed.

The federal antidilution act prohibits the commercial use of another person's famous mark where the junior use causes "dilution of the distinctive quality of the mark." 15 U.S.C. § 1125(c) (1). Dilution is defined as "the lessening of the capacity of a famous mark to identify and distinguish goods or services, regardless of the presence or absence of (1) competition between the owner of the famous mark and other parties, or (2) likelihood of confusion, mistake, or deception." 15 U.S.C. 1127. Similarly, "a likelihood of injury to business reputation or dilution of the distinctive quality of a mark or trade name" will entitle plaintiff to prevail on its state law claim of dilution, "notwithstanding the absence of competition between the parties or the absence of confusion as to the source of goods or services." N.Y. Gen. Bus. Law § 360-1.

It is undisputed that Hilfiger's marks have the requisite fame and distinction to warrant protection under the antidilution statutes. See *N.Y. Stock Exch.,* 293 F.3d 550, 555-58. The remaining issue is whether Nature Labs' use is likely to dilute the marks. Traditionally, dilution under state law has involved "either the blurring of a mark's product identification or the tarnishment of the affirmative associations a mark has come to convey." *Deere,* 41 F.3d at 42-43 (quoting *Mead Data Central, Inc. v. Toyota Motor Sales, U.S.A., Inc.,* 875 F.2d 1026, 1031 (2d Cir.1989)). These same claims have been held to be actionable under the newer federal provision as well. See *N.Y. Stock Exch.,* 69 F. Supp. 2d at 489.

1. Blurring

"[D]ilution by 'blurring' may occur where the defendant uses or modifies the plaintiff's trademark to identify the defendant's goods and services, raising the possibility that the mark will lose its ability to serve as a unique identifier of the plaintiff's product." *Deere,* 41 F.3d at 43. It *422 typically involves "the whittling away of an established trademark's selling power through its unauthorized use by others upon dissimilar products." *Id.* (citation omitted).

Although a likelihood of confusion is not necessary to find dilution, and indeed may be inconsistent with such a finding, many of the factors relevant to a likelihood of confusion are also relevant to a likelihood of dilution. *See* Restatement (Third) of Unfair Competition § 25 cmt. f; *see also N.Y. Stock Exch.,* 293 F.3d 550, 558; *Nabisco,* 191 F.3d at 217-222; *Yankee Publ'g,* 809 F. Supp. at 282. In this case, the above discussion of the confusion factors also disposes of Hilfiger's blurring claim. *See id.* Rather than result in this type of dilution, Nature Labs' spoof, like other obvious parodies, "tends to increase public identification of a plaintiff's mark with the plaintiff." *Jordache,* 828 F.2d at 1490 (citation omitted); *see Hormel,* 73 F.3d at 506. That is, "the use of famous marks in parodies causes no loss of distinctiveness, since the success of the use depends upon the continued association of the mark with the plaintiff." *Yankee Publ'g,* 809 F. Supp. at 282 (citation omitted). This may be true even when the parody is itself part of a trademark use. *See, e.g., N.Y. Stock Exch.,* 293 F.3d 550, 558; Denicola, *supra,* at 188-89 (citing cases and explaining: "The presence of a famous mark on certain products may have little diluting effect, particularly where it is obvious that the defendant intends the public to associate the use with the true owner.... [T]he joke itself reinforces the public's association of the mark with the plaintiff.") In this instance, the possibility of dilution by blurring is remote. Rather, as in the case of the "Petley Flea Bag" stickers, "the broad humor defendant employs serves to prevent the type of blurring which might result from a more subtle or insidious effort at humor at plaintiff's expense." *Tetley,* 556 F. Supp. at 794. Given the nature of the challenged use, then, and the utter lack of evidence that the selling power of Hilfiger's marks has been diminished, no rational trier of fact could conclude that Nature Labs' pet perfume is likely to impair the identification of Hilfiger's marks with its products.

2. Tarnishment

"Tarnishment'" generally arises when the plaintiff's trademark is linked to products of shoddy quality, or is portrayed in an unwholesome or unsavory context likely to evoke unflattering thoughts about the owner's product. *Deere,* 41 F.3d at 43. The reputation of the trademark is harmed and its value reduced "because the public will associate the lack of quality or prestige in the defendant's goods with the plaintiff's unrelated goods," or because the mark ceases to serve as a "wholesome identifier of the owner's products." *Id.*

In the present case, Hilfiger has submitted no evidence on whether there is a disparity in quality between its own fragrance and the pet perfume. Rather, it complains merely that "Nature Labs' use of 'Tommy Hilfiger' and an imitation of the Hilfiger Flag Design to sell cologne for dogs projects an image at odds with Hilfiger's reputation for high-quality fragrance products for humans." (Pl. Supp. Mem. at 4-5) Plaintiff is correct in pointing out that "tarnishment is not limited to seamy conduct," *see Hormel,* 73 F.3d at 507, and that it is "enough that the image projected by *423 the defendant's mark and services [is] at odds with the image projected by the plaintiff's mark and services," Pl. Supp. Mem. at 4; *see N.Y. Stock Exch.,* 293 F.3d 550, 558. However, "[t]he sina qua non of tarnishment is a finding that plaintiff's mark will suffer negative associations through defendant's use." *Hormel,* 73 F.3d at 507. Here, plaintiff has not put forth any evidence supporting such a conclusion, nor would I expect to find any. *See Tetley,* 556 F. Supp. at 794. Although the *Grey* Court speculated that DOGIVA and CATIVA animal treats would likely tarnish GODIVA chocolates for humans, 650 F. Supp. at 1175, I find that no rational jury could reach the same animal-unfriendly conclusion here. There is nothing to suggest that a designer label has anything to lose from mere association with pets, particularly where the entire association is a light-hearted if somewhat heavy-handed parody. I agree with the conclusion of the district court in *Jordache:* "When the association is essentially a harmless, clean pun, which merely parodies or pokes fun at the plaintiff's mark, tarnishment is not likely." *Jordache Enters. v. Hogg Wyld, Ltd.,* 625 F. Supp. 48, 57 (D.N.M.1985), *aff'd,* 828 F.2d 1482 (10th Cir.1987); *see also McCarthy* §31:155 (quoting *id.*). Even *Deere,* the case upon which Hilfiger principally relies, notes: "Not every alteration will constitute dilution, and more leeway for alterations is appropriate in the context of satiric expression and humorous ads for noncompeting products." *Deere,* 41 F.3d at 45; *see also Hormel,* 73 F.3d at 507-08 (holding that a benign parody product that was not in direct competition with plaintiff's product was unlikely to cause dilution). That observation applies in this case, and I find for defendant on plaintiff's dilution claim.

C. False Advertising

Plaintiff's final claim is for false advertising, based on the comparative statement on the Timmy Holedigger label that reads, "If you like Tommy Hilfiger, your pet will love Timmy Holedigger." Hilfiger alleges that the asserted similarity between the scent of Timmy Hilfiger and the fragrance products sold under the Hilfiger trademarks is a "false and misleading claim." (Pl. Supp. Mem. at 15).

Comparative advertising is often the basis for a false advertising claim, *see McCarthy* §27:59, yet the analysis of any such claim must begin with the recognition that comparative advertising is not only permissible, but encouraged. Such advertisements serve the "beneficial purpose of imparting factual information about the relative merits of competing products." *Deere,* 41 F.3d at 44. It has repeatedly been held that one may copy the unpatented formula of another's product and may use that product's trademark in its advertising to identify the product it has copied. *See Calvin Klein Cosmetics Corp. v. Parfums de Coeur, Ltd.,* 824 F.2d 665, 668 (8th Cir.1987); *Smith v. Chanel, Inc.,* 402 F.2d 562, 563 (9th Cir.1968), and its progeny. Indeed, courts have upheld so-called "like/love" slogans such as the one at issue here. *See id.; Diversified Mktg., Inc. v. Estee Lauder, Inc.,* 705 F. Supp. 128 (S.D.N.Y.1988). The only limitations the Lanham Act imposes on these slogans are that the advertiser cannot make false claims about the similarity of the products involved, and that the advertiser cannot use another product's mark in a way that is likely to confuse consumers about the source of the advertiser's product. *See Saxony Prods., Inc. v. Guerlain, Inc.,* 513 F.2d 716, 722 (9th Cir.1975); *Charles of the Ritz,* 636 F. Supp. at 435. Liability on the latter theory has been discussed and rejected, *see supra* p. 13-14 & n. 5, because the parodic context in which the statement appears sufficiently cures any consumer confusion. The subject claim here rests on Hilfiger's assertion that the advertisement is untruthful.

Once again, that the statement in question is attached to a parody product is relevant to the applicability of the Lanham Act's proscription of false claims. Although Nature Labs asserts that its claim is true, it is hard to imagine anyone relying on the truth of Nature Labs' statement in the same way one does when trying to buy a lower-cost copy of a product in the typical "like/love" case. A statement drawing a likeness between the buyer's own taste and that of his or her pet is unverifiable puff. The injury plaintiff will suffer, and upon which standing to bring this claim is based, is not as clear as in other comparative advertising cases, where the parties are competitors. *Cf. Ortho Pharmaceutical Corp. v. Cosprophar, Inc.*, 32 F.3d 690, 694-697 (2d Cir.1994) (discussing standing requirements and citing relevant case law). To put the point in the form of a question, is Hilfiger likely to be damaged by a diversion in sales, either through pet-owners ceasing to use Hilfiger products on their pets or starting to use pet perfume on themselves? Somehow, I don't think so. Nevertheless, the Second Circuit has held, albeit in the context of competing products, that harm will be presumed in cases of false comparative advertising that mentions plaintiff's product by name. *See McNeilab, Inc. v. Am. Home Prods. Corp.*, 848 F.2d 34, 38 (2d Cir.1988). I will therefore apply that presumption here.

Turning to the merits then, the relevant portion of the Lanham Act prohibits any "false or misleading description of fact, or false or misleading representation of fact, which . . . in commercial advertising or promotion, misrepresents the nature, characteristics, qualities, or geographic origins of [the advertiser's] goods." 15 U.S.C. § 1125(a). To prevail, a plaintiff must show either: (1) that an advertisement is literally false; or (2) that the advertisement, though literally true, is likely to mislead or confuse consumers. *See S.C. Johnson & Son, Inc. v. Clorox Co.*, 241 F.3d 232, 238 (2d Cir. 2001).

Hilfiger rests its claim of falsity upon the deposition testimony of Nature Labs' John Harris, in which Harris admitted never having done a comparison or chemical analysis of the two products. (Harris Dep. at 56) In making its pet perfume, Nature Labs buys its fragrances from several third parties and mixes it with alcohol to achieve the desired scent. The testing of the product consists of Harris's spraying the product on himself. (*Id.* at 105-06) However, where an advertiser makes a simple claim of equivalence, as is the case here, it is not enough to show that the claim is unsubstantiated. Rather, plaintiff must show affirmatively that the statement is false. *See Castrol, Inc. v. Quaker State Corp.*, 977 F.2d 57, 62-63 (2d Cir.1992) (citing *Procter & Gamble Co. v. Chesebrough-Pond's Inc.*, 747 F.2d 114, 119 (2d Cir.1984)). The only other evidence on the scent of the pet perfume is Harris's testimony that the Tommy/Timmy Holedigger cologne smells like his recollection of the scent of Hilfiger cologne. (Harris Dep. at 56) Plaintiff offers no evidence as to the composition or olfactory impression of the two perfumes, and therefore plaintiff's claim of literal falsity fails as a matter of law.

To the extent plaintiff is not relying on literal falsity, and instead is arguing that the statement is misleading, plaintiff still fails to meet its burden. To prevail on this theory, plaintiff is required to "produce consumer surveys or some surrogate to prove whether consumers expect the advertising claim to be substantiated and whether they expect the level of substantiation to be greater than that which the defendant has performed." *McCarthy* § 21:61 (citing *Sandoz Pharm. Corp. v. Richardson-Vicks,*

Inc., 902 F.2d 222 (3d Cir.1990)); *Johnson & Johnson-Merck Consumer Pharm. Co. v. Rhone-Poulenc* *425 *Rorer Pharm., Inc.*, 19 F.3d 125 (3d Cir. 1994); *see also L & F Prods. v. Procter & Gamble Co.*, 45 F.3d 709, 711 (2d Cir.1995) (explaining that extrinsic evidence must confirm that a commercial is likely to mislead consumers); *Coors Brewing Co. v. Anheuser-Busch Cos., Inc.*, 802 F. Supp. 965, 969 (S.D.N.Y.1992) (same). Plaintiff has not offered any such evidence. Because plaintiff has not put forth a genuine issue as to a material fact, there is no triable dispute, and summary judgment for defendant is proper.

* * *

For the reasons set forth above, defendant's motion for summary judgment is granted. As the Ninth Circuit recently counseled both parties in a bitterly contested trademark parody case, plaintiff is "advised to chill." *Mattel, Inc. v. MCA Records, Inc.*, No. 296 F.3d at 908 (9th Cir.2002).

SO ORDERED.

Notes

1. The Court observed: "I do not find that a statement advertising that if *you* like Hilfiger, *your pet* will love Holedigger" raises an issue of fact on confusion. Do you think a survey might have been advisable to determine whether the advertisement may have created a likelihood of confusion, association, or affiliation between Tommy Hilfiger and Nature Labs?

2. The Court noted that Nature Labs' intentional copying of Tommy Hilfiger's marks does not show that defendant acted with the bad faith intent relevant in trademark cases—that is, an intent to capitalize on consumer deception or hitch a free ride on plaintiff's goodwill. How could Tommy Hilfiger have established bad faith in a parody case?

Louis Vuitton Malletier, S.A. v. My Other Bag, Inc.

674 F. App'x 16 (2d Cir. 2016)

CALABRESI, Circuit Judge; RAGGI, Circuit Judge; LYNCH, Circuit Judge.

Plaintiff Louis Vuitton Malletier, S.A. ("LV") appeals from an award of summary judgment in favor of My Other Bag, Inc. ("MOB") on LV's claims under federal and state trademark and copyright law. See 15 U.S.C. §§ 1114, 1125; 17 U.S.C. § 501; N.Y. Gen. Bus. Law § 360-l. We review an award of summary judgment de novo, construing the evidence in the light most favorable to the non-moving party and drawing all reasonable inferences in its favor. *See, e.g., Cross Commerce Media, Inc. v. Collective, Inc.*, 841 F.3d 155, 162 (2d Cir. 2016). We assume the parties' familiarity with the facts and record of prior proceedings, which we reference only as necessary to explain our decision to affirm for substantially the reasons stated by the district court in its thorough and well-reasoned opinion. *See Louis Vuitton Malletier, S.A. v. My Other Bag, Inc.*, 156 F. Supp. 3d 425 (S.D.N.Y. 2016).

1. Trademark Infringement

LV submits that the district court ignored or discounted favorable record evidence during its application of the non-exclusive, eight-factor Polaroid balancing test, *see Polaroid Corp. v. Polarad Electronics Corp.*, 287 F.2d 492 (2d Cir. 1961), and thereby wrongly concluded that there was no likelihood of consumer confusion between LV's and MOB's products. The argument fails because, whether we review the district court's findings as to each Polaroid factor deferentially, *see Playtex Prods., Inc. v. Ga.-Pac. Corp.*, 390 F.3d 158, 162 (2d Cir. 2004), or *de novo, see generally Kelly-Brown v. Winfrey*, No. 15-697-CV, 2016 WL 4945415, at *2 n.3 (2d Cir. Sept. 16, 2016), we reach the same conclusion. Specifically, obvious differences in MOB's mimicking of LV's mark, the lack of market proximity between the products at issue, and minimal, unconvincing evidence of consumer confusion compel a judgment in favor of MOB on LV's trademark infringement claim. Accordingly, we affirm this part of the summary judgment award to MOB.

2. Trademark Dilution

LV argues that the district court erred in finding as a matter of law that the use of its marks on MOB's tote bags was parodic, bringing it within the "fair use" exclusion from dilution liability. *See* 15 U.S.C. § 1125(c)(3). Whether parody is properly identified before or after conducting the six-factor dilution analysis stated in § 1125(c)(2)(B), *see generally Starbucks Corp. v. Wolfe's Borough Coffee, Inc.*, 588 F.3d 97, 112 (2d Cir. 2009) (assuming without deciding that factor analysis should be conducted first), the district court correctly awarded judgment to MOB.

"A parody must convey two simultaneous—and contradictory—messages: that it is the original, but also that it is not the original and is instead a parody." *Hormel Foods Corp. v. Jim Henson Prods., Inc.*, 73 F.3d 497, 503 (2d Cir. 1996) (*quoting Cliffs Notes, Inc. v. Bantam Doubleday Dell Publ'g Grp., Inc.*, 886 F.2d 490, 495 (2d Cir. 1989)). MOB's bags do precisely that. At the same time that they mimic LV's designs and handbags in a way that is recognizable, they do so as a drawing on a product that is such a conscious departure from LV's image of luxury—in combination with the slogan "My other bag"—as to convey that MOB's tote bags are not LV handbags. The fact that the joke on LV's luxury image is gentle, and possibly even complimentary to LV, does not preclude it from being a parody. *See Louis Vuitton Malletier, S.A. v. My Other Bag, Inc.*, 156 F. Supp. 3d at 435–38; *see also L.L. Bean, Inc. v. Drake Publishers, Inc.*, 811 F.2d 26, 34 (1st Cir. 1987) ("[A] trademark parody reminds us that we are free to laugh at the images and associations linked with the mark . [or provides] entertainment conveyed by juxtaposing the irreverent representation of the trademark with the idealized image created by the mark's owner."). Indeed, a parody of LV's luxury image is the very point of MOB's plebian product. That distinguishes this case from ones cited by LV where a trademark was used merely to "promote" or "sell" goods and services, which is impermissible. *See Starbucks Corp. v. Wolfe's Borough Coffee, Inc.*, 588 F.3d at 115 (using "Charbucks" to identify coffee blend as one competing at same level and quality as Starbucks);

Harley Davidson, Inc. v. Grottanelli, 164 F.3d 806, 813 (2d Cir. 1999) (using Harley-Davidson logo to advertise motorcycle repair shop).

LV nevertheless contends that MOB is not entitled to a fair-use dilution defense because MOB uses LV's marks as a "designation of source." 15 U.S.C. § 1125(c)(3)(A). The district court, however, determined that the testimony of MOB's CEO, upon which LV principally relies to support this argument, unambiguously refers to the likelihood of consumer confusion, not the designation of source. *See Louis Vuitton Malletier, S.A. v. My Other Bag, Inc.*, 156 F. Supp. 3d at 437–38 (*citing J.A.* 350–51). Our review of the transcript does not suggest otherwise. In any event, the nature of MOB's business—it sells quite ordinary tote bags with drawings of various luxury-brand handbags, not just LV's, printed thereon—and the presence of "My other bag," an undisputed designation of source, on one side of each bag, independently support summary judgment for MOB on this designation-of-source issue.

Accordingly, we affirm the award of summary judgment to MOB on LV's federal trademark-dilution claim. We likewise affirm summary judgment to MOB on LV's state-law dilution claim. While N.Y. Gen. Bus. Law § 360-l does not provide an explicit fair-use defense, the manifest parodic use here precludes the requisite finding that the marks are "substantially similar." *See Starbucks Corp. v. Wolfe's Borough Coffee, Inc.*, 588 F.3d at 114 (internal quotation marks omitted).

3. Copyright Infringement

MOB's parodic use of LV's designs produces a "new expression [and] message" that constitutes transformative use. *Campbell v. Acuff-Rose Music, Inc.*, 510 U.S. at 579 (alterations, citations, and internal quotation marks omitted); *accord TCA Television Corp. v. McCollum*, 839 F.3d 168, 180 (2d Cir. 2016). Like the district court, we conclude that the remaining fair-use factors either weigh in MOB's favor or are irrelevant, *see Louis Vuitton Malletier, S.A. v. My Other Bag, Inc.*, 156 F. Supp. 3d at 444–45, and LV's arguments to the contrary largely repeat or echo those we have already rejected.

Accordingly, we affirm the award of summary judgment to MOB on LV's copyright claim.

4. Conclusion

We have considered LV's remaining arguments and conclude that they are without merit. Accordingly, the judgment of the district court is AFFIRMED.

Notes

1. Following the Second Circuit's decision, Louis Vuitton filed a petition for certiorari with the following Question Presented: "Whether the Second Circuit's test for determining if the unauthorized use of a famous mark constitutes parody is inconsistent with the Trademark Dilution Revision Act?" In its petition for certiorari, Louis Vuitton wrote that: "The Second Circuit's decision . . . vastly expands the fair-use exception beyond the narrow bounds that Congress intended, leaving famous marks vulnerable to widespread dilution through the production of

imitation products marketed under the guise of 'parody.'" The Supreme Court did not grant the petition. Do you agree with that decision?

2. Louis Vuitton contended in its petition for certiorari that the circuit courts of appeal, including the Fourth Circuit and Second Circuit, "have repeatedly confused the concepts of trademark dilution and trademark infringement when making parody determinations in dilution cases." Specifically, Louis Vuitton contended that in a case of dilution by blurring under the TDRA, the question of whether the parody "convey[ed] two simultaneous—and contradictory—messages: that it is the original, but also that it is not the original and is instead a parody" is not the proper test because in a case of dilution it is irrelevant whether consumers would confuse the two marks at issue. Have the parody cases involving trademark dilution claims been uniformly decided?

The following case arose from a toy company bringing a declaratory judgment action to resolve the issue of dilution before it mass-produced its goods. Consider whether this was a wise decision.

MGA Entertainment, Inc. v. Louis Vuitton Malletier, S.A.

2019 U.S. Dist. LEXIS 81397 (C.D. Cal. May 14, 2019)

WALTER, District Judge.

Statement of Decision Granting Motion to Dismiss Pursuant to Fed. R. CIV. P. 12(B)(1)

On April 19, 2019, Defendant Louis Vuitton Malletier, S.A.S. ("Louis Vuitton") filed a Motion to Dismiss Plaintiff MGA Entertainment, Inc.'s ("MGA") First Amended Complaint in its entirety. On April 29, 2019, MGA filed its Opposition. On May 6, 2019, Louis Vuitton filed a Reply. After considering the moving, opposing, and reply papers, and the arguments therein, the Court rules that MGA failed to establish that an actual controversy exists between the parties. As a result, the Court hereby dismisses MGA's First Amended Complaint for lack of jurisdiction pursuant to Fed. R. Civ. P. 12(b)(1) without leave to amend.

I. Background

On April 5, 2019, MGA filed a First Amended Complaint against Louis Vuitton seeking a declaratory judgment that MGA's toy product in no way violates Louis Vuitton's intellectual property rights. MGA is a California corporation that develops and distributes children's toys, including the "Bratz" dolls and a "handbag shaped toy container" referred to as "Pooey Puitton." (First Am. Compl. (Dkt. No. 35) ¶¶ 5, 10, 11, 13.) MGA alleges that on or around December 7, 2018, Louis Vuitton filed an action in a French court alleging that the Pooey Puitton name (the "Pooey Name") and product (the "Pooey Product") infringe upon and disparage certain E.U. trademarks owned by Louis Vuitton, and seeking orders from the court permitting the seizure of Pooey Products from E.U. businesses that had purchased them. (*Id.* ¶¶ 17, 19.) Louis Vuitton and MGA are now engaged in a lawsuit in France in which Louis Vuitton seeks relief in France for MGA's claimed violation of Louis Vuitton's E.U. trademark rights. (*Id.* ¶¶ 22-26.) In its action here, MGA claims that by filing an action in France alleging violation of its E.U. trademarks, Louis Vuitton has asserted claims against MGA and its customers in the United States related to U.S. trademarks, which MGA claims are "identical" to those asserted in the French proceedings. (*Id.* ¶ 30.)

The First Amended Complaint additionally alleges that there is an actual controversy between the parties because Louis Vuitton "has a history of not respecting parody rights" and "filing vexatious lawsuits" related to its trademarks. (*Id.* ¶ 60.) MGA refers to three such cases concerning unrelated companies and products. (*Id.* ¶¶ 61-62.) On this basis, MGA concludes that an "actual, present, and justiciable controversy has arisen between Plaintiff and Defendants concerning their respective rights." (*Id.* ¶ 69.)

MGA asks the Court to declare that: (a) MGA's use of the Pooey Name and the Pooey Product does not infringe or dilute Louis Vuitton's trademarks; (b) the Pooey Name and the Pooey Product are protected as fair use under 15 U.S.C. § 1125(c)(3)(A); (c) the Pooey Name and the Pooey Product are protected as parody under 15 U.S.C. § 1125(c)(3)(A)(ii); and (d) MGA may continue to market and distribute the Pooey Product and may continue to use the Pooey Name. (*Id.* at Prayer for Relief.)

Louis Vuitton now moves to dismiss pursuant to Fed. R. Civ. P. 12(b)(1) on the grounds that MGA's First Amended Complaint fails to plead that an actual controversy exists under the laws of the United States sufficient to establish subject matter jurisdiction under the Declaratory Judgment Act ("DJA").

II. Legal Standard

Article III § 2 of the United States Constitution limits the jurisdiction of federal courts to "Cases" and "Controversies" between parties. Therefore, the plaintiff must establish that an actual case or controversy exists before a federal court can exercise subject matter jurisdiction in any case. *See, e.g., Lujan v. Defs. of Wildlife*, 504 U.S. 555, 560-61 (1992).

The same rule applies where, as here, the plaintiff seeks a declaratory judgment. The DJA states, "[i]n a case of *actual controversy* within its jurisdiction . . . any court of the United States, upon the filing of an appropriate pleading, may declare the rights and other legal relations of any interested party seeking such declaration." 28 U.S.C. § 2201(a) (emphasis added). "[T]he phrase 'case of actual controversy' in the [DJA] refers to the type of 'Cases' and 'Controversies' that are justiciable under Article III." *MedImmune, Inc. v. Genentech, Inc.*, 549 U.S. 118, 127 (2007).

To meet the "actual controversy" standard of the DJA, as required to invoke the Court's jurisdiction, a plaintiff must allege facts showing that there is a dispute between the parties that is: "definite and concrete, touching the legal relations of parties having adverse legal interests; and that it be real and substantial and admit of specific relief through a decree of a conclusive character, as distinguished from an opinion advising what the law would be upon a hypothetical state of facts." *Id.* (internal quotation marks and citation omitted).

The plaintiff bears the burden of establishing that the Court has jurisdiction. *Kokkonen v. Guardian Life Ins. Co. of Am.*, 511 U.S. 375, 377 (1994). To invoke federal subject matter jurisdiction, a plaintiff "must allege facts, not mere legal conclusions" sufficient to establish grounds for the Court's jurisdiction. *Leite v. Crane Co.*, 749 F.3d 1117, 1121 (9th Cir. 2014) (citing *Bell Atl. Corp. v. Twombly,* 550 U.S. 544 (2007) and *Ashcroft v. Iqbal,* 556 U.S. 662 (2009)).

A Rule 12(b)(1) motion to dismiss for lack of subject matter jurisdiction "may be facial or factual. In a facial attack, the challenger asserts that the allegations contained in a complaint are insufficient on their face to invoke federal jurisdiction." *Safe Air for Everyone v. Meyer,* 373 F.3d 1035, 1039 (9th Cir. 2004) (internal citation omitted). "The district court resolves a facial attack as it would a motion to dismiss under Rule 12(b)(6): Accepting the plaintiff's allegations as true and drawing all reasonable inferences in the plaintiff's favor, the court determines whether the allegations are sufficient as a legal matter to invoke the court's jurisdiction." *Leite,* 749 F.3d at 1121. But "the Court is not required to accept mere conclusory allegations nor does the Court necessarily assume the truth of legal conclusions merely because they are cast in the form of factual allegations." *Cattie v. Wal-Mart Stores, Inc.*, 504 F. Supp. 2d 939, 943 (S.D. Cal. 2007).

Finally, where a motion to dismiss is granted, the Court must decide whether to grant leave to amend. While leave to amend should generally be freely granted, *DeSoto v. Yellow Freight System, Inc.*, 957 F.2d 655, 658 (9th Cir. 1992), a Court need not grant leave to amend in cases where "the pleadings before the court demonstrate that further amendment would be futile." *Rutman Wine Co. v. E. & J. Gallo Winery,* 829 F.2d 729, 738 (9th Cir. 1987).

III. Discussion

The allegations of MGA's First Amended Complaint fail to establish that an actual controversy exists under U.S. laws to establish jurisdiction under the DJA.

A. MGA's Assertion that a Claim about E.U. Rights is a Claim about U.S. Rights is Unsupported.

MGA argues that by filing an action in France concerning E.U. trademark registrations, Louis Vuitton has asserted claims against MGA in the United States concerning Louis Vuitton's U.S. trademark registrations. (First Am. Compl. ¶ 30.) The Court disagrees.

It is a fundamental tenet of trademark law that "a trademark has a separate legal existence in each country and receives the protection afforded by the laws of that country." *Am. Circuit Breaker Corp. v. Or. Breakers Inc.*, 406 F.3d 577, 582 (9th Cir. 2005) (internal citation omitted); *see also Person's Co., Ltd. v. Christman,* 900 F.2d 1565, 1568-69 (Fed. Cir. 1990). Because of the jurisdictionally bound nature of trademarks, a foreign court's determination whether a product infringes trademarks registered under that country's laws has no relevance to or effect on whether a product infringes U.S. trademarks. *Calzaturificio Rangoni S.p.A. v. U.S. Shoe Corp.*, 868 F. Supp. 1414, 1418 (S.D.N.Y. 1994). For the same reason, "when trade-mark rights within the United States are being litigated in an American court, the decisions of foreign courts concerning the respective trade-mark rights of the parties are irrelevant and inadmissible." *Fuji Photo Film Co, Inc. v. Shinohara Shoji Kabushiki Kaisha*, 754 F.2d 591, 599 (5th Cir. 1985) (internal citation omitted).

Here, MGA alleges that "[a]s a result of Louis Vuitton's filing of the French Action, . . . Louis Vuitton has asserted claims against MGA and its customers in the United States based upon its identical registrations for the LV Word Mark and LV Design Mark in the United States, and with the USPTO." (First Am. Compl. ¶ 30.) By law, however, E.U. and U.S. trademark rights are separate and distinct. *Am. Circuit Breaker*, 406 F.3d at 582. What may constitute impermissible action by MGA under E.U. trademark law may be permissible in the U.S. or *vice versa*. Furthermore, any determination that the French court may make regarding Pooey Puitton and Louis Vuitton's E.U. trademark rights has no relevance to any question of U.S. law, U.S. trademark registrations, or the parties' U.S. rights. *Fuji Photo*, 754 F.2d at 599. Accordingly, an assertion of E.U. trademark rights is *not* an assertion of U.S. trademark rights. The fact that the E.U. marks and U.S. marks may appear visually similar or identical does not eliminate this distinction.

In addition, MGA fails to plead facts that Louis Vuitton has asserted its U.S. trademark rights. MGA does *not* allege that Louis Vuitton is seeking to enforce its U.S. marks in the French proceedings. The First Amended Complaint does not allege that Louis Vuitton has ever communicated with MGA about the U.S. marks, claimed infringement or dilution of the U.S. marks, threatened or filed litigation asserting the U.S. marks, or taken any concrete action at all related to the Pooey Product and the Pooey Name in the U.S. and Louis Vuitton's U.S. marks. In its Opposition, MGA references post-complaint meet-and-confer discussions between the parties where Louis Vuitton stated it does not intend to bring suit in the United States related to the Pooey Puitton product and argues that this statement shows an actual controversy. (Opposition (Dkt. No. 42) at 8.) This argument does not follow, and in any event, consideration of such post-complaint events is improper in determining subject matter jurisdiction here. *Innovative Therapies, Inc. v. Kinetic Concepts, Inc.*, 599 F.3d 1377, 1383-84 (Fed. Cir. 2010).

B. The Foreign Action Does Not Show an Actual Controversy.

Numerous courts have ruled that a claim pending elsewhere of violation of foreign intellectual property rights standing alone does not support the finding of an actual controversy between the same parties related to U.S. intellectual property rights. *See, e.g., Avon Prods., Inc. v. Moroccanoil, Inc.*, 2013 WL 795652, *3-4 (S.D.N.Y. Mar. 4, 2013); *Schutte Bagclosures Inc. v. Kwik Lok Corp.*, 48 F. Supp. 3d 675, 691-93 (S.D.N.Y. 2014); *San DiskCorp. v. Audio MPEG, Inc.*, No. C-06-02655 RMW, 2007 WL 30598, *3 (N.D. Cal. Jan. 3, 2007); *Studex Corp. v. Blomdahl Med. Innovation AB*, 355 F. Supp. 2d 3, 8-9 (D.D.C. 2004).

Here, MGA claims that Louis Vuitton's French lawsuit against MGA regarding E.U. trademark rights establishes an actual controversy exists concerning the Pooey Product and Pooey Name and Louis Vuitton's U.S. marks. But, as the cases cited above establish, litigation concerning foreign rights standing alone does not support the finding of an actual controversy here, and the Court will not find otherwise.

C. MGA's Decision-Making and Contractual Agreements Do Not Evidence an Actual Controversy.

MGA's allegations that it makes decisions about the Pooey Name and Pooey Product in the United States and in the Central District of California, and that its agreements with customers are governed by California and U.S. law, do not change the fact that the only outstanding dispute between the parties is one pending in a French court concerning E.U. trademark rights. That action has no connection to Louis Vuitton's U.S. trademarks, which are MGA's only claimed basis for the Court's subject matter jurisdiction in this case. (*See* First Am. Compl. ¶ 2.) MGA's contracts with its customers are similarly irrelevant to whether there is an actual controversy in the United States between MGA and Louis Vuitton, as those contracts have no connection to a claimed dispute between the parties here.

MGA also argues in Opposition that there may be a "chilling effect" on its actions in the United States based on Louis Vuitton's institution of an action in France. (Opposition at 10.) But this subjective concern on MGA's part does not evidence that the parties have taken "adverse positions" regarding Louis Vuitton's U.S. trademarks, or that their "conflict of interests" regarding Louis Vuitton's U.S. trademarks are "real and immediate," such that an actual controversy exists as to those trademarks. *Societe de Conditionnement en Aluminium v. Hunter Eng'g Co., Inc.*, 655 F.2d 938, 943 (9th Cir. 1981).

D. MGA's Allegations about Other Cases, Companies, and Products are Irrelevant.

MGA's attempt to create a controversy between the parties by alleging that Louis Vuitton has a "history of not respecting parody rights in the United States and filing vexatious lawsuits against such protected parody," First Am. Compl. ¶ 60, is similarly unavailing. *See SanDisk,* 2007 WL 30598, at *5 (contentions that Defendant was "litigious" did not support finding actual case or controversy). Rather than looking at past behavior concerning other unrelated companies and products to determine whether there is an actual controversy here, the Court need look only to the fact that Louis Vuitton has *not* sued MGA based on its trademark rights in the U.S., while it has initiated proceedings in France. These past events do not support the finding of a case or controversy.

E. MGA Seeks an Impermissible Advisory Opinion.

MGA's First Amended Complaint is also improper in that it seeks a broad advisory order that is not limited to the Louis Vuitton trademarks identified in the First Amended Complaint, nor to a decision regarding MGA's rights in relation to Louis Vuitton. (*See* First Am. Compl. at Prayer for Relief.) Instead, by, among other things, asking for a judgment that "MGA may continue to market and distribute its Pooey Product, and may continue to use the Pooey Name in associate with the Pooey Product" (*id.* at Prayer for Relief, ¶ D), MGA seeks a judicial endorsement of its product against legal challenges of any kind. The requested relief is an example of an advisory opinion that courts will not allow. *See Veoh Networks, Inc. v. UMG Recordings, Inc.*, 522 F. Supp. 2d 1265, 1270 (S.D. Cal. 2007). Though MGA disclaims in its Opposition that it intended to seek such broad relief (Opposition at 11-12), the plain language of the First Amended Complaint speaks for itself.

IV. Conclusion

MGA's First Amended Complaint fails to allege sufficient facts to establish that an actual controversy exists between the parties as required for jurisdiction under the Declaratory Judgment Act. Because there are no additional facts that could be alleged that would cure the defects in the First Amended Complaint, no leave to amend is granted. *Doe v. U.S.*, 58 F.3d 494, 497 (9th Cir. 1995).

Good cause appearing thereof, IT IS HEREBY ORDERED THAT:

f1. Louis Vuitton's Motion to Dismiss MGA's First Amended Complaint is GRANTED without leave to amend; and

2. All claims for relief against Louis Vuitton are hereby DISMISSED with prejudice.

Notes

1. Do you think the Pooey Puitton name and Pooey Product would be protected as a parody under United States law?

2. Do you think that the tee shirt below, which resulted in a lawsuit (*Luxury Goods International v. Jeanine Heller*) in the United States District Court of the Southern District of New York, is an actionable parody?

Chapter 6

Design and Utility Patents

Barry Lewin

The fashion world has expanded from focusing primarily on style and comfort to also encompassing specialized technology, and now includes a variety of wearable products and accessories and the processes for making and using those goods. Examples of embedded technology in fashion include elements for diagnosing or treating medical issues, technology configured for collecting or utilizing data to improve a person's lifestyle, or advanced materials for providing improved comfort to athletes as health or environmental conditions change.

Patent protection in the fashion world has been somewhat limited. Historically, fashion designers were primarily concerned with protecting their novel designs and enforcing those protected designs against others, so design patents were most common. However, the usefulness of patent protection and enforcement is gaining significance in the fashion world due to the use of innovative materials and manufacturing processes, functionality being built into designs, and the speed at which others can incorporate new designs in their products.

A. Patents in General

Patents are prescribed in the U.S. Constitution (Art. I, Sect. 8) and the patent function in the United States is reserved to the federal government (no patents are granted by the states or territories of the United States). An agency of the Commerce Department, the United States Patent and Trademark Office ("USPTO") handles all U.S. applications for patents. To request a patent, one applies to the USPTO, which examines the application relative to statutes prescribed by Congress and related case law. In general, to obtain patent protection, the application must meet criteria including novelty and non-obviousness over prior inventions.

There are two relevant types of patents: design and utility patents. A design patent protects ornamental appearance while a utility patent protects functional elements of useful goods, systems, materials, and processes. In other words, utility patents protect novel functional aspects of a given technology—a protection distinct from the protection afforded by design patents. A patent provides its owners with a limited monopoly, including the right to exclude others from practicing the invention. Design patent protection lasts about 15 years and utility patent protection can last about 20 years. Once the term of a design or utility patent expires, the patent is no longer infringeable, it enters the "public domain," and becomes available for everyone's use. A design or utility patent term is not renewable (unlike trademark protection). This converging of technology with appearance has resulted in the same product commonly being the subject of both utility and design patents.

Design patents and utility patents can be harder to obtain than trademark or copyright registrations. To achieve the limited monopoly of a patent, the subject matter of an application must meet three fundamental criteria (among others):

1. Novel—meaning the first to bring the invention to the attention of a patent office anywhere in the world;
2. Not Obvious—as compared with published or disclosed designs in the marketplace, in patents, or otherwise published; and
3. Ornamental or Useful—the design is primarily ornamental for design patent applications or useful for utility patent applications.

Upon application, a USPTO Examiner, typically a person who handles applications in this technical field, conducts an extensive search for earlier published and relevant references ("prior art") in order to determine if the present invention meets the novelty and non-obviousness criteria (among others) for patentability. The process can be highly interactive over several years for a utility patent and typically takes about a year or two for a design patent. In addition, the criteria for patentability change frequently—the USPTO rules change, court interpretations of statutes happen regularly, and Congress amends the statutes from time to time, often reflecting changing technology. Although these hurdles may seem tremendous, applicants continue to seek patent protection because of the value patents can bring.

Due in part to the highly technical nature of procuring a valuable patent involving both technology and the law, many applicants seek representation from an experienced patent attorney. A patent attorney is someone who is licensed and admitted to practice at the USPTO, requiring that the attorney be admitted to the bar in at least one state and pass a separate USPTO exam (the patent bar exam), which can only be taken by someone with adequate academic training in science, math, or engineering.

The validity of an issued patent may later be challenged. For instance, a patent holder may bring a claim against a potential infringer, who may counter that the patent fails to meet one or more of the three criteria, among other reasons. A patent may be invalidated if a court determines that one or more of the criteria was not satisfied.

While a patent application is pending in the USPTO, its owner generally marks the product with "Patent Pending" to notify others of the possibility of a patent. When the patent is issued, the marking should change, reflecting the patent protection. It is imperative to mark the patented goods because failure to do so may limit or preclude damages recoverable from an infringer. In the event that the product is not marked, a court may hold that the infringement damages will start from when the infringer had "notice." Filing an infringement action also constitutes notice. When the product is not marked, the patent holder may only recover from the date that "notice" was given, even if the infringer was profiting from the product for years.

B. Design Patents

Although popular perceptions and news reports typically refer to utility patents, design patents have been more common in the fashion world. Typical fashion objects protectable by design patent include the appearance of eyeglass frames, handbags, watches, footwear, jewelry, perfume bottles, and even dishes and cutlery.

Under 35 U.S.C. § 171(a), "whoever invents any new, original and ornamental design for an article of manufacture may obtain a patent . . . ." To obtain a design patent, sometimes referred to as a "picture patent," the design must be embodied in the article of manufacture. The design must be ornamental in nature and if the design is dictated by the performance of the article, it may be considered "functional" and therefore ineligible for design patent protection.

A design patent applicant files an application with clear and complete drawings showing views of the product from multiple directions (usually six or more orientations), and the scope of protection in the granted patent is based on these views. In some cases, shading is used, for example, to show curvature. It is imperative to file drawings with care since "design patents are typically claimed as shown in drawings, and claim construction must be adapted to a pictorial setting." *Crocs, Inc. v. International Trade Commission*, 598 F.3d 1294, 1302 (Fed. Cir. 2010).

Although utility patents are rapidly becoming more common in fashion, design patent protection is usually preferred and continues to be used in part because of its comparatively low cost and rapid examination in the USPTO. When fashion companies ready a new design, they would (and still) often file for design patent protection in selected jurisdictions, typically filing in at least one jurisdiction before the product is publicly released. The timing for filing can be based on the desired locales of patent protection. While the U.S. allows filing within a year of first public disclosure, other jurisdictions require filing before public disclosure.

Importantly, a design patent can protect the appearance of the entirety or just select components of a product. For example, an applicant can apply for protection for the overall design of a watch, the watch face alone, and the band alone with separate design patents. An advantage of this strategy is to ensure that if a competitor copies one component of the watch, the patent holder has patent protection on at least that single component. However, the protection provided by a design patent is only as broad in scope as the views shown in the patent (not the applicant's product), so it is possible to broaden coverage by not precisely matching the design but rather, filing an application that encompasses the design.

1. Design Patent Infringement

A design patent is infringed "if in the eye of an ordinary observer, giving such attention as a purchaser usually gives, two designs are substantially the same, if the resemblance is such as to deceive such an observer, inducing him to purchase one supposing the other." *Egyptian Goddess, Inc. v. Swisa, Inc.*, 543 F.3d 665, 670 (Fed. Cir. 2008). As with utility patents (discussed below), the patent holder must prove infringement of a design patent by a preponderance of the evidence. *Id.* at 679. If the claimed and accused designs are "sufficiently distinct" and "plainly dissimilar," the patentee fails to meet its burden of proving infringement as a matter of law. *Id.* at 678. Where the claimed and accused designs are not plainly dissimilar, the inquiry may benefit from comparing the claimed and accused designs with prior art to identify differences that are not noticeable in the abstract but would be significant to the hypothetical ordinary observer familiar with the prior art. *Id.*

In a design patent infringement claim, a trier of fact must consider the ornamental aspects of the design as a whole and not merely isolated portions of the patented design. *In re Salmon*, 705 F.2d 1579, 1582 (Fed. Cir. 1983). An element-by-element comparison in an ordinary observer inquiry is a procedural error. *Amini Innovation Corp. v. Anthony Cal., Inc.*, 439 F.3d 1365, 1372 (Fed. Cir. 2006).

Potential remedies for a prevailing design patent holder in an infringement action may include a permanent injunction against future infringement, profits earned by the infringer, and the patent-holder's damages.

High Point Design, LLC v. Buyer's Direct, Inc.

621 F. App'x 632 (Fed. Cir. 2015)

CHEN, Circuit Judge.

This is the second time this case has been appealed to our court. In *High Point Design LLC v. Buyers Direct, Inc.*, 730 F.3d 1301 (Fed. Cir. 2013) ("*High Point I*"), we reversed the United States District Court for the Southern District of New York's grant of summary judgment of invalidity of the design patent belonging to Buyers Direct, Inc. (BDI). We ruled that the district court made various errors in finding the claimed design obvious, including that it applied the wrong legal standard and failed to adequately explain how it reached the conclusion that the prior art created "basically the same" visual impression as the patented design. *Id.* at 1313-14. We also vacated the district court's dismissal of BDI's trade dress infringement claim because there was insufficient basis for this court to review the district court's decision to deny BDI the opportunity to amend the complaint. *Id.* at 1319-20.

On remand, the district court again granted summary judgment, finding that: (1) the asserted patent was anticipated; (2) the accused products did not infringe; (3) BDI was not entitled to additional discovery on infringement issues; and (4) BDI failed to show "good cause" for allowing its amendments to the complaint after the deadline in the scheduling order. *High Point Design LLC v. Buyer's Direct Inc.*, No. 11 CIV. 4530 KBF, 2014 U.S. Dist. LEXIS 41290, 2014 WL 1244558, at *7-9 (S.D.N.Y. Mar. 26, 2014) ("*Remand Order*").

BDI challenges each of these determinations on appeal. For the reasons set forth below, we reverse summary judgment of invalidity, affirm summary judgment of non-infringement, affirm the denial of BDI's motion for additional discovery, and affirm the denial of BDI's motion to amend the complaint.

I. Background

The background of the case is set forth in *High Point I* and the *Remand Order*. We recount below only the facts pertinent to the issues on appeal.

BDI owns a design patent for the ornamental appearance of a fuzzy slipper, U.S. Patent No. D598,183 (the D'183 patent). The D'183 patent is entitled "Slipper," and recites one claim for "the ornamental design for a slipper, as shown and described" in eight figures. Exemplary Figures 1 and 4 are reproduced below:

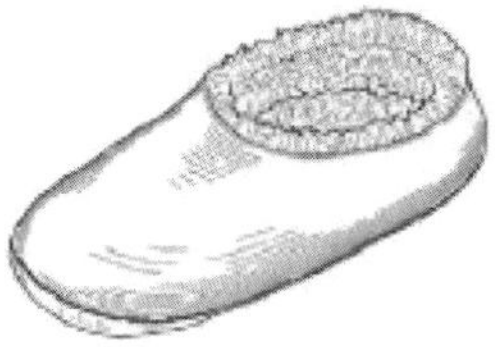

Fig. 1

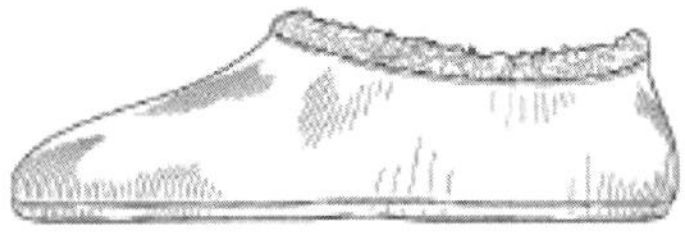

Fig. 4

The claimed design discloses two embodiments for the slipper soles. One embodiment has a sole with two groups of raised dots (Figure 7 on the left), and the other has a sole with a smooth bottom (Figure 8 on the right).

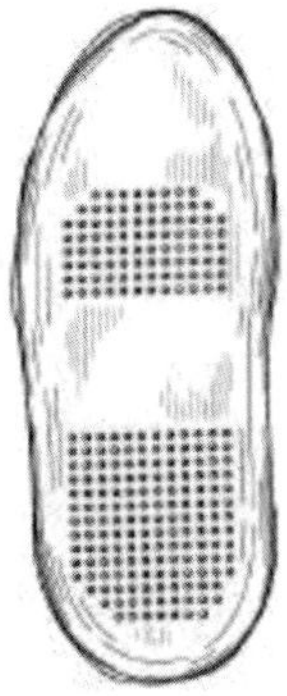

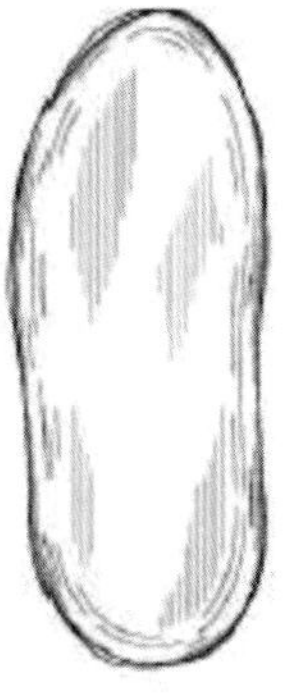

A.

BDI manufactures a slipper called the SNOOZIE® (Snoozie), which it contends is an embodiment of the design disclosed in the D'183 patent. An exemplary Snoozie slipper is shown below:

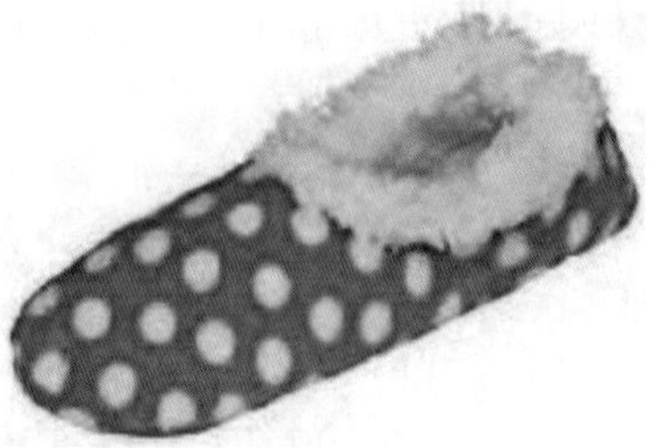

High Point Design LLC (High Point) manufactures and distributes the accused FUZZY BABBA® slipper (Fuzzy Babba). Fuzzy Babba slippers are sold through various retailers, including Meijer, Sears, and Wal-mart (collectively Retailers) and are alleged to compete with Snoozie. An exemplary Fuzzy Babba slipper is shown below:

After learning about the Fuzzy Babba slippers, BDI sent a cease and desist letter to High Point asserting design patent infringement. In response, High Point filed a complaint in district court seeking declaratory judgment that the design of the accused slipper does not infringe the D'183 patent, and that the patent is invalid and/or unenforceable. BDI then counterclaimed for patent infringement and infringement of its trade dress for Snoozie. BDI also filed a third-party complaint which alleged that the Retailers infringe the D'183 patent and BDI's trade dress by selling Fuzzy Babba slippers.

B.

On February 28, 2012, the district court issued a scheduling order which set March 16, 2012, as the deadline for parties to amend their pleadings. BDI did not move to amend its counterclaims by that date. Four days after the deadline, on March 20, 2012, High Point filed motions seeking summary judgment of invalidity and non-infringement of the D'183 patent, and judgment on the pleadings with respect to BDI's trade dress claim.

BDI opposed the motion, including with its briefing an amended complaint that provided added detail describing the particular trade dress at issue in its trade dress claim.

The district court granted High Point's motion for summary judgment of invalidity, finding the patented design obvious over the prior art. *High Point Design LLC v. Buyer's Direct, Inc.*, No. 11 CIV. 4530 KBF, 2012 U.S. Dist. LEXIS 70193, 2012 WL 1820565, at *5 (S.D.N.Y. May 15, 2012) ("*2012 Order*"). The district court based its determination on two primary references: the Laurel Hill and the Penta slippers, both of which were sold at one point in time by Woolrich (collectively the Woolrich Prior Art).

Laurel Hill

Penta

The district court also dismissed BDI's trade dress claim as inadequate under the pleading requirements of Rule 12(b)(6) of the Federal Rules of Civil Procedure (Federal Rules). *Id.* at *6. In particular, the district court found BDI failed to set forth the specific characteristics and scope of the trade dress at issue as required by Second Circuit law. *Id.* (citing *Sherwood 48 Assoc. v. Sony Corp. of Am.*, 76 Fed. Appx. 389, 391 (2d Cir. 2003)). Accordingly, the district court entered final judgment in favor of High Point. *2012 Order*, 2012 U.S. Dist. LEXIS 70193, 2012 WL 1820565, at *6.

BDI appealed the district court's grant of summary judgment and the dismissal of its trade dress infringement claim.

C.

In *High Point I*, we held that the district court's obviousness analysis was flawed for a number of reasons. We determined that the district court wrongly used an "ordinary observer" standard, instead of the appropriate "ordinary designer" test for obviousness. *High Point I*, 730 F.3d at 1313. We also found that the district court's verbal description of the D'183 patent translated the scope of the patented design at "too high a level of abstraction" and failed to focus on the distinctive visual appearance of the design. *Id.* at 1314 (quoting *Apple, Inc. v. Samsung Elecs. Co.*, 678 F.3d 1314, 1331-32 (Fed. Cir. 2012)). We also found that the district court failed to sufficiently explain its determination that the Woolrich Prior Art created "basically the same" visual impression as the claimed design. *High Point I*, 730 F.3d at 1314.

We instructed the district court on remand to (i) apply the "ordinary designer" test for obviousness, *id.* at 1313; (ii) add sufficient detail to its verbal description of the claimed design "to evoke a visual image consonant with that design[,]" *id.* at 1314; and (iii) perform a side-by-side comparison of the D'183 patent design and the Woolrich Prior Art to determine if they create the same visual impression, *id.*

D.

On remand, the district court again granted summary judgment of invalidity. This time the district court found that the D'183 patent was anticipated by the Woolrich Prior Art. The district court offered the following description of the claimed design in support of its decision:

> To an ordinary observer, the '183 Patent is the design of a slipper with a formed body, a protrusion of fuzz or fluff, and a sole with some solidity. The outside of the slipper appears durable and looks to be made of a relatively tough material; the inside looks soft, plush, and made of a warm material. The sole appears to be fairly thick and looks sturdy.

Remand Order, 2014 U.S. Dist. LEXIS 41290, 2014 WL 1244558, at *6.

Addressing each of the prior art designs in turn, the district court first determined that the Laurel Hill anticipated because it also had "a structured body, a soft-looking fluff surrounding the opening of the slipper, and a sole that appears durable and fairly thick." *Id.* The district court then found that the Penta also anticipated, concluding that the Penta was even more similar to the D'183 patent than the Laurel Hill. The court found that the Penta "conveys the visual effect of a slipper, the body and sole of which have some defined shape and solidity but which has a protrusion of fluff or fuzz emanating from the foot opening." *Id.* at *7. Although the district court noted that a close study of the patented and prior art designs revealed differences, those differences were "minor" and insufficient to defeat anticipation. *Id.*

The district court also ruled in favor of High Point on grounds that the Fuzzy Babba slipper did not infringe the patented design. In particular, the district court found:

> The Fuzzy Babba conveys the visual effect of an entirely soft and malleable body with an indistinguishable sole; it is soft and malleable all around. In contrast, the visual effect of the '183 Patent is of a formed body and sole with some solidity; and a body distinct from the sole.

Id.

Having found the D'183 patent invalid, not infringed, and the trade dress claim properly dismissed, the district court entered final judgment in favor of High Point. BDI timely appealed. We have jurisdiction under 28 U.S.C. § 1295(a).

II. Discussion

We apply regional circuit law in reviewing a district court's grant of summary judgment. *Broadcast Innovation L.L.C. v. Charter Commc'ns, Inc.*, 420 F.3d 1364, 1366 (Fed. Cir. 2005). The Second Circuit reviews a grant of summary judgment without deference. *Kuebel v. Black & Decker Inc.*, 643 F.3d 352, 358 (2d Cir. 2011). All evidence is construed in the light most favorable to the non-movant and all reasonable inferences are drawn in that party's favor. *Id.* Summary judgment is appropriate when no "reasonable jury could return a verdict for the nonmoving party." *Anderson v. Liberty Lobby, Inc.*, 477 U.S. 242, 248, 106 S. Ct. 2505, 91 L. Ed. 2d 202 (1986).

A. Invalidity

We turn first to the district court's grant of summary judgment on anticipation. Design patents are presumed to be valid. 35 U.S.C. § 282(a). A party seeking to invalidate a patent on the basis of anticipation must do so by clear and convincing evidence. *See Catalina Lighting, Inc. v. Lamps Plus, Inc.*, 295 F.3d 1277, 1288 (Fed. Cir. 2002). Design patent anticipation requires a showing that a single prior art reference is "identical in all material respects" to the claimed invention. *Door-Master Corp. v. Yorktowne, Inc.*, 256 F.3d 1308, 1312 (Fed. Cir. 2001) (quoting *Hupp v. Siroflex of Am., Inc.*, 122 F.3d 1456, 1461 (Fed. Cir. 1997)). In other words, the two designs must be substantially the same. *See Door-Master*, 256 F.3d at 1312, 1313 (applying design patent infringement test from *Gorham Mfg. Co. v. White*, 81 U.S. 511, 528, 20 L. Ed. 731 (1871), as the test for anticipation). Two designs are substantially the same "if the resemblance is such as to deceive [an ordinary observer], inducing him to purchase one supposing it to be the other[.]" *Gorham*, 81 U.S. at 528. Anticipation is a question of fact. *Int'l Seaway Trading Corp. v. Walgreens Corp.*, 589 F.3d 1233, 1237 (Fed. Cir. 2009). Summary judgment is proper only when the evidence underlying anticipation is clear and convincing such that no reasonable fact-finder could find otherwise. *See SRAM Corp. v. AD-II Eng'g, Inc.*, 465 F.3d 1351, 1357 (Fed. Cir. 2006).

Viewing all evidence in the light most favorable to the non-moving party—BDI—we conclude that a reasonable jury could have found there was not clear and convincing evidence of anticipation.

In *High Point I*, we instructed that on remand, the district court should "add sufficient detail to its verbal description of the claimed design to evoke a visual image consonant with [the] claimed design." 730 F.3d at 1314. We also instructed that the district court should perform a side-by-side comparison of the claimed and prior art designs as part of the proper obviousness determination. *Id.* Notably, we cautioned that there appeared to be "genuine issues of material fact as to whether the Woolrich Prior Art are, in fact, proper primary references" for obviousness purposes under 35 U.S.C. § 103. *Id.*

On remand, the district court did not perform a side-by-side comparison, but concluded that the claimed and prior art designs share the "same characteristics" because they share "a structured body, a soft-looking fluff surrounding the opening of the slipper, and a sole that appears durable and fairly thick." *Remand Order*, 2014 WL 1244558, at *6; *see also id.* at *7.

We find again that the district court fundamentally erred in its analysis by analyzing the designs from "too high a level of abstraction" and failing to focus "on the distinctive visual appearances of the reference and the claimed design." *High Point I*, 730 F.3d at 1314 (quoting *Apple*, 678 F.3d at 1331-32). Specifically, the court's description does little more than point out the main concepts of the claimed design: a structured slipper having fuzzy material at the foot opening. *See Durling v. Spectrum Furniture Co.*, 101 F.3d 100, 104 (Fed. Cir. 1996) ("By focusing on the design concept of [the patented] design rather than its visual appearance, the district court erred."). In doing so, the court failed to properly consider the ornamental aspects of the designs at issue. There are numerous such features in the body, the fuzzy material, and the sole of the designs, all of which were overlooked in the district court's analysis.

For example, there are meaningful differences between the curvatures of the slipper body designs. The body of the patented design has a distinct 'S' curve between the foot opening and the front of the slipper as viewed from the side, which ends in a downward slope toward the front of the body. By contrast, the Laurel Hill has a prominent upward curve near the front. The Penta is also different because it has a noticeably flatter, more even slope from the foot opening towards the front.

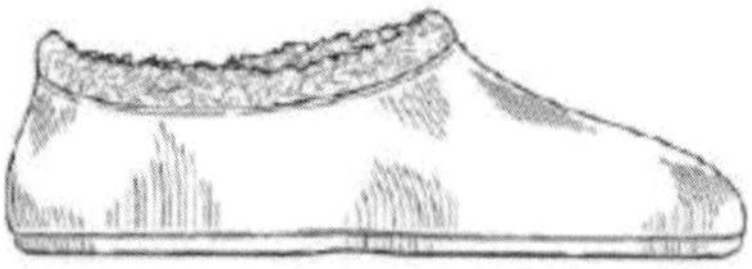

D'183 patent, Figure 5

Laurel Hill Prior Art

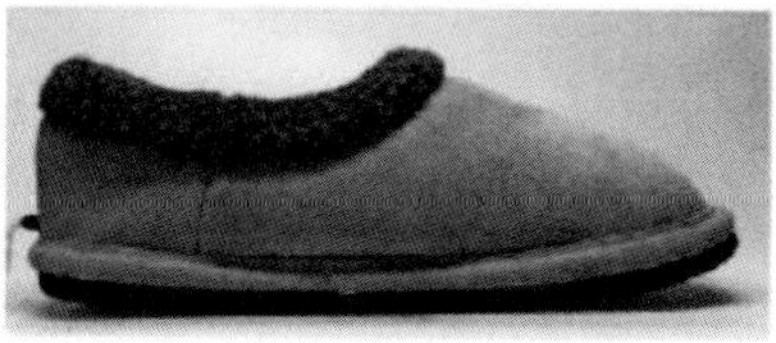

Penta Prior Art

There are also clear differences between the protruding fuzz of the claimed and prior art designs. In particular, the Woolrich Prior Art appears to differ from the claims in that both prior art slippers have a pronounced fleece overlap oriented outward and which obscures the top edge of the foot opening. By contrast, no such overlap is visible in the patented design.

We also find that the district court failed to take into consideration the substantial differences between the ornamental aspects of the soles of the claimed design and the prior art designs. As we stated in *Contessa Food Prods., Inc. v. Conagra, Inc.*, "[o]ur precedent makes clear that all of the ornamental features illustrated in the figures must be considered in evaluating design patent infringement." 282 F.3d 1370, 1378 (Fed. Cir. 2002), *abrogated on other grounds by Egyptian Goddess, Inc. v. Swisa, Inc.*, 543 F.3d 665, 672-79 (Fed. Cir. 2008).

The district court did not address the ornamental aspects of the soles in the *Remand Order*, but stated in the *2012 Order* that "[t]he only difference between the slippers relates to the sole of the slippers, which is quite minor in the context of the overall slipper." 2012 U.S. Dist. LEXIS 70193, 2012 WL 1820565, at *4. We disagree. There are unmistakable differences between the sole design of the D'183 patent and the Woolrich Prior Art. The patent claims one embodiment, shown in Figure 7, where the sole has dots. Those dots are arranged in a uniformly spaced pattern of rows and columns in two separate groups. One group is positioned closer to the front of the slipper, and narrows slightly toward the toe area. The other group is placed closer to the rear, and has a corresponding taper toward the rear area. The other embodiment, shown in Figure 8, has a smooth sole. Neither of the Woolrich Prior Art designs has either of these design components.

The prior art designs instead each have their own distinct ornamental designs. The Laurel Hill sole has embedded within it images of four trees and two moose. The Laurel Hill also has a grooved border not present in the claimed design. The Penta sole has a large "WOOLRICH" image imprinted thereon and is also decorated with a distinct pattern. Like the Laurel Hill—but unlike the claimed design—the Penta also has a grooved border.

As we cautioned in *High Point I*, there appeared to be genuine issues of material fact regarding whether the Woolrich Prior Art properly served as base references under this court's obviousness law. 730 F.3d at 1314. We now similarly hold that the evidence is not so clear and convincing such that a reasonable fact-finder could not find for BDI on anticipation. For these reasons, we reverse summary judgment of invalidity.

B. Infringement

We turn next to the district court's grant of summary judgment of non-infringement. Infringement is a question of fact, *Lockheed Martin Corp. v. Space Sys./Loral, Inc.*, 324 F.3d 1308, 1318 (Fed. Cir. 2003), and must be proved by a preponderance of the evidence, *Egyptian Goddess*, 543 F.3d at 678. Summary judgment of non-infringement is appropriate when no reasonable fact-finder could find the accused design substantially similar to the claimed design. *See Elmer v. ICC Fabricating, Inc.*, 67 F.3d 1571, 1578 (Fed. Cir. 1995).

Infringement of design patents is judged by the same test as anticipation—whether two designs are "substantially the same." *See Egyptian Goddess*, 543 F.3d at 678 (adopting test set forth in *Gorham*, 81 U.S. at 528 as sole test for design patent infringement). Under *Egyptian Goddess*, where the claimed and accused designs are "sufficiently distinct" and "plainly dissimilar," the patentee does not meet its burden of proving infringement. *Id.* Only if the claimed and accused designs are not plainly dissimilar does the inquiry potentially benefit from comparison of the claimed and the accused designs in with the prior art. *Id.* We agree with the district court that it is not necessary to resort to a comparison with the prior art in ruling on infringement here.

The district court conducted a side-by-side comparison between the claimed design and the accused Fuzzy Babba slippers, and concluded that "the Fuzzy Babba's appearance evokes a soft, gentle image, while the D'183 patent appears robust and durable." *Remand Order*, 2014 WL 1244558, at *7. Finding that a consumer would not confuse the two designs, the court then granted summary judgment of non-infringement. *Id.* at *7-8. We agree.

Accused Fuzzy Babba design

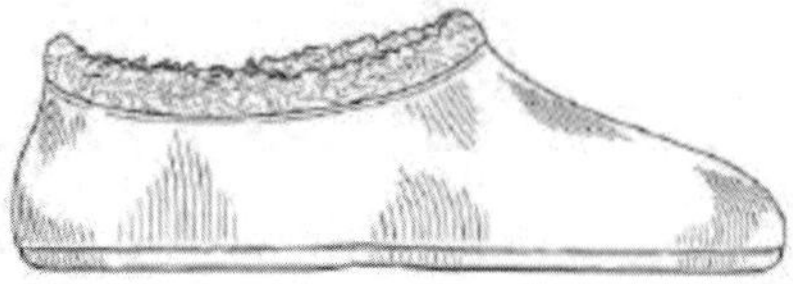

D'183 patent, Figure 5

We conclude that the patented and accused designs bring to mind different impressions. The Fuzzy Babba design appears soft and formless, whereas the claimed design appears structured and formed. These differences are reflected in the ornamental aspects of each of the designs. For example, the side profile of the Fuzzy Babba shows a relatively smooth, downward slope from the rear toward the front area of the slipper. By contrast, the D'183 patent design has a relatively defined, curved opening that is lower in the middle and higher at the edges. Further, the Fuzzy Babba has a relatively straight rear line, whereas the rear of claimed design bulges outward. The front areas of the two designs are also substantially dissimilar. The Fuzzy Babba has a relatively flatly sloping side profile, whereas the patented design has a curved profile, roughly following in an 'S' curve shape.

As we did with respect to invalidity, we also find that there are meaningful differences in the soles which affect the overall visual effect of the two designs. *See Source Search Techs., LLC v. LendingTree, LLC*, 588 F.3d 1063, 1075 (Fed. Cir. 2009) ("It is axiomatic that claims are construed the same way for both invalidity and infringement." (citing *Amgen Inc. v. Hoechst Marion Roussel, Inc.*, 314 F.3d 1313, 1330 (Fed. Cir. 2003)). Unlike the D'183 patent design, the Fuzzy has a continuous distribution of dots throughout almost the entire length of the sole. These dots are of a constant width and in one group, in contrast to the varying width of dot columns displayed in Figure 7, and in further contrast to the embodiment in Figure 8 that has a smooth sole and no dots.

We recognize that both designs essentially consist of a slipper with a fuzzy portion extending upward out of the foot opening. Such high-level similarities, however, are not sufficient to demonstrate infringement. *See, e.g., Apple*, 678 F.3d at 1332 (finding error where district court looked to "general concept" of a tablet, as opposed to the distinctive "visual appearance" of the claimed design); *Durling*, 101 F.3d at 104.

BDI also argues that the district court erred by not performing a comparison of the accused Fuzzy Babba slipper to BDI's alleged commercial embodiment, the Snoozie. We have long-cautioned that it is generally improper to determine infringement by comparing an accused product with the patentee's purported commercial embodiment. *See, e.g., Sun Hill Indus., Inc. v. Easter Unlimited, Inc.*, 48 F.3d 1193,

1196 (Fed. Cir. 1995) *abrogated on other grounds by Egyptian Goddess*, 543 F.3d at 672-79.

If a patentee is able to show that there is no substantial difference between the claimed design and the purported commercial embodiment, a comparison between that embodiment and the accused design is *permissible. See L.A. Gear, Inc. v. Thom McAn Shoe Co.*, 988 F.2d 1117, 1125-26 (Fed. Cir. 1993) ("When the patented design and the design of the article sold by the patentee are substantially the same, it is not error to compare the patentee's and the accused articles directly[.]"); *Lee v. Dayton-Hudson Corp.*, 838 F.2d 1186, 1189 (Fed. Cir. 1988). Contrary to BDI's suggestion, however, we have never mandated such comparisons and decline to do so here. The proper test for infringement is performed by measuring the accused products against the claimed design. *Payless Shoesource, Inc. v. Reebok Int'l Ltd.*, 998 F.2d 985, 990 (Fed. Cir. 1993).

BDI also argues that the district court erred by failing to take into account how the accused products appeared as worn. We disagree. Even as worn, there are meaningful differences in the visual impression between the two designs. The Fuzzy Babba lacks the distinctive 'S' curve of the front area visible in Figure 4 of the claimed design. Moreover, the protrusion of fuzz in the Fuzzy Babba remains thicker toward the back then toward the front of the foot opening. And critically, there remain the aforementioned differences in the soles of the two designs.

For all these reasons, we affirm the district court's grant of summary judgment of non-infringement.

III. Conclusion

Because a reasonable fact-finder could conclude that there was not clear and convincing evidence that the D'183 patent is anticipated by the Woolrich Prior Art, we reverse summary judgment of invalidity. And because there can be no genuine dispute that the claimed and accused Fuzzy Babba designs are plainly dissimilar, we affirm summary judgment of non-infringement. We also affirm the district court's denial of BDI's motion for additional discovery and the denial of BDI's motion to amend the complaint.

AFFIRMED IN PART, REVERSED IN PART

Notes

1. First, unlike most other areas of the law, there is only one court designated for handling appeals in patent cases. The Court of Appeals for the Federal Circuit ("CAFC"), located in Washington, D.C., handles all appeals related to patent law from all district courts in the United States. This case is an example of an appeal that came to the CAFC.

2. Infringement of a design patent, as described in the case, requires an analysis of the potentially infringing product to the granted patent, not to the accuser's product. Consequently, it is important that the figures used in the patent application

describe a product at least as broad as the applicant's product so as to encompass variations of the product.

3. A design patent can include multiple embodiments of a product. As shown in *High Point Design, LLC*, the patent shows two embodiments—one with raised dots and one without. The potential infringer need not have products with both designs—only one is sufficient.

4. In this case, the applicant chose to broaden the coverage by applying for a design that was exclusive of the polka dot design and the precise texture of the fuzziness of the exterior. By excluding these elements and leaving the exterior as shown, the exterior of many slippers could rely on the patent, so long as the shape and fuzzy opening existed at the upper side and the bottom had either the dot design or a blank design.

5. Even though a patent is granted by the USPTO, that is not the final word on the patent's validity; the courts can determine that a patent is invalid. When one is sued or threatened to be sued for infringement, the party charged with infringement can sue first for a Declaratory Judgment of non-infringement and/or invalidity, as in this case.

6. To obtain patent protection, the design must be novel (that is, not anticipated by a prior design) and not obvious over prior inventions. In this case, High Point brought several prior designs to the Court's attention. Do you agree with the Court's analysis regarding the prior art references?

7. Finally, the actual design, despite being a comparatively simple slipper, has a number of component pieces which the Court viewed collectively in comparison to the potentially infringing product. The *Gorham* case, among others, refers to the "Ordinary Observer" test to determine infringement in a design patent case. Note that standard is used here in determining infringement.

C. Utility Patents

A utility patent provides powerful protection for the functionality embedded in a product, system, or process. For example, a utility patent may be granted for a new hinge mechanism for glasses, new clasp on handbags, novel opening in a boot, or the assembly process for them. A utility patent also protects a new process or technique such as the process of making a fabric. Due to fashion designers incorporating increasingly complex technologies into the items they design (such as smart glasses or fashion articles with sensors), utility patents are growing rapidly in importance in the industry.

Like design patents, utility patents must be filed with the USPTO within one year of the first public disclosure of the good. The United States is a party to treaties (relative to both design and utility patents) allowing applicants to file applications in multiple jurisdictions in order to obtain multi-country rights. Other jurisdictions require that an application be filed before any public disclosure (an "absolute bar"). By leveraging one of the treaties, one can overcome the absolute bar by filing in one jurisdiction, such as the United States, before public disclosure and claiming the filing date of the earlier application as a priority date.

A utility patent application includes: (1) a detailed description of the invention (the "specification"), which may contain figures such as drawings of a product or flow charts, and (2) numbered sentences articulating the scope of protection (the "claims"). The specification must be written at a level of detail "to enable a workman or other person skilled in the art or manufacture . . . to make, construct, or use the same, to the end that the public may have the full benefit thereof, after the expiration of the patent term." *Bonito Boats v. Thunder Craft Boats*, 489 U.S. 141, 147 (1989) (quoting the Patent Act of 1790).

The United States allows an earlier provisional application, without the requirement for claims, as one way of establishing a priority date. Once filed, the applicant has a one-year window to file a formal or non-provisional application inclusive of claims. Applicants often take advantage of initially filing the provisional application to test the waters. Failure to file during this one-year window effectively abandons the application.

Once a non-provisional application is filed, the application is assigned to a USPTO Examiner who conducts a prior art search and compares the claims to relevant prior art. The applicant (or an attorney licensed by the USPTO) can interact with the Examiner over time by, for example, amending claims to overcome prior art. But any amendment must be consistent with the originally filed specification, even with the content of an earlier filed provisional application, in order to continue to claim the benefit of its filing date. The claims require extremely careful drafting because they articulate the bounds of the innovation to the public.

Like a design patent, the validity of a granted utility patent may be challenged later. A court may invalidate a patent if it determines that one of the criteria, such as novelty or obviousness, is not satisfied.

1. Utility Patent Infringement

According to 35 U.S.C. § 271(a), "whoever without authority makes, uses, offers to sell, or sells any patented invention, within the United States or imports into the United States any patented invention during the term of the patent therefor, infringes the patent." In general, there are two steps in determining infringement. First, the claim must be properly construed to determine its scope and meaning. The claim terms may be defined in the specification or in the claims themselves. However, construing a claim term can be difficult due to potential ambiguities and undefined terms. Second, once properly construed, the claim must be compared to the accused device or process. While claim construction is a question of law, infringement is a question of fact.

Two types of infringement can be found: literal or through the doctrine of equivalents. Literal infringement results when each of the claim limitations is present in the accused device, with the initial burden of proof on the patent holder. Under the doctrine of equivalents, the patent holder still holds the burden and needs to make a similar showing. The legal test, articulated in *Warner-Jenkinson Co. v. Hilton Davis Chem. Co.*, is "[d]oes the accused product or process contain elements identical or equivalent to each claimed element of the patented invention?" *Warner-Jenkinson Co. v. Hilton Davis Chem. Co.*, 520 U.S. 17, 40 (1997). For example, if a patent claims the use of a knife for cutting and the accused device uses a different type of blade for the same function, there may be infringement under the doctrine of equivalents.

A prevailing patent owner in a utility patent infringement action may obtain injunctive relief and recover damages to adequately compensate for the infringement.

QR Spex, Inc. v. Motorola Inc.

588 F. Supp. 2d 1240 (C.D. Cal. 2008)

CARNEY, District Judge.

Plaintiff QR Spex Inc. ("QR Spex") alleges that Defendants Motorola Inc., Oakley Inc., Oakley Sales Corp., and Oakley Direct, Inc. (collectively "Oakley") are infringing its United States Patent No. 6,769,767 (the "'767 Patent"). Specifically, QR Spex alleges that two pairs of Oakley Eyewear—the O ROKR and the O ROKR Pro (collectively "Oakley Eyewear") infringe Claim 1 of the '767 Patent. Claim 1 of the '767 Patent, an independent claim, discloses an eyewear comprising of a frame and a Bluetooth transceiver that is "embedded" in that frame.

Oakley now moves for partial summary judgment contending that its eyewear do not infringe Claim 1 of the '767 Patent because the Bluetooth transceivers in the Oakley Eyewear are not embedded within the frame. The Court agrees. The Bluetooth transceivers in the Oakley Eyewear are attached to the frames by clips, screws, posts, and ridges. The Bluetooth transceivers can be easily removed or replaced. They are not permanently set in the frame as Claim 1 of the '767 Patent requires. Consequently, the Oakley Eyewear do not literally infringe the '767 Patent.

Nor do the Oakley Eyewear infringe Claim 1 of the '767 Patent under the doctrine of equivalents. First, the Oakley Eyewear do not perform the same function in the same way as the eyewear claimed in the '767 Patent. Specifically, the ability to easily remove the Bluetooth transceivers from the Oakley Eyewear without destroying the eyewear is a substantial difference from the eyewear claimed in the '767 Patent. Second, QR Spex narrowed its claims in the patent prosecution process to claim only eyewear with a Bluetooth transceiver embedded in the frame. It is now, therefore, estopped from claiming infringement against any and every pair of glasses integrating a Bluetooth transceiver. QR Spex cannot recapture what it gave up during the patent prosecution process.

I. Factual Background

Oakley Inc. and its related companies design, manufacture, and sell sunglasses and other eyewear, including several models of eyewear that have integrated MP3 players and Bluetooth technology. (Declaration of Carlos Reyes P 2 ("Reyes Decl."); Second Amended Compl. PP 4-5.) Motorola designs, manufactures, and sells wireless communications products. (Fourth Amended Counterclaim P 5.) The Oakley Eyewear are the result of Oakley Inc. and Motorola's collaboration. The Oakley Eyewear are sunglasses with a slightly futuristic appearance. They have earbud-style headphones attached to each temple on swiveling arms. A Bluetooth transceiver on a printed circuit board is placed in an indentation in the right temple of the eyewear. (Decl. of Clinton Cowen ("Cowen Decl.") PP 13, 16.) The transceiver and circuit board are held in place by a combination of ridges, clips, and posts inside the temple, and a screw-on plastic cover that goes over the indentation, creating a chamber that protects the Bluetooth apparatus and holds it inside the glasses. (Cowen Decl. P 13; Reyes Decl. P 11.) The Bluetooth transceiver can then create a wireless network with equipment like an MP3 player or cellular phone, allowing a person wearing the Oakley Eyewear to listen to music wirelessly or take telephone calls through his or her sunglasses.

QR Spex is a patent holding company that seeks to license its patent portfolio to other companies. (Decl. of Gregory Swab ("Swab Decl.") P 2.) In April 2000, QR Spex contracted with another company, Frog Designs, to design eyewear with integrated radio transceivers. *(Id.* P 3.) The product of that collaboration was patented in the '767 patent. *(Id.* PP 5, 6.) QR Spex has not brought any eyewear to market. As described in the '767 patent and figures included in that document, QR Spex's claimed eyewear includes detachable temples with various electronic components embedded within them. ('767 Patent figs.2a-2e.) QR Spex designed its eyewear to allow a user to swap temples depending on which function the user wanted the eyewear to perform including: functioning as headphones, television sets, or child or baby monitors. ('767 Patent col.6-7.) One of the primary applications of QR Spex's claimed eyewear would be to create a Bluetooth network to allow a user to listen to music wirelessly from an MP3 player, as in the Oakley Eyewear. ('767 Patent. col.6 ll.18-44.) The '767 Patent repeatedly describes the Bluetooth transceiver as co-molded within one of the temples of QR Spex's claimed eyewear, while its figures and specification show and describe a transceiver permanently set in a cavity, without a possibility of disassembling the eyewear to remove it. *(See, e.g.,* '767 Patent col.5 ll.48-50.)

QR Spex narrowed the scope of the '767 Patent during prosecution. At one point, Claim 1 of the '767 Patent described an invention simply comprising eyewear and a transceiver. (Decl. of Phillip T. Bruns ("Bruns Decl.") Ex. 6 at 5.) In response to the Patent and Trademark Office's December 11, 2003 rejection of its claims, QR Spex amended Claim 1 to specify a Bluetooth transceiver that would be "embedded" in the frame of the glasses. (Bruns Decl. Ex. 7 at 2.) QR Spex made these changes to accommodate the Patent and Trademark Office's finding that, as originally written, the eyewear described in Claim 1 was anticipated by the U.S. Patent No. 6,629,076 (the "'076 Patent"). (Bruns Decl. Ex. 6 at 3.) The '076 Patent described eyeglasses that would use a wireless connection to display information about a speaker's tone and volume graphically on the lenses of a speaker's glasses. In arguments accompanying its amendment of Claim 1, QR Spex inventors stated that "because the transceiver is *embedded* in the frame of the eyewear, the eyewear itself becomes a wireless communications device communicating with other wireless devices." (Bruns Decl. Ex. 7 at 7.)

QR Spex also cited U.S. Patent No. 6,091,546 (the '546 Patent), as prior art by QR Spex in the background of the '767 Patent. The invention described in the '546 Patent integrates a transceiver in a similar way as the eyewear claimed in the '767 Patent does, and it does not characterize its method of integration as embedded. The '546 Patent claims an "eyeglass interface system . . . wherein at least one of the first and second temples is hollow and the interface circuitry comprises a multi-chip module disposed within the at least one of the first and second temples." ('546 Patent col.12 at ll.64-67.) The '546 Patent further shows that its communications circuitry is placed inside a cavity in the temple and enclosed by a cover attached to the frame by four screws. ('546 Patent fig.15.) QR Spex described the '546 Patent as disclosing electronics that were "mounted on" the frame. ('767 Patent col.1 ll.31-33.) In the '767 Patent, QR Spex does not describe the electronic equipment in its claimed eyewear as "disposed" or as "mounted upon" as in the '546 Patent. QR Spex describes the Bluetooth transceiver in the eyewear claimed in the '767 patent as "embedded." ('767 Patent, col.8 ll.1-7.)

II. The Patent-in-Suit

The '767 Patent claims a pair of glasses with a Bluetooth transceiver embedded within the temples of their frames. Claim 1 of the '767 Patent is the only asserted independent claim at issue in this motion. It claims:

> *An eyewear comprising:*
>
> *a frame; and*
>
> *a Bluetooth transceiver for short distance wireless communication, wherein said Bluetooth transceiver is embedded in said frame and wherein said Bluetooth transceiver is configured to form an ad hoc wireless network with a plurality of devices.*

('767 Patent, col.8 ll.1-10.)

IV. Construction of Claim 1 of the '767 Patent

The Court construes that the term embedded to mean "permanently set in the frame" of the eyewear. The Court's construction is based on the plain language of Claim 1 of the '767 Patent and additional information contained in the '767 Patent, including the specification.

The ordinary meaning of Claim 1's language is "readily apparent," so "claim construction in [this case] involves little more than the application of the widely accepted meaning of commonly understood words." *Phillips,* 415 F.3d at 1314 (citation omitted). Claim 1 of the '767 Patent requires that a "Bluetooth transceiver is embedded in said frame" of the eyewear. ('767 Patent col.8 ll.6-7.) The plain language of Claim 1 requires that the Bluetooth transceiver be permanently set in the frame of the eyewear. This construction, as opposed to the Bluetooth transceiver merely being attached, clipped in, or screwed down to the frame, is further supported by other language and information in the '767 Patent.

For instance, the specification of the '767 Patent consistently refers to the Bluetooth transceiver being "molded" or "co-molded" into the eyewear: "A battery powering the transceiver and other co-molded devices can also be co-molded within one of the temples. . . ." ('767 Patent col.2 ll.53-57.) The "Brief Description of Drawings" describes eyewear with transceivers "co-molded" within the frame: "FIG. 2e is a diagram showing the hinge, connector and circuitry such [as a] Bluetooth PCB before being molded into the temple." ('767 Patent col.3 ll.27-29.) The '767 Patent's "Detailed Description" of the QR Spex eyewear also suggests that the transceiver is permanently set in the frame:

> Temple 20 has co-molded within its body an apparatus 36. Apparatus 36 can be, for example, an audio device, a camera, a speaker, a microphone, and a display device such as a liquid crystal or an alarm. The apparatus includes electrical circuitry for operation in an electronics package such as a Bluetooth module with PCB [Printed Circuit Board].

('767 Patent col.5 ll.48-53.) These descriptions imply that the Bluetooth transceiver cannot be removed because co-molded manufacturing means that the material of the frame is molded around the transceivers, and then hardened.

The figures in the '767 Patent also support the Court's construction of the word "embedded." Figures 2a and 2c show the "apparatus," which would include the Bluetooth transceiver, fully embedded within the frames of the eyewear; no seams or screws are visible to suggest that it could be removed without breaking open the frames. Figure 2a shows the transceiver to be permanently set within the frames of the glasses without indicating seams or screws that would facilitate one's ability to remove the transceiver without breaking the frames. ('767 Patent fig.2a.) Figure 2c further illustrates a fully fabricated eyeglass stem, in which the surrounding plastic material has filled in all the space around the transceiver without seams, leaving it set permanently in place. ('767 Patent fig.2c.) Figure 2e shows the transceiver placed within the frame prior to the completion of the fabrication of the eyewear. In figure 2e, the transceiver is exposed, sandwiched between two thin, flat, pieces of material. ('767 Patent at fig.2e.) As depicted in the figure, the transceiver cannot be removed without damaging the sandwiching materials. Figures 8 and 9 show the Bluetooth transceiver seamlessly placed within the frame; while figures 9 and 10 show the earphone components that are meant to be removable being removed, there is no such illustration of the removability of the Bluetooth transceiver. All of the figures in the '767 Patent have this attribute in common: there is nothing in them that indicates one would be able to remove or separate the Bluetooth transceiver from the temples without destroying the structure of the frames in the process. Each figure depicts transceivers permanently set in the frames.

The '767 patent's discussion of the likely methods of manufacturing the eyewear is also instructive:

> The eyewear is manufactured in a process to create electrical components contained throughout the entire frames and temples. Electrical components discussed above and electrical conductors are embedded in the temple and frame portions for the purpose of supplying electrical energy to the various components. In one method some or all of the components, including the conductive wires are co-molded into the temples and frames. This is an in-process method where the components are inserted into the temple and frame tools. The mold cycle is started, plastic material flows into the core and covity of the tool, and the components are permanently set in the rigid temples and frames.

('767 Patent col.7 ll.39-51.) This paragraph describes the primary production method that the patent repeatedly sets forth: co-molding the plastic frames around the electronic apparatus so as to embed it within the frame. It also describes the production method's object: to embed—or "permanently set"—the components within the frame.

The easy interchangeability of the temples of the eyewear claimed in the '767 patent also suggest that the term embedded should be construed as permanently set in the frame of the eyewear. The claimed eyewear is described as having detachable temples that can be switched to change the electronic functions of the eyeglasses:

> The invention contemplates eyewear with interchangeable temples housing a transceiver enabled with small-range wireless network technology, which allows the provided eyewear to form small-range ad-hoc networks with other devices equipped with similar transceivers.
>
> The eyewear includes a frame and connected to the frame are two temples. The temples are connected to the frame hinges.... The temples can be removed by pulling the connector apart, and a temple with a different apparatus within it can be inserted in place of the removed temples.

('767 Patent col. 2 ll.43-58) The patent not only discusses the Bluetooth transceiver as being housed in one of these detachable, interchangeable temples; it also discusses the possibility of embedding other communications devices, including child monitors, audio devices, cameras, speakers, microphones, or displays within other interchangeable temples. *(Id.)* If the transceiver in the claimed eyewear were to malfunction, one would simply replace that temple with a new interchangeable temple with a new transceiver. With such easily interchangeable temples, there would be no reason to be able to access or remove a Bluetooth transceiver from its position embedded within the frame of the temple. The easy interchangeability of the temples in this design makes it more practical for QR Spex to set the transceiver permanently within the frame.

QR Spex suggests that the meaning of embedded should be construed as "fixed firmly or snugly in the frame." (Pl's Op. Brf. at 1.) Because this construction is largely unsupported by the '767 Patent itself—unlike the Court's construction, which is taken directly from the text of the '767 Patent—QR Spex largely relies on extrinsic evidence to argue for its preferred construction. Courts disfavor extrinsic evidence as unreliable for multiple reasons. *Phillips,* 415 F.3d at 1318-19. For instance, extrinsic evidence is not relied on by the patentee during the prosecution process so it has only marginal relevance to explaining the scope and meaning of the claims of the patent. Considering extrinsic evidence also allows the parties to submit a wide variety of evidence of disparate quality, leaving the Court to determine what pieces are probative. *Id.* Extrinsic evidence may also distort the meaning of the words in the patent, undermining the patent system's function of providing public notice. *Id.* QR Spex's extrinsic evidence here has these reliability problems. In any event, the Court finds no reason to resort to QR Spex's extrinsic evidence because the meaning of the word embedded is readily apparent from the intrinsic record.

Before turning to the issue of infringement, the Court would be remiss if it did not address the primary intrinsic argument QR Spex makes in support of its proposed construction of "embedded." This argument is based on a misguided interpretation of a section outlining a possible manufacturing method for its claimed eyewear. The language QR Spex relies on, which immediately follows the description of the co-molded method, states:

> Alternatively, the method of manufacture may be that some or all of the components, including the conductive wires, are assembled into piece parts that make up the temples and frames. The piece parts that make up the temples and frames are designed and injection molded to facilitate easy insertion and assembly of mechanical and electrical components. Further, a combination of the co-molded and assembled components may be used to maximize efficiency.

('767 Patent col.7 ll.51-60.) Although QR Spex argues that this paragraph supports the proposition that that the word embedded means "fixed firmly or snugly in the frame," this is not the case. Something inserted or assembled into the frame can be permanently fixed just as something co-molded is permanently fixed. The description of the manufacturing method is silent as to whether the transceiver is fixed within the frame firmly, permanently, or at all. This language says nothing about how the transceiver is actually set in the frame.

V. The Oakley Eyewear do not Literally Infringe Claim 1 of the '767 Patent

"Literal infringement of a claim exists when each of the claim limitations reads on, or in other words is found in, the accused device." *Allen Engineering Corp. v.*

Bartell Industries, Inc., 299 F.3d 1336, 1345 (Fed. Cir. 2002) (citations and quotations omitted). In *Bai v. L & L Wings,* the Federal Circuit held that a "target game" did not infringe on a patent of a different "target game" because the patent claimed a game with a hemispherical target, and the allegedly infringing game had a target that was partially flat. *Bai v. L & L Wings,* 160 F.3d 1350 (Fed. Cir. 1998.) The Federal Circuit construed hemispherical as "less than a sphere, but . . . nevertheless, a part of a sphere" and held that the accused target game did not literally infringe because it was predominantly flat. *Id.* at 1354. Similarly, the Court's construction of the word embedded leads to the inescapable conclusion that the Oakley Eyewear do not literally infringe Claim 1 of the '767 Patent.

Unlike the transceiver in the eyewear claimed in the '767 Patent, which was co-molded or inserted into a detachable frame so as to be permanently set in the frame, the transceivers in the Oakley Eyewear are attached to the frame via plastic connectors and ridges, and then held in place by a cover secured by screws. (Cowen Decl. PP 13-14.) Any person could remove the printed circuit board including the transceiver in two easy steps by: (1) unscrewing the cover; and (2) unfastening the connectors. Then, a new transceiver could be attached without damaging the frame. Because the transceiver can be taken out and replaced without damaging a pair of the Oakley Eyewear, the Bluetooth transceiver is not permanently set in the frame. It is merely attached to the frame and can be detached. Furthermore, after removal of the transceiver, the cover of the area that once contained the transceiver can be screwed back on, and the eyewear would remain intact.

The way the Bluetooth transceivers are integrated into the Oakley Eyewear is a marked departure from the embedded integration of the transceiver in the eyewear claimed in the '767 Patent. Because that transceiver is permanently set in the frame of the eyewear, removing the transceiver from that eyewear would require more than a screwdriver. Removing the transceiver from the eyewear would result in the eyewear's destruction. No reasonable jury could find that the Oakley Eyewear, with its impermanent, removable, Bluetooth transceiver, directly infringes Claim 1 of the '767 Patent, which requires the eyewear to contain a permanent—embedded—transceiver.

VI. The Oakley Eyewear do not Infringe the '767 Patent Under the Doctrine of Equivalents

The Oakley Eyewear also do not infringe Claim 1 of the '767 Patent under the doctrine of equivalents. For the doctrine of equivalents to apply, there must be only insubstantial differences between a missing claim element and corresponding aspects of the accused device. *See Sage Prods., Inc. v. Devon Indus., Inc.,* 126 F.3d 1420, 1423 (Fed. Cir. 1997). In no circumstances may the doctrine of equivalents be "allowed such broad play as to effectively eliminate [a claim] element in its entirety." *Warner-Jenkinson Co. v. Hilton Davis Chem. Co.,* 520 U.S. 17, 29, 117 S. Ct. 1040, 137 L. Ed. 2d 146 (1997). If any of the claim limitations is totally absent in an accused device, the doctrine of equivalents is inapplicable. *See DeMarini Sports, Inc. v. Worth, Inc.,* 239 F.3d 1314, 1332 (Fed. Cir. 2001). In other words, the plaintiff alleging infringement must establish that the accused product meets every limitation of the patent claim. *See Warner-Jenkinson*, 520 U.S. at 29 ("Each element contained in a patent claim is deemed material to defining the scope of the patented invention. . . ."); *see also Freedman Seating Co. v. Am. Seating Co.*, 420 F.3d 1350, 1358 (Fed. Cir. 2005) (citing *Warner-Jenkinson*, 520 U.S. at 29) ("[A]n element of an accused product or process is not, as a matter of law, equivalent to a limitation of [a] claimed invention if such a finding would entirely vitiate the limitation.").

The doctrine of equivalents allows patentees to protect against infringement by "insubstantial alterations" not captured in the patent claim that entail only "trivial changes." *Festo Corp. v. Shoketsu Kinzoku Kogyo Kabushiki Co., Ltd.*, 535 U.S. 722, 733, 122 S. Ct. 1831, 152 L. Ed. 2d 944 (2002). Whether a product infringes under the doctrine of equivalents is a question of fact for the jury unless the evidence is such that no reasonable jury could determine two elements to be equivalent. *See Warner-Jenkinson Co., Inc. v. Hilton Davis Chem. Co.*, 520 U.S. 17, 39 n.8, 117 S. Ct. 1040, 137 L. Ed. 2d 146 (1997).

To determine whether an invention infringes under the doctrine of equivalents, a court analyzes whether the accused device and the claimed invention in the patent perform substantially the same function in substantially the same way with substantially the same result. *Stumbo v. Eastman Outdoors*, 508 F.3d 1358, 1364 (Fed. Cir. 2007) ("A finding of infringement under the doctrine of equivalents requires a showing that the difference between the claimed invention and the accused product was insubstantial. One way of doing so is by showing on a limitation-by-limitation basis that the accused product performs substantially the same function in substantially the same way with substantially the same result as each claim limitation of the patented product.") (citations omitted). The Federal Circuit in *Stumbo* determined that the doors to one collapsible hunting blind did not infringe the doors of another collapsible hunting blind under the doctrine of equivalents because the doors to each blind were designed in substantially different ways. *Stumbo*, 508 F.3d at 1365. In that case, the plaintiff's hunting blind's entrance was a zippable vertical slit in the fabric of the hunting blind while the defendant's entrance was a triangular flap of fabric: both allowed entrance and egress to the hunting blind, but both allowed it in substantially different ways. *Id.* at 1360-61, 1365. The plaintiff's one-zipper hunting blind door had to be flexed open to allow entrance and closed itself, while the defendant's two-zipper door required no flexing and could remain open by rolling up the flap. *Id.* at 1365.

In this case, the Oakley Eyewear achieve their function of integrating Bluetooth transceivers with eyeglasses in a substantially different way than the eyewear described in Claim 1 of the '767 Patent. The eyewear disclosed in Claim 1 integrates a Bluetooth transceiver into eyeglasses by embedding a transceiver into a removable, interchangeable temple, either by co-molding or inserting the transceiver into the temple, so that it cannot be removed. With the transceiver fixed inside the interchangeable temple, the temple snaps onto the front portion of the eyeglasses. If one transceiver fails, the entire temple can be replaced. In contrast, the transceivers in the Oakley Eyewear are placed inside a cavity in the temple, and snap into place using plastic posts and clips. (Reyes Decl. P 11.) The transceiver is then protected and held into place by a soft pad and a plastic cover, secured by two screws. *(Id.)* In this method, the transceiver itself (and the printed circuit board it is affixed to) can be removed from the eyewear and replaced or repaired, or taken out altogether, without affecting the overall function of the eyewear. This is a substantial difference in design, construction, and function from the eyewear claimed in the '767 Patent.

QR Spex is also estopped from arguing that the Oakley Eyewear infringe Claim 1 of the '767 Patent under the doctrine of equivalents. QR Spex narrowed its claims in the patent prosecution process, precluding it from claiming infringement against any pair of eyewear integrating a Bluetooth transceiver, except eyewear with a Bluetooth transceiver embedded in its frame. When a patentee originally claims subject matter in a patent, but then narrows the claim in response to a rejection of the patent application, it is presumed that the patentee is estopped from raising the doctrine of equivalents on any matter surrendered between the original and the narrower amended claims. *Festo Corp. v. Shoketsu Kinzoku Kogyo Kabushiki Co., Ltd.* 344 F.3d 1359, 1366-67 (Fed. Cir. 2003). A narrowing amendment can occur either by amending an existing limitation or by adding a limitation. *Honeywell Int'l Inc. v. Hamilton Sundstrand Corp.*, 370 F.3d 1131, 1140 (Fed. Cir. 2004). The United States Supreme Court has stated that prosecution history estoppel is an important part of insuring the integrity of the patent system by narrowing the application of the doctrine of equivalents:

> Prosecution history estoppel ensures that the doctrine of equivalents remains tied to its underlying purpose. Where the original application once embraced the purported equivalent but the patentee narrowed his claims to obtain the patent or to protect its validity, the patentee cannot assert that he lacked the words to describe the subject matter in question. The doctrine of equivalents is premised on language's inability to capture the essence of innovation, but a prior application describing the precise element at issue undercuts that premise. In that instance the prosecution history has established that the inventor turned his attention to the subject matter in question, knew the words for both the broader and narrower claim, and affirmatively chose the latter.

Festo Corp. v. Shoketsu Kinzoku Kogyo Kabushiki Co., Ltd., 535 U.S. 722, 734, 122 S. Ct. 1831, 152 L. Ed. 2d 944 (2002). For example, in *Biagro Western Sales, Inc. v. Grow More Inc.*, the plaintiff was subject to prosecution history estoppel when it narrowed its claims to distinguish them from prior art. *Biagro Western Sales, Inc. v. Grow More Inc.*, 423 F.3d 1296, 1305-1306 (Fed. Cir. 2005). The Federal Circuit found that Biagro surrendered claims to alternative formulations of its fertilizer with respect to proportions of phosphorous-containing acid or salt because it specified a range for those chemicals in order to get the Patent and Trademark office to issue its patent. *Id.*

Here, QR Spex narrowed its claim from one encompassing all eyewear with attached transceivers to a claim encompassing only eyewear with Bluetooth transceivers embedded within the frame. In its "Response to Office Action" to the United States Patent and Trademark Offices on January 13, 2007, QR Spex amended Claim 1 as follows:

1. An eyewear comprising:

> *a frame; and*
>
> *a Bluetooth transceiver for short-distance wireless communication, wherein said Bluetooth transceiver is embedded in said frame, and wherein said Bluetooth transceiver is configured to form an ad hoc wireless network with a plurality of devices.*

(Nelson Decl. Ex. 7, Response to Office Action, at 2.) Before the January 13, 2007 response, Claim 1 claimed "An eyewear comprising a transceiver for short-distance wireless communication, said transceiver is configured to form an ad hoc wireless network with a plurality of devices." QR Spex initially claimed all eyeglasses with integrated transceivers. QR Spex narrowed this claim to refer specifically to eyewear with a Bluetooth transceiver embedded within a frame. The narrowing not only specified the type of transceiver required, it also specified the method by which it is to be integrated into the eyewear claimed in the '767 Patent. QR Spex narrowed its claim to specify only one method of integrating a Bluetooth transceiver with a pair of glasses. Because of this, QR Spex is now estopped from arguing that any method of integrating a Bluetooth transceiver and eyewear infringes under the doctrine of equivalents. QR Spex cannot recapture what it surrendered. It can only argue infringement as to eyewear that has a Bluetooth transceiver embedded or permanently set in the frame.

QR Spex argues that its amendment to add "embedded in said frame" bears no more than a tangential relation to the equivalent in question. If a party can show that "the rationale underlying the narrowing amendment bears no more than a tangential relation to the equivalent in question," then it can rebut the presumption of prosecution estoppel. *Festo,* 535 U.S. at 740. On remand, the Federal Circuit further refined what it means for a narrowing amendment to be tangential:

> In other words, this criterion asks whether the reason for the narrowing amendment was peripheral, or not directly relevant, to the alleged equivalent. Although we cannot anticipate the instances of mere tangentialness that may arise, we can say that an amendment made to avoid prior art that contains the equivalent in question is not tangential; it is central to allowance of the claim.... [T]he inquiry into whether a patentee can rebut the *Festo* presumption under the "tangential" criterion focuses on the patentee's objectively apparent reason for the narrowing amendment.

Festo, 344 F.3d at 1369.

QR Spex argues that its addition of the limitation embedded merely specified that the eyewear and transceiver were integrated as one device and did not specify any method of integration. QR Spex's argument of no tangential relation is not persuasive. Its amendment surrendered a much broader scope. The amendment was made in direct response to the Patent and Trademark Office's rejection over the '076 Patent. In its brief opposing summary judgment for non-infringement, QR Spex specifically admitted that "adding the limitation that the transceiver was embedded in the frame . . . was intended to narrow the scope of Claim 1 and its dependent claims by narrowing the relationship between the frame and the transceiver to one where the later is fixed firmly within the former." *(Id.* at 13-14.) Later in the same brief, QR Spex makes the contradictory argument that it merely made its amendment—adding the word embedded—to show that the transceiver was integrated into the eyewear, not to specify the method by which it integrated the transceiver into the eyewear. However, the text of Claim 1already claimed a device that integrated a transceiver into eyewear before QR Spex added the term embedded. Claim 1 originally disclosed "an eyewear comprising a transceiver." Making a change to specify that the transceiver is embedded in the eyewear describes *how* the transceiver is set in the eyewear. It has very little to do with claiming integration. QR Spex's narrowing of Claim 1 so the Patent and Trademark Office would issue the '767 Patent is not tangential. It was made to avoid the prior art.

VII. Conclusion

For all the reasons set forth above, the Court finds that the accused Oakley Eyewear do not infringe the '767 Patent either literally or under the doctrine of equivalents. Accordingly, the Court grants partial summary judgment of non infringement in favor of Defendants.

Notes

1. This case centers on a utility patent directed to technology-enabled eyewear. In a utility patent, the claims define the metes and bounds of the invention and, at times, the words of the claim need to be properly construed so as to truly understand the scope of the claim and whether infringement might exist.

2. Claim construction begins with the word or term's "ordinary and customary meaning" and may include intrinsic evidence and, as needed, extrinsic evidence. *See Markman v. Westview Instruments, Inc.,* 517 U.S. 370 (1996). Intrinsic evidence includes what is in the public record, particularly the claims themselves and the specification. Because a patent applicant can be his or her own lexicographer, and because of the importance of clarity in the specification, the meaning can often be found in the specification. Extrinsic evidence may be included, but is considered less reliable.

3. As noted in the case, claim construction is a matter of law. What are the implications of this?

4. When it comes to infringement, there may be either or both of literal infringement and infringement under the doctrine of equivalents.

5. Another consideration in determining claim scope (and possible infringement) is prosecution history estoppel. If, in the course of interacting with the USPTO, explanations or amendments resulted in, for example, narrowing scope or articulating distinctions, these narrowing limitations or distinctions can be used in

determining claim construction and/or infringement, even infringement under the doctrine of equivalents.

6. Such a narrowing limitation became the key item in determining infringement in this case.

2. Alternative Recourse: ITC

Because fashion is an international industry, U.S. companies and designers often need to defend patents and other intellectual property against foreign companies. However, this may be difficult and inconvenient to do because the foreign companies are not subject to personal jurisdiction in U.S. courts. A solution is to pursue action through the International Trade Commission ("ITC"). The ITC has the authority to determine patent infringement issues under 19 U.S.C. § 1337 when infringement occurs with importation into the United States. The ITC is tasked with blocking importation of infringing articles.

A patent holder may bring actions before both a federal district court and the ITC to challenge an alleged infringer's imports. Upon a finding of patent infringement, the ITC may impose two remedies. First, it may issue either a general or limited exclusion order to the specific parties in the investigation before the ITC, directing U.S. Customs and Border Protection to bar entry of infringing products. Second, the ITC may issue a cease-and-desist order to a specific party barring importation and other activities, such as sales and distribution of imported infringing products. For an example of an action at the ITC, *see Crocs, Inc. v. International Trade Commission*, 598 F.3d 1291 (2010).

Figure 1

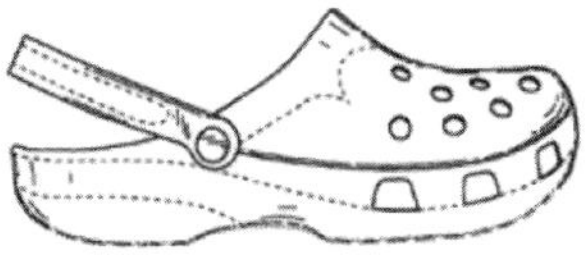

Figure 2

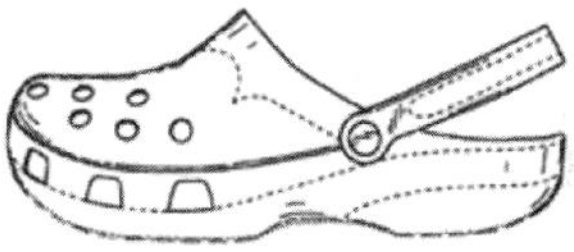

Figure 3

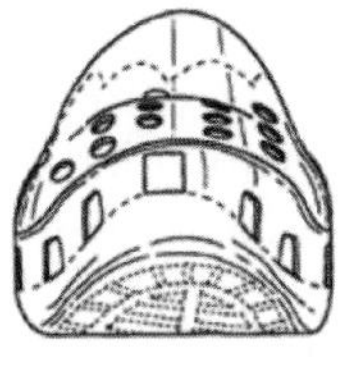

Figure 4

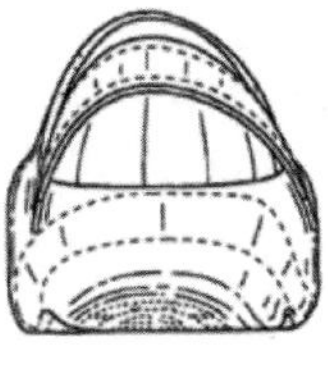

Figure 5

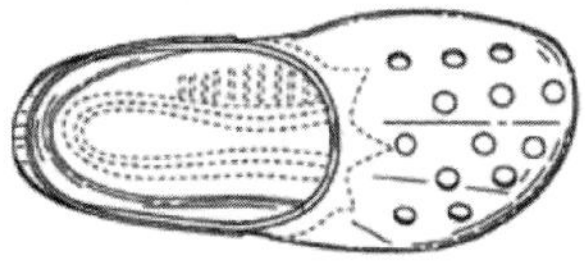

Figure 6

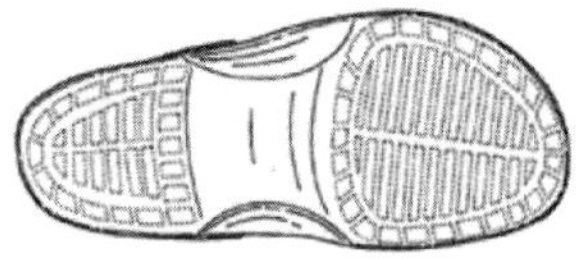

Figure 7

These are the parent drawings for '789 patent, called "Footwear" for which Crocs claimed "an ornamental footwear design."

Source: U.S. Patent Office. http://www.cafc.uscourts.gov/images/stories/opinions-orders/08-1596.pdf at page 4, and http://www.jdsupra.com/legalnews/crocs-v-international-trade-commission-47815/.

Crocs, Inc. v. International Trade Commission

598 F.3d 1294 (Fed. Cir. 2010)

RADER, Circuit Judge.

I.

Crocs is the assignee of the '858 and '789 patents. Crocs's '858 patent, entitled "Breathable Footwear Pieces," issued on February 7, 2006, based on a filing in 2003. The asserted claims of the '858 patent, independent claims 1 and 2, cover foam footwear having a foam base section—an upper portion ("upper") and a sole—and a foam strap. A pair of connectors ties the foam strap to the base section. This connection creates frictional forces that keep the strap in an ideal position at the rear of the base section.

Crocs filed a complaint and an amended complaint on March 31, 2006 and April 27, 2006, respectively. Crocs's amended complaint alleged unfair competition under 19 U.S.C. § 1337 by respondents due to importation into the United States of foam footwear. Crocs asserted that the imported footwear infringes claims 1 and 2 of the '858 patent, the design in the '789 patent, and Crocs's trade dress. Crocs later withdrew its trade dress complaint. The complaint named eleven respondents. After some settlements and some determinations of non-infringement, five respondents remained in the investigation: (1) Collective; (2) Double Diamond; (3) Effervescent; (4) Gen-X; and (5) Holey Soles. They make accused products in Asia and import them into the United States.

Crocs filed a motion for summary determination of infringement of the '789 patent. Respondents answered with motions for summary determination of non-infringement of the '789 patent. On November 7, 2006, the presiding administrative law judge granted respondents' motions for summary determination of non-infringement of the '789 patent. On review, the Commission issued an Order of Vacatur and Remand of Initial Determination on February 15, 2007. On remand, the administrative judge held an evidentiary hearing from September 7 through 14, 2007.

On April 11, 2008, the administrative judge concluded that the respondents did not violate section 1337. Specifically, the administrative judge found that the '789 patent was not infringed and that Crocs's products, its Beach, Cayman, and Kids Cayman shoes, did not satisfy the technical prong of the domestic industry requirement. In reaching this latter decision, the administrative judge found that Crocs's own products did not practice the patent. Turning to the utility patent, the administrative judge found that claims 1 and 2 of the '858 patent would have been obvious under 35 U.S.C. § 103 in light of two pieces of prior art: (1) the Aqua Clog (the base section of claims 1 and 2 of the '858 patent); and (2) U.S. Patent No. 6,237,249 (the "Aguerre '249 patent").

With respect to the design patent, the '789 patent, the administrative judge provided a detailed verbal claim construction:

> In summary, when the '789 patent is considered as a whole, the visual impression created by the claimed design includes: footwear having a foot opening with a strap that may or may not include any patterning, is attached to the body of the footwear by two round connectors, is of uniform width between the two round connectors, has a wrench-head like shape at the point of attachment, and extends to the heel of the shoe; with round holes on the roof of the upper placed in a systematic pattern; with trapezoid-shaped holes evenly spaced around the sidewall of the upper including the front portion; with a relatively flat sole (except for upward curvature in the toe and heel) that may or may not contain tread on the upper and lower portions of the sole, but if tread exists, does not cover the entire sole, and scalloped indentations that extend from the side of the sole in the middle portion that curve toward each other.

Based on this description, the administrative judge found the Holey Soles and Gen-X accused products did not infringe because their strap is not of uniform thickness and does not extend to the heel of the shoe. The same reasoning excused the Collective and Effervescent accused products from infringement but the administrative judge added the further explanation that these imports did not have round holes in the upper portion. He found that the Double Diamond accused products did not infringe because each of the accused products has at least one of the following: a strap that does not have uniform thickness and does not extend to the heel of the shoe; holes in the upper that are not round; holes in the upper that are placed in a web-shaped, not systematic, pattern; or a tread pattern that covers the entire sole.

Crocs, CLI, and the Commission investigative attorney ("IA") filed petitions for review with the Commission. On June 18, 2008, the Commission agreed to review the following issues: (1) the findings concerning non-infringement of the '789 patent and the lack of satisfaction of the technical prong of the domestic industry requirement; and (2) the finding of invalidity with respect to the '858 patent. The Commission did not review any other issues.

On July 25, 2008, the Commission affirmed the finding of no infringement and no domestic industry for the '789 patent, and obviousness for the '858 patent. The Commission augmented the discussion in the initial determination about non-infringement of the '789 patent and lack of satisfaction of the technical prong of the domestic industry requirement by finding that the accused shoes and Crocs's shoes lacked even spacing of ventilator holes around the front (toe) portion of the upper as shown in the '789 patent design.

For obviousness of the '858 patent, the Commission found that the administrative judge properly concluded that the principal remaining difference between the prior art and the claimed invention is the use of foam for the strap. The Commission upheld the administrative judge's finding that the prior art showed foam straps. Finally, on secondary considerations of non-obviousness, the Commission found that Crocs did not show a nexus between its claimed shoes and their commercial success. The Commission, unlike the administrative judge, did find that at least one respondent copied Crocs's commercially available shoe. The Commission held that the evidence of copying, however, did not disturb the prima facie case of obviousness.

Crocs appeals the Commission's final determination. Collective and Gen-X were dismissed as intervenors from the appeal. Double Diamond, Effervescent, and Holey Soles are the remaining intervenors.

III.

This court reviews the Commission's legal determinations without deference and its factual findings for substantial evidence. Substantial evidence is "such relevant evidence as a reasonable mind might accept as adequate to support a conclusion." *Universal Camera Corp. v. NLRB*, 340 U.S. 474, 477, 71 S. Ct. 456, 95 L. Ed. 456 (1951).

A.

This court has cautioned, and continues to caution, trial courts about excessive reliance on a detailed verbal description in a design infringement case. *See, e.g., Egyptian Goddess, Inc. v. Swisa, Inc.*, 543 F.3d 665, 679 (Fed. Cir. 2008). In *Egyptian Goddess*, this court warned that misplaced reliance on a detailed verbal description of the claimed design risks undue emphasis on particular features of the design rather than examination of the design as a whole. In many cases, the considerable effort in fashioning a detailed verbal description does not contribute enough to the infringement analysis to justify the endeavor. Depictions of the claimed design in words can easily distract from the proper infringement analysis of the ornamental patterns and drawings.

Design patents are typically claimed as shown in drawings, and claim construction must be adapted to a pictorial setting. Thus, an illustration depicts a design better "than it could be by any description and a description would probably not be intelligible without the illustration." *Dobson v. Dornan*, 118 U.S. 10, 14, 6 S. Ct. 946, 30 L. Ed. 63, 1886 Dec. Comm'r Pat. 202 (1886). "[A]s a rule, the illustration in the drawing views is its own best description." *Manual of Patent Examining Procedure* § 1503.01 (8th ed. 2006).

This case shows the dangers of reliance on a detailed verbal claim construction. The claim construction focused on particular features of the '789 patent design and led the administrative judge and the Commission away from consideration of the design as a whole. This error is apparent in the Commission's explicit reference to two details required by the written claim construction but not by the '789 drawings: (1) a strap of uniform width, and (2) holes evenly spaced around the sidewall of the upper. As shown in Figure 1 of the '789 patent, the strap bulges to a greater width at the middle of the strap on the far left of the figure. Thus, the design figure does not require a strap of uniform width between the two round connectors. Also, as shown in Figure 4 of the 789 patent, the holes are not evenly spaced. Figure 4 shows a gap in the spacing (particularly towards the big toe). Nonetheless, the written claim description required uniform strap width and uniform hole spacing—contrary to the claimed invention. This error distorts the infringement analysis by the ordinary observer viewing the design as a whole. The administrative judge and the Commission needed to apply the ordinary observer test to "the design shown in Figures 1-7."

B.

In determining whether an accused product infringes a patented design, this court applies the "ordinary observer" test, without any "point of novelty" perspective. *Egyptian Goddess*, 543 F.3d at 678. To show infringement under the proper test, an ordinary observer, familiar with the prior art designs, would be deceived into believing that the accused product is the same as the patented design. When the differences between the claimed and accused designs are viewed in light of the prior art, the attention of the hypothetical ordinary observer may be drawn to those aspects of the claimed design that differ from the prior art. *Id.* If the claimed design is close to the prior art designs, small differences between the accused design and the claimed design assume more importance to the eye of the hypothetical ordinary observer. *Id.* The ordinary observer, however, will likely attach importance to those differences depending on the overall effect of those differences on the design. *Id.* Even if the claimed design simply combines old features in the prior art, it may still create an overall appearance deceptively similar to the accused design. In that case, this court will uphold a finding of infringement. In other words, "the deception that arises is a result of the similarities in the overall design, not of similarities in ornamental features in isolation." *Amini Innovation*, 439 F.3d at 1371. The ordinary observer test applies to the patented design in its entirety, as it is claimed. "[M]inor differences between a patented design and an accused article's design cannot, and shall not, prevent a finding of infringement." *Payless Shoesource*, 998 F.2d at 991 (quoting *Litton Sys. Inc. v. Whirlpool*, 728 F.2d 1423, 1444 (Fed. Cir. 1984)).

Turning to this case, the Commission placed undue emphasis on particular details of its written description of the patented design. Those details became a mistaken checklist for infringement. Without a view to the design as a whole, the Commission used minor differences between the patented design and the accused products to prevent a finding of infringement. In other words, the concentration on small differences in isolation distracted from the overall impression of the claimed ornamental features.

The proper comparison requires a side-by-side view of the drawings of the '789 patent design and the accused products.

These side-by-side comparisons of the '789 patent design and the accused products suggest that an ordinary observer, familiar with the prior art designs, would be deceived into believing the accused products are the same as the patented design. In one comparison after another, the shoes appear nearly identical. If the claimed design and the accused designs were arrayed in matching colors and mixed up randomly, this court is not confident that an ordinary observer could properly restore them to their original order without very careful and prolonged effort.

One of the overall effects of the design is the interaction between the strap assembly portion and the base portion of the shoes where the strap is attached to the base. Multiple major design lines and curves converge at that point creating a focal point attracting the eye of the ordinary observer when viewing the overall effect of the design. Another overall effect of the design is a visual theme of rounded curves and ellipses throughout the design, including the strap forming a sort of continuation of the sidewall of the base to create a visually continuous ring encircling the entire shoe. Other examples of rounded curves or ellipses in the design are the ellipses formed by the strap and the foot opening in the base. Both the claimed design and the accused designs have these overall effects.

In any event, this court perceives that the accused products embody the overall effect of the '789 design in sufficient detail and clarity to cause market confusion. Thus, the accused products infringe the '789 design.

C.

One requirement of a patent-based section 1337 action is that a domestic industry "relating to the articles protected by the patent . . . exists or is in the process of being established." 19 U.S.C. § 1337(a)(2) (2006). To determine the relationship between a domestic industry and protected articles (the "technical prong" of the domestic industry requirement), the Commission determines whether the industry produces articles covered by the asserted claims. The test for the technical prong of the industry requirement "is essentially the same as that for infringement, i.e., a comparison of domestic products to the asserted claims." *Alloc, Inc. v. Int'l Trade Comm'n*, 342 F.3d 1361, 1375 (Fed. Cir. 2003). In other words, the technical prong requires proof that the patent claims cover the articles of manufacture that establish the domestic industry. Put simply, the complainant must practice its own patent.

Because the test for the technical prong is essentially the same as for infringement, this court uses the ordinary observer test to compare Crocs's own shoe products to the '789 patent design. This court has stated that test above. Once again, the test applies best in a side-by-side comparison of the drawings of the '789 patent design and the Crocs products.

The Crocs Cayman and Kids Cayman shoes are practically identical to the Crocs Beach shoe, so this court uses only that product for comparison.

As illustrated by the side-by-side comparison of the '789 patent design and the Crocs Beach shoe, an ordinary observer, familiar with the prior art designs, would consider the Crocs shoes the same as the patented design. The overall effects of the design in the '789 patent and the Crocs shoes are the same. One of the overall effects of the design present in both the '789 patent and Crocs shoes is the focal point where multiple major design lines and curves converge at the point where the strap is attached to the base. Another is the visual theme of rounded curves and ellipses throughout both designs. Crocs's shoes embody the overall effect of the '789 design in light of the prior art; they "infringe" the '789 design. Thus, Crocs satisfies the technical prong of the domestic industry requirement.

IV.

Obviousness is a question of law based on underlying factual inquiries including: (1) the scope and content of the prior art; (2) the level of ordinary skill in the art; (3) the differences between the prior art and the claimed invention; and (4) the extent of any objective indicia of non-obviousness

The record shows that the prior art would actually discourage and teach away from the use of foam straps. An ordinary artisan in this field would not add a foam strap to the foam Aqua Clog because foam was likely to stretch and deform, in addition to causing discomfort for a wearer. The prior art depicts foam as unsuitable for straps. A firm inelastic material like foam was likely to cause abrasions at the back of the foot. In addition, foam had another deficient property. Foam, according to the prior art, did not have a good memory, meaning that the stretching of normal use would likely cause the material to elongate or compress. These deformations would defeat the strap long before the normal life span of the footwear combination. Thus, the prior art only used a non-elastic material for attaching footwear in combination with a buckle or another mechanism that could adjust the length of the strap for a comfortable fit and for a reduction in stretching and deformation.

Despite the prior art warnings against inelastic and non-adjustable foam straps, the '858 patent employed foam without a buckle or some other similar adjustment mechanism. Moreover the '858 patent riveted the inelastic foam directly to the base of the footwear. This claimed feature defied the prior art's caution against the poor characteristics of a foam strap. Indeed, no prior art reference disclosed a foam strap riveted to a shoe.

The record shows that Crocs's expert testified that artisans of ordinary skill in this art thought that foam shoe components connected through perforations such as by stitching or riveting were excessively prone to tearing. The Commission unreasonably determined that foam straps were known in the art without acknowledging that those prior art references rendered the material out of place for use as a strap. Thus, the Commission could not properly conclude that a person of ordinary skill would use foam to attach a foam base portion to a wearer.

The Commission also held that choosing foam as the material for a strap for a shoe that is otherwise made of foam is a logical modification because it produces a shoe of uniform composition. To the contrary, a foam strap is not a logical modification because foam was known to be an unsuitable material that was prone to tearing. One of ordinary skill would have no reason to use foam straps in combination with a foam base portion. Thus, the new combination would not have been obvious at the time of the invention of the '858 patent.

Even if the '858 patent was a combination of known elements according to their established functions—which it is not as foam straps were not in the prior art—it yields more than predictable results; thus, it is non-obvious.

The inventor of the '858 patent, Scott Seamans, testified that the unique frictional forces that develop between the foam components keep the strap in place so that it can maintain the shoe in the correct position on the foot without constant contact with the wearer's Achilles. Instead of pushing the foot forward into the shoe—like prior art straps that are elastic or length adjustable—the '858 patent's passive restraint system allows the strap to "lend support" only when necessary to keep the shoe positioned correctly on the foot. This feature facilitates a loose anatomical fit that makes the claimed invention more comfortable than prior art products.

The administrative judge recognized this distinction between the '858 invention and the Aguerre '249 patent:

Now, it is true that the strap disclosed in the Aguerre '249 patent was made of material other than foam and was adjustable and elastic so that it held the foot snugly in the shoe. By contrast, the '858 patent discloses a firm foam strap that acts as a passive restraint to the Achilles portion of the foot and can be set in various fixed position[s] because of the friction created by the *direct contact* between the upper portion of the base and the strap.

Thus, the prior art did not include any hint or suggestion or even commonsense reason to include the passive restraint system of the '858 patent at the time of the invention. The prior art, in fact, taught away from the passive restraint system. Because this claimed feature of the invention yielded more than predictable results, the '858 patent for this reason also would not have been obvious at the time of invention.

Secondary considerations "can be the most probative evidence of non-obviousness in the record, and enables the . . . court to avert the trap of hindsight." *Custom Accessories, Inc. v. Jeffrey-Allan Indus., Inc.*, 807 F.2d 955, 960 (Fed. Cir. 1986). Judge Learned Hand appreciated the importance of secondary considerations:

> In appraising an inventor's contribution to the art, as we have often said, the most reliable test is to look at the situation before and after it appears. Courts, made up of laymen as they must be, are likely either to underrate, or to overrate, the difficulties in making new and profitable discoveries in fields with which they cannot be familiar; and, so far as it is available, they had best appraise the originality involved by the circumstances which preceded, attended and succeeded the appearance of the invention. We have repeatedly declared that in our judgment this analysis [evidence of secondary considerations] is more reliable than prior conclusions drawn from vaporous, and almost inevitably self-dependent, general propositions. *Safety Car Heating & Lighting Co. v. Gen. Elec. Co.*, 155 F.2d 937, 939 (2d Cir. 1946).

The Commission found that three models of Crocs shoes practice claims 1 and 2 of the '858 patent: the Beach, Cayman, and Kids Cayman shoes. It found that those three models of Crocs shoes have enjoyed a great deal of commercial success. A prima facie case of nexus is made when the patentee shows both that there is commercial success, and that the product that is commercially successful is the invention disclosed and claimed in the patent. Once the patentee demonstrates a prima facie nexus, the burden of coming forward with evidence in rebuttal shifts to the challenger.

Because the Commission found, based on substantial evidence, that Crocs shoes practice the '858 patent and that the Crocs shoes were commercially successful, Crocs established a prima facie case of nexus. The record discloses little or no evidence to rebut this prima facie case of nexus. This court is aware that many market forces unrelated to the inventiveness of the patent may influence commercial success, but the intervenors must make a convincing case that those market forces indeed were the likely cause of the success. This record does not show any effort to make that rebuttal case. In the absence of a rebuttal, Crocs may add its commercial success to its proofs of non-obviousness. This court gives even more credit to the administrative judge's finding of substantial industry praise for the claimed invention and the products covered by the claimed invention. Still another objective measure tips the scale farther in the direction of non-obviousness, namely the Commission's finding of copying. Copying may indeed be another form of flattering praise for inventive features. In the absence of any record evidence attributing these secondary considerations to causes other than the claimed invention, Crocs may rely on this added support for non-obviousness.

In light of the prior art teaching away from the claimed invention and the claimed features that do not appear in the prior art, this court detects several reasons at the time of the invention that an ordinary artisan would not have been motivated even to try, let alone make, this inventive combination. In addition, the secondary considerations supply additional evidence of non-obviousness. Thus, this court reverses the Commission's holding that the '858 patent would have been obvious and easily attainable at the time of invention.

V.

For the foregoing reasons, this court reverses the Commission's determination that the '789 patent was not infringed, that Crocs did not satisfy the technical prong of the domestic industry requirement of section 1337 relating to the '789 patent, and that the '858 patent would have been obvious. This court remands the investigation to the Commission for a determination of infringement of the '858 patent and any appropriate remedies.

REVERSED AND REMANDED.

Notes

1. This case illustrates the benefits of patents in the fashion world and various forms of enforcement of those patents.

2. In addition, this case illustrates the global nature of the fashion world.

3. A U.S. company may wish to defend its patent (or other intellectual property rights) against foreign entities that are not subject to personal jurisdiction in the

United States. To do so, it can choose to proceed in an action in the ITC of the United States.

4. One result of such a proceeding is that the U.S. company can block importation of infringing goods. To block importation, the U.S. company needs to prove that it is entitled to the claimed intellectual property rights. This case is an example of an appeal from the ITC, which goes to the CAFC.

5. In this case, the CAFC begins its analysis by reviewing the ITC by addressing the design patent in question.

6. The ITC's analysis resulted in a determination that defendants had not infringed the Crocs '789 design patent (patents are referred to by the last three digits of the patent number). The CAFC reversed, and unlike the analysis at the ITC, the CAFC compared the product being imported to the pictures in the design patent, rather than the verbal descriptions of the design of the allegedly infringing products, opining, "a picture is worth a thousand words." Does such a comparison favor the patent holder or alleged infringer?

Chapter 7

Counterfeiting and Gray Market Goods

Robertson D. Beckerlegge

A. Introduction

Counterfeiting is not going away. What was once confined to illicit shopping districts around the world, such as Canal Street in New York City, has ballooned into a global, multibillion-dollar business. It's no longer just whispers of "Louis Vuitton," "Gucci," and "Rolex," on some street corner, but it's millions of illegal shipments, large and small. And counterfeiting impacts more than just luxury brands; it has expanded today to affect virtually all large fashion brands and has become a highly profitable global business. The numbers are almost too big to be believable. The following are not typos:

- In Fiscal Year 2019, U.S. Customs and Border Protection ("Customs") conducted 27,599 Intellectual Property Rights ("IPR") seizures of goods that, if genuine, would have been worth approximately $1.5 billion.
- Customs found these goods among approximately 28.7 million shipping containers, 144 million express mail shipments, and 463 million packages coming into the United States.
- China and Hong Kong accounted for 83 percent of all 2019 IPR seizures.
- Of types of goods, apparel/accessories accounted for 14 percent of seizures; foot wear, 12 percent; watches/jewelry, 15 percent; and handbags/wallets, 13 percent.

While Customs works diligently, it can't possibly keep up with the volume of goods coming into the United States. If the above is what Customs seized in FY 2019, imagine what is making it through to consumers.

At the geopolitical level, the issue of counterfeiting is addressed by high-level trade negotiations through the Office of the United States Trade Representative ("USTR"), which issues a yearly Special 301 Report that identifies countries that do not provide adequate intellectual property protection for its citizens and to U.S. citizens and that are often manufacturers and exporters of counterfeit goods. These countries are identified as Priority Watch List and Watch List Countries. The problem is as regimes and governments change, counterfeiting typically rises and falls in terms of prioritization. While some governments say the right things in publicized sound bites, they do little to stem the flow of counterfeits when counterfeiting can be a key component of their economy. The Trump administration issued its Memorandum on Combating Trafficking in Counterfeit and Pirated Goods in April 2019, focusing on curbing online counterfeiting with a report to follow. It remains to be seen what actions, if any, will be taken and what enforcement efforts will evolve. Economically, counterfeits directly deprive brand owners of revenue due to substitution of counterfeits for genuine articles and governments' tax proceeds. But legally, counterfeiting decreases brand value due to overexposure and harm to a brand's carefully cultivated image of exclusivity.

B. Laws Governing Counterfeiting

Trademark counterfeiting is the act of manufacturing or distributing a product bearing a mark identical to, or substantially indistinguishable from, a registered trademark. This chapter discusses federal civil and criminal as well as state laws relating to counterfeiting and enforcement.

The term "knockoff" is sometimes inaccurately used as a synonym for "counterfeit." The term "knockoff" in the fashion industry simply refers to any article that imitates or copies another article. While some copies are legal and others are infringements, an egregious form of trademark infringement is deemed counterfeiting. The differences between counterfeiting and ordinary trademark infringement are: (a) counterfeiting applies when the copy is substantially identical to the authentic mark; and (b) punitive civil remedies (such as seizures and treble damages) become available as well as criminal penalties.

1. Federal Laws Relating to Counterfeiting

The importance of expanding intellectual property protection to penalize counterfeiters is seen in the legislative history of developing federal counterfeiting laws. The Lanham Act of 1946 ("Lanham Act") was enacted "to protect persons engaged in commerce against false advertising and unfair competition" and defines counterfeiting as the act of producing, offering for sale, selling, or distributing a product or service with "a spurious mark which is identical with, or substantially indistinguishable from, a registered mark." Brand owners relied on the Lanham Act in actions against counterfeiters prior to 1984 by pursuing civil anticounterfeiting litigation under provisions against unfair competition.

15 U.S.C. § 1114

(1) Any person who shall, without the consent of the registrant—

> (a) use in commerce any reproduction, counterfeit, copy, or colorable imitation of a registered mark in connection with the sale, offering for sale, distribution, or advertising of any goods or services on or in connection with which such use is likely to cause confusion, or to cause mistake, or to deceive; or

(b) reproduce, counterfeit, copy, or colorably imitate a registered mark and apply such reproduction, counterfeit, copy, or colorable imitation to labels, signs, prints, packages, wrappers, receptacles or advertisements intended to be used in commerce upon or in connection with the sale, offering for sale, distribution, or advertising of goods or services on or in connection with which such use is likely to cause confusion, or to cause mistake, or to deceive,

shall be liable in a civil action by the registrant for the remedies hereinafter provided. Under subsection (b) hereof, the registrant shall not be entitled to recover profits or damages unless the acts have been committed with knowledge that such imitation is intended to be used to cause confusion, or to cause mistake, or to deceive.

Though the Lanham Act provided a basis for enjoining counterfeiters, awarding monetary relief and possibly conducting seizures of counterfeit goods, it does little to deter the typical counterfeiter driven by the lucrative counterfeit market.

Under federal law an extraordinary remedy, the *ex parte* civil seizure order, is available against counterfeiters:

15 U.S.C. § 1116

(d) Civil actions arising out of use of counterfeit marks

(1)

(A) In the case of a civil action arising under section 1114(1)(a) of this title or section 220506 of Title 36 with respect to a violation that consists of using a counterfeit mark in connection with the sale, offering for sale, or distribution of goods or services, the court may, upon ex parte application, grant an order under subsection (a) of this section pursuant to this subsection providing for the seizure of goods and counterfeit marks involved in such violation and the means of making such marks, and records documenting the manufacture, sale, or receipt of things involved in such violation.

(B) As used in this subsection the term "counterfeit mark" means—

(i) a counterfeit of a mark that is registered on the principal register in the United States Patent and Trademark Office for such goods or services sold, offered for sale, or distributed and that is in use, whether or not the person against whom relief is sought knew such mark was so registered; or

(ii) a spurious designation that is identical with, or substantially indistinguishable from, a designation as to which the remedies of this chapter are made available by reason of section 220506 of Title 36;

but such term does not include any mark or designation used on or in connection with goods or services of which the manufacture or producer was, at the time of the manufacture or production in question authorized to use the mark or designation for the type of goods or services so manufactured or produced, by the holder of the right to use such mark or designation.

[The United States Attorney must be notified of any proposed application for a civil seizure:]

(2) The court shall not receive an application under this subsection unless the applicant has given such notice of the application as is reasonable under the circumstances to the United States attorney for the judicial district in which such order is sought. Such attorney may participate in the proceedings arising under such application if such proceedings may affect evidence of an offense against the United States. The court may deny such application if the court determines that the public interest in a potential prosecution so requires.

[The proposed order must be carefully drafted consistent with the statute since this seizure order essentially allows a brand owner to assume the role of law enforcement:]

(3) The application for an order under this subsection shall—

(A) be based on an affidavit or the verified complaint establishing facts sufficient to support the findings of fact and conclusions of law required for such order; and

(B) contain the additional information required by paragraph (5) of this subsection to be set forth in such order.

(4) The court shall not grant such an application unless—

(A) the person obtaining an order under this subsection provides the security determined adequate by the court for the payment of such damages as any person may be entitled to recover as a result of a wrongful seizure or wrongful attempted seizure under this subsection; and

(B) the court finds that it clearly appears from specific facts that—

(i) an order other than an ex parte seizure order is not adequate to achieve the purposes of section 1114 of this title;

(ii) the applicant has not publicized the requested seizure;

(iii) the applicant is likely to succeed in showing that the person against whom seizure would be ordered used a counterfeit mark in connection with the sale, offering for sale, or distribution of goods or services;

(iv) an immediate and irreparable injury will occur if such seizure is not ordered;

(v) the matter to be seized will be located at the place identified in the application;

(vi) the harm to the applicant of denying the application outweighs the harm to the legitimate interests of the person against whom seizure would be ordered of granting the application; and

(vii) the person against whom seizure would be ordered, or persons acting in concert with such person, would destroy, move, hide, or otherwise make such matter inaccessible to the court, if the applicant were to proceed on notice to such person.

(5) An order under this subsection shall set forth—

(A) the findings of fact and conclusions of law required for the order;

(B) a particular description of the matter to be seized, and a description of each place at which such matter is to be seized;

(C) the time period, which shall end not later than seven days after the date on which such order is issued, during which the seizure is to be made;

(D) the amount of security required to be provided under this subsection; and

(E) a date for the hearing required under paragraph (10) of this subsection.

(6) The court shall take appropriate action to protect the person against whom an order under this subsection is directed from publicity, by or at the behest of the plaintiff, about such order and any seizure under such order.

(7) Any materials seized under this subsection shall be taken into the custody of the court. For seizures made under this section, the court shall enter an appropriate protective order with respect to discovery and use of any records or information that has been seized. The protective order shall provide for appropriate procedures to ensure that confidential, private, proprietary, or privileged information contained in such records is not improperly disclosed or used.

(8) An order under this subsection, together with the supporting documents, shall be sealed until the person against whom the order is directed has an opportunity to contest such order, except that any person against whom such order is issued shall have access to such order and supporting documents after the seizure has been carried out.

(9) The court shall order that service of a copy of the order under this subsection shall be made by a Federal law enforcement officer (such as a United States marshal or an officer or agent of the United States Customs Service, Secret Service, Federal Bureau of Investigation, or Post Office) or may be made by a State or local law enforcement officer, who, upon making service, shall carry out the seizure under the order. The court shall issue orders, when appropriate, to protect the defendant from undue damage from the

disclosure of trade secrets or other confidential information during the course of the seizure, including, when appropriate, orders restricting the access of the applicant (or any agent or employee of the applicant) to such secrets or information.

(10)

(A) The court shall hold a hearing, unless waived by all the parties, on the date set by the court in the order of seizure. That date shall be not sooner than ten days after the order is issued and not later than fifteen days after the order is issued, unless the applicant for the order shows good cause for another date or unless the party against whom such order is directed consents to another date for such hearing. At such hearing the party obtaining the order shall have the burden to prove that the facts supporting findings of fact and conclusions of law necessary to support such order are still in effect. If that party fails to meet that burden, the seizure order shall be dissolved or modified appropriately.

(B) In connection with a hearing under this paragraph, the court may make such orders modifying the time limits for discovery under the Rules of Civil Procedure as may be necessary to prevent the frustration of the purposes of such hearing.

[Wrongful seizure can be damaging to a brand owner:]

(11) A person who suffers damage by reason of a wrongful seizure under this subsection has a cause of action against the applicant for the order under which such seizure was made, and shall be entitled to recover such relief as may be appropriate, including damages for lost profits, cost of materials, loss of good will, and punitive damages in instances where the seizure was sought in bad faith, and, unless the court finds extenuating circumstances, to recover a reasonable attorney's fee. The court in its discretion may award prejudgment interest on relief recovered under this paragraph, at an annual interest rate established under section 6621(a)(2) of Title 26, commencing on the date of service of the claimant's pleading setting forth the claim under this paragraph and ending on the date such recovery is granted, or for such shorter time as the court deems appropriate.

2. Civil Seizure

One of the most important tools that fashion companies employ to battle counterfeiters is the civil seizure. Fashion houses typically use outside counsel and private investigators to obtain information on the location of a counterfeiter's warehouse or administrative headquarters. With this evidence, the brand owner obtains an *ex parte* order to seize the contents of the locations in question. Not only can civil seizures provide valuable proof of the extent of counterfeit operations, they also allow counterfeit inventory to be taken off the market and destroyed.

Plaintiffs must use reliable investigators with experience in the industry to help build their case. They won't overstep legal boundaries in their efforts to identify the counterfeiters and make evidentiary buys. In addition, plaintiffs must make sure they have the evidence before seeking a seizure order. Many judges are not familiar with seizure orders in the civil context. They often have many questions. Plaintiffs must be prepared to make their case with supporting, contemporaneous evidence and the investigator may have to testify at a preliminary hearing. Plaintiffs need the assistance of law enforcement to carry out the *ex parte* civil seizure and must know the rules of the relevant branch, the forms required, and the associated cost.

The trademark owner is acting *ex parte* so a court will be extra vigilant before granting such a request. The seizure cannot be publicized in advance and the trademark owner must be able to demonstrate likelihood of success on the merits. The trademark owner should be prepared to show immediate and irreparable injury and the specific locations where counterfeit products were sold and where the seizures will occur. And the trademark owner must be able to demonstrate that the harm to the brand outweighs any potential harm to the counterfeiter and therefore the seizure action should be granted. When seeking a seizure order plaintiffs must: (i) notify the U.S. Attorney's Office; (ii) make sure to include a client affidavit concerning the trademarks; (iii) file the case under seal; (iv) submit evidence that the target(s) of the seizure are likely to destroy/move/hide the counterfeit goods if the proceeding was on notice; and (v) post a bond in case of wrongful seizure.

Cartier International B.V. v. Ben-Menachem

2008 WL 64005 (S.D.N.Y. Jan. 3, 2008)

SWEET, District Judge.

Prior Proceedings

The Plaintiffs commenced this action on May 23, 2006, and a temporary restraining order, seizure order, and order for expedited discovery, asset restraint and to show cause for a preliminary injunction was issued and was executed.

Following an evidentiary hearing unopposed by Defendants, this Court entered a Preliminary Injunction against Defendants which required, *inter alia,* that:

> Defendants shall deliver to Plaintiffs' attorneys, within two (2) days from the date of this Order, all of the documents, records, things and other items seized by Plaintiffs' representatives during their execution of the Order....

The Plaintiffs sought discovery and, after efforts described below, the Plaintiffs requested removal of the action from the trial calendar and filed the instant motion for summary judgment.

The Plaintiffs have been engaged for many years in the business of manufacturing and distributing various types of high-quality luxury products, including, *inter alia,* watches, watch buckles, bracelets, scarves, handbags, lighters, pens, belts, belt buckles, letter openers, and eyewear under a number of trademarks and trade names ("Plaintiffs' Products"). Plaintiffs own the entire right, title and interest in and to Plaintiffs' federally registered trademarks (the "Plaintiffs' Marks"), most of which are incontestable.

Plaintiffs have used and are currently using the registered Plaintiffs' Marks in commerce in the United States and throughout the world in connection with their sale of Plaintiffs' Products. Over the years, Plaintiffs have enjoyed extraordinary success by designing, developing, and marketing an extensive line of luxury goods, which are known for their unique shapes, styles, and overall appearances.

Plaintiffs manufacture, merchandise, and market all of Plaintiffs' Products with a concern for design, artistry, workmanship, and material quality, as well as their projected image, goodwill and long-term growth. Plaintiffs have earned a reputation for high-quality luxury products. The Plaintiffs' policy is that only high-quality goods be produced under Plaintiffs' Marks and they maintain quality control over the manufacture, sale, and servicing of Plaintiffs' Products throughout the United States and the world.

Each year, Plaintiffs spend millions of dollars in advertising, promoting, and developing Plaintiffs' Marks throughout the world. As a result, products bearing Plaintiffs' Marks are closely associated with Plaintiffs' reputation in the eyes of the public, customers, and the luxury goods industry. Plaintiffs' Marks have come to symbolize Plaintiffs' enormous goodwill and are invaluable assets of Plaintiffs.

Investigations commenced in 2005 by Plaintiffs' representatives revealed that Defendants have imported, exported, distributed, advertised, offered for sale, and sold counterfeit watches bearing Plaintiffs' Marks, including A. Lange & Sohne, Cartier, Lanieres, Baignoire, Tortue, Tankissime, Panthere, Pasha de Cartier, 21 Chronoscaph, Santos de Cartier, Divan, Dunhill, Vacheron Constantin, Jaeger-Lecoultre, IWC, Montblanc, Piaget, Luminor, and Panerai (the "Counterfeit Products") through, among other locations, approximately fifteen websites (the "Websites"), including but not limited to those located at: kingreplica.com, swisskingdom.com, vertexo.com, davidluxury.com, davidsluxury.com, replicakingdom .com, and watches-boutique.com.

Defendants Ilan Ben-Menachem ("Ilan"), Aviv Ben-Menachem ("Aviv"), David Ben-Menachem ("David"), and Chana Ben-Menachem ("Chana") operated the Websites, and operated the following Defendant counterfeiting entities (the "Defendant Businesses"): King Replica, Davids Luxury, Replica Kingdom a/k/a Swiss Kingdom, Branded Luxury d/b/a BS Gifts, Vertexo, Inc., Avilan Marketing LLC, and Travel Derech Tslecha ("Travel").

The Defendants operated the Websites and Defendant Businesses and sold and distributed the Counterfeit Products from their home at 939 East 13th Street, Brooklyn, New York, 11230 (the "Premises"), as well as other locations. The Defendants had been operating their Websites since at least May 2004 and through their Websites and Defendant Businesses, advertised, offered for sale, and sold counterfeit watches bearing copies of Plaintiffs' Marks and designed to look exactly like genuine Plaintiffs' Products. Plaintiffs did not in any way authorize or consent to the Defendants' sale of the Counterfeit Products.

The Websites displayed photographs of watches bearing exact duplicates of Plaintiffs' Marks and designed to look like genuine Plaintiffs' Products. The "Contact Us" page of the Website located at kingreplica.com (the "King Replica Website") listed for customer service the telephone number: 206-333-0050. An investigator for Plaintiffs called this telephone number and received a message that he had reached Branded Luxury customer service.

A database search for the King Replica Website revealed fifteen domain names listed on the same server, including the following watch-related websites: replicakingdom.com, davidsluxury.com, davidluxury.com, and watches-boutique .com. A WhoIs database search for replicakingdom.com listed the following contact information: Ilan Ben-Menachem, 939 East 13th Street, Brooklyn, NY, 11230, Tel: 917-370-3154, Email: apogee91@gmail.com. A domain name system report for replicakingdom.com confirmed that the host master email address was apogee91 @gmail.com.

On August 10, 2005, an investigator for Plaintiffs accessed the King Replica Website and ordered a watch bearing Plaintiffs' Cartier Marks for $246.00. On August 11, 2005, Plaintiffs' investigator received an email from "David Angelino" at sales@ kingreplica.com inquiring whether he wanted the male Cartier Tank watch. Plaintiffs' investigator responded, requesting a male Cartier Tank watch. On August 23, 2005, Plaintiffs' investigator received a package with an EMS/China Posting Tracking sticker on it bearing a return address in Chinese (the "Package").

The Package contained a white box bearing the mark Cartier. Inside the white box was a red leather box bearing the mark Cartier. The box contained one men's silver watch in the Cartier Tank design and bearing the mark Cartier on the watch face, watch back, and wristband clasp (the contents of the Package are collectively referred to herein as the "Counterfeit Watch"). Upon inspection, Plaintiffs' representative confirmed that the Counterfeit Watch is not a genuine Plaintiffs' watch but rather an inferior counterfeit replication. On August 23, 2005, Plaintiffs' investigator noted a credit card charge of $246.00, the price paid for the Counterfeit Watch.

Pursuant to the Order, Plaintiffs' investigators and attorneys, accompanied by a police officer, arrived at the Premises to conduct a seizure. They were met at the front door of the Premises by a woman who stated that no one else was present, and that she did not know anything about a counterfeit watch operation. After gaining entry to the house, Plaintiffs' representatives discovered that a young man, two teenage girls, and a preteen boy, all apparently residents of the house, and a housekeeper were inside. The young man refused to identify himself, but picture identification discovered later that he was Defendant Aviv Ben-Menachem. Plaintiffs' attorney advised Aviv to call his attorney, as well as Defendants Ilan, Chana, and David. Aviv replied that he could not reach any of them.

Throughout Plaintiffs' execution of the Order, Aviv behaved in an aggressive and threatening manner towards Plaintiffs' representatives. At the urging of Plaintiffs' representatives, Aviv called 9-1-1, leading to the arrival of five additional uniformed police officers at the Premises. These officers confirmed that Aviv must cooperate with Plaintiffs' representatives in their execution of the Order. Aviv proceeded to follow Plaintiffs' representatives around the house, attempting to hide evidence, and generally disrupting the seizure and execution of the Order.

Plaintiffs' representatives collected several watches and watch boxes bearing Plaintiffs' Marks, one entire banker's box and separate file folder of documents relating to Defendants' counterfeit watch business, and two computer towers and a laptop computer likely used in Defendants' counterfeit watch business. Among the documents collected by Plaintiffs' representatives were documents that demonstrated: (a) that Defendants were selling large quantities of replica watches on the Websites; (b) that Defendants were corresponding with entities and individuals in Hong Kong and China to import and distribute Counterfeit Products; (c) that Defendants had set up off-shore accounts and foreign corporations, including in Panama; (d) that Defendant Ilan Ben-Menachem reported an income of $800,000 in 2005; and (e) that Defendants were selling several hundred thousand dollars of counterfeit watches, including the Counterfeit Products, monthly. Plaintiffs' representatives photographed and placed evidence tags on watches bearing Plaintiffs' Marks presumed to be Counterfeit Products.

When one of Plaintiffs' investigators was nearly finished with boxing and tagging as evidence watches bearing Plaintiffs' Marks and documents relating to Defendants' counterfeit watch business, he was alone on the first floor of the house. Plaintiffs' investigator had in his possession at this time a banker's box and file folder of documents, a laptop, two computer towers, and an evidence bag containing ten watches bearing Plaintiffs' Marks and several watch boxes. He was then confronted by Aviv and an unidentified man seen earlier outside the Premises. Aviv and the unidentified man approached Plaintiffs' investigator, pushed him, and tried to hit him. The unidentified man grabbed the folder of documents and ran from the room. Plaintiffs' investigator clutched the box of documents firmly as Aviv and the unidentified man, who had returned to the room, tried to push Plaintiffs' investigator to the ground, and tried to wrest the box of documents from his hands. Aviv and the unidentified man succeeded in ripping the box of documents, sending documents flying, and gathered the ripped box and documents and ran out the front door.

The police officer accompanying Plaintiffs' representatives had taken possession of a lockbox located in the Travel Derech Tslecha office in the basement of the house. Defendant Chana Ben-Menachem arrived at the house and began to attack the police officer holding the lockbox. Chana then tried to grab the evidence bag described above. Plaintiffs' representatives and the police officers tried to prevent Chana from taking the bag. The laptop computer and evidence bag were then placed on the coffee table just inside the front door on the first floor.

Chana then handed one of Plaintiffs' attorneys a cordless phone and informed him that her attorney, Asher White, was on the line and wished to confer. Plaintiffs' attorney began to speak with White about the Plaintiffs' execution of the Order. While the police officers (totaling approximately ten, uniformed and undercover) were speaking with Plaintiffs' representatives on the front porch and Plaintiffs' attorney was speaking with Defendants' attorney, Chana locked the front door of the house and drew the blinds. She refused to open the door when the police officers knocked. When uniformed police officers regained entry to the house, Plaintiffs' representatives noticed that the evidence bag and the laptop computer, which had all been on the coffee table just inside the doorway, were missing. Plaintiffs' representatives were not able to recover from the house the documents, laptop computer, or the evidence bag of watches bearing Plaintiffs' Marks described above, or the lockbox described above, and were forced to leave the Premises without this evidence.

Pursuant to the Order, Plaintiffs' investigators and attorney, accompanied by a police officer, also entered the premises of 1367 Coney Island Avenue, Brooklyn, NY, to conduct a seizure. This location had been used by Defendants as an office to operate their counterfeit watch business. At 1367 Coney Island Avenue, Plaintiffs' representatives seized approximately one folder of business records relating to Defendants' counterfeit watch business, as well as a postal scale, shipping labels, and envelopes. Documents seized at 1367 Coney Island Avenue corroborate the documents gathered by Plaintiffs' representatives at the Premises but absconded with by Defendants.

Documents seized at 1367 Coney Island Avenue included evidence of:

(a) a wire transfer in the amount of $36,250.00 from Defendant Avilan Marketing LLC into an off-shore account in the name of Defendant Chana Ben-Menachem;

(b) a merchant application to Credicorp Bank on behalf of Luxury Goods, Inc., identified on the application as a corporation existing in Panama City, Panama, to provide credit card processing for the website bagsnstyle.com. The merchant application estimates a monthly sales volume on the website of $600,000. This application was faxed to Credicorp Bank from Defendant Travel Derech Tslecha.

White asked Plaintiffs' counsel to forgo filing a Motion for Contempt and represented to Plaintiffs' counsel that Defendants would return all documents and things hidden by Defendants during the execution of the Order. On May 31, 2006, White informed Plaintiffs' counsel that Defendants had provided to him what Defendants represented were all of the documents and things collected by Plaintiffs' representatives during the execution of the Order. White confirmed that these items included the evidence bag of Counterfeit Products collected by Plaintiffs' representatives. Later on May 31, 2006, Plaintiffs' messenger retrieved the items described above from White's office and delivered them to Plaintiffs' counsel.

The items retrieved from White's office consisted of a banker's box, approximately one-eighth full of documents, two computer towers, and a laptop computer. The banker's box appeared to be the same box used by Plaintiffs' representatives to gather documents during the execution of the Order. The box had writing on the top identifying where in the Premises the collected documents were found. The box also appeared to be ripped and bent in a way that comports with the struggle over the box between Plaintiffs' investigator and Aviv and the unknown man.

The documents retrieved from White's office, however, did not include the folder of documents collected by Plaintiffs' representatives during the execution of the Order and taken back by Defendants. White did not provide to Plaintiffs' counsel any of the watches or watch boxes bearing Plaintiffs' Marks that had been collected by Plaintiffs' representatives and put into an evidence bag during the execution of the Order. Additionally, a large number of files, including those in folders bearing the name "Cartier" and other of Plaintiffs' brands, had been deleted from the laptop provided by White. After Plaintiffs' counsel reviewed the items retrieved from White, he telephoned White and told him of the missing documents and items. White confirmed that those items comprised everything that had been provided to him by Defendants.

On November 1, 2006, Defendants Aviv, Ilan, Avilan Marketing LLC, Branded Luxury, Davids Luxury, King Replica, Replica Kingdom, and Vertexo, Inc. filed an opposition to Plaintiffs' Motion for Contempt.

Aviv admitted in his sworn declaration to taking items from Plaintiffs' representatives during the execution of the Order. He also admitted to disposing of the watches and watch boxes bearing Plaintiffs' Marks collected by Plaintiffs' representatives despite the fact that he had been served by the Order and was already represented by counsel. Ilan and Aviv, King Replica, Davids Luxury, Branded Luxury d/b/a BS Gifts, Avilan Marketing LLC, and Vertexo, Inc. admitted in interrogatory responses to disposing of the Counterfeit Products described above and that they refused to comply with the Order and deliberately prevented Plaintiffs from executing the Order by (a) physically attacking Plaintiffs' representatives, (b) barring access to the Premises, (c) concealing the Counterfeit Products, and (d) forcibly taking back documents and items that had been identified and collected by Plaintiffs pursuant to the Order.

Aviv admitted he knew that the Counterfeit Products collected by Plaintiffs' representatives during execution of the Order "were replica watches" and that he and Ilan were in the watch business selling replica watches.

The June 15 Order additionally required that:

> Defendants shall deliver to Plaintiffs' attorneys, within ten (10) days from the date of this Order, copies of all accountant's reports, bank statements, tax returns, certificates of deposit, notes, bonds, checking accounts, trust accounts, money market or GNMA accounts, savings accounts or other financial institution records or documentation showing investments or

deposits, and documents indicating title to any real or personal property in each of the Defendants' actual or constructive possession or control.

Defendants have not provided to Plaintiffs any information about overseas accounts in the names of David and Chana or any information about funds transferred into those accounts.

On December 12, 2006, Plaintiffs served counsel for Ilan, Aviv, King Replica, Replica Kingdom a/k/a Swiss Kingdom, Davids Luxury, Branded Luxury d/b/a BS Gifts, Avilan Marketing LLC, and Vertexo, Inc. with Plaintiffs' First Requests for the Production of Documents and Things and Plaintiffs' First Set of Interrogatories ("Plaintiffs' Interrogatories"), returnable January 2, 2007. The response to Plaintiffs' Interrogatories admits that watches were acquired from a source in China.

David has admitted that funds were wired to China from the Travel account to purchase merchandise at the request of Aviv and Ilan. Aviv and Ilan, along with their companies, admitted to attempting to start overseas businesses and to having foreign contacts, including contacts with companies in the United Kingdom, Hong Kong, the Philippines, and Panama.

Though Aviv and Ilan, and the Defendant Businesses (excluding Defendant Travel Derech Tslecha), including Defendant Avilan Marketing, deny forming foreign entities and opening foreign accounts, financial records obtained by Plaintiffs' subpoenas show that Defendant Avilan Marketing transferred over $200,000 to overseas accounts maintained by David and Chana. Defendants have refused to provide any information about these accounts. The response to Plaintiffs' Interrogatories admits that "Bagsnstyle.com" operated on servers of Defendants. Though "LaPeree.com," "LaPeree Distribution Center," and "LaPeree Malls" are mentioned on Defendants' website replicakingdom.com, the response to Plaintiffs' Interrogatories denies knowledge of any such entities.

White filed a Motion to be Relieved as Counsel, citing his clients' non-communication, on February 27, 2007. The Court granted this motion on March 26, 2007.

David has admitted that he and Chana, his wife, "set up the account" and gave approximately $150,000 to their sons, Ilan and Aviv, to start the counterfeiting operations. Financial records obtained by Plaintiffs' subpoenas confirm that David and Chana maintain overseas accounts and received large transfers from Defendant Avilan Marketing LLC.

Records obtained by Plaintiffs' subpoena to Central Bancard LLC shows two different merchant accounts opened by David and Chana. The application for the Branded Luxury Merchant Account indicated that Defendant Branded Luxury is a sole proprietorship wholly-owned by David Ben-Menachem. This application provided Travel Derech Tslecha as a merchant reference and "Hanna" as the contact person. The Branded Luxury Merchant Account application described the merchandise being sold as "watches" and shows that the online store is located at www.kingreplica.com.

The two computer towers seized by Plaintiffs' representatives during execution of the May 23 Order contain document folders containing document files related to counterfeit watches, intermingled with David's academic papers. These documents include: a copy of defendant David's New York driver's license next to a copy of a cancelled check from the Branded Luxury Checking Account; a memorandum from David to Central Bancard LLC entitled "How I Will Avoid Chargebacks in the Future"; and a compilation of standard correspondence to buyers of counterfeit watches. Some of these form letters are from Aviv at the 1367 Coney Island Avenue address, others from "B. Luxury" at 130 Church Street, others from "David Angelino" and others from "David Moreno".

Defendants are Liable for Trademark Counterfeiting and Infringement

The Lanham Act imposes liability upon on a person who sells, offers for sale, advertises or distributes goods using a counterfeit of a registered trademark, regardless of "whether or not the person against whom relief is sought knew such mark was so registered," 15 U.S.C. § 1116(d)(B)(i).

Plaintiffs have established their ownership and registration with the United States Patent and Trademark Office of the Plaintiffs' Marks. In the course of this action, Plaintiffs have identified nineteen different registered trademarks which Defendants have counterfeited: A. LANGE & SOHNE, BAIGNOIRE, CARTIER, DIVAN, DUNHILL, IWC, JAEGER-LECOULTRE, LANIERES, LUMINOR, MONTBLANC, PANERAI, PANTHERE, PASHA DE CARTIER, PIAGET, SANTOS DE CARTIER, TANKISSIME, TORTUE, VACHERON CONSTANTIN, and 21 CHRONOSCAPH.

The Plaintiffs have also established that Defendants were importing, distributing, advertising, offering for sale, and selling counterfeit reproductions of Plaintiffs' Marks likely to cause consumer confusion. In cases involving counterfeit marks, this Court has found it unnecessary to perform a *Polaroid* examination because counterfeit marks are inherently confusing.

David and Chana and Travel Derech Tslecha continue to deny knowledge of the counterfeiting business operating from their home, although they admit that they were actively involved. Their denials, however, are not credible and are not supported by any evidentiary submission. David and Chana were: (1) the owners and residents of the home in which counterfeit operations occurred openly; (2) direct financial beneficiaries of the counterfeiting operations, in part through deposits into their off-shore accounts; and (3) are the parents of admitted counterfeiters Ilan and Aviv. Documents relating to Counterfeit Products and Defendants' Websites, including a document authored by David, were found in David's computer folders, David and Chana jointly owned a bank account with admitted counterfeiting entity Defendant Branded Luxury, withdrawals from bank accounts of admitted counterfeiting entities were deposited into the purported business account of Travel, Branded Luxury is a sole proprietorship of David, and transfers of funds overseas from the Travel account were made at the behest of Ilan and Aviv.

Since a seller bears strict liability for violations of the Lanham Act, even an "innocent" individual who sells goods bearing an infringing mark is liable for trademark infringement—intent is not required. Even if David and Chana and Travel were not directly involved in the sale of the Counterfeit Products, they remain liable for contributory trademark infringement because they chose to be willfully blind to the counterfeiting business operated by two of their sons from the Ben-Menachem home, also the location of the Travel office, which involved David's computer and Defendants' bank accounts.

Even if the denials of David and Chana were to be accepted as plausible, the facts establish that David and Chana and Travel were "willfully blind" to the activities and not only failed to investigate, but also assisted their co-Defendants' sales of the Counterfeit Products. Accordingly, David and Chana and Travel are at the very least liable for contributory trademark infringement.

Defendants are Liable for Federal Unfair Competition and State and Common Law Claims

Because Plaintiffs have presented a successful claim of federal trademark infringement, Defendants are also found liable for federal unfair competition under Section 1125(a).

The same acts that constitute trademark counterfeiting and unfair competition under federal laws give rise to Plaintiffs' claims of common law trademark infringement and unfair competition, as well as unfair competition under New York law. Unfair competition under New York law additionally requires evidence of bad faith. However, a presumption of bad faith attaches to the use of a counterfeit mark. Defendants' sale of the Counterfeit Products serves to establish bad faith under New York law, and therefore summary judgment is appropriate as to these claims.

Defendants Are Liable for Statutory Damages

Because counterfeiters' records are frequently non-existent, inadequate or deceptively kept, making proving actual damages in these cases difficult, if not impossible, the Lanham Act permits a statutory damage award in lieu of an award of actual damages resulting from the use of counterfeit marks. The Act permits an award not less than $500 or more than $100,000 per counterfeit mark per type of goods or services sold, offered for sale, or distributed, as the court considers just. If the court finds that the use of the counterfeit mark was willful, the court may award damages in an amount not more than $1,000,000 per counterfeit mark per type of goods sold, offered for sale, or distributed.

Plaintiffs have diligently attempted to discover the full extent of Defendants' counterfeiting activities. For several months, Defendants refused to provide any information, claiming that they had produced all documents in their possession to Plaintiffs' counsel. After Plaintiffs were forced to subpoena voluminous records from financial institutions, it became apparent that the documents provided by Defendants are incomplete and thus there is no way to determine actual damages. Statutory damages are therefore appropriate in this case.

Courts have wide discretion in setting an amount of statutory damages. In awarding statutory damages, courts consider a variety of factors, including whether a defendant's conduct was willful, lost revenue and harm to the plaintiff, the value of the plaintiff's marks, the defendant's cooperation in providing information on the value of the infringing material, and the deterrent effect on the defendant and others.

Plaintiffs seek enhanced statutory damages in light of the evidence that Defendants' conduct was "willful" under Section 1117(c). However, the Court concludes that standard statutory damages in the amount of $50,000 for each of Plaintiffs' nineteen Marks counterfeited by Defendants will be sufficient to meet the goals of the statute, including compensating the Plaintiffs and deterring future violations.

Defendants Are Liable for Costs and Attorneys' Fees

Having prevailed on its claims for willful infringement and unfair competition, Plaintiffs are entitled to an award of costs and reasonable attorney's fees.

Defendants Are Permanently Enjoined

Plaintiffs have shown that they are entitled to a permanent injunction based on: (1) actual success on the merits, and (2) irreparable harm. Plaintiffs have established that Defendants have violated the Lanham Act by engaging in the counterfeiting activities described in the Complaint and, therefore, the Plaintiffs are granted entry of a permanent injunction.

Conclusion

Summary judgment against Defendants is granted for importing, distributing, advertising, selling, and offering for sale the Counterfeit Products, and permanently enjoining Defendants' counterfeiting and infringing activities as set forth in the Complaint, and awarding Plaintiffs statutory damages against Defendants in the amount of $950,000, as well as costs and attorneys' fees. Plaintiffs will submit judgment on notice, as well as a supporting affidavit with respect to attorneys' fees.

Notes

1. This case describes a typical online counterfeit operation, run out of a home in Brooklyn, New York, by four family members operating various websites. Plaintiffs' private investigator made "buys" of counterfeit Cartier watches from the websites. The investigation led to civil seizures of counterfeit goods, books, and records outlining the scope of Defendants' business and leading to the source of the counterfeit goods in China and Hong Kong and to off-shore bank accounts in Panama. Though Defendants absconded with key documents in the course of the seizure, the key benefit of a civil seizure is that plaintiffs can immediately obtain evidence tying defendants to the distribution of counterfeit goods, evidence of overseas bank accounts and profits made from these illegal sales, and other valuable evidence, including copies of documents related to other counterfeit litigation involving Defendants. Such evidence would have disappeared if Defendants were simply named in a lawsuit.

2. In counterfeit cases, the eight-factor analysis of *Polaroid Corp. v. Polarad Electronics Corp.*, 287 F.2d 492 (1961) is not required, since confusing the consumer is the only point of selling counterfeit goods. Counterfeit sellers bear strict liability for violations of the Lanham Act, thus brand owners do not need to prove "intent."

3. The Court awarded Plaintiffs $950,000 in statutory damages against Defendants. Most successful judgments in counterfeit cases are uncollectable because individuals and companies that engage in the sale of counterfeit goods are often judgment-proof. However, Cartier was fortunate here in uncovering assets that could be seized to satisfy the judgment.

4. Further, suggested reading: *Shell Co., Ltd v. Los Frailes Service Station, Inc.*, 596 F. Supp. 2d 193 (D.D.R. 2008); *Philip Morris USA, Inc. v. Lee* 547 F. Supp. 2d 685 (W.D. Tex. 2008); *Cartier, Inc. v. Symbolix, Inc.*, 544 F. Supp. 2d 316 (S.D.N.Y. 2008); *Coach, Inc. v. Sassy Couture*, 2012 WL 162366 (W.D. Tex. Jan. 19, 2012); *Koon Chun Hing Kee Soy & Sauce Factory, Ltd. v. Star Management, Inc.*, 628 F. Supp. 2d 312 (E.D.N.Y. 2009).

3. Support of Government Agencies

Numerous government agencies, as well as state and local law enforcement, all work to combat counterfeiting. U.S. Customs and Border Protection (defined in Section A of this Chapter as "Customs"), Immigration and Customs Enforcement ("ICE"), and Homeland Security Investigations ("HSI") conduct investigations at the borders and at various ports throughout the country. Customs is authorized to seize and destroy imported merchandise bearing counterfeit trademarks or otherwise dispose of counterfeit merchandise. But it is more than just Customs, ICE, and HSI. The Federal Bureau of Investigation, U.S. Postal Inspection Service, Secret Service, Internal Revenue Service, Bureau of Alcohol, Tobacco, Firearms and Explosives, and U.S. Marshals' Service all play roles. And this is not an exhaustive list. All agencies have counterfeiting on their radar as the problem grows.

The most important thing a brand owner can do and the only way Customs will be on the lookout for counterfeits is to *record* its trademarks with Customs. "Recordation" enables Customs to seize counterfeit goods at airports and seaports. The trademark must be registered with the United States Patent and Trademark Office ("USPTO") and the Customs' recordation expires when the USPTO registration expires. There is a fee of $190 (per mark per class recorded). This is the best $190 a trademark owner can spend.

After a brand owner records its trademarks, it must train Customs officers and law enforcement on how to identify counterfeits. There are a number of opportunities at major ports of entry year to year where brand owners can train the authorities on how to identify counterfeits. Brand owners should have materials it can share with law enforcement. Even if it is just highlights or key distinguishing features, brand owners usually see an uptick in seizures after training law enforcement. Also, a brand owner or outside counsel must be responsive to Customs' inquiries.

Nothing causes a Customs official to lose interest in a brand more quickly than if the official doesn't get a response to his or her questions. A brand owner must get back to the official with whatever information he or she needs.

Gucci America, Inc. v. Duty Free Apparel, Ltd.

286 F. Supp. 2d 284 (S.D.N.Y. 2003)

MARRERO, District Judge.

Decision and Order

Plaintiff Gucci America, Inc. ("Gucci") alleges that defendants Duty Free Apparel Ltd. ("DFA") and Harvest Wrap, Inc. ("Harvest Wrap") sold counterfeit Gucci merchandise in violation of federal and state law. Gucci seeks an entry of partial summary judgment on the issue of liability for its federal claims against all four defendants: DFA, DFA President Joel Soren ("Soren"), Harvest Wrap, and Harvest Wrap owner Kurt Davidsen ("Davidsen") (collectively, "Defendants"). Gucci also seeks to enjoin Defendants from selling counterfeit Gucci merchandise in the future.

I. Background

Gucci owns the trademark and trade name "GUCCI" and various "G" and "GG" logos and designs. These trademarks are associated with various articles of jewelry, watches, handbags, wallets, and accessories. DFA, a Manhattan retailer of designer merchandise and accessories, sold a "Gucci" wallet to a Gucci investigator for $150 on August 14, 2000. That same day, DFA sold to another Gucci investigator a "Gucci" handbag for $350. In May 2001, an assistant for Gucci's outside counsel purchased a "Gucci" handbag from DFA's website for $415.

After Gucci initiated this lawsuit, DFA identified Harvest Wrap as its source for "Gucci" goods, and Gucci added Harvest Wrap as a defendant. At some point in late 2002, Harvest Wrap sold several "Gucci" backpacks to Sherry Dvorkin ("Dvorkin"), who is in the business of selling women's accessories through private sales, including sales on the internet. Gucci subpoenaed Dvorkin to appear at a deposition in connection with this lawsuit. She testified that she purchased over $50,000 worth of merchandise from Harvest Wrap in several cash transactions with Davidsen. An invoice of her transactions indicates that she purchased 173 "Gucci" backpacks and 44 "Gucci" pouch bags, along with 24 "Fendi mamma bags" and 503 "Prada key chains." She turned over to Gucci's lawyers two of the "Gucci" backpacks she obtained from Harvest Wrap, along with the invoice.

Gucci's expert, Luciano Chiarelli ("Chiarelli"), has determined that all five of the above "Gucci" items which Gucci obtained for this lawsuit—the wallet and two handbags from DFA and the two backpacks from Harvest Wrap—are counterfeit. Chiarelli has been associated with Gucci since 1969 and has been head of the Quality Control department since 1995. He has participated in numerous federal cases on Gucci's behalf. The purchasers of the "Gucci" items at issue stated that they immediately marked and turned over the items to Gucci's lawyers, and Chiarelli's report indicates that he received those marked items from Gucci's lawyers for the purpose of evaluating their authenticity.

Gucci supplies its leather goods assembly factories with the component parts and the necessary materials for assembly. Those factories then must account for all of these materials. Assembled items must meet Gucci's quality control standards before being sold to the public. Those items that do not meet the standards are either destroyed, or, if the defects are minor, the items are marked as "seconds" and sent to Gucci's outlet store in Florence, Italy.

Chiarelli obtained authentic component parts from Gucci suppliers and compared those parts with the components of the items at issue here. Chiarelli's report identifies various deviations in each of the five items. For example, Chiarelli asserts that one of the handbags contains a gold-colored closure and buckle, which has never been used on that particular style of bag, and the Gucci logo on the backpacks is different from the genuine logo. The items in evidence are not marked as "seconds."

DFA states that it no longer sells items from Harvest Wrap. DFA and Soren consent to an injunction, but they object to certain parts of Gucci's formulation of the proposed order.

Harvest Wrap concedes selling backpacks to Dvorkin, but it denies that any of the five items at issue came from Harvest Wrap, as it only sells authentic goods. Alternatively, Harvest wrap asserts that there is at least an issue of fact as to whether the items are in fact counterfeit.

III. Discussion

A. Liability

For both Lanham Act claims, Gucci must demonstrate (1) that it has a valid mark that is entitled to protection under the Act and (2) that Defendants' actions are likely to cause confusion as to the origin of the mark. The parties do not dispute the validity of Gucci's mark, and thus the Court's resolution of this motion will turn on the likelihood of confusion.

In this case, however, the Court need not undertake a factor-by-factor analysis under *Polaroid* because counterfeits, by their very nature, cause confusion. Indeed, confusing the customer is the whole purpose of creating counterfeit goods. *Cf. Polo Fashions, Inc. v. Craftex, Inc.*, 816 F.2d 145, 148 (4th Cir.1987) ("Where, as here, one produces counterfeit goods in an apparent attempt to capitalize upon the popularity of, and demand for, another's product, there is a presumption of a likelihood of confusion."). Thus, the Court need only determine the more fundamental question of whether there are items to be confused in the first place—that is, whether the items at issue here are, in fact, counterfeit and whether Defendants sold those items. Harvest Wrap asserts that there are genuine issues facts as to both questions. The Court disagrees.

Gucci's expert Chiarelli explained both his credentials and the bases for his conclusion that the five items in question are counterfeit. As stated above,

Chiarelli identified several deviations in each of the five items at issue, and Gucci has accounted for the chain of custody of the items from the sellers to Chiarelli. Defendants have produced no evidence, expert or otherwise, that sufficiently refutes Chiarelli's findings. The Court concludes that, with this evidence alone, no reasonable juror would fail to hold Defendants liable. Thus, the Court concludes that Gucci has made a *prima facie* case that it is entitled to summary judgment.

Harvest Wrap responds, first, by asserting that there are fact issues as to the authenticity of the bags. It points out that Chiarelli failed to perform a side-by-side comparison with fully-assembled Gucci items, and that Chiarelli has failed to foreclose the possibility that the alleged deviations occurred sometime *after* the bags were authentically manufactured. Harvest Wrap points out that the items could have been irregular but authentic Gucci merchandise, or diverted overstock merchandise.

Harvest Wrap next questions the chain of custody of the items. Harvest Wrap denies having supplied the three items purchased from DFA because, as the depositions indicate, the Harvest Wrap-DFA relationship began after those bags were sold. Harvest Wrap acknowledges that Davidsen met with Dvorkin and sold her "Gucci" backpacks, but Harvest Wrap disputes virtually every other aspect of Dvorkin's story. Specifically, Harvest Wrap contends that the invoice Dvorkin has produced is a complete forgery. Harvest Wrap supplied a sample real invoice, which appears somewhat different. Davidsen indicated at his deposition that he sold Dvorkin *only* "Gucci" backpacks, not any pouch bags nor any items from other designers. He also asserted that he only sold her around 70 to 80 bags for about $100 each, as opposed to the over $50,000 worth of merchandise indicated on the invoice. Davidsen testified that the transaction took place later in the month of November 2002, instead of the date indicated on Dvorkin's invoice, November 6, 2002. Harvest Wrap also highlights various inconsistencies in Dvorkin's testimony, as a means to call into question her credibility in general. All of this evidence is apparently intended to show that there is an issue of fact as to whether Harvest Wrap actually sold the allegedly counterfeit backpacks now at issue.

It is notable that Harvest Wrap failed to produce any affirmative evidence that the items in evidence are actually authentic, either through an expert or through an explanation of their origins. Harvest Wrap entirely fails to account for the specific deviations contained in Chiarelli's report.

Moreover, Harvest Wrap fails to offer specific evidence supporting its hypothesis that these particular bags escaped the Gucci's rigorous quality control measures. To be sure, the Court recognizes that Gucci's quality control measures are likely not foolproof and that authentically-manufactured Gucci items containing deviations may wind up in the retail market. However, Harvest Wrap cannot defeat a *prima facie* case of summary judgment based on the mere speculation that this unlikely possibility came about in this particular case.

Harvest Wrap's argument regarding Dvorkin's custody of the two backpacks is likewise unavailing because it rests on speculation. Harvest Wrap concedes that, sometime in late November 2002, it sold Dvorkin backpacks of the same style as those at issue. It asserts that there is a genuine issue of fact as to whether Dvorkin handed over a *different* set of backpacks to Gucci's attorneys. The only evidence Harvest Wrap offers in support of that hypothesis is the obviously question-begging assertion that it only sells genuine merchandise. Harvest Wrap's disputes over the timing and quantity of the transaction, and of the authenticity of the invoice, are simply immaterial because Harvest Wrap concedes that it sold Dvorkin at least two backpacks of the same style as the two at issue. In short, Harvest Wrap has no evidentiary basis to counter Dvorkin's testimony that she bought the backpacks from Harvest Wrap. The notion that Dvorkin substituted Harvest Wrap's genuine merchandise with another set of counterfeit merchandise is pure speculation and will not defeat a motion for summary judgment.

Finally, Harvest Wrap asserts that whether or not it is in the business of selling counterfeit goods—as opposed to merely having sold two counterfeit items—is an issue of material fact which should preclude summary judgment. The Court disagrees. The plain language of the relevant statutes does not require that the plaintiff prove that a defendant committed the infringement in any particular amount, or with any amount of regularity.

B. Injunction

To obtain a permanent injunction, Gucci must demonstrate (1) actual success on the merits and (2) irreparable harm. The preceding discussion establishes Gucci's success on the merits, and in this Circuit, a showing of likelihood of confusion establishes irreparable harm. Accordingly, Gucci is entitled to a permanent injunction enjoining Defendants from further trademark infringement against Gucci.

For the reasons discussed above, it is hereby

ORDERED that the motion of plaintiff Gucci America, Inc. ("Gucci") for entry of partial summary judgment of liability for violation of the Lanham Act, 15 U.S.C. §§ 1114(1), 1125(a), as against defendants Duty Free Apparel, Ltd., Joel Soren, Harvest Wrap, Inc., and Kurt Davidsen (collectively, "Defendants") is GRANTED; it is further

ORDERED that Defendants, their agents, and employees are hereby permanently enjoined from selling, offering for sale, advertising or distributing any counterfeit goods bearing any Gucci trademark, and from infringing on any Gucci trademarks.

Fendi Adele, S.R.L. v. Ashley Reed Trading, Inc.

507 F. App'x 26 (2d Cir. 2013)

KATZMANN, Circuit Judge; PARKER, Circuit Judge; WESLEY, Circuit Judge.

Summary Order

Defendants-Appellants-Cross-Appellees Ashley Reed Trading, Inc., Scott Ressler, and James Ressler (collectively, "Ashley Reed") appeal a June 30, 2011, judgment of the United States District Court for the Southern District of New York (Berman, *J.*).

On summary judgment, the district court held Ashley Reed liable for trademark counterfeiting, false designation of origin, and trademark dilution under the Lanham Act, and for unfair competition and trademark dilution under New York state law. The district court awarded Plaintiffs-Appellees-Cross-Appellants Fendi Adele S.R.L., Fendi S.R.L., and Fendi North America, Inc. (collectively, "Fendi") $12,324,062.66 in trebled damages, prejudgment interest, costs, and attorneys' fees. Specifically, because it found willful infringement, the court ordered the disgorgement of Ashley Reed's profits from selling Fendi-branded products in 2005 and 2006.

On appeal, Ashley Reed contends that the district court erred by (1) rejecting its affirmative defenses of acquiescence and laches, (2) admitting Leonardo Minerva's testimony that Fendi-branded products sold by Ashley Reed were counterfeit, (3) finding Ashley Reed liable for infringement that occurred before 2005, (4) deciding on summary judgment that Ashley Reed's infringement was willful despite disputed questions of fact, and (5) failing to deduct Ashley Reed's costs from its gross revenue when calculating its profits. James Ressler separately argues that the district court erred by refusing to stay his deposition pending completion of criminal proceedings against him. On cross-appeal, Fendi challenges the district court's decision to award damages based only on Ashley Reed's 2005 and 2006 profits even though the court appeared to find the defendants liable from 2001 to 2004 as well. We assume the parties' familiarity with the underlying facts and procedural history of this case, as well as the issues on appeal.

We review a district court's grant of summary judgment *de novo.* The moving party must offer concrete evidence showing the absence of a disputed issue of material fact, and then the burden shifts to the nonmoving party to present specific evidence showing a genuine dispute.

We first address Ashley Reed's contention that the affirmative defenses of acquiescence and laches should have barred Fendi's claims. To prove acquiescence, a defendant must demonstrate that the plaintiff actively consented. Active consent means "conduct on the plaintiff's part that amount [s] to an assurance to the defendant, express or implied, that the plaintiff would not assert his trademark rights against the defendant." Laches will bar a plaintiff's claim when a defendant has been prejudiced by a plaintiff's unreasonable delay in bringing suit; no affirmative consent is required because the unreasonable delay implies consent. Here, the parties agree that Ashley Reed bears the burden of proof.

Ashley Reed failed to prove either defense. There is no evidence that Fendi actively consented to infringement by Ashley Reed. Although Fendi remained silent for several years after the 2001 meetings between the parties, Fendi was entitled to investigate and was under no obligation to respond. Ashley Reed was on notice that Fendi believed it was selling infringing products. Moreover, Ashley Reed presented no evidence that Fendi unreasonably delayed in filing suit. On the contrary, Fendi sued promptly after discovering counterfeit handbags that it could prove were sold by Ashley Reed.

We next turn to Ashley Reed's argument that the district court erred in considering Leonardo Minerva's deposition testimony, which Ashley Reed contends was inadmissible. The district court has wide discretion in determining which evidence is admissible. Given this highly deferential standard of review, we cannot say it was "manifest error" for the district court to conclude that Minerva's testimony was based on sufficient personal knowledge. Although Minerva's assistant performed the initial inspections of the allegedly counterfeit items and drafted the reports, Minerva testified that he reviewed each report, discussed them with his assistant, made revisions as necessary, and approved each report.

Ashley Reed does not dispute that Minerva's testimony—if admissible—establishes its liability for infringement during 2005 and 2006. However, it argues that a trial was necessary to determine whether it infringed Fendi's trademarks before 2005 because there was no direct proof that it infringed during that period. Given that Ashley Reed was buying products with fabricated Fendi invoices as early as 2000, it strains credulity to believe that none of these products were counterfeit. The district court did not err in resolving Ashley Reed's liability for the entire 2001 to 2006 period on summary judgment.

Once liability is established, Fendi's entitlement to Ashley Reed's profits depends upon whether the infringement was willful. Fendi argues that it does not need to prove willfulness, relying on decisions from some of our sister circuits holding that a 1999 amendment to the Lanham Act changed the governing rule. However, we need not resolve the question because, assuming *arguendo* that Fendi is still required to prove willfulness, the district court properly concluded on summary judgment that Ashley Reed willfully infringed Fendi's trademarks.

To prove willfulness, a plaintiff must show (1) that the defendant was actually aware of the infringing activity, or (2) that the defendant's actions were the result of reckless disregard or willful blindness. In the context of a trademark infringement action, willful blindness means that a defendant knew it might be selling infringing goods but nevertheless intentionally shielded itself from discovering the truth. Despite Ashley Reed's claims, willful blindness can be proven on summary judgment; a finding of actual knowledge is not required.

Ashley Reed argues that the district court ignored reasonable inferences that should have been drawn in its favor and, in doing so, improperly resolved disputed questions of material fact. However, given the evidence, no reasonable jury could have credited these proposed inferences. Under these circumstances, a reasonable jury could not conclude that Ashley Reed acted with sufficient care to ensure that its goods were not counterfeit given that they were on notice of the goods' possibly counterfeit nature. Similarly, a reasonable jury could not credit Scott Ressler's testimony that he conducted side-by-side comparisons to ensure his products' authenticity given the lack of records and obvious differences—according to Mr. Minerva—between the counterfeit goods and genuine Fendi products. Even if we credited Scott Ressler's testimony that a Fendi inspector assured him that certain goods from certain suppliers would be authentic, Ashley Reed does not contend that it purchased all of its Fendi-branded products through those channels. Additionally, the other evidence establishes that the defendants exhibited willful blindness with respect to the goods it acquired through other channels. Therefore, the district court correctly concluded that Ashley Reed's infringement was willful as a matter of law.

The final two issues both relate to the calculation of damages. The district court used Ashley Reed's revenues from selling Fendi-branded products as a proxy for its profit and did not subtract any of the costs Ashley Reed might have expended in acquiring the bags or operating its business. Ashley Reed argues that this was error. However, a defendant bears the burden to prove any "deductions" from its gross revenue in calculating profits, and Ashley Reed failed to present any specific evidence of its costs.

On cross-appeal, Fendi contends that it was entitled to recover Ashley Reed's profits from 2000 to 2006 but that the district court's award only covered 2005 and 2006. We agree that the damage award seems facially inconsistent with the court's apparent conclusion that Fendi had proven infringement during the entire 2001 to 2006 period. Under these circumstances, we vacate the current damage award and remand to the district court for a determination in the first instance of whether it would be equitable to award damages only for 2005 and 2006.

For the reasons stated herein, the district court's decision is **AFFIRMED IN PART, VACATED IN PART,** and **REMANDED.**

Notes

1. Where counterfeiters are legitimate businesses with assets, as in the above two cases, witnesses and documents proving liability and damages are less likely to disappear. Thus, traditional civil actions (not civil seizures) may be appropriate and can yield significant judgments, as in the *Fendi* case. On the other hand, such defendants will have the resources to hire lawyers who will lodge creative defenses as demonstrated in both the *Gucci* and *Fendi* cases above.

2. In the *Fendi* case, Ashley Reed was found to be willfully blind as a matter of law on summary judgment. Ashley Reed, at that time a large U.S. retail chain, failed to inquire about the authenticity and source of the goods it purchased for sale in its stores; it failed to question invoices that have been sanitized of information that would indicate the source of the goods and failed to maintain key records and financial documents. Most damaging of all, it returned counterfeit merchandise to its supplier rather than cooperating with Fendi and turning over counterfeit product to Fendi. This happens time and time again where retailers fail to authenticate. Blockchain technology may help with this problem and will be a growing avenue for brand protection in the future.

3. Fendi has also sued another discount retailer, Burlington Coat Factory, for similar deeds and Burlington was enjoined from selling any product purporting to be Fendi without Fendi's express consent. *See Fendi Adele S.R.L. v. Burlington Coat Factory Warehouse Corp.*, 642 F. Supp. 2d 276 (S.D.N.Y. 2009).

Coach, Inc. v. Fashion Paradise, LLC

2012 U.S. Dist. LEXIS 7429 (D.N.J. Jan. 20, 2012)

SIMANDLE, Chief Judge.

Opinion

I. Introduction

This matter comes before the Court on the motion of Plaintiffs Coach, Inc. and Coach Services, Inc.'s ("Coach" or "Plaintiffs") for default judgment as against Defendants Fashion Paradise, LLC, and Naman Rafi ("Defendants"). For the reasons expressed below, the Court will grant Plaintiffs' motion.

I. Background

A. Facts

Coach is a manufacturer and distributor of luxury fashion accessories. Coach sells its goods through its own specialty retail stores, department stores, catalogs, and via the Internet throughout the United States. Coach owns a number of trademarks, trade dresses, and design elements/copyrights that it uses on its products.

Based on information obtained from a private investigator and Coach staff, Coach alleges that Defendants Fashion Paradise, LLC, and registered owner Naman Rafi have sold counterfeit Coach items at the store located at 2607-A Boardwalk, Atlantic City, New Jersey. For example, Defendants sold a $16.04 imitation of a $98.00 Coach belt that bore three Coach trademarks. Neither Fashion Paradise, LLC, nor Naman Rafi have been given permission to use the Coach trademarks.

B. Procedure

On September 22, 2010, the Plaintiffs filed a ten-count complaint against Defendants and ten John Does presenting claims of trademark counterfeiting, trademark infringement, trade dress infringement, false designation of origin and false advertising, trademark dilution, copyright infringement, trademark counterfeiting, unfair competition, common law trademark infringement, and unjust enrichment.

Despite being properly served, the Defendants have failed to respond to the Amended Complaint. Plaintiffs now move the Court to enter a default judgment against Defendants and seek a permanent injunction, statutory damages, and an award of attorney fees, investigator fees, and costs.

III. Discussion

Fed.R.Civ.P. 55(b)(2) authorizes the entry of a default judgment against a party that has defaulted. However, default judgment is not a right. The decision about whether default judgment is proper is primarily within the discretion of the district court.

A. Standard of Review

Once a party has defaulted, the consequence is that the factual allegations of the complaint, except those relating to the amount of damages, will be taken as true.

Entry of default judgment where damages are not a sum certain requires an application to the Court to prove, *inter alia*, damages.

B. Sufficiency of Causes of Action

In the present case, the Defendants failed to appear or otherwise defend, and the Clerk of the Court entered a default. The first issue is whether the Plaintiffs have stated a sufficient cause of action. The Court determines that Coach has established Defendants' liability for the purposes of this default judgment motion.

a. Trademark Infringement (15 U.S.C. § 1114(1)(a)) and False Designation (15 U.S.C. § 1125(a)(1)(A))

Trademark infringement (Count II) and false designation (Count IV) are measured by identical standards. The record must show: (1) the plaintiff has a valid and legally protectable mark, (2) the plaintiff owns the mark, and (3) the defendant's use of the mark causes a likelihood of confusion.

The first two elements are satisfied by the Plaintiffs' registration and ownership of the relevant trademarks. The third element is also satisfied. In the Amended Complaint and through exhibits, the record has uncontested assertions and evidence that are sufficient to show a likelihood of confusion between the counterfeit belt and the genuine Coach product.

b. Trademark Counterfeiting (15 U.S.C. § 1114(1)(a))

To establish trademark counterfeiting (Count I) the record must show (1) the defendant infringed a registered trademark in violation of the Lanham Act, and (2) the defendant intentionally used the trademark knowing it was counterfeit or was willfully blind to such use. The Third Circuit has stated that "willful" infringement involves an intent to infringe or a deliberate disregard of a mark holder's rights. Such willful conduct can be shown through deliberate and unnecessary duplicating of a plaintiff's mark in a way that was calculated to appropriate or otherwise benefit from the good will the plaintiff had nurtured.

Here, both elements of trademark counterfeiting are met. It has already been established that Defendants infringed the "Coach Op Art" trademark, the "Signature C" trademark, and the "Coach" trademark. In addition, The Court infers from the sale of the infringing belt bearing the unmistakable Coach logo that the counterfeiting here meets the Third Circuit standard of willfulness.

2. State Claims

Plaintiffs have asserted four state law claims: trademark counterfeiting; unfair competition; common law trademark infringement; and unjust enrichment. As discussed below, the state common law claims were sufficiently stated, and because federal liability has already been established, state statutory liability is also met.

a. State Statutory Claims

Because Plaintiffs have sufficiently stated their federal claims for trademark counterfeiting, the Plaintiffs have also stated a claim for trademark counterfeiting and unfair competition under [New Jersey state law].

c. Unjust Enrichment

Finally, the Plaintiffs have stated a claim under New Jersey common law for unjust enrichment. Here the Defendants were profiting from counterfeit items based on Coach's reputation. It would be unjust for the Defendants to enrich themselves without compensating the Plaintiffs, so a cause of action for unjust enrichment has been established.

C. Default Judgment

Before imposing the extreme sanction of default judgment, district courts must make explicit factual findings as to (1) whether the party subject to default has a meritorious defense, (2) the prejudice suffered by the party seeking default, and (3) the culpability of the party subject to default.

The current record does not show any meritorious defenses. Because the Defendants did not respond, the Court cannot determine whether the Defendants had meritorious defenses that are not reflected in the record.

D. Remedies

1. Lanham Act Statutory Damages

The Lanham Act provides that a plaintiff can elect to recover either actual damages based on the defendant's profits and the plaintiff's damages or statutory damages. The Plaintiffs have elected to recover statutory damages. As discussed below, after considering past awards in this District, the point of sale, the extent of sales, and the lack of evidence concerning Plaintiffs' losses, the Court will award $450,000 in statutory damages for Defendants' Lanham Act violations.

For statutory damages under the Lanham Act, the plaintiff may recover not less than $1,000 or more than $200,000 per counterfeit mark per type of goods or services sold, offered for sale, or distributed, as the court considers just. If the use of the counterfeit mark was willful, the maximum increases to $2,000,000 per mark per type of good. As stated above, for use to be willful, a defendant must show an aura of indifference to plaintiff's rights or a deliberate and unnecessary duplicating of a plaintiff's mark in a way that was calculated to appropriate or otherwise benefit from the good will the plaintiff had nurtured.

In the instant case, five types of goods were sold by the Defendant that carried counterfeit Coach marks: handbags, wallets, scarves, belts and shoes. Three Coach trademarks were infringed: "Coach Op Art"; "Signature C" and "Coach". Plaintiffs have produced some evidence of the scale of Defendants' operations, which included "approximately 50 handbags, 15 wallets, 10 scarves, 5 belts and 3 pairs of shoes, all bearing Coach trademarks and designs." All these items were observed by a private investigator on a single day in Defendants' Fashion Paradise store on August 30, 2010.

Because there are five types of goods and three marks, the total statutory damage amount must be not less than $15,000 nor more than $30,000,000. The Plaintiffs have requested one hundred times the minimum statutory damages, $100,000 per mark per good for a total of $1,500,000.

In fixing the amount of statutory damages, the Court will follow the approach of *Platypus Wear* which considered the following factors:

> (1) the expenses saved and the profits reaped; (2) the revenues lost by the plaintiff; (3) the value of the copyright; (4) the deterrent effect on others besides the defendant; (5) whether the defendant's conduct was innocent or willful; (6) whether a defendant has cooperated in providing particular records from which to assess the value of the infringing material produced; and (7) the potential for discouraging the defendant.

In considering these factors, the Court will award $30,000 per infringement for a total of $450,000, thirty times the minimum statutory damages. This amount is within the guidelines established by Congress, takes into account Defendants' culpability, and is significant enough to serve as compensation to the Plaintiffs and a deterrent to both the Defendant and others. This award also acknowledges that the sales took place at a small shop on the boardwalk rather than the Internet. In addition, this amount takes into account Defendant Naman Rafi's repeated unlawful conduct in using Plaintiffs' trademarks.

3. Costs and Attorney Fees

In addition to statutory damages, Plaintiffs ask for both attorney fees and costs, which their evidence shows to be $5,435.00 for attorney fees, $147.43 for investigative fees, and $552.66 for costs.

The costs of actions brought under § 43(a), § 43(d), or a willful violation under § 43(c) of the Lanham Act can be recovered pursuant to § 35(a) (codified at 15 U.S.C. § 1117(a)). In "exceptional cases" the court may award reasonable attorney fees. "Exceptional" has been interpreted by the Court to mean involving culpable conduct. Because this case involved the culpable conduct of Defendants, attorney fees and costs will be awarded to the Plaintiffs.

4. Permanent Injunction

The Supreme Court requires that any plaintiff seeking a permanent injunction to show: (1) that it has suffered an irreparable injury; (2) that remedies available at law, such as monetary damages, are inadequate to compensate for that injury; (3) that, considering the balance of hardships between the plaintiff and defendant, a remedy in equity is warranted; and (4) that the public interest would not be disserved by a permanent injunction.

a. Irreparable Injury

Because a likelihood of confusion has been shown, the requirement of irreparable harm has been met.

b. Inadequacy of Remedies at Law

A remedy at law would be inadequate to compensate the Plaintiffs.

c. Balancing of Hardships

The only hardship imposed upon the Defendants is that they obey the law. On the other hand if an injunction were not issued then Plaintiffs suffer the hardships that gave rise to this suit: loss of reputation and sales.

d. Public Interest

Issuing an injunction will serve the public interest goals of preventing consumer confusion and the trademark holder's property interest.

In sum, the Court will grant $450,000 in statutory damages under the Lanham Act, $5,435.00 for attorney fees, $147.43 for investigative fees, and $552.66 for costs, bringing Plaintiffs' total recovery from Defendants to $456,135.09. In addition, the Court will permanently enjoin Fashion Paradise, LLC, and Naman Rafi from infringing Plaintiffs' trademarks and copyrights in the future and require them to surrender to Plaintiffs all infringing products they currently possess.

For the foregoing reasons the Court will grant the Plaintiffs' motion for default judgment, award a default judgment of $456,135.09, and issue a permanent injunction. The accompanying order for default judgment and permanent injunction shall be entered.

Notes

1. Frequently, defendant counterfeiters in civil counterfeiting actions do not appear or defend, so plaintiff brand owners seek large default judgments against them. The challenge is enforcement of such judgments since counterfeiters rarely can be found or have assets which can be readily located. (Later in this chapter we discuss contributory/third party liability.) Such defendants are often identified as "John Does" because they cannot be identified or use false names. Even absent a defendant's appearance, willfulness can be inferred.

2. Lanham Act statutory damages are useful in a case involving defaulting defendants where no defense has been submitted. In the Coach case, the court awarded $450,000 in statutory damages together with costs, including the private investigator fees and attorney's fees.

4. Importation, Smuggling, and Trafficking

Counterfeiting is a crime under federal law and under 46 state criminal statutes. In 1984, Congress passed the Trademark Counterfeiting Act, 18 U.S.C. § 2320, creating federal criminal penalties for trafficking in counterfeit goods or services. Thereafter, growth of the counterfeit goods trade led Congress to pass the Anti-counterfeiting Consumer Protection Act of 1996, adding counterfeiting as a "racketeering activity" under RICO. Under this Act an intentional trafficker can be fined up to $2 million or imprisoned for up to 10 years or both.

Those fines and penalties were increased on March 16, 2006, when President Bush signed into effect H.R. 32, the "Stop Counterfeiting in Manufactured Goods

Act" and the most significant anticounterfeiting legislation in more than 20 years. This Act establishes prison terms of up to 20 years and fines of up to $15 million. It also includes mandatory forfeiture, destruction, and restitution provisions as well as restricting the shipment of falsified labels or packaging and reimbursement to the brands harmed.

On October 13, 2008, President Bush signed the PRO-IP Act ("Prioritizing Resources and Organization for Intellectual Property Act of 2008"), HR 4279, S 3325, which provided increased resources for the Department of Justice programs to combat Intellectual Property theft, creating stiffer criminal and civil penalties, creating a new White House Coordination Office, and providing more funding to hire additional FBI officers to investigate. Additionally, it authorizes $25 million annually to train law enforcement and educate the public on how to combat counterfeit activity.

18 U.S.C. § 2320

Anticounterfeiting Consumer Protection Act of 1996

Trafficking in Counterfeit Goods or Services

(a) Offenses.—Whoever intentionally—

(1) traffics in goods or services and knowingly uses a counterfeit mark on or in connection with such goods or services,

(2) traffics in labels, patches, stickers, wrappers, badges, emblems, medallions, charms, boxes, containers, cans, cases, hangtags, documentation, or packaging of any type or nature, knowing that a counterfeit mark has been applied thereto, the use of which is likely to cause confusion, to cause mistake, or to deceive, . . .

or attempts or conspires to violate any of paragraphs (1) through (4) shall be punished as provided in subsection (b).

(b) Penalties.—

(1) In general.—Whoever commits an offense under subsection (a)—

(A) if an individual, shall be fined not more than $2,000,000 or imprisoned not more than 10 years, or both, and, if a person other than an individual, shall be fined not more than $5,000,000; and

(B) for a second or subsequent offense under subsection (a), if an individual, shall be fined not more than $5,000,000 or imprisoned not more than 20 years, or both, and if other than an individual, shall be fined not more than $15,000,000.

(c) Forfeiture and destruction of property; restitution.—Forfeiture, destruction, and restitution relating to this section shall be subject to section 2323, to the extent provided in that section, in addition to any other similar remedies provided by law.

(d) Defenses.—All defenses, affirmative defenses, and limitations on remedies that would be applicable in an action under the Lanham Act shall be applicable in a prosecution under this section. In a prosecution under this section, the defendant shall have the burden of proof, by a preponderance of the evidence, of any such affirmative defense.

* * *

(f) Definitions.—For the purposes of this section—

(1) the term "counterfeit mark" means—

(A) a spurious mark—

(i) that is used in connection with trafficking in any goods, services, labels, patches, stickers, wrappers, badges, emblems, medallions, charms, boxes, containers, cans, cases, hangtags, documentation, or packaging of any type or nature;

(ii) that is identical with, or substantially indistinguishable from, a mark registered on the principal register in the United States Patent and Trademark Office and in use, whether or not the defendant knew such mark was so registered;

(iii) that is applied to or used in connection with the goods or services for which the mark is registered with the United States Patent and Trademark Office, or is applied to or consists of a label, patch, sticker, wrapper, badge, emblem, medallion, charm, box, container, can, case, hangtag, documentation, or packaging of any type or nature that is designed, marketed, or otherwise intended to be used on or in connection with the goods or services for which the mark is registered in the United States Patent and Trademark Office; and

(iv) the use of which is likely to cause confusion, to cause mistake, or to deceive.

18 U.S.C. § 1961

Definitions

As used in this chapter—

(1) "racketeering activity" means (B) any act which is indictable under any of the following provisions of title 18, United States Code: sections 471, 472, and 473 (relating to counterfeiting), section 2319 (relating to criminal infringement of a copyright), section 2319A (relating to unauthorized fixation of and trafficking in sound recordings and music videos of live musical performances), section 2320 (relating to trafficking in goods or services bearing counterfeit mark).

United States v. Chong Lam

677 F.3d 190 (4th Cir. 2012)

DUNCAN, Circuit Judge.

Opinion

A jury convicted appellants Chong Lam and Siu Yung Chan (collectively "Appellants") of conspiracy to traffic in counterfeit goods, trafficking in counterfeit goods, and smuggling goods into the United States. The counterfeiting convictions were based on the jury's determination that a mark displayed on goods Appellants imported into the United States was a counterfeit of a trademark registered to fashion designer Burberry Ltd. ("Burberry"), depicting its signature plaid pattern (the "Burberry Check mark"). On appeal, Appellants advance various challenges to their convictions for trafficking in counterfeit goods.

I.

A.

The convictions in this case arise out of Appellants' participation in the manufacture, import, and sale of handbags and wallets bearing counterfeit trademarks. Since 1999, Appellants have owned or otherwise controlled at least 10 companies incorporated in the United States that engaged in the importation of both legitimate and counterfeit handbags and wallets. Lam also had authority over at least three companies located in China and Hong Kong that engaged in the manufacture and export of such goods. Appellants transferred significant amounts of money among these various enterprises.

Between 2002 and 2005, [U.S. Customs and Border Protection ("CBP")] issued seizure notices to a number of the corporations controlled by Appellants, each time informing the individual company that certain goods it had imported into the United States were being seized because CBP had determined that the goods were labeled with what were likely counterfeit trademarks. The marks CBP identified as counterfeit were copies of legitimate marks registered to various luxury handbag and wallet manufacturers, including Burberry. CBP found a layer of legitimate merchandise on the top and bottom of each container, followed by a cardboard divider, concealing the goods bearing allegedly counterfeit marks within the interior of the container. CBP seized goods displaying marks it determined were likely counterfeit. These goods form the basis for the charges brought against Appellants.

B.

Appellants filed a motion in limine seeking to have the district court declare the phrase "substantially indistinguishable," as used in 18 U.S.C. § 2320, unconstitutionally vague. The district court denied the motion.

C.

Burberry registered the Burberry Check mark—a mark depicting Burberry's signature plaid pattern, created by intersecting red, white, black, and grey lines against a tan background—with the United States Patent and Trademark Office ("USPTO") in 1996. Burberry also has a registered trademark for an equestrian knight symbol (the "Burberry Equestrian mark"). The government introduced into evidence examples of authentic Burberry handbags displaying the Burberry Check mark and authentic handbags displaying the combination of the Burberry Check mark and the Burberry Equestrian mark.

The government introduced a number of samples of the goods seized from Norfolk that bore the allegedly counterfeit Burberry Check mark. Significantly, these wallets and handbags displayed Appellants' so-called Marco mark—the above-described pattern, which consisted of a plaid pattern similar to the Burberry Check mark with an equestrian knight superimposed over it.

At several points during the trial, the government suggested that whether an allegedly counterfeit mark was substantially indistinguishable from a legitimate mark should be analyzed from the viewpoint of a hypothetical "reasonable consumer of ordinary intelligence." The government made such statements at least twice during its cross-examination of Appellants' witnesses. During closing argument, the government also asserted several times that the jury should look to "the perspective of the average person" in comparing the goods. The district court sustained Appellants' objections to these comments as incorrect statements of the law.

In response to Appellants' objections and directly following the government's closing argument, the district court instructed the jury as follows:

> Obviously, you are to be guided by the instructions on the law that the court will provide to you. A lot of the lawyers have made references to what the law is or what they think it might be. But these instructions, I hope, will clear up, if there was some confusion.... Listen to me when it comes to what the law is.

At the beginning of formal jury instructions, the district court further informed the jury that "it is your sworn duty to follow the law as I am now in the process of defining for you. You must follow all of my instructions as a whole."

With regard to whether the mark on Appellants' goods was a counterfeit of the Burberry Check mark, the district court instructed the jury:

> You have to determine whether or not the mark that is alleged to be counterfeit is identical to or substantially indistinguishable from the mark that is registered on the same goods in the Principal Register of the [USPTO]. In order to carry out your responsibility as it relates to that part of these instructions, you have to compare the marks, the mark on the alleged to be counterfeit and the mark that is the genuine mark.
>
> Now, you do that, and you make a decision. This is based on your side-by-side comparison, use of your own eyes, and any other evidence that came into the record that might help you in that task. But it is for you to decide. If you decide that the mark is not identical or substantially indistinguishable, that pretty much ends the inquiry. That means it is not counterfeit.

During deliberations, the jury submitted a question to the district court, asking if "when comparing the Marco plaid on the purses seized in Norfolk to the [Burberry Check mark], should we consider the presence of the Marco knight?" The district court responded:

> You have heard evidence and argument that you can accept certain facts. On the one hand, the defendants presented evidence and argued that you accept as a fact that the plaid plus the Marco knight is a composite mark that should be compared as a composite mark with the [Burberry Check mark]. On the other hand, the government has put on evidence and argued that the plaid pattern alone on the alleged counterfeit bag is violative, meaning substantially indistinguishable, from the [Burberry Check mark]. Depending on the way you find facts, you may consider the Marco knight in comparing the marks. That's not the province of the court, it's the province of the jury. Of course, the defendants also contend that the plaid by itself is not substantially indistinguishable and therefore not counterfeit.

Appellants did not object to this response.

The jury found Appellants guilty of conspiracy to traffic in counterfeit goods, trafficking in counterfeit goods, and smuggling goods into the United States.

D.

Appellants renewed their motion for acquittal, and moved for a new trial.

The district court considered Appellants' argument that remarks made by the government necessitated a new trial. It held that the government's comments were improper because, in its estimation, they incorrectly stated the perspective from which the jurors were to consider whether a mark was counterfeit. It next considered the six factors our circuit takes into account when determining whether a prosecutor's comments were so prejudicial that they deprived a defendant of a fair trial: (1) whether the government's remarks mislead the jury, (2) whether they were extensive, (3) the strength of the evidence supporting conviction absent the comments, (4) whether the government deliberately made the comments to mislead the jury, (5) whether the defendant invited the comments, and (6) the presence of a curative instruction. After thoroughly reviewing the trial transcript, the district court found that, although the government's comments were misleading and extensive, and Appellants did not invite the comments, the government did not make the comments with the purpose of deliberately misleading the jury. It also found that the government presented enough evidence to support Appellants' convictions in the absence of the misleading remarks. Finally, the district court considered its curative instructions, finding that they removed any prejudice the government's comments created. Appellants timely appealed.

II.

Appellants' principal contention as to why the evidence was insufficient to allow a jury to conclude that the mark displayed on their goods was a counterfeit is that it consists of a plaid background and equestrian knight overlay, whereas the Burberry Check mark does not include an equestrian knight. They assert that "no rational jury would conclude that a mark with a knight integrated onto it was a counterfeit of a mark without a knight." We disagree, finding that the marks are similar enough to allow a reasonable jury to draw such a conclusion—especially in light of the evidence demonstrating that Burberry often sells goods displaying the Burberry Check mark and the Burberry Equestrian mark together.

A mark does not have to be an exact replica of a registered trademark to be deemed a counterfeit. As stated, § 2320 defines a counterfeit mark as "identical to *or* substantially indistinguishable from" a registered trademark. This court has only once held that two marks were so divergent that, as a matter of law, no rational jury could find one was a counterfeit of the other. In a civil counterfeiting case under the Lanham Act, we found that a dog toy manufacturer's use of the name "Chewy Vuiton" and a monogram design featuring the letters "CV" was, as a matter of law, not substantially indistinguishable from the trademarked "Louis Vuitton" and "LV" designs owned by Louis Vuitton Malletier. *See Louis Vuitton Malletier S.A. v. Haute Diggity Dog, LLC,* 507 F.3d 252, 269 (4th Cir.2007). We based our decision upon marked differences between the legitimate and allegedly counterfeit goods, including their distinct names, the different letters used in the respective monograms, their divergent design and color patterns, and that the allegedly counterfeit mark was displayed on dog toys, rather than handbags. *See id.* ("In selling 'Chewy Vuiton' dog toys, Haute Diggity Dog is not selling knock-off LOUIS VUITTON handbags with a counterfeit LV mark, and no reasonable trier of fact could so conclude."). Thus, our case law suggests that a good displaying an allegedly counterfeit trademark must possess pronounced differences from a legitimate trademarked good for us to declare that no rational jury could find that it was a counterfeit.

Here, viewing the evidence in the light most favorable to the government, we find that Appellants' mark was similar enough to the legitimate Burberry mark that we cannot say, as a matter of law, that no rational jury could conclude Appellants' mark was a counterfeit. We base this holding on the similarity of the two marks. The plaid pattern displayed on Appellants' goods differs only slightly from the Burberry Check mark—in color and in the shape of the boxes formed by the stripes. Moreover, although the Burberry Check mark does not include an equestrian knight, it is undisputed that Burberry has obtained trademark protection for an equestrian knight mark, and that it often sells handbags and other goods displaying a combination of the two marks.

Appellants next contend that the district court erred when, in response to the jury's question, it instructed the jury to decide for itself whether to consider the knight in determining whether Appellants' mark was a counterfeit. Appellants concede that they did not object to this statement at trial. We therefore review the district court's instruction for plain error.

Here, Appellants have not met the high standard required to convince us to exercise our discretion. Their only contention as to why the district court's instruction was error is that, as a matter of law, the jury was required to consider the presence of the knight in addition to the plaid pattern when comparing Appellants' goods to those bearing the legitimate Burberry mark. Appellants point to no case law, and we have found none, that supports this proposition. They therefore provide us with no basis on which we could conclude that the district court erred. Even if the district court's instruction was erroneous, however, we cannot say the error was plain unless Appellants establish it was "obvious or clear under current law."

Appellants next contend that § 2320 is unconstitutionally vague. Specifically, they assert that the statute's definition of a "counterfeit mark" as "a spurious mark . . . that is identical with, or substantially indistinguishable from" a mark registered on the principal register in the [USPTO]" does not clearly explain how similar a mark must be for it to be considered counterfeit. Thus, Appellants contend, the statute encourages arbitrary enforcement.

Finally, they claim, as they did before the district court, that a retrial is necessitated by the government's allegedly improper comments at trial. Specifically, Appellants argue that prosecutors, at several points during the trial, misstated the perspective the jury should use when determining whether the mark displayed on their goods was a counterfeit, implying that the jury should consider a hypothetical "average person on the street" rather than using its own judgment. These misstatements, Appellants contend, were so prejudicial that they deprived them of a fair trial.

Rule 33 allows a district court to "[u]pon the defendant's motion, . . . vacate any judgment and grant a new trial if the interest of justice so requires." Fed.R.Crim.P. 33(a). Here, the district court agreed that prosecutors had misstated the law and found that such comments were prejudicial. It nevertheless denied Appellants' Rule 33 motion, however, finding that any prejudice was cured by the district court's correct statement of the law and its instructions to the jury to apply the law as stated by the court, not the attorneys. A prosecutor's statements at trial constitute reversible error only if they were (1) improper and (2) "prejudicially affected the defendant's substantial rights so as to deprive the defendant of a fair trial." In light of the district court's comprehensive analysis and the deferential standard of review, we focus on the presence of curative instructions, which formed the basis of the district court's decision.

Assuming without deciding that the government's comments were improper and prejudicial, we find that the district court did not abuse its discretion by concluding that its curative instructions were sufficient to ensure Appellants were afforded a fair trial. At trial, the district court instructed the jury twice—including immediately following the government's allegedly improper closing argument—that it was required to apply the law as the district court described it, not as the lawyers stated it. It also provided the jury with lengthy instructions regarding the perspective it was to use when determining whether the plaid used on Appellants' goods was a counterfeit of the Burberry Check mark. It emphasized that the determination was to be based on a "side-by-side comparison [and] use of [their] own eyes." It also stated that if the jury "decide[d] the mark [was] not identical or substantially indistinguishable," it must find in favor of Appellants. We do not believe it was an abuse of discretion for the district court to presume the jury followed these detailed instructions—a presumption our precedent requires.

As such, we conclude that it was well within the district court's discretion to deny Appellants' request for a new trial, particularly given the heightened showing we require of defendants before we will grant the drastic relief of affording them a new trial.

With all due respect to our dissenting colleague, we believe the standard of review—and the fact that the decision to grant a new trial is itself highly discretionary—requires this conclusion. We first note that the dissent focused on advancing two assertions that we have assumed, for the sake of argument, are true: that the prosecution's remarks were improper and that they prejudiced Appellants. Because we assume the validity of both of these conclusions, we take no issue with this portion of the dissent.

The dissent expresses the view that the district court's instructions to the jury were insufficient to cure the prejudice caused by the government's comments. It also takes issue with the district court's statement that the jury could consider "other evidence that came into the record" in determining whether the two marks were substantially indistinguishable—in addition to a "side by side comparison" and their "own eyes." It further opines that the district court should have explicitly instructed the jury regarding the limited effect of certain testimony. The question before us, however, is not whether we would have instructed the jury differently—as the dissent no doubt would have—because our review is not de novo. Rather, we consider whether the district court abused its discretion. Our review of the record indicates that the district court undertook a thoughtful and comprehensive review of the remarks made by the prosecution, the effect of those comments, and its responses to those comments—which included two instructions to follow the law as stated by the court, and not the lawyers, and specific instructions to the jury to determine whether the marks were substantially indistinguishable by performing a "side by side comparison," by using their "own eyes," and to make the decision on their own.

III.

For the foregoing reasons, the judgment of the district court is

AFFIRMED.

FLOYD, Circuit Judge, concurring in part, dissenting in part, and dissenting from the judgment:

On no fewer than eight occasions during its closing and rebuttal arguments, the government misstated the legal standard governing the key issue disputed by the parties at trial—whether the genuine and allegedly counterfeit marks were "substantially indistinguishable." Six of these misstatements occurred after the district court sustained the first of four defense objections to the remarks. Nevertheless, the district court denied Lam and Chan's Rule 33 motion for a new trial, concluding that, although the statements were prejudicial, the court's curative instruction negated the prejudice. Because I believe that these statements deprived Appellants of a fair trial, and because I think the district court abused its discretion in concluding they did not, I respectfully dissent in part from the majority opinion.

I.

At trial, Lam and Chan did not contest that they engaged in the conduct alleged by the government—that is, that they imported handbags bearing the "Marco mark." Rather, the central issue disputed by the parties was whether Appellants' Marco mark was "substantially indistinguishable" from the registered Burberry Check mark.

Yet during closing and rebuttal arguments, government counsel repeatedly misstated the standard governing this key issue. He instructed the jurors to assume the perspective of the average consumer who failed to conduct a side-by-side examination of the marks, specifically directing them to adopt the view of two government witnesses in place of their own conclusions regarding the marks. Despite numerous defense objections sustained by the district court, the prosecutor continued to assert this erroneous legal standard.

A.

Government counsel first addressed the issue of the standard for evaluating whether the marks were substantially indistinguishable in his closing argument. That determination, the prosecutor informed the jury, should be made "from the standpoint of the average purchaser."

In total, the government told the jury to adopt the perspective of the average consumer on no fewer than eight distinct occasions during closing arguments. By my count, six of these comments occurred after the first sustained objection. The defense entered four objections, three of which the district court sustained. Yet the government carried on in making the erroneous statements and never sought clarification from the district court regarding the nature of its error.

B.

As the majority notes, the district court provided several instructions that, it concluded, cured the prejudice caused by the government's statements. First, the district court instructed the jurors generally that they should listen to the court, not the lawyers, regarding "what the law is."

C.

Following their convictions, Lam and Chan filed a motion under Federal Rule of Criminal Procedure 33 seeking a new trial on the ground that the government's improper statements constituted reversible prosecutorial misconduct. The district court concluded that the government's remarks were both improper and prejudicial. Nevertheless, it denied Appellants' motion because it found that its instructions to the jury cured this prejudice.

II.

The government first urges that, contrary to the district court's conclusion, its statements were not improper and, as a result, this court need not review the district court's finding with respect to prejudice. I disagree.

The district court found that the prosecutor's remarks were improper in two ways. First, the government's comments regarding the standard for evaluating whether two marks are substantially indistinguishable were erroneous because, in instructing the jurors that this determination should be made from the perspective of the average consumer, the prosecutor told the jury that they should not rely on their own visual examination to make this factual finding. Second, the government improperly cited testimony to establish whether an average consumer would find the marks substantially indistinguishable. This testimony, however, could be used to prove only the likelihood-of-confusion element.

Use of the "ocular test" is particularly apt where a jury is available to undertake the comparison. Thus, the government erred in instructing the jurors that they should not conduct a visual comparison and that, after hearing evidence at trial, they were no longer positioned to make the requisite factual determination.

In addition, the district court correctly found that the government erred in directing the jury to adopt the views of Bartko and Abel on this issue. The district court allowed these witnesses' testimony because it was relevant to the likelihood-of-confusion issue. Yet the government repeatedly and extensively invoked their testimony for the purpose of establishing that the marks were substantially indistinguishable. This was, as the district court found, improper.

I must next consider the district court's determination regarding whether the improper remarks caused prejudice depriving Lam and Chan of a fair trial. Whether the marks were substantially indistinguishable was the central issue disputed by the parties at trial. The government not only misstated the relevant legal standard but also suggested that the jurors should adopt the view of government witnesses in place of their own. Accordingly, the government's statements were highly likely to mislead the jury.

Moreover, the remarks were extensive, particularly during the government's rebuttal argument, in which the prosecutor cited the average-consumer standard no fewer than seven times. The prosecutor also spoke at length on two occasions about why he believed the jurors had become too sophisticated to judge the evidence correctly. The improper remarks pervaded the government's argument, and the district court correctly found they were extensive.

The district court clearly erred in concluding that the prosecutor's statements were not deliberate. The district court found that the prosecutor did not deliberately seek to mislead the jury because he genuinely believed that he had set forth the correct standard on the "substantially indistinguishable" element. Where, however, a prosecutor continues to make an incorrect statement of the law after the district court has sustained repeated objections to that statement, notifying the prosecutor of the error, the court should, in my opinion, infer some degree of deliberateness. To be clear, I do not disturb the district court's finding that, when the prosecutor began to speak, he believed that his statements accurately reflected the law. But a prosecutor's refusal to acknowledge his error after multiple sustained objections should be viewed as deliberate, and a court should deduce from his decision to soldier on a deliberate attempt to mislead the jury.

C.

Despite finding that the government's remarks were prejudicial, the district court held that its curative instructions were sufficient to cure the prejudice. The majority, too, has treated this factor as determinative. I cannot share their view that the district court's instructions dispelled the prejudice and ensured Lam and Chan received a fair trial.

The district court noted that it provided general curative instructions that the jury should follow the directions of the court, rather than the lawyers, as to the applicable law. In light of the pervasive and highly misleading nature of the prosecutor's comments, I have no difficulty concluding that these general instructions were insufficient to cure the prejudice. Furthermore, contrary to the district court's finding, I cannot agree that the court's specific instruction on the "substantially indistinguishable" element was sufficient to dissipate the prejudicial effect of the prosecutor's remarks. The district court did tell the jury to compare the allegedly counterfeit mark with the Burberry mark. But it went on to instruct the jury that it should base its determination of this element not only on the jurors' "side-by-side comparison" of the marks, but also on "any other evidence that came into the record."

Thus, the district court allowed the jurors to rely on any and all evidence introduced at trial and failed to focus the jurors on the "ocular test." Most notably, at no time did the district court limit the jurors' use of [n]or did the district court disabuse the jurors of the notion that they had gathered too much expertise to make the indistinguishability determination based on their own perceptions.

The district court's instructions, therefore, failed to counter several of the serious errors that the court had identified in the prosecutor's statements.

III

Ultimately, considering all factors relevant to the determination of prejudice, I am compelled to conclude that the government's highly misleading and erroneous statements regarding a central issue disputed at trial prejudiced Lam and Chan, depriving them of the fair trial to which they are entitled. Moreover, I find that the district court abused its discretion in finding that its instructions to the jury cured this prejudice. Accordingly, with all due respect to the district court and my esteemed colleagues, I dissent.

Notes

1. The key issue is determining whether a product is a counterfeit. The alleged counterfeit must bear a trademark that is "identical or substantially indistinguishable" from the authentic trademark. This is a much stricter standard than that used for determining trademark infringement, under which the mark in question must

only be "confusingly similar" to the plaintiff's trademark. In both cases, the question is one of determining the degree of similarity. In order to hold that there has been an infringement, the court must find that the similarity is sufficient to confuse potential customers. With counterfeiting, the similarity must be so great that the ordinary consumer is unable to tell the trademarks apart or can only do so with great difficulty.

2. Deciding whether a given trademark is a counterfeit is not difficult when the two trademarks involved are so similar as to be identical. The question becomes more difficult in a case like *United States v. Lam*, in which the products are very similar but there is some degree of difference. If a court or a jury determines that the trademarks in question are somewhat similar but it is still easy to tell them apart, then we are no longer dealing with a counterfeit, though the similarity may still be sufficient for a finding of trademark infringement.

3. Consider the practical and procedural context of this case. Federal criminal prosecutions of counterfeit cases are extremely rare. However, the defendants apparently ran a sophisticated and profitable counterfeiting operation, using a number of shell companies to conceal their operations from the authorities. Evidence was presented at trial to indicate that defendants often imported goods in such a way that their counterfeits or alleged counterfeits were hidden inside or underneath other products, clearly in order to evade Customs scrutiny. (We have seen counterfeit watches imported in boxes of roofing tiles or clothing with the counterfeit labeling hidden under generic labeling removed after the merchandise clears Customs.) Is it possible that such suspicious behavior may have predisposed the jury to believe that the defendants were "bad guys" and therefore probably guilty of counterfeiting in this case? Consider also that defendants went through two trials (the first trial ended in a mistrial) and now have raised a number of sophisticated legal arguments on appeal, indicating a very well-financed legal defense team. What inferences about the defendants' business operations might you draw from this state of affairs?

5. State Laws

Many states have enacted criminal trademark counterfeiting laws that can be used to prosecute counterfeiters. In New York, Penal Law §§ 165.71, 165.72, 165.73 and 165.74 make it an A misdemeanor or E or C felony to sell or offer for sale goods that bear a counterfeit trademark if the defendant acts "with the intent to deceive or defraud some other person or with the intent to evade a lawful restriction [of] sale" and the destruction of the goods thereof.

Proving that the defendant knew he was selling a counterfeit can be accomplished in a number of ways: (1) prior arrest for same offense, (2) low price of goods or (3) statement from defendant or arresting officer. N.Y. Penal Law § 165.70 provides the underlying definitions of the aforementioned sections. A number of states have also adopted legislation that treats civil actions for trademark counterfeiting differently from civil actions for ordinary infringement.

Compare these provisions with the California statute below.

Cal. Penal Code § 350
Counterfeit of registered mark; offenses; punishment

(a) Any person who willfully manufactures, intentionally sells, or knowingly possesses for sale any counterfeit mark registered with the Secretary of State or registered on the Principal Register of the United States Patent and Trademark Office, shall, upon conviction, be punishable as follows:

(1) When the offense involves less than 1,000 of the articles described in this subdivision, with a total retail or fair market value less than that required for grand theft as defined in Section 487, and if the person is an individual, he or she shall be punished by a fine of not more than ten thousand dollars ($10,000), or by imprisonment in a county jail for not more than one year, or by both that fine and imprisonment; or, if the person is a business entity, by a fine of not more than two hundred thousand dollars ($200,000).

(2) When the offense involves 1,000 or more of the articles described in this subdivision, or has a total retail or fair market value equal to or greater than that required for grand theft as defined in Section 487, and if the person is an individual, he or she shall be punished by imprisonment in a county jail not to exceed one year, or pursuant to subdivision (h) of Section 1170 for 16 months, or two or three years, or by a fine not to exceed five hundred thousand dollars ($500,000), or by both that imprisonment and fine; or, if the person is a business entity, by a fine not to exceed one million dollars ($1,000,000).

6. The Gray Market and the First Sale Doctrine

"Gray market" products are goods manufactured under authorization from the trademark owner, legally purchased outside the United States from authorized distributors, which are then imported by persons other than the trademark holder and without the mark-holder's permission. Prices for authentic products often vary from country to country, which creates an incentive for third parties to purchase product legally from authorized dealers in countries where the products are less expensive and sell those products to unauthorized retailers in countries where the products are more expensive (this is also known as "parallel importing"). Gray market sales enable unauthorized retailers to undercut the prices of authorized retailers. Although gray market transactions are often legal, brand owners have sought a variety of means for preventing them; one such means, as we see in the case below, is the use of quality-control codes (known as unique production codes or "UPCs") on product packaging.

Zino Davidoff SA v. CVS Corp.

571 F.3d 238 (2d Cir. 2009)

LEVAL, Circuit Judge.

Defendant CVS Corporation, a retail drugstore chain, appeals from the order of the United States District Court for the Southern District of New York (Karas, *J.*), granting to plaintiff Zino Davidoff SA ("Davidoff"), a Swiss corporation, a preliminary injunction which enjoined CVS from dealing in any way in trademarked goods of the plaintiff with Davidoff's unique production code ("UPC") removed. The district court found that the plaintiff was likely to succeed on the merits of its trademark infringement claim because the UPC acts as a quality control mechanism which enables Davidoff to protect the reputation of its trademarks by identifying counterfeits and by protecting against defects.

Background

Davidoff has been a well-regarded brand for high-end luxury goods for personal consumption since 1911. In 1988, Davidoff launched DAVIDOFF COOL WATER, a cologne for men, followed by a COOL WATER fragrance for women in 1997. Davidoff holds valid uncontested trademarks for all of the COOL WATER products at issue in this case. The COOL WATER fragrances are manufactured and marketed by Coty Inc. ("Coty") and its subsidiaries, under license from Davidoff.

Davidoff and Coty together have developed a comprehensive quality assurance and anti-counterfeiting program. Part of this program involves the placement of a unique production code on the bottom of each COOL WATER fragrance bottle and on the bottom of its corresponding package. As its name suggests, the UPC is a multi-digit code unique to each unit. Embedded within the code is a variety of information about that particular unit, such as the time and place of production, the production line, ingredients used, etc.

Davidoff's use of the UPC plays an important role in fighting counterfeits. Because of the high expense involved in placing a unique number on each unit, counterfeiters will generally either omit such a number from their packaging or repeatedly use sets of fake numbers on a series of counterfeit units. The UPC system therefore facilitates the spotting of counterfeit units by allowing investigators to make a determination based on the absence of a UPC on the packaging or the use of a repeating and, thus, fake UPC number. Also, the identification of a fake UPC number allows investigators to search for other fakes merely by identifying products bearing the same fake number. Furthermore, Davidoff's own investigators are not the only recipients of these benefits. Davidoff regularly instructs its retailers and officers of U.S. Customs and Border Protection ("Customs") in the use of the UPC system and relays information regarding fake UPC numbers known to be used by counterfeiters. Armed with this knowledge, Customs and retailers are more easily able to check newly-received COOL WATER shipments and set aside suspected counterfeits.

Use of the UPC system also assists Davidoff's ability to protect its brand against quality slippage in genuine authorized products. When a quality problem surfaces, the UPC identifies the place of manufacture, the batch which produced the defect, and other identifying information. This information helps Davidoff both to recall already distributed product that may share the defect and to prevent further recurrence of the defect. The ability derived from the use of the UPC helps Davidoff assure that its marks will not appear on defective product and thus preserve and protect the value of its trademarks.

In an effort to maintain the prestige of its brand, Davidoff limits sales of COOL WATER products to luxury retailers and has declined to sell to CVS. Though not an authorized retailer, CVS is nonetheless able to secure stock of COOL WATER from outside of Davidoff's normal distribution channels. Davidoff products are among CVS's top-selling fragrances. Some of the COOL WATER fragrances sold by CVS have been found to be counterfeit. In addition, some of the COOL WATER stock purchased by CVS that is not counterfeit consists of gray-market goods, meaning "goods that are manufactured [under authorization from the trademark owner], are legally purchased [outside the United States] from authorized distributors, and are then imported by persons other than the trademark holder and without the mark-holder's permission." *Olympus Corp. v. United States,* 792 F.2d 315, 317 (2d Cir.1986).

On two occasions, in 1998 and 2005, Davidoff discovered that counterfeit COOL WATER products were being sold at CVS. On both occasions, Davidoff sent cease-and-desist letters to CVS and provided information to CVS on how to identify counterfeits based on the product's UPC. CVS assured Davidoff that it would conduct an inventory review, remove all counterfeit products, and source only from authorized distributors. Despite these assurances, Davidoff discovered in 2006 that CVS was continuing to sell counterfeit COOL WATER fragrances. Davidoff then brought this action against CVS alleging trademark infringement, unfair competition, and trademark dilution. Davidoff's original complaint sought relief only as to CVS's marketing of counterfeit Davidoff products. On December 22, 2006, the district court granted a temporary restraining order and authorized Davidoff to inspect all undistributed products in CVS's inventory bearing the Davidoff mark.

During the course of this inspection, Davidoff discovered that, in the case of 16,600 items in CVS's inventory, the UPCs on the packages and labels affixed to the bottle had been removed. The codes had been removed through a variety of techniques, including cutting the portion of the box or label exhibiting the UPC, using chemicals to wipe away the UPC on the label, and grinding away the bottom of the bottles to remove the UPC. It was apparent in many instances that the packaging had been opened.

Davidoff amended its complaint to include also claims for relief based upon CVS's sale of Davidoff products with the UPC removed. On March 2, 2007, CVS voluntarily agreed to halt the sale of counterfeit Davidoff products, but not the products with the codes removed. Davidoff then moved for a preliminary injunction forbidding the sale of all its trademarked goods with code removed. The court granted Davidoff's motion. *Zino Davidoff SA v. CVS Corp.*, No. 06-cv-15332, 2007 WL 1933932 (S.D.N.Y. July 2, 2007). The court reasoned that removal of the codes from Davidoff's trademarked product impaired Davidoff's marks by interfering with the trademark owner's ability to identify counterfeit goods and to control the quality of its legitimate products by identifying and recalling defective products. The court thus concluded that Davidoff was likely to succeed on the merits of its trademark infringement claims on the theory that CVS's sale of Davidoff's trademarked products with the codes removed constituted trademark infringement. CVS brought this appeal.

Discussion

We review a district court's grant of a preliminary injunction for abuse of discretion.

In cases involving claims of trademark infringement and dilution, as in other types of cases, a party seeking a preliminary injunction must demonstrate (1) the likelihood of irreparable injury in the absence of such an injunction, and (2) either (a) likelihood of success on the merits or (b) sufficiently serious questions going to the merits to make them a fair ground for litigation plus a balance of hardships tipping decidedly toward the party requesting the preliminary relief.

CVS argues that Davidoff failed to establish a likelihood of success on the merits and would not suffer irreparable harm in the absence of an injunction. We disagree and affirm the district court's grant of a preliminary injunction.

I. Trademark Infringement

CVS contends that the district court erred in ruling that Davidoff is likely to succeed on the merits of its trademark infringement claims. CVS asserts that the goods with the codes removed are gray-market goods—*i.e.*, genuine Davidoff goods sold by Davidoff through authorized channels in other countries and subsequently imported by others into the United States. Because these goods are sold in their original packaging with the Davidoff trademarks clearly visible and unaltered, CVS contends that the removal of the codes does not negate their genuineness or constitute infringement. CVS's argument misses the point. The fact that the goods in question may be gray-market goods does not furnish CVS with a valid defense. The question before us is not whether, or under what circumstances, the sale of gray-market goods infringes their trademark. The district court did not justify its grant of a preliminary injunction by the proposition that the goods authorized by Davidoff for sale in another country are not genuine when sold in the United States. The injunction was justified rather on the basis that the removal of Davidoff's codes interfered unlawfully with Davidoff's trademark rights regardless of whether the goods were originally authorized by Davidoff for sale in the United States or elsewhere.

CVS argues that neither the plain text nor the legislative history of the Lanham Act supports the district court's conclusion that a retailer may be found liable for trademark infringement for selling a genuine product in its original packaging with the registered trademark intact, simply because the mark holder's production code has been altered or removed. In support of its argument, CVS points to past failed legislative attempts seeking to amend the Lanham Act to include a prohibition on the alteration or removal of production codes.

To the extent CVS's argument rests on the failed efforts to amend the governing statutes, we reject it. The Supreme Court has cautioned that "failed legislative proposals are a particularly dangerous ground on which to rest an interpretation of a prior statute." *Central Bank of Denver, N.A. v. First Interstate Bank of Denver, N.A.*, 511 U.S. 164, 187, 114 S.Ct. 1439, 128 L.Ed.2d 119 (1994).

In our view, furthermore, the district court correctly found that Davidoff was likely to succeed on the merits in its contention that CVS's sales of its products with the UPC removed constituted trademark infringement. We recognize that, as a general rule, the Lanham Act does not impose liability for "the sale of genuine goods bearing a true mark even though the sale is not authorized by the mark owner" because such a sale does not inherently cause confusion or dilution. However, we have held that goods are not genuine if they do not conform to the trademark holder's quality control standards, or if they differ materially from the product authorized by the trademark holder for sale, *Original Appalachian Artworks, Inc. v. Granada Elecs., Inc.*, 816 F.2d 68, 73 (2d Cir.1987).

Where the alleged infringer has interfered with the trademark holder's ability to control quality, the trademark holder's claim is not defeated because of failure to show that the goods sold were defective. That is because the interference with the trademark holder's legitimate steps to control quality unreasonably subjects the trademark holder to the risk of injury to the reputation of its mark. "One of the most valuable and important protections afforded by the Lanham Act is the right to control the quality of the goods manufactured and sold under the holder's trademark." *El Greco Leather Prods. Co. v. Shoe World, Inc.*, 806 F.2d 392, 395 (2d Cir.1986). In attaching its mark to its goods over time, a holder assures consumers that the goods conform to the mark holder's quality standards. Reputation for quality, whether good or bad, becomes associated with a mark in the minds of consumers. Many consumers are willing to pay more to buy goods bearing a mark which experience has taught the consumer represents an assurance of high quality.

Davidoff asserts that its codes serve as a control of quality in two ways: (1) the codes permit the easy detection of counterfeits, and (2) they improve Davidoff's ability to identify defective products, effectuate a targeted recall, and remedy production defects. A trademark holder is entitled to an injunction against one who would subvert its quality control measures upon a showing that (i) the asserted quality control procedures are established, legitimate, substantial, and non-pretextual, (ii) it abides by these procedures, and (iii) sales of products that fail to conform to these procedures will diminish the value of the mark. *Id.* at 6. The district court found that these requirements were met. We agree.

1. Detection of Counterfeits

Because the creation of unique production codes for each package is expensive, counterfeiters often either omit the UPC altogether or use sets of identical bogus codes on numerous packages. Davidoff's evidence showed that the UPC system facilitates its ability to identify counterfeit Davidoff products by allowing it to scan for products which either lack a UPC or exhibit a UPC known to be used by counterfeiters. The district court found that Davidoff regularly trains retailers, private investigators, and U.S. Customs to use UPCs in this manner to identify and seize counterfeit goods. As a result, it determined that the first two prongs of the *Warner-Lambert* formulation were met because the procedures were "legitimate, substantial, and nonpretextual" and Davidoff "abides by these procedures." The district court concluded that the third prong was also met because the loss of these protections against counterfeits would expose Davidoff to a higher incidence of substantial sales of counterfeit goods, which are invariably non-conforming and inferior, and thus harm Davidoff's reputation and diminish the value of its trademark.

CVS argues that the presence or absence of a UPC on a particular unit of a Davidoff product does not prove the unit's authenticity or lack thereof, and as a result, cannot be considered a legitimate quality control procedure. The argument again misses the point. The code system enhances the effectiveness of Davidoff's ability to detect and prevent the sale of counterfeits. Removal of the codes makes it more difficult to detect counterfeits. Regardless of whether the presence or absence of a code on an individual unit of Davidoff product establishes the authenticity of that unit, the removal of the codes exposes Davidoff to an increased risk that any given unit sold at retail will be counterfeit. Davidoff adequately showed that the affixation of the code is a legitimate, substantial, non-pretextual procedure to detect counterfeits, that it abides by the procedure, and that removal of the codes exposes it to a realistic risk of increased incidence of counterfeits with resultant damage to the reputation of its mark. That showing was sufficient to support the court's grant of the preliminary injunction.

2. Identification of Defective Products and Effective Recall

The district court also based its finding on the role Davidoff's code system plans to help protect against quality defects in genuine Davidoff products. Embedded within the UPC numbers are several pieces of information about the product, including where and when it was produced and ingredients used. Davidoff showed that this information could assist its quality controls in several ways. When a defect in quality is discovered in a particular item, reference to the code helps identify the source of the problem and thus facilitates correction. Furthermore, when a quality problem is discovered, the code system permits easy, rapid identification of affected product already in the chain of distribution, so as to facilitate a targeted recall that will remove the defective goods from the channels of commerce while leaving unaffected goods in place.

CVS contends the code system is merely pretextual. First, CVS notes that the UPC is minimized in small print at the bottom of the box and bottle, and Davidoff's retailers and customers are not made aware of it. Second, CVS points out that Davidoff has never enacted a targeted recall of the type that the UPC system is allegedly designed to facilitate. Thus, CVS contends that Davidoff's quality control claims are pretextual and that the true purpose of the UPC system is to allow Davidoff to search out gray-market goods.

These arguments are not convincing. Whether Davidoff's retailers and consumers are aware of how to obtain information from the UPC number is of no significance. The codes are designed to assist Davidoff and its agents in quality control and the detection of counterfeits as described above. Whether consumers and/or retailers understand the codes is irrelevant to the codes' performance of their function. Moreover, if the need arose, Davidoff could seek the assistance of retailers and consumers by instructing them to look for units whose UPC numbers are associated with the problem.

The testimony of Davidoff's Vice President for Regulatory Affairs and Quality Assurance revealed that Davidoff had, on multiple occasions, relied on the UPC system to assist with quality issues, including under-filled or over-filled bottles, defective dispensers, and improper packaging. The fact that none of these instances resulted in a large-scale recall does not help CVS. To the contrary, an important benefit of the UPC system is that it permits Davidoff to keep recalls small and targeted.

Nor does the fact that the UPC system also may allow Davidoff to ensnare distributors operating outside the authorized distribution and retail network and to identify importers of gray-market goods defeat its claim. What matters is whether Davidoff's codes are a bona fide control device upon which Davidoff actually relies. If the codes served only to help Davidoff exert control over the distribution and sales network, different questions would arise. But the mere fact that the UPC system provides Davidoff additional benefits that may be unrelated to quality control does not negate its legitimate function in protecting Davidoff's marks from quality defects and counterfeiting.

CVS also argues Davidoff has not shown that any of CVS's sales involved inferior product. CVS notes that the purpose of the injunction in *Warner-Lambert* was to protect the mark holder against distribution of stale, inferior cough drops. *See Warner-Lambert,* 86 F.3d at 7–8 & n. 1. It contends no such issue is at stake here.

For at least two reasons, CVS's argument is meritless. First, such proof is unnecessary. In *El Greco,* we clearly articulated that, for purposes of analyzing trademark infringement involving interference with quality control procedures, "the actual quality of the goods is irrelevant; it is the control of quality that a trademark holder is entitled to maintain." *El Greco,* 806 F.2d at 395. The mark holder is entitled to protection against acts that subvert its ability to protect the reputation of its marks by exercising quality controls.

Second, it is untrue that none of CVS's sales of product with code removed involve inferior product. Characteristically, sellers of luxury goods, such as fragrances, go to great length and expense to present the trademarked merchandise in appealing packaging. For a seller to damage the packaging by cutting away portions or applying acids to blur markings detracts from the value of the product. The evidence showed that removal of the UPC required tampering—the cutting of packaging, the application of chemicals to wipe away the labeling, and the grinding of the bottles—all of which is visible to a consumer. It is a logical inference that consumers may regard a product whose packaging has been tampered as inferior and perhaps suspicious. Mutilation of packaging to conceal markings may lead the consumer to suspect that the item is stolen merchandise, or is defective and has been diverted from a recall, or is otherwise untrustworthy. Furthermore, fragrances are often purchased to be offered as romantic gifts. Mutilated packaging makes the item less appealing to such a purchaser, who runs the risk that the gift will be viewed by the recipient as a sketchy, cheap purchase from an illicit source or of the sort given by Tony Soprano to Carmela. In short, trademarked goods whose luxury packaging is damaged are materially different from those that are intact.

Thus, Davidoff is likely to succeed in its trademark infringement claim not only on the basis of CVS's interference with Davidoff's quality controls but because CVS is selling under Davidoff's mark goods that are materially different from Davidoff's genuine trademarked product. In the context of gray-market goods, in comparing the trademark holder's product with the gray-market product, we apply a low threshold of materiality, requiring no more than a slight difference which consumers would likely deem relevant when considering a purchase of the product. The damage to the packaging furnishes an additional basis, over and above the detriment to the mark holder's ability to detect counterfeits and to guard against defects, to justify the grant of the preliminary injunction.

II. Irreparable Injury

A plaintiff who establishes that an infringer's use of its trademark creates a likelihood of consumer confusion generally is entitled to a presumption of irreparable injury. The district court found that Davidoff had established a likelihood of confusion and was thus entitled to this presumption. CVS argues on appeal that the district court did not adduce evidence sufficient for it to conclude that consumers were likely to be confused by CVS's sale of decoded gray-market Davidoff products. We disagree. Even without the benefit of a presumption, Davidoff's evidence showed a likelihood that the absence of codes increased the risk that consumers would unwittingly purchase counterfeit or defective product because of the disabling of Davidoff's device to guard against these things.

Conclusion

The district court's order for a preliminary injunction is hereby AFFIRMED.

Notes

1. Carefully cultivated distribution is key to maintaining the prestige of a luxury brand. Gucci, Burberry, and Chanel products cannot be found in Walmart or similar "big box" stores. Similarly, Davidoff limited sales of its COOL WATER products to luxury retailers, declining to sell to defendant CVS. Nevertheless, CVS was able to obtain Davidoff product through the "gray market." Obtaining authentic product in this way is not illegal. When Costco was able to obtain authentic Calvin Klein jeans through the gray market, the trademark holder, Calvin Klein, Inc., had no cause of action against Costco and thus could not require Costco to reveal its source of the authentic but gray market product. However, where, as in the Davidoff case, counterfeit product is mixed with authentic product, Davidoff might have recourse to seek the source of all unauthorized product.

2. The fact that COOL WATER, a fragrance, is applied to the skin and thus constitutes a health risk if tampered with or if counterfeit clearly influenced Judge Leval's decision in this case. Health and safety is always a top governmental priority. UPCs are multi-digit codes that allow a manufacturer to track various production and distribution information for each unit of its product and to promptly recall products that harm consumers. Defendant CVS's tampering with Davidoff's UPC code interferes with Davidoff's ability to conduct targeted recalls of defective products so as to protect consumers from harm.

3. The Lanham Act does not impose liability for the sale of genuine goods bearing a true mark even when the goods are not authorized by the mark owner, because such a sale does not cause confusion or dilution. If CVS had not altered the UPC code (interfering with Davidoff's ability to control quality) or mixed counterfeit goods with gray market goods, Davidoff would have no cause of action against CVS. If that were the case, Davidoff's only option would be to buy from CVS all the gray market product on its shelves, an expensive solution.

4. The Court also points out that Davidoff enforced its product security by training retailers, private investigators, and Customs in using those codes to identify and seize counterfeit goods and that CVS's removal of such codes exposed Davidoff to increased risk of counterfeit.

5. In affirming the preliminary injunction, the Second Circuit found that regardless of whether units with removed UPCs were legitimate, gray market, or counterfeit goods, selling Davidoff goods without the UPCs could constitute trademark infringement. The court rejected CVS's assertion that Davidoff failed to show that any of CVS's sales involved inferior products, finding: (i) that such proof was unnecessary because Davidoff showed that removing the UPCs undermined its control of quality and (ii) that CVS's sale of COOL WATER units without UPC labels involved the sale of inferior products because removing the labels required mutilating packages and bottles in ways that would undermine consumer trust in the luxury product.

7. The International Trade Commission as a Venue

The International Trade Commission ("ITC") is an alternative option for a brand owner to seek redress against counterfeiters. Brand owners may file a complaint with the ITC under Section 337 of the Tariff Act of 1930, which prohibits "unfair acts in the importation of articles in the United States" and also prohibits "the importation of articles in the U.S. which infringe valid U.S. patents, copyrights and trademarks." Once the complaint is filed, the ITC has 30 days to decide if an investigation should begin on the basis of the complaint. The investigation begins by assignment to an administrative law judge ("ALJ"), who conducts an on-the-record evidentiary hearing where the complainants, respondents, and Commission Investigative Attorney may all present evidence. After the hearing, the ALJ will issue an initial determination subject to full ITC review. (The ITC forum is traditionally used in connection with patent infringement, trade secrets, and gray goods. However, ITC under Section 337 may also be used in trademark counterfeits claims.)

To prove a violation of Section 337, the complainant must establish four factors: (1) unfair competition or unfair act; (2) importation into the United States of the debated products; (3) the existence of a domestic industry regarding said products; and (4) that the alleged or unfair act has caused or threatens to cause injury. The "domestic industry" requirement can be satisfied by a two-pronged test: (1) economic; (2) technical, or by showing a complainant's investment in licensing. Section 337 cases take anywhere from 12 to 18 months, which is a quicker alternative to litigation.

The ITC may grant an exclusion order prohibiting importation, cease-and-desist orders, or both against the accused items. These orders are effective when issued and become final after 60 days unless the President disapproves for policy reasons. Temporary exclusion or cease-and-desist orders are other options available for 90 to 150 days if the complainant can prove irreparable harm in the absence of such relief. No monetary damages are available as remedies from the ITC. For monetary damages, the complainant must file suit in a United States District Court. The complainant is allowed to file parallel suits in the ITC and the United States District Court.

In re Certain Handbags, Luggage, Accessories and Packaging Thereof

Inv. No. 337-TA-754, USITC (Mar. 5, 2012)
(Initial and Recommended Determination)

BULLOCK, Chief Administrative Law Judge.

Complainants Louis Vuitton Malletier S.A. and Louis Vuitton U.S. Manufacturing, Inc. ("Louis Vuitton") filed a motion for summary determination of violation of section 337 and further moved for the issuance of a general exclusion order. On August 30, 2011, the Commission Investigative Staff ("Staff") filed a response in support of the motion. The undersigned denied Louis Vuitton's motion, determining it had been filed late without good cause. The Commission reversed and remanded for consideration of Louis Vuitton's summary determination motion and request for entry of a general exclusion order, or alternatively, to provide Louis Vuitton with the opportunity for an evidentiary hearing.

I. Background

Louis Vuitton filed a complaint alleging violations of section 337 based on the importation into the United States, the sale for importation and the sale within the United States after importation of certain handbags, luggage, accessories, and packaging thereof on December 3, 2010.

On December 29, 2010, the Commission voted to institute this Investigation and on January 5, 2011, the Notice of Investigation was published in the Federal Register. The Commission instituted this Investigation to determine whether there is a violation of section 337 in the importation into the United States, the sale for importation, or the sale within the United States after importation of certain handbags, luggage, accessories and packaging thereof that infringe various U.S. Trademark Registrations of Louis Vuitton and whether an industry in the United States exists as required by subsection (a)(2) of section 337.

During the course of this Investigation, all of the respondents have settled or been found in default. None of the Defaulting Respondents have contested Louis Vuitton's allegations that they have violated and continue to violate section 337. The only active party in this Investigation, other than Louis Vuitton, is Staff.

II. Violation of Section 337

A. Standard for Summary Determination

Because the Respondents remaining in this Investigation defaulted, they have waived the right to contest Louis Vuitton's allegations.

B. Trademark Infringement

Louis Vuitton asserts that handbags, luggage, accessories and packaging thereof manufactured, imported into, and/or sold in the United States by the Defaulting Respondents infringe seven of Louis Vuitton's trademarks covering the toile monogram. The toile monogram mark was created in 1896 and features an "entwined LV monogram and various design motifs displayed in a repeated fashion, at regularly spaced intervals, in horizontal lines covering the entire surface of the products on which the mark is used." The 297,594 mark covers the entire toile monogram. The components of the toile monogram are covered individually by the 1,519,828 mark (the interlocked LV), the 2,177,828 mark (the pinwheel design), the 2,773,107 mark (the diamond with inset pinwheel), and the 2,181,753 mark (the circle with inset flower design). The 1,653,663 and 1,643,625 marks relate to the yellow color of the components of the toile monogram and the deep chestnut color of the background.

Louis Vuitton divides the accused products into three groups: "the counterfeit monogram," "the knock off monogram design," and "the additional infringement." The counterfeit monogram is allegedly an exact copy of the toile monogram mark. The knock-off monogram design features "a horizontal pattern of interlocking initials and geometric shapes in repeated fashion, at regularly spaced intervals, covering the entire surface of the products." The accused products typically employ Louis Vuitton's traditional chestnut and yellow color combination. The additional infringement contains the same repeating pattern of geometric shapes as the knock-off monogram design, but also includes a slightly distorted overlapping LV.

Trademark infringement is analyzed under a two prong test: first, we look to see whether Complainants' mark merits protection, and second, whether Respondents' use of a similar mark is likely to cause consumer confusion. *Louis Vuitton Malletier v. Dooney & Bourke, Inc.*, 454 F.3d 108, 115 (2d. Cir. 2006). In support of its motion for summary determination of trademark infringement, Louis Vuitton offers declarations from (1) Eric Lichtmess, Director of Advertising for Louis Vuitton North America; (2) Kenneth Klug, Director of Criminal Enforcement, North America for Louis Vuitton Malletier S.A.; and (3) Michael J. Allan, Counsel for Louis Vuitton. Appended to each declaration are photos of authentic products, photos of the accused products, invoices, and screenshots of the websites of some of the named respondents.

1. Valid Enforceable Mark

Under the Lanham Act, federal registration is prima facie evidence of validity, ownership and the exclusive right to use a mark. Federal registration of a mark becomes conclusive evidence of validity, ownership and exclusive right to use if (1) a registered mark is used continuously for five years after registration; (2) there has been no final decision adverse to the registrant's claim of ownership; and (3) an affidavit of incontestability is submitted to the Patent and Trademark Office.

The toile monogram marks consist of seven registered trademarks that have each been on the Principal Register for more than five years. None of the toile monogram marks have been invalidated in any U.S. court or administrative proceeding. Accordingly, the undersigned finds that the asserted marks are valid and enforceable.

2. Likelihood of Confusion

a. Counterfeit Marks

Analysis of the likelihood of confusion between authentic and counterfeit marks is unnecessary because counterfeits inherently cause confusion. *Chanel, Inc. v. Gardner*, 07 Civ. 6679, 2011 U.S. Dist. LEXIS 6088, at 12 (S.D.N.Y Jan. 21, 2011); *Gucci Am. Inc. v. Duty Free Apparel, Ltd.*, 286 F. Supp. 2d 284, 287 (S.D.N.Y. 2003) ("Indeed, confusing the consumer is the whole purpose of creating counterfeit goods."). To prevail on its claim that the toile monogram marks have been counterfeited, Louis Vuitton must prove that the Defaulting Respondents sold products bearing a mark identical to, or substantially indistinguishable from, the registered marks.

Louis Vuitton and Staff contend that "there is no question" that T&T sold counterfeit products in the United States. The undersigned agrees. The evidence shows that T&T is expressly engaged in the business of selling counterfeit Louis Vuitton products on its website. Because T&T sold products bearing marks indistinguishable from Louis Vuitton's toile monogram marks, the undersigned finds that there is no genuine issue of material fact with respect to whether T&T has counterfeited Louis Vuitton's toile monogram marks.

b. Infringing Marks

The test for trademark infringement is whether the accused mark is "likely to cause confusion, or to cause mistake or to deceive." 15 U.S.C. § 1114(1). To determine whether a reasonable consumer is likely to be confused as to the source or sponsorship of the products, the Commission balances the following factors:

i. Similarity of Marks

Louis Vuitton and Staff contend that the marks on the Defaulting Respondents' products are "plainly similar in overall appearance and commercial impression" to the toile monogram marks because they feature similar geometric patterns and color combinations as the genuine products. After examining photographs of the accused and authentic products, the undersigned concludes that both the "knock-off monogram" and the "additional infringement monogram" create a commercial impression similar to that of Louis Vuitton's registered marks. The Defaulting Respondents' products all feature repeated geometric designs evocative of Louis Vuitton's toile monogram marks and use the chestnut and yellow color combination.

Though the shapes used on the accused handbags differ from those composing the toile monogram marks, exact identity is not required when goods fall within the same category of product. *Burlington Coat Factory Warehouse Corp.*, 426 F.3d at 583 n.3. The undersigned finds that the similarity in overall commercial impression between the Defaulting Respondents' products and Louis Vuitton's products weighs in favor of a finding of likelihood of confusion.

ii. Intent

The intent to derive benefit from the reputation of the asserted trademarks constitutes strong evidence of confusion. A lack of intent to derive a benefit from the reputation of a trademark, however, is largely irrelevant in determining likelihood of confusion. Louis Vuitton argues that the "overwhelming evidence of intent alone is sufficient to render a finding of trademark infringement." The undersigned disagrees. Accordingly, the undersigned accords this factor no weight in the likelihood of confusion analysis.

iii. Manner of Marketing, Degree of Care, and Post-Purchase Confusion

Louis Vuitton ignores the Restatement factor addressing the manner of marketing of the accused and authentic goods, and dismisses the factor focusing on purchaser sophistication in a single sentence, stating it is "largely irrelevant in a post-purchase confusion case." This sentence is the first and only time that Louis Vuitton addresses post-purchase confusion in its entire motion. Because the manner of marketing and degree of care factors focus on point of sale confusion, they are generally inapplicable in cases of post-purchase confusion where the actionable harm is confusion among the general public viewing the mark after purchase. Louis Vuitton, despite its burden on summary determination to demonstrate it is entitled to relief, sets forth no argument as to post-purchase confusion and offers no evidence relating to its existence. Thus, the undersigned declines to make any findings related to the existence of post-purchase confusion.

iv. Actual Confusion

Though not required to prevail on its trademark infringement claim, actual confusion is routinely considered by the Commission as proof of trademark infringement as it is "undoubtedly the best evidence of likelihood of confusion." Louis Vuitton and Staff contend that there is "substantial evidence" of actual confusion on the record. The undersigned concludes, however, that the evidence of actual confusion is unconvincing. Because actual confusion is not required for a finding of trademark infringement, the undersigned accords this factor no weight in the likelihood of confusion analysis. *Louis Vuitton Malletier S.A. v. Haute Diggity Dogg, LLC*, 507 F.3d 252, 263 (4th Cir. 2007).

v. Strength of the Mark

Strong and famous marks are afforded wider latitude of legal protection. The strength and fame of the toile monogram marks is beyond dispute. Louis Vuitton has been using the mark consistently for over a century on luxury handbags, luggage, and accessories. The undersigned finds that the strength and fame of the toile monogram marks weighs in favor of a likelihood of confusion.

vi. Conclusion on Likelihood of Confusion

Because the toile monogram marks are valid and enforceable and the Defaulting Respondents' use creates a likelihood of confusion, the undersigned finds that Louis Vuitton is entitled to summary determination of trademark infringement.

C. Importation

To prove a violation of section 337, Louis Vuitton must show by "reliable, probative and substantial evidence" that the Defaulting Respondents imported, sold for importation or sold after importation into the United States the accused products bearing the marks at issue. Louis Vuitton and Staff contend that no genuine issue of material fact exists as to whether the Defaulting Respondents imported or sold the accused products.

Louis Vuitton argues that importation has been established by the fact that the Defaulting Respondents defaulted. Indeed, "the facts alleged in the complaint will be presumed to be true with respect to the defaulting respondent." Louis Vuitton and Staff further contend that the record is replete with evidence that each of the Defaulting Respondents have sold infringing merchandise after importation. Louis Vuitton has provided invoices for, and photographs of, the infringing handbags it purchased from the Defaulting Respondents. In view of the above, the undersigned finds that Louis Vuitton has satisfied its burden of establishing importation.

D. Conclusion

For the reasons stated hereinabove, there is no genuine issue of material fact relating to any element of a section 337 violation and Louis Vuitton is entitled to summary determination as a matter of law.

RECOMMENDED DETERMINATION ON REMEDY AND BOND

I. Remedy and Bonding

A. General Exclusion Order

As detailed herein, Louis Vuitton has offered substantial evidence of a pattern of violation of Section 337 and the near impossibility of accurately identifying the sources of the infringing products. Accordingly, the undersigned finds that a general exclusion order is warranted.

Louis Vuitton and Staff assert that the prevalence of infringing merchandise in the marketplace is evidence of a pattern of trademark violation. Louis Vuitton notes that infringing products are found virtually everywhere in the United States, from Los Angeles, CA to Deny, NH. Infringing products have been found in stores, kiosks, flea markets, and trade shows in the United States, and are routinely offered for sale on major internet sites, including Overstock.com and eBay.com. The undersigned agrees that the overwhelming presence of counterfeit and infringing goods in the United States and the existence of countless sellers of the accused products support a finding of widespread violation.

The undersigned finds that a pattern of violation of section 337 is further evinced by Louis Vuitton's extensive civil and criminal enforcement activities within the United States. Continued infringement despite Louis Vuitton's diligence in policing its marks provides ample support for a finding of widespread violation.

Regarding the difficulty faced in identifying the source of counterfeit and infringing goods, Louis Vuitton argues that because many of the respondents in this Investigation defaulted and did not participate in discovery, source identification is "virtually impossible." Staff submits that this difficulty is exacerbated by the fact that companies involved in selling the infringing goods frequently change their name and corporate form. Louis Vuitton also notes that counterfeit and infringing products are routinely sold on the internet, which facilitates anonymity and allows infringers to evade U.S. law enforcement.

The undersigned agrees with Staff and Louis Vuitton that the "difficult to identify" component is satisfied. Indeed, identifying the source of the infringing products is next to impossible, as even the respondents that participated in this Investigation could not identify the manufacturers and distributers of the infringing merchandise they sold. Because a pattern of violation of section 337 is present and it is difficult to accurately identify the sources of the infringing products, the undersigned recommends that the Commission issue a general exclusion order.

B. Bond During Presidential Review

Since none of the Defaulting Respondents participated in discovery, reliable price information is not available. In similar circumstances, the Commission has set the bond at 100% of the entered value of the imported infringing products. The undersigned finds that there is insufficient reliable price information to set a bond based on price differential and recommends a bond of 100% during the Presidential review period.

SO ORDERED.

8. Third-Party Liability: Indirect Infringement and Counterfeiting

Although deep in the chapter, this is the meat of a brand owner's remedies. Frequently the counterfeiter has minimal or little money to pay a judgment. But that does not mean the litigation is futile. This is where third-party/contributory liability comes into play. A trademark or copyright holder may pursue an infringement action against a third party such as auction sites, banks, credit card companies, internet registrars, payment processors, web hosts, search engine optimizers, flea market owners, landlords, or online marketplace owners that rent space to counterfeiters, and Internet Service Providers ("ISPs") who indirectly aid in violating the Lanham Act or Copyright Act under theories of vicarious or contributory liability. Such third parties almost always have greater financial resources. There is no specific language in the Copyright or Lanham Acts allowing a course of action for contributory or vicarious liability. However, the Supreme Court in *Inwood Laboratories, Inc. v. Ives Laboratories, Inc.*, 456 U.S. 844 (1982), recognized that liability for trademark infringement extends beyond those who mislabel goods with another's mark.

Don't confuse contributory and vicarious liability. Both are secondary liability (third-party liability) in that the defendant is not the actual counterfeiter, but is helping the actual counterfeiter in some way that opens them up to liability. Contributory liability is when the defendant does not control the infringer but knowingly assists or somehow provides the means for the infringement. Vicarious liability is when the direct infringer is an agent or business partner of the defendant and a plaintiff needs to prove such a relationship exists.

a. Suits Against Landlords/Flea Market Owners

Landlords and flea market owners may be held contributorily liable for infringement that occurs on their real property if first placed on notice. If the landlord fails to take action to correct it, the landlord can be held liable under the *Inwood Laboratories* test. However, if the landlord does not have knowledge of infringement and therefore does not investigate the alleged actions, the landlord may not be liable for infringement because he lacks the knowledge element required for contributory infringement. A brand owner should not bother to bring an action for contributory infringement if the target is not on notice. Once on notice, make another buy confirming the illegal activity continues and file the action.

Coach, Inc. v. Goodfellow

717 F.3d 498 (6th Cir. 2013)

McKEAGUE, Circuit Judge.

Opinion

This case presents a question the Sixth Circuit has not directly addressed: Can a flea market operator be held contributorially liable for trademark infringement by vendors?

Plaintiffs brought suit under the Lanham Act, alleging a Memphis flea market operator is liable for sales of counterfeit products at his flea market. The district court granted plaintiffs' motion for summary judgment on liability, entered judgment on the jury's damages verdict of $5,040,000, and awarded attorney's fees and costs to plaintiffs in the amount of $186,666.61. Defendant argues on appeal that the Lanham Act does not provide for contributory liability for trademark infringement by third persons and that this is not an "exceptional case" warranting attorney's fees.

I. Background

Plaintiffs Coach, Inc. and Coach Services, Inc. (hereinafter "Coach") are in the business of designing, marketing, and selling products such as handbags, briefcases, leather goods, eyewear, and footwear. Coach owns an extensive portfolio of trademarks. Defendant Frederick Goodfellow, d/b/a The Southwest Flea Market ("Goodfellow"), at all times relevant owned and operated a flea market as a sole proprietorship in Memphis. Goodfellow controlled, managed, and oversaw the day-to-day operations of the flea market. The flea market rented seventy-five to one hundred booths to vendors at the rate of $15 per day Thursday through Sunday each week. The flea market also rented storage containers to vendors for storage of their goods.

On January 15, 2010, Coach sent a letter to Goodfellow, notifying him of counterfeit sales of Coach products at the flea market, advising him of the potential violation of both federal and state laws, and demanding that all sales of counterfeit Coach products cease. On March 26, 2010, Goodfellow received another letter, this time from the Shelby County Office of the District Attorney General. The letter notified Goodfellow that counterfeit sales of Coach items were continuing at the flea market. The letter also stated that Goodfellow was in willful disregard of the law. On April 23, 2010, law enforcement officers raided the flea market and seized counterfeit Coach products.

In June 2010, Coach filed this action against Goodfellow and the flea market demanding the sale of counterfeit Coach products be stopped. After a Coach investigator discovered continuing sales of counterfeit Coach products in February 2011, law enforcement officers conducted another raid on March 4, 2011. Yet another raid was conducted on June 23, 2011, this time involving approximately 150 local, state and federal officers and various Coach investigators. More than 4,600 counterfeit Coach products were seized and the flea market was permanently shut down.

Goodfellow admitted knowing that vendors continued to sell counterfeit Coach products at the flea market between the time he received the first letter from Coach in January 2010 and the time he received the letter from the District Attorney in March 2010. Goodfellow also admitted that he was aware of the multiple raids, and he knew that arrests were made during these raids. The flea market's employees never received any training to identify counterfeit goods. Johnson did not remember any vendors having been expelled or rejected for selling counterfeit products. Neither Goodfellow nor Johnson inspected vendors' goods or questioned them as to whether their goods were counterfeit or authentic. The flea market did not have a license to sell Coach products and neither Goodfellow nor Johnson asked vendors if they had licenses. Nor were vendors required to sign a statement agreeing, as a condition of renting a booth, that they would not sell counterfeit products.

There was some evidence of remedial measures. Goodfellow distributed pamphlets to vendors, posted copies of a "counterfeit is prohibit" sign, and called a meeting with vendors to address the selling of counterfeit goods. However, the pamphlets were distributed randomly and incompletely; the signs that were posted were actually intended to address a growing problem with counterfeit currency, not counterfeit products; attendance at the meeting with vendors, scheduled on a day when the flea market was not open for business, was voluntary and attended only by some vendors; and communication was frustrated by language differences, as many of the vendors were from West Africa.

In the complaint, Coach alleged that Goodfellow was liable for the sale of counterfeit products and infringement of Coach's trademarks. Coach filed a motion for partial summary judgment on the issue of liability on October 11, 2011. Goodfellow failed to respond to Coach's motion. On February 21, 2012, the district court, without conducting a hearing, granted partial summary judgment to Coach on the issue of contributory liability. Despite Goodfellow's failure to respond, the court viewed the record in the light most favorable to him as non-movant, but still held that Goodfellow was contributorially liable for sales of counterfeit Coach products by his vendors.

On March 1, 2012, Goodfellow moved to set aside the order granting partial summary judgment. Goodfellow asked for relief from judgment because notice of the motion for partial summary judgment had been misplaced by his attorney and because Coach's counsel had filed notice of intent to strike the motion for partial summary judgment on January 20, 2012. While setting forth these grounds for his failure to timely respond, Goodfellow's motion offered no argument on the merits. The district court denied Goodfellow's motion. Goodfellow's liability having thus been established, the district court conducted a jury trial to determine Coach's damages. On March 20, 2012, Coach was awarded $5,040,000 in damages. The jury found that Goodfellow willfully infringed Coach's trademarks. The jury awarded $240,000 per mark for twenty-one total infringed marks. In granting Coach's ensuing motion for attorney's fees, awarding Coach $186,666.61 in fees and costs, the district court noted that the Lanham Act allows for award of attorney's fees to the prevailing party in exceptional cases. The court determined the case was exceptional because Goodfellow failed to litigate the liability issue at all and because the jury found his infringement to be willful.

II. Analysis

A. Secondary Liability for Trademark Infringement

Goodfellow appears to frame the claim of error on appeal as a question of law, contending the Lanham Act does not provide for contributory liability for trademark infringement by third persons. In substance, however, his claim is in the nature of a challenge to the sufficiency of the evidence to support liability in this case.

Ordinarily, we will not address issues raised for the first time on appeal. Inasmuch as adjudication by default is disfavored and this case affords opportunity to provide guidance on contributory trademark infringement, we take up the merits of the district court's ruling notwithstanding Goodfellow's default below.

In relevant part, the Lanham Act addresses trademark counterfeiting and infringement as follows:

> Any person who shall, without the consent of the registrant . . . use in commerce any reproduction, counterfeit, copy, or colorable imitation of a registered mark in connection with the sale, offering for sale, distribution, or advertising of any goods or services on or in connection with which such use is likely to cause confusion, or to cause mistake, or to deceive . . . shall be liable in a civil action by the registrant for the remedies hereinafter provided.15 U.S.C. § 1114(1)(a).

A party proves trademark infringement by showing (1) that it owns a trademark, (2) that the infringer used the mark in commerce without authorization, and (3) that the use of the alleged infringing trademark "is likely to cause confusion among consumers regarding the origin of the goods offered by the parties." There is no dispute in this case as to whether infringement occurred. The legal question presented is whether Goodfellow is properly held liable for the infringing acts of others.

Goodfellow contends the district erred by holding him liable for trademark infringement because there was no showing that he and the infringing vendors were in a partnership relationship or had authority to bind one another or exercised joint ownership or control. On this point Goodfellow is right: the record does not show that he and the vendors were in such a relationship as would justify recognition of *vicarious* liability for infringement. Vicarious liability is a species of secondary liability, but not the one applied here by the district court. Rather, the district court held Goodfellow was subject to *contributory* liability for vendors' trademark infringements.

This form of secondary liability was first recognized by the Supreme Court in *Inwood Laboratories, Inc. v. Ives Laboratories, Inc.*, 456 U.S. 844, 102 S.Ct. 2182, 72 L. Ed.2d 606 (1982). The Court determined that liability under the Lanham Act may be imposed on those who facilitate trademark infringement, stating that where a "distributor intentionally induces another to infringe a trademark, or if it continues to supply its product to one whom it knows or has reason to know is engaging in trademark infringement, [it] is contributorially responsible for any harm done as a result of the deceit." Although the Lanham Act refers only to direct trademark infringers, *Inwood* established that liability may also be imposed on those who facilitate the infringement.

The teaching of *Inwood* has been applied to flea market operators, rendering them subject to liability for trademark infringement by vendors. In *Hard Rock Cafe Licensing Corp. v. Concession Services, Inc.*, 955 F.2d 1143 (7th Cir.1992), the Seventh Circuit held that a flea market operator can be liable for trademark violations by its vendors if it knew or had reason to know of them. *Id.* at 1149. Although there was no proof that the flea market operator in *Hard Rock Cafe* had actual knowledge that its vendors were selling counterfeit products, the court held that knowledge could be established and contributory liability could be imposed if the flea market operator was shown to be "willfully blind" to ongoing violations. *Id.* The court defined as willfully blind one who suspects wrongdoing and deliberately fails to investigate. *Id.* Thus, per *Hard Rock Cafe*, a flea market operator who deliberately fails to investigate suspected infringing activity by vendors and facilitates ongoing infringement by permitting such vendors to use flea market resources may be subject to contributory liability.

Similarly, in *Fonovisa, Inc. v. Cherry Auction, Inc.*, 76 F.3d 259 (9th Cir.1996), a flea market operator knew that its vendors were selling counterfeit music recordings both before and after law enforcement officers raided the flea market and seized counterfeit recordings. *Id.* at 261. The Ninth Circuit adopted *Hard Rock Cafe*'s application of *Inwood*, holding that the flea market operator was liable for contributory trademark infringement because it knew or had reason to know of the infringing activity. *Id.* at 264–65 (observing that a flea market operator "can not disregard its vendors' blatant trademark infringements with impunity"). Other circuits have also applied this reasoning to internet marketplaces, concluding that the marketplace may be liable for contributory trademark infringement if it knew or had reason to know identified vendors were engaging in infringing activity. *See Rosetta Stone*, 676 F.3d at 163–65; *Tiffany (NJ), Inc. v. eBay, Inc.*, 600 F.3d 93, 105–10 (2d Cir.2010).

Here, Goodfellow, provider of a product or service, i.e., rental booths and storage units for vendors, continued to supply these resources to vendors who he knew or had reason to know were engaging in trademark infringement. Goodfellow's actual knowledge of the counterfeit sales is established by several items. He received a letter from Coach on January 15, 2010, which he signed, advising that counterfeit Coach products were being sold at Goodfellow's flea market. Goodfellow also received a second letter, this time from the district attorney, dated March 26, 2010, again stating that counterfeit Coach products were being sold at his flea market and advising Goodfellow that he was willfully violating state and federal law. Goodfellow received notice of the lawsuit filed by Coach on June 6, 2010, informing him of his potential liability for the counterfeit Coach products. Moreover, law enforcement officers raided the flea market on April 23, 2010, March 4, 2011, and June 23, 2011. Some of the raids were conducted after Coach filed this lawsuit against Goodfellow. Because Goodfellow continued to rent spaces at his flea market to vendors that he knew, or should have known, were engaging in infringing activity, and because these facts are sufficient to support a finding of contributory liability under *Inwood* as applied in other circuits, we find no error in the district court's ruling.

Goodfellow does not dispute that he was on notice of infringing activity, but maintains he responded reasonably. He contends that his remedial measures were analogous to those taken by the defendant in *Tiffany*, where the Second Circuit affirmed judgment in favor of the defendant, eBay. The *Tiffany* court found that eBay was not liable for trademark infringement for counterfeit merchandise sold on eBay's website because eBay promptly removed all listings that Tiffany challenged as counterfeit and spent millions of dollars taking affirmative steps toward the removal and monitoring of counterfeit Tiffany merchandise. *Tiffany*, 600 F.3d at 103. These remedial steps went well beyond those taken by Goodfellow. Additionally, the court in *Tiffany* found that eBay was not liable for contributory trademark infringement because eBay only had general knowledge of counterfeit sales through its website, holding that contemporary knowledge of particular listings would have been necessary to support contributory liability. *Id.* at 107–08. The present facts are distinguishable from those presented in *Tiffany* in that Goodfellow had actual knowledge that the infringing activity was occurring at his flea market over a lengthy period of time and even knew that particular vendors were selling counterfeit Coach products. Yet, throughout this sustained period of time, Goodfellow failed to deny access to offending vendors or take other reasonable measures to prevent use of flea market resources for unlawful purposes, and failed even to undertake a reasonable investigation.

Furthermore, some evidence of Goodfellow's remedial measures was presented only in the jury trial on damages, not in opposition to the motion for partial summary judgment. Because Goodfellow is bound by the record developed at the time of the summary judgment ruling, evidence of remedial measures presented in the damages trial is not properly considered on appeal. Yet, even if the full factual record were considered, Goodfellow's efforts do not compare with those taken by eBay in *Tiffany*. *See also Coach, Inc. v. Gata Corp.*, 2011 WL 2358671 (D.N.H. June 9, 2011) (distinguishing *Tiffany*, awarding summary judgment to Coach, and imposing contributory liability on defendant flea market operator under facts nearly identical to those presented here).

Although Goodfellow attempted to notify vendors that selling counterfeit goods was prohibited through the distribution of pamphlets and by holding a voluntary meeting with some vendors, he admitted knowing that vendors continued to sell products that Coach charged were counterfeit both before and after Coach filed this lawsuit. Goodfellow claims he thought the Coach products offered for sale in plain sight were authentic. Yet, he admitted that the flea market did not have a license to sell Coach products and he never inquired whether the vendors' goods were licensed or authentic despite receiving actual notice of sales of counterfeit products. Additionally, Goodfellow rented spaces at his flea market to vendors he knew, or should have known, were engaging in infringing activity.

Thus, even if we consider all the evidence of remedial measures, it fails to undermine the district court's conclusion that Goodfellow engaged in "ostrich-like practices." Goodfellow continued to supply flea market resources to vendors with knowledge of and willful blindness toward ongoing infringing activities, thereby facilitating continued infringing activity. The facts are sufficient to support a finding of contributory liability under the prevailing standards established by the Supreme Court as applied in other circuits, authorities which we find persuasive.

B. Attorney's Fees

The district court awarded attorney's fees and costs to Coach in the amount of \$186,666.61. The court noted that the Lanham Act allows award of attorney's fees to the prevailing party in exceptional cases.

Goodfellow insists this is not an exceptional case. He does not specifically challenge the amount of the award, but contends that no award is warranted. He maintains he acted in good faith and that the law under which he is held liable was not clearly established at the time of the infringing activities.

The district court held this case was exceptional because Goodfellow knew or had reason to know that his vendors were engaging in infringing activity, he failed to litigate the issue of liability, and the jury found his conduct willful. Goodfellow had actual notice of ongoing infringing activity. Despite such knowledge, Goodfellow continued to facilitate the infringing activity by providing space and facilities at his flea market to infringing vendors. The district court was well within its discretion in finding that Goodfellow's intentional, deliberate, or willful ignorance of actual notice of infringing activity made out an "exceptional case," permitting award of attorney's fees to the prevailing party under the Lanham Act.

III. Conclusion

The district court did not err in ruling that Goodfellow was contributorially liable for vendors' infringements. Nor did the district court abuse its discretion in holding that Goodfellow's actions were willful, constituting an exceptional case warranting an award of attorney's fees to Coach. Accordingly, the judgment of the district court is **AFFIRMED.**

Notes

1. The flea market case above opens the door to applying to well-settled trademark infringement secondary liability concepts for copyright infringement, an outgrowth of the dance hall cases and agency principles of *respondeat superior.* Flea

market owners can only be found vicariously liable for trademark infringement where their owners have the right and ability to supervise the infringing activity and have a direct financial interest in such activity. However, a flea market operator may be found liable for contributory liability where it knew or had reason to know of the infringing activity. That knowledge can be established by fashion brands by routinely notifying flea market owners of the identities of vendors selling counterfeits at their markets after raids or investigations. This requires that brands conduct follow-up visits to those markets to confirm compliance.

2. In September 2019, Michael Kors filed suit against a flea market operator in New Haven, Connecticut. Check the docket and see where this case goes.

Third-party liability can also be extended to credit card processing companies enabling online money transfers to counterfeiters from buyers.

Gucci America, Inc. v. Frontline Processing Corp.

721 F. Supp. 2d 228 (S.D.N.Y. 2010)

BAER, JR., District Judge.

Opinion & Order

Gucci America, Inc. is a well-known manufacturer of luxury goods. The company holds a variety of trademarks in its products and designs, and invests substantial capital in ensuring that the marks maintain a reputation for quality. Seeking to capitalize on the popularity of Gucci products, certain internet merchants have sold "replica," counterfeit Gucci products that infringe Gucci marks at significantly lower prices and of lower quality. Gucci recently concluded a successful litigation against one such merchant that operated a website called TheBagAddiction.com. The owners of the website admitted that they sold counterfeit Gucci products to customers across the country through the website. In its continuing effort to root out and prevent infringement of its trademarks, Gucci now brings suit against three entities, which while a step down in the "food chain," allegedly ensured that TheBagAddiction.com was able to sell these counterfeit products. These defendants allegedly established the credit card processing services used to complete the online sales of fake Gucci items. The three defendants have jointly moved to dismiss the case for lack of personal jurisdiction and for failure to state a claim.

I. Background

Gucci America, Inc. ("Plaintiff" or "Gucci") is a New York company, with its principal place of business in New York City. It is the sole, exclusive distributor in the United States of items labeled with the "Gucci Marks," including leather goods, jewelry, home products, and clothing. The Gucci Marks are a series of marks—the Gucci name, the Gucci crest, the "non-interlocking GG monogram," the "repeating GG design," etc.—registered by Gucci with the United States Patent and Trademark Office. According to Plaintiff, the marks are well-known and recognizable in the United States and around the world. Gucci promotes the marks widely, and relies on "strict quality control standards" for its products" and as a result has achieved and retains a reputation for quality. The company spends hundreds of millions of dollars to advertise and promote its products and marks, and enjoys billions in sales of the Gucci products.

This case arises out of Plaintiff's attempts to eliminate online sales of counterfeit products and the unauthorized use of the Gucci Marks. In *Gucci America, Inc., et al. v. Laurette Company, Inc., et al.*, No. 08 Civ. 5065(LAK), Gucci brought suit in this District against certain defendants, collectively known as the "Laurette Counterfeiters" or "Laurette," for the sale of counterfeit Gucci products on a website called "TheBagAddiction.com." Through this website, the Laurette Counterfeiters sold a variety of "replica" luxury products, and, in particular, sold replica Gucci products under the Gucci name, with the various Gucci registered trademarks, and at fractions of the retail price for an authentic version. The website itself was replete with the use of the Gucci name and trademarks. According to Plaintiff, the Laurette Counterfeiters "openly boasted" about the sale of counterfeit products, because the website expressly noted that the products were not authentic but rather "mirror images" of Gucci products. Though they are inferior in quality and workmanship, they appear to the naked eye to be similar if not identical to Gucci products. Eventually, Laurette consented to the entry of judgment and admitted liability for counterfeiting activities.

Plaintiff now seeks to bring the present action against three companies, Durango Merchant Services, Frontline Processing Corporation, and Woodforest National Bank, who allegedly assisted the Laurette Counterfeiters and other similar website operators. Durango Merchant Services ("Durango") is a Wyoming corporation with its business address in Durango, Colorado. According to Defendants, Durango has only five employees, and has no offices, no employees, and no property located in New York. Frontline Processing Corporation ("Frontline") is a Nevada corporation with its principal place of business in Bozeman, Montana. Similar to Durango, Defendants claim that Frontline has no office, no employees, and no property in New York. A small minority of the businesses it has worked with maintain addresses in New York. Finally, Woodforest National Bank ("Woodforest") is a bank organized under the laws of the United States, with its business address in The Woodlands, Texas. Like the other two defendants, Woodforest claims to have no New York offices or property in New York, while a small percentage of its business comes from New York-based clients. Gucci alleges that Woodforest provides some of its services through an affiliate with an office in New York, Merchants' Choice Card Services Corporation ("MCCS"), though Woodforest disputes the nature of the relationship.

A summary explanation of the credit card transaction process is necessary. A customer will initiate the process when he or she purchases a product from the merchant with a credit card. Once the credit card information is "swiped" on a terminal, or entered on a website, the merchant terminal transmits an authorization request to the merchant's "acquiring bank," who in this case was Frontline and

Woodforest. The acquiring bank sends the credit card request through an electronic network to the cardholder's issuing bank. Based on the cardholder's credit limit or other factors, the issuing bank will send a message back through the network to the acquiring bank, who forwards it back to the merchant, which states that the merchant should either approve or decline the transaction. If approved, the merchant will complete the transaction and the acquiring bank will credit the merchant's account with the appropriate amount of funds. This entire process typically takes a matter of seconds. Some days to months after the sale is completed, the acquiring bank will submit the transaction information to the issuing bank, which will seek payment from the cardholder and settle with the acquiring bank.

Gucci's overarching theory of the case is that Durango arranged for web companies that sold counterfeit Gucci products to establish credit card processing services with companies like Woodforest and Frontline. These processors then provided the credit card services necessary for the sale of the faux Gucci items. The complaint focuses largely on the allegedly representative conduct of Defendants with the Laurette Counterfeiters. According to Plaintiff, Durango acted as an agent for the defendant credit card processing companies to locate potential customers, including the Laurette Counterfeiters and other similar infringing online operations. Durango collected a referral fee for bringing together these online merchants with banks and companies like Frontline and Woodforest. Durango's website billed the company as specializing in services for "High Risk Merchant Accounts," including those who sell "Replica Products." Gucci alleges that the Laurette Counterfeiters entered into a "Merchant Service Agreement" with Durango through one of its sales representatives, Nathan Counley and, through this relationship, "procur[ed] merchant accounts with credit card processing agencies, including Defendants Frontline and Woodforest." Gucci asserts that, through email and other documents, Durango was aware that TheBagAddiction.com sold counterfeit "replica" Gucci products and nevertheless chose to do business with them.

Frontline began to provide credit card processing services to TheBagAddiction.com in September 2006. The relationship was precipitated by an application completed by the Laurette Counterfeiters through the assistance of Durango; Counley was listed as a sales agent for Frontline on the application. Once the service was established, Frontline processed Visa, MasterCard, Discover, and American Express credit card transactions for goods sold by the Laurette Counterfeiters. Frontline deducted a fee, or discount rate, based on the transactions it processed. As part of its services, Frontline would investigate "chargebacks"—a credit card charge that is disputed by a customer—made in connection with orders from the website. When faced with a chargeback, Laurette allegedly gave detailed documentation to Frontline, including a description of the item purchased and the price that was paid. Since Frontline credited Laurette's account after a credit card transaction was authorized, but before it received any final payment from the issuing bank, it required Laurette to keep a "reserve account" for chargebacks. The account allegedly totaled in excess $40,000 by the time it was shut down in June 2008. Allegedly funded "solely through the proceeds from counterfeit goods sold on" the website, Frontline supposedly took possession of these funds when TheBagAddiction.com was shut down. Gucci also alleges that Frontline charged a higher transaction fee, or discount rate, for processing credit cards for high risk merchants, such as "replica" merchants like the Laurette Counterfeiters. Frontline was the only credit card processor used by the Laurette Counterfeiters for TheBagAddiction.com from September 2006 to November 2006, and Laurette continued to use Frontline until they were shut down in June 2008. According to Plaintiff, Laurette's sales of counterfeit Gucci products from September 2006 to June 2008 totaled in excess of $500,000.

Laurette allegedly sought to do business with Woodforest because of the high discount rate it was charged by Frontline. The Laurette Counterfeiters applied for an account with Woodforest in November 2006; again Counley from Durango was listed on the application, this time as Woodforest's sales agent. As part of the process, Woodforest employees reviewed the application and completed an "Internet Merchant Review Checklist." The checklist required the employee to review the website and confirm that it contained a "complete description" of the goods offered, and pages of the website were printed in support of this review. Gucci alleges that Woodforest, through its employee, printed a number of pages from TheBagAddiction.com that displayed the Gucci Marks and counterfeit Gucci products. A second-level review of the website was allegedly performed after Woodforest accepted the application. An employee or agent would complete a purchase on the website and request a refund; this process was repeated regularly over the relationship with the online merchant. Woodforest began processing credit card transactions—Visa, MasterCard and American Express—for the Laurette Counterfeiters in November 2006, and continued to provide these services until June 2008 when the website was shut down. Like Frontline, Woodforest also investigated chargebacks and received relevant documentation from Laurette, though Gucci claims that MCCS was responsible for processing the chargeback requests. Also akin to Frontline, Woodforest charged a higher discount rate for replica merchants like Laurette. Woodforest allegedly processed over $1 million in transactions for counterfeit items, and made over $30,000 from the fees on these transactions.

Gucci maintains that the credit card processing services established by these three defendants was essential to the Laurette Counterfeiters' sale of counterfeit Gucci products. Defendants jointly moved to dismiss these claims based on a purported lack of personal jurisdiction, and because Plaintiff has failed to state a claim.

II. Discussion

A. Personal Jurisdiction

1. Legal Standard

On a motion to dismiss for lack of personal jurisdiction, the plaintiff bears the burden of showing that the court has jurisdiction over the defendants. Personal jurisdiction is necessarily a fact-sensitive inquiry dependent on the particulars of the case before the court.

2. The Defendants Are Amenable To Jurisdiction Under New York Law

New York's long-arm jurisdiction statute provides for service of process for defendants based on both general and specific jurisdictional grounds. The jurisdictional facts presently before this Court indicate that jurisdiction is clearly available for a tortious act committed outside the state that causes injury within the state. Gucci alleges that each of the defendants is liable, either directly, as a contributor, or vicariously, for the trademark infringement and counterfeiting committed by the Laurette Counterfeiters and other similar online enterprises. A plaintiff "need not actually prove that defendant committed a tort" to satisfy the first element of § 302(a)(3)(ii), "but rather need only state a colorable cause of action." Trademark infringement is a tort for jurisdictional purposes, and the situs of this tort is considered to be where the website, or servers which maintain the website, are located. The present factual allegations indicate that TheBagAddiction.com website was operated from outside of New York, specifically in California. Since I find that Gucci has stated a plausible claim for contributory liability for trademark infringement, *see infra*, the first and second elements have been satisfied.

The pleadings are sufficient to demonstrate injury to a person or property within New York. Gucci is a New York corporation with its principal place of business in New York City. It claims injury based on the confusion and lost sales created in the market by the counterfeits, as well as the harm from the diminished reputation for the marks due to the inferior quality of the counterfeits. Gucci specifically alleges sales of counterfeit goods to New York-based consumers. Injury within a state "includes harm to a business in the New York market in the form of lost sales or customers." Moreover, courts in this district have specifically held that an allegation of trademark infringement by a New York-based corporate plaintiff that alleges harm in New York is sufficient to satisfy this element.

Fourth, it is clear that each of the three defendants derive substantial revenue from interstate or international commerce. Gucci generally alleges that Durango, Woodforest, and Nationwide hold themselves out as national, if not international, companies that derive substantial revenue from interstate or international commerce. Using the Defendants' relationship with Laurette as an example, they note that over 15,000 orders totaling more than $2 million was processed during the period in which they were serviced by Frontline and Woodforest, as established by Durango. The allegations suffice to show that none of these businesses operate on a purely local basis and derive sufficient revenue in interstate commerce to satisfy jurisdiction.

The trickiest element, and primary source of contention with regard to jurisdiction, is whether or not each or any of the defendants expected or reasonably should have expected consequences in New York. The test for whether a defendant expects or should reasonably expect his act to have consequences within the State is an objective one. This foreseeability requirement "relates to the forum consequences generally and not to the specific event which produced injury within the state." In other words, it "requires that a defendant foresee that its tortious act will have some consequences in New York, although not necessarily the exact consequences that occurred." The purpose of this element is to "ensure some link between a defendant and New York State to make it reasonable to require a defendant to come to New York to answer for tortious conduct committed elsewhere."

Gucci has pled sufficient facts to demonstrate that each of the three defendants expected or should have expected that their business relationships with companies like Laurette, who sold counterfeit goods over the internet without restriction to any particular state, would have consequences in New York. Durango bills itself as a nationwide and international service that connects merchants, particularly high-risk online merchants, to credit card processing entities like Woodforest and Frontline. Moreover, Durango concededly has clients in New York, albeit a small number of them. Gucci has pled sufficient concrete facts to indicate that Durango knew that its services were utilized in New York. Here, Durango, as a national service that works with companies that transact goods over the internet to states including New York, should have been aware that it could be hauled into court in this forum based on their alleged contributory liability for their clients' infringing conduct.

Gucci's allegations with regard to Woodforest and Frontline likewise establish that these two entities expected or should have expected consequences in this forum. Both companies hold themselves out as nationwide operations and both have clients in New York (although they stress that these clients are few in number). In addition, both maintain relationships with New York-based organizations as part of their credit card processing businesses.

3. Jurisdiction Satisfies Constitutional Due Process

(a) Minimum Contacts & Purposeful Availment

Specific jurisdiction is determined by first asking if the claim arises out of or relates to defendants' contacts with the state, and then showing defendants purposefully availed itself of the privilege of doing business in the forum so that defendant could reasonably foresee being haled into the forum's courts. Gucci's allegations are sufficient to demonstrate that all defendants have both minimum contacts with New York and purposefully availed themselves of the privileges of doing business in this state.

(b) Reasonableness

To satisfy due process, Gucci must also demonstrate that the assertion of jurisdiction "comports with traditional notions of fair play and substantial justice—that is, whether it is reasonable under the circumstances of the case." Five factors are considered to determine the reasonableness of jurisdiction: (1) the burden of jurisdiction on the defendant; (2) the interest of the forum in adjudicating the case; (3) the plaintiff's interest in convenient and effective relief; (4) the judicial system's interest in obtaining the most efficient resolution of the dispute; and (5) the shared interests of the states in furthering social substantive policies. The facts as alleged here indicate that jurisdiction would be reasonable in this case.

B. Trademark Infringement Liability

1. Standard of review

To survive a motion to dismiss, a plaintiff must "plead enough facts to state a claim to relief that is plausible on its face."

Gucci offers three theories of liability to hold Defendants accountable for the infringing sales of counterfeit products by others: direct, vicarious, and contributory liability.

2. Direct and Vicarious Liability

Gucci has not put forth sufficient factual allegations to support trademark infringement claims based on either direct or vicarious theories of liability. Direct liability for trademark infringement requires a valid mark entitled to protection under the Lanham Act, and that the defendant used the mark in commerce in connection with the sale or advertising of goods or services, without the plaintiff's consent. In addition, Plaintiff must show that the Defendant's use of the mark is likely to cause confusion. The problem for Gucci is that there is no indication that any of the defendants actually "used the mark in commerce." Knowledge alone of another party's sale of counterfeit or infringing items is insufficient to support direct liability, and there are otherwise no factual allegations that Durango, Woodforest, or Frontline themselves advertised or sold infringing goods.

Gucci's allegations are also unable to support a claim for vicarious liability. Vicarious trademark infringement, a theory of liability considered elsewhere but not yet the subject of a decision by this Circuit, "requires a finding that the defendant and the infringer have an apparent or actual partnership, have authority to bind one another in transactions with third parties or exercise joint ownership or control over the infringing product." *Hard Rock Cafe Licensing Corp. v. Concession Servs., Inc.*, 955 F.2d 1143, 1150 (7th Cir.1992). While Defendants may have sufficient control over the sale of counterfeit goods to support contributory liability, the facts alleged do not support an inference that they had the type of control over a company like Laurette as a whole, i.e. akin to joint ownership, necessary for vicarious liability.

3. Contributory Liability

Gucci's only plausible theory of liability here is contributory trademark infringement. The Supreme Court has determined that liability can extend "beyond those who actually mislabel goods with the mark of another." *Inwood Lab., Inc. v. Ives Lab., Inc.*, 456 U.S. 844, 853, 102 S.Ct. 2182, 72 L.Ed.2d 606 (1982). Gucci can proceed with its action against Defendants if it can show that they (1) intentionally induced the website to infringe through the sale of counterfeit goods or (2) knowingly supplied services to websites and had sufficient control over infringing activity to merit liability.

(a) Intentional Inducement

A party can be held liable for trademark infringement if it intentionally induces another to engage in trademark infringement. With regards to the role played by Durango, Plaintiff's inducement theory is supported by sufficient factual allegations. Durango's website reaches out to "high risk merchant accounts," including those who sell "replica products." The website further boasts that 95% of merchant accounts are approved and that Durango "specialize[s] in hard to acquire accounts." Similar to the companies that promise the extension of credit or loans to those who are rejected by traditional lending institutions for having bad credit, Gucci's complaint suggests that Durango bills itself as a company that sets up a certain quality of business with credit card processing services that accept these "high risk" clients. These allegations can fairly be construed as Durango's attempt to induce less savory businesses, like those who sell counterfeit "replicas" of luxury goods. Moreover, Gucci alleges that Durango's sales representative, Nathan Counley, specifically discussed Laurette's difficulty in finding a credit card processor because they were "replica" merchants, which Gucci argues was synonymous on the internet for a counterfeiter. Durango "communicated an inducing message to [its] . . . users," and while there is of yet no evidence that they expressly sought out counterfeiters, Gucci has pled sufficient facts to infer that Durango crafted "advertisement[s] or solicitation[s] that broadcast a message designed to stimulate others to commit violations." Finally, Gucci alleges that Counley and Durango helped the Laurette Counterfeiters set up a system to avoid chargebacks, which required customers to check a box that said "I understand these are replicas." This suggests "affirmative steps taken to foster infringement" or "that Defendants promoted their payment system as a means to infringe."

On the other hand, Gucci has failed to plausibly support a claim that either Woodforest or Frontline intentionally induced Laurette to sell counterfeit products. Durango, not Woodforest or Frontline, helped set up the Laurette Counterfeiters with credit card processing services. Though both companies allegedly advertised for high risk merchants, they did not bring Laurette to the table the way Durango allegedly did. Gucci notes that they both charged higher fees for processing high risk merchants, and that Frontline reviewed the language of the aforementioned acknowledgement of receipt of a replica product. These claims, however, are not enough to suggest that either Woodforest or Frontline took the affirmative steps necessary to foster infringement.

(b) Control and knowledge

Even if a defendant does not seek out and intentionally induce a third-party to commit trademark infringement, it may still be held liable for the infringement if it supplied services with knowledge or by willfully shutting its eyes to the infringing conduct, while it had sufficient control over the instrumentality used to infringe.

Here, Gucci has made substantial factual allegations about the knowledge of all three defendants. These allegations at the very least provide a strong inference that each knew that Laurette traded in counterfeit products, or were willfully blind to that fact. As described previously, Durango allegedly held itself out to high risk replica merchants. Its sales agent, Counley, traded emails with the Laurette Counterfeiters who expressly told him that they were unable to get credit card services because they sold "replica" items. Counley later wrote back to say he had found a U.S. bank that "can do replica accounts now." Surely, a connection between an inability to get the services needed to transact goods online and the sale of replicas should have attracted Durango's attention.

Frontline likewise is alleged to have sufficient knowledge of trademark infringement by the Laurette Counterfeiters. According to Gucci, Laurette completed an application to obtain Frontline's services, and Nathan Counley, though a Durango employee, is listed as Frontline's sales agent. Counley "acted as Frontline's agent in soliciting and directing credit card processing business from replica merchants like the Laurette Counterfeiters" and therefore Frontline may be charged with his knowledge, including his understanding of Laurette's difficulty to obtain services for selling replicas. Gucci alleges that the "replica acknowledgment" described above that was created for the Laurette website with Counley's assistance was also reviewed by Frontline, who made suggestions as to where they should place this warning on the website. Even more significantly, Frontline allegedly performed its own investigation of products sold through TheBagAddiction.com as part of Frontline's chargeback reviews. When faced with a chargeback, Gucci claims that Frontline received supporting documentation from Laurette that included information about the specific item ordered, including a description of the item purchased. Not only did Frontline allegedly review the specific item description, Plaintiff also claims that the relatively small price tag for the item, as well as specific complaints from customers who made chargebacks about not receiving what the website purported to sell, e.g. a product made of genuine leather, should have alerted Frontline that these were infringing products. These fact-specific claims are enough to at least infer that Frontline knew or consciously avoided knowing that the counterfeit products were sold on TheBagAddiction.com

Gucci claims that Woodforest's situation is similar to Frontline. As was the case with Frontline, Counley represented himself on Laurette's application as Woodforest's sales agent. The application itself said that Laurette was a "wholesale/retail designer [of] handbags," and listed the supplier as a Chinese bag manufacturer rather than Gucci. Gucci also claims that Woodforest specifically reviewed the website and the products listed on it as part of its initial decision to do business with Laurette. A Woodforest employee allegedly completed an "Internet Merchant Review Checklist," which required him or her to review the website and confirm whether it contained a complete description of the goods offered. Based on these claims and the website images provided by Plaintiff, even a cursory review of the TheBagAddiction.com would indicate that they claimed to sell replica Gucci products. Indeed, Plaintiff alleges that Woodforest printed out a number of pages that displayed goods that were for sale, including counterfeit Gucci products, and maintained these pages as part of their business records. Woodforest would also perform a second-level review, performed repeatedly after it accepted the business, where an employee would complete a purchase and request a refund. Finally, like Frontline, Woodforest investigated chargeback disputes and received supporting documentation that allegedly should have tipped them off to the infringing conduct. These claims are more than sufficient to suggest, at this stage of the litigation, that Woodforest knew or shielded themselves from the knowledge that Laurette was selling counterfeit Gucci products with their credit card processing system.

The most significant dispute between the parties with regard to contributory liability is whether any or all of the Defendants had sufficient control over Laurette and TheBagAddiction.com website to render them liable for the web merchant's counterfeiting practices. Although the concept of control arose out of the flea market context and is based on common law landlord-tenant tort principles, the concept of control is not limited to that context.

Here, Plaintiff provides sufficient factual allegations to establish a claim that Woodforest and Frontline had some control over the directly infringing third-party, but fails to provide enough facts to show control on the part of Durango. Though Gucci has made an adequate showing of intentional inducement by Durango, there is little indication that they had much control over the website's sales process. Durango appears to be the veritable middleman in this case. Though there allegedly was an ongoing relationship between Durango and the Laurette Counterfeiters, Gucci provides little indication that once Laurette received services from Frontline and Woodforest, Durango had any particular ability to stop or prohibit sales. Plaintiff's allegations suggest both inducement and knowledge, but "procuring merchant accounts with credit card processing agencies," does not demonstrate that Durango could thereafter prevent the sale of any or all of the counterfeit products.

In contrast, Gucci's complaint indicates that Frontline and Woodforest's credit card processing services are a necessary element for the transaction of counterfeit goods online, and were essential to sales from TheBagAddiction.com. Without the credit card processing operation set up by these two defendants, Gucci alleges that TheBagAddiction.com would largely have been unable to sell its counterfeit Gucci products. By processing these transactions, both companies allegedly earned significant revenue from the transaction fees they charged. Though both Frontline and Woodforest insist they are middlemen with no ability to prevent a transaction, they do not dispute that they could have simply refused to do business with "replica" internet merchants, just like the flea market purveyor who refuses to provide a booth to a counterfeiter.

Frontline and Woodforest insist that these allegations are insufficient because they do not allege direct or complete control over the website itself. However, the ability to literally shut down the website is not needed given the facts of this case. The circuits that have considered this issue look for control and monitoring over the "instrumentality used . . . to infringe the plaintiff's mark." Based on Gucci's claims, the instrumentality in this case is the combination of the website and the credit card network, since both are allegedly necessary elements for the infringing act—the sale and distribution of the counterfeit good.

Rather, Gucci's allegations indicate that they are concerned primarily with the sale of tangible counterfeit goods to customers around the country, which allegedly could not be accomplished without Woodforest and Frontline's ability to process the credit card-based purchases. This action resembles cases with defendants who helped consummate infringing transactions by delivering the counterfeit or infringing goods to the customer.

* * *

Gucci has sufficiently alleged facts to support personal jurisdiction and its trademark claims against Durango, Woodforest, and Frontline. Although Plaintiff has not sufficiently pled facts to support either direct or vicarious theories of liability, claims against all three defendants may proceed based on a contributory liability theory. The factual allegations are sufficient to infer that Durango intentionally induced trademark infringement, and that Woodforest and Frontline exerted sufficient control over the infringing transactions and knowingly provided its services to a counterfeiter.

III. Conclusion

For the foregoing reasons, Defendant's motion to dismiss is DENIED.

SO ORDERED.

Notes

1. The procedural context of this case was defendants' motion to dismiss pursuant to Federal Rule of Civil Procedure 12(b)(2)(6) and 12(b) for lack of personal jurisdiction and failure to state a claim. On the lack of personal jurisdiction claim, defendants attempted to assert that, under traditional concepts of New York's long-arm jurisdiction, plaintiff does not possess personal jurisdiction over defendants because they did not have offices or property in New York, i.e., the requisite "contacts" with New York. The Court found that under New York's long-arm jurisdiction statute, defendants' tortious acts—trademark infringement conducted outside the state—caused injury within the state of New York. There is no question that with respect to website businesses, serving any customers regardless of where they are located, it is foreseeable that counterfeit product would enter the New York market. After the court denied defendants' motion to dismiss, this case quickly settled.

2. The court in *Gucci* remarks that credit cards serve as the primary engine of electronic commerce. The defendant credit card processing companies in this case marketed their services to high-risk online merchants, selling "replicas" of genuine Gucci products. Is it likely that the court's analysis in this case could be applied to more mainstream credit card processing companies like PayPal? Or to Visa or Mastercard? Can you anticipate further extension of third-party liability to other online services?

3. Look at the International Anticounterfeiting Coalition's Rogue Block and Market Safe programs. Do they work? Does eBay's VeRO program work? Also look at Amazon's Project Zero—does it work? What makes one better than the other?

How does the next case, *Tiffany v. eBay*, distinguish these cases?

Tiffany (NJ) Inc. v. eBay Inc.

600 F.3d 93 (2d Cir. 2010)

SACK, Circuit Judge.

Opinion

eBay, Inc. ("eBay"), through its eponymous online marketplace, has revolutionized the online sale of goods, especially used goods. It has facilitated the buying and selling by hundreds of millions of people and entities, to their benefit and eBay's profit. But that marketplace is sometimes employed by users as a means to perpetrate fraud by selling counterfeit goods.

Plaintiffs Tiffany (NJ) Inc. and Tiffany and Company (together, "Tiffany") have created and cultivated a brand of jewelry bespeaking high-end quality and style. Based on Tiffany's concern that some use eBay's website to sell counterfeit Tiffany merchandise, Tiffany has instituted this action against eBay, asserting various causes of action—sounding in trademark infringement, trademark dilution and false advertising—arising from eBay's advertising and listing practices. For the reasons set forth below, we affirm the district court's judgment with respect to Tiffany's claims of trademark infringement and dilution but remand for further proceedings with respect to Tiffany's false advertising claim.

Background

By opinion dated July 14, 2008, following a week-long bench trial, the United States District Court for the Southern District of New York (Richard J. Sullivan, *Judge*) set forth its findings of fact and conclusions of law. *Tiffany (NJ) Inc. v. eBay, Inc.*, 576 F.Supp.2d 463 (S.D.N.Y.2008) ("*Tiffany*").

eBay

eBay is the proprietor of www.ebay.com, an Internet-based marketplace that allows those who register with it to purchase goods from and sell goods to one another. It connects buyers and sellers and enables transactions, which are carried out directly between eBay members. In its auction and listing services, it "provides the venue for the sale of goods and support for the transactions, but it does not itself sell the items" listed for sale on the site, nor does it ever take physical possession of them. Thus, "eBay generally does not know whether or when an item is delivered to the buyer."

eBay has been enormously successful. More than six million new listings are posted on its site daily. At any given time it contains some 100 million listings.

eBay generates revenue by charging sellers to use its listing services. For any listing, it charges an "insertion fee" based on the auction's starting price for the goods being sold and ranges from $0.20 to $4.80. For any completed sale, it charges a "final value fee" that ranges from 5.25% to 10% of the final sale price of the item. Sellers have the option of purchasing, at additional cost, features "to differentiate their listings, such as a border or bold-faced type."

eBay also generates revenue through a company named PayPal, which it owns and which allows users to process their purchases. PayPal deducts, as a fee for each transaction that it processes, 1.9% to 2.9% of the transaction amount, plus $0.30. This gives eBay an added incentive to increase both the volume and the price of the goods sold on its website.

Tiffany

Tiffany is a world-famous purveyor of, among other things, branded jewelry. Since 2000, all new Tiffany jewelry sold in the United States has been available exclusively through Tiffany's retail stores, catalogs, and website, and through its Corporate Sales Department. It does not use liquidators, sell overstock merchandise, or put its goods on sale at discounted prices. It does not—nor can it, for that matter—control the "legitimate secondary market in authentic Tiffany silvery jewelry," i.e., the market for second-hand Tiffany wares.

Sometime before 2004, Tiffany became aware that counterfeit Tiffany merchandise was being sold on eBay's site. Prior to and during the course of this litigation, Tiffany conducted two surveys known as "Buying Programs," one in 2004 and another in 2005, in an attempt to assess the extent of this practice. Under those programs, Tiffany bought various items on eBay and then inspected and evaluated them to determine how many were counterfeit. Tiffany found that 73.1% of the purported Tiffany goods purchased in the 2004 Buying Program and 75.5% of those purchased in the 2005 Buying Program were counterfeit. The district court concluded, however, that the Buying Programs were methodologically flawed and of questionable value, and provided limited evidence as to the total percentage of counterfeit goods available on eBay at any given time. The court nonetheless decided that during the period in which the Buying Programs were in effect, a significant portion of the 'Tiffany' sterling silver jewelry listed on the eBay website was counterfeit, and that eBay knew that some portion of the Tiffany goods sold on its website might be counterfeit. The court found, however, that a "substantial number of authentic Tiffany goods are also sold on eBay."

Reducing or eliminating the sale of all second-hand Tiffany goods, including genuine Tiffany pieces, through eBay's website would benefit Tiffany in at least one sense: It would diminish the competition in the market for genuine Tiffany merchandise. The immediate effect would be loss of revenue to eBay, even though there might be a countervailing gain by eBay resulting from increased consumer confidence about the bona fides of other goods sold through its website.

Anti-Counterfeiting Measures

Because eBay facilitates many sales of Tiffany goods, genuine and otherwise, and obtains revenue on every transaction, it generates substantial revenues from the sale of purported Tiffany goods, some of which are counterfeit. eBay's Jewelry & Watches category manager estimated that, between April 2000 and June 2004, eBay earned $4.1 million in revenue from completed listings with 'Tiffany' in the listing title in the Jewelry & Watches category. Although eBay was generating revenue from all sales of goods on its site, including counterfeit goods, the district court found eBay to have an interest in eliminating counterfeit Tiffany merchandise from eBay to preserve the reputation of its website as a safe place to do business. During the last six weeks of 2004, 125 consumers complained to eBay about purchasing 'Tiffany' items through the eBay website that they believed to be counterfeit.

Notwithstanding these limitations, eBay spent as much as $20 million each year on tools to promote trust and safety on its website. For example, eBay and PayPal set up "buyer protection programs," under which, in certain circumstances, the buyer would be reimbursed for the cost of items purchased on eBay that were discovered not to be genuine. eBay also established a "Trust and Safety" department, with some 4,000 employees "devoted to trust and safety" issues, including over 200 who "focus exclusively on combating infringement" and 70 who "work exclusively with law enforcement."

By May 2002, eBay had implemented a "fraud engine," "which is principally dedicated to ferreting out illegal listings, including counterfeit listings." eBay had theretofore employed manual searches for keywords in listings in an effort to identify blatant instances of potentially infringing . . . activity. The fraud engine uses rules and complex models that automatically search for activity that violates eBay policies. In addition to general filters, the fraud engine incorporates "Tiffany-specific filters," including "approximately 90 different keywords" designed to help distinguish between genuine and counterfeit Tiffany goods. During the period in dispute, eBay also "periodically conducted [manual] reviews of listings in an effort to remove those that might be selling counterfeit goods, including Tiffany goods."

For nearly a decade, including the period at issue, eBay has also maintained and administered the "Verified Rights Owner ('VeRO') Program"—a "'notice-and-takedown' system" allowing owners of intellectual property rights, including Tiffany, to "report to eBay any listing offering potentially infringing items, so that eBay could remove such reported listings." Any such rights-holder with a "good-faith belief that [a particular listed] item infringed on a copyright or a trademark" could report the item to eBay, using a "Notice Of Claimed Infringement form or NOCI form." During the period under consideration, eBay's practice was to remove reported listings within twenty-four hours of receiving a NOCI, but eBay in fact deleted seventy to eighty percent of them within twelve hours of notification.

On receipt of a NOCI, if the auction or sale had not ended, eBay would, in addition to removing the listing, cancel the bids and inform the seller of the reason for the cancellation. If bidding had ended, eBay would retroactively cancel the transaction. In the event of a cancelled auction, eBay would refund the fees it had been paid in connection with the auction.

In some circumstances, eBay would reimburse the buyer for the cost of a purchased item, provided the buyer presented evidence that the purchased item was counterfeit. During the relevant time period, the district court found, eBay never refused to remove a reported Tiffany listing, acted in good faith in responding to Tiffany's NOCIs, and always provided Tiffany with the seller's contact information.

In addition, eBay has allowed rights owners such as Tiffany to create an "About Me" webpage on eBay's website "to inform eBay users about their products, intellectual property rights, and legal positions." eBay does not exercise control over the content of those pages in a manner material to the issues before us.

Tiffany, not eBay, maintains the Tiffany "About Me" page. With the headline "**BUYER BEWARE,**" the page begins: "**Most of the purported TIFFANY & CO. silver jewelry and packaging available on eBay is counterfeit.**" It also says, *inter alia*:

> The only way you can be certain that you are purchasing a genuine TIFFANY & CO. product is to purchase it from a Tiffany & Co. retail store, via our website (www.tiffany.com) or through a Tiffany & Co. catalogue. Tiffany & Co. stores do not authenticate merchandise. A good jeweler or appraiser may be able to do this for you.

In 2003 or early 2004, eBay began to use special warning messages when a seller attempted to list a Tiffany item. These messages instructed the seller to make sure that the item was authentic Tiffany merchandise and informed the seller that eBay does not tolerate the listing of replica, counterfeit, or otherwise unauthorized items and that violation of this policy could result in suspension of the seller's account. The messages also provided a link to Tiffany's "About Me" page with its "buyer beware" disclaimer. If the seller "continued to list an item despite the warning, the listing was flagged for review."

In addition to cancelling particular suspicious transactions, eBay has also suspended from its website hundreds of thousands of sellers every year, tens of thousands of whom were suspected of having engaged in infringing conduct.

By late 2006, eBay had implemented additional anti-fraud measures: delaying the ability of buyers to view listings of certain brand names, including Tiffany's, for 6 to 12 hours so as to give rights-holders such as Tiffany more time to review those listings; developing the ability to assess the number of items listed in a given listing; and restricting one-day and three-day auctions and cross-border trading for some brand-name items.

The district court concluded that eBay consistently took steps to improve its technology and develop anti-fraud measures as such measures became technologically feasible and reasonably available.

eBay's Advertising

At the same time that eBay was attempting to reduce the sale of counterfeit items on its website, it actively sought to promote sales of premium and branded jewelry, including Tiffany merchandise, on its site. Among other things, eBay "advised its sellers to take advantage of the demand for Tiffany merchandise as part of a broader effort to grow the Jewelry & Watches category." And prior to 2003, eBay advertised the availability of Tiffany merchandise on its site. eBay's advertisements trumpeted "Mother's Day Gifts!," a "Fall FASHION BRAND BLOWOUT," "Jewelry Best Sellers," "GREAT BRANDS, GREAT PRICES," or "Top Valentine's Deals," among other promotions. It encouraged the viewer to "GET THE FINER THINGS." These advertisements provided the reader with hyperlinks, at least one of each of which was related to Tiffany merchandise—"Tiffany," "Tiffany & Co. under $150," "Tiffany & Co," "Tiffany Rings," or "Tiffany & Co. under $50."

eBay also purchased sponsored-link advertisements on various search engines to promote the availability of Tiffany items on its website.

Procedural History

By amended complaint dated July 15, 2004, Tiffany initiated this action. It alleged, *inter alia,* that eBay's conduct—i.e., facilitating and advertising the sale of "Tiffany" goods that turned out to be counterfeit—constituted direct and contributory trademark infringement, trademark dilution, and false advertising. On July 14, 2008, following a bench trial, the district court, in a thorough and thoughtful opinion, set forth its findings of fact and conclusions of law, deciding in favor of eBay on all claims.

Tiffany appeals from the district court's judgment for eBay.

Discussion

We review the district court's findings of fact for clear error and its conclusions of law *de novo.*

I. Direct Trademark Infringement

Tiffany alleges that eBay infringed its trademark. The district court described this as a claim of "direct trademark infringement," and we adopt that terminology. We analyze such a claim "under a familiar two-prong test. The test looks first to whether the plaintiff's mark is entitled to protection, and second to whether the defendant's use of the mark is likely to cause consumers confusion as to the origin or sponsorship of the defendant's goods."

In the district court, Tiffany argued that eBay had directly infringed its mark by using it on eBay's website and by purchasing sponsored links containing the mark on Google and Yahoo! Tiffany also argued that eBay and the sellers of the counterfeit goods using its site were jointly and severally liable. The district court rejected these arguments on the ground that eBay's use of Tiffany's mark was protected by the doctrine of nominative fair use.

The doctrine of nominative fair use allows a defendant to use a plaintiff's trademark to identify the plaintiff's goods so long as there is no likelihood of confusion about the source of the defendant's product or the mark-holder's sponsorship or affiliation.

While a trademark conveys an exclusive right to the use of a mark in commerce in the area reserved, that right generally does not prevent one who trades a branded product from accurately describing it by its brand name, so long as the trader does not create confusion by implying an affiliation with the owner of the product.

We agree with the district court that eBay's use of Tiffany's mark on its website and in sponsored links was lawful. eBay used the mark to describe accurately the genuine Tiffany goods offered for sale on its website. And none of eBay's uses of the mark suggested that Tiffany affiliated itself with eBay or endorsed the sale of its products through eBay's website.

We conclude that eBay's use of Tiffany's mark in the described manner did not constitute direct trademark infringement.

II. Contributory Trademark Infringement

The more difficult issue, and the one that the parties have properly focused our attention on, is whether eBay is liable for contributory trademark infringement—i.e., for culpably facilitating the infringing conduct of the counterfeiting vendors.

A. Principles

Contributory trademark infringement is a judicially created doctrine that derives from the common law of torts. *See, e.g., Hard Rock Café Licensing Corp. v. Concession Servs., Inc.*, 955 F.2d 1143, 1148 (7th Cir.1992);.

Speaking more generally, the Ninth Circuit concluded that *Inwood*'s test for contributory trademark infringement applies to a service provider if he or she exercises sufficient control over the infringing conduct.

The limited case law leaves the law of contributory trademark infringement ill-defined. We are apparently the first to consider its application to an online marketplace.

B. Discussion

1. Does Inwood Apply?

Inwood*'s test for contributory trademark infringement governs.*

2. Is eBay Liable Under Inwood?

When applying *Inwood* to service providers, there are two ways in which a defendant may become contributorially liable for the infringing conduct of another: first, if the service provider "intentionally induces another to infringe a trademark," and second, if the service provider "continues to supply its [service] to one whom it knows or has reason to know is engaging in trademark infringement." Tiffany does not argue that eBay induced the sale of counterfeit Tiffany goods on its website—the circumstances addressed by the first part of the *Inwood* test. It argues instead, under the second part of the *Inwood* test, that eBay continued to supply its services to the sellers of counterfeit Tiffany goods while knowing or having reason to know that such sellers were infringing Tiffany's mark.

The district court rejected this argument. First, it concluded that to the extent the NOCIs that Tiffany submitted gave eBay reason to know that particular listings were for counterfeit goods, eBay did not continue to carry those listings once it learned that they were specious. The court found that eBay's practice was promptly to remove the challenged listing from its website, warn sellers and buyers, cancel fees it earned from that listing, and direct buyers not to consummate the sale of the disputed item. The court therefore declined to hold eBay contributorily liable for the infringing conduct of those sellers. Tiffany disagrees vigorously with the district court's further determination that eBay lacked sufficient knowledge of trademark infringement by sellers behind other, non-terminated listings to provide a basis for *Inwood* liability. Tiffany argued in the district court that eBay knew, or at least had reason to know, that counterfeit Tiffany goods were being sold ubiquitously on its website. As evidence, it pointed to, *inter alia*, the demand letters it sent to eBay in 2003 and 2004, the results of its Buying Programs that it shared with eBay, the thousands of NOCIs it filed with eBay alleging its good faith belief that certain listings were counterfeit, and the various complaints eBay received from buyers claiming that they had purchased one or more counterfeit Tiffany items through eBay's website. Tiffany argued that taken together, this evidence established eBay's knowledge of the widespread sale of counterfeit Tiffany products on its website. Tiffany urged that eBay be held contributorily liable on the basis that despite that knowledge, it continued to make its services available to infringing sellers.

The district court concluded that while eBay clearly possessed general knowledge as to counterfeiting on its website, such generalized knowledge is insufficient under the *Inwood* test to impose upon eBay an affirmative duty to remedy the problem.

Accordingly, the district court concluded that for Tiffany to establish eBay's contributory liability, Tiffany would have to show that eBay "knew or had reason to know of specific instances of actual infringement" beyond those that it addressed upon learning of them. Tiffany failed to make such a showing.

On appeal, Tiffany argues that the distinction drawn by the district court between eBay's general knowledge of the sale of counterfeit Tiffany goods through its website, and its specific knowledge as to which particular sellers were making such sales, is a "false" one not required by the law. Tiffany posits that the only relevant question is whether all of the knowledge, when taken together, puts eBay on notice that there is a substantial problem of trademark infringement. If so and if it fails to act, eBay is liable for contributory trademark infringement.

We agree with the district court. For contributory trademark infringement liability to lie, a service provider must have more than a general knowledge or reason to know that its service is being used to sell counterfeit goods. Some contemporary knowledge of which particular listings are infringing or will infringe in the future is necessary.

Tiffany's demand letters and Buying Programs did not identify particular sellers who Tiffany thought were then offering or would offer counterfeit goods. And although the NOCIs and buyer complaints gave eBay reason to know that certain sellers had been selling counterfeits, those sellers' listings were removed and repeat offenders were suspended from the eBay site. Thus Tiffany failed to demonstrate that eBay was supplying its service to individuals who it knew or had reason to know were selling counterfeit Tiffany goods.

Accordingly, we affirm the judgment of the district court insofar as it holds that eBay is not contributorily liable for trademark infringement.

3. Willful Blindness.

Tiffany and its amici express their concern that if eBay is not held liable except when specific counterfeit listings are brought to its attention, eBay will have no incentive to root out such listings from its website. They argue that this will effectively require Tiffany and similarly situated retailers to police eBay's website—and many others like it "24 hours a day, and 365 days a year." They urge that this is a burden that most mark holders cannot afford to bear.

First, and most obviously, we are interpreting the law and applying it to the facts of this case. We could not, even if we thought it wise, revise the existing law in order to better serve one party's interests at the expense of the other's.

But we are also disposed to think, and the record suggests, that private market forces give eBay and those operating similar businesses a strong incentive to minimize the counterfeit goods sold on their websites. eBay received many complaints from users claiming to have been duped into buying counterfeit Tiffany products sold on eBay. The risk of alienating these users gives eBay a reason to identify and remove counterfeit listings. Indeed, it has spent millions of dollars in that effort.

Moreover, we agree with the district court that if eBay had reason to suspect that counterfeit Tiffany goods were being sold through its website, and intentionally shielded itself from discovering the offending listings or the identity of the sellers behind them, eBay might very well have been charged with knowledge of those sales sufficient to satisfy *Inwood*'s "knows or has reason to know" prong. A service provider is not, we think, permitted willful blindness. When it has reason to suspect that users of its service are infringing a protected mark, it may not shield itself from learning of the particular infringing transactions by looking the other way.

eBay appears to concede that it knew as a general matter that counterfeit Tiffany products were listed and sold through its website. Without more, however, this knowledge is insufficient to trigger liability under *Inwood.*

III. Trademark Dilution

A. Principles

"Dilution by blurring" is an "association arising from the similarity between a mark or trade name and a famous mark that impairs the distinctiveness of the famous mark." *Id.* § 1125(c)(2)(B). It can occur "regardless of the presence or absence of actual or likely confusion, of competition, or of actual economic injury." Some classic examples of blurring include hypothetical anomalies as Dupont shoes, Buick aspirin tablets, Schlitz varnish, Kodak pianos, Bulova gowns, and so forth. It is not a question of confusion; few consumers would likely confuse the source of a Kodak camera with the source of a "Kodak" piano. Dilution by blurring refers instead to the whittling away of the established trademark's selling power and value through its unauthorized use by others.

Federal law identifies a non-exhaustive list of six factors that courts "may consider" when determining whether a mark is likely to cause dilution by blurring. These are: (1) the degree of similarity between the mark or trade name and the famous mark (2) the degree of inherent or acquired distinctiveness of the famous mark (3) "[t]he extent to which the owner of the famous mark is engaging in substantially exclusive use of the mark"; (4) "[t]he degree of recognition of the famous mark"; (5) "[w]hether the user of the mark or trade name intended to create an association with the famous mark"; and (6) "[a]ny actual association between the mark or trade name and the famous mark."

In contrast to dilution by blurring, "dilution by tarnishment" is an "association arising from the similarity between a mark or trade name and a famous mark that harms the reputation of the famous mark." 15 U.S.C. § 1125(c)(2)(C). This generally arises when the plaintiff's trademark is linked to products of shoddy quality, or is portrayed in an unwholesome or unsavory context likely to evoke unflattering thoughts about the owner's product.

New York State law also provides for protection against both dilution by blurring and tarnishment.

B. Discussion

The district court rejected Tiffany's dilution by blurring claim on the ground that eBay never used the TIFFANY Marks in an effort to create an association with its own product, but instead, used the marks directly to advertise and identify the availability of authentic Tiffany merchandise on the eBay website. The court concluded that just as the dilution by blurring claim fails because eBay has never used the Tiffany Marks to refer to eBay's own product, the dilution by tarnishment claim also fails.

We agree. There is no second mark or product at issue here to blur with or to tarnish "Tiffany."

Tiffany argues that counterfeiting dilutes the value of its product. Perhaps. But insofar as eBay did not itself sell the goods at issue, it did not itself engage in dilution.

IV. False Advertising

Finally, Tiffany claims that eBay engaged in false advertising in violation of federal law.

A. Principles

Section 43(a) of the Lanham Act prohibits any person from, "in commercial advertising or promotion, misrepresent[ing] the nature, characteristics, qualities, or geographic origin of his or her or another person's goods, services, or commercial activities." 15 U.S.C. § 1125(a)(1)(B).

Where an advertising claim is literally false, the court may enjoin the use of the claim without reference to the advertisement's impact on the buying public. To succeed in a likelihood-of-confusion case where the statement at issue is not literally false, however, a plaintiff "must demonstrate, by extrinsic evidence, that the challenged commercials tend to mislead or confuse consumers," and must "demonstrate that a statistically significant part of the commercial audience holds the false belief allegedly communicated by the challenged advertisement."

B. Discussion

eBay advertised the sale of Tiffany goods on its website in various ways. Among other things, eBay provided hyperlinks to "Tiffany," "Tiffany & Co. under $150," "Tiffany & Co.," "Tiffany Rings," and "Tiffany & Co. under $50."

eBay also purchased advertising space on search engines, in some instances providing a link to eBay's site and exhorting the reader to "Find **tiffany** items at low prices." Pl.'s Ex. 1065 (bold face type in original). Yet the district court found, and eBay does not deny, that "eBay certainly ha" generalized knowledge that Tiffany products sold on eBay were often counterfeit." *Tiffany,* 576 F.Supp.2d at 520–21. Tiffany argues that because eBay advertised the sale of Tiffany goods on its website, and because many of those goods were in fact counterfeit, eBay should be liable for false advertising.

The district court rejected this argument. The court first concluded that the advertisements at issue were not literally false "[b]ecause authentic Tiffany merchandise is sold on eBay's website," even if counterfeit Tiffany products are sold there, too.

The court then considered whether the advertisements, though not literally false, were nonetheless misleading. It concluded they were not for three reasons. First, the court found that eBay's use of Tiffany's mark in its advertising was "protected, nominative fair use." Second, the court found that "Tiffany has not proven that eBay had specific knowledge as to the illicit nature of individual listings," implying that such knowledge would be necessary to sustain a false advertising claim. Finally, the court reasoned that "to the extent that the advertising was false, the falsity was the responsibility of third party sellers, not eBay."

We agree with the district court that eBay's advertisements were not literally false inasmuch as genuine Tiffany merchandise was offered for sale through eBay's website. But we are unable to affirm on the record before us the district court's further conclusion that eBay's advertisements were not "likely to mislead or confuse consumers." *Time Warner Cable,* 497 F.3d at 153.

As noted, to evaluate Tiffany's claim that eBay's advertisements misled consumers, a court must determine whether extrinsic evidence indicates that the challenged advertisements were misleading or confusing. The reasons the district court gave for rejecting Tiffany's claim do not seem to reflect this determination, though. The court's first rationale was that eBay's advertisements were nominative fair use of Tiffany's mark.

But, even if that is so, it does not follow that eBay did not use the mark in a misleading advertisement. It may, after all, constitute fair use for Brand X Coffee to use the trademark of its competitor, Brand Y Coffee, in an advertisement stating that "In a blind taste test, 9 out of 10 New Yorkers said they preferred Brand X Coffee to Brand Y Coffee." But if 9 out of 10 New Yorkers in a statistically significant sample did *not* say they preferred X to Y, or if they were paid to say that they did, then the advertisement would nonetheless be literally false in the first example, or misleading in the second.

There is a similar difficulty with the district court's reliance on the fact that eBay did not know which particular listings on its website offered counterfeit Tiffany goods. That is relevant, as we have said, to whether eBay committed contributory trademark infringement. But it sheds little light on whether the advertisements were misleading insofar as they implied the genuineness of Tiffany goods on eBay's site.

Finally, the district court reasoned that if eBay's advertisements were misleading, that was only because the sellers of counterfeits made them so by offering inauthentic Tiffany goods. Again, this consideration is relevant to Tiffany's direct infringement claim, but less relevant, if relevant at all, here. It is true that eBay did not itself sell counterfeit Tiffany goods; only the fraudulent vendors did, and that is in part why we conclude that eBay did not infringe Tiffany's mark. But eBay did affirmatively advertise the goods sold through its site as Tiffany merchandise. The law requires us to hold eBay accountable for the words that it chose insofar as they misled or confused consumers.

eBay and its amici warn of the deterrent effect that will grip online advertisers who are unable to confirm the authenticity of all of the goods they advertise for sale. We rather doubt that the consequences will be so dire. An online advertiser such as eBay need not cease its advertisements for a kind of goods only because it knows that not all of those goods are authentic. A disclaimer might suffice. But the law prohibits an advertisement that implies that all of the goods offered on a defendant's website are genuine when in fact, as here, a sizeable proportion of them are not.

Rather than vacate the judgment of the district court as to Tiffany's false advertising claim, we think it prudent to remand the cause so that the district court, with its greater familiarity with the evidence, can reconsider the claim in light of what we have said. The case is therefore remanded, for further proceedings for the limited purpose of the district court's re-examination of the false advertising claim in accordance with this opinion.

Conclusion

For the foregoing reasons, we affirm the judgment of the district court with respect to the claims of trademark infringement and dilution. Employing a *Jacobson* remand, we return the cause to the district court for further proceedings with respect to Tiffany's false advertising claim.

Notes

1. Auction sites like eBay have routinely escaped liability in the United States for the infringing activities of their users except in certain limited circumstances, and it is up to brand owners to combat their own online counterfeit problems.

2. This case was litigated over a six-year period in the midst of what was at that time the worst economic crisis since the Great Depression. If you were the judge's law clerk, and relieved that eBay had some responsibility beyond its VeRO program in stopping the sale of Tiffany counterfeits on its site, what sort of remedy would you recommend? eBay's successful business model included fees earned from transactions and conducting seminars and workshops to educate sellers in growing their business, marketing, and even government lobbying regarding regulations and legislation affecting their sales. This model encouraged entrepreneurs in an economy that had experienced massive job losses.

3. On remand, the District Court finally closed the case, finding that eBay was not liable for false advertising, finding that consumers were not misled by eBay's advertisements. Tiffany had relied on the declarations of three eBay customers who believed they bought counterfeit goods on eBay, testimony from a Tiffany employee that the company had received numerous emails complaining about counterfeit Tiffany products on eBay, and 125 emails sent to eBay by customers complaining about counterfeit Tiffany products. Tiffany did not appeal this ruling. In order to prove consumer confusion, brands must produce actual evidence of consumer confusion based on the advertisements at issue.

4. Many amicus briefs were filed on Tiffany's behalf, including briefs filed by the Council of Fashion Designers of America, Inc., the trade organization that represents U.S. designers; the International Anticounterfeiting Coalition; and Coty, Inc. However, Google, Inc., Amazon.com, Inc., Yahoo, Inc., and numerous trade organizations representing the interests of internet "players" also filed amicus briefs for eBay.

5. On September 3, 2010, in France, the Paris Court of Appeal affirmed eBay's liability for the sale of Louis Vuitton counterfeits through its online auction site but reduced the previous damage award of $7.3 million.

6. Brand owners should educate consumers about unauthorized sellers by posting, on their own websites, which stores, retailers, or websites are authorized sellers of their products. This information, together with education about counterfeit goods, may at least steer consumers away from eBay or unauthorized websites that may sell counterfeits.

C.I.P. Enforcement Abroad

The greater part of counterfeit fashion items imported into the United States are manufactured in China. Brand owners are often frustrated by the seeming lack of will by Chinese authorities to enforce anticounterfeiting laws. Legal scholars have described China's historic economic model as promoting a culture of copying. China has been a regular "member" of the Primary Watch List of the Special 301 Report.

C. Ethical Issues — Use of Private Investigators

Brand owners need investigators. Brand owners may not even get to trial if an *ex parte* seizure stops the problem. The investigators research manufacturers and sellers. They make the buys supporting a brand owner's legal actions. They testify when called upon by a judge. And they must do all of this without violating ethical rules. Brand owners must use a reliable, known investigator experienced with counterfeiting matters. Experienced investigators know how to play within the rules, not overstep legal boundaries and ethical rules, and can be counted upon to testify succinctly and clearly should a need for their testimony arise. When seeking a seizure order, a brand owner must prepare the investigator to testify. Frequently the judge knows the law but wants to hear directly from the investigator what steps were taken and why an item is counterfeit. Having trained investigators available to testify increases the likelihood of success of a civil seizure order.

Lawyers hire undercover investigators to disguise their identity for the purposes of soliciting information about a person or organization to gain evidence for an ongoing case. Since undercover investigators cannot perform their job without disguising who they really are, are lawyers ethically allowed to hire someone who purposely fails to disclose their identity? As it turns out, courts and ethics committees are grappling with this issue, but depending on the authority and context you seek, the answer could be yes. To further understand this issue, let's take a closer look at the Model Rules of Professional Conduct since these are the rules that govern the professional responsibilities lawyers have to their profession.

- Model Rule 4.1(a) states that a lawyer shall not "make a false statement of material fact or law to a third person."[1] The commentary to this rule points out that if a lawyer affirms another person's false statement that is a material fact, it constitutes prohibited conduct.[2]
- Model Rule 8.4 prohibits lawyers from engaging in dishonest, fraudulent, or deceitful conduct.[3]

---

1. Model Code of Prof'l Conduct r. 4.1(a) (Am. Bar Ass'n 2019).
2. *See* Model Code of Prof'l Conduct r. 4.1(a) cmt. [1] (Am. Bar. Ass'n 2019).
3. Model Code of Prof'l Conduct r. 8.4 (Am. Bar Ass'n 2019).

- Model Rule 5.3 states that a lawyer cannot ethically have someone else indirectly perform acts on their behalf that the Model Rules prohibit.[4]

This raises the question: if an undercover investigator misrepresents his/her identity while under the supervision of a lawyer, would such misrepresentation constitute a material fact that would subject the lawyer to disciplinary action under Rule 5.3? The American Bar Association (ABA) has not provided an opinion directly addressing the ethical considerations of lawyer-supervised undercover investigators. This lack of guidance has led to disagreements between what the Rules say and what is considered permitted conduct. There is no doubt some of this discord can be traced back to an unwillingness to call government lawyers who use undercover investigators unethically. This is because some courts explicitly allow government lawyers and prosecutors to direct or supervise the use of undercover investigators.

Furthermore, there are some courts and ethics commissions that allow private lawyers to direct or supervise undercover investigations without going against the Model Rules' prohibited conduct. For instance, in *Gidatex v. Campaniello Imports, Ltd.* for a trademark infringement action, the court found that the plaintiff's lawyers' usage of undercover investigators posing as customers in the defendant's store was not unethical conduct.[5] The court stated that the undercover investigators did not cause "the sales clerks . . . [to make] statements they otherwise would not have made" and was an accepted investigative technique that would make unfair business practices hard to uncover without such use.[6] Moreover, the Professional Ethics Committee of the New York County Lawyers' Association announced that it is not unethical in certain circumstances for a non-government lawyer to use a non-lawyer investigator whom the lawyer knows employs dissemblance in the investigation.[7] The use of investigators is permitted only in the following circumstances: "(i) the investigation relates to a violation of civil or intellectual property rights and the lawyer has a good faith belief that such a violation is taking place or will take place imminently, or the dissemblance is expressly authorized by law; (ii) the evidence is not reasonably available through other lawful means; (iii) the conduct of the supervising lawyer and investigator do not otherwise violate the ethical rules or applicable law; and (iv) the dissemblance does not unlawfully or unethically violate the rights of third parties."[8]

It is also worth looking into the conduct of investigators and lawyers during the scope of communications throughout an undercover investigation. Model Rule 4.2 prohibits a lawyer from communicating about the subject of representation with a

---

4. Model Code of Prof'l Conduct r. 5.3 (Am. Bar Ass'n 2019).

5. Gidatex, S.r.l. v. Campaniello Imports, Ltd., 82 F. Supp. 2d 119, 126 (S.D.N.Y. 1999) ("The use of private investigators, posing as consumers and speaking to nominal parties who are not involved in any aspect of the litigation, does not constitute an end-run around the attorney/client privilege").

6. *Id.*

7. New York Cty. Lawyers' Ass'n Comm. on Prof'l Ethics, Formal Op. 737 (2007).

8. John K. Villa, *The Ethics of Using Undercover Investigators*, 28 ACC Docket 86 (2010).

person the lawyer knows is represented by counsel, unless the lawyer has consent or is authorized by law or a court order to do so.[9] Under this rule, a represented person includes anyone with managerial authority, anyone with authority to obligate the organization in question, or any person whose conduct can be imputed to the organization for purposes of civil or criminal liability. This Rule is important because undercover investigators are often sent to communicate with an opposing party and, most of the time, the opposing party's lawyer is not present. To this end, one court stated that "there is a discernable continuum in the cases from clearly impermissible to clearly permissible conduct."[10] For example, if an undercover investigator speaks to the president of an opposing party's company with the intent of eliciting information for pending litigation, this constitutes impermissible conduct. However, contact with low-level employees by an investigator who poses as a customer and engages in ordinary business transactions, as in *Gidatex*, is seen as ethically permissible conduct. Finally, Rule 4.3 provides that when a lawyer reasonably knows that an unrepresented person misunderstands the lawyer's role in a matter, the lawyer is required to make reasonable efforts to correct the misunderstanding by identifying who they represent and how their interests are adverse.[11] Some authorities construe this rule to mean only where lawyers represent their client and speak to the adverse parties directly, but on the other hand, one court has held that this Rule is inapplicable since both the lawyer and investigator are acting in the capacity of lawyers.[12]

Rolex Watch, U.S.A., Inc. v. Michel Co.

179 F.3d 704 (9th Cir. 1999)

TASHIMA, Circuit Judge.

Order Denying Motion to Dismiss, Denying Motion to Exclude Evidence

Defendants, Micha Mottale and Michel Co., renew their motion to dismiss and motion to exclude evidence. Plaintiff opposes. Having fully considered the papers submitted and the oral argument presented, the Court denies Defendants' motion to dismiss and motion to exclude.

Background

On May 3, 1996, Plaintiff, Rolex Watch U.S.A., Inc., filed a complaint against Defendants alleging, inter alia, trademark counterfeiting and infringement. In an order filed June 24, 1996, the parties entered a stipulated preliminary injunction. As part of that order, Defendants were restrained from using Rolex trademarks or colorable imitations in connection with advertising or sale of non-Rolex items, from using such marks in a manner likely to cause confusion, mistake, or deception, from

9. Model Code of Prof'l Conduct r. 4.2 (Am. Bar Ass'n 2019).
10. Hill v. Shell Oil Co., 209 F. Supp. 2d 876, 880 (N.D. Ill. 2002).
11. Model Code of Prof'l Conduct r. 4.3 (Am. Bar Ass'n 2019).
12. Villa, *supra* note 8.

passing off products not entirely Rolex as Rolex products, and from possessing, delivering, or selling items falsely bearing Rolex trademarks.

In preparation for trial, Plaintiff's counsel hired an investigator, Mr. Jack Smalley, to observe the conduct of Defendants and to purchase items in the normal course of business. Upon learning of Mr. Smalley's contacts with Defendants, Defendants moved to exclude evidence and dismiss the complaint for Plaintiff's counsels' violations of California Rule of Professional Conduct 2-100. Plaintiff opposed Defendants' motions.

Mr. Smalley's testimony at trial shows that he has attended International Watch and Jewelry Guild shows and observed Defendant Mottale. On October 26, 1996, Mr. Smalley attended a trade show in New York City. Mr. Smalley approached Defendant Mottale with a Rolex watch, inquired if Defendant had a dial and a diamond bezel he could install on the watch, and purchased a diamond dial and diamond bezel from Defendant. At that time, Defendant advised Mr. Smalley that he could contact him by phone if he wished to purchase other items. On November 15, 1996, Mr. Smalley called Defendant by phone and ordered a non-Rolex ladies replacement band and a men's Datejust watch with diamond dial, diamond bezel, and a replacement band. During the course of Mr. Smalley's contacts with Defendant Mottale, he did not discuss the instant law suit or ask questions regarding the law suit.

Defendants renew their motions to dismiss and to exclude the testimony of and evidence produced by Mr. Smalley. In addition, Defendants request that if the Court denies the motion to dismiss, that the Court strike Plaintiff's prayer for damages and attorneys' fees. The parties have filed supplemental memoranda in the matter.

Discussion

Defendants contend that Plaintiff counsels' use of an investigator to contact and purchase items from Defendants, without the knowledge and consent of Defendants' counsel, constitutes a violation of California Rule of Professional Conduct 2-100:

> While representing a client, a member shall not communicate directly or indirectly about the subject of the representation with a party the member knows to be represented by another lawyer in the matter, unless the member has the consent of the other lawyer. Cal. R. Prof. Cond. 2-100(a).

Rule 2-100 should be given a reasonable, common sense interpretation, and should not be given a broad or liberal interpretation which would stretch the rule so as to cover situations which were not contemplated by the rule. The purpose of Rule 2-100 is to preserve the attorney-client relationship from an opposing attorney's intrusion and interference.

Mr. Smalley as an agent of Plaintiff's counsel, is prohibited from communicating about the subject of the representation with Defendant Mottale because Rule

2-100 prohibits communication by direct or indirect means. The issue, therefore, is whether the contacts made by Mr. Smalley constitute communication "about the subject of the representation."

Having carefully considered the arguments presented by the parties and the testimony and evidence presented, the Court finds that Plaintiff's counsel did not violate Rule 2-100. Defendants are in the business of selling watches and accessories. The testimony of Mr. Smalley reveals that he approached Defendants for information regarding items Defendants offered for sale and to purchase certain of those items. The evidence indicates that Mr. Smalley was another one of Defendants' patrons. Mr. Smalley may be an investigator for Plaintiff's counsel, but his interaction with Defendants was no different than the contact that any of Defendants' other customers have. Mr. Smalley's employment status as an investigator for Plaintiff's counsel does not transform his contacts as a customer into communication about a represented matter.

Moreover, Mr. Smalley's contacts with Defendants did not threaten Defendant's attorney-client relationship or interfere with confidential attorney-client communications. The conduct of Mr. Smalley as a customer can no more be said to interfere with the attorney-client relationship than any of Defendants' other everyday, formal customer transactions. To interpret Rule 2-100 to cover the contacts made by Mr. Smalley would be to stretch the rule to cover transactions freely made in the open marketplace, a situation not reasonably contemplated by the rule. Therefore, the Court finds that the contacts made by Mr. Smalley would be to stretch the rule to cover transactions freely made in the open marketplace, a situation not reasonably contemplated by the rule. Therefore, the Court finds that the contacts made by Mr. Smalley do not constitute communications about the subject of the representation within the meaning of Rule 2-100.

The Court also notes that Defendants are subject to a preliminary injunction. If Rule 2-100 prohibited Plaintiff from interacting with Defendants in the normal course of Defendants' business, Plaintiff would effectively be precluded from testing Defendants' compliance with the preliminary injunction. It appears to be a common practice for plaintiffs in trademark and patent infringement cases to test a defendant's compliance with court-imposed injunctions. *See, e.g., Rolex U.S.A., Inc. v. Hoffman*, 717 F. Supp. 942 (D. Mass. 1989). Rule 2-100 would have the unintended and opposite effect of transforming Plaintiff's suit and preliminary injunction into a shield for Defendants to continue alleged infringing conduct. Such an interpretation could not have been intended, and the Court declines to prohibit Plaintiff from testing Defendant's compliance with the Court's orders.

Conclusion

Having fully considered the papers submitted in the matter and the argument presented by the counsel, the Court finds that Plaintiff's counsel have not violated California Rule of Professional Conduct 2-100 and Defendants' motions to dismiss and exclude evidence are denied.

Note

Rolex hired a reliable, known investigator who understood how not to overstep legal boundaries and ethical rules. It also prepared its investigator to testify succinctly, increasing its likelihood of success on the ethical issue.

D. Suits against ISPs

Often ISPs provide their clients with more than just access to the web and access to an email account. More likely than not, these clients can upload files and make them accessible to the general public. When the client is an infringer or counterfeiter, brand owners need a remedy. Although the client may not be easy to locate, the ISP is. The infringer is often "judgment-proof," but the ISP may be a deeper pocket. Nevertheless, this creates additional policing responsibilities for brand owners.

Louis Vuitton Malletier, S.A. v. Akanoc Solutions, Inc.

658 F.3d 936 (9th Cir. 2011)

GOULD, Circuit Judge.

Opinion

Louis Vuitton Malletier, S.A., sued Managed Solutions Group, Inc. ("MSG"), Akanoc Solutions, Inc., and Steven Chen (collectively "Defendants") for contributory copyright and trademark infringement, contending that Defendants were liable for their role in hosting websites that directly infringed Louis Vuitton's trademarks and copyrights. After a trial, a jury found Defendants liable and awarded damages against each defendant. In response to Defendants' motion for judgment as a matter of law, the district court set aside the jury's verdict and award against MSG. The district court otherwise denied the motion.

Appellants Akanoc and Chen appeal the jury verdict, contending that the district court erred in instructing the jury and in denying their post-trial motion for judgment as a matter of law. Louis Vuitton cross-appeals the district court's order granting judgment as a matter of law in favor of MSG.

Among other questions, we must decide whether the district court properly instructed the jury on awarding damages as to each defendant.

I. Facts and Procedural History

Louis Vuitton is the sole and exclusive United States distributor of its merchandise, which includes a variety of luxury goods bearing its trademarks and copyrighted designs. To guard the reputation and exclusivity of its brand and to otherwise maintain its rights, Louis Vuitton polices its intellectual property, including its trademarks and copyrights, through various monitoring and enforcement strategies.

In late 2006, Louis Vuitton discovered websites selling goods that it believed infringed its copyrights and trademarks. The websites did not sell merchandise directly; instead, they listed an email address that interested parties could use to initiate a transaction. Upon further investigation Louis Vuitton discovered that the websites were using IP addresses assigned to defendants MSG and Akanoc.

MSG and Akanoc were in the "web hosting" business. Chen managed both MSG and Akanoc, which were based in San Jose, California. According to Defendants, MSG leased servers, bandwidth, and some IP addresses to Akanoc. Akanoc, in turn, operated the servers and otherwise ran the business. Akanoc leased packages of server space, bandwidth, and IP addresses to its customers. Some of Akanoc's customers were located outside the United States. According to Louis Vuitton, the customers who directly infringed the trademarks and copyrights were based in China.

From 2006 to 2007, Louis Vuitton sent Defendants at least eighteen Notices of Infringement ("NOIs") documenting trademark and copyright infringement occurring on numerous websites hosted by Defendants. The NOIs demanded that Defendants either remove the infringing content from their servers or require their customers to do so. Louis Vuitton received no response from Defendants. Although Defendants asserted that they took regular steps to curb any infringement by websites using their servers, Defendants were not able to identify any action taken in response to the notices sent by Louis Vuitton, and the websites continued to operate using servers and IP addresses owned by Defendants.

Louis Vuitton sued Defendants in the Northern District of California, alleging contributory copyright and trademark infringement under federal law. Louis Vuitton contended that Defendants had actual knowledge of the websites' activities, that Defendants knowingly avoided learning the full extent of the infringing activities and deliberately disregarded Louis Vuitton's notifications, that Defendants knowingly enabled the infringing conduct by hosting the websites and willfully permitting websites to display the products, and that Louis Vuitton suffered irreparable harm and damage as a result of Defendants' conduct.

The case went to trial and the jury returned a verdict for Louis Vuitton, holding Akanoc, MSG, and Chen liable for contributory infringement of thirteen of Louis Vuitton's trademarks, and of two of Louis Vuitton's copyrights. The jury also found that Defendants acted willfully. The jury awarded $10,500,000 in statutory damages for willful contributory trademark infringement of the thirteen trademarks against each defendant, for a total of $31,500,000. The jury also awarded $300,000 in statutory damages for willful copyright infringement of the two copyrights against each defendant, for a total of $900,000.

After the verdict, Defendants moved for judgment as a matter of law, requesting among other things that the court discard the jury verdict. The district court granted the post-trial motion as to MSG, concluding that there was no evidence indicating that MSG sold domain names, operated the servers, or did anything more than own and lease the hardware operated by Akanoc and Chen. The district court denied the motion as to Akanoc and Chen, awarded statutory damages, and entered a permanent injunction restricting them from engaging in similar conduct. Akanoc and Chen timely appealed. Louis Vuitton cross-appealed the district court's order granting judgment as a matter of law in favor of MSG.

II. Standards of Review

We review de novo a district court's decision to grant or deny judgment as a matter of law.

III. Discussion

A. The Cross-Appeal

Louis Vuitton contends that the district court erred when it set aside the jury's verdict against MSG. We disagree. The jury's verdict as to MSG was not supported by "substantial evidence."

With regard to both contributory copyright and trademark infringement, the district court's verdict form asked the jury to determine whether each defendant, while knowing that its customers were using its services to directly infringe Louis Vuitton's intellectual property rights, "had reasonable means to withdraw its services so that they could not be used to directly infringe but continued to provide its services." We agree with the district court that no evidence presented at trial showed that MSG operated the servers that hosted the direct infringers' websites. Even assuming that the direct infringers could be construed as MSG's customers, Louis Vuitton presented no evidence that MSG had reasonable means to withdraw services to the direct infringers.

B. Appellants' Motion for Judgment as a Matter of Law

Appellants Akanoc and Chen urge that the district court erred in denying their post-trial motion for judgment as a matter of law. However, in reviewing the particular issues of substantive law raised by Appellants as described below, we have concluded that the jury had sufficient facts before it to find Appellants liable as a matter of law, and therefore the district court did not err in denying Appellants' motion for judgment as a matter of law.

C. Jury Instructions

1. Contributory Trademark Infringement

To prevail on its claim of contributory trademark infringement, Louis Vuitton had to establish that Appellants continued to supply its services to one who it knew or had reason to know was engaging in trademark infringement. Because Appellants provided services rather than a product, Louis Vuitton also needed to establish that Appellants had "[d]irect control and monitoring of the instrumentality used by a third party to infringe" Louis Vuitton's marks.

Appellants contend that the district court did not instruct the jury about the proper scope of the "means of infringement." According to Appellants, the servers and internet services they provided and operated were not the "means of infringement"; instead, they maintain, the websites selling the infringing goods were the sole means of infringement. Appellants claim that the jury instructions failed to distinguish between the servers or services provided by Appellants and the websites maintained by Appellants' customers. But websites are not ethereal; while they exist, virtually, in cyberspace, they would not exist at all without physical roots in servers and internet services. As the district court held, Appellants "physically host websites on their servers and route internet traffic to and from those websites. This service is the Internet equivalent of leasing real estate." *Louis Vuitton Malletier, S.A. v. Akanoc Solutions, Inc.*, 591 F.Supp.2d 1098, 1112 (N.D.Cal.2008).

Appellants also contend that the jury instructions were erroneous because, in their view, "contribution to infringement must be intentional for liability to arise." We disagree. Plaintiffs asserting contributory trademark infringement claims must prove that defendants provided their services with actual or constructive knowledge that the users of their services were engaging in trademark infringement. An express finding of intent is not required.

D. Damages

1. Contributory Trademark Infringement

a. Statutory Damages

Appellants contend that 15 U.S.C. § 1117(c) does not authorize statutory damages against contributory infringers. Appellants assert that statutory damages cannot be awarded against contributory infringers because the statute defines infringement in terms of the unauthorized "use" of a counterfeit mark. But § 1117(c) does not require defendants to "use ... [the] counterfeit mark." It applies so long as the "case *involves* such use." At bottom, Appellants urge us to hold that a defendant may avoid the consequences of contributory liability (i.e., statutory damages) simply by claiming that the infringing acts (the unauthorized uses) were committed by others. But holding a defendant liable for the unauthorized acts of another is a primary purpose of the doctrine of contributory trademark liability.

b. Likelihood of Confusion

The district court instructed the jury that "[t]here is a likelihood of confusion ... when the offending mark is a counterfeit mark, or a mark virtually identical to a previously registered mark coupled with the intent to pass off or borrow from established good will." Appellants urge that this instruction misstates the law. But the district court's instruction specified that the presumption arises when intent to cause confusion is coupled with the use of a counterfeit mark or a mark virtually identical to a previously registered mark. This formulation accurately tracks the law. We have approvingly cited Judge Learned Hand's formulation of the presumption:

> [T]he late comer who deliberately copies the dress of his competitors already in the field, must at least prove that his effort has been futile.... He may indeed succeed in showing that it was; that, however bad his purpose, it will fail in execution; if he

does, he will win. . . . But such an intent raises a presumption that customers will be deceived. *HMH Publ'g Co. v. Brincat,* 504 F.2d 713, 720 n. 12 (9th Cir.1974).

c. Definition of "Counterfeit Mark"

To claim statutory damages under 15 U.S.C. § 1117(c), Louis Vuitton had to prove that the goods trafficked by the direct infringers were "counterfeit" as that term is defined in § 1116(d). Section 1116(d) specifies that a counterfeit mark for purposes of § 1117(c) is "a counterfeit of a mark that is registered on the principal register in the United States Patent and Trademark Office for such goods or services sold, offered for sale, or distributed and that is in use, whether or not the person against whom relief is sought knew such mark was so registered." § 1116(d)(1)(B)(i). Appellants contend that the district court erred because the jury instructions did not define the term "counterfeit mark."

This contention has no merit. Section 1116(d) requires that the mark in question be (1) a non-genuine mark identical to the registered, genuine mark of another, where (2) the genuine mark was registered for use on the same goods to which the infringer applied the mark. The district court's Closing Instructions and Supplemental Instruction Number 1 adequately explained this requirement.

Substantial evidence supports the jury's verdict.

2. The Damage Awards

Under 17 U.S.C. § 504(c), the statutory maximum for willful copyright infringement is $150,000 "for all infringements involved in the action, with respect to any one work, for which any one infringer is liable individually, or for which any two or more infringers are liable jointly and severally." Under 15 U.S.C. § 1117(c)(2), the statutory maximum for willful trademark infringement involving counterfeit marks now is $2,000,000 "per counterfeit mark per type of goods or services sold, offered for sale, or distributed, as the court considers just." But the statutory maximum at the outset of litigation in this case was $1,000,000, not $2,000,000, and the parties agreed to abide by the lower amount. The jury awarded statutory damages of $10,500,000 per defendant for willful contributory infringement of thirteen of Louis Vuitton's trademarks and $300,000 per defendant for willful contributory infringement of two of Louis Vuitton's copyrights. §§ 504(c), 1117(c)(2). The district court held that these awards did not violate the statutory maximums, noting that the total award "amounts to approximately $807,692 per trademark per Defendant and $150,000 per copyright per Defendant." The court did not specify whether the awards were separate awards for which Appellants were separately liable, or if Appellants were jointly and severally liable for the full amount.

With respect to damages for contributory trademark infringement, logic compels the same result. Like 17 U.S.C. § 504(c), 15 U.S.C. § 1117(c) entitles a plaintiff to *an* award, not multiple awards. A learned treatise counsels that "[t]he body of case law developed to interpret the similar statutory damages provision in copyright law should prove helpful in applying the counterfeit statutory damages option." J. Thomas McCarthy, *McCarthy on Trademarks & Unfair Competition* § 30:95

(4th ed.1996) (footnotes omitted). Louis Vuitton cites no authority to the contrary. When combined, the awards of $10,500,000 per defendant exceed the statutory maximum.

Because it is clear from the jury verdict form that the jury found each defendant liable for $10,500,000 in calculated statutory damages for contributory trademark infringement and $300,000 in calculated statutory damages for contributory copyright infringement, a new trial on the issue of damages is unnecessary. Instead, the damages as established by the jury may be implemented by making Akanoc and Chen jointly and severally liable for single awards in those amounts.

E. Conclusion

For the reasons expressed above, we affirm the district court on all issues of liability raised by the appeal and cross-appeal. But we vacate the judgment and remand with instructions that the district court award statutory damages in the amount of $10,500,000 for contributory trademark infringement and $300,000 for contributory copyright infringement, for which Akanoc and Chen shall be jointly and severally liable. The parties shall bear their own costs.

VACATED AND REMANDED WITH INSTRUCTIONS.

E. Real Property Law and Anticounterfeiting

In New York, brand owners have another remedy against landlords who knowingly refuse to evict tenants selling counterfeit goods under New York Real Property Law Section 231.

New York Real Property Law § 231

§ 231. Lease, when void; liability of landlord where premises are occupied for unlawful purpose

1. Whenever the lessee or occupant other than the owner of any building or premises, shall use or occupy the same, or any part thereof, for any illegal trade, manufacture or other business, the lease or agreement for the letting or occupancy of such building or premises, or any part thereof shall thereupon become void, and the landlord of such lessee or occupant may enter upon the premises so let or occupied.

2. The owner of real property, knowingly leasing or giving possession of the same to be used or occupied, wholly or partly, for any unlawful trade, manufacture or business, or knowingly permitting the same to be so used, is liable severally, and also jointly with one or more of the tenants or occupants thereof, for any damage resulting from such unlawful use, occupancy, trade, manufacture or business.

* * *

6. Any owner or tenant, including a tenant of one or more rooms of an apartment house, tenement house or multiple dwelling of any premises within two hundred feet

of the demised real property, may commence an action or proceeding in supreme court to enjoin the continued unlawful trade, manufacture or other business in such premises.

Omega SA v. 375 Canal LLC

324 F.R.D. 47 (S.D.N.Y. 2018)

[This is one of the most recent cases on landlord liability. Here, after a jury trial, the jury returned a verdict for $1.1 million as the landlord acted with willful blindness to the ongoing counterfeiting at its property and continued to lease the property, allowing the activity to continue despite being on notice.

In the following case, the Civil Court of the State of New York addressed the issue of whether the crime of trademark counterfeiting constitutes an illegal use under this statute.]

1165 Broadway Corp. v. Dayana of N.Y. Sportswear, Inc.

166 Misc. 2d 939 (N.Y. Civ. Ct. 1995)

BRANSTEN, Justice.

Opinion

At the request of the New York County District Attorney's Office, petitioner landlord, 1165 Broadway Corp. (hereinafter Petitioner), commenced these four summary holdover proceedings against the above-named respondent tenants (hereinafter Respondents) pursuant to Real Property Law § 231 (1) and RPAPL 715 (1), on the novel grounds that respondents were utilizing the commercial premises identified in each petition for the illegal manufacture and sale of counterfeit trademark apparel and sportswear.

Petitioner seeks possession of different rooms located at 1165 Broadway, New York, New York, after police officers purportedly recovered counterfeit goods in each premises valued in excess of $1,000 upon the execution of separate search warrants. Petitioner asserts that Respondents' possession for sale of said counterfeit trademark items is an illegal trade, manufacture, or business which renders the leases between the parties void pursuant to Real Property Law § 231 and which entitles petitioner to immediate possession in this summary proceeding instituted pursuant to RPAPL 715.

Applicability of Real Property Law § 231 (1) and RPAPL 715 (1)

Now, in this motion to dismiss each petition, all four respondents appear by the same attorney who submits that the Legislature did not intend Real Property Law § 231 (1) and RPAPL 715 (1) to be utilized when the allegations are that a premises is being used for the illegal manufacture and sale of counterfeit trademark goods. Respondents maintain that the use of Real Property Law § 231 (1) and RPAPL 715 (1) upon such grounds would be an expansive and impermissible application of these statutes, asserting that these statutes should be applied only where premises are being utilized to promote social and moral wrongs dangerous to the health or safety of other tenants in a given building and/or the neighborhood at large.

It is true that many courts have recognized RPAPL 715 (1)'s vital importance as a tool in the protection of owners, tenants and entire neighborhoods from the dangers of illegal activity such as drug dealing, prostitution and gambling. A reading of the statute, however, reveals that its application cannot be limited to only those illegal businesses which detrimentally impact on the quality of life in a given building or neighborhood.

Real Property Law § 231 (1) is a substantive statute which defines instances when a lease can be treated as void. "Whenever the lessee or occupant other than the owner of any building or premises, shall use or occupy the same, or any part thereof, *for any illegal trade, manufacture or other business,* the lease or agreement for the letting or occupancy of such building or premises, or any part thereof shall thereupon become void, and the landlord of such lessee or occupant may enter upon the premises so let or occupied." (Real Property Law § 231 [1] [emphasis added].)

RPAPL 715 (1) is both a substantive and procedural statute which grants conditional standing to various interested individuals and enforcement entities to maintain a summary proceeding for the recovery of real property where said property is: "used or occupied in whole or in part as a bawdy-house, or house or place of assignation for lewd persons, or for purposes of prostitution, *or for any illegal trade, business or manufacture.*" (RPAPL 715 [1] The language in both Real Property Law § 231 (1) and RPAPL 715 (1) is clear and unambiguous in proscribing "any illegal trade, manufacture or business" (Real Property Law § 231 [1]) without reference to the moral turpitude of any given conduct or the impact of such conduct on other tenants or on a neighborhood. Indeed, neither Real Property Law § 231 (1) nor RPAPL 715 (1) places restrictions or qualifications on the term "any illegal trade, business or manufacture" (RPAPL 715 [1]) in its respective text.

The intent or purpose of a statute must be derived from the plain meaning of the words and may not be declared by any other construction where the language of the statute is clear and unambiguous. Accordingly, in interpreting the meaning of an unambiguous statute, legislative intent need not be scrutinized.

The proscription against the use of a premises for "any illegal trade, manufacture or business" found in both Real Property Law § 231 (1) and RPAPL 715 (1) is plain. It certainly includes any enterprise operated in violation of the Penal Law. In the within matters, petitioner has alleged that respondents are utilizing their commercial premises in violation of Penal Law § 165.72, known as trademark counterfeiting in the second degree, a class E felony.

In 1992, the Legislature added the crimes of trademark counterfeiting to the Penal Law. (*See,* Penal Law §§ 165.70–165.74.) In his Practice Commentaries, William C. Donnino notes that: "[The Legislature] believed that prosecution of those who specialize in fraud by the use of counterfeit trademarks would be facilitated by creation of a crime specifically tailored to cover such conduct." (Donnino, Supp Practice Commentaries, McKinney's Cons Laws of NY, Book 39, Penal Law § 165.70, 1995 Pocket Part, at 105.) Notwithstanding the fact that the Legislature has specifically outlawed trademark counterfeiting, respondents ask this court to ignore the Penal Law and substitute its own tailored definition of illegality based on the impact a given activity has on other tenants or on the quality of life in a given neighborhood. Respondents' argument is clearly misplaced.

By their very terms, these statutes were specifically intended to address *any* illegal business, trade or manufacture and should not be interpreted to arbitrarily exclude those illegal businesses which fail to directly impact on the health, morals, welfare or safety of the public.

Although this court finds that these statutes are specifically applicable to the facts alleged herein, the potential reach of these statutes is not as broad as Respondents would contend. There is a distinction between the illegal use of a premises which violates Real Property Law § 231 (1) and RPAPL 715 (1) and the commission of illegal acts within a premises which do not. To present a valid cause of action under these statutes, a premises must be *used* for an illegal *trade, business* or *manufacture.*

The words "business," "trade" and "manufacture" themselves present a limitation to the potential reach of Real Property Law § 231 (1) and RPAPL 715 (1). For example, the personal use of illegal drugs within a premises, even if habitual and customary, does not constitute an illegal use of that premises for purposes of Real Property Law § 231 (1) and RPAPL 715 (1) because such conduct does not amount to a commercial activity or enterprise.

Similarly, the requirement that a premises be "used" for illegal business activity also presents a significant limitation to the reach of these statutes because the "use" of a premises imports not an isolated act but conduct with some measure of continuity. Therefore, an isolated use of a premises even in the commission of the most heinous of crimes, such as murder or rape, would not constitute an "illegal use" of a premises for purposes of these statutes.

On the other hand, it is clear that any commercial enterprise operating and utilizing a premises in violation of the Penal Law is an "illegal" business which subjects the lessee of the premises to eviction proceedings under Real Property Law § 231 (1) and RPAPL 715 (1) upon proof that the tenant engaged, or even acquiesced in said illegal use.

Indeed, although these statutes have been typically applied to recover premises utilized for prostitution, gambling and narcotics, they have also been applied to recover premises used for other illegal enterprises, including the storage and distribution of fireworks in violation of the Administrative Code of the City of New York, the sale and distribution of obscene material in violation of Penal Law § 235.05, the operation of a lodging or rooming house in violation of the former

Tenement Housing Law and the current Multiple Dwelling Law, and the selling of liquor in violation of the National Prohibition Act.

In 1921, with the repeal of many sections of the Code of Civil Procedure, the "bawdy-house" law became part of the Civil Practice Act. Thus, Code of Civil Procedure § 2231 (5) became Civil Practice Act § 1410 (5). The substantive language of the statute, however, remained unchanged.

Through these years, the persons entitled to bring eviction proceedings in "bawdy-house" cases grew. At first, only the landlord could bring such an action (L 1868, ch 764, § 61). In 1880, the Legislature expanded the right to a neighbor of the premises (L 1880, ch 178, § 2237). In 1913, those within "200 feet" of the premises (L 1913, ch 448, § 2237), another tenant in the same apartment or tenement house, or a domestic corporation holding certification from the board of charities were authorized to institute a proceeding (Code Civ Pro § 2237, later Civ Prac Act § 1417). In 1939, agencies licensed by the State Board of Social Welfare were also included in the growing list of entities with potential standing to bring eviction proceedings under the "bawdy-house" law (Civ Prac Act § 1417).

In 1947, the Legislature provided, for the first time, that "any duly authorized law enforcement agency of the state . . . under a duty to enforce the provisions of the Penal Law" be added to the list of individuals or agencies authorized to bring civil suit for dispossession. (L 1947, ch 284, § 1417.) Significantly, at the same time, the Legislature expanded the right of neighboring tenants and designated agencies to bring an action for removal of a tenant who was using the premises to conduct "any illegal trade, business or manufacture", and gave that right to law enforcement as well.

Contrary to Respondents' contention, nothing in the case law or legislative history prevents application of Real Property Law § 231 (1) and RPAPL 715 (1) to the facts herein. Indeed, a plain reading of the statute, the case law and the legislative history supports a nonrestrictive application of Real Property Law § 231 (1) and RPAPL 715 (1) to *any* illegal business, trade or manufacture. Accordingly, Respondents' motion to dismiss the petition is denied because there is no basis to conclude that an illegal business involving sale and storage of counterfeit goods should not be covered by Real Property Law § 231 (1) and RPAPL 715 (1).

Conclusion

Based on the foregoing, the court finds that the petitions are sufficiently pleaded and state a valid cause of action under both Real Property Law § 231 (1) and RPAPL 715 (1).

Note

While neither specific to landlords or New York property laws generally, if you have ever wondered about the legitimacy of "our version of" fragrances and how sellers can (or cannot) get away with such marketing, check out *Coty Inc. v. Excell Brands*, LLC, 277 F. Supp. 3d 425 (S.D.N.Y. 2017).

F. The Future of Anticounterfeiting and the Internet

This is the new Wild West of counterfeiting. Brands must move quickly, but so do the counterfeiters. It could be described as twenty-first-century whack-a-mole. What was once confined to back alleys, flea markets, and the like is now simply a click or two away. And frequently those clicks lead to a website operated from abroad. So how do brands deal with this? In a first-of-its-kind case, two brands collaborated to take on and take down Chinese websites selling counterfeits.

North Face Apparel Corp. v. Fujian Sharing Import & Export Ltd.

2011 U.S. Dist. LEXIS 158807 (S.D.N.Y. June 24, 2011)

HELLERSTEIN, District Judge.

Order Denying on Reconsideration Plaintiffs' Motion to Hold Public Interest Registry in Contempt of this Court's December 2, 2010, and December 20, 2010, Orders

On June 13, 2011, plaintiffs The North Face Apparel Corp. and PRL USA Holdings, Inc. and non-party Public Interest Registry appeared before me for oral argument on plaintiffs' motion, by order to show cause, to hold Public Interest Registry in contempt of this court's orders dated December 2, 2010, and December 20, 2010. Ruling from the bench, I granted plaintiffs' motion, subject to a ten-day stay to allow Public Interest Registry an opportunity either to comply with my December 2 and December 20 orders or to seek, from the United States Court of Appeals for the Second Circuit, a stay pending appeal. Immediately after oral argument, I issued a summary order that memorialized my oral ruling.

On June 21, 2011, I *sua sponte* enlarged by ten days the stay, which otherwise would have expired on June 23, 2011, and advised the parties that I was reviewing the appropriateness of my order.

On further consideration, I have come to the belief that the relief I ordered, however advisable it might have been generally, was not responsive to plaintiffs' motion to hold Public Interest Registry in contempt. For the reasons stated below, I vacate my June 13, 2011, ruling and deny plaintiffs' motion.

Plaintiffs initiated the underlying lawsuit in March 2010. Defendants comprise an online counterfeiting ring, based in China, that manufactures, markets, distributes, offers for sale, and sells, through a large number of "rogue websites," counterfeits of plaintiffs' goods that falsely bear plaintiffs' famous and well-regarded trademarks. In carrying out their counterfeiting activities, defendants have registered and used a wide array of Internet domain names that contain plaintiffs' trademarks. The websites associated with defendants' infringing domain names are set up to look like the websites for authorized online retail stores that sell plaintiffs' genuine goods. No sooner does one website become disabled than defendants are able to shift their business to a new website, succeeding in this way to continue in their counterfeiting business, one step ahead of the processes of law.

In the underlying lawsuit, plaintiffs alleged claims for federal trademark counterfeiting and infringement, unfair competition and false designation of origin, and cybersquatting. Plaintiffs have sought, and obtained, preliminary and permanent injunctive relief, trying vainly to stop defendants from counterfeiting.

I entered a default judgment and a permanent injunction against defendants in September 2010, after defendants had failed to appear or respond to plaintiffs' complaint. On plaintiffs' motion, on December 2, 2010, I entered an Amended Default Judgment and Permanent Injunction. In spite of this court's having awarded tens of millions of dollars in damages and injunctive relief in plaintiffs' favor, and despite this court's having found defendants in civil contempt, defendants persist, to this day, in their counterfeiting activities.

Public Interest Registry, a non-profit corporation formed under Pennsylvania law with a sole place of business in Reston, Virginia, manages the registry for, and maintains an authoritative database of, all ".org" domain names on the Internet. Public Interest Registry was neither served with process nor joined as a party in the underlying lawsuit.

On May 2, 2011, plaintiffs moved, by order to show cause, to hold Public Interest Registry in contempt, not of the Amended Default Judgment and Permanent Injunction, but rather of this court's orders dated December 2, 2010, and December 20, 2010. The December 2 order is styled a "Temporary Restraining Order Disabling Defendants' Websites, Asset Restraining Order, and Order to Show Cause Why Defendants Should Not Be Held in Contempt of this Court's Prior Order and Why the Order Should Not Be Modified." The December 2 order requires Public Interest Registry, in relevant part, to "temporarily disable the[] domain names [owned and controlled by Defendants] and make them inactive and untransferable pending further order from th[e] Court." The order dated December 20, 2010, styled an "Order for Contempt," requires Public Interest Registry to "disable Defendants' [d]omain [n]ames and make them inactive and untransferable, unless and until Plaintiffs request that any given domain name be re-activated" and, in addition, to "immediately transfer the Defendants' [i]nfringing [d]omain[] [names] to the ownership and control of Plaintiffs, through the registrar of Plaintiffs' choosing." Thus, both orders, the December 2 order and the December 20 order, require Public Interest Registry affirmatively to perform one or more acts.

The law is clear that a court may not require a person over whom it has not acquired valid in personam jurisdiction to perform an act. Squeez-A-Purse Corp. v. Stiller, 31 F.R.D. 261, 263 (S.D.N.Y. 1962). As Judge Learned Hand, writing for the Second Circuit, explained,

> [N]o court can make a decree which will bind any one but a party; a court of equity is as much so limited as a court of law; it cannot lawfully enjoin the world at large, no matter how broadly it words its decree. If it assumes to

> do so, the decree is *pro tanto brutum fulmen*, and the persons enjoined are free to ignore it. It is not vested with sovereign powers to declare conduct unlawful; its jurisdiction is limited to those over whom it gets personal service, and who therefore can have their day in court.

Alemite Mfg. Corp. v. Staff, 42 F.2d 832, 832-33 (2d Cir. 1930). Because Public Interest Registry was not joined as a party in the underlying lawsuit, and was not an "officer[], agent[], servant[], employee[], [or] attorney[]" of any defendant, see Fed. R. Civ. P. 65(d)(1)(A)-(B), I lacked the authority to order Public Interest Registry affirmatively to act, i.e., to disable or otherwise render inactive defendants' infringing domain names and transfer them to plaintiffs' ownership and control. Public Interest Registry cannot be held in contempt of my December 2 or December 20 orders for having failed to do what I lacked the authority to require it to do in the first instance.

At oral argument, Plaintiffs proceeded on a different theory, that Public Interest Registry had aided and abetted defendants in violating this court's orders. See Alemite Mfg., 42 F.2d at 833 ("[T]he only occasion when a person not a party may be punished, is when he has helped to bring about, not merely what the decree has forbidden, because it may have gone too far, but what it has power to forbid, an act of a party."). Although I lacked the power, under the December 2 and December 20 orders, to require Public Interest Registry to take down defendants' websites, I had the power and authority to enjoin it from aiding and abetting, or participating, in defendants' unlawful activities.

Public Interest Registry, for example, cannot continue to make the connections that enable customers attracted to defendants' websites to access those websites. Physically, such a connection is made when a customer types one of defendants' domain names ending in ".org ," such as "officialpolos.org," into an Internet browser window or clicks on a hyperlink that corresponds to such a domain name. Public Interest Registry's server responds to the customer's initiated message by supplying the link that connects the customer to the appropriate second-level domain name server, which, in turn, directs the customer to the specific website he or she addressed. See GlobalSantaFe Corp. v. Globalsantafe.com, 250 F. Supp. 2d 610, 618-19 (E.D. Va. 2003).

The system that allows Public Interest Registry to continue to make these connections is kept current by entities known as domain name registrars. "A domain name is created when it is registered with the appropriate registry operator"— here, Public Interest Registry, which maintains the authoritative database of all " .org" domain names. Coal. for ICANN Transparency Inc. v. VeriSign, Inc., 464 F. Supp. 2d 948, 952 (N.D. Cal. 2006), rev'd on other grounds, 567 F.3d 1084 (9th Cir. 2009). Public Interest Registry receives instructions for domain name registrations and registration renewals from domain name registrars who act, in turn, on the instructions of a member of the public. See id. Thus, the public, through domain name registrars, gains access to the ".org" registry system managed by Public Interest Registry. Apparently, the registrars who acted for defendants with respect to their infringing domain names are located overseas, beyond the reach of this court's jurisdiction.

My injunction, once served on Public Interest Registry, should have alerted it to no longer play its role in allowing customers to connect to defendant counterfeiters' websites, for Public Interest Registry would, by continuing to do so, commit an unlawful act, by aiding and abetting in defendants' unlawful counterfeiting activities in violation of United States law. Furthermore, Public Interest Registry should no longer have accepted transmissions of registration information from registrars who had received defendants' orders for domain name registrations and registration renewals because my injunction advised that defendants' domain names had been used to advertise and sell counterfeits of plaintiffs' goods.

Plaintiffs may, if they wish, renew their motion to make clear that the scope of the permanent injunction against defendants applies to Public Interest Registry for aiding and abetting, and participating, in defendants' unlawful activities. For, if Public Interest Registry continues to connect customers to defendant counterfeiters' websites, and continues to permit the registration and renewal of defendants' infringing domain names, Public Interest Registry will itself have violated the permanent injunction against defendants.

For the reasons stated, I vacate my ruling of June 13, 2011, which granted plaintiffs' motion to hold Public Interest Registry in contempt, and I hereby deny plaintiffs' motion. The Clerk shall mark the motion (Doc. No. 36) terminated. Plaintiffs may, if they wish, renew their motion in the manner indicated above.

SO ORDERED.

A number of other brands have used a similar model to go after foreign, primarily Chinese, websites hawking counterfeit goods online. While the awards are impressive, the ability to collect monetarily has diminished over time. But there is still value in the shutting down of the websites. Successful suits listing dozens of foreign websites continue to be brought today. A number of brands file suit primarily in federal courts in Illinois and Florida naming dozens of websites per complaint seeking to take down various domain names that are really nothing more than websites selling cheap knockoffs of the genuine brand.

Gucci America, Inc. v. Weixing Li

135 F. Supp. 3d 87 (S.D.N.Y. 2015)

Opinion and Order

SULLIVAN, District Judge.

On June 25, 2010, Plaintiffs Gucci America, Inc., and certain of its affiliates ("Gucci") commenced this trademark infringement action against the owners and operators of a Chinese website dedicated to the sale of imitation handbags and other counterfeit items bearing Gucci's trademarks. (Doc. No. 1.) Now before the

Court is Gucci's motion to compel nonparty Bank of China ("BOC") to comply with subpoenas requesting the production of account documents relating to all Defendants. (Doc. No. 135.) For the reasons set forth below, the motion is granted.

I. Background

The Court presumes the parties' familiarity with the facts underlying this case, which were thoroughly discussed in the Court's August 23, 2011 Memorandum and Order (Doc. No. 75 ("August 23 Order")) and May 18, 2012 Memorandum and Order (Doc. No. 98 ("May 18 Order")). However, to provide context, the Court briefly recites the facts and procedural history below.

Gucci is a distributor of luxury handbags, clothing, jewelry, fragrances, and home products. In or around June 2010, Gucci discovered that Defendants and their affiliates were offering for sale on the internet counterfeit versions of Gucci's products. On June 25, 2010, Gucci initiated this action against certain Defendants pursuant to the Lanham Act, 15 U.S.C. § 1051 *et seq.*, and related state-law causes of action. Gucci amended its complaint to add additional Defendants on October 4, 2010 (Doc. No. 18) and on March 10, 2011 (Doc. No. 55).

On July 12, 2010, the Court issued a preliminary injunction (the "Injunction"), which froze Defendants' assets and enjoined Defendants from manufacturing, distributing, marketing, or selling counterfeit goods. (Doc. No. 12.) Because Gucci had obtained evidence that certain Defendants had wired the proceeds of the counterfeit sales to accounts at the Chinese headquarters of BOC (the "Head Office"), the Injunction also provided that "any banks . . . who receive actual notice of this order . . . are, without prior approval of the Court, restrained and enjoined from transferring, disposing of, or secreting any money, stocks, bonds, real or personal property, or other assets of Defendants." (*Id.* at 6.) The Injunction also provided that "any third party receiving a subpoena pursuant to this Order shall produce documents responsive to such requests within ten (10) days of service of such subpoena." (*Id.* at 9.)

Pursuant to the Injunction, Gucci served a subpoena on BOC on July 16, 2010 (the "2010 Subpoena") in accordance with Rule 45 of the Federal Rules of Civil Procedure, requesting documents pertaining to any BOC accounts maintained by Defendants and defining "ACCOUNTS" to include "all . . . accounts at [BOC] held by Defendants; including, but not limited to" two specifically named BOC accounts. (Doc. No. 28-5 at 4.) The 2010 Subpoena also requested "documents associated with any open or closed checking, savings, money market accounts, and certificates of deposit held in the name of any of the Defendants, including but not limited to" the two named BOC accounts. (*Id.* at 6.) Shortly before filing the Second Amended Complaint, Gucci served BOC with a second subpoena on February 23, 2011 (the "2011 Subpoena"), making some new requests for information but largely repeating the same requests contained in the 2010 Subpoena. (Doc. No. 109-4.) Although again seeking documents pertaining to "any" BOC accounts maintained by any of the Defendants, the 2011 Subpoena specifically identified the same two accounts identified in the 2010 Subpoena, along with six additional accounts. (*Id.*)

In a supplemental submission, Gucci identified one other account, bringing the total number of BOC accounts connected to Defendants to nine. (Doc. No. 58-9.)

On August 23, 2011, the Court granted Gucci's motion to compel BOC to comply with the 2010 Subpoena and the asset freeze provisions of the Injunction, and denied BOC's cross-motion to modify the Injunction so as to exclude assets held by BOC in any of its locations in China. (August 23 Order at 1.) On September 12, 2011, the Court denied BOC's motion for leave to appeal, as well as BOC's request for an additional twenty-one days to comply with the August 23 Order. (Doc. No. 79.) In response to the Court's September 12 Order, BOC produced documents relating to only the two accounts identified in the 2010 Subpoena, and refused to produce information regarding other accounts held by Defendants. (Doc. No. 116 at 3.) According to Gucci, BOC's production was also incomplete as to even those two accounts, since it did not include "documents reflecting deposits and withdrawals into the account[s], such as monthly account statement[s], even though these were among the documents [that] Gucci specifically requested." (Doc. No. 111 at 9.)

On November 30, 2011, BOC filed a motion for reconsideration of the Court's August 23 Order, based principally on a November 3, 2011 letter that BOC received from the People's Bank of China ("PBOC") and the China Banking Regulatory Commission ("CBRC"). In the letter, PBOC and CBRC set forth their views as to the application of Chinese bank secrecy laws to disclosures of customer information outside of China, China's commitment to using Hague Convention procedures for document requests, and the likelihood of sanctions being imposed on BOC in China as a result of its compliance with the August 23 Order. (Doc. No. 91-9.) On May 18, 2012, the Court issued its Memorandum and Order denying the motion for reconsideration. (May 18 Order at 1.) BOC thereafter appealed the Court's August 23 and May 18 Orders to the Second Circuit. (Doc. Nos. 80 & 99.)

On September 17, 2014, the Second Circuit affirmed the Court's Injunction but vacated its August 23 and May 18 Orders in light of the Supreme Court's opinion on general personal jurisdiction in *Daimler AG v. Bauman*, —— U.S. ——, 134 S. Ct. 746, 187 L.Ed.2d 624 (2014), which postdated the Court's August 23 and May 18 Orders. *Gucci Am., Inc. v. Weixing Li*, 768 F.3d 122 (2d Cir.2014) ("*Gucci II*"). The Second Circuit remanded the case to this Court to consider in the first instance whether the Court has specific personal jurisdiction over BOC, and, if so, whether exercising such jurisdiction is consistent with principles of comity in light of recent Chinese court decisions. *Id.* at 145.

On December 1, 2014, Gucci filed its motion to compel BOC's compliance with the 2010 and 2011 Subpoenas (Doc. No. 135) and an accompanying memorandum of law (Doc. No. 136 ("Mem.")). BOC filed its memorandum of law in opposition to the motion to compel on January 23, 2015 (Doc. No. 141 ("Opp.")), and Gucci filed its reply memorandum of law on February 6, 2015 (Doc. No. 146 ("Rep.")). After the matter was fully submitted, the parties submitted additional letters relating to recent cases they argue are relevant to the motion before the Court. (Doc. Nos. 152, 154, 155, 156 & 157.) The matter was thus fully briefed as of September 10, 2015.

II. Discussion

As noted above, the Second Circuit has directed the Court on remand to consider (1) whether it has specific personal jurisdiction over BOC justifying an order to compel it to produce the documents called for in the 2010 and 2011 Subpoenas, and, if so, (2) whether recent decisions from Chinese courts alter the Court's previous comity analysis pursuant to § 442 of the Restatement (Third) of Foreign Relations Law. For the reasons set forth below, the Court concludes that it has specific personal jurisdiction over BOC and that the § 442 factors still strongly support ordering BOC to comply with the 2010 and 2011 Subpoenas.

A. Specific Personal Jurisdiction

A district court must have personal jurisdiction over a nonparty to compel it to comply with a Rule 45 subpoena. *See, e.g., First Am. Corp. v. Price Waterhouse LLP,* 154 F.3d 16, 20 (2d Cir.1998); *In re Sealed Case,* 141 F.3d 337, 341 (D.C.Cir.1998); *In re Application to Enforce Admin. Subpoenas Duces Tecum of the S.E.C. v. Knowles,* 87 F.3d 413, 418 (10th Cir.1996). Federal courts must satisfy three primary requirements to lawfully exercise personal jurisdiction over an entity: (1) the entity must have been properly served, (2) the court must have a statutory basis for exercising personal jurisdiction, and (3) the exercise of personal jurisdiction must comport with constitutional due process. *Licci ex rel. Licci v. Lebanese Canadian Bank, SAL,* 673 F.3d 50, 59–60 (2d Cir.2012) ("*Licci II*"). Here it is undisputed that BOC was properly served at its New York branch. (August 23 Order at 5.) Accordingly, the Court will address the second and third "primary requirements" under *Licci II*—namely, whether the Court has a statutory basis for exercising jurisdiction, and whether doing so comports with constitutional due process.

1. Statutory Basis for Personal Jurisdiction

A federal statute or the law of the state in which the court is located can provide the statutory basis for personal jurisdiction. *See Licci II,* 673 F.3d at 60. New York's long-arm statute provides that a court "may exercise personal jurisdiction over any non-domiciliary . . . who in person or through an agent . . . transacts any business within the state" so long as the plaintiff's "cause of action aris[es] from" that "transact[ion]." N.Y. C.P.L.R. § 302(a)(1); *see also Licci II,* 673 F.3d at 60. Accordingly, before exercising personal jurisdiction over an entity, "a court must decide (1) whether the defendant transacts any business in New York and, if so, (2) whether this cause of action arises from such a business transaction." *Licci II,* 673 F.3d at 60 (quoting *Best Van Lines, Inc. v. Walker,* 490 F.3d 239, 246 (2d Cir.2007)) (internal quotation marks omitted).

The New York Court of Appeals has noted that, in the banking context, the first prong of the § 302(a)(1) inquiry "may be complicated by the nature of inter-bank activity, especially given the widespread use of correspondent accounts nominally in New York to facilitate the flow of money worldwide, often for transactions that otherwise have no other connection to New York, or indeed the United States." *Licci ex rel. Licci v. Lebanese Canadian Bank, SAL,* 20 N.Y.3d 327, 338, 960 N.Y.S.2d 695,

984 N.E.2d 893 (2012) ("*Licci III*"). Notwithstanding this potential complication, the New York Court of Appeals has held that "complaints alleging a foreign bank's repeated use of a correspondent account in New York on behalf of a client" are sufficient to "show purposeful availment of New York's dependable and transparent banking system, the dollar as a stable and fungible currency, and the predictable jurisdictional and commercial law of New York and the United States." *Id.* at 339, 960 N.Y.S.2d 695, 984 N.E.2d 893.

With respect to the second prong of the § 302(a)(1) jurisdictional analysis, the New York Court of Appeals requires that "in light of all the circumstances, there must be an *articulable nexus* or *substantial relationship* between the business transaction and the claim asserted." *Id.* (citations and internal quotation marks omitted) (emphasis added). Notably, New York does not require a *causal relationship* between the business transaction and the claim asserted; it is enough that "the latter is not completely unmoored from the former." *Id.* Considering this analysis in the subpoena context, the Second Circuit in this action endorsed a focus on "the connection between the nonparty's contacts with the forum and the discovery order at issue." *Gucci II*, 768 F.3d at 141–42 (citing *Knowles*, 87 F.3d at 418).

In answering a certified question from the Second Circuit, the New York Court of Appeals in *Licci III* applied its § 302(a)(1) analysis to a foreign bank in a strikingly similar situation to that of BOC here. There, the foreign bank "did not operate branches or offices, or maintain employees, in the United States," *Licci III*, 20 N.Y.3d at 332, 960 N.Y.S.2d 695, 984 N.E.2d 893, but it nevertheless executed dozens of U.S. dollar-denominated wire transfers through a correspondent account it maintained with a domestic bank in New York, *id.* at 340, 960 N.Y.S.2d 695, 984 N.E.2d 893. In so doing, the plaintiffs alleged, the foreign bank provided financial support for a terrorist group. *Id.* The New York Court of Appeals held that "the fact that [the foreign bank] used a New York account 'dozens' of times indicates desirability and a lack of coincidence," which demonstrates a transaction of business in New York. *Id.* The court also held that the plaintiffs had shown "an articulable nexus or substantial relationship between the transaction and the alleged breaches" because the foreign bank "did not route a transfer for a terrorist group once or twice by mistake," but rather "deliberately used a New York account again and again to effect its support of [the terrorist group]." *Id.*

Here, BOC's New York conduct is, if anything, even more substantial, deliberate, and recurring than that of the foreign bank in the *Licci* cases (collectively "*Licci*"). As a result, the Court has no trouble concluding that Gucci satisfies the first prong of § 302(a)(1). Unlike the bank in *Licci*, BOC owns multiple real properties in New York and maintains two branches that are staffed with employees. (Doc. No. 138, Declaration of Robert L. Weigel, dated Dec. 1, 2014 ("Weigel Decl."), Exs. 14–15.) Moreover, BOC's Head Office opened a correspondent account at JPMorgan Chase Bank ("Chase") in New York to facilitate transfers directly from Chase customers to BOC customers. (Weigel Decl., Exs. 2–8, 17.) This relationship enables BOC to boast that its New York branches are the "principal U.S. dollar clearing channel of

[BOC] worldwide," and that BOC is "the first choice of U.S. dollar wire transfers to and from China." (Weigel Decl., Ex. 17.) Such marketing apparently captivated Defendants, who used BOC nearly a dozen times to transfer what Gucci alleges are ill-gotten gains denominated in U.S. dollars from the United States to China. (Weigel Decl., Exs. 2–12.)

Furthermore, with respect to the second prong of the § 302(a)(1) analysis, there is a strong relationship between BOC's New York conduct and Gucci's subpoena requests. Specifically, Gucci alleges that Defendants' use of BOC's correspondent account at Chase and BOC's relationship with Chase in New York to effectuate wire transfers between the United States and China were crucial components of their counterfeiting operation. Gucci's 2010 and 2011 Subpoenas seek information about those very transfers, as well as Defendants' relationship with BOC. Clearly, there is more than "an articulable nexus" between BOC's New York business activity and Gucci's discovery requests.

BOC's efforts to distinguish *Licci* are unpersuasive. BOC asserts that "there is a vast difference between a bank's purposeful *use* of a correspondent account in the United States to *make* illegal payments for a client, as in *Licci,* and BOC's passive receipt of transfers that [D]efendants and Chase Bank initiated and routed to BOC." (Opp. at 14 (emphasis in original).) But BOC mischaracterizes *Licci.* The Second Circuit and New York Court of Appeals emphasized that frequent and deliberate *use* of a domestic correspondent account to execute international wire transfers was enough to constitute transacting business in New York; neither court said anything about the *Licci* foreign bank knowingly making illegal payments, much less that such knowing complicity was required to establish jurisdiction pursuant to § 302(a)(1). *See Licci III,* 20 N.Y.3d at 338–39, 960 N.Y.S.2d 695, 984 N.E.2d 893; *Licci ex rel. Licci v. Lebanese Canadian Bank, SAL,* 732 F.3d 161, 168 (2d Cir.2013) ("*Licci IV*"). Here, there can be no real dispute that BOC frequently and deliberately *used* its New York correspondent account with Chase to effectuate wire transfers for its U.S. clients, including, critically, Defendants in this action. BOC did not simply "maintain" a correspondent account with Chase in New York that was used "once or twice by mistake" or "coincidental[ly]" by Defendants. To the contrary, BOC encouraged its clients to rely on its relationships with Chase so that they could effectuate frequent wire transfers from the United States to China, which is exactly what Defendants did here. *Licci III,* 20 N.Y.3d at 340, 960 N.Y.S.2d 695, 984 N.E.2d 893.

Moreover, the cases that BOC relies on to support its argument that "receiving a transfer of funds, whether via a U.S. correspondent account or through wire services, does not subject the recipient to personal jurisdiction" (Opp. at 15), are equally inapplicable to the instant facts. None of those cases involved a foreign bank deliberately thrusting itself into the New York financial market by establishing a New York office and a correspondent account with a New York bank to repeatedly facilitate the transfer of money from its clients' bank accounts in the United States to their accounts abroad. Rather, the cases either involved banks with no New York operations that passively received money via a New York correspondent account, *see e.g., Rushaid v. Pictet & Cie,* 127 A.D.3d 610, 9 N.Y.S.3d 16, 17 (2015) and *Leema Enterprises, Inc. v. Willi,* 575 F.Supp. 1533, 1537 (S.D.N.Y.1983), or, even less applicable, concerned non-banks that received wire transfers from an account that happened to be associated with a New York or U.S. bank, *see e.g., Ballard v. Walker,* No. 11-cv-5874 (LLS), 2013 WL 6501234, *3 (S.D.N.Y. Dec. 11, 2013), *Gargano v. Cayman National Corp.,* 2010 WL 2245034, at *6 (D.Mass. June 2, 2010), and *Canadian Group Underwriters Insurance Co. v. M/V "Arctic Trader",* No. 96-cv-9242 (DAB), 1998 WL 730334, at *3–4 (S.D.N.Y. Oct. 19, 1998).

Here, BOC is a bank that is in the business of providing banking services to individuals in China and the United States. (Weigel Decl., Ex. 13.) Critical to serving those clients is the existence of a correspondent account at a reputable New York bank to conduct secure, efficient, and quick wire transfers. BOC cannot credibly compare itself to a passive recipient of a few one-off wire transfers that by pure happenstance were routed through a domestic correspondent bank account.

Finally, BOC asserts that Gucci cannot demonstrate the requisite nexus between BOC's New York-based conduct and the Subpoenas, since the information sought by Gucci is in fact located in China and the active task of crediting Defendants' Chinese bank accounts took place in China. (Opp. at 10–11, 14.) However, the Second Circuit in *Licci* directly addressed and rejected the argument that the effects of the entity's in-forum conduct must also take place in New York for jurisdiction to be proper. In fact, the Second Circuit concluded that "[s]o long as [the entity's] in-forum activity sufficiently reflects the [entity's] 'purposeful availment' of the privilege of carrying on its activities here, minimum contacts are established, even if the effects of the [entity's] entire course of conduct are felt elsewhere." *Licci IV,* 732 F.3d at 173. Thus, the fact that BOC's deliberate conduct in New York produced effects in China—such as causing China-based BOC employees to make book entries to Defendants' Chinese bank accounts to reflect wire transfers—does nothing to undermine the nexus between BOC's New York-based conduct and the 2010 and 2011 Subpoenas.

BOC's argument that the information that Gucci seeks is physically located in China, not New York, is equally unavailing. BOC seems to be invoking a species of the "separate entity rule," which "provides that even when a bank garnishee with a New York branch is subject to personal jurisdiction, its other branches are to be treated as separate entities for certain purposes." *Motorola Credit Corp. v. Standard Chartered Bank,* 24 N.Y.3d 149, 158, 996 N.Y.S.2d 594 (2014). However, "where the remedy sought is . . . a subpoena, the separate entity rule has not barred enforcement;" rather, "only personal jurisdiction over the legal entity, the bank and its branches, is necessary." *CE Int'l Res. Holdings, LLC v. S.A. Minerals Ltd. P'ship,* No. 12-cv-8087 (SN), 2013 WL 2661037, at *17 (S.D.N.Y. June 12, 2013) (citing *United States v. First Nat'l City Bank,* 379 U.S. 378, 384, 85 S.Ct. 528, 13 L. Ed.2d 365 (1965)); *see also Eitzen Bulk A/S v. Bank of India,* 827 F.Supp.2d 234, 239–41 (S.D.N.Y.2011). Therefore, it is clear that the Court has a statutory basis to exercise personal jurisdiction over BOC.

Citing the amended Rule 45, which provides that "[a] subpoena may be served at any place within the United States," Fed.R.Civ.P. 45(b)(2), the Second Circuit suggested that the Court may consider BOC's contacts nationwide in evaluating personal jurisdiction. *See Gucci II,* 768 F.3d at 142 n. 21. However, because the Court finds that it has personal jurisdiction over BOC under New York's long-arm statute, the Court need not determine whether BOC's nationwide contacts with the United States are relevant to the personal jurisdiction analysis.

2. Constitutional Due Process

When assessing whether the exercise of specific personal jurisdiction over an entity is constitutionally proper, courts must apply a two-step test: first, they must determine whether the entity has sufficient "minimum contacts" with the forum, and second, they must find that the exercise of jurisdiction under the circumstances was "reasonable." *Licci IV,* 732 F.3d at 170; *Metro. Life Ins. Co. v. Robertson-Ceco Corp.,* 84 F.3d 560, 567 (2d Cir.1996). Determining whether an entity has sufficient "minimum contacts" with a forum turns on whether the entity" 'purposefully directed' [its] activities at . . . the forum and [whether] the litigation results from alleged injuries that 'arise out of or relate to' those activities." *Burger King Corp. v. Rudzewicz,* 471 U.S. 462, 472, 105 S.Ct. 2174, 85 L.Ed.2d 528 (1985) (citations omitted). Once the threshold showing of "minimum contacts" is met, the party objecting to jurisdiction must present "a compelling case that the presence of some other considerations would render jurisdiction unreasonable." *Bank Brussels Lambert v. Fiddler Gonzalez & Rodriguez,* 305 F.3d 120, 129 (2d Cir.2002) (Sotomayor, J.) (quoting *Metro. Life Ins. Co.,* 84 F.3d at 568). Reduced to its essence, the "reasonableness" of exercising jurisdiction depends on whether doing so would comport with "fair play and substantial justice." *Burger King Corp.,* 471 U.S. at 476, 105 S.Ct. 2174.

As an initial matter, the Second Circuit noted in *Licci IV* that it would be "rare" and "unusual" for a court to find that an entity's conduct satisfied § 302(a)(1), "yet, in connection with the same transaction of business," that the entity did not have sufficient minimum contacts with New York or that the exercise of personal jurisdiction would be otherwise unreasonable. *Licci IV,* 732 F.3d at 170. The court further observed that it was aware of no such decisions in the Second Circuit. *Id.* Therefore, in light of the Court's prior finding that it has statutory personal jurisdiction over BOC for the enforcement of the Subpoenas pursuant to § 302(a)(1), it would be "unusual," and in fact unprecedented in this Circuit, if the Court's exercise of personal jurisdiction over BOC did not comport with due process. Nevertheless, the Court will specifically assess whether BOC has sufficient "minimum contacts" with New York and whether the exercise of jurisdiction in this action is otherwise "reasonable."

a. Minimum Contacts

Court often analyze the "minimum contacts" inquiry as two separate prongs: (1) the "purposeful availment" prong, whereby the court determines whether the entity deliberately directed its conduct at the forum, and (2) the "relatedness" prong, whereby the court determines whether the controversy at issue arose out of or related to the entity's in-forum conduct. *See, e.g., Chew v. Dietrich,* 143 F.3d 24, 27–29(2d Cir.1998); *Nowak v. Tak How Inv., Ltd.,* 94 F.3d 708, 713 (1st Cir.1996).

As the Court has already noted, BOC's in-forum conduct is deliberate and recurring, not "random, isolated, or fortuitous." *Licci IV,* 732 F.3d at 171 (quoting *Keeton v. Hustler Magazine, Inc.,* 465 U.S. 770, 774, 104 S.Ct. 1473, 79 L.Ed.2d 790(1984)). BOC's Head Office opened a correspondent account at Chase in New York to facilitate transfers directly from Chase customers to BOC customers, thereby enabling BOC to assert that its New York branches are the "principal U.S. dollar clearing channel of [BOC] worldwide" and that it is "the first choice of U.S. dollar wire transfers to and from China." (Weigel Decl., Ex. 17.) There is also no dispute that BOC's New York branches are "mainly funded by deposits from various third parties in China as well as in the United States," are "designated as the U.S. dollar funding pool within [BOC]'s global operations," provide "U.S. dollar funding . . . to other [BOC] foreign branches and affiliates," and "manage[ ] the liquidity for other U.S. branches." (Weigel Decl., Ex. 13.) As noted above, BOC owns multiple real properties in New York (Weigel Decl., Exs. 14–15), and it has initiated multiple lawsuits in the Southern District of New York (*see, e.g.,* Mem. at 10 n. 5). Accordingly, as the Court observed in its August 23 Order, it is clear that BOC "has purposely chosen to do business in New York and has availed itself of the myriad benefits that come with establishing a presence in the United States' premier financial center." (August 23 Order at 11.)

Once again, the *Licci* decisions demonstrate that BOC had the requisite "minimum contacts" with New York. In *Licci IV,* the Second Circuit concluded that "the selection and repeated use of New York's banking system . . . constitutes 'purposeful availment of the privilege of doing business in New York.'" *Licci IV,* 732 F.3d at 171(quoting *Bank Brussels Lambert,* 305 F.3d at 127) (alterations omitted). Like the foreign bank in *Licci,* BOC selected Chase in New York to be its correspondent bank to give it access to "New York's dependable and transparent banking system, the dollar as a stable and fungible currency, and the predictable jurisdictional and commercial law of New York and the United States." *Licci III,* 20 N.Y.3d at 339, 960 N.Y.S.2d 695, 984 N.E.2d 893. Clearly, BOC could have chosen to process Defendants' U.S. dollar-denominated wire transfers through correspondent accounts elsewhere, or chosen to have its Head Office establish a correspondent account elsewhere, but it did not. *See Licci IV,* 732 F.3d at 171. Thus, BOC's arguments that it did not purposefully avail itself of the privilege of conducting business in New York are as unpersuasive here as they were when considered in connection with the § 302(a)(1) analysis above.

Relatedness, the second prong of the minimum contacts inquiry, is a sliding-scale test: when an entity has only limited contacts with a forum, relatedness requires that "the plaintiff's injury was proximately caused by those contacts," but when an entity's contacts with the forum "are more substantial," it is not unreasonable to exercise personal jurisdiction "even though the acts within the state are not the proximate cause of the plaintiff's injury." *Chew,* 143 F.3d at 29; *see also S.E.C. v. Straub,* 921 F.Supp.2d 244, 254 n. 6 (S.D.N.Y.2013) (recognizing that *Chew* established a sliding-scale analysis for assessing relatedness). For an entity's contacts to fall on the "more substantial" end of the sliding scale test, the contacts need not rise to the level that would establish general jurisdiction. *See Del Ponte v. Universal City Dev. Partners, Ltd.,* No. 07-cv-2360 (KMK), 2008 WL 169358, at *10(S.D.N.Y. Jan. 16, 2008) (concluding that a defendant's contacts with New York placed it on the "more substantial" end of the spectrum because it repeatedly sent its principals on business trips to New York and it purchased a large portion of its products from New York suppliers). And when an entity's contacts with the forum are "more substantial," courts have determined that it is sufficient that those contacts be a "but for" cause of the plaintiff's injury, rather than the "proximate cause" of the injury. *In re LIBOR-Based Fin. Instruments Antitrust Litig.,* No. 11-mdl-2262 (NRB), 2015 WL 4634541, at *23 (S.D.N.Y. Aug. 4, 2015). Finally, the Second Circuit in this action endorsed the Tenth Circuit's approach to applying the relatedness inquiry in the context of a subpoena, which focused on "the connection between the nonparty's contacts with the forum and the discovery order at issue." *Gucci II,* 768 F.3d at 141–42 (citing *Knowles,* 87 F.3d at 418).

Under the *Chew* sliding scale, BOC's contacts with New York are sufficiently "substantial" that they need only be a "but for" cause of Gucci's 2010 and 2011 Subpoenas. As noted previously, BOC has significant operations, employees, and physical locations in New York, actively solicits business and customers in New York, and has deliberate and recurring contacts with New York. Furthermore, BOC provides extensive services to its clients in New York, including a correspondent account at Chase that its Head Office established to facilitate U.S. dollar-denominated transfers. Therefore, contrary to BOC's assertions, BOC bears little resemblance to the defendants in *SPV OSUS Ltd. v. UBS AG*—which were "foreign banks alleged to have provided services to foreign investment funds, acting entirely abroad and with only sporadic or indirect contacts with the United States," with no physical presence or employees in New York, and which did not "directly or purposefully solicit, market, or otherwise seek out business from potential customers located in the United States." 114 F.Supp.3d 161, 168–70, No. 15-cv-619 (JSR), 2015 WL 4394955, at *5–6 (S.D.N.Y. July 20, 2015).On the record before it, the Court has little difficulty concluding that BOC's New York contacts are a "but for" cause of Gucci's document requests. Gucci's Subpoenas are premised on the fact that Defendants' proceeds from the sale of counterfeit goods were transferred through BOC's correspondent account in New York. As such, there is a substantial nexus between (1) the motion to compel BOC to comply with Gucci's Subpoenas, which focus on Defendants who allegedly sold counterfeit goods on the internet in violation of the Lanham Act and utilized New York banks as part of that scheme, and (2) BOC's contacts with New York.

Accordingly, the Court finds that BOC purposefully availed itself of this forum and that its conduct was sufficiently related to the subpoena enforcement action that is the subject of this dispute. The Court thus concludes that BOC has sufficient minimum contacts with New York for the Court to have personal jurisdiction over Gucci's motion to compel.

b. Reasonableness

In determining whether the exercise of personal jurisdiction would comport with "traditional notions of fair play and substantial justice," courts consider five factors: (1) "the burden that the exercise of jurisdiction will impose on the [entity]," (2) "the interests of the forum state in adjudicating the case," (3) "the plaintiff's interest in obtaining convenient and effective relief," (4) "the interstate judicial system's interest in obtaining the most efficient resolution of the controversy," and (5) "the shared interest of the states in furthering substantive social policies." *Bank Brussels Lambert,* 305 F.3d at 129 (citations omitted). When the entity that may be subject to personal jurisdiction is a foreign one, courts consider the *international* judicial system's interest in efficiency and the shared interests of the *nations* in advancing substantive policies. *See Asahi Metal Indus. Co. v. Superior Court of Cal., Solano Cty.,* 480 U.S. 102, 115, 107 S.Ct. 1026, 94 L.Ed.2d 92 (1987). Here, it is clear that BOC, as the party objecting to jurisdiction, has not carried its burden of making "a compelling case" that jurisdiction is unreasonable. *Bank Brussels Lambert,* 305 F.3d at 129.

The burden on BOC of submitting to jurisdiction in New York is minimal. BOC has been litigating this action in New York since June 2010. Moreover, BOC has initiated multiple lawsuits in the Southern District of New York and maintains physical operations here. In addition, "the conveniences of modern communication and transportation ease" any burden BOC might experience from further contesting the 2010 and 2011 Subpoenas. *Licci IV,* 732 F.3d at 174 (quoting *Metro. Life Ins.,* 84 F.3d at 574). Indeed, the fact that the controversy at issue involves subpoena compliance, and not BOC's own liability, gives BOC even less "cause to complain of an outrage to fair play." *First Am. Corp.,* 154 F.3d at 20. Although BOC asks the Court to consider the fact that granting Gucci's motion would force BOC to violate Chinese law (Doc. No. 141 at 16), BOC cites to no other courts that have considered such arguments in the context of assessing the reasonableness of an exercise of personal jurisdiction, as opposed to a separate and subsequent comity analysis, and the Court declines to be the first. In fact, in a case that BOC cites to support its contention, the court specifically *declined* to consider any potential "clash between the forum law and the substantive policies of another state" as part of the personal jurisdiction analysis. *Ballard v. Savage,* 65 F.3d 1495, 1501 (9th Cir.1995); *see also United States v. Int'l Bhd. of Teamsters,* 945 F.Supp. 609, 623(S.D.N.Y.1996) (considering the conflict of two nations' laws only in the comity analysis, not the personal jurisdiction due process analysis). With respect to the burden factor, courts tend to focus their inquiry on the logistical difficulties facing a foreign entity forced to litigate in a given forum, such as the distance the entity would have to travel and the entity's unfamiliarity with the forum. *See Wiwa v. Royal Dutch Petroleum Co.,* 226 F.3d 88, 99 (2d Cir.2000). Here, it is clear that such burdens are minimal or non-existent, since BOC is physically present in the forum, no stranger to litigation in it, and already represented by able New York counsel.

With respect to the forum's interest in adjudicating the dispute, courts do not "compare the interests of the sovereigns" but rather "determine whether the forum state *has* an interest." *Nowak,* 94 F.3d at 718 (emphasis in original). Here, New York as the forum state has a "manifest interest in providing effective means of redress for its residents." *Chloe v. Queen Bee of Beverly Hills, LLC,* 616 F.3d 158, 173 (2d Cir.2010) (quoting *Burger King,* 471 U.S. at 483, 105 S.Ct. 2174). Several Plaintiffs, including Gucci and Yves Saint Laurent America, Inc., are incorporated in New York and have their principal place of business here. (Doc. No. 55 ¶¶ 6 & 9.) Furthermore, the U.S. dollar-denominated transfers of allegedly ill-gotten gains were routed through New York. Finally, New York has a strong interest in litigants' compliance with their discovery obligations, such as subpoenas, to ensure an efficient and effective judicial process, *see, e.g., Hickman v. Taylor,* 329 U.S. 495, 501, 67 S.Ct. 385, 91 L. Ed. 451 (1947), and it is clear that New York and the United States "ha[ve] a powerful interest in enforcing the acts of Congress, especially those, such as the Lanham Act, that are designed to protect intellectual property rights and prevent customer confusion," (August 23 Order at 11).

As for "the plaintiff's interest in obtaining convenient and effective relief," *Bank Brussels Lambert,* 305 F.3d at 129, there can be no doubt that Gucci has a strong interest in BOC complying with the 2010 and 2011 Subpoenas because, as the Court already found, "the documents sought by the Subpoena[s] are likely to provide the most fruitful avenue for discovering the identity of additional infringers" and "the most effective measure of the revenues generated by Defendants." (August 23 Order at 6.) Because "there exists substantial doubt that [Gucci] could adequately resolve the dispute" by other means, *Nowak,* 94 F.3d at 718, Gucci's interests in obtaining its desired relief in its desired forum are even greater. (*See* August 23 Order at 10 (casting doubt on the viability of a Hague Convention request yielding Gucci the information it seeks).)

With respect to the international judicial system's interest in obtaining the most efficient resolution to the controversy, the Court's retention of jurisdiction over this action would undoubtedly provide the fastest and most practical means of resolving this dispute. The Court is already intimately familiar with the parties, facts, and legal issues, *see Ballard,* 65 F.3d at 1502, and BOC has already partially complied with Gucci's document requests. Forcing Gucci to initiate this process in China would be significantly less efficient, extremely time consuming, and potentially fruitless. (August 23 Order at 10.)

Finally, a balancing of the substantive social policies at issue further supports exercising personal jurisdiction. As the Court already concluded in its original §442 comity analysis under the "balance of national interests" factor, Gucci's interest in compelling BOC to comply with the 2010 and 2011 Subpoenas and the United States' interest in enforcing the Lanham Act clearly outweigh BOC's interest in resisting compliance and China's interest in its bank secrecy laws. (August 23 Order at 11; *see also infra* Section II.B.) BOC has failed to identify any compelling substantive social policies not raised in its earlier comity briefing that would alter the Court's conclusion on this factor.

Accordingly, having carefully considered each of the factors discussed above, the Court concludes that the exercise of personal jurisdiction over BOC to compel it to comply with the 2010 and 2011 Subpoenas is consistent with "fair play and substantial justice," *Burger King*, 471 U.S. at 476, 105 S.Ct. 2174, and comports with due process.

B. Comity

In its August 23 Order, the Court conducted a detailed comity analysis and concluded that a balancing of the § 442 factors strongly supported ordering BOC to comply with Gucci's document requests. (August 23 Order at 13.) The Second Circuit upheld this conclusion, holding that there was "no abuse of discretion in this analysis" and that "BOC's arguments to the contrary are without merit." *Gucci II*, 768 F.3d at 141. However, the Second Circuit also directed the Court to "consider the question of comity again" in light of recent Chinese court cases involving BOC. *Id.* at 142.

The Court's initial comity analysis considered seven factors. Five of those factors came from § 442(1)(c): (i) "the importance to the investigation or litigation of the documents or other information requested;" (ii) "the degree of specificity of the request;" (iii) "whether the information originated in the United States;" (iv) "the availability of alternative means of securing the information;" and (v) "the extent to which noncompliance with the request would undermine important interests of the United States, or compliance with the request would undermine important interests of the state where the information is located." Two additional factors that the Court considered included "the hardship of compliance on the party or witness from whom discovery is sought" and "the good faith of the party resisting discovery." (August 23 Order at 6 (quoting *Minpeco S.A. v. Conticommodity Servs., Inc.*, 116 F.R.D. 517, 523 (S.D.N.Y.1987)).) After carefully considering the various factors and interests, the Court concluded that a balancing of the factors "strongly weighs in favor" of granting Gucci's motion to compel. The Court noted that this result was particularly necessary in light of (1) "[BOC's] failure to demonstrate an actual likelihood that compliance with the Subpoena would result in criminal or civil liability in China," (2) "[BOC's] failure to put forward credible, non-speculative evidence that requests made through the Hague Convention represent a viable alternative method of obtaining discovery," (3) "the clear and obvious harm caused by counterfeiters to mark holders such as [Gucci]," and (4) "the fact that such counterfeiters have deliberately utilized institutions such as [BOC] to thwart Congress and the reach of the Lanham Act." (August 23 Order at 13.)

The Second Circuit directed the Court to "consider the question of comity again in light of the newly available December 4, 2013 Judgment of the Second Intermediate People's Court of Beijing Municipality, and any subsequent judgments it finds relevant." (Doc. No. 127 at 44.) After the Second Intermediate People's Court of Beijing Municipality issued the December 4, 2013 Civil Judgment (Doc. No. 142, Declaration of Yuqing Zhang, dated Jan. 22, 2015 ("Zhang Decl."), Ex. 10 ("Beijing Intermediate Court Judgment")), BOC appealed the Beijing Intermediate Court Judgment to the Higher People's Court of Beijing Municipality. On June 20, 2014, the Higher People's Court issued a Civil Judgment, upholding the Beijing Intermediate Court Judgment. (Zhang Decl., Ex. 11 ("Beijing High Court Judgment").) Accordingly, the Court will consider how both the Beijing Intermediate Court Judgment and Beijing High Court Judgment (the "Beijing judgments") affect the §442 comity analysis.

The controversy underlying the Beijing judgments is a private civil suit between BOC and some of the Defendants in this action. Specifically, the plaintiffs in that action—who are Defendants here—alleged that BOC unlawfully froze their bank accounts as a result of the litigation before this Court, and argued that the terms and conditions of their account opening documents did not permit BOC to suspend their banking services. (Beijing Intermediate Court Judgment at 2–3.) Consequently, the account holders sought an order directing BOC to lift the account freezes and to pay all litigation costs associated with the case. (*Id.* at 2.)

The Beijing Intermediate Court held that BOC "failed to produce evidence to prove that [the plaintiffs] actually made any operation with malicious intent, or defamed or damaged the reputation of the bank, or maliciously attacked the electronic banking system of the bank," which the Beijing Intermediate Court found was the necessary prerequisite for BOC to freeze the plaintiffs' bank accounts. (*Id.* at 6–7.) The Beijing Intermediate Court further noted that the action before this Court "is still on-going and pending," "no judgment has taken effect in China," and BOC "failed to produce evidence sufficient to prove that it has justifiable reason ... to cease to provide services" to the account holders. (*Id.* at 7.) The Beijing Intermediate Court therefore concluded that BOC had no contractual or legal basis for suspending the plaintiffs' accounts and ordered BOC to resume providing banking services to the account holders. (*Id.*)

On appeal, the Beijing High Court noted that under Chinese commercial banking law, "the lawful business operation of a commercial bank [should be] free from interference of any entity or individual," "a commercial bank shall protect the lawful interest of depositors from being damaged by any entity or individual," and "personal savings deposit business with commercial banks shall be based on the principles of voluntary deposit, free withdraw[al], deposit bearing interest, and the confidentiality for the depositor." (Beijing High Court Judgment at 8.) After *de novo* review of the Beijing Intermediate Court Judgment (Doc. 137, Declaration of Donald Clarke, dated Dec. 1, 2014 ("Clarke Decl.") ¶ 13), the Beijing High Court held that BOC "failed to produce evidence to prove that [the account holders] violated any contractually agreed terms, [that BOC] unilaterally terminated services for their bank accounts, [and] thus there is no contractual or legal basis for BOC to unilaterally stop financial service and suspend usage of the accounts."

(*Id.*) The Beijing High Court Judgment directed BOC to pay 140 renminbi in court fees (approximately $22.00 at current exchange rates) and upheld the Beijing Intermediate Court's injunction. (*Id.*)

As an initial matter, it is important to note that the Beijing judgments impact only a few of the seven factors the Court considered. Nothing in the Beijing judgments changes the Court's conclusion that: (i) "the documents requested in the Subpoena[s] are important to the instant litigation," (ii) "the Subpoena[s] [are] sufficiently specific," and (iv) "Hague Convention requests in circumstances similar to those presented here are not a viable alternative method of securing the information [Gucci] seek[s]." (August 23 Order at 6–10.) The only factors that the Beijing judgments could affect are (v) "the extent to which noncompliance with the request would undermine important interests of the United States, or compliance with the request would undermine important interests of the state where the information is located," and "the hardship of compliance on the party or witness from whom discovery is sought." The Court will consider each in turn.

Because the Second Circuit explicitly cabined the Court's reconsideration of its comity analysis to the Beijing Intermediate Court Judgment and "any subsequent judgments it finds relevant," such as the Beijing High Court Judgment, the Court does not consider the numerous arguments the parties raise with respect to the Court's comity analysis that have nothing to do with the Beijing judgments. (*See* Mem. at 23–24; Opp. at 23–24; Rep. at 8–9.) In any event, most of the parties' arguments are simply rehashes of ones previously made in connection with the Court's initial comity analysis.

With respect to the balancing of national interests, the Court noted that while China has bank secrecy laws that prevent disclosure of an individual's account information without consent, such protection can be waived by several different public bodies. (August 23 Order at 10 (discussing declaration of BOC's Chinese bank law expert).) Accordingly, the Court concluded that "China's bank secrecy laws merely confer an individual privilege on customers rather than reflect a national policy entitled to substantial deference." (*Id.* at 11.) Weighing against China's interests, the Court concluded that the United States "has a powerful interest in enforcing the acts of Congress, especially those, such as the Lanham Act, that are designed to protect intellectual property rights and prevent consumer confusion." (*Id.*) Overall, the Court determined that this factor "clearly weighs in favor of" Gucci. (*Id.*)

The Beijing judgments, if anything, shift the balance of national interests more firmly toward the United States because they acknowledge that BOC had broad contractual rights over its customers' account information, such as the power to suspend or terminate service in certain circumstances. (Clarke Decl. ¶¶ 16–18.) That BOC did not sufficiently prove the existence of those circumstances does not change the fact that the Beijing judgments recognized BOC as lawfully having that authority. The Beijing judgments do not provide any support for BOC's assertion that China's bank secrecy laws are rigidly enforced or a matter of strong state policy that trump the United States' interest in enforcing the Lanham Act. Accordingly, the Court concludes that this factor "clearly weighs in favor of" Gucci.

As for the hardship of compliance, the Court initially found that this factor weighed in favor of Gucci because it concluded that BOC's representations that it would face significant criminal and civil liability from complying with the 2010 Subpoena were unduly speculative. Specifically, the Court determined that the Chinese cases that purportedly demonstrated that Chinese courts take customer bank account secrecy seriously did not in fact support BOC's assertion that compliance with the 2010 Subpoena would subject BOC or its employees to heavy fines or incarceration. (August 23 Order at 11–12.) In fact, the Court concluded that BOC could point to no case where a Chinese bank was subjected to liability for disclosing the type of bank account information sought by Gucci. (*Id.* at 12.) In light of the speculative nature of BOC's professed hardship, the Court determined that the factor supported granting the motion to compel.

Once again, the Beijing judgments only provide further support for Gucci's case. The controversy underlying the Beijing judgments was a simple, private contract case. The Beijing Intermediate Court and Beijing High Court merely concluded that BOC had not sufficiently proven grounds upon which it could lawfully freeze the plaintiffs' bank accounts. Nothing in the Beijing judgments suggests that China has an ironclad requirement of bank secrecy or that disclosure of the information requested by the 2010 and 2011 Subpoenas would expose BOC and its employees to serious criminal or civil liability in China. Even BOC's own Chinese bank law expert does not opine that the Beijing judgments demonstrate that China has a strong national policy against disclosure of bank client information (*see* Zhang Decl. ¶¶ 30–35), whereas Gucci's Chinese bank law expert expressly states that the Beijing judgments do not change his opinion that "there is no strong state policy affording a high degree of protection to clients of Chinese banks" and that "BOC and its officers are unlikely to be prosecuted for complying with the Court's orders in this case" (Clarke 2014 Decl. ¶¶ 14–15). Put simply, the Beijing judgments, which resulted in BOC paying the equivalent of $22.00 in court fees, do nothing to change the Court's prior conclusion that BOC's contention that compliance with the 2010 and 2011 Subpoenas would subject it to serious criminal and civil liability is unduly speculative.

Because the Court previously found that a balancing of the § 442 factors "strongly weighs in favor of" granting Gucci's motion to compel, and the Beijing judgments actually strengthen that determination, the Court reaffirms its comity analysis and concludes that ordering BOC to comply with the 2010 and 2011 Subpoenas is consistent with § 442 of the Restatement (Third) of Foreign Relations Law.

III. Conclusion

For the reasons set forth above, the Court concludes that it has specific personal jurisdiction over BOC with respect to the 2010 and 2011 Subpoenas and that exercising such jurisdiction comports with due process and principles of comity. Accordingly, Plaintiffs' motion to compel is granted. IT IS HEREBY ORDERED THAT BOC shall produce all documents requested in the 2010 and 2011 Subpoenas as they pertain to all Defendants, including but not limited to (1) all documents and communications regarding Defendants or their accounts, (2) all documents associated with any accounts or deposits held in any Defendants' name, and (3) all documents relating to any checks, money orders, or other negotiable instruments purchased by Defendant. For clarification, "all Defendants" covers all Defendants who have been named in this action, including those in the Second Amended Complaint: Wenying Guo, Xiaochao Shang, Lei Xu, Fengyuan Zhao, Liqun Zhao, Ming Zhao, and Peiyuan Zhao. IT IS FURTHER ORDERED THAT Plaintiffs shall submit a letter to the Court by October 15, 2015 apprising the Court of BOC's compliance with the 2010 and 2011 Subpoenas. The Clerk of Court is respectfully directed to terminate the motion located at docket number 135.

SO ORDERED.

This case is a great example of how a brand owner went above and beyond to stop counterfeiting. While it required an intense jurisdictional analysis and comity played a role, ultimately Gucci successfully obtained discovery in an effort to enforce its trademark rights against Chinese counterfeiters transferring funds out of the United States to China. While the bank failed to comply and was sanctioned, the Second Circuit refused to stay the sanctions and the parties settled.

The government, specifically the IPR Center, working with ICE and HSI, does its part as well. Through Operation In Our Sights, the U.S. government "targets websites and their operators that distribute counterfeit and pirated items over the internet, including counterfeit pharmaceuticals and pirated movies, television shows, music, software, electronics, and other merchandise as well as products that threaten public health and safety." The government works to seize domain names and, once seized, display a notification that the website has been seized by federal authorities.

The laws concerning anticounterfeiting and the internet are and will continue to be in a perpetual state of flux. Government priorities play a role. Trade wars play a role. Monopolies and potential future regulation play a role. And every case is fact-specific. In addition, it is not just counterfeiting through illicit foreign websites that is problematic, but counterfeits being offered through otherwise legitimate businesses. See the following cases for examples of how brands have tried to bring the fight to the most notorious online retailer, Alibaba.

Atmos Nation LLC v. Alibaba Group Holding Ltd.

2016 U.S. Dist. LEXIS 33228 (S.D. Fla. Mar. 15, 2016)

MOORE, Chief District Judge.

Order Granting Defendant alibaba.com, Inc.'s Motion to Dismiss the Second Amended Complaint Pursuant to Rule 12(B)(2)

This cause is before the Court on Defendant Alibaba.com, Inc.'s Motion to Dismiss the Second Amended Complaint Pursuant to Rule 12(b)(2) [D.E. 44]. For the reasons explained below, the motion is granted.

I. Background

This is an action for trademark infringement brought by Plaintiff Atmos Nation LLC ("Atmos"), the owner of a brand of portable vaporizers, against several Alibaba entities, including Defendant Alibaba.com, Inc., and various independent third-party merchants. In its Second Amended Complaint ("SAC") [D.E. 21], Atmos asserts claims for trademark infringement, trademark counterfeiting, contributory trademark infringement and counterfeiting, and false representation under the Lanham Act, 15 U.S.C. § 1051 *et seq.*; unfair competition under the Florida Deceptive and Unfair Trade Practices Act, Fla. Stat. § 501.201 *et seq.*; and unjust enrichment. *See* SAC ¶¶ 274-316. As relief, Atmos seeks preliminary and permanent injunctive relief, monetary damages, and other appropriate redress. *See id.* at 4.

The SAC alleges that Atmos designs, markets, and sells portable vaporizers under its Atmos brand. *See id.* ¶ 81. The gist of Atmos' action concerns the alleged sale of counterfeit vaporizers bearing the Atmos brand by independent third-party merchants (the "Merchant Defendants") on the Alibaba platforms, Alibaba.com, AliExpress.com, and Taobao.com (collectively, the "Alibaba Platforms"). *See id.* ¶¶ 75-76, 81, 93, 95. Atmos alleges that some of these sales were made to a purchaser in Florida. *Id.* ¶¶ 178-82, 188-93, 199-202, 208-12, 218-21, 227-31, 237-41, 247-51, 257-61.

Atmos identifies the specific Alibaba entities it claims are responsible for operating the Alibaba Platforms. According to the SAC, Defendant Alibaba.com Hong Kong Limited "operates the websites www.alibaba.com and www.aliexpress .com," and Defendant Taobao China Holding Ltd. "is the operating entity for the overseas business of Taobao Marketplace and Tmall platforms." *Id.* ¶¶ 16, 25. The pleading then sweeps in several other Alibaba entities—including Alibaba.com, Inc.—by alleging that they are collectively responsible for allowing the Merchant Defendants to list and sell counterfeit Atmos vaporizers on the Alibaba Platforms. *See id.* ¶¶ 75-76, 81, 93, 95.

Alibaba.com, Inc. does not operate or exercise any control over the content of the Alibaba Platforms. *See* Decl. of Michael Lee, dated Dec. 10, 2015 ("Lee Decl.") ¶ 9. [D.E. 44-1].[2] Nor does it manufacture, sell, or deliver any of the products displayed on the Alibaba Platforms, or own, control, or take possession of them. *See id.* ¶ 10. Rather, Alibaba.com, Inc. is a business-to-business e-commerce company that focuses on technology maintenance, marketing, and administrative services. *See id.* ¶ 8; SAC ¶ 21. It provides marketing services to promote the brand awareness of the Alibaba Platforms through trade show exhibitions, event marketing, online display advertising, search engine marketing, affiliate marketing, social media marketing, cross promotional business partnerships, and public relations. *See* Lee Decl. ¶ 11.

2. A motion to dismiss for lack of personal jurisdiction is inherently a matter requiring the resolution of factual issues outside of the pleadings, and the court may consider all pertinent documentation submitted by the parties in deciding the motion. *Energy Brands Inc. v. Spiritual Brands, Inc.*, 571 F. Supp. 2d 458, 463 (S.D.N.Y. 2008).

Alibaba.com, Inc. has no presence in Florida. It is incorporated in Delaware and has its only office in San Mateo, California. *See* SAC ¶ 56; Lee Decl. ¶ 2. It does not have any offices or employees in Florida. *See* Lee Decl. ¶ 4. It does not have any contracts to supply goods or services to companies or individuals in Florida. *See* Lee Decl. ¶ 5. It does not direct any marketing services to Florida and, since 2012, has not sent any employees to Florida.[3] *See id.* ¶ 6, 12.

II. Discussion

Alibaba.com, Inc. moves to dismiss this action under Rule 12(b)(2) for lack of personal jurisdiction. Atmos argues that this Court has personal jurisdiction over the Alibaba entities, including Alibaba.com, Inc., on the grounds that there is both general and specific personal jurisdiction under Florida's long arm statute.[4] *See* SAC ¶¶ 46, 48(a). Atmos, however, fails to show how or why this Court has jurisdiction over Alibaba.com, Inc., relying instead on general assertions about the cumulative conduct of the "ALIBABA Defendants." *See, e.g.*, SAC ¶¶ 46, 48. As shown more fully below, because Alibaba.com, Inc. neither operates nor controls any of the Alibaba Platforms, nor has any presence in Florida, the Court lacks personal jurisdiction over it. For those reasons, Alibaba.com, Inc.'s Motion to Dismiss is granted.

A. General Principles Governing Personal Jurisdiction

Because federal courts ordinarily follow state law in determining the bounds of their jurisdiction over persons, *Daimler AG v. Bauman*, 134 S. Ct. 746, 753, 187 L. Ed. 2d 624 (2014), a federal court sitting in Florida must conduct a two-step inquiry to determine whether it has personal jurisdiction over a non-resident defendant. The court must determine "(1) whether personal jurisdiction exists over the nonresident defendant . . . under Florida's long-arm statute, and (2) if so, whether that exercise of jurisdiction would violate the Due Process Clause of the Fourteenth Amendment to the U.S. Constitution." *Louis Vuitton Malletier, S.A. v. Mosseri*, 736 F.3d 1339, 1350 (11th Cir. 2013).

Under Florida's long-arm statute, Fla. Stat. § 48.193, a non-resident defendant can be subject to personal jurisdiction in two ways. First, a Florida court can exercise general personal jurisdiction—that is, jurisdiction over any claims against a defendant, whether or not they involve the defendant's activities in Florida—if the

---

3. In 2011 and 2012, representatives of Alibaba.com, Inc. visited Florida to attend five trade shows, but none of these trade shows involved portable vaporizers or any other tobacco/smoking products. *See id.* ¶ 6.

4. The SAC also asserts jurisdiction under the federal long-arm statute, Fed. R. Civ. P. 4(k). *See* SAC ¶ 48(b). Rule 4(k), however, does not apply to Alibaba.com, Inc., a U.S. domiciliary incorporated in Delaware with a principal place of business in California. *See Merial Ltd. v. Cipla Ltd.*, 681 F.3d 1283, 1293-94 (Fed. Cir. 2012) ("Rule 4(k)(2) was adopted to provide a forum for federal claims in situations where a foreign defendant lacks substantial contacts with any single state but has sufficient contacts with the United States as a whole to satisfy due process standards and justify the application of federal law."); *see also Barrocos of Florida, Inc. v. Elmassian*, No. 11-CV-22393, 2012 U.S. Dist. LEXIS 64948, 2012 WL 1622988, at *6 (S.D. Fla. May 9, 2012).

defendant engages in "substantial and not isolated activity" in Florida. *Schulman v. Inst. for Shipboard Educ.*, 624 F. App'x 1002, 1005 (11th Cir. 2015). Second, a Florida court can exercise specific personal jurisdiction—that is, jurisdiction over suits that arise out of or relate to a defendant's contacts with Florida——if the claim asserted against the defendant arises from the defendant's contacts with Florida, and those contacts fall within one of nine statutorily enumerated categories set forth in section 48.193(1)(a). *Id.*

If the requirements of the long-arm statute are satisfied, then the court must determine whether the defendant has established sufficient "minimum contacts" with the State of Florida, such that the exercise of jurisdiction over the defendant would not offend "traditional notions of fair play and substantial justice." *Int'l Shoe Co. v. State of Wash., Office of Unemployment Comp. & Placement*, 326 U.S. 310, 316, 66 S. Ct. 154, 90 L. Ed. 95 (1945).

The plaintiff bears the initial burden of pleading sufficient material facts to make out a prima facie case of jurisdiction. *See Future Tech. Today, Inc., v. OSF Healthcare Systems*, 218 F.3d 1247, 1249 (11th Cir. 2000). If the plaintiff does so, the burden shifts to the defendant to contradict the plaintiff's allegations by affidavits or other competent evidence. *See Posner v. Essex Ins. Co.*, 178 F.3d 1209, 1214-15 (11th Cir. 1999). To the extent the defendant's proffered evidence does not contradict the plaintiff's jurisdictional allegations, the allegations must be accepted as true. *See id.* at 1215 (citation omitted). But to the extent the defendant does contradict the plaintiff's allegations, the burden shifts back to the plaintiff, this time requiring the plaintiff to prove—not merely allege—jurisdiction by affidavits, testimony, or other documents. *See id.* at 1214-15.

B. The Court Does Not Have General Jurisdiction Over Alibaba.com, Inc.

Alibaba.com, Inc. does not fall within the general jurisdiction of this Court. The reach of Florida's general jurisdiction provision, Fla. Stat. § 48.193(2), extends to the limits on personal jurisdiction imposed by the Due Process Clause of the Fourteenth Amendment. *Fraser v. Smith*, 594 F.3d 842, 846 (11th Cir. 2010). "A court may assert general jurisdiction over foreign (sister-state or foreign-country) corporations," without offending due process, only "when their affiliations with the State are so 'continuous and systematic' as to render them essentially at home in the forum State." *Goodyear Dunlop Tires Operations, S.A. v. Brown*, 564 U.S. 915, 131 S. Ct. 2846, 2851, 180 L. Ed. 2d 796 (2011) (quoting *Int'l Shoe Co.*, 326 U.S. at 317). Only in an "exceptional" case will "a corporation's operations in a forum other than its formal place of incorporation or principal place of business" be "so substantial and of such a nature as to render the corporation at home in that State." *Daimler*, 134 S. Ct. at 761 n.19. Accordingly, "[a] foreign corporation cannot be subject to general jurisdiction in a forum unless the corporation's activities in the forum closely approximate the activities that ordinarily characterize a corporation's place of incorporation or principal place of business." *Carmouche v. Tamborlee Mgmt., Inc.*, 789 F.3d 1201, 1205 (11th Cir. 2015).

Alibaba.com, Inc. is hardly at home in Florida. As noted above, and as Atmos acknowledges, Alibaba.com, Inc. is incorporated in Delaware and has its only office in San Mateo, California. *See* SAC ¶¶ 21, 56. Alibaba.com, Inc. does not have any employees in Florida; does not direct its marketing services to Florida or tailor its marketing services for individuals or businesses in Florida; does not have any contracts to supply goods or services to any companies or individuals in Florida; and, since 2012, has not sent any employees to Florida. *See* Lee Decl. ¶¶ 3-5, 12. Accordingly, the Court lacks general jurisdiction over Alibaba.com, Inc. *See, e.g., Hard Candy, LLC v. Hard Candy Fitness, LLC*, 106 F. Supp. 3d 1231, 2015 WL 3377906, at *18 (S.D. Fla. 2015) (finding no general jurisdiction under the Florida long-arm statute where the defendants were not incorporated in Florida, were not residents of Florida, did not have a principal places of business in Florida, and did not have continuous and systematic contacts with Florida).

C. The Court Does Not Have Specific Jurisdiction Over Alibaba.com, Inc.

Nor does the Court have personal jurisdiction over Alibaba.com, Inc. To determine whether specific jurisdiction exists over a defendant, the court must determine whether the requirements of Florida's long-arm statute are satisfied, and, if so, whether the requirements of due process are satisfied. *See Madara v. Hall*, 916 F.2d 1510, 1514 (11th Cir. 1990). Atmos fails to make either showing.

i. Atmos Fails To Establish Personal Jurisdiction Under Florida's Long-Arm Statute

Atmos' assertion of specific jurisdiction under Florida's long-arm statute fails. In an effort to establish specific jurisdiction over Alibaba.com, Inc., Atmos relies on Florida Statute 48.193(1)(a)(2) and (6).[5] *See* SAC ¶ 48(a). Subparagraph (2) provides for jurisdiction over a non-resident defendant where the defendant "commit[ed] a tortious act within this state." Fla. Stat. § 48.193(1)(a)(2). Subparagraph (6) allows for jurisdiction where a non-resident defendant

> [c]aus[ed] injury to persons or property within this state arising out of an act or omission . . . outside this state, if, at or about the time of the injury, either: a. The defendant was engaged in solicitation or service activities within this state; or b. Products, materials, or things processed, serviced, or manufactured by the defendant anywhere were used or consumed within this state in the ordinary course of commerce, trade, or use.

Fla. Stat. § 48.193(1)(a)(6). Both provisions require that the defendant's conduct somehow impact a person or entity within the State of Florida—either by

5. Atmos actually cites Florida Statute 48.193(1)(b) and (f). These citations, however, appear to be to a prior version of the statute, which was amended on July 1, 2013. *See* 2013 Fla. Sess. Law Serv. Ch. 2013-164 (C.S.S.B. 186). The Court therefore construes the SAC as if it had cited to the statutory provisions currently in effect.

committing a tort in Florida or at least causing an injury in Florida. Atmos does not allege that Alibaba.com, Inc. did either, nor could it.

Atmos' assertion of jurisdiction over the Alibaba entities is premised on the alleged sale of counterfeit goods on the Alibaba Platforms into Florida., which Atmos maintains constituted tortious acts and/or caused injury sufficient to establish personal jurisdiction in Florida. *See* SAC ¶¶ 48, 178-182, 188-193, 199-202, 208-212, 218-221, 227-231, 237-241, 247-251, 257-261. With respect to Alibaba.com, Inc., however, because that entity has no involvement with the operation of or control over the Alibaba Platforms; does not process, service, or manufacture any goods listed for sale; and has had only *de minimis* contacts with Florida wholly unrelated to the sale of portable vaporizers, Atmos cannot establish that Alibaba.com, Inc. has committed any tortious acts in Florida, or caused any injury in Florida, through the Alibaba Platforms. *See United Techs. Corp. v. Mazer*, 556 F.3d 1260, 1280 (11th Cir. 2009) (affirming the district court's finding that it lacked jurisdiction where the defendant's refutation of facts asserted by the plaintiff sufficiently negated allegations tying the defendant to tortious conduct in Florida); *Reflection Mfg., LLC v. I.S.A. Corp.*, No. 6:10-CV-1951-ORL, 2011 U.S. Dist. LEXIS 34154, 2011 WL 972570, at *9 (M.D. Fla. Mar. 18, 2011) (holding that a finding of jurisdiction under section 48.193(1)(a)(6) (formerly § 48.193(1)(f)(1)-(2)) was inappropriate where the defendant was not engaged in solicitation or service activities in Florida).[6] Accordingly, the Court lacks specific jurisdiction over Alibaba.com, Inc.

The Court rejects Atmos' contention that "[t]he ALIBABA Defendants help facilitate every transaction on their site via the Post Buying Request System. . . ." [D.E. 48 at 6]. This claim ignores the distinction acknowledged in the SAC, and confirmed by the Lee Declaration, that only certain of the entities Atmos lumps together as the "ALIBABA Defendants" actually operate the Alibaba Platforms, and that Alibaba .com, Inc. is not one of them. *See* SAC ¶¶ 16, 25; Lee Decl. ¶ 9. In that way, Atmos incorrectly conflates the functions of the various "ALIBABA Defendants" to impute the alleged conduct of the other entities onto Alibaba.com, Inc.

The Court also rejects Atmos' characterization that Alibaba.com, Inc.'s marketing efforts and search engine optimization "play[] a pivotal role in targeting Florida consumers and businesses" and "are essential to ensure that Florida Consumers and Businesses are targeted." [D.E. 48 at 3, 6, 8]. These allegations are nowhere in the SAC, are entirely uncorroborated, and are contradicted by the Lee Declaration,

---

6. There are conflicting decisions among Florida courts regarding whether a tortious act committed outside the state resulting in injury inside the state subjects the actor to jurisdiction in Florida pursuant to Florida Statute 48.193(1)(a)(2) (or its predecessor, Florida Statute 48.193(1)(b)). *See Posner v. Essex Ins. Co.*, 178 F.3d 1209, 1216 (11th Cir. 1999) (noting that the courts are "deeply divided on the issue"); *Jack Pickard Dodge, Inc. v. Yarbrough*, 352 So. 2d 130, 134 (Fla. 1977) (finding no jurisdiction where the injury occurred in Florida, but the alleged tortious act was the servicing, outside of the state, of a vehicle that caused the injury). Here, under either standard, there is no jurisdiction over Alibaba.com, Inc., as it does not operate the Alibaba Platforms and is not alleged to have committed—nor did it commit—a tortious act in Florida.

which states that "Alibaba.com, Inc. has not carried out any marketing activity that was directed to or specifically tailored for individuals or businesses in the [S]tate of Florida," and, since 2012, has not sent a single employee into the State of Florida. Lee Decl. ¶¶ 4, 6.

Moreover, Atmos' reliance on a pair of defamation cases, *Internet Solutions Corp. v. Marshall*, 39 So. 3d 1201 (Fla. 2010), and *Calder v. Jones*, 465 U.S. 783, 790, 104 S. Ct. 1482, 79 L. Ed. 2d 804 (1984), is misplaced. Unlike these defamation cases, where the statement itself is what causes the injury, here, there is no claim that any of Alibaba.com, Inc.'s advertising or marketing efforts defamed or caused any injury to Atmos. Rather, the claim is that non-affiliated, China-based parties, referred to in the SAC as the "Merchant Defendants," sold counterfeit Atmos products using the Alibaba Platforms——which Alibaba.com, Inc. undisputably does not operate or control.

In sum, because Alibaba.com, Inc. has no involvement with the operation of or control over the Alibaba Platforms; does not process, service, or manufacture any goods listed for sale; and has had only *de minimis* contacts with the State of Florida, Atmos cannot establish that Alibaba.com, Inc. has committed any tortious acts in Florida. Accordingly, the Court finds no basis for the assertion of specific jurisdiction over Alibaba.com, Inc.

ii. Exercising Personal Jurisdiction Over Alibaba.com, Inc. Would Not Comport With Due Process

Even if a basis for jurisdiction existed under Florida's long-arm statute, the exercise of personal jurisdiction over Alibaba.com, Inc. would violate due process. "The exercise of personal jurisdiction comports with due process if the non-resident defendant has established 'certain minimum contacts with the forum such that the maintenance of the suit does not offend traditional notions of fair play and substantial justice.'" *Fraser*, 594 F.3d at 846 (citations and quotations omitted). The minimum-contacts test for specific jurisdiction has three elements: (1) "the defendant must have contacts related to or giving rise to the plaintiff's cause of action"; (2) "the defendant must, through those contacts, have purposefully availed itself of forum benefits"; and (3) "the defendant's contacts with the forum must be such that it could reasonably anticipate being haled into court there." *Id.* at 850.

Alibaba.com, Inc. does not have sufficient contact with Florida to justify jurisdiction here. As explained above, Alibaba.com, Inc. does not operate, design, or control any of the Alibaba Platforms. Additionally, Alibaba.com, Inc.'s attendance at five trade shows involving products wholly unrelated to vaporizers several years ago is insufficient to confer jurisdiction, particularly where no employees have been sent to Florida in the past three years. *See Kertesz v. Net Transactions, Ltd.*, 635 F. Supp. 2d 1339 (S.D. Fla. 2009) ("Nor does the attendance by [the defendant's] representatives at a Florida trade show or [the defendant's] representatives' one or two visits to Florida rise to the level of continuous and systematic contacts."). In short, because Alibaba.com, Inc. does not have any presence in the State of Florida, it "could not reasonably have anticipated being hauled into court in Florida," where it "does not conduct business . . . [and] has no offices, employees, assets or leases." *See F&G Research, Inc. v. Dynapoint (Taiwan), Inc.*, No. 06-60904-CIV, 2007 U.S. Dist. LEXIS 97040, 2007 WL 5175171, at *5 (S.D. Fla. Apr. 13, 2007).

At least one other court has reached the same conclusion in a virtually identical case. In *P.S. Products, Inc. v. Alibaba.com, Inc.*, the District Court for the Eastern District of Arkansas held that Alibaba.com, Inc.'s relationship with the Alibaba platform did not establish enough minimum contacts to give rise to jurisdiction in Arkansas. *See id.*, 2011 U.S. Dist. LEXIS 25948, 2011 WL 861164, at *3. The court based its decision on, among other reasons, the fact that Alibaba.com, Inc. did not operate, design, or exercise any control over the Alibaba platform and did not have any contracts with residents in Arkansas. *See id.* (finding that the plaintiff had "failed to prove by a preponderance of the evidence that the Court has personal jurisdiction over the Defendant Alibaba.com, Inc. based upon its relationship with the Website").

Accordingly, because Alibaba.com, Inc. does not have sufficient contact with Florida, the assertion of jurisdiction over it in this state would not comport with due process.

iii. Atomos' Claim That Alibaba.com, Inc. Is An Alter Ego Of Other Defendants Does Not Justify Jurisdiction In Florida

Atmos' attempt to establish personal jurisdiction over Alibaba.com, Inc. by piercing the corporate veil is equally unavailing. Atmos alleges that the Alibaba Defendants are all alter egos of each other. SAC ¶ 61. In support of this allegation, Atmos claims that the "ALIBABA Defendants" "operate as a single unit, sharing common ownership, [under] the Alibaba Group[,]" constituting a "single operating and reporting segment," and are "agent[s]" of each other, "maintain common office spaces and addresses among its various entities," and are "financially dependent" upon the Alibaba Group. SAC ¶¶ 61-64.

Black-letter law forbids equating a subsidiary with its parent absent extraordinary justification to pierce a corporate veil. *See, e.g., Goodyear Dunlop Tires Operations, S.A. v. Brown*, 564 U.S. 915, 131 S. Ct. 2846, 2857, 180 L. Ed. 2d 796 (2011). The Eleventh Circuit has made clear that "a parent and a subsidiary are separate and distinct corporate entities, and the presence of one in a forum state may not necessarily be attributed to the other." *Consol. Dev. Corp. v. Sherritt, Inc.*, 216 F.3d 1286, 1293 (11th Cir. 2000). Personal jurisdiction may be assumed over another corporate entity only if the plaintiff can demonstrate "(1) that the subsidiary is a mere instrumentality of the parent; and (2) improper conduct." *Peruyero v. Airbus S.A.S.*, 83 F. Supp. 3d 1283, 1289 (S.D. Fla. 2014). A parent uses a subsidiary as a "mere instrumentality" when it directs and controls the business operations and sets the policies of the subsidiary, *Hermetic Seal Corp. v. Savoy Elecs., Inc.*, 290 F. Supp. 240, 243 (S.D. Fla. 1967), while a parent engages in "improper conduct" if it uses the subsidiary "to mislead creditors or to perpetrate a fraud upon them" or "as a means of evading liability." *Dania Jai-Alai Palace, Inc. v. Sykes*, 450 So. 2d 1114, 1119-20 (Fla. 1984).

Atmos has not sufficiently pleaded either element. None of Atmos' allegations even suggest that any of the Alibaba Defendants used Alibaba.com, Inc. as a "mere instrumentality." Nor do Atmos' allegations indicate any improper conduct by Alibaba.com, Inc. Atmos does not allege that Alibaba.com, Inc. was created for any improper purpose, or that Alibaba.com, Inc. or any of the other Alibaba entities used or had any intent to use Alibaba.com, Inc. for any improper purpose. At most, Plaintiff's alter ego theory amounts to a claim that the various Alibaba entities are related to each other and act together in certain respects——which is not enough to justify personal jurisdiction. *See, e.g., Mother Doe I v. Maktoum*, 632 F. Supp. 2d 1130, 1142 (S.D. Fla. 2007) ("The fact that Defendants may have involvement, even extensive involvement, with corporations that do business in Florida is not sufficient, in and of itself, to establish that Defendants themselves are subject to the personal jurisdiction of a Florida court."). Accordingly, the Court finds no basis to exercise personal jurisdiction over Alibaba.com, Inc. by virtue of its relationship with the other Alibaba defendants.[7]

III. Conclusion

For the foregoing reasons, it is ordered and adjudged that Defendant Alibaba .com, Inc.'s Motion to Dismiss the Second Amended Complaint Pursuant to Rule 12(b)(2) [D.E. 44] is granted. This case is dismissed for lack of personal jurisdiction as to Alibaba.com, Inc.

Cepia, L.L.C. v. Alibaba Group Holding Ltd.

2011 U.S. Dist. LEXIS 129126 (E.D. Mo. Nov. 8, 2011)

LIMBAUGH, JR., District Judge.

Memorandum and Order

Plaintiff has filed a multicount trademark infringement complaint raising claims of trademark infringement, trade dress infringement, false advertising, false designation of origin, copyright infringement, unfair competition, and dilution. This matter is before the Court on Defendant Alibaba Group Holding Limited's motion to dismiss for lack of personal jurisdiction filed June 7, 2011 and Defendant Alibaba.Com Hong Kong Limited's motion to dismiss for lack of personal jurisdiction, filed June 7, 2011. Extensive responsive pleadings have now all been filed and this matter is ripe for disposition.

I. Background

Plaintiff Cepia, LLC is a limited liability company organized under the laws of Missouri, with its principal place of business in St. Louis, Missouri. Plaintiff develops, manufactures, and sells various children's toy lines. Plaintiff's most successful line to date and the subject of this lawsuit is the ZhuZhu Pets line which can best be described as motorized animal toys. Plaintiff launched ZhuZhu Pets in 2009 and

7. Indeed, Atmos concedes as much by seemingly abandoning this argument in its opposition.

was recognized as "Toy of the Year" by the Toy Industry Association in the same year. Plaintiff later extended distribution beyond the United States to Europe, Asia, Australia, New Zealand, and North and South America. In addition to expanding its geographic distribution, Plaintiff extended the ZhuZhu Pets line to include a wide variety of similar and supporting products. In 2010, Plaintiff successfully registered the mark "ZhuZhu Pets," along with the ZhuZhu Pets logo, with the United States Patent and Trademark Office. Plaintiff also is the owner of several copyrights related to ZhuZhu Pet product design and packaging.

Defendant Alibaba.Com Hong Kong Limited (hereinafter Alibaba.Com) is a Hong Kong corporation with its principal place of business in Wanchai, Hong Kong. Alibaba.Com is a subsidiary of Alibaba Group Holding Limited, a Cayman Islands corporation. Alibaba.Com maintains websites in the United States and elsewhere that allow a variety of third party sellers to display products for sale to consumers in one central internet location. Alibaba.Com maintains no physical presence of any kind in Missouri beyond the operation of its websites. Alibaba.Com generally does not offer products of its own creation for sale; instead facilitating commercial transactions between buyers and sellers online through its global websites. Alibaba .Com operates as an online marketplace where various third party sellers can list their products for sale, often purchased by wholesale buyers. Alibaba.Com has two "paid users" in Missouri, as well as 1,211[1] third party suppliers who identify themselves as being located in Missouri.[2] Alibaba.Com permits visitors to search for products either based upon pre-determined product category listings or based upon search terms provided by individual visitors. During the relevant period, Alibaba.Com provided a link viewable on its home page that directed visitors to a page built specifically for ZhuZhu Pet merchandise. The ZhuZhu Pet link existed on Alibaba.Com's home page regardless of any search terms a visitor may or may not have provided.

Alibaba Group Holding Limited (hereinafter Alibaba Holding) is a Cayman Islands Corporation with its principal place of business in Hong Kong. Alibaba Holding is a holding company that owns a number of internet business, including Alibaba.Com. Alibaba Holding owns the domain name "alibaba.com" and owns the marks "Alibaba" and "Aliexpress." Alibaba Holding is the majority shareholder of Alibaba.Com. Additionally, Alibaba.Com and Alibaba Holding share the same chairman of their separate boards of directors. Alibaba Holding maintains no presence of any kind in Missouri beyond its ownership interests in Alibaba.Com and Alibaba Holding's intellectual property used by Alibaba.Com.

Plaintiff contends Alibaba.Com unlawfully uses Plaintiff's ZhuZhu Pet related intellectual property, including the ZhuZhu Pet name, logo, packaging and

1. The parties disagree as to the number of third party suppliers in Missouri. Plaintiff contends there are over 2,000; Defendant contends there are 1,211. For the purposes of these motions only the Court will assume Alibaba.Com has 1,211 suppliers in Missouri.

2. None of the third party suppliers who identify themselves as being located in Missouri sell ZhuZhu Pet related merchandise.

product depictions to facilitate the sale of counterfeit and unauthorized ZhuZhu Pet merchandise. Plaintiff contends Alibaba.Com maintained, during the relevant time period, a link on the subject website taking visitors to a ZhuZhuPet microsite featuring ZhuZhu Pet products for sale from various sellers. According to Plaintiff, none of the sellers are authorized ZhuZhu Pet suppliers, and nearly all of the offered merchandise is counterfeit or otherwise unauthorized by Plaintiff.

II. Applicable Legal Standard—Motion to Dismiss

In ruling on a motion to dismiss, a court must view the facts alleged in the complaint in the light most favorable to the plaintiff. *Scheuer v. Rhodes*, 416 U.S. 232, 94 S. Ct. 1683, 40 L. Ed. 2d 90 (1974); *Conley v. Gibson*, 355 U.S. 41, 45-46, 78 S. Ct. 99, 2 L. Ed. 2d 80 (1957); *Toombs v. Bell*, 798 F.2d 297, 298 (8th Cir. 1986). When personal jurisdiction is challenged by a defendant, the plaintiff bears the burden to show that jurisdiction exists. *KV Pharmaceutical Co. v. J. Uriach & CIA, S.A.*; 648 F.3d 588, 591-92 (8th Cir. 2011); *Viasystems, Inc. v. EBM-Papst St. Georgen GmbH & Co., KG*, 646 F.3d 589, 592 (8th Cir. 2011); *Miller v. Nippon Carbon Co., Ltd.*, 528 F.3d 1087, 1090 (8th Cir. 2008); *Dever v. Hentzen Coatings, Inc.*, 380 F.3d 1070, 1072-73 (8th Cir. 2004); *Epps v. Stewart Information Servs. Corp.*, 327 F.3d 642, 647 (8th Cir. 2003); *Burlington Indus. v. Maples Indus.*, 97 F.3d 1100, 1102 (8th Cir. 1996); *Gould v. P.T. Krakatau Steel*, 957 F.2d 573, 575 (8th Cir. 1992); *Enterprise Rent-A-Car Co. v. Stowell*, 137 F.Supp.2d 1151, 1154 (E.D. Mo. 2001). To successfully survive a motion to dismiss challenging personal jurisdiction, a plaintiff must make a *prima facie* showing of personal jurisdiction over the challenging defendant. *KV Pharmaceutical*, 648 F.3d at 591 ("To survive a motion to dismiss for lack of personal jurisdiction, a plaintiff must make a prima facie showing that personal jurisdiction exists . . ."); *Steinbuch v. Cutler*, 518 F.3d 580, 585 (8th Cir. 2008) ("To survive a motion to dismiss, the plaintiff must state sufficient facts in the complaint to support a reasonable inference that defendant's may be subjected to jurisdiction in the forum state."); *Dever*, 380 F.3d at 1072-73 (plaintiff must produce some evidence; conclusory allegations are insufficient to sustain the *prima facie* showing); *Epps*, 327 F.3d at 647; *Clune v. Alimak AB*, 233 F.3d 538, 541 (8th Cir. 2000); *Falkirk Mining Co. v. Japan Steel Works*, 906 F.2d 369, 373 (8th Cir. 1990); *Enterprise Rent-A-Car*, 137 F.Supp.2d at 1154 (*citing Digi-Tel Holdings v. Proteq Telcoms.*, 89 F.3d 519, 522 (8th Cir. 1996)). A plaintiff's *prima facie* showing "must be tested, not by pleadings alone, but by affidavits and exhibits" presented in support or in opposition to the motion. *KV Pharmaceutical*, 648 F.3d at 592; *Miller*, 528 F.3d at 1090 (*citing Dever*, 380 F.3d at 1072); *Dever*, 380 F.3d at 1072 (citations omitted); *see Stevens v. Redwing*, 146 F.3d 538, 543 (8th Cir. 1998) (when considering whether personal jurisdiction exists under Missouri long arm statute, court may inquire by affidavits or otherwise into facts as they exist). Although a court must view evidence in a light most favorable to the plaintiff and resolve factual conflicts in the plaintiff's favor; the party seeking to establish the court's personal jurisdiction carries the burden of proof, and the burden does not shift to the party challenging jurisdiction. *Viasystems*, 646 F.3d at 592; *Epps*, 327 F.3d at 647.

III. Discussion

In order for a federal court to exercise personal jurisdiction over a non-resident defendant two prerequisites must be satisfied. *Johnson v. Arden*, 614 F.3d 785, 794 (8th Cir. 2010); *see KV Pharmaceutical*, 648 F.3d at 592. Firstly, the forum state's long arm statute must be satisfied. *Viasystems*, 646 F.3d at 593; *Johnson*, 614 F.3d at 794. Secondly, the Court must determine whether the defendant has sufficient contacts with the forum state to satisfy due process concerns of the Fourteenth Amendment. *Johnson*, 614 F.3d at 794; *Miller*, 528 F.3d at 1090; *Stanton v. St. Jude Medical*, 340 F.3d 690, 693 (8th Cir. 2003); *St. Jude Medical, Inc. v. Lifecare Int'l*, 250 F.3d 587, 591 (8th Cir. 2001); *Clune*, 233 F.3d at 541; *Redwing*, 146 F.3d at 543l; *Burlington Indus.*, 97 F.3d at 1102. The Eighth Circuit Court of Appeals suggests the due process and long arm statute inquiries should be analyzed separately. *Viasystems*, 646 F.3d at 593 n.2 (*citing Bryant v. Smith Interior Design Grp.*, 310 S.W.3d 227, 231 (Mo. 2010)).[3]

The reach of Missouri's long arm statute is a question of Missouri law. *See Scullin Steel Co. v. National Railway Utilization Corp.*, 676 F.2d 309, 311 (8th Cir. 1982). Accordingly, the Court must accept the interpretation given the statute by the Missouri Supreme Court. *See id.* Missouri's long arm statute provides for personal jurisdiction over any person or firm who, *inter alia*, either in person or through an agent transacts business, makes a contract, or commits a tort within Missouri. Mo. Rev. Stat. § 506.500.1(1)-(3). Missouri's long-arm statute has been interpreted as covering "extraterritorial acts that yield consequences in Missouri." *Furminator v. Wahba*, No. 4:10-CV-01941, 2011 U.S. Dist. LEXIS 96695, 2011 WL 3847390 at *2 (August 29, 2011) (*quoting Bryant v. Smith Interior Design Grp., Inc.*, 310 S.W.3d 227, 232 (Mo. 2010)).

The second prerequisite—minimum contacts—is based on the notion that "those who live or operate primarily outside a State have a due process right not to be subjected to judgment in its courts as a general matter." *J. McIntyre Mach. Ltd. v. Nicastro*, 131 S.Ct. 2780, 2787, 180 L. Ed. 2d 765 (2011). Due process requires that a plaintiff show that a non-resident have "minimum contacts" with the forum state and that the maintenance of the lawsuit does not offend "traditional notions of fair play and substantial justice." *Id.*; *World-Wide Volkswagen Corp. v. Woodson*, 444 U.S. 286, 291-92, 100 S. Ct. 559, 62 L. Ed. 2d 490 (1980); *Int'l Shoe Co. v. Washington*, 326 U.S. 310, 316, 66 S. Ct. 154, 90 L. Ed. 95 (1945); *see Asahi Metal Indus. Co. v. Superior Court of California, Solano County*, 480 U.S. 102, 109-112, 107 S. Ct. 1026, 94 L. Ed. 2d 92 (1987); *Miller*, at 1090-1091; *Steinbuch*; at 585-86; *Stanton v. St. Jude Medical*, 340 F.3d at 693; *Epps*, 327 F.3d at 647-48; *Clune*, 233 F.3d at 541-42 (*citing International Shoe Co. v. Washington*, 326 U.S. 310, 66 S. Ct. 154, 90 L. Ed. 95); *Burlington Indus.*, 97 F.3d at 1102 (*citing World-Wide Volkswagen*,

---

3. At the time the parties briefed their arguments in this matter, precedent indicated only a due process inquiry was required. Since the parties briefed this issue, the Eighth Circuit in *Viasystems* indicated a two-part inquiry, testing both the application of the state long arm statute and due process, is necessary. *Viasystems*, 646 F.3d at 593 n.2.

444 U.S. at 291-92); *Guinness Import Co. v. Mark VII Distributors*, 153 F.3d 607, 614 (8th Cir. 1998); *Enterprise Rent-A-Car.* at 1155 (*citing Int'l Shoe*, 326 U.S. at 310). A defendant's contacts with the forum state must be sufficient so that a non-resident defendant should reasonably anticipate being haled into court there. *World-Wide Volkswagen*, 444 U.S. at 297; *Stanton*, 340 F.3d at 694; *Epps*, 327 F.3d at 648. Minimum contacts can cover a plethora of activities; however, sufficient minimum contacts "requires some act by which the defendant 'purposely avails itself of the privilege of conducting activities within the forum State, thus invoking the benefits and protections of its laws.'" *Nicastro*, 131 S.Ct. at 2787 (*quoting Hanson v. Denckla*, 357 U.S. 235, 253, 78 S. Ct. 1228, 2 L. Ed. 2d 1283 (1958)); *see Miller*, 528 F.3d at 1091; *Steinbuch*, 518 F.3d at 586; *Romak USA v. Rich*, 384 F.3d 979, 984 (8th Cir. 2004); *Dever*, 380 F.3d at 1073; *Stanton*, 340 F.3d at 693; *Epps*, 327 F.3d at 648-49; *Guinness Import*, 153 F.3d at 614.

The "'purposeful availment' requirement ensures that a defendant will not be haled into a jurisdiction solely as the result of 'random,' 'fortuitous,' or 'attenuated' contacts or of the 'unilateral activity of another party or a third person.'" *Stanton*, 340 F.3d at 693-94 (*quoting Burger King*, 471 U.S. at 475 (citations omitted)); *see also Epps*, 327 F.3d at 648; *Guinness Import*, 153 F.3d at 614. "Jurisdiction is proper, however, where the contacts proximately result from actions by the defendant himself that create a 'substantial connection' with the forum state." *Stanton*, 340 F.3d at 694 (*quoting Burger King*, 471 U.S. at 475). That is, "jurisdiction is viable only if the injury giving rise to the lawsuit occurred within or had some connection to the forum state. In other words, the cause of action must 'arise out of' or 'relate to' a defendant's activities within a state." *Romak USA*, 384 F.3d at 984 (internal citations omitted).

Based on the due process standard espoused by *World-Wide Volkswagen* and *International Shoe* and their progeny, the Eighth Circuit Court of Appeals established a five factor test to determine the sufficiency of a non-resident defendant's contacts with the forum state. *Romak USA*, 384 F.3d at 984; *but see Bryant*; 310 S.W.3d at 233 n.4 (noting that the five factor test is "simply a tool . . .", not a required test for personal jurisdiction). The five factors utilized by the Eighth Circuit Court of Appeals are: 1) the nature and quality of contacts with the forum state; 2) the quantity of the contacts; 3) the relation of the cause of action to the contacts; 4) the interest of the forum state in providing a forum for its residents; and 5) convenience of the parties. *Romak USA*, 384 F.3d at 984; *Dever*, 380 F.3d at 1073-74; *Stanton*, 340 F.3d at 694; *Epps*, 327 F.3d at 648; *Guinness Import*, 153 F.3d at 614; *Burlington Indus.*, 97 F.3d at 1102; *see also Prods. Plus, Inc. v. Clean Green, Inc.*, 112 S.W.3d 120, 124 (Mo.App. 2002). The first three factors are of "primary importance", while the last two factors are of "secondary importance" and as such are not determinative of personal jurisdiction. *Romak USA*, 384 F.3d at 984; *Dever*, 380 F.3d at 1074; *Stanton*, 340 F.3d at 694; *Guinness Import*, 153 F.3d at 614.

Furthermore, with respect to the third factor, the Supreme Court has differentiated between general and specific jurisdiction. *Helicopteros Nacionales de*

Colombia, S.A. v. Hall, 466 U.S. 408, 414, 104 S. Ct. 1868, 80 L. Ed. 2d 404 (1984); *see also Viasystems*, 646 F.3d at 589. "'Specific jurisdiction refers to jurisdiction over causes of action arising from or related to a defendant's actions within the forum state, while [g]eneral jurisdiction . . . refers to the power of a state to adjudicate any cause of action involving a particular defendant, regardless of where the cause of action arose.'" *Viasystems*, 646 F.3d at 593 (*quoting Miller*, 528 F.3d at 1091) (alteration in original) (omission in original)). General personal jurisdiction may be exercised if a defendant has maintained systematic and continuous presence in a forum state such that it has purposefully availed itself of the privileges of a particular state's laws to the point where exercising jurisdiction does not offend traditional notions of fair play or substantial justice. *Nicastro*, 131 S.Ct. at 2787; *World-Wide Volkswagen*, 444 U.S. at 291-92; *Steinbuch*, 518 F.3d at 586. Unlike specific personal jurisdiction, general personal jurisdiction does not require a direct relationship between the defendant's contacts with the forum and the plaintiff's cause of action. *See Steinbuch*, 518 F.3d at 586.

A. Alibaba Holding

Plaintiff first argues Alibaba Holding is subject to the jurisdiction of this Court because Alibaba Holding owns the domain name www.alibaba.com, certain trade names and other intellectual property in connection with its subsidiary Defendant Alibaba.Com, and due to Alibaba.Com's allegedly tortious acts. Few Missouri courts have addressed the issue of whether the Missouri long arm statute reaches a parent company due to the alleged tortious conduct of a subsidiary. In *Weicht v. Suburban Newspapers of Greater St. Louis, Inc.*, the Missouri Court of Appeals narrowly addressed whether a parent corporation was subject to personal jurisdiction in Missouri for actions of a subsidiary which occurred in Missouri. 32 S.W.3d 592 (Mo. App. 2000). The Missouri Court of Appeals held the parent company did not have sufficient minimum contacts with Missouri to support jurisdiction pursuant to the Missouri long arm statute because the parent did not commit the allegedly tortious acts in Missouri, and the plaintiff had not shown the subsidiary was acting as an agent of the parent. *Id.* at 601-02.

In a similar vein, the Eighth Circuit held that a North Carolina corporation was not subject to personal jurisdiction in a Nebraska Court based upon a subsidiary's conduct in Nebraska. *Peterson v. U-Haul. Co.*, 409 F.2d 1174 (8th Cir. 1969) (applying Nebraska's long arm statute). Nebraska's long arm statute provided jurisdiction was proper in Nebraska so long as a party either conducted business in Nebraska or committed a tortious act in Nebraska. *Id.* at 1183. Nebraska's long arm statute is substantially similar to Missouri's long arm statute, in that both statutes confer jurisdiction over parties that either conduct business or commit a tort with the forum state. *See* Mo. Rev. St. § 506.500(1)-(3); *Peterson*, 409 F.2d at 1183. In determining whether or not a Nebraska District Court had jurisdiction over a North Carolina company based upon business conducted by a Nebraska subsidiary, the Eighth Circuit Court of Appeals explained "the doing business of a subsidiary corporation in a state does not without more confer jurisdiction over the nonresident parent corporation." *Peterson*, 409 F.2d at 1184; *see Cannon Mfg. v. Cudahy Packing Co.*, 267 U.S. 333, 334-37, 45 S. Ct. 250, 69 L. Ed. 634 (1925).

Plaintiff next argues that a parent company may become subject to the jurisdiction of a forum based upon a symbiotic relationship with a subsidiary, citing *Anderson v. Dassault Aviation*, 361 F.3d 449 (8th Cir. 2004). In *Dassault*, the Eighth Circuit Court of Appeals held a parent corporation which completed manufacture of a majority of its products through a subsidiary located in Arkansas was subject to personal jurisdiction in Arkansas based upon "a close, synergistic relationship that is not an abuse of the corporate organizational form." *Id.* at 453. *Dassault*, however, is distinguishable from the present case. *Dassault* involved a parent company knowingly sending a majority of its products to a subsidiary in Arkansas for completion before the products were distributed to purchasers. The present case involves only the use of trademarks and other intellectual property on web sites viewable, but not based, in Missouri. While Alibaba Holding certainly derives a benefit from Alibaba.com's use of trademarks owned by Alibaba Holding, the relationship between parent and subsidiary does not approach the same level of symbiosis found in *Dassault*.

Further, in *Viasystems, Inc. v. EBM-Papst St. Georgen GmbH & Co., KG*, the Eighth Circuit cautioned against the misapplication of *Dassault*. 646 F.3d 589, 596 (8th Cir. 2011). The Eighth Circuit explained that determining whether or not a parent purposefully directed products at a forum state and attributing the conduct of a subsidiary to a parent within a given forum should be "conceptually separate" inquiries. *Id.* The Eighth Circuit Court of Appeals opined that attribution of subsidiary conduct to a parent entity for jurisdictional purposes requires a degree of parental control and domination. *Id.* Although not quantifying the degree of parental control and domination required, the Eighth Circuit equated the parental relationship necessary to attribute the conduct of a subsidiary to its parent corporation with the alter ego relationship required by *Epps v. Stewart Information Services Corp.*, 327 F.3d 642, 649 (8th Cir. 2003). In *Epps*, the Eighth Circuit Court of Appeals stated that jurisdiction over a non-resident parent corporation can be based on the actions of a resident subsidiary corporation "only if the parent so controlled and dominated the affairs of the subsidiary that the latter's corporate existence was disregarded so as to cause the residential corporation to act as the nonresidential corporate defendant's alter ego." *Id.*

Plaintiff has failed to sufficiently show the level of control needed to attribute Alibaba.Com's conduct to Alibaba Holding. Plaintiff points to use of the same name and logo, together with Alibaba.Com and Alibaba Holding having the same chairman of each entity's separate boards of directors, as evidence of parental control. Such an arrangement does not reach the level of control as set forth in *Epps*. Beyond the parental relationship and ownership interests in domain names and trademarks indicated previously, Alibaba Holding does no business in Missouri. Alibaba Holding has never entered into any contract in Missouri, and is not registered to conduct business in Missouri with the Missouri Secretary of State. Plaintiff alleges that Alibaba Holding committed various state law torts and Lanham

Act violations relating to trademark infringement and dilution. However, Plaintiff has asserted only that the allegedly infringing acts were performed by Alibaba.Com, not Alibaba Holding. Finally, Plaintiff has failed to sufficiently argue that Alibaba .Com is either an agent or an alter-ego of Alibaba Holding so as to subject Alibaba Holding to personal jurisdiction in Missouri. Therefore, Alibaba Holding's contacts with Missouri are insufficient to meet the jurisdictional requirements of Missouri's long arm statute.

Plaintiff alternatively argues Alibaba Holding is subject to the jurisdiction of the Court based upon Federal Rule of Civil Procedure 4(k)(2). Rule 4(k)(2) provides that jurisdiction over claims arising under federal law is proper if: "(A) the defendant is not subject to any state's courts general jurisdiction; and (B) exercising jurisdiction is consistent with the United States Constitution and laws." Fed. R. Civ. P. 4(k)(2). The propriety of exercising jurisdiction under Rule 4(k)(2) is measured based upon a defendant's contacts with the United States as a whole to satisfy the due process concerns of the Fifth Amendment. *1st Tech., LLC v. Digital Gaming Solutions S.A.*, 2009 U.S. Dist. LEXIS 27786, 2009 WL 879463 at *6 (E.D. Mo. 2009) (*citing Odilla Mutaka Mwani v. Osama Bin Laden*, 417 F.3d 1, 368 U.S. App. D.C. 1 (D.C. Cir. 2005)). Due process analysis concerning jurisdiction under Rule 4(k)(2) must be focused on whether the "defendant purposely directed its activities at residents of the forum, and whether litigation results from alleged injuries that arise out of, or relate to those activities." *Id.* Again, Plaintiff has not shown Alibaba Holding has purposely directed its activities at Missouri. Further, Plaintiff has failed to show the conduct giving rise to this lawsuit is attributable to Alibaba Holding and not its subsidiary company Defendant Alibaba.Com. Therefore, jurisdiction under Federal Rule of Civil Procedure 4(k)(2) is not proper in this case.

For the reasons set forth above, Defendant Alibaba Holding's motion to dismiss pursuant to Rule 12(b)(2) of the Federal Rules of Civil Procedure will be granted.

B. Alibaba.Com

Alibaba.Com is within reach of Missouri's long arm statute. Violations of the Lanham Act and related state law violations of which Alibaba.Com is accused are tortious acts. *See Furminator*, No. 4:10-CV-01941, 2011 U.S. Dist. LEXIS 96695, 2011 WL 3847390 (Aug. 29, 2011). Tortious acts aimed at citizens of Missouri are sufficient to satisfy Missouri's long arm statute. *See id.* Plaintiff, a limited liability company organized under Missouri law with its principal place of business in Missouri, is a Missouri citizen. Alibaba.Com's allegedly tortious conduct allegedly injured Plaintiff's intellectual property and business interests in Missouri. Furthermore, Alibaba.Com's relationships with its 1,211 third party suppliers in Missouri qualify as transacting business within the state. *See* Mo. Rev. Stat. § 506.500(1). As a result, Missouri's long arm statute is satisfied.

Having concluded that Alibaba.Com's conduct brings it within reach of Missouri's long arm statute, the Court turns to consider whether asserting personal jurisdiction over Defendant Alibaba.Com comports with due process. Jurisdiction will be proper if it is consistent with principles of due process espoused by *World-Wide Volkswagen* and its progeny. In determining whether sufficient minimum contacts exist to exercise personal jurisdiction over Defendant Alibaba.Com, the Court considers the five factor test used by the Eighth Circuit in determining whether or not Alibaba .Com's contacts with Missouri are sufficient to support personal jurisdiction. *See Steinbuch*, 518 F.3d at 586. The first three factors of the Eighth Circuit test each support the existence of personal jurisdiction. Firstly, Alibaba.Com operates a web site accessible in Missouri that is designed to generate commercial profits. Alibaba .Com allegedly infringed upon the intellectual property of Plaintiff in operating the subject website for profit, which was accessible from Missouri. Secondly, taking the evidence in a light most favorable to the Plaintiff, there are at least 1,211 third party sellers from Missouri that have entered into business relationships with Alibaba .Com to sell their products on the subject website. Alibaba.Com has at least two paid "users" in Missouri and unknown quantity of unpaid users of Alibaba.Com presumably in Missouri.

Third, without determining whether there is a sufficient connection between Alibaba.Com's contacts with Missouri and Plaintiff's cause of action that would support specific personal jurisdiction, the evidence amply supports a finding of general personal jurisdiction over Alibaba.Com. At the heart of determining whether the exercise of general personal jurisdiction is consistent with the principles of due process is a determination of whether the defendant has purposefully availed itself of the privileges of a particular state's laws such that exercising jurisdiction does not offend traditional notions of fair play or substantial justice. *Nicastro*, 131 S.Ct. at 2787; *World-Wide Volkswagen*, 498 U.S. at 291-92. Alibaba.Com's contacts with Missouri are not fleeting or isolated. Alibaba.Com maintains significant business relationships with over 1,200 persons or entities in Missouri on an ongoing basis. These relationships, combined with similar relationships across the world, are what allow Alibaba.Com to operate. In short, Alibaba.Com's commercial relationships with third party sellers are a critical aspect of its operation. Further, Alibaba.Com's commercial relationships with third party sellers are not a one time event, but rather a continuing critical component of its business. Alibaba.Com maintains 1,211 such relationships with suppliers in Missouri. Accordingly, Alibaba.Com's contacts with Missouri are systematic and continuous in such a manner that supports general personal jurisdiction. By maintaining systematic and continuous commercial relationships with at least 1,211 people or entities in Missouri, Alibaba.Com, has purposefully availed itself of Missouri's laws. As a result, it is reasonable that Alibaba .Com may be haled into court in Missouri without offending traditional notions of fair play or substantial justice. Therefore, exercising general personal jurisdiction over Alibaba.Com is consistent with principles of due process.

Finally, the supplemental fourth and fifth factors further support the Court's finding of personal jurisdiction. Plaintiff is a Missouri citizen. Missouri has an interest in allowing its citizens to assert their rights and protect against allegedly tortious invasions of their intellectual property and business interests by foreign defendants. As for convenience, although Defendant Alibaba.Com is a Hong Kong Corporation, it maintains significant business relationships in the United States and Missouri. Thus, it cannot be said that litigation in Missouri poses a significant inconvenience to Alibaba.Com.

An analysis of the five factor test put forward by the Eighth Circuit Court of Appeals and an examination of the fundamental principles governing personal jurisdiction indicate that Alibaba.Com has sufficient contacts with Missouri to allow the Court to exercise general personal jurisdiction over Alibaba.Com

Accordingly, Alibaba.Com's motion to dismiss pursuant to Rule 12(b)(2) of the Federal Rules of Civil Procedure will be denied.

Accordingly,

IT IS HEREBY ORDERED that Alibaba Group Holding Limited's motion to dismiss due to lack of personal jurisdiction is **GRANTED.**

IT IS FINALLY ORDERED that Alibaba.Com Hong Kong Limited's motion to dismiss due to lack of personal jurisdiction is **DENIED.**

What works? What doesn't and what does it mean for the future of how brands fight against online counterfeiting? How can brand owners successfully hold Alibaba accountable? As Alibaba's size and reach grow, will it become more susceptible to U.S. jurisdiction? Additional suggested reading includes: *Carson Optical Inc. v. eBay, Inc.*, 202 F. Supp. 3d 247 (E.D.N.Y. 2016) and *H-D U.S.A., LLC v. SunFrog, LLC*, 282 F. Supp. 3d 1055 (E.D. Wis. 2017).

G. Conclusion

There is no counterfeiting silver bullet. There will always be an appetite for the next hot item at a greatly reduced price. Brands, especially luxury brands, must remain vigilant and proactive to protect their image, their consumers, and their intellectual property. While online counterfeiting continues to grow, traditional brick-and-mortar counterfeiting will always have a place. Gone are the days when guidebooks would tell you where to go on Canal Street in New York City to get the best fakes, but if a consumer really wants the look and doesn't want to pay for it, that consumer will find a way. The proliferation of online counterfeits has only increased consumer access. It is up to the brands to make counterfeiting a priority even when the CFO down the hall doesn't want to spend the money. Without enforcement, a brand could be irreversibly damaged.

Chapter 8

Fashion Licensing and Collaborations

Sherry L. Jetter
With special thanks to Simone A. Dvoskin

"Fashion is indelibly connected with time. It not only reflects and represents the spirit of the times, but it also changes and develops with the times."[1]

—Andrew Bolton, Head Curator
The Costume Institute of the Metropolitan Museum of Art

A. Introduction

Halston, Pierre Cardin, Oleg Cassini. Donna Karan, Ralph Lauren, Tommy Hilfiger, Calvin Klein. Prada, Gucci, Louis Vuitton, Christian Dior, Chanel. Stella McCartney, Kate Moss, Sarah Jessica Parker. Roger Federer, Shaquille O'Neal, LeBron James, Michael Jordan. Nordstrom, Target, Topshop. There is a common thread among these beacons in the fashion industry, iconic luxury brands, lauded celebrities, star athletes, and powerhouse retailers—*fashion licensing and collaborations.*

A tenet, if not a cornerstone, in the fashion industry is the business of licensing and strategic collaborations. Essentially, two or more distinct entities operating separate businesses in the fashion arena enter into an alliance to leverage and monetize their respective stature, influence, and strengths—either as a high-profile brand, public persona, reputable retailer, or a best-of-breed manufacturer. The ultimate collaborative goal is to cultivate and sustain joint venture relationships to design, manufacture, market, and sell products or services that will broaden and elevate the reputation of a brand and its related trademarks, as well as the strategic collaborative partner.[2] Fundamentally, the heart of these brand-building relationships is fashioned upon (no pun intended) the basics of trademark law—identification of source and transparency to consumers.

1. Vanessa Friedman, *The Met's Next Big Fashion Show Revealed*, N.Y. Times (Nov. 7, 2019).

2. *See generally* Jacob Jacoby & David Mazursky, *Linking Brand and Retailer Images—Do the Potential Risks Outweigh the Potential Benefits?*, 60 J. Retailing 105 (1984) (discussing the association of retailer images and manufacturer (or brand) images, supporting a thesis that the party with the least favorable image may have that image enhanced).

This chapter will discuss the significance of licensing as a business model for fashion companies, the motivations behind and structure of license agreements, including drafting notes, and the origins of such collaborations. It will also explore how the traditional licensing landscape in the fashion industry has evolved with the entry of "pure-play" brand management collectives and the phenomenon of collaborations between celebrities, brands, big-box department stores, and influencers, who in their own right have taken fashion licensing by storm. A number of high-profile seminal cases involving disputes that arose out of these distinct relationships will be highlighted, which arguably had and will have a significant impact upon the business of modern-day licensing and collaborations on the fashion stage. (Pay close attention to the footnotes as well, as they contain useful anecdotes!)

1. Valuable Brand—The Bedrock of Licensing and Collaborations in the Fashion Industry

> *"At the end of the day, consumers will buy the products that they like from the brands they trust. . . . Licensing provides opportunities for brands to reach a broader audience by leveraging the properties consumers already love."*[3]

There are countless consumer brands that typically contain a name, term, symbol, or design that, over time, consumers come to identify with the source and the quality of the product or service, hence establishing a trademark or service mark.

In the fashion industry, a *valuable brand* takes on particular significance and meaning, especially when linked to the essence of luxury. The names or trademarks associated with a high-profile fashion brand can potentially become as marketable as the products they sell. This is the *value* and therein lies the key to a successful business of licensing in the fashion industry.[4]

What is a "fashion brand"? Consider the following elements:

- A fashion brand is its face in the marketplace;
- It's what consumers know, believe, and come to expect;
- It adds emotion, trust, and value, cultivating a relationship with consumers;
- It creates an aspirational lifestyle;
- It comes to represent a company's vision;
- It's the crown jewel—a company's most valuable asset.

---

3. Alexandra Pastore, *License Global Honors Disruptors of Brand Licensing*, WWD 16 (Dec. 13, 2019) (quoting Amanda Cioletti, content director at License Global).

4. Arifoglu & Tang, *Extending Luxury Brands via Licensing and Umbrella Branding: Control, Competition, and Reference Group Effects* 2 (July 23, 2019) (unpublished manuscript) (on file with the UCLA Anderson School of Management).

All, if not most, fashion law practitioners will stand behind the proposition that a successful licensing program for a fashion company is based upon a valuable brand.[5]

What is the essence of a license agreement in the fashion industry? Consider the following elements:

- Granting the right to use:
- A legally protected trademark, name, graphic, logo, slogan, likeness, or other intellectual property;[6]
- In connection with the production and distribution of a specific product category or providing a service;
- For a prescribed period;
- In a specific geographic area;
- In exchange for a defined payment or series of payments in the form of royalties and/or fees.

All of the foregoing issues between a licensor and licensee will be synthesized and memorialized in a trademark license agreement (product category), retail store license agreement (retail development and operations), or license and distribution agreement (geographic expansion) between the parties.[7]

It is important to note that licensing and collaboration relationships in the fashion/luxury business commonly entail other agreements, which define different aspects of these partnerships. The common touchstone, however, is that these agreements are rooted in the same principle—the licensed right to use a fashion company's trademarks. Consider the following:

a. Design Services Agreements

Design Services Agreements are often used by licensors as corresponding agreements to a trademark product license agreement and are commonly entered into in tandem. Design Services Agreements serve a unique purpose. As we will further probe in this chapter, a standard trademark license agreement in the fashion industry must contemplate and secure a licensor's control over the creative process, design,[8]

---

5. For an in-depth analysis of how the issues involved in licensing and branding are interrelated, *see generally* Douglas Hand, *When Licensing and Branding Meet*, *in* INSIDE THE MINDS: NAVIGATING FASHION LAW 251 (Thomson Reuters/Aspatore ed., 2012).

6. In the fashion business, the license typically contemplates the grant of trademark rights by a fashion designer, brand, or celebrity.

7. The terms of a license and distribution agreement are very similar to those of a trademark product license agreement. They differ only in that a license and distribution agreement does not include the right to *manufacture* products. Therefore, this chapter will predominantly focus on trademark product license agreements and retail store license agreements as they relate to the business of fashion. *See* Section G, The Art of Drafting a License Agreement, *infra*.

8. In some licensing arrangements, the creative and design process is solely in the hands of the licensor; in other cases these functions in the development of licensed products are provided jointly

and quality of the licensed products.[9] However, a Design Services Agreement goes further. It contemplates creative and design direction that a licensor agrees to provide in order to enable a licensee to develop, create, design, and manufacture the licensed products. Tangibly, the licensor provides the licensee with "design concepts" that will allow the licensee to develop the composition of each seasonal collection for the licensed brand(s). Under a Design Services Agreement, a licensee is granted a "design license" for the use of the design concepts and, in consideration, the licensee pays a "design fee," which is based upon a percentage of the sales of the licensed products, similar to a royalty payment under a trademark product license agreement.

b. License and Distribution Agreements

As opposed to granting a broad license with the right to manufacture a product bearing a fashion company's trademark(s) along with related rights to distribute, market, promote, and sell the licensed product, *license and distribution agreements* only grant a licensee the right to use a licensor's trademark(s) in order to import, distribute, market, and sell, at wholesale, branded products *in a specific geographic territory.* License and distribution agreements are typically used when a company wants to expand into foreign territories. In most cases, strategically similar to international retail store licenses, the expertise of a local expert in the business is required, based upon its relationship with customers in the territory for wholesale distribution (i.e., independent retailers), marketing strength in the territory, and knowledge of local customs and applicable laws. The terms and conditions of a license and distribution agreement are very similar to a trademark license agreement for the manufacture and sale of a specific product, yet differ in that the rights granted do not include the right to manufacture the products that it sells. This unique distribution relationship between a licensor and licensee calls for the "distributor licensee" to purchase licensed products either from the licensor's product licensees or from the licensor directly.

c. Intercompany License Agreements

Licensing arrangements in the fashion industry call to mind the joining of forces between *unrelated* parties, each with its unique business experience and acumen, which will be used to leverage and build a viable business around an in-demand brand. Yet consider the following—*what mechanism can a fashion company use*

---

by the licensor and licensee. *See also* Hand, *supra* note 5 (analyzing the "design approval process" in fashion licensing, noting that "[f]rom [a] licensor's perspective, 'sole and absolute discretion' in rendering the approval is the goal while the licensee will argue for a 'commercially reasonable' standard and further seek to have approval 'deemed' to have occurred if the licensor does not proffer a specific approval or rejection. Deemed approval negotiation can be a bloody sport, a tortured mechanism in which the licensor has a period to render the approval after the design or sample is submitted with confirmed delivery.").

9. Quality control is integral to a brand owner's obligations to maintain its trademark rights. *See* Section H, The Paradigm of Naked Licensing, *infra*.

internally to increase the value of its trademarks and manage and extend the world-wide breadth of its brands? The answer—*intercompany license agreements.*

Intercompany license agreements can be an effective tool that allows a brand to control its international distribution stream as well as manage its intellectual property. Structurally, a brand typically "houses" its intellectual property, including its trademark portfolio, in a specific entity within its organization. Let's call that the "*trademark holding company.*" The trademark holding company becomes the "licensor" of the brand's trademarks and the recipient of the licensing fee or royalty income. Fashion companies often form new or use existing affiliated entities or subsidiaries (for our purposes, an "*Interco*") and enter into intercompany license agreements between its trademark holding company and an Interco, giving the Interco the right to use the brand's trademarks in order to distribute licensed products in a specific territory. In another scenario, intercompany license agreements are used when an organization chooses to migrate all or part of its trademark portfolio to a foreign trademark holding company for strategic business purposes, which often contemplates tax savings on royalty income. The company would use its international Interco network as a licensing conduit to manufacture, distribute, market, and sell its products. This strategy needs to be executed as an arm's-length business transaction. Similar to license agreements with unrelated third parties, intercompany license agreements must include language that expressly defines the trademark holding company as the licensor, obligations of quality control, and brand supervision, so as not to be considered a "naked license."[10]

d. Collaboration and Influencer Agreements

As further explored in Section K of this chapter, over the past decade, the advertising and marketing landscape in the fashion industry has evolved to embrace collaborations between different fashion, luxury, sports, celebrity, and other lifestyle brands, as well as relationships with social media personalities commonly known as "influencers" or "brand ambassadors." These unions, which often result in "co-branding," seek to broaden the audience and style of each brand and also deliver a specific brand message. The integral legal issues pertaining to these ventures echo traditional fashion licensing arrangements, e.g., the use of a brand owner's trademarks, sustaining brand integrity, and ultimate ownership of intellectual property (which include influencer online posts). When entering into such agreements, the parties must also be aware of any government regulations that would dictate the parties' behavior. For example, influencers who have "material connections" with brands and are compensated, either by payment or in kind, in consideration for their endorsements, are regulated by the Federal Trade Commission ("FTC").[11]

---

10. *See generally* Section H, The Paradigm of Naked Licensing, *infra*.

11. In recent years, the FTC has been following and scrutinizing influencer testimonials in this space to monitor adherence to the commission's principle of truth-in-advertising and honest endorsements to assure that there is clear and conspicuous disclosure to consumers about the

B. Why License?

Licensing can be a seductive, and perhaps necessary, prospect for a fashion company, a high-profile brand, or a burgeoning designer. When done strategically and with integrity, a licensing business model has the potential to elevate and successfully exploit the market power and commercial value of a brand.[12]

A licensing arrangement is a symbiotic relationship. For a licensor, the fundamental interest is the ability to exploit a licensee's sourcing, manufacturing, distribution, sales and marketing capabilities, and infrastructure. In the case of licensed retail stores, and in particular internationally, a licensor can benefit from the local expertise of an influential fashion retailer who has forged relationships with landlords for prime real estate and can assume the responsibility for all aspects of the operation and management of a retail store under a license from a coveted fashion brand. For a licensee, on the other hand, it can greatly benefit from the strength of the brand and related consumer recognition. This benefit should not be taken lightly, as it takes years of ardent work and a substantial capital investment to build and establish brand awareness and ultimate value, especially on a worldwide basis. When a licensee enters into a relationship with a strong, well-known brand, it inherits this brand recognition and obtains market power for the licensed products it is going to manufacture, distribute, market, and sell, or for the retailer that is going to operate a fashion-branded retail store. If done strategically and in tandem with the licensor's vision, such a licensee is primed to breed a robust and lucrative business.

It has been thought that entering into licensing arrangements in the fashion business is an uncomplicated, relatively easy avenue to create brand value. This would be achieved by expanding rapidly and economically into new product categories, market segments, and geographical locations—"[a] win-win, cash in your hand-right-now proposition."[13] But let's take a closer look at the licensing relationship between

---

relationship, or "material connection" (which includes a personal, family, or employment relationship or a financial relationship—such as a brand paying or giving free or discounted products or services) between the influencer and the company or brand. The FTC's enforcement activity in the arena of influencer endorsements is rooted in its *Guides Concerning the Use of Endorsements and Testimonials in Advertising,* 16 C.F.R. § 255 (2009), *available at* www.ftc.gov/opa/2009/10/endortest.shtm (last visited Dec. 30, 2019). *See also generally,* FTC, The FTC's Endorsement Guides: What People Are Asking (Sept. 2017), https://www.ftc.gov/tips-advice/business-center/guidance/ftcs-endorsement-guides-what-people-are-asking; FTC, Disclosures 101 for Social Media Influencers (Nov. 2019), https://www.ftc.gov/tips-advice/business-center/guidance/disclosures-101-social-media-influencers. Companies should also take a proactive approach to avoid becoming a target of FTC enforcement and train, provide guidelines, and monitor its programs in connection with compensated influencers.

12. Celebrities and influencers alike have also sought out fashion licensing and collaborations as a promotional and lucrative means to advance their fame. *See* Section K, Collaborations in the Fashion Business, *infra.*

13. Diana Pemberton-Sikes, *Should You License Your Designs?*, FashionJobReview.com (2005), *available at* https://web.archive.org/web/20130218201559/http://fashionjobreview.com:80/License_Your_Designs.html.

a brand owner/licensor and manufacturer/licensee and explore the nuances. It is a marriage of sorts, which can lead to fruitful longevity and success[14] or, alternatively, go down a path of discord, distress, and ultimate failure. There is an unavoidable factor, as further discussed below—*risk*. It is essential that the integrity and value of the licensed trademarks, which can take years to establish, are not compromised or diluted when a brand is essentially in the hands of a third party.[15] Ultimately, the key to success is the balance between the licensor's control over the design and quality of the licensed products and the licensee's talent, expertise, and commitment to "translate the personality, the stylistic features, the codes and values of a brand into the product."[16]

So, why license? Research has shown that year-over-year royalty income for fashion brands has increased, generating approximately $32.2 billion of annual retail sales.[17] Given this well-established and growing phenomenon, at some point in the stages of development of almost every fashion company, they will turn to licensing as a sensible, if not commercially attractive, business model to elevate their brand.

The business model of licensing in the fashion industry is based upon the fundamental principle of leveraging the value of an established trademark by expanding into new product categories and geographic territories to exploit product offerings and regions complementary to the brand's image.[18] Yet there are other significant factors that motivate a fashion company to license its trademarks:

- Strengthen brand value when challenged with limited internal resources and staffing capabilities;
- Create a lucrative revenue stream with minimal capital expenditure or investment by the brand owner;
- Shift the business risks to a third party, e.g., manufacturing expenses, liquidation of inventory;

---

14. For example, Marcolin Group, a leading eyewear manufacturer and licensee with a healthy stable of influential luxury consumer brands including Bally, Longines, Omega, Adidas, and BMW, recently extended its license with fashion designer Tom Ford that began in 2004, to 2029. *See* Luisa Zargani, *Marcolin's CEO on Industry's Changing Scenario*, WWD 1, 4 (Nov. 13, 2019). For a general overview of Marcolin Group's business, design collaborations and vision for growth, *see* WWD Studios, *Eye-Catching Style*, WWD 22 (Dec. 2, 2019).

15. There is also a theory that there are two countervailing forces in fashion licensing, especially for luxury brands. Given their strong brand image, luxury brands become a strong platform to easily expand into new product categories that "aspirational" customers will be able to afford, such as lower-end branded merchandise and, as a result, may lose the niche customers who were attracted to the brand due to its high-end products and exclusivity. *See generally* Arifoglu & Tang, *supra* note 4.

16. *See* Zargani, *supra* note 14 (quoting Massimo Renon, CEO of Marcolin Group).

17. *Global Sales of Licensed Products and Services Reach US $280.3 Billion, Fifth Straight Year of Growth for the Licensing Industry*, LICENSING INT'L (June 4, 2019), https://licensinginternational.org/news/global-sales-of-licensed-products-and-services-reach-us-280-3-billion-fifth-straight-year-of-growth-for-the-licensing-industry/.

18. Hand, *supra* note 5.

- Brand expansion into new products or services that are not the brand owner's core competency; and
- Brand expansion into new geographic territories requiring local expertise and an established distribution network.[19]

For example, a typical licensing program for a fashion apparel brand will initially launch with complementary line extensions, such as eyewear, fragrance, watches and jewelry, handbags, leather goods, and footwear. As a fashion company's licensing program gains momentum and profitability, it is not uncommon for the company to branch out into a broader range of product categories, such as children's wear, home furnishings, and bed and bath products. Some luxury design houses have even ventured into the food and beverage and hospitality businesses, such as Ralph Lauren with branded restaurants, and both Bulgari and Giorgio Armani with branded hotels.

The number of licensing arrangements that a fashion brand has at a particular time is essentially based upon its business strategy and growth plans. Yet there is a considerable challenge: seamlessness. A brand owner who engages in an aggressive licensing program is challenged by making such arrangements indistinguishable to the consumer, who otherwise relies on the integrity of the trademark that the product (or even a retail store) bears and is not aware that it may be manufactured (or operated, in the case of retail) by a third party. The quality of the products and services must be consistent. A good example of this is Michael Kors, who has entered into several licensing arrangements over the longevity of its business including, but not limited to, watches, jewelry, eyewear, accessories, fragrance, and footwear. It also opened third-party licensed retail stores throughout the world. Yet the consistency of the quality of Michael Kors' products and retail store services has, to date, not faltered.

C. Peeling Back the Onion—A History: The Phenomenon of Licensing in the Fashion Industry

"Desirability rather than necessity have always driven fashion and the current cult for branded merchandise reflects that a designer's name may be just as marketable as his or her Collection. Desirability can be instilled into quite ordinary and unexceptional products once a brand or a 'marque' has been established. T-shirts, jeans, perfumes and sunglasses can all become 'must-have'

19. It is important to note that when granting international licenses, a company must consider the issue of "recordation." Some countries maintain a legal requirement that trademark licenses be recorded if the right to use a registered trademark is granted to a national resident licensee. In this context, local counsel should be contacted. The United States does not require a trademark license to be recorded with the United States Patent and Trademark Office.

items (with the appropriate price tags) by the addition of a Designer name or a logo."[20]

Licensing as a prudent business model in the fashion industry was instituted decades ago, rooted in the commercial exploitation of status-laden high-end designer names. As we will see in the case below, *Otis F. Wood v. Lucy, Lady Duff-Gordon*,[21] as early as 1916 celebrity and status often went hand-in-hand with licensing. In the 1940s, haute couture brands began to realize the potential financial gain in licensing their famous names, whether to start their own fragrance companies or when experiencing cash flow problems, forcing them to explore licensing to reap the benefits of an instant injection of cash flow without the heavy costs of manufacturing.[22]

Pioneers in the business of licensing in the fashion industry led the way, starting in the 1940s:[23]

- **Coco Chanel**—first fragrance license for "CHANEL No. 5";
- **Christian Dior**—the first licensing deal in fashion history;
- **Pierre Cardin**—"the man who became a label" and first couturier to sign a license for ready-to-wear, off-the-rack dresses.[24]

Over the years, the fashion industry has evolved into a complex welding of brand image, aspiration, famous personalities, and charisma. The most successful fashion companies exploit the magic of associating their brand with an iconic founding designer. For example, for more than five decades and until today, Ralph Lauren products elicit a distinct association with its legendary founder.[25]

Such was the case of the British fashion designer, Lady Duff-Gordon, who, at the turn of the twentieth century, paved the way for the now well-established genre of "fashion celebrities." Known by her trade name "Lucile," Lady Duff-Gordon capitalized upon her international fame and successfully exploited the fact that consumers grew to trust and associate her product endorsements with value. As the court notes below, Lady Duff-Gordon turned to licensing her name and "turned this vogue into money."[26] This is the essence of the business of trademark licensing

---

20. Anita Hunter, *Conspicuous Consumption*, New Millennium (1997), *available at* https://garfnet.org.uk/new_mill/autumn97/ah_cons.htm.

21. Wood v. Lucy, Lady Duff-Gordon, 222 N.Y. 88 (1917).

22. *See generally*, Hunter, *supra* note 20.

23. *Id.*

24. *Id.* (In Cardin's words, "Everyone was copying my clothes, so why shouldn't I do the ready-to-wear." For Cardin, licensing became an unwieldy conundrum from the 1960s through the 1980s, with products ranging from chocolate to carpets. The company held more than 800 product licenses. Although generating substantial licensing income, the brand ultimately lost credibility and its cachet.)

25. *See* Very Ralph (HBO Documentary Films 2019); *see also* Lisa Lockwood, *Ralph Lauren Doc Ready for Big Reveal*, WWD 1, 8–9 (Oct. 23, 2019); Kristen Tauer, *"Very Ralph" Documentary Premieres at the Met*, WWD 20 (Oct. 25, 2019).

26. Wood v. Lucy, Lady Duff-Gordon, 222 N.Y. 88, 90 (1917).

in the fashion industry. In *Otis F. Wood v. Lucy, Lady Duff-Gordon*,[27] we are introduced to the classic example of a fashion license agreement and essential terms that are necessary to promote yet protect a brand, the breadth of the rights granted to a licensee, and how any ambiguity in drafting such contracts can lead to misunderstandings and discord between a licensor and licensee.

Wood v. Lucy, Lady Duff-Gordon

118 N.E. 214 (N.Y. 1917)

CARDOZO, Justice.

The defendant styles herself as "a creator of fashions." Her favor helps a sale. Manufacturers of dresses, millinery and like articles are glad to pay for a certificate of her approval. The things which she designs, fabrics, parasols, and whatnot have a new value in the public mind when issued in her name. She employed the plaintiff to help her turn this vogue into money. He was to have the exclusive right, subject always to her approval, to place her endorsement on the designs of others. He was also to have the exclusive right to place her own designs on sale or to license others to market them. In return, she was to have one-half of "all profits and revenues" derived from any contracts he might make. The exclusive right was to last at least one year from April 1, 1915, and thereafter from year to year unless terminated by notice of ninety days. The plaintiff says that he kept the contract on his part and that the defendant broke it. She placed her endorsement on fabrics, dresses, and millinery without his knowledge, and withheld the profits. He sues her for the damages and the case comes here for demurrer.

The agreement of employment is signed by both parties. It has a wealth of recitals. The defendant insists, however, that it lacks the elements of a contract. She says that the plaintiff does not bind himself to anything. It is true that he does not promise in so many words that he will use reasonable efforts to place the defendant's endorsements and market her designs. We think, however, that such a promise is fairly implied. The law has outgrown its primitive stage of formalism when the precise word was the sovereign talisman, and every slip was fatal. It takes a broader view today. A promise may be lacking, and yet the whole writing may be "instinct with an obligation," imperfectly expressed. If that is so, there is a contract.

The implication of a promise here finds support in many circumstances. The defendant gave an exclusive privilege. She was to have no right for at least a year to place her own endorsement or market her own designs except through the agency of the plaintiff. The acceptance of the exclusive agency was an assumption of its duties. Many other terms of the agreement point the same way. We are told at the outset by way of recital that "the said Otis F. Wood possesses a business organization adapted to the placing of such endorsements as the said Lucy, Lady Duff Gordon has approved." The implication is that the plaintiff's business organization will be used

27. *Id.*

for the purpose for which it is adapted. But the terms of the defendant's compensation are even more significant. Her sole compensation for the grant of an exclusive agency is to be one-half of all profits resulting from the plaintiff's efforts. Unless he gave his efforts, she could never get anything. Without an implied promise, the transaction cannot have such business "efficiency as both parties must have intended that at all events it should have." But the contract does not stop there. The plaintiff goes on to promise that he will account monthly for all the money received by him and that he will take out all such patents and copyrights and trademarks as may in his judgment be necessary to protect the rights and articles affected by the agreement. It is true, of course, as the Appellate Division has said, that he was under no duty to try to market designs or to place certificates of endorsement, his promise to account for profits or take out copyrights would be valueless. But in determining the intention of the parties, the promise has a value. It helps to enforce the conclusion that the plaintiff had some duties. His promise to pay the defendant one-half of the profits and revenues from the exclusive agency and to render accounts monthly was a promise to use reasonable efforts to bring profits and revenues into existence.

The judgment of the Appellate Division should be reversed, and the order of the special Term affirmed, with costs in the Appellate Division and in this court.

CUDDEBACK, MCLAUGHLIN, and ANDREWS, Justices, concur. HISCOCK, Chief Justice, and CHASE and CRANE, Justices, dissent.

Order reversed, etc.

Notes

1. In essence, *Wood v. Lady Duff-Gordon* exemplifies the underperformance of a licensee who was granted exclusive rights to the Lady Duff brand. How did they end up in court? Otis Wood sold virtually no products under the Lady Duff brand. It came to light that, in 1916, Duff-Gordon signed a competitive contract with Sears Roebuck and Company, who tremendously outperformed Otis Wood. Unfortunately, the Court ultimately determined that this arrangement caused Duff-Gordon to be in breach of contract.

2. *Query—could Duff-Gordon have contractually protected herself and, in drafting the contract agreement, inserted provisions for the contingency of Wood's lack of performance?* Consider a strategy that affords a licensor the right to terminate a license agreement under such circumstances, allowing it to extricate itself from a failing business without breaching its contractual obligations.

3. Ironically, almost a century later, this case is analogous to the litigation between Macy's, J.C. Penney, and Martha Stewart. Ms. Stewart, a famous brand unto herself, was under an "exclusive" license with Macy's when she covertly entered into another licensing arrangement with J.C. Penney. *See, generally Macy's Inc. v. J.C. Penney Corporation, Inc.; Macy's, Inc. v. Martha Stewart Living Omnimedia, Inc.*, Supreme Court of New York County, 45 Misc. 3d 274 (2014) and discussion regarding same, *infra*, Section J, Licensing Disputes: A Licensee's Perspective.

D. Fashion Licensing and Brand Integrity: The Perils — From Class to Mass

He was considered to be the single most influential figure in the history of American fashion. He was the first American designer turned celebrity—a superstar. His notoriety grew into an international presence. He defined an era and reigned over the glamour of the fashion industry. He was Halston. *Yet his empire unraveled.*

Halston (born Roy Halston Frowick) emerged on the New York fashion scene in the late 1950s as the head of the custom millinery department of Bergdorf Goodman, a legacy and exclusive fashion department store, with its notable presence on New York City's Fifth Avenue. One of Halston's most well-known accolades was designing pillbox hats for Jacqueline Kennedy.[28] He was a self-made success[29] and ultimately defined his own signature style as an apparel fashion designer for celebrities. In the 1970s and 1980s Halston's brand grew to capture the essence of American fashion. At the height of his career he embraced trademark licensing as a business model, expanding his couture and ready-to-wear lines to an impressive licensing portfolio ranging from fragrances, footwear, handbags, accessories, and housewares to uniforms for Avis and the United States athletes at the 1976 Olympic Games.[30]

As is common to reputable brands, Halston licensed his well-established trademark in connection with relevant product line extensions. However, Halston went beyond licensing and made some unwise business alliances that resulted in selling his business and himself along with it. He lost control of his company and the use of his name—the famous Halston trademark that he zealously nurtured for more than three decades.[31] Perhaps Halston's worst decision was to agree to sign a $1 billion licensing deal with J.C. Penney to design a ready-to-wear collection. As a result, Bergdorf Goodman, which catapulted Halston into his career and carried his label for 20 years, no longer carried Halston products because "the designer's

---

28. For an overview of Halston's career, *see generally* HALSTON (CNN Films 2019), (a documentary chronicling Halston's fame, career, rise, and fall); *see also* Lisa Belkin, *The Prisoner of 7th Avenue: How Halston Lost the Right to His Own Name*, N.Y. Times (Mar. 15, 1987), https://www.nytimes.com/1987/03/15/magazine/no-headline-650887.html; Matthew Ponsford, *The Rise and Fall of Halston, The Man Who Redefined American Fashion* CNN (Aug. 6, 2019), https://www.cnn.com/style/article/halston-american-fashion/index.html.

29. Roy Halston Frowick was born on April 23, 1932 in Des Moines, Iowa, and after starting a business creating hats for notable personalities, he moved to New York in 1957. *See* Belkin, *supra* note 28.

30. HALSTON (CNN Films 2019); Belkin, *supra* note 28; Ponsford, *supra* note 28.

31. Since the sale of the Halston business and its trademark in 1973 to the company Norton Simon, Inc., it went through multiple acquisitions, ultimately being purchased by Revlon in 1986, the sixth organization to own the business and brand. *See generally*, Belkin, *supra* note 28; *see also Halston: A Brand's Lifetime*, Wall St. J. (Sept. 8, 2008), https://www.wsj.com/articles/SB122064202376704587.

association with Penney had diluted his cachet."[32] Perhaps this was the beginning of the end.[33] There have been several attempts to revive the Halston line under various iterations of Halston marks by owners that kept changing hands.[34] The current owner, Xcel Brands Inc.,[35] purchased the trademarks H by Halston and H Halston in 2014 and built a QVC and department store business. Committed to recapture the original essence of *Halston,* in 2019, Xcel Brands Inc. acquired the Halston and Halston Heritage trademarks intending to attract a higher-end market to be sold online as well as in upscale department stores.[36]

Halston epitomizes both the zenith and nadir of licensing in the fashion industry. But then there is Gucci.

Gucci's legacy can be considered the *resurgence* of a luxury lifestyle brand.[37] In the 1980s and 1990s, Gucci, well-known for the utmost of quality and exclusivity, was headed down the rabbit hole of "over-licensing." During that period, several luxury brands instituted extensive licensing programs and created so-called "diffusion lines"[38] to increase profits and growth on an international scale. Unfortunately, if not well-managed, such a strategy can backfire and cause a brand to suffer, losing its exclusive allure and causing brand dilution.

That was Gucci's story. Originally a saddler company and known for unsurpassed design and quality of leather goods and footwear that were affordable only to a niche aristocratic customer, Gucci sought an aggressive licensing program as the avenue to ameliorate declining sales in the 1980s. It expanded into the mass market with attenuated product categories affordable to "aspirational customers."[39] At one point, Gucci licensed its brand name to a myriad of licensees who produced more than 22,000 products, from alcohol and disposable lighters to key chains and dog food. The brand's identity was badly damaged, having become associated with department

---

32. Belkin, *supra* note 28.

33. *See* Jacoby & Mazursky, *supra* note 2, at 105–06 ("[H]ow does a consumer react when he or she learns that J.C. Penney will be carrying the Halston line of designer clothes? Does the combined impression reflect favorably upon both the manufacturer/brand and the retailer, or is there potential for one (or both) of the linked parties to be adversely affected by such an association?").

34. *See* Constance White, *Reviving the Halston Legacy*, N.Y. Times (Apr. 1, 1997).

35. *See* Xcel Brands, https://www.xcelbrands.com/ (last visited Nov. 17, 2019).

36. *See* Evan Clark, *Xcel Brings Halston Back Together*, WWD (Feb. 13, 2019).

37. "Lifestyle brand" is a term of art used in the fashion industry. It connotes the epitome of a brand's product range, as each category of a product pervades into the lifestyle of the consumer. For example, Ralph Lauren, together with its iconic polo pony logo, is considered to be the quintessential lifestyle brand, as its products range from men's, women's, and children's apparel, outerwear, footwear and accessories, to leather goods, fragrances, eyewear, home furnishings, watches, jewelry, and restaurants.

38. "Diffusion lines" are product lines of apparel, accessories, footwear, etc., that include a fashion designer's or luxury brand's original trademark for a high-end products, but are geared to lesser expensive products that are more affordable to the mass market, e.g., Marc by Marc Jacobs, Lauren by Ralph Lauren, and Michael by Michael Kors.

39. *See generally* Arifoglu & Tang, *supra* note 4.

stores and drug stores.[40] Gucci executives came to realize that if the company wanted to rebuild and maintain its heritage as a luxury brand, over-licensing licensing would be its demise. In the 1990s, it dramatically changed its strategy under the guidance of its then-chief executive officer, Domenic Del Sole, and bought back, as well as terminated, licenses. In Del Sole's words, "[i]f you are really committed to resurrecting a brand for a long term you do need to have control over distribution. So licensing doesn't work."[41] This led to a remarkable turnaround. Gradually, Gucci regained its high-end status and chic brand image of exclusivity by limiting the number of its licenses and instituting tighter control over its licensees.

Today, Gucci is at the top of its game and on the cutting edge. This luxury powerhouse turned 90 in 2011 and at that time was committed "[t]o give Gucci a chance to be Gucci" and go back to its roots as jet-set glamour and its aura of exclusivity.[42] Yet Gucci realizes, along with its ongoing rich heritage, it cannot live in the past and must move forward in a current way to remain competitive. It has aggressively embraced e-commerce, social media, the Gucci Art Lab,[43] Gucci 9 Hudson,[44] and strategic collaborations.[45] These efforts have not been unrecognized. In 2019 Gucci was ranked as the fastest-growing luxury brand by the London-based marketing consultant, Interbrand, and was noted as an "iconic mover," transforming the way customers interact with its brand.[46] And Gucci's reach continues to go beyond its roots. It is exploring digital strategies in partnership with Tencent, a global leader "in driving technological innovations to support the upgrading of industries and to create the best value for consumers"[47] and, together with Tencent, recently created native content in a short film series called "*Gucci Inspiration Map.*" In 2019 Gucci was ranked by Tribe Dynamics, a data firm best known for tracking media value, as number 1 out of 10 fashion brands, recording more than $26.7 million in earned

---

40. *Id.*

41. *See* Eric Wilson, *After Calvin, Some Wonder if Licensing is a No-Brands Land*, WWD (Aug. 1, 2000).

42. *See* Luisa Zargani, *Patrizio di Marco's Directive*, WWD 16 (Feb. 23, 2011).

43. *See* Natali Theodosi, *Interbrand Ranks Gucci Fastest-Growing Luxury Brand*, WWD 10 (Oct. 18, 2019).

44. *See* Sharon Edelson, *Gucci on the Hudson, Where Customer Service is Center Stage*, WWD 3 (Nov. 14, 2019).

45. For example, Gucci has entered into unique collaborations with Farfetch, an online luxury and designer multi-brand retailer. *See* Chavie Lieber, *Farfetch Teams with Gucci for "Communities' Initiatives*, Bus. of Fashion (May 31, 2019) ("'Gucci Open House' goes live on Farfetch Communities.... It's an eight-month series that takes users [of Farfetch] into the homes and lives of different Gucci diehards. The content has been created by Gucci's digital marketing team, and gives shoppers a peek at how these superfans integrate Gucci into their [lives] everyday. This isn't Farfetch's first partnership with Gucci. The two companies teamed up in 2017 to offer 90-minute delivery in certain cities."). Gucci's bold foray into what used to be uncharted waters is illustrated by its recent collaboration—Disney x Gucci. *See* Sandra Salibian, *Big Year*, WWD 12 (Jan. 3, 2020).

46. *See* Natalie Theodosi, *Interbrand Ranks Gucci Fastest-Growing Luxury Brand*, WWD 10 (Oct. 18, 2019).

47. *See generally*, Luisa Zargani, *Gucci, Tencent Form Partnership*, WWD 2 (Dec. 2, 2019) (also quoting Martin Lau, president of Tencent).

media value.[48] This is a remarkable feat for a brand, once associated with drug stores, that is soon to reach its centennial as an archetypal, world-renowned, luxury lifestyle brand.

E. Choosing a Licensing Partner—Wisely

A licensor-licensee relationship is a marriage of sorts, built upon honesty and promises to respect the value that each party brings to the table. Yet a licensor is obligated not to let its licensee stray and allow the licensee to get a free ride on the success of a brand while failing to live up to its obligation to quality standards.

There are a number of factors that a brand owner should consider with vigilance when choosing a licensing partner:

- A best-of-breed manufacturer/distributor—an expert and leader in the industry;
- Willing to invest in the brand—money, dedicated management, and strategic marketing efforts;
- Understands the licensor's brand positioning and business model, reinforced by an appropriate distribution network;
- Shares the same vision for the development and growth of the licensed business and support of the brand's integrity;
- Financially stable and, if necessary, willing to give appropriate guarantees;
- Has a record of compliance with all applicable laws (labor, safety, customs, etc.) and maintains set policies to maintain quality standards.

Given these significant considerations, each having the unique ability to affect the growth and enhancement of a brand's value, perhaps the essential factors for a licensor and licensee to clearly define are: (i) understanding brand positioning, (ii) agreement upon appropriate distribution channels, (iii) maintaining product quality, and (iv) sharing the same vision for the strategic growth of the licensed business. Yet, despite the best efforts on the part of both parties to achieve such clarity and alignment, conflicting incentives between a licensor and licensee may develop and muddy the waters of a once-harmonious licensing relationship. Pressured to meet financial obligations under a license agreement, a licensee may "reinterpret" the terms of the license agreement and produce lower-quality products at less expensive wholesale price points and distribute to retail outlets that were not originally contemplated by the parties. From a licensee's perspective, it is complying with its contractual obligations to meet financial goals (e.g., minimum sales and minimum royalty obligations). However, despite the short-term profitability of this agenda, inevitably it will undermine the prestige of the licensed trademarks.

---

48. *Id.*

The case of *Calvin Klein Trademark Trust v. Wachner*, set forth below,[49] is a classic example of such a conundrum. Here we examine a dispute wherein a famed fashion company, named for its celebrity designer, Calvin Klein, was poised to develop and proliferate a profitable jeans business, but allegedly suffered diminished brand value due to its trusted licensee's unilateral decision to cut corners and skimp on the quality of the licensed jeanswear products.[50] Calvin Klein sued Warnaco, at one time a powerhouse manufacturer in the apparel business, and painted a disturbing picture of an underhanded scheme by its long-term licensee to reduce the wholesale price points of the Calvin Klein jeans product line in order to sell to subpar distribution streams, allegedly in contravention of the terms of the license agreement.

Calvin Klein's action against Warnaco had a jarring effect on the business of licensing in the fashion industry.[51] This case was ultimately settled out of court, so we turn to study the complaint below as it raises the issues that are at the crux of the delicate relationship between a licensor and licensee.[52]

Calvin Klein Trademark Trust v. Wachner

198 F.R.D. 53 (S.D.N.Y. 2000)

RAKOFF, Judge.

Complaint

Nature of The Action

1. Plaintiffs CK Trust and CKI bring this action to protect the integrity of the "CALVIN KLEIN", "CK/CALVIN KLEIN", "CK/CALVIN KLEIN JEANS", and "CK" trademarks (referred to collectively as the "Marks"), and for related relief.

2. The Marks reflect the creative vision of Mr. Calvin Klein, and are among the most respected and well-known designer brands in the world. The CK Trust (the Marks' registered owner), CKI, and CKI's licensees have invested substantial effort and resources over many years in developing and protecting the Marks. Misuse or misappropriation of the Marks harms not only CKI, the CK Trust, and its licensees; it also harms the public that places its trust and confidence in products that bear the Marks, expecting that those products embody the design standards and quality that have historically been associated with the Marks.

3. Defendants—various companies controlled by defendant Linda Wachner (referred to collectively as "Warnaco"), and Wachner herself—have become a

49. Calvin Klein Trademark Trust v. Wachner, 198 F.R.D. 53 (S.D.N.Y. 2000).

50. *Id.*

51. For an in-depth analysis of the significance of this case and a thorough assessment of licensing in the fashion industry and the designer marketplace, see Susan Fournier & Jessica Boer, *Calvin Klein, Inc. v. Warnaco Group, Inc.*, Harvard Business School Case 503-011 (2002).

52. As is typical with complaints, the language is phrased with flailing, if not barely controlled, outrage, and the long recitation of offenses is one-sided. *See also* Wathne Imports Ltd. v. PRL USA, Inc., No. 157356/2015 (N.Y. Sup. Ct. Sept. 8, 2015).

cancer on the value and integrity of the Marks. Plaintiffs therefore seek preliminary injunctive relief barring Defendants from further infringing or diluting the Marks or breaching their various licenses, permanent equitable relief in the form of termination and forfeiture of those licenses, and damages.

4. Pursuant to various agreements between the CK Trust, CKI, and Warnaco, Warnaco has, *inter alia,* (a) licenses to make and distribute Jeanswear (as defined below and in the Jeanswear License) and men's accessories bearing the Marks, and (b) the right to operate Calvin Klein Outlet Stores and underwear stores selling products bearing the Marks.

5. Yet, as the other brands that Warnaco controls have faltered and Wachner's business empire has deteriorated, Wachner has caused Warnaco to repudiate that basic understanding—and breach fiduciary and contractual duties owed to Plaintiffs—by embarking on a program of discounting and mass-marketing of products bearing the Marks, with the intention of maximizing short-term cash flow regardless of the long-term damage to the Marks, CKI, CKI's licensees, and the public that values the Marks as a quality designer brand. Defendants have:

> (a) infringed and diluted the Marks by producing large volumes of goods for sale to unauthorized and inappropriate distribution channels, and by producing goods that were not approved by CKI and not consistent with CKI's design and quality standards;
>
> (b) breached their fiduciary duties by self-dealing (*e.g.*, selling other brands that Warnaco controls in Calvin Klein Outlet Stores); misrepresentation (*e.g.*, claiming that shipments of special-cut, first-quality goods to unapproved and inappropriate distributors comprised only excess inventory, mark-downs, irregulars, seconds, or close-outs); and malfeasance (*e.g.*, trying to pass off other designers' products as Calvin Klein product samples);
>
> (c) breached various fiduciary and contractual obligations by failing to exploit licensed products in various markets, abandoning product lines, failing to appoint required personnel to develop the Marks, and repeatedly ignoring or interfering with design timetables, marketing guidelines, and quality control standards.

* * *

Statement of Facts

The March 1994 Transaction Creates a Fiduciary Relationship Between the Parties

21. In March 1994, the parties entered into a series of agreements pursuant to which the CK Trust became the registered owner of the Marks and all goodwill related thereto; CKI and Warnaco, Inc. became the beneficial owners of the CK Trust; and Warnaco obtained licenses to sell certain products bearing the Marks, subject to quality, advertising, and distribution standards determined by CKI and enforceable by the CK Trust or CKI as the Trust's agent.

* * *

Defendants Acquire the Jeanswear License and the Store License Agreement, and Promise to "Clean Up" Distribution

28. According to the Jeanswear License, Designer Holdings and licensees or sublicensees thereof, were required to operate what is known in the fashion industry as a fullprice, wholesale business — not a discount or mass-merchandising operation. As of 1997, CKI complained to Calvin Klein Jeanswear Co. with respect to certain sales to unauthorized discounters and jobbers (intermediaries who resell goods to third parties for retail sales without restriction as to outlets or territories) who had not been approved by CKI and who were not appropriate channels of distribution for either first-quality or close-out articles.

* * *

30. In or about September 1997, Warnaco acquired a controlling share of Designer Holdings, and acquired the balance of the company before the end of the year. Warnaco thereby assumed all the rights and obligations of Calvin Klein Jeanswear Co., and all the obligations for compliance with the Jeanswear License. Warnaco's obligations as a Jeanswear licensee were also subject to the Quality Assurance Agreement between Warnaco, CKI, and the CK Trust.

31. During or shortly after its acquisition of Designer Holdings in late 1997, Warnaco became aware of Calvin Klein Jeanswear Co.'s practice of selling first-quality Jeanswear through unauthorized channels of distribution, including Costco Wholesale Corporation ("Costco"), a warehouse membership club, and jobbers.

32. Wachner promised CKI and the public in late 1997 and early 1998 that Warnaco would "clean up" what it claimed were inherited problems with its distribution channels, in order to preserve and maintain the quality and integrity of the Marks. Wachner acknowledged that sales to unapproved off-price discounters constituted a breach of the Jeanswear License, and specifically asked CKI that Warnaco not be held in breach while it tried to "clean up" distribution. As part of that effort, and in connection with a settlement pending litigation, Warnaco in late 1997 requested CKI's permission to make what it described as a one-time sale of overstock inventory to Costco.

33. CKI, like many other designers of full-price retail designer products, approved of occasional sales of overstocked items, or close-outs of seasonal items, through discount chains such as Marshall's or Loehmann's, but had never given permission for sales to a warehouse-style mass-marketer such as Costco. Warnaco's request for permission to make what it described as a one-time sale of overstocked inventory to Costco was an acknowledgment that Costco was not an appropriate distribution channel, and that Warnaco needed CKI's approval to sell any products to Costco.

34. Based on Warnaco's representations, CKI approved the one-time sale to Costco.

Despite CKI's Protests, Defendants Continue to Distribute Jeanswear Through Unauthorized and Inappropriate Channels

36. Despite Wachner's public and private representations, however, Warnaco continued to make substantial sales to Costco after that "one-time" sale. Wachner and her senior executive have actively solicited orders from Costco and other, similarly

inappropriate discounters and mass-merchandisers, and have tried to misrepresent and conceal the nature and volume of those unauthorized sales from CKI.

37. Warnaco's licenses and agreements for goods bearing the Marks acknowledge that proper and authorized channels of distribution are critical to maintaining the quality, prestige, value, and reputation of the Marks. Section 2.3 of the Quality Assurance Agreement sets forth overall distribution standards which govern the distribution of all Calvin Klein goods:

> In order to maintain the reputations, image and prestige of the Trademarks, the distribution patterns of CKI, Warnaco and their respective successors shall consist of those retail outlets determined from time to time whose location, source, merchandising and overall operations are consistent with the high quality of goods sold under the Trademarks and the reputation, image and prestige of the Trademarks.

38. And Section 4.3 of the Jeanswear License provides that only those channels CKI was then using, or would approve as consistent with existing channels, could be used to sell Calvin Klein goods:

> In order to maintain the reputation, image and prestige of the Licensed Marks, [Warnaco's] distribution patterns (a) shall consist of those retail outlets whose location, merchandising and overall operations *are consistent with the quality of Articles and the reputation, image and prestige of the Licensed Marks,* and/or (b) *shall be consistent with [CKI's] past practices,* and (c) may include those authorized distribution channels in which apparel products manufactured by [CKI] and its licensees and sublicensees bearing the mark CALVIN KLEIN have been or are being sold and such *other distribution channels as CKI shall approve.*

39. Costco, BJ's, and Sam's Club operate membership warehouses nationwide and offer a range of merchandise at reduced prices based on high volume sales and rapid inventory turnover. When the parties entered into the Quality Assurance Agreement and the Jeanswear License, Costco, BJ's, and Sam's Club were not authorized outlets for *any* distribution of *any* Jeanswear products—not close-outs of first-quality products; not mark downs; not seconds; and not irregulars. And since 1997, CKI has never approved Costco, BJ's, or Sam's Club as appropriate channels of regular distribution for close-outs, seconds, or irregulars of Calvin Klein goods—much less sales of first-quality goods.

* * *

42. Warnaco has caused a deterioration in the quality of the off-price distribution channels by specifically directing the business towards the mass merchandising segment of the market, including warehouse outlet stores such as Costco, Sam's Club, and BJ's.

Wachner's Deliberate Decision to Transform the Products into Mass-Market, Discounted Items

43. As Warnaco's sales of its other brands deteriorated sharply in 1999, the pressure on Wachner to increase unapproved sales of Calvin Klein products only

grew. On at least one occasion in 1999, at Wachner's personal direction, Warnaco took a large order of first-quality goods for sale to Costco. And by late 1999, Wachner herself became personally involved in taking purchase orders from Costco for Jeanswear. In addition to Jeanswear, Warnaco also distributed men's accessories through discount warehouses and other unauthorized channels during 1999.

* * *

57. As a direct result of Warnaco's unauthorized distribution practices, Dillard's Department Stores, Inc., Nordstrom, Inc., and Neiman Marcus have canceled certain Calvin Klein product lines, and Federated Department stores has notified CKI that it would not expand the Calvin Klein Men's line that it carries.

Defendants' Sale of Unapproved Products and Interference with the Design Process

58. Warnaco, through Wachner herself or through individuals acting under her direction and control, has engaged in a pattern of conduct involving frequent and significant design "injections"—*i.e.*, designs, alterations, or changes that were not developed as part of the regular design process and schedule. While there is nothing wrong with an injection that is made as part of a regular design process and approved by CKI, Wachner has abused the process in various ways:

(a) Wachner has standing orders to her employees to regularly "inject" products, styles and designs, regardless of whether those injections are shown to or approved by CKI, as is required under the parties' agreements;

(b) Wachner routinely intervenes in the design process, substituting her personal whims (about the fabric, color, cut, or style of a product) for the specifications developed by CKI as part of the creative design process contemplated in the parties' agreements; and

(c) Wachner's interventions, under-staffing, and mis-staffing (*e.g.*, hiring designers as merchandisers) delay the design process to the point that plans are often delayed or incomplete, presentations to buyers are bungled and unprofessional, and the creative process intended by the parties' agreement is hopelessly disrupted.

* * *

Defendants' Breaches of the Store License Agreement

76. Warnaco has breached its most basic obligation under the Store License Agreement by selling quantities of Calvin Klein Outlet Stores on Calvin Klein goods, such as Speedo and Chaps by Ralph Lauren, in Calvin Klein Outlet Stores. The reason for these breaches is simple self-dealing: Wachner has been the chief executive officer of Authentic Fitness, maker of Speedo products, since 1991, and Warnaco is a Chaps by Ralph Lauren licensee.

* * *

94. In sum, Wachner has caused Defendants to engage in a deliberate and concerted pattern of conduct that has breached fiduciary and contractual obligations,

tarnished the reputation and prestige of the Marks, infringed Plaintiffs' rights in the Marks, and interfered with CKI's relationship with retailers, other licensees, and suppliers, all with the apparent goal of increasing Warnaco's short-term gains at the expense of Plaintiffs' interests and purporting to exercise control over the Marks. Plaintiffs therefore bring this action to remedy Defendants' repeated, malicious, and substantial breaches of their contractual and fiduciary obligations, and to stop any further harm to the Marks and to CKI's business.

95. Besides damages, a constructive trust, termination of the licenses and forfeiture of Warnaco's interests in the CK Trust, Plaintiffs seek to enjoin Wachner's and Warnaco's pattern of infringement, dilution and misuse of the Marks and their continuing breaches of fiduciary duties owed to Plaintiffs. Plaintiffs bring this action against Wachner and the companies she controls jointly and severally because Wachner has acted and continues to act in a manner designed for her personal enrichment, has caused Defendants to conspire between and among themselves to commit the acts described above, and has treated each of the Defendants as her personal fiefdom, running each without regard for corporate formalities required for treatment as a separate corporate entity, and as her alter egos.

* * *

Claims for Relief

Count I

Trademark Infringement

(by CK Trust and CKI against all Defendants)

104. Warnaco has repeatedly engaged in unauthorized distribution of Jeanswear through inappropriate channels of distribution such as Costco, Sam's Club and BJ's; repeatedly distributed unauthorized articles bearing one or more of the Marks by making unauthorized changes to CKI-designed articles; "dumped" or caused to be "dumped" unapproved Calvin Klein articles knowing, or having reason to know, that such unapproved articles would be sold on the "gray market", typically through inappropriate channels of distribution which may be outside Calvin Klein Jeanswear Co.'s authorized territory; and operated outlet stores without approval of their design or merchandise—all of which actions have foreseeably caused the purchasing public to believe, incorrectly, that such unapproved and unauthorized changes, and unauthorized channels of distribution, were approved, sanctioned or otherwise endorsed by the source of approved goods sold under the Marks.

105. The foregoing conduct of Warnaco constitutes the use, without the consent of the registrant, of a copy of the registered Marks in connection with the sale, offering for sale, distribution and advertising of products on or in connection with which such use is likely to cause confusion, or to cause mistake or to deceive as to the sponsorship or approval of CK Trust, the ultimate source of all quality standards for authorized goods bearing the Marks.

* * *

117. CKI and the CK Trust are entitled to preliminary and permanent injunctive relief enjoining Defendants from (1) distributing Calvin Klein Jeanswear and men's accessories bearing one or more of the Marks to Costco, Sam's Club, BJ's and other unauthorized channels of distribution that are inconsistent with the quality, value, prestige, and reputation of the Marks; and (2) marketing, promoting, advertising or selling any non-Off-Price Articles, as that term is defined in the Store License Agreement, in "Calvin Klein Outlet Stores".

Count III

Trademark Dilution

15 U.S.C. § 1125(c) and N.Y. Gen. Bus. Law § 360-1

(CK Trust and CKI against Defendants)

123. Defendants, as shown by their continued knowing violations of the various trademark agreements and many misrepresentations, willfully intended to trade on the CK Trust's reputation embodied in the Marks, and to cause dilution of the famous Marks for their own short term benefit to the long-term detriment of the integrity and value of the famous Marks.

* * *

Count IV

Breach of Fiduciary Duty

(By CK Trust and CKI against Wachner, Warnaco Group, and Warnaco, Inc. (the "Fiduciary Defendants")

135. Over CKI's objections, the Fiduciary Defendants, through Wachner, have engaged in distribution and merchandising practices that directly benefit the Fiduciary Defendants, and in particular, Wachner, to the detriment of CKI, the CK Trust, and the Marks.

* * *

Notes

1. *Calvin Klein v. Wachner* is pivotal in the ever-expanding body of notable licensing disputes in the fashion industry. It demonstrates how a long-term licensing relationship that began with zeal and a united vision for brand and product development can take a turn for the worse. This dispute provides an ideal example of what a licensor must keep at the forefront when policing its licensees—quality of the licensed products and the importance of selective distribution channels in order to maintain a brand's integrity.

2. Another important takeaway from this dispute is the motivation behind trademark licensing in the fashion industry and, sometimes, the countervailing interests between a licensor and licensee. Here we see the quintessential "rub"—revenue growth to meet a licensee's financial obligations under the license agreement while preserving the licensor's brand equity and value in the licensed trademarks. From a

licensor's perspective, the "brand lives on," and the long-term strategy is to maintain the prestige and heritage of the brand's trademarks. Licensees, on the other hand, often see their role as temporary and are motivated by a short-term incentive to seek immediate profitability, which if not carefully managed by a brand owner, can lead to jeopardizing product quality and unauthorized distribution practices. If not remedied immediately, the value and goodwill of the licensed trademarks, which have taken years for a fashion company to build—often at a great expense—may be eroded.

3. In analyzing the licensing arrangement between Calvin Klein and Warnaco, consider whether Calvin Klein abdicated any if its control over the manufacturing process and ultimate quality of the licensed product that was sold into allegedly unauthorized distribution streams. *How strong was Calvin Klein's case?* As noted above, the parties ultimately settled out of court on the eve of trial, and ironically, several years later, both companies were acquired by Phillips-Van Heusen ("PVH"), which put all of the controversy between Calvin Klein and Warnaco to rest.

4. And the beat goes on: Recently, Swatch Group, the world's largest Swiss watchmaker and licensee for several fashion and luxury brands, decided to end its 22-year exclusive licensing collaboration with the Calvin Klein brand upon the expiration of their license agreement in 2021, allegedly due to discord between long-term licensing partners. Hence another demonstration of the souring of a long-term licensing arrangement in the fashion industry between two prominent players. *See* Joelle Diderich, *Swatch to Let Calvin Klein Deal to Expire*, WWD 3 (Oct. 23, 2019). *The question remains—how to preserve established and time-honored licensing arrangements when the parties' respective businesses go through growth and financial challenges and they no longer see eye-to-eye?*

F. New Kids on the Block—Brand Management and Licensing Companies

The business of licensing in the fashion industry evolves constantly. Enter brand management and licensing companies. Traditional trademark licensing in the fashion industry has been taken by storm by this different breed of licensors.

What are *brand management and licensing companies*? These organizations purely own the intellectual property, and often the assets, of brands that they acquire (for our purposes, let's call them "*pure-play brand management/licensing companies*"). Most pure-play brand management/licensing companies start out by purchasing one fashion brand and expand exponentially to amass stables of consumer brands, from luxury to streetwear, celebrity legends, and renowned retailers, in order to establish a diversified trademark portfolio.[53]

53. Although initially predominantly fashion and luxury brands that include apparel, footwear, accessories, and home furnishings, the intellectual property assets of brand management/licensing

A catalyst for many acquisitions by pure-play brand management/licensing companies are bankruptcy filings by heritage fashion brands. It is also common for pure-play/brand management/licensing companies to pursue and revive distressed or waning significant fashion brands that, without such an acquisition, could not afford the wherewithal to support a viable business. Pure-play brand management/licensing companies strategically partner with manufacturers, retailers, personalities, and influencers to exploit their acquired intellectual property assets through various business models based upon the platform of strategic licensing and collaborations to maximize brand equity.[54]

So who are these trailblazers? The following companies are considered to be the frontrunners in the landscape of pure-play brand management/licensing, each with its own unique approach to exploit a business model that is growing rapidly.[55]

- *Iconix Brands Group (Iconix)*—Iconix was the first pure-play brand management/licensing company, operating for more than four decades, and owner of a varied and wide portfolio of famous brands, including Mossimo, Mudd Jeans, Danskin, London Fog, Candie's, Cannon, and fashion brands by Madonna and other celebrities.[56]
- *Marquee Brands (Marquee)*—Marquee is a privately held pure-play brand management/licensing company, with a mission to manage a portfolio of established global fashion and consumer products to foster organic growth

companies have expanded into celebrity, sports, and entertainment brands. Compare the business model of "pure-play" brand management and licensing companies to "lifestyle brand collectives" or "luxury conglomerates" that, in addition to owning a robust portfolio of brands, design, manufacture, merchandise, manage, and market and advertise their intellectual property, from brick and mortar and wholesale to social media and digital platforms. *See, e.g.*, Capri Holdings Limited, http://www.capriholdings.com/ (last visited Nov. 17, 2019); Centric Brands, https://www.centricbrands.com/ (last visited Nov. 17, 2019); Kering, https://www.kering.com/en/ (last visited Nov. 17, 2019); LVMH, https://www.lvmh.com/ (last visited Nov. 17, 2019); Tapestry, https://www.tapestry.com/ (last visited Nov. 17, 2019); Xcel Brands, https://www.xcelbrands.com/ (last visited Nov. 17, 2019), PVH, https://www.pvh.com/(last visited Nov. 26, 2019)*; see also* Evan Clark, *PVH Looking for Deals in the New* Year, WWD 2 (Nov. 26, 2019); Lisa Lockwood, *Zac Posen Trademark Reportedly Sold to Centric Brands*, WWD 2 (Dec.19, 2019); Mimosa Spencer, *LVMH Adds Tiffany in $16.2B Deal*, WWD 6 (Nov. 26, 2019).

54. Such partnerships typically include alliances in the areas of design and marketing, e-commerce, social media, digital platforms, and emerging media. *See* Section K, Collaborations in the Fashion Business, *infra*.

55. For example, the pure-play brand management/licensing companies Marquee Brands, Sequential Brands Group, and WHP Global vied to purchase the Joseph Abboud brand from its previous owner, Tailored Brands; the sale went to WHP Global for $115 million in March 2020. *See* Jean E. Palmieri, *Licensing Firms Circling Joseph Abboud Brand*, WWD 3 (Dec. 17, 2019); Tailored Brands, Inc., *Tailored Brands Closes the Sale of the Joseph Abboud Trademarks to WHP Global for $115 Million*, Tailored Brands (Mar. 5, 2020), https://ir.tailoredbrands.com/press-releases/detail/1885.

56. For a full profile of Iconix Brands, its business model, brand portfolio, licensing arrangements, and collaborations, *see generally* Iconix Brand Group, *available at* www.iconixbrands.com (last visited Nov. 2, 2019).

through brand extensions that are consistent with the identity and original heritage of the brands that it owns. Marquee's notable portfolio includes Bruno Magli, BCBGMAXAZRIA, Body Glove, Emeril Lagasse, and Martha Stewart.[57]

- *Sequential Brands Group (Sequential)*— Sequential is a publicly traded company that has aggressively developed sustainable relationships with licensees to promote, protect, and activate its brand portfolio, which includes, among other popular brands, Jessica Simpson, Joe's, Ellen Tracey, Avia, and Caribbean Joe.[58]
- *Authentic Brands Group (ABG)*—ABG may be considered to be the leader of the pack.[59] It has taken this powerhouse, initially a start-up business focused on celebrity icons Elvis Presley and Marilyn Monroe, less than 10 years to establish an impressive portfolio of more than 50 global lifestyle brands spanning the sectors of fashion, luxury, sports, active, home, and entertainment. Notable ABG brands also include Sports Illustrated, Michael Jackson, Shaquille O'Neal, Nautica, Aeropostale, Juicy Couture, Jones New York, Vince Camuto, Frye, Nine West, Judith Leiber, Spyder, Hind, Tretorn, Vision Street Wear, and Volcom.[60] Most recently, ABG acquired the intellectual property and assets of Barneys New York (Barneys), a beacon fashion retail institution, best known for its edgy and avant-garde fashion sense, in a highly publicized bid once Barneys filed for Chapter 11.[61]

Given the success of the pure-play brand management/licensing company business model illustrated above, such forces are bound to continue to grow and have a significant impact on the world of fashion licensing and collaborations. Still, this long-standing

57. For a full profile of Marquee Brands, its business model, brand portfolio, licensing arrangements and collaborations, *see generally*, Marquee Brands, *available at* www.marqueebrands.com (last visited Nov. 2, 2019).

58. For a full profile of Sequential's business model, brand portfolio, licensing arrangements and collaborations, *see generally*, Sequential Brands Group, *available at* www.sequentialbrandsgroup.com (last visited Nov. 2, 2019).

59. According to License Global, as of May 29, 2019, ABG was ranked as the fifth-largest licensing company by retail sales, amounting to $9 billion in 2018. *See* Amanda Cioletti, *Top 150 Global Licensors: The New Class*, License Global T3-T4, T9 (Aug. 2019), *available at* www.licenseglobal.com; *see also* Jean E. Palmieri, *Jamie Salter on Plans for SI and Eyeing Reebok Buy,* WWD (July 22, 2019).

60. For a full profile of ABG, its business model, brand portfolio, licensing arrangements, and collaborations, *see generally* Authentic Brands Group, *available at* www.authenticbrandsgroup.com (last visited Nov. 2, 2019).

61. Unique to this transaction is that ABG plans to license the Barneys trademark to Hudson's Bay Co. to operate Barneys departments within Saks Fifth Avenue stores. The fate of Barneys' retail stores is yet to be determined. For further details about this transaction, *see generally* Bloomberg, *Gucci and Prada Take Up Light of Workers in Barneys Bankruptcy,* Bus. Of Fashion (Oct. 30, 2019); David Moin & Evan Clark, *Barneys New York: What Went Wrong*, WWD 4 (Nov. 4, 2019); Jean Palmieri et al., *The New Barneys New York,* WWD 5 (Nov. 4, 2019); Sindhu Sundar et al., *Barneys Saga Nears Finish with ABG On Top*, WWD (Nov. 1, 2019); Sindhu Sundar et al., *Daniella Vitale Out at Barneys as ABG Takes the Reins*, WWD (Nov. 1, 2019), https://wwd.com/business-news/retail/barneys-end-liquidation-authentic-brands-bankruptcy-retail-1203360736; Sindhu Sundar et al., *Has ABG Won the Barneys Race*? WWD 2 (Oct. 25, 2019).

business model, deep-rooted in the culture of the fashion industry, comes down to basics. The primary goals of such endeavors are: expansion into new product categories and geographical locations; maximizing brand value; and maintaining the integrity of licensed trademarks. This will ultimately be realized through strategic business negotiations that result in terms that that are beneficial to a licensor and licensee and memorialized in well-drafted licenses and collaboration agreements.

G. The Art of Drafting a License Agreement

In the fashion industry, a license agreement constitutes the definitive written contract that sets forth the commitment between a licensor and licensee to monetize the commercial value of the licensor's brand and its related trademarks.

A *licensor* is the owner of proprietary intellectual property. A *licensee* is a carefully chosen business partner—entrusted, by an express grant of rights, to commercialize, either through a product, retail store, or geographic location, a licensor's trademarks (and other intellectual property), and maintain the goodwill and stature associated therewith. To this end, a license agreement sets forth the negotiated terms and conditions under which a licensee, who pays a licensor to receive the *license* (typically in the form of *royalties*), will manufacture, market, distribute, and sell specific products. In addition to trademarks, license agreements in the fashion industry may also include a license for the use of a licensor's other intellectual property, e.g., copyrights, trade secrets, patents, and designs. A grant of such rights should be specified in the license agreement. For example, a copyrighted image may only be reproduced and used in connection with a line of streetwear, which includes hoodies, sweatshirts, t-shirts, and sweatpants.

A license agreement is a living instrument and needs to define the rights and obligations of the parties throughout the *term* of the agreement. It should be mutually beneficial and include definitive guidelines that the parties will use, often for a significant period, to achieve the agreed-upon vision for the growth and monetization of the licensed brand. While many fashion industry license agreements are structured similarly and contain common provisions, they vary significantly based upon the intricacies of the business contemplated under a specific license. Ultimately, however, a licensing relationship will fail unless the understanding of both parties regarding the end-to-end strategic direction is aligned.

There is an art to drafting a license agreement in the fashion industry. The challenge is to clearly and unambiguously express in writing an equitable balance between the business goals and respective legal obligations of each party. There are strategic considerations from the perspective of both the licensor and licensee. Most importantly, the drafting of an effective license agreement requires careful foresight, as the business environment can change during the term of the license and affect the obligations of the parties, especially impacting the financial commitments of a licensee. The license agreement should provide for such contingencies to avoid disputes down the road.[62] It is often said that once a license agreement is executed, the parties will put the document in a file and never take it out again. But this cannot be said with certainty.[63] Both parties must contemplate potential differences that may arise that would necessitate "dusting off" the license agreement to analyze the respective rights and obligations of the parties. Such considerations are heightened in the event of an unexpected termination or, for that matter, when the license agreement expires according to its terms.[64] Plainly said, it is essential that the parties fully understand the implications of their business commitment.

A new licensing initiative is often propelled with excitement and optimism for commercial success and a long-lasting relationship between the parties. However, there are inherent competing interests between a licensor and a licensee. Consider the following:

- The design-driven focus of the licensor versus commercial marketability of the licensed products sold by the licensee.
- A licensee's focus to realize immediate profitability to meet its financial obligations under the license agreement versus a licensor's focus on the prestige of the brand's trademarks, appropriate distribution channels, and maintaining brand integrity.[65]
- The declining investment in the brand by the licensee as the term of the license agreement winds down versus the licensor's focus on the longevity of the brand.

Although apparently in sync from the outset, a licensor and licensee may experience some disharmony during their relationship. *How can this be anticipated and addressed when drafting a license agreement?* Attorneys who are experts in the field of licensing in the fashion industry, either as in-house counsel or specialists in private practice, play a critical role.[66] In order to draft an operative license agreement with checks and balances that address these issues, a licensing attorney must work closely with management, business, and design teams to understand the strategy for the brand and licensed business, the proposed business terms, and assess the risks and potential liabilities. To be most effective, it is suggested that counsel be involved early on in negotiations. Counsel can also be instrumental in the due diligence

---

62. *See, e.g.,* Wathne Imports Ltd. v. PRL USA, Inc., No. 157356/2015 (N.Y. Sup. Ct. Sept. 8, 2015).

63. *See generally* Section J, Licensing Disputes: A Licensee's Perspective, *infra*.

64. For clarification, when a license agreement expires "according to its terms," it means that the negotiated Term of the license agreement expires and there are no further renewal options.

65. *See generally* Calvin Klein Trademark Trust v. Wachner, 198 F.R.D. 53 (S.D.N.Y. 2000).

66. It is important to note that some brand owners engage a licensing agent to be involved in the venture. An agent may be tasked to develop a strategic licensing plan, identify appropriate licensing partners, broker the deal and negotiate terms, and remain involved in the relationship to monitor the performance of the licensee. However, there are pros and cons to such a relationship, e.g., an agent is incentivized by receiving a commission once a deal closes and the business starts to generate revenues, which may influence the agent's judgment and potential conflicts of interest can arise. *See* Hand, *supra* note 5.

process to determine if a potential licensee is financially stable and suitable to take on this important venture.

Given this innate dichotomy between the interests of a licensor and licensee, consider the following strategic approach to drafting an effective license agreement for a fashion brand:

Stage 1—Initial Negotiations of the Business Terms

The initial negotiations of the business terms of a potential licensing relationship between a brand owner and a manufacturer, a retail store operator, or a distributor is a fundamental and a critical stage. It is at this nascent point where the brand owner defines the scope of the license grant and what it foresees as the permissible limits of exploiting the intellectual property rights that are to be granted. This sparks the dialogue between the parties to determine whether they see eye-to-eye on the direction of the licensed business. It allows the parties to understand the temperament of the other and determine whether there are synergies between their respective business practices. If negotiations start out with difficulty and antagonism, this may be a tell-tale sign that the parties should rethink their potential relationship. It is not unusual for there to be some incongruity, posturing, and "push and pull" during initial negotiations, but this initial stage can be a litmus test to see whether the parties can compromise amenably to reach a resolution that meets both parties' interests.

Stage 2—Entering into a Term Sheet or Memorandum of Understanding

As noted above, in order to achieve a successful licensing endeavor, a licensor and licensee must be of the same understanding regarding the scope of the license and their respective obligations thereunder. To this end, parties typically enter into a term sheet or a memorandum of understanding ("MOU") before negotiating a conclusive license agreement. This, too, is a critical part of the negotiation process. Term sheets and MOUs are negotiable instruments, which should be relatively brief and address integral business issues such as: the scope of the license; exclusivity and reservation of rights by the licensor; royalty compensation; advertising commitments and payments; the term of the agreement and renewal options (if any); and any definitions of terms that may lead to contention, such as "net sales." It is also not unusual for term sheets and MOUs to include an exclusive negotiation period (e.g., 60 to 90 days), within which the parties are restricted from negotiating with another third party to enter into a licensing arrangement that is the subject of the negotiations at hand. Other common binding clauses include confidentiality and nonsolicitation of the other parties' employees whom the parties may encounter during the negotiation process.

A term sheet and MOU can also have a subliminal effect upon the underlying licensor-licensee relationship. As the parties take their negotiations to the next level with the intent to ink a term sheet or MOU, it allows the licensor and licensee to witness each other "in action" when negotiating a written agreement. The parties can assess the other's style and approach to such business practices and further evaluate the synergies between them. Similar to initial negotiation discussions, if the negotiation of a term sheet or MOU results in arduous discord on the fundamental business terms, then the parties should seriously consider concluding negotiations and parting ways. Alternatively, if the parties can agree on a term sheet or MOU, the business perimeters of the license agreement are set and can facilitate the process of negotiating a full license agreement. Most importantly, a term sheet and MOU should be drafted with the unequivocal and express stipulation on the part of both parties that this document is nonbinding and does not constitute a final definitive agreement between the parties, except for those terms that they mutually decide would expose one or both of the parties to a risk or liability if negotiations break down, such as exclusive negotiation period, confidentiality, and nonsolicitation of employees.

Stage 3—The Nuts and Bolts of a License Agreement

The fashion industry is a niche business and there are strategic "nuts and bolts" provisions that should be included in a well-drafted license agreement. Trademark license agreements for the manufacture of a product category are most common, both domestically and internationally. Retail store licenses and license and distribution agreements, on the other hand, are predominantly used internationally, where the local expertise of the licensee is critical.[67]

As legal practitioners, we consider *all* of the terms of a license agreement to be key, as they frame and govern the relationship between the licensor and a licensee. Still, there are some terms and conditions that are considered "*material.*" Why so? First, such terms must be adhered to as they are essential to successfully execute the business contemplated under the license agreement, e.g., the manufacture of licensed products that are up to the quality standards of the brand image. Second, a term is considered "material" if it impacts the proprietary rights of a party, e.g., the unauthorized use of the licensed trademarks. Finally, noncompliance with a material term can trigger a breach and potentially the termination of the license agreement. We explore this later in this chapter.

There are some provisions in a license agreement that can be considered "neglected stepchildren" that should not, however, be taken for granted. For example, "*Recitals*" or "*Whereas*" clauses, which appear in most, if not all, license agreements, are often overlooked yet they serve a significant purpose. These initial clauses explain the context, background, and underlying purpose of the license agreement, e.g., they identify the parties and their expertise; what brought the parties together; and what they intend to achieve in this relationship. These clauses should be drafted in simple, plain language so if there ever is any litigation, a judge and a jury can easily understand the context of the relationship between the parties, which can be critical.

---

67. In addition to seeking a foreign licensee's expertise, some countries require an operator of a business to be a resident national. In such case, a licensor would be required to work with a foreign licensee.

Typically, the language in Whereas clauses or Recitals is not legally binding. However, in an infamous legal battle between two dominant companies in the fashion industry, Ralph Lauren and Jones Apparel Group, over the term of the Lauren brand license agreement, the court in fact considered the Whereas clauses in its ruling. "The recitals of a contract indicate only the background, and ordinarily form no part of the real contract. Where the recital in an agreement is so inconsistent with the covenant or promise that they cannot be harmonized, the latter, if unambiguous, must prevail, because it is the most important."[68]

The same could be said for the "*Definitions*" provision, which to some appears to be extensive and cumbersome. Yet this depends on the complexity of the agreement. A simple agreement will not necessarily need to have a separate section devoted to definitions, as the definitions can be given when distinct terms are first encountered in the text of the document. License agreements in the fashion industry tend to differ. They are detailed, complex, and use terms that are part of a vernacular that is specific to this niche business and its practices. In the context of license agreements in the fashion business, a Definitions clause sets forth "defined terms" that are used throughout the license agreement and can act as a dictionary of sorts that defines critical terms that influence the transaction and take precedence over any other common meaning of the word or terms used in everyday language. If drafted skillfully and with precision, Definitions can be used as evidence of the parties' meeting of the minds if a dispute arises.

For example, in a trademark product license agreement the definition of "*net sales*" will vary in almost every instance. Typically, the definition of net sales allows for specific deductions from *gross sales* (the gross amount that is invoiced and billed to customers, e.g., department stores), including, but not limited to, credits for returns; trade discounts (e.g., prompt payment); sales taxes collected by the licensee from the purchaser of the licensed products; and insurance, shipping, and handling costs. Similarly, the products to be manufactured under the licensed marks, the designated territory, and the approved distribution network need to be defined clearly, since the crux of the transaction is based on these terms.

In principal, however, perhaps the most important provisions of a license agreement are those that define *the nature and scope of the license being granted* by *the licensor to the licensee.* (For our purposes, we will refer to them as the "grant provisions.") Consider the following:

- Purpose of the license that is being granted, e.g., the right to manufacture, distribute, promote, and sell the licensed product(s);
- Intellectual property being licensed, e.g., specifying the trademarks and related logos;
- Categories of products or services, e.g., eyewear, a branded retail store;

68. *See* Jones Apparel Group, Inc. v. Polo Ralph Lauren Corp., 3 Misc. 3d 1107(A) (N.Y. Sup. Ct. 2004).

- Geographic territory of distribution and sale, e.g., United States, Canada, and Europe;
- Designated wholesale distribution channels, e.g., better department stores, limited sales to off-price outlets;[69]
- Exclusivity perimeters of the license granted, e.g., children's apparel (excluding footwear), within the defined geographical territory;
- Extent of the licensee's rights and rights reserved by the licensor;[70] and
- Defined standards and procedures binding upon both parties to ensure the quality and prestige of the licensed products.

Drafting Notes:

Precision and clarity—an elementary concept when drafting all terms of a license agreement, especially when drafting the grant provisions, yet not easily achieved. Given this challenge, it is not surprising that ambiguity in drafting has proven to be at the heart of disputes between licensors and licensees.[71] Strategically, it is a best practice to define and limit the scope of the license and draft these provisions as narrowly as possible to avoid unwarranted use of the rights granted. The respective rights of the parties, however, should be set forth in detailed provisions of the license agreement to similarly avoid ambiguity.

Carve Outs—when a licensor retains certain rights as they relate to the grant of a license, it is known as a "carve out." Most license agreements include a carve out for rights that are specifically retained by the licensor and not granted to the licensee, e.g., the right to license other third parties to use the licensed trademarks in connection with licensed products in another territory or in connection with products other than licensed products; the right for the licensor (or a third party) to operate e-commerce websites or other direct-to-consumer businesses bearing the licensed trademarks. Some license agreements address this issue with a broad "catch all" provision that states, "*all rights not granted to licensee hereunder are retained by licensor.*" Although seemingly helpful, such a broad provision can be considered ambiguous and lead to disputes as to which rights are retained. It is a best practice to

---

69. Many license agreements include an attached schedule naming the specific stores that are approved by the licensor, and conversely, those stores that are prohibited and not included in the distribution network.

70. *See* The Levy Group, Inc. v. L.C. Licensing Group and Liz Claiborne, Inc., 2010 N.Y. Misc. LEXIS 6816 (N.Y. Sup. Ct. 2010) ("[l]icensor retains and reserves the right to use and exploit, and to grant to any other Person to use and exploit, any Licensed Mark . . . and any designs, names or other items supplied by Licensor hereunder in connection with any and all products and services, other than Merchandise bearing the Licensed Marks. . . .").

71. *See* Calvin Klein Trademark Trust v. Wachner, 198 F.R.D. 53 (S.D.N.Y. 2000); *see also* Section J, Licensing Disputes: A Licensee's Perspective, *infra* (highlighting cases between licensees and licensors for breach of contract allegedly for noncompliance with the license grant provisions of the agreement).

use such a "catch all" provision together with an express reservation of specifically defined rights.

As stated above, *all* terms of a license agreement can be considered essential in order to successfully navigate licensing relationships. Yet, what would licensing practitioners consider to be the *material* terms of a license agreement? Consider the following:

1. License Grant and Rights Reserved by Licensor

The *license grant* is the fundamental provision of a license agreement. It sets forth the purpose and scope of the license arrangement and the perimeters of the licensor-licensee relationship. Given the significance of this provision, *the grant should include only those rights necessary for the licensee to perform its obligations under the agreement.* Let's explore this in detail.

It is not uncommon for the license grant to be concise stating, for example, *"In accordance with the terms and conditions of this Agreement, Licensor hereby grants to Licensee, and Licensee hereby accepts, the License."* Yet, in its simplicity, this is a powerful provision. The definition of "License" is typically robust and includes other defined terms that are used throughout the agreement. Together, these defined terms set forth the nature and extent of the license grant. Consider the following: *"License shall mean the exclusive right to manufacture, sell, distribute and promote Eyewear Products under the Trademarks in the Territory and the non-exclusive right to use the IP Rights in connection therewith."*[72] Hence, the definition of "License" in and of itself is the coalescence of the core elements of a license grant.

The license grant section should include a provision that explicitly states the rights that are retained by the licensor and are not granted to the licensee, maintaining the licensor's continuing rights in the licensed intellectual property. This unequivocally allows the licensor to grant others (including its other licensees, its own affiliates, and subsidiaries) the right to use any such intellectual property in any manner, except to the extent of the rights granted to the licensee under the subject license agreement. For example, there should be explicit language that reserves the right for the licensor to grant licenses to other entities for the use of the licensed intellectual property in connection with other product categories and in the same or different territories, gaining the benefit of the expertise of other specialized manufacturers. Underscoring this reserved right, a license agreement may go on to state that the licensee shall not have the right to operate free-standing retail stores, in-store concessions, internet e-commerce websites, or any other

72. Drafting note: The terms "Licensed Products," "Eyewear Products," "Trademarks," "IP Rights," and "Territory" would be defined in the Definitions section of a license agreement. Due to the importance of the license grant provisions, it is also a best practice for license agreements to include schedules that specifically list the elements of these grants, e.g., Trademarks, IP Rights, Territory, and distribution channels (including approved full price and off-price retail accounts).

direct-to-consumer distribution channels in connection with the licensed products, having the licensee acknowledge that such rights are reserved by the licensor. In the case of direct-to-consumer sales, the licensor, or one of its "retail licensees," will purchase the licensed products from the "product licensee." The parties will then negotiate the price at which the licensed products will be purchased, which is typically at a discount from the wholesale price at which the product licensee sells the licensed products to its retail accounts. Such terms may be included in license agreements with both the product licensee and the retail licensee.

In a similar vein, the definition of "License" will usually indicate whether or not the grant is exclusive or nonexclusive. In most cases, exclusive licensing rights are granted to licensees who manufacture a specific product category or a licensee that has been granted the right to distribute and sell in a defined geographic territory. Yet careful drafting will necessitate that a licensee's rights of exclusivity will be subject to the licensor's reservation of rights.[73]

The license grant section and its related provisions should also address whether or not a licensee has *sublicensing rights,* meaning whether a licensee is permitted to re-grant or sublicense any of the rights granted to it in the first instance under the license agreement to a third party in connection with the performance of a licensee's obligations. It is uncommon for sublicensing rights to be granted outright, as a licensor specifically chooses its licensee for its expertise. Typically, a license agreement will contain an express prohibition on sublicensing, with an exception only for sublicensees that are preapproved by a licensor, and even in such an instance, a licensor will want to review and approve the sublicense agreement, as the financial terms affect the ultimate royalty that a licensor receives as well as terms that affect quality control, trademark protection, and the ultimate integrity of the brand. Most importantly, if sublicensing rights are granted, a licensee should be held responsible and fully indemnify a licensor for any of the sublicensee's acts or omissions that result in a loss or liability to a licensor.

Yet it is not only a licensor's world. As noted earlier in this chapter, a license agreement should be mutually beneficial between the parties. A licensee that embraces its rights and obligations under a license agreement makes a substantial commitment of time, money, and resources to foster the growth and stature of the brand on behalf of a licensor. In exchange, the parties may agree that a licensee should have certain advantageous rights. For example, if minimum sales volumes are met and a licensee is not otherwise in default, a licensee may be granted the right

73. Most manufacturers of a specific product line have a "stable" of fashion brands, e.g., Estee Lauder for fragrance and beauty and EssilorLuxottica for eyewear. It is not uncommon to see license agreements that prohibit licensees from manufacturing and selling products that are the subject of their license agreement for a direct competitor of a licensor. This can be a heavily negotiated point of contention. In such a case the resolution will depend upon leverage—whose business has more clout in the industry to have its demands met, the licensor or licensee?

to renew a license agreement. We will revisit this concept again in this chapter when we discuss the Term and Termination provisions below.

Another significant advantage that may be extended to an effective licensee is the ability to add future product extensions or expansion into new territories. Such rights are commonly offered in the form of (i) a *right of first negotiation*, whereby a licensee is granted the right to approach a licensor seeking to add specified products or territories to the license; (ii) a *right of first offer*, that would obligate a licensor to offer new product categories or territories to a licensee before offering them to third parties; or (iii) a *right of first refusal*, which would obligate a licensor, when approached by a third party for a new product category or territory, to offer its licensee the same license terms proposed by such third party, and a licensee has the first right to accept or reject those terms.

Each licensor-licensee relationship will vary with respect to the "first right" that their license agreement will contemplate. Yet such provisions evidence good faith and fair dealing between the parties. Each model typically requires a period of negotiation between a licensor and licensee, including submission of business and marketing plans, sales projections, minimum sales and royalty payment obligations, and advertising commitments. If the parties cannot reach an agreement, ultimately a licensor will be free to enter into licensing relationships with one or more third parties covering the new products or territories.

Finally, there are clauses that are not necessarily widely found in fashion industry license agreements, but if included, would typically be found in the grant provision section. For example:

- *Buyout Provision*: Some licensors and licensees negotiate a "buyout" of the business of a license agreement by a licensor after a specific period (which is at least after the initial term and typically when a licensee has a right of renewal). This would allow a licensor to operate the business contemplated under the license agreement directly and all of the rights granted to a licensee under the license agreement would revert to a licensor. This would also contemplate a financial component and an agreed-upon formula to put a value on the business and its assets and inventory to compensate the licensee and arrive at a fair purchase price. This provision would typically be found in trademark product license agreements.
- *Purchase Option*: Similar to a buyout provision, a purchase option is commonly seen in retail store license agreements. This negotiated term gives the licensor the option to purchase one or all of the free-standing retail stores that are owned and operated by the licensee. This option cannot be exercised immediately, but would allow the licensee to have operated the store(s) for a number of years during the term. If such option is exercised, there would similarly be a negotiated financial formula. Typically, a licensor would be required to purchase all of the assets and inventory related to the store(s), as well as assume a licensee's obligations that it had in connection with operating the store(s), e.g., real property leases(s).

2. Term

Most, if not all, license agreements contain a "*term*" provision, which sets forth the duration of a licensing relationship. Specifically, it provides for the commencement date of the license, the meaning of a "*contract year*," and when the agreement expires (unless earlier terminated by the parties) including provisions for potential renewals, as further discussed below. In essence, the term provision is the gatekeeper of the time periods that dictate compliance with the parties' respective obligations.

From the perspective of building a sustainable licensing business, the materiality of this provision takes on particular significance. Essentially, it comes down to the vision for the business, leverage, and whether the parties have ever been involved in a prior venture. A term provision often includes *renewal terms*, based upon a licensee's performance and meeting sales and other similar performance benchmarks. The term of a license agreement can vary based upon the nature of the licensing relationship. For example, a licensor may want a relatively short initial term of three to five years if this is a first-time license to assess the licensee's performance ability. On the other hand, a licensee that is investing heavily in building the licensed business (e.g., infrastructure, marketing, design and personnel) would prefer a longer term so as to see a return on its investment. For example, Calvin Klein's jeanswear license with Warnaco contemplated a 40-year term, with an option to renew for 10 additional years.[74] In a recent case, Marcolin Group entered into a 29-year term eyewear license agreement with designer Tom Ford, considered to be one of the longest terms in this industry.[75]

After the expiration of the initial term, a license agreement may provide for one or a succession of renewal periods. It is common to see "automatic renewals," which provide the licensee with the right to renew the license agreement upon written notice to the licensor of its intent to renew within a designated period if the licensee achieves its performance obligations and is otherwise in compliance with the material terms of the license agreement. Alternatively, if the license agreement does not provide for an automatic renewal, the parties may agree to meet in good faith within a reasonable time prior to the term's expiration to discuss and negotiate the terms of a possible renewal of the license.

3. Design, Approval, Production Process, and Quality Control of Licensed Products

There are a bundle of obligations that run back and forth between a licensor and licensee related to the process of design through production of the licensed products. This process is a collaborative, if not critical, effort between a licensor and licensee, starting with the first sketch or design concept and resulting in a branded

74. *See* Fournier & Boer, *supra* note 51, at 18, 21.
75. *See supra* note 14.

product that is commercially available to consumers. The roles and responsibilities connected to each stage will vary brand-by-brand based upon the category of the licensed product(s) and the respective expertise of the parties, but there is one ultimate goal that is shared—meeting production and delivery deadlines. Notwithstanding the foregoing, the ultimate obligation for quality control rests with a licensor, and the license agreement should explicitly reflect that the licensor retains approval rights and the right to control the entire design process.[76] Yet, "[t]he licensor's right to approve designs and samples is meaningless if the quality demonstrated in the samples is not maintained throughout the process."[77]

Consider the following stages as they relate to design, approval, production, and quality control that are widely embraced and included as material terms in a license agreement:[78]

(i) A licensor will provide a licensee with design concepts and inspiration for seasonal collections of licensed products;[79] the parties set specified times each season to meet to finalize the designs, adhering to a "design calendar," which is often attached as a schedule to the license agreement;

(ii) A licensee creates prototype samples, also known as "preproduction samples" of the finished licensed products for a licensor's review and approval; in some cases this also involves in-person design meetings or line reviews between the licensee and licensor in order to secure a licensor's approval. An essential element of this process is a licensor's control not only over the design of the licensed products, but the materials used, overall quality, and the manufacturing process. As with most license agreements, the mechanisms for obtaining a licensor's approval vary between fashion companies.

(iii) The mechanism that a licensor puts in place for its review and approval process in a license agreement is one component of its vital obligation to exercise quality control over the products manufactured, distributed, marketed,

---

76. For a discussion on the obligations of a trademark owner to police the use of its trademarks and the danger of losing its rights if it fails to do so, *see generally* Section H, The Paradigm of Naked Licensing, *infra*.

77. Hand, *supra* note 5.

78. *See also Gucci Am., Inc. v. Guess?, Inc.*, 868 F. Supp. 2d 202 (S.D.N.Y. 2012) (discussing a specific design and approval process put in place by Guess? to monitor its licensees).

79. Drafting Note: Throughout this chapter, we have underscored that the essence of a license agreement is that of the granting of the right to use proprietary intellectual property owned by a licensor in connection with manufacturing, distributing, and marketing products or retail services. The licensed intellectual property would include all design concepts and other such related materials that the licensor provides to the licensee. A wisely drafted license agreement would address this issue and include apt protective language, e.g., "*Licensor shall provide to Licensee the overall concepts and inspiration for each seasonal collection. Any and all materials that Licensor may provide to Licensee or use in connection with such seasonal concepts and inspirations, or otherwise in connection with the design of Licensed Products, shall remain the sole property of Licensor and shall be used by Licensee solely in connection with the Licensed Products.*"

and sold by its licensees. Depending upon the leverage between the licensor and licensee, some license agreements provide that a licensor's failure to respond by a specified time will be deemed a rejection of the prototypes on the part of the licensor; on the other hand, some license agreements provide that failure of the licensor to respond by a specified time indicates the licensor's approval of the prototypes. Once samples are approved, it is taken as an indication that the licensee can commence production of the licensed products.

A licensor's approval of a prototype or sample of a licensed product also typically includes approval of the marketing materials, packaging, labels, tags, and any other materials upon which or in connection with which a licensee intends to display the licensed trademarks and intellectual property. It is also not unusual for a fashion or luxury brand to require its licensee, at the licensee's expense, to provide a dedicated design staff and dedicated management, marketing, and sales personnel to run the licensed business.

Finally, a licensor should reserve the right, upon notice to a licensee and during normal business hours, to inspect the relevant manufacturing plants. This is another important element of a licensor's obligation to control the quality of the licensed products and integrity of the brand. Differing from the design and manufacturing process, such inspections allow a licensor to see firsthand whether best industry standards are being met (e.g., child or slave labor) and compliance with applicable local laws (e.g., environmental laws, worker safety). It is a best practice to include a provision in the license agreement to require a licensee to use best efforts to monitor its own, as well as its third-party contractors', facilities, as well as the business practices of its suppliers. An infraction of the foregoing is dangerous prospect for any fashion brand and may very likely cause negative press and publicity. Any such incident will undeniably tarnish a brand's reputation and diminish the goodwill of its trademarks, which takes years to establish. If not controlled, a licensee's bad acts can lead to a brand's demise.

4. Advertising, Marketing, and Promotion

It's the sizzle and buzz—in the fashion industry, a company's notoriety and brand value hinge upon captivating advertising, cutting-edge marketing, and superstar promotion.

Reputation—it can make or break a fashion company's business. When it comes to licensing initiatives, a license agreement should address the manner in which the licensee is required to advertise, market, and promote the brand, and dictate the perimeters within which it is authorized to do so. A licensor's control over this essential aspect of the licensed business is imperative from the perspective of sustaining brand integrity, and analogous to its legal duty to control and monitor the quality of the products or services that bear its trademarks. Further, advertising, marketing, and promotion have a financial impact, both upon a licensee's obligation to "contribute" and/or "spend" toward such efforts, as well as the overall effect on the future revenues of the licensed business and the brand generally.

Each licensor takes a different approach. It is common that a license agreement will provide that a licensee is required to pay, on an annual basis, an agreed-upon amount or a percentage of its projected net sales, as a contribution to support a licensor's "institutional image advertising campaign," meaning seasonal advertising campaigns that are created by a licensor, at its direction and in its sole discretion, to promote its overall brand image and all of its branded products (including those manufactured and sold by its other licensees). Additionally, a licensor may require that a licensee spend a percentage of its projected net sales annually on promotional and trade marketing activities, which may include cooperative advertising in conjunction with approved retailers to whom the licensed products are sold. In this case, as opposed to institutional advertising, the licensee is responsible for the content, appearance, production, and distribution of such marketing materials. However, the license agreement will typically provide that the licensee shall not produce, distribute, or otherwise use any such materials without a licensor's prior approval.[80]

Certain licensing arrangements for a product line contemplate and provide for a joint investment in advertising and marketing by a licensor and licensee. For example, when a product line is launched, the parties may share equally in such efforts for an agreed-upon amount of funds and designated period. It is also typical for a licensor to obligate a product licensee to construct or designate showroom space to display the licensed products for retail buyers. A license agreement should stipulate the precise terms of agreement and understanding between the parties under such arrangements.

5. Sales and Distribution of Licensed Products

After reading and analyzing *Calvin Klein Trademark Trust v. Wachner*[81] in Section E, Choosing a Licensing Partner—Wisely, it is plain to see that channels of distribution of licensed products are tremendously important when it comes to the meeting of the minds between a licensor and licensee. Strategic considerations must be made regarding brand positioning, elevation of brand value, and maintenance of brand integrity. When drafting a license agreement between a brand owner and a manufacturer/distributor, these issues should be at the forefront of negotiations. The parties' mutual understanding as to the appropriate distribution channels for the licensed products should be fully agreed upon prior to entering into the final license agreement, and perhaps, memorialized in a term sheet or MOU. A trademark license agreement typically includes provisions that dictate channels

80. Other promotional activities may include events in association with a celebrity or public figure.

81. 198 F.R.D. 53 (S.D.N.Y. 2000).

of distribution, which also relate to a licensee's obligation to develop, exploit, and maintain a market in the territory for the licensed products and adherence to an approved business plan.

It is essential that a trademark license agreement clearly define permitted retail outlets for the sale of licensed products. (Such sales would be at a wholesale price point and are sometimes referred to as "*wholesale accounts.*") A license may broadly designate "department stores," "specialty stores," "off-price accounts" and a licensor's retail stores—both owned and operated by a licensor or its third-party licensees as permitted wholesale accounts; however, it is common that "schedules" attached to the license agreement are used and set forth the actual names of such stores as the approved channels of distribution.[82] It is also quite common for a licensor to require all wholesale accounts to meet "qualitative criteria," meaning professional qualifications and business methods that reflect and uphold the stature of a brand, which are also set forth on a schedule to the agreement.

Most, if not all, licensors accept the practice among product licensees in the fashion business to sell off excess inventory, which may include returns, at a discounted percentage off of the wholesale price. As with wholesale accounts, the discount channel of distribution, as well as the percentage markdown, must be approved in advance by a licensor. To avoid ambiguity, a license agreement will likely provide such dictates. Although seemingly of less importance in the overall scheme of the development of a successful wholesale business, sales to off-priced accounts must be closely monitored. An overabundant presence in this market may effectively tarnish a brand's image. In its best efforts to control a licensee's off-price sales activities, a licensor will typically put a "cap" on such sales, e.g., only 20 percent of the amount of a licensee's total sales during a calendar quarter may be sold to approved off-price accounts. Non-compliance with the off-price cap can trigger a default and the termination of the license agreement. Regardless of the channel of distributions, these provisions of a license agreement are meant to ensure that a brand and its related trademarks are represented in a consistent, cohesive, and appropriate manner across all permitted wholesale platforms.

6. Compensation, Reporting, and Audit

Leverage. This element of negotiation permeates the terms and conditions of a license agreement. Be it the power of a famous brand or the renowned expertise of a wholesale manufacturer, retail store operator, or pure-play licensing company, leverage is perhaps the most integral component when it comes to negotiating a licensor's compensation. Royalty payments (often termed *royalties*) are the most common form of compensation paid by a licensee for a license.

---

82. A licensor should retain the right to review this schedule from time to time and add or remove wholesale accounts in its sole discretion if it believes that such outlets do not represent the prestige of the brand and the licensed trademarks.

Royalties can be structured in a number of ways, the most common of which is based on a percentage of a revenue stream, specifically gross or net sales of the licensed products. As noted above, trademark license agreements are typically based on wholesale net sales, the calculation of which allows for certain deductions from its gross sales, including discounts and returns. Deductions can be looked at as a form of "expenses" that a licensee is required pay, which reduce its income from the sale of licensed products. Thus, the definition of net sales is fundamental to a licensor's compensation. Leverage will come into play in the negotiations since a licensee will want to negotiate the greatest amount of deductions to lower royalty payments and a licensor will push to limit the amount of deductions. Keen drafting is essential and should enumerate the allowed deductions as well as deductions that are not allowed.

Similarly, a company's leverage over its licensing partner will dictate the amount of a licensee's royalty obligations. Still, a mature licensor with leverage over its licensee wants its licensee to be successful and does not want to sabotage a viable and potentially profitable licensing relationship by overwhelming and potentially unattainable financial commitments. From the perspective of a licensee, however, a more established company that has leverage over its licensor will be determined to have the lowest royalty rate that it can possibly negotiate. The percentage royalty rate in the fashion industry can range anywhere from 5 to 15 percent, and such payments are typically made on a quarterly basis. The agreement can be structured in a manner where the royalty rate is fixed throughout the term or it can be "tiered," meaning the royalty rate increases or decreases, which sometimes depends upon sales volume. For example, a licensor with longevity and strong brand identity may require an eight percent royalty rate in years 1 and 2 of the term and in year 3, the royalty rate will increase to 10 percent. Alternatively, when a licensee meets its minimum annual sales obligations, which increase year over year, the royalty rate may decrease. This incentivizes a licensee to generate increased manufacturing, distribution, and sale of licensed products.[83]

A sophisticated licensor will require a licensee to pay *guaranteed minimum royalties* on an annual basis. As opposed to percentage or "earned" royalties, guaranteed minimum royalties are set payments to be made to a licensor annually, commonly on a prepaid quarterly basis, regardless of the amount of licensed products sold and revenues earned by a licensee. If a licensee's sales income and earned royalty payments meet or exceed the guaranteed minimum royalties, a licensee can offset the earned royalty payments due to a licensor against prepaid guaranteed minimum royalties. For example, if the guaranteed minimum royalty is $1,000,000 in a given contract year, a licensee will make four quarterly payments in the amount of $250,000 at the beginning of each quarter. At the end of the quarter, a licensee will account for its

83. Guaranteed minimum net sales and guaranteed minimum royalties typically reflect projected revenues for the licensed product categories during the term on an annual basis, agreed upon by the parties and set forth in a formal business plan.

earned royalties. If the earned royalties are greater than $250,000 for that quarter, a licensee can offset the earned royalty quarterly payment against the guaranteed minimum royalty payment, and only pay a licensor the difference. Conversely, if a licensee's earned royalties fall below $250,000 for the quarter, a licensor will have benefited from the set quarterly fee that it maintains in full.

David and Goliath? Not really. There is an equitable rationale to support a guaranteed minimum royalty obligation. It incentivizes a licensee to exploit the license and build a strong business, manufacture well-supplied products, and generate sales. If a licensee underperforms, a licensor should not be penalized. Indeed, by entering into a licensing relationship, a licensor takes itself out of the market for a number of years and cannot easily enter into another licensing relationship if its current licensee fails to adequately monetize a brand's value. Guaranteed minimum royalties make a licensee whole and allows it to realize some income from the recognition and worth if its trademarks—its most valuable asset.[84]

How does a licensor monitor this fairly complex financial arrangement with a licensee? The onus is on the licensee. License agreements should include reporting and accounting provisions, pursuant to which the licensee is required to report detailed sales and royalty activities on a quarterly basis. Such statements would include the following itemized information: gross sales, merchandise returns, credits, discounts and trade allowances, other deductions from sales, a calculation of net sales, and computation of the amounts due to a licensor. In the case of international license agreements with multiple territories, a licensor will typically require that such reporting be made on a country-by-country basis and the currency in which the royalty payments are to be made is that of a licensor, converted based upon an independent conversion source, e.g., the Central Bank of Europe or *The Wall Street Journal*. A licensee should be required to keep such records for a period of two to three years. To verify a licensee's reporting, a licensor is typically granted "audit rights," allowing for the periodic examination (usually one time per calendar year during the term) of a licensee's books and records, at a licensor's expense, as they relate to the licensed products. It is not unusual for the parties to negotiate and agree that if such examination discloses an underpayment of fees in excess of an agreed-upon percentage (e.g., three percent), a licensee will be responsible to pay the costs of the audit.

7. Termination—Cause and Effect

Termination—the death knell of a licensing relationship or a blessing in disguise? Despite the optimism of a successful business relationship, there are times when the parties' practices or the profitability of the venture do not align with the original

84. A licensor with a famous and desirable brand may have the leverage to negotiate an up-front lump sum payment upon executing a license agreement, especially if a licensor is being courted by a number of licensees. Such payments are usually applied, in whole or in part, to future royalty payments.

business plan.[85] Prudent businesspeople will rely on licensing counsel to draft termination provisions that will address these contingencies. Termination of a license does not necessarily have to be fraught with contention. If drafted tactically, the parties can part ways equitably and amicably.

Case in point—a famous fashion company and a leading manufacturer of watches entered into an exclusive worldwide product license agreement. The term of the license was for a period of 10 years. The parties negotiated an *early termination provision*, whereby the license agreement could be terminated unilaterally by either party by written notice if, by the end of the fifth contract year, the net sales of the licensed products did not reach a projected designated threshold. If the early termination provision is called into play, the license agreement will expire by its terms. The inclusion of the early termination provision gives the parties a reasonable mechanism to navigate the separation under these circumstances.

Generally, however, the termination clause should provide a roadmap indicating those acts that clearly constitute a breach and the related consequences. As noted earlier in this chapter, certain "material breaches" may a trigger a licensor's immediate termination rights. However, in order to maintain business continuity, it is not necessarily in the parties' best interests to have their relationship come to an abrupt end. Most license agreements provide for a "cure period" for certain material breaches, within which the licensee is afforded a period of time, upon written notice by the licensor, to rectify the infraction and keep the license in force.

Following are examples of what would be considered "noncurable" breaches and terminable upon notice, in the licensor's sole discretion:

- Failure to meet minimum sales requirements;
- Licensee challenges the title or any rights of a licensor in and to the licensed trademarks or its other intellectual property;
- If a controlling equity interest in a licensee is sold or acquired by a competitor of the licensor.

In addition, license agreements typically consider a licensee's bankruptcy or insolvency as grounds for automatic termination if a licensee is adjudicated bankrupt. However, such a provision is not easily enforceable.[86]

Following are examples of what would be considered "curable" material breaches:[87]

---

85. *See* Calvin Klein Trademark Trust v. Wachner, 198 F.R.D. 53 (S.D.N.Y. 2000).

86. *See infra* notes 105, 108 (discussing the recent decision of the Supreme Court of the United States in *Mission Product Holdings, Inc. v. Tempnology LLC*, ruling that when a trademark license agreement, as an executory contract, is rejected by a trustee in bankruptcy, the licensor-licensee relationship continues and hence the contract and contractual rights remain in force); *see also generally* Section I, Bankruptcy in the Fashion Industry: The Fate of a Licensing Arrangement, *infra*.

87. The cure period varies based upon the severity of the breach. It is typical to see a period of 5 days to 30 days, which will be negotiated by the parties.

- Failure to make timely royalty payments;
- Failure to meet reporting requirements;
- Failure to fulfill quality obligations;
- Unauthorized sales of licensed products;
- Licensee challenges the title or any rights of a licensor in and to the licensed trademarks or its other intellectual property;
- Licensee's material breach of any of its representations or warranties under the agreement.

You may ask—*is a licensee the underdog, without the same rights to terminate as a licensor?* The short answer is *maybe*. It is not unusual to find most license agreements devoid of a provision for termination by a licensee. However, an astute attorney should realize that it is only equitable if a licensee is afforded the right to terminate upon a licensor's breach of its material obligations. There are perhaps two grounds on which a licensee may be able to argue this point: (i) if the licensor sells, distributes, or authorizes others to sell the licensed products in violation of a licensee's exclusive rights under the agreement, and (ii) if a licensor materially breached any of its representations or warranties under the license agreement. If agreed to, licensee's right to terminate will most likely be subject to a lengthy cure period within which a licensor is permitted to right its wrong.

Upon termination or expiration of the agreement for any reason, a license agreement will characteristically broadly state that all rights that have been granted to the licensee will immediately terminate and revert to the licensor, and the licensee shall cease the use of the licensed trademarks and other intellectual property. Yet to dissolve the relationship and provide for a smooth transition of the licensed business, the license agreement needs to be clear as to the post-termination rights and obligations of the parties.

Following are critical provisions to be addressed upon termination or expiration:

Royalties: All accrued and unpaid royalty payments must be made by the licensee; if terminated due to breach prior to the expiration by its terms, the license should provide that the minimum royalty payments for the remainder of the term will be accelerated and payment is due immediately.

Inventory: The licensee must provide a detailed written accounting of the amount of inventory of licensed products (including related works in progress, materials on hand, and noncancelable orders) in its or any sublicensees' possession; a licensor may negotiate the purchase of all or part of said inventory, or otherwise finish production of the works in progress to become salable licensed products.

Sell-off Period: Typically, a license agreement will provide for a winding down or "sell-off period," typically three to six months, of the remaining inventory that has not been purchased by a licensor. During the sell-off period, all of the terms and conditions of the license agreement remain in effect (e.g., royalty payments, territorial restrictions, accounting, and reporting).

Terms that Survive Termination: Although a license agreement may terminate or expire, there are provisions that should remain in force and effect after the parties separate. A "survival clause" is necessary in a license agreement to protect the parties' respective interests, e.g., payment of outstanding royalties, agreement by a licensee not to challenge a licensor's trademark of other intellectual property rights, confidentiality, representations and warranties, and indemnification from any claims or losses resulting from a breach.

8. Retail Store License Agreement

In the Introduction to this chapter and in Section B, Why License, we touched upon retail store licensing arrangements as another strategic opportunity for a fashion company to monetize and leverage the strength of its trademarks and forge greater worldwide brand recognition. In this section we will study this business model further in light of the material terms of a retail store license agreement.

There are a few, yet distinct, differences between a retail store license agreement and a product license agreement. Essentially, both grant a licensee the right to exploit a company's trademarks in order to commercialize and expand the breadth of a brand owner's global footprint in a specified territory. However, the nature and scope of these license agreements differ. How so?

A retail store licensee provides a *service*—the operation of one or more branded retail stores within a designated territory, for a specified period, for the retail sale of a licensor's branded products to consumers. Each licensed store is typically required to sell only products that bear a licensor's trademark and represent the brand. The spin on this business proposition is "retail," which affects the nature of the grant of rights, and a licensee's attendant compliance with design and operation dictates any financial obligations.

Grant of Rights. As with a trademark product license, the grant of rights in a retail license agreement should be narrowly drafted. When a fashion company enters into a retail store operations relationship, it is allowing a third party to orchestrate its retail presence in a territory, typically on an exclusive basis.[88] This can be a precarious situation if not scrupulously approached by both parties. A licensor must maintain control over the use of its trademarks by a licensee. Conversely, it is essential for a licensee to carefully review the grant terms to be certain that the grant is sufficiently broad to support a licensor's objectives. Still, as we have seen, a licensor may expressly carve out certain rights that it reserves. For example, the grant of a retail license may expressly exclude direct mail, the internet, and all other

88. Depending on a company's business model and strategic planning, intercompany license agreements are sometimes used for retail store licenses as well.

direct-to-consumer channels; duty-free stores; and U.S. military post exchanges. Sometimes, a retail store license agreement extends to "shops," which, in the fashion business, means a retail shop located within a visually defined area in a department store (sometimes referred to as a "shop-in-shop" or "concession") that is dedicated to the sale of a company's products exclusively, displays its trademarks, and is designed using fixtures, signage, etc. that replicate and exemplify the brand's image.

Compliance. Key elements of a licensee's compliance obligations under a retail store license relate to a store's name, site, and design. A retail store licensee is typically obligated to use a licensor's proprietary "tradename," under which a store will be operated embodied in a particular "tradestyle," i.e., the type style, type size, color scheme, and format, specified by a licensor. To ensure consistency with a licensor's other retail stores operated worldwide, a retail store license agreement should also clearly define a licensor's right to choose the site/location of the retail space and to monitor and approve all aspects of a licensee's execution of the development, construction, design, and decoration of a licensed store. Most retail store license agreements put significant emphasis on a licensee's obligation to conform to the physical "look and feel" of a retail store that has become an identifiable signature of a brand, reflected in the consistent use of particular fixtures, fittings, color schemes, displays, and signage, even to the extent of designating or having approval rights over the architect and general contractor.

Adherence to the conduct of operations is similarly underscored, as a licensor, in most cases, will require all inventory be purchased directly from a licensor or its corporate affiliates or approved distributors (which may also be a licensor's product licensees). A licensor will also typically negotiate for its approval rights over the product assortment, inventory levels, and merchandise mix. Management and store personnel should not be overlooked; the manner in which a customer is treated and customer service is a reflection of a brand and its credibility. A licensor will most certainly require that a licensee operate each store in a "first-class" manner so as not to injure or diminish the value of a licensor's brand, trademarks, or reputation. The ultimate goal of these efforts is a fully integrated worldwide retail store network that upholds the integrity of the brand and, to a consumer, appears to be owned and operated by a licensor. *Query: would you consider this to be analogous to a licensor's intrinsic obligation under a product license to expressly retain approval rights and control over the design process, the quality of the licensed products and distribution channels? If so, why?*

Financial Obligations/Purchase Option. In retail store license agreements, consideration for the license can be structured: (i) by the payment of royalties based upon a percentage of revenue from the sale of products calculated on *retail sales* (as opposed to wholesale sales), or (ii) direct payment to a licensor for products that are manufactured by a licensor or its subsidiaries at a percentage discount of the regular wholesale price. Depending on the line or specific product categories, the discount typically ranges from 50 to 25 percent. The theory with respect to the latter is that if a licensee is purchasing the products directly from its licensor, the licensor should not be entitled to both payment for the goods and a percentage royalty from sales.

9. Intellectual Property

> *As between Licensor and Licensee, the Trademarks and IP Rights (including IP Rights in all materials of any kind created by on behalf of Licensee hereunder) and the goodwill appurtenant thereto are the sole and exclusive property of Licensor. Licensee acknowledges that all uses of the Trademarks and IP Rights hereunder and all the goodwill attached or which shall become attached to the Trademarks and IP Rights in connection with the manufacture, sale, distribution, promotion and advertisement of the Licensed Products shall inure solely to Licensor's benefit.*[89]

As evidenced by the foregoing provision, a fashion license agreement should include definitive provisions that protect a licensor's rights in and to the licensed intellectual property. Following are some additional examples commonly found in such agreements:

- The trademarks and other intellectual property shall be used solely in connection with the licensed products and shall use and display the trademarks only in such form and manner as specifically provided or approved by a licensor.
- A licensee will not challenge a licensor's ownership of or the validity of any of the licensed trademarks or other intellectual property.
- A licensee shall not do anything or authorize anyone to do anything that will adversely affect a licensor's ownership rights of the licensed trademarks and other intellectual property or reduce or dilute their value or distinctiveness or disparage or detract from their reputation and prestige.
- A licensor, in its sole discretion, will determine whether any of the licensed trademarks or other intellectual property should be registered (bearing all costs in connection therewith, including maintenance and renewal fees).
- A licensee will not seek to register any of the licensed trademarks or other intellectual property, or any trademark that is confusingly similar thereto.

A schedule listing all of the licensed marks is typically annexed to a trademark license agreement, including pending trademark applications and registrations. New applications that are filed by, or registrations that are issued to, a licensor during the term of the license agreement will typically be incorporated into the schedule.

In furtherance of its intellectual property rights, a licensor should reserve the right to take any and all enforcement actions that it deems advisable when challenged

89. This provision, or a version thereof, typically appears in most license agreements. The captioned terms are typically defined in the license agreement.

with infringement.[90] A license agreement should provide that a licensee is obligated to notify a licensor promptly upon learning of any suspected infringement; however, a licensor should not be obligated to take any action. For example, there may be situations where a licensor decides that, economically, litigation is not a prudent means to enforce its rights. Notwithstanding the foregoing, a licensor should be held responsible to take reasonable steps necessary to protect the licensed trademarks and attendant goodwill. Such an obligation falls within a licensor's charge to police its trademarks that are subject to a license agreement. We will explore this principle further in the Section H, The Paradigm of Naked Licensing. Ultimately, however, an enforcement program should be devised. Leverage, once again, can play a part to determine which party is responsible for the costs associated with enforcement efforts. It is not unusual for a licensee to bear all or a portion of such fees when a licensor is the owner of a well-established, high-profile, and coveted brand.

10. Representations and Warranties

This provision serves as an affirmation of the certainties upon which the parties rely as they venture into a licensing arrangement. Both a licensor and licensee, respectively, make representations and warranties to the other party. The materiality of this provision is evident, as a breach of a representation or warranty can trigger termination as well as indemnification obligations, which will be discussed below. Following are examples of a licensor's representations and warranties: (i) it has the right and authority to grant the rights, including the right to use the licensed trademarks, to its licensee under the terms of the agreement; (ii) it has not granted, and will not grant, a third party a license to use the licensed trademarks in connection with the licensed products in the territory during the term of the license agreement; and (iii) to the best of its knowledge, it is the exclusive owner of the licensed trademarks (and other intellectual property) and it will continue to prosecute, maintain, and enforce the underlying registrations and applications, unless, in its reasonable business judgment, there is no reason to do so.

Similarly, a licensee may represent and warrant the following: (i) that it is a valid company organized in good standing in the jurisdiction of incorporation; (ii) that it is financially sound and has adequate resources to manufacture, distribute, market, and sell the licensed products in the territory; (iii) it has the full right and power to enter into the license agreement and perform its designated obligations; (iv) the license agreement does not conflict with the rights of any third party with whom a licensee is currently bound by contract; (v) it is not currently and has not filed for bankruptcy protection; and (vi) it will use its best efforts to market and sell the licensed products and will perform its obligations under the license agreement in compliance with applicable law.

90. In some instances, a licensor will extend the exclusive rights to a licensee to enforce the licensed trademarks, e.g., in an intercompany license agreement, where the licensee is a corporate affiliate and is tasked to assume such efforts.

11. Indemnification/Insurance

Indemnification is another key provision that should be included in a fashion license agreement. Coupled with the representations and warranties clause, it addresses the risks and potential liabilities inherent in a licensing arrangement and the respective parties' obligations in the face of such exigencies. This can be considered a "risk shifting provision"—each party respectively assumes responsibility for liabilities that arise under certain conditions and compensates the party who suffers a loss or liability due to the acts or omissions of the indemnifying party.

A licensor will seek to negotiate a very limited indemnification provision, while a licensee may want reciprocal indemnifications. What does this illustrate? *Leverage.* When a licensor has the upper hand, it is common that it will agree to a single indemnity—to indemnify a licensee for losses or liabilities that it may suffer as a result of a claim by a third party that a licensee's use of the licensed trademarks or other intellectual property, solely in accordance with the terms of the agreement, infringes upon such third party's rights.

On the other hand, a licensee's indemnification obligation is typically broad and may encompass the following: *any losses or liabilities that a licensor may suffer as a result of a licensee's acts or omissions under the license agreement.* In essence, a licensee will indemnify and compensate a licensor (and its affiliates, parents, subsidiaries, officers, directors, and employees) for any third-party claims that will result in a financial liability due to a licensee's breach of the license agreement. Still, a license agreement should also specify certain contingencies that will trigger a licensee's indemnification obligation. For example, (i) the manufacture, labeling, sale, distribution, or advertisement of the licensed products, including product liability; and (ii) workplace misconduct or personal injury arising out of workplace safety issues, in a licensee's, or its affiliates' or agents', office(s) alleged by any of licensees' design staff or other employees that are dedicated to the development, design, distribution, promotion, and sale of the licensed products.

To assure that the indemnification provision has "teeth" and is effective, a license agreement ordinarily requires that a licensee[91] obtain and maintain insurance coverage throughout the term of the agreement in certain designated amounts for each incident and names a licensor as an additional insured under the policy.

12. Other Provisions

There are other material provisions that should be included in a fashion license agreement that address issues of particular importance to the parties.

---

91. It is rare that such a provision is reciprocal. A licensee is the party, as the manufacturer of the licensed products, in the appropriate position to address and cover the risks of product liability, including safety and other related manufacturing issues and implications.

For example:

- *Confidentiality*: Each of the parties should hold in confidence, and not use or disclose, the confidential information of the other party, as well as the terms and conditions of the license agreement between them. Moreover, a licensee should take all reasonable precautions to protect the secrecy of the designs and the related materials used to manufacture the licensed products prior to their commercial distribution.
- *Nonsolicitation*: Upon termination or expiration of the agreement, neither party can solicit or hire the employees of the other for a designated period, without the prior approval of the other party.
- *Assignability:* Most fashion license agreements will provide that the agreement is of a personal nature with respect to the license that is granted. Therefore, a licensor will restrict a licensee from sublicensing, assigning, or transferring its rights without the prior written approval of a licensor. This restriction also may extend to a change of control or ownership of the licensee.
- *Governing Law, Jurisdiction, and Dispute Resolution*: The law of the state or country that will govern the interpretation of the terms of the license agreement should be specified, e.g., New York, Delaware, Italy. Similarly, the parties should agree upon the venue in which any action may be brought and the manner in which the parties will handle an unresolvable dispute, e.g., private arbitration or litigation in a specific jurisdiction.

If a licensor and licensee stay true to the foregoing nuts and bolts of their license agreement, they will likely not fall prey to the pitfalls of "naked licensing," as we will explore in the next section.

H. The Paradigm of Naked Licensing

Sometimes they never learn: A trademark owner, excited about a licensing opportunity with lucrative prospects, may be tempted to shift the entire burden of operating the business to a licensee and fail to perform its legal duty to dictate and control the use of its trademark. This may elicit a severe consequence—abandonment of the trademark.

Regardless of all of the terms and conditions that are negotiated between a brand owner and its selected licensee to secure an even-handed and equitable license agreement, the paramount obligation falls upon the shoulders of the licensor as the owner of the trademark. Legally, a licensor has the duty to control the use of its trademarks so as to assure consumers that its branded products are manufactured under quality standards that have been instituted and supervised by the licensor.[92]

---

92. *See generally* 3 J. Thomas McCarthy, McCarthy on Trademarks and Unfair Competition § 18:48 (5th ed. 2019) ("When that duty is not adequately discharged, the licensed

This also leads to the expectation that that each of a licensor's licensees are bound by the same dictates of quality and maintenance of the integrity of the brand.[93]

As we will see in the case of *Eva's Bridal Ltd. v. Halanick Enterprises.*[94] set forth below, a licensor cannot turn a blind eye once it licenses its trademarks. Contractual and actual control must be exercised over a licensee. Lacking such basic actions on the part of a trademark owner constitutes uncontrolled licensing, also called "naked licensing" under United States trademark law. Naked licensing occurs when a trademark owner has licensed to a third party the right to manufacture products or provide services under its trademarks or brands and then fails to monitor and control the quality of the products manufactured, distributed, and sold by the licensee or the services that the licensee provides.

For decades, courts have required trademark owners to police their marks that are licensed to third parties, the mechanism for which is typically set forth in the terms and conditions of a well-drafted license agreement. For example, most trademark licenses are drafted to avoid such a result by requiring samples of all licensed products to be periodically submitted to the licensor for approval and quality control.[95] These court decisions consistently relate back to trademark law fundamentals—a trademark or service mark is an indicator that identifies and distinguishes a single source of good or services. Consumers, when deciding to purchase a product or service, should be afforded the ability to rely on the significance of the origins of the product or service that bears the brand name and the attendant standard of quality.[96]

The consequences of uncontrolled or naked licensing can be devastating to a trademark owner, resulting in what is considered "abandonment" of the mark; it can even lead to the cancellation of an uncontested trademark, the status of which has been attained by many famous fashion brands. The Lanham Act is clear as it discusses "abandonment," stating that a mark is "abandoned" by any act or omission by the trademark owner that causes the designation "to lose its significance as a mark."[97]

---

mark carries the potential for customer deception: the antithesis of a valid trademark"); *see also* Dawn Donut Co. v. Hart's Food Stores, Inc., 267 F.2d 358, 367 (2d Cir. 1959).

93. *See generally* McCarthy, *supra* note 92, § 18:48 ("Without adequate control by the trademark owner, the nature and quality of goods and services sold by licensees under the mark will inevitably vary from the level of quality that the mark conveys to buyers . . . Multiple sources selling goods or services of varying types and quality under a single mark without adequate central control by the trademark owner is contrary to the basic definition of the purpose and meaning of a 'trademark' or 'service mark.'").

94. 639 F.3d 788 (7th Cir. 2011).

95. *See supra* text accompanying notes 76–77.

96. *See generally* McCarthy, *supra* note 92, § 18:48 ("A trademark carries with it a message that the trademark owner is controlling the nature and quality of the goods or services sold under the mark. Without quality control, this message is false because without control of quality, the goods or services are not truly 'genuine.' This dissonance and deception erodes the significance of the designation as an accurate indication of origin: a trademark.").

97. Lanham Act § 45, 15 U.S.C. § 1127 ("Abandonment of a Mark" defined). The registration of a mark can be canceled if the mark has become "abandoned." Lanham Act § 14(c), 15 U.S.C.

> Uncontrolled or "naked" licensing may result in the trademark ceasing to function as a symbol of quality and controlled source. This effect has often been characterized as "abandonment" of the trademark. Of all the courts, the Ninth Circuit has stated this the most forcefully: "We have previously declared that naked licensing is 'inherently deceptive and constitutes abandonment of any rights to the trademark by the licensor.'"[98]

Uncontrolled licensing can only be seen as an abdication of a trademark owner's responsibility to its customers, unfortunately with dire consequences. As noted above, courts have held that the effect of naked licensing may cause a trademark to lose its meaning, be deceptive to the public, and that the trademark owner has abandoned the trademark, *in which case the owner would be estopped from asserting rights to the trademark.*[99] This is precisely the problem that Eva Sweis encountered in the case below.

Eva's Bridal Ltd. v. Halanick Enterprises, Inc.

639 F.3d 788 (7th Cir. 2011)

EASTERBROOK, Chief Judge.

In 1966 Eva Sweis established in Chicago a shop that she called "Eva's Bridal." It sold dresses for brides and bridal parties. The venture was a success; Sweis allowed her children to open their own shops under the same name. The business passed to Said and Nancy Ghusein (née Sweis), who operate an "Eva's Bridal" shop in Oak Lawn, one of Chicago's suburbs. They have continued the pattern of licensing the name to relatives. Three years after opening a shop in Orland Park, another of Chicago's suburbs, Said and Nancy Ghusein sold that operation to Nayef Ghusein for $10. The agreement required Nayef to pay $75,000 a year for the right to use the "Eva's Bridal" name and marks.

The license agreement expired in 2002. Nayef and his corporation Halanick Enterprises have continued to operate the store under the Eva's Bridal name (see http://www.evasbridalsoforlandpark.com/) but no longer remit a royalty. In 2007 Said and his firm Eva's Bridal Ltd. filed this suit under the Lanham Act, contending that Nayef and Halanick have violated the Act by using the "Eva's Bridal" mark without payment (or, for that matter, a current license agreement). See 15 U.S.C. §§ 1117, 1125(a).

The district judge did not decide whether plaintiffs waited too long before suing. Instead the court dismissed the suit, 2010 U.S. Dist. LEXIS 79186 (N.D.Ill. Aug. 4,

---

§ 1064(c). "Abandonment" is a statutory defense to a mark whose registration is "incontestable." Lanham Act § 33(b)(2), 15 U.S.C. § 1115(b)(2).

98. McCarthy, *supra* note 92, § 18:48 (quoting FreecycleSunnyvale v. Freecycle Network, 626 F.3d 509, 515–16 (9th Cir. 2010)).

99. *See generally id.* (citing Heaton Distribution Co. v. Union Tank Car Co., 387 F.2d 477 (8th Cir. 1967)) (emphasis added).

2010), on the ground that plaintiffs abandoned the "Eva's Bridal" mark by engaging in naked licensing—that is, by allowing others to use the mark without exercising "reasonable control over the nature and quality of the goods, services, or business on which the [mark] is used by the licensee". *Restatement (Third) of Unfair Competition* § 33 (1995); see also *id.* § 30 (discussing abandonment); *TMT North America, Inc. v. Magic Touch GmbH,* 124 F.3d 876, 885–87 (7th Cir.1997). The written agreement did not require Nayef and Halanick to operate the Orland Park store in any particular way and did not give the licensor any power of supervision over how the business was conducted. Nancy conceded during her deposition that she and her husband Said never tried to control any aspect of how defendants' shop operated or how the mark was used. The district judge concluded that the mark has been abandoned and that defendants therefore may use it without payment.

Plaintiffs do not dispute the proposition that a naked license abandons a mark. Instead they observe that many decisions say that a licensor must supervise to ensure quality control, and they insist that they have never doubted the high standards of Nayef and his firm, so they had no reason to superintend any aspects of defendants' business. Plaintiffs maintain that Nayef and Halanick sell dresses from the same designers that the shop carried when it opened in 1988 and when ownership changed in 1991. Because consumers care about who designs and makes the clothing, which determines how the dresses look when worn, plaintiffs maintain that there was no need for any form of regulation. Doubtless consumers also care about the quality of service, whether the dressing rooms are clean and the staff helpful, whether alterations are performed accurately and on time, and so forth—matters about which plaintiffs left defendants to their own devices—but it is not necessary to decide which aspects of a retail bridal business contribute most to customers' satisfaction.

This argument that licensors may relinquish all control of licensees that operate "high quality" businesses misunderstands what judicial decisions and the *Restatement* mean when they speak about "quality." There is no rule that trademark proprietors must ensure "high quality" goods—or that "high quality" permits unsupervised licensing. "Kentucky Fried Chicken" is a valid mark, see *Kentucky Fried Chicken Corp. v. Diversified Packaging Corp.,* 549 F.2d 368 (5th Cir.1977), though neither that chain nor any other fast-food franchise receives a star (or even a mention) in the *Guide Michelin.* The sort of supervision required for a trademark license is the sort that produces *consistent* quality. "Trademarks [are] indications of consistent and predictable quality assured through the trademark owner's control over the use of the designation". *Restatement* § 33 comment b. See also William M. Landes & Richard A. Posner, *The Economic Structure of Intellectual Property Law* 166–68, 184–86 (2003).

A person who visits one Kentucky Fried Chicken outlet finds that it has much the same ambiance and menu as any other. A visitor to any Burger King likewise enjoys a comforting familiarity and knows that the place will not be remotely like a Kentucky Fried Chicken outlet (and is sure to differ from Hardee's, Wendy's, and

Applebee's too). The trademark's function is to tell shoppers what to expect—and who to blame if a given outlet falls short. The licensor's reputation is at stake in every outlet, so it invests to the extent required to keep the consumer satisfied by ensuring a repeatable experience. See generally *Two Pesos, Inc. v. Taco Cabana, Inc.*, 505 U.S. 763, 112 S.Ct. 2753, 120 L.Ed.2d 615 (1992).

How much control is enough? The licensor's self-interest largely determines the answer. Courts are apt to ask whether "the control retained by the licensor [is] sufficient under the circumstances to insure that the licensee's goods or services would meet the expectations created by the presence of the trademark." *Restatement* § 33 comment a (summarizing doctrine); see also *id.* at Reporter's Note comment c (collecting authority, which we need not set out). It isn't necessary to be more specific here, because plaintiffs did not retain *any* control—not via the license agreement, not via course of performance. A person who visited Eva's Bridal of Oak Lawn and then Eva's Bridal of Orland Park might not have found a common ambiance or means of doing business. And though the shops may have had many designers in common, this would not distinguish an "Eva's Bridal" shop from any other bridal shop; the trademark would not be doing any work if identical dresses could be purchased at Macy's or Nordstrom, and the "Eva's Bridal" shops were dissimilar except for some products that many retailers carried. Safeway could not license its marks to a corner grocery store, while retaining no control over inventory, appearance, or business methods, just because every grocery store is sure to have Coca-Cola and Wheaties on the shelf.

Trademark law requires that "decision making authority over quality remains with the owner of the mark." *Restatement* § 33 comment c. How much authority is enough can't be answered generally; the nature of the business, and customers' expectations, both matter. Ours is the extreme case: plaintiffs had, and exercised, *no* authority over the appearance and operations of defendants' business, or even over what inventory to carry or avoid. That is the paradigm of a naked license.

AFFIRMED.

Notes

1. *Eva's Bridal* is the seminal case in the fashion industry that demonstrates the abandonment, and arguably the assignment, of a trademark as a result of entering into a license agreement that lacked the necessary controls over its licensee's use of the licensed mark and continuing to allow the licensee to use the mark without supervision once the license had expired. It is interesting to note that the district judge did not decide this case on whether the plaintiffs waited too long to sue the defendants for royalty payments once the license expired. Rather, the case was dismissed on the grounds of the abandonment of the "Eva's Bridal" mark by engaging in naked licensing. The written license agreement between the parties did not include or impose any obligations upon the defendants to operate the Eva's Bridal store under the licensed mark in any particular manner, nor did it afford the licensor any rights to supervise over how the business was conducted. How does such

an agreement in Eva's Bridal compare with the discussion on Retail Store License Agreements in the fashion industry? *See* Section G, The Art of Drafting a License Agreement, *supra*.

2. What is "reasonable control?" In its decision, the Court relied on Restatement (Third) of Unfair Competition § 33 (1995), which states in pertinent part:

> The owner of a trademark, trade name, collective mark or certification mark may license another to use the designation. If the licensor exercises ***reasonable control*** over the nature and quality of the goods, services, or business on which the designation is used by the licensee, any rights in the designation arising from the licensee's use accrue to the benefit of the licensor. Failure of the licensor to exercise reasonable control over the use of the designation by the licensee can result in the abandonment of the designation.[100]

Comment [b] to the Restatement also states in pertinent part:

> An uncontrolled or 'naked' license allows use of the trademark on good or services for which the trademark owner *cannot offer a meaningful assurance of quality*. . . . The significance of a trademark as an accurate indication of source or sponsorship is not threatened unless there is a substantial uncontrolled use by licensees. Thus, if the uncontrolled use continues for only a short time, or represents only an insignificant proportion of the total use of the mark, a court will not ordinarily find abandonment.[101]

The court went on to point out that "[the] sort of supervision required for a trademark license is the sort that produces *consistent* quality" and again, relying on Restatement (Third) § 33, "[t]rademarks are indications of consistent and predictable quality assured by the trademark owner's control over the user of the designation." The court, however, did not go as far as to define "reasonable control"; rather, it provided some ambiguity in the rhetorical question of how much control is enough, stating that "[t]he licensor's self-interest largely determines the answer."

Do you think the court provided sufficient precedent in this case? Do you think the court ruled fairly?

3. Compare this case to *Robert Trent Jones II, Inc., and Robert Trent Jones Licensing Group, LLC v. GFSI, Inc., d/b/a/ Gear for Sports, Inc.*, 37 F. Supp. 2d 1061 (N.D. Cal. 2008), in which the licensor sued the licensee for selling products in unauthorized distribution streams. The license agreement included three provisions that were designed to preserve the integrity of the licensor's brand by limiting the channels of distribution, excluding mass retailers, clubs, or discount stores, and restricting the sale of defective product. In light of the foregoing, would you consider this "reasonable control?" How do you think this case was decided?

---

100. American Law Institute, Restatement (3d) of Unfair Competition § 33 (1995) (emphasis added).

101. *Id.* at § 33 comment [b] (emphasis added).

I. Bankruptcy in the Fashion Industry: The Fate of a Licensing Arrangement

In the fashion/luxury brand industry, like any other industry, with success comes financial hardship due to fierce competition, the change in the landscape of the fashion retail business, and the reality of today's digital world. As a result, several brands in the fashion business have sought relief through filing for bankruptcy, often through Chapter 11 of the U.S. Bankruptcy Code. Although such a filing allows a financially troubled company to seek protection from its creditors, reorganize its debts, and hopefully continue its business operations through a reorganization (and avoid liquidation), serious consideration must be given to the effect of bankruptcy on parties to a trademark license agreement. This was a conundrum for years, until the Supreme Court of the United States issued its decision in *Mission Product Holdings, Inc. v. Tempnology LLC* on May 20, 2019,[102] which addressed the bankruptcy filing by a debtor licensor, Mission Product Holdings, Inc., who rejected the trademark license agreement with its non-debtor licensee, Tempnology, LLC, under § 365(a) of the Bankruptcy Code, with the intention to terminate Tempnology's right to continue using the licensed mark and operating under the license agreement.[103]

Formerly, there was ambiguity as to the respective rights and obligations of a licensor and licensee that were parties to a trademark license agreement in bankruptcy. This is due to the fact that the Bankruptcy Code does not include trademarks or similar rights in its definition of "intellectual property" and, as a result, trademarks have not been afforded the same protection in bankruptcy as patents and copyrights, which, *inter alia*, are included in the definition.[104] Presumably, as addressed by the Supreme Court in its opinion, this was because of the unique nature of trademark licenses, which require ongoing quality control efforts and oversight by the licensor, otherwise the trademark itself may be deemed abandoned.[105] Federal

---

102. 139 S. Ct. 1652 (2019).

103. A trademark license is considered an "executory contract," i.e., a contract for which performance remains due to some extent on both sides. A company that files for bankruptcy, known as the debtor, (or the debtor's trustee in bankruptcy) has the right to reject an executory contract, which effectively terminates the agreement, leaving the nondebtor party in a precarious position. In *Mission Product*, the nondebtor licensee would not have had the option to retain its rights under a license rejected by the debtor licensor. But, as further discussed herein, the Supreme Court ruled otherwise.

104. 11 U.S.C. § 101(35A) ("The term 'intellectual property' means (A) trade secret; (B) invention, process, design, or plant protected under title 35; (C) patent application; (D) plant variety; (E) work of authorship protected under title 17; or (F) mask work protected under chapter 9 of title 17; to the extent protected by applicable nonbankruptcy law.").

105. For a general discussion of a trademark owner's obligations to maintain quality control over of the use of its trademarks by a licensee and what would trigger abandonment of a mark, *see* Section H, The Paradigm of Naked Licensing, *supra*.

courts have been split on the issue at hand. This Supreme Court ruling has now given resolution and guidance to the judiciary.

The case of *Mission Product Holdings, Inc. v. Tempnology, LLC* is set forth below. Pay close attention to the Court's reasoning and how it reached its ultimate ruling that the nondebtor licensee is entitled to continue to use licensed marks that are subject to a trademark license with a debtor licensee.[106]

Mission Product Holdings, Inc. v. Tempnology, LLC

139 S. Ct. 1652 (2019)

Justice KAGAN delivered the opinion of the Court.

Section 365 of the Bankruptcy Code enables a debtor to "reject any executory contract"—meaning a contract that neither party has finished performing. 11 U.S.C. § 365(a). The section further provides that a debtor's rejection of a contract under that authority "constitutes a breach of such contract." § 365(g).

Today we consider the meaning of those provisions in the context of a trademark licensing agreement. The question is whether the debtor-licensor's rejection of that contract deprives the licensee of its rights to use the trademark. We hold it does not. A rejection breaches a contract but does not rescind it. And that means all the rights that would ordinarily survive a contract breach, including those conveyed here, remain in place.

I

This case arises from a licensing agreement gone wrong. Respondent Tempnology, LLC, manufactured clothing and accessories designed to stay cool when used in exercise. It marketed those products under the brand name "Coolcore," using trademarks (*e.g.*, logos and labels) to distinguish the gear from other athletic apparel. In 2012, Tempnology entered into a contract with petitioner Mission Product Holdings, Inc. *See* App. 203–255. The agreement gave Mission an exclusive license to distribute certain Coolcore products in the United States. And more important here, it granted Mission a non-exclusive license to use the Coolcore trademarks, both in the United States and around the world. The agreement was set to expire in July 2016. But in September 2015, Tempnology filed a petition for Chapter 11 bankruptcy. And it soon afterward asked the Bankruptcy Court to allow it to "reject" the licensing agreement. § 365(a).

Chapter 11 of the Bankruptcy Code sets out a framework for reorganizing a bankrupt business. See §§ 1101–1174. The filing of a petition creates a bankruptcy estate consisting of all the debtor's assets and rights. See § 541. The estate is the pot out of which creditors' claims are paid. It is administered by either a trustee or, as in this case, the debtor itself. See §§ 1101, 1107.

---

106. For an overall discussion of the ramifications of this decision on trademark licensing practices, *see generally* Milton Springut, *Supreme Court Bankruptcy Decision Has Major Impact on Trademarks and Licenses*, N.Y.L.J. (June 12, 2019), https://www.law.com/newyorklawjournal/2019/06/12/supreme-court-bankruptcy-decision-has-major-impact-on-trademarks-and-licenses/.

Section 365(a) of the Code provides that a "trustee [or debtor], subject to the court's approval, may assume or reject any executory contract." § 365(a). A contract is executory if "performance remains due to some extent on both sides." *NLRB v. Bildisco & Bildisco*, 465 U. S. 513, 522, n. 6, 104 S.Ct. 1188, 79 L.Ed.2d 482 (1984) (internal quotation marks omitted). Such an agreement represents both an asset (the debtor's right to the counterparty's future performance) and a liability (the debtor's own obligations to perform). Section 365(a) enables the debtor (or its trustee), upon entering bankruptcy, to decide whether the contract is a good deal for the estate going forward. If so, the debtor will want to assume the contract, fulfilling its obligations while benefiting from the counterparty's performance. But if not, the debtor will want to reject the contract, repudiating any further performance of its duties. The bankruptcy court will generally approve that choice, under the deferential "business judgment" rule. *Id.*, at 523, 104 S.Ct. 1188.

According to Section 365(g), "the rejection of an executory contract[ ] constitutes a breach of such contract." As both parties here agree, the counterparty thus has a claim against the estate for damages resulting from the debtor's nonperformance. See Brief for Petitioner 17, 19; Brief for Respondent 30–31. But such a claim is unlikely to ever be paid in full. That is because the debtor's breach is deemed to occur "immediately before the date of the filing of the [bankruptcy] petition," rather than on the actual post-petition rejection date. § 365(g)(1). By thus giving the counterparty a pre-petition claim, Section 365(g) places that party in the same boat as the debtor's unsecured creditors, who in a typical bankruptcy may receive only cents on the dollar. See *Bildisco*, 465 U. S. at 531–532, 104 S.Ct. 1188 (noting the higher priority of post-petition claims).

In this case, the Bankruptcy Court (per usual) approved Tempnology's proposed rejection of its executory licensing agreement with Mission. See App. to Pet. for Cert. 83–84. That meant, as laid out above, two things on which the parties agree. First, Tempnology could stop performing under the contract. And second, Mission could assert (for whatever it might be worth) a pre-petition claim in the bankruptcy proceeding for damages resulting from Tempnology's nonperformance.

But Tempnology thought still another consequence ensued, and it returned to the Bankruptcy Court for a declaratory judgment confirming its view. According to Tempnology, its rejection of the contract also terminated the rights it had granted Mission to use the Coolcore trademarks. Tempnology based its argument on a negative inference. See Motion in No. 15-11400 (Bkrtcy. Ct. NH), pp. 9–14. Several provisions in Section 365 state that a counterparty to specific kinds of agreements may keep exercising contractual rights after a debtor's rejection. For example, Section 365(h) provides that if a bankrupt landlord rejects a lease, the tenant need not move out; instead, she may stay and pay rent (just as she did before) until the lease term expires. And still closer to home, Section 365(n) sets out a similar rule for some types of intellectual property licenses: If the debtor-licensor rejects the agreement, the licensee can continue to use the property (typically, a patent), so long as it makes whatever payments the contract demands. But Tempnology pointed out that neither Section 365(n) nor any similar provision covers trademark licenses. So, it reasoned, in that sort of contract a different rule must apply: The debtor's rejection must extinguish the rights that the agreement had conferred on the trademark licensee. The Bankruptcy Court agreed. See *In re Tempnology, LLC*, 541 B. R. 1 (Bkrtcy. Ct. NH 2015). It held, relying on the same "negative inference," that Tempnology's rejection of the licensing agreement revoked Mission's right to use the Coolcore marks. *Id.*, at 7.

The Bankruptcy Appellate Panel reversed, relying heavily on a decision of the Court of Appeals for the Seventh Circuit about the effects of rejection on trademark licensing agreements. See *In re Tempnology, LLC*, 559 B. R. 809, 820–823 (Bkrtcy. App. Panel CA1 2016); *Sunbeam Products, Inc. v. Chicago Am. Mfg., LLC*, 686 F. 3d 372, 376–377 (CA7 2012). Rather than reason backward from Section 365(n) or similar provisions, the Panel focused on Section 365(g)'s statement that rejection of a contract "constitutes a breach." Outside bankruptcy, the court explained, the breach of an agreement does not eliminate rights the contract had already conferred on the non-breaching party. See 559 B. R. at 820. So neither could a rejection of an agreement in bankruptcy have that effect. A rejection "convert[s]" a "debtor's unfulfilled obligations" to a pre-petition damages claim. *Id.*, at 822 (quoting *Sunbeam*, 686 F. 3d at 377). But it does not "terminate the contract" or "vaporize[ ]" the counterparty's rights. 559 B. R. at 820, 822 (quoting *Sunbeam*, 686 F. 3d at 377). Mission could thus continue to use the Coolcore trademarks.

But the Court of Appeals for the First Circuit rejected the Panel's and Seventh Circuit's view, and reinstated the Bankruptcy Court decision terminating Mission's license. See *In re Tempnology, LLC*, 879 F. 3d 389 (2018). The majority first endorsed that court's inference from Section 365(n) and similar provisions. It next reasoned that special features of trademark law counsel against allowing a licensee to retain rights to a mark after the licensing agreement's rejection. Under that body of law, the majority stated, the trademark owner's "[f]ailure to monitor and exercise [quality] control" over goods associated with a trademark "jeopardiz[es] the continued validity of [its] own trademark rights." *Id.*, at 402. So if (the majority continued) a licensee can keep using a mark after an agreement's rejection, the licensor will need to carry on its monitoring activities. And according to the majority, that would frustrate "Congress's principal aim in providing for rejection": to "release the debtor's estate from burdensome obligations." *Ibid.* (internal quotation marks omitted). Judge Torruella dissented, mainly for the Seventh Circuit's reasons. See *id.*, at 405–407.

We granted certiorari to resolve the division between the First and Seventh Circuits. 586 U. S.——, 139 S.Ct. 397, 202 L.Ed.2d 309 (2018). We now affirm the Seventh's reasoning and reverse the decision below.[107]

---

107. In its briefing before this Court, Mission contends that its exclusive distribution rights survived the licensing agreement's rejection for the same reason as its trademark rights did. See Brief for Petitioner 40–44; supra, at 1658. But the First Circuit held that Mission had waived that

II

Before reaching the merits, we pause to consider Tempnology's claim that this case is moot. Under settled law, we may dismiss the case for that reason only if "it is impossible for a court to grant any effectual relief whatever" to Mission assuming it prevails. *Chafin v. Chafin*, 568 U. S. 165, 172, 133 S.Ct. 1017, 185 L.Ed.2d 1 (2013) (internal quotation marks omitted). That demanding standard is not met here.

Mission has presented a claim for money damages—essentially lost profits—arising from its inability to use the Coolcore trademarks between the time Tempnology rejected the licensing agreement and its scheduled expiration date. See Reply Brief 22, and n. 8. Such claims, if at all plausible, ensure a live controversy. See *Memphis Light, Gas & Water Div. v. Craft*, 436 U. S. 1, 8–9, 98 S.Ct. 1554, 56 L.Ed.2d 30 (1978). For better or worse, nothing so shows a continuing stake in a dispute's outcome as a demand for dollars and cents. See 13C C. Wright, A. Miller & E. Cooper, Federal Practice and Procedure § 3533.3, p. 2 (3d ed. 2008) (Wright & Miller) ("[A] case is not moot so long as a claim for monetary relief survives"). Ultimate recovery on that demand may be uncertain or even unlikely for any number of reasons, in this case as in others. But that is of no moment. If there is any chance of money changing hands, Mission's suit remains live. See *Chafin*, 568 U. S. at 172, 133 S.Ct. 1017.

Tempnology makes a flurry of arguments about why Mission is not entitled to damages, but none so clearly precludes recovery as to make this case moot. First, Tempnology contends that Mission suffered no injury because it "never used the trademark[s] during [the post-rejection] period." Brief for Respondent 24; see Tr. of Oral Arg. 33. But that gets things backward. Mission's non-use of the marks during that time is precisely what gives rise to its damages claim; had it employed the marks, it would not have lost any profits. So next, Tempnology argues that Mission's non-use was its own "choice," for which damages cannot lie. See *id.*, at 26. But recall that the Bankruptcy Court held that Mission *could not* use the marks after rejection (and its decision remained in effect through the agreement's expiration). See *supra*, at 1659. And although (as Tempnology counters) the court issued "no injunction," Brief for Respondent 26, that difference does not matter: Mission need not have flouted a crystal-clear ruling and courted yet more legal trouble to preserve its claim. Cf. 13B Wright & Miller § 3533.2.2, at 852 ("[C]ompliance [with a judicial decision] does not moot [a case] if it remains possible to undo the effects of compliance," as through compensation). So last, Tempnology claims that it bears no blame (and thus should not have to pay) for Mission's injury because all it did was "ask[ ] the court to make a ruling." Tr. of Oral Arg. 34–35. But whether Tempnology did anything to Mission amounting to a legal wrong is a prototypical merits question, which no court has addressed and which has no obvious answer. That means it is no reason to find this case moot.

---

argument, see 879 F.3d at 401, and we have no reason to doubt that conclusion. Our decision thus affects only Mission's trademark rights.

And so too for Tempnology's further argument that Mission will be unable to convert any judgment in its favor to hard cash. Here, Tempnology notes that the bankruptcy estate has recently distributed all of its assets, leaving nothing to satisfy Mission's judgment. See Brief for Respondent 27. But courts often adjudicate disputes whose "practical impact" is unsure at best, as when "a defendant is insolvent." *Chafin*, 568 U. S. at 175, 133 S.Ct. 1017. And Mission notes that if it prevails, it can seek the unwinding of prior distributions to get its fair share of the estate. See Reply Brief 23. So although this suit "may not make [Mission] rich," or even better off, it remains a live controversy—allowing us to proceed. *Chafin*, 568 U. S. at 176, 133 S. Ct. 1017.

III

What is the effect of a debtor's (or trustee's) rejection of a contract under Section 365 of the Bankruptcy Code? The parties and courts of appeals have offered us two starkly different answers. According to one view, a rejection has the same consequence as a contract breach outside bankruptcy: It gives the counterparty a claim for damages, while leaving intact the rights the counterparty has received under the contract. According to the other view, a rejection (except in a few spheres) has more the effect of a contract rescission in the non-bankruptcy world: Though also allowing a damages claim, the rejection terminates the whole agreement along with all rights it conferred. Today, we hold that both Section 365's text and fundamental principles of bankruptcy law command the first, rejection-as-breach approach. We reject the competing claim that by specifically enabling the counterparties in some contracts to retain rights after rejection, Congress showed that it wanted the counterparties in all other contracts to lose their rights. And we reject an argument for the rescission approach turning on the distinctive features of trademark licenses. Rejection of a contract—any contract—in bankruptcy operates not as a rescission but as a breach.

A

We start with the text of the Code's principal provisions on rejection—and find that it does much of the work. As noted earlier, Section 365(a) gives a debtor the option, subject to court approval, to "assume or reject any executory contract." See *supra*, at 1658. And Section 365(g) describes what rejection means. Rejection "constitutes a breach of [an executory] contract," deemed to occur "immediately before the date of the filing of the petition." See *supra*, at 1658. Or said more pithily for current purposes, a rejection is a breach. And "breach" is neither a defined nor a specialized bankruptcy term. It means in the Code what it means in contract law outside bankruptcy. See *Field v. Mans*, 516 U. S. 59, 69, 116 S.Ct. 437, 133 L.Ed.2d 351 (1995) (Congress generally meant for the Bankruptcy Code to "incorporate the established meaning" of "terms that have accumulated settled meaning" (internal quotation marks omitted)). So the first place to go in divining the effects of rejection is to non-bankruptcy contract law, which can tell us the effects of breach.

Consider a made-up executory contract to see how the law of breach works outside bankruptcy. A dealer leases a photocopier to a law firm, while agreeing to service it every month; in exchange, the firm commits to pay a monthly fee. During the lease term, the dealer decides to stop servicing the machine, thus breaching the agreement in a material way. The law firm now has a choice (assuming no special contract term or state law). The firm can keep up its side of the bargain, continuing to pay for use of the copier, while suing the dealer for damages from the service breach. Or the firm can call the whole deal off, halting its own payments and returning the copier, while suing for any damages incurred. See 13 R. Lord, Williston on Contracts §39:32, pp. 701–702 (4th ed. 2013) ("[W]hen a contract is breached in the course of performance, the injured party may elect to continue the contract or refuse to perform further"). But to repeat: The choice to terminate the agreement and send back the copier is for the *law firm*. By contrast, the *dealer* has no ability, based on its own breach, to terminate the agreement. Or otherwise said, the dealer cannot get back the copier just by refusing to show up for a service appointment. The contract gave the law firm continuing rights in the copier, which the dealer cannot unilaterally revoke.

And now to return to bankruptcy: If the rejection of the photocopier contract "constitutes a breach," as the Code says, then the same results should follow (save for one twist as to timing). Assume here that the dealer files a Chapter 11 petition and decides to reject its agreement with the law firm. That means, as above, that the dealer will stop servicing the copier. It means, too, that the law firm has an option about how to respond—continue the contract or walk away, while suing for whatever damages go with its choice. (Here is where the twist comes in: Because the rejection is deemed to occur "immediately before" bankruptcy, the firm's damages suit is treated as a pre-petition claim on the estate, which will likely receive only cents on the dollar. See *supra*, at 1658–1659.) And most important, it means that assuming the law firm wants to keep using the copier, the dealer cannot take it back. A rejection does not terminate the contract. When it occurs, the debtor and counterparty do not go back to their pre-contract positions. Instead, the counterparty retains the rights it has received under the agreement. As after a breach, so too after a rejection, those rights survive.

All of this, it will hardly surprise you to learn, is not just about photocopier leases. Sections 365(a) and (g) speak broadly, to "any executory contract[s]." Many licensing agreements involving trademarks or other property are of that kind (including, all agree, the Tempnology-Mission contract). The licensor not only grants a license, but also provides associated goods or services during its term; the licensee pays continuing royalties or fees. If the licensor breaches the agreement outside bankruptcy (again, barring any special contract term or state law), everything said above goes. In particular, the breach does not revoke the license or stop the licensee from doing what it allows. See, *e.g.*, *Sunbeam*, 686 F. 3d at 376 ("Outside of bankruptcy, a licensor's breach does not terminate a licensee's right to use [the licensed] intellectual property"). And because rejection "constitutes a breach," §365(g), the same consequences follow in bankruptcy. The debtor can stop performing its remaining obligations under the agreement. But the debtor cannot rescind the license already conveyed. So the licensee can continue to do whatever the license authorizes.

In preserving those rights, Section 365 reflects a general bankruptcy rule: The estate cannot possess anything more than the debtor itself did outside bankruptcy. See *Board of Trade of Chicago v. Johnson*, 264 U. S. 1, 15, 44 S.Ct. 232, 68 L.Ed. 533 (1924) (establishing that principle); § 541(a)(1) (defining the estate to include the "interests *of the debtor* in property" (emphasis added)). As one bankruptcy scholar has put the point: Whatever "limitation[s] on the debtor's property [apply] outside of bankruptcy[ ] appl[y] inside of bankruptcy as well. A debtor's property does not shrink by happenstance of bankruptcy, but it does not expand, either." D. Baird, Elements of Bankruptcy 97 (6th ed. 2014). So if the not-yet debtor was subject to a counterparty's contractual right (say, to retain a copier or use a trademark), so too is the trustee or debtor once the bankruptcy petition has been filed. The rejection-as-breach rule (but *not* the rejection-as-rescission rule) ensures that result. By insisting that the same counterparty rights survive rejection as survive breach, the rule prevents a debtor in bankruptcy from recapturing interests it had given up.

And conversely, the rejection-as-rescission approach would circumvent the Code's stringent limits on "avoidance" actions—the exceptional cases in which trustees (or debtors) may indeed unwind pre-bankruptcy transfers that undermine the bankruptcy process. The most notable example is for fraudulent conveyances—usually, something-for-nothing transfers that deplete the estate (and so cheat creditors) on the eve of bankruptcy. See § 548(a). A trustee's avoidance powers are laid out in a discrete set of sections in the Code, see §§ 544–553, far away from Section 365. And they can be invoked in only narrow circumstances—unlike the power of rejection, which may be exercised for any plausible economic reason. See, *e.g.*, § 548(a) (describing the requirements for avoiding fraudulent transfers); *supra*, at 1658–1659. If trustees (or debtors) could use rejection to rescind previously granted interests, then rejection would become functionally equivalent to avoidance. Both, that is, would roll back a prior transfer. And that result would subvert everything the Code does to keep avoidances cabined—so they do not threaten the rule that the estate can take only what the debtor possessed before filing. Again, then, core tenets of bankruptcy law push in the same direction as Section 365's text: Rejection is breach, and has only its consequences.

B

Tempnology's main argument to the contrary, here as in the courts below, rests on a negative inference. See Brief for Respondent 33–41; *supra*, at 1658–1659. Several provisions of Section 365, Tempnology notes, "identif[y] categories of contracts under which a counterparty" may retain specified contract rights "notwithstanding rejection." Brief for Respondent 34. Sections 365(h) and (i) make clear that certain purchasers and lessees of real property and timeshare interests can continue to exercise rights after a debtor has rejected the lease or sales contract. See § 365(h)(1) (real-property leases); § 365(i) (real-property sales contracts); §§ 365(h)(2), (i) (timeshare interests). And Section 365(n) similarly provides that licensees of some intellectual property—but not trademarks—retain contractual rights after rejection. See § 365(n); § 101(35A); *supra,* at 1659. Tempnology argues from those provisions that the ordinary consequence of rejection must be something different—*i.e.,* the termination, rather than survival, of contractual rights previously granted. Otherwise, Tempnology concludes, the statute's "general rule" would "swallow the exceptions." Brief for Respondent 19.

But that argument pays too little heed to the main provisions governing rejection and too much to subsidiary ones. On the one hand, it offers no account of how to read Section 365(g) (recall, rejection "constitutes a breach") to say essentially its opposite (*i.e.,* that rejection and breach have divergent consequences). On the other hand, it treats as a neat, reticulated scheme of "narrowly tailored exception[s]," *id.,* at 36 (emphasis deleted), what history reveals to be anything but. Each of the provisions Tempnology highlights emerged at a different time, over a span of half a century. See, *e.g.,* 52 Stat. 881 (1938) (real-property leases); § 1(b), 102 Stat. 2538 (1988) (intellectual property). And each responded to a discrete problem—as often as not, correcting a judicial ruling of just the kind Tempnology urges. See Andrew, Executory Contracts in Bankruptcy, 59 U. Colo. L. Rev. 845, 911–912, 916–919 (1988) (identifying judicial decisions that the provisions overturned); compare, *e.g., In re Sombrero Reef Club, Inc.,* 18 B. R. 612, 618–619 (Bkrtcy. Ct. SD Fla. 1982), with, *e.g.,* §§ 365(h)(2), (i). Read as generously as possible to Tempnology, this mash-up of legislative interventions says nothing much of anything about the content of Section 365(g)'s general rule. Read less generously, it affirmatively refutes Tempnology's rendition. As one bankruptcy scholar noted after an exhaustive review of the history: "What the legislative record [reflects] is that whenever Congress has been confronted with the consequences of the [view that rejection terminates all contractual rights], it has expressed its disapproval." Andrew, 59 U. Colo. L. Rev., at 928. On that account, Congress enacted the provisions, as and when needed, to reinforce or clarify the general rule that contractual rights survive rejection.[108]

Consider more closely, for example, Congress's enactment of Section 365(n), which addresses certain intellectual property licensing agreements. No one disputes how that provision came about. In *Lubrizol Enterprises v. Richmond Metal Finishers,* the Fourth Circuit held that a debtor's rejection of an executory contract worked to revoke its grant of a patent license. See 756 F. 2d 1043, 1045–1048 (1985). In other words, *Lubrizol* adopted the same rule for patent licenses that the First Circuit announced for trademark licenses here. Congress sprang into action, drafting Section 365(n) to

---

108. At the same time, Congress took the opportunity when drafting those provisions to fill in certain details, generally left to state law, about the post-rejection relationship between the debtor and counterparty. *See, e.g.,* Andrew, *Executory Contracts in Bankruptcy,* 59 U. Colo. L. Rev. 845, 903, n. 200 (1988) (describing Congress's addition of subsidiary rules for real property leases in Section 365(h)); Brief for United States as Amicus Curiae 29 (noting that Congress similarly set out detailed rules for patent licenses in Section 365(n)). The provisions are therefore not redundant of Section 365(g): Each sets out a remedial scheme embellishing on or tweaking the general rejection-as-breach rule.

reverse *Lubrizol* and ensure the continuation of patent (and some other intellectual property) licensees' rights. See 102 Stat. 2538 (1988); S. Rep. No. 100-505, pp. 2–4 (1988) (explaining that Section 365(n) "corrects [*Lubrizol's*] perception" that "Section 365 was ever intended to be a mechanism for stripping innocent licensee[s] of rights"). As Tempnology highlights, that provision does not cover trademark licensing agreements, which continue to fall, along with most other contracts, within Section 365(g)'s general rule. See Brief for Respondent 38. But what of that? Even put aside the claim that Section 365(n) is part of a pattern—that Congress whacked Tempnology's view of rejection wherever it raised its head. See *supra*, at 1664. Still, Congress's repudiation of *Lubrizol* for patent contracts does not show any intent to *ratify* that decision's approach for almost all others. Which is to say that no negative inference arises. Congress did nothing in adding Section 365(n) to alter the natural reading of Section 365(g)—that rejection and breach have the same results.

Tempnology's remaining argument turns on the way special features of trademark law may affect the fulfillment of the Code's goals. Like the First Circuit below, Tempnology here focuses on a trademark licensor's duty to monitor and "exercise quality control over the goods and services sold" under a license. Brief for Respondent 20; see *supra*, at 1659–1660. Absent those efforts to keep up quality, the mark will naturally decline in value and may eventually become altogether invalid. See 3 J. McCarthy, Trademarks and Unfair Competition § 18:48, pp. 18–129, 18–133 (5th ed. 2018). So (Tempnology argues) unless rejection of a trademark licensing agreement terminates the licensee's rights to use the mark, the debtor will have to choose between expending scarce resources on quality control and risking the loss of a valuable asset. See Brief for Respondent 59. "Either choice," Tempnology concludes, "would impede a [debtor's] ability to reorganize," thus "undermining a fundamental purpose of the Code." *Id.*, at 59–60.

To begin with, that argument is a mismatch with Tempnology's reading of Section 365. The argument is trademark-specific. But Tempnology's reading of Section 365 is not. Remember, Tempnology construes that section to mean that a debtor's rejection of a contract terminates the counterparty's rights "unless the contract falls within an express statutory exception." *Id.*, at 27–28; see *supra*, at 1663–1664. That construction treats trademark agreements identically to most other contracts; the only agreements getting different treatment are those falling within the discrete provisions just discussed. And indeed, Tempnology could not have discovered, however hard it looked, any trademark-specific rule in Section 365. That section's special provisions, as all agree, do not mention trademarks; and the general provisions speak, well, generally. So Tempnology is essentially arguing that distinctive features of trademarks should persuade us to adopt a construction of Section 365 that will govern not just trademark agreements, but pretty nearly every executory contract. However serious Tempnology's trademark-related concerns, that would allow the tail to wag the Doberman.

And even putting aside that incongruity, Tempnology's plea to facilitate trademark licensors' reorganizations cannot overcome what Sections 365(a) and

(g) direct. The Code of course aims to make reorganizations possible. But it does not permit anything and everything that might advance that goal. See, *e.g.*, *Florida Dept. of Revenue v. Piccadilly Cafeterias, Inc.*, 554 U. S. 33, 51, 128 S.Ct. 2326, 171 L. Ed.2d 203 (2008) (observing that in enacting Chapter 11, Congress did not have "a single purpose," but "str[uck] a balance" among multiple competing interests (internal quotation marks omitted)). Here, Section 365 provides a debtor like Tempnology with a powerful tool: Through rejection, the debtor can escape all of its future contract obligations, without having to pay much of anything in return. See *supra,* at 1658–1659. But in allowing rejection of those contractual duties, Section 365 does not grant the debtor an exemption from all the burdens that generally applicable law—whether involving contracts or trademarks—imposes on property owners. See 28 U.S.C. §959(b) (requiring a trustee to manage the estate in accordance with applicable law). Nor does Section 365 relieve the debtor of the need, against the backdrop of that law, to make economic decisions about preserving the estate's value—such as whether to invest the resources needed to maintain a trademark. In thus delineating the burdens that a debtor may and may not escape, Congress also weighed (among other things) the legitimate interests and expectations of the debtor's counterparties. The resulting balance may indeed impede some reorganizations, of trademark licensors and others. But that is only to say that Section 365's edict that rejection is breach expresses a more complex set of aims than Tempnology acknowledges.

IV

For the reasons stated above, we hold that under Section 365, a debtor's rejection of an executory contract in bankruptcy has the same effect as a breach outside bankruptcy. Such an act cannot rescind rights that the contract previously granted. Here, that construction of Section 365 means that the debtor-licensor's rejection cannot revoke the trademark license.

We accordingly reverse the judgment of the Court of Appeals and remand the case for further proceedings consistent with this opinion.

It is so ordered.

SOTOMAYOR, Justice (concurring).

I agree with the Court that a debtor's choice to reject an executory contact under 11 U.S.C. §365(a) functions as a breach of the contract rather than unwinding the rejected contract as if it never existed. *Ante*, at 1661–1663. This result follows from traditional bankruptcy principles and from the general rule set out in §365(g) of the Bankruptcy Code. I also agree that no specific aspects of trademark law compel a contrary rule that equates rejection with rescission. I therefore join the Court's opinion in full. I write separately to highlight two potentially significant features of today's holding.

First, the Court does not decide that every trademark licensee has the unfettered right to continue using licensed marks postrejection. The Court granted certiorari to decide whether rejection "terminates rights of the licensee that would survive the licensor's breach under applicable nonbankruptcy law." Pet. for Cert. i. The answer is no, for the reasons the Court explains. But the baseline inquiry remains whether the licensee's rights would survive a breach under applicable nonbankruptcy law. Special terms in a licensing contract or state law could bear on that question in individual cases. See *ante*, at 1661–1663; Brief for American Intellectual Property Law Association as *Amicus Curiae* 20–25 (discussing examples of contract terms that could potentially lead a bankruptcy court to limit licensee rights postrejection).

Second, the Court's holding confirms that trademark licensees' postrejection rights and remedies are more expansive in some respects than those possessed by licensees of other types of intellectual property. Those variances stem from § 365(n), one of several subject-specific provisions in the Bankruptcy Code that "embellis[h] on or twea[k]" the general rejection rule. *Ante*, at 1664, n. 2. Section 365(n)—which applies to patents, copyrights, and four other types of intellectual property, but not to trademarks, § 101(35A)—alters the general rejection rule in several respects. For example, a covered licensee that chooses to retain its rights postrejection must make all of its royalty payments; the licensee has no right to deduct damages from its payments even if it otherwise could have done so under nonbankruptcy law. § 365(n)(2)(C)(i). This provision and others in § 365(n) mean that the covered intellectual property types are governed by different rules than trademark licenses.

Although these differences may prove significant for individual licensors and licensees, they do not alter the outcome here. The Court rightly rejects Tempnology's argument that the presence of § 365(n) changes what § 365(g) says. As the Senate Report accompanying § 365(n) explained, the bill did not "address or intend any inference to be drawn concerning the treatment of executory contracts" under § 365's general rule. S. Rep. No. 100-505, p. 5 (1988); see *ante*, at 1664–1665. To the extent trademark licensees are treated differently from licensees of other forms of intellectual property, that outcome leaves Congress with the option to tailor a provision for trademark licenses, as it has repeatedly in other contexts. See *ante*, at 1664–1665.

With these observations, I join the Court's opinion.

GORSUCH, Justice (dissenting).

This Court is not in the business of deciding abstract questions, no matter how interesting. Under the Constitution, our power extends only to deciding "Cases" and "Controversies" where the outcome matters to real parties in the real world. Art. III, § 2. Because it's unclear whether we have anything like that here, I would dismiss the petition as improvidently granted.

This case began when Mission licensed the right to use certain of Tempnology's trademarks. After Tempnology entered bankruptcy, it sought and won from a bankruptcy court an order declaring that Mission could no longer use those trademarks. On appeal and now in this Court, Mission seeks a ruling that the bankruptcy court's declaration was wrong. But whoever is right about that, it isn't clear how it would make a difference: After the bankruptcy court ruled, the license agreement expired by its own terms, so nothing we might say here could restore Mission's ability to use Tempnology's trademarks.

Recognizing that its original case seems to have become moot, Mission attempts an alternative theory in briefing before us. Now Mission says that if it prevails here it will, on remand, seek money damages from Tempnology's estate for the profits it lost when, out of respect for the bankruptcy court's order, it refrained from using the trademarks while its license still existed.

But it's far from clear whether even this theory can keep the case alive. A damages claim "suffices to avoid mootness only if viable," which means damages must at least be "legally available for [the alleged] wrong." 13C C. Wright, A. Miller, & E. Cooper, Federal Practice and Procedure § 3533.3, p. 22 (3d ed. 2008). Yet, as far as Mission has told us, Tempnology did nothing that could lawfully give rise to a damages claim. After all, when Tempnology asked the bankruptcy court to issue a declaratory ruling on a question of law, it was exercising its protected "First Amendment right to petition the Government for redress of grievances." *Bill Johnson's Restaurants, Inc. v. NLRB*, 461 U. S. 731, 741, 103 S.Ct. 2161, 76 L.Ed.2d 277 (1983). And petitioning a court normally isn't an actionable wrong that can give rise to a claim for damages. Absent a claim of malice (which Mission hasn't suggested would have any basis here), the ordinary rule is that "'no action lies against a party for resort to civil courts'" or for "the assertion of a legal argument." *Lucsik v. Board of Ed. of Brunswick City School Dist.*, 621 F. 2d 841, 842 (CA6 1980) (*per curiam*); *see, e.g., W. R. Grace & Co. v. Rubber Workers*, 461 U. S. 757, 770, n. 14, 103 S.Ct. 2177, 76 L.Ed.2d 298 (1983); *Russell v. Farley*, 105 U. S. 433, 437–438, 26 L.Ed. 1060 (1882).

Maybe Mission's able lawyers will conjure something better on remand. But, so far at least, the company hasn't come close to articulating a viable legal theory on which a claim for damages could succeed. And where our jurisdiction is so much in doubt, I would decline to proceed to the merits. If the legal questions here are of sufficient importance, a live case presenting them will come along soon enough; there is no need to press the bounds of our constitutional authority to reach them today.

Notes

1. In *Mission Product Holdings, Inc. v. Tempnology, LLC*, the Supreme Court creatively applied basic principles of contract law to the dictates of the Bankruptcy Code to determine that a debtor's rejection of an executory contract (a contract for which performance obligations remain due on both sides), and in this case a trademark license, constitutes a breach rather than a rescission. The Court held that a debtor's rejection of an executory contract under Section 365 of the Bankruptcy Code has the same effect as a breach of that contract outside of bankruptcy—such an act on the part of a licensor cannot rescind rights that the contract previously granted. Does this decision appear to be based upon equitable grounds? Do you agree with the Court's decision?

2. Trademark License Drafting. Counsel representing both licensors and licensees in trademark licensing transactions need to be aware of this decision and the likely

impact it will have on trademark licensing practices. Consider the importance of preserving the trademark, i.e., quality control, maintenance of trademark registrations, and consistent monitoring of the licensor-licensee relationship, which in essence are the respective obligations of both parties. The Supreme Court's *Mission Product* decision is a step in the right direction, standing for the principle that the licensor-licensee relationship continues even after a trademark license is rejected by a bankruptcy trustee. As there are no governing statutes in this regard, strategic contract drafting is necessary to afford such protection. (See Justice Sotomayor's concurrence, which underscores the importance of contract drafting to account for this occurrence within the four corners of the agreement.) How could the license terms in a trademark licensing agreement be drafted to protect these interests of both parties in the event of bankruptcy?

J. Licensing Disputes: A Licensee's Perspective

> *Discourage litigation. Persuade your neighbors to compromise whenever you can . . .*
>
> —Abraham Lincoln

> *If someone tries to steal your watch, by all means fight them off. If someone sues you for your watch, hand it over and be glad you got away so lightly.*
>
> —John Clifford Mortimer

Litigation is a hefty price to pay for a falling-out between a licensor and a licensee. Not only are the parties reaching deep into their pockets to fund their lawsuit, the rift between them becomes publicly known and tends to be a significant distraction from business operations. The following cases illustrate high-profile court battles relating to fashion licensing arrangements, typically initiated by a licensee.[109] Although each case is factually unique, the common recurring cause of action appears to be a breach of contract by the licensor based upon term and termination, exclusivity rights, the covenant of good faith and fair dealing, fraud, and deceptive trade practices.

Levy Group, Inc. v. L.C. Licensing, Inc.

2010 N.Y. Misc. LEXIS 6816 (N.Y. Sup. Ct. 2010)

KAPNICK, Judge.

In this action arising out of the rights to the world-famous "Liz Claiborne" and "Claiborne" Marks, plaintiff The Levy Group ("Levy") seeks to recover damages against defendants L.C. Licensing, Inc. ("LCL") and Liz Claiborne, Inc. ("Claiborne") for: (i) breach of contract (first cause of action); (ii) breach of the covenant of good

---

109. As noted above, there have been claims brought by licensors against their licensees based upon quality and distribution. *See* Eva's Bridal, Ltd. v. Halanick Enters., 639 F.3d 788 (7th 2011); Calvin Klein Trademark Trust v. Wachner, 198 F.R.D. 53 (S.D.N.Y. 2000).

faith and fair dealing (second cause of action); and (iii) promissory estoppel (third cause of action) and against defendant Claiborne only for (iv) tortious interference with contract (fourth cause of action).

Defendants LCL and Claiborne now move, under motion sequence number 001, for an order pursuant to CPLR 3211(a) (1) and (a) (7) dismissing the plaintiff's Complaint in its entirety on the grounds that there is a defense founded upon documentary evidence and for failure to state a cause of action.

Background

On December 1, 1997, Levy and LCL entered into an agreement (the "License Agreement") granting Levy the exclusive right to sell and distribute men's and women's outerwear and rainwear (the "Merchandise") bearing Liz Claiborne Marks (the "Marks") throughout the United States and Puerto Rico. On April 29, 2002, the License Agreement was amended (the "Third Amendment") to grant the plaintiff the right to renew the License Agreement every five years until December 31, 2028 and to renegotiate royalty payments and sales minimums. In 2008, plaintiff exercised the option to renew the License Agreement for another five years.

The License Agreement provides in the Preamble that the "licensee is desirous of associating its products with the (Marks) so as to obtain the benefit of the goodwill associated therewith." Paragraph 34 of the License Agreement (*Licensor's Approval or Consent*) provides that:

> [t]he parties hereby agree and acknowledge that the highest standards and reputation and established image, prestige and goodwill within the 'better zone' for women's apparel products (as such term is understood in the industry) are associated with the "Liz Claiborne" name, the [Marks] and with the businesses and products of [LCL} and their respective affiliates and licensees, and that the operations of the license granted hereunder and the Person who own the license or any equity interest in Licensee will reflect upon and affect such standards, reputation, image, prestige and goodwill. Accordingly, [Plaintiff] agrees and acknowledges that any approval or consent of Licensor is required hereunder . . . may be based upon subjective standards intended to maintain such standards, reputation, image, prestige and goodwill, and the quality and reputation of Liz Merchandise.

Other references to the "high quality", "prestige" and "goodwill" associated with the Marks are found throughout the License Agreement in sections delineating acknowledgments, restrictions or requirements on the part of plaintiff only. License Agreement § 2.1 provides in relevant part that:

> [l]icensor retains and reserves any and all rights to use and exploit, and to grant to any other Person the right to use and exploit, any Licensed Mark . . . and any designs, names or other items supplied by Licensor hereunder in connection with any and all products and services, other than Merchandise bearing the Licensed Marks . . .

The Complaint alleges that prior to entering into the Third Amendment, Levy had had discussions with a major Claiborne competitor regarding a license to design, manufacture and sell the competitor's outerwear in lieu of renewing the License Agreement. Levy claims that in order to induce it to renew the License Agreement, Claiborne agreed, *inter alia*, to extend the length of the Agreement, and that plaintiff relied on Claiborne's continued obligation to protect the prestige and reputation associated with the Marks and its continued right to sell the Merchandise to a network of "better zone" department stores.

The Complaint further alleges that as a result of many years of effort and investment, Levy has developed a large network of "better zone" retailers which purchase large volumes of the Merchandise. "Better zone" is a clothing industry term referring to stores associated with higher quality, reputation and prices, such as Macy's and Dillards.

Notwithstanding all this, on October 7, 2009, Claiborne entered into an agreement with J.C. Penney Corporation ("JC Penney") granting it the exclusive worldwide license to use the Marks in connection with certain products, not including the Merchandise (the "Penney License").

The Complaint alleges that JC Penney is not considered a "better zone" retailer and that the defendants previously required Levy under the Second Amendment to the License Agreement (the "Second Amendment") to use the less prestigious "Crazy Horse" trademark, also owned by Claiborne, rather than the Marks if Levy wished to sell Merchandise to JC Penney.

According to the Complaint, now that the Marks will appear on items sold in JC Penney, "better zone" retailers will no longer purchase plaintiff's Merchandise. Moreover, JC Penney is under no obligation to purchase the Merchandise from Levy, and even if it did, it could not match the volume of sales which Levy had previously developed with the "better zone" retailers. Furthermore, Levy's margin of profit on any sales to JC Penney would be lower because it is not a "better zone" retailer. The Complaint alleges that all of these factors will result in a decline in net sales of tens of millions of dollars annually and will make it more difficult, if not impossible, for Levy to meet its net sales minimums that trigger its right to renew the License Agreement.

Discussion

I. Breach of Contract

Defendants argue that plaintiff's breach of contract claim should be dismissed on the grounds that the written contract conclusively establishes a defense as a matter of law. Specifically, defendants contend that § 2.1 of the License Agreement grants defendants broad rights to license the Marks to any person so long as it does not include the Merchandise. Moreover, § 1.3 of the License Agreement provides that it was "understood and agreed that Licensor retains all rights of creation and exploitation with respect to all other products other than Merchandise . . . ," and the Penney License includes a specific carve-out for defendants' pre-existing licensees, including the license with Levy.

In addition, defendants assert that nothing in the plain language of the License Agreement either obligates defendants to maintain the "reputation and prestige" of the Marks by not entering into an agreement similar to the Penney License, or grants Levy the unequivocal right to sell exclusively to "better zone" stores. On the contrary, defendants argue that the terms of the Agreement cited by Levy in the Complaint, such as § 2.4, are designed to police the conduct of Levy as LCL's licensee, not to create any duty on the part of the defendants to maintain the "reputation and prestige" of the Marks as "better zone" brands, as Levy claims.

Plaintiff argues in opposition that (i) the repeated references to the Marks' value, prestige and goodwill throughout the License Agreement, (ii) the Bilateral Acknowledgment in Paragraph 34 and (iii) the License Agreement's statement of plaintiff's desire to benefit from the goodwill associated with the Marks collectively express an obligation on the part of Claiborne to protect the Marks' "better zone" standards. Plaintiff argues that it was this obligation which triggered the defendants' breach.

However, the License Agreement here was negotiated by sophisticated and well-counseled parties, and under such circumstance, the Courts are extremely reluctant to interpret an agreement as impliedly stating something which the parties have neglected to specifically include. It is a basic contract principle that when parties set down their agreement in a clear, complete document, their writing should be enforced according to its terms.

Paragraph 2.1 of the License Agreement contains clear and unambiguous language in favor of Claiborne's right to license the Marks to any Person, with a carve-out for the Merchandise. While plaintiff argues that the License Agreement obligates Claiborne to protect the Marks' high quality and standards, there is no provision which specifically provides for this obligation.

Certainly, as plaintiff points out, references to the reputation and prestige of the Marks are peppered throughout the License Agreement, yet, none of these references imposes an obligation to maintain those standards upon Claiborne. To the contrary, those references are found in sections which impose obligations on Levy. Even the plain language of the Bilateral Acknowledgment in Paragraph 34, in which both parties acknowledge the high standards associated with the Marks, describes only the subjective standards which Claiborne may use in exercising its rights of approval or consent in regard to Levy's use of the Marks.

If restrictions upon Claiborne's actions which might harm the value of the Marks were contemplated by the parties to the Agreement, those restrictions should have been clearly and expressly included in the License Agreement.

Paragraph 2.1 of the License Agreement *expressly* reserves LCL's rights to license the Marks to "any other Person." The defendants have simply exercised a clearly expressed right reserved to them in the License Agreement. Thus, that portion of defendants' motion seeking to dismiss the breach of contract claim is granted.

II. Breach of the Covenant of Good Faith and Fair Dealing

In New York, all contracts imply a covenant of good faith and fair dealing in the course of performance. This covenant embraces a pledge that neither party shall do anything which will have the effect of destroying or injuring the right of the other party to receive the fruits of the contract. While the duties of good faith and fair dealing do not imply obligations inconsistent with other terms of the contractual relationship, they do encompass any promises which a reasonable person in the position of the promisee would be justified in understanding were included.

Nonetheless, defendants argue that the plaintiff's claim for breach of the covenant of good faith and fair dealing should be dismissed in the instant case because it is duplicative of plaintiff's claim for breach of contract—namely, the execution of the JCPenney lease—and involves the same purported injury—namely, the profits Levy alleges it will lose from reduced sales to "better zone" retailers.

Plaintiff alternatively argues that it has stated a claim for breach of the covenant of good faith and fair dealing by alleging that defendants, by entering into the Penney license which permits the Claiborne Marks to be sold on items in JCPenney, after previously requiring Levy to use the less prestigious Claiborne trademark "Crazy Horse" it if wished to sell its merchandise to JCPenney, have potentially destroyed Levy's "better zone" business and deprived Levy of the benefit of "the fruits of the contract."

However, plaintiff's claim for breach of the implied covenant of good faith and fair dealing seeks to nullify an express and unambiguous term of the License Agreement, namely, LCL's right to grant to "any other Person", whether in or out of the "better zone", a license for the use of the Marks with respect to products other than outerwear. The implied covenant cannot be construed so broadly as effectively to nullify other express terms of a contract, or to create independent contractual rights.

Accordingly, that portion of defendants' motion seeking to dismiss the implied covenant claim is granted.

Notes

1. In *Levy Group v. L.C. Licensing*, the licensee, an outerwear manufacturer, sued the owner of the Liz Claiborne marks for entering into a license agreement with a department store that the licensee did not consider a "better zone" retailer. The licensee alleged in its complaint that by entering into a license agreement with J.C. Penney, the licensor breached the agreement with the licensee by not maintaining the prestige and reputation of the Liz Claiborne marks, which would ultimately result in a decline in net sales for the licensee.

2. In *Levy Group v. L.C. Licensing*, the court refused to alter an agreement executed by sophisticated business parties. There was clear language in the agreement reserving the right to license the Liz Claiborne trademarks to "any other Person." The court refused to "nullify an express and unambiguous term of the License Agreement."

3. *Exclusive versus Nonexclusive Licenses.* An exclusive license gives a licensee the exclusive right to use a licensor's trademark in connection with certain goods or services in a particular region. Exclusive licenses can also give a licensee "the right by agreement with the owner of the trademark to exclude even him from selling in their territory." *Quabaug Rubber Co. v. Fabiano Shoe Co.*, 567 F.2d 154, 159 (1st Cir. 1977). Unless a licensor grants a licensee an exclusive license, a licensor will also have the ability to license its mark to another third-party licensee. Therefore, licensors often include language in license agreements, such as the one found in *Levy Group v. L.C. Licensing*, that gives the licensor the right to license the mark to any person.

Jones Apparel Group, Inc. v. Polo Ralph Lauren Corp.

3 Misc. 3d 1107(A) (N.Y. Sup. Ct. 2004)

LOWE, Judge.

Jones Apparel Group, Inc. (Jones Apparel) designs, manufactures, and markets apparel, footwear and accessories. It sells clothing under a number of nationally recognized brands, including Jones New York, Evan-Picone, Rena Rowan, and Nine West. Jones Apparel also designs, manufactures and sells clothing under trademarks owned by the Polo Ralph Lauren Corporation.

Polo is the publicly held business of designer Ralph Lauren. In 1995, Jones Apparel, and its subsidiary, Jones Investment, Co., Inc., entered into a series of four agreements with Polo, by which Jones obtained the exclusive rights within the United States and Canada to produce lines of clothing under several labels, including the "Lauren" label (the Lauren Agreements).

The Lauren Agreements include two license agreements, one pertaining to the United States and the other pertaining to Canada; and two associated "design service agreements," one for the United States and the other for Canada. Jones Apparel is party to the licensing and design service agreements pertaining to the United States, and Jones Investment is party to the licensing and design service agreements pertaining to Canada. Each of the four Lauren Agreements permits Polo to terminate it in the event of specified default conditions, such as Jones' non-payment of royalties or Jones' bankruptcy. The Lauren Agreements also contain "cross-default" provisions, whereby a default under the license agreement would trigger a default under the design services agreement, and vice versa. In addition, the Lauren Agreements contain provisions providing that a default under the United States agreements would trigger a default under the Canada agreements.

The Lauren Agreements also have analogous "cross-expiration provisions." Under these provisions, the expirations of the United States license agreement would result in the expiration of the United States design services agreement, and the expiration of the Canada license agreement would result in the expiration of the Canada design services agreement, and vice versa. Under another section, the expiration of the United States license agreement would result in the expiration of the Canada license agreement.

However, while the cross-default/expiration provisions in the Lauren Agreements provide that a default or expiration of either of the United States agreements results in a default or expiration of the Canada agreements, the reverse is not provided for. Thus, a default under, or expiration of, any of the Canada agreements does not trigger a default under, or expiration of, the United States agreements.

As originally executed in 1995, the terms of the Lauren Agreements ran through December 31, 2001. However, those agreements gave Jones the option to extend them for an additional three years, through December 31, 2004, if sales of the Lauren lines met specified minimum sales levels during 2000. The lines of clothing Jones Apparel designs and produces for Polo have been extremely profitable. Jones' sales of Lauren clothing within the United States and Canada accounted for well over $500 million in sales during both 2001 and 2002.

Jones alleges that in 1998, Polo approached Jones with the proposal that Jones and Polo enter into licensing and design services agreements with respect to a new line of clothing to be aimed at younger women. The line would be marketed under the "Ralph/Ralph Lauren" or "Ralph by Ralph Lauren" label (the Ralph Line). As with the Lauren line, the Ralph line would be designed and manufactured by Jones.

Jones agreed, and on May 11, 1998 Jones and Polo executed four license and design agreements for the Ralph Line (the Ralph Agreements). The Ralph Agreements include two license agreements, with respect to products bearing the "Ralph/Ralph Lauren" trademark in the United States and Canada, respectively, and two design services agreements, with respect to Ralph products in the United States and Canada, respectively.

On that same day, the parties also executed a "Cross-Default and Term Extension Agreement." Jones contends that to compensate Jones for the risk associated with agreeing to take on this new, untested venture, Polo agreed to extend the renewal terms of the Lauren agreements by two years, such that the agreements, once renewed, would not expire until December 31, 2006, rather than December 31, 2004, as provided for under the Lauren Agreements. The Cross-Default and Term Extension Agreement provides, in part as follows:

> 1. In the event the term of the Lauren License is renewed in the manner set forth in paragraph 8 thereof, the "Renewal Term" (as defined therein) shall expire on December 31, 2006 instead of December 31, 2004, and the term of the Lauren Design Agreement shall be similarly extended in accordance with its terms.
>
> 2. In the event the term of the Lauren Canada License is renewed in the manner set forth in paragraph 8 thereof, the "Renewal Term" (as defined therein) shall expire on December 31, 2006 instead of December 31, 2004, and the term of the Lauren Canada Design Agreement shall be similarly extended in accordance with its terms.
>
> 3. Any Event of Default under any of the above-referenced agreements shall constitute an Event of Default under all of the above-referenced agreements,

> and except as may otherwise be agreed upon in a writing signed by the relevant parties, the termination or expiration of any of the above-referenced agreements shall result in the simultaneous termination or expiration of all of the above referenced agreements.

Sales of the Lauren line for the year 2000 met the minimum levels specified for renewal in paragraph 8 of the Lauren Licenses. Accordingly, in 2001, Jones exercised its option to extend the terms of the Lauren Agreements through December 31, 2006, as provided by the Cross-Default and Term Extension Agreement.

However, sales under the Ralph label were not as successful. Those sales fell below the minimum levels that would allow renewal of those agreements beyond December 31, 2003. By letter dated December 6, 2002, Polo took the position that, by virtue of the third sentence of the Cross-Default Agreement, the expiration of the Ralph Agreements automatically triggered the expiration of the Lauren Agreements, and that the Lauren Agreements would, therefore, expire on December 31, 2003. Polo asserted that the term "above-referenced agreements" in the third sentence of the Cross-Default Agreement refers not only to the Lauren Agreements, but also to the agreements referenced in the recitals. Those recitals list, in a "whereas" clause, all of the agreements that Jones and Polo were parties to. On December 16, 2002, Jones wrote a letter to Polo, rejecting Polo's interpretation of the Cross-Default Agreement. In early June 2003, Jones and Polo each commenced action against the other.

Polo seeks a declaratory judgment that the Lauren Agreements terminate as of December 31, 2003, and that after that date all rights granted to Jones in the Lauren Agreements revert to Polo. Polo also seeks an injunction, preventing Jones from any use of the rights granted in the Lauren Agreement.

The Motion to Dismiss and the Motion and Cross Motion for Summary Judgment

Polo contends that the Lauren Agreements have expired based upon a reading of the term "above-referenced agreements" in the third sentence of the Cross-Default And Term Extension Agreement. Polo asserts that "above-referenced agreements" includes not only the four Lauren Agreements, which are the subject matter of the operative part of the agreement, but also to the four Ralph Agreements. Jones contends that the Cross-Default and Extension Agreement was intended to do two things: (1) to extend the expiration of the Lauren Agreements, and (2) to provide that if there were a default in the Canada agreements, the U.S. agreements would expire as well.

It is well settled that the issue of whether an agreement is ambiguous is a question of law. Ambiguity is to be determined by looking within the four corners of the document and not to outside sources. As a matter of basic contract law, the Cross-Default and Term Extension Agreement is not ambiguous. The operative portion of the agreement lists only the two United States Lauren Agreements and the two Canada Lauren Agreements. The recitals of a contract indicate only the background, and ordinarily form no part of the real contract. Where the recital in an agreement is so inconsistent with the covenant or promise that they cannot be harmonized, the latter, if unambiguous, must prevail, because it is the most important.

Further, in interpreting a contract the court should examine the entire contract and consider the relation of the parties and the circumstances under which it was executed. Here, given the relation of the parties, its strains credulity that Jones would risk continuation of its very profitable Lauren line on the success of an untried new line. Further, given that the parties had agreed to extend the expiration dates of the Lauren line, possibly as consideration for entering into the new Ralph line, it would make no sense for them to simultaneously provide for expiration of that profitable line.

Therefore, Polo's motion to dismiss the first cause of action is denied. Jones['] motion to dismiss the complaint is granted. Polo's cross-motion for summary judgment in its favor is denied.

Notes

1. In *Jones Apparel Group v. Polo Ralph Lauren*, the court applied principles of basic contract law, finding that the terms of the agreements between the parties were not ambiguous. In doing so the court gave deference to the relationship of the parties and the circumstances under which Jones and Polo executed the agreements.

2. In granting Jones' motion to dismiss, the court viewed the extension of the Lauren Agreements as Jones' consideration for agreeing to produce lines of clothing under an untried, new label. Do you think a two-year extension to the Lauren Agreements was proper consideration for Jones' willingness to market Ralph Lauren's untried new brand?

3. The Lauren Agreements originally did not include the language that a default under, or expiration of, any of the Canada agreements would trigger a default under, or expiration of, the U.S. agreements, even though the reverse was provided for. Although this discrepancy in the original agreement was corrected by the parties in the Cross-Default and Term Extension Agreement, an important detail such as this one that is not included in an agreement can result in unexpected and costly litigation.

4. In a dispute between a licensee and licensor, the court's inquiry about consumer likelihood of confusion is different from a traditional trademark infringement case because the ownership of a valid mark is not an issue. In a licensing dispute, there is no need to compare the designer's marks or products with the licensee's because they are identical by virtue of the agreement the parties entered into. However, a dispute between a licensee and licensor may arise when a licensee breaches an agreement by engaging in the unauthorized use of a licensor's trademark. Such unauthorized use of a licensor's trademark can arise when a licensee sells apparel and other merchandise bearing the licensor's mark to unauthorized distribution channels. "Where a licensee persists in the unauthorized use of a licensor's trademark, courts have found that the continued use alone establishes a likelihood of consumer

confusion." *Robert Trent Jones II, Inc. v. GFSI, Inc.*, 537 F. Supp. 2d 1061 (N.D. Cal. 2008); *Sun Microsystems v. Microsoft Corp.*, 999 F. Supp. 1301, 1311 (N.D. Cal. 1998) (citing *Paisa, Inc. v. N & G Auto, Inc.*, 928 F. Supp. 1009, 1012 n. 4 (C.D. Cal. 1996); *Hollywood Athletic Club*, 938 F. Supp. at 614–15 (C.D. Cal. 1996)).

Macy's, Inc. v. J.C. Penney Corp.

45 Misc. 3d 274 (N.Y. Sup. Ct. 2014)

OING, Judge.

The Stakes

These consolidated actions involve three of this country's largest retailers, one with a marquee name recognized as a retail giant, one that is a household name struggling to survive, but recently turning the corner, and one company whose namesake is known worldwide as the decorating doyenne. In spite of all the publicity and notoriety that this matter has garnered, these actions, at bottom, straightforward disputes involving breach of contract and tortious interference with contract.

What sets these disputes apart are the stakes. The issues presented by these actions affect economic issues such as, but not limited to, employment, manufacturing, and distribution, both domestically and internationally.

The Parties

Plaintiff, Macy's, Inc. ("Macy's"), is a Delaware corporation with corporate offices in New York and Ohio, and is a national chain of department stores operating more than 850 department stores in 45 states. It also has a significant internet presence operating under the names "Macy's" and "Bloomingdale's."

Plaintiff, Macy's Merchandising Group, Inc. ("MMG"), is a Delaware corporation with its principal place of business in New York. MMG is a wholly-owned subsidiary and affiliate of Macy's, and is responsible for the design, development and marketing of Macy's private label brands and certain licensed brands.

Defendant, J.C. Penney Corporation, Inc. ("JCP"), is a Delaware corporation with its principal place of business in Texas. JCP operates more than 1,100 department stores throughout the Unites States and Puerto Rico, and has a significant internet presence operating under the name "J.C. Penney."

Former defendant, Martha Stewart Living Omnimedia, Inc. ("MSLO"), is a Delaware corporation with its principal place of business in New York. MSLO is a diversified media and merchandising company founded by Martha Stewart in February 1997. Martha Stewart is the public face of MSLO. Following trial but before my decision, Macy's discontinued its action against MSLO.

Findings of Fact

The Origins of the Macy's/MSLO Agreement

By the early 1980s, Martha Stewart had become well known in the domestic arts through newspaper columns, cookbooks, and television appearances. With her celebrity status rising, Ms. Stewart in 1987 contracted with Kmart to serve as its consultant and spokeswoman. Ten years later, Ms. Stewart's company, MSLO, entered into a contract with Kmart for the sale of Martha Stewart-labeled merchandise in bed and bath, housewares, holiday and outdoor categories under the brand name "Martha Stewart Everyday." Her merchandise soon after became the dominant brand at Kmart. That business relationship, however, began to sour. Over the ensuing years, Kmart sought to reduce MSLO's royalty payments, and MSLO became increasingly concerned with the appearance of Kmart's stores and quality of the merchandise bearing Ms. Stewart's name.

In 2002, both Kmart and Ms. Stewart encountered their own difficulties. Kmart filed for Chapter 11 bankruptcy and the United States Securities and Exchange Commission began investigating Ms. Stewart for alleged insider trading violations. By the middle of 2003, as a result of a criminal indictment, Ms. Stewart resigned as MSLO's chairwoman and Chief Executive Officer. In March 2004, the United States government obtained a conviction against Ms. Stewart for obstruction of justice and other felony counts. She began a period of incarceration later that year. In that same time period, Ms. Stewart engaged Charles Koppelman to look after MSLO during her prison term. With the Kmart business relationship deteriorating, Mr. Koppelman, who has experience in running troubled corporations, reached out to Terry Lundgren, Macy's CEO, to gauge Macy's interest in a proposed licensing arrangement for home merchandise with MSLO. The overtures went nowhere.

In 2005, Robin Marino, MSLO's new president of merchandising, reached out to Macy's again. Ms. Marino began her career at Macy's after college, and worked her way up through the ranks in her 11 years at Macy's. She wanted to move the MSLO brand upscale and believed Macy's would be an ideal partner. This time Macy's did not reject the overtures. The parties' negotiations bore fruit, but only after protracted and lengthy discussions. Ms. Marino led the negotiations for MSLO; Janet Grove, MMG's chairperson, and Leonard Marcus, its president and Chief Operating Officer, led the negotiations for Macy's.

Macy's had many concerns. To begin, there were significant risks in entering into a relationship with MSLO because the Martha Stewart brand had been associated with low-price, low-quality goods as a result of MSLO's association with Kmart, and because of Ms. Stewart's trial and conviction for securities law violations. Also, Macy's had concerns that there had been no business model for successfully bringing a mass-market brand upscale of the likes of Martha Stewart. Mr. Marcus was skeptical of the volume of sales MSLO could generate at Macy's; skeptical of the ability to move the Martha Stewart brand upscale; and ever skeptical and concerned that if Macy's succeeded in moving the brand upscale MSLO would seek to take advantage of that success, brought on by Macy's singular efforts, to sell its designs to a broader market. Indeed, the contemplated business arrangement had Macy's taking on all the financial risks, *i.e.*, product demand reduction, consumer dissatisfaction. To call Mr. Marcus a "doubting Thomas" about the impending business relationship would be putting it mildly.

After months of negotiations, the parties were able to settle on the terms of a license and promotion agreement (the "Macy's/MSLO agreement"). Broadly speaking, the terms included a minimum annual royalty; a condition that once the Kmart deal expired Macy's would have full exclusivity in the categories set forth in the Macy's/MSLO agreement; and Macy's would have the unilateral right to renew the Macy's/MSLO agreement for a term of up to 20 years. The essence of the deal, however, was exclusivity:

> Q. So, Mr. Marcus, what were your negotiations about exclusivity?
>
> A. What we discussed was that Mr. Koppelman and Robin Marino knew how strongly we felt that if we went into a deal, Macy's could be the only person where Martha Stewart product in our categories could be sold, that she would design for us, but it had to be totally exclusive for us, and that we couldn't ask for total exclusivity, we carved out these categories, so Mr. Koppelman then said: We can't give you everything because we want to have—we already have some deals in place and, two, there are certain categories where Macy's doesn't do a lot of business, so we carved out categories and said—cookware, as an example, so anything to do with cookware was going to be exclusive to Macy's.
>
> Q. Now, when you say "exclusive to Macy's," what do you mean?
>
> A. That customer—the only place you can buy it would be at a Macy's, that we would be the—they would design it, we would be the only ones who could manufacture it, we could be the only ones to distribute it, we could be the only one to retail it and promote it, and they would come to Macy's.

As for design exclusivity, Mr. Marcus gave the following testimony:

> Q. Now, did MSLO ever ask for the right to design in your categories for anybody else?
>
> A. Never. It would have been a deal breaker. The whole concept was, they were going to bring the whole—from the very first discussion, Martha brings incredible design talent, Macy's brings incredible manufacturing sourcing and distribution expertise and store expertise and customer marketing, and it's a win/win for both companies. That was at the very heart from the Day One they give us their designs, they never would have—they never asked to design for anyone else, and frankly that would have been another show stopper, that wouldn't have done the deal.

Macy's Launches the Martha Stewart Collection

In September 2007, with much fanfare and excitement, Macy's unveiled its new venture with MSLO. At its iconic flagship store in Herald Square, Macy's devoted its entire window display to Martha Stewart, and spent substantial monies to bring its store in line with Ms. Stewart's tastes. In that regard, Macy's painted the store walls "Martha blue" and added new fixtures. Macy's featured Ms. Stewart on Macy's website and advertised Macy's new venture with Ms. Stewart in a number of ways.

Macy's "wanted to create a whole world, a whole world shop of Martha Stewart". Despite the excitement, the first 18 months of sales were disappointing—"a disaster". Nonetheless, Macy's continued to work with MSLO to get through the growing pains and to add more advertising monies to attract consumers. The efforts bore fruit. Every year since 2008, sales for the Martha Stewart Collection have increased annually so that it has become the leading brand in Macy's Home store. All appeared to be well.

The Genesis of the JCP/MSLO Agreement

Notwithstanding MSLO's strength and success in merchandising, it suffered heavy losses in its media business. In order to stabilize its finances and to obtain further financing, MSLO's board of directors ("MSLO board") established a special committee in the spring of 2011 to explore "strategic partnerships." The special committee retained The Blackstone Group ("Blackstone") to lead the search. MSLO did not confer with Macy's about a strategic partnership.

Coincidentally, on June 14, 2011, JCP announced that it had hired Ron Johnson as its new CEO. Mr. Johnson, with the support of JCP's board of directors ("JCP board"), had a new vision for the company. In that regard, he was drawing on his extensive experience in merchandising at Target, and his successful development and implementation of the Apple Store. To that end, he viewed Martha Stewart as the key to that vision, and testified that she would be a "game changer" for JCP. He also believed that Martha Stewart's influence on the Home industry has been tremendous and greater than any single designer in the Home apparel industry. Indeed, Ms. Stewart herself attested that she provides MSLO "guidance, overall strategy, overall design sensibility, and likability of designs" and is "the uber designer, uber leader, uber teacher" for MSLO. Holding those firm beliefs, Mr. Johnson set off to land Martha Stewart.

On August 8, 2011, with Blackstone's assistance, Mr. Johnson met Ms. Stewart for the first time. MSLO never sought permission from Macy's to meet with JCP. Accompanying Ms. Stewart was Lisa Gersh, MSLO's new CEO. Ms. Stewart characterized Mr. Johnson's statements made during the meeting as "very flattering," and "very appealing" and, more importantly for MSLO's purposes, eagerly agreed with Macy's counsel's description of the meeting as being very "enticing". What was plainly obvious to Mr. Johnson and his JCP team was the fact that the sole obstacle to their planned business relationship with MSLO was the Macy's/MSLO agreement. Indeed, the "impediment" was that the Macy's/MSLO agreement covered the same product categories that JCP wanted to develop with MSLO, and that the Macy's/MSLO agreement purportedly gave Macy's exclusivity over these categories. Indeed, in an August 17, 2011 email, Mr. Johnson wrote to Daniel Walker, another JCP executive:

> I'm feeling awesome about grand strategy. I need to pull off Martha. She wants to do it . . . I need to propose a deal so she can go to Terry L Lundgren at Macy's and break their agreement. That is the only issue in way of success at this point.

In reply, Mr. Walker emailed, "getting Martha landed will give you the cornerstone that you'll need." Mr. Johnson was also aware of Macy's unilateral renewal right, which was quickly approaching its deadline in January 2012. To that end, he wrote an August 14, 2011 email to Steve Roth, another JCP board member: "Macy's deal is key. We need to find a way to break the renewal right in Spring 2013." Mr. Roth agreed.

JCP's Grand Strategy

Prior to hiring Mr. Johnson, JCP had contracted with Sephora to open shops inside JCP. Sephora had already operated many free-standing retail stores, and JCP modeled the shops inside its stores on fixtures and inventory after the Sephora stores. Mr. Johnson wanted to take this "store within a store" concept to another level. His vision of JCP's "grand strategy" was to have JCP stores organized by brand shops, and he testified that this strategy was undertaken to reinvent JCP stores by opening individual stores and boutiques inside them. JCP planned to have one hundred such shops, with twenty in the Home area alone. The anchor for these shops would be a Martha Stewart shop, which was particularly critical because of its established appeal. According to Mr. Johnson, that appeal would drive foot traffic and produce "halo sales," *i.e.*, consumers buying other items.

The Loophole

Despite the perceived contractual obstacle, with the assistance of Blackstone, JCP's negotiations with MSLO were progressing well enough for Mr. Johnson to write an August 31, 2011 email to Steve Seabolt, another JCP executive:

> The ball is in her court now to talk to Macy's about a break in a tight, exclusive agreement they have with her. This will be a difficult issue as they see JCP as their primary competitor.

Thus, Mr. Johnson was of the belief that MSLO would have to negotiate with Macy's to resolve what MSLO could agree to do in a contract with JCP. He was optimistic that Macy's would support MSLO's new relationship with JCP to the point of writing in an email to Steve Seabolt, a JCP executive, "Terry L [Lundgren] is a good friend and will want to support her". Subsequent events would demonstrate that Mr. Johnson was overly optimistic.

In late August 2011, MSLO hired Daniel Taitz, a former law partner of Ms. Gersh, as its general counsel. With an understanding of JCP's grand strategy, he theorized that opening a Martha Stewart shop within a JCP store would be permitted under the Macy's/MSLO agreement. He told JCP of his interpretation and understanding of the Macy's/ MSLO agreement.

On September 20, 2011, Mr. Johnson met again with Ms. Stewart and Ms. Gersh, who told him of Mr. Taitz's theory. In an email of the same date, Mr. Johnson wrote to his team:

> A big breakthrough . . . Martha's lawyers have determined that they can do Martha Stewart Stores which include "Stores within a Store" . . . so like

> Sephora we have a path should Terry [Lundgren] not be amenable. We should obviously validate all this but they are exceedingly interested in making this happen.

Confidence in this interpretation, however, was tepid. In reviewing the "MSLO Store" provision set forth in the Macy's/MSLO agreement, Katheryn Burchett, JCP's senior vice president of merchandising and marketing integration and one of JCP's lead negotiators, became concerned that the Martha Stewart store within a store exception might not hold up. Mr. Taitz thought otherwise. In response to why MSLO did not want to indemnify JCP, he believed that the "likelihood that someone would later view this as a breach was a very low probability," but he thought that "it was a very high probability that Macy's would attack it." He held firm the belief that MSLO could open a store within JCP and not run afoul of the Macy's/MSLO agreement. Simply stated, Mr. Taitz's testimony is that MSLO is right, but that Macy's would not like it. As to the latter sentiment, he could not be more accurate. The former sentiment is less absolute as the unfolding events would later prove.

In the midst of these quickly developing events, JCP and MSLO decided to approach The Home Depot, one of MSLO's major retail partners, for consent, which they obtained. That was not the same approach taken with Macy's. Charles Koppelman, who viewed MSLO's relationship with Macy's as intimate and trusting, growing out of their mutual objectives to build their businesses, advised MSLO and Ms. Stewart to inform Macy's as they did with The Home Depot, and thought that not to do so would be a mistake. MSLO and Ms. Stewart did not heed his advice. In November 2011, MSLO and JCP agreed that Macy's would not be told until after they signed their agreement. Hindsight is always "twenty/twenty" vision—MSLO and Ms. Stewart should have heeded Mr. Koppelman's wise counsel.

The Dramatic Fallout

On December 6, 2011, JCP and MSLO entered into a licensing agreement, with JCP board's approval. Ms. Stewart broke the news to Mr. Lundgren on the evening of December 6. To say that Macy's was shocked and surprised would be an understatement. His testimony is as follows:

> Q. Tell the court if you could what happened.
>
> A. I was traveling that day. I landed and had a message from my assistant who said: Please call Ms. Stewart. She would like to talk to you tonight. And this was about—I landed something like 6:00 p.m., so I called her right away. And she put me on the speakerphone with her relatively new president Lisa Gersh, I had never met her, but she was the president, the two of them, and she started talking to me about this new relationship that she was about to announce the next morning, and she said it will be with J.C. Penney, and they have taken an interest in her company.
>
> And I was completely shocked and blown away by what she was saying to me. It was so far from anything that I could ever imagine. I was in complete shock, and I was totally disappointed, why she would. And I said: Why

> wouldn't you bring this to me? Why wouldn't you come and talk to me about this? I mean, Martha, we're business partners, we're friends. I think. And: Well, I couldn't do it, she said, because it was confidential, we had a confidential agreement with Penney's, so I was not allowed to talk to you. That was her response.
>
> And so then she went back to—and it seemed to me like she was reading a document when she was on the phone. So I said, you know—which sounded like it was prepared by lawyers frankly, and so I said, after some minutes, I finally said: This conversation is over, and I hung up the phone. I can't remember ever hanging up on anyone in my life, but that's how frustrated and disappointed I was with Martha Stewart with that phone call, and so I did hang up on her.
>
> Q. Did she say the effect that this would have on Macy's?
>
> A. She said this was going to be good for Macy's. I think that's when I hung up actually, because the thought of how this could be good for Macy's was just so far away from anything that I could comprehend and still could comprehend. I think that's the point when I hung up.

Macy's counsel then read the following to Mr. Lundgren, which was an email Mr. Lundgren wrote to Jim Slucewski, Macy's communications person, right after his telephone conversation with Ms. Stewart:

> "They will open Martha shops in their stores and do an online catalogue with crafts and other Martha products. She hopes we will continue to support her. I told her I was shocked, appalled and disgusted that she would not come to us first with the opportunity to counter, especially since her business problems have nothing to do with us. We have done everything for her and been totally loyal. She said they had to do something since the company is failing, with negative earnings, and she couldn't talk to us during the process since it was confidential. She wants to come in and talk face to face, but I told her I was busy with the board meeting and need time to digest this."
>
> Q. How were you feeling as you wrote this e-mail?
>
> A. As the words say, I was very upset. This was such a shock to me, and I was certain it was going to be a shock to my executive team who had this relationship with the company and with Martha herself. So I was literally sick to my stomach about this. It was just something I couldn't imagine.

The entire Macy's team shared those sentiments when they heard the news. Laurene Gandolfo, MMG's Executive Vice President for Home Private Brands, who worked primarily with MSLO, bluntly stated, "I felt like somebody just stabbed me in the heart, and I didn't know why."

On December 7, 2011, JCP and MSLO publicly announced their new business relationship: MSLO had entered into what it called a "strategic alliance" with JCP.

Pursuant to this "strategic alliance," JCP would purchase a 16.6% equity stake in MSLO and receive two seats on the MSLO board in exchange for a $38.5 million investment in the company. MSLO and JCP also announced their above-mentioned licensing agreement, dated December 6, 2011.

The Aftermath

JCP's view of what had transpired over those last two days can be described as nothing short of sophomoric. Incredibly, ignoring the seriousness of what had just transpired, Mr. Johnson wrote to William Ackman and Steven Roth, JCP board members who controlled the largest and second largest blocks of JCP shares, respectively, the following emails:

To Mr. Ackman:

> Media good as well. We put Terry [Lundgren] in a corner. Normally when that happens and you get someone on the defensive they make bad decisions. This is good.

To Mr. Roth:

> Terry clearly stewing . . . he might simply walk. I'm inclined to let the press run and let him stew for a bit. The more this is seen as brilliant for JCP and Martha the more he won't want to interfere. He will say "go to the masses . . . I'm too good for her." Thank you for your help on getting this accomplished.

A number of other emails from that time period among senior executives at JCP—Mr. Johnson, Steve Lawrence, and Michael Francis—expressed unabashed giddiness at the discomfort they thought the JCP/MSLO agreement would bring to Macy's:

From Steve Lawrence to Mr. Johnson:

> I appreciate your support and I am excited to be part of the team that will re-shape department store retail. On a side note, sounds like Macy's is pretty unhappy with the Martha deal . . . :-(

From Mr. Johnson to Steve Lawrence:

> I am so sad. It is always good to be playing offense. I like the fact that we have everyone watching and paying attention. I'm sure Macy's is in shock and it must be a bit embarrassing. They look asleep at the wheel.

From Mr. Johnson to Michael Francis:

> Terry might have a headache tonight . . . wait until 1/24. It will be a full on migraine:)

From Mr. Francis to Mr. Johnson:

> I think Terry is more likely to race past migraine into grand mal seizure!

Such childish behavior displayed by these individuals is unbecoming of top executives of a major corporation, and is nothing to be proud of, particularly given the stakes. Putting that behavior aside, the clear aim of such incredible pressure was to push Macy's and Mr. Lundgren in the direction that they had taken with Liz Claiborne, namely, to walk away from Macy's' right of renewal with MSLO, which is why JCP and MSLO provided for sales to begin in February 2013, immediately after the expiration of the first five year term of the Macy's/MSLO agreement. Unbeknownst to Mr. Lundgren and Macy's, Mr. Johnson's attitude towards them with respect to JCP's budding relationship with MSLO was take it or leave it. Mr. Johnson aptly described the scene as making JCP's "offensive so strong" that Macy's would "simply pick up their toys and go home". JCP and Mr. Johnson could not have been more wrong.

Faced with this Hobson's choice, Mr. Lundgren exercised Macy's renewal right, which Ms. Stewart expressly accepted, and commenced litigation against MSLO and JCP to enforce and protect Macy's contractual rights.

The Claims

Macy's asserted two causes of action against MSLO: 1) breach of contract in that MSLO, in derogation of its duty of good faith and fair dealing, challenged Macy's unilateral renewal rights pursuant to the Macy's Agreement; and 2) breach of contract in that MSLO disclosed to JCP confidential information in violation of section 22(a) of the Macy's Agreement.

As against JCP, Macy's asserted three causes of action: 1) tortious interference with Macy's contract by inducing MSLO to challenge Macy's unilateral renewal rights under the Macy's Agreement; 2) tortious interference with section 22(a) of the Macy's Agreement by inducing MSLO to disclose to JCP confidential information; and 3) unfair competition.

Strange Bedfellows

After entering into the JCP/MSLO agreement, and subsequent to Macy's commencement of its action against MSLO, JCP and MSLO took steps to implement the terms of their agreement. In particular, they began conceptualizing and designing the MSLO Store within JCP. By spring of 2012, Black, Inc., a design firm, had created conceptual designs for a large, four-walled, freestanding, prominently branded Martha Stewart store inside JCP with sections dedicated to Martha Stewart kitchen, bedding, and bath products.

In addition, the product development process "started right away". Between December 2011 and July 2012, MSLO developed and provided JCP approximately 900 designs for products within Macy's Exclusive Product Categories. The parties do not dispute that when MSLO created those designs, and when JCP received them, both MSLO and JCP intended that the designed products would be branded with a Martha Stewart trademark pursuant to the JCP/MSLO agreement.

At the same time, while all this activity was going on between MSLO and JCP, MSLO continued to work closely with Macy's to develop designs for Macy's 2013 season, providing all the designs that Macy's requested and needed. In fact, shortly before trial of these actions began, Ms. Gandolfo informed Patsy Pollack, MSLO's senior executive vice president of merchandising, that the 2012 design presentations were the best that she had ever seen from MSLO.

The Judicial Proceedings—July and August 2012
Preliminary Injunction

On July 13, 2012, after oral argument, I granted Macy's motion for a preliminary injunction against MSLO. Specifically, I enjoined and restrained MSLO during the pendency of Macy's action against it from performing under the agreement between MSLO and J.C. Penney Corporation, Inc.

On August 30, 2012, I heard arguments on Macy's motion for a preliminary injunction against JCP. During oral argument, I was compelled to make the following observation:

> Three blue chip companies on the stock exchange, publicly traded companies that are really . . . part of the fabric of this country . . . go into this nasty fight right now about contracts. Not only are vendors confused, but you have workers and employees that are concerned as to what is going on.
>
> J.C. Penney right now is fighting to survive. You turn the pages of the Financial Times or the financial news and Mr. Johnson is batting away, trying to resurrect J.C. Penney.

In the end, I denied Macy's motion for a preliminary injunction against JCP, particularly in view of JCP's voluntary agreement to abide by the terms of the preliminary injunction issued against MSLO.

The April 2013 Preliminary Injunction

In accordance with my preliminary injunction order, and JCP's agreement to abide by that order, JCP stopped orders for "Martha Stewart" branded products in the Exclusive Product Categories, but began a process for placing orders to manufacture the products branded with the "jcp Everyday" mark along with the "Double House" logo (the "JCP products").

On April 12, 2013, at the close of Macy's case-in-chief, Macy's made another application for a preliminary injunction against JCP, which was necessitated because JCP sought to sell the JCP products. Macy's also sought additional injunctive reliefs against MSLO.

As for MSLO, I granted Macy's motion to the extent of incorporating my prior preliminary injunction order it obtained against MSLO.

Trial Proceedings

I heard closing arguments on August 1, 2013. The place settings have dramatically changed since that time.

The Game Changer

While this matter was *sub judice,* two significant events took place. MSLO and JCP agreed that JCP would no longer manufacture and sell products designed by

MSLO—branded or unbranded—in the Exclusive Product Categories. Put simply, JCP's deal with MSLO was over.

The other significant event was Macy's decision to settle its dispute with MSLO.

Macy's, however, has not been as magnanimous with JCP. Macy's continues to assert that JCP is liable to it for tortious interference with its contract with MSLO.

Analysis

The Relevant Terms of the Macy's/MSLO Agreement

The Macy's/MSLO agreement provided for an initial five-year term, a unilateral renewal right to Macy's for an additional five-year term, and five additional two-year renewal terms. While the agreement granted Macy's a license for certain Martha Stewart marks and certain designs created by MSLO in collaboration with Macy's, MSLO retained ownership of its designs and its intellectual property.

Section 1 defines "exclusive product category" as items set forth in Exhibit A to the agreement: soft home (bedding, bath & kitchen textiles), housewares (dinnerware, tabletop & gadgets), home decor (candles & frames), and cookware. That section also sets forth the definitions of key terms. "Exclusive Product" means "those products in the Exclusive Product Categories that are branded under the Trademark, manufactured by [Macy's], and marketed and sold by [Macy's] or, under the conditions set forth herein, through an MSLO DTC Channel."

The key sections that are at the heart of this dispute are section 2, entitled "Grant; Exclusivity," which provides Macy's with licensing rights over the Martha Stewart marks, and section 4, entitled "Product Development and Design," which directs that "as an integral part of this Agreement" MSLO shall develop both "designs" and "concepts" for goods in Macy's Exclusive Product Categories. That section further directs that MSLO undertake this work "in collaboration with [Macy's]" and that "each Party's design personnel shall work in cooperation with each other and with the manufacturing personnel of [Macy's]."

The exclusivity granted by MSLO to Macy's is subject to section 8, entitled "Manufacturing, Production, Projections and Distribution," which provides, *inter alia*, for the operation of a MSLO Store. Lastly, section 18, entitled "Additional Covenants," sets forth, *inter alia*, MSLO's non-compete obligations. Specifically, with the exception of an MSLO Store, section 18(b) prohibits MSLO from entering in any agreement with "any department store or manufacturer or other retailer of department store merchandise" to compete with Macy's within the Exclusive Product Categories.

The Relevant Terms of the JCP/MSLO Agreement

The JCP/MSLO agreement provides that JCP would commence selling MSLO designed products bearing the Martha Stewart marks in JCP department stores and through an independent e-commerce site that MSLO and JCP would jointly develop. The agreement, like the Macy's/MSLO agreement, provides for MSLO to design and JCP to source and sell Martha Stewart-branded products in the Macy's exclusive product categories as well as in certain non exclusive product lines. According to a press release, these products would be sold in "distinct Martha Stewart retail stores inside the majority of J.C. Penney department stores," and "J.C. Penney [would] market and source the products". The press release further stated that MSLO "expected to receive in excess of $200 million from J.C. Penney over the initial 10-year contract period".

The JCP/MSLO agreement also provides that JCP would pay for the design and construction of "MSLO Stores," which would then be a focal point for the JCP Home Store in approximately 600 JCP department stores. Additionally, the agreement provides that with respect to these stores JCP has the sole right to hire and terminate employees, that JCP would bear the expenses of the MSLO Stores, and that MSLO agrees not to open any MSLO Store that sells kitchen products or other products in any category that becomes exclusive to JCP. More specifically, JCP would source the Martha Stewart goods, own the inventory, and sell the products in a space owned or leased by JCP, employ the sales personnel, book the revenue from the sales of products in the Martha Stewart stores, and essentially bear all the risks.

A careful review of the Macy's/MSLO and JCP/MSLO agreements demonstrates that they are irreconcilable and incompatible—both claim to have exclusivity over virtually the same product categories. In light of this conundrum, the question then is whether JCP can be held liable for tortious interference with Macy's contract with MSLO.

I. Tortious Interference Claim

In order to establish this claim, Macy's must prove 1) that it had a valid contract with MSLO, 2) that JCP had knowledge of Macy's contract with MSLO, the specific terms of which need not have been known by JCP, 3) that JCP intentionally induced MSLO to breach its contract with Macy's, 4) that MSLO breached its contract with Macy's, 5) that MSLO would not have breached its contract with Macy's absent JCP's conduct, and 6) that Macy's sustained damages.

Although MSLO did not actually "break" its contract with Macy's, which facially undermines Macy's tort claim against JCP, the questions to be decided are whether by entering into the JCP/MSLO agreement MSLO breached certain terms set forth in the Macy's/MSLO agreement, and whether JCP induced MSLO to enter the JCP/MSLO agreement. Of course, the threshold issue is whether there was a breach because without it Macy's tort claim must fail.

A. MSLO's and JCP's Omnibus defenses

(i) The Good For Macy's Defense

MSLO's attempted justification that the JCP/MSLO agreement creating a "strategic alliance" with JCP would be "good for Macy's" is pure sophistry. Indeed, when Ms. Stewart made that point to Mr. Lundgren, his reaction was simple—he hung up on her. Likewise, Mr. Marcus testified that he recalled Ms. Gersh telling him that "some people believe" sales at Macy's "will actually go up" as a result of the "strategic alliance," but that he was unwilling to accept that "illogical" argument—as he explained, if a customer "can go to Penney's or . . . to Macy's" to buy the same product, "[h]ow is that not going to hurt sales?". Under these circumstances, I easily reject this defense.

(ii) Macy's breached the Macy's/MSLO agreement

If the "good for Macy's defense" is incredible, the next argument that Macy's breached the parties' agreement is disingenuous. Here, the trial evidence clearly establishes that MSLO did not enter into the JCP/MSLO agreement on the ground that Macy's was in breach of the Macy's/MSLO agreement, and MSLO raised this defense only after Macy's commenced this action against it. Indeed, if this defense were tenable, MSLO could have blocked Macy's January 23, 2012 renewal—section 3(b)(i) bars Macy's renewal if it were in breach of the agreement. Rather, the trial evidence demonstrates that MSLO and Ms. Stewart were pleased with the renewal, publicly stating: MSLO has had a "very excellent relationship with Macy's", "[w]e love working with" Macy's, "Macy's has been a very nice partner" and MSLO's relationship with Macy's "should continue" into the future. Indeed, shortly after the renewal, Ms. Stewart proudly stated on CNBC that Macy's extended its contract with MSLO, and that it "now runs through 2018." With these undeniably consistent statements indicating that Macy's was not in breach of the Macy's/MSLO agreement, I reject this defense.

B. Breach of Contract

Although the parties focused much of their witnesses' testimony and trial evidence on what Macy's and MSLO wanted, intended, or believed to be the "essence" of the Macy's/MSLO agreement when the contract was negotiated, none of this evidence is relevant to the interpretation of the contract unless I first find that the agreement is ambiguous. The principle is well settled that parol evidence of what the parties intended cannot be considered when interpreting an unambiguous contract.

Whether a contract is ambiguous is, of course, a question of law for a court. A contract is ambiguous only if on its face it is reasonably susceptible of more than one interpretation. Only when a contract is found to be ambiguous will a court look to extrinsic evidence to resolve the ambiguity. If the contract on its face is reasonably susceptible to only one meaning, a court is not free to alter the contract to reflect its personal notions of fairness and equity. Here, Macy's and MSLO agree that the Macy's/MSLO agreement is unambiguous.

(i) The Store within a Store Exception

MSLO and JCP's foundational argument that the JCP/MSLO agreement did not violate the terms of the Macy's/MSLO agreement rests on the interpretation of the term "MSLO Store." MSLO and JCP forcefully argue that the Macy's/MSLO agreement provides a carve-out from exclusivity for an MSLO Store, and that JCP's creation of MSLO Stores within JCP stores is therefore permissible.

To be sure, the Macy's/MSLO agreement permits MSLO to compete with Macy's in limited circumstances under certain conditions, namely, by way of an MSLO

Store. The question is whether the "MSLO Store" contemplated in the JCP/MSLO agreement falls within this permissible exception. The parties overlook the obvious in arguing this issue.

An MSLO Store is defined as "any retail store branded with Martha Stewart Marks or Stewart Property that is owned or operated by MSLO or an Affiliate of MSLO or that otherwise prominently features Martha Stewart Marks or Stewart Property." Whether or not the MSLO Store in the JCP/MSLO agreement is a "retail store" is not dispositive. Indeed, contrary to Macy's argument, the MSLO Store contemplated by the JCP/MSLO agreement has all the indicia of a retail store, *i.e.*, four walls, cash registers, store counters, salespersons. Further, although it is not "owned or operated by MSLO or an Affiliate of MSLO," it does "otherwise prominently feature[] Martha Stewart Marks or Stewart Property." Ostensibly, under Mr. Taitz's historical account, the MSLO Store contemplated by the JCP/MSLO agreement is permissible under the Macy's/MSLO agreement. Not so fast.

Here, with respect to the operational aspect, MSLO's and JCP's relationship under the JCP/MSLO agreement would operate in essentially an identical manner to the way Macy's and MSLO operated pursuant to their agreement. In that regard, MSLO would collaborate with JCP on the design process, product assortment, packaging and advertising for the licensed goods in exchange for royalties calculated as a percentage of sales, but JCP would manufacture the goods, own the goods, design and construct the display areas, stock the shelves, control the displays, employ the sales personnel, own the sales space, and book the sales and revenues. Indeed, Mr. Johnson testified as much: MSLO would not own or rent retail space from JCP; JCP, not MSLO, would source the goods; JCP would hire the staff; JCP would own the goods sold in the stores and maintain the inventory; JCP would book the sales as revenue; JCP would price the goods; JCP would decide when products would go on sale; and JCP would bear all risk of loss.

I find this operational framework for the MSLO Store violates section 18(b), entitled "Non-Competition by MSLO," of the Macy's/MSLO agreement. Although the Macy's/MSLO agreement contemplates potential competition between MSLO and Macy's by way of an MSLO Store, section 18(b) is clear and unambiguous—it prohibits MSLO from entering into any agreement "with any department store . . . that promotes the sale of any items . . . within the Exclusive Product Categories that are branded with the Trademark or any Martha Stewart Mark."

(ii) Exclusivity of Designs

To be clear, the evidence clearly demonstrates that the Macy's/MSLO agreement is not and never has been a personal service contract. It is and has always been a licensing agreement providing Macy's with the exclusive right to exploit the Martha Stewart trademark in certain circumstances. Also, there is no dispute that Macy's does not own the designs, but that MSLO always retained ownership of its designs and its intellectual property. Indeed, the Macy's/MSLO agreement provides Macy's with the exclusive right to license and use the Martha Stewart trademark for

Exclusive Products within the Exclusive Product Categories. Exclusive Products are defined as products in the Exclusive Product Categories that are Martha Stewart branded.

MSLO and JCP argue that the Macy's/MSLO agreement did not give Macy's the exclusive right to MSLO's designs for products in the Exclusive Product Categories that will not bear any Martha Stewart mark. Contrary to their position, for the reasons that follow, whether or not a product falling within the Exclusive Product Category bears a Martha Stewart mark is not relevant to the disposition of the issue of design exclusivity. The critical issue is whether Macy's has exclusivity over designs produced by MSLO in the Exclusive Product Categories—before a product is considered for branding or not. This issue is sharply disputed.

MSLO argues that there is no wording in the agreement that provides that MSLO can only design for Macy's and cannot design for others. In fact, MSLO and JCP argue that the Macy's/MSLO agreement contains no prohibition on MSLO designing for JCP and JCP selling products in the Exclusive Product Categories branded with the "jcp Everyday" mark, or on designing products that were not developed in collaboration with Macy's "in accordance with the merchandising plan mutually agreed to by" Macy's and MSLO.

While not explicitly precluding MSLOs design arrangement with JCP, that arrangement clearly violates section 18(b)'s non-compete provisions. Section 4, entitled "Product Development and Design," covers MSLO's activities in the area of the Exclusive Product Categories. That section requires MSLO to establish:

> . . . concepts, designs and product selections in collaboration with [Macy's] (the "*Design Direction*") for the Exclusive Products and any Branded Non-Exclusive Products to be manufactured by [Macy's] (together, the "*Macy's Manufactured Products*") and each Party's design personnel shall work in cooperation with each other and with the manufacturing personnel of [Macy's] (including, without limitation, [Macy's] vendors of Exclusive Products) to design and create Macy's Manufactured Products consistent with the Design Direction established by MSLO in collaboration with [Macy's]. . . . (emphasis in the original).

This collaborative and cooperative structure is critical to implementing section 2(a)(iii). Thus, MSLO is required to provide all designs "developed by MSLO in connection with" the design and conceptual activities of section 4. Further, section 2(b)(ii) expressly prohibits MSLO from entering into any agreement allowing anyone else to use its product designs in regard to its section 4 activities (*i.e.*, the "Licensed Property") in connection with the manufacture, marketing, distribution, and sale of any items in the Exclusive Product Categories, regardless of branding.

After reading and reviewing these sections collectively, the simple fact is that the Macy's/MSLO agreement provides for exclusivity of items in the Exclusive Product Categories.

Nonetheless, MSLO argues:

> Macy's argument that Section 4 should be read to *imply* a sweeping bar on MSLO's design activities for other partners cannot be reconciled with the 28-page Agreement, which is extremely detailed and explicit about what the parties can and cannot do. It is inconceivable that the parties to this carefully drawn contract would agree to something as momentous as a categorical ban on MSLO designing in the Exclusive Product Categories—that is, a provision precluding MSLO from an entire area of potential business growth—and then not explicitly say that, but leave it to *post hoc* inference and implication.

In making this argument, MSLO apparently suffers a memory lapse with respect to Macy's concerns during the 2005 negotiations, *i.e.,* all the above-noted significant risks that Macy's had to undertake in entering into a relationship with MSLO. Clearly, this restriction was not inconceivable. Moreover, as the parties concede that the Macy's/MSLO agreement is unambiguous, I cannot draw any inference from the absence of such a provision, but must accept the terms as written.

In a last-ditch effort, JCP posits that Macy's and MSLO's pre-dispute course of dealing proves that the parties always understood that MSLO could design products within the "Exclusive Product Categories" for others, under names unrelated to Martha Stewart. As evidence, JCP points to the fact that "since at least 2008, MSLO has designed products in the Exclusive Product Categories for [celebrity chef] Emeril Lagasse under the name 'Emeril' without complaint from Macy's". JCP further points out that although Macy's was aware that the Emeril brand was owned and controlled by MSLO (Trial Tr. 683:13–18) it never raised any complaints that MSLO was designing those products in violation of the Macy's/MSLO agreement. JCP, thus, reasons that Macy's silence "is plain: Macy's did not complain because 'Emeril' was not sold using a Martha Stewart Mark" (JCP Post-Trial Brief, p. 28). JCP's argument is unavailing. In taking this position, JCP overlooks the clear "No Waiver of Rights" provision found in Macy's/MSLO Agreement.

In short, whether Macy's did or did not object to MSLO designing items for the Emeril brand has no bearing on the instant dispute. Thus, I find that the Macy's/MSLO agreement provides Macy's with exclusivity over MSLO's designs in the Exclusive Product Categories, and that by entering into the JCP/MSLO agreement MSLO breached its contractual obligation owed to Macy's pursuant to their agreement.

C. Inducement of the Breach

Having determined that there is a breach, the next issue to resolve is whether JCP induced it. The preponderance of trial evidence overwhelmingly establishes that JCP intentionally induced MSLO to enter into their agreement, and that MSLO would not have done so absent JCP's conduct. Specifically, JCP offered Ms. Stewart both flattery and large financial inducements. Mr. Johnson told Ms. Stewart that she was not realizing her potential with Macy's, and that JCP could "take her to a whole new level", and "rightfully place Martha where she belongs as the unquestioned authority for living of our generation". JCP told her that no one else could offer what JCP was offering. And, as soon as MSLO informed JCP that its financial proposals were too low, and that MSLO "would not give up Macy's for relatively little gain", JCP immediately improved its offer to get MSLO to do the deal.

Although the procurement of the breach was intentional, the critical issue is whether Macy's has proven that the breach herein would not have occurred but for JCP's activities. The uncontested facts underscore how "over the top" Mr. Johnson's and his team's conduct and relentless efforts were in JCP's pursuit of MSLO and Ms. Stewart—conduct and efforts that the JCP board endorsed. Under these circumstances, the preponderance of the evidence compels me to find that JCP's "inducement exceeded the minimum level of ethical behavior in the marketplace," and, as such, was improper. Macy's has established JCP's liability for tortious interference with its contract with MSLO.

II. Remedies/Damages

Damages

In July 2012, I enjoined MSLO from allowing JCP to sell goods in the Exclusive Product Categories with a Martha Stewart Brand in an MSLO Store located within a JCP store. Given that MSLO and JCP have complied with that directive, Macy's suffered no lost profits on that theory.

As to Macy's other claimed damages, the only one that bears consideration is the dispute over the 900 designs, which MSLO prepared for JCP pursuant to the JCP/MSLO agreement. The question is how much of those designs, if any, were influenced from the knowledge MSLO obtained through its collaborative relationship with Macy's and used in its collaboration with JCP. That issue will necessarily require discovery concerning the 900 designs to determine what influence, if any, did Macy's collaborative efforts with MSLO have on MSLO's designs for JCP. Accordingly, this damage issue is respectfully referred to a Special Referee/Judicial Hearing Officer to hear and report.

If one were to say that a finding of no liability for punitive damages would be to let JCP get off easy, consider the following facts.

Mr. Lundgren and Macy's, the loyal and unsuspecting partners, have been vindicated. JCP terminated Mr. Johnson on April 8, 2013, before this trial ended, a casualty of his own hubris. JCP, its board of directors, and its top executives were publicly ridiculed and humiliated as a consequence of this trial. Their grand strategy was a colossal and abject retail failure. The termination of JCP's "strategic alliance" with MSLO and Ms. Stewart underscored how ill-conceived it was, to the point where it placed JCP on the verge of financial collapse. I find that these significant facts are a sufficient deterrent to JCP and other companies from acting in a similar way in the future. Based on the foregoing, I find that Macy's failed to prove by "clear, unequivocal and convincing evidence" that it is entitled to a punitive damage award against JCP.

Accordingly, it is

ORDERED and ADJUDGED that defendant, J.C. Penney, tortiously interfered with plaintiffs', Macy's, Inc. and Macy's Merchandising Group, Inc., agreement with defendant, Martha Stewart Living Omnimedia, Inc.

Notes

1. The definitions of "exclusive" and "store" are at the heart of the Martha Stewart/Macy's/J.C. Penney case. Macy's financial risk in entering into the Macy's/MSLO license agreement after Ms. Stewart's criminal conviction and jail term and after MSLO's declining sales at Kmart, her former partner, were motivations underlying Macy's requirement of long-term exclusivity. The risk paid off for Macy's with sales of the Martha Stewart collection increasing annually. Robin Marino, Martha Stewart's president of merchandising in 2005, at the time the license agreement was entered into, had come up through the Macy's training program as a young merchant and was able to convince Macy's to take this risk with Martha Stewart.

2. In 2011, J.C. Penney hired a new CEO, Ron Johnson, who was well known for his "successful development and implementation of the Apple Store" and for brilliant merchandising at Target, which at that time was the star of the "big box" stores (like Walmart and Kmart). Without notifying Macy's, Martha Stewart retained The Blackstone Group to explore "strategic partnerships" in order to further strengthen the brand. Mr. Johnson met with Ms. Stewart and the new CEO of MSLO with the goal of proposing "a deal so she can go to" Macy's and "break their agreement." With Macy's right to renew the Martha Stewart license agreement fast approaching, Mr. Johnson pulled out all the stops to land Martha Stewart as a cornerstone of his vision of 20 home product shop-in-shops in the new J.C. Penney anchored by Martha Stewart.

3. The crucial "carve out" provision in MSLO/Macy's license agreement permitted MSLO to sell through Martha Stewart branded "stores." Martha Stewart's new General Counsel opined that the definition of "store" included the J.C. Penney shop-in-shop concept. J.C. Penney's grand plan to "reshape department store retail" with the shop-in-shop concept did not materialize and Mr. Johnson left the company. The emails between the parties, extensively quoted by Judge Oing, were characterized as "childish" and "unbecoming of top executives of a major corporation . . . given the status between J.C. Penney board members and Mr. Johnson."

4. When drafting language related to termination of a license agreement, the licensor/brand owner must contemplate the time it may take to identify and set up a new licensee, including time to review designs and samples. In this case, Martha Stewart announced its new license with J.C. Penney on December 6, 2011, breaking the news to Macy's that day. The design process between the two companies overlapped, leading to claims related to disclosure of confidential information related to such designs. Were designs created for Macy's shared with J.C. Penney?

K. Collaborations in the Fashion Business

"All the world's a stage,
And all the men and women merely players;
They have their exits and their entrances;
And one man in his time plays many parts,
His acts being seven ages."

—William Shakespeare, *As You Like It*

Trademark licensing has been, and continues to be, the established business model embraced by fashion companies to exploit and monetize the strength of their brands. Over the years, however, classic licensing in the fashion industry has evolved. Brand owners, fashion houses, and retailers alike have sought another means to effectively achieve a similar goal—"collaborations." Collaborations can be thought of as co-branding, where two distinct players—perhaps, even, from different industries—come together to leverage their brand value and commercial strength to develop products branded with their respective trademarks.

A stunning example is the collaboration between two influential powerhouses, with rich legacies in their respective industries—Prada and Adidas. These two timeless iconic brands joined forces, each bringing their unique expertise to launch a long-term collaboration to "investigate the realms of heritage, technology and innovation—and to challenge conventional wisdom through unexpected strategies."[110] Prada and Adidas are leveraging their brand value in the luxury and sportswear industries, respectfully, to design, manufacture, promote, and sell fashion-forward products under the label "Prada for Adidas," and on social media announced the hashtag #pradaforadidas.[111]

And Dior is not too far behind in the luxury-sports industry collaborations. Recently, Christian Dior, the famous atelier founded in 1947, and now a luxury brand that is among the crown jewels of LVMH Moet Hënnessy Louis Vuitton,[112] collaborated with megabrand Nike and its Air Jordan line to create the Air Jordan 1 High OG Dior sneaker. Although launching initially with this one product, it appears that this is just the beginning of a unique partnership.[113]

Collaborations, however, are not necessarily a new phenomenon in the fashion industry. As early as 1965, Yves Saint Laurent collaborated on a dress series using Mondrian art,[114] and Andy Warhol collaborated with Campbell's Soup Company on

---

110. *See* Luisa Zargani, *Prada, Adidas Partner Up on Long-Term Collaboration,* WWD 1 (Nov. 8, 2019).

111. *Id.* at 13. *See also* Luisa Zargani, *Prada and Adidas Unveil First Set of Bag, Sneakers,* WWD 5 (Nov. 25, 2019).

112. *See* LVMH, https://www.lvmh.com/ (last visited Nov. 17, 2019).

113. *See* Obi Anyanwu, *Dior, Jordan Debut Collaboration Sneakers,* WWD 24 (Dec. 4, 2019).

114. *1966: Homage to Pop Art,* Musée Yves Saint Laurent Paris, https://museeyslparis.com/en/biography/hommage-au-pop-art (last visited Oct. 22, 2019).

the "Souper Dress" collection, which was a line of A-line dresses covered from neck to hemline in images of the Campbell's soup cans Warhol photographed.[115] Strategically, collaborations such as the unlikely marriage between an established luxury brand and legendary artist, or between a food company and a pop artist extraordinaire to form a fashion collection, spark intrigue, exclusivity, and appeal. That is the essence of collaborations in the fashion industry as a brand-building business model.[116]

Collaborations in the fashion industry boast celebrity and there is an allure to entering into such ventures. Indeed, Tommy Hilfiger was awarded *Collaborator of the Year* by Footwear News, acknowledging the celebrity fashion designer for his numerous collaborative collections with actresses, singers, and models including Zendaya, Gigi Hadid, and several hip hop and rock groups.[117] Brands exploit collaborations in this manner to enter into new markets as well. For example, Adidas, whose collaboration with Prada established a footprint in Italy with a luxury fashion house,[118] plans to obtain a "bigger chunk of the American market" by launching a high-profile product line with Beyoncé, consisting of performance and athleisure wear.[119] Such collaborations breed hunger. It is the company's vision "to be the best sports brand in the world, and to do that, we have to win in America."[120]

Typically, such collaborations are built upon limited edition lines, also known as "capsule collections,"[121] promoting a partnership between a retailer and a famous brand

---

115. *See The Marriage of Art and Fashion*, ARTDEX BLOG (Mar. 6, 2017), https://www.blog.artdex.com/art-world/marriage-art-fashion/.

116. Other classic examples of collaborations or co-branding deals between fashion houses, famous brands, and retailers include Stella McCartney for Adidas, Richard Chai for Original Penguin by Munsingwear, Florsheim by Duckie Brown, Karl Lagerfeld for Macy's, Lanvin for H&M, Rodarte for Target. Collaborations are also popular with companies completely outside of the fashion industry, e.g., Nike-Apple, Lexus-Coach, Adidas-Porsche. *See generally* Hand, *supra* note 5.

117. *See* Thomas Walle, *FN Achievement Awards Honor Kerby Jean-Raymond, J Balvin,* WWD 19 (Dec. 5, 2019).

118. *See supra* note 111.

119. *See* Jean E. Palmieri & Rosemary Feitelberg, *Adidas Seeking Higher Profile in American Market*, WWD 5 (Dec. 6, 2019). Adidas also has a robust stable with celebrity collections including Pharrell Williams, Kanye West, and Stella McCartney. *Id. See also* Kellie Ell, *Luxury Growing Place in The Ath-leisure Ecosystem,* WWD 4 (Jan. 2, 2020) (discussing the extension of mainstream athleisure brands into the luxury market and Adidas' athleisurewear collaborations with Stella McCartney and Ivy Park, Beyoncé's line).

120. Palmieri & Feitelberg, *supra* note 120 (quoting Zion Armstrong, Adidas' North American president).

121. *See, e.g.*, Joelle Diderich & Obi Anyanwu, *The Next "League of Legends" Champions Will Wear Louis Vuitton*, WWD 5 (Sept. 23, 2019) (Louis Vuitton has collaborated with streetwear brand Supreme to create a capsule ready-to-wear collection and a trophy case in connection with the League of Legends World Championship); Sharon Edelson, *Zadig & Voltaire Hooks Up With Kate Moss for Handbag Line and More*, WWD 6 (Aug. 26, 2019) (Zadig & Voltaire has partnered with Kate Moss for a handbag collection, Zadig & Voltaire x Kate Moss); Luisa Zargani, *Fendi to Introduce Capsule with Nicki Minaj*, WWD 2 (Sept. 9, 2019) (Fendi has introduced a capsule collection with Nicki Minaj called Fendi Prints On).

or persona, especially musicians, models, and actors. A retailer will likely look to collaborations to grow its customer demographic while its celebrity partner may look to exploit her personal fame to enter into a new business arena and to develop a fashion brand.[122] It is also common for companies to partner with famous athletes who may appeal to a certain segment and unique customer—for example, Shaquille O'Neal's XLG line for big and tall apparel exclusively for J.C. Penney;[123] Roger Federer for Rolex's "Every Rolex Tells a Story" campaign;[124] and Julian Edelman's capsule collection for Joe's Jeans.[125] Often, retailers and fashion companies seek to partner with celebrities who organically "fit in" with the company's brand image, which beckons instantaneous magnetism and a genuine endorsement of the products that are the focus of the collaboration. This has been evidenced by supermodel Kate Moss' multiple international collections for Topshop,[126] actress Zoe Kravitz's six-lipstick line Rouge Pur Couture for YSL Beauté promoting the expression of female individuality,[127] and rapper/art collector

---

122. In recent times, we have seen celebrities turn their names into trademarks, sometimes through licensing arrangements and others through collaborations, and used in connection with the development of a fashion business in several product categories. *See, e.g.*, Bloomberg, *How Jessica Simpson Built a Billion-Dollar Fashion Empire*, Bus. of Fashion (Apr. 7, 2015, 9:00 AM), https://www.businessoffashion.com/community/voices/discussions/are-celebrity-labels-good-for-fashion/how-jessica-simpson-built-a-billion-dollar-fashion-empire (Jessica Simpson developed a line of apparel, among many other product categories, that targets women of nearly all segments in the marketplace); Alexandra Gibbs, *Kate Hudson on Fabletics: I Wanted to Create a Brand That Was More about Lifestyle than Fitness*, CNBC (Apr. 20, 2018, 8:06 AM), https://www.cnbc.com/2018/04/20/actor-and-businesswoman-kate-hudson-on-fabletics-and-taking-business-risks.html (Kate Hudson for Fabletics, who developed a brand of athletic wear); Natalie Robehmed, *How Rihanna Created A $600 Million Fortune—And Became The World's Richest Female Musician*, Forbes (June 4, 2019, 8:38 AM), https://www.forbes.com/sites/natalierobehmed/2019/06/04/rihanna-worth-fenty-beauty/ (Rihanna, for Fenty, who went on to develop a lingerie, makeup, and apparel line in collaboration with LVMH); UNKNWN, https://www.unknwn.com (last visited Oct. 25, 2019) (LeBron James for Unknwn, launching and associating his name as a Miami-based designer, street, and lifestyle retail destination for men and women). Unknwn recently collaborated with award-winning menswear fashion designer, Thom Brown, known to have a long-standing relationship with the NBA superstar, on a capsule collection to launch in December 2019. *See* Obi Anyanwu, *Joining Lebron's Team*, WWD 23 (Oct. 25, 2019).

123. JCPenney Company, *JCPenney Elevates Big & Tall with Shaquille O'Neal Partnership*, JCPenney Company Blog (Mar. 27, 2018), https://companyblog.jcpnewsroom.com/2018/03/27/jcpenney-elevates-big-tall-with-shaquille-oneal-partnership/.

124. *Every Rolex Tells a Story: Roger Federer*, Rolex, https://www.rolex.com/every-rolex-tells-a-story/roger-federer-rolex-watch.html (last visited Oct. 22, 2019).

125. Abby Bielagus, *Get Inside Julian Edelman's Pants*, Boston Mag. (Mar. 1, 2019, 4:57 PM), https://www.bostonmagazine.com/life-style/2019/03/01/julian-edelman-joes-jeans/.

126. *See* Julia Neel, *Moss, Topshop Set New Collection*, WWD 2 (Oct. 7, 2013); WWD Staff, *Topshop Kisses Kate: U.K. Retailer to Launch Fashion Line by Moss*, WWD 1–5 (Sept. 20, 2006).

127. Rachel Lubitz, *Zoë Kravitz's First Move At YSL Was Naming a Lipstick After Her Dog*, Refinery29 (Aug. 21, 2019, 1:00 PM), https://www.refinery29.com/en-us/2019/08/240953/zoe-kravitz-ysl-beauty-lipstick-collection.

Swizz Beatz' multiple collaborations with Bally and Faith Connexion promoting the integration of fashion and art.[128]

1. The Quintessential Collaborator: Sarah Jessica Parker: From Actor to Lifestyle Brand

Best known for playing the writer and "fashionista" Carrie Bradshaw on *Sex and the City*, Sarah Jessica Parker is an exemplary model of successful collaborations and licensing partnerships in the fashion industry, ultimately becoming a fashion icon and establishing a lifestyle brand.

Sarah Jessica Parker made her mark in fashion by establishing her eponymous brand, *SJP by Sarah Jessica Parker*.[129] Her foray into the business was with fragrances and in 2005 Parker partnered with Coty and International Flavors and Fragrances to launch *Lovely*.[130] Since then she has gone on through strategic licensing arrangements to establish *SJP by Sarah Jessica Parker* as a lifestyle brand with, in addition to fragrances, having footwear, apparel, bridal, handbags and accessories, eyewear, candles, and wines bear her trademark. Parker has collaborated with other famous brands as a model image, creative director, and designer. The following timeline highlights her journey and the footprint that she has made in the fashion industry:

2004	Starred in Gap's fall campaign
2005	Launched *Lovely by Sarah Jessica Parker* fragrance
2007	Designed Steve & Barry's *Bitten Sarah Jessica Parker* collection Launched *Covet Sarah Jessica Parker* fragrance
2009	Launched *SJP NYC* fragrance
2010	Appointed Halston Heritage President and Chief Creative Officer Collaborated with Hallmark for greeting cards, stationery, and giftwrap capsule
2014	Partnered with George Malkemus III to start SJP Collection footwear line for SJP by Sarah Jessica Parker • *This has become the focal product line of her namesake brand*
2015	Developed handbag and candle collections for SJP by Sarah Jessica Parker Designed *SJP x Tome* pump collection
2016	Formed literary imprint in collaboration with Hogarth Launched *Stash* fragrance Designed "little black dress" line exclusively with Nordstrom, called *SJP LBD*
2017	Designed *Gap | Sarah Jessica Parker* kidswear collection

128. *See* Joelle Diderich, *The Beat Goes On*, WWD 27 (June 18, 2018); Andrew Nodell, *Old School Style: Swizz Beatz x Bally Celebrate Design Collaboration*, WWD (July 13, 2017), https://wwd.com/eye/parties/old-school-style-swizz-beatz-x-bally-celebrate-design-collaboration-10946036/.

129. *See* SJP by Sarah Jessica Parker, https://sjpbysarahjessicaparker.com/ (last visited Oct. 22, 2019).

130. Over the past 15 years, Parker went on to launch other fragrance products, including Covet, SJP NYC, Stash, and Born Lovely.

2018 ◈ Launched bridal ready-to-wear line with Gilt Bridal: *SJP by Sarah Jessica Parker Bridal*
Partnered with Intimissimi to promote lingerie and pajama product lines
Launched *Born Lovely* fragrance

2019 ◈ Designed new style of sunglasses in *Sunglass Hut x SJP* collaboration
Launched sauvignon blanc and rosé wine collection with Invivo Wines: *Invivo X, SJP*

2. Influencers: The Next Frontier of Collaborations in the Fashion Industry

A decade ago, fashion companies collaborated with celebrities famous for acting, modeling, athletics, and music. Enter 2010, and "influencers" have become the new celebrity, pervading the landscape of collaborations. Influencers have anywhere from thousands to millions of followers on social media, and the more followers, the more likely they are to influence consumers—hence the term "influencer." They are viewed as a hot commodity by brands because of the potential to increase eyeballs on their products and enter new markets.

Influencing is the new wave of brand-building. For companies in the modern age, it is important to keep up to date with consumers' needs and preferences; today, the preference is to obtain information through social media, so influencers are taking priority over supermodels in magazines, who influenced consumers prior to the Instagram age. Consumers choose what is important to them and seek out influencers and brands who share the same values.

Most influencers want to work with brands that share their vision and values because they don't want to alienate their followers and lose subscribers. Raina Penchansky, founder and chief creative officer of influencer management agency Digital Brand Architects, said:

> 2018 was a year when brands finally started to realize that they need to listen to the influencer as opposed to dictating the creative and the tone. If you're working with an influencer, let them guide the content. Creative briefs are fantastic, but you need to let the influencer guide what their message is. They know how to speak to their audience, they know what their audience wants in terms of content, they know how to work well with brands. We saw a shift this year in brands finally coming around to that. You see it in the [return on investment] in terms of how brands are able to more effectively work with talent.[131]

131. Alexa Tietjen, *WWD Yearbook #9: 2018's Biggest Influencer News*, WWD (Dec. 12, 2018) https://wwd.com/business-news/business-features/2018-biggest-influencer-news-1202929420/#9 (quoting Raina Penchansky).

Successful influencer marketing has prompted both retailers and brands to offer influencers the opportunity to launch their own brands for collaboration purposes. Nordstrom was one of the first retailers to realize how much power influencers have over their followers' shopping habits, and to give influencers their own lines after finding success with capsule collections.[132] For example, Something Navy began as a blog by Arielle Charnas out of a passion for fashion, and it has become a big name in the industry, in no small part due to Charnas's collaboration with Nordstrom. In 2017, Nordstrom launched a capsule collection with Something Navy and Nordstrom line Treasure and Bond, which brought in $1 million in one day. In light of the extraordinary success, Nordstrom gave Charnas a stand-alone Something Navy line, which, on the day of the line's launch, crashed Nordstrom's website. Nordstrom realized the value in Charnas's loyal following—she had built it by engaging her followers with Instagram stories about the design process and posting polls for them to make various design decisions—which led to high conversion rates for purchasing product, ultimately resulting in high sales figures.[133] Nordstrom also collaborated with Rachel Parcell of Pink Peonies to expand her personal dress line with sales exclusively at Nordstrom stores and its e-commerce platform; Blair Eadie of Atlantic-Pacific on Nordstrom's Halogen line; and Chriselle Lim, which followed the Something Navy model to launch the influencer's own brand.[134]

Retailers including Nordstrom, Express,[135] and others see the potential in working with influencers to increase business for mutual benefit.[136]

The beauty business is riding on the coattails of the fashion industry's pioneering ingenuity to collaborate with influencers. "Influencer brands are a

132. Katie Richards, *"Nordstrom is a Unicorn": How the Department Store Finds Success with Influencer Collabs*, Glossy (June 3, 2019), https://www.glossy.co/fashion/nordstrom-is-a-unicorn-how-the-department-store-finds-success-with-influencer-collabs.

133. *Id.*

134. *Id.*

135. Kellie Ell, *Express x Negin Mirsalehi Collection Debuts Online*, WWD 10 (Sept. 5, 2019).

136. The need for sustainability is a hot button issue coming to the forefront from the influencer model. Consumers want more sustainable practices for the companies producing their products than are currently in place. They follow and engage with brands that showcase sensitivity toward the environment, and companies are taking note of the ecological desires of potential customers. Brands are at different levels of sustainability, and those that are trying to improve their corporate social responsibility can, and should, collaborate with brands and companies that have succeeded in green practices. Some brands, like Eileen Fisher and Stella McCartney, have been committed to sustainable practices for a long time, and new brands are emerging as "sustainable" because of the gap in the industry. Even so, brands such as Reformation want to collaborate with other brands to create a more sustainable fashion community. Founder and chief executive officer of Reformation, Yael Aflalo, said, "The industry is in need of some serious systemic change and we want to be a part of solutions to clean up the industry, whether that's helping to develop new closed-loop fibers, ensuring living wages for our factory workers or innovating more-efficient dye practices." Kaley Roshitsh, *Reformation, New Balance Team for Sustainable Sneaker*, WWD 8 (Oct. 4, 2019) (quoting Yael Aflalo). Collaborations are the key in developing a more sustainable fashion future, as a traditional licensing arrangement would not help a brand transform its ecological footprint.

rising phenomenon in the beauty space and are garnering a lot of interest most recently . . . when Coty Inc. purchased a majority stake in Kylie Jenner's cosmetics business for $600 million."[137] Beauty startups as well are using influencers as their foray into the business and, in some cases, as a sole marketing tool. A prime example is the beauty brand Rowse—a burgeoning Madrid-based company that is "the eco juggernaut with plant-based products" that are "raw and sustainable." Rowse is the brainchild of Spanish lifestyle influencer Nuria Val and seasoned beauty executive Gabriela Salord. The company launched purely on a digital platform based upon the "influencer community."[138] The brand has invested in "no paid marketing" and looks to collaborations as its current business model.[139]

3. IP Rights in Collaboration Deals—How to Draft the Appropriate Agreement

When considering the approach and strategy to drafting a collaboration (or co-branding) agreement, there may be some similarities to a traditional license agreement between a brand owner and a manufacturer/licensee.[140] However, unique to collaborations in the fashion industry is the inherent dynamic that each party to the co-venture owns its own intellectual property, typically in the form of a trademark or copyright. This integral factor needs to be addressed in the drafting of a collaboration agreement.

Nonetheless, the grant of a license in some manner still governs a collaboration arrangement. This agreement can be drafted "in one of two ways: the holder of one trademark, X, licenses it to the owner of another, Y, and the owner of Y produces and markets the XY brand; or the holder[s] of trademark[s] X and . . . Y each license their respective trademarks to a newly formed" entity, specifically formed to carry out the business of the co-venture, which ultimately manufactures and markets the XY brand.[141]

Ultimately, the co-branding agreement should set forth, with specificity, how each of the respective parties' trademarks (or logos) are to be displayed and

137. Jennifer Weil, *Rowse: A Newfangled Influencer Beauty Brand,* WWD 3 (Dec.10, 2019).

138. *Id.*

139. *Id.* Rowse is unique in that, in addition to influencers, the company considers its customers as collaborators, stating that its first 10,000 fans are the brand's "ambassadors." Rowse continues to expand its business organically based upon a social media platform. *Id.*

140. *See generally* Section G, The Art of Drafting a License Agreement, *supra.*

141. Hand, *supra* note 5 ("The former structure has the trappings of a traditional license, in which the holder of trademark X takes on the role of licensor and the holder of trademark Y takes on the role of licensee. The latter structure is a joint venture structure, as detailed above, but in this case with two separate licenses, which can make the arrangement more of a pure 50/50 joint venture and therefore easier to negotiate. In either case, it is important that each party acknowledge the other party's ownership of their existing trademark as well as ensure that the other party does not have rights to take the co-brand into product categories that would create confusion with the existing product offering.").

physically placed in conjunction with one another on the products that are the subject of the collaboration, as well as any marketing or public relations materials, including social media posts, photographs or any televised commercials.

When drafting a collaboration agreement, the parties should also contemplate any new trademark(s) or logo(s) that might arise out of the combination of the two co-branded trademarks. If ownership issues of such a new mark are not contemplated and vetted (e.g., the parties agree not to file for registration of a joint mark, or the parties agree that they each have some respective residual rights to the new mark, perhaps in a different product category, and the parties agree to respective rights upon the termination of such an agreement) this could lead to contention between the parties, which is in contravention of the original collaborative venture.[142]

However, sometimes the magnetism, let alone glamour, of collaborations in the fashion industry can lead to a dangerous path of unauthorized use and trademark infringement, particularly with regard to celebrities' and their rights of publicity. Such is the case of *Ariana Grande v. Forever 21*, which is set forth below.

Grande-Butera v. Forever 21, Inc.[143]

No. 2:19-cv-07600 (C.D. Cal. Sept. 2, 2019)

ARIANA GRANDE-BUTERA, p/k/a ARIANA GRANDE, an individual; and GRANDARI, INC., a Florida Corporation, Plaintiffs, v. FOREVER 21, INC., a California Corporation; RILEY ROSE LLC, a California Company; and DOES 1-10, inclusive, Defendants.

Complaint for Damages

1. Violation of California Civil Code Section 3344 (Cal. Civ. Code § 3344);
2. Violation of Common Law Right of Publicity;
3. False Endorsement under the Lanham Act (15 U.S.C. § 1125(a));
4. Trademark Infringement (15 U.S.C. § 1114(1)(a));
5. Common Law Trademark Infringement; and
6. Copyright Infringement (17 U.S.C. § 501).

Unlimited Civil Case

* * *

Plaintiffs Ariana Grande-Butera, p/k/a/ "Ariana Grande" and GrandAri Inc. allege as follows:

---

142. See *id.* for a general discussion on the interplay of traditional fashion law license agreements and collaboration agreements.

143. Complaint for Damages & Demand for Jury Trial, Grande-Butera v. Forever 21, Inc., No. 2:19-cv-07600 (C.D. Cal. Sept. 2, 2019), ECF No. 1.

Introduction

1. Ariana Grande is an internationally renowned singer, songwriter and actress who, through years of hard work and dedication to her craft, has developed a personal brand and global following unparalleled by any of her peers. Indeed, Ms. Grande is one of the most successful artists in pop culture today, has the largest social media following of any female celebrity in the world. Given her stature and influence, Ms. Grande is highly sought after by companies hoping to secure her endorsement of their products, and those companies are willing pay enormous sums of money to engage Ms. Grande to help promote their brands. Even a single social media post by Ms. Grande can garner fees of several hundred thousand dollars, and her longer-term endorsement arrangements command fees in the millions of dollars.

2. Hoping to benefit from Ms. Grande's celebrity and influence, in or around early 2019, Forever 21, Inc. ("Forever 21") sought her endorsement of its clothing and accessory products, which she explicitly declined due to Forever 21's unwillingness to pay the fair market value for a celebrity of Ms. Grande's stature. Fearing irrelevance in a rapidly evolving market with increasing competition from other fast fashion brands, rather than pay Ms. Grande, Forever 21 and Riley Rose, the beauty company started by the daughters of Forever 21's founders (collectively, "Defendants"), instead stole her name, likeness, and other intellectual property to promote their brands for free.

3. Forever 21's and Riley Rose's unauthorized use of Ms. Grande's name, image, likeness, and music to promote their brands and products are blatant and willful violations of her statutory and common law rights of publicity, and constitute infringement of Plaintiffs' copyrights and trademarks under the Copyright Act and Lanham Act, respectively. By this action, Plaintiffs seek an award of actual damages, the disgorgement of Forever 21's ill-gotten profits, and an award of punitive damages to deter Forever 21 and Riley Rose from future violations of Plaintiffs' personal and intellectual property rights.

Jurisdiction and Venue

4. The Court has original jurisdiction pursuant to 28 U.S.C. §§ 1331 and 1338(a). This is a civil action arising under federal law, the Lanham Act of 1946 as amended (codified at 15 U.S.C. §§ 1051, et seq.). The pendent state law claims are so related to the federal claims that they form part of the same case or controversy pursuant to Article III of the United States Constitution. The court therefore has supplemental jurisdiction over those claims pursuant to 28 U.S.C. § 1367(a).

5. Venue is proper in this judicial district pursuant to 28 U.S.C. § 1391(b) for several independent reasons, including that: Defendants "reside" in this judicial district for venue purposes under 28 U.S.C. § 1391(c)(2); a substantial part of the events or omissions giving rise to the claims occurred in this district; and a substantial part of property that is the subject of the action is situated in this district.

Parties

6. Plaintiffs Ariana Grande-Butera is an individual and resident of Los Angeles County, California.

7. Plaintiffs GrandAri Inc. is a Florida corporation with its principal place of business in Los Angeles, California.

8. Plaintiffs are informed and believe, and based thereon allege, that Defendant Forever 21 is a California corporation, with its principal place of business in Los Angeles, California.

9. Plaintiffs are informed and believe, and based thereon allege, that Defendant Riley Rose is a California-based limited liability company, with its principal place of business in Los Angeles, California.

General Allegations
I. Ms. Grande's Fame and Influence

10. Ariana Grande is one of the biggest stars in pop culture today. As a Grammy Award-winning singer, songwriter, and actor, Ms. Grande has not only performed at sold-out stadium tours all over the world, but her music and videos have amassed over 30 billion streams on platforms such as YouTube, Spotify, and Apple Music, making her the most listened-to female artist on the latter two.

11. Ms. Grande's career continues to defy norms and break records in the music industry. All five of Ms. Grande's full-length albums have been certified platinum by the Recording Industry Association of America ("RIAA"), and she is the first artist to have the lead singles from each studio album debut within the top ten in the United States.

12. Upon the release of her fifth album Thank U, Next in 2019, Ms. Grande again broke a string of records. The album's title track, Thank U, Next, debuted at number one on the US Billboard Hot 100, and held the record for the most-played song in a single day by a female artist on Spotify. The track was dethroned from the top spot by Ms. Grande's other singles, 7 Rings and Break Up with Your Girlfriend, I'm Bored, making Ms. Grande the first female artist to replace herself at number one on the charts, and the first solo artist to simultaneously hold the top three spots on the Billboard Hot 100 chart.

13. Ms. Grande's fame, following, and social influence are equally unparalleled and record-breaking. As of February 2019, Ms. Grande became the most-followed woman on Instagram in the world, amassing more than 160 million Instagram followers; a title she continues to hold through the date of filing this Complaint. Ms. Grande has another 64 million followers on Twitter.

14. TIME Magazine named Ms. Grande one of "The 25 Most Influential People on the Internet" in 2019, and one of "The 100 Most Influential People in the World" in both 2016 and 2019. Billboard recognized Ms. Grande as the "Woman of the Year" in 2018 after she hosted the One Love Manchester benefit, which helped raise

$29 million dollars for the victims of a suicide bombing attack outside an arena in Manchester, England, where Ms. Grande had just finished performing.

15. Ms. Grande's success and star power have enabled her to expand her career beyond the music industry through various commercial endorsement deals. Still, Ms. Grande is selective of the brands with whom she chooses to partner, and frequently turns down endorsement proposals. And when she does choose to collaborate with a company or endorse its products or services, Ms. Grande often works closely with third-parties to curate products and images that coincide with her personal brand.

16. Ms. Grande's control over the use of her name, image, likeness, and intellectual property in promoting third-party products and services is critical to safeguard her reputation, and to prevent the public from being misled into believing that she has associated herself with a product or service that she does not, in fact, endorse.

17. As alleged in further detail below, in complete disregard of Plaintiffs' intellectual property rights and rights of publicity, Defendants have repeatedly and willfully used Ms. Grande's name, image, likeness, and music without authorization to generate renewed interest in their brands and social media platforms, and to elicit sales of their products.

II. Forever 21's Declining Success

18. Plaintiffs are informed and believe, and based thereon allege, that Forever 21 is a privately-owned clothing retailer with approximately 815 stores in 57 countries around the world. With over 30,000 employees, Forever 21 sells clothing, shoes, handbags, and accessories, among other things, to mostly women and girls ranging in age from 14 to 24.

19. Since being founded in 1984, Forever 21 has become a staple in nearly every shopping mall around the world by capitalizing on its then-revolutionary techniques of rapidly producing inexpensive clothing, making it one of the most well-known "fast fashion" brands in the world.

20. Indeed, Forever 21's annual revenue totaled approximately $3.4 billion in 2017. Recently, however, Forever 21 has faced competition from new online fast fashion companies which do not have the practical limitations and financial burdens that come with brick-and-mortar stores. As a result of Forever 21's online competition, Defendant Forever 21 is reportedly experiencing a financial downturn and has been looking for ways to develop its business, including by expanding its brand into beauty products and cosmetics by launching the beauty boutique, Riley Rose in 2017.

21. Riley Rose founders Esther and Linda Chang, daughters of Forever 21 founder and CEO, Do Wan Chang, reportedly stated that "Forever 21 and Riley Rose have a similar customer base," but that the goal when creating Riley Rose was to make something "very trendy and Instagram-worthy" as the ultimate "homage

to millennials."[144] The beauty boutique sells makeup, skincare, haircare and home décor through its website, www.rileyrose.com, and via 13 storefronts in shopping malls across the United States.

III. Defendants Resort to Unlawful Conduct as a Desperate Attempt to Stay Relevant and Profitable

22. Following the record-breaking release of Ms. Grande's single *Thank U, Next* on or around November 3, 2018, and in anticipation of the album's release in February 2019, Forever 21 contacted Ms. Grande's representatives to discuss the possibility of having her endorse the fast fashion Forever 21 brand given that Ms. Grande's fans are squarely within Forever 21's target market.

23. Notably, the endorsement deal Forever 21 sought with Ms. Grande centered around social media marketing, including, but not limited to, Twitter posts, Instagram posts, and Instagram stories.[145]

24. The importance and influence derived from social media marketing to consumers in today's market cannot be overstated. Indeed, platforms such as Instagram and Twitter are premier forms of marketing for most companies today, and paying influential celebrities with large social media followings such as Ms. Grande is the modern-day equivalent of buying television ads 20 years ago.

25. Given her stature, influence, and social media following, the market value for even a single Instagram post by Ms. Grande is well into the six figures, and she commands in the mid-seven figures to over eight figures for longer-term endorsement deals, marketing campaigns, and/or licensing deals for use of her name and likeness.

26. Negotiations between Forever 21 and Ms. Grande's representatives took place in or around December 2018 and January 2019, but the proposed endorsement deal never came to fruition because the amounts that Forever 21 offered to pay for the right to use Ms. Grande's name and likeness were insufficient for an artist of her stature. Ms. Grande's representatives communicated as much to Forever 21.

27. Rather than pay for that right as the law requires, Defendants simply stole it by launching a misleading campaign across its website and social media platforms primarily in January and February 2019. The campaign capitalized on the concurrent success of Ms. Grande's album *Thank U, Next* by publishing at least 30 unauthorized images and videos misappropriating Ms. Grande's name, image, likeness, and music in order to create the false perception of her endorsement....

---

144. Mau, Dhani, How New Beauty Store Riley Rose Was Designed to Be the Ultimate 'Homage to Millennials,' FASHIONISTA, Feb. 4, 2018, (last accessed Aug. 30, 2019 at https://fashionista.com/2017/10/riley-rose-forever-21-beauty-store).

145. An "Instagram story" is a picture and/or video, potentially set to music, posted onto an Instagram account holder's page for up to 24 hours. Account holders can also permanently archive Instagram stories by posting them onto their page as "Highlights."

28. As part of Defendants' unauthorized marketing campaign, Defendants also falsely suggested Ms. Grande's endorsement by hiring a look-alike model and posting photos of that model in clothing and accessories that resemble clothing worn in Ms. Grande's music videos and that the public immediately associates with Ms. Grande.[146]

29. Defendants did not simply use a model with a similar look and hairstyle; they used [1] a model who looks strikingly similar to Ms. Grande, [2] wearing a similar hairstyle to the one Ms. Grande wore in the *7 Rings* video, [3] dressed in a top designed to look like a top worn by Ms. Grande in numerous well-known photographs (including photographs of Ms. Grande that Forever 21 wrongfully posted on its Instagram feed, depicted above), [4] wearing a distinctive hair accessory worn by Ms. Grande in the *7 Rings* video and numerous well-known photographs, [5] using a pose that is virtually identical to the pose in which Ms. Grande was photographed, [6] in certain instances, with *7 Rings* audio played over the post, [7] in certain instances, with the distinctive "7" from the *7 Rings* video displayed in the background, [8] in certain instances intermixed with photographs of Ms. Grande herself (which photographs Forever 21 again had no authorization to post); and, [9] in certain instances, coupled with captions containing lyrics from Ms. Grande's song *7 Rings*.

* * *

31. The resemblance is uncanny and Forever 21's intent was clear: to suggest to the viewing public that Ms. Grande endorsed Forever 21, its products, and was affiliated with Forever 21.

32. When Ms. Grande discovered the infringement on or around February 23, 2019, she immediately contacted her attorneys and agents, including representatives of Bravado International Group Merchandising Services, Inc. ("Bravado"), her exclusive licensee for certain of her intellectual property in the apparel industry. Shortly thereafter, Ms. Grande's representatives demanded that Forever 21 take down all unauthorized uses of Ms. Grande's name, likeness, and intellectual property.

33. Despite their stated agreement to do so, Defendants did not remove all of the unauthorized content. Outside counsel for Ms. Grande contacted Forever 21 again on or around March 15, 2019 and on or around April 3, 2019 to demand that the unauthorized and infringing uses of Ms. Grande's name, image, likeness, and music cease and desist immediately.

34. Defendants' infringing and unauthorized posts remained on Forever 21's and Riley Rose's social media accounts until at least April 17, 2019. As a result, Defendants improperly misappropriated and profited from Ms. Grande's influence and star-power for approximately 14 weeks.[147]

146. Videos of Defendants' alleged infringement of Ms. Grande's music and videos will be submitted to the Court separately.

147. Defendants began their use of Ms. Grande's name, image, likeness and music on November 30, 2018, and failed to remove all unauthorized content until at least April 17, 2019.

First Claim for Relief
(Violation of Cal. Civ. Code § 3344—Against All Defendants)

35. Ms. Grande incorporates all prior allegations of this Complaint by this reference.

36. Ms. Grande is the owner of the rights of publicity in her name, image, likeness, and persona necessary for endorsement deals.

37. Defendants have willfully and without authorization used Ms. Grande's name, image, likeness, and persona for commercial purposes, to advertise the Forever 21 and Riley Rose brands, and to promote the sale of clothing, accessories and beauty products on Forever 21's and Riley Rose's social media platforms and website.

38. Defendants' unauthorized use of Ms. Grande's name, image, likeness, and persona constitute a commercial misappropriation in violation of Section 3344 of the California Civil Code.

39. As a direct and proximate result of Defendants' wrongful conduct, Ms. Grande has suffered, and will continue to suffer, damages in an amount to be proven at trial, but in no event less than $10 million.

40. Defendants have further been unjustly enriched by their misappropriation of Ms. Grande's statutory right of publicity. Accordingly, Ms. Grande is entitled to restitution of all income, profits, and other benefits resulting from Defendants' conduct, in an amount to be determined according to proof at trial.

41. Defendants' actions as alleged above were malicious, oppressive, and fraudulent, and done with the intent to injure Ms. Grande and with a willful and conscious disregard for Ms. Grande's rights. As a result, Ms. Grande is entitled to recover from Defendants punitive and exemplary damages in an amount sufficient to punish and deter them and others from engaging in such acts in the future.

Second Claim for Relief
(Violation of Common Law Right of Publicity—Against All Defendants)

42. Ms. Grande incorporates all prior allegations of this Complaint by this reference.

43. Ms. Grande is the owner of the common law rights of publicity in her name, image, likeness, and persona necessary for endorsement deals.

44. Defendants have willfully and without authorization used Ms. Grande's name, image, likeness, and persona for commercial purposes, to advertise the Forever 21 and Riley Rose brands, and to promote the sale of clothing, accessories, and beauty products on Defendants' social media platforms and websites.

45. The unauthorized use of Ms. Grande's likeness also includes at least 13 instances wherein Forever 21 falsely suggested Ms. Grande's endorsement by hiring a look-alike model and posting photos of that model in clothing and accessories that resemble clothing and accessories worn in Ms. Grande's music videos, and that the public immediately associates with Ms. Grande.

46. Defendants' unauthorized use of Ms. Grande's name, image, likeness, and persona constitutes a violation of California's common law right of publicity.

47. As a direct and proximate result of Defendants' wrongful conduct, Ms. Grande has suffered, and will continue to suffer, damages in an amount to be proven at trial, but in no event less than $10 million.

48. Defendants have further been unjustly enriched by its infringement of Ms. Grande's common law right of publicity. Accordingly, Ms. Grande is entitled to restitution of all income, profits, and other benefits resulting from Forever 21's conduct, in an amount to be determined according to proof at trial.

49. Defendants' actions as alleged above were malicious, oppressive, and fraudulent, and done with the intent to injure Ms. Grande and with a willful and conscious disregard for Ms. Grande's rights. As a result, Ms. Grande is entitled to recover from Defendants punitive and exemplary damages in an amount sufficient to punish and deter Defendants and others from engaging in such acts in the future.

Third Claim for Relief
(False Endorsement (15 U.S.C. § 1125(a))—Against All Defendants)

50. Ms. Grande incorporates all prior allegations of this Complaint by this reference.

51. Ms. Grande is the owner of the statutory and common law rights associated with Ms. Grande's name, image, likeness, and persona necessary for endorsement deals, including her right to decide whether to associate her name, image, likeness, or persona with any third-party for purposes relating to sponsorship and/or endorsement.

52. Defendants' used distinctive attributes of Ms. Grande's persona, including her name, image, and likeness without permission by posting on to Defendants' website, www.forever21.com, and the Instagram accounts @forever21 and @riley rose, images of Ms. Grande and/or a look-alike model dressed in clothing and accessories strikingly similar to the clothing and accessories worn by Ms. Grande in her iconic *7 Rings* music video, and posed in positions nearly identical to poses made by Ms. Grande in the *7 Rings* video, and that the public readily associates with Ms. Grande.

53. Defendants' unauthorized uses constitute false or misleading representations of fact to falsely imply the endorsement of Defendants' businesses and products by Ms. Grande.

54. Defendants' unauthorized uses of Ms. Grande's persona are likely to confuse and deceive consumers as to Ms. Grande's sponsorship and/or endorsement of Forever 21's and Riley Rose's brands. Specifically, Defendants' use of Ms. Grande's name, image, and likeness is likely to cause consumers to mistakenly believe that Ms. Grande is associated with Forever 21 and Riley Rose, or that she sponsors or endorses Defendants' products, websites, or social media accounts.

55. As a direct and proximate result of the acts of false endorsement set forth above, Ms. Grande has suffered actual damages in an amount to be proven at trial, but in no event less than $10 million. Ms. Grande is entitled to the full range of relief available under the Lanham Act, 15 U.S.C. § 1117, including, without limitation, an award of actual damages and the disgorgement of Defendants' profits arising from their false or misleading acts. Defendants' conduct further renders this an "exceptional" case within the meaning of the Lanham Act, thus entitling Ms. Grande to an award of attorneys' fees and costs.

56. Ms. Grande is informed and believes, and based thereon alleges, that Defendants committed the unauthorized acts described above knowing that is likely to cause consumers to falsely believe that Ms. Grande endorses Defendants' brands and products. Defendants have thus willfully, knowingly, and maliciously deceived and confused the relevant consuming public, such that Ms. Grande is entitled to an award of treble damages.

Fourth Claim for Relief
(Trademark Infringement (15 U.S.C. § 1114(1))—Against All Defendants)

57. Plaintiffs incorporate all prior allegations of this Complaint by this reference.

58. Plaintiffs have extensively used the trademark ARIANA GRANDE in commerce in connection with a myriad of products and services, including Plaintiffs' advertising and promotion of Ms. Grande's fragrance line, as well as through endorsement of third-party products in the entertainment and fashion industries.

59. Plaintiffs own several federally registered trademarks in Ms. Grande's name, including without limitation: (1) U.S. Registration No. 4,965,758 for the use of ARIANA GRANDE in connection with "perfume" and "fragranced body care;" (2) Int'l Registration No. 1,477,022 for use of ARIANA GRANDE THANK U, NEXT in connection with "perfume" and "fragranced body care;" (3) U.S. Registration No. 4,932,682 for the use of ARIANA GRANDE in connection with clothing and apparel; (4) U.S. Registration NO. 4,297,601 for the use of ARIANA GRANDE in connection with "Entertainment services, namely, . . . musical performances, musical videos, related film clips, photographs, and other multimedia materials featuring Ariana Grande;" and (5) U.S. Serial No. 87,472,487 for the use of ARIANA GRANDE in connection with "the field of music and entertainment," "clothing," "handbags," "jewelry accessories," "licensing of intellectual property," and "entertainment services, namely, . . . music, film, television, celebrity and popular culture provided over the internet," (collectively, the "Registered Marks"). . . .

60. The Registered Marks are valid trademarks owned by Plaintiffs. Additionally, by virtue of Plaintiffs' longstanding and continuous use of the Registered Marks in commerce, Plaintiffs have acquired a valid common law trademark in Ms. Grande's name. The public has come to recognize the Registered Marks as exclusively identifying Ms. Grande, and the marks are famous worldwide.

61. Defendants infringed Plaintiffs' registered and common law trademarks by using these marks on their social media accounts, including the Instagram accounts @forever21 and @rileyrose, to promote Defendants' brands and sale of clothing, accessories, and beauty products.

62. Defendants' unauthorized use of Plaintiffs' registered and common law trademarks are likely to confuse and deceive consumers as to the origin, sponsorship, and/or endorsement of the Forever 21 and Riley Rose brands and products. Specifically, Defendants' use of Ms. Grande's name and Plaintiffs' mark are likely to cause consumers to mistakenly believe that Ms. Grande is associated with Forever 21 and Riley Rose, or that she sponsors or endorses Defendants' products, websites, or social media accounts.

63. As a direct and proximate result of the acts of trademark infringement set forth above, Plaintiffs have suffered actual damages in an amount to be proven at trial, but in no event less than $10 million. Plaintiffs are entitled to the full range of relief available under the Lanham Act, 15 U.S.C. § 1117, including, without limitation, an award of actual damages and the disgorgement of Defendants' profits arising from the acts of trademark infringement. Defendants' conduct further renders this an "exceptional" case within the meaning of the Lanham Act, thus entitling Plaintiffs to an award of attorneys' fees and costs.

64. Plaintiffs are informed and believe, and based thereon allege, that Defendants committed the infringement described above knowing that its unauthorized use of the ARIANA GRANDE and ARIANA GRANDE THANK U, NEXT trademarks is likely to cause consumer confusion. Defendants have thus willfully, knowingly, and maliciously deceived and confused the relevant consuming public, such that Plaintiffs are entitled to an award of treble damages.

Fifth Claim for Relief
(Common Law Trademark Infringement—Against All Defendants)

65. Plaintiffs incorporate all prior allegations of this Complaint by this reference.

66. Plaintiffs own valid common law trademarks in ARIANA GRANDE and ARIANA GRANDE THANK U, NEXT for use in connection with a wide variety of products and services, including without limitation the promotion of products and services in the entertainment, fashion, and beauty industries. The Registered Trademarks are likewise valid trademarks owned by Plaintiffs.

67. The public has come to recognize the ARIANA GRANDE and ARIANA GRANDE THANK U, NEXT marks as exclusively identifying Ms. Grande, and the marks are famous worldwide.

68. Defendants have infringed Plaintiffs' trademarks by using these marks on their social media platforms, including the Instagram accounts @forever21 and @rileyrose, to promote Defendants' brands and products.

69. Defendants' unauthorized use of Plaintiffs' trademarks is likely to confuse and deceive consumers as to the origin, sponsorship, and/or endorsement of the Forever 21 and Riley Rose brands, websites, social media accounts, and products. Specifically, Defendants' use of Plaintiffs' marks is likely to cause consumers to mistakenly believe that Ms. Grande is associated with Forever 21 and/or Riley Rose, or that she sponsors or endorses Defendants' products.

70. As a direct and proximate result of the acts of trademark infringement set forth above, Plaintiffs have suffered actual damages in an amount to be proven at trial, but in no event less than $10 million.

71. Plaintiffs are informed and believe, and based thereon allege, that Defendants committed the infringement described above knowing that its unauthorized use of the ARIANA GRANDE and ARIANA GRANDE THANK U, NEXT marks is likely to cause consumer confusion. Defendants have thus willfully, knowingly, and maliciously deceived and confused the relevant consuming public, such that Plaintiffs are entitled to an award of treble damages.

72. Plaintiffs are further informed and believe, and based thereon allege, that Defendants acted with fraud, oppression, or malice in infringing Plaintiffs' marks as alleged above. As such, in addition to the other relief sought herein, Plaintiffs are entitled to an award of punitive damages.

Sixth Claim for Relief
(Copyright Infringement—Against All Defendants)

73. In addition to the wrongful use of Ms. Grande's right of publicity and Plaintiffs' trademarks, Forever 21 and Riley Rose simultaneously infringed Ms. Grande's copyrights by publishing images, lyrics, and audiovisual clips from Ms. Grande's copyrighted songs: (1) *7 Rings*; (2) *Thank U, Next*; and (3) *Break Up With Your Girlfriend, I'm Bored.*

74. Ms. Grande holds either the federally registered copyright or the beneficial interest and approval rights for each of the three songs infringed by Forever 21 and/or Riley Rose, including without limitation: (1) U.S. Registration No. PA0002154953 for the audio clip of song *Thank U, Next*; (2) U.S. Registration No. PA0002164214 for the audiovisual clip of *Thank U, Next*; (3) U.S. Registration No. PA0002191175 for the audio clip of song *7 Rings*; (4) U.S. Registration No. PA002177521 for the audiovisual clip of *7 Rings*; and (5) U.S. Registration No. PA0002182759 for the audiovisual clip of *Break Up With Your Girlfriend, I'm Bored*, (collectively the "Copyrighted Works"). . . .

75. Defendants unlawfully copied the Copyrighted Works by publishing (1) audio clips from Ms. Grande's song *7 Rings*; (2) audiovisual clips from her music videos for both *7 Rings* and *Thank U, Next*; and (3) song lyrics from Ms. Grande's songs *7 Rings*, *Thank U, Next*, and *Break Up With Your Girlfriend, I'm Bored.*

76. As a direct and proximate result of the acts of copyright infringement set forth above, Ms. Grande has suffered actual damages in an amount to be proven at

trial, but in no event less than $600,000 dollars. Ms. Grande is entitled to the full range of relief available under the Copyright Act, U.S.C. § 504(a)(1), (b), including, without limitation, an award of actual damages and the disgorgement of Defendants' profits arising from the acts of copyright infringement. Defendants' conduct entitles Ms. Grande to an award of attorneys' fees and costs. 17 U.S.C. § 505.

Prayer for Relief

WHEREFORE, Plaintiffs pray for judgment as follows:

1. On all claims for relief, for an award of compensatory and treble damages in an amount to be proven, but in no event less than $10 million;

2. On all claims for relief, for the disgorgement of Forever 21's and Riley Rose's profits attributable to the infringement of Plaintiffs' intellectual property rights and rights of publicity;

3. On the First and Second Claims for Relief, for an award of punitive damages in an amount sufficient to deter unlawful conduct by Forever 21 and Riley Rose in the future;

4. For a permanent injunction restraining and enjoining Defendants from using Ms. Grande's name, images, likeness, persona, copyrights and Plaintiffs' trademarks;

5. For pre-judgment and post-judgment interest according to proof and to the maximum extent allowed by law;

6. For attorneys' fees and costs; and

7. For such other and further relief as the Court may deem just and proper.

Notes

1. *Ariana Grande v. Forever 21* arose out of failed negotiations for a collaboration between Ariana Grande, one of the biggest stars in pop culture today, and Forever 21, a clothing retailer, who reportedly was experiencing a financial downturn. It exemplifies the potential halo effect of collaborations between retailers on the one hand, and artists and celebrities on the other. This arguably drove Forever 21 to use Ms. Grande's name, likeness, and image allegedly without permission and then use her music, allegedly without prior authorization, in order to develop and market a line of clothing.

2. This case also illustrates the various causes of action that an artist or celebrity may bring when negotiations for collaborations do not work out, and regardless, the other party proceeds with the alleged unauthorized exploitation of the persona and intellectual property of the celebrity: commercial misappropriation violating California Civil Code § 3344; violating California's common law rights of publicity; false endorsement violating the Lanham Act (15 U.S.C. § 1125(a)); trademark infringement violating the Lanham Act (15 U.S.C. § 1114(1)); trademark infringement violating the common law; and copyright infringement violating the Copyright Act (17 U.S.C. § 501).

3. Forever 21 filed for Chapter 11 bankruptcy on September 29, 2019, just a few weeks after this lawsuit was filed. Is it possible that the retailer used their seemingly unauthorized actions as a ploy for publicity and potential increase in sales, knowing that a bankruptcy filing would be an impediment to lawsuit proceedings?

4. Another case in point underscoring an infamous collaboration between a retailer and celebrity dates back to 2015, when the pop star and fashion phenomenon Rihanna (Robyn Rihanna Fenty) successfully sued fashion retailer Topshop in the United Kingdom for selling t-shirts featuring her likeness and image without her authorization. Ironically, Topshop owned the copyright to the image, which it purchased from an independent photographer. However, the retailer never received a license or any other form of permission from the celebrity. It's interesting to note that both the lower court and appellate court decisions were based on the grounds that Topshop's actions constituted "passing off" and false representations that these products were endorsed by Rihanna, whereas in the United States such cases are typically brought by celebrities based upon an infringement of the right of publicity. *See Fenty v. Arcadia Group Brands Ltd.* [2013] EWHC (Ch) 2310, [2014] E.C.D.R. 3, aff'd, [2015] EWCA (Civ) 3, [2015] F.S.R. 14 (Eng.).

L. What Will the Future Bring?

Licensing and collaborations in the fashion industry have a very rich history. As we look back on the evolution of these two vital business models, we have come to see that licensing and collaborations, when done prudently and strategically, have ultimately become the foundation to support building and maintaining brand value—for iconic fashion designers, luxury brands, burgeoning fashion businesses, celebrities, personalities, influencers, brand management, and licensing companies, and established apparel and accessories manufacturers alike. There is no doubt that this fascinating cross section of business and law in the fashion industry will continue to evolve in the wake of the ever-expanding world of social media and digital technology and its effects upon corporate strategic growth and consumer response.[148] It has even been proffered that the next channel for luxury brands is to enter into the online gaming business, which as of 2019 was a $150 billion industry and projected to reach $180 billion by 2021, to engage a new demographic

148. Digital technology in the fashion industry has outpaced traditional brand building with consumers, even among the strongest brands in the industry. Digitization allows consumers to immediately purchase products and services online when they want, how they want, and through whatever channel they want to obtain them. *See* Barry Libert & Megan Beck, *Software and Platforms Are Eating the Fashion Industry,* WWD 19 (Aug. 5, 2019). For example, Stitch Fix is a leader in this space, providing online personalized styling for its customers to help them save time and find the clothes that they love through technology. *See generally* Stitch Fix, www.stitchfix.com (last visited Nov. 17, 2019). Heritage designers have also followed this lead. Ralph Lauren has also turned to digitization of its line to have a better reach and penetrate a wide customer base. *See* Kaley Roshish, *Ralph Lauren to Digitize Its Line*, WWD 9 (Nov. 4, 2019).

and younger generation of customers.[149] It appears that this trend has already taken traction; "[f]rom Hermès' mobile app H-pitchhh to Dior and Guerlain's branded interactive games, heritage brands from around the world are embracing gaming platforms with the hopes of increasing engagement to seduce millennial consumers."[150] Indeed, Louis Vuitton recently dipped its toe into gaming waters by entering into a two-year partnership with a popular multiplayer online video game "League of Legends."[151]

Yet from a legal perspective the traditional intellectual property and commercial transactional issues relating to quality control and assurance, brand integrity, licensing arrangements, exclusivity, good faith and fair dealing, and legitimate collaborations between retailers, influencers, and famous personalities, do not vary. The obligations on each of the players that delve into such relationships seeking to elevate and foster the longevity of a brand's footprint remain the same.

---

149. *See* In Focus: Business Insights, *Is It Time for Luxury Brands to Get Their Game On?*, WWD 20 (Dec. 5, 2019).

150. *Id.* (quoting Steven Ekstract, brand director of the Global Licensing Group, a unit of Informa). "Millennials and Gen Z are the new luxury consumers—they grew up with video games and are comfortable with game play. Most importantly, luxury and gaming are all about fantasy. People don't buy luxury products for need; they buy luxury products to fulfill their dreams. Luxury products create an emotional connection with the consumer that makes them feel more attractive, more intelligent, more successful." *Id.*

151. *See* Alexandra Pastore, *A New Class of Influencers Have Their Game Faces On*, WWD 15 (Dec. 9, 2019) (discussing how the online gaming industry shows promise for luxury brand partnerships).

Chapter 9

Advertising

Olivera Medenica and Julie Zerbo
With special thanks to Sixtine Bousquet and Molly Webber

A. Introduction

Creating and clearing content for marketing campaigns is a painstaking process that requires an understanding of traditional intellectual property considerations and thorough familiarity with the parameters of what can and cannot be said about the product itself. The visual manner in which the product is portrayed is as important as what is said about it. The challenging legal questions raised in this context are further complicated by the fact that advertisers have moved away from traditional advertising campaigns and embraced alternative means of promotion such as social media and influencer marketing. These platform-driven tools add yet another level of intricacy to a field already fraught with legal complexity. Fashion advertisers should thus, both in traditional advertising and viral marketing campaigns, carefully consider how the campaign is implemented and to what extent privacy considerations are triggered through the collection of consumer information.

This chapter provides a broad overview of some of these issues, and examines advertising campaigns through the lens of traditional advertising, as well as social media and influencer marketing.

B. What Constitutes Advertising?

If "advertising law" applied only to a print or television ad, advertisers would have free rein to make all kinds of misrepresentations about products or services outside of that limited context. Courts and the Federal Trade Commission ("FTC") have taken a broad view of what constitutes "advertising" to include any communications to the public to promote the advertiser's products or services. This means that any statement by an advertiser describing the products or services should be closely scrutinized for legal compliance. This includes product packaging, product display, website copy, social media statements by brands or influencers, point-of-sale materials, oral communications by sales staff, catalogs, print and television ads, product placement, conference and event sponsorships, and viral marketing campaigns. As discussed below, failure to scrutinize such materials for legal compliance can result in a significant regulatory challenge by federal, state, or local authorities—or a costly lawsuit by a disgruntled consumer or competitor.

C. Regulatory Framework Governing Fashion Advertising

In the United States, advertising is regulated at the federal, state, and local levels, as well as by self-regulatory organizations. The major federal regulatory body regulating advertising is the FTC, whose work is mainly performed by the Bureau of Consumer Protection. While the FTC has broad authority to prohibit "unfair or deceptive acts or practices" (15 U.S.C. §45), it particularly focuses on the regulation of advertising to children, social media and online advertising, telemarketing, advertising of certain specific goods (e.g., dietary supplements, tobacco, drugs, etc.), and eco-marketing. The FTC tends to address cases that involve substantial public interest. The sanctions that the FTC may impose range from a request to cease unlawful activities to corrective advertising and disclosures, to the imposition of civil penalties.

Advertising is also regulated at the state, county, and city levels with various administrative and civil codes, or business and professional codes, that address advertisements deemed deceptive or unfair. Typically, state or local laws are based on federal legislation such as the Federal Trade Commission Act ("FTC Act") or the Uniform Deceptive Trade Practices Act. Consumers typically file complaints with the state, county, or city Attorney General or with the state, county, or city Department of Consumer Affairs.

Self-regulatory organizations, such as the Better Business Bureau ("BBB") and its National Advertising Division ("NAD"), as well as the National Advertising Review Council ("NARC"), are also powerful mechanisms to control false or deceptive advertising. These organizations are responsible for monitoring and reviewing advertising campaigns and for addressing and resolving complaints between advertisers, consumers, and competitors.

1. Claims

Statements and representations made about a product or service in advertising that constitute "claims" must be materially true and not misleading. Claims can be express or implied; statements deemed "puffery" are not claims. "Puffery," however, has a narrow definition and most representations either fall under the express or implied category.

Pursuant to the FTC Act, an advertising claim must be: (1) truthful and nondeceptive; (2) backed by evidence; and (3) cannot be unfair. According to the FTC, an ad is deceptive if it contains a statement (or omits information) that is likely to mislead consumers acting reasonably under the circumstances and such statement, or omission, is material to a consumer's decision to buy or use the product. *See Deception Policy Statement, appended to Cliffdale Associates, Inc.*, 103 F.T.C. 110, 174 (1984), *cited with approval in Kraft, Inc. v. FTC*, 970 F.2d 314 (7th Cir. 1992), *cert. denied*, 507 U.S. 909 (1993). An ad is unfair if it causes or is likely to cause substantial consumer injury, which a consumer could not reasonably avoid and it is not outweighed by the benefit to consumers. *Unfairness Policy Statement, appended to International Harvester Co.*, 104 F.T.C. 949, 1070 (1984); *see also* 15 U.S.C. § 45(n). Advertisers must have a reasonable basis for making objective claims before the claims are disseminated. *Pfizer, Inc.*, 81 F.T.C. 23 (1972), *infra*. An advertiser must possess at least the level of substantiation expressly or impliedly claimed in the ad. *See, e.g., Honeywell, Inc.*, 126 F.T.C. 202 (1998).

The FTC provides that advertisements must be, when appropriate, backed by scientific evidence. Those standards are applied to whatever media the advertisement is published in and to every claim made in the advertisement.

a. Express Claims

An express claim is a statement about or depiction of a product or service that is plain and direct. For example, an advertisement stating that a shirt is "wrinkle free" constitutes an express claim that must be substantiated by the advertiser. Similarly, an advertisement that shows a man washing a shirt, hanging it to dry, and tossing it on, wrinkle free, constitutes a pictorial express claim that must be substantiated as well.

There is no set process to substantiate a claim, but the level of substantiation depends on the type of claim that is being made. For example, if an ad states that "a clinical study showed . . . ," then the advertiser must substantiate accordingly.

If, however, a claim does not specify the level of substantiation upon which the advertiser relied, then the advertiser must have a reasonable basis for making the claim. In *Pfizer Inc.*, 81 F.T.C. 23 (1972), the FTC identified several factors advertisers should consider when establishing a reasonable basis for making a claim: (1) type of product; (2) type of claim; (3) consumer benefit from a truthful claim; (4) ease of developing substantiation for the claim; (5) consequences of a false claim; and (6) amount of substantiation experts in the relevant field believe is reasonable. Thus, a claim stating that a shirt is made of "light and breathable" material may require less substantiation than a claim stating that the shirt provides SPF 50 sun block protection.

While advertisers may include disclosures to modify a claim, those disclosures cannot contradict the claim being made and must be clear and conspicuous. In *Pfizer Inc.*, 81 F.T.C. 23 (1972), the FTC entered an order against Pfizer, finding that without a reasonable basis to substantiate its claims, Pfizer violated § 5 of the FTC Act. In coming to its conclusion, the FTC evaluated the aforementioned factors and found that given the nature of the product in question—a sunburn product—as well as Pfizer's promises that such product had pain-relieving properties that soothed sunburned skin by anesthetizing sensitive nerves, Pfizer had engaged in deceptive trade practices, as such claims were wholly unsubstantiated by any scientific findings.

b. Implied Claims

An implied claim is a statement about or depiction of a product or service that is indirect. For example, a depiction of a woman unable to fit into a pair of jeans, but magically being able to do so after putting on shapewear, constitutes an indirect claim that the shapewear will make you feel and look thinner. In ascertaining the claim being made, the FTC looks at the overall net impression of an ad, and not just the plain language of a claim. If reasonable consumers would take a particular meaning from the ad, then the FTC will conclude that an implied claim was made by the advertiser. It is thus necessary to evaluate the entire ad, beyond mere literal statements, to determine whether there are additional implied claims made by the advertiser.

c. Puffery

Puffery statements in fashion advertising include statements that cannot be proven one way or another because they are so exaggerated. A puffery statement is, by nature, not likely to be believed or relied upon by reasonable consumers. A puffery claim need not to be materially true and non-misleading and does not need any substantiation. So, for example, "this shapewear will make you the most beautiful woman in the world" might be puffery but "this shapewear will make you lose two dress sizes" might not be. *See, e.g., Coty, Inc.* (Sally Hansen Complete Manicure), Report #5201, NAD/CARU Case Reports (August 2010) (claim that "All 5 Steps of a Manicure in 1 Bottle" deemed puffery because no consumer could reasonably interpret the claim to mean that a nail polish could perform all of the physical tasks associated with a manicure).

In the present case, the NAD has been tasked with independently assessing certain messages conveyed by Coty, Inc. for its Sally Hansen Complete Manicure nail polish through print, point-of-purchase, and internet advertising claims. The main claim at issue, "All 5 Steps of a Salon Manicure in 1 Bottle," appears in a print advertisement, next to a picture of many women's fingers wearing a myriad of nail polish colors.

Coty, Inc. (Sally Hansen Complete Manicure)*

NAD Case No. 5201 (Aug. 5, 2010)

Challenger: O.P.I., Inc.

In the absence of reliable consumer perception evidence, NAD steps into the role of the consumer to independently assess the messages reasonably conveyed by the challenged advertising.

Basis of Inquiry: Print, point-of-purchase ("POS) and internet advertising claims made by Coty, Inc., for its Sally Hansen Complete Manicure nail polish were challenged by O.P.I., Inc. ("the challenger"), a competing nail polish manufacturer. The claims at issue include:

> "9 out of 10 Salon professionals preferred our formula to the leading salon brand."
>
> "All 5 Steps of a Salon Manicure in 1 Bottle"

Implied claim "The new Sally Hansen product line is actually available in and used by a significant number of salon professionals in a salon setting."

In the print advertisement, next to a picture of many women's fingers wearing a myriad of nail polish colors, appears the main claim "All 5 Steps of a Salon Manicure in 1 Bottle." The five steps of a salon manicure are enumerated as (1) base coat; (2) strengthener; (3) growth treatment; (4) color; and (5) top coat. The claim "9 out of 10 Salon professionals preferred our formula to the leading salon brand" runs underneath the list of the five manicure steps.

Challenger's Position:

I. "9 Out Of 10 Salon Professionals Preferred Our Formula To The Leading Salon Brand" Claim

The challenger explained that it produces nail care products, including nail lacquers ("polish"), strengtheners, base coats and top coats. The bulk of its business is in its professional lacquer line, OPI Nail Lacquers, sold only in nail salons and is the leading salon brand with 50% market share. The challenger also sells a nail polish called Nicole by OPI in retail stores. The advertiser is the leading mass marketed retail nail polish and its products are not sold in salons.

A. Preference Claim

The challenger argued that the study that the advertiser submitted to support its claim that "*9 out of 10 Salon professionals preferred our formula to the leading salon brand*" was fatally flawed for several reasons. The challenger took issue with the size and geographical diversity of the study panel, which consisted of twenty-five nail technicians from eight different cities, Atlanta, Georgia; Dartmouth, Massachusetts; Vernon Hills, Illinois; Montclair, California; St. Louis, Missouri; Tucson, Arizona; Denton, Texas; and Lakewood, Colorado. The challenger argued that the sample was too small to support the strong "*9 out of 10*" claim, noting that one or two changes in respondents' preferences would dramatically change the percentages. Further, the eight cities used in the study only included two areas in the eastern U.S. with the remaining cities located in the western region markets, and as such, was not diverse enough to produce sufficiently reliable results. The challenger also objected to the advertiser limiting the panelists to those who purchased nail products at an open to the public beauty supply store, where the challenger maintained its product is not sold. As a result, manicurists working at salons, which purchase only at outlets available to salons exclusively[,] were intentionally excluded from the survey. The challenger maintained that this criterion excluded seventy percent of manicurists, whom the challenger maintained were most likely veteran manicurists.[1] The challenger also argued that potential panelists were deselected if they stated preference for the OPI brand in the salon or for personal use.

1. A 2009-2010 survey by Nails Magazine demonstrated that fewer than 4% of nail technicians reported that they frequently use "OTC beauty supply stores" as sources for purchasing nail polishes.

Next, the challenger asserted that the advertiser's attempt to blind the polish bottles by filing off the raised OPI logo on the cap was ineffective. The challenger argued that OPI has a distinctive trade dress including the cap and brush and salon professionals were likely to recognize the bottle. OPI, through its experts, asserted that the proper blinding technique would have been to place both the advertiser's and challenger's nail polishes in stock bottles with stock caps.[2]

With regard to the methodology of the study, the challenger argued that the most critical deficiency of the study was that the advertiser tested its "5-in-1" formula as a substitute for a salon manicure against the challenger's professional OPI nail enamel with no base or top coat. Through its expert, the challenger maintained that this rendered the study meaningless because all OPI professional enamels are used in salons as intended—with top and base coats. The challenger argued that the advertiser's preference claim would have no appeal to consumers if it truthfully disclosed that the claim was based on performance of a "5-in-1" product against nail enamel only and not a full salon manicure.[3]

The challenger maintained that this deficiency was compounded by the fact that the respondents wore each nail polish for three days—a time period that would favor an initially shinier polish but not long enough to assess other material nail enamel performance attributes, such as resistance to chipping and fading.[4] Base coats, the challenger explained, enhance the adhesion and longevity of the colored nail coating and also prevent the color from staining the underlying nail plate. As base coats are standalone products, formulators may disregard the question of gloss and surface hardness, and bias the resin mixture to maximize its adhesive properties. Thus, the advertiser's study is too short in duration to meaningfully study the longevity performance of either nail polish. Salon professionals judge a nail polish's performance based on how well it wears between visits and therefore an assessment made after only three days is not an accurate predictor of performance. Moreover, three days is not a consumer relevant time period; according to a 2004 Gallup study of Women's Nail Care Practices, no respondent had a salon manicure performed more than six times per month.

The challenger further argued that the study suffered from an order bias that benefitted the advertiser's product. A total of seventeen out of twenty-five

---

2. OPI also reported that the OPI brush could be removed from the cap and therefore the brush could be placed inside a stock bottle cap.

3. The base coat acts to even out the nail plate and help the polish adhere while also preventing the polish from staining the nail. The top coat seals the colored polish to help prevent chipping and adds shine.

4. The challenger pointed out that the survey instructions directed respondents to apply sample to clean, dry nails, remove it three days later and apply the second for three more days. Also, the challenger maintained that from the study that it could not confirm whether the two colors selected to test were color equivalents because the advertiser did not identify the tested shades.

respondents sampled the challenger's product first.[5] The challenger also asserted that the questionnaire employed excessive probing that further biased the results in the advertiser's favor. For example, in its paired preference questions, the advertiser queried, "which product do you prefer for applying?" as well as "which product do you prefer for ease of application?" and then "which brush do you prefer?" The challenger argued that the advertiser had essentially asked the same question three times. The challenger maintained that these questions favored the advertiser because of the eighteen respondents who selected Complete as their overall preferred product, nine cited the brush as reason for their selection.[6]

B. The Implied Claim

The challenger argued that consumers can reasonably interpret the claim that "*9 Out Of 10 Salon Professionals Preferred Our Formula To The Leading Salon Brand*" to mean that Complete nail polish is widely used in salons by salon professionals.

In response to the advertiser's argument that the distinctions between salon products and mass market products have little meaning for consumers, the challenger argued that it must have meaning[,] otherwise the advertiser would not have chosen to advertise the "9 out of 10" preference claim. The challenger also took issue with the advertiser's argument that the fact that one prefers a product does not mean that one uses that product, primarily because the question from the survey questionnaire relied upon by the advertiser for its "9 out of 10" claim was "which product would you prefer to use in [your] salon on clients?"

The challenger noted that the advertiser had not submitted any evidence to support this reasonable interpretation of its claim. The challenger contended that the 2009 survey cited by the advertiser that purports to demonstrate that eighteen percent of consumers have used an unspecified Sally Hansen product in salons at least once during a one-year period, is not sufficient to support its implied claim. The same data shows that only about twenty-two percent of salon users have ever brought their own products to a salon. Assuming the reliability of this data, the

---

5. The challenger argued that this represented a bias of "overall preference" of 82% from the second position.

6. The challenger argued that the advertiser's laboratory mechanical testing that it also was similarly unavailing. According to the challenger, the mechanical tests (i.e., cupping test, reverse impact test and the slip angle test) comparing the strength of aluminum treated with Complete nail polish versus a "competitive salon product" was not consumer relevant because it was not performed on human nail surfaces. Further, the several tests that the advertiser performed were irrelevant to nail enamel performance. For example, the challenger argued that the cupping test determines the deformability of a substrate by applying pressure on the underside of a surface with a steel indenter to determine at what point cracks form in the coating. The challenger maintained that in the real world this would be equivalent to driving a steel rod through a finger to see when the nail polish cracks. Similarly, the reverse impact test assesses the deformation of a substrate when subjected to falling weight. In the slip angle test, two coated panels are placed horizontally facing one another while lifting the bottom panel to asses[s] the angle at which the top breaks free. The challenger maintained that none of these tests reflected consumer relevant nail enamel performances.

challenger argued that this is not evidence of professional use of the Sally Hansen products in salons but rather evidence that people may sometimes bring their own nail polish to a salon.

II. "All 5 Steps of a Manicure in 1 Bottle" Claim.

The challenger maintained that the claim *"All 5 Steps of a Manicure in 1 Bottle"* reasonably conveys the message that the results of the nail treatment from Complete nail polish are comparable to results one would derive from a salon visit. The 5 steps—as defined by Coty, Inc.—are base coat, enamel, growth treatment, strengthener and top coat. The advertiser provided a formulation comparison chart that purported to compare ingredients of Complete nail polish with the advertiser's stand-alone base and top coats, strengthener, hardener and growth treatment products. The challenger argued that a product ingredient list cannot establish product efficacy or prove performance capability as compared to a salon manicure.[7]

The challenger maintained that simply adding base coat ingredients to nail enamel [cannot] equal the results of a salon manicure because of the function the base coat plays in a manicure. The base coat—which is applied before the enamel—acts as a barrier between the enamel and the nail surface to prevent staining. Combining the base coat and enamel ingredients will not provide the same protection as a base coat which is applied first, allowed to dry and then enamel applied over the base coat. The challenger argued that the advertiser did not submit any evidence regarding the protection again staining of the nail plate offered by Complete nail polish.

The challenger further argued that there is no evidence that Complete nail polish has a growth treatment ingredient. The advertiser has a separate growth product and the key ingredient that promotes nail growth is called "Spirulina Maxima Extract." The challenger noted that Complete nail polish does not contain Spirulina Maxima extract. Further, the challenger maintained that the advertiser conceded that Complete does not contain a growth treatment, but instead contains a nail hardener which helps promote nail growth. The challenger argued that the advertiser is misleading consumers because it is counting one ingredient as two steps (growth treatment and hardener) in claim *"All 5 Steps of a Manicure in 1 Bottle."*

Advertiser's Position:

I. "9 Out Of 10 Salon Professionals Preferred Our Formula To The Leading Salon Brand" Claim

A. Preference Claim

The advertiser maintained that its express preference claim is substantiated by an in-depth, multiday, blinded clinical study of the preferences between Complete and

7. OPI argued that Coty, Inc.'s lab mechanical testing was similarly unavailing. According to OPI, the mechanical tests comparing the strength of aluminum treated with Complete nail polish versus a leading salon brand was not consumer relevant because it was not performed on human nail surfaces. Further, the several tests that Coty, Inc. performed were irrelevant to nail enamel performance.

OPI nail polishes amongst twenty-five salon professionals from eight cities across the United States. An independent research company conducted the study and, the advertiser contended, the results demonstrated an overwhelming preference for Complete nail polish over OPI that was statistically significant at the ninety-five percent confidence level.

The twenty-five salon professional respondents were provided with an OPI and a Complete nail enamel sample in similar colors.[8] Some respondents were given two pink shades and others two red shades in blinded bottles. They were instructed to apply and wear one product for three days, remove it and then wear the other nail enamel for three days. At the end of six days the respondents completed a series of eleven survey questions that addressed performance aspects of nail enamel products—*e.g.*, ease of application, formula consistency, color intensity, shine and resistance to chipping. For each question, respondents were given the option of stating their preference between the two products or selecting a "no preference" option. The advertiser maintained that OPI was not found to be the preferred product in response to any one of the [] questions. The final question, which the advertiser relied upon to support its "9 out of 10" claim, was "which product would you prefer to use in [your] salon?" Out of twenty-five people, nineteen stated a preference for Complete nail polish, two preferred OPI and four had no preference.

In response to the challenger's criticism that the OPI nail enamel was not applied according to typical usage, the advertiser rejoined that OPI nail enamel does not have any instructions on the label. The advertiser further argued that consumers typically do not use base or top coats when they paint their nails at home. In support of this position, the advertiser submitted, through its expert, a survey that purported to demonstrate, among other things, that women do not apply base and top coats as part of at-home manicures.[9] Additionally, the study surveyed salon professionals whom the advertiser maintained possessed the expertise to evaluate the performance of two nail polish products without base and top coats. From a testing point of view, the products must be applied in the same manner so that salon professionals could directly compare Complete to OPI nail polishes under similar conditions.

The advertiser also maintained that the blinding of the OPI nail polish bottles was appropriate. The advertiser filed off the "OPI" engraved on the top of the challenger's OPI bottle, instead of transferring the polish to a stock bottle, because the brush and feel of the cap is an important aspect of the overall nail polishing experience. Further, had the OPI brush not been used, the challenger would have argued that its absence also biased the results in the advertiser's favor. The advertiser also contended that it did not completely exclude salon professionals . . . during the screening questionnaire that stated that OPI was their favorite brand, it simply

8. The name of the OPI shades were unreported.

9. This survey was submitted confidentially under NAD Rules & Procedures.

capped the number of those who stated an express preference for OPI to fifty percent of the panel. In any event, after the study was completed, one hundred percent of the respondents who expressed an OPI preference in the screening questionnaire selected Complete nail polish as their overall preference.[10]

B. The Implied Claim

The advertiser, through its expert, disputed the reasonableness of consumers taking away the message that the new Sally Hansen product line is actually purchased and used by a significant number of salon professionals in a salon setting. The advertiser's expert asserted that the implied claim is illogical as the concept of purchasing the product in a "salon setting" is wholly independent from the use of Complete nail polish in a salon setting.

In any event, the advertiser argued that it can support the alleged implied claim. The advertiser explained that it represents over fifty-five percent of the mass retail market for nail care products in the United States. As a result, the advertiser maintained that while its products are not sold in salons, many consumers use Sally Hansen products in professional salon settings. The advertiser submitted tracking data from an advertising agency that demonstrated that twenty-two percent of nail salon patrons bring their own nail polish when they go to get to a manicure regardless of the salon's preference to use a particular brand. Given its penetration, the advertiser argued, it is a fair inference that many salon customers are using the Complete nail polish at professional salons.

II. "All 5 Steps of a Manicure in 1 Bottle" Claim

The advertiser explained that it clearly defines in the text of the advertisements the five steps of a salon manicure as (1) base coat; (2) strengthener; (3) growth treatment; (4) color; and (5) top coat provided by its Complete nail polish. In other words, rather than using multiple bottles of different formulas for each of the five functions, Complete nail polish combines them all in one product. The advertiser disagreed with the challenger that the steps to a salon manicure are universally understood as preparation of the hand, nail plate and cuticle and then application of a base coat, nail polish and top coat.

The advertiser also argued that the claim "*All 5 Steps of a Manicure in 1 Bottle*" is puffery—vague, subjective and fanciful. The advertiser maintained that no consumer could reasonably believe that Complete nail enamel would clean nails,

---

10. Complete was preferred in all specific categories as well, including application ease, brush, consistency, high intensity color, resistance to wear and chipping. Coty, Inc. also submitted, in confidence to NAD, the final report from a second QRS survey, that was conducted from March 10, 2010 to March 11, 2010. As the survey was conducted after the challenged advertising was distributed, Coty, Inc. did not submit the second survey as substantiation for the challenged advertising, but claimed that it would use it to support preference claims going forward. Coty, Inc. maintained the second survey addressed the flaws of the first survey in that it had a larger sample size, eliminated the "no preference" option and forced the respondent to select a preference and randomized the order of nail enamels.

moisturize the hand, cut the cuticles and buff the nail. Indeed, no reasonable consumer would believe that the "5 Steps" in the advertisement refers to anything other than the application of enamel to nail.

In support of its claim that Complete nail polish provides "5 Steps in 1," the advertiser submitted a list of the ingredients in Complete which it asserted are known to perform more or one of these functions.[11] With regard to the challenger's criticism that Complete does not contain an ingredient for nail growth, the advertiser argued that Complete contains corallina officinalis extract (coral extract) and hydrolyzed conchiolin protein, which are known for strengthening nails and Vitamin E for conditioning and flexibility. According to the advertiser, these materials are present in the base even after it dries and provides a protective finish that is strengthening, provides protection and therefore supports natural nail growth.

Decision:

I. "9 Out Of 10 Salon Professionals Preferred Our Formula To The Leading Salon Brand" Claim

A. Preference Claim

In support of its "9 Out Of 10 Salon Professionals Preferred Our Formula To The Leading Salon Brand" the advertiser submitted a study of the preferences between Complete and OPI mauve and red nail polishes amongst twenty-five salon professionals.[12] The advertiser conducted its study in eight markets: Atlanta, Georgia; Dartmouth, Massachusetts; Vernon Hills, Illinois; Montclair, California; St. Louis, Missouri; Tucson, Arizona; Denton, Texas; and Lakewood, Colorado. The participants were instructed to apply two coats of one nail enamel product to clean, dry nails on the morning of day one. No base or top coats were applied to either nail enamel. The participants wore the enamel without touching it up until the end of the third day. After removing the first enamel, the respondents answered a series of questions about the first product and then applied the second product in the same manner as the first product and again wore it without any reapplication for three days. After removing the second product, the respondents answered questions about the second product and then answered a series of twelve questions regarding which product they preferred.[13] The advertiser based its "9 out of 10" claim on the answer to the last question, "which product would you use in the salon with your clients?"

---

11. The advertiser also submitted the results from a series of mechanical tests that comparing the adhesion, cupping, impact resistance, gloss, slip angle and hardness of OPI versus Complete Salon Manicure that purports to demonstrate performance parity in these categories.

12. The advertiser has the initial burden of presenting a reasonable basis for its claims. In support of its claim. *See, e.g.*, Domino's Pizza, Inc. (Oven Baked Sandwiches), Report #5023, *NAD/CARU Case Reports* (May 2009).

13. The questions were (1) overall which product do you prefer?; (2) which product do you prefer for overall appearance on your nails?; (3) which product do you prefer for ease of application?; (4) which product do you prefer for applying?; (5) which brush do you prefer? (6) which consistency do you prefer?; (7) which dry time do you prefer?; (8) which product do you prefer for shine?; (9) which product do you prefer for resistance to wear?; (10) which product do you prefer for resistance

While the challenger addressed what it believed was a myriad of methodological flaws with the advertiser's study, it identified as the most problematic aspect of the study that the OPI nail enamel was not applied with base and top coats as is typical in a salon setting. There was no dispute between the parties that, in a salon, nail technicians apply base and top coats on their customers' nails and that these additional coats enhance nail polish adhesion to the nail plate, protect the nail from staining, prevent chipping and wear and also add shine. The advertiser responded that the OPI polish was applied as consumers would apply it at home, *i.e.*, consumers typically do not use base or top coats when they paint their own nails. The advertiser submitted two surveys that it purports demonstrate that women do not apply base and top coats for at-home manicures.

NAD was troubled by the fact that the study compared the advertiser's nail polish—that has base, color and top coats all in on bottle—to the challenger's professional polish that was only colored enamel and was intended to be used with separate applications of base and top coats. NAD has previously found, across all product categories, that performance studies are fatally flawed if products are not tested according to usage instructions.[14] Although OPI nail polish for professional use does not have instructions on the bottle, no argument was made to contradict the basic premise that salon manicures include base and top coats. Indeed, the challenged advertising itself defines a salon manicure as including base and top coats.

NAD considered but did not find availing the advertiser's arguments that consumers supposedly do not use base and top coats for at-home manicures and therefore the study correctly applied the polishes as consumers would typically use them in the home.[15] In the context in which it appears,[16] the claim "*9 Out Of*

---

to chipping? (11) which product do you prefer for ease of removal?; and (12) which product would you use in the salon with your clients?

14. North American Green/Mulch& Seed Innovation (HydraCX2), Report #4854, NAD/CARU Case Reports (May 2008); Avon Products, Inc. (CELLU-SCULPT Anti-Cellulite Slimming Treatment), Report #4124, NAD/CARU Case Reports (January 2004) (holding that the home use study, which instructed participants to apply the product for "at least 5 minutes each time" twice a day was not in accordance with the product's use instructions which, though indicating that the product should be applied twice daily, did not specify the length of application time); Mission Pharmacal (Citracal), Report #3472, NAD/CARU Case Reports (July 1998) (holding that the advertiser's testing, administered at inappropriately high dosages and under fasting conditions, contravened Os-Cal's product use instructions); Amden Corporation (Smile White Tooth Whitening System), Report #4048, NAD/CARU Case Reports (July 2003) (holding that product testing submitted as substantiation for a performance claim should illustrate that the product was tested according to the product's use instructions).

15. NAD noted that the OPI-sponsored survey Nail Application Survey submitted with Coty, Inc.'s expert's supplemental declaration found that 95.1% of people surveyed responded that they polish their nails at home. The survey also then reported that 39.3% of people always apply a base coat at home and 21.4% very frequently apply a base coat. Only 5.4% never applied a base coat. The percentages were very similar for top coats, at 39.3%, 30.4% and 0.0%, respectively. The other survey, Coty's Nail Care Category Assessment Survey, which was submitted confidentially, reported similar data.

16. In the print advertisement, next to a picture of many women's fingers wearing a myriad of nail polish colors, appears the main claim "*All 5 Steps of a Salon Manicure in 1 Bottle*." The five steps

10 Salon Professionals Preferred Our Formula To The Leading Salon Brand" suggests that, both expressly and by implication, professionals assessed Complete nail polish as compared to a salon brand as used in a professional manicure. That this was the advertiser's intended message is made clear by the fact [that] it based its claim on the responses to the question "which product would you use in the salon on your clients?" As the advertiser defined a salon manicure as including top and base coats, its testing should have at least included base and top coats on the challenger's nail enamel. This is a significant and critical flaw when coupled with the fact the participants only wore each nail enamel for three days which, in addition to not being a consumer relevant time period, is not long enough to properly assess nail enamel performance attributes, such as resistance to chipping and fading.[17]

NAD was also concerned that the sample size of twenty-five people was too small to support such a strong claim.[18] This concern was compounded by several other factors that NAD believes that had the potential to introduce bias into the study. More specifically, NAD questioned whether the eight markets that the advertiser tested in (Atlanta, Georgia; Dartmouth, Massachusetts; Vernon Hills, Illinois; Montclair, California; St. Louis, Missouri; Tucson, Arizona; Denton, Texas; and Lakewood, Colorado) were representative of the universe of national salon technicians. For example, only one town in the northeastern U.S. was included and it was not a large urban area.[19] Second, the advertiser's study failed to randomly rotate which enamel was tested first, and in fact seventeen out of twenty-five respondents used the challenger's product first. It is recognized that respondents may be more likely to select a product based on the order in which it was used in the study versus an actual preference for the product.[20] Although order effects may be small, "no general formula is available that can adjust values to correct for order effects," and

---

of a salon manicure are enumerated as (1) base coat; (2) strengthener; (3) growth treatment; (4) color; and (5) top coat. The claim "*9 out of 10 Salon professionals preferred our formula to the leading salon brand*" runs underneath the list of the five manicure steps.

17. The respondents were not told that they were comparing a simple enamel to a multi-function nail product which featured ingredients that improve adhesion, prevent wear and chipping and increase shine.

18. See L'Oreal USA (L'Oreal Excellence Crème), Report #49938, NAD/CARU Case Reports (December 2008) (study determined to be insufficient where it excluded users of L'Oreal Excellence Crème, a hair dye with the largest market share). NAD was also concerned that the number of colors tested was too small to support such a broad claim.

19. See L'Oreal USA (L'Oreal Excellence Crème), Report #, NAD/CARU Case Reports (2009) (general discussion of past cases where under inclusive sample frame has invalidated study). An explanation of how the cities in the advertiser's study were chosen and whether or not the excluded population was likely to react differently from the included population may have alleviated this concern is in-line with sound methodological practices. See Reference Manual on Scientific Evidence, Shari Diamond, J.D. , et al, Reference Guide on Survey Research (2d Ed.) at p. 241. If the sample is drawn from an under inclusive universe, there is generally no way to know how the unrepresented members would have responded. Ibid.

20. Reference Manual on Scientific Evidence, Shari Diamond, J.D. , et al, Reference Guide on Survey Research (2d Ed.) at p. 255. It is also difficult to assess whether a question suffers from a primacy (likelihood of selecting first option) or recency effect (likelihood of selecting last option). Thus, the order should be rotated equally to eliminate doubt. Ibid.

given the extremely small sample size of the study, a small order bias may have a large impact on the final results.

Lastly, NAD was concerned about the effectiveness of blinding the challenger's product by filing off the "OPI" logo. The filing appeared to be ragged and NAD noted that the OPI cap has a distinctive long, tapered shape.[21] The advertiser maintained that it filed the logo off because the nail polish brushes are unique to each manufacturer and an important part of the nail polishing experience. NAD noted that the OPI brush is removable from the cap and as such could have been included in a neutral bottle.[22] In sum, the small sample size combined with the potential for bias in the study, especially in the aggregate, and the flawed methodology rendered its results insufficiently reliable to support the advertiser's "*9 Out Of 10 Salon Professionals Preferred Our Formula To The Leading Salon Brand*" claim.[23]

Consequently, NAD recommended that the advertiser discontinue the claim "*9 Out Of 10 Salon Professionals Preferred Our Formula To The Leading Salon Brand.*"

B. The Implied Claim

In the absence of reliable consumer perception evidence, NAD stepped into the role of the consumer and independently assessed the messages reasonably conveyed by the challenged advertising.[24] NAD determined that at least one reasonable interpretation of the "9 out of 10" preference claim is that Complete nail polish is actually available in, preferred by and used by a significant number of salon professionals in a salon setting.[25]

---

21. The advertiser argued that recognition of the OPI bottle should have biased the results in favor of the challenger. However, the very problem with the effect of methodological flaws in studies is that they cannot be accounted for and one cannot simply guess as to how the conclusions would have been different if not for the error in design.

22. In its second submission Coty, Inc. submitted, in confidence to the NAD, the final report of a second study that it claimed addressed the concerns raised in this case, was statistically significant to the 99% confidence level and that it intends to use this study to support its preference claims going forward. NAD determined however, that while the study had a larger sample size, that it still suffered from many of the flaws, including but not limited to the most critical flaw, the failure to add base and top coats to the challenger's nail enamel during a two-day time period. Also, the survey eliminated the "no preference" option, which NAD also determined to be a fatal flaw as respondents were forced to possibly artificially choose one product or another. NAD's concern regarding the "no preference" option in the first survey was not that there was such an option, but rather that the "no preference" responses were excluded from the data set. NAD had further concerns regarding the number of colors tested and the blinding techniques.

23. Although the study was deemed insufficient in its entirety, an argument was also raised by the challenger that the "9 out of 10" claim was also insufficient because the advertiser did not count two "no preference" responses to the final survey question and therefore, at best, the advertiser only could support a "7 out of 10" claim. Given the methodological flaws with the survey, NAD determined that the advertiser's study also does not provide a reasonable basis for a "7 out of 10" claim.

24. *See e.g.*, Pfizer, Inc., (Zantac 150), Report #4437, *NAD/CARU Case Reports* (January 2006).

25. General Mills, Inc. (Pillsbury Toaster Strudel Frozen Toaster Pastries), Report # 4867, *NAD/CARU Case Reports* (June 2008) (in the context of the challenged advertising, where a boy is eating

The advertiser asserted that the implied message was supported by a survey that demonstrated that eighteen percent of consumers have used a Sally Hansen product (the advertiser has several Sally Hansen lines of nail enamel at various price points) in a salon.[26] The challenger countered that this is not evidence of professional use but rather evidence that people may sometimes bring their own nail polish to a salon. NAD determined that . . . whether or not consumers bring a Sally Hansen product to a salon, using a product or having an experience with a product is not synonymous with preferring a product. In any event, the implied message is that salon professionals prefer and use Complete in a salon setting and not whether consumers bring their favorite nail polish to the salon, a message that is not supported by the message in the record.[27] Therefore, NAD determined that the advertiser did not have evidence sufficient to support the implied claim, although this issue is moot in light of the fact that NAD recommended that the advertiser discontinue the underl[y]ing preference claim.

II. "All 5 Steps of a Manicure in 1 Bottle" Claim

Having recommended that the advertiser discontinue its salon professional preference claim, NAD considered the claim "*All 5 Steps of a Manicure in 1 Bottle*" in a monadic setting. The claim that it is a manicure in a bottle is fanciful and NAD agrees with the advertiser that no consumer could reasonably believe that Complete nail enamel would, as the challenger suggested, clean and buff the nails, moisturize the hand and cut the cuticles. Rather, NAD found that consumers would understand [the] "5 Steps" claim to be a reference to the attributes of the product as described in the challenged advertising: (1) base coat; (2) strengthener; (3) growth treatment; (4) color; and (5) top coat.[28] NAD determined that the advertiser's product ingredient list[,] which included ingredients that have been recognized to provide the listed attributes[,] provided a reasonable basis for its claim "*All 5 Steps of a Manicure in 1 Bottle*."[29]

---

a toaster strudel and nodding approvingly, the claim "the one kids want to eat" is an implied taste preference claim).

26. Both parties discussed that a "gray market" exists in the nail enamel profession where sometimes professional nail polishes end up on drug store shelves without the consent of the manufacturer, primarily in New York City. NAD did not discount the possibility that a renegade salon could sell the advertiser's Sally Hansen line. Nothing in the record however suggests that this is more than an aberration.

27. Coty, Inc. maintained that OPI was arguing that an advertiser could never make a prospective preference claim. NAD disagrees. NAD has permitted a "doctor endorsed" claim for such a product where the survey was reliable and the claim narrowly tailored. The Proctor & Gamble Company (Secret Clinical Strength), Report # 4682, NAD/CARU Case Reports (June 2007).

28. With regard to OPI's argument that Coty, Inc. is misleading consumers because it is counting one function as two steps, NAD noted that Complete nail polish contains corallina officinalis extract, hydrolyzed conchiolin protein, and Vitamin E that provides a protective finish that strengthens, provides protection and therefore supports natural growth.

29. Coty, Inc. also submitted the results from a series of mechanical tests to demonstrate that Complete performed at a comparable level with OPI nail polish. The underlying documentation of

Conclusion:

NAD recommended the advertiser discontinue its "*9 out of 10 Salon professionals preferred our formula to the leading salon brand*" claim because the surveys were not sufficiently reliable to provide a basis for the advertiser's claim. NAD also determined at least one reasonable interpretation of the unqualified "9 out of 10" preference claim is that Complete nail polish is actually available in, preferred by and used by a significant number of salon professionals in a salon setting, a message not supported by the evidence in the record.

Lastly, NAD determined that the advertiser had provided a reasonable basis for its monadic claim that Complete has "*All 5 Steps of a Salon Manicure in 1 Bottle.*"

Notes

1. Why do you think the NAD was created? Why not defer to the FTC?

2. Why did the NAD determine that the statement "All 5 Steps of a Manicure in 1 Bottle" is puffery? Why wouldn't a consumer reasonably believe the statement to be accurate?

3. Compare with "9 out of 10 Salon professionals preferred our formula to the leading salon brand"—why isn't that puffery? What if the advertiser had said "all salon professionals prefer our formula"? Is that puffery?

2. Performance Demonstrations

An advertiser must possess substantiation for the claims it makes in its advertising prior to dissemination. A product should thus not be featured in a manner that involves digital or temporal alterations, or distorted in such a way that it impacts the product's performance. This includes product demonstration and performance claims made in broadcast, print, and internet advertising, as well as on product packaging. So, for example, "before" and "after" pictures showing a nail growth of 1.5 inches within a month after applying the advertiser's topical nail product is deceptive without substantiation where nails typically grow 1.5 inches per year. Similarly, having a woman dip and vigorously move around her perfectly manicured nails in a casserole dish of rocks only to come out with the same perfect nails constitutes an unqualified promise of product performance if there is no substantiation. *See Ontel Products Corporation*, NAD, Case #5701.

In the present case, the NAD has been tasked with independently assessing certain product demonstrations and performance claims made in broadcast, print, and internet advertising, as well as on product packaging, by Ontel Products Corporation for its Pink Armor nail gel product, which have been challenged by Coty Inc., a competing manufacturer of nail products. Namely, Ontel's claims include "before" and "after" photographs/product demonstrations, as well as express claims

---

the tests, however, including any evidence as to how these tests are consumer relevant, are not in the record.

including, but not limited to, "Your nails won't peel, chip or crack no matter what the attack," "Rock Hard Finish," and "Guaranteed to transform cracked, brittle and weak nails into healthy, stronger, brighter nails with just one coat, once a week."

Ontel Products Corp. (Pink Armor Nail Gel)*

NAD Case No. 5701 (Mar. 27, 2014)

Challenger: Coty Inc.

It is well-established that an advertiser must possess substantiation for claims made in its advertising prior to their dissemination. "Before" and "after" photographs are product performance claims and, therefore, they must be supported, accurate and representative of the level of product efficacy that a reasonable consumer can expect to achieve.

Basis of Inquiry: Product demonstrations and performance claims made in broadcast, print and Internet advertising, as well as on product packaging, by Ontel Products Corporation for its Pink Armor nail gel product were challenged by Coty Inc., a competing manufacturer of nail products. The following claims formed the basis of NAD's inquiry:

"Before" and "after" photographs/product demonstrations

Express Claims:

"Your nails won't peel, chip or crack no matter what the attack."

"Rock Hard Finish."

"[G]uaranteed to transform cracked, brittle and weak nails into healthy, stronger, brighter nails with just one coat, once a week."

"[W]ith just one coat, once a week, [i]t's like getting a professional nail treatment at home manicure at home!"

Challenger's Position:

I. "Before" and "after" photographs/product demonstrations

The challenger argued that the product demonstrations are deceptive for the following reasons: 1) they drastically misrepresent the rate at which nails grow—while nail growth varies, nails typically grow 1.5 inches *per year* (or one-tenth an inch each month) thus nails are incapable of growing to the lengths depicted in the challenged advertisements in just one month; 2) the comparative demonstrations falsely represent how a consumer's fingernails will appear after using the Pink Armor nail gel product because the "after" photo in the demonstrations show meticulously manicured, polished and painted nails, a look that cannot be achieved solely by using the product; and 3) they imply that Pink Armor is capable of healing diseased fingernails and inflamed cuticles, health conditions for which Pink Armor (a purely cosmetic product) has no effect. The challenger maintained that it conducted a four-week internal study[,] which shows that Pink Armor's only effect was to make nails slightly shinier[,] which belies the dramatic results depicted in the challenged demonstrations.

In support of its position, the challenger referred to FTC and NAD precedent on "before" and "after" product demonstrations[,] which make clear they must accurately depict product performance. The challenger rejected the advertiser's argument that the "before" and "after" photographs are puffery. Rather, they constitute actual product performance claims, creating expectations that consumers can transform short, broken and diseased nails into longer, stronger, healthier nails impervious to any chipping or cracking simply by using Pink Armor Nail Gel. The challenger argued that the comparative demonstrations are false and misleading because the fingernails that appear in the "after" photographs have been artificially enhanced using various polishing, coloring and manicuring techniques. The challenger noted that the inclusion of the "dramatization" disclosure in some of the comparative demonstrations is both incorrect and misleading because the results depicted are not achievable.

The challenger maintained that the advertiser's evidence is comprised solely of anecdotal evidence (consumer feedback) and, as such, is insufficient to support the challenged demonstrations and claims. As for the advertiser's reliance on the ingredient, keratin, to support its claims, the challenger maintained that while keratin helps support nail growth, there is no evidence that it can produce the results depicted in the comparative demonstrations or that it can heal damaged or diseased nails.

The challenger asserted that the challenged television commercial includes a computer-generated "graphic simulation" which purports to demonstrate how the product works. The simulation shows a woman applying Pink Armor to a fingernail[,] which begins to glimmer upon contact as the voiceover states "the Keratin Gel goes deep down to repair and restore, helping battered nails recover faster." Concomitantly, the inside of the woman's nail is shown where the nail cells appear to be healing[,] after which the outside of the nail is shown with a glimmering pink color and white tip. Coty Inc. argued that this graphic simulation is factually and scientifically inaccurate because the product cannot and does not go "deep down" to repair or restore the nail because it is merely a nail protectant and the cells of the nail plate are already dead.

II. Express Claims: "Your nails won't peel, chip or crack no matter what the attack"; "Rock Hard Finish"; "[G]uaranteed to transform cracked, brittle and weak nails into healthy, stronger, brighter nails with just one coat, once a week"; "[W]ith just one coat, once a week, [i]t's like getting a professional nail treatment at home manuicure at home!"

The challenger argued that the television commercial also features a demonstration in which a woman places her manicured fingernails in a casserole dish of rocks and moves her hand vigorously around the dish and, upon removing her hand, reveals her perfect nails and states that by using Pink Armor "your nails won't peel, chip or crack no matter what the attack." The image of this demonstration is also shown on the advertiser's website alongside the claim that Pink Armor provides a "Rock Hard Finish." Taken together, the advertiser maintained that the demonstration is literally false because Pink Armor Nail Gel alone cannot confer the strength and protection depicted in the demonstration, adding that the woman in the commercial is clearly wearing nail polish and/or other coating on her fingernails to shield her nails from damage. The accompanying claims are likewise false because they communicate the unsupported message that consumers who use Pink Armor will never experience any peeling, chipping or cracking.

The challenger also argued that the advertiser's claim that consumers need only apply "one coat [of the product], once a week," shown in the television commercial and on the advertiser's website, is unsupported because it directly contravenes its own product use instructions (specifically, an insert in the package), which instruct users to "[a]pply *2 coats* of Pink Armor to [their] bare natural nails" on a weekly basis. (emphasis added.) The instructions also encourage users to "[a]pply a fresh coat regularly for enhanced results" and note that "[f]or touchups, you can recoat over dry Pink Armor at anytime," further demonstrating that the "one coat [of the product], once a week" claim is unsupported.

The challenger maintained that the challenged claims do not constitute puffery. The challenger maintained that the advertiser's reliance on the Sally Hansen Complete Manicure case[30] to support its argument that these claims are puffery is misplaced. In that case, the challenged claim "All 5 Steps of a Manicure in 1 Bottle" was appropriately deemed to be puffery because no consumer could reasonably interpret the claim to mean that a nail polish could perform all of the physical tasks associated with a manicure. Here, however, the challenged claims are unqualified promises of product performance[,] which are reinforced by a demonstration where a woman runs her hand through a dish of rocks without damaging any of her perfectly manicured nails[,] as well as other images of miraculously transformed nails.

The challenger argued that the advertiser's proposed revisions, including the addition of the term "dramatization" to the "before" and "after" photographs on its website, is not sufficient to correct the inaccurate messages conveyed. Further, the advertiser's proposed modification of its website copy from "with just one coat, once a week, [i]t's like getting a professional nail treatment" to "two coats, once a week, [i]t's like getting a professional nail treatment" is similarly unsupported because it has failed to provide any evidence that two coats of Pink Armor can provide the results depicted in the challenged advertising.[31]

---

30. Coty Inc. (Sally Hansen Complete Manicure), Report #5201, NAD/CARU Case Reports (August 2010).

31. The similar claim is "Pink Armor is ... [g]uaranteed to transform cracked, brittle and weak nails into healthy, stronger, brighter nails with just one coat, once a week." The challenger also noted that the advertiser's proposed modification ("two coats, once a week, [i]t's like getting a professional nail treatment") is also insufficient because neither the television commercial nor the

Advertiser's Position:

The advertiser argued that its product packaging clearly and conspicuously states that the "before" and "after" photographs are dramatizations. The advertiser maintained that these dramatizations constitute puffery because consumers are accustomed to seeing dramatizations in advertising. The advertiser argued that the "before" photographs do not show yellow, diseased fingernails and that the "after" photographs feature fingernails that have only been filed with an emery board and coated with Pink Armor nail gel. The advertiser also argued that claims such as "won't peel, chip or crack no matter what the attack" and "Rock Hard Finish" also constitute puffery.[32]

The advertiser maintained that the challenged comparative demonstrations and express claims are supported by positive testimonials from uncompensated consumers who used Pink Armor and reported that their nails were stronger, healthier and growing more quickly after weeks of use.[33] The advertiser also argued that its claims are further supported by the keratin in its product, which is widely regarded in the nail industry as strengthening nails and supporting nail growth. The advertiser also noted that the target audience of the challenged advertisements is not a vulnerable one as would be the case for weight loss or hair loss products.

The advertiser agreed to make the following modifications to its advertising: 1) adding the term "dramatization" to the "before" and "after" photographs to avoid any potential consumer confusion; 2) revising its website to state a) that the product should be used for four consecutive weeks to obtain the desired outcome; and b) that two coats should be applied each time in accordance with product use instructions; and 3) revising the YouTube page for its Pink Armor product to include the same disclosures that appear on the Pink Armor website.

Decision:

I. "Before" and "after" photographs/product demonstrations

It is well established that an advertiser must possess substantiation for claims made in its advertising prior to their dissemination.[34] "Before" and "after" photo-

---

website includes a disclosure indicating that a consumer must use Pink Armor for four consecutive weeks to achieve the dramatized (i.e., unattainable) results. Although this disclosure appears on the product packaging, the advertiser has provided no explanation as to why it should not appear on its website and in its television commercial. The challenger also argued that the proposed change failed to address the similar claim ("one coat [of the product], once a week") that continues to appear in the challenged television commercial which will confuse consumers especially when the commercial appears in isolation.

32. The advertiser maintained that the challenged commercial is no longer running on television and will be shown exclusively on its website.

33. The advertiser maintained that there are over 150 customer reviews with an average of 4-5 stars.

34. Too Faced Cosmetics (Lip Injection Extreme Lip Plumping Treatment), Report #4276, NAD/CARU Case Reports (January 2005). *See also* FTC Policy Statement Regarding Advertising Substantiation, Appended to Thompson Medical Co., 104 F.T.C. 648, 839 (1984), aff'd, 791 F.2d 189 (D.C. Cir. 1986), cert. denied, 479 U.S. 1086 (1987) (noting that the reasonable basis doctrine

graphs are product performance claims and, therefore, they must be supported, accurate and representative of the level of product efficacy that a reasonable consumer can expect to achieve.[35] Further, actual product testing is the most direct and affirmative means by which to assess a product's performance capability.[36]

The front and side panels of the Pink Armor Nail Gel product package prominently feature "before" and after" photographs. The "before" photographs feature a woman's short and visibly damaged or diseased fingernails. In contrast, the "after" photographs depict perfectly manicured, shiny, noticeably longer and pink fingernails after four weeks of use—in fact, the "after" photograph on the side panel features what appears to be a perfectly manicured *artificial* nail.[37] The "dramatization" disclaimer appears below the photographs.

In the challenged television commercial, there are many "before" and "after" photographs depicting a visibly short and damaged/diseased nail in the "before" photograph and a noticeably longer, pink and well-manicured nail in the "after" photograph. These photographs appear in conjunction with the following: 1) consumer testimonials promoting Pink Armor Nail Gel's efficacy,[38] 2) a demonstration of the announcer putting her hands into a bowl filled with rocks and moving her hands around vigorously to show that with Pink Armor, her nails "won't chip, peel or crack whatever the attack," and 3) a depiction of the keratin rich gel penetrating deep into the nail bed to "help battered nails recover faster."

The advertiser submitted no product testing in support of its "before" and "after" photographs/product demonstrations or its performance claims. Instead, the advertiser submitted an affidavit from the commercial's producer explaining the following: 1) the four individuals featured in the on-screen testimonials were instructed to use the product twice a week for four to six weeks and not to get a manicure for the duration of product use; 2) the video was shot after four to six weeks of product use; 3) the individuals in the commercial were not compensated; and 4) their testimonials are based on their personal experience using the product. The advertiser also submitted product reviews from Amazon.com of satisfied users as further support for "before" and "after" product demonstrations.

It is well established that endorsements and testimonials cannot replace reliable evidence as support for advertising claims, notwithstanding that they may reflect

---

requires that firms have substantiation before disseminating a claim), at http://www.ftc.gov/ftc-policy-statement-regarding-advertising-substantiation.

35. Lifestyle Lift Holdings, Inc. (Lifestyle Lift®), Report #4654, NAD/CARU Case Reports (April 2007).

36. Preval® (ActiFade™ Complete Age-Defying System), Report #4747, NAD/CARU Case Reports (November 2007).

37. Similarly, the back of the product packaging also features what appear to be perfectly manicured *artificial* nails.

38. Testimonials include "no splitting and healthy nails"; "my nails have become longer and stronger with Pink Armor" and "Pink Armor is supposed to repair, seal and strengthen and it absolutely does."

the honest opinions of satisfied users.[39] The FTC's Endorsements and Testimonials Guides clarify that "[a]n advertisement employing endorsements by one or more consumers about the performance of an advertised product or service will be interpreted as representing that the product or service is effective for the purpose depicted in the advertisement. Therefore, the advertiser must possess and rely upon adequate substantiation, including, when appropriate, competent and reliable scientific evidence, to support such claims made through endorsements in the same manner the advertiser would be required to do if it had made the representation directly, *i.e.*, without using endorsements. Consumer endorsements themselves are not competent and reliable scientific evidence."[40] The Guides also state that "[i]f the advertiser does not have substantiation that the endorser's experience is representative of what consumers will generally achieve, the advertisement should clearly and conspicuously disclose the generally expected performance in the depicted circumstances, and the advertiser must possess and rely on adequate substantiation for that representation."[41]

Regardless of how heartfelt the testimonials of the users in the commercial (or those satisfied customers on Amazon.com) are, they are no substitute for reliable product testing demonstrating that consumers who use the product as instructed will achieve results similar to the nails depicted in the "after" photos on the product packaging and in the commercial. Further, the advertiser provided no evidence to counter the challenger's argument regarding typical nail growth (namely, 1.5 inches per year, or one-tenth an inch per month), which is significantly less than what is depicted in the "before" and "after" photographs/product demonstrations. Similarly, the producer affidavit is not proof of what consumers can typically expect to achieve when using the product according to its use instructions.

As for the "dramatization" disclaimer on the product packaging and the advertiser's website, NAD has determined that dramatizations, while an acceptable means of conveying a message, must nonetheless be accurate and substantiated.[42]

---

39. Alde Associates, LLC (daniPro Nail Polish), Report #5565, NAD/CARU Case Reports (March 2013).

40. Guides Concerning the Use of Endorsements and Testimonials in Advertising, 16 CFR §255.2(a), at http://www.ftc.gov/sites/default/files/attachments/press-releases/ftc-publishes-final-guides-governing-endorsementstestimonials/091005revisedendorsementguides.pdf.

41. *Id.* at 16 CFR §255.2(b).

42. Natural White, Inc. (Rapid White® Tooth Whitening System), Report #3995, NAD/CARU Case Reports (January 2003) (noting that the depicted "before" and "after" depictions could reasonably be interpreted to mean that consumers could anticipate similar dramatic results after using Rapid White); see also Church & Dwight Co., Inc. (Arm & Hammer® Liquid Laundry Detergents), Report #5658, NAD/CARU Case Reports (December 2013), fn. 72 (noting that while the term "Dramatization" is shown onscreen during the challenged television commercial, there is no evidence that consumers would understand the advertiser's intended message that "Dramatization" refers both to the fact that the product is not actually manufactured by pouring baking soda back into the bottle, as well as the fact that the "two scoops" claim and imagery merely characterize the presence of a functionally significant amount of baking soda in the 4X concentrated products).

Just recently, the FTC, in a case it settled against Nissan North America, Inc., made clear that a false product demonstration (which was shown in conjunction with a mice-type super which states "Fictionalization. Do Not Attempt") violated Section 5(a) of the FTC Act.[43]

Here, the advertiser's use of the "dramatization" disclaimer in connection with the "before" and "after" photographs on the product packaging and in the Internet advertising does not insulate it from its responsibility to provide evidence that consumers will typically achieve nails similar to those depicted in the "after" photograph when using the product according to its use instructions.

With respect to the depiction of visual simulation of the keratin penetrating the nail bed to heal damaged or diseased nails, even assuming as true that keratin when applied to the surface of the nail is known to strengthen nails, there is no evidence in the record that keratin works systemically, *i.e.*, that it can penetrate the nail bed, which is comprised of *dead* cells, and repair or heal damaged or diseased nails.

For all the foregoing reasons, NAD recommended that the "before" and "after" photographs and the visual simulation of the keratin penetrating the nail bed be discontinued.[44]

II. Express Claims: "Your nails won't peel, chip or crack no matter what the attack"; "Rock Hard Finish"; "[G]uaranteed to transform cracked, brittle and weak nails into healthy, stronger, brighter nails with just one coat, once a week"; "[W]ith just one coat, once a week, [i]t's like getting a professional nail treatment at home manicure at home!"

NAD considered the advertiser's puffery arguments, noting that statements that are mere puffing do not require substantiation. In determining whether claims constitute puffery, NAD looks to the following factors: (1) whether the representations concern general matters that cannot be proven or disproved, (2) whether the statements are distinguishable from representations of specific characteristics that are

---

43. In the commercial, a Nissan Frontier pickup truck is shown speeding up a steep hill to rescue a dune buggy that is trapped in sand atop the hill, ultimately pushing the dune buggy over the hill. Before the Nissan Frontier is shown, a mice-type super which states "Fictionalization. Do Not Attempt" appears. The narrator subsequently states "[t]he mid-size Nissan Frontier with full-size horsepower and torque. Innovation for doers, innovation for all." In reality, however, Nissan failed to accurately represent the performance of the actual, unaltered Nissan Frontier under the depicted conditions because the Nissan Frontier and the dune buggy were pulled to the top of the hill by cable and the sand dune is significantly less steep than depicted. In the Matter of Nissan North America. Inc., Complaint, at ¶¶ 5, 7, 8.

44. NAD advised the advertiser that any depiction of product performance must be supported by reliable and robust product testing prior to the dissemination of such depictions in any future advertising. While the challenger submitted in-house testing to demonstrate that the "before" and "after" photographs exaggerate the product's efficacy, NAD did not need review this testing because the advertiser failed to provide a reasonable basis to support the challenged claims and product demonstrations.

measurable by research or test, or (3) whether the wording uses expressions of opinion that will be discounted by the buyer.[45]

Product performance claims, unlike puffery, must be supported by reliable product testing.[46] NAD noted that Pink Armor Nail Gel has many sets of product use instructions. The instructions on the product packaging make no reference to the number of times one must apply Pink Armor while the product insert, titled "Read Before First Use!," states "Apply 2 coats of Pink Armor to your bare nails—allow to dry thoroughly between coats. Remove once weekly with any nail polish remover and repeat."[47] In contrast, the challenged commercial and the advertiser's website promote the product's efficacy based on the product being applied with "one coat, once a week." Regardless of how often applied or the number of coats, the advertiser has failed to provide *any* product testing to support the challenged performance claims. Specifically, the claim "Your nails won't peel, chip or crack no matter what the attack" is an objectively provable performance claim and is reinforced by the depiction of the announcer inserting her manicured nails into a rock bed and moving her hands around in it. Similarly, "[G]uaranteed to transform cracked, brittle and weak nails into healthy, stronger, brighter nails with just one coat, once a week" is also an objectively provable performance claim which is reinforced by "before" and "after" photographs[,] with which it is shown.

In contrast, NAD determined that the claims "Rock Hard Finish" and "[W]ith just one coat, once a week, it's like getting a professional nail treatment at home manicure at home!" constitute permissible advertiser puffing because no reasonable consumers would expect their nails to be as hard as a rock (even when shown in conjunction with a woman moving her manicured nails around vigorously in a rock bed) or that they could get a professional manicure (which involves a multi-step cleaning and shaping process) simply by using Pink Armor Nail Gel.[48]

Accordingly, NAD recommended that the advertiser discontinue the unsupported performance claims "Your nails won't peel, chip or crack no matter what the attack" (together with the depiction of the woman moving her nails around vigorously in the rock bed) and "[G]uaranteed to transform cracked, brittle and weak nails into healthy, stronger, brighter nails with just one coat, once a week."

---

45. Envirocon Technologies, Inc. (Lemi Shine® Performance Booster and Lemi Shine® Rinse Agent), Report #5543, NAD/CARU Case Reports (January 2013).

46. Preval® (ActiFade™ Complete Age-Defying System), Report #4747, NAD/CARU Case Reports (November 2007).

47. The product packaging states: "Apply Pink Armor directly to your natural nails. You may re-coat at anytime. Can be removed with any nail polish remover."

48. NAD noted that the advertiser agreed to modify the claim and "[W]ith just one coat, once a week, [i]t's like getting a professional nail treatment at home manicure at home!" to state "two coats, once a week, [i]t's like getting a professional nail treatment."

Conclusion:

NAD recommended that, given the lack of reliable supporting evidence in the record, the "before" and "after" photographs and the visual simulation of the keratin penetrating the nail bed be discontinued.

NAD determined that the claims "Rock Hard Finish" and "[W]ith just one coat, once a week, [i]t's like getting a professional nail treatment at home manicure at home!" constitute permissible advertiser puffing. However, NAD recommended that the advertiser discontinue the unsupported product performance claims "Your nails won't peel, chip or crack no matter what the attack" (together with the depiction of the woman moving her nails around vigorously in the rock bed) and "[G]uaranteed to transform cracked, brittle and weak nails into healthy, stronger, brighter nails with just one coat, once a week."

Notes

1. Why was Pink Armor's reliance on the Sally Hansen case misplaced?

2. Would a consumer believe the performance presentation to be puffery? Why?

3. What could Pink Armor have done differently?

When dealing with product performance, endorsement and testimonials are not reliable evidence as support for advertising claims. On the contrary, such evidence will merely reinforce the advertiser's statement that the product or service is effective for the purposes for which it was depicted in the advertisement. In other words, an advertiser must obtain adequate substantiation, such as competent and reliable scientific evidence, to support the claims made in the demonstration in the same manner as it would have to do if the representation was made directly. *See also FTC Policy Statement Regarding Advertising Substantiation—Appended to Thompson Medical Co.*, 104 F.T.C. 648, 839 (1984).

3. Other Advertising Claims

There are a number of other advertising claims that advertisers must be aware of when making claims about certain products. Included below are the most salient ones pertaining to the apparel and beauty industry.

a. Wool Products Labeling Act

The Wool Products Labeling Act (15 U.S.C. § 68) was enacted in 1939 and requires labels on wool products disclosing (1) the manufacturer's or marketer's name, (2) the country where the product was processed or manufactured, and (3) information about the fiber content of the item. For example, if a sweater is made of wool, then it can be labeled as 100 percent wool, assuming it contains only wool. If a sweater contains cashmere mixed with sheep's wool, then the label must accurately disclose the content (e.g., 70 percent wool, 30 percent cashmere). The label on the garment must be consistent with other representations made on a garment. For example, a coat could not have a sleeve label stating "Fine Cashmere Garment" but be otherwise labeled "50% Cashmere and 50% Wool."

b. Labeling and Advertising Cotton Products

The Textile Fiber Identification Act ("Textile Act"), and the Textile Labeling Rules ("Textile Rules") provide mandatory content disclosures in the labeling, invoicing, and advertising of textile fiber products, including cotton. According to the Textile Rules, businesses advertising or selling clothing or household items containing cotton must label the products reflecting the fabric content accurately. Textile Rules cover fibers, yarns, and fabrics, and household textile products made from them, like clothing and accessories, draperies, floor coverings, furnishings, and beddings.

Any product covered by the Textile Act and Textile Rules must include a fiber content statement listing the generic name of each fiber that equals five percent or more of the product's weight, in order of predominance, and the percentage of the product's weight represented by each fiber. So, for example, 65 percent polyester and 35 percent cotton. 15 U.S.C. § 70b(b)(1)-(2) and § 68b(a)(2)(A); 16 C.F.R. § 303.16(a)(1) and § 300.3(a)(1).

c. Sustainability and Green Products

The FTC published its "Green Guides," 16 C.F.R. Part 260, guidelines that are designed to help marketers avoid making environmental claims that are unfair or deceptive under Section 5 of the FTC Act.

The Green Guides were first issued in 1992 and were revised in 1996, 1998, and 2012. The guidance they provide includes: (1) general principles that apply to all environmental marketing claims; (2) how consumers are likely to interpret particular claims and how marketers can substantiate these claims; and (3) how marketers can qualify their claims to avoid deceiving consumers. The Guides include guidance on advertisers' use of product certifications and seals of approval, claims about materials and energy sources that are "renewable," and "carbon offset" claims.

Pursuant to the Green Guides, an advertiser should be careful not to make broad, unqualified general environmental benefit claims like "green" or "eco-friendly." Advertisers should try to include claims with specific environmental benefits. However, if a trade-off of having a specific claim negates the general claim, then the specific claim may not be substantiated. For example, it may be deceptive to claim "green, made with recycled content" where the environmental cost of using recycled content outweighs the environmental benefit of using it.

When using certifications and seals of approvals, advertisers are subject to the FTC's Endorsement Guidelines (16 C.F.R. Part 255), which govern the use of endorsements and testimonials in advertising, and must disclose if there is any material connection with the certifying organization. Moreover, advertisers must clearly convey the basis for the certification when using environmental certifications or seals.

If claiming that a product is made from recycled content, then such material must have been recovered or diverted from the waste stream during the manufacturing process or after consumer use. Moreover, if the product is partly made with recycled content, the advertiser should clearly state this and include a disclaimer (e.g., "Made from 30% recycled material").

See e.g., United States v. Nordstrom, Inc., No. 1:15-cv-2130 (Nordstrom, Bed Bath & Beyond, Backcountry.com, and JC Penney to pay penalties totaling $1.3 million for falsely labeling rayon textiles as made of "bamboo").

United States v. Nordstrom, Inc.

Case No. 1:15-cv-2130 (D.D.C. Dec. 9, 2015)

Complaint for Civil Penalties, Injunctive, and Other Relief

Plaintiff, the United States of America, acting upon the notification and authorization to the Attorney General by the Federal Trade Commission ("FTC" or "Commission"), for its complaint alleges that:

1. Plaintiff brings this action under Sections 5(a)(1), 5(m)(1)(B), 13(b), and 16(a) of the Federal Trade Commission Act as amended ("FTC Act"), 15 U.S.C. §§45(a)(1), 45(m)(1)(B), 53(b), and 56(a), to obtain monetary civil penalties, injunctive, and other relief for Defendant's violations of the Textile Fiber Products Identification Act ("Textile Act"), 15 U.S.C. §70 et seq., the Rules and Regulations Under the Textile Fiber Products Identification Act, 16 C.F.R. Part 303 ("Textile Rules"), and injunctive relief for violations of Section 5(a)(1) of the FTC Act, 15 U.S.C. §45(a)(1).

Jurisdiction And Venue

2. This Court has jurisdiction over this matter pursuant to 28 U.S.C. §§1331, 1337(a), 1345, and 1355, and 15 U.S.C. §§45(m)(1)(B), 53(b), and 56(a). This action arises under 15 U.S.C. §45(a).

3. Venue in this District is proper under 15 U.S.C. §53(b) and 28 U.S.C. §§1391(b) and (c) and 1395(a).

Defendant

4. Defendant Nordstrom, Inc. is a Washington corporation with its principal place of business at 1617 Sixth Avenue, Seattle, Washington 98101. At all times material to this complaint, Defendant has participated in the acts and practices described in this complaint. Defendant transacts business in this district, including through its websites, www.nordstrom.com and www.nordstromrack.com, and through its retail stores at 1800 L Street NW, Washington, DC 20036, and 5333 Wisconsin Avenue, Friendship Heights, DC 20015.

Commerce

5. At all times material to this complaint, Defendant has maintained a substantial course of trade in or affecting commerce, as "commerce" is defined in Section 4 of the FTC Act, 15 U.S.C. §44

Defendant's Business Practices

6. Defendant markets and sells textile fiber products throughout the United States on its websites and through brick-and-mortar stores.

7. Defendant manufactures, markets, and sells textile fiber products under its own private label, Nordstrom. Defendant also markets and sells retail textile products, which it purchases from a vendor and then resells.

8. In advertisements for textile products marketed and sold on its websites, www.nordstrom.com and www.nordstromrack.com, Defendant makes or has made various claims concerning the fiber content of those textile products.

9. On the www.nordstrom.com website, Defendant has marketed and sold its own private-label "Bamboo Blend Over The Knee Socks" and described the product as "[f]ine-gauge socks blended with oh-so-soft bamboo fibers," but admitted in the fiber content that the product is actually "78% rayon from bamboo, 20% polyester, 2% spandex." Due to its size and location, consumers are not likely to notice and understand this contradictory admission[.]

10. On the www.nordstrom.com and www.nordstromrack.com websites, Defendant has also claimed, without qualification, that the textile fiber in retail products it markets and sells is "bamboo":

a. For example, Defendant markets and sells a "Gypsy05 Bamboo Racerback Hi-Lo Dress" and lists the fiber content as "100% bamboo[";]

b. Defendant also markets and sells a "Degree Six Clothing The Bamboo Long Sleeve Tee" and lists the fiber content as "60% bamboo, 40% sorona[";]

c. Defendant also markets and sells the "Barefoot Dreams Hooded Top & Track Pants Set (Baby)," describing the product as "[m]ade of soft cotton and bamboo," and listing the fiber content as "60% bamboo, 40% cotton["; and]

d. Defendant also markets and sells the "Nicole Miller 'Neon Jaguar' Scarf" and lists the fiber content as 100% bamboo[.]"

11. Defendant also has made "bamboo" claims for retail textile products it markets and sells with contradictory fiber content information. In these advertisements, as with the "Nordstrom Bamboo Blend Over the Knee Sock" described above, Defendant makes large, prominent "bamboo" claims—often in the product title—and repeats those claims near the product image. Elsewhere in the advertisement, Defendant contradicts those "bamboo" claims by admitting that the product actually is rayon. But, as a result of its size and location, consumers are not likely to notice and understand the contradictory admission.

a. For example, Defendant markets the "California Creative Republic 'Bamboo' Hooded Jumpsuit" and describes the product as a "supersoft stretch blend of cotton and bamboo-derived fibers." Well below the product image and button to purchase the product, where consumers will not see it without scrolling down on the webpage, Defendant lists the fiber content as "47% rayon from bamboo, 47% cotton, 6% spandex[.]"

b. Defendant also markets and sells the "Aden + Anais Bamboo Daydream Blanket," describing the product as "[b]amboo-fiber muslin," but listing the fiber content as "100% rayon from bamboo fiber[.]"

12. In addition, on its www.nordstrom.com and www.nordstromrack.com websites, Defendant has marketed and sold textile fiber products labeled as "bamboo."

a. For example, on February 25, 2015, the Commission purchased the "Nicole Miller Neon Jaguar Scarf" from www.nordstrom.com. The label affixed to the scarf states that the product is "100% bamboo[.]"

b. Similarly, on March 17, 2015, the Commission purchased the "Gypsy05 Bamboo Waterfall Cami" from www.nordstromrack.com. The label affixed to the "cami" states that it is "93% bamboo 7% spandex[.]"

c. On March 17, 2015, the Commission also purchased the "Barefoot Dreams Hooded Top & Track Pants Set (Baby)" from www.nordstromrack.com. The hangtag attached to the product states that it is "made of soft cotton and bamboo[.]" . . . Similarly, the label affixed to the product states that the fiber content is "60% bamboo 40% cotton[.]"

13. As defined by the Textile Act and Rules, textile fiber products marketed and sold by Defendant as bamboo, including those described in paragraphs 8 through 12 above, are rayon and not actual bamboo fiber woven into fabric.

14. Rayon is the generic name for a type of regenerated or manufactured fiber made from cellulose. Rayon is manufactured by taking purified cellulose from a plant source, also called a cellulose precursor, and converting it into a viscous solution by dissolving it in one or more chemicals, such as sodium hydroxide. The chemical solution is then forced through spinnerets and into an acidic bath where it solidifies into fibers.

15. Many plant sources may be used as cellulose precursors for rayon fabric, including cotton linters (short cotton fibers), wood pulp, and bamboo. Regardless of the source of the cellulose, the manufacturing process involves the use of hazardous chemicals, and the resulting fiber is rayon and not cotton, wood, or bamboo fiber. *See* 40 C.F.R. Part 63 ("National Emission Standards for Hazardous Air Pollutants for Cellulose Products Manufacturing").

16. "[H]azardous air pollutants (HAP) emitted from cellulose products manufacturing operations" include carbon disulfide, carbonyl sulfide, ethylene oxide, methanol, methyl chloride, propylene oxide, and toluene. 40 C.F.R. § 63.5480.

17. Pursuant to the Textile Act and Rules, textile products must be labeled and advertised using the proper generic fiber names recognized or established by the Commission. Manufactured textile products composed, in whole or in part, of

regenerated cellulose fiber must be labeled and advertised using a generic fiber name such as rayon.

Prior Commission Proceedings Concerning Textile Fiber Product Misrepresentations

18. In August 2009, the Commission announced three settlements and one administrative action against marketers that improperly labeled and advertised rayon textile products as "bamboo." In addition to publicly announcing these cases, the Commission issued a Business Alert to remind marketers of the need to label and advertise textile products properly and to clarify that "bamboo" is not a proper generic fiber name for manufactured rayon textile fibers. The Commission disseminated the press release announcing the four cases and the Business Alert widely throughout the marketplace.

19. On January 27, 2010, the Commission sent Defendant a letter ("Warning Letter"), by express mail, informing Defendant that certain acts or practices in connection with the advertising and labeling of textile fiber products may violate the Textile Act and the Textile Rules and are unfair or deceptive under Section 5 of the FTC Act, 15 U.S.C. § 45(a)(1).

20. Defendant received the Warning Letter in February 2010.

21. Enclosed with the Warning Letter was a synopsis of previous litigated decisions issued by the Commission, as well as instructions to contact Commission staff or to visit the Commission's website at http://www.ftc.gov/bamboo to obtain complete copies of the Textile Act, Textile Rules, and the Commission's Final Orders and Opinions in the proceedings described in the synopsis.

22. As detailed in the synopsis enclosed in the Warning Letter, in a series of litigated decisions, the Commission determined, among other things, that:

a. Both manufacturers and sellers of textile fiber products must comply with the Textile Act and the Textile Rules, *see H. Myerson Sons, et al.*, 78 F.T.C. 464 (1971); *Taylor-Friedsam Co., et al.*, 69 F.T.C. 483 (1966); *Transair, Inc., et al.*, 60 F.T.C. 694 (1962); and

b. It is an unfair or deceptive act or practice to falsely or deceptively stamp, tag, label, invoice, advertise, or otherwise identify any textile fiber product regarding the name or amount of constituent fibers contained therein, *see Verrazzano Trading Corp., et al.*, 91 F.T.C. 888 (1978); *H. Myerson Sons, et al.*, 78 F.T.C. 464 (1971); *TaylorFriedsam Co., et al.*, 69 F.T.C. 483 (1966); *Transair, Inc., et al.*, 60 F.T.C. 694 (1962).

23. The Warning Letter also notified Defendant of its potential liability for civil penalties under Section 5(m)(1)(B) of the FTC Act, 15 U.S.C. § 45(m)(1)(B), for knowingly engaging in acts or practices determined by the Commission to be unfair or deceptive and unlawful, as described in Paragraph 22 of this Complaint.

24. Despite the Commission's public announcements and the Warning Letter, Defendant has marketed and sold rayon textile fiber products advertised and

labeled as "bamboo," including by engaging in practices such as those described in Paragraphs 8 through 12 above.

25. The practices described in Paragraphs 8 through 12 above are violations of the Textile Act and the Textile Rules, and are deceptive acts or practices in violation of Section 5(a)(1) of the FTC Act, 15 U.S.C. § 45(a)(1).

26. In January 2013, the Commission announced four settlements with large, national marketers that received the January 2010 Warning Letter and thereafter allegedly engaged in improperly labeling and advertising of rayon textile products as "bamboo." In those settlements, the defendants agreed to pay a total of $1,026,000.00 in civil penalties and agreed to injunctive relief relating to labeling and advertising of "bamboo" textile products. In addition to publicly announcing these cases, the Commission reminded marketers of the Business Alert it previously issued regarding the need to label and advertise textile products, and specifically "bamboo" products, properly. The press release announcing the four cases was disseminated widely throughout the marketplace.

Violations Of The Textile Act And The Textile Rules

27. The Textile Act governs, *inter alia*, the labeling and advertising of textile fiber products manufactured, sold, advertised, or offered for sale in commerce. *See* 15 U.S.C. § 70a.

28. Under the Textile Act, a textile fiber product is "misbranded if it is falsely or deceptively stamped, tagged, labeled, invoiced, advertised, or otherwise identified as to the name or amount of constituent fibers contained therein." 15 U.S.C. § 70b(a).

29. Pursuant to section 70e(c) of the Textile Act, 15 U.S.C. § 70e(c), the Commission promulgated the Textile Rules, which state:

a. All textile fiber products must carry affixed labels stating the recognized generic names of the constituent fibers, 16 C.F.R. §§ 303.15; 303.16(a)(1);

b. No generic name for a manufactured fiber may be used until such generic name has been "established or otherwise recognized by the Commission," 16 C.F.R. § 303.8;

c. "[w]ords, coined words, symbols or depictions, (a) which constitute or imply the name or designation of a fiber which is not present in the product . . . [may] not be used in such a manner as to represent or imply that such fiber is present in the product." 16 C.F.R. § 303.18. Any term used in advertising, including internet advertising, that constitutes or connotes the name or presence of a textile fiber is deemed to be an implication of fiber content, 16 C.F.R. § 303.40; and

d. Any information or representation included in advertising or labeling of a textile fiber product that is not required under the Textile Act or the Textile Rules "shall in no way be false, deceptive, or misleading as to fiber content and shall not include any names, terms, or representations prohibited by the

[Textile] Act and regulations." 16 C.F.R. § 303.42(b); 16 C.F.R. § 303.41(d); see also 16 C.F.R. § 303.17.

30. A violation either of the Textile Act or of the Textile Rules constitutes an unfair or deceptive act or practice in violation of the FTC Act. See 15 U.S.C. §§ 70a and 70e.

Count I: Misrepresented Or Mislabeled Textile Products

31. As set forth in Paragraphs 8 through 12, Defendant

a. Markets and sells or has marketed and sold textile fiber products labeled as "bamboo;" and

b. Advertises or has advertised the fiber content of textile fiber products using the terms "bamboo" and "bamboo fiber."

32. In truth and in fact, as set forth in Paragraph 13, in numerous instances these textile fiber products are not bamboo fiber but instead rayon, a regenerated cellulose fiber.

33. Therefore, through the means described in Paragraphs 8 through 12, Defendant has introduced, advertised, offered for sale, or sold retail textile fiber products that are mislabeled or falsely or deceptively advertised, in violation of Sections 70a and 70b of the Textile Act, 15 U.S.C. §§ 70a and 70b, and Sections 303.6, 303.8, 303.16, 303.17, 303.18, 303.33, 303.34, 303.40, 303.41, and 303.42 of the Textile Rules, 16 C.F.R. Part 303.

34. Defendant's violations of the Textile Act and of the Textile Rules constitute deceptive acts or practices, in or affecting commerce, in violation of Section 5(a) of the FTC Act. *See* 15 U.S.C. §§ 70a and 70e.

Violations Of Prior Commission Determinations Concerning Unfair Or Deceptive Acts Or Practices In Commerce

35. Pursuant to Section 5(m)(1)(B) of the FTC Act, 15 U.S.C. § 45(m)(1)(B), if the Commission has determined in a proceeding under section 5(b) of the FTC Act, 15 U.S.C. § 45(b), that an act or practice is unfair or deceptive by issuing a final cease and desist order other than a consent order, then a person, partnership, or corporation which engages in such act or practice with actual knowledge that such act or practice is unfair or deceptive shall be liable for a civil penalty of not more than $16,000 for each violation.

36. In prior litigated decisions, the Commission has determined that it is an unfair or deceptive act or practice to offer for sale or sell textile fiber products that are falsely or deceptively labeled as to the name or amount of constituent fiber contained therein. The Commission also has determined that it is an unfair or deceptive act or practice to falsely or deceptively advertise textile fiber products including, but not limited to, falsely or deceptively advertising the name or amount of constituent fiber contained within a textile fiber product. See Paragraph 22.

Count II: Violations of Section 5(m)(1)(B)

37. As set forth in Paragraphs 19 through 23, at least since receiving the Warning Letter in February 2010, Defendant has had actual knowledge that offering for sale or selling falsely or deceptively labeled textile products and that falsely or deceptively advertising textile fiber products are unfair or deceptive acts or practices subject to civil penalties.

38. As set forth in Paragraphs 8 through 12, Defendant has offered for sale and sold textile products labeled as "bamboo" and has represented, directly or indirectly, expressly or by implication, that certain textile fiber products it advertises and sells are "bamboo."

39. In truth and in fact, as set forth in Paragraph 13, in numerous instances these textile fiber products are not bamboo fiber but instead rayon, a regenerated cellulose fiber.

40. Defendant has engaged in the acts and practices described in Paragraphs 38 and 39 with the actual knowledge, as set forth in Paragraph 37, that such acts and practices have been determined by the Commission in a final cease and desist order, other than a consent order, to be unfair and deceptive under Section 5(a) of the FTC Act. Defendant, therefore, has violated Section 5(m)(1)(B) of the FTC Act.15 U.S.C.§ 45(m)(1)(B).

Consumer Injury

41. Consumers have suffered and will continue to suffer substantial injury as a result of Defendant's violations of the FTC Act and the Textile Act and Rules. In addition, Defendant has been unjustly enriched as a result of its unlawful acts or practices. Absent injunctive relief by this Court, Defendant is likely to continue to injure consumers, reap unjust enrichment, and harm the public interest.

Civil Penalties and Injunctive Relief

42. Violations of the Textile Act constitute deceptive acts or practices, in or affecting commerce, in violation of Section 5(a) of the FTC Act. See 15 U.S.C. §§ 70a and 70e. The FTC "is authorized and directed to prevent any person from violating the provisions of [the Textile Act] in the same manner, by the same means, and with the same jurisdiction, powers, and duties as though all applicable terms and provisions of the [FTC Act] were incorporated" therein, and any "person violating the [Textile Act] shall be subject to the penalties" provided in the FTC Act. 15 U.S.C. § 70e(b).

43. Under Section 13(b) of the FTC Act, 15 U.S.C. § 53(b), this Court is authorized to issue a permanent injunction to restrain violations of the FTC Act, as well as such ancillary relief as is necessary.

44. Section 5(m)(1)(B) of the FTC Act, 15 U.S.C. § 45(m)(1)(B), authorizes the Court to award monetary civil penalties of not more than $16,000 for each violation of prior Commission determinations concerning unfair and deceptive acts or practices in commerce, as described in Paragraphs 18-25 and 37-40. 45.

45. Pursuant to Section 5(m)(1)(B) of the FTC Act, for the purpose of computing civil penalties, each and every instance that Defendant has introduced, advertised, offered for sale, or sold a misbranded retail textile fiber product, since February 2010, constitutes an act or practice that the Commission has determined in a prior proceeding to be unfair or deceptive.

Prayer For Relief

WHEREFORE, Plaintiff, pursuant to 15 U.S.C. §§45(a)(1), 45(m)(1)(B), and 53(b) and the Court's own equitable powers, requests that the Court:

1. Enter judgment against Defendant and in favor of Plaintiff for each violation of the Textile Act and the Textile Rules alleged in this complaint;

2. Award Plaintiff monetary civil penalties pursuant to 15 U.S.C. §45(m)(1)(B);

3. Enter a permanent injunction to prevent future violations of the Textile Act and the Textile Rules; and

4. Award Plaintiff the costs of bringing this action, as well as such other and additional relief as the Court may determine to be just and proper.

Notes

1. What should Nordstrom have done differently to avoid FTC action?

2. Pursuant to the Textile Act, can Nordstrom state that it is using bamboo at all?

3. How likely is it that a consumer would understand use of the word "bamboo" to be a branding term as opposed to a descriptive one?

d. CAN-SPAM

The CAN-SPAM Act is a law setting the rules for commercial email by establishing the requirements for commercial messages, giving recipients the right to require a company to stop emailing them and creating penalties in case of violations.

The CAM-SPAM Act applies to all commercial messages, which are defined as "any electronic mail message the primary purpose of which is the commercial advertisement or promotion of a commercial product or service."

The CAN-SPAM Act forbids the use of false or misleading header information, deceptive subject lines, and requires the sender to identify the message as an ad. In addition, the sender must inform recipients where the sender is located, explain how to opt out of receiving future email from the sender, promptly honor opt-out requests and monitor what others are doing on the sender's behalf.

Each email in violation of the CAN-SPAM Act is subject to penalties up to $42,530.

e. Care Labeling

The FTC enforces the Care Labeling Rule, which requires manufacturers and importers to attach care instructions to garments.

The term "manufacturers" covers: (1) manufacturers and importers of textile wearing apparel, (2) manufacturers and importers of piece goods sold to consumers for making wearing apparel, and (3) any person or organization that directs or controls the manufacturing or importing of textile wearing apparel or piece goods for making wearing apparel. The term "garment" includes all textile apparel worn to cover or protect the body (with the exception of shoes, gloves, hats, bels, handkerchiefs, belts, suspenders, neckties, non-woven garments made for one-time use) and piece goods sold for making apparel at home (except marked manufacturers' remnants of up to 10 yards when the fiber content is not known and cannot be determined easily and trim up to five inches wide).

Covered manufacturers and importers must provide complete instruction about regular care for the garment or provide warnings if the garment cannot be cleaned without harm, ensure that if followed, care labeling instruction will cause no substantial harm to the product and warn consumers about certain procedures that they may assume to be consistent with the instructions on the label but that would harm the product.

Labels for clothing must have washing or dry-cleaning instructions. Washing instructions include five elements: (1) washing by hand or by machine, (2) bleaching, (3) drying, (4) ironing, and (5) warning (if a certain care product would harm the garment). The FTC has addressed this issue and penalized companies for using inaccurate labels on its clothing. In *Tommy Hilfiger U.S.A.*, 99 Civ. 1957 (1999), the FTC filed a complaint against Tommy Hilfiger for violating the Care Labeling Rule. The complaint alleged that the company had sold garments with inaccurate labeling, which did not properly describe "what regular care is needed for the ordinary use of the product." Consequently, when the labeling instructions were followed, the clothing bled and faded. The parties eventually settled and Tommy Hilfiger paid a civil penalty of $300,000.00—the highest penalty ever sought by the FTC in a care labeling case.

United States v. Tommy Hilfiger U.S.A., Inc.

No. 99-cv-1957 (S.D.N.Y. Mar. 17, 1999)

Complaint

Plaintiff, the United States of America, acting upon notification and authorization to the Attorney General by the Federal Trade Commission ("Commission") for its complaint alleges that:

1. Plaintiff brings this action under Sections 5(a)(1), 5(m)(1)(A), 9, 13(b) and 16(a) of the Federal Trade Commission Act ("FTC Act"), 15 U.S.C. §§45(a)(1), 45(m)(1)(A), 49, 53(b) and 56(a) to obtain monetary civil penalties and injunctive and other relief for defendant's alleged violations of the Commission's Trade Regulation Rule Concerning the Care Labeling of Textile Wearing Apparel, 16 C.F.R. Part 423 ("the Care Labeling Rule").

2. The Court has jurisdiction over this matter under 28 U.S.C. §§ 1331, 1337(a), 1345, and 1355 and under 15 U.S.C. §§ 45(m)(1)(A), 49, 53(b) and 56(a). This action arises under 15 U.S.C. § 45(a)(1).

3. Venue in the Southern District of New York is proper under 15 U.S.C. § 53(b) and under 28 U.S.C. §§ 1391(b-c) and 1395(a).

4. Defendant Tommy Hilfiger U.S.A., Inc. is a Delaware corporation with its office and principal place of business located within the Southern District of New York at 25 West 39th Street, 13th Floor, New York, NY 10018. Defendant Tommy Hilfiger U.S.A., Inc. resides and transacts business in the Southern District of New York.

5. At all times during which the acts or practices alleged herein occurred, defendant Tommy Hilfiger U.S.A., Inc. was engaged in the business of directing or controlling the manufacturing of textile wearing apparel (as "textile wearing apparel" is defined in Section 423.1 of the Care Labeling Rule, 16 C.F.R. § 423.1), importing textile wearing apparel and offering for sale and selling such apparel throughout the United States, in or affecting commerce, as "commerce" is defined in Section 4 of the FTC Act, 15 U.S.C. § 44.

6. The Care Labeling Rule, promulgated by the Commission on December 9, 1971, was amended by the Commission in 1983 under Section 18 of the FTC Act, 15 U.S.C. § 57a. The amended Rule became effective on January 2, 1984, and has since that date remained in full force and effect.

7. In some instances in the five years preceding the date of the filing of this complaint, in connection with the sale of textile wearing apparel in or affecting commerce, as "commerce" is defined in Section 4 of the FTC Act, 15 U.S.C. § 44, defendant has violated Section 423.6(b) of the Care Labeling Rule, 16 C.F.R. § 423.6(b), which requires that the "care label" (as that term is defined in Section 423.1 of the Care Labeling Rule, 16 C.F.R. § 423.1) must state a regular care procedure needed for the ordinary use of the product. In particular, in some instances the care procedure recommended on the care label resulted in dye bleeding from one portion of the garment to another, in fading, or in other damage to the garment.

8. In some instances in the five years preceding the date of the filing of this complaint, in connection with the sale of textile wearing apparel in or affecting commerce, defendant has violated Section 423.6(c) of the Care Labeling Rule, 16 C.F.R. § 423.6(c), which requires a manufacturer or importer to possess, prior to sale, a reasonable basis for all care information disclosed to purchasers on the care label, including any warnings.

9. Section 5(a)(1) of the FTC Act, 15 U.S.C. § 45(a)(1), provides that "unfair or deceptive acts or practices in or affecting commerce, are hereby declared unlawful."

10. Pursuant to Section 18(d)(3) of the FTC Act, 15 U.S.C. § 57a(d)(3), a violation of the Care Labeling Rule constitutes an unfair or deceptive act or practice in violation of Section 5(a)(1) of the FTC Act, 15 U.S.C. § 45(a)(1).

11. By engaging in the acts and practices alleged in Paragraphs 7 and 8 above, defendant has violated Section 5(a)(1) of the FTC Act, 15 U.S.C. § 45(a)(1).

12. Defendant, having knowledge of the Care Labeling Rule as set forth in Section 5(m)(1)(A) of the FTC Act, 15 U.S.C. § 45(m)(1)(A), has violated the Rule as alleged above.

13. Each sale or attempted sale, during the five years preceding the filing of this complaint, of a garment in which defendant has violated the Care Labeling Rule, in one or more of the ways described above, constitutes a separate violation for which plaintiff seeks monetary civil penalties.

14. Section 5(m)(1)(A) of the FTC Act, 15 U.S.C. § 45(m)(1)(A), authorizes this Court to award monetary civil penalties of not more than $10,000 for each such violation of the Care Labeling Rule that occurred prior to November 20, 1996. Section 4 of the Federal Civil Penalties Inflation Adjustment Act of 1990, 28 U.S.C. § 2461, as amended, authorizes the Court to award monetary civil penalties of not more than $11,000 for each such violation of the Care Labeling Rule that occurred on or after November 20, 1996.

15. Under Section 13(b) of the FTC Act, 15 U.S.C. § 53(b), this Court is authorized to issue a permanent injunction against defendant's violating the FTC Act, as well as such ancillary relief as may be just and proper.

Prayer

WHEREFORE, plaintiff requests that this Court, pursuant to 15 U.S.C. §§ 45(a)(1), 45(m)(1)(A), 49 and 53(b) and the Court's own equity powers:

1. Enter judgment against the defendant and in favor of the plaintiff for each violation alleged in this complaint;

2. Award plaintiff monetary civil penalties from defendant for each violation of the Care Labeling Rule alleged in this complaint;

3. Enjoin defendant from violating the Care Labeling Rule;

4. Order defendant to retain adequate records of the care instructions on each item of textile wearing apparel sold by defendant, adequate records of the reasonable basis for each such care instruction, and other records relating to the adequacy of the care instructions for a period of five years from the last date on which the item was shipped to a retail store; and

5. Award such other relief as the Court may deem to be just and proper.

CONSENT DECREE

No. 99-cv-1957 (Mar. 29, 1999)

WHEREAS: Plaintiff, the United States of America, has commenced this action by filing the Complaint herein; defendant has waived service of the Summons and Complaint; the parties have been represented by the attorneys whose names appear hereafter; and the parties have agreed to the settlement of any violations of the

Federal Trade Commission's Trade Regulation Rule Concerning the Care Labeling of Textile Wearing Apparel that occurred in the five years preceding the date of the filing of the Complaint, as alleged in the Complaint, upon the following terms and conditions, without adjudication of any issue of fact or law and without defendant admitting liability for any of the matters alleged in the Complaint;

THEREFORE, on the joint motion of plaintiff and defendant, it is hereby ORDERED, ADJUDGED, and DECREED as follows:

1. This Court has jurisdiction of the subject matter and of the parties.

2. The Complaint states a claim upon which relief may be granted against the defendant under Sections 5(a)(1), 5(m)(1)(A), 9, 13(b) and 16(a) of the Federal Trade Commission Act, 15 U.S.C. §§45(a)(1), 45(m)(1)(A), 49, 53(b) and 56(a).

3. Defendant Tommy Hilfiger U.S.A., Inc., its successors and assigns, shall pay to plaintiff a civil penalty, pursuant to Section 5(m)(1)(A) of the Federal Trade Commission Act, 15 U.S.C. §45(m)(1)(A), in the amount of $300,000.00.

4. Defendant shall make the payment required by Paragraph 3 within five (5) days of the date defendant receives notice from plaintiff of entry of this Consent Decree by electronic fund transfer in accordance with instructions provided by The Office of Consumer Litigation, Civil Division, U.S. Department of Justice, Washington, DC 20530.

5. In the event of any default in payment, which default continues for ten (10) days beyond the due date of payment, the entire unpaid penalty, together with interest, as computed pursuant to 28 U.S.C. § 1961, from the date of default to the date of payment, shall immediately become due and payable.

6. Defendant is hereby required, in accordance with 31 U.S.C. §7701, to furnish to the Federal Trade Commission its taxpayer identification number, which shall be used for purposes of collecting and reporting on any delinquent amount arising out of defendant's relationship with the government.

7. Defendant, its successors and assigns, and its officers, agents, servants, employees and attorneys, and all persons in active concert or participation with any one or more of them who receive actual notice of this Consent Decree by personal service or otherwise, directly or through any corporation, subsidiary, division, or other device, shall comply with all provisions of the Federal Trade Commission's Trade Regulation Rule Concerning the Care Labeling of Textile Wearing Apparel ("the Care Labeling Rule"), 16 C.F.R. Part 423, or as the Rule may hereafter be amended. A copy of the Care Labeling Rule is attached hereto as "Appendix A" and incorporated herein as if fully set forth verbatim.

8. Defendant shall provide for a toll-free telephone number to be placed on defendant's care labels, stating in effect "For Product Care Information, Call 1-800-XXX-XXXX." With respect to items of textile wearing apparel that, pursuant to §423.8 of the Care Labeling Rule, are exempt from care labeling but for which

product care information is required, the toll-free telephone number shall be placed in conjunction with the care information provided pursuant to § 423.8(c). Defendant may implement the use of care labels containing the toll-free product care telephone number after its existing inventory of care labels is depleted.

9. Defendant, its successors and assigns, shall within thirty (30) days of the entry of this Consent Decree, provide a copy of this Consent Decree, the Care Labeling Rule and the Statement of Basis and Purpose for that Rule to each of its officers and directors and to all supervisory personnel responsible for compliance with the Care Labeling Rule, secure from each such person a signed statement acknowledging receipt of a copy of this Consent Decree and shall, within ten (10) days of complying with this Paragraph, file an affidavit with the Court and serve the Federal Trade Commission by mailing a copy thereof to the Associate Director, Division of Enforcement, Bureau of Consumer Protection, Federal Trade Commission, Washington, DC 20580, setting forth the fact and manner of their compliance including the name and title of each person to whom a copy of the Consent Decree has been provided.

10. Defendant, its successors and assigns, shall maintain the following: a record of the instructions on the care labels on all items of textile wearing apparel offered for sale by defendant; a record of any and all care instructions appearing on hangtags attached to textile wearing apparel offered for sale by defendant; a record of the reasonable basis for each such care instruction; copies of all test reports relating to the care of any textile wearing apparel offered for sale by defendant (including tests of any component thereof), and either the actual items that were tested, or a photograph or a duplicate thereof; all correspondence to and from customers, suppliers and consumers relating to the accuracy, adequacy or completeness of the care instructions or any harm to textile wearing apparel which might have been caused by the inaccuracy, inadequacy or incompleteness of the care instructions; and employee manuals, memoranda, correspondence or other documents containing instructions, explanations, policies or procedures, relating to defendant's compliance with any provision of this Decree. All such documents and things shall be maintained for five (5) years from the date defendant last ships the textile wearing apparel at issue to its customers. Defendant shall have the right to destroy all such documents and things thereafter, unless defendant has received notification from the Federal Trade Commission. Within forty-five (45) days after receipt of a written request, defendant shall make such documents and things available for inspection and copying by Federal Trade Commission staff during defendant's regular business hours at defendant's offices.

11. Defendant, its successors and assigns, shall notify the Associate Director, Division of Enforcement, Bureau of Consumer Protection, Federal Trade Commission, Washington, DC 20580, thirty (30) days, or as soon as practicable thereafter, prior to any change in defendant's business, including, but not limited to, merger, incorporation, dissolution, assignment, sale resulting in the emergence of a

successor corporation, the creation or dissolution of a subsidiary or parent, or any other change that may affect defendant's obligations under this Consent Decree.

12. This Court shall retain jurisdiction of this matter for the purposes of enabling any of the parties to this Consent Decree to apply to the Court at any time for such further orders or directives as may be necessary or appropriate for the interpretation or modification of this Consent Decree, for the enforcement of compliance therewith, or for the punishment of violations thereof.

JUDGMENT IS THEREFORE ENTERED in favor of plaintiff against defendant, pursuant to all of the terms and conditions recited above.

Notes

1. What is a consent decree and when is it effective?

2. How is the Consent Decree favorable to Tommy Hilfiger?

3. What is the purpose of the Care Labeling Rule? What should Tommy Hilfiger do to avoid future FTC actions?

f. Made in the USA Standard

There are no laws that require products sold in the United States to be marked or labeled as "Made in the USA" with the exception of automobile, textile, wool, and fur products. Advertisers may choose to state "Made in the USA" for other products, but if they do, the FTC's "Made in the USA" policy applies.

The FTC's "Made in the USA" rules apply to all products advertised or sold in the United States. A "Made in the USA" claim can be either express or implied. So for example, a statement that "Our products are American-made" would be express, but an ad featuring U.S. flags, or references to U.S. locations of factories may constitute an implied statement that the products are "Made in the USA."

"Made in the USA" means that "all or virtually all" of the product has been made in the United States. Products "Made in the USA" should not contain foreign content unless it is negligible. When an advertiser makes an unqualified claim that the product is "Made in the USA," the advertiser should have a reasonable basis to support that claim at the time it is made. This includes the use of reliable evidence showing that is the case, such as use of factories or materials located in the United States.

In *David Paz v. AG Adriano Goldschmied, Inc. et al.*, 3:14-cv-01372 (S.D. Cal), plaintiffs brought a consumer class action suit against AG Adriano Goldschmied, a luxury denim manufacturer, claiming the company had falsely marketed its expensive jeans as "Made in the USA." While the jeans boasted a "Made in the USA" label, various components of the jeans, including the fabric, thread, buttons, and zipper were actually manufactured outside of the United States. In the complaint, the Plaintiffs claimed that they relied on the "Made in the USA" label in choosing to pay a higher price for the jeans and that they would have typically paid less for jeans made in a foreign country. The parties eventually settled.

Paz v. AG Adriano Goldschmied, Inc.

No. 3:14-cv-01372 (S.D. Cal. June 4, 2014)

Complaint for:

(1) Violation of Consumers Legal Remedies Act (California Civil Code Section 1750 et seq.);

(2) Violation of Business & Professions Code Sections 17200 et seq. (California Unfair Competition Law); and

(3) Violation of Business & Professions Code Section 17533.7 (California False "Made in USA" Claim).

COMES NOW, plaintiff DAVID PAZ ("Plaintiff"), as an individual and on behalf of the general public and all others similarly situated, by his undersigned attorneys, alleges as follows:

Nature of the Case

1. This is a putative class action case brought on behalf of all purchasers of AG Adriano Goldschmied, Inc. apparel products manufactured, distributed, marketed, and/or sold by defendants AG Adriano Goldschmied, Inc. ("AGAG") and Nordstrom, Inc. ("Nordstrom") in California. AGAG, Nordstrom, and the DOE defendants are collectively hereinafter referred to as the "Defendants." Through an unlawful, deceptive and unfair course of conduct, Defendants manufactured, marketed, and/or sold to California consumers a variety of AGAG apparel products with the false designation and representation that the AGAG apparel was "Made in U.S.A."

2. The "Made in U.S.A." claim is prominently printed on the apparel products themselves.[49] However, the offending apparel products are substantially made, manufactured or produced from <u>component parts</u> that are manufactured outside of the United States in violation of California law and/or federal law.

3. On information and belief, major components of the apparel products, including but not limited to the fabric, thread, buttons, subcomponents of the zipper assembly, and/or rivets are manufactured *outside the United States.*

Parties

4. Plaintiff is an individual residing in San Diego, California.

5. Defendant AG Adriano Goldschmied, Inc. ("AGAG") is a corporation that is organized and exists under the laws of the State of California. . . .

6. AGAG is a leading designer and manufacturer of men's and women's denim jean products. On information and belief, AGAG sells jeans, shorts, skirts and

---

49. Plaintiff intends to seek class wide relief on behalf of all California purchasers of any AGAG apparel product that was labeled as "Made in U.S.A." but incorporated foreign-made component parts in violation of California and/or federal law—not just the specific brand of men's jeans purchased by Plaintiff.

dresses, maternity wear, knits, woven, sweaters, and jackets for women; and jeans, shorts, knits, woven, sweaters, and jackets, as well as fabrics for men. AGAG sells its products through its own stores, online, and through high-end retailers such as Nordstrom, Inc. It has retail store locations in Atlantic City, Miami, Beverly Hills, Costa Mesa, San Francisco, New York, St. Louis, and Tokyo. One of the products AGAG manufacturers and sells to California retailers is THE PROTÉGÉ brand jean purchased by Plaintiff at a San Diego Nordstrom store on or about May 16, 2014.

7. Defendant NORDSTROM, INC. (hereinafter "Nordstrom" or "Defendant") is a Washington corporation doing business under and by virtue of the laws of the State of California. Nordstrom's principal place of business is 1700 Seventh Avenue, Seattle, WA 98101. Nordstrom may be served with process in this matter by serving its California registered agent for service of process, CT Corporation System, 818 West Seventh Street, 2nd Floor, Los Angeles, CA 90017.

8. On information and belief, Nordstrom is a fashion specialty retailer that offers apparel, shoes, cosmetics, and accessories for women, men, and children in the United States. The Protégé brand jean was purchased by Plaintiff at a Nordstrom retail store.

9. Plaintiff is ignorant of the true names and capacities of the defendants sued herein as DOES 1-100, inclusive; therefore, Plaintiff sues these defendants by such fictitious names. Plaintiff is informed and believes that each of the fictitious named defendants are legally responsible in some manner for the occurrences herein alleged, assisted in and about the wrongs complained herein by providing financial support, advice, resources or other assistance. Plaintiff will amend the complaint to allege their true names and capacities when ascertained.

10. Plaintiff is informed and believes that all defendants were agents, servants and employees of their co-defendants, and in doing the things hereinafter mentioned, were acting within the scope of their authority as such agents, servants and employees with the permission and consent of their co-defendants.

Jurisdiction and Venue

11. This Court has jurisdiction over this matter pursuant to CAFA because the amount in controversy in this matter exceeds $5,000,000.00 as to all Class Members, inclusive of attorneys' fees and costs, and injunctive relief. 28 U.S.C. Sections 1332(d), 1453, and 1711–1715.

12. Venue in this judicial district is proper under 28 U.S.C. §§ 1391(b) and 1391(c) in that this is the judicial district in which a substantial part of the acts and omissions giving rise to the claims occurred.

General Allegations Common to All Causes of Action

13. Plaintiff realleges and incorporates herein by reference all of the allegations contained in Paragraphs 1 through 12, inclusive, of this complaint as though fully set forth herein.

14. Defendants manufacture, market, and/or sell AGAG apparel products that have printed on the product itself and the product packaging that the products are "Made in U.S.A."

15. Contrary to the representation, the AGAG apparel products are substantially and/or partially made, manufactured or produced with component parts that are manufactured outside of the United States. Based upon information and belief, the foreign component parts included in The Protégé jeans (and presumably all other offending AGAG apparel products) are the fabric, thread, buttons, rivets, and/or certain subcomponents of the zipper assembly. For other models of jeans, Plaintiff is informed and believes that the fabric, thread, buttons, rivets, and/or certain subcomponents of the zipper assembly are made outside of the United States as well.

16. Defendants market, and continue to market, and represent to the general public that its AGAG apparel products are "Made in U.S.A." In addition, Defendants fraudulently concealed the material facts at issue herein by failing to disclose 100% of the truth to the California general public regarding the country of origin of AGAG apparel products. The disclosure of this information was necessary in order to make Defendants' representation not misleading. Defendants possess superior knowledge of the true facts, which were not disclosed, thereby tolling the running of any applicable statute of limitations.

17. Consumers are particularly vulnerable to these deceptive and fraudulent practices. Most consumers possess very limited knowledge of the likelihood that products, including the component parts therein, claimed to be made in the United States are in fact made in foreign countries. This is a material factor in many individuals' purchasing decisions, as they believe they are supporting American companies and American jobs.

18. Consumers generally believe that "Made in U.S.A." products are higher quality than their foreign-manufactured counterparts. Due to Defendants' scheme to defraud the market, members of the general public were fraudulently induced to purchase Defendants' products at inflated prices. On information and belief, and during the entirety of the relevant four-year statutory time period, Defendants charged excess monies for AGAG apparel products, in comparison to their competitors, based on the false "Made in U.S.A." designation. California and federal laws are designed to protect consumers from this type of false representation and predatory conduct. Defendants' scheme to defraud consumers is ongoing and will victimize consumers each and every day until altered by judicial intervention.

The Plaintiff Transaction

19. On or about May 16, 2014, Plaintiff purchased The Protégé brand jeans at a Nordstrom store in San Diego. At the time of purchase, the product itself was marked with a "Made in U.S.A." country of origin designation when the product actually contains component parts made outside of the United States. Accordingly, Defendants are not entitled to lawfully make a "Made in U.S.A." representation on the product.

20. In each case when Plaintiff, and Class Members, purchased a Class Product,[50] they relied upon Defendants' "Made in U.S.A." representation in their purchasing decision, which is typical of most U.S. consumers, and they were deceived as a result of Defendants' actions. These purchasing decisions were supported by the "Made in U.S.A." representation made by Defendants, which is absent from most of Defendants' competitors. Plaintiff believed at the time he purchased The Protégé that he was supporting U.S. jobs and the U.S. economy.

21. Plaintiff suffered an "injury in fact" because Plaintiff's money was taken by Defendants as a result of Defendants' false "MADE IN USA" claims set forth on The Protégé. Furthermore, he suffered an "injury in fact" by paying for something he believed was genuinely manufactured in the USA, when it was not.

22. U.S. made component parts are subject to strict regulatory requirements, such as environmental, labor, and safety standards. Foreign made component parts are not subject to the same U.S. manufacturing standards and are often inherently of lower quality than their U.S. made counterparts. Foreign made component parts are also routinely less reliable and durable than their U.S. made counterparts. As such, The Protégé is of inferior quality due to AGAG's decision to include foreign made component parts within.

23. As such, the offending AGAG apparel products, made with foreign made component parts, are of inferior quality, less reliable, and fail more often than if the product was truly made from 100% American made component parts. Essentially, THE PROTÉGÉ is not worth the purchase price paid. The precise amount of damages will be proven at time of trial, in large part, by expert testimony.

24. Plaintiff and Class Members were undoubtedly injured as a result of Defendants' false "Made in U.S.A." representations that are at issue in this litigation.

Class Allegations

25. Plaintiff realleges and incorporates herein by reference all of the allegations contained in Paragraphs 1 through 24, inclusive, of this complaint as though fully set forth herein.

26. Plaintiff brings this action, as set forth below, against Defendants, pursuant to Rules 23(a), 23(b)(1), 23(b)(2), and 23(b)(3) of the Federal Rules of Civil Procedure ("Fed. R. Civ. P."), individually and on behalf of a class consisting of all persons in the United States who purchased one or more of Defendants' AGAG apparel products during the relevant four-year statutory time period that bore a "Made in U.S.A." country of origin designation but that contained foreign-made component parts (the "Class"). Excluded from the Class are the Court and its employees; Defendants; any parent, subsidiary, or affiliate of Defendants; and all employees

50. The term "Class Products" is defined as any AGAG manufactured or labeled product that was sold in California during the past four years with a "Made in U.S.A." or equivalent country of origin label but that incorporated foreign-made component parts.

and directors who are or have been employed by Defendants during the relevant time period.

Definition of the Subclass

27. Subclass members are all of Defendants' California customers who purchased AGAG apparel products that were labeled as "MADE IN U.S.A. OF IMPORTED FABRIC" that contained foreign-made component parts beyond the fabric (e.g., rivets, thread, buttons, and/or subcomponents of the zipper assembly) during the relevant four-year statutory time period (hereinafter the "Sub-Class Products").

Class Action Requirements

28. The numerosity requirement of Fed. R. Civ. P. 23(a)(1) is satisfied for each of the foregoing Classes because the members of each Class are so numerous and geographically dispersed that joinder of all Class members is impracticable. Plaintiff currently believes that there are at hundreds of thousands of members of each Class located in the State of California.

29. Common questions of fact and law exist here, satisfying the requirement of Rule 23(a)(2), including but not limited to:

a. Whether Defendants participated in, or committed the wrongful conduct alleged herein;

b. Whether Defendants' acts, transactions, or course of conduct constitute the violations of law alleged herein;

c. Whether the members of the Class and the Sub-Class sustained and/or continue to sustain damages by reason of Defendants' conduct, and, if so, the proper measure and appropriate formula to be applied in determining such damages; and

d. Whether the members of the Class and the Sub-Class are entitled to injunctive or other equitable relief.

30. Plaintiff's claims are typical of the claims of all other members of the Class and the Sub-Class and involve the same violations of law by Defendants as other Class members' claims. Plaintiff and members of the Class and Sub-Class also sustained damages arising out of Defendants' common course of conduct complained herein. Accordingly, Plaintiff satisfies the "typicality" requirements of Fed. R. Civ. P. 23(a)(3) with respect to the Class and Sub-Class.

31. Plaintiff will fairly and adequately protect the interests of the other members of the Class and Sub-Class, and has no interests that are antagonistic to or which conflict with those of the other members of those Classes. Plaintiff is committed to the vigorous prosecution of this action and has retained competent counsel experienced in litigation of this nature to represent themselves and the other members of the Class and Sub-Class; as such, the requirements of Rule 23(a)(4) are satisfied.

32. Absent a representative class action, members of the Class and the Sub-Class would continue to suffer the harm described herein, for which they would have

no remedy. Even if separate actions could be brought by individual purchasers, the resulting multiplicity of lawsuits would cause undue hardship and expense for both the Court and the litigants, as well as create a risk of inconsistent rulings and adjudications that might be dispositive of the interests of similarly situated purchasers, substantially impeding their ability to protect their interests, while establishing incompatible standards of conduct for Defendants. The proposed Class, and, respectively, the members of the Sub-Class, thus satisfy the requirements of Fed. R. Civ. P. 23(b)(1).

33. Defendants ha[ve] acted or refused to act on grounds generally applicable to Plaintiff and the other members of the Class, and, respectively, the members of the Sub-Class, thereby rendering class certification and injunctive relief with respect to the Class as a whole and the Sub-Class appropriate. Certification under Fed. R. Civ. P. 23(b)(2) is proper in this regard.

34. As discussed above, numerous common questions of fact and law exist. These questions predominate over the individual questions presented in this action. The predominance requirement of Rule 23(b)(3) is thus satisfied.

35. A class action is the superior method for the fair and efficient adjudication of this controversy, because joinder of all members of the Class, and, respectively, the Sub-Class, is impracticable. Because the damages suffered by individual members of the Class, and, respectively, the Sub-Class, may be relatively small, the expense and burden of litigation would prevent class members from individually redressing the wrongs done to them. Where, as here, the size and nature of individual Class members' claims would allow few, if any, members of those Classes to seek legal redress against Defendants for the wrongs complained of herein, a representative class action is both the appropriate vehicle by which to adjudicate these claims and is essential to the interests of justice. Furthermore, a class action regarding the issues in this action creates no significant problems of manageability. The superiority and manageability requirements of Rule 23(b)(3) are thus satisfied.

First Claim For Relief

(Violation of California Consumers Legal Remedies Act Against All Defendants)

36. Plaintiff realleges and incorporates herein by reference all of the allegations contained in Paragaphsl through 35, inclusive, of this complaint as though fully set forth herein.

37. California Civil Code Section 1750 et seq. (entitled the Consumers Legal Remedies Act) provides a list of "unfair or deceptive" practices in a "transaction" relating to the sale of "goods" or "services" to a "consumer." The Legislature's intent in promulgating the Consumers Legal Remedies Act is expressed in Civil Code Section 1760, which provides, inter alia, that its terms are to be:

> [C]onstrued liberally and applied to promote its underlying purposes, which are to protect consumers against unfair and deceptive business practices and to provide efficient and economical procedures to secure such protection.

38. Defendants' AGAG apparel products constituted "goods" as defined in Civil Code Section 1761(a).

39. Plaintiff, and Class members, are each a "Consumer" as defined in Civil Code Section 1761(d).

40. Each of Plaintiff's purchases of Defendants' AGAG apparel products constituted a "transaction" as defined in Civil Code Section 1761(e).

41. Civil Code Section 1770(a)(4) and (9) provides that "[t]he following unfair methods of competition and unfair or deceptive acts or practices undertaken by any person in a transaction intended to result or which results in the sale or lease of goods or services to any consumer are unlawful: Using deceptive representations or designations of geographic origin in connection with goods or services [and] [a]dvertising goods or services with intent not to sell them as advertised."

42. Defendants violated Civil Code Section 1770(a)(4) and (9) by marketing and representing that their AGAG apparel products are "Made in U.S.A." when they actually contain component parts that are manufactured outside of the United States.

43. It is alleged on information and belief that Defendants' violations of the Consumer's Legal Remedies Act set forth herein were done with awareness of the fact that the conduct alleged was wrongful and were motivated solely for increased profit. It is also alleged on information and belief that Defendants did these acts knowing the harm that would result to Plaintiff and that Defendants did these acts notwithstanding that knowledge.

44. As a direct and proximate result of Defendants' violations of the Consumers Legal Remedies Act, Plaintiff and Class members are entitled to the following remedies as against Defendants: (a) a declaration that Defendants violated the Consumers Legal Remedies Act, and (b) an injunction preventing Defendants' unlawful actions.

45. Plaintiff suffered an "injury in fact" because Plaintiff's money was taken by Defendants as a result of Defendants' false "Made in U.S.A." claims set forth on the AGAG apparel products.

46. Plaintiff and Class Members were undoubtedly injured as a result of Defendants' false "MADE IN USA" representations that are at issue in this litigation.

Second Claim For Relief

(Violation of Business & Prof. Code Section 17200 Et Seq. Against All Defendants)

47. Plaintiff realleges and incorporates herein by reference all of the allegations contained in Paragraphs 1 through 46, inclusive, of this complaint as though fully set forth herein.

48. Business & Professions Code section 17200 *et seq.* provides that unfair competition means and includes "any unlawful, unfair or fraudulent business act or practice and unfair, deceptive, untrue or misleading marketing."

49. By and through their conduct, including the conduct detailed above, Defendants engaged in activities which constitute unlawful, unfair, and fraudulent business practices prohibited by Business & Professions Code Section 17200 *et seq.* Beginning at an exact date unknown as yet and continuing up through the present, Defendants committed acts of unfair competition, including those described above, by engaging in a pattern of "unlawful" business practices, within the meaning of Business & Professions Code Section 17200 *et seq.*, by manufacturing, distributing, marketing AGAG apparel products with a false country of origin designation and violating Section 17533.7 by falsely claiming that the products referenced herein are "Made in U.S.A." when they actually contain component parts manufactured *outside of the United States.*

50. Beginning at an exact date unknown as yet and continuing up through the present, Defendants committed acts of unfair competition that are prohibited by Business and Professions Code section 17200 et seq. Defendants engaged in a pattern of "unfair" business practices that violate the wording and intent of the statutes, by engaging in practices that threaten an incipient violation of law or violate the policy or spirit of laws because their effects are comparable to or the same as a violation of the law by manufacturing, distributing, and marketing their AGAG apparel products with a false country of origin designation, and by violating Section 17533.7 by falsely claiming that their AGAG apparel products referenced herein are "Made in U.S.A." when they actually contain component parts manufactured outside of the United States.

51. Alternatively, Defendants engaged in a pattern of "unfair" business practices that violate the wording and intent of the statutes, by engaging in practices that are immoral, unethical, oppressive or unscrupulous, the utility (if any) of which conduct is far outweighed by the harm done to consumers and public policy by manufacturing, distributing, marketing, and advertising AGAG apparel products with the false claim that the products referenced herein are "Made in U.S.A."

52. Alternatively, Defendants engaged in a pattern of "unfair" business practices that violate the wording and intent of the statutes, by engaging in practices, including manufacturing, distributing, marketing, and advertising AGAG apparel products with the false claim that the products referenced herein are "Made in U.S.A.," wherein: (1) the injury to the consumer was substantial; (2) the injury was not outweighed by any countervailing benefits to consumers or competition; and (3) the injury was of the kind that the consumers themselves could not reasonably have avoided.

53. Beginning at an exact date unknown as yet and continuing up through the present, Defendants committed acts of unfair competition, including those described above, prohibited by Business and Professions Code section 17200 et seq. by engaging in a pattern of "fraudulent" business practices within the meaning of Business & Professions Code section 17200 et seq., by manufacturing, distributing, marketing AGAG apparel products with a false country of origin designation and violating Section 17533.7 by falsely claiming that the products referenced herein are "Made in U.S.A."

54. Defendants engaged in these unlawful, unfair and fraudulent business practices for the primary purpose of collecting unlawful and unauthorized monies from Plaintiff and all others similarly situated; thereby unjustly enriching Defendants.

55. As a result of the repeated violations described herein, Defendants received and continue to receive unearned commercial benefits at the expense of their competitors and the public.

56. Defendants' unlawful, unfair and fraudulent business practices presents a continuing threat to the public in that Defendants continues to engage in unlawful conduct.

57. Such acts and omissions are unlawful and/or unfair and/or fraudulent and constitute a violation of Business & Professions Code section 17200 et seq. Plaintiff reserves the right to identify additional violations by Defendants as may be established through discovery.

58. As a direct and legal result of their unlawful, unfair and fraudulent conduct described herein, Defendants have been and will be unjustly enriched by the receipt of ill-gotten gains from customers, including Plaintiff, who unwittingly provided their money to Defendants based on Defendants' fraudulent country of origin designation.

59. Plaintiff suffered an "injury in fact" because Plaintiff's money was taken by Defendants as a result of Defendant's false "Made in U.S.A." claims set forth on the AGAG apparel products.

60. In prosecuting this action for the enforcement of important rights affecting the public interest, Plaintiff seeks the recovery of attorneys' fees, which is available to a prevailing plaintiff in class action cases such as this.

Third Claim For Relief

(Violation of Business & Professions Code § 17533.7 Against All Defendants)

61. Plaintiff realleges and incorporates herein by reference all of the allegations contained in Paragaphsl through 60, inclusive, of this complaint as though fully set forth herein.

62. Business & Professions Code Section 17533.7 provides:

> It is unlawful for any person, firm, corporation or association to sell or offer for sale in this State any merchandise on which merchandise or on its container there appears the words "Made in U.S.A." "Made in America," "U.S.A.," or similar words when the merchandise or **any article, unit, or part thereof**, has been entirely or substantially made, manufactured, or produced outside of the United States. (emphasis added).

63. Defendants (both AGAG and Nordstrom) [violated] Business & Professions Code Section 17533.7 by selling and offering to sell merchandise in the State of California with the "Made in U.S.A." country of origin designation as fully set forth herein. The merchandise at issue in this case actually contains component parts that are manufactured outside of the United States in violation of California and federal law.

64. It is alleged on information and belief that Defendants' violations of Business & Professions Code Section 17533.7 were done with awareness of the fact that the conduct alleged was wrongful and were motivated solely for increased profit. It is also alleged on information and belief that Defendants did these acts knowing the harm that would result to Plaintiff and that Defendants did these acts notwithstanding that knowledge.

65. As a direct and proximate result of Defendants' violations of Business & Professions Code Section 17533.7, Plaintiff and Class members are entitled to restitution of excess monies paid to Defendants by Plaintiff and Class members relating to the false "Made in U.S.A." claims on Defendants' AGAG apparel products.

66. Plaintiff suffered an "injury in fact" because Plaintiff's money was taken by Defendants as a result of Defendants' false "Made in U.S.A." claims set forth on the AGAG apparel products.

67. In prosecuting this action for the enforcement of important rights affecting the public interest, Plaintiff seeks the recovery of attorneys' fees, which is available to a prevailing plaintiff in class action cases such as this.

Prayer

WHEREFORE, Plaintiffs, on behalf of themselves, collectively on behalf of the Class, and respectively on behalf of the Sub-Class, respectfully request the following relief:

1. That the Court determine that this action may be maintained as a class action by certifying this case as a California class action as to both the Class and Sub-Class;

2. That the Court certify Plaintiff to serve as a class representative in this case;

3. That Defendants' wrongful conduct alleged herein be adjudged and decreed to violate the consumer protection statutory claims asserted herein;

4. That Plaintiff and each of the other members of the Class and each of the Sub-Class recover the amounts by which Defendants have been unjustly enriched;

5. That Defendants be enjoined from continuing the wrongful conduct alleged herein and required to comply with all applicable law;

6. That Plaintiff and each of the other members of the Class and each of the Sub-Class recover their costs of suit, including reasonable attorneys' fees and expenses as provided by law; and

7. That Plaintiff and each of the other members of Class and each of the Sub-Class be granted such other and further relief as the nature of the case may require or as this Court deems just and proper.

* * *

Final Judgment and Injunction

No. 3:14-cv-01372 (S.D. Cal. Oct. 28, 2016)

Plaintiff David Paz, both individually and on behalf of all members of the class, and Defendant AG Adriano Goldschmied, Inc. ("AGAG") through its attorneys of record, having stipulated to the entry of this Final Judgment and Injunction (the "Judgment") without the taking of proof, without trial or adjudication of any fact or law herein, without the judgment constituting evidence of or an admission by AGAG regarding any issue of fact or law alleged in the Complaint herein, and without AGAG admitting any liability, and good cause appearing therefore:

IT IS HEREBY ORDERED, ADJUDGED, AND DECREED THAT:

This action is brought under California and federal law, and this Court has jurisdiction over the allegations and subject matter of the operative complaint on file herein.

This Court has personal jurisdiction over the parties to this action, including the Class Members (as defined below).

This Judgment has been reviewed by this Court, and this Court finds that it has been entered into in good faith and to be in all respects suitable and equitable.

The injunctive provisions of this Judgment are applicable to AGAG, including its successors in interest and the assigns of all or substantially all of the assets of their business; their directors, officers, employees, agents, managers, members, and principals (collectively, the "Enjoined Parties").

Federal Rule of Civil Procedure 23(c), the members of the Class is comprised of all persons in California who purchased a "Made in USA" or "Made in USA of Imported Fabric" labeled Class Product between June 04, 2010 to December 31, 2015 and who do not timely exercise his or her right to opt out of participation in the settlement (the "Class Members").

<u>Permanent Injunction</u>. Without admitting any liability or wrongdoing whatsoever, pursuant to California Business and Professions Code Sections 17203, the Enjoined Parties, and each of them, shall be enjoined and restrained from directly or indirectly doing or performing any and all of the following acts or practices: representing, labeling, advertising, selling, offering for sale, and/or distributing any of the AGAG Class Products in the list attached to the Settlement Agreement as Exhibit G, with a "Made in USA", "Made in USA of Imported Fabric", or similar designation unless it complies with the requirements of California Business & Professions Code Section 17533.7 and the requirements of the FTC pertaining to country of origin labeling.

<u>Restitution to Class Members</u>. Without admitting any liability or wrongdoing whatsoever, AGAG shall send to each Class Member who timely submitted a properly completed, signed claim form (received either online or by mail) that is not rejected by the Claims Administrator or Defendant, a pair of AGAG pants, valued at approximately $160.00, or a $20.00 promotional gift code, for each qualifying Class Product purchased during the Class Period.

This Court retains jurisdiction for the purpose of enabling any party to this Judgment to apply to this Court at any time for such further orders and directions as may be necessary or appropriate for the construction or carrying out of this

Judgment, for the modification of any of the provisions hereof, for the enforcement of compliance herewith, and for the punishment of violations hereof.

The parties agree to negotiate in good faith to try to resolve any disputes that may arise relating to this Judgment. Plaintiff shall give Defendant twenty (20) days' notice before filing an application or other pleading seeking contempt of court or other sanctions for any purported violation of this Judgment.

Nothing in this Judgment shall be deemed to permit or authorize any violation of the laws, rules, or regulations of California and/or the other 49 states and the District of Columbia or otherwise be construed to relieve Defendant of any duty to comply with any applicable laws, rules, or regulations.

This Judgment is a final resolution and disposition of all those matters, claims, and causes of action alleged in the Complaint herein. This Judgment shall have a res judicata effect that bars Plaintiff and all Class Members from bringing and asserting any action, claim, demand, or cause of action against Defendant, its predecessors, heirs, representatives, assigns, agents, distributors, customers, retailers, or employees, past and present, alleging any violation of: (1) California Business & Professions Code §§ 17200, et seq.; (2) California Business & Professions Code § 17533.7, (3) California Civil Code § 1770 et seq.; and (4) any other California law arising out of their conduct related to representing, labeling, advertising, selling, offering for sale, and/or distributing AGAG apparel products with an unqualified "Made in USA", "Made in USA of Imported Fabric", or similar designation when the product or any article, unit, or part therein, was made, manufactured, or produced outside of the United States.

This Judgment shall take effect immediately upon entry thereof, without further notice to Defendant.

The Court finds that an attorneys' fees award of $175,000.00 is fair and reasonable and awards same to Class Counsel. This award shall be inclusive of Class Counsel's costs and expenses.

The Court further awards Plaintiff David Paz an incentive award of $5,000.00, which the Court finds to be fair and reasonable.

The attorneys' fees award, reimbursement of expenses, and the Plaintiff incentive award shall be paid within ten (10) business days after the date of this Judgment. If not so paid, then interest on such award, fees and expenses shall accrue from the date of this Judgment until paid at the maximum rate allowed by law.

The Clerk shall enter this Judgment forthwith.

Notes

1. How is mislabeling a form of misrepresentation?

2. What is the threshold to determine if AGAG apparel can be labeled as "Made in the USA" while incorporating any foreign-made component? How is this distinguishable from a "Made in the USA of Imported Fabric" label?

3. What is the benefit of litigating this case or similar cases as class actions as opposed to separate lawsuits filed by individual plaintiffs?

Similarly, in *Marko Djoric v. Justin Brands, Inc.*, BC574927, the parties settled after a class action suit was filed against the makers of Chippewa footwear for falsely advertising their products—whose inner leather linings were from China—as "Made in the USA." Justin Brands additionally agreed to revise its product packaging and labeling accordingly.

In *Huber et al. v. Shinola/Detroit, LLC*, 1:16-cv-06465, Shinola was forced to change its advertising campaigns to read "Built in Detroit using Swiss and imported Parts." Originally, the company had been advertising its watches as "Made in America" and using the slogan "Where American is Made." The FTC ruled that although the company was based in Detroit, such representations about the source of its products were misleading. These cases have created precedent for companies whose products are manufactured in the United States but utilize foreign materials and components.

g. Feather or Down Products

Under the FTC Act, advertising claims about feather and down products must be truthful, nondeceptive and substantiated. A product may not indicate that it contains only down or feather unless it is true. When a product label states a specific percentage of down or other plumage, there may be a deviation of no more than five percent. Moreover, when a label identifies a particular species of feather, only a modest deviation is acceptable because of unavoidable manufacturing variation. The FTC can seek the following remedies against a company using false or deceptive labels for feather and down products. First, the FTC can issue cease-and-desist orders to stop running the deceptive ads or engaging in the deceptive practice, to substantiate claims in future ads, and to report to FTC staff about its compliance with the order. Violation of such order could lead to a penalty up to $42,530 per violation. Second, the FTC can condemn a company to civil penalties for knowingly engaging in deceptive practices. Finally, in some cases the FTC has required full or partial refunds to all consumers who brought the product.

h. Fur Products Labeling Act (Fur Rules)

The Fur Products Labeling Act (15 U.S.C. § 69) requires fur manufacturers and retailers to label fur products with certain information such as the animal's type, the name of the manufacturer, and the garment's country of origin. Manufacturers, importers, distributors, and retailers are responsible for complying with the Fur Rules and may be subject to civil or criminal penalties for selling mislabeled products. Sellers may protect themselves from liability under the Act and Rules for selling misbranded fur products by asking their U.S. supplier of fur products for a guaranty of compliance with the federal Fur Products Labeling Act ("FPLA") and Fur Rules and relying on the guaranty in good faith.

Online retailers are no exception to the Fur Rules and must also ensure that the products on their website have accurate descriptions and are correctly advertised. In the *Matter of The Neiman Marcus Group, Inc.*, C-4407, the FTC settled with upscale retailer Neiman Marcus after it had misrepresented various products as "faux fur." Specifically, the Neiman Marcus website advertised an Alice + Olivia coat and a Burberry jacket as having fake fur when, in fact, the items themselves contained labels indicating they were made with real fur. The FTC action also alleged that Neiman Marcus advertised one particular product on its website—a Stuart Weitzman shoe—as having fake fur, while other forms of advertising, including the Neiman Marcus catalog, advertised the shoes as having "dyed mink" and "rabbit fur."

In re Neiman Marcus Group, Inc.

No. C-4407 (F.T.C. Aug. 6, 2013)

Complaint

Pursuant to the provisions of the Federal Trade Commission Act, as amended, 15 U.S.C. §41 *et seq.*, and by virtue of the authority vested in it by said Act, the Federal Trade Commission ("Commission"), having reason to believe that Neiman Marcus Group, Inc. ("Neiman Marcus" or "respondent") has violated the provisions of the Federal Trade Commission Act, 15 U.S.C. §41 *et seq.*, the Fur Products Labeling Act, 15 U.S.C. §69 *et seq.* and the Rules and Regulations Under the Fur Products Labeling Act, 16 C.F.R. Part 301, and it appearing to the Commission that this proceeding is in the public interest, alleges:

1. Respondent is a Delaware corporation with its principal office or place of business at 1618 Main St., Dallas, TX 75201.

2. The acts and practices of respondent alleged in this complaint have been in or affecting commerce, as commerce is defined in Section 4 of the Federal Trade Commission Act, 15 U.S.C. §44, and Section 2(j) of the Fur Products Labeling Act, 15 U.S.C. §69(j).

3. Respondent has advertised, offered for sale, sold, and distributed fur products, as that term is defined in Section 2(d) of the Fur Products Labeling Act, 15 U.S.C. §69(d). Respondent advertises and offers fur products for sale through the Internet sites www.neimanmarcus.com and www.bergdorfgoodman.com.

4. In May 2009, Commission staff closed an investigation into whether respondent Neiman Marcus had falsely advertised coats as having faux fur that in fact contained real fur. In closing the investigation, staff relied in part on respondent's assurances that it had reached an agreement with a third-party vendor to label products as containing either real fur or other material.

Conduct

5. From approximately October 5, 2009, until approximately November 16, 2012, respondent disseminated, or caused to be disseminated, advertisements for fur products, including, but not limited to, a Burberry Outerwear Jacket ("Outerwear

Jacket"), a Stuart Weitzman Ballerina Flat ("Ballerina Flat"), and an Alice + Olivia Kyah Faux-Fur Collar Coat ('Kyah Coat").

Outerwear Jacket False Advertising

6. From approximately October 5, 2009, until October 30, 2009, respondent disseminated, or cause[d] to be disseminated, the advertisement attached as Exhibit A. This advertisement from www.neimanmarcus.com contained the following statements (emphasis added):

> Outerwear Jacket
>
> Cardinal red. Allover quilted topstitching. **Black faux-fur** hood with snap-tab detail; zip/snap front. Long sleeves with zip cuff detail. Tonal belt at natural waist. Zip pockets. A-line. Polyester/polyamide. Made in Italy of imported material.

7. The Outerwear Jacket had an attached label disclosing that it in fact contained "real fur."

8. From October 5, 2009, until October 30, 2009, respondent sold at least five Outerwear Jackets via its website for a total revenue of at least $6,475.

Ballerina Flat False Advertising

9. From approximately August 3, 2011, until approximately December 1, 2011, respondent disseminated, or caused to be disseminated, the advertisement attached as Exhibit B. This advertisement from www.neimanmarcus.com contained the following statements (emphasis added):

> A cute fur ornament decorates the toe of this basic ballerina flat by Stuart Weitzman.
>
> Sport suede upper.
>
> **Faux fur (cotton/viscose)** pom on round toe.
>
> Imported of Spanish and Italian material.

Respondent's www.bergdorfgoodman.com internet site carried a similar advertisement beginning on August 20, 2011.

10. From approximately August 14, 2011, until approximately December 1, 2011, respondent disseminated, or caused to be disseminated, the catalog advertisement for the Ballerina Flat attached as Exhibit C, which contained the following statements (emphasis added):

> Black or cola "Furball" ballet flat with **dyed mink** (Spain) pouf, rubber sole, and 1/2" wedge heel.

11. From approximately November 27, 2011, until approximately December 1, 2011, respondent mailed to its customers a "stuffer" attached as Exhibit D that described the product as containing a "dyed mink (Spain) pouf" (emphasis added).

12. The vendor of the Ballerina Flat had notified respondent that the product contained real rabbit fur before July 25, 2011.

13. From approximately August 3 to December 1, 2011, respondent sold at least 292 Ballerina Flats via its websites, catalog, and mailers for a total revenue of at least $85,000.

Kyah Coat False Advertising

14. From approximately August 9, 2012, until approximately November 16, 2012, respondent disseminated, or caused to be disseminated, the advertisement attached as Exhibit E. This advertisement from www.neimanmarcus.com contained the following statements (emphasis added):

> Kyah Faux Fur-Collar Coat: Glam up your professional looks with the Alice + Olivia Kyah coat, which features a plush **faux-fur** collar.
>
> Crepe with **faux-fur (polyester/viscose)** collar.
>
> Self-tie waist.
>
> Long sleeves.
>
> Arched hem falls below hip.
>
> Virgin wool/cashmere/polyester.
>
> Dry clean.
>
> Imported.

15. The Kyah Coat had an attached label disclosing that its collar was in fact "real fur."

16. From approximately August 9, 2012, until approximately November 16, 2012, respondent sold at least 19 Kyah Coats via its website for a total revenue of at least $15,162.

Count I

17. Through the means described in Paragraphs 6, 9, and 14, respondent represented, expressly or by implication, that the fur in the Outerwear Jacket, Ballerina Flat, and Kyah Coat was faux or fake. In truth and in fact, those products contained real fur. Therefore, the representations set forth in Paragraphs 6, 9, and 14 were false, deceptive, or misleading.

18. Through the means described in Paragraphs 10 and 11, respondent represented, expressly or by implication, that the fur in the Ballerina Flat was mink fur. In truth and in fact, the Ballerina Flat contained rabbit fur. Therefore, the representations set forth in Paragraphs 10 and 11 were false, deceptive, or misleading.

19. Respondent's practices, as alleged in this complaint, constitute unfair or deceptive acts or practices in or affecting commerce in violation of Section 5(a) of the Federal Trade Commission Act, 15 U.S.C. § 45(a), and false advertising in violation of Section 5(a)(5) of the Fur Products Labeling Act, 15 U.S.C. §§ 69c(a)(5), and Sections 301.2(c) and 301.49 of the Rules and Regulations Under the Fur Products Labeling Act, 16 C.F.R. §§ 301.2(c) and 301.49. Pursuant to Sections 3(a) and 3(c) of the Fur Products Labeling Act, 15 U.S.C. § 69a(a) and 69a(c), the false advertising

of fur products, within the meaning of the Fur Products Labeling Act and the Rules and Regulations Under Fur Products Labeling Act, is unlawful and an unfair and deceptive act or practice, in commerce, under the Federal Trade Commission Act, 15 U.S.C. § 41, *et seq.*

Count II

20. Through the means described in paragraphs 6, 9-11, and 14, respondent did not disclose the name of the animal that produced the fur in the Outerwear Jacket, Ballerina Flat, and Kyah Coat as set forth in the Fur Products Name Guide, 16 C.F.R. § 301.0.

21. Through the means described in paragraphs 6, 9, and 14, respondent did not disclose the country of origin for the fur in the Outerwear Jacket, Ballerina Flat, and Kyah Coat.

22. Respondent's practices, as alleged in this complaint, constitute unfair or deceptive acts or practices in or affecting commerce in violation of Section 5(a) of the Federal Trade Commission Act, 15 U.S.C. § 45(a), and false advertising in violation of Sections 5(a)(1), 5(a)(5), and 5(a)(6) of the Fur Products Labeling Act, 15 U.S.C. §§ 69c(a)(1),(5), and (6), and Sections 301.2(c) and 301.49 of the Rules and Regulations Under the Fur Products Labeling Act, 16 C.F.R. §§ 301.2(c) and 301.49. Pursuant to Sections 3(a) and 3(c) of the Fur Products Labeling Act, 15 U.S.C. § 69a(a) and 69a(c), the false advertising of fur products, within the meaning of the Fur Products Labeling Act and the Rules and Regulations Under Fur Products Labeling Act, is unlawful and an unfair and deceptive act or practice, in commerce, under the Federal Trade Commission Act, 15 U.S.C. § 41, et seq.

WHEREFORE, THE PREMISES CONSIDERED, the Federal Trade Commission has caused this Complaint to be signed by its Secretary and its official seal to be hereto affixed, at Washington, D.C., this eighteenth day of July, 2013.

By the Commission.

Decision and Order

The Federal Trade Commission ("Commission"), having initiated an investigation of certain acts and practices of the Respondent named in the caption hereof, and the Respondent having been furnished thereafter with a copy of a draft of a Complaint which the Bureau of Consumer Protection proposed to present to the Commission for its consideration and which, if issued, would charge the Respondent with violations of the Federal Trade Commission Act and the Fur Products Labeling Act; and

The Respondent, its attorney, and counsel for the Commission having thereafter executed an Agreement Containing Consent Order ("Consent Agreement"), which includes: a statement by Respondent that it neither admits nor denies any of the allegations in the draft complaint, except as specifically stated in the Consent Agreement, and, only for purposes of this action, admits the facts necessary to establish jurisdiction; and waivers and other provisions as required by the Commission's Rules; and

The Commission having thereafter considered the matter and having determined that it had reason to believe that the Respondent has violated the Federal Trade Commission Act, and that a complaint should issue stating its charges in that respect, and having thereupon accepted the executed consent agreement and placed such agreement on the public record for a period of thirty (30) days for the receipt and consideration of public comments, and having duly considered the comments received from interested persons pursuant to Commission Rule 2.34, 16 C.F.R. §2.34, now in further conformity with the procedure prescribed in Commission Rule 2.34, the Commission hereby issues its complaint, makes the following jurisdictional findings, and enters the following order:

1. Respondent The Neiman Marcus Group, Inc., is a Delaware corporation with its principal office or place of business at 1618 Main St., Dallas, TX 75201.

2. The Federal Trade Commission has jurisdiction of the subject matter of this proceeding and of the Respondent, and the proceeding is in the public interest.

Order

Definitions

For purposes of this order, the following definitions shall apply:

1. "Respondent" shall mean The Neiman Marcus Group, Inc., its successors and assigns, subsidiaries and divisions, and their officers, agents, representatives, and employees.

2. "Commerce" shall mean commerce among the several States or with foreign nations, or in any Territory of the United States or in the District of Columbia, or between any such Territory and another, or between any such Territory and any State or foreign nation, or between the District of Columbia and any State or Territory or foreign nation.

3. "Covered product" shall mean any article of clothing or covering for any part of the body that (a) is made in whole or in part of fur or used fur or (b) respondent advertises as containing fake or faux fur.

4. "Fur" shall mean any animal skin or part thereof with hair, fleece, or fur fibers attached thereto, either in its raw or processed state, but shall not include such skins as are to be converted into leather or which in processing shall have the hair, fleece, or fur fiber completely removed.

5. "Fur product" shall mean any article of clothing or covering for any part of the body made in whole or in part of fur or used fur.

I.

IT IS ORDERED that, subject to the guaranty provisions of the Fur Products Labeling Act ("Fur Act"), 15 U.S.C. §69 et seq., and the Rules and Regulations Under the Fur Products Labeling Act ("Fur Rules"), 16 C.F.R. Part 301, Respondent, directly or through any person, partnership, corporation, subsidiary, division, trade name, or other device, in connection with the labeling, advertising, promotion, offering for sale, sale, or distribution of any fur product in any advertisement disseminated through the mail, on any website, or in any catalog, in or affecting commerce, is hereby permanently restrained and enjoined from engaging in, causing other persons to engage in, or assisting other persons to engage in, violations of the Fur Act and the Fur Rules, including, but not limited to, falsely or deceptively advertising any fur product by misrepresenting or failing to disclose:

A. That the fur in any fur product is faux or fake;

B. The name or names (as set forth in the Fur Products Name Guide, 16 C.F.R. § 301.0) of the animal or animals that produced the fur, and such qualifying statement as may be required pursuant to 15 U.S.C. § 69e(c);

C. That the fur is used fur or that the fur product contains used fur when such is the fact;

D. That the fur product or fur is bleached, dyed, or otherwise artificially colored fur when such is the fact;

E. That the fur product is composed in whole or in substantial part of paws, tails, bellies, or waste fur when such is the fact; and

F. The name of the country of origin of any imported furs or those contained in the fur product.

Provided that, in the event the Fur Act or Fur Rules are amended or modified:

1. Respondent shall comply fully and completely with all applicable requirements thereof, on and after the effective date of any such act or rule; and

2. That nothing in this Paragraph shall impose upon Respondent obligations beyond what is required under the amended or modified version of the Fur Act or Rules.

Provided further that if Respondent (1) cannot legally obtain a guaranty when it takes an ownership interest in a fur product, (2) does not embellish or misrepresent claims provided by the manufacturer about that product, and (3) does not sell the product as a private label product, then Respondent shall be liable for a violation of this Paragraph only if it knew or should have known that the marketing or sale of the product would violate this Paragraph.

II.

IT IS FURTHER ORDERED that Respondent shall maintain and, upon request, make available to the Commission, for inspection and copying, all records that will demonstrate compliance with the requirements of this order, including, but not limited to:

A. All acknowledgments of receipt of order obtained pursuant to Paragraph III.B.

B. For three (3) years after the last date of dissemination of any representation by Respondent about any covered product in any advertisement disseminated through the mail, on any website, or in any catalog;

1. All advertisements and promotional materials containing the representation;
2. All materials that were relied upon in disseminating the representation;
3. All tests, reports, studies, surveys, demonstrations, or other evidence in the possession or control of any of the persons covered by Paragraph III.A that contradict, qualify, or call into question the representation, or the basis relied upon for the representation; and
4. All complaints and other communications with consumers that call into question the representation, or the basis relied upon for the representation, in connection with a specific product purchased by a specific consumer, and all communications with governmental or consumer protection organizations that contradict, qualify, or call into question the representation, or the basis relied upon for the representation.

III.

IT IS FURTHER ORDERED that Respondent shall:

A. For a period of three (3) years, deliver a copy of this order to all employees, agents, and representatives having responsibilities with respect to Respondent's marketing or advertising of any covered product in any advertisement disseminated through the mail, on any website, or in any catalog and to any manager or officer in the chain of command of such employees, agents, and representatives, within thirty (30) days after (1) the date of service of this order, or (2) the person assumes a position covered by this paragraph.

B. Secure from each person receiving this order pursuant to this paragraph a signed and dated statement acknowledging receipt of this order.

IV.

IT IS FURTHER ORDERED that Respondent shall notify the Commission in connection with compliance with this order as follows:

A. At least thirty (30) days prior to any change in the corporation that may affect compliance obligations arising under this order, including, but not limited to, a dissolution, assignment, sale, merger, or other action, that would result in the emergence of a successor corporation; the creation or dissolution of a subsidiary, parent, or affiliate that engages in any acts or practices subject to this order; the proposed filing of a bankruptcy petition; or a change in the corporate name or address. Provided that, with respect to any proposed change in the corporation about which Respondent learns less than thirty (30) days prior to the date such action is to take place, Respondent shall notify the Commission as soon as is practicable after obtaining such knowledge.

B. Within sixty (60) days after the date of service of this order, file with the Commission a true and accurate report, in writing, setting forth in detail the manner and form of its own compliance with this order. Within ten (10) days of receipt of written notice from a representative of the Commission, it shall submit additional true and accurate written reports.

C. Unless otherwise directed by a representative of the Commission in writing, all notices required by this Part shall be emailed to Debrief@ftc.gov or sent by overnight courier (not the U.S. Postal Service) to: Associate Director for Enforcement, Bureau of Consumer Protection, Federal Trade Commission, 600 Pennsylvania Avenue NW, Washington, DC 20580. The subject line must begin: FTC v. The Neiman Marcus Group, Inc., File Number 0823199, Docket Number C-4407.

V.

IT IS FURTHER ORDERED that this order will terminate on July 18, 2033, or twenty (20) years from the most recent date that the United States or the Commission files a complaint (with or without an accompanying consent decree) in federal court alleging any violation of the order, whichever comes later. Provided that the filing of such a complaint will not affect the duration of:

A. Any Part in this order that terminates in less than twenty (20) years;

B. This order, if such complaint is filed after the order has terminated pursuant to this Part. Provided, further, that if such complaint is dismissed, or a federal court rules that the Respondent did not violate any provision of the order, and the dismissal or ruling is either not appealed or upheld on appeal, then the order will terminate according to this Part as though the complaint had never been filed, except that the order will not terminate between the date such complaint is filed and the later of the deadline for appealing such dismissal or ruling and the date such dismissal or ruling is upheld on appeal.

By the Commission.

Notes

1. What is the significance in identifying the type of animal the fur is from?

2. Would there be a strong claim against Neiman Marcus if both the website and catalog advertisements were identical, both advertising faux fur while the items themselves contain labels indicating real fur? Would the claim against Neiman Marcus be stronger if both advertisements stated real fur while the items themselves contained labels indicating faux fur?

3. How does a court determine "faux fur" versus real animal fur?

Accurately identifying the type of animal is essential to ensure compliance with the Fur Rules. In *The Humane Society of the United States v. Andrew & Suzanne Co.*, 2008 CA 008285 B, The Humane Society filed suit against Macy's, accusing it of selling a coat falsely advertised as having imitation rabbit fur. When the Humane Society purchased the coat, the labels indicated the coat was made with "genuine raccoon fur." As the coat was made in China, one of the major questions was whether the coat was in fact made with raccoon fur or if it was made with the fur of raccoon dog, a type of dog whose fur resembles that of a raccoon.

Humane Society of the United States v. Andrew & Suzanne Co.

No. 2008 CA 008285 B (D.C. Super. Nov. 24, 2008)

Complaint

Introduction

Plaintiff The Humane Society of the United States ("The HSUS"), in its own and in a representative capacity, on behalf of all its members, alleges unlawful trade practices pursuant to the District of Columbia Consumer Protection Procedures Act ("CPPA"), D.C. Code Ann. § 28-3901 *et seq.*, and files this Complaint with jury demand. This action for statutory penalties and injunctive relief arises from Defendants' marketing and sale in the District of Columbia of falsely advertised and/or falsely labeled fur-trimmed garments in violation of the CPPA, the federal Fur Products Labeling Act ("FPLA"), 15 U.S.C. § 69 *et seq.*, and the Federal Trade Commission Act ("FTCA"), 15 U.S.C. § 41 *et seq.*

As described herein, Defendants have been manufacturing, distributing, marketing, and selling fur-trimmed garments advertised and/or labeled as "faux fur," when they are, in fact, derived from real animal fur. Defendants have also been manufacturing, distributing, marketing, and selling fur-trimmed garments advertised and/or labeled as raccoon, coyote, or rabbit fur, when, in fact, they are made from the wholly distinct species of raccoon dog—a member of the canine family. Such actions not only mislead humane-conscious consumers into unknowingly purchasing real fur products but also further increase consumer confusion over the type and origin of fur that is used on garments.

Accordingly, Defendants' deceptive advertising and labeling practices constitute an unlawful trade practice and therefore violate the CPPA. D.C. Code Ann. § 28-3904(a), (d), (e), (f) ("It shall be a violation of this chapter, whether or not any consumer is in fact misled, deceived or damaged thereby, for any person to: (a) represent that goods or services have ... characteristics ... that they do not have; ... (d) represent that goods or services are of particular standard, quality, grade, style, or model, if in fact they are of another; (e) misrepresent as to a material fact which has a tendency to mislead; ... [or] (f) fail to state a material fact if such failure tends to mislead").

Such deceptive advertising and labeling also violates the FPLA and the FTCA, and therefore constitutes an unlawful trade practice under the CPPA. 15 U.S.C. § 69a(a) ("introduction, or manufacture for introduction, into commerce, or the sale, advertising or offering for sale in commerce, or the transportation or distribution in commerce, of any fur product which is misbranded or falsely advertised ... is unlawful and shall be an unfair method of competition, and an unfair and deceptive act or practice, in commerce under the Federal Trade Commission Act (15 U.S.C. § 41 *et seq.)"); D.C. CODE ANN. § 28-3904(x) (unlawful for any person to "sell consumer goods in a condition or manner not consistent with that warranted by . . . operation or requirement of federal law").

All such statutory violations are actionable by way of the cause of action available to organizational plaintiffs, such as The Humane Society of the United States, under section 28-3905(k)(1) of the CPPA. D.C. CODE ANN. § 28-3905(k)(1).

Jurisdiction and Venue

1. The Court has subject matter jurisdiction over statutory claims in this matter pursuant to D.C. CODE ANN. § 28-3905(k)(1). The Court has personal jurisdiction over Defendants pursuant to D.C. CODE ANN. §§ 13-334(a) and 13-423(a)(1), because the allegations and claims for relief herein arise from Defendants' "transaction of business" and "doing business" in the District of Columbia.

2. As a result of Defendants' purposeful and substantial advertising, marketing, distribution, and selling of fur-trimmed garments in the District of Columbia—either through online websites and/or retail stores that are located in the District of Columbia—Defendants have established sufficient contacts with the District of Columbia such that it is reasonable for Defendants to reasonably anticipate being subject to action in the courts of the District of Columbia.

3. Venue is proper in the District of Columbia because Plaintiff The HSUS's headquarters are in the District of Columbia and this action relates to Defendants' activities within the District of Columbia.

The Parties

4. Plaintiff The HSUS is the nation's largest animal protection organization with over 29,000 members and constituents in the District of Columbia and over 10.5 million members and constituents nationwide. The HSUS is a non-profit organization headquartered in the District of Columbia and since 1954 has been working to protect all animals through education, investigation, litigation, legislation, advocacy, and field work. In particular, The HSUS's Fur-Free Campaign works to end the killing of animals for fur and fur trim by promoting humane alternatives to animal fur. The false and deceptive advertising and labeling described herein injures The HSUS and its members by misleading fur-free consumers into buying real fur products and increasing consumer confusion over the type and origin of fur-trimmed garments sold at retail, thereby injuring The HSUS's organizational mission and its members, including those that reside in the District of Columbia, as described further below.

5. Defendant Andrew & Suzanne Company, Inc., doing business as "Andrew Marc," is incorporated in the State of New York and is headquartered in New York, NY. As of February 11, 2008, Andrew & Suzanne Company, Inc. operates as a wholly owned subsidiary of G-III Leather Fashions, Inc. Andrew Marc is an American design company that designs, manufactures, and distributes upscale clothing under the brand names Andrew Marc and Marc New York. Defendant Andrew Marc regularly

conducts business in the District of Columbia by distributing garments that are sold to consumers at retail stores throughout the District of Columbia, including Bloomingdale's (a retail division of Macy's, Inc.), Lord & Taylor, Neiman Marcus, and Saks Fifth Avenue. Andrew Marc also markets and sells its collection directly to consumers in the District of Columbia through its website, www.andrewmarc.com.

6. Defendant Dillard's, Inc. ("Dillard's") is incorporated in the State of Delaware and its headquarters are located in Little Rock, AR. Dillard's operates approximately 330 retail department stores located primarily in the southeastern, southwestern, and midwestern areas of the United States and offers a mix of name brand and private label merchandise, including house brand Preston & York. Defendant Dillard's regularly conducts business in the District of Columbia by marketing and selling its merchandise directly to consumers in the District of Columbia through its website, www.dillards.com.

7. Defendant Lord & Taylor, LLC ("Lord & Taylor") is a limited liability corporation incorporated in the State of Delaware and headquartered in New York, NY. Lord & Taylor is an upscale department store retailer that operates 47 retail locations and sells luxury apparel, jewelry, and accessories, including designer brands Andrew Marc and Marc New York. Lord & Taylor regularly conducts business in the District of Columbia by selling and marketing merchandise to D.C. residents and consumers through its department store at 5255 Western Avenue, Washington, DC 20015, and at nearby stores located in Alexandria, VA, McLean, VA, and Kensington, MD. Defendant Lord & Taylor also markets and sells its merchandise directly to consumers in the District of Columbia through its online store, www.lordandtaylor.com. Lord & Taylor also frequently advertises to residents and consumers in the District of Columbia in *The Washington Post,* primarily using "run of paper" ("ROP") display advertising, which allows the newspaper to place Lord & Taylor ads anywhere within the paper. For example, several Lord & Taylor advertisements were displayed in the recent November 16, 2008 print edition of *The Washington Post.*

8. Defendant Macy's, Inc. ("Macy's") is incorporated in the State of Delaware and its principal headquarters are located in Cincinnati, OH. Macy's is one of America's largest retailers, operating 40 Bloomingdale's department stores and more than 810 Macy's department stores. Defendant Macy's regularly conducts business in the District of Columbia by selling merchandise at several retail stores throughout the greater D.C. metropolitan area, including a Macy's department store located in downtown Washington, DC at 1201 G Street, NW, and nearby stores in Arlington, VA, McLean, VA, and Bethesda, MD. Macy's also regularly conducts business in the District of Columbia by selling and marketing merchandise to D.C. residents and consumers at Bloomingdale's department stores located in nearby Chevy Chase, MD—located just over the District border at 5300 Western Avenue—McLean, VA and Kensington, MD. Defendant Macy's also markets and sells its merchandise directly to consumers in the District of Columbia through its online

stores, www.macys.com and www.bloomingdales.com, and a direct mail catalogue, Bloomingdale's By Mail. Macy's, Inc. also frequently advertises to residents and consumers in the District of Columbia in *The Washington Post,* primarily using ROP advertising to display both Macy's and Bloomingdale's advertisements. For example, several Macy's advertisements were displayed in the recent November 16, 2008 print edition of *The Washington Post.*

9. Defendant Neiman Marcus Group, Inc. ("Neiman Marcus") is incorporated in the State of Delaware and headquartered in Dallas, TX. Neiman Marcus is a luxury retailer that operates 39 flagship stores in the United States. It sells upscale apparel, jewelry, clothing accessories, and home goods, including designer brands Andrew Marc and Marc New York. Neiman Marcus regularly conducts business in the District of Columbia by selling and marketing merchandise to D.C. residents and consumers through its department store at 5300 Wisconsin Avenue, NW, Washington, DC 20015, and at another nearby store in McLean, VA. Defendant Neiman Marcus also markets and sells its merchandise directly to consumers in the District of Columbia through its website, www.neimanmarcus.com, and a direct mail print catalog. Neiman Marcus also frequently advertises to residents and consumers in the District of Columbia in *The Washington Post,* primarily using ROP display advertising.

10. Defendant Saks Incorporated, incorporated in Delaware and headquartered in New York, NY, is a luxury retailer that sells upscale clothing, accessories, jewelry, and housewares—including designer brands Andrew Marc and Marc New York—at over 54 "Saks Fifth Avenue" department stores. Saks Fifth Avenue regularly conducts business in the District of Columbia by selling and marketing merchandise to D.C. residents and consumers through its retail department store located at 5300 Wisconsin Avenue, NW, Washington, DC 20015, and at other stores located in nearby McLean, VA, Woodbridge, VA, and Chevy Chase, MD. Defendant Saks Fifth Avenue also markets and sells its merchandise directly to consumers in the District of Columbia through its online store, www.saks.com. Saks Fifth Avenue also frequently advertises to residents and consumers in the District of Columbia in *The Washington Post,* primarily using ROP display advertising. For example, a recent Saks Fifth Avenue advertisement was displayed in the November 16, 2008 print edition of *The Washington Post.*

Legal Framework

A. District of Columbia Consumer Protection Procedures Act

11. The CPPA provides:

> A person, whether acting for the interests of itself, its members, or the general public, may bring an action under this chapter in the Superior Court of the District of Columbia seeking relief from the use by any person of a trade practice in violation of the law of the District of Columbia. . . .

D.C. Code Ann. § 28-3905(k)(1).

12. It is a violation of District of Columbia law, and therefore an unlawful trade practice under the CPPA, *id.*, *"whether or not any consumer is in fact misled, deceived or damaged thereby,"* for any person to:

> (a) represent that goods or services have a source, sponsorship, approval, certification, accessories, characteristics, ingredients, uses, benefits, or quantities that they do not have;
>
> . . .
>
> (d) represent that goods or services are of particular standard, quality, grade, style, or model, if in fact they are of another;
>
> (e) misrepresent as to a material fact which has a tendency to mislead;
>
> (f) fail to state a material fact if such failure tends to mislead; [or]
>
> . . .
>
> (x) sell consumer goods in a condition or manner not consistent with that warranted by . . . operation or requirement of *federal law.*"

Id. § 28-3904 (emphasis added).

13. Additionally, "the CPPA's extensive enforcement mechanisms apply not only to the unlawful trade practices proscribed by § 28-3904, but to all other statutory and common law prohibitions." *Osbourne v. Capital City Mortgage Corp.*, 727 A.2d 322, 325-26 (D.C. 1999).

14. The CPPA allows for treble damages, or $1,500 per violation, whichever is greater, as well as reasonable attorney's fees, punitive damages, an injunction against the unlawful trade practice, "additional relief as may be necessary to restore the consumer money or property . . . which may have been acquired by means of the unlawful trade practice," and "any other relief the court deems proper." D.C. Code Ann. § 28-3905(k)(1).

B. Federal Fur Products Labeling Act

15. Section 3(a) of the federal Fur Products Labeling Act ("FPLA") provides:

> The introduction, or manufacture for introduction, into commerce, or the sale, advertising or offering for sale in commerce, or the transportation or distribution in commerce, of any fur product which is *misbranded or falsely or deceptively advertised . . . is unlawful and shall be an unfair method of competition, and an unfair and deceptive act or practice,* in commerce under the Federal Trade Commission Act (15 U.S.C. § 41 *et seq).*

15 U.S.C. § 69a(a) (emphasis added).

16. Pursuant to section 4 of the FPLA, "a fur product shall be considered to be misbranded"—

> (1) if it is falsely or deceptively labeled or otherwise falsely or deceptively identified, or if the label contains any form of misrepresentation or deception, directly or by implication, with respect to such fur product;

(2) if there is not affixed to the fur product a label showing in words and figures plainly legible -

(A) the name or names (as set forth in the Fur Products Name Guide) of the animal or animals that produced the fur, and such qualifying statement as may be required pursuant to section 69e(c) of this title;

(B) that the fur product contains or is composed of used fur, when such is the fact;

(C) that the fur product contains or is composed of bleached, dyed, or otherwise artificially colored fur, when such is the fact;

(D) that the fur product is composed in whole or in substantial part of paws, tails, bellies, or waste fur, when such is the fact;

(E) the name, or other identification issued and registered by the Commission, of one or more of the persons who manufacture such fur product for introduction into commerce, introduce it into commerce, sell it in commerce, advertise or offer it for sale in commerce, or transport or distribute it in commerce;

(F) the name of the country of origin of any imported furs used in the fur product;

(3) if the label required by paragraph (2)(A) of this section sets forth the name or names of any animal or animals other than the name or names provided for in such paragraph.

Id. § 69b.

17. Section 5(a) of the FPLA also provides that "a fur product shall be considered to be falsely or deceptively advertised if any advertisement, representation, public announcement, or notice which is intended to aid, promote, or assist directly or indirectly in the sale or offering for sale of such fur product or fur":

(1) does not show the name or names . . . of the animal or animals that produced the fur . . . ;

. . .

(5) contains any form of misrepresentation or deception, directly or by implication, with respect to such fur product or fur; or

(6) does not show the name of the country of origin of any imported furs or those contained in a fur product.

Id. § 69c(a).

C. Federal Trade Commission Act

18. The FTCA declares that "[u]nfair methods of competition in or affecting commerce, and unfair or deceptive acts or practices in or affecting commerce, are hereby declared unlawful." 15 U.S.C. § 45(a)(1).

19. As described above, "[t]he introduction, or manufacture for introduction, into commerce, or the sale, advertising or offering for sale in commerce, or the transportation or distribution in commerce, of any product which is misbranded or falsely or deceptively advertised or invoiced" is a violation of the FPLA and is therefore "unlawful and shall be an unfair method of competition, and an unfair, and deceptive act or practice, in commerce under the [FTCA]." *Id.* § 69a(a).

Facts Giving Rise To Plaintiffs Claims For Relief

A. The Inhumane Fur Trade

20. Due to the lack of animal welfare protection and a surplus of cheap labor, China has become the leading pelt producer and manufacturer of fur garments in the world. Mark Rissi *et al.*, Fun Fur? A Report on the Chinese Fur Industry 2–4 (2005), *available at* http://www.careforthewild.com/files/furreport05. pdf. Roughly half of all fur garments entering the United States come from China, where a large number of dogs, cats, raccoon dogs, and other domestic and wild species are raised inhumanely for their fur. *Id.* at 5.

21. A 2004–2005 investigation conducted by Swiss Animal Protection SAP, Care for the Wild International, and EAST International documented the horrifying conditions of Chinese fur farms. *Id.* at 5-11. The report states that animals are frequently housed in small mesh cages, where they exhibit pathological behaviors, including self-mutilation and infanticide. *Id.* at 5-7. The report further notes that in preparation for skinning, fur farm animals are removed from their cages with a capture pole and are either swung head-first into the ground or are repeatedly beaten with a metal or wooden stick so they are stunned or immobilized. *Id.* at 6. However, according to the report, a significant number of the animals remain fully conscious while they are skinned alive. *Id.* at 9. The report notes that, in several cases, after the skin was removed, breathing, eyelid movements, and heartbeat were apparent for up to five to ten minutes. *Id.*

22. A significant amount of China's fur is derived from the raccoon dog species, as it is estimated that there are over 1.5 million raccoon dogs in China being raised for their fur. *Id.* at 3. Raccoon dogs are a member of the dog family whose fur resembles the common raccoon, even though raccoon dogs are an entirely different species from the common raccoon (*Procyon lotor*). The raccoon dog's scientific name is *Nyctereutes procyonoides* and it is taxonomically classified under the Family Canidae. University of Michigan Museum of Zoology, Animal Diversity Web, *at* http://animaldiversity.ummz.umich.edu/site/accounts/information/Nyctereutes _ procyonoides.html (last accessed November 18, 2008).

23. Although the FPLA's Name Guide requires raccoon dog fur products to be labeled as "Asiatic Raccoon," 16 C.F.R. § 301.0, in light of the stigma attached to fur products derived from members of the canine family and the growing consumer demand for faux fur, many clothing companies elect to confuse and mislead consumers by marketing and selling raccoon dog-trimmed garments as either faux fur or common raccoon fur. *See* The HSUS, WHAT IS THAT THEY'RE WEARING 4

(1998) (HSUS investigators posing as American buyers "were told by a middleman in the Chinese fur trade that any label could be put in any garment or fur product, depending on the preference of the buyer").

24. In addition to China's exploitation of raccoon dogs, a 1997–1998 investigation conducted by The HSUS also documented the often inhumane killing of two million domestic dogs and cats for their fur, including the live skinning of animals. The HSUS, WHAT IS THAT THEY'RE WEARING (1998). As a result of this investigation, Congress enacted the Dog and Cat Protection Act of 2000, 19 U.S.C. § 1308, which was intended to prohibit the trade in domestic dog and cat fur. However, some garments derived from domestic dog fur continue to enter the United States because of widespread problems with false advertising and mislabeling of fur garments in the fashion industry.

B. Defendants' Deceptive Advertising and/or Labeling of Real Fur Products, Including Canine Fur, as Faux Fur

25. In September 2007, Bloomingdale's, a retail division of Defendant Macy's, Inc., advertised an Aqua house brand "faux fur lined" jacket on its online website, www.bloomingdales.com. However, after purchase and receipt by an HSUS representative, it was discovered that the garment's labels stated "rabbit fur," even though it was advertised as faux. On December 19, 2007, mass spectrometry tests confirmed that this jacket, advertised as faux fur, was, in fact, trimmed in genuine rabbit fur.

26. In September 2008, it was again discovered that Bloomingdale's, a retail division of Defendant Macy's, Inc., advertised a Marc New York brand fur-trimmed jacket as "faux fur" on its online website. However, upon purchase and receipt by an HSUS representative and resident of the District of the Columbia, it was discovered that the garment, advertised as faux fur, was labeled as genuine "Asiatic raccoon" fur—the FPLA Name Guide term for raccoon dog, which is a member of the canine family.

27. In November 2007, Defendant Dillard's advertised a Preston & York house brand jacket as having "removable faux-fur trim" on its online website, www.dillards.com. However, after purchase and receipt by an HSUS representative, it was discovered that the garment, advertised as faux fur, contained two conflicting labels—an external hangtag identifying the fur trim as "genuine fox fur" and an internal label identifying the fur trim as "genuine natural raccoon." On December 14, 2007, mass spectrometry tests confirmed that this coat, advertised as faux but labeled as genuine fox and raccoon fur, was actually trimmed with genuine raccoon fur.

28. In November 2007, Defendant Neiman Marcus, through their online website, www.neimanmarcus.com, advertised an Adam*Eve brand jacket as having a "faux fur-trim collar." However, upon purchase and receipt by an HSUS representative, it was discovered that the garment's label identified the fur trim as "100% rabbit fur" even though it was advertised as faux fur. On December 19, 2007, mass spectrometry

tests reported that this garment, advertised as faux fur, was actually trimmed with genuine rabbit fur.

29. In December 2007, Defendant Saks Fifth Avenue's website, www.saksfifthavenue.com, advertised a Burberry brand coat as having a "detachable faux fur collar." However, after purchase by an HSUS representative, it was discovered that not only was the coat unlabeled, mass spectrometry testing conducted on December 19, 2007, confirmed that this jacket, advertised as faux fur, tested positive for genuine rabbit fur.

30. In November 2007, an HSUS representative purchased an Andrew Marc brand fur-trimmed jacket from Defendant Neiman Marcus' retail department store at Tysons Corner Center in McLean, VA, that was labeled as "trim: polyester 100%." However, on December 14, 2007, mass spectrometry tests reported that this garment, labeled as containing fake polyester fur, was actually trimmed with genuine raccoon dog fur.

31. In December 2007, an HSUS representative purchased a Marc New York brand garment from Defendant Lord & Taylor's retail department store at the White Flint Mall in Kensington, MD. This fur-trimmed jacket was similarly labeled as "trim: polyester 100%." However, on December 19, 2007, mass spectrometry tests confirmed that this garment, labeled as faux polyester fur, instead contained both genuine rabbit and raccoon dog fur.

C. Defendants' Deceptive Advertising and/or Labeling of Canine Fur Products as Raccoon, Fox, or Rabbit

32. In October 2008, Defendant Andrew Marc advertised and sold a jacket as being trimmed in genuine "raccoon" on its website, www.andrewmarc.com. However, upon purchase and receipt by an HSUS representative and resident of the District of Columbia, it was discovered that the garment contained two conflicting labels—the first identifying the fur trim as "natural raccoon fur" but the second identifying the trim as "real Asiatic raccoon"—the FPLA Name Guide term for raccoon dog, which is a member of the canine family and a wholly distinct species from the common raccoon.

33. On November 16, 2007, Defendant Dillard's advertised a Preston & York house brand jacket as having a "genuine raccoon-trimmed collar" on its website, www.dillards.com. Upon purchase and receipt, an HSUS representative found that the garment's label also stated "trim: genuine dyed racoon [sic] fur." However, on December 14, 2007, mass spectrometry tests reported that this jacket, advertised and labeled as containing genuine raccoon fur, was actually trimmed with the wholly distinct species of raccoon dog fur.

34. In November 2008, Defendant Lord & Taylor advertised a Marc New York brand fur-trimmed jacket as genuine common "raccoon." However, upon purchase and receipt by an HSUS representative and resident of the District of Columbia, it was discovered that the garment, advertised as common raccoon, was instead labeled as "Asiatic raccoon"—the FPLA Name Guide term for raccoon dog, which is a member of the canine family and a wholly distinct species from the common raccoon.

35. In October 2008, Defendant Neiman Marcus advertised a Weekend Max Mara brand coat on its website, www.neimanmarcus.com, as being trimmed in "fox" fur. However, upon purchase and receipt by an HSUS representative and resident of the District of Columbia, it was discovered that the garment, advertised as fox fur, was instead labeled as "Asiatic raccoon"—the FPLA Name Guide term for raccoon dog, which is a member of the canine family.

36. In October 2008, Defendant Saks Fifth Avenue's website, www.saksfifthavenue.com, advertised a Weekend Max Mara brand jacket as being trimmed in "fox" fur. However, upon purchase and receipt by an HSUS representative and resident of the District of Columbia, it was discovered the garment contained two conflicting labels—an external hang tag identifying the trim as "faux fur" and an internal label identifying the trim as "Asiatic raccoon," which is the FPLA Name Guide term for raccoon dog.

D. Harm to District of Columbia Consumers and Plaintiffs Members

37. Plaintiff has purchased Defendants' fur-trimmed garments that are advertised and sold to residents and consumers in the District of Columbia through online websites and/or retail stores that are located in or near the District of Columbia.

38. On information and belief, based on representations made by Defendants in their advertising or labeling, consumers in the District of Columbia believe that Defendants' fur-trimmed garments are "faux fur," when the fur is, in fact, derived from real animal fur, such as raccoon dog fur, a member of the canine family.

39. On information and belief, based on representations made by Defendants in their advertising or labeling, consumers in the District of Columbia believe that Defendants' fur-trimmed garments are derived from one particular animal—such as raccoon, fox, or rabbit—when, in fact, they are derived from raccoon dog, a member of the canine family.

40. On information and belief, consumers in the District of Columbia have purchased clothing—in reasonable reliance on Defendants' deceptive advertising and labeling—that they otherwise would not have purchased.

41. Consumer surveys show that consumers consider animal welfare when making purchasing decisions and are often willing to switch to animal-free products. For example, according to recently published Gallup poll data, a sizeable and significant percentage of Americans find that buying or wearing animal fur is "morally wrong."

42. Defendants' advertising—particularly with respect to "faux fur" advertisements—is directed at and targets the specific class of consumers who are deeply concerned with the welfare of animals, such as Plaintiffs members, and who specifically attempt to buy products that are produced in a way that does not negatively impact animal welfare, and, as such, are more vulnerable and susceptible to being misled by the representations.

43. Consumers are unable to tell upon purchasing Defendants' garments that they have been deceived, because it is extremely difficult to differentiate faux fur from real

animal fur or raccoon dog fur from common raccoon fur, fox fur, or rabbit fur. The result is that consumers—especially humane-conscious and fur-free consumers, such as Plaintiffs members—will continue to be deceived and induced to purchase Defendants' garments as long as the false advertisements and labels continue.

44. Most consumers, including Plaintiffs members, do not find out that they have been deceived by falsely advertised or falsely labeled fur-trimmed garments until they learn about the actual type of fur from which the trim is derived from third party sources, such as advocacy groups like Plaintiff and the media.

45. On information and belief, District of Columbia residents and consumers have been and will continue to be injured by Defendants' conduct because they purchase fur-trimmed clothing that Defendants manufacture, distribute, sell, advertise, and label as being "faux" when, in fact, the clothing is made from real animal fur, including raccoon dog fur. As such, consumers have suffered and will continue to suffer actual and present economic damage as a result of Defendants' actions because they have expended funds to purchase garments that they otherwise would not have purchased.

46. On information and belief, District of Columbia residents and consumers have been and will continue to be injured by Defendants' conduct because they purchase fur-trimmed clothing that Defendants manufacture, distribute, sell, advertise, and label as being derived from one particular type animal fur—such as the common raccoon, fox, or rabbit—when, in fact, the garments are made from raccoon dog fur. As such, consumers have suffered and will continue to suffer actual and present economic damage as a result of Defendants' actions because they have expended funds to purchase garments that they otherwise would not have purchased.

47. Because more than 75 million fur-bearing animals are killed annually for the purpose of obtaining their pelts for fashion, The HSUS's Fur-Free Campaign works to end the killing of animals for fur and fur trim by educating consumers on the inhumane fur trade and the availability of fur-free choices. Defendants' actions impair and frustrate The HSUS's ability to pursue its goals, because Defendants' deceptive advertising and labeling requires The HSUS to divert its limited organizational and programmatic resources to combat Defendants' misleading actions by informing the public and its members about the actual type of fur that is used on Defendants' garments. These resources would otherwise be spent on programmatic and advocacy activities to prevent other cruelty to animals, in furtherance of The HSUS's goals. The HSUS's injuries will be redressed if The HSUS prevails in this action, because if Defendants cease their deceptive advertising and labeling, The HSUS will not be required to divert its resources to combat such misleading advertising and labeling by having to inform the public about the actual type of fur that is used on Defendants' garments.

48. Additionally, The HSUS's members are particularly susceptible to being misled by Defendants' deceptive advertising and labeling because they are deeply concerned with the welfare of animals and seek out products that are produced in

a way that does not negatively impact welfare. The HSUS members who seek out fur-free and humane conscious garments and who live in the District of Columbia have been and will continue to be injured by Defendants' actions, as described in paragraphs 37-47 above. These injuries will be redressed if The HSUS prevails in this action.

Plaintiff's Claims for Relief

Count 1

Violations of the D.C. Consumer Protection Procedures Act Based on Misrepresentations and Failure to State a Material Fact

49. Plaintiff incorporates by reference all the preceding paragraphs as fully set forth herein.

50. Plaintiff brings Claim One in its individual and representative capacity against Defendants on Plaintiffs own behalf, on behalf of its members, and on behalf of affected consumers and the general public, pursuant to section 28-3905(k)(1) of the CPPA, which provides that any "person, whether acting for the interests of itself, its members, or the general public, may bring an action under this chapter in the Superior Court of the District of Columbia seeking relief from the use by any person of a trade practice in violation of a law of the District of Columbia." D.C. CODE ANN. § 28-3905(k)(1).

51. By falsely advertising and/or falsely labeling fur products as "faux fur" when they are, in fact, derived from real animal fur, Defendants have "represent[ed] that goods . . . have a source, . . . [or] characteristics . . . that they do not have"; "represent[ed] that goods . . . are of particular standard, quality, grade, style, or model, if in fact they are of another"; "misrepresent [ed] as to a material fact which has a tendency to mislead"; and "fail[ed] to state a material fact if such failure tends to mislead." D.C. CODE ANN. § 28-3904(a), (d), (e), (f).

52. In addition, by falsely advertising and/or falsely labeling fur-trimmed garments as common raccoon, fox, or rabbit fur when they are, in fact, derived from the wholly distinct species of raccoon dog—a member of the canine family—Defendants have "represent[ed] that goods . . . have a source, . . . [or] characteristics . . . that they do not have"; "represent[ed] that goods . . . are of particular standard, quality, grade, style, or model, if in fact they are of another"; "misrepresent[ed] as to a material fact which has a tendency to mislead"; and "fail[ed] to state a material fact if such failure tends to mislead." D.C. CODE ANN. § 28-3904(a), (d), (e), (f).

53. These unlawful trade practices have caused and will continue to cause Plaintiff injuries as described in paragraphs 37-48.

Count 2

Violations of the D.C. Consumer Protection Procedures Act Based on Violations of the Federal Fur Products Labeling Act and Federal Trade Commission Act

54. Plaintiff hereby incorporates by reference all the preceding paragraphs as if fully set forth herein.

55. Plaintiff brings Claim Two in its individual and representative capacity against Defendants on Plaintiffs own behalf, on behalf of its members, and on behalf of affected consumers and the general public, pursuant to section 28-3905(k)(1) of the CPPA, which provides that any "person, whether acting for the interests of itself, its members, or the general public, may bring an action under this chapter in the Superior Court of the District of Columbia seeking relief from the use by any person of a trade practice in violation of a law of the District of Columbia." D.C. Code Ann. § 28-3905(k)(1).

56. It is unlawful under the CPPA to "sell consumer goods in a condition or manner not consistent with that warranted by . . . operation or requirement of federal law." *Id.* § 28-3904(x).

57. The federal Fur Products Labeling Act and Federal Trade Commission Act prohibit false or deceptive advertising and labeling. Pursuant to section 3(a) of the FLPA, "[t]he introduction, or manufacture for introduction, into commerce, or the sale, advertising, or offering for sale in commerce, or the transportation or distribution in commerce, of any fur product which is misbranded or falsely or deceptively advertised . . . is unlawful and shall be an unfair method of competition, and an unfair and deceptive act or practice, in commerce under the Federal Trade Commission Act (15 U.S.C. § 41 *et seq).*" 15 U.S.C. § 69a(a); *see also id.* § 45(a)(1) ("[u]nfair methods of competition in or affecting commerce, and unfair or deceptive acts or practices in or affecting commerce, are hereby declared unlawful").

58. Section 5(a) of the FPLA provides that "a fur product or fur shall be considered to be falsely or deceptively advertised if any advertisement, representation, public announcement, or notice which is intended to aid, promote, or assist directly or indirectly in the sale or offering for sale of such fur product or fur — (1) does not show the name or names . . . of the animal or animals that produced the fur . . . ;" "(5) contains the name or names of any animal or animals other than the name or names specified in paragraph (1) of this subsection, or contains any form of misrepresentation or deception, indirectly or by implication, with respect to such fur product or fur;" or "(6) does not show the name of the country or origin of any imported furs or those contained in a fur product." *Id.* § 69c(a).

59. Section 4 of the FLPA further provides that "fur product shall be considered to be misbranded" if it is (1) "falsely or deceptively labeled"; (2) "if there is not affixed to the fur product a label showing in words and figures plainly legible (A) the name or names (as set forth in the Fur Products Name Guide) of the animal"; or (3) "if the label required by paragraph (2)(A) of this section sets forth the name or names of any animal or animals other than the name or names provided for in such paragraph." *Id.* § 69b.

60. In the instant case, a number of the Defendants sold fur-trimmed garments that were deceptively advertised. For instance, Macy's, Inc. (through its retail division Bloomingdale's), Dillard's, Neiman Marcus, and Saks Fifth Avenue advertised and sold fur-trimmed garments as "faux fur" on their online stores, rather than

correctly advertising the garments as genuine rabbit, genuine raccoon, or genuine raccoon dog fur, which are the actual "name or names . . . of the animal or animals that produced the fur." *Id.* § 69c(a)(1). In addition, Andrew Marc, Dillard's, Lord & Taylor, Neiman Marcus, and Saks Fifth Avenue advertised and sold fur-trimmed garments as either common raccoon or fox fur, rather than correctly advertising the garments as raccoon dog—a member of the canine family and a wholly distinct species from common raccoon—which is "the name . . . of the animal . . . that produced the fur." *Id.* § 69c(a)(1). Therefore, these garments "shall be considered to be falsely or deceptively advertised" in violation of the FPLA. *Id.* § 69c(a); *see also id.* § 69a(a) ("[t]he introduction, or manufacture for introduction, into commerce, or the sale, advertising, or offering for sale in commerce, or the transportation or distribution in commerce, of any fur product which is . . . falsely or deceptively advertised . . . is unlawful and shall be an unfair method of competition, and an unfair and deceptive act or practice, in commerce under the Federal Trade Commission Act (15 U.S.C. § 41 *et seq).*"

61. A number of the Defendants also manufactured, distributed, or sold fur-trimmed garments that were falsely labeled. For instance, Andrew Marc, Dillard's, Lord & Taylor, Neiman Marcus, and Saks Fifth Avenue manufactured, distributed, or sold garments that were labeled as either faux fur or common raccoon or fox fur when, in fact, these fur-trimmed garments were derived from real raccoon dog—a member of the canine family and a wholly distinct species from the common raccoon. Therefore, these garments "shall be considered to be misbranded," *id.* § 69b, in violation of the FPLA because they are "falsely or deceptively labeled or otherwise falsely or deceptively identified," *id.* § 69b(1), and "set[] forth the name . . . of [an] animal other than name [of the animal that produced the fur]," *id.* § 69b(3). *See also id.* § 69a(a) ("[t]he introduction, or manufacture for introduction, into commerce, or the sale, advertising, or offering for sale in commerce, or the transportation or distribution in commerce, of any fur product which is misbranded . . . is unlawful and shall be an unfair method of competition, and an unfair and deceptive act or practice, in commerce under the Federal Trade Commission Act (15 U.S.C. § 41 *et seq).*"

62. Accordingly, these Defendants have violated the CPPA because it is unlawful to "sell consumer goods in a condition or manner not consistent with that warranted by .. operation or requirement of federal law." D.C. Code Ann. § 28-3904(x).

63. These unlawful trade practices have caused and will continue to cause Plaintiff injuries as described in paragraphs 37-48.

Relief Requested

WHEREFORE, Plaintiff, individually and in its representative capacity, requests judgment and the following relief:

A. Declaratory judgment that each and every one of Defendant's acts alleged above violates the D.C. Consumer Protection Procedures Act, D.C. Code Ann. § 28-3904(a), (d), (e), (f), (x);

B. All appropriate injunctive relief, including an Order that Defendants permanently cease and desist from unlawful trade practices, namely the manufacturing, distributing, selling, and marketing of falsely advertised and falsely labeled fur and fur-trimmed garments, *id.* §28-3905(k)(1)(D);

C. Additional relief as may be necessary to restore the consumer the money or property which may have been acquired by means of the unlawful trade practice, *id.* §28-3905(k)(1)(E);

D. Reasonable attorney's fees and costs, *id.* §28-2905(k)(1)(B); and

E. Such other relief as the Court deems proper, *id.* §28-3905(k)(1)(F).

Notes

1. Pursuant to the federal Fur Products Labeling Act, what are the implications of labeling a product as genuine?

2. What is the FTC's distinction between mislabeling and misadvertising?

3. How can relief for a claim of false advertising of fur versus false labeling of fur differ?

In addition to the Fur Rules, several U.S. cities have banned fur altogether. In 2017, the city of Berkeley, California, passed an ordinance prohibiting the sale of fur from all species of fur-bearing animals. In March 2018, San Francisco's Board of Supervisors unanimously voted to ban fur within city limits. A few months later, Los Angeles City Council members voted to ban the sale and manufacturing of fur by 2020.

4. Native Advertising

The term "native advertising" refers to a method of delivering digital advertising content that bears a similarity to the news, feature articles, product reviews, entertainment, and other material that surround it online. The FTC has taken the position that where consumers are unable to differentiate advertising from other content, such as news, then the advertising is likely deceptive or constitutes an unfair practice. To address these issues, the FTC has issued an Enforcement Policy Statement on Deceptively Formatted Advertisements that explains how the Commission applies truth-in-advertising standards to native advertising.

To determine whether an advertisement is deceptive, the Commission looks at the advertisement as a whole and the impression that it conveys to consumers. The overall context of the ad is examined, such as text, images, sounds, and format in which the ad is conveyed. The Commission also takes into consideration any clarifying information necessary to prevent deception. If a consumer is misled as to the nature of the ad and believes that the content comes from an impartial source, then the ad will be deemed deceptive. For example, an ad that deceptively copies the format of news programming would likely be deemed deceptive. Similarly, if there is an undisclosed material connection between an advertiser and endorser, the ad will also be deemed deceptive. For more on FTC endorsement and disclosure guidelines in the context of social media influencers, refer to Section E of this chapter.

When using disclosures in native advertising, they must be clearly visible to the consumer so as not to mislead the consumer into believing the content is impartial content. In doing so, the disclosures should be: (1) in clear and unambiguous language; (2) as close as possible to the native ads to which they relate; (3) in a font and color that is easy to read; (4) in a shade that stands out against the background; (5) for video ads, on the screen long enough to be noticed, read, and understood; and (6) for audio disclosures, read at a cadence that is easy for consumers to follow and in words consumers will understand.

The FTC has taken action not just against advertisers, but against all other parties who helped create the content. This includes ad agencies and operators of affiliate advertising networks. *See, e.g.,* Enforcement Policy Statement, https://www.ftc.gov/public-statements/2015/12/commission-enforcement-policy-statement-deceptively-formatted; *In the Matter of Lord & Taylor, LLC* (Docket No. C-4576) (FTC charged Lord & Taylor with deceiving consumers by paying for native advertisements, including a seemingly objective article in the online publication *Nylon* and a *Nylon* Instagram post, without disclosing that the posts actually were paid promotions for the company's 2015 Design Lab clothing collection); *American Media, Inc.* (SHAPE Water Boosters), NAD/CARU Case #5665 (December 2013) (In an issue of *SHAPE* magazine, which included news articles reporting on developments in health and fitness technologies, *SHAPE* included an article under the caption "News" that discussed the importance of staying hydrated and recommended the Water Boosters product. The NAD concluded that *SHAPE* should "clearly and conspicuously" designate content as advertising when it advertises *SHAPE*-branded products).

In re Lord & Taylor, LLC

No. C-4576 (F.T.C. May 20, 2016)

Complaint

The Federal Trade Commission, having reason to believe that Lord & Taylor, LLC, a limited liability company ("Respondent"), has violated the provisions of the Federal Trade Commission Act, and it appearing to the Commission that this proceeding is in the public interest, alleges:

1. Respondent Lord & Taylor is a New York limited liability company with its principal office or place of business at 424 5th Avenue, New York, NY, 10018.

2. Respondent has manufactured, advertised, labeled, offered for sale, sold, and distributed women's, men's, and children's apparel, accessories, cosmetics, and other retail merchandise to consumers.

3. The acts and practices of Respondent alleged in this complaint have been in or affecting commerce, as "commerce" is defined in Section 4 of the Federal Trade Commission Act.

Lord & Taylor's Design Lab Instagram Campaign

4. In the Fall of 2014, Respondent Lord & Taylor developed plans to promote its new Design Lab collection, a private label clothing line aimed at women ages 18-35. Respondent's Design Lab marketing plan included a comprehensive social media campaign ("product bomb") launched at the end of March 2015. The campaign was comprised of Lord & Taylor-branded blog posts, photos, video uploads, native advertising editorials in online fashion magazines, and use of a team of fashion influencers recruited for their fashion style and extensive base of followers on social media platforms, all focused on a single article of clothing, the Design Lab Paisley Asymmetrical Dress.

5. Lord & Taylor gifted the Paisley Asymmetrical Dress to 50 select fashion influencers who were paid, in amounts ranging from $1,000 to $4,000, to post on the social media platform Instagram one photo of themselves wearing the Design Lab dress during a specified timeframe during the weekend of March 27–28, 2015. While the influencers were given the freedom to style the dress in any way they saw fit, Lord & Taylor contractually obligated them to exclusively mention the company using the "@lordandtaylor" Instagram user designation and the campaign hashtag "#DesignLab" in the photo caption. The influencers also were required to tag their photos of the dress using the "@lordandtaylor" Instagram designation.

6. Although Lord & Taylor's Design Lab influencer contracts detailed the manner in which Respondent was to be mentioned in each Instagram posting, the contracts did not require the influencers to disclose in their postings that Respondent had compensated them, nor did Respondent otherwise obligate the influencers to disclose that they had been compensated.

7. In advance of the March 27–28, 2015 Design Lab debut, Respondent's representatives pre-approved each of the influencers' Instagram posts to ensure that the required campaign hashtag and the @lordandtaylor Instagram user designation were included in the photo captions. Respondent also made certain other stylistic edits to the influencers' proposed text. None of the Instagram posts presented to Respondent for pre-approval included a disclosure that the influencer had received the dress for free, that she had been compensated for the post, or that the post was a part of a Lord & Taylor advertising campaign. Respondent Lord & Taylor did not edit any of the 50 posts to add such disclosures. *See* Exhibit A (representative Design Lab Instagram posts from the weekend of March 27–28, 2015).

8. The Design Lab Instagram campaign reached 11.4 million individual Instagram users, resulted in 328,000 brand engagements with Lord & Taylor's own Instagram user handle (such as likes, comments, or re-postings), and the dress subsequently sold out.

9. Respondent's Design Lab debut also included strategic placement of Lord & Taylor-edited Instagram posts and an article in online fashion magazines. One such magazine was Nylon, a pop culture and fashion publication owned by Nylon Media, LLC, the company that represented the majority of the fashion influencers involved

in Respondent's Design Lab Instagram campaign. Nylon posted a photo of the Paisley Asymmetrical Dress, along with a Lord & Taylor-edited caption, on its Instagram account during the product bomb weekend. *See* Exhibit B (Nylon.com Design Lab Instagram Post). Although paid for, reviewed, and pre-approved by Lord & Taylor, Nylon's Instagram post failed to disclose that Lord & Taylor had paid for the posting.

10. Nylon Magazine also ran an article about the Design Lab collection in its online magazine on March 31, 2015. Under the terms of its contract with Nylon Magazine, Lord & Taylor reviewed and pre-approved the paid-for Nylon Design Lab article, yet the article did not disclose or otherwise make clear this commercial arrangement. *See* Exhibit C (Nylon.com Design Lab magazine article).

Count I

Misrepresentations About the Design Lab Instagram Postings

11. Through the means described in Paragraphs 4 through 7, Respondent represented, directly or indirectly, expressly or by implication, that the 50 Instagram images and captions reflected the independent statements of impartial fashion influencers.

12. In fact, the 50 Instagram images and captions did not reflect the independent statements of impartial fashion influencers. Respondent's influencers specifically created the postings as part of an advertising campaign to promote sales of Respondent's Design Lab collection. Therefore, the representation set forth in Paragraph 11 is false or misleading.

Count II

Failure to Disclose Influencers' Material Connection to Lord & Taylor

13. Through the means described in Paragraphs 4 through 7, Respondent represented, directly or indirectly, expressly or by implication, that the 50 Instagram images and captions posted on March 27 and 28, 2015 about the Paisley Asymmetrical Dress reflected the opinions of individuals with expertise in new trends in fashion. In numerous instances, Respondent failed to disclose or disclose adequately that these individuals were paid endorsers for Respondent. These facts would be material to consumers in their decision to purchase the Paisley Asymmetrical Dress. The failure to disclose these facts, in light of the representation made, was and is, a deceptive practice.

Count III

Misrepresentations About the Nylon Instagram Post and the March 31, 2015 Nylon Magazine Article

14. Through the means described in Paragraphs 9 and 10, Respondent represented, directly or indirectly, expressly or by implication, that the article that appeared on the March 31, 2015 Nylon Magazine website and the Design Lab posting on Nylon's Instagram account, were independent statements and opinions regarding the launch of Respondent's Design Lab collection.

15. In fact, neither the Nylon Magazine article nor the Nylon Instagram post were independent statements or opinions regarding Respondent's Design Lab collection; they were paid commercial advertising. Therefore, the representation set forth in Paragraph 14 is false or misleading.

16. The acts and practices of Respondent as alleged in this complaint constitute unfair or deceptive acts or practices in or affecting commerce in violation of Section 5(a) of the FTC Act, 15 U.S.C. § 45(a).

THEREFORE, the Federal Trade Commission this twentieth day of May, 2016, has issued this Complaint against Respondent.

By the Commission.

Order

Definitions

For purposes of this order, the following definitions shall apply:

1. Unless otherwise specified, "Respondent" shall mean Lord & Taylor, LLC, a limited liability company, its successors and assigns, and its officers, agents, representatives, and employees.

2. "Clear(ly) and conspicuous(ly)" means that a required disclosure is difficult to miss (*i.e.*, easily noticeable) and easily understandable by ordinary consumers, including in all of the following ways:

a. In any communication that is solely visual or solely audible, the disclosure must be made through the same means through which the communication is presented. In any communication made through both visual and audible means, the disclosure must be presented simultaneously in both the visual and audible portions of the communication even if the representation requiring the disclosure is made in only one means.

b. A visual disclosure, by its size, contrast, location, the length of time it appears, and other characteristics, must stand out from any accompanying text or other visual elements so that it is easily noticed, read, and understood.

c. An audible disclosure, including by streaming video, must be delivered in a volume, speed, and cadence sufficient for ordinary consumers to easily hear and understand it.

d. In any communication using an interactive electronic medium, such as the Internet or software, the disclosure must be unavoidable.

e. The disclosure must use diction and syntax understandable to ordinary consumers and must appear in each language in which the representation that requires the disclosure appears.

f. The disclosure must comply with these requirements in each medium through which it is received, including all electronic devices.

g. The disclosure must not be contradicted or mitigated by, or inconsistent with, anything else in the communication.

h. When the representation or sales practice targets a specific audience, such as children, the elderly, or the terminally ill, "ordinary consumers" includes reasonable members of that group.

3. "Close proximity" means that the disclosure is very near the triggering endorsement or representation. In an interactive electronic medium (such as a mobile app or other computer program), a visual disclosure that cannot be viewed at the same time and in the same viewable area as the triggering endorsement or representation, on the technology used by ordinary consumers, is not in close proximity. A disclosure made through a hyperlink, pop-up, interstitial, or other similar technique is not in close proximity to the triggering endorsement or representation. A disclosure made on a different printed page than the triggering endorsement or representation is not in close proximity.

4. "Commerce" means as defined in Section 4 of the Federal Trade Commission Act, 15 U.S.C. §44.

5. "Endorsement" means any advertising message (including verbal statements, demonstrations, or depictions of the name, signature, likeness, or other identifying personal characteristics of an individual or the name or seal of an organization) that consumers are likely to believe reflects the opinions, beliefs, findings, or experiences of a party other than the sponsoring advertiser, even if the views expressed by that party are identical to those of the sponsoring advertiser.

6. "Endorser" means an individual or organization that provides an endorsement.

7. "Influencer Campaign" means any arrangement whereby, in connection with the advertising, promotion, offering for sale, sale, or distribution of any product or service, Respondent engages an endorser (also known as an Influencer) to create, publish, or otherwise disseminate an endorsement and the endorser has a material connection to Respondent, or any other person or entity acting on Respondent's behalf.

8. "Material connection" means any relationship that materially affects the weight or credibility of any endorsement and that would not be reasonably expected by consumers.

I.

IT IS ORDERED that Respondent, directly or through any corporation, partnership, subsidiary, division, or other device, in connection with the advertising, labeling, promotion, offering for sale, sale, or distribution of any product or service, in or affecting commerce, shall not misrepresent, in any manner, expressly or by implication, that an endorser of such product or service is an independent user or ordinary consumer of the product or service.

II.

IT IS FURTHER ORDERED that Respondent, directly or through any corporation, partnership, subsidiary, division, or other device, in connection with the advertising, labeling, promotion, offering for sale, sale, or distribution of any product or service, in or affecting commerce, by means of an endorsement of such product or service, shall clearly and conspicuously, and in close proximity to the representation, disclose a material connection, if one exists, between such endorser and Respondent.

III.

IT IS FURTHER ORDERED that Respondent, and its successors and assigns, shall not misrepresent, in any manner, expressly or by implication, that paid commercial advertising is a statement or opinion from an independent or objective publisher or source.

IV.

IT IS FURTHER ORDERED that Respondent, directly or through any corporation, partnership, subsidiary, division, or other device, in connection with the advertising, labeling, promotion, offering for sale, sale, or distribution of any product or service, in or affecting commerce, by means of an endorsement by an endorser with a material connection to Respondent, shall take steps sufficient to ensure compliance with Parts I and II of this order. Such steps shall include, at a minimum:

A. Providing each such endorser with a clear statement of his or her responsibility to disclose, clearly and conspicuously, in any print, radio, television, online, or digital advertisement or communication, including but not limited to Instagram or blog posts, the endorser's material connection to Respondent, and obtaining from each such endorser a signed and dated statement acknowledging receipt of that statement and expressly agreeing to comply with it;

B. Establishing, implementing, and there after maintaining a system to monitor and review the representations and disclosures of endorsers, made as part of an Influencer Campaign, with material connections to Respondent to ensure compliance with Parts I and II of this order. The system shall include, at a minimum, monitoring and reviewing its endorsers' print, radio, television, online, or digital advertisements or communications made as part of an Influencer Campaign;

C. Immediately terminating any endorser with a material connection to Respondent who Respondent reasonably concludes:

1. Has misrepresented, in any manner, his or her independence and impartiality; or
2. Has failed to disclose, clearly and conspicuously, and in close proximity to the representation, a material connection between such endorser and Respondent;

Provided, however, that Respondent may provide an endorser with one notice of a failure to disclose and an opportunity to cure the disclosure prior to terminating the endorser if Respondent reasonably concludes that the failure to disclose was inadvertent; Respondent shall inform any endorser to whom it has provided a notice of a failure to disclose a material connection that any subsequent failure to disclose will result in immediate termination; and

D. Creating, and thereafter maintaining, reports sufficient to show the results of the monitoring required by subpart B of this Part of the order.

V.

IT IS FURTHER ORDERED that Respondent, and its successors and assigns, shall, for five (5) years after the last date of dissemination of any representation or endorsement covered by this order, maintain and upon reasonable notice make available to the Federal Trade Commission for inspection and copying:

A. All advertisements and promotional materials containing the representation or endorsement;

B. All contracts and written communications concerning or relating to the disclosures required by Part II of this order with any endorser engaged by Respondent, or any other person or entity acting on Respondent's behalf, to participate in any Influencer Campaign;

C. Any documents that comprise or relate to complaints or inquiries related to the subject matter of this order, whether received directly, indirectly, or through any third party, that concern any endorsement made or disseminated by Respondent, or on behalf of Respondent, and any responses to those complaints or inquiries;

D. Any documents reasonably necessary to demonstrate full compliance with each provision of this order, including but not limited to, all documents obtained, created, generated, or which in any way relate to the requirements, provisions, terms of this order, and all reports submitted to the Commission pursuant to this order;

E. Any documents that contradict, qualify, or call into question Respondent's compliance with this order; and

F. All acknowledgments of receipt of this order obtained pursuant to Part VI.

VI.

IT IS FURTHER ORDERED that Respondent, and its successors and assigns, shall deliver a copy of this order to all current and future principals, officers, and directors, and to all current and future managers, employees, agents, and representatives having responsibilities with respect to the subject matter of this order, and shall secure from each person a signed and dated statement acknowledging receipt of this order. Respondent shall deliver this order to such current personnel within thirty (30) days after the date of service of this order and to future personnel within thirty (30) days after the person assumes such position or responsibilities.

VII.

IT IS FURTHER ORDERED that Respondent, and its successors and assigns, shall notify the Commission at least thirty (30) days prior to any change in the corporation that may affect compliance obligations arising under this order, including, but not limited to, dissolution, assignment, sale, merger, or other action that would result in the emergence of a successor corporation; the creation or dissolution of a subsidiary, parent, or related entity that engages in any acts or practices subject to this order; the proposed filing of a bankruptcy petition; or a change in the corporate name or address. Provided, however, that, with respect to any proposed change in the corporation about which Respondent learns less than thirty (30) days prior to the date such action is to take place, Respondent shall notify the Commission as soon as is practicable after obtaining such knowledge. Unless otherwise directed by a representative of the Commission in writing, these reports shall be emailed to Debrief@ftc.gov or sent by overnight courier (not the U.S. Postal Service) to: Associate Director for Enforcement, Bureau of Consumer Protection, Federal Trade Commission, 600 Pennsylvania Avenue, NW, Washington, D.C. 20580. The subject line must begin: *In re Lord & Taylor.*

VIII.

IT IS FURTHER ORDERED that Respondent, and its successors and assigns, within ninety (90) days after the date of service of this order, shall file with the Commission a true and accurate report, in writing, setting forth in detail the manner and form of its compliance with this order. Within ten (10) days of receipt of written notice from a representative of the Commission, it shall submit additional true and accurate written reports. Unless otherwise directed by a representative of the Commission in writing, these reports shall be emailed to Debrief@ftc.gov or sent by overnight courier (not the U.S. Postal Service) to: Associate Director for Enforcement, Bureau of Consumer Protection, Federal Trade Commission, 600 Pennsylvania Avenue, NW, Washington, D.C. 20580. The subject line must begin: *In re Lord & Taylor.*

IX.

This order will terminate on May 20, 2036, or twenty (20) years from the most recent date that the United States or the Federal Trade Commission files a complaint (with or without an accompanying consent decree) in federal court alleging any violation of the order, whichever comes later; provided, however, that the filing of such a complaint will not affect the duration of:

A. Any Part in this order that terminates in less than twenty (20) years; and

B. This order if such complaint is filed after the order has terminated pursuant to this Part.

Provided, further, that if such complaint is dismissed or a federal court rules that Respondent did not violate any provision of the order, and the dismissal or ruling is either not appealed or upheld on appeal, then the order will terminate according to this Part as though the complaint had never been filed, except that the order will not terminate between the date such complaint is filed and the later of the deadline for appealing such dismissal or ruling and the date such dismissal or ruling is upheld on appeal.

By the Commission.

Notes

1. Why do you think the FTC chose not to include the individual influencers in its investigation of the Design Lab campaign? Should it have?

2. Do you think that the terms of the FTC's settlement with Lord & Taylor were strong enough to deter advertising missteps by retailers?

3. With the settlement in mind, what terms would you include in an endorsement contract for an influencer hired to promote Lord & Taylor if you were the company's general counsel?

American Media, Inc. (Shape Water Boosters)*

NAD Case No. 5665 (Dec. 18, 2013)

Challenger: National Advertising Division

Advertising that appears in a format that makes it look like editorial content has the potential to mislead or confuse consumers because consumers may attach a different weight or significance to editorial content than to pure advertising content.

Basis of Inquiry: As part of its routine monitoring program, NAD reviewed an article in Shape Magazine, published by American Media, Inc. (the "advertiser" or "AMI"), which promoted the benefits of SHAPE-branded products in a context that appeared to be an editorial news article. NAD was concerned that promoting SHAPE-Branded products in a format that makes it look like editorial content blurs the line between editorial content and advertising in a way that can confuse consumers.

Implied Claim:

Embedded within what appeared to be an editorial article in shape magazine about the health value of hydration was an advertisement for Shape Water Boosters. NAD was concerned that consumers may give more credence to the advertiser's objective claims about the product's attributes because of the context in which the claims appeared.

Advertiser's Position:

American Media, Inc. ("AMI") is the owner and publisher of SHAPE magazine and other popular, life-style publications. A SHAPE-branded product, "SHAPE Water Boosters—was promoted in an article in the September 2013 issue of SHAPE magazine. The advertiser contended that SHAPE readers are sophisticated, well-educated and experienced consumers and are likely to understand that a product sold under the SHAPE trade name is connected to SHAPE magazine and its publisher.

The advertiser advised and documented to NAD that the typical reader of Shape magazine is an established, professional woman, who is highly educated, with a college or more advanced degree, and a concomitant significant income. AMI contended that its sophisticated readers have significant experience about how to make decisions about consumer products, arguing that its readers can and do understand the SHAPE-branded products are connected to SHAPE magazine. Because the relationship between the magazine and SHAPE-branded products is obvious, AMI argued that it is under no further obligation to define the promotion of its product separately as an advertisement. AMI argued that its magazines can promote themselves or their associated product lines as long as consumers understand the relationship between the magazine and the service or product, referring NAD's attention to the FTC Guidelines for endorsements and testimonials. AMI contended that where a consumer understands the relationship between a product and the reviewer's relationship to the product, no disclosure is necessary.

Because SHAPE Magazine and SHAPE Water Boosters share the same branded and trademarked name, AMI maintained that the relationship between the product and the publisher is clear. In fact, the advertiser maintained that the decision to brand the Water Boosters and other products with the SHAPE trademark was to leverage the SHAPE magazine's brand equity and benefit from consumer awareness of SHAPE magazine. Further, the advertiser argued that its recommendation of SHAPE Water Boosters within an article on hydration does not change the obvious connection between the advertiser and the product. It contended that product recommendations are ubiquitous in SHAPE magazine, where information content often contains product recommendations. AMI advised NAD that readers buy the magazine to learn about healthy products, beauty tips and supplies, hot trends and designer clothing, healthy life-style choices, and fitness advice. It contended it would be odd if it could not recommend its own products in the same manner as other companies' products in editorial content.

AMI further contended that the context of the advertisement makes clear that SHAPE is promoting its own products. The editor's note on page 22 of the September issue explains:

> Whether you're a superstar athlete like Maria [Sharapova] or simply a super-busy everywoman, it's no secret that you need a well-rounded diet to stay healthy and strong. But unfortunately, many women don't get enough nutrients from what they eat and drink. While the simple solution is to supplement your diet with protein powder, vitamins, and the like, SHAPE recognized there was a gaping hole in the market: Products that truly addressed the nutritional needs of the active woman simply weren't available. To that void, *we've* launched a line of products made to do just that. The first are featured on page 134, but there's much more to come—see the pic below for a sneak peek. We'll be sure to keep you posted. (Emphasis added.)

Additionally, there are two full page advertisements for SHAPE Nutritionals and specifically SHAPE Water Boosters on pages 120 and 123 of the September issue. The advertiser argued that these messages can be viewed as disclosures made in the context of the advertising for SHAPE Water Boosters or as evidence that

SHAPE magazine was in no way trying to hide the relationship between SHAPE magazine and its branded products. The advertiser submitted that its audience of well-educated women is unlikely to be misled as to the connection between the magazine, its publisher and the SHAPE-branded products.

Decision:

NAD opened this monitoring case because of a concern that an article in SHAPE magazine captioned "news" that focused on the importance of hydration promoted the benefits of SHAPE Water Boosters which blurred the line between advertising and editorial content in a way which could confuse consumers. SHAPE magazine is well-known for providing information related to health and fitness. The September 2013 issue of SHAPE Magazine also introduces new SHAPE- branded products including SHAPE Water Boosters. News articles in the September 2013 issue included an article reporting on a recent study on the benefits of combining changes in both diet and exercise to lose weight; three new choices for protective wear glasses or goggles for fitness activities; and an article recommending four technology tools for reducing stress. An article titled, *Water Works*, bearing the caption "News" discussed the importance of staying hydrated and recommends SHAPE Water Boosters as an aid to staying hydrated, "The obvious solution is to stick with water, but about 20 percent of Americans reportedly don't like the taste. If that sounds like you, check out the new SHAPE Water Boosters . . . Just a single squeeze . . . adds delicious flavor—but not calories—along with a concentrated punch of nutrients that offer some important bonus benefits."[51] NAD considered whether the context in which SHAPE recommended its SHAPE-branded product could mislead or confuse consumers to believe that the recommendation is an independent editorial assessment.

NAD has often expressed concern about advertising in deceptive formats, particularly when the content in question recommends a product or service.[52] Advertising that appears in an editorial context has the potential to mislead or confuse consumers because consumers may attach a different weight or significance to editorial content than to pure advertising content.[53] In 1968, the FTC considered

51. The advertising in question makes claims about the benefits of SHAPE Water Boosters, and thus is not like a product placement where no objective claims about product attributes are made. See http://www.ftc.gov/os/closings/staff/050210productplacemen.pdf. (Reviewing product placement and brand integration programs and determining if such promotion could mislead consumers, the FTC noted that "the rationale for disclosing that an advertiser paid for a product placement (i.e. that consumers will give more credence to objective claims about a product's attributes when made by a party independent from the advertiser), is absent.")

52. *See generally eSalon (Custom Formulated Hair Color)*, #5645 *NAD/CARU Case Reports* (October 2013); *NourishLife (SpeechNutrients Speak)*, #5620 *NAD/CARU Case* Reports (August 2013); *Herbal Groups Inc. (Prostalex Plus)*, NAD/CARU Case Reports, Report #5005 (July 2009) (citing *JS&A Group*, 54 F.Reg 12593, March 28, 1989, Corporation ordered to cease and desist from "misrepresenting, either directly or indirectly, that an advertisement is an independent consumer or news program and not a paid advertisement.")

53. The FTC has advised that advertising can be deceptive if, (1) there is a representation or omission of information that is likely to mislead the consumer acting reasonably under the

a restaurant review that appeared as a news article. The FTC reviewed "the question of whether it is deceptive to publish an advertisement in the format of a news article without disclosing it is an advertisement" and concluded that "since the column consists of a series of commercial messages which are paid for by the advertisers, the Commission is of the opinion that it will be necessary to clearly and conspicuously disclose it is an advertisement."[54]

Here, the advertiser argued that because consumers are aware of the connection between the magazine and the SHAPE-branded product, it has no obligation to disclose that its promotion of SHAPE-Branded products is advertising. The advertiser directed NAD's attention to the FTC Guidelines to Endorsements and Testimonials and maintained that the connection between the content and the magazine is obvious to consumers.[55] NAD does not disagree. NAD's concern, however, was not the disclosure of a financial connection between SHAPE Magazine and SHAPE-Branded products. Rather, NAD was concerned that the "*Water Works*" article was formatted and titled and appeared to be a news article yet it promoted SHAPE Water Boosters as part of the news. The article was preceded by the headline "News" and included information about the importance of hydration and recommended SHAPE Water Boosters as a healthful way to stay hydrated. Although consumers reading SHAPE magazine may be aware that SHAPE Water Boosters are related to SHAPE magazine, those same consumers can reasonably attach different weight to recommendations made in an editorial context than recommendations made in an advertising context. Put another way, consumers may reasonably believe that editorial recommendations in SHAPE magazine are independent of the influence of a sponsoring advertiser.

NAD considered, but was not persuaded by, the advertiser's argument that the editor's note on page 32 of the magazine and disclosed the connection between SHAPE Magazine and SHAPE Water Boosters was sufficient to alert consumers that the article was an advertisement.[56] NAD precedent is clear that effective disclosures

---

circumstances; and (2) the representation or omission is 'material'—defined as "likely to affect the consumer's conduct or decision with regard to a product or service." FTC Letter to Commercial Alert, http://www.ftc.gov/os/closings/staff/050210productplacemen.pdf, quoting FTC Deception Policy Statement, *appended to Cliffdale Associates, Inc.*, 103 F.T.C. 110, 175 (1984).

54. FTC Advisory Opinion No. 191, http://www.ftc.gov/os/decisions/docs/Vol%2073/ftcd-vol73(JANUARY- JUNE1968)PAGES1289-END.pdf.; *see also In the Matter of JS&A Group, Inc.*, 111 F.T.C. 522 (1989).

55. The FTC Guidelines to Endorsements and Testimonials, http://ftc.gov/os/2009/10/091005revisedendorsementguides.pdf, define as endorsement as "any advertising message ... that consumers are likely to believe reflects the opinions, beliefs, findings, or experiences of a party other than the sponsoring advertiser, even if the views expressed by that party are identical to those of the sponsoring advertiser.

56. NAD noted that SHAPE Water Boosters were promoted in separate, clearly delineated advertisements, including on pages 120 and 123.

must be in close proximity to the main claim, meaning that they can be read at the same time a consumer reviews the claim.[57]

As the advertiser aptly pointed out, SHAPE's well-educated and sophisticated readership "have become accustomed to [the informational/endorsement] format and expect and utilize the recommendations in the magazines they purchase to help them make validated lifestyle decisions." Readers, however, generally attach different significance to recommendations made in an editorial news article than they would if the same recommendations were made in an advertising format. For all of the foregoing reasons, NAD recommended that the advertiser clearly and conspicuously designate content as advertising when it promotes SHAPE-branded products.

Conclusion

NAD recommended that the advertiser clearly and conspicuously designate content as advertising when it advertises SHAPE-branded products.

Notes

1. According to the NAD, how should advertising content format be distinguished from editorial content to avoid confusion?

2. Is it reasonable to expect consumers to identify advertising content regardless of its format?

3. In terms of the SHAPE Water Boosters, why do you think that that NAD was unpersuaded by SHAPE's assertion that the magazine's readership can distinguish between editorial and sponsored content?

D. Creating and Clearing Content for Marketing Campaigns

When using third-party content in an advertisement, there are a number of clearance and permission issues that may arise, including copyright, trademark, privacy, and right to publicity. Care must be taken to properly identify third-party content included in the advertisement and obtain third-party permission to use such content. Failure to do so can result in costly damages and legal fees when

57. *Digital Capital Advisors (Representative Transactions)*, Report #5593 *NAD/CARU Case Reports* (May 2013); *3M Company (Nexcare Comfort Ultra Fabric Bandages)*, Report # 4596 *NAD Case Reports* (November 2006); *Windmill Health Products (Chitosol Chitosan Fat Binding Diet System)*, Report # 3900 at 5 *NAD Case Reports* (April 2002); see also http://www.ftc.gov/os/2013/03/130312dotcomdisclosures.pdf at 8; http://www.business.ftc.gov/documents/bus71-ftcs-revised-endorsement-guideswhat-people-are-asking. ("As for where to place a disclosure, the guiding principle is that it has to be clear and conspicuous. Putting disclosures in obscure places—for example, buried on an ABOUT US or GENERAL INFO page, behind a poorly labeled hyperlink or in a terms of service agreement—isn't good enough. The average person who visits your site must be able to notice your disclosure, read it and understand it.").

faced with a potential infringement claim, not to mention removal of the infringing content from public dissemination.

1. Copyright, Trademark, and Unfair Competition

Copyright or trademark claims may arise from using protected visual, sound, or audiovisual material in the background of an advertisement. This may include artwork, songs, movies, television shows, books, magazines, photographs, or architecture. Unless a license or assignment is granted by the owners of such rights, the unauthorized use may give rise to infringement claims. The more attention is placed on these protected materials, the greater the risk associated with using them without permission from the owner.

An advertiser may obtain rights to use third-party content by entering into a written agreement such as a license, assignment, or work made for hire. A license agreement typically grants rights in a copyright, trademark, or a person's name or image for a specific purpose, while an assignment agreement transfers all or a substantial part of the rights to a protected work. A work made for hire is only applicable to a limited category of works created by an employee or freelancer as defined under the Copyright Act (17 U.S.C. § 101). Whether a work is a work made for hire is not always a straightforward analysis and may lead to significant ownership disputes. A work made for hire is either a work made by an employee within the scope of employment, or a work specially ordered or commissioned for use. In the latter category, the Copyright Act specifically enumerates what constitutes a commissioned work and expressly provides that there must be a written instrument signed by both parties that the work is to be considered a work for hire. The better practice is for both employees and independent contractors to execute an agreement that includes a work for hire clause, as well as an assignment so as to assure proper ownership from the time of creation.

Trademark claims arise out of the use of branded material in the advertisement when the inclusion of that material is likely to confuse the public and/or cause the public to mistakenly perceive a relationship or endorsement between the mark and the advertiser. Trademarks include brand names, logos, slogans, product designs, product configurations, and some architectural elements. For example, in *Louis Vuitton Malletier, S.A. v. Hyundai Motor America*, 10-cv-1611 (S.D.N.Y. 2012), Louis Vuitton brought an infringement suit against Hyundai for featuring a four-second clip of a basketball covered in their famous Toile-Monogram in the 30-second 2010 Super Bowl advertisement.

Louis Vuitton Malletier, S.A. v. Hyundai Motor America

2012 U.S. Dist. LEXIS 42795 (S.D.N.Y. Mar. 22, 2012)

CASTEL, District Judge.

During the post-game show of the 2010 Super Bowl, defendant Hyundai Motor America ("Hyundai") debuted a commercial that its counsel describes as "a humorous, socio-economic commentary on luxury defined by a premium price tag, rather than by the value to the consumer." The ad, which would eventually air five times over the course of a month, included a one-second shot of a basketball decorated with a distinctive pattern resembling the famous trademarks of plaintiff Louis Vuitton Malletier, S.A. ("Louis Vuitton").

Louis Vuitton has asserted trademark and unfair competition claims under New York and federal law, alleging that the commercial diluted and infringed its marks. Discovery in this case is now closed. Louis Vuitton moves for summary judgment on its trademark dilution claims as to liability only, and Hyundai has moved for summary judgment in its favor on all claims.

For the reasons explained, Louis Vuitton's motion is granted and Hyundai's motion is denied.

Background

The following facts are either undisputed or described in the light most favorable to Hyundai as the non-movant. *See, e.g., Costello v. City of Burlington,* 632 F.3d 41, 45 (2d Cir.2011).[58]

A. Hyundai's Use of Louis Vuitton Markings in the "Luxury" Ad.

Hyundai's thirty-second commercial goes by the name "Luxury." (It consists of brief vignettes that show "policemen eating caviar in a patrol car; large yachts parked beside modest homes; blue-collar workers eating lobster during their lunch break; a four-second scene of an inner-city basketball game played on a lavish marble court with a gold hoop; and a ten-second scene of the Sonata driving down a street lined with chandeliers and red-carpet crosswalks.")

The commercial's "scene of an inner-city basketball game" features "a basketball bearing marks similar, but not identical," to the Louis Vuitton marks. Louis Vuitton characterizes the vignette as "a street-yard basketball scene in which it would use a basketball with markings copied from the design and colors of the [Louis Vuitton] Marks, altering them only slightly."

The Louis Vuitton marks are known as the "toile monogram." As described by Hyundai, it "consists of a repeating pattern design of the letters 'LV and flower-like symbols on a chestnut-brown background." In the cease-and-desist letter that it would send to Hyundai after the ad's initial broadcast, Louis Vuitton described the marks as having "three distinctive elemental designs—a pinwheel design, a diamond with an inset pinwheel design, and a circle with an inset flower design. . . ." Louis Vuitton first registered this mark with the United States Patent and Trademark Office in 1932, and subsequently registered the mark's individual elements.

58. The background section addresses facts pertaining to Louis Vuitton's motion for summary judgment, and therefore describes the facts in the light most favorable to Hyundai as the non-movant. When addressing Hyundai's motion for summary judgment, the record is construed in the light most favorable to Louis Vuitton as the non-movant.

The most prominent alteration in the "Luxury" ad was the substitution of the letters "LZ" for "LV," although Hyundai made small modifications to the other elements of the mark, including slight alterations to their proportions.

According to Hyundai, the commercial sought to "emphasize" the "style, quality and amenities" of the 2011 Sonata, "a mid-sized Sedan priced at approximately $20,000." As described by Hyundai, the "Luxury" ad

> sought to redefine the concept of luxury by communicating to consumers that Sonata offered "luxury for all." The Commercial attempted to accomplish this goal by poking fun at the silliness of luxury-as-exclusivity by juxtaposing symbols of luxury with everyday life (for example, large yachts parked beside modest homes).

As further explained by Hyundai, "The symbols of 'old' luxury, including the [Louis Vuitton] Marks, were used as part of the Commercial's humorous social commentary on the need to redefine luxury during a recession. . . . The commercial poked fun at these symbols of 'old' luxury to distinguish them from [Hyundai] in an effort to challenge consumers to rethink what it means for a product to be luxurious." In Hyundai's view, the ad sought "to distinguish [Louis Vuitton] from the common-sense Sonata."

Hyundai does not dispute that the Louis Vuitton marks "are famous and distinctive" as "widely recognized luxury marks," and are "viewed by some as the most valuable luxury brand in the world." While the parties set forth slight and immaterial differences in their characterizations of the basketball's design, they agree that the ball was intended to evoke "the original Louis Vuitton Toile Monogram. . . ." Christopher J. Perry, a former marketing executive at Hyundai, confirmed in a Rule 30(b)(6) deposition that Hyundai worked to "genericize[ ] the Louis Vuitton marks" so "that they remained very similar" to the brown-and-gold marks of Louis Vuitton. Perry said that "the brown and gold of [Louis Vuitton]" were intended to give the basketball a "more stylized and luxurious look to it," and that these colors were "a distinctive special reference" that was "tied to Louis Vuitton." At deposition, Perry testified as follows:

> Q: [Y]ou wanted to create an association with Louis Vuitton, isn't that true?
>
> Mr. Perry: With luxury. Yes.
>
> Q: Right. Because in your view Louis Vuitton is very, very distinctive and a sign of luxury, correct?
>
> Hyundai counsel: [Objection.]
>
> Mr. Perry: Louis Vuitton, the brown and gold convey luxury.

Liz Boone, an account executive at the advertising firm overseeing the "Luxury" ad, confirmed that the design was intended to evoke "Louis Vuitton in particular." She testified that the design "came out of somebody's imagination, so there was nobody to go seek permission from." According to Hyundai, its advertising firm designed the basketball pattern in hopes of "evoking luxury" through the "telltale signs of high-end fashion goods." Joel Ewanick, a former Hyundai marketing executive, testified in deposition that Hyundai designed "a brown basketball as you'd expect with some gold emblems on it to represent luxury definitely laddering and borrowing equity from Louis Vuitton. And I believe we changed as much as we could to make it so it wasn't a complete logo. But [we] tried to make it look like that so we would get that quick reference to luxury and people would get the luxury reference quickly. It was the simplest thing."

The "Luxury" ad was motivated in part by a desire on the part of Hyundai to change its brand image among consumers. As described by Hyundai, "among those who highly considered but did not purchase an earlier model of the Sonata, brand reputation and resale value were the main reasons for rejection." As Ewanick testified:

> The Hyundai brand is one with significant deficiencies when you ask consumers what they think about safety, what you think about amenities, what you think about styling, what you think about performance. . . . But I would say generally speaking the idea was to reframe the way people looked at Hyundai, the brand, and specifically through the eyes of the Sonata. . . . As I recall, the one that you're referring to with the Louis Vuitton in it had a reference to luxury and how there's an immense amount of amenities that you would get in a Sonata that you would expect to find in luxury brands.

Ewanick, who had been at Hyundai at the time the ad was developed, testified that it was "[c]orrect" to say that Hyundai "used the Louis Vuitton[-]like marks in order to raise the image of the Hyundai brand in the mind of the consumer[.]"

Elsewhere, Hyundai states that it "objects to [Louis Vuitton's] implication that the sole and immediate purpose of the campaign was to sell cars. Rather, the admissible evidence demonstrates [Hyundai's] goal to build consideration and awareness and try to change the brand perception long term."

B. Hyundai Previously Sought, But Did Not Receive, Permission to Display Several Luxury Marks in Its Commercial.

Before going forward with the final version of "Luxury," Hyundai requested permission from numerous companies to display their luxury marks in a commercial. Hyundai's outside advertising firm contacted thirteen companies to see whether they would permit Hyundai to use their brands free of charge. In a never-broadcast vignette, Hyundai displayed "a vending machine that dispensed luxury handbags. . . ." Six brands (Chanel, Prada, Coach, Yves Saint Laurent, Chloe, Gucci and Ferragamo) expressly declined consent. Others (Fendi, Chloe,[59] Dolce & Gabbana, Marc Jacobs, Burberry and Louis Vuitton) never responded to the request. As described by Hyundai's counsel, "it does not appear" that its outside advertising firm "ever spoke with anyone at [Louis Vuitton] about this Commercial." An e-mail

59. Presumably in error, Hyundai lists Chloe as both expressly declining and never responding to the request.

of November 19, 2009 sent within Hyundai's outside advertising firm states that as to permission from Louis Vuitton: "have not been able to get a return phone call-email has not been sent." A separate e-mail in the chain states: "Unfortunately we have not found one who would be open to participating yet."

C. Hyundai's Continued Airing of "Luxury."

The "Luxury" ad first ran during the Superbowl post-game show of February 7, 2010, following the New Orleans Saints' 31–17 victory over the Indianapolis Colts. On February 12, 2010, Louis Vuitton sent Hyundai a cease-and-desist letter objecting to the inclusion of Louis Vuitton imagery in the "Luxury" ad. By then, Hyundai had already arranged for "Luxury" to air three times during the NBA All-Star Game weekend, over February 12–14, 2010. Hyundai executives decided to wait for an opinion from legal counsel before taking action on the ad, and went forward with the plan to run the ad during the NBA programming.

Louis Vuitton commenced this litigation on March 1, 2010. Hyundai executives "took the complaint under advisement," and again aired the commercial during the 9 p.m. hour of the Academy Awards on March 7, 2010.

D. Procedural History.

Louis Vuitton commenced this action on March 1, 2010. On April 19, 2010, Louis Vuitton filed an Amended Complaint that asserts five causes of action. Count I asserts trademark dilution by blurring and/or tarnishment under the Lanham Act, 15 U.S.C. § 1125(c); Count II asserts trademark dilution under New York General Business Law § 360-*l;* Counts III and V assert trademark infringement under the Lanham Act, 15 U.S.C. § 1125(a)(1) (A) and 1114(1); and Count IV asserts common-law unfair competition under New York law.

Louis Vuitton moves for summary judgment in its favor only as to liability under Counts I and II, including willfulness for any dilution. Hyundai moves for summary judgment in its favor on all five counts.

Summary Judgment Standard

Summary judgment "shall" be granted "if the movant shows that there is no genuine dispute as to any material fact and the movant is entitled to judgment as a matter of law." Rule 56(a), Fed.R.Civ.P. It is the initial burden of a movant on a summary judgment motion to come forward with evidence on each material element of his claim or defense, sufficient to demonstrate that he or she is entitled to relief as a matter of law. *Vt. Teddy Bear Co. v. 1-800 Beargram Co.,* 373 F.3d 241, 244 (2d Cir.2004). In raising a triable issue of fact, the non-movant carries only "a limited burden of production," but nevertheless "must 'demonstrate more than some metaphysical doubt as to the material facts,' and come forward with 'specific facts showing that there is a genuine issue for trial.' "*Powell v. Nat'l Bd. of Med. Exam'rs,* 364 F.3d 79, 84 (2d Cir.2004) (quoting *Aslanidis v. U.S. Lines, Inc.,* 7 F.3d 1067, 1072 (2d Cir.1993)).

A fact is material if it "might affect the outcome of the suit under the governing law," meaning that "the evidence is such that a reasonable jury could return a verdict for the nonmoving party." *Anderson v. Liberty Lobby, Inc.,* 477 U.S. 242, 248, 106 S. Ct. 2505, 91 L.Ed.2d 202 (1986). The Court must view the evidence in the light most favorable to the non-moving party and draw all reasonable inferences in its favor, and may grant summary judgment only when no reasonable trier of fact could find in favor of the nonmoving party. *Costello,* 632 F.3d at 45; *accord Matsushita Elec. Indus. Co. v. Zenith Radio Corp.,* 475 U.S. 574, 585–88, 106 S.Ct. 1348, 89 L.Ed.2d 538, (1986). In reviewing a motion for summary judgment, the court may scrutinize the record, and grant or deny summary judgment as the record warrants. Rule 56(c)(3). In the absence of any disputed material fact, summary judgment is appropriate. Rule 56(a).

"A party opposing summary judgment does not show the existence of a genuine issue of fact to be tried merely by making assertions that are conclusory or based on speculation." *Major League Baseball Properties, Inc. v. Salvino, Inc.,* 542 F.3d 290, 310 (2d Cir.2008) (internal citation omitted); *see also Anderson,* 477 U .S. at 249–50 (summary judgment may be granted if the opposing evidence is "merely colorable" or "not significantly probative") (citations omitted). An opposing party's facts "must be material and of a substantial nature, not fanciful, frivolous, gauzy, spurious, irrelevant, gossamer inferences, conjectural, speculative, nor merely suspicions." *Contemporary Mission, Inc. v. U.S. Postal Serv.,* 648 F.2d 97, 107 n. 14 (2d Cir.1981) (quotation marks omitted).

Discussion

I. Summary Judgment is Granted to Louis Vuitton on Its Claims of Dilution by Blurring.

At 15 U.S.C. § 1125(c)(1), the Trademark Dilution Revision Act of 2006 (the "TDRA") states:

> Subject to the principles of equity, the owner of a famous mark that is distinctive, inherently or through acquired distinctiveness, shall be entitled to an injunction against another person who, at any time after the owner's mark has become famous, commences use of a mark or trade name in commerce that is likely to cause dilution by blurring or dilution by tarnishment of the famous mark, regardless of the presence or absence of actual or likely confusion, of competition, or of actual economic injury.

Although this provision speaks only of injunctive relief, at 15 U.S.C. § 1125(c)(5)(B), the statute separately provides for money damages under 15 U.S.C. § 1117(a), in the event of a willful violation. *See generally Sporty's Farm LLC v. Sportsman's Market, Inc.,* 202 F.3d 489, 500 (2d Cir.2000) (discussing willfulness requirement).

The federal anti-dilution statute "is designed solely for the benefit of sellers. Its purpose is to protect the owners of famous marks from the kind of dilution that is permitted by the trademark laws when a junior user uses the same mark in a non-confusing way in an unrelated area of commerce." *TCPIP Holding Co. v. Haar Commc'ns, Inc.*, 244 F.3d 88, 95 (2d Cir., 2001). It applies "regardless of the absence of competition or confusion." *Id.* In addition, the 2006 amendments eliminated a requirement that a plaintiff prove actual dilution: under the TDRA, a plaintiff need establish only likely dilution. *See, e.g., Burberry Ltd. v. Euro Moda, Inc.*, 2009 WL 1675080, at *8–9 (S.D.N.Y. June 10, 2009) (comparing TDRA with prior anti-dilution provisions).

There are two types of dilution: blurring and tarnishment. "[B]lurring is an 'association arising from the similarity between a mark or trade name and a famous mark that impairs the distinctiveness of the famous mark.' "*Starbucks Corp. v. Wolfe's Borough Coffee, Inc.*, 588 F.3d 97, 105 (2d Cir.2009) (quoting 15 U.S.C. § 1125(c)(2)(B)); *see also Tiffany (NJ) Inc. v. eBay Inc.*, 600 F.3d 93, 111 (2d Cir.2010) (blurring is "the whittling away of [the] established trademark's selling power through its unauthorized use by others.") (alteration in original; quotation marks omitted). As noted, the statute states that blurring may occur regardless of actual or likely confusion, competition or economic injury. *Starbucks*, 588 F.3d at 105 (citing 15 U.S.C. § 1125(c)(1)). "Some classic examples of blurring include 'hypothetical anomalies as Dupont shoes, Buick aspirin tablets, Schlitz varnish, Kodak pianos, Bulova gowns, and so forth.' " *Id.* (quoting *Mead,* 875 F.2d at 1031). As discussed below, the TDRA sets forth six non-exclusive factors that go toward blurring. 15 U.S.C. § 1125(c)(2)(B).

The TDRA also includes a fair use provision:

> The following shall not be actionable as dilution by blurring or dilution by tarnishment under this subsection:
>
> (A) Any fair use, including a nominative or descriptive fair use, or facilitation of such fair use, of a famous mark by another person other than as a designation of source for the person's own goods or services, including use in connection with—
>
> (i) advertising or promotion that permits consumers to compare goods or services; or
>
> (ii) identifying and parodying, criticizing, or commenting upon the famous mark owner or the goods or services of the famous mark owner.

15 U.S.C. § 1125(c)(3). Hyundai argues, among other things, that the "Luxury" ad qualifies as fair use under section 1125(c)(3) (A)(ii).

To date, the Second Circuit's most comprehensive discussion of the TDRA is set forth in *Starbucks Corp.*, 588 F.3d at 105–13. In that case, the coffee retailer Starbucks brought dilution claims against a company that marketed and sold a coffee branded "Charbucks Blend" and "Mister Charbucks." *Id.* at 103. The Charbucks logo did not resemble the Starbucks marks. *Id.* at 103, 106–07. Following a bench trial in which the district court concluded that defendants had not diluted the Starbucks marks, the Second Circuit affirmed in part, vacated in part and remanded, noting that the district court did not consider each of the six TDRA blurring factors, 15 U.S.C. § 1125(c)(2)(B), and instead placed undue weight solely on the marks' lack of similarity. *Id.* at 107–09.

A. Louis Vuitton Has Established Blurring Under the TDRA.

The TDRA sets forth six non-exclusive factors that go toward dilution by blurring. They are: (i) the degree of similarity between defendant's mark and the famous mark; (ii) the distinctiveness of the famous mark; (iii) whether the famous mark's owner "is engaging in substantially exclusive use of the mark;" (iv) the degree of recognition of the famous mark; (v) whether the defendant intended to create an association with the famous mark; and (vi) actual association between the defendant's mark and the famous mark. 15 U.S.C. § 1125(c)(2)(B). *Starbucks* explained that no single factor is outcome-determinative, and concluded that a district court erred by focusing on the similarity of marks to the exclusion of other factors. 588 F.3d at 108–09.

1. The Marks Have a High Degree of Similarity

Under the TDRA, to successfully prove blurring, a plaintiff need not establish "substantial similarity," and a court considers the "degree of similarity" as one of six probative factors. *See Starbucks,* 588 F.3d at 107–08 (comparing TDRA criteria to previous dilution standard). "Still, a finding that two marks lack similarity is probative." *Miss Universe, L.P. v. Villegas,* 672 F.Supp.2d 575, 593 (S.D.N.Y.2009).

The Louis Vuitton marks and the basketball design in "Luxury" are virtually indistinguishable. They feature highly similar geometric designs stamped in gold, set against a brown background. When closely scrutinized, the design in the Hyundai commercial includes the stylized initials "LZ," as opposed to Louis Vuitton's "LV." The "LZ" and the "LV" are portrayed in similar script and design.

As set forth in *Starbucks,* the context of the marks' use is central to a similarity analysis. 588 F.3d at 106–07. Hyundai argues that, rather than making a side-by-side comparison of the designs, the context of "Luxury" underscores the dissimilarities between Hyundai and Louis Vuitton. In this case, however, the brief appearance of the Louis Vuitton-like marks heightens the similarities. Absent exceedingly close scrutiny, the component elements of the Louis Vuitton Toile Monogram, and their overall effect, are virtually indistinguishable from Hyundai's stylized basketball design. Indeed, the brevity of the basketball's appearance in the "Luxury" ad, totaling approximately one second, renders it more difficult to assess the minor differences between the Louis Vuitton marks and Hyundai's alterations. This similarity was intended by Hyundai. As Ewanick testified, the ball's design was intended to "register luxury with the snap of the fingers." Considered in context, the ball's fleeting appearance in "Luxury" heightens the similarities between Louis Vuitton's marks and the Hyundai design.

Hyundai also argues that because Louis Vuitton does not produce sporting items or automobiles, there is no similarity between the marks. It asserts that "[a] rational person" viewing the "Luxury" ad would view "the couture basketball" as "utterly distinct from the ever-practical Sonata." In support of its motion, Louis Vuitton submits evidence that it has sold limited-edition soccer balls in honor of the 1998 World Cup in France,[60] soccer cleats, a croquet set, "petanque balls," golf bags and tennis bags. Vuitton also notes that it "has enjoyed a strong association with the automobile industry for nearly one hundred years," and has submitted a color photocopy of a book titled "Louis Vuitton: The Art of the Automobile." The photo-intensive book asserts claims such as, "[t]he paths of the Louis Vuitton company and the automobile world have often crossed," and offers detailed accounts of "the Louis Vuitton Classic," a series of annual events that includes awards to rare and vintage automobiles. Hyundai does not contend that the book is inadmissible hearsay, only that its sales volume in the United States is not set forth in the record. Drawing every favorable inference in favor of Hyundai, and assuming that the sales volume and public awareness of Louis Vuitton's sports- and auto-related products in the United States are limited to a niche market, the record nevertheless indicates that Louis Vuitton has had an ongoing, if limited, presence in the sales and marketing of sports- and auto-related goods. In this respect, Hyundai has not come forward with facts to support its dissimilarity argument.

Louis Vuitton has submitted evidence that the "Luxury" basketball design is highly similar to its own famous marks, and Hyundai has not come forward with evidence that would permit a reasonable juror to conclude otherwise.

2. The Louis Vuitton Marks Are Distinct.

The greater a mark's distinctiveness, the higher its degree of protection under dilution law. *Nabisco, Inc. v. PF Brands, Inc.*, 191 F.3d 208, 217 (2d Cir.1999), *abrogated on other grounds, Moseley v. V Secret Catalogue, Inc.*, 537 U.S. 418, 123 S.Ct. 1115, 155 L.Ed.2d 1 (2003).

Hyundai acknowledges that the Louis Vuitton marks "are famous and distinctive" as "widely recognized luxury marks," and are "viewed by some as the most valuable luxury brand in the world." They are entitled to a high degree of protection. *Cf. Louis Vuitton Malletier v. Dooney & Bourke, Inc.*, 454 F.3d 108, 116 (2d Cir.2006) (concluding that a "new Multicolore" of the Louis Vuitton Toile mark was "inherently distinctive"); *Burberry Ltd.*, 2009 WL 1675080, at *10–13 (concluding that Burberry's luxury markings were distinct).

3. Louis Vuitton Exercises Exclusive Use of the Marks.

Louis Vuitton has set forth evidence that in 2009, it "initiated" 9,489 anti-counterfeiting raids and 26,843 anti-counterfeiting procedures. In 2010, it sent 499 cease-and-desist letters in response to Customs Seizure Notices, after sending 217 such letters in 2009. Hyundai does not challenge this evidence.

---

60. The record includes a photograph from the January 28, 1999 edition of the Los Angeles Times showing basketball star Shaquille O'Neal wearing a Lakers jersey and posing with five Louis Vuitton soccer balls.

Hyundai, however, contends that Louis Vuitton has permitted unlicensed, third-party uses of its marks. It asserts that the Black Eyed Peas featured Louis Vuitton marks in the music video for "My Humps," and that musicians Dwight Yoakam and Jim Jones have featured the marks in their promotional material. Louis Vuitton notes that it sent a cease-and-desist letter in response to the "My Humps" video, and states that it was unaware of the other artists' uses until they were raised in a deposition. Hyundai also asserts that, under a licensing agreement, Louis Vuitton permits the jewelry company Tiffany & Co. to manufacture and sell pendants resembling a Louis Vuitton mark, and that Louis Vuitton provides celebrities with its products for promotional purposes.

Viewing the evidence in a light most favorable to Hyundai, the record indicates that, at most, Louis Vuitton had two minor lapses in enforcement, when it was unaware that two musicians incorporated the company's marks in promotional materials. Louis Vuitton responded to the "My Humps" video with a cease-and-desist letter, requires royalties for the Tiffany pendant, and consciously elects to provide its products to celebrities as a marketing strategy. Additionally, Louis Vuitton also has submitted a record that reflects aggressive anti-counterfeiting measures. Based on the record, Louis Vuitton has set forth evidence supporting its exclusive use of its marks, and Hyundai has failed to come forward with evidence that Louis Vuitton does not maintain exclusive use of its marks.

4. The Louis Vuitton Mark Has a High Degree of Recognition.

Hyundai does not dispute that Louis Vuitton's marks "are widely recognized luxury marks."

5. Hyundai Intended to Create an Association with Louis Vuitton.

The intent to associate with a famous mark weighs in favor of dilution. *Starbucks*, 58 F.3d at 109. Evidence of an intent to associate with the mark does not require evidence of bad faith. *Id.*

As conceded by Hyundai's counsel, "The parties do not dispute that [Hyundai] intended to create an association with the [Louis Vuitton] Marks and the luxury they convey." Several deponents who worked on the "Luxury" ad testified that Hyundai and its outside advertising firms specifically intended to create an association with Louis Vuitton. In the Rule 30(b)(6) deposition taken of Hyundai, Perry testified that the brown-and-gold colors were selected because they "are tied to Louis Vuitton" and that the "genericized" marks "remained very similar to the original Louis Vuitton marks."[61] When asked whether he wanted to create an association with Louis Vuitton, Perry answered, "With luxury. Yes."\Boone answered in the affirmative

61. In trademark law, the word "generic" may be used as a term of art that refers to a mark with a broad meaning over a range of products, and is therefore ineligible for trademark protection. *See, e.g., Harley-Davidson, Inc. v. Grottanelli,* 164 F.3d 806, 810–11 (2d Cir.1999) (discussing "hog" as generic term for motorcycles). When the word "genericize" was used to describe the markings, I do not understand it to imply an effort to make the Louis Vuitton marks generic in this sense.

when asked whether the marks were designed to evoke "Louis Vuitton in particular."\When asked whether Hyundai "used Louis Vuitton[-]like marks in order to raise the image of the Hyundai brand in the mind of the consumer," Ewanick answered, "Correct." Ewanick also testified, "I believe it was a brown basketball as you'd expect with some gold emblems on it to represent luxury definitely laddering and borrowing equity from Louis Vuitton."

In opposition to the motion, Hyundai notes that there is no dispute that Hyundai "intended to create an association with the [Louis Vuitton] Marks and the luxury they convey." It asserts, however, that any such association was "expressive" in nature, and that the basketball design imperfectly copied the Louis Vuitton marks, such that the Louis Vuitton marks could not be impaired as a matter of law. As discussed below, the "Luxury" ad is not expressive in the sense that the word is used in trademark law, and Hyundai's argument about lack of impairment to the Louis Vuitton marks is *ipse dixit* not supported by citation to the record.

Louis Vuitton has come forward with evidence of an intent to associate by Hyundai, which Hyundai has admitted, subject to certain unsupported qualifications. This factor weighs in favor of Louis Vuitton.

6. Louis Vuitton Has Submitted Probative Evidence of Actual Association Between the Marks.

The TDRA's sixth blurring factor weighs "[a]ny actual association between the mark or trade name and the famous mark." 15 U.S.C. § 1125(c)(2)(B)(vi).

To prove actual association, a plaintiff must establish that defendant's mark "conjure[s] an association with the senior [mark]," thereby "lessen[ing] the distinctiveness of the senior mark." *Nabisco,* 191 F.3d at 218. "[T]he absence of actual or even of a likelihood of confusion does not undermine evidence of trademark dilution." *Starbucks,* 588 F.3d at 109. In *Starbucks,* the Second Circuit noted that the plaintiff submitted results of a telephone survey reflecting that 3.1% of respondents viewed Starbucks as the possible source of a coffee that called itself "Charbucks." *Id.* Overall, 30.5% of consumers said that Starbucks was "the first thing that comes to mind" upon hearing the word "Charbucks." *Id.* The Second Circuit concluded that the district court erred by concluding that no evidence supported a conclusion of "actual association," noting that the statute does not equate association with confusion. *Id.* at 110 (citing *Nabisco,* 191 F.3d at 221 (the absence of confusion "has no probative value" in dilution analysis)). On remand, the district court concluded that the survey results "constitute evidence of actual association," but that because the survey did not present the marks in their full contexts and the surveys reflected relatively low levels of confusion, "the actual association factor weighs no more than minimally in Plaintiff's favor." *Starbucks Corp. v. Wolfe's Borough Coffee, Inc.,* 2011 WL 6747431, at *4 (S.D.N.Y. Dec. 23, 2011).

In support of its assertion of actual association, Louis Vuitton cites the research of Hyundai's own expert, Dr. Jerry Wind. From January 7 to 19, 2011, Wind conducted a double-blind survey using a test group that was shown the "Luxury" ad and a control group that was shown the same ad without the stylized basketball. Participants were asked a series of questions about the ad. The study tested among the general population, and, separately, a subset of prospective Hyundai Sonata purchasers.

When asked to identify the brands shown in "Luxury," 19% of Wind's test-group participants cited Louis Vuitton. Ninety percent of test-group petitioners said that they noticed the basketball, and 30% stated that the basketball reminded them of Louis Vuitton. Fifty-eight percent of the test group noticed "a pattern or design on the basketball." When asked to list which brand or product was advertised in the commercial, seventy-nine percent of the test group cited Hyundai first, and five percent mentioned Louis Vuitton first.[62] None of the respondents said that it made them think less favorably of Louis Vuitton. Only two percent of respondents in the test group believed that Hyundai and Louis Vuitton were affiliated. Nine percent of the test-group respondents said that the basketball made them more likely to buy a Hyundai Sonata.

Louis Vuitton's expert, John R. Hauser, SC.D., conducted a double-blind internet survey from April 9 to 17, 2011. The survey used both a control group and a test group, with the control group shown a video that replaced the stylized "Luxury" basketball with a standard orange basketball. Seventy-two percent of test-group participants noticed the basketball design (compared to five percent of control-group respondents) and fifteen percent of the test-group recognized the design as belonging to Louis Vuitton; twenty-nine percent of all test-group respondents recognized it as some type of luxury mark. Hauser states that the fifteen-percent recognition is consistent with the percentage of the buying public that is aware of the Louis Vuitton mark. Among those who recognized the design as Louis Vuitton's, sixty-two percent believed that Louis Vuitton authorized Hyundai's use of the mark. Large percentages of both the test group and control group interpreted the ad as promoting Hyundai's luxury qualities.

Louis Vuitton also cites to messages that appeared on the social networking site Twitter, which purport to show public responses to Louis Vuitton's role in the "Luxury" ad. For example, on February 14, 2010, during the weekend of the NBA All-Star game, Twitter user kailanhindsman wrote, "I think a Louis vuitton football or basketball would be gangsta." That same day, Dhat_Kid_DiCE wrote on Twitter, "Dyd yall See tht Louis Vuitton Basketball? Lols iWant ^___^". By way of another example, MrExclusive1990 on Twitter wrote, "were they just playing ball with a LV basketball lol."[63]

---

62. Other participants believed that the commercial advertised non-specified car manufacturers, caviar, lobsters, basketballs, yachts, Spalding, the police or chandeliers.

63. Louis Vuitton's memorandum of law and Local Rule 56.1 statement make generalized assertions that, in certain focus groups, the participants' oral responses reflect confusion about Louis Vuitton's role in the ad. The precise nature of the focus group responses is not explained. Unhelpfully, Louis Vuitton has submitted hours-long, apparently unedited DVDs of these focus groups, which do not form a basis for this Court's decision.

Hyundai argues that Louis Vuitton has a "'conspicuous absence' of survey evidence," but plaintiff's record in support of summary judgment includes both its own expert's report, as well as the report of Hyundai's expert. (Def Mem. at 16.) Hyundai also argues that the Wind survey indicates that "only" nineteen percent of unguided test-group participants recognized Louis Vuitton's appearance in the "Luxury" ad. However, in light of the *Starbucks* opinions in both the Second Circuit and this District, the survey results present evidence of association. 588 F.3d at 109. As also emphasized by *Starbucks*. Louis Vuitton is not required to prove actual consumer confusion, as in a trademark-infringement case. 588 F.3d at 109, 2011 WL 6747431, at *4. The ultimate question in blurring is whether a famous mark's power has been whittled away by unauthorized use, or whether an association blurs the famous mark's distinctiveness. *Starbucks,* 588 F.3d at 105: *Tiffany (NJ),* 600 F.3d at 111. According to Louis Vuitton's expert, among those who recognized the Louis Vuitton mark, sixty-two percent believed the ad was approved by Louis Vuitton. This is probative and relevant survey evidence that participants associated Louis Vuitton with Hyundai. Moreover, the nineteen-percent figure emphasized by Hyundai also is relevant and probative evidence that participants associated Louis Vuitton with the "Luxury" ad. Finally, while I afford limited weight to the Twitter postings, they provide some evidence of actual association. *Cf. New York City Triathlon, LLC v. NYC Triathlon Club, Inc.,* 704 F.Supp.2d 305, 319, 323 (S.D.N.Y.2010) (e-mail from sophisticated consumer was probative of actual association).

Hyundai's evidence in opposition consists of the assertions that the focus group responses are unreliable. As noted, the Court has not relied on the oral comments of the focus groups. It also relies on one aspect of the Wind survey, which Hyundai itself commissioned, in which 19% of respondents cited the presence of Louis Vuitton's logo, a figure that Hyundai contends is too low to constitute evidence of actual association. It is statistically significant that 19% of survey respondents, without prompting, identified Louis Vuitton as a brand shown in the ad, as is the 30% of participants who, when asked in Hyundai's survey to focus their attention on the basketball, said that it reminded them of Louis Vuitton.

Louis Vuitton has come forward with evidence of actual association and Hyundai, in the face of that evidence, has failed to come forward with evidence that would permit a reasonable factfinder to conclude otherwise.

7. Weighing the Six Statutory Factors, Louis Vuitton Has Set Forth Evidence in Its Favor on Each and Hyundai Has Not Come Forward with Relevant Evidence in Its Favor.

The plaintiff has come forward with evidence in support of each statutory factors at 15 U.S.C. § 1125(c)(2)(B). The defendant has failed to come forward with evidence that, if believed, would enable a reasonable jury to find in its favor.

Hyundai has admitted that Louis Vuitton's marks are both distinct and well recognized. 15 U.S.C. § 1125(c)(2)(B)(ii) & (iv). As previously noted, the greater a mark's distinctiveness, the higher the degree of protection afforded under anti-dilution law. *Nabisco,* 191 F.3d at 217.

Louis Vuitton also has set forth considerable evidence, including the statements of Hyundai's Rule 30(b)(6) witness, that Hyundai intended to create an association with Louis Vuitton—indeed, that the purpose behind the basketball design was to invoke just such an association, 15 U.S.C. § 1125(c)(2)(B)(v).

As to Louis Vuitton's exclusive use of the marks, Hyundai has offered evidence that two recording artists used Louis Vuitton marks in promotional images; Louis Vuitton asserted that it was unaware of those uses until they were cited in deposition. By contrast, Louis Vuitton has set forth a record going toward aggressive enforcement of counterfeiting, and the other instances cited by Hyundai (the marks' appearance in the "My Humps" video and Tiffany's use of a Louis Vuitton mark) led to a cease-and-desist letter and a royalties agreement. Louis Vuitton has set forth evidence supporting its exclusive use of its marks, and Hyundai has failed to come forward with evidence that Louis Vuitton did not maintain exclusive use of its marks. 15 U.S.C. § 1125(c)(2)(B)(iii).

As to the similarity between Louis Vuitton's marks and the designs on the basketball, they are virtually indistinguishable. Viewed in context of the commercial, the brevity of the basketball's appearance, if anything, renders it more difficult to distinguish between the original Louis Vuitton marks and the minor variations made by Hyundai to "genericize" the marks. Louis Vuitton also has set forth some evidence that it has maintained a limited, if ongoing, presence in niche sports and automobile products. The degree of similarity between the marks is high. 15 U .S.C. § 1125(c)(2)(B)(i).

Lastly, Louis Vuitton has come forward with significant, probative evidence reflecting actual association between its famous marks and the stylized basketball in the "Luxury" ad. 15 U.S.C. § 1125(c)(2)(B)(vi). Each party's expert conducted surveys as to consumer perceptions of Louis Vuitton's role in the "Luxury" advertisement. When asked an open-ended question as to the brands identified in the ad, Hyundai's study concluded that 19% of respondents identified Louis Vuitton; Louis Vuitton's expert found a rate of 15%. When participants were asked to focus on the basketball, Hyundai's expert concluded that 30% of respondents associated the design with Louis Vuitton. Sixty-two percent of those familiar with the Louis Vuitton marks believed that Hyundai received permission to use them in the "Luxury" ad. Louis Vuitton also has submitted some evidence from social networking users that reflect interest and enthusiasm about a Louis Vuitton basketball. The record as to actual association with Louis Vuitton is substantial and unrebutted.

Viewed in its entirety, Louis Vuitton has set forth evidence that satisfies each of the TDRA's six blurring factors. It also bears emphasizing that these factors go toward the ultimate question of "whether an *association,* arising from the similarity of subject marks, 'impairs the distinctiveness of the famous mark.'

"*Starbucks,* 588 F.3d at 109 (emphasis in original; quoting 15 U.S.C. § 1125(c)(2)(B)); *see also Tiffany (NJ*), 600 F.3d at 111 (blurring is "the whittling away" of a famous mark "through its unauthorized use by others."). The blurring inquiry does not require two companies to be in direct competition. *TCPIP Holding Co.,* 244 F.3d at 95. Moreover, the text of the TDRA looks to whether "use of a mark or trade name in commerce is *likely* to cause dilution by blurring. . . ." 15 U.S.C. § 1125(c)(1) (emphasis added); *see also v. Secret Catalogue, Inc. v. Moseley,* 605 F.3d 382, 388 (6th Cir.2010) ("The phrase 'likely to cause dilution' used in the new statute . . . significantly changes the meaning of the law from 'causes actual harm' under the preexisting law.").

Relying on *Tiffany (NJ) Inc. v. eBay Inc.,* 600 F.3d at 112, Hyundai argues that it cannot be liable under the TDRA because it did not use the Louis Vuitton marks to designate its own products—presumably, for instance, a hypothetical product such as the Louis Vuitton Sonata, or the actual sale of Louis Vuitton-style basketballs. *Tiffany* held that the online auction site eBay could not be liable for trademark dilution when it displayed the famous Tiffany mark "to advertise and identify the availability of authentic Tiffany merchandise on the eBay website." 600 F.3d at 112. Tiffany also argued that eBay facilitated the sale of counterfeit Tiffany products, but the Second Circuit noted that eBay did not itself "sell the goods at issue." *Id.*

By contrast, in this case, Louis Vuitton has set forth evidence that Hyundai utilized the Louis Vuitton marks for its own branding goals, and, in the minds of some consumers, created actual association between Hyundai and Louis Vuitton. It did so without authorization from Louis Vuitton. Unlike *Tiffany,* Hyundai, as the ad's creators testified, was "definitely laddering and borrowing equity from Louis Vuitton." Hyundai argues that the dilution claim must fail because "[t]he pattern was not used to designate [Hyundai's] own goods, services, or business," but that argument conflates dilution with a false designation of origins claim under 15 U.S.C. § 1125(a). *Tiffany* does not stand for the proposition that a viable blurring claim arises only when a mark designates an item's origins.

Louis Vuitton has come forward with substantial, probative evidence in its favor on each of the six factors of 15 U.S.C. § 1125(c)(2)(B), and that Hyundai has not come forward with evidence that would permit a reasonable juror to find in its favor. Louis Vuitton has established blurring under the TDRA as a matter of law.[64]

8. Louis Vuitton Has Established Willfulness.

To be eligible for money damages under the TDRA, a defendant must have "willfully intended to trade on the recognition of the famous mark." 15 U.S.C.

64. Because I conclude that Louis Vuitton has satisfied its summary judgment burden on blurring, I need not reach the issue of dilution by tarnishment. The Amended Complaint sets forth both dilution theories in a single count and does not assert that separate damages arose based on tarnishment.

§ 1125(c)(5)(B)(i). A damages award is "subject to the discretion of the court and the principles of equity." 15 U.S.C. § 1125(c)(5).

As discussed, the record is replete with statements that Hyundai intentionally used the Louis Vuitton marks for purposes of promoting the Sonata, Hyundai witnesses confirmed that the marks were intended to evoke "Louis Vuitton in particular" and that Hyundai used the marks "in order to raise the image of the Hyundai brand in the mind of the consumer[.]" When counsel asked Perry whether he "wanted to create an association with Louis Vuitton," Perry answered, "With luxury. Yes." The basketball was designed to "represent luxury definitely laddering and borrowing equity from Louis Vuitton."

Moreover, the record reflects awareness on the part of Hyundai that it believed it needed permission to use other companies' luxury brands as part of the commercial, through evidence that Hyundai sought permission from numerous companies to use their marks in its campaign. Hyundai sought out permission from thirteen companies to use their brands, and six of them expressly declined. Others, including Louis Vuitton, never responded to the request. When no response came from Louis Vuitton, Hyundai nevertheless proceeded to use the "genericized" Louis Vuitton mark.

Even with Louis Vuitton's cease-and-desist letter in hand, Hyundai proceeded to run the ad through the NBA All-Star Weekend and, following commencement of this action, the Academy Awards. According to Hyundai, its management "took the complaint under advisement, but ultimately determined there was no reason, legal or otherwise, not to run the Commercial as planned in the Academy Awards." When asked at deposition whether the ad's quality "was more important a consideration than anything else you were aware of" in deciding to run it during the Academy Awards, Perry responded, "Yeah. I mean, there was issues obviously. The litigation was an issue. It was a good ad."

The deliberate alteration to the Louis Vuitton marks also demonstrates a consciousness that Hyundai could not lawfully use the marks. Perry confirmed in the Rule 30(b)(6) deposition that Louis Vuitton "genericized" the marks but ensured that "they remained very similar" to the Louis Vuitton design. The coloring was "a distinctive special reference" to Louis Vuitton. Boone testified that the design was intended to evoke "Louis Vuitton in particular," but also that Hyundai's design "came out of somebody's imagination, so there was nobody to go seek permission from." Such testimony reflects the conscious intent within Hyundai to ladder and borrow from the equity of Louis Vuitton marks while also circumventing any obligation to seek Louis Vuitton's permission

In opposition, Hyundai counters that it acted with an expressive intent, and that its willfulness should be decided by a jury. The expressive intent of the ad is more appropriately directed to its fair use defense. Plaintiff has come forward with substantial, probative evidence of Hyundai's willfulness, and Hyundai has not come forward with evidence that would permit a reasonable juror to find in its favor on willfulness.

B. Louis Vuitton Has Established Blurring Under New York Law

New York has adopted an anti-dilution law that is similar, but not identical to the federal statute. It states:

> Likelihood of injury to business reputation or of dilution of the distinctive quality of a mark or trade name shall be a ground for injunctive relief in cases of infringement of a mark registered or not registered or in cases of unfair competition, notwithstanding the absence of competition between the parties or the absence of confusion as to the source of goods or services.

N.Y. Gen. Bus. L. § 360-*l*.[65] New York law does not require a mark to be famous, and it "does not permit a dilution claim unless the marks are 'substantially' similar." *Tiffany,* 600 F.3d at 111 (comparing New York and federal anti-dilution law); *see also Biosafe-One, Inc. v. Hawks,* 639 F.Supp.2d 358, 367 (S.D.N.Y.2009) (Chin, J.) (a plaintiff suing under the New York statute must prove "'(1) that it possess[es] a strong mark one which has a distinctive quality or has acquired a secondary meaning such that the trade name has become so associated in the public's mind with the [plaintiff] that it identifies goods sold by that entity as distinguished from goods sold by others, and (2) a likelihood of dilution by either blurring or tarnishment.'") (quoting *Matter of Fireman's Ass'n of State of N.Y. v. French Am. Sch. of N.Y.,* 41 A.D.3d 925, 928, 839 N.Y.S.2d 238 (3d Dep't 2007) (internal citations and quotations omitted)). To determine dilution by blurring, New York dilution law looks to "(i) the similarity of the marks; (ii) the similarity of the products covered; (iii) the sophistication of the consumers; (iv) the existence of predatory intent; (v) the renown of the senior mark; and (vi) the renown of the junior mark." New York Stock *Exchange, Inc. v. New York, New York Hotel LLC,* 29.3 F.3d 550, 558 (2d Cir.2002).

Louis Vuitton argues that it has established points first, fourth and fifth in support of its motion on the federal claim. As to the similarities between the products covered, it cites to its sale of sports-related items and its ties to the automobile industry. Louis Vuitton also argues that while its consumers are sophisticated, because the basketball's markings are nearly identical to the Louis Vuitton marks, the factor either is neutral or tips in Louis Vuitton's favor. Lastly, it argues that the renown of the junior mark is irrelevant here, because the basketball was shown in a commercial and was not a product for sale.

In opposition, Hyundai does not separately address the evidence as it pertains to New York's dilution law. It merely argues in a footnote that because Louis Vuitton is not entitled to summary judgment on its federal dilution claim, it is

---

65. Section 360-*l* speaks only of injunctive relief and is silent as to the availability of damages, although the Second Department has indicated that they may be awarded. *See Out of Box Promotions, LLC v-Koschitzki,* 55 A.D.3d 575, 578, 866 N.Y.S.2d 677 (2d Dep't 2008). Neither party has addressed whether the statute provides for damages, and I need not resolve the issue at this time.

not entitled to summary judgment on its state-law claim. It also argues that there is not substantial similarity between the marks. As previously discussed, however, the Louis Vuitton marks are virtually indistinguishable from the design of the "Luxury" basketball.

With no opposing evidence submitted by Hyundai other than that which it submitted on the federal blurring claim (as to which summary judgment is granted in plaintiff's favor) this Court concludes that factors first, fourth and fifth weigh in Louis Vuitton's favor. Given that Louis Vuitton has periodically produced and marketed sports-related items, this Court concludes that the second factor weighs slightly in Louis Vuitton's favor. The third and sixth factors are neutral.

Based on the record, summary judgment is granted to plaintiff on its New York law claim for dilution by blurring.

C. Hyundai Has Not Come Forward with Evidence That Would Permit a Jury to Find Fair Use Protection.

1. Overview of the TDRA's Text.

"Statutory analysis necessarily begins with the plain meaning of a law's text and, absent ambiguity, will generally end there." *Walters v. Industrial & Commercial Bank of China, Ltd.*, 651 F.3d 280, 290 (2d Cir.2011) (quotation marks omitted). An application of Hyundai's fair use defense must be grounded in the text of the TDRA, which states:

> (3) Exclusions
>
> The following shall not be actionable as dilution by blurring or dilution by tarnishment under this subsection:
>
> (A) Any fair use, including a nominative or descriptive fair use, or facilitation of such fair use, of a famous mark by another person other than as a designation of source for the person's own goods or services, including use in connection with—
>
> (i) advertising or promotion that permits consumers to compare goods or services; or
>
> (ii) identifying and parodying, criticizing, or commenting upon the famous mark owner or the goods or services of the famous mark owner,
>
> (B) All forms of news reporting and news commentary.
>
> (C) Any noncommercial use of a mark.

15 U.S.C. § 1125(c)(3). Hyundai asserts that any use of the Louis Vuitton marks "include[ed] use in connection with . . . identifying, parodying, criticizing, or commenting upon the famous mark owner or the goods and services of the famous mark owner." *Id.* § 1125(c)(3)(A)-(ii). Because "[a]ny noncommercial use of the mark" "shall not be actionable," *id.* § 1125(c)(3) (C), the text of the statute contemplates that fair use may apply in a commercial context.

As Hyundai notes, "there is limited case law discussing the fair use exception of the TDRA." In *Starbucks,* the Second Circuit first concluded that the Charbucks logo did not fall within the TDRA's fair-use framework because it designated the origins of goods, *see* 15 U.S.C. § 1125(c)(3) (A), but then considered whether its parodic qualities lessened the likelihood of blurring. 588 F.3d at 111–13. It concluded that because the Charbucks marks were, "at most, a subtle satire" of Starbucks, they did not qualify as a parody or "effect an 'increase [in] public identification [of the Starbucks Marks with Starbucks].' " *Id.* at 113 (alterations in original; quoting *Hormel Foods Corp. v. Jim Henson Productions, Inc.,* 73 F.3d 497, 506 (2d Cir.1996)).

2. The Record Includes Express Evidence that Hyundai Intended No Parody, Criticism or Comment Upon Louis Vuitton.

Through deposition testimony and in submissions by counsel, Hyundai has disclaimed any intention to parody, criticize or comment upon Louis Vuitton. Rather, it contends that the basketball design in the "Luxury" ad reflects a broader social comment, one that embodies "an effort to challenge consumers to rethink what it means for a product to be luxurious."

The text of the TDRA expressly states that fair use applies if dilution has arisen due to "use in connection with . . . identifying and parodying, criticizing, or commenting upon the famous mark owner or the goods or services of the famous mark owner." 15 U.S.C. § 1125(c)(3)(A)(ii) (emphasis added). Because Hyundai has disclaimed any comment, criticism or parody of Louis Vuitton, the "Luxury" ad does not, as a matter of law, qualify for fair use under the TDRA.

Louis Vuitton has directed the Court to deposition testimony in which individuals involved in the ad's creation state that the ad contains no comment on Louis Vuitton. In the Rule 30(b)(6) deposition, Perry testified as follows:

Q. Okay. Why didn't you just use the [un-altered] Louis Vuitton marks?

A. I don't recall the-Innocean came back to us and suggested adjustments.

Q. Well, why didn't you say, gee, to make the association even stronger, let's just use the Louis Vuitton marks?

A. The intent of the spot wasn't to-was to portray these over-the-top overwhelming luxury ideas.

Q. Right. And, in fact, you weren't commenting in any way or giving any commentary on Louis Vuitton, were you?

[Defense counsel]: Objection to the form. You may answer.

A. No.

Q. And the point here was not to actually make fun of Louis Vuitton or criticize Louis Vuitton, was it?

[Defense counsel]: Objection to the form.

A. That is correct.

Q. So why not use the Louis Vuitton marks themselves?

[Defense counsel]: Asked and answered. You may answer.

A. I suppose we could have. We opted not to. It wasn't the intent to try to—the intent wasn't specific to—the same reason why we didn't use specific brands on any of the other things we did. It was just to convey luxury. And to your point that the brown and gold conveyed luxury.

Q. The intent wasn't to say anything about Louis Vuitton, was it?

[Defense counsel]: Asked and answered.

A. Correct

Similarly, Perry testified that any commentary in the "Luxury" ad was of a broad, societal nature, and not directed to any item or brand. He stated:

Q. Well, were you trying to provide commentary on the specific things that are shown in the course of the commercial?

A. No.

Q. No. You were—you were trying to give a kind of general social comment, correct?

A. That's correct.

Q. And am I correct that the individual scenes that you used within the course of the commercial, you could use one, you could use another. It's just a matter of sort of decisions of which ones you liked best, right?

[Defense counsel]: Objection to the form of the question. You may answer.

A. Yes.

* * *

Q. In fact, you could have—had you wanted to, you could have continued to do the ad and have it make sense without any additional basketball scene at all; isn't that true?

A. Yes.

Boone, an account executive at the advertising firm that oversaw the "Luxury" ad, also testified that the ad contained no comment directed toward Louis Vuitton or its marks:

Q. So what other than Louis Vuitton were you attempting to have consumers take away from the basketball with these markings on it?

A. That was just one teeny, tiny piece of the commercial that was meant to signify luxury. . . . It was a 30-second commercial that in its totality at the end of watching that commercial they would say, oh, this commercial is about communicating that Hyundai is a vehicle that provides luxury to all, that we're bringing luxury-you don't have to spend gazillions of dollars to have luxury, that this car-it was about the car, about communicating the Hyundai product. We weren't trying to at all promote Louis Vuitton. That was not our objective. We wanted to sell Hyundais through this over-arching communication about that you can get luxury at an affordable price, that was what we were trying to do.

Q. You weren't commenting on Louis Vuitton in any way, were you?

[Defense counsel]: Object to the form of the question.

A. Can you be more specific with your question?

Q. I'm just asking you were you attempting through the commercial to comment on Louis Vuitton?

A. No.

Q. I'm sorry?

A. No.

Q. Were you in some ways trying to criticize Louis Vuitton?

A. No.

Q. Were you in some ways trying to make fun of Louis Vuitton?

A. No.

Q. Were you in any way trying to compare the Hyundai with Louis Vuitton?

A. No.

Q. And it's your position that this wasn't about Louis Vuitton at all, this basketball, is that correct?

A. Correct.

In opposition to Louis Vuitton's motion, Hyundai does not direct the Court to evidence that contradicts this testimony. It does not, for example, cite to testimony or other evidence in which other persons involved in the process explained an intention to parody or comment upon Louis Vuitton. Indeed, in its memorandum of law, Hyundai does not even address this evidence. Its opposition instead turns on discussion of legal authorities that do not apply the TDRA, with little engagement of the record cited by Louis Vuitton and minimal discussion of the statutory text.

Moreover, Hyundai's counsel states that the "Luxury" ad makes no comment on Louis Vuitton: "The symbols of 'old' luxury, including the [Louis Vuitton] Marks, were used as part of the Commercial's humorous social commentary on the need to redefine luxury during a recession, *even though the Commercial's overall intent was not to comment directly on [Louis Vuitton] or the other luxury symbols.*" It also states that "[a]lthough the Commercial was *not intended as a direct attack on any of the luxury products shown,* [Hyundai] used these items as part of a humorous social commentary on the current definition of luxury itself, which was a contrast to the 'luxury for all' offered by the Sonata."

In its opposition brief, Hyundai's counsel also states:

> Surely the Commercial could have been made by evoking a different designer's marks on the basketball (*e.g.*, Gucci, Fendi, etc.). Yet, *some* symbol of luxury had to be chosen to make the basketball an integral part of the basketball vignette; for commentary purposes, HMA chose LVM, the number one luxury brand in 2010.

Yet Hyundai does not suggest that Louis Vuitton or these other marks were the object of parody, comment or criticism, but instead that these brands were proxies for its broader observation about an "old" luxury that stands in contrast with the Sonata line. They were not comment, criticism or parody "upon the famous mark owner or the goods or services of the famous mark owner." 15 U.S.C. § 1125(c)(3)(A)(ii).

Louis Vuitton has come forward with evidence that the "Luxury" ad is not a comment, criticism or parody of Louis Vuitton. Hyundai has cited no evidence to the contrary. In addition, even Hyundai's counsel states that "the Commercial's overall intent was not to comment directly on [Louis Vuitton] or the other luxury symbols," but rather, to make a generalized statement that contrasts the Sonata with "old" luxury.

Based on this record, I conclude that no reasonable trier of fact could conclude that the Louis Vuitton-style marks shown in the "Luxury" ad could constitute "use in connection with . . . identifying and parodying, criticizing, or commenting upon the famous mark owner or the goods or services of the famous mark owner." 15 U.S.C. § 1125(c)(3)(A)(ii).

3. The Authorities Cited by the Parties Do Not Support Hyundai's Fair Use Argument.

Hyundai's fair use argument is resolved by the text of the TDRA. Both parties have, however, extensively briefed authority discussing fair use in other contexts. Even if the statute's text did not resolve Hyundai's argument, the authority cited by Hyundai would not support its claim to fair use. In discussing this authority, I am mindful that several of the decisions arose from bench trials or preliminary injunction motions, and therefore may be distinguishable. Certain other decisions explore fair use under the Copyright Act, 17 U.S.C. § 107, the text of which varies from the fair-use provision of the TDRA.

First, as under the TDRA, the Second Circuit previously concluded that to apply trademark fair use, any comment or parody must be directed to the plaintiff's mark. *See, e.g., Harley-Davidson,* 164 F.3d at 813 (the parody exception does not apply when the purported parody "makes no comment" on the original mark, and "simply uses it somewhat humorously to promote [its] own products and services. . . ."). As discussed, Hyundai has stated that the "Luxury" ad makes no comment upon Louis Vuitton.

Second, and relatedly, courts have rejected fair-use arguments that assert a use directed toward expansive social criticism, as opposed to a targeted comment or parody of the original. Applying the Copyright Act, *Rogers v. Koons,* 960 F.2d 301, 310 (2d Cir.1992), stated that absent a requirement that "the copied work must be, at least in part, an object of the parody," "there would be no real limitation on the copier's use of another's copyrighted work to make a statement on some aspect of society at large."

Third, the TDRA extends protection to "[a]ny noncommercial use of a mark," while simultaneously protecting a use "identifying and parodying, criticizing, or commenting upon the famous mark." 15 U.S.C §§ 1125(c)(3)(A)(ii) & 1125(c)(3)(C). As such, the TDRA contemplates the protection of parody, criticism or comment for commercial use. In other contexts, however, courts have concluded that the promotional use of a senior mark weighs against fair use protections. *See, e.g., Harley-Davidson,* 164 F.3d at 813: *Deere & Company v. MTD Products, Inc.,* 41 F.3d 39, 44–45 (2d Cir.1994) (promotional ads are not "worthy purposes of expression," but done "simply to sell products," a "purpose that can easily be achieved in other ways."). Given that Hyundai was "definitely laddering and borrowing equity from Louis Vuitton" and did so for the purpose of advertising the Sonata, under Second Circuit authority pre-dating the TDRA, Hyundai's promotional purpose would weigh against fair use protection.

Fourth, in opposition to Louis Vuitton's motion and in support of its own summary judgment motion, Hyundai heavily relies on authority that concluded, as a matter of law, that a defendant's use of a mark constituted parody or comment.[66] Courts have, however, not applied fair use when the defendant's mark is instead "a subtle satire" of the original. *Starbucks,* 588 F.3d at 113. The instances of parody that Hyundai cites involve over-the-top, unmistakable parodies of an original. *See, e.g., Cliffs Notes, Inc. v. Bantam Doubleday Dell Publishing Grp., Inc.,* 886 F.2d 490, 496–97 (2d Cir.1989) (variations in coloring, content and the labeling "a satire" alerted consumer of difference between parody and original); *Hormel Foods,* 73 F.3d at 501, 503 (an "an unclean 'grotesque' boar" puppet bears no resemblance to luncheon meat, and "consumers are likely to see the name 'Spa'am' as the joke it was intended to be."); *Tommy Hilfiger Licensing. Inc. v. Nature Labs. LLC,* 221 F.Supp.2d 410, 422 (S.D.N.Y.2002) (Mukasey, J.) (pet perfume called "Timmy Holedigger" was an "obvious parod[y]" of Tommy Hilfiger brand); *Louis Vuitton Malletier S.A. v. Haute Diggity Dog, LLC,* 507 F.3d 252, 260–61 (4th Cir.2007) (reciting "immediate[ ]" differences between dog chew toy and Louis Vuitton products). Even if Hyundai had not expressly disavowed comment, criticism or parody directed to Louis Vuitton, the cases identifying such clear-cut instances of fair use do not go toward the existence of triable issues of fact in the "Luxury" ad.

66. "Parody or satire, as we understand it, is when one artist, for comic effect or social commentary, closely imitates the style of another artist and in so doing creates a new art work that makes ridiculous the style and expression of the original." *Rogers,* 960 F.2d at 309–10.

Therefore, even if Hyundai's fair use argument was not resolved by the text of the TDRA, the authorities extensively briefed by the parties would not support a different result.

II. Hyundai's Motion for Summary Judgment is Denied.

Hyundai has moved for summary judgment in its favor on all claims asserted by Louis Vuitton. In addition to its trademark dilution claims, Louis Vuitton asserts trademark infringement claims under 15 U.S.C. §§ 1125(a)(1)(A) & 1114(a), and common-law unfair competition under New York law. The elements of a federal trademark-infringement claim and a New York unfair competition claim are "almost indistinguishable," except that New York requires an additional element of bad faith. *Grout Shield Distribs., LLC v. Elio E. Salvo, Inc.,*——F.Supp.2d——, 2011 WL 5560296, at *11 n. 15 (E.D.N.Y. Nov.16, 2011) (citing *U.S. Polo Ass'n, Inc. v. PRL USA Holdings, Inc.,* 800 F.Supp.2d 515 (S.D.N.Y.2011)).

The Lanham Act provides for a trademark-infringement claim if unapproved use of a mark is likely to cause confusion as to affiliation, sponsorship, or approval. 15 U.S.C. § 1125(a)(1)(A); *see generally Dallas Cowboys Cheerleaders, Inc. v. Pussycat Cinema, Ltd.,* 604 F.2d 200, 204 (2d Cir.1979) (reviewing infringement claim as it relates to affiliation, sponsorship or approval). To a large extent, both parties' submissions have failed to focus on the key issue plaintiff's trademark infringement claims: Whether prospective purchasers of Hyundai Sonatas incorrectly perceived Louis Vuitton to have sponsored, associated or affiliated with Hyundai based on the "Luxury" ad. *See, e.g., Dallas Cowboys Cheerleaders,* 604 F.2d at 204–05. The evidence and theory of liability in this context is likely to be significantly different than in many trademark actions, where allegedly confusing marks are employed by head-to-head competitors, *see, e.g., Starbucks,* 588 F.3d at 114 & n. 6, or even, as in *Tommy Hilfiger,* 221 F.Supp.2d at 416–21, where the allegedly infringing mark is displayed on products available for purchase, by the general public. In its motion for summary judgment, Hyundai often strays from the issue of whether Hyundai Sonata consumers have made misinformed purchasing decisions based on Louis Vuitton's role in the "Luxury" ad, and instead focuses heavily on the ad's purportedly expressive nature and the protections that should be afforded to it.

For the reasons explained, I conclude that Hyundai has not met the initial summary judgment burden of coming forward with facts that, if undisputed, would entitle it to judgment as a matter of law. *See Vt. Teddy Bear,* 373 F.3d at 244, In reviewing Hyundai's motion for summary judgment, I construe the record in the light most favorable to Louis Vuitton as the non-movant and draw all reasonable inferences in its favor. *Costello,* 632 F.3d at 45.

A. Weighing Consumer Confusion under Polaroid.

In *Polaroid Corp. v. Polarad Elecs., Corp.,* 287 F.2d 492, 495 (2d Cir.1961), Judge Friendly, writing for the panel, set forth eight factors to be considered in determining the likelihood of confusion. They are: (1) the strength of the mark; (2) the similarity of the parties' marks; (3) the proximity of the parties' products in the marketplace; (4) the likelihood that the plaintiff will "bridge the gap" between the products; (5) evidence of actual consumer confusion; (6) whether the defendant acted with bad faith in adopting the mark; (7) the defendant's product quality; and (8) consumer sophistication. A court is not "limited to consideration of only these factors." *Louis Vuitton Malletier,* 454 F.3d at 118. No single *Polaroid* factor is dispositive. *Nabisco, Inc. v. Warner Lambert Co.,* 220 F.3d 43, 46 (2d Cir.2000).

1. Strength of the Mark.

Hyundai asserts that Louis Vuitton's "undeniably strong" mark weighs against consumer confusion. It relies on *Yankee Publishing Inc. v. News America Publishing Inc.,* 809 F.Supp. 267, 271–73 (S.D.N.Y.1992), in which, at the conclusion of a bench trial, Judge Leval observed that a strong mark lessens the likelihood of confusion when consumers encounter the mark as a clear joke-in that case, a cover of New York magazine issue that was a "very recognizable takeoff" on the Old Farmer's Almanac. As previously discussed, however, the design of the "Luxury" basketball and the Louis Vuitton marks are not obviously different, and the "jest or commentary" reflected in the marks' use is less apparent than what Judge Leval found at the conclusion of a bench trial. *See also Starbucks,* 588 F.3d at 116 (a mark's strength weighs against confusion only "in the limited circumstance where the defendants' mark is a clear parody and there is widespread familiarity with the parody.") Moreover, Hyundai makes no citations to the record in support of this prong, but asserts, *ipse dixit,* that there is no confusion about the source of the Louis Vuitton marks in the "Luxury" ad. This is insufficient to establish its entitlement to summary judgment. *See Vt. Teddy Bear,* 373 F.3d at 244.

Hyundai has not established that the undisputed strength of Louis Vuitton's mark weighs in Hyundai's favor.

2. Similarity of the Marks.

As previously discussed, the modified marks in the "Luxury" ad closely resemble the Louis Vuitton marks, a similarity made all the more difficult to distinguish by the ball's brief appearance in the commercial. Additionally, as noted, Louis Vuitton has submitted some evidence that it has produced sports items, include niche, high-end products. Based on this record, Hyundai has not established that the marks are dissimilar. This factor does not weigh in Hyundai's favor.

3. Competitive Proximity.

Based upon the record submitted by the parties, there is virtually no competitive proximity between Louis Vuitton's luxury consumer goods and Hyundai's automobiles. Even noting Louis Vuitton's association with high-end vehicles, as depicted in "Louis Vuitton: The Art of the Automobile," its role apparently has been limited to sponsorships of certain shows and awards that honor rare car models. Similarly, as discussed, Louis Vuitton has set forth evidence that it has sold certain sports products, but not that it has sold any basketball-related items.

Therefore, construing the evidence in a light most favorable to Louis Vuitton as the non-movant, I conclude that the competitive proximity of Hyundai's vehicles and Louis Vuitton's luxury products is minimal to non-existent, and that this factor weighs in Hyundai's favor.

4. "Bridging the Gap."

"Bridging the gap refers to the senior user's interest in preserving avenues of expansion and entering into related fields." *Hormel Foods,* 73 F.3d at 504 (quotation marks omitted). There is no evidence that Louis Vuitton intends to further bridge the gap between luxury consumer goods and automobiles. As Hyundai notes, Louis Vuitton has no marks registered for use in automobiles. Counsel to Louis Vuitton states that certain other luxury brands, such as Gucci, have co-sponsored automobiles in recent years, but Louis Vuitton does not assert that it intends to do the same. As to bridging the gap to sports-related items, as discussed, Louis Vuitton has had a limited presence in the production and sale of items such as golf bags and certain soccer-related products. Louis Vuitton does not assert that it has an interest in further expanding to this market or entering into related fields. *See generally Hormel Foods,* 73 F.3d at 504. Similarly, there is no evidence that Hyundai intends to expand into products such as handbags.

Because Louis Vuitton has not come forward with evidence that it is likely to bridge the gap, this factor weighs in Hyundai's favor.

5. Actual Confusion

"[E]vidence of actual confusion regarding affiliation or sponsorship is also entirely relevant to the ultimate likelihood-of-confusion inquiry." *Morningside Group Ltd. v. Morningside Capital Group, LLC,* 182 F.3d 133, 141 (2d Cir.1999). "'The public's belief that the mark's owner sponsored or otherwise approved the use of the trademark satisfies the confusion requirement.' " *Starbucks,* 588 F.3d at 114. (quoting *Star Indus., Inc. v. Bacardi & Co.,* 412 F.3d 373, 384 (2d Cir.2005)).

In *Dallas Cowboys Cheerleaders,* 604 F.2d at 204, the defendant, which owned an adult-movie theater, argued that there could be no instance of confusion as to whether an adult film "originated with" plaintiff Dallas Cowboys Cheerleaders, Inc. based on the film's display of marks highly similar to those used by the well-known cheerleading squad. The Second Circuit stated that confusion was not limited to the film's origination, and instead could arise if the public believed that the plaintiff "sponsored or otherwise approved the use of the trademark"—in that case, a slightly altered version of a cheerleading uniform. *Id.* at 205. According to the Second Circuit, "the uniform depicted in 'Debbie Does Dallas' unquestionably brings to mind the Dallas Cowboys Cheerleaders. Indeed, it is hard to believe that anyone who had seen defendants' sexually depraved film could ever thereafter disassociate it from plaintiffs cheerleaders." *Id.*;[67] *see also Lois Sportswear, U.S.A., Inc. v. Levi*

67. In affirming the district court's conclusion of actual confusion, the court in *Dallas Cowboys Cheerleaders* did not rely on survey evidence or a record of consumer mis impressions so much as its own impression concerning the marks' similarity and the film's effect on the consuming public. *Id.* To some extent, it appears to have blended an analysis of actual confusion in the trademark

Strauss & Co., 799 F.2d 867, 872 (2d Cir.1986) (discussing confusion as to whether consumers perceived the plaintiff to have consented to defendant's use of unique stitching pattern).

Thus, in this case, actual confusion is narrowly focused on the issue of whether prospective Hyundai Sonata consumers incorrectly perceived Louis Vuitton to have affiliated with, associated with or sponsored the Hyundai "Luxury" ad.

As discussed in Hyundai's dilution claim, various postings on Twitter misapprehended the authenticity of the Louis Vuitton-like basketball. Other posts mentioned Louis Vuitton's apparent nexus with Hyundai. A poster named rebelscholar wrote, "Did I just see a Louis Vuitton basketball in a Hyundai commercial? ? ?" post by syntheticgent stated, "That luxury hyndai sonata commercial is hard body. LV basketball wit marble & gold backboard was so sick!" Finally, superbetch10 stated, "in one of Hyundai's ad, there is a guy holding a basketball with the LV logo." Certain other Twitter posts mentioned both brands, but did so in the context of remarking on this litigation, thereby reflecting an express awareness that Louis Vuitton had *not* sponsored or affiliated with the ad.[68] While anecdotal and limited, the postings to Twitter reflect some actual confusion as to Louis Vuitton's role in the Hyundai ad, in the same fashion as letters or phone calls. At the same time, Louis Vuitton's Rule 30(b)(6) witness testified that no consumer contacted Louis Vuitton about the commercial.[69]

The parties dispute the relevance and methodologies of one another's consumer surveys. "To be probative and meaningful . . . surveys . . . must rely upon responses by potential consumers of the products in question." *Universal City Studios, Inc. v. Nintendo Co., Ltd.,* 746 F.2d 112, 118 (2d Cir.1984) (quotation marks omitted; ellipsis in original). When a senior user asserts that its mark has been unlawfully used by a defendant, the relevant survey universe is the prospective purchasers of the defendant's products. *See Sterling Drug. Inc. v. Bayer AG,* 14 F.3d 733, 741 (2d Cir.1994) (discussing varying universes of survey participants as determined by plaintiff's theory of liability). In this case, the relevant universe would consist of prospective Hyundai Sonata purchasers, and the relevant underlying issue is whether that population erroneously believed that Louis Vuitton sponsored, affiliated or associated with Hyundai. *See id.*

According to Hyundai's expert, a net eight percent of likely Hyundai Sonata consumers either believed that Hyundai and Louis Vuitton were affiliated in the

---

infringement context with tarnishment in the dilution context. *Id.* (noting harm to reputation caused by likely association with adult film).

68. For instance, PurseBlog commented, "Anyone else notice the Hyundai commercial that LV is suing them over is still airing? The basketball does resemble LV much more on TV."

69. Louis Vuitton again relies on the responses of certain focus groups, but as previously discussed, its Rule 56.1 Statement and related submissions have provided no basis to meaningfully weigh the focus group evidence, and the Court declines to independently review the apparently lengthy videos of the groups that are included in the record.

"Luxury" ad, or that Louis Vuitton granted permission to use its marks. Ten percent stated that they were more likely to purchase a Honda Sonata as a result of the basketball in "Luxury." Hyundai asserts that these figures reflect an absence of actual confusion.

Louis Vuitton points out certain flaws in the Wind survey. They note that the basketball showed to the control group was a chestnut-brown color. Indeed, by depicting the ball in an atypical color that mimics the Louis Vuitton marks, a reasonable trier of fact may question the control's credibility. In addition, Wind asked participants, "In creating the commercial, do you think the company that produces the advertised brand or product [X] got or was required to get permission from any other company or brand?" As Louis Vuitton notes, the question is not only compound, but requires participants to draw a legal conclusion as to Hyundai's obligations. In *Louis Vuitton Malletier. S.A. v. Dooney & Bourke, Inc.*, 340 F.Supp.2d 415, 444–45 & 445 n. 161 (S.D.N.Y.2004), *vacated in part on other, grounds*, 454 F.3d 108 (2d Cir.2007), Judge Scheindlin concluded that a consumer-confusion study premised on a similar question "carr[ied] little weight," and cited other district courts that reached the same conclusion.[70]

To the extent that Louis Vuitton cites its own expert's opinions in opposition, that evidence is not directed to likely Hyundai Sonata purchasers and instead looks to the misapprehension among all participants who recognized the Louis Vuitton mark. While such views may be relevant in the dilution context—where the inquiry is directed toward perceptions of the senior mark and the whittling away of the senior mark's power—they carry little or no weight under the relevant survey universe as defined by *Sterling Drug*, 14 F.3d at 741, and do not shed light on the ultimate issue of whether prospective Hyundai purchasers mistakenly believed that Louis Vuitton sponsored, approved or affiliated with the "Luxury" ad.

For the reasons discussed, the Hyundai survey, while probative on association, contains flaws that are better assessed by a jury on the issue of actual confusion. Louis Vuitton's arguably most probative evidence is a scattering of Twitter postings by unknown users, and the research of its own expert is not probative of actual confusion under Second Circuit authority. On this record, neither party has submitted evidence that permits the Court to identify the presence or absence of actual confusion as a matter of law.

6. Bad Faith.

The bad faith prong looks to "whether the defendant adopted its mark with the intention of capitalizing on plaintiffs reputation and goodwill and any confusion between his and the senior user's product." *The Sports Authority, Inc. v. Prime Hospitality Corp.*, 89 F.3d 955, 964 (2d Cir.1996) (quotation marks omitted). As previously noted, Ewanick stated that the basketball in the "Luxury" ad was intended "to

70. There, the disputed survey asked respondents whether the defendant "needed to get permission or a license from the company whose bags were shown in the ad." 340 F.Supp.2d at 444–45.

represent luxury definitely laddering and borrowing equity from Louis Vuitton." Several other witnesses testified that the basketball design was intended to closely resemble the Louis Vuitton marks.

As also noted, when Hyundai's advertising firm sought permission from thirteen luxury brands to use their marks in an advertisement, six expressly declined and the others, including Louis Vuitton, never responded. This provides some evidence that Hyundai believed that it needed permission to use the Louis Vuitton mark, but elected to proceed with the stylized basketball anyway.

Lastly, when Louis Vuitton requested that Hyundai stop airing the ad, Hyundai elected to go forward with its planned broadcast, even after commencement of this litigation.

In light of the foregoing, I conclude that Hyundai has not established as a matter of law that the bad-faith prong weighs in its favor.

7. Product Quality.

As previously discussed, there is minimal competitive proximity between Louis Vuitton and Hyundai. Louis Vuitton nevertheless contends that because of divergent product quality, it is harmed by any confusion of its mark's association with Hyundai, noting that Hyundai "aspires" to be a luxury brand, but is not comparable to Louis Vuitton.

Assuming the accuracy of Louis Vuitton's characterization of Hyundai, it is nevertheless the case that the dissimilarity between plaintiff's luxury consumer goods and defendant's automobiles are unlikely to cause confusion "because the products are not otherwise related as to makeup, usage, etc." *Hormel*, 73 F.3d at 505. I therefore agree with Hyundai's argument that this factor is irrelevant to determining consumer confusion.

8. Consumer Sophistication

Given the expense of purchasing a new automobile and the market niche for Louis Vuitton's luxury products, the consumers of both Louis Vuitton products and Hyundai Sonatas are likely to be highly sophisticated and attentive to their respective purchases. *See, e .g., Arrow Fastener Co. v. Stanley Works*, 59 F.3d 384, 399 (2d Cir.1995) (detailed purchasing process for pneumatic staplers supports consumer sophistication); *Louis Vuitton Malletier v. Dooney & Bourke, Inc.*, 561 F. Supp.2d 368, 389 (S.D.N.Y.2008) ("It cannot be reasonably disputed that consumers of products offered by . . . Louis Vuitton . . . are sophisticated and discerning.").

Based on this record, I cannot conclude, as a matter of law, that consumer sophistication weighs in favor of either party. Because of the close similarity between the Louis Vuitton marks and the basketball design, a sophisticated consumer could plausibly conclude that the design in the "Luxury" ad originated with Louis Vuitton. A sophisticated consumer also could be more likely than others to distinguish between the marks.

Hyundai has not come forward with evidence that establishes this prong in its favor as a matter of law.

9. Hyundai's First Amendment Arguments.

As noted, courts are not limited to the *Polaroid* factors when weighing the likelihood of consumer confusion. *Louis Vuitton Malletier,* 454 F.3d at 118. I briefly address Hyundai's First Amendment arguments as specifically directed to plaintiff's trademark-infringement and unfair-competition claims.

Similar to its argument asserting a fair use defense under the TDRA, Hyundai's motion for summary judgment on Louis Vuitton's trademark-infringement claim is interspersed with contentions as to the "Luxury" ad's expressive value and humorous intentions. It contends that the ad's expressive value weighs in Hyundai's favor on points of the marks' strength, similarity of the marks and bad faith. As previously noted, however, any comment in the "Luxury" ad is far more subtle than, for example, the parody that inheres in a Muppet depicting an unkempt boar, *Hormel Foods,* 73 F.3d at 503, or a pet perfume that directly pokes fun at a high-end fashion label, *Tommy Hilfiger,* 221 F.Supp.2d at 415, 422. Moreover, Hyundai has acknowledged that it intended to make no comment on the Louis Vuitton mark, but instead offered a broader social critique. The Second Circuit has deemed such motivations unworthy of protection. *Rogers,* 960 F.2d at 310.

Therefore, based on the record and the law of this Circuit, I conclude that any intended expression in the "Luxury" ad does not weigh in Hyundai's favor.

10. Weighing the Factors.

As noted, I conclude that the minimal competitive proximity and likelihood of bridging the gap weigh in favor of Hyundai. Hyundai also has established that any difference in product quality is not material to assessing consumer confusion. On the point of actual confusion, the evidence provided by both parties, while somewhat probative, is insufficient to determine as a matter of law whether this prong favors Hyundai. On all other *Polaroid* factors, Hyundai has failed to set forth evidence that entitle it to judgment in its favor as a matter of law.

The *Polaroid* factors guide a court in reaching the ultimate question of whether there is a likelihood of consumer confusion. *See, e.g., Morningside Grp.,* 182 F.3d at 142 (good faith is not alone dispositive to the ultimate issue of consumer confusion); *Lee Myles Auto Grp., LLC v. Fiorello,* 2010 WL 3466687, at *3 (S.D.N.Y. Aug.25, 2010) ("The *Polaroid* factors must be considered in the context of how each factor supports or undermines the ultimate issue of whether a consumer will be confused by the disputed marks."). They are not to be applied using "some rigid formula," and "[e]ach case" may "present[ ] its own peculiar circumstances." *Lois Sportswear,* 799 F.2d at 872. Hyundai has not made any effort to explain how a balancing of the factors should be applied in this case, and asserts only that because all factors should weigh in its favor, there is no likelihood of confusion, especially "against the backdrop of First Amendment principles." It does not argue that the Court should place special emphasis on the lack of competitive proximity between Louis Vuitton or Hyundai, or emphasize the lack of evidence that Louis Vuitton intends to "bridge the gap" at some point in the future.

In balancing the *Polaroid* factors, I conclude that Hyundai has not established that it is entitled to judgment as a matter of law on Louis Vuitton's trademark infringement claims. Hyundai's motion for summary judgment is therefore denied.

B. Hyundai's Motion as to Damages is Denied.

As noted, 15 U.S.C. § 1125(c)(5)(B)(i) allows for damages only if a defendant "willfully intended to trade on the recognition of the famous mark."

Hyundai argues that, even in the event that Louis Vuitton can establish willfulness, the record would not permit a reasonable juror to conclude "that even one" Sonata sale resulted from the stylized basketball in the "Luxury" ad. Hyundai argues that the "Luxury" ad was "just a first step in a buying process," and that the evidence is too attenuated to attribute any sales to the ad. In opposition, Louis Vuitton argues that "the simplest measure" of damages is for a jury to award it "the roughly $3.2 million" that Hyundai spent to produce and air the ad. Louis Vuitton also cites to the report of its damages expert, Laura Stamm, who has opined that the Louis Vuitton-like designs were "integral" to the "Luxury" ad, that the ad caused a spike in visits to Hyundai's website, and that "approximately $14.5 million" in profits "can be attributed to the dilutive and infringing advertisement. . . ." Hyundai asserts that Stamm's conclusions are unreliable because they are extrapolations based on studies of year-long advertising campaigns that do not compare to the "Luxury" ad's limited run. Based on the record and the parties' contentions, a finder of fact is best positioned to determine how much credit should be afforded to Stamm's research, or whether, as Hyundai contends, her views are "simply not plausible."

Conclusion

Louis Vuitton's motion for summary judgment in its favor on liability on Counts I and II of the Amended Complaint is GRANTED.

Hyundai's motion for summary judgment is DENIED.

SO ORDERED.

Notes

1. How do you think the judge viewed Hyundai's risk-taking in showing the commercial after receiving the cease-and-desist letter? After receiving the complaint?

2. What advice would you have given Hyundai after receipt of Louis Vuitton's cease-and-desist letter?

When dealing with physical locations, an advertiser must secure permission from the property owner, through a location release, for a photo or film shoot. The purpose of this agreement is to designate the parties' respective rights and duties with respect to the use of the location and depiction of the premises. In addition, an advertiser should determine whether any architectural works, as well as any designs upon such architectural works, are subject to copyright protection. The Copyright Act protects architectural works created on or after December 1, 1990. The Copyright Act also protects unconstructed architectural works embodied in unpublished plans or drawings on December 1, 1990, if the design was constructed on or before December 31, 2002. Thus, for example, houses, office buildings, churches, and museums are subject to copyright protection. Architectural works or depictions of such works may, in some instances, also be subject to a trademark claim. It is important to note that any element affixed or otherwise separable from the building or architectural work may be subject to copyright or trademark claims.

2. Right of Publicity

A right of publicity allows a person to control and profit from the commercial use of their identity. The personal traits that are protected under the right of publicity claim are the name, image, voice, and miscellaneous traits of an individual. Therefore, advertising the name, image, voice, or any identifying traits of an individual, whether alive or deceased, must be done with the permission of that individual or, if they are deceased, their heirs or estate. Not every state has post-mortem rights, therefore it is important to determine the scope of protection provided under pertinent state laws.

To succeed on a right to publicity claim, the individual's identity must be identifiable or recognizable, have commercial value, and their likeness must have been used for a commercial purpose without their permission. If an advertisement incorrectly suggests an endorsement of the product, it can lead to a trademark or false association claim.

See, e.g., Heigl v. Duane Reade, Inc., No. 1:14-CV-2502 (S.D.N.Y. 2014); *Kim Kardashian v. The Gap, Inc.*, No. 2:11-CV-06568 (C.D. Cal. 2011); *Monge v. Maya Magazines, Inc.*, 688 F.3d 1164 (9th Cir., 2012) (fair use analysis of celebrity photos); *Ariana Grande-Butera v. Forever 21, Inc.*, and *Riley Rose LLC*, 2:19-cv-07600 (C.D. Cal.); *Kimsaprincess, Inc. and Kim Kardashian West v. Missguided USA (Finance) Inc.*, and *Missguided Limited*, 2:19-cv-01258 (C.D. Cal).

Heigl v. Duane Reade, Inc.

No. 1:14-cv-02502-ER (S.D.N.Y. Apr. 9, 2014)

Complaint . . .

Plaintiff Katherine Heigl, by her attorneys Ballard Spahr LLP, for her complaint in this action against Defendant Duane Reade, Inc., alleges as follows:

Nature of the Action

1. The actress Katherine Heigl, who has starred in the television series *Grey's Anatomy* and in films including *27 Dresses* and *The Ugly Truth*, was recently

photographed without her consent by *paparazzi* in New York City leaving a Duane Reade pharmacy. Duane Reade then misused and misappropriated the photograph for its own commercial advertising, distributing the photo with Duane Reade's own promotional slogans on its *Twitter* and *Facebook* accounts, all without Ms. Heigl's knowledge or approval. Duane Reade has ignored a written demand that it stop this unlawful activity, and brazenly continues to exploit Ms. Heigl's image for commercial gain, despite her strenuous objection.

2. For its continuing willful violation of the law, Duane Reade is liable for not less than $6 million in compensatory and punitive or treble damages. While the harm to Ms. Heigl is substantial, she intends to donate all monies recovered in this lawsuit to a charitable foundation, the Jason Debus Heigl Foundation. The Foundation focuses on animal welfare through animal relocation, humane education, grant giving, and training for companion animals.

3. Duane Reade's actions make it liable for (i) violation of the Lanham Act, 15 U.S.C. § 1051 *et seq.;* (ii) violation of Plaintiff's right of privacy and publicity under Sections 50 and 51 of the New York Civil Rights Law; and (iii) unfair competition under New York law. Each of these claims arises from Duane Reade's unauthorized use, done knowingly and willfully, of Ms. Heigl's name, picture, image, and likeness for commercial advertising and other trade purposes within New York State and elsewhere.

The Parties

4. As set forth further below, Plaintiff Katherine Heigl ("Plaintiff") is a major motion picture and television actress, celebrity, producer and philanthropist, whose persona has substantial financial and other value. She is a citizen of the State of Utah.

5. Defendant Duane Reade, Inc. ("Defendant" or "Duane Reade") is a Delaware corporation with its principal place of business in New York City at 40 Wall Street, New York, New York 10005. On information and belief, Defendant is a leading retail pharmacy chain in New York State and the New York City tri-state area in terms of number of locations, customer base, and amount of revenue. Defendant heavily advertises itself, its products and its services widely in all media, including via the Internet and social media, using, for example, Facebook and Twitter to reach millions of customers.

Jurisdiction And Venue

6. The Court has subject matter jurisdiction over this action pursuant to 15 U.S.C. § 1121 (actions arising under the Federal Trademark Act), 28 U.S.C. § 1331 (federal question), 28 U.S.C. § 1338 (civil action arising under statutory trademark law and related unfair competition claims), and under 28 U.S.C. § 1332(a) (diversity) because the amount in controversy exceeds $75,000 (exclusive of interest and costs) and the dispute is between citizens of different states. Jurisdiction exists over the state law claims pursuant to 28 U.S.C. § 1367(a) (supplemental jurisdiction).

7. This Court has jurisdiction over Defendant because Defendant is, and at all times relevant to this action has been, doing business in the State of New York, having continuous and systematic business contacts with New York carried out with a fair measure of permanence and continuity here. In particular, Defendant's business headquarters and principal place of business are located in New York City, and Defendant is registered with the New York Department of State, Division of Corporations, to do business in New York State.

8. Venue is proper in the Southern District of New York pursuant to 28 U.S.C. § 1391(b) and (c) because Defendant resides in this District, being subject to personal jurisdiction here, and because a substantial part of the events giving rise to Plaintiff's claims in this action occurred in this District.

Facts

Katherine Heigl's Creation, Use and Promotion of Her Valuable Professional Persona

9. Plaintiff is a highly successful television and motion picture actress, producer and celebrity. She has starred in the major motion pictures *27 Dresses, The Ugly Truth, Knocked Up, Life As We Know It,* and *New Year's Eve,* among others. According to the film industry web-site www.boxofficemojo.com, Plaintiff's films have grossed over one billion dollars worldwide. Plaintiff also has appeared in numerous television programs and series, starring in the highly successful long-running television series, *Grey's Anatomy,* for which Plaintiff received a Primetime Emmy Award for Outstanding Supporting Actress in a Drama Series for her role as the character Dr. lzzie Stevens. Plaintiff was a member of the *Grey's Anatomy* cast that received the Screen Actors Guild Award for Outstanding Performance by an Ensemble in a Drama Series, and has twice been nominated for a Golden Globe Award. Plaintiff recently completed filming three motion pictures that will be released in 2014 and 2015 and has been in New York City during the period her likeness was misappropriated by Defendant while starring in a one-hour pilot for NBC. Plaintiff continues to be in high demand in the entertainment industry.

10. In addition to her celebrity in the entertainment world, Plaintiff is a founder of, and grants selected use of her name and likeness to, the non-profit Jason Debus Heigl Foundation (the "Foundation"). The Foundation maintains a website at www.jasonheiglfoundation.org.

11. As a consequence of her work in the entertainment and philanthropic worlds, Plaintiff is a highly recognized celebrity. Plaintiff maintains a Twitter account with over 754,000 followers (@KatieHeigl). A recent search for "Katherine Heigl" on the Google search engine returned over 3.2 million results.

12. Plaintiff's picture, image and likeness enjoy wide-spread recognition and monetary value. To prevent any diminution of that value, Plaintiff has carefully and deliberately protected her valuable professional name, picture, image, likeness, and persona—that is, her legally-recognized right of privacy and publicity—from exploitation through unauthorized commercial advertising. Accordingly, when

Plaintiff chooses to endorse a product or service, she is highly selective and well compensated.

13. Furthermore, in connection with the Foundation, Plaintiff carefully authorizes and controls the use of her name, picture, image and likeness for charitable fundraising purposes and other activities of the Foundation.

14. Plaintiff was never approached by and did not authorize Defendant to license or use Plaintiff's name, picture or image for any purpose, including commercial advertising, sponsorship or endorsement.

Duane Reade's Use of Social Media For Its Advertising in New York and Elsewhere

15. Duane Reade engages in commercial advertising of its company, goods, and services using social media sites, including Facebook, Twitter, Pinterest, and others.

16. Defendant's Twitter account can be found at www.twitter.com, with the user name @DuaneReade. A printout of its Twitter home page created on March 31, 2014 is attached hereto as Exhibit A. It is 36 pages and includes Defendant's commercial advertising postings ("Tweets") going back to March 14, 2014. Defendant's Twitter account has 2.02 million followers, and states in the identification headline that "Duane Reade is the largest and most recognized drugstore chain in the New York Metropolitan area serving customers since 1960." As of April 1, 2014, Defendant has tweeted advertising messages to its two-million-plus followers over 19,900 times. (Ex. A, p. 1).

17. Defendant links its Internet and social media sites to maximize the commercial advertising impact of Defendant's Internet marketing program. Defendant's Twitter account includes a link to Defendant's Facebook account, found at facebook.com/duanereade. Defendant's home page on the Internet, found at www.duanereade.com, includes prominent graphical links to Facebook, Twitter, Pinterest, and other sites under the banner headline "Get Social with Duane Reade."

18. The purpose of Defendant's social media activities is commercial advertising aimed at attracting customers and revenue, especially social media savvy customers in the coveted young adult demographics. As a finalist for an advertising industry "Shorty Award" (http://industry.shortyawards.com), Duane Reade boasted that its online "Get Social with Duane Reade" campaign is intended to "drive awareness, engagement and increase sales at all retail stores using digital marketing strategies," and that its social media presence "[a]chieved 4 billion+ impressions across the social web. This is huge especially for a regional drugstore chain. To achieve the same number of impressions in USA Today, an ad spend of 2,249 full-page ads priced at over $467 Million would be necessary." Duane Reade also boasts that "DR is now the most widely followed drugstore in the world, dominating the social media landscape and stealing the voice from their national competitors."

19. Defendant's Tweets predominantly promote commercial advertisements for a wide range of its products and services. For example, on March 14, 2014, Defendant

tweeted *"Crunch, crunch Munch! It's National Potato Chip Day! Enjoy!"* followed by a link to an advertisement for Defendant's own "DeLish" label food product. (Ex. A, p. 35). In another representative commercial advertisement Tweet on March 17, 2014, Defendant tweeted *"Experience the best of beauty from around the world at #DuaneReade LOOK Boutique March 17-21 See .flyer for info,"* with a link to an advertisement for beauty products. (Ex. A, p. 31).

20. Defendant's Twitter page typically relies on short text tweets, followed by hyperlinks to full page photographic advertisements for products and services. Defendant's calculated social media advertising methods only occasionally use large photographs immediately visible along with a tweet to make an extra impression upon consumers. Such photos typically include pictures of Defendant's products accompanied by links to product ads, such as Duane Reade food products (Ex. A, pp. 17, 19, 20), other products sold by Duane Reade (Ex. A, p. 27), and Duane Reade store premises (Ex. A, p. 22).

Defendant's Actions in Violation of Plaintiff's Valuable Rights

21. On or about March 18, 2014, Defendant posted a Tweet accompanied by a large and prominently displayed photograph of Plaintiff, stating *"Love a quick #DuaneReade run? Even @KatieHeigl can't resist shopping #NYC's favorite drugstore."* (Ex. A, p. 25–26).

22. Clicking on the Plaintiff's featured photograph in the March 18, 2014 Tweet automatically expands to a full-size photograph of Plaintiff, with the same Tweet text, attached hereto as Exhibit B (the "Heigl Photograph").

23. On or about March 18, 2014, Defendant posted the Heigl Photograph on Defendant's Facebook page, under the "Photo Album" section with the heading "Duane Reade's Photos ·Duane Reade's Page." The Facebook posting included a new and revised text, making it clear that @KatieHeigl was indeed the famous actress Katherine Heigl, and highlighting that Defendant's false advertising message—that Plaintiff endorses Duane Reade—was the sole reason for Duane Reade to prominently feature the photograph. Capitalizing on their original unauthorized Tweet to maximum advantage on their Facebook page, Defendant changed "favorite drugstore" to "most convenient drugstore" to drive home the commercial message: *"Don't you just love a quick #Duane Reade run? Even Katherine Heigl can't resist shopping at #NYC's most convenient drugstore!"* Copies of the Face book text and Heigl Photograph posting are attached hereto as Exhibit C.

24. The Heigl Photograph is a typical "Paparazzi" shot, depicting Plaintiff walking on the street in New York City, in a private moment looking away from the camera, apparently exiting a Duane Reade location and carrying Duane Reade shopping bags. The photograph posted on the Twitter home page shows Plaintiff from the waist up. The Heigl Photograph accessed via links on Twitter and Facebook shows a full-length image of Plaintiff.

25. The Heigl Photograph's lower right corner includes a logo "Just Jared," and the Facebook posting (Ex. C) references the source of the Heigl Photograph to the

website "Just Jared," as follows: "*Image via: justjared.com/photo-gallery/3073133 /katherine-heigl- signs-with-wmeleaves-caa/02.*"

26. On information and belief, Just Jared is a celebrity news website specializing in so-called Paparazzi photographs of celebrities in candid moments. The website www.justjared.com includes the Heigl Photograph, and several others taken the same moment (including a photo of Nancy Heigl), as part of a news story dated March 17, 2014, entitled "Katherine Heigl Signs With WME After Leaving Creative Artists Agency." A copy of the Just Jared news article and photographs is attached hereto as Exhibit D. Clicking on the Just Jared photos leads to a full-size version of the Heigl Photograph, attached hereto as Exhibit E.

27. On information and belief, Defendant obtained a Paparazzi photograph originally published by Just Jared as part of Just Jared's news reporting on Katherine Heigl's career, and Defendant misappropriated and purloined the photograph for use completely unrelated to its original news context, by stripping the photo of its original editorial context. Defendant's actions involved multiple uses on multiple Internet websites, and constituted an unauthorized publication for commercial advertisement and "endorsement" by Plaintiff of Duane Reade.

28. Duane Reade's Facebook page "Photo Album" link directs viewers to a collection of photographs that include product and merchandise depictions. This page featured Plaintiff, very prominently, as the only celebrity among product and other photos. This use and depiction was calculated to attract consumers to the Duane Reade brand by falsely implying that Plaintiff endorses Defendant. A copy of Defendant's Facebook Photo Album page showing this prominent use of Plaintiff's image is attached hereto as Exhibit F.

29. On information and belief, Duane Reade's Twitter account normally includes only occasional Duane Reade products or store premises photographs displayed as the user scrolls through the Tweet postings. But among recent photographs, Plaintiff's image stands out as the only celebrity image, thereby designed to exploit Plaintiff's image to suggest false cachet for Defendant's Twitter page and imply falsely that Plaintiff endorses Defendant. On information and belief, Defendant has singled out Plaintiff simply because she happened to be a customer on one occasion at a Duane Reade store, and a photograph of that occasion happened to be included in reporting on entertainment-industry news.

30. Use of Plaintiff's image under these circumstances improperly exploited Plaintiff's name and likeness, as a celebrity, for Defendant's commercial advertising and purposes of trade, without authorization. Such use was done knowingly and willfully, as evidenced by Defendant's manipulation of and changes to the Duane Reade advertising messages in the captions, after Defendant had intentionally stripped out all evidence of the original news context to the Heigl Photograph.

31. Indeed, Duane Reade's infringing and illegal acts required multiple, discrete steps, including, on information and belief, (i) purloining and misappropriating the Heigl Photograph from the Just Jared entertainment news web-site; (ii) eliminating

all news reporting aspects of the original posting; (iii) then posting the Heigl Photograph on Twitter with a text advertisement for Defendant, including a link to the full size Heigl Photograph; and (iv) finally, posting the Heigl Photograph on Facebook on Defendant's Photo Album with a revised and improved advertising message, and again omitting any news reporting aspects of the original use of the photograph of Plaintiff.

32. Defendant's actions were at all times intentional and knowing and in bad faith. At no time did Defendant seek or obtain any authorization from Plaintiff for Defendant's use of the Heigl Photograph. Defendant has improperly sought to transform news photography into unauthorized commercial advertising and endorsements for its own benefit.

33. On or about March 19, 2014, Plaintiff's counsel sent a cease and desist letter to Defendant, demanding that Defendant cease its illegal acts and respond immediately. Defendant ignored Plaintiff's demands.

First Claim (Section 43(a) of the Lanham Act)

34. Plaintiff repeats, realleges, and incorporates by reference the allegations of paragraphs I through 33 above as if fully set forth herein.

35. Defendant has in commerce made a false or misleading representation of fact in connection with goods or services that is likely to cause consumer confusion as to the origin, sponsorship, or approval of the goods or services.

36. Defendant's commercial advertising campaigns on the Internet and in social media are aimed and occur across state lines in the New York metropolitan area, including New York, New Jersey, Connecticut, and via the Internet to all fifty states and internationally.

37. Plaintiff has not authorized Defendant to use her valuable name, picture, image, or likeness.

38. Defendant's use of Plaintiff's name, picture, image, and likeness falsely implies that Plaintiff sponsors, endorses, or is affiliated with Defendant's goods and services and is likely to cause consumer confusion, and therefore constitutes false advertising and unfair competition.

39. Defendant's acts have been willful, knowing, deliberate, and intended to benefit Defendant at Plaintiff's expense.

40. As a direct and proximate result of Defendant's unlawful acts, Plaintiff has been, and continues to be, damaged. Plaintiff has suffered economic and reputational injury flowing directly from Defendant's unlawful acts, including reputational injury resulting from false endorsement of Defendant's services and products which deprived Plaintiff of her valuable right to select what endorsements to grant, including and how those endorsements are presented to and perceived by the public, as evidenced by comments on Defendant's Twitter page and elsewhere, all of which directly damage Plaintiff's ability to control and negotiate endorsement agreements and her valuable rights.

41. Plaintiff is entitled to recover from Defendant compensatory damages, Defendant's profits resulting from its unlawful conduct, treble damages and reasonable attorney fees and costs in such amounts to be determined at trial.

42. Furthermore, Plaintiff has no adequate remedy at law to compensate her fully for the injury caused by Defendant's unlawful acts and which would be caused by any further infringement of Plaintiff's rights. Accordingly, the Court should enjoin Defendant from committing future unlawful acts and infringements as alleged here.

Second Claim (Violation of New York Civil Rights Law Sections 50 and 51)

43. Plaintiff repeats, realleges, and incorporates by reference the allegations of paragraphs 1 through 33 above as if fully set forth herein.

44. Defendant has used Plaintiff's name, picture, image and likeness within the State of New York for advertising purposes or for the purpose of trade without Plaintiff's consent.

45. Defendant's use of Plaintiff's name, picture, image and likeness was willful, malicious and in conscious disregard of Plaintiff's rights.

46. Defendant's conduct violates Plaintiff's rights under Sections 50 and 51 of the Civil Rights Law of the State of New York.

47. As a result of Defendant's unauthorized use of Plaintiff's name, picture, image, and likeness, Plaintiff has been, and continues to be, damaged.

48. Defendant received a cease and desist letter from Plaintiff's counsel but continues to intentionally ignore Plaintiff's legal rights and to profit therefrom.

49. Defendant has purposefully used Plaintiff's name, picture, Image, and likeness in a manner that it knew to be unlawful pursuant to Sections 50 and 51 of the New York Civil Rights Law. Defendant knew it was required to obtain Plaintiff's consent for its use of her name and the Heigl Photograph. Defendant never sought such consent.

50. Plaintiff is entitled to recover from Defendant all damages for her injuries sustained by reason of Defendant's unlawful actions, as well as exemplary and punitive damages, under Section 51 of the New York Civil Rights Law in such amounts to be determined at trial.

51. Furthermore, Plaintiff has no adequate remedy at law to compensate her fully for the injury caused by Defendant's unlawful acts and which would be caused by any further infringement of Plaintiff's rights. Accordingly, the Court should enjoin Defendant from committing future unlawful acts and infringements as alleged here.

Third Claim (Common Law Unfair Competition)

52. Plaintiff repeats, realleges, and incorporates by reference the allegations of paragraphs 1 through 33 above as if fully set forth herein.

53. Defendant's actions alleged herein constitute unfair competition within the State of New York and in violation of New York law because Defendant acted

intentionally to mislead and confuse consumers, or caused a likelihood of consumer confusion, and acted in bad faith.

54. Plaintiff carefully monitors and controls the valuable commercial use of her name, picture, image, and likeness.

55. Defendant's recent Facebook and Twitter pages prominently feature the Heigl Photograph and Plaintiff's name in a manner that misleads and confuses consumers.

56. Defendant acted in bad faith by first misappropriating the Heigl Photograph, then using it stripped of its original news-reporting function to falsely imply that Plaintiff's valuable endorsement rights were granted to Defendant—even though they were not—and by using Plaintiff's name in conjunction with at least two advertising messages and multiple links to commercial advertising for Defendant's products and services.

57. As a direct and proximate result of Defendant's acts of unfair competition, Plaintiff has been, and continues to be, damaged, and is entitled to recover from Defendant damages in such amount to be determined at trial. Defendant's acts of unfair competition were willful, malicious and in conscious disregard of Plaintiff's rights, entitling Plaintiff to recover punitive damages.

58. Furthermore, Plaintiff has no adequate remedy at law to compensate her fully for the injury caused by Defendant's unlawful acts and which would be caused by any further infringement of Plaintiff's rights. Accordingly, the Court should enjoin Defendant from committing future unlawful acts and infringements as alleged here.

Relief Requested

WHEREFORE, Plaintiff respectfully demands judgment against Defendant as follows:

(a) on the First Claim under Section 43(a) of the Lanham Act, awarding Plaintiff (i) compensatory damages in an amount to be determined at trial; (ii) the amount of Defendant's profits resulting from its unlawful conduct; (iii) treble damages as authorized by statute; and (iv) reasonable attorney fees and costs as also authorized by statute;

(b) on the Second Claim for violation of New York Civil Rights Law Sections 50 and 51, awarding Plaintiff (i) damages for her injuries sustained by reason of Plaintiff's unlawful actions; (ii) exemplary and punitive damages; and (iii) reasonable attorney fees and costs;

(c) on the Third Claim for unfair competition, awarding Plaintiff(i) compensatory damages in an amount to be determined at trial; and (ii) exemplary and punitive damages;

(d) on each of the First, Second and Third Claims, permanently enjoining Defendant, and its agents, officers, servants, employees, successors and assigns and all others acting in concert or privity with Defendant, from using, imitating, or copying Plaintiff's name, picture, image, or likeness in connection with any promotion, advertisement, display, sale, or circulation of any services or products, including commercial advertising use, whether express or implied, on the Internet or social media in any form; and

(e) awarding such other and further relief as this Court deems just and proper.

* * *

Notes

1. This case was settled by Duane Reade's agreement to pay an undisclosed sum to Heigl's favorite charity.

2. What could Duane Reade have done to obtain permission to use the photo? What is the likelihood that it would have obtained such permission?

3. Draft a brief set of rules for your marketing department on the use of celebrity photos.

Kim Kardashian West v. Missguided Ltd.

No. 2:19-cv-01258 (C.D. Cal. Feb. 20, 2019)

Complaint for:

(1) **Violation of Statutory Right of Publicity (Cal. Civ. Code § 3344);**

(2) **Violation of Common Law Right of Publicity;**

(3) **False Designation of Origin (15 U.S.C. § 1125(a));**

(4) **Trademark Infringement (15 U.S.C. § 1114(1));**

(5) **Common Law Trademark Infringement**

* * *

Plaintiffs Kimsaprincess, Inc. and Kim Kardashian West (individually and collectively, "Plaintiffs" or "Kardashian") alleges as follows:

Introduction

1. Kim Kardashian West is a television celebrity, model, and spokesperson. Kardashian has been immensely successful in developing and promoting her own fashion, beauty, and other products that have sold under the famous "Kardashian" name and related trademarks. In addition, she has been highly sought after for many years, and continuing to this day, as a paid spokesperson for third-party products. With Kardashian enjoying one of the largest social media followings of *any* celebrity in the world, companies pay enormous sums of money to engage Kardashian to help promote their brands. Even a single social media post by Kardashian can fetch fees of several hundred thousand dollars, and her longer-term endorsement arrangements regularly garner fees in the millions of dollars.

2. While most companies understand and respect Kardashian's right to control and approve any use of her name and likeness in the promotion of products, other companies have sought out ways to leverage her celebrity status and social media following without seeking her consent, thus effectively turning her into an unwitting and unwilling spokesperson of their products. In the instant case, Defendants Missguided USA (Finance) Inc. and Missguided Limited (collectively, "Defendants" or "Missguided") have made this sort of unlawful misappropriation of Kardashian's persona—and that of many other celebrities as well—a cornerstone of their marketing and sales strategy.

3. Like other "fast fashion" companies, Missguided, which sells clothing throughout the world on its www.missguidedus.com website (among others), has become notorious for "knocking off" the clothing worn by celebrities like Kardashian. But Missguided does not merely replicate the looks of these celebrities as seen on red carpets, in paparazzi photos, and in social media posts. Missguided systematically uses the names and images of Kardashian and other celebrities to advertise and spark interest in its website and clothing. Missguided's website and social media pages are riddled with images of and references to Kardashian that are designed to promote the www.missguidedus.com website and to elicit sales of clothing that are purportedly "inspired by" Kardashian. Missguided's use of Kardashian's name and likeness is so pervasive that consumers have begun to erroneously and mistakenly conclude that she is affiliated with Missguided and is working with the company to knock off the clothing that fashion designers have created for her.

4. Missguided's unauthorized use of Kardashian's trademarked name and likeness to promote its website and products is a blatant and willful violation of her statutory and common law rights of publicity, and it further constitutes trademark infringement in violation of the Lanham Act and California common law. By this action, Kardashian seeks a permanent injunction restraining Missguided's unlawful misappropriation of her persona and trademarks, and she seeks an award of actual damages, the disgorgement of Missguided's ill-gotten profits, and an award of punitive damages to deter Missguided from future violations of her intellectual property rights.

Jurisdiction And Venue

5. The Court has original jurisdiction pursuant to 28 U.S.C. §§ 1331 and 1338(a). This is a civil action arising under federal law, the Lanham Act of 1946 as amended (codified at 15 U.S.C. §§ 1051, et seq.). The pendent state law claims are so related to the federal claims that they form part of the same case or controversy pursuant to Article III of the United States Constitution. The court therefore has supplemental jurisdiction over those claims pursuant to 28 U.S.C. § 1367(a).

6. Venue is proper in this judicial district pursuant to 28 U.S.C. § 1391(b) for several independent reasons, including that: Defendant "resides" in this judicial district for venue purposes under 28 U.S.C. § 1391(c)(2); a substantial part of the

events or omissions giving rise to the claims occurred in this district; and a substantial part of property that is the subject of the action is situated in this district.

Parties

7. Plaintiff Kimsaprincess, Inc. is a California corporation with its principal place of business in Los Angeles County, California.

8. Plaintiff Kim Kardashian West is an individual residing in Los Angeles County, California.

9. Plaintiffs are informed and believe, and based thereon allege, that Defendant Missguided USA (Finance) Inc. ("Missguided USA") is a Delaware Corporation. At this time, Plaintiffs are unaware of Missguided USA's principal place of business.

10. Plaintiffs are informed and believe, and based thereon allege, that Defendant Missguided Limited ("Missguided UK") is a corporation organized and existing under the laws of the United Kingdom, with its principal place of business in Manchester, United Kingdom.

11. Defendants Missguided USA and Missguided UK are collectively referred to herein as "Missguided."

Allegations Common To All Claims For Relief

12. Kardashian is a world-famous television celebrity, model, and spokesperson. For over a decade, she has been featured on the reality television series *Keeping Up With The Kardashians*, which is broadcast in over 160 countries. Kardashian now enjoys one of the largest social media followings of *any* celebrity anywhere in the world, including more than 120 million followers on Instagram, and close to 60 million followers on Twitter.

13. Kardashian promotes and sells a variety of products through her own companies, including a cosmetics line sold under the "KKW Beauty" mark and a fragrance line sold under the "KKW Fragrance" mark. Further, Kardashian is in high demand as a paid spokesperson for third-party products. Because of her popularity and reach on social media, companies routinely pay Kardashian *millions* of dollars in fees to serve as a celebrity endorser.

14. Kardashian is selective of the third-party companies with whom she chooses to partner. She frequently turns down endorsement deals. And when she does sign on as a spokesperson for third-party products or services, she often works closely with these partners to develop particular products for her endorsement. Kardashian's control over the use of her name, likeness, and trademarks in promoting third-party products and services is absolutely critical to safeguard her reputation, and to prevent the public from being misled into believing that she has associated herself with some product or service that she does not endorse.

15. As alleged in further detail below, in total disregard of Kardashian's trademark rights and rights of publicity, Defendants have repeatedly used Kardashian's name and image without authorization to generate interest in their brand and website, and to elicit sales of their products.

16. Missguided operates several websites that sell clothing, including the website www.missguidedus.com. Missguided specializes in "fast" and inexpensive clothing designs, which are often derivative of other companies' designs if not blatant knock-offs. Missguided has become particularly well-known for copying designs worn by famous celebrities, which it then offers for sale on its sites within days—sometimes even hours—of the celebrity appearing in the clothing.

17. Missguided has not only knocked-off the clothing of other designers, but it has unabashedly misappropriated the rights of celebrities like Kardashian in selling these knock-offs on its websites. Missguided's U.S. website has included entire pages that are devoted solely to the sale of clothing inspired by Kardashian, and on which Kardashian's name and likeness are prominently used *without her permission* to promote the products. . . .

18. Other pages from Missguided's U.S. website have featured both Kardashian *and* her famous sisters, using *all* of their names and likenesses without authorization to promote Missguided's knock-off clothing[.]

19. [T]hese website pages do not merely report on Kardashian's style or fashions. Missguided is using Kardashian's name and image for the *express* purpose of promoting and selling products on the site. Indeed, the web pages depicted above, and others like them on the Missguided website, contain direct links to pages on the site where clothing can be purchased. In the first example shown above, visitors to the site are specifically prompted to click a "Shop Kim K." link, where they can buy clothing copied from Kardashian's prior looks.

20. On its social media platforms as well, including Instagram, Missguided has repeatedly used Kardashian's name and likeness without permission to promote its sale of clothing on the www.missguidedus.com website. Recently, for example, after Kardashian posted a photo on Instagram of a dress that was made for her . . . , Missguided quickly responded with its own Instagram post . . . boasting that it would be ripping off the design within "a few days"[.] Missguided purposefully inserted Kardashian's Instagram username (@kimkardashian) into its post to capitalize on her celebrity status and social media following in promoting the sale of its upcoming product.

21. [A]nother example in which Missguided used (without authorization) Kardashian's name and image [is] in an Instagram post in order to promote a dress that it was selling on its website[.]

22. Additionally, Missguided has routinely posted other photos of Kardashian on its Instagram feed—at times together with her husband and children—that do not specifically solicit sales of a particular item of clothing as do the preceding examples, but which function nevertheless to advertise Missguided's brand and website. The whole of Missguided's Instagram page is devoted to the advertising of its website and the clothing sold there. Many of Missguided's posts on the feed, including those shown above, promote clothing that is available on www.missguidedus.com; and frequently, Missguided's Instagram posts contain direct links to pages on the

site where clothing can be purchased. The entirety of the Instagram page, therefore, is an advertisement for the Missguided brand, website, and products; and accordingly, Missguided's Instagram posts depicting images of Kardashian and using her name are clearly intended to, and have the effect, of promoting Missguided's brand and products. In fact, Missguided has gone so far to as to emboss its "M" logo on photographs of Kardashian and her family to promote its site and products. . . .

23. Missguided has so systematically misappropriated Kardashian's name and likeness that the consuming public is likely to and has come to the mistaken conclusion that she is affiliated with Missguided and is working hand in hand with the company to create "fast fashion" versions of her clothing. A website entitled "The Fashion Law" (www.thefashionlaw.com) recently published an article entitled *Kim K and Missguided: Fast Fashion at its Quickest or a Marketing Ploy in Disguise*? The article referenced the speed with which Missguided had been able to post images of a knock-off version of the gold dress worn by Kardashian . . . , and it proffered that this may well be the result of "a coordinated marketing ploy between the mega-influencer [Kardashian] and the millennial-centric fashion company." In the same article, the author referred to other commentators who had hypothesized (incorrectly) that Missguided's quick turnaround of a knock-off of Kardashian's dress was as "an example of 'a thinly veiled collab' at play between Missguided and Kim K."

First Claim For Relief

(Violation of Cal. Civ. Code § 3344—Against All Defendants)

24. Plaintiffs incorporate all prior allegations of this Complaint by this reference.

25. Plaintiffs are the owners of all rights of publicity in Kardashian's name, image, likeness, and persona.

26. Missguided has willfully and without authorization used Kardashian's name, image, likeness, and persona for commercial purposes, to advertise the Missguided brand and website, and to promote the sale of clothing on Missguided's site.

27. Missguided's unauthorized use of Kardashian's name, image, likeness, and persona constitutes a commercial misappropriation in violation of Section 3344 of the California Civil Code.

28. As a direct and proximate result of Missguided's wrongful conduct, Plaintiffs have suffered, and will continue to suffer, damages in an amount to be proven at trial, but in no event less than $10 million.

29. Missguided has further been unjustly enriched by its misappropriation of Kardashian's statutory right of publicity. Accordingly, Plaintiffs are entitled to restitution of all income, profits, and other benefits resulting from Missguided's conduct, in an amount to be determined according to proof at trial.

30. Missguided's actions as alleged above were malicious, oppressive, and fraudulent, and done with the intent to injure Plaintiffs and with a willful and conscious disregard for Plaintiffs' rights. As a result, Plaintiffs are entitled to recover from

Missguided punitive and exemplary damages in an amount sufficient to punish and deter it and others from engaging in such acts in the future.

31. Missguided's actions have further caused and will continue to cause irreparable injury to Plaintiffs that cannot be remedied by an award of monetary damages alone. Plaintiffs are therefore entitled to preliminary and permanent injunctive relief preventing the continuing infringement of their rights of publicity.

Second Claim For Relief

(Violation of Common Law Right of Publicity—Against All Defendants)

32. Plaintiffs incorporate all prior allegations of this Complaint by this reference.

33. Plaintiffs are the owners of all common law rights of publicity in Kardashian's name, image, likeness, and persona.

34. Missguided has willfully and without authorization used Kardashian's name, image, likeness, and persona for commercial purposes, to advertise the Missguided brand and website, and to promote the sale of clothing on Missguided's site.

35. Missguided's unauthorized use of Kardashian's name, image, likeness, and persona constitutes a violation of California's common law right of publicity.

36. As a direct and proximate result of Missguided's wrongful conduct, Plaintiffs have suffered, and will continue to suffer, damages in an amount to be proven at trial, but in no event less than $10 million.

37. Missguided has further been unjustly enriched by its infringement of Kardashian's common law right of publicity. Accordingly, Plaintiffs are entitled to restitution of all income, profits, and other benefits resulting from Missguided's conduct, in an amount to be determined according to proof at trial.

38. Missguided's actions as alleged above were malicious, oppressive, and fraudulent, and done with the intent to injure Plaintiffs and with a willful and conscious disregard for Plaintiffs' rights. As a result, Plaintiffs are entitled to recover from Missguided punitive and exemplary damages in an amount sufficient to punish and deter it and others from engaging in such acts in the future.

39. Missguided's actions have further caused and will continue to cause irreparable injury to Plaintiffs that cannot be remedied by an award for monetary damages alone. Plaintiffs are therefore entitled to preliminary and permanent injunctive relief preventing the continuing infringement of their rights of publicity.

Third Claim For Relief

(False Designation of Origin (15 U.S.C. § 1125(a))—Against All Defendants)

40. Plaintiffs incorporate all prior allegations of this Complaint by this reference.

41. For many years, Plaintiffs have extensively used the trademarks KIM KARDASHIAN and KIM KARDASHIAN WEST in commerce in connection with a myriad of products and services, including Kardashian's advertising and promotion of third-party products in the fashion and beauty industries.

42. Plaintiffs are further the owners of several federally registered trademarks in Kardashian's name, including without limitation: (1) U.S. Registration No. 4,989,420 for the use of KIM KARDASHIAN WEST in Int'l Class 41 in connection with "Entertainment in the nature of providing information by means of a global computer network in the fields of entertainment and pop culture; entertainment services, namely, personal appearances by a celebrity, actress and model."; (2) U.S. Registration No. 4,978,865 for the use of KIM KARDASHIAN WEST in Int'l Class 35 in connection with "Advertising services, namely, promoting the brands, goods and services of others; endorsement services, namely, promoting the goods and services of others"; and (3) U.S. Registration No. 4,516,079 for the use of KIM KARDASHIAN in Int'l Class 35 in connection with "Advertising services, namely, promoting the brands, goods and services of others; endorsement services, namely, promoting the goods and services of others" (collectively, the "Registered Marks").

43. The Registered Marks are valid trademarks owned by Plaintiffs. Additionally, by virtue of Plaintiffs' longstanding and continuous use of the marks KIM KARDASHIAN and KIM KARDASHIAN WEST in commerce, Plaintiffs have acquired valid common law trademarks in these names. The public has come to recognize these marks as exclusively identifying Plaintiffs, and the marks are famous worldwide.

44. Missguided has infringed and is continuing to infringe Plaintiffs' registered and common law trademarks by using these marks on its websites, including the www.missguidedus.com website, to promote Missguided's brand and sale of clothing. Missguided has further infringed and is continuing to infringe Plaintiffs' marks by using them on social media, including in Instagram posts, to promote its Missguided brand and websites and the products sold on those sites.

45. Missguided's unauthorized use of Plaintiff's registered and common law trademarks is likely to confuse and deceive consumers as to the origin, sponsorship, and/or endorsement of the Missguided brand, website, and products. Specifically, Missguided's use of Plaintiffs' marks is likely to cause consumers to mistakenly believe that Plaintiffs are associated with Missguided, or that they sponsor or endorse Missguided and its websites. And in fact, consumers have *already* expressed such confusion, suggesting in social media posts and online articles that Plaintiffs must be in a "collaboration" with Missguided.

46. As a direct and proximate result of the acts of trademark infringement set forth above, Plaintiffs have suffered actual damages in an amount to be proven at trial, but in no event less than $10 million. Plaintiffs are entitled to the full range of relief available under the Lanham Act, 15 U.S.C. § 1117, including, without limitation, an award of actual damages and the disgorgement of Missguided's profits arising from the acts of trademark infringement. Missguided's conduct further renders this an "exceptional" case within the meaning of the Lanham Act, thus entitling Plaintiffs to an award of attorneys' fees and costs.

47. Plaintiffs are informed and believe, and based thereon allege, that Missguided has committed the infringement described above knowing that its unauthorized

use of the KIM KARDASHIAN and KIM KARDASHIAN WEST trademarks is likely to cause consumer confusion. Missguided has thus willfully, knowingly, and maliciously deceived and confused the relevant consuming public, such that Plaintiffs are entitled to an award of treble damages.

48. Missguided's actions have further caused and will continue to cause irreparable injury to Plaintiffs that cannot be remedied by an award of monetary damages alone. Plaintiffs are therefore entitled to preliminary and permanent injunctive relief preventing the continuing infringement of their trademark rights.

Fourth Claim For Relief

(Trademark Infringement (15 U.S.C. § 1114(1))—Against All Defendants)

49. Plaintiffs incorporate all prior allegations of this Complaint by this reference.

50. The Registered Trademarks are valid marks owned by Plaintiffs.

51. Missguided has infringed the Registered Trademarks as alleged in detail above by using those marks (or confusingly similar variations thereof) in a manner likely to cause confusion or mistake as to Plaintiffs' association with or sponsorship or endorsement of Missguided and its website and products.

52. As a direct and proximate result of the acts of trademark infringement set forth above, Plaintiffs have suffered actual damages in an amount to be proven at trial, but in no event less than $10 million. Plaintiffs are entitled to the full range of relief available under the Lanham Act, 15 U.S.C. § 1117, including, without limitation, an award of actual damages and the disgorgement of Missguided's profits arising from the acts of trademark infringement. Missguided's conduct further renders this an "exceptional" case within the meaning of the Lanham Act, thus entitling Plaintiffs to an award of attorneys' fees and costs.

53. Plaintiffs are informed and believe, and based thereon allege, that Missguided has committed the infringement described above knowing that its unauthorized use of the Registered Trademarks is likely to cause consumer confusion. Missguided has thus willfully, knowingly, and maliciously deceived and confused the relevant consuming public, such that Plaintiffs are entitled to an award of treble damages.

54. Missguided's actions have further caused and will continue to cause irreparable injury to Plaintiffs that cannot be remedied by an award of monetary damages alone. Plaintiffs are therefore entitled to preliminary and permanent injunctive relief preventing the continuing infringement of their trademark rights.

Fifth Claim For Relief

(Common Law Trademark Infringement—Against All Defendants)

55. Plaintiffs incorporate all prior allegations of this Complaint by this reference.

56. Plaintiffs own valid common law trademarks in KIM KARDASHIAN and KIM KARDASHIAN WEST for use in connection with a wide variety of products and services, including without limitation the promotion of products and services

in the fashion and beauty industries. The Registered Trademarks are likewise valid trademarks owned by Plaintiffs.

57. The public has come to recognize the KIM KARDASHIAN and KIM KARDASHIAN WEST marks as exclusively identifying Plaintiffs, and the marks are famous worldwide.

58. Missguided has infringed and is continuing to infringe Plaintiffs' trademarks by using these marks on its websites, including the www.missguidedus.com website, to promote Missguided's brand and sale of clothing. Missguided has further infringed and is continuing to infringe Plaintiffs' marks by using them on social media, including in Instagram posts, to promote its Missguided brand and websites, as well as the products sold on those sites.

59. Missguided's unauthorized use of Plaintiff's trademarks is likely to confuse and deceive consumers as to the origin, sponsorship, and/or endorsement of the Missguided brand, website, and products. Specifically, Missguided's use of Plaintiffs' marks is likely to cause consumers to mistakenly believe that Plaintiffs are associated with Missguided, or that they sponsor or endorse Missguided and its websites. And in fact, consumers have *already* expressed such confusion, suggesting in social media posts and online articles that Plaintiffs must be in a "collaboration" with Missguided.

60. As a direct and proximate result of the acts of trademark infringement set forth above, Plaintiffs have suffered actual damages in an amount to be proven at trial, but in no event less than $10 million.

61. Plaintiffs are informed and believe, and based thereon allege, that Missguided has committed the infringement described above knowing that its unauthorized use of the KIM KARDASHIAN and KIM KARDASHIAN WEST trademarks is likely to cause consumer confusion. Missguided has thus willfully, knowingly, and maliciously deceived and confused the relevant consuming public, such that Plaintiffs are entitled to an award of treble damages.

62. Plaintiffs are further informed and believe, and based thereon allege, that Missguided has acted with fraud, oppression, or malice in infringing Plaintiffs' marks as alleged above. As such, in addition to the other relief sought herein, Plaintiffs are entitled to an award of punitive damages.

63. Missguided's actions have further caused and will continue to cause irreparable injury to Plaintiffs that cannot be remedied by an award of monetary damages alone. Plaintiffs are therefore entitled to preliminary and permanent injunctive relief preventing the continuing infringement of their trademark rights.

WHEREFORE, Plaintiffs pray for judgment as follows:

A. On all claims for relief, for an award of compensatory and treble damages in an amount to be proven, but in no event less than $10 million;

B. On all claims for relief, for the disgorgement of Missguided's profits attributable to the infringement of Plaintiffs' trademarks and rights of publicity;

C. On the First, Second, and Fifth Claims for Relief, for an award of punitive damages in an amount sufficient to deter unlawful conduct by Missguided in the future;

D. For a preliminary and permanent injunction restraining and enjoining Missguided from using Plaintiffs' name, images, likeness, persona, and trademarks;

E. For pre-judgment and post-judgment interest according to proof and to the maximum extent allowed by law;

F. For attorneys' fees and costs; and

G. For such other and further relief as the Court may deem just and proper.

Default Judgment

(July 2, 2019)

PHILLIPS, Chief U.S. District Judge.

TO ALL PARTIES AND THEIR ATTORNEYS OF RECORD:

Defendant Mis[s]guided USA Finance Inc. has failed to appear, plead, or otherwise defend in this action, and default was entered on March 29, 2019.... Counsel for Plaintiffs requested judgment against Mis[s]guided USA and filed a proper motion and declaration in accordance with Federal Rule of Civil Procedure 55(a) and (b).... Pursuant to the Court's Order Granting in Part Plaintiffs' Motion for Default Judgment, judgment is hereby entered in favor of Plaintiffs and against Mis[s]guided USA in the amount of $2,700,000.00 in damages and $59,600.00 in attorneys' fees. Furthermore, Mis[s]guided USA is hereby permanently enjoined from using Plaintiffs' trademarks in connection with the sale, marketing or distribution of its products.

IT IS SO ORDERED.

Notes

1. This generous award in favor of plaintiff is probably uncollectible, having resulted from a default. What is the benefit to plaintiff of having a judgment like this?

2. Why do you think Kim Kardashian is more litigious than many other celebrities when it comes to the unauthorized use of her likeness?

3. Do you think the holding would have been different if Missguided merely posted the images in question of Kim Kardashian on its website, and not on Instagram as well?

4. How would you classify the role Instagram plays within the market of fashion advertising today?

3. Talent/Union Issues

Advertisers often want to include talent in their advertisement and thus draft creative services agreements with models, actors, and other talent who appear in the advertising campaign. These agreements may include not only termination, representation and warranty provisions but must also address any talent union concerns. Fashion companies and advertising agencies may be signatories to industry guild agreements such as the Screen Actors Guild (SAG) commercials code, the American Federation of Television and Radio Artists (AFTRA) and the American Federation of Musicians (AFM). These guilds require that signatories hire only guild members to perform in advertisements, pay at least minimum fees to the talent for their performance and an additional fee to the applicable guild's pension and health funds at a set percentage. Talent and union issues arise also in the context of using prerecorded music, for example, where the singer and musicians need to be adequately compensated, even if the advertiser never hired musicians for recording the advertisement in the first place.

If the company is not a signatory to any guild or if the advertisement falls outside the jurisdiction of the guilds, the agreement with the talent must contain a provision stating that the advertiser is buying out all of the talent's right in the advertising and so the talent will not receive any residual fees for her performance.

E. Influencer and Social Media Marketing

The FTC requires that endorsements and product placements from influencers—individuals who have the ability to affect consumers' purchasing decisions and/or to give rise to greater brand awareness as a result of their authority, knowledge, position, or relationship with their audience, most commonly on social media platforms—that are the result of a connection that consumers would not reasonably expect, be clearly disclosed as marketing messages. The government entity's rules regarding influencers and social and digital media are set out in its Dot Com Disclosures Guide and its revised Endorsement Guides, which were respectively released in March 2013 and September 2017, to address current marketing techniques, such as blogging and influencer marketing.

According to the Dot Com Disclosures Guide, "Consumer protection laws apply equally to marketers across all mediums, whether delivered on a desktop computer, a mobile device, or more traditional media such as television, radio, or print." This means that ads must be disclosed as such, and "advertisers should ensure that the disclosure is clear and conspicuous on all devices and platforms that consumers may use to view the ad."

In addition to traditional advertising messages, endorsements must also be disclosed. The FTC's Endorsement Guides define an endorsement "as any advertising message . . . that consumers are likely to believe reflects the opinions, beliefs, findings, or experiences of a party other than the sponsoring advertiser, even if the views expressed by that party are identical to those of the sponsoring advertiser." This could include anything from verbal or written messages to photos posted on social media. As the FTC has stated, "Simply posting a picture of a product on social media . . . or a video of you using [a product] could convey that you like and approve of the product," and would thus amount to an endorsement.

In addition to requiring that endorsements "reflect the honest opinions, findings, beliefs, or experience of the endorser," any endorsement messages that result from a connection between an influencer and a brand that "might affect the weight or credibility that consumers give the endorsement" must be fully disclosed. Such a connection may be that the influencer/endorser is being compensated to endorse a product, including but not limited to payment with cash or other form of compensation, or that the influencer/endorser maintains an ownership stake in the company.

The FTC requires that such connections be "clearly and conspicuously made," either by way of plain language or easily identifiable hashtags, such as #ad or #sponsored. While the FTC has not explicitly provided an exhaustive list of proper disclosures, it has stated that "many consumers will not understand a disclosure like "#sp," "Thanks [Brand]," or "#partner" in an Instagram post to mean that the post is sponsored." Moreover, it has stated that "when multiple tags, hashtags, or links are used, readers may just skip over them, especially when they appear at the end of a long post—meaning that a disclosure placed in such a string is not likely to be conspicuous."

The FTC has also stated that in order to make a disclosure "clear and conspicuous," it should be placed "as close as possible to the triggering claim" and should not require a user to "scroll" to find a disclosure.

The responsibility for proper disclosure falls on both advertisers and endorsers/influencers, alike, and both parties may be subject to liability for false or unsubstantiated statements made through endorsements, or for failing to disclose material connections between themselves.

In letters dated April 2017 and September 2017, the FTC alerted various brands, influencers, and celebrities of the disclosure rules and reminded them that they must clearly and conspicuously disclose their relationships when promoting or endorsing products through social media.

The letters came after enforcement action by the FTC against Cole Haan in 2014 in connection with a promotional contest in which Cole Haan instructed participants to post images of Cole Haan shoes to their Pinterest boards with the hashtag #WanderingSole for a chance win a $1,000 shopping spree. Because Cole Haan did not require participants to properly disclose their participation in the contest, the FTC determined that the pins were undisclosed endorsements.

Letter from FTC to Cole Haan

Mar. 20, 2014

As you know, the staff of the Federal Trade Commission's Division of Advertising Practices has conducted an investigation into whether your client, Cole Haan, Inc., violated Section 5 of the Federal Trade Commission Act, 15 U.S.C. § 45, in connection with its Wandering Sole Pinterest Contest.

The contest rules instructed contestants to create Pinterest[71] boards titled "Wandering Sole." The contest rules further required that a board include five shoe images from Cole Haan's Wandering Sole Pinterest Board as well as five images of the contestants' "favorite places to wander." Finally, contestants were instructed to use "#WanderingSole" in each pin description. Cole Haan promised to award a $1,000 shopping spree to the contestant with the most creative entry.

We believe that participants' pins featuring Cole Haan products were endorsements of the Cole Haan products, and the fact that the pins were incentivized by the opportunity to win a $1000 shopping spree would not reasonably be expected by consumers who saw the pins. Moreover, we were concerned that Cole Haan did not instruct contestants to label their pins and Pinterest boards to make it clear that they had pinned Cole Haan products as part of a contest.

We do not believe that the "#WanderingSole" hashtag adequately communicated the financial incentive- a material connection- between contestants and Cole Haan.

Section 5 of the FTC Act requires the disclosure of a material connection between a marketer and an endorser when their relationship is not otherwise apparent from the context of the communication that contains the endorsement. Under the circumstances set out above, entry into a contest to receive a significant prize in exchange for endorsing a product through social media constitutes a material connection that would not reasonably be expected by viewers of the endorsement.

Upon review of this matter, we have determined not to recommend enforcement action at this time. We considered a number of factors in reaching this decision. First, we have not previously publicly addressed whether entry into a contest is a form of material connection, nor have we explicitly addressed whether a pin on Pinterest may constitute an endorsement. Second, the contest ran for a limited length of time and drew a relatively small number of contestants. Finally, Cole Haan has since adopted a social media policy that adequately addresses our concerns. The FTC staff expects that Cole Haan will take reasonable steps to monitor social media influencers' compliance with the obligation to disclose material connections when endorsing its products.

Our decision not to pursue enforcement action is not to be construed as a determination that a violation may not have occurred, just as the pendency of an investigation should not be construed as a determination that a violation has occurred. The Commission reserves the right to take further action as the public interest may warrant.

---

71. Pinterest is a social media site where users can save and organize images knows as "pins" in collections known as "boards." Pinterest users may "follow" other Pinterest users, and the Pinterest home page displays a chronological "feed" of pins from boards and pinners that the user has chosen to follow. Also, users can run searches for pins by entering search terms. All Pinterest boards are public by default.

Notes

1. According to the FTC, what constitutes a material connection?

2. The FTC's guidelines note that disclosures may vary depending on the social media platform in play. What are some of the important things that brands need to be aware of from one platform to another?

3. The FTC decided not to pursue enforcement action against Cole Haan for this violation. Do you think the implementation of Cole Haan's social media policy is sufficient to prevent further violations?

4. Do you think that a pin on Pinterest constitutes an endorsement in today's social media landscape? How about a "follow" on Instagram?

A year later, the FTC investigated Lord & Taylor over an undisclosed influencer marketing campaign for its Design Lab collection, in which the retailer paid 50 online fashion "influencers" to post Instagram pictures of themselves wearing the same paisley dress from the new collection, but failed to disclose they had given each influencer the dress, as well as thousands of dollars, in exchange for their endorsement. *See In the Matter of Lord & Taylor, LLC, supra.*

See FTC Letters to influencers and celebrities: https://www.ftc.gov/system/files/documents/foia_requests/2b-2017-00801_instagram_influencers_95_pgs.pdf; *Gregory M. Messer v. Kendall Jenner* 1:19-ap-1347 (Fyre Fest related lawsuit that notes that Jenner was paid to post on Instagram but failed to include FTC disclosure language).

Letter from Public Citizen, Commercial Alert, Campaign for a Commercial-Free Childhood and Center for Digital Democracy to the Federal Trade Commission

Sept. 7, 2016

Public Citizen, Campaign for a Commercial-Free Childhood and the Center for Digital Democracy wrote a letter to the FTC on September 7, 2016 requesting the agency to investigate and bring enforcement actions related to non-disclosed advertising practices by "influencers" on Instagram. They summarized the status of endorsement rules and influencers' non-compliance of the rules, as excerpted below:

> A longstanding, core principal of fair advertising law in the United States is that people have a right to know when they are being advertised to. With that knowledge, consumers can hopefully apply the appropriate emotional and intellectual filters to advertisements, discounting puffery and claims of authenticity. By contrast, disguised advertisements are inherently deceptive, because consumers do not know to apply appropriate screens. The issue is acute with disguised ads featuring paid endorsements, where deceived consumers believe admired celebrities are making genuine, self-directed and enthusiastic endorsements of brands, not realizing that those celebrities are instead paid and may not even use the touted brand.

Although FTC policy regarding disguised advertising is well established, and reiterated in recent enforcement guidelines, we are deeply concerned that the agency is failing to keep pace with developments in the social media space. The result is that consumers, especially young consumers, are being deceived on vast scale. Social media norms are evolving so that practices that contravene clear FTC policy are considered by many advertisers and influencers to be routine and non-objectionable. Advertisers often assert that "everyone knows" that paid endorsements are pervasive in social media, though there is no evidence to support this assertion, particularly among young consumers. An important part of an FTC enforcement initiative must be to shift the center-of-gravity on social media so that advertisers take affirmative steps to ensure they comply with FTC rules designed to protect consumers from trickery and deception.

The FTC's Policy on Endorsements

The Federal Trade Commission (FTC) considers an "endorsement" to occur when an endorser is paid to advocate for a product, such as when a TV host is paid to proclaim that they love Donut King.[72] In the recent past, the FTC has done significant work on regulating "endorsements." In recent years, the FTC has clarified rules on paid endorsements and native advertisements on the Internet, specifying in its enforcement statement the need for more explicit and simultaneous disclosure of all advertisements.[73] The FTC has expressed concerns about the growing trend of native advertisements on search engines, news websites, and social media, as the advertisements sometimes appear indistinguishable from regular content. The specific recommendations focused on the proximity, placement, prominence, and clarity of meaning of the disclosures. Disclosure language like "Promoted by [X]" and "Sponsored by [X]" is discouraged due to possible ambiguity, with the agency directing the use of words like "Advertisement" or "Ad" instead.[74] While the FTC noted that all parties involved with marketing have the responsibility to follow the rules, they stated that the particular onus of obedience was on the marketers.[75]

---

72. Federal Trade Commission.. {2009). Guides Concerning the. Use of Endorsements and Testimonials. in Advertising. Retrieved from https://www.ftc.gov/sites/default/files/attachments/press-releases/ftc-publishes-final-guides-governing endorsements-testimonials/091005revisedendorsementguides.pdf. Federal Trade Commission. (2015). Commission Enforcement Policy Statement on Deceptively Formatted Advertisements. Retrieved from https://www.ftc.gov/system/files/documents/public statements/896923/151222deceptiveenforcement.pdf. See also Federal Trade Commission. (2015). The FTC's endorsement guides: What people are asking. Retrieved from https://www.ftc.gov/system/flles/documents/public_statements/896923/151222deceptiveenforcement.pdf.

73. Federal Trade Commission. (2015). Native advertising: A guide for businesses. Retrieved from https://www.ftc.gov/tips-advice/business-center/guidance/native-advertising-guide-businesses

74. *Id.*

75. *Id.*

The FTC has taken enforcement action against disguised ads in social media. In May of 2015, the FTC approved a final consent order against Lord & Taylor for, among other things, paying 50 models to post a picture of themselves wearing a Lord & Taylor dress on Instagram without disclosure of payment.[76] In the final consent order, the FTC stated that paid endorsers must disclose when they have been paid to endorse.[77] It is important to note that the final consent order did not penalize the individual models, but instead disciplined Lord & Taylor, the marketer.[78] Similarly, in September of 2015, the FTC settled with Machinima, Inc. for failing to disclose that they had paid endorsers to promote the Xbox One system and Xbox One games.[79]

Evidence of Non-Compliance with FTC Policy

Non-disclosed native advertising, or advertisements that appear to be regular content, is no longer a minor and isolated phenomenon. Non-disclosed native advertising has become a burgeoning and immensely profitable industry. Companies pay "influencers," or social media users with a large following, to post endorsements of their products without disclosure.[80] While there is evidence of the illicit "influencer" market on Twitter and Snapchat, the "influencer" industry on Instagram represents one of the most prominent and ethically egregious violations of FTC policy.

Public Citizen conducted an investigation of the disclosure practices among movie stars, reality TV personalities, famous athletes, fitness gurus, fashion icons and pop musicians. The investigation revealed 113 "influencers" who endorsed a product without disclosure; based on industry norms, our presumption is that all or most of these influencers were compensated for their endorsements.[81] This investigation was by no means exhaustive as the total number of illicit endorsements would likely be too high to measure manually. Many of the celebrities cited in the investigation are role models for children and teens. From Rihanna (pop music star) advertising Puma to Kim Kardashian (famous for the teen reality show *Keeping Up with the Kardashians)* endorsing Express Smile (a teeth-whitening

76. Federal Trade Commission. (2016). FTC Approves final Lord & Taylor order prohibiting deceptive advertising. Retrieved from https://www.ftc.gov/news-events/press-releases/2016/05/ftc-approves-final-lord-taylor-order-prohibiting deceptive.

77. *Id.*

78. *Id.*

79. Federal Trade Commission. (2015). Xbox One promoter settles FTC charges that it deceived consumers with endorsement videos posted by paid 'influencers.' Retrieved from https://www.ftc.gov/news-events/press releases/2015/09/xbox-one- promoter-settles-ftc-charges-it-deceived-consumers.

80. Saiidi, U. (2016). The power of lnstagram: Brands eye more social media influencers. Retrieved from http://www.enbe.com/2016/05/20/the-power-of-instagram-brands-eye-more-social-media-influencers.html.

81. See Appendix A for cxamples.

company), these idols have a primarily young and impressionable audience. Other celebrities who have endorsed products without disclosure include musicians in the pop band One Direction and actresses from Nickelodeon shows (e.g. Victoria Justice).[82]

The noncompliant "influencers" mentioned above are not outliers. They represent a growing trend of deceptive native advertising that disproportionately targets young people. "Influencers" almost always are role models that young people tend to emulate in personal tastes, behavior, and purchasing decisions. As a result of the lack of enforcement of FTC policy, millions of consumers, many of whom are minors, are unknowingly being influenced by corporations through the ostensibly benign medium of their own role models.

The cosmetics and weight loss industries are prominent employers of influencers, marketing products ranging from skin cream to teeth whitening kits to herbal teas promising weight loss. The "influencers" in this case are overwhelmingly reality TV stars idolized by young girls and teens, a demographic especially susceptible to advertising preying off of unrealistic standards of beauty.[83] Weight loss companies such as Fab Fit Fun and Flat Tummy Tea appear to employ dozens of celebrities and influencers to endorse their goods without any disclosure.[84]

This problem has reached epidemic proportions. One agent who casts influencers estimates that there are 100,000 Instagram "influencers" paid to endorse, a vast majority of who do not disclose their advertisements.[85]

Notes

1. Do you think that the FTC imposes stronger consequences within enforcement actions for influencers failing to include proper disclosure language on Instagram posts featuring cosmetics and weight loss products? What about medication?

---

82. Please consult above list for specific endorsements.

83. Renfrew Center Foundation. (2013). From Barbies to Blush—New Survey Reveals Young Girls Are Wearing Makeup Earlier Than Ever to Hide Their Insecurities. Retrieved from http://www.prnewswire.com/news-releases/from-barbies-to-blush---new-survey-reveals-young-girls-are-wearing-makeup-earlier-than-ever-to-hide-their-insecurities-192318071.html.

84. See Appendix B for screenshots of Fab Fit Fun and Flat Tummy Tea Instagram posts. The pictures were obtained from a search of the respective companies' Instagram profile "hashtag" mentions. A majority of the Instagram posts shown in the screenshots display celebrities illicitly endorsing their products. See also Brown, K. Here's how much celebrities make in the Instagram product placement machine. Retrieved from http://jezebel.com/heres-how-much-celebrities-make-in-the· instagram-produc-1740632946.

85. Chafkin, M. (2016). Why Snapchat's influencer economy runs on hot tubs, selfies, and whey protein. Retrieved from http://www.bloomberg.com/features/2016-arsenictv-snapchat-influencer-economy/.

2. Is the FTC the only government agency that has the authority to take action against brands and influencers over improperly disclosed commercial posts? What other agencies have the ability to do so?

3. Do you think an influencer writing "#ad" on an Instagram post impacts their user engagement per post or total number of followers?

Gregory M. Messer, as Chapter 7 Trustee of the Estate of Fyre Festival LLC v. Kendall Jenner Inc.

No. 1:19-ap-01347-MG (Bankr. S.D.N.Y. Aug. 28, 2019)

Complaint Seeking The Avoidance And Recovery Of Fraudulent Transfers

Gregory M. Messer, the Chapter 7 Trustee (the "Trustee" or "Plaintiff") of the estate of Fyre Festival LLC ("Fyre Festival" or the "Debtor"), by and through his counsel, Klestadt Winters Jureller Southard & Stevens, LLP, as and for his complaint (the "Complaint") herein against Kendall Jenner Inc. and Kendall Jenner (collectively, "Jenner" or the "Defendants"), upon information and belief, alleges as follows:

Preliminary Statement

William Z. McFarland, a/k/a Billy McFarland ("McFarland") and his business partner, hip hop artist Jeffrey Atkins, a/k/a Ja Rule ("Ja Rule"), started Fyre Media Inc. ("Fyre Media") in early 2016 with the intention of creating and promoting a software application for booking entertainment. In or around late-summer 2016, the two conceived of the "Fyre Festival" (the "Festival"), which was to be a unique destination concert experience in the Caribbean aimed at young millennials and featuring a number of top musical acts. The Festival was scheduled over two weekends in April and May 2017 in the Exumas, Bahamas, and was intended to, among other things, promote Fyre Media's booking application. The Festival was self-described in an offering memorandum designed to solicit investments as follows:

Overview

Fyre Festival leverages our global access to talent and
our understanding of the millennial demographic to create
THE CULTURAL EXPERIENCE OF THE DECADE.
Fyre Festival is a rich experience that emboldens
our quest to connect to a diverse set of influencers.
For two weekends in April and May, the curious and adventurous come
together on a private **Exuma island**:
Fyre Festival will feature **music** from the greatest talents in the world,
immersive experiences through art, theater, and a weekend long **treasure hunt**; as well as **informative discussions** with some of the brightest minds
in the world. Fyre will be defined by its ability to connect: the ultimate in
a tasteful experience.

(emphasis in original).

The Festival was promoted on Instagram, Twitter and other social media outlets by numerous "influencers" including socialite and model Defendant Kendall Jenner, as well as a number of other famous models like Bella Hadid and Emily Ratajkowski. Ticket buyers were promised an exotic island adventure with luxury accommodations, gourmet food, the hottest musical acts and celebrity attendees. The unique social media marketing method employed by Fyre Festival tapped in on the power of FOMO (short for "fear of missing out") and was extraordinarily successful amongst millennials, resulting in significant ticket sales.

When concertgoers arrived at the Festival on April 27, 2017, they "were met with total disorganization and chaos."[86] None of the promised musical acts showed up or performed. The luxury accommodations turned out to be FEMA disaster relief tents. The gourmet food consisted of the now infamous cheese sandwich served in a Styrofoam container that was even joked about by Tina Fey during her opening monologue at the 2019 Academy Awards.[87] Feral dogs roamed the site and no models or celebrities, including Jenner and others that promoted the Festival and/or told their social media followers that they would be there, were in attendance. The disaster that became of the Festival is now infamous, capturing the attention of popular culture and spawning two separate documentaries on Hulu and Netflix.

McFarland raised and spent over $16 million in connection with the failed Festival, at least that the Trustee has identified thus far.[88] Nearly all of those funds were deposited into and disbursed from accounts held by Fyre Media, Fyre Festival's parent company (Fyre Media and Fyre Festival collectively, the "Fyre Entities"), or transferred by Fyre Media to McFarland and then disbursed by McFarland. Most of the funds were borrowed from individuals and institutions that were defrauded by McFarland. Among many other things, McFarland promised investors significant returns and told them that Fyre Festival owned land in Exuma worth $8.4 million and had over $14 million in receivables, none of which was true. McFarland is now serving a six-year sentence in federal prison and owes over $26 million in restitution on account of his frauds.

86. This description was given by the Bahamas Ministry of Tourism on April 28, 2017. The full statement is available at https://www.bahamas.com/article/bahamas-ministry-tourism-statement-fyre-festival.

87. Ms. Fey said to the crowd, "hey everybody, look under your seats, you are all getting one of those cheese sandwiches from the Fyre Festival."

88. Accounts of the amounts of money raised and spent vary. The United States Securities and Exchange Commission (the "SEC") and the United States Attorney claim that over $16.5 million was raised from defrauded investors in Fyre Festival, plus an additional approximately $8 million raised from defrauded investors for Fyre Media. The Trustee's investigation has identified approximately $12.5 million raised from defrauded investors and creditors of Fyre Festival, approximately $1.4 million raised from ticket sales, approximately $1.5 million raised from a company for advances on prospective future ticket sales, and approximately $1 million raised from sales on prepaid wrist bands from Festival attendees. Funds raised for the Festival would most often be deposited into Fyre Media accounts, then transferred directly to recipients or transferred to McFarland's personal accounts before finally reaching the ultimate recipient.

McFarland used much of the funds raised from defrauded investors and ticketholders to fund legitimate expenses of the doomed Festival. However, significant amounts were recklessly spent in continuation of McFarland's schemes. Just by way of example, significant amounts were spent on musical acts that never showed up (including $500,000 to Blink 182), over $2.25 million to influencers that promoted the Festival on social media without indicating to their followers and the public that they were paid for promoting the Festival (including $275,000 to Jenner for a single social media post), over $500,000 to the company that shot and edited Fyre Festival ads and Festival footage which ultimately used that footage to produce a profitable and popular documentary panning the Festival (without sharing any of the proceeds of that documentary with those victimized by McFarland), and over $1.8 million for prepaid private flights to and from the Festival that never happened.

By the instant Complaint, the Trustee seeks the avoidance of $275,000 paid to Jenner for just making the following single post to her Instagram account promoting the Festival:

[The post featured a grayscale image of Jenner and another model clad in bikinis and holding palm leaves covering their heads, walking along the water on a beach. An orange square overlays the black and white photo, which, in height, covers the span from the bottom third of the models' faces to their knees. The image is captioned: "So hyped to announce my G.O.O.D. Music Family as the first headliners for @fyrefestival. Get tix now at fyrefestival.com. VIP access for my followers . . . use my promo code KJONFYRE for the next 24 hours to get on the list for the artists and talent afterparty on Fyre Cay. #fyrefestival"]

Jenner did not indicate to the public that she was paid to promote the Festival. Further, Jenner's reference to her "G.O.O.D. Music Family" as "headliners" at the Festival, intentionally led certain members of the public and ticket purchasers to believe that Jenner's brother in law, famous musician and GOOD Music record label founder Kanye West, may be or would be performing at the Festival. In fact, Mr. West was never going to perform at the Festival. This conduct demonstrates a clear lack of good faith on Jenner's part.

The Trustee asserts that the Transfers are avoidable as actual fraudulent transfers as they were made in continuation of McFarland's fraud which involved duping investors, creditors and the public into investing in Fyre Festival and purchasing tickets to the doomed Festival.

Introduction

1. On July 7, 2017 (the "Petition Date"), an involuntary petition under chapter 7 of Title 11 of the United States Code (the "Bankruptcy Code") was filed against Fyre Festival by alleged creditors John Nemeth, Raul Jimenez and Andrew Newman.

2. On August 29, 2017, the Court entered the Order for Relief in Fyre Festival's case [Docket No. 4].

3. The Order for Relief directed Fyre Festival to file all schedules, statements, lists and a creditors' matrix within fourteen (14) days of its entry, or September 12, 2017,

and on December 13, 2017, the Court entered an order designating McFarland as the person responsible for performing Fyre Festival's duties under the Bankruptcy Code [Docket No. 26], which gave McFarland a further extension until December 27, 2017 to file the required documents with the Court. To date, McFarland has not filed the required bankruptcy schedules or statement of financial affairs, testified at a meeting of creditors, or performed any other duties as required by the Bankruptcy Code and the Court's Orders.

4. On or around August 31, 2017, Gregory M. Messer was appointed interim trustee of Fyre Festival's estate. On or about November 17, 2017, the Trustee presided over the first meeting of creditors pursuant to section 341(a) of the Bankruptcy Code and duly qualified and became the permanent trustee herein by operation of section 702(d) of the Bankruptcy Code.

Basis For Relief

5. This adversary proceeding is brought pursuant to 11 U.S.C. §§ 544, 548 and 550, Rule 7001(1) of the Federal Rules of Bankruptcy Procedure (the "Bankruptcy Rules"), and § 276 of the New York Debtor and Creditor Law.

6. This adversary proceeding relates to the bankruptcy case of *In re Fyre Festival LLC, Debtor*, Case No. 17-11883 (Bankr. S.D.N.Y. Jul. 7, 2017) (the "Bankruptcy Case") which is pending under Chapter 7 of the Bankruptcy Code in the United States Bankruptcy Court for the Southern District of New York before the Honorable Martin Glenn, United States Bankruptcy Judge (the "Bankruptcy Court").

7. The Bankruptcy Court has jurisdiction over this adversary proceeding by virtue of 28 U.S.C. §§ 157(a) and (b), and 1334(b), and the "Amended Standing Order of Reference" of the United States District Court for the Southern District of New York (Preska, C.J.), dated January 31, 2012. This Court has jurisdiction over the pendent state law claims pursuant to 28 U.S.C. § 1367.

8. Plaintiff consents to the entry of final orders or judgments by the Bankruptcy Court with respect to all matters and claims raised by this Complaint.

9. Venue is proper in this district pursuant to 28 U.S.C. § 1409(a) because this proceeding arises in a case under the Bankruptcy Code pending in this district.

Parties

10. Gregory M. Messer is a member of the panel of private Chapter 7 trustees established by the United States Trustee pursuant to 28 U.S.C. § 586(a)(1). The Trustee is the permanent Chapter 7 trustee of Fyre Festival and its bankruptcy estate and is empowered to bring this action. The Trustee maintains an address for the conduct of business at 26 Court Street, Brooklyn, New York 11242.

11. Fyre Festival is a limited liability company formed on or around December 14, 2016 and existing under the laws of the State of Delaware. Fyre Festival's registered office within the State of Delaware is 1209 Orange Street, Wilmington, Delaware 19801. During its operation and prior to becoming a debtor under the Bankruptcy

Code, Fyre Festival maintained offices at 52 Lispenard Street, TH1, New York, New York 10013. Fyre Festival is the wholly-owned subsidiary of Fyre Media.

12. Fyre Media is a corporation formed on or around March 3, 2016 and existing under the laws of the State of Delaware. Fyre Media maintains an address for the service of process of c/o CT Corporation Systems, 28 Liberty St., New York, New York 10005, and c/o CT Corporation Systems, 111 8th Avenue, 13th Floor, New York, New York 10011. During its operation, Fyre Media maintained offices at 52 Lispenard Street, TH1, New York, New York 10013.

13. McFarland is an individual with a current address at Inmate No. 91186-054, FCI Otisville, Federal Correctional Institution, P.O. Box 1000, Otisville, New York 10963.

14. Kendall Jenner Inc. is a corporation with an office for the conduct of business at in Woodland Hills, California.

15. Kendall Jenner is an individual who resides in the State of California and maintains an office for the conduct of business in Woodland Hills, California.

Facts Common to All Causes of Action

A. Fyre Festival—Origin to Disaster

16. In or around 2013, McFarland, then 22 years old, founded Magnises Inc., a company that marketed an invitation-only charge card. The Magnises card was marketed as the "black card" for millennials and was supposed to entitle card holders to exclusive tickets, events and experiences.

17. In or around March 2016, McFarland and Ja Rule founded Fyre Media, a digital media company, to develop, launch and manage a software application to be, in its words, "the first global marketplace for seamless and secure live entertainment booking."

18. The concept for Fyre Media's business and platform was created by some combination of McFarland and Ja Rule. McFarland served as Fyre Media's Chief Executive Officer.

19. In mid- to late-2016, McFarland and Ja Rule conceived of and began promoting the Festival as a unique concert experience that would take place in Exuma over the course of two weekends in April and May of 2017.

20. Tickets to the Festival were billed as "exclusive" and purported to cost between $1,200 and $100,000 per ticket or ticket package. In promotional materials, the Festival was called "the cultural experience of the decade" which included travel via private jet from Miami to the Bahamas, VIP accommodations and A-list musical performances.

21. Fyre Festival promised attendees that the Festival would feature top musical talent including Blink 182, Pusha T, Tyga, Major Lazer, Disclosure, Migos, and Kaytranada, among many others.

22. The Festival was promoted through celebrities and influencers on social media including Defendant Jenner, Bella Hadid, Emily Ratajkowski, Elsa Hosk,

Lais Ribeiro, Hailey Baldwin (n/k/a Hailey Bieber), Rose Bertram, Gizele Oliveira, Chanel Iman, and Shanina Shaik.

23. Many of the models that promoted the Festival were featured in a promotional video shot and released in or around December 2016 (the "Promotional Video"),[89] which promised "an immersive music festival" that "exceeds all expectations" to take place "over two transformative weekends" in April and May 2017 "on a remote and private island in the Exumas" that was "once owned by Pablo Escobar."

24. Many of the models and influencers posted a simple orange tile with a link to the Promotional Video to their Instagram accounts at the same time in order to disrupt users' news feeds and draw attention to the Festival, like this post from Bella Hadid:

[The post was an orange square covering the image space allotted. The caption reads: "CANT wait for #FyreFestival Coming soon (ribbon emoji) (microphone with musical notes emoji) fyrefestival.com (race flag emoji) (race flag emoji) (race flag emoji)]

25. A majority if not all of the models and influencers that were paid to promote the Festival, including Jenner, did not indicate to their fans and followers that they were paid to advertise and promote the Festival. Nor did they inform their fans and followers that they ultimately decided not to attend the Festival because of problems with the Festival of which they and their agencies were uniquely aware.

26. Through the advertisements and promotions, McFarland and other employees of the Fyre Entities intentionally led the public to believe that the Festival would be filled with famous models on an exotic private island with "first-class culinary experiences and a luxury atmosphere."

27. When attendees began arriving on Great Exuma for the Festival on April 27, 2017, they were met with chaos.

28. The luxury accommodations promised to Festival attendees were actually FEMA disaster relief tents with plastic-wrapped mattresses, which, regardless of quality, were grossly insufficient in number to house the number of attendees. The gourmet food consisted of the now infamous cheese sandwich. Ferrell dogs roamed the site. Attendees' luggage was dumped out of trucks with no organization. No Fyre Festival personnel had answers for the confused attendees.

29. At 3:06 pm on April 27, 2017, the band Blink 182, which was supposed to be one of the headliners for the Festival, tweeted:

> Regrettably, and after much careful and difficult consideration, we want to let you know that we won't be performing at Fyre Fest in the Bahamas this weekend and next weekend. We're not confident that we would have what we need to give you the quality of performances we always give our fans.

30. Blink 182 had already been paid $500,000 when it cancelled at the last minute. The band has retained those funds. In its cancellation tweet, the band did

89. The promotional video is available at https://www.youtube.com/watch?v=mz5kY3RsmKo.

not disclose to its fans and others any of the problems that it was having with Fyre Festival and its management, or that the Festival appeared to be in serious trouble.

31. Finally, on the morning of April 28, 2017, Fyre Festival announced on Twitter, "after assessing the situation this morning and looking at best options for our guests, we cannot move forward as we hoped we could. . . ."

32. Attendees had significant difficulty getting off the island once they were there, and many were locked in the airport for a night while they waited for return flights.

33. The Bahamas Ministry of Tourism released this statement on April 28th, describing the chaotic event:[90]

> We are extremely disappointed in the way the events unfolded yesterday with the Fyre Festival. We offer a heartfelt apology to all who traveled to our country for this event. Tourism is our number one industry and it is our aim to deliver world- class experiences and events. Hundreds of visitors to Exuma were met with total disorganization and chaos. The organizers of Fyre recently asked the Ministry of Tourism for support for their private event. The Ministry of Tourism is not an official sponsor of Fyre Festival. Given the magnitude of this undertaking, the MOT lent its support as we do with all international events. We offered advice and assisted with communications with other government agencies. The event organizers assured us that all measures were taken to ensure a safe and successful event but clearly they did not have the capacity to execute an event of this scale. A team of Ministry of Tourism representatives is on the island to assist with the organization of a safe return of all Fyre Festival visitors. It is our hope that the Fyre Festival visitors would consider returning to the Islands Of The Bahamas in the future to truly experience all of our beauty.

34. In the aftermath of the Festival, both Hulu and Netflix released documentaries about the Festival—Hulu's *Fyre Fraud*, released on January 14, 2019, and Netflix's *Fyre: The Greatest Party That Never Happened*, released on January 18, 2019. Both documentaries chronical McFarland's frauds and the disaster that became of the Festival.

B. Fyre Festival Raised Funds by Defrauding Lenders, Investors and Ticketholders

35. McFarland raised money for the Festival by defrauding investors, lenders and ticket purchasers. Fyre Festival raised and expended not less than $16.5 million according to the SEC and United States Attorney.

36. McFarland acted as the primary solicitor of investments in Fyre Festival via investment contracts, which gave investors the rights to profits in the Festival's commercial enterprises.

---

90. Statement available at: https://www.bahamas.com/article/bahamas-ministry-tourism-statement-fyre-festival.

37. In offering documents and other communications with Fyre Festival investors, McFarland:

a) Made false statements concerning Fyre Festival's assets;

b) Falsified financial data;

c) Made false claims of affiliations with talent;

d) Created a fraudulent brokerage statement in order to suggest to investors and banks that McFarland personally possessed collateral sufficient to securitize investments; and

e) Claimed that he would obtain event cancellation insurance for the Festival, which he never did.

38. In January 2017, McFarland created a Private Placement Memorandum (the "PPM") concerning Fyre Media and Fyre Festival, which was widely distributed to existing and prospective investors in early 2017.

39. The PPM included, on Fyre Festival's balance sheet as of January 1, 2017, assets including accounts receivable of $14,827,382.97 and "BlackPoint Exuma Land" valued at $8,400,000. These assets did not exist. Certain investors relied on the claimed existence of these assets in making their investment decision.

40. In response to requests from certain existing and prospective Fyre Festival investors that their investments be collateralized, McFarland created a fake brokerage statement, which showed that McFarland owned $2.56 million in shares in the common stock of Facebook, Inc. ("Facebook"). In fact, McFarland owned just $1,499 worth of Facebook shares, a tiny fraction of the shares indicated by the fake brokerage statement.

41. McFarland attached the fake brokerage statement to certain executed investor agreements and made numerous misstatements concerning his fictitious shares of Facebook in emails and texts to other prospective investors.

42. In early 2017, in an effort to keep the struggling Fyre Festival afloat, McFarland sought millions of dollars in personal loans from two banks. To attempt to induce the banks to grant him loans, McFarland provided false information in his loan applications, including representations inflating his net worth and reiterating the false claim that he owned $2.56 million worth of Facebook stock.

43. McFarland also provided one of the banks with a copy of the fake brokerage statement, as well as a fraudulent Fyre Media income statement, which grossly inflated the company's revenue and income.

44. Although both of McFarland's loan applications ultimately were denied, he told potential investors that the loans had been approved and that monies from these loans could serve as collateral for their investments.

45. As an inducement to invest in Fyre Festival, McFarland also falsely communicated to actual and prospective investors that they would have the rights to payouts from Fyre Festival event cancellation policies if the festival did not proceed

as planned. In reality, however, McFarland never obtained any event cancellation policies for the Festival.

46. McFarland's false statements confirming the purported existence of these policies were material to the decision of at least one investor to invest in Fyre Festival.

47. McFarland also falsely told investors that a number of stars—including Justin Bieber and Drake—would perform at the Fyre Festival, when, in fact, no such agreements were ever reached. McFarland persisted in these false representations regarding artists, despite requests to desist by the artists' agents.

48. McFarland and Fyre Festival representatives made numerous misrepresentations to ticket purchasers in order to induce them to purchase tickets and attend the Festival. Fyre Festival received in excess of $1.4 million from ticket sales, plus an additional $1.5 million from a ticket vendor for advance ticket sales.

49. When Fyre Festival was desperate for money to fund the doomed Festival, it informed ticket purchasers by email that:

> Fyre Festival is a cashless festival designed to be experienced with your digitally- enabled Fyre Band, a wristband that acts as your festival ID and password- protected payment method. ATMs will not be available at either event site, so plan ahead if you think you'll want cash on hand in case of emergency.

50. In the one week leading up to the Festival, Fyre Festival actively encouraged ticketholders to put significant amounts onto their prepaid wristbands (the "Fyre Bands"), recommending $300 per attendee per day, and sent emails to attendees who had already put significant funds on their Fyre Bands telling them that they should "top off" the amount on their Fyre Bands ahead of the Festival. In just one week, Fyre Festival raised over $1 million in prepayments from ticketholders on their Fyre Bands.

C. McFarland's Criminal Conduct and Admission of Fraud

51. On October 2, 2017, McFarland was charged by the United States Attorney with wire fraud in connection with allegedly defrauding investors in the Festival and Fyre Media. See *United States v. William McFarland*, Case no. 17-cr-00600 (NRB) (S.D.N.Y. Oct. 2, 2017) (the "McFarland Criminal Action").

52. On March 6, 2018, McFarland pled guilty to, among other things, wire fraud. In connection with his plea, McFarland testified as follows:

> In an attempt to promote the digital application [of Fyre Media], I conceived and launched the idea for a music festival, the Fyre Festival. While my intention for the Fyre Festival was legitimate, I grossly underestimated the resources that it would take to execute an event of the magnitude that I had come up with.
>
> So in an attempt to raise the funds that I deemed necessary to execute the event, I lied to investors about various aspects of Fyre Media and my personal finances. These lies included false documents and information that I am aware were transmitted across interstate lines.

> In addition, on or about April 2017, I engaged in a fraudulent scheme in connection with a ticket vendor. Specifically I provided false information to the vendor about Fyre Media's financial condition before entering into a guarantee agreement that induced the vendor to pay $2 million for a block of advance tickets in order to help fund the Fyre Festival.

McFarland Criminal Action, Dkt. No. 35, transcript of Mar. 2, 2019 hearing, pp.12–13.

53. Before being sentenced on the original charges in connection with the Fyre Entities, on June 12, 2018, McFarland was arrested and charged for a second time in connection with another alleged ticket-selling scheme.

54. On July 26, 2018, McFarland pled guilty to, among other things, wire fraud and bank fraud while on pretrial release in connection with the new charges.

55. As set forth in greater detail in the government's sentencing memorandum, "[w]ith Fyre Media in 2016 and Fyre Festival in 2017, McFarland's lies about the rapid growth and incredible financial success of the Fyre companies led roughly 80 investors to lose over $24 million." The Government's Sentencing Memorandum, Docket No. 63 in Case No. 17-cv- 00600, p. 23 (S.D.N.Y. Oct. 3, 2018).

56. In sentencing McFarland, the Honorable Naomi Reice Buchwald, United States District Judge, noted:

> While defendant has argued that he committed these crimes because he suffers from certain psychological conditions which explain his actions, I reject that evaluation. Rather, it is my conclusion, based on all the submissions which I've carefully considered, that the defendant is a serial fraudster, and that to date his fraud, like a circle, has no end.
>
> Beyond his statement in Court today, which I do not know exactly how to evaluate, the absence prior to today of any moral recognition of the wrongfulness of his conduct is at the heart of the need for specific deterrence. It is also clear that Mr. McFarland has actually been dishonest most of his life. He started out with small scams which have grown over time.

McFarland Criminal Action, Dkt. No. 69, p.55, LL.6-18 (Oct. 11, 2018).

57. On October 16, 2018, the United States District Court for the Southern District of New York entered judgment against McFarland, which included a term of six (6) years in federal prison and forfeiture to the United States in the amount of $26,191,306.28, the amount that McFarland raised from defrauded lenders and investors in the Fyre Entities.

D. The Transfer of Fyre Festival Funds in, to and Through Fyre Media and McFarland's Accounts

58. Fyre Festival maintained only two financial accounts—escrow accounts for the benefit of a flight vendor at First Western Trust Bank (account nos. ending in 0793 and 2468) (the "Air Travel Accounts"). The Air Travel Accounts were established and used exclusively in connection with the booking of and payment for flights, a requirement of the Federal Aviation Administration.

59. The Air Travel Accounts were funded with at least $1.8 million in Festival Funds (as defined below), including by three transfers—$1.22 million from McFarland that he received from Fyre Media, $313,000 from Fyre Media, and $240,000 directly from defrauded investor Carola Jain.

60. All other funds raised and expended by Fyre Festival were deposited into and disbursed directly from accounts maintained by Fyre Media and McFarland.

61. Not less than $14,415,346.60 of Fyre Festival's funds (together with any funds borrowed by, invested in, received for the account of, or otherwise belonging to Fyre Festival, the "Festival Funds") were transferred to, deposited into and disbursed from Fyre Media's bank accounts (collectively, the "Festival to Media Transfers"). The Festival to Media Transfers include $10,471,000 in transfers by investors in and lenders to Fyre Festival, $1,404,531.86 in revenues from ticket purchasers, $1,500,000 from a company that paid for advance ticket sales, and $1,039,814.77 from ticket purchasers for amounts put on their Fyre Bands.

62. Fyre Media then made transfers of Festival Funds to McFarland (collectively, the "Festival to McFarland Transfers", and together with the Festival to Media Transfers, the "Insider Fraudulent Transfers"). The Festival to McFarland Transfers from January 1, 2017 to April 30, 2017 were not less than $10,993,267.51.

E. Use of Fyre Festival Funds

63. Much of the Festival Funds were used to pay vendors and service providers which provided legitimate and necessary services to the Fyre Festival.

64. However, much of the Festival Funds were used to pay musical acts that never showed up or performed at the Festival, models and influencers such as defendant Jenner who promoted the Festival at significant cost without disclosing to the public that they were paid for promoting the Festival, a production company that ultimately used the footage to co-produce a profitable Netflix documentary, a $187,250 deposit to a catering company that never provided food to the Festival, and over $1.8 million for flights that never took place. These parties received Festival Funds at the unfair expense of Fyre Festival's defrauded investors, creditors and ticketholders. These expenditures are collectively referred to herein as the "Festival Fraudulent Transfers").

65. McFarland commingled in his personal account his assets and the assets of Fyre Festival, Fyre Media and possibly other entities under his control. During the period where the Festival to McFarland Transfers were made, McFarland spent not less than $315,645.87 on personal expenses including a luxury penthouse apartment, interior design and home furnishings, hotel stays, dining and entertainment, transportation, clothing and other things.

66. Other Festival Funds were simply used to make "preferential transfers" to certain of Fyre Festival's creditors, which should be recovered by the Trustee for the benefit of all of the creditors of Fyre Festival (collectively, the "Festival Preferential Transfers").

67. The Trustee has commenced an action against Fyre Media and McFarland seeking the avoidance in the first instance of the Insider Fraudulent Transfers as

well as the exclusive right to pursue the recovery of any Festival Fraudulent Transfers and Festival Preferential Transfers.

F. Jenner's Relationship with Fyre Festival and the Instant Transfers

68. Jenner is a famous model and social media influencer. According to Forbes, Jenner is the highest paid model in the world with earnings exceeding $22.5 million for the year ending June 2018.

69. The Fyre Entities entered into an agreement with Jenner pursuant to which Jenner was required to make a single social media post promoting the Festival (the "Promotional Post") in exchange for $250,000.

70. In connection with the agreement between the Fyre Entities and Jenner, the following Transfers totaling $275,000.00 were made to or for the benefit of Jenner:

Date	Transferor	Amount	Initial Transferee	Potential Ultimate Transferee or Beneficiary
01/3/2017	Fyre Media	$250,000.00	Kendall Jenner Inc.	Kendall Jenner
01/12/2017	Fyre Media	$25,000.00		

(as defined above, the "Transfers").

71. It is unknown to the Trustee why the Transfers exceeded the amount required under the agreement.

72. Following receipt of the first $250,000 Transfer, on or around January 5, 2017, Jenner made the following Promotional Post to her Instagram page:

[The post was a grayscale image of Jenner and another model clad in bikinis and holding palm leaves covering their heads, walking along the water on a beach. An orange square overlayed the photo, which, in height, covered the span from the bottom third of the models' faces to their knees. The image was captioned: "So hyped to announce my G.O.O.D. Music Family as the first headliners for @fyrefestival. Get tix now at fyrefestival.com. VIP access for my followers . . . use my promo code KJONFYRE for the next 24 hours to get on the list for the artists and talent after-party on Fyre Cay. #fyrefestival"]

73. Following the Promotional Post, Jenner received the additional $25,000.

74. The Promotional Post has been removed from Jenner's Instagram page.

75. The Promotional Post failed to include any indication that Jenner was paid to promote the Festival pursuant to the guidelines of the Federal Trade Commission, which require as follows:

> When there exists a connection between the endorser and the seller of the advertised product that might materially affect the weight or credibility of the endorsement (i.e., the connection is not reasonably expected by the audience), such connection must be fully disclosed.

116 C.F.R. § 255.5.

76. The Promotional Post successfully promoted the fantasy that the Festival would be populated with models and beautiful people and that fans would be missing out if they were not there.

77. Based upon the language used by Jenner in the Promotional Post, certain members of the public reasonably believed that Jenner's brother in law and GOOD Music record label founder Kanye West would be performing at the Festival. In fact, Mr. West never agreed to perform at the Festival.

78. Jenner never informed the public that she either had no intention of attending the Festival, or that she ultimately determined not to attend the Festival.

79. At least two years after the Festival was scheduled to occur, Jenner reportedly said this to the New York Times when asked about her promotion of the Festival: "[y]ou get reached out to by people to, whether it be to promote or help or whatever, and you never know how these things are going to turn out, sometimes it's a risk" and "I definitely do as much research as I can, but sometimes there isn't much research you can do because it's a starting brand and you kind of have to have faith in it and hope it will work out the way people say it will."

80. Jenner has retained the full value of the Transfers and the funds received from the Fyre Entities.

As and For a First Cause of Action
(Fraudulent Transfers—Actual Fraud—11 U.S.C. §§ 544(b), 548(a)(1)(A) and 550; And N.Y. Debtor and Creditor Law § 276)
(Against All Defendants)

81. Plaintiff repeats and re-alleges each and every allegation set forth in paragraphs 1 through 80 of this Complaint as if fully set forth at length herein.

82. Each of the Transfers was made from Festival Funds.

83. Each of the Transfers constituted a transfer of an interest of Fyre Festival within the meaning of section 101(54) of the Bankruptcy Code.

84. Each of the Transfers was to or for the benefit of the Defendants as set forth above.

85. Fyre Festival was at all times undercapitalized and incapable of putting on the Festival in the manner promised to ticketholders, or repaying the funds borrowed from lenders to the Fyre Festival, or returning investments made in the Fyre Festival.

86. McFarland admitted to his fraudulent scheme in connection with his guilty plea in the McFarland Criminal Action and has been sentenced to and is serving a 6-year term in federal prison as a result of his wrongful conduct.

87. A judgment of restitution in favor of the United States has been entered against McFarland in the amount of $26,191,306.28 on account of the funds raised by McFarland through his fraudulent conduct.

88. The Transfers were made in continuation of McFarland's scheme to defraud investors, lenders, and ticket purchasers of the Fyre Festival.

89. The Transfers were made with actual intent by Fyre Festival to hinder, delay, and/or defraud Fyre Festival's existing creditors, ticket holders and investors, and individuals and entities to which Fyre Festival would become obligated.

90. All of the Transfers were made within two (2) years of the Petition Date.

91. There are creditors that hold unsecured claims against Fyre Festival allowable under Section 502 of the Bankruptcy Code that were creditors at the time each of the Transfers were made.

92. Based upon the foregoing, the Trustee is entitled to an order and judgment against each of the Defendants avoiding the Transfers in the full amount of $275,000, making each jointly and severally liable for the return of the Transfers, and awarding prejudgment interest and attorneys' fees.

WHEREFORE, the Trustee demands judgment against each of the Defendants avoiding the Transfers in the full amount of $275,000, making each jointly and severally liable for the return of the Transfers, and awarding prejudgment interest and attorneys' fees, and requests that the Court grant him such other and further relief as this Court deems just.

Notes

1. Should the FTC implement stronger consequences within enforcement actions for celebrity influencers for failing to include FTC disclosure language on Instagram or is it more likely that consumers assume that their posts are sponsored? Does it matter?

2. Is it reasonable for the FTC to hold influencers liable for good faith promotional posts?

3. Assume that Kendall Jenner was *not* paid to promote Fyre Fest on her Instagram account, and was only compensated to travel to the Exumas to make an appearance in the Fyre Fest promotion photo shoot and video. If she decided to post about Fyre Fest on her Instagram account thereafter, would she have to include disclosure language? Does a material connection exist?

As a result of deceptive advertisements, particularly in the realm of social media, the FTC released advertising disclosures guidelines for online influencers on November 5, 2019.

Disclosures 101 for Social Media Influencers

FTC (Nov. 5, 2019)

* * *

One key [to complying with the law when recommending or endorsing products] is to make a good disclosure of your relationship to the brand.

* * *

If you endorse a product through social media, your endorsement message should make it obvious when you have a relationship ("material connection") with the brand. A "material connection" to the brand includes a personal, family, or employment relationship or a financial relationship—such as the brand paying you or giving you free or discounted products or services.

Telling your followers about these kinds of relationships is important because it helps keep your recommendations honest and truthful, and it allows people to weigh the value of your endorsements.

As an influencer, it's your responsibility to make these disclosures, to be familiar with the Endorsement Guides, and to comply with laws against deceptive ads. Don't rely on others to do it for you.

When to Disclose

- Disclose when you have any financial, employment, personal, or family relationship with a brand.
    - Financial relationships aren't limited to money. Disclose the relationship if you got anything of value to mention a product.
    - If a brand gives you free or discounted products or other perks and then you mention one of its products, make a disclosure even if you weren't asked to mention that product.
    - Don't assume your followers already know about your brand relationships.
    - Make disclosures even if you think your evaluations are unbiased.
- Keep in mind that tags, likes, pins, and similar ways of showing you like a brand or product are endorsements.
- If posting from abroad, U.S. law applies if it's reasonably foreseeable that the post will affect U.S. consumers. Foreign laws might also apply.
- If you have no brand relationship and are just telling people about a product you bought and happen to like, you don't need to declare that you don't have a brand relationship.

How to Disclose

Make sure people will see and understand the disclosure.

- Place it so it's hard to miss.
    - The disclosure should be placed with the endorsement message itself.
    - Disclosures are likely to be missed if they appear only on an ABOUT ME or profile page, at the end of posts or videos, or anywhere that requires a person to click MORE.
    - Don't mix your disclosure into a group of hashtags or links.

  - If your endorsement is in a picture on a platform like Snapchat and Instagram Stories, superimpose the disclosure over the picture and make sure viewers have enough time to notice and read it.
  - If making an endorsement in a video, the disclosure should be in the video and not just in the description uploaded with the video. Viewers are more likely to notice disclosures made in both audio and video. Some viewers may watch without sound and others may not notice superimposed words.
  - If making an endorsement in a live stream, the disclosure should be repeated periodically so viewers who only see part of the stream will get the disclosure.
- Use simple and clear language.
  - Simple explanations like "Thanks to Acme brand for the free product" are often enough if placed in a way that is hard to miss.
  - So are terms like "advertisement," "ad," and "sponsored."
  - On a space-limited platform like Twitter, the terms "AcmePartner" or "Acme Ambassador" (where Acme is the brand name) are also options.
  - It's fine (but not necessary) to include a hashtag with the disclosure, such as #ad or #sponsored.
  - Don't use vague or confusing terms like "sp," "spon," or "collab," or stand-alone terms like "thanks" or "ambassador," and stay away from other abbreviations and shorthand when possible.
- The disclosure should be in the same language as the endorsement itself.
- Don't assume that a platform's disclosure tool is good enough, but consider using it in addition to your own, good disclosure.

What Else to Know

- You can't talk about your experience with a product you haven't tried.
- If you're paid to talk about a product and thought it was terrible, you can't say it's terrific.
- You can't make up claims about a product that would require proof the advertiser doesn't have—such as scientific proof that a product can treat a health condition.

F. Collection of Information and Privacy Considerations

1. COPPA and Marketing to Children

The Children's Online Privacy Protection Act ("COPPA") protects children under the age of 13 years old from sharing personal information on the internet without express parental consent. Along with parental consent, COPPA also requires that websites post a clear and comprehensive online privacy policy explaining how they collect personal information from children, provide parents with access to the information collected from their children with the option to delete such information, and give parents the option to prevent further collection of information.

COPPA is enforced by the FTC, which has taken law enforcement actions against companies that failed to comply with the provisions. The fines for violations continue to rise. Currently, operators who violate the rule are liable for civil penalties of up to $42,530 per violation. To illustrate the rise in penalties, in 2009, Iconix Brand Group, Inc. settled with the FTC for a fine of $250,000 for violating COPPA and as recently as August 30, 2019, Google reportedly settled to pay between $150–200 million for violating COPPA by collecting information from children under 13 years of age and targeting advertisements to them without their parents' permission.

2. Federal and State Regulatory Framework for Privacy

When companies tell consumers they will safeguard their personal information, the FTC can and does take law enforcement action to make sure that companies live up to these promises. The FTC has brought legal actions against organizations that have violated consumers' privacy rights, or misled them by failing to maintain security for sensitive consumer information, or caused substantial consumer injury. In many of these cases, the FTC has charged the defendants with violating Section 5 of the FTC Act, which bars unfair and deceptive acts and practices in or affecting commerce. In addition to the FTC Act, the agency also enforces other federal laws relating to consumers' privacy and security.

G. Conclusion

As this chapter plainly demonstrates, marketing a product to consumers can be fraught with pitfalls for the unwary brand owner. Advertisers must carefully map out each advertising campaign so as to ensure no misrepresentations are made about a product's performance, no third-party rights are infringed, and each relationship is sufficiently transparent so as not to mislead the consuming public. It is a challenging and ever-evolving area of the law, where public interest dictates the parameters of an advertiser's commercial message, and third-party property rights define its budget. It is the advertiser's role to entertain, motivate, and move us to purchase a product; it is the lawyer's task to ensure they do so within legal, permissible parameters.

Chapter 10

Employment Law Issues in Fashion

Lee S. Sporn and Tiffani McDonough Solomon

A. Introduction

Employment law issues in the fashion industry vary widely and include such topics as employment discrimination, harassment, wage and hour compliance, non-competition agreements, disability accommodation, and medical leave issues, and the creation and implementation of workplace policies, such as dress code policies. This chapter presents an overview of common employment law issues facing the fashion and retail industries.

B. Overview of Discrimination Laws

Federal employment discrimination laws protect employees from discrimination and retaliation based on various protected characteristics such as race, gender, age, religion, pregnancy, and disability. These laws apply to all terms and conditions of employment—including, but not limited to, hiring, placement, promotion, termination, layoff, recall, transfer, leaves of absence, compensation, and training.

1. Title VII of the Civil Rights Act of 1964

Title VII of the Civil Rights Act of 1964 ("Title VII") prohibits discrimination on the basis of race, color, sex, national origin, and religion ("protected classes" or "protected characteristics"). Title VII makes it illegal to retaliate against a person because the person complained about discrimination, filed a charge of discrimination, or participated in an employment discrimination investigation or lawsuit. Many state and local laws provide greater protections than Title VII. For example, California's Fair Employment and Housing Act ("FEHA") and the New York City Human Rights Law ("NYHRL") include gender identity and sexual orientation as protected categories.

Title VII also prohibits harassment based upon a protected characteristic. In its most basic form, harassment is physical, verbal, or nonverbal conduct that unreasonably interferes with an employee's job performance or creates an intimidating, hostile, or offensive work environment. Harassment is considered unlawful when the unwelcome conduct is based on a protected characteristic.

Under Title VII, a plaintiff seeking to recover for harassment must proceed under one of two theories: (1) harassment by reason of a hostile work environment; or (2) quid pro quo harassment. A hostile work environment claim under Title VII requires a showing that the harassment was sufficiently severe or pervasive to alter the conditions of the victim's employment and create an abusive working environment, and that a specific basis exists for imputing the objectionable conduct to the employer.

In order to establish a prima facie case of quid pro quo sexual harassment, a plaintiff must present evidence that the plaintiff was subjected to unwelcome sexual conduct and that the reaction to that conduct was then used as a basis for decisions, either actual or threatened, affecting compensation, terms, conditions, or privileges of employment. Quid pro quo harassment is literally a "this for that" harassment.

Employers may also be liable for harassment by nonemployees such as vendors, consultants, or customers if the employer has knowledge of the harassment and fails to act. As such, fashion companies must investigate and take all complaints of harassment seriously, even an employee's complaint involving a top client or customer. In the latter situation, if there is merit to the complaint and a client is unlawfully harassing an employee, the company may have to direct the client to cease patronizing the company's stores.

Finally, Title VII also requires that employers reasonably accommodate applicants' and employees' sincerely held religious practices, unless doing so would impose an undue hardship on the operation of the employer's business. This issue is of particular importance to the fashion industry because fashion companies are selling an image—one carefully honed and consistently reinforced. Employees of fashion companies (particularly, but by no means exclusively, customer-facing employees) are generally seen as ambassadors of the brand, and so fashion employers care deeply about how they look. Dress codes, as well as image and grooming policies, have been repeatedly attacked as a form of discrimination, with inconsistent results. When an appearance policy is a pretext to discriminate, or has the impact of discriminating, against individuals in a protected class, antidiscrimination laws are implicated.

2. The Pregnancy Discrimination Act

The Pregnancy Discrimination Act ("PDA") amended Title VII to include discrimination on the basis of pregnancy, childbirth, or related medical conditions. Under the PDA, women who are pregnant or affected by pregnancy-related conditions must be treated in the same manner as other applicants or employees with similar abilities or limitations. It is also unlawful to retaliate against an individual for opposing employment practices that discriminate based on pregnancy or for filing a discrimination charge, testifying, or participating in any way in an investigation, proceeding, or litigation involving pregnancy discrimination.

Several state and local jurisdictions (e.g., California, New Jersey, New York City, Philadelphia) have pregnancy accommodation laws that expressly require employers to provide reasonable workplace accommodations to pregnant employees absent a showing of undue hardship on the employer's business. These laws cover accommodations of symptoms such as morning sickness and fatigue. Common potential accommodations for pregnant employees include:

- more frequent restroom breaks;
- periodic rest for those who stand for long periods;
- assistance with manual labor;
- leave for a period of disability arising from childbirth;
- reassignment to a vacant position; and
- job restructuring.

3. The Age Discrimination in Employment Act of 1967

The Age Discrimination in Employment Act of 1967 ("ADEA") protects employees who are 40 years old or older from discrimination because of age. The law also makes it illegal to retaliate against a person because the person complained about discrimination, filed a charge of discrimination, or participated in an employment discrimination investigation or lawsuit.

4. Americans with Disabilities Act

The Americans with Disabilities Act ("ADA") makes it illegal to discriminate against a qualified person with a disability. The law also makes it illegal to retaliate against a person because the person complained about discrimination, filed a charge of discrimination, or participated in an employment discrimination investigation or lawsuit.

Further, the ADA requires that employers reasonably accommodate the known physical or mental limitations of an otherwise qualified individual with a disability who is an applicant or employee, unless doing so would impose an undue hardship on the operation of the employer's business. "Reasonable accommodation" means an employer must take steps to enable a qualified individual with a disability to perform the essential functions of the position. Examples of "reasonable accommodations" include:

- Job restructuring;
- Modifying work schedules or reducing hours;
- Reassigning an employee to a vacant position;
- Making existing facilities readily accessible;

- Acquiring or modifying equipment or devices; or
- Providing a leave of absence.

"Reasonable accommodations" do not include:

- Eliminating or reallocating an essential function of a job;
- Lowering production standards of quality or quantity; or
- Providing items for general daily living not specific to the requirements of the job (e.g., contact lenses).

An employer's obligation to provide an accommodation is generally prompted by a request from the employee or applicant that triggers the "interactive process." Interestingly, the ADA itself does not mention the term "interactive process" with respect to reasonable accommodations; however, the ADA's regulations state that: "To determine the appropriate reasonable accommodation it may be necessary for the covered entity to initiate an informal, interactive process with the qualified individual with a disability in need of accommodation. This process should identify the precise limitations resulting from the disability and the potential reasonable accommodations that could overcome those limitations."

The ADA does not require employers to speculate about the accommodation needs of employees and applicants; rather, the individual requesting the accommodation has an obligation to provide the employer with enough information about the disability to determine a reasonable accommodation. An employer then has an obligation to explore a potential accommodation and provide the employee with an appropriate reasonable accommodation. Both the employer and the individual seeking accommodation must participate in the interactive process in good faith.

Finally, the "association" provision of the ADA prohibits employment discrimination against a person, whether or not he or she has a disability, because of his or her known relationship or association with a person with a known disability. This means that an employer is prohibited from making adverse employment decisions based on unfounded concerns about the known disability of a family member or anyone else with whom the applicant or employee has a relationship or association.

5. Requirement to Exhaust Administrative Remedies

In order to assert a Title VII, PDA, ADA, or ADEA claim, the plaintiff must have first exhausted their administrative remedies with respect to the claim by filing a charge with the Equal Employment Opportunity Commission ("EEOC") or equivalent state agency. The purpose behind filing a charge with the EEOC is to give the Commission an opportunity to investigate and try to resolve the controversy through conciliation before allowing the aggrieved party to pursue a lawsuit. There are strict time limits for filing a charge. Where the discrimination took place can determine how long you have to file a charge. Generally the filing deadline is 180 calendar days unless the state or local agency enforces a state or local law that prohibits employment discrimination on the same basis; then the filing deadline is extended to 300 calendar days. The rules are slightly different for age discrimination charges. For age discrimination, the filing deadline is only extended to 300 days if there is a state law prohibiting age discrimination in employment and a state agency or authority enforcing that law. The deadline is not extended if only a local law prohibits age discrimination. The filing deadlines may be extended by state law. For example, in California, the Stop Harassment and Reporting Extension (SHARE) Act extends the deadline to file a discrimination complaint with the state agency to three years.

6. The Equal Pay Act of 1963

The Equal Pay Act of 1963 ("EPA") makes it illegal to pay different wages based on gender if the employees perform equal work in the same workplace. The law also makes it illegal to retaliate against a person because the person complained about discrimination, filed a charge of discrimination, or participated in an employment discrimination investigation or lawsuit. Several states and local jurisdictions are enacting far more expansive equal pay laws. For example, Oregon law prohibits pay discrimination on the basis of race, color, religion, sex, sexual orientation, national origin, marital status, veteran status, disability, and age.

7. The Family and Medical Leave Act

The Family and Medical Leave Act (FMLA) applies to all companies with 50 or more employees. These employers must provide an eligible employee with up to 12 weeks of unpaid leave each year for any of the following reasons:

- For the birth and care of the newborn child of an employee;
- For placement with the employee of a child for adoption or foster care;
- To care for an immediate family member (i.e., spouse, child, or parent) with a serious health condition; or
- To take medical leave when the employee is unable to work because of a serious health condition.

Employees are eligible for leave if they have worked for their employer at least 12 months, at least 1,250 hours over the past 12 months, and work at a location where the company employs 50 or more employees within 75 miles.

Several states such as New York, California, New Jersey, and Washington D.C. have more generous laws that mandate paid family leave and/or additional leave time.

C. Discrimination Case Studies

1. Sexual Harassment Case Study

Mendez-Nouel v. Gucci America, Inc.

2012 U.S. Dist. LEXIS 160530 (S.D.N.Y. Nov. 8, 2012)

Opinion & Order

ENGELMAYER, District Judge.

Plaintiff Adolfo Mendez-Nouel, a former clothing salesperson at Gucci America, Inc. ("Gucci"), claims that during his employment he was subjected to a hostile work environment on account of his sex and sexual orientation, and that he was retaliated against for complaining about that environment, in violation of Title VII of the Civil Rights Act of 1964 ("Title VII"), 42 U.S.C. § 2000e *et seq.*, the New York State Human Rights Law ("NYSHRL"), N.Y. Exec. Law § 290 *et seq.*, and the New York City Human Rights Law ("NYCHRL"), N.Y. City Admin. Code § 8-101 *et seq.* Gucci now moves for summary judgment against Mendez-Nouel's complaint. For the following reasons, the Court grants Gucci's motion for summary judgment as to Mendez-Nouel's Title VII and NYSHRL claims and declines to exercise supplemental jurisdiction over his NYCHRL claims.

I. Background and Undisputed Facts

On November 12, 2007, Mendez-Nouel was hired by Gucci as a Sales Associate in the Women's Ready-to-Wear ("WRTW") Department in Gucci's flagship Fifth Avenue, Manhattan Store. Mendez-Nouel initially reported to Ami Garbiras; in September 2008, after Garbiras was promoted, David Gray was hired as the WRTW manager. The WRTW manager, in turn, reported to the store manager, who was Mark Mitsukawa at the time Mendez-Nouel was hired; in summer 2008 Michael Daly replaced Mitsukawa.

During Mendez-Nouel's tenure, at least four documented incidents occurred as to which he was either formally reprimanded or informally spoken to about his conduct at or in relation to the workplace. These incidents, the facts of which are undisputed, are as follows:

In March 2008, Mendez-Nouel was extensively quoted in a *New York Times* article about Gucci; Mendez-Nouel's then-manager, Mitsukawa, spoke to him, and cautioned him to refrain from speaking to the press about internal corporate matters.

In May or June 2008, Mendez-Nouel became embroiled in a dispute with a co-worker. This disagreement led the co-worker to request a meeting between Mendez-Nouel, the co-worker, and the WRTW assistant manager, at which the dispute was resolved.

In summer 2008, Mendez-Nouel had another dispute with a co-worker, this time about the proper crediting for a clothing sale. Although Mendez-Nouel did not raise the issue directly with the co-worker, he approached managers to dispute how a sale was credited as between him and the co-worker. During the episode, Mendez-Nouel said he "just want[ed] to go home"; the assistant manager told him that if he did not want to remain in Gucci's employ, he could leave.

In September 2008, during a store inventory, Mendez-Nouel shouted "Mets suck!" over a balcony in the store, yelling to a co-worker below. Daly, the store manager, heard this outburst, as did an outside auditor. Gray, Mendez-Nouel's direct supervisor, reprimanded him for this incident and placed a "Memo to File" in his personnel file. Mendez-Nouel concedes that this incident merited discipline by Gray; he apologized to Daly for his conduct.

In addition, during early 2009, Mendez-Nouel was warned several times about other incidents, including hanging up the phone on a customer, shoving a garment at a customer in a rude fashion, and appearing dejected on the sales floor. Mendez-Nouel concedes that management approached him and raised concerns about these incidents; however, he disputes that the incidents themselves occurred. Mendez-Nouel instead claims that the underlying incidents were fabricated as a pretext to justify terminating him. Mendez-Nouel does admit, however, that on February 20, 2009, immediately after he allegedly hung up on the customer, he left his post on the sales floor, retired to the employee locker room, and broke down in tears. He also admits that he feared for his job at this time.

On February 23, 2009, Mendez-Nouel attended a meeting with his manager, Gray, a Gucci HR representative, and the store's assistant manager. At that meeting, management discussed the incidents for which Mendez-Nouel had recently been disciplined (those which Mendez-Nouel claims did not occur), and asked Mendez-Nouel whether he was committed to his job at Gucci. Mendez-Nouel stated that he was distracted by personal issues outside work, including a recent unsuccessful audition for a movie and a possibility that his wife was pregnant, but he stated that he was committed to his job. Three days later, on February 26, 2009, Mendez-Nouel sent an email to Lori Strober-Lewin, the HR representative who had been present at the February 23 meeting, to formally complain about alleged harassment by his immediate supervisor, Gray, and the store manager, Daly. Mendez-Nouel claimed that he was (1) touched by Daly, (2) subjected to inappropriate comments by Gray, and (3) retaliated against for failing to accept the touching or to participate in inappropriate conversations. Although Mendez-Nouel asserts that he had once made an offhand remark to a co-worker to the effect that Daly had touched him in an unwelcome manner, the February 26, 2009 complaint was his first formal statement to HR about alleged harassment. Gucci quickly launched an investigation into Mendez-Nouel's complaint.

On March 4, 2009, as part of that investigation, Mendez-Nouel met with Strober-Lewin, Gucci's HR representative, and Gucci's regional manager (Daly's immediate supervisor). Strober-Lewin took notes at this meeting. These reflect that Mendez-Nouel acknowledged that business was slow, and that he felt he was "next in line" to be terminated.

After the meeting, Mendez-Nouel went to lunch; upon his return, he was observed to be shaking and out of breath. A fellow employee called an ambulance, and Mendez-Nouel was diagnosed with a panic attack.

On March 5, 2009—the day after Mendez-Nouel's panic attack at the store—a co-worker, Meryam Kabsy, called HR representative Strober-Lewin. Kabsy expressed concern over Mendez-Nouel's condition and behavior. Kabsy stated that she believed Mendez-Nouel's recent agitation was creating a dangerous situation at the workplace. Kabsy also told HR that Mendez-Nouel had said to her that "something big was going to happen" but he "couldn't tell her" what it was. Kabsy also informed HR that Mendez-Nouel had related to her a story from his childhood in which he had shot somebody with a BB gun.

Strober-Lewin also interviewed two other co-workers of Mendez-Nouel's. As reflected in her report, these co-workers related other provocative statements that Mendez-Nouel had made in the workplace. These included that: (1) "People are ungrateful and something big is going to happen and he knows about it but they don't"; (2) "people had become bad towards each other and people don't understand life until something bad happens" and "something big should happen so people will care about each other"; (3) Mendez-Nouel "would make jokes about shooting and would point his finger to himself. He would talk about shooting people and he would read the internet and talk about the world and how it should end and start over. He said somebody should be shot"; and (4) Mendez-Nouel had made comments about the world coming to an end, or the destruction of the world, around the time of the 2008 presidential election.

On March 6, 2009, after speaking with various employees, Gucci's HR department determined that numerous employees were concerned about Mendez-Nouel's references to shooting and violence. It decided to suspend Mendez-Nouel pending further investigation. A contemporaneous e-mail from Gucci's global HR director, explaining the decision, stated:

> [W]e have had three employees inform us today that they are seriously concerned about their safety as Adolfo has made numerous comments about shooting people (not employees but people in general) and that Michael Daly, David Gray and Gucci will "get what's coming to them and something big is going to happen." He sounds seriously disturbed and I made the decision at this time to suspend him until further notice.

After the suspension, HR continued investigating Mendez-Nouel's behavior. Strober-Lewin, the HR employee, spoke with three other co-workers who had not previously been interviewed. Her investigation report reflects that those witnesses attributed the following statements to Mendez-Nouel: (1) two co-workers stated, consistent with the earlier interviews, that Mendez-Nouel had said that "something big was going to happen"; and (2) another co-worker also stated that Mendez-Nouel went on "tirades" and "if you disagreed with him you were on his list." A third co-worker expressed "relief" that Mendez-Nouel was no longer on the sales floor.

On March 18, 2009, Strober-Lewin interviewed Mendez-Nouel by telephone as part of the investigation. On March 19, 2009, following the additional interviews, Gucci terminated Mendez-Nouel's employment.

II. Procedural History

After his termination, Mendez-Nouel filed an administrative complaint with the Equal Employment Opportunity Commission, claiming that his rights under Title VII had been violated. On March 15, 2010, the EEOC issued plaintiff a "right to sue" letter. On April 22, 2010, Mendez-Nouel filed this lawsuit. Mendez-Nouel claims that he was subject to a hostile work environment on account of his sex (male) and sexual orientation (heterosexual) when: (1) Gray, his direct manager, made a number of sexually-charged comments on the sales floor; and (2) Daly, the store manager, touched him on the shoulders and back. As to Gray, Mendez-Nouel alleges that Gray said on at least two occasions that Mendez-Nouel was "gay inside" and that Gray "bet [Mendez-Nouel was] gay." Mendez-Nouel also asserts that Gray would say that men in the store were "hot" and that he would "do that guy." Gray also allegedly would relate stories of his nights out at gay clubs, including at least one episode where Gray was "pole dancing" or engaging in other sexualized behavior. Mendez-Nouel also complains of an instance in which Gray described a YouTube video he had seen. In that video, Anna Nicole Smith is drawn as a smurf character and said "you should smell my smurph"; Mendez-Nouel states that he understood this to be a reference to female genitalia. Mendez-Nouel states that he was uncomfortable when Gray made such comments, and that he did not participate in the sexualized banter.

As to Daly, Mendez-Nouel asserts that in or around September 2008, Daly, whom Mendez-Nouel alleges to be homosexual, approached him from behind, grabbed his shoulders, and gave them a brief massage; Mendez-Nouel alleges that at the conclusion of the massage, Daly ran his hand down Mendez-Nouel's back, stopping above the buttocks. Mendez-Nouel also alleges that, also in or about September 2008, Daly gave him a second brief shoulder rub.

In addition to claiming a hostile work environment, Mendez-Nouel also claims that he was retaliated against, in two ways. First, he claims that he was denied a day off during the Christmas season, but that a co-worker who did join in Gray's sexual banter was given a day off during that time period. Second, he claims that he was terminated in March 2009 in retaliation for his February 26, 2009 complaint about his alleged harassment at the hands of Gray and Daly.

On May 4, 2012, following discovery, the Court held a pre-motion conference regarding Gucci's proposed motion for summary judgment. On June 8, 2012, Gucci filed the instant motion. On July 13, 2012, Mendez-Nouel filed his opposition. On July 27, 2012, Gucci filed its reply. On September 4, 2012, the Court held oral argument on this motion.

* * *

IV. Applicable Legal Standard

Summary judgment may be granted only where the submissions, taken together, "show [ ] that there is no genuine dispute as to any material fact and the movant is entitled to judgment as a matter of law." Fed.R.Civ.P. 56(a). The movant bears the burden of demonstrating the absence of a material factual question; in making this determination, the court must view all facts "in the light most favorable" to the non-movant. *Celotex Corp. v. Catrett,* 477 U.S. 317, 323, 106 S.Ct. 2548, 91 L.Ed.2d 265 (1986); *see also Holcomb v. Iona Coll.,* 521 F.3d 130, 132 (2d Cir.2008). "A party may not rely on mere speculation or conjecture as to the true nature of the facts to overcome a motion for summary judgment," because "conclusory allegations or denials cannot by themselves create a genuine issue of material fact where none would otherwise exist." *Hicks v. Baines,* 593 F.3d 159, 166 (2d Cir.2010) (citation omitted). "Only disputes over facts that might affect the outcome of the suit under the governing law" will preclude a grant of summary judgment. *Anderson v. Liberty Lobby, Inc.,* 477 U.S. 242, 248, 106 S.Ct. 2505, 91 L.Ed.2d 202 (1986).

In cases alleging discrimination or retaliation, courts must use "an extra measure of caution" in determining whether to grant summary judgment "because direct evidence of discriminatory intent is rare and such intent often must be inferred from circumstantial evidence found in affidavits and depositions." *Schiano v. Quality Payroll Sys., Inc.,* 445 F.3d 597, 603 (2d Cir.2006) (citation omitted). However, "the salutary purposes of summary judgment—avoiding protracted, expensive and harassing trials—apply no less to discrimination cases." *Weinstock v. Columbia Univ.,* 224 F.3d 33, 41 (2d Cir.2000) (citation omitted). Thus, in such cases, "a plaintiff must provide more than conclusory allegations to resist a motion for summary judgment." *Holcomb,* 521 F.3d at 137.

Mendez-Nouel's claims logically divide between his substantive claims of sex and sexual orientation discrimination and harassment (based on the comments and conduct of Gray and Daly) and his claims of retaliation. The Court addresses these categories of claims in turn.

V. Mendez-Nouel's Substantive Claims Under Title VII and the NYSHRL

In claiming discrimination and harassment, Mendez-Nouel alleges that Gray's comments and Daly's touching of him were directed at him on the basis of his gender and/or his sexual orientation, and that these actions together created a hostile work environment. As noted, Mendez-Nouel brings claims under Title VII, the NYSHRL, and the NYCHRL. The Court analyzes the substantive claims under Title VII and the NYSHRL together, because the substantive standards for liability under these statutes are coextensive. Measured against the standards, it is clear that the evidence, even when viewed in the light most favorable to Mendez-Nouel, is insufficient to support claims under Title VII and the NYSHRL.

A. Whether the Allegedly-Harassing Comments or Actions Were Directed at Mendez-Nouel Because of his Sex or Sexual Orientation

"It is axiomatic that mistreatment at work, [including] subjection to a hostile work environment . . . is actionable under Title VII only when it occurs because of an employee's sex." *Brown v. Henderson,* 257 F.3d 246, 252 (2d Cir.2001) (citing *Oncale v. Sundowner Offshore Servs., Inc.,* 523 U.S. 75, 79–80, 118 S.Ct. 998, 140 L.Ed.2d 201 (1998)); *see also Alfano v. Costello,* 294 F.3d 365, 377 (2d Cir.2002)("It is . . . important in hostile work environment cases to exclude from consideration personnel decisions that lack a linkage or correlation to the claimed ground of discrimination."). In cases of alleged same-sex harassment, the Court must "distinguish between simple teasing or roughhousing among members of the same sex, and conduct which a reasonable person in the plaintiff's position would find severely hostile or abusive." *Oncale,* 523 U.S. at 81–82. "The prohibition of harassment on the basis of sex requires neither asexuality nor androgyny in the workplace; it forbids only behavior so objectively offensive as to alter the 'conditions' of the victim's employment." *Id.*

Accordingly, in same-sex harassment cases, courts in this Circuit, drawing upon the Supreme Court's decision in *Oncale,* have "suggested three evidentiary routes to prove gender-based discrimination in a same-sex harassment case: (1) evidence that the harasser is homosexual and that the harassment is motivated by sexual desire; (2) evidence that the harasser was motivated by general hostility to employees of victim's sex; [or] (3) comparative evidence that the harasser treated employees of both sexes differently." *Borski v. Staten Island Rapid Transit,* No. 04-cv-3614, 2006 U.S. Dist. LEXIS 89242, at *9–10, 2006 WL 3681142 (E.D.N.Y. Dec. 11, 2006).

The Court now applies these standards to Daly's touching of Mendez-Nouel and to Gray's comments to him.

1. Daly's Alleged Touching of Mendez-Nouel

Mendez-Nouel asserts that he has raised a triable issue of fact as to whether Daly, whom he alleges is gay, touched Mendez-Nouel out of "sexual desire." But the actions of which Mendez-Nouel complains — two brief shoulder rubs (one of which concluded with Daly running his hand down Mendez-Nouel's back), both of which occurred in a public place and were unaccompanied by any suggestive comments — are not evocative of such desire. Indeed, claims of discrimination premised on far more suggestive conduct have been found wanting. *See, e.g., Soliman v. Deutsche Bank,* No. 03-cv-104, 2004 U.S. Dist. LEXIS 9087, at *32, 2004 WL 1124689 (S.D.N.Y. May 20, 2004) (no inference of desire where supervisor treated plaintiff "favorably, touched his arm, touched his shoulders in meetings when describing their relationship as 'close' . . . sat close to him, commented that he was a 'good looking guy,' told [plaintiff] he was gay, invited him to social events and an allegedly 'gay' bar on two occasions, [and] asked him about his personal life"); *Moran v. Fashion Inst. of Tech.,* No. 00-cv-1275, 2002 U.S. Dist. LEXIS 19387, at *18, 2002 WL 31288272 (S.D.N.Y. Oct. 7, 2002) (supervisor's conduct of lingering next to plaintiff, touching him on the arm or shoulder and complimenting him on his appearance was "not inherently sexual"). Nor were the areas of Mendez-Nouel's body that Daly allegedly touched (his shoulder and back) "gender-specific body parts" which could reasonably give rise to the inference that Daly touched them *because* of their sexual significance. *See Redd v. N.Y. State Div. of Parole,* 678 F.3d 166, 179 (2d Cir.2012) (vacating grant of summary judgment where alleged female on female harassment included allegations that defendant had repeatedly groped plaintiff's breasts).

Mendez-Nouel's argument against summary judgment assumes the conclusion that Daly *must* have had the requisite "sexual desire" because Daly touched him. But the fact that Daly may be gay, without more, does not imbue his every touch with the "sexual desire" necessary to sustain a harassment claim. And there is no evidence that Daly made any sexualized, flirtatious, or innuendo-laden comment to Mendez-Nouel, or confided in others that he was attracted to Mendez-Nouel. Further, it is undisputed that Daly touched or hugged Gucci employees of both sexes, thus rendering unreasonable any inference that Daly touched only those to whom he was attracted on the basis of gender. Mendez-Nouel has done nothing to distinguish the episodes complained of from the other, categorically non-sexual episodes in which Daly touched female employees.

Accordingly, on the record at summary judgment, a reasonable jury could not find that Daly touched Mendez-Nouel because of "sexual desire" without engaging in "unsubstantiated speculation." *Jeffreys v. City of N.Y.*, 426 F.3d 549, 554 (2d Cir.2005) (quoting *Fujitsu Ltd. v. Fed. Express Corp.*, 247 F.3d 423, 428 (2d Cir.2001)). To the extent Mendez-Nouel's claims of discrimination are based on Daly's having touched him, he has failed to carry his burden to show a genuine issue of fact as to whether Daly touched him because of his sex or sexual orientation.

2. Gray's Alleged Comments in Mendez-Nouel's Presence

Gray's comments towards Mendez Nouel, as alleged, fall into five discrete categories. As to four of them, Mendez-Nouel has similarly failed to adduce evidence tending to show that Gray directed comments of a sexual nature towards him because of his sex or sexual orientation. As to one category of comments, however, Mendez-Nouel has carried his burden to come forward with evidence that the comments were directed at him because of his sex and sexual orientation.

Specifically, Mendez-Nouel takes issue with five categories of comments allegedly made by Gray:

1. Gray allegedly told Mendez-Nouel, on several occasions, "You know what, I know you're gay inside. You are so gay. You just don't know it."

2. Gray often made comments about other men's appearances, saying things like "that guy is hot" or "I would totally do that guy."

3. Gray would commonly relate stories of his night life, including "sex-based exploits," including stories of a party including pole dancing, and two male employees kissing in the bathroom at the company Christmas party.

4. Once, Gray told employees a story about a YouTube video depicting Anna Nicole Smith, as a smurf, in which the smurf referred to female genitalia. During this conversation, Gray allegedly also commented that he believed Anna Nicole Smith and her lawyer were having a homosexual relationship.

5. Gray tried to steer every conversation towards a discussion about homosexuality or gay pride.

Significantly, Mendez-Nouel concedes that Gray talked about personal or sexual matters "in front of everybody," both male and female, homosexual and heterosexual employees. As to the categories of comments identified above as # 2, # 3, # 4, and # 5, that concession, without more, defeats the inference he asks the Court to draw that the comments were made in Mendez-Nouel's presence because of his sex or sexual orientation. And Mendez-Nouel has not identified any evidence in support of his assertion that these comments were directed at Mendez-Nouel because of his gender or sexual orientation.

However, the first category of comments by Gray—that Mendez-Nouel was "gay inside" and just didn't "know it"—is different. On its face, these statements are reasonably interpreted as having been directed at Mendez-Nouel because he is a male who asserts he is heterosexual but is in fact homosexual, *i.e.,* directed to Mendez-Nouel because of Mendez-Nouel's sex and sexual orientation (actual or perceived). Accordingly, were Mendez-Nouel's claim of a hostile work environment to go to trial, these statements, but not those falling within categories # 2 through # 5, could be put before a jury as probative evidence.

B. Whether the Alleged Harassment Constitutes a Hostile Work Environment

Mendez-Nouel claims that Daly's touching and Gray's comments combined to expose him to a hostile work environment. A hostile work environment claim under Title VII:

[R]equires a showing [1] that the harassment was "sufficiently severe or pervasive to alter the conditions of the victim's employment and create an abusive working environment," and [2] that a specific basis exists for imputing the objectionable conduct to the employer. *Perry v. Ethan Allen, Inc.,* 115 F.3d 143, 149 (2d Cir.1997). The plaintiff must show that the workplace was so severely permeated with discriminatory intimidation, ridicule, and insult that the terms and conditions of her employment were thereby altered. *Leibovitz v. N.Y. City Transit Auth.,* 252 F.3d 179, 188 (2d Cir.2001). This test has objective and subjective elements: the misconduct shown must be "severe or pervasive enough to create an objectively hostile or abusive work environment," and the victim must also subjectively perceive that environment to be abusive. *Harris v. Forklift Sys., Inc.,* 510 U.S. 17, 21, 114 S.Ct. 367, 126 L.Ed.2d 295 (1993). As a general rule, incidents must be more than "episodic; they must be sufficiently continuous and concerted in order to be deemed pervasive." *Perry,*115 F.3d at 149. Isolated acts, unless very serious, do not meet the threshold of severity or pervasiveness. *Brennan,* 192 F.3d at 318; *see also Faragher v. City of Boca Raton,* 524 U.S. 775, 788, 118 S.Ct. 2275, 141 L.Ed.2d 662 (1998) (noting that "we have made it clear that conduct must be extreme to amount to a change in the terms and conditions of employment").

In analyzing a hostile work environment claim, the Court is "required to look to the record as a whole and assess the totality of the circumstances, considering a variety of factors, including the frequency of the discriminatory conduct; its severity; whether it is physically threatening or humiliating, or a mere offensive utterance; and whether it unreasonably interferes with an employee's work performance." *Gorzynski v. JetBlue Airways Corp.,* 596 F.3d 93, 102 (2d Cir.2010). Analyzed under this rubric, neither Daly's touching, nor Gray's comments, nor the two together suffice to create a genuine issue of fact as to whether Mendez-Nouel suffered a hostile work environment.

1. Daly's Alleged Touching of Mendez-Nouel

As noted above, Mendez-Nouel alleges that Daly twice grabbed his shoulders, each time for less than five seconds. On one of those occasions, Daly allegedly ran his hand down Mendez-Nouel's back. These events can only be characterized as "episodic" and "isolated," and do not constitute the "concerted" or "continuous" course of harassment that Title VII and the NYSHRL require. *Alfano,* 294 F.3d at 374.

Mendez-Nouel attempts to salvage these claims by arguing—correctly—that many cases have found that a small number of serious incidents can qualify as sufficiently serious to raise a genuine issue of fact as to whether a work environment was hostile. As Gucci rightly observes, however, the facts of those cases are a far cry from those presented here. *See Cruz v. Coach,* 202 F.3d 560 (2d Cir.2000) (harasser said women should be "barefoot and pregnant," leered at the victim, and repeatedly backed victim into a wall in a threatening manner); *Tomka v. Seiler Corp.,* 66 F.3d 1295 (2d Cir.1995) (victim was allegedly raped by three co-workers); *Kotcher v. Rosa & Sullivan Appliance Ctr.,* 957 F.2d 59 (2d Cir.1992) (harasser made numerous comments about victim's breasts, and pretended to masturbate behind plaintiffs' backs); *Breeding v. Cendant Corp.,* No. 01-cv-11563, 2003 U.S. Dist. LEXIS 6558, 2003 WL 1907971 (S.D.N.Y. Apr. 17, 2003) (harasser made comments about victim engaging in "wild sex," demonstrated sexual positions in front of co-workers, and asked on a conference call whether victim was wearing a "garter belt, panties, and stockings"). This line of case law thus does not salvage Mendez-Nouel's claims. His allegations about Daly do not come close to constituting a hostile work environment under Title VII or the NYSHRL.

2. Gray's Alleged Comments to Mendez-Nouel

Gray's comments to Mendez-Nouel also do not suffice to constitute a hostile work environment under Title VII or the NYSHRL. As an initial matter, the Court has already found that only one set of Gray's alleged comments can reasonably be said to have been motivated by Mendez-Nouel's sex or sexual orientation. Gray's several statements to Mendez-Nouel—to the effect that, "You know what, I know you're gay inside. You are so gay. You just don't know it"—viewed alone, cannot prevent summary judgment for Gucci on Mendez-Nouel's Title VII and NYSHRL claims. However, even if the Court considered all of Gray's alleged comments together—and, it bears repeating, there is no evidence whatsoever that the vast majority of them were directed at Mendez-Nouel because of his sex or sexual orientation—they would still be insufficient to be actionable. That is because these comments, even viewed together, lack the pervasiveness, ridicule, or intimidation necessary to create a hostile work environment for purposes of Title VII. "Conduct that can be categorized as a few isolated incidents, teasing, casual comments or sporadic conversation will not be deemed to create a hostile work environment." *Davis-Bell v. Columbia Univ.,* No. 10-cv-4362, 2012 U.S. Dist. LEXIS 38490, at *38, 2012 WL 946680 (S.D.N.Y. Mar. 19, 2012). Further, that Mendez-Nouel may have taken offense at Gray's comments does not mean that he was being discriminated against on the basis of sex or sexual orientation. *Cf. Fox v. Sierra Dev. Co.,* 876 F.Supp. 1169, 1176 (D.Nev.1995) ("Pictures, literature and discussions of homosexual conduct do not inherently intimidate, ridicule, or insult men. [. . .] That an otherwise reasonable man might be highly offended by homosexual depictions is not enough. He must reasonably feel the homosexual depictions strike at his gender or attack him because of his gender. . . .").

Notably, courts in this Circuit have found far more serious non-physical conduct to fall short of creating a hostile work environment. *See, e.g., Marshall v. N.Y. City Bd. of Elections,* 322 F. App'x 17 (2d Cir.2009) (summary order) (finding no hostile work environment where homosexual supervisor showed plaintiff a "sexual device he had purchased for his partner," even though plaintiff "may have been legitimately offended" by such talk); *Murray v. Visiting Nurse Servs.,* 528 F.Supp.2d 257, 278–79 (S.D.N.Y.2007) (male-to-male statements in the workplace such as "you're such a bitch," "good morning ladies," "when are you going to come out of the closet," and "are you ladies going to the parade?" insufficient to defeat summary judgment on hostile work environment claim).

In sum, Gray's comments, while inappropriate, fail, as a matter of law, to form the basis of a finding of a hostile work environment for purposes of Title VII and the NYSHRL.

3. Daly's Touching and Gray's Comments In Combination

Mindful of its obligation to "look to the record as a whole and assess the totality of the circumstances," *Gorzynski,* 596 F.3d at 102, the Court also considers whether Daly's episodic touching and Gray's sporadic comments combined to create an arguably hostile work environment.

On review of the record as a whole, and in line with numerous other cases from within this Circuit, the Court readily concludes that they do not. *See, e.g., Dayes v. Pace Univ.,* No. 98-cv-3675, 2000 U.S. Dist. LEXIS 3698, at *2–3, *11–12, 2000 WL 307382 (S.D.N.Y. Mar. 24, 2000), *aff'd,* 2 F. App'x 204 (2d Cir.2001) (granting summary judgment to defendant where plaintiff was subject to six sexual comments, multiple requests for dates, was screamed at by a supervisor, and was touched on the back); *Lucas v. S. Nassau Cmty. Hosp.,* 54 F.Supp.2d 141, 147–48 (E.D.N.Y.1998) (denying NYSHRL hostile work environment claim where supervisor brushed against plaintiff three times, touched plaintiff three times, briefly touched plaintiff's back or shoulders five to seven other times, asked about the color of plaintiff's underwear, said plaintiff wanted to "go to bed" with her, and said "fuck you" to plaintiff on two occasions); *Ricard v. Kraft Gen. Foods, Inc.,* No. 92-cv-2256, 1993 U.S. Dist. LEXIS 21062, at *9, 1993 WL 385129 (S.D.N.Y. Mar. 16, 1993), *aff'd,* 17 F.3d 1426 (2d Cir.1994) (four sexually-oriented incidents insufficient to withstand summary judgment). The episodes Mendez-Nouel complains of are simply too episodic, insufficiently serious, and, most important, insufficiently tied to his gender or sexual orientation, to have materially altered the conditions of Mendez-Nouel's employment on the basis of any protected classification. Gucci's motion as to Mendez Nouel's substantive Title VII and NYSHRL claim is, therefore, granted in its entirety.

VI. Mendez-Nouel's Claims of Retaliation Under Title VII and the NYSHRL

Mendez-Nouel also claims that Gucci retaliated against him for his February 26, 2009 complaint against Daly and Gray by placing him on administrative leave and ultimately terminating his employment.

Under Title VII, it is unlawful for an employer to discriminate against an employee because that employee "has opposed any practice made an unlawful employment practice by this subchapter, or because he has made a charge, testified, assisted, or participated in any manner in an investigation, proceeding, or hearing under this subchapter." 42 U.S.C. § 2000e-3(a). The statute thus "prohibits an employer from taking 'materially adverse' action against an employee because the employee opposed conduct that Title VII forbids or the employee otherwise engaged in protected activity." *Tepperwien v. Entergy Nuclear Operations, Inc.*, 663 F.3d 556, 567 (2d Cir.2011). Title VII and the NYSHRL are therefore violated when "a retaliatory motive plays a part in adverse employment actions toward an employee, whether or not it was the sole cause." *Cosgrove v. Sears, Roebuck & Co.*, 9 F.3d 1033, 1039 (2d Cir.1993).

In adjudicating retaliation claims, courts follow the "familiar burden-shifting framework" of *McDonnell Douglas [Corp. v. Green*, 411 U.S. 792, 93 S.Ct. 1817, 36 L. Ed.2d 668 (1973)]." To prove a prima facie case of retaliation, a plaintiff must establish: (1) that she participated in a protected activity; (2) that participation in the protected activity was known to the employer; (3) that the employer thereafter subjected her to a materially adverse employment action; and (4) that there was a causal connection between the protected activity and the adverse employment action. *See Kaytor v. Elec. Boat Corp.*, 609 F.3d 537, 552 (2d Cir.2010). The burden of proof at the prima facie stage has been characterized as "de minimis." *Hicks v. Baines*, 593 F.3d 159, 166 (2d Cir.2010).

If this initial burden is met, "a presumption of retaliation arises," and the burden shifts to "the employer to articulate a legitimate, non-retaliatory reason for the adverse employment action." *Id.* If and when the employer meets that burden of production, "'the *McDonnell Douglas* framework . . . disappear[s] and the sole remaining issue . . . [is] discrimination *vel non.*' " *Holtz v. Rockefeller & Co.*, 258 F.3d 62, 77 (2d Cir.2001) (quoting *Reeves v. Sanderson Plumbing Prods., Inc.*, 530 U.S. 133, 142–43, 120 S.Ct. 2097, 147 L.Ed.2d 105 (2000)). The plaintiff must then prove the ultimate issues without any "benefit of . . . intermediate burdens and presumptions." *Id.; see also Holcomb*, 521 F.3d at 138. The plaintiff may satisfy this burden by showing "pretext," *i.e.*, that the employer's proffered reason was false, *see, e.g., Reeves*, 530 U.S. at 143, 147; but even in the absence of such a showing, a plaintiff may prevail by demonstrating that "an employment decision was motivated both by legitimate and illegitimate reasons," *Holcomb*, 521 F.3d at 141–42; *see, e.g., Reeves*, 530 U.S. at 147 ("Proof that the defendant's explanation is unworthy of credence is simply one form of circumstantial evidence that is probative of intentional discrimination. . . .") *Holtz*, 258 F.3d at 78.

However, "if the record conclusively reveal[s][a] nondiscriminatory reason for the employer's decision, or if the plaintiff create[s] only a weak issue of fact [as to pretext] and there [i]s abundant and uncontroverted independent evidence that no discrimination ha[s] occurred," then the employer is entitled to judgment as a matter of law. *Reeves,* 530 U.S. at 148.

Applying these principles to the record at summary judgment, the Court finds that Mendez-Nouel has, at the very best, created a "weak issue of fact" as to pretext, which, measured against the abundant and indeed overwhelming evidence offered by Gucci as to its basis for putting Mendez-Nouel on leave and then terminating him, is insufficient to withstand Gucci's motion for summary judgment. *Reeves,* 530 U.S. at 148; *Richardson,* 532 F.3d at 125–26.

Mendez-Nouel makes two primary arguments to show pretext. First, he claims that the temporal proximity between his complaint (February 26, 2009) and his suspension (March 6, 2009) and termination (March 19, 2009) could permit a fact finder to find that those employment actions were pretextual. Second, he argues that inconsistencies and/or errors in Gucci's report of the pre-termination investigation could validly lead a fact finder to conclude that the entire exercise was a sham—a façade to enable Gucci to cover up his retaliatory termination. Neither argument withstands analysis.

1. The Facts Do Not Permit an Inference of Pretext Based on the Temporal Proximity of His Complaint and Gucci's Adverse Actions

Mendez-Nouel observes, correctly, that the "causal connection needed for a proof of a retaliation claim can be established indirectly by showing that the protected activity was closely followed in time by the adverse action." Pl. Br. 19 (quoting *Cifra v. G.E. Co.,* 252 F.3d 205, 217 (2d Cir.2001)). However, such a causal inference may be negated—or, put differently, the causal chain broken—where an intervening event post-dating the protected conduct provides an independent basis for the adverse action, or where the uncontroverted evidence otherwise renders the inference unreasonable in the case at hand. *See Thompson v. Morris Heights Health Ctr.,* No. 09-cv-7239, 2012 U.S. Dist. LEXIS 49165, at *28, 2012 WL 1145964 (S.D.N.Y. Apr. 6, 2012).

Here, it is undisputed that less than two weeks after Mendez-Nouel complained of Daly's and Gray's alleged harassment, Mendez-Nouel's co-worker Meryam Kabsy complained to Gucci's HR representative, Strober-Lewin, that she was concerned about his mental state and felt the situation was "dangerous." Although Mendez-Nouel challenges the process and outcome of the investigation that followed this complaint, as discussed *infra,* there is no dispute that Kabsy's complaint was made, or that it triggered the investigation which led to Mendez-Nouel's suspension and termination. In light of these undisputed facts, a jury could not fairly draw an inference of pretext based on the short passage of time between Mendez-Nouel's protected activity (his complaint) and his suspension and termination.

2. Mendez-Nouel's Criticisms of the Investigation Report Are Insufficient to Give Rise to a Genuine Issue of Material Fact

Mendez-Nouel's other basis for claiming pretext consists of various procedural or substantive challenges to Gucci's investigation of Kabsy's complaint. Specifically, Mendez-Nouel claims that the investigation suffered from the following defects:

1. Gucci's human resources employees created a record allegedly based on the statements of Mendez-Nouel's co-workers, but, in discovery in this case, some co-workers denied making certain statements attributed to them, and the report exaggerated other statements or took them out of context.

2. Gucci made its decision to terminate Mendez-Nouel before speaking with him.

3. Gucci's reasons for terminating Mendez-Nouel were "fabricated" and "intentionally ignored mitigating information."

4. After Mendez-Nouel's termination, Gucci now claims his termination was justified based on additional reasons not mentioned in his termination letter.

5. Mendez-Nouel was a good, productive sales employee (and therefore, presumably, his termination was not merited).

None of these asserted deficiencies, when viewed in light of the evidence in record at summary judgment, would permit a reasonable juror to find Gucci's investigation to have been pretextual.... Accordingly, Gucci's motion for summary judgment against Mendez-Nouel's retaliation claims under Title VII and the NYSHRL are granted as well.

* * *

Conclusion

For the foregoing reasons, Gucci's motion is granted as to Mendez-Nouel's claims under Title VII and the NYSHRL. The Clerk of Court is directed to enter judgment in Gucci's favor as to those claims. Because the Court declines to exercise supplemental jurisdiction over Mendez-Nouel's NYCHRL claims, they are dismissed without prejudice.

SO ORDERED.

Notes

1. Do you agree with the court's analysis of plaintiff's claims? Why or why not?

2. Research the standard under the NYCHRL. Do plaintiff's claims rise to the level of discrimination under the NYCHRL standard?

3. At the time of publication of this text, in *Bostock v. Clayton County, Georgia*, No. 17-1618 (decided June 15, 2020), the Supreme Court finally resolved a circuit court split, holding that Title VII does prohibit discrimination against individuals based on sexual orientation or transgender status. The court said that: "[a]t bottom, these cases involve no more than the straight-forward application of legal terms with plain and settled meanings. For an employer to discriminate against

employees for being homosexual or transgender, the employer must intentionally discriminate against individual men and women in part because of sex. That has always been prohibited by Title VII's plain terms—and that 'should be the end of the analysis.'" 883 F. 3d, at 135 (Cabranes, J., concurring in judgment).

2. Employer Dress Code Policies Case Studies

Equal Employment Opportunity Commission v. Abercrombie & Fitch Stores, Inc.

575 U.S. 768 (2015)

Opinion

Justice SCALIA delivered the opinion of the Court.

Title VII of the Civil Rights Act of 1964 prohibits a prospective employer from refusing to hire an applicant in order to avoid accommodating a religious practice that it could accommodate without undue hardship. The question presented is whether this prohibition applies only where an applicant has informed the employer of his need for an accommodation.

I

We summarize the facts in the light most favorable to the Equal Employment Opportunity Commission (EEOC), against whom the Tenth Circuit granted summary judgment. Respondent Abercrombie & Fitch Stores, Inc., operates several lines of clothing stores, each with its own "style." Consistent with the image Abercrombie seeks to project for each store, the company imposes a Look Policy that governs its employees' dress. The Look Policy prohibits "caps"—a term the Policy does not define—as too informal for Abercrombie's desired image.

Samantha Elauf is a practicing Muslim who, consistent with her understanding of her religion's requirements, wears a headscarf. She applied for a position in an Abercrombie store, and was interviewed by Heather Cooke, the store's assistant manager. Using Abercrombie's ordinary system for evaluating applicants, Cooke gave Elauf a rating that qualified her to be hired; Cooke was concerned, however, that Elauf's headscarf would conflict with the store's Look Policy.

Cooke sought the store manager's guidance to clarify whether the headscarf was a forbidden "cap." When this yielded no answer, Cooke turned to Randall Johnson, the district manager. Cooke informed Johnson that she believed Elauf wore her headscarf because of her faith. Johnson told Cooke that Elauf's headscarf would violate the Look Policy, as would all other headwear, religious or otherwise, and directed Cooke not to hire Elauf.

The EEOC sued Abercrombie on Elauf's behalf, claiming that its refusal to hire Elauf violated Title VII. The District Court granted the EEOC summary judgment on the issue of liability, 798 F.Supp.2d 1272 (N.D.Okla.2011), held a trial on damages, and awarded $20,000. The Tenth Circuit reversed and awarded Abercrombie summary judgment. 731 F.3d 1106 (2013). It concluded that ordinarily an employer cannot be liable under Title VII for failing to accommodate a religious practice until the applicant (or employee) provides the employer with actual knowledge of his need for an accommodation. *Id.*, at 1131. We granted certiorari. 573 U.S.——, 135 S.Ct. 44, 189 L.Ed.2d 897 (2014).

II

Title VII of the Civil Rights Act of 1964 78 Stat. 253, as amended, prohibits two categories of employment practices. It is unlawful for an employer:

"(1) to fail or refuse to hire or to discharge any individual, or otherwise to discriminate against any individual with respect to his compensation, terms, conditions, or privileges of employment, because of such individual's race, color, religion, sex, or national origin; or

(2) to limit, segregate, or classify his employees or applicants for employment in any way which would deprive or tend to deprive any individual of employment opportunities or otherwise adversely affect his status as an employee, because of such individual's race, color, religion, sex, or national origin." 42 U.S.C. § 2000e-2(a).

These two proscriptions, often referred to as the "disparate treatment" (or "intentional discrimination") provision and the "disparate impact" provision, are the only causes of action under Title VII. The word "religion" is defined to "includ[e] all aspects of religious observance and practice, as well as belief, unless an employer demonstrates that he is unable to reasonably accommodate to" a "religious observance or practice without undue hardship on the conduct of the employer's business." § 2000e(j).[1]

Abercrombie's primary argument is that an applicant cannot show disparate treatment without first showing that an employer has "actual knowledge" of the applicant's need for an accommodation. We disagree. Instead, an applicant need only show that his need for an accommodation was a motivating factor in the employer's decision.[2]

---

1. For brevity's sake, we will in the balance of this opinion usually omit reference to the § 2000e(j) "undue hardship" defense to the accommodation requirement, discussing the requirement as though it is absolute.

2. The concurrence mysteriously concludes that it is not the plaintiff's burden to prove failure to accommodate. Post, at 2036. But of course that is the plaintiff's burden, if failure to hire "because of" the plaintiff's "religious practice" is the gravamen of the complaint. Failing to hire for that reason is synonymous with refusing to accommodate the religious practice. To accuse the employer of the one is to accuse him of the other. If he is willing to "accommodate"—which means nothing more than allowing the plaintiff to engage in her religious practice despite the employer's normal rules to the contrary—adverse action "because of" the religious practice is not shown. "The clause that begins with the word 'unless,' " as the concurrence describes it, *ibid.*, has no function except to place upon the employer the burden of establishing an "undue hardship" defense. The concurrence provides no example, not even an unrealistic hypothetical one, of a claim of failure to hire because of religious practice that does not say the employer refused to permit ("failed to accommodate") the religious practice. In the nature of things, there cannot be one.

The disparate-treatment provision forbids employers to: (1) "fail . . . to hire" an applicant (2) "because of" (3) "such individual's . . . religion" (which includes his religious practice). Here, of course, Abercrombie (1) failed to hire Elauf. The parties concede that (if Elauf sincerely believes that her religion so requires) Elauf's wearing of a headscarf is (3) a "religious practice." All that remains is whether she was not hired (2) "because of" her religious practice.

The term "because of" appears frequently in antidiscrimination laws. It typically imports, at a minimum, the traditional standard of but-for causation. *University of Tex. Southwestern Medical Center v. Nassar,* 570 U.S. ——, 133 S.Ct. 2517, 186 L. Ed.2d 503 (2013). Title VII relaxes this standard, however, to prohibit even making a protected characteristic a "motivating factor" in an employment decision. 42 U.S.C. § 2000e-2(m). "Because of" in § 2000e-2(a)(1) links the forbidden consideration to each of the verbs preceding it; an individual's actual religious practice may not be a motivating factor in failing to hire, in refusing to hire, and so on.

It is significant that § 2000e-2(a)(1) does not impose a knowledge requirement. As Abercrombie acknowledges, some antidiscrimination statutes do. For example, the Americans with Disabilities Act of 1990 defines discrimination to include an employer's failure to make "reasonable accommodations to the *known* physical or mental limitations" of an applicant. § 12112(b)(5)(A) (emphasis added). Title VII contains no such limitation.

Instead, the intentional discrimination provision prohibits certain *motives,* regardless of the state of the actor's knowledge. Motive and knowledge are separate concepts. An employer who has actual knowledge of the need for an accommodation does not violate Title VII by refusing to hire an applicant if avoiding that accommodation is not his *motive.* Conversely, an employer who acts with the motive of avoiding accommodation may violate Title VII even if he has no more than an unsubstantiated suspicion that accommodation would be needed.

Thus, the rule for disparate-treatment claims based on a failure to accommodate a religious practice is straightforward: An employer may not make an applicant's religious practice, confirmed or otherwise, a factor in employment decisions. For example, suppose that an employer thinks (though he does not know for certain) that a job applicant may be an orthodox Jew who will observe the Sabbath, and thus be unable to work on Saturdays. If the applicant actually requires an accommodation of that religious practice, and the employer's desire to avoid the prospective accommodation is a motivating factor in his decision, the employer violates Title VII.

Abercrombie urges this Court to adopt the Tenth Circuit's rule "allocat[ing] the burden of raising a religious conflict." Brief for Respondent 46. This would require the employer to have actual knowledge of a conflict between an applicant's religious practice and a work rule. The problem with this approach is the one that inheres in most incorrect interpretations of statutes: It asks us to add words to the law to produce what is thought to be a desirable result. That is Congress's province. We construe Title VII's silence as exactly that: silence. Its disparate-treatment provision prohibits actions taken with the *motive* of avoiding the need for accommodating a religious practice. A request for accommodation, or the employer's certainty that the practice exists, may make it easier to infer motive, but is not a necessary condition of liability.

Abercrombie argues in the alternative that a claim based on a failure to accommodate an applicant's religious practice must be raised as a disparate-impact claim, not a disparate-treatment claim. We think not. That might have been true if Congress had limited the meaning of "religion" in Title VII to religious *belief*—so that discriminating against a particular religious *practice* would not be disparate treatment though it might have disparate impact. In fact, however, Congress defined "religion," for Title VII's purposes, as "includ[ing] all aspects of religious observance and practice, as well as belief." 42 U.S.C. § 2000e(j). Thus, religious practice is one of the protected characteristics that cannot be accorded disparate treatment and must be accommodated. Nor does the statute limit disparate-treatment claims to only those employer policies that treat religious practices less favorably than similar secular practices. Abercrombie's argument that a neutral policy cannot constitute "intentional discrimination" may make sense in other contexts. But Title VII does not demand mere neutrality with regard to religious practices—that they be treated no worse than other practices. Rather, it gives them favored treatment, affirmatively obligating employers not "to fail or refuse to hire or discharge any individual . . . because of such individual's" "religious observance and practice." An employer is surely entitled to have, for example, a no-headwear policy as an ordinary matter. But when an applicant requires an accommodation as an "aspec[t] of religious . . . practice," it is no response that the subsequent "fail[ure] . . . to hire" was due to an otherwise-neutral policy. Title VII requires otherwise-neutral policies to give way to the need for an accommodation.

* * *

The Tenth Circuit misinterpreted Title VII's requirements in granting summary judgment. We reverse its judgment and remand the case for further consideration consistent with this opinion.

It is so ordered.

Note

Justice Scalia's opinion addresses an employer's impermissible motive, in making a hiring decision, to avoid the need for a religious accommodation to a Muslim woman required by her religion to wear a headscarf. More recently, in early 2019 the New York City Commission on Human Rights issued legal enforcement guidance stating that: "Anti-Black bias also includes discrimination based on characteristics and cultural practices associated with being Black, including prohibitions on natural hair or hairstyles most closely associated with Black people." In July 2019, California adopted legislation known as the CROWN Act ("Creating a Respectful and Open Workplace") prohibiting purportedly race-neutral appearance policies that disproportionately impact individuals in a protected class. These recent efforts would appear simply to codify ample precedent that a facially neutral appearance policy that disparately impacts individuals in a protected class (whether intentionally or not) is impermissible. What room is left, then, for a company to create dress codes and appearance policies that treat men and women differently and require employees to conform to the idealized image that the employer seeks to project?

Schiavo v. Marina District Development Co.

442 N.J. Super. 346 (2015)

Opinion

LIHOTZ, P.J.A.D.

Plaintiffs, twenty-one women who are present or former employees of defendant Marina District Development Company, LLC, operating as the Borgata Casino Hotel & Spa, appeal from the summary judgment dismissal of their complaint alleging violations of the New Jersey Law Against Discrimination (LAD), *N.J.S.A.* 10:5-1 to -49, as informed by Title VII of the Civil Rights Act of 1964 (Title VII), 42 *U.S.C.A.* §§ 2000e to 2000e-17. Plaintiffs allege defendant's adoption and application of personal appearance standards (the PAS) subjected them to illegal gender stereotyping, sexual harassment, disparate treatment, disparate impact, and as to some plaintiffs, resulted in adverse employment actions.

The motion judge found the provisions of the challenged PAS, to which plaintiffs specifically consented to abide when accepting employment in defendant's program known as "the BorgataBabes," were reasonable in light of casino industry standards and customer expectations. Therefore, the PAS requirements were permitted by *N.J.S.A.* 10:5–12(p), a provision allowing an employer to establish reasonable employee appearance standards. Further, the judge rejected as unsupported plaintiffs' assertions of disparate treatment and enforcement between male and female BorgataBabes. Accordingly, he concluded plaintiffs failed to sustain the alleged LAD violations. The judge granted defendant's motions against each plaintiff for summary judgment and dismissed all claims.

On appeal, plaintiffs argue the motion judge inappropriately engaged in factfinding. Further, they challenge his interpretation of *N.J.S.A.* 10:5–12(p), and maintain the evidence was sufficient to allow a jury to conclude plaintiffs were victims of gender stereotyping, sexual harassment, and disparate impact in contravention of the LAD. Defendant not only refutes these arguments, requesting we affirm the motion judge's determinations, but also argues plaintiffs' claims are barred by the statute of limitations or, otherwise, precluded by laches and estoppel.

Amici, the National Employment Lawyers Association of New Jersey (NELA) and the New Jersey Association for Justice (NJAFJ), concur with plaintiffs' position summary judgment was prematurely granted. . . .

Following our review, we affirm in part and reverse in part. We have considered plaintiffs' claims and conclude all facial discrimination challenges to the PAS are time-barred or unsupported. We also conclude the LAD does not encompass allegations of discrimination based on weight, appearance, or sex appeal. However, we determine the motion judge erred in concluding the record was insufficient to present a prima facie claim of sexual harassment hostile work environment discrimination. Certain plaintiffs, whose lack of compliance resulted from documented medical conditions or post-pregnancy conditions, have presented a material dispute of facts regarding defendant's application of the PAS weight standard resulting in harassment because of their gender. As to those claims, summary judgment is reversed and the matter remanded. As to all other claims, for the reasons discussed in our opinion, we affirm.

I.

In order to provide context to the claims raised in plaintiffs' complaint, we must provide an overview of the BorgataBabes program and the challenged PAS, as amended in 2005. Thereafter, we generally identify the facts asserted to support the various LAD claims, examining together similar allegations of groups of plaintiffs. In our legal discussion, we recite the standards guiding our review, including the requisites of the LAD and, as appropriate, federal jurisprudence. Finally, we apply these principles to the facts presented in the record.

A.

"The market in Atlantic City changed forever in 2003 with the opening of the Borgata, the city's first Las Vegas[-]style resort. The 2,000-room facility was the first casino to open in over a decade and it quickly became the largest grossing property in the city." *A Brief History of the Casino Control Commission,* St. of N.J. Casino Control Commission, http://www.nj.gov/casinos/about/history/ (last visited Aug. 30, 2015). Defendant's business decision to differentiate itself from the existing Atlantic City casinos included the creation of the "BorgataBabes," a specialized group of costumed beverage servers.[1] The BorgataBabes reflected "the fun, upscale, sensual, international image that is consistent with the Borgata brand" bringing "Las Vegas[-]style to Atlantic City." All Babes were expected to comply with the "Five Fs": "Fun, Friendly, Focused, Fresh, and Fast."

Defendant's recruiting brochure described its image of the BorgataBabes this way:

"They're beautiful. They're charming. And they're bringing drinks.

She moves toward you like a movie star, her smile melting the ice in your bourbon and water. His ice blue eyes set the olive in your friend's martini spinning. You forget your own name. She kindly remembers it for you. You become the most important person in the room. And relax in the knowledge that there are no calories in eye candy.

Part fashion model, part beverage server, part charming host and hostess. All impossibly lovely. The sensational BorgataBabes are the new ambassadors of

1. The parties agree all BorgataBabes were costumed beverage servers, but not all costumed beverage servers were BorgataBabes.

hospitality representing our beautiful hotel casino and spa in Atlantic City. On a scale of 1 to 10, elevens all.

Eyes, hair, smile, costumes as close to absolute perfection as perfection gets. BorgataBabes do look fabulous, no question. But once you can breathe again, prepare to be taken to another level by the BorgataBabe attitude. The memory of their warm, inviting, upbeat personalities will remain with you long after the vision has faded from your dreams.

ARE YOU A BABE?"

Of the more than 4000 male and female applicants for approximately 200 placements, the final candidates underwent two rigorous interviews, and a twenty-minute audition in-costume. The audition notification, sent to those who were chosen following the interviews, made clear "[p]ersonal appearance in costume" was one evaluative criteria and the audition required "performing" mock customer scenarios. Chosen candidates were also advised of the PAS requirements, which required male and female Babes be physically fit, with their weight proportionate to height, and display a clean, healthy smile. Female BorgataBabes were to have a natural hourglass shape; males were to have a natural "V" shape with broad shoulders and a slim waist. Women were to have hair that was clean and naturally styled, and tasteful, professional makeup that complimented their facial features. Men were to be either clean shaven or have neatly trimmed and sculpted facial hair. BorgataBabes were to deliver excellent customer service and create a feeling of "upscale classiness, sensuality, and confidence to build customer loyalty." Defendant maintained the PAS was designed to maximize its ability to maintain and preserve the image defendant seeks to project to the public.

The men and women chosen as BorgataBabes contractually agreed to adhere to these strict personal appearance and conduct standards. The final candidates were sent a notice, which attached the PAS, recited the terms of engagement, and stated: "During your employment, you must maintain approximately the same physical appearance in the assigned costume. You must appear to be comfortable while wearing the assigned costume for which you were fitted. . . ."

In keeping with its objective to create a Las Vegas-style casino image and atmosphere, employees hired as BorgataBabes wore distinctive, custom-fitted costumes, designed by Zac Posen. All Babes were fitted with costumes issued by defendant's wardrobe department. Unlike other employees, BorgataBabes enjoyed the use of the "Babe Lounge," which was a "private, Hollywood-style dressing room"; an extra forty-five minutes of paid time to change into costume and complete their personal grooming; photo opportunities; gratuitous spa and fitness center access; and reimbursement for gym memberships, nutritionists, and personal trainers.

In late 2004, defendant sought to modify the PAS to interpose a compliance standard which defendant believed would allow it "to enforce the PAS in an objective manner." On February 18, 2005, defendant announced this PAS "clarification" to the original requirement to "maintain approximately the same physical appearance" as when hired. Specifically, the PAS change sought to elucidate the "weight proportioned to height" standard. Under the modified PAS, barring medical reasons, BorgataBabes could not increase their baseline weight, as established when hired, by more than 7% (weight standard). "[Defendant] selected the 7% standard because it reasonably approximated a change of one clothing size and because it was consistent with the scientific definition of a clinically significant weight gain."

Twenty of the twenty-one plaintiffs worked for defendant prior to the issuance of the clarifying PAS. In February 2005, all BorgataBabes were weighed to establish a baseline. Each of the plaintiffs executed the modified PAS, which included the new weight standard and stated non-compliance with the standard would result in termination. On the document, immediately above each plaintiff's signature, appears this statement, in bold capital letters: "I read and fully understand that costume requirements, personal appearance and weight standard[,] and the personal grooming standards, as set forth herein, are expectations and ongoing requirements for all costumed beverage servers." Several plaintiffs executed the modified PAS adding the words "under protest." Many testified they believed failure to accept the PAS would evoke termination.

The PAS did not provide a fixed schedule for weigh-ins, such as the first of each month or every quarter. Rather, weigh-ins were "periodic," to occur "including, but not limited to" when a BorgataBabe "requires a costume size change or whenever he/she returns from any leave of absence." Other weigh-ins were arbitrary and occurred when managers from the beverage and talent departments concluded a BorgataBabe's costume was ill-fitting. The PAS explained the procedures followed when an associate exceeded the weight limit, allowing a period for compliance, and detailed consequences and discipline for non-compliance. The PAS also explained that employees could request exceptions from enforcement because of a "bona fide medical condition" or pregnancy.

Much of the deposition testimony of defendant's management employees was devoted to the enforcement of the weight standard in the PAS. Between February 2005 and December 2010, stipulated by all parties as the relevant time period for review, 686 female and 46 male associates were subject to the PAS, of which 25 women and no men were suspended for failure to comply with the weight standard.

B.

On August 20, 2008, Jacqueline Schiavo filed the first complaint challenging the PAS and alleged its enforcement against women as violative of the LAD. Subsequently filed complaints by other plaintiffs were consolidated by the Law Division under the first filed docket number.[6]

6. Following Schiavo's filing, substantially similar complaints were filed as follows: Patricia Taylor on September 10, 2008; Kimberly Johnson on September 19, 2008; Zorayma Rivera on

Collectively, plaintiffs object to the PAS weight standard as gender stereotyping and gender role discrimination in violation of the LAD. Further, they allege defendant's sexual harassment and gender stereotyping created a hostile work environment. Individual plaintiffs allege facts asserting LAD violations arising from defendant's administration of the weight standard, maintaining defendant engaged in harassing, sexually suggestive, and gender biased conduct. The underlying facts experienced by each plaintiff are set forth in individual counts of the complaint.

Generally, each of these nine plaintiffs were suspended for different periods when defendant determined each exceeded the 7% weight gain limit: Askins, Garcia, Schiavo, Vaisyte, Higbee, Taylor, Rivera, Lopez, and Nelson. Askins, Garcia, Schiavo, and Vaisyte were suspended, but thereafter complied and remained employed with defendant as of June 2012. In lieu of termination following non-compliance with the PAS weight standard, Higbee and Taylor chose to transfer to a non-PAS position and ultimately separated from employment within a year of transfer. Rivera and Lopez suffered documented medical conditions affecting weight control. Nelson resigned following an inability to meet the PAS weight standard following a pregnancy.

The remaining plaintiffs were never suspended for non-compliance with the PAS. Barrella was given a medical allowance. Booker and B. Johnson experienced post-pregnancy weight gain. Booker returned to compliance, but Johnson resigned when notified she remained out of compliance one-year after her child was born. McDonnell, Werthmann, and Leonardis were found to be non-compliant at times, but each successfully returned to the designated weight range, without suspension. Estrada, K. Johnson, Kennelly, Nouel, Williams, and Wilson at all times met the PAS weight standard.

In addition to the gender stereotyping and harassment claims, plaintiffs allege the PAS weight standard was not equally applied to male BorgataBabes. Plaintiffs' allegations include statements told to them by men who were not weighed or who purchased a black shirt or pants similar to their nondescript outfit to avoid requesting a new costume. A few plaintiffs knew or dated males who were unconcerned with the PAS weight standard and others testified they saw male bartenders who they felt gained weight.

Defendant admits no male BorgataBabe was suspended for noncompliance with the PAS weight standard. The record contains information regarding one male

---

September 19, 2008; Noelia Lopez, Cindy Nelson, Latoya Wilson, Amy Askins, and Brandi Johnson on January 8, 2009; Williams joined Lopez, Nelson, Wilson, Askins, and B. Johnson in an amended complaint filed on January 20, 2009; and Tara Kennelly, Andrea Cimino, Aimee Barrella, Jacquelyn McDonnell, Misty Gale, Terri Estrada, Melissa Werthmann, Danielle Leonardis, Morta Vaisyte, Marcella Booker, Wendy Garcia, Carol Cohen, Kelly Higbee, Nancy Carfagno, Natasha Bucceroni, and Tania Nouel on September 22, 2009. Various orders consolidated these matters under the lead docket number of Schiavo's complaint. Further, the consolidated first amended complaint eliminated several of these plaintiffs.

BorgataBabe disciplined when found not wearing the issued costume. Defendant also produced a chart, summarizing the weighing of male associates, recording baseline weights of forty-three men in February 2005, or their date of hire. The chart also records five male Babes who were reweighed prior to 2008, when this action originated.

The summary judgment record also includes expert reports submitted by plaintiffs and defendant. Dr. Christopher Erath, an economist with a specialized interest in labor economics and econometrics, opined on behalf of defendant "that application of conventional statistical standards and tests yields no statistical evidence consistent with plaintiffs' allegation that the PAS had a disparate impact upon female Costumed Associates." Plaintiffs' expert Dr. Alan J. Salzberg, an economist and statistician, suggested, given the small percentage of male BorgataBabes, the tests performed by Erath were not statistically meaningful.

II.

We recognize the "major public policy . . . enshrined in the LAD," *Alexander v. Seton Hall Univ.*, 204 *N.J.* 219, 227, 8 *A.*3d 198 (2010), which proclaims all individuals

"shall have the opportunity to obtain employment . . . without discrimination because of race, creed, color, national origin, ancestry, age, marital status, affectional or sexual orientation, familial status, disability, nationality, sex, gender identity or expression . . . , subject only to conditions and limitations applicable alike to all persons. This opportunity is recognized as and declared to be a civil right."

[*N.J.S.A.* 10:5-4.]

See also N.J.S.A. 10:5-3 (stating Legislature's commitment of state's public interest to eliminate practices of discrimination).

"Without doubt, the LAD 'unequivocally expresses a legislative intent to prohibit discrimination in all aspects of the employment relationship, including hiring and firing, compensation, the terms and conditions of employment, and retirement.'" *Alexander, supra*,204 *N.J.* at 227–28, 8 *A.*3d 198 (quoting *Nini v. Mercer Cty. Cmty. Coll.*, 202 *N.J.* 98, 106–07, 995 *A.*2d 1094 (2010)). "Those commands provide the force underlying the frequent case law refrain that 'the clear public policy of this State is to eradicate invidious discrimination from the workplace.'" *Id.* at 228, 8 *A.*3d 198 (quoting *Craig v. Suburban Cablevision, Inc.*, 140 *N.J.* 623, 630, 660 *A.*2d 505 (1995)).

"Because of its remedial purpose, the LAD should be construed liberally. . . ." *Zive v. Stanley Roberts, Inc.*, 182 N.J. 436, 446, 867 *A.*2d 1133 (2005). However, "the LAD acknowledges the authority of employers to manage their own businesses" and "prevents only unlawful discrimination against [protected] individuals. . . ." *Ibid.* (emphasis omitted).

It is also well-settled that a plaintiff bears the burden to establish a prima facie case showing he or she was a victim of discrimination by an employer. *Victor v. State*, 203 *N.J.* 383, 408, 4 *A.*3d 126 (2010). Typically, a prima facie case of employment discrimination based on sex is established when a plaintiff demonstrates by a preponderance of the evidence that he or she (1) is a member of a designated protected class; (2) who was qualified for and performing the essential functions of the job; but (3) suffered termination or other adverse employment action; and (4) others not in the protected class did not suffer similar adverse employment actions. *Id.* at 409, 4 *A.*3d 126. However, "[t]here is no single prima facie case that applies to all employment discrimination claims. Instead, the elements of the prima facie case vary depending upon the particular cause of action." *Id.* at 408, 4 *A.*3d 126.

As noted, all plaintiffs allege sexual harassment hostile work environment, disparate treatment, disparate impact, and gender stereotyping. "Identifying the elements of the prima facie case that are unique to the particular discrimination claim is critical to its evaluation." *Id.* at 410, 4 *A.*3d 126.

The test for hostile work environment sexual harassment claims, irrespective of a defendant's effort to dispute the evidence, requires "a female plaintiff allege conduct that occurred because of her sex and that a reasonable woman would consider sufficiently severe or pervasive to alter the conditions of employment and create an intimidating, hostile, or offensive working environment." *Lehmann v. Toys 'R' Us, Inc.*, 132 *N.J.* 587, 603–04, 626 *A.*2d 445 (1993).

Our Court has stated the proofs required for a disparate impact claim are based upon those required under federal law. *Gerety v. Atl. City Hilton Casino Resort,* 184 *N.J.* 391, 400, 877 *A.*2d 1233 (2005); *see also* 42 *U.S.C.A.* § 2000e-2(k)(1). "[C]laims that stress 'disparate impact' . . . involve [ ] employment practices that are facially neutral in their treatment of different groups but that in fact fall more harshly on one group than another and cannot be justified by business necessity." *Gerety, supra,* 184 *N.J.* at 398, 877 *A.*2d 1233 . . . .

The LAD "forbids the use of any employment criterion, even one neutral on its face and not intended to be discriminatory, if, in fact, the criterion causes discrimination as measured by the impact on a person or group entitled to equal opportunity." *Garcia v. Gloor,* 618 *F.*2d 264, 270 (5th Cir.1980), *cert. denied,* 449 *U.S.* 1113, 101 *S.Ct.* 923, 66 *L.Ed.*2d 842 (1981) . . . . "However, there is no disparate impact if the rule is one that the affected employee can readily observe and nonobservance is a matter of individual preference." *Garcia, supra,* 618 *F.*2d at 270. "An adverse effect on a single employee, or even a few employees, is not sufficient to establish disparate impact." *Massarsky v. Gen. Motors Corp.*, 706 *F.*2d 111, 121 (3d Cir.), *cert. denied,* 464 *U.S.* 937, 104 *S.Ct.* 348, 78 *L.Ed.*2d 314 (1983) . . . .

III.

With these principles in mind, we consider the sufficiency of the evidence to form a prima facie cause of action alleging prohibited discriminatory conduct to survive summary judgment dismissal.

Generally, plaintiffs allege (1) the PAS on its face was discriminatory, in violation of the LAD, and outside the bounds of reasonable appearance standards as provided in *N.J.S.A.* 10:5-12(p); (2) the PAS weight standard imposed unlawful gender stereotyping; (3) defendant's disparate enforcement of the PAS weight standard resulted in gender bias sexual harassment; (4) the PAS weight standard had a disparate impact upon females; and (5) defendant's conduct in enforcing the PAS created a hostile work environment.

McDonnell's complaint alleges defendant designed and enforced the PAS to have a disparate impact on female BorgataBabes based on their gender and female BorgataBabes suffered disparate treatment under the policy, which was an act of gender stereotyping. She was never suspended and her position was never affected; rather, she challenges the PAS as facially discriminatory.

Whether the PAS generally and the weight standard specifically are actionable as sex discrimination requires consideration of additional legal principles. "Courts have recognized that the appearance of a company's employees may contribute greatly to the company's image and success with the public and thus that a reasonable dress or grooming code is a proper management prerogative." *Craft v. Metromedia, Inc.*, 766 *F.*2d 1205, 1215 (8th Cir.1985), *cert. denied*, 475 *U.S.* 1058, 106 *S.Ct.* 1285, 89 *L.Ed.*2d 592 (1986). Moreover, there is no protected class based solely on one's weight.[8] The LAD addresses no such category nor does Title VII "proscribe discrimination based upon an employee's excessive weight. . . ." *Taylor v. Small*, 350 *F.*3d 1286, 1292 (D.C.Cir.2003).

The LAD addresses appearance at *N.J.S.A.* 10:5-12(p):

"Nothing in the provisions of this section shall affect the ability of an employer to require employees to adhere to reasonable workplace appearance, grooming and dress standards not precluded by other provisions of State or federal law, except that an employer shall allow an employee to appear, groom and dress consistent with the employee's gender identity or expression."

No reported New Jersey case has considered a challenge under this subsection of the LAD. We note other jurisdictions have reviewed allegations of discrimination by an employer's appearance standards to determine whether the challenged policies fall within an employer's imposition of reasonable appearance and grooming policies, or cross the line and violate legislative proscriptions against discrimination. The reported authority makes clear such a determination is fact-sensitive. We recite these examples as illustrative of the law's evolution, and they are not meant to be exhaustive.

In *Bellissimo v. Westinghouse Electric Corporation*, 764 *F.*2d 175, 178, 182 (3d Cir.1985), *cert. denied*, 475 *U.S.* 1035, 106 *S.Ct.* 1244, 89 *L.Ed.*2d 353 (1986), the court reversed a finding of sex discrimination under Title VII where the plaintiff alleged she was criticized because her attire was non-conforming to the defendant's sex-specific dress code. The court noted "[d]ress codes . . . are permissible under Title VII as long as they, like other work rules, are enforced evenhandedly between

8. Neither McDonnell nor any other plaintiff has alleged their weight represents a physical handicap requiring accommodation, which entails a different LAD analysis. See *Viscik v. Fowler Equip. Co.*, 173 N.J. 1, 15–16, 800 A.2d 826 (2002).

men and women, even though the specific requirements may differ." *Id.* at 181. Accordingly, policies need not be exactly the same for each gender, but will be considered evenhanded for the purposes of Title VII when they contain similar restrictions for both sexes. *Ibid.* In rejecting the plaintiff's arguments, the court stated:

"Perhaps no facet of business life is more important than a company's place in public estimation. That the image created by its employees dealing with the public when on company assignment affects its relations is so well known that we may take judicial notice of an employer's proper desire to achieve favorable acceptance."

[*Ibid.* (quoting *Fagan v. Nat'l Cash Register Co.,* 481 *F.*2d 1115, 1124–25 (D.C.Cir.1973)).]

In *Price Waterhouse,* an employer's sex-based evaluation, not related to performance or ability, resulted from a decision to deny a partnership promotion to the plaintiff, a female senior manager, who was perceived as less than feminine. *Price Waterhouse, supra,* 490 *U.S.* at 258, 109 *S.Ct.* at 1795, 104 *L.Ed.*2d at 293. The United States Supreme Court concluded a discriminatory motive affected the plaintiff's employment opportunity and represented illegal gender stereotyping, a form of discrimination under Title VII, observing:

"we are beyond the day when an employer could evaluate employees by assuming or insisting that they matched the stereotype associated with their group, for in forbidding employers to discriminate against individuals because of their sex, Congress intended to strike at the entire spectrum of disparate treatment of men and women resulting from sex stereotypes."

[*Id.* at 251, 109 *S.Ct.* at 1791, 104 *L.Ed.*2d at 288 (citation and internal quotation marks omitted).]

At issue in *Delta Air Lines v. New York State Division of Human Rights,* 229 *A.D.*2d 132, 134, 652 *N.Y.S.*2d 253 (N.Y.App.Div.1996), *aff'd* 91 *N.Y.*2d 65, 666 *N.Y.S.*2d 1004, 689 *N.E.*2d 898 (1997), was whether the airline's use of weight standards when hiring flight attendants constituted, among other things, gender discrimination. The airline argued the height and weight standards were permissible nondiscriminatory grooming standards. *Id.* at 134–35, 652 *N.Y.S.*2d 253. The Supreme Court of New York, Appellate Division, determined plaintiffs' challenge to the airline's weight guidelines was also not actionable as establishing sex discrimination, stating:

"[I]n the matter at bar, there is no evidence in the record that Delta intended to deprive one sex of equal opportunity or treatment, or that the weight requirements were somehow applied in a discriminatory manner. In fact, Delta has submitted evidence that approximately 90% of its flight attendants are female, thereby erasing petitioners' claim that the weight charts were somehow utilized to discriminate against women, insofar as no disparate impact toward females can be shown whatsoever. Therefore, petitioners' claim of sex discrimination fails."

[*Id.* at 141, 652 *N.Y.S.*2d 253.]

A similar Title VII challenge was presented in *Frank v. United Airlines, Inc.*, 216 *F.*3d 845, 847 (9th Cir.2000), where the class of plaintiffs challenged the employer's use of maximum weight requirements as imposing different standards upon female flight attendants and their male counterparts. The plaintiffs argued the employer's policy was facially discriminatory and was enforced in a discriminatory manner. *Ibid.* The plaintiffs proved the weight charts addressed medium-framed women, but large-framed men. *Id.* at 854. That difference in treatment was facially discriminatory as it applied less favorable treatment to one gender over the other. *Ibid.* The sex-differentiated weight standard was determined to be invalid because it imposed unequal burdens on men and women, which was unjustified as a bona fide occupational qualification. *Id.* at 855. *Jespersen v. Harrah's Operating Co.*, 444 *F.*3d 1104 (9th Cir.2006), addressed a plaintiff's challenge to a casino's "comprehensive uniform, appearance and grooming standards for all bartenders," which differentiated between men and women by prohibiting men from, but requiring women to, wear make-up. *Id.* at 1105, 1107. The plaintiff challenged the make-up requirement as placing an unequal burden on women and as sex stereotyping. *Id.* at 1106. The court held Title VII requires an employer's actions be intentionally discriminatory or have "a discriminatory effect on the basis of gender." *Id.* at 1108–09. Affirming the summary judgment dismissal of the plaintiff's complaint, the court concluded, "a sex-based difference in appearance standards alone, without any further showing of disparate effects," will not create a prima facie case of discriminatory treatment. *Id.* at 1109. The court also found the different grooming standards for men and women did not impose a more onerous standard for one gender. *Id.* at 1111.

Further, the court rejected the plaintiff's argument that the make-up requirement was sex stereotyping, noting: "If we were to do so, we would come perilously close to holding that every grooming, apparel, or appearance requirement that an individual finds personally offensive, or in conflict with his or her own self-image, can create a triable issue of sex discrimination." *Id.* at 1112. *See also Fountain v. Safeway Stores, Inc.*, 555 *F.*2d 753, 755–56 (9th Cir.1977) (stating an employer's regulations, which required male and female employees to conform to different grooming and dress standards, alone were not sex discrimination under Title VII).

A general principle gleaned from the cited authorities is: When an employer's "reasonable workplace appearance, grooming and dress standards" comply with State or federal law prohibiting discrimination, even if they contain sex-specific language, the policies do not violate Title VII, and by extension, the LAD. *See Rivera v. Trump Plaza Hotel & Casino*, 305 *N.J.Super.* 596, 602–03, 702 *A.*2d 1359 (App.Div.1997) (citing federal decisions uniformly rejecting challenges to an employer's hair length policy because hair length is not constitutionally or statutorily protected). Mindful of the objectives of achieving equal employment opportunities and removing barriers that favor an identifiable group over others, we undertake review of the fact-sensitive issue of whether the PAS discriminated against women on its face.

McDonnell contends the trial judge erred in relying on subsection *N.J.S.A.* 10:5-12(p) as legitimizing the PAS weight standard arguing he "ignored the portion of the subsection that addresses gender identity or expression." Further, she suggests the motion judge ignored the language of subsection (a), which impacts and contours the parameters of subsection (p).

The PAS applied to both male and female associates. Although defining different but analogous general gender appearance standards, the PAS weight standard imposed the same 7% above baseline weight increase for men as for women. The policy recognized pregnancy, a gender specific condition, in the category of bona fide medical conditions representing an exception to enforcement. We find these provisions are not facially discriminatory. Unlike the weight charts in *Frank* and subsequent airline cases, the PAS did not impose a designated weight for associates of a certain height, or use differing standards to determine whether weight of males and females met defined limits. Rather, the PAS accepted an associate's baseline weight as of the date of adoption and mandated weight gain or loss must not exceed 7% of that baseline.

All plaintiffs individually expressed dislike for, or struggled to comply with, the weight standard. However, this does not demonstrate the facially neutral policy more adversely affects women than men. In addition to plaintiffs' subjective response, their evidence challenging the PAS appears to rely on sheer numbers: They argue because a disproportionately higher number of female BorgataBabes were disciplined, this proves the weight standard unequally affected women. However, such simple statistical disparities are insufficient to show the weight standard was facially discriminatory. *See Watson v. Fort Worth Bank & Trust,* 487 *U.S.*977, 994, 108 *S.Ct.* 2777, 101 *L.Ed.*2d 827 (1988).

Here, no expert evidence explained how the PAS weight standard, which was neutral on its face, posed an unequal burden on one gender over the other. Also, no proof supports the contention the PAS weight standard adversely affected female over male applicants for positions or advancement. Further, nothing reveals defendant's reliance on a 7% increase as representing a clinically significant weight gain was erroneous or disproportionately burdensome to women.

We also cannot find the use of the differentiated costumes for male and female BorgataBabes actionable. *See Hayden v. Greensburg Cmty. Sch. Corp.,* 743 *F.*3d 569, 578 (7th Cir.2014) (discussing federal authority governing differential grooming standards for males and females). All associates, whether male or female, are required to wear costumes as a condition of employment; women were not singled out. *See Carroll v. Talman Fed. Sav. & Loan Ass'n of Chicago,* 604 *F.*2d 1028, 1032–33 (7th Cir.1979) (rejecting as discriminatory employer's policy that women alone wear uniforms), *cert. denied,* 445 *U.S.* 929, 100 *S.Ct.* 1316, 63 *L.Ed.*2d 762 (1980).[10]

"Although the prohibitions against discrimination in employment based on sex extend not only to hiring but to conditions and privileges of employment . . . , we

10. We need not address the BorgataBabes calendar. No evidence reflects this was mandated as part of plaintiffs' or any other associate's employment. Calendar participation was voluntary.

do not believe that an employer unlawfully discriminates when he establishes a reasonable grooming policy which may be said to differentiate between male and female. Employers, particularly those whose business involves contact with the public should be free to express and act upon a concern with the image which their employees communicate by their appearance and demeanor."

[*Matter of Page Airways v. N.Y. State Div. of Human Rights,* 39 *N.Y.*2d 877, 386 *N.Y.S.*2d 223, 352 *N.E.*2d 140, 140–41 (1976)(citations omitted).]

The record contains only photographs of the female BorgataBabes wearing the designated costume, which is form fitting, skimpy, and reminiscent of a Las Vegas-themed casino. The record states the men wore a tight-fitted club shirt and fitted pants. Although McDonnell correctly asserts the BorgataBabe costume stereotypes the hour-glass figure of the female, she ignores the expressed business differentiation in the role of a BorgataBabe from other casino associates.

This is not a case similar to *Equal Employment Opportunity Commission v. Sage Realty Corp.,* 507 *F.Supp.* 599, 602–04 (S.D.N.Y.1981), where a lobby attendant was required to wear a short, revealing outfit, resembling an American flag, to commemorate the Bicentennial. There, when the plaintiff refused to continue to wear the uniform because it provoked sexualized comments, her employment was terminated. *Id.* at 607. The court rejected the employer's claim the uniform fell within reasonable appearance standards, noting the lobby attendant's job was to greet and direct those who entered the building, making the sexually provocative "uniform" inappropriate to the employment task. *Id.* at 608–09. Here, defendant's business was to provide customers entertainment and the BorgataBabes' costumes aided the Las Vegas-style casino theme.

The record shows the BorgataBabe position comprised more than a job serving drinks and washing glasses. From its inception, an element of performance and a public appearance component was part of the described BorgataBabe position. The record does not dispute the BorgataBabes appeared as the face of the casino outside the casino floor. Further, based on their designated role on behalf of defendant BorgataBabes were provided lower and more flexible hours, more beneficial earning opportunities, and perquisites of employment not extended to defendant's other associates. These facts demonstrate the business specialization of the BorgataBabes among defendant's associates.

We generally agree customer preferences cannot justify discriminatory hiring or the use of stereotyping gender roles in employment positions. *See Fernandez v. Wynn Oil Co.,* 653 *F.*2d 1273, 1277 (9th Cir.1981); *Diaz v. Pan Am. World Airways, Inc.,*442 *F.*2d 385, 389 (5th Cir.), *cert. denied,* 404 *U.S.* 950, 92 *S.Ct.* 275, 30 *L.Ed.*2d 267 (1971). However, the hiring of BorgataBabes was not gender restricted and the record contains no evidence female BorgataBabes' assignments or earning ability were compromised because of their gender.

Moreover, the entertainment nature of the casino and its associates distinguishes it from a restaurant or tavern that serves customers drinks. Notably, the casino has several restaurants and cocktail lounges. Also, plaintiffs acknowledge non-PAS positions serving drinks were available in casino areas not designated for the BorgataBabe positions. As a casino, defendant's entertainment business distinguishes this matter from other cases, as the costume may lend authenticity to the intended entertainment atmosphere. *See, e.g., Wilson v. S.W. Airlines Co.*, 517 *F.Supp.* 292, 302–03 (N.D.Tex.1981) (rejecting airline's Title VII defense to policy limiting flight attendant and ticketing positions to women based on their sex appeal to attract male business travelers, reasoning the essential business of the airline was to transport their customers); *Sage Realty, supra*, 507 *F.Supp.* at 602–04 finding sexually provocative uniform unrelated to business of lobby hostess for real estate firm violated Title VII).

We also reject plaintiffs' contention the discriminatory impact of the PAS was "obvious and self-evident." The facts in this record offer no evidence defendant's use of the weight standard or differentiated costumes deprived women employment, earning opportunities, or privileges of employment. Indisputably, the PAS reflects defendant's overemphasis on appearance, including weight. Nevertheless, that alone is not actionable as illegal discrimination under the LAD. While we understand plaintiffs' desire to require a unisex, gender-neutral costume, which eliminates all sex-based distinctions among BorgataBabes, we cannot conclude the LAD mandates this result.

We conclude on this record the evidence fails to present a cognizable claim of facial discrimination based on defendant's PAS weight policy. We cannot read the LAD to bar as discriminatory an employer's appearance policy requiring an associate, representing a casino business to the public, must remain fit and within a stated weight range, such as required by the PAS. *See Marks v. Nat'l Commc'ns Ass'n*, 72 *F.Supp.*2d 322, 330 (S.D.N.Y.1999) (finding employer's preference for physically fit employees to have direct interaction with customers did not violate Title VII); *Alam v. Reno Hilton Corp.*, 819 *F.Supp.* 905, 913–14 (D.Nev.1993).

C.

Plaintiffs next assert defendant discriminated against women when implementing and enforcing the PAS. Plaintiffs cite testimony some of them were told "male costumed associates . . . were not weighed"; some observed men "who gained significant amounts of weight without being subject to a weigh-in [or the] subsequent requirement to come into conformance with the PAS"; and others noted men "were able to purchase their own pants, rather than wear the Borgata costume."

Plaintiffs insist the motion judge failed to accept these facts as true for summary judgment purposes. They challenge as error his rejection of their proofs, which he characterized as anecdotal or hearsay.

Grooming policies applicable to all, but not evenhandedly enforced between men and women, may disadvantage one gender over the other and violate the LAD. *See, e.g., Marks, supra*, 72 *F.Supp.*2d at 330. In this matter, to prove disparate treatment, plaintiffs must provide admissible evidence showing men were treated as if exempt from the rules.

The record demonstrates all associates—male and female—were weighed when the PAS was modified to include the weight standard. Defendant's documentation records the baseline weights for employees subject to the PAS. The evidence also reveals few men were reweighed and none were disciplined.

Plaintiffs argue the motion judge erroneously failed to accord all favorable inferences to plaintiffs' testimony on this issue, which is asserted to be competent evidence of discriminatory treatment. Although plaintiffs' testimony of their own personal experiences is admissible and competent to prove a prima facie case of discrimination, statements of opinion or belief regarding male associates' experiences is not cognizable evidence to support their claims. *See Cinelli v. U.S. Energy Partners,* 77 *F.Supp.*2d 566, 572–73, 575–76 (D.N.J.1999) ("An issue is 'genuine' if it is supported by evidence upon which a reasonable jury could return a verdict for the nonmoving party.").

Testimony relating what some men said or a plaintiff's observation of what she considered a significant weight gain by a male is not competent proof. Nor is the fact that some men were not concerned about their weight demonstrative that these same men needed to be concerned. Plaintiffs' suggestions they never saw men weighed is refuted by defendant's documentary evidence. Even the statements that some plaintiffs saw male associates with "big bellies" lacks foundation and additional context necessary to show a violation of the PAS occurred. Further, plaintiffs offer no direct evidence from a male associate subject to the PAS explaining defendant ignored that he gained more than 7% of his baseline weight. Overall, plaintiffs' proofs alone are deficient. Absent accompanying competent proof, plaintiffs' claims of disparate enforcement of the PAS fails.

D.

The asserted hostile work environment gender stereotyping claims relate to the use of the female costume and the PAS weight standard to maintain the stereotypical image of a woman. Plaintiffs contend "the BorgataBabes are used as nothing more than sex objects by the casino, required to adhere to a stereotype of overt and aggressive feminine sexuality." Plaintiffs maintain male BorgataBabes are not sexualized or marketed in the same way as females. They rely on *Jespersen* to suggest the LAD prohibits an employer's policy making women "conform to a commonly-accepted stereotypical image of what women should wear." *Jespersen, supra,* 444 *F.*3d at 1112.

First, discussing gender stereotyping, the United States Supreme Court in *Price Waterhouse* stated:

"In saying that gender played a motivating part in an employment decision, we mean that, if we asked the employer at the moment of the decision what its reasons were and if we received a truthful response, one of those reasons would be that the applicant or employee was a woman. In the specific context of sex stereotyping, an employer who acts on the basis of a belief that a woman cannot be aggressive, or that she must not be, has acted on the basis of gender."

[*Price Waterhouse, supra,* 490 *U.S.* at 250, 109 *S.Ct.* at 1790–91, 104 *L.Ed.*2d at 287–88.]

Second, to date, New Jersey courts reviewing gender stereotyping discrimination claims have considered harassment of plaintiffs who were thought to insufficiently exhibit traits perceived to be assigned to their gender. In *Zalewski v. Overlook Hospital,* 300 *N.J.Super.*202, 203, 692 *A.*2d 131 (Law Div.1996), the plaintiff was harassed by coworkers who believed he was a virgin. Characterizing "gender stereotyping" as "the assigning of certain behavior characteristics as appropriate for women and for men but not for the other sex," *id.*at 203 n. 1, 692 *A.*2d 131, the Law Division judge concluded the LAD clearly prohibited any sexual harassment resulting in a hostile work environment, including discrimination based on gender stereotyping. *Id.* at 211, 692 *A.*2d 131.

This court in *Enriquez,* which concerned a transsexual female, concluded "sex discrimination under the LAD includes gender discrimination so as to protect [a] plaintiff from gender stereotyping and discrimination for transforming herself from a man to a woman." *Enriquez, supra,* 342 *N.J.Super.* at 515–16, 777 *A.*2d 365. Further, "[d]istinctions must be made on the basis of merit, rather than skin color, age, sex or gender, or any other measure that obscures a person's individual humanity and worth." *Id.* at 526–27, 777 *A.*2d 365.

We reiterate not all sex-based differentiations are actionable and "standards that appropriately differentiate between the genders are not facially discriminatory." *Jespersen, supra,* 444 *F.*3d at 1109–10. Essentially, the law "does not demand that things that are different in fact be treated the same" or that we "pretend that there are no physiological differences between men and women." *State v. Vogt,* 341 *N.J.Super.* 407, 418, 775 *A.*2d 551 (App.Div.2001).

We do not deny the PAS costume and physical fitness standards imposed what many would label an "archaic stereotype" of male and female physiques. Interestingly, there was disagreement among plaintiffs on the appropriateness of the BorgataBabes costume. Some found it too revealing and offensive. Others had no complaints. However, as *Jespersen* and *Price Waterhouse* clarify, actionable conduct results when these stereotypes are shown to be accompanied by a burden on one sex over the other or are otherwise used to interfere with employment opportunities of the discriminated group. We cannot find support for the latter essential elements among the facts in this record.

Regarding the weight standard, plaintiffs claim the 7% limit imposes "a stereotype of feminine sexual appeal and sexuality of the sort envisioned [in] *Jespersen* " as actionable. We cannot agree with such a generalization. We have discussed the differentiated role of the BorgataBabes from other associates, and their costumes added to that distinction and defendant's entertainment setting. We cannot agree with plaintiffs that their personal reactions to the weight standard evince proven gender stereotype disparities. Overall, discipline for non-compliance with the equally applicable PAS 7% weight standard by both men and women was very rare. Defendant's evidence reflected only twenty-five of 686 women, or 3%, were disciplined, and none of the forty-six men were disciplined.

E.

The trial judge's dismissal of the alleged sexual harassment hostile work environment discrimination claims based on defendant's conduct in enforcing the weight standard of the PAS is cited as erroneous. Plaintiffs assert they suffered severe and pervasive discriminatory comments and treatment by supervisors charged with enforcing the PAS weight standard because they were women, thereby creating a hostile, intimidating, and abusive work environment. More specifically, plaintiffs allege defendant engaged in conduct that amounted to sexual stereotyping sexual harassment while enforcing the PAS.

Defendant rejects these arguments, maintaining any discipline under the PAS resulted because of plaintiffs' weight, not their sex. This general denial does not squarely meet the myriad of factual assertions of harassing conduct. The record includes evidence of several plaintiffs who experienced discriminatory interactions following pregnancies or documented medical conditions, most of which were specific only to women, in the course of enforcing the weight standard.

Following our review, we agree material factual disputes regarding harassment experienced by some plaintiffs made summary judgment dismissal of their claims unwarranted. It is important to understand that although all plaintiffs couched their testimony in the context of enforcement of the PAS, the claims are not discriminatory because of weight per se, but because of a gender specific characteristic such as pregnancy or a medical condition such that the weight comments actually targeted women. In essence, but for the subjected plaintiffs' sex, they would not have been the object of the harassment. . . .

Additional evidence reinforces similar hostile work environment allegations, unmitigated by defendant's management. Schiavo complained to Preston Patterson, the Beverage Manager, when another employee was snorting like a pig toward certain female associates; Patterson did not take action. Werthmann related Patterson's comment to the BorgataBabes: "Don't anybody get pregnant. I don't want to hear anything about anybody's family or kids." The record shows only women suffered such harassment. It is obvious similar comments were not directed toward men.

Several discriminatory hostile work environment LAD claims do not need proof of overt sexual conduct in the workplace. *Muench v. Twp. of Haddon*, 255 *N.J.Super.* 288, 292, 605 *A.*2d 242 (App.Div.1992). Harassment based on gender is sufficient. *Ibid.* Although we have found enforcement of the PAS weight standard alone may not violate the LAD, the complained of conduct reflects a pattern of discriminatory comments toward women suffering medical conditions or returning from maternity leave that present a prima facie cause of action. As *Lehmann* states: "discrimination itself *is* the harm that the LAD seeks to eradicate. . . ." *Lehmann, supra,* 132 *N.J.* at 610, 626 *A.*2d 445 (emphasis in original). "[I]t is the harasser's conduct, not the plaintiff's injury, that must be severe or pervasive." *Ibid.* "Severity and workplace hostility are measured by surrounding circumstances." *Taylor v. Metzger,* 152 *N.J.* 490, 506, 706 *A.*2d 685 (1998).

The record evidence of management and supervisors' conduct, when viewed in a light most favorable to plaintiffs, presents a prima facie showing of harassment against women because of their gender, which "a reasonable woman would consider sufficiently severe or pervasive to alter the conditions of employment and create an intimidating, hostile, or offensive working environment." *Lehmann, supra,* 132 *N.J.* at 603–04, 626 *A.*2d 445. Incidents not obviously based on a plaintiff's sex must be prima facie shown to be because of her sex. *Ivan v. Cnty. of Middlesex,* 595 *F.Supp.*2d 425, 454 (D.N.J.2009). The evidence here is adequate to create a substantial dispute of material facts that the harassment alleged was gender based, defeating summary judgment. *Taylor, supra,* 152 *N.J.* at 508, 706 *A.*2d 685.

The record also contains some evidence of reported sexual harassment by customers and sexually harassing comments and actions by other associates, which although reported, went unaddressed by supervisors. Defendant's evidence included a sexual harassment prevention policy and a hotline to make such reports. The Supreme Court recently addressed evaluation of an employer's defense to claims of sexual harassment in *Aguas v. State,* 220 *N.J.* 494, 107 *A.*3d 1250 (2015). *Aguas* provided a framework for analyzing claims and defenses offered regarding sexual harassment hostile work environment claims. *Id.* at 499–500, 107 *A.*3d 1250. With respect to direct claims for negligence or recklessness, the Court's discussion, anchored in *Restatement [(Second) of Agency]* § 219(2)(b), provided: "[A]n employer's implementation and enforcement of an effective anti-harassment policy, or its failure to maintain such a policy, is a critical factor in determining negligence and recklessness claims under *Restatement (Second) of Agency* § 219(2)(b)." *Aguas, supra,* 220 *N.J.* at 499, 107 *A.*3d 1250.

To prevail on a direct claim alleging defendant's negligence, a plaintiff bears the burden to show a defendant negligently created a discriminatory work environment by "faili[ng] to exercise due care with respect to sexual discrimination in the workplace, that [the defendant's] breach of the duty of care caused the plaintiff's harm, and that [plaintiff] sustained damages." *Id.* at 512, 107 *A.*3d 1250. To defend against such a claim as discussed in *Aguas,* defendant may prove:

"[T]he existence of: (1) formal policies prohibiting harassment in the workplace; (2) complaint structures for employees' use, both formal and informal in nature; (3) anti-harassment training, which must be mandatory for supervisors and managers, and must be available to all employees of the organization; (4) the existence of effective sensing or monitoring mechanisms to check the trustworthiness of the policies and complaint structures; and (5) an unequivocal commitment from the highest levels of the employer that harassment would not be tolerated, and demonstration of that policy commitment by consistent practice."

Id. at 513, 107 *A.*3d 1250 (quoting *Gaines v. Bellino,* 173 *N.J.* 301, 313, 801 *A.*2d 322 (2002)).

Based on our review of the record evidence, some plaintiffs have alleged facts sufficient to demonstrate that the PAS weight standards were enforced in a harassing manner against women because of their gender, creating a hostile work environment. Defendant's response noting accommodations were given to women fails to specifically address the alleged harassing acts. On those claims summary judgment was prematurely entered.

IV.

For the reasons discussed in our opinion . . . [t]he record does not support discriminatory gender stereotyping by the use of sex-specific costumes or the provisions of the PAS. Further, no disparate impact is shown on these facts by the adoption of defendant's grooming and personal appearance policies. However, the record does include adequate evidence some plaintiffs' alleged facts sufficient to demonstrate defendant's enforcement of the weight policy was applied in a discriminatory harassing manner, targeting women returning from maternity and medical leave. Despite defendant's "accommodations" of these documented conditions, allegations have been presented showing the policy was used to harass these women. Collectively, the alleged acts adequately suggest a prima facie claim of sexual harassment hostile work environment.

We reverse the summary judgment dismissal of the hostile work environment claims based on the conduct surrounding the identified plaintiffs, and we remand for further proceedings. We affirm the summary judgment dismissal of all other claims for the reasons stated in our opinion.

Affirmed in part as modified. Reversed and remanded in part.

Notes

1. The *Schiavo* opinion concludes that appearance policies "need not be exactly the same for each gender, but will be considered evenhanded for the purposes of Title VII when they contain similar restrictions for both sexes." Imagine you represent a fashion company that makes only collections of women's apparel, and your client wants to adopt a dress policy for retail employees that requires female employees to dress in the company's clothing from head to toe, and male employees to wear their own black slacks, black shoes and a white dress shirt. What advice would you give?

2. Assume your client adopts the policy described in the paragraph above, and an employee explains to her manager that she is uncomfortable wearing the collection dresses the company requires, but is perfectly happy to wear the clothes required to be worn by men, and would therefore like to comply with the male dress code instead. The store manager asks you whether you can refuse the request. What advice would you give?

3. The *Schiavo* opinion also suggests that being overweight (assuming in the particular case that it is not a disability) or unattractive does not put a prospective employee in a protected class. If your fashion company client wants to make it clear

to its hiring managers that overweight and unattractive applicants are to be rejected, what advice would you give? What recommendations would you make in order to achieve the client's goal while minimizing the risk of liability?

D. Noncompete Provisions in Employment Contracts

Fashion companies use noncompete agreements to prevent rivals from poaching employees who have unique skills and/or access to valuable confidential company information. Courts generally disfavor the use of noncompete agreements because they restrict the free market in labor and essentially interfere with an individual's ability to earn a living. Some jurisdictions place significant limitations on the use of noncompete agreements, while others, such as California, ban the use of these agreements altogether.

1. Noncompete Case Study

Estee Lauder Cos. v. Batra

430 F. Supp. 2d 158 (S.D.N.Y. 2006)

Opinion

SWEET, District Judge.

Plaintiff Estee Lauder Companies, Inc. ("Estee Lauder") has moved by order to show cause for a temporary restraining order and preliminary injunction pursuant to Rule 65, Fed.R.Civ.P., to restrain defendant Shashi Batra ("Batra") from breaching the terms of his Confidentiality, Non-solicitation, and Non-competition Agreement with Estee Lauder (the "Non-compete Agreement") and from engaging in employment with N.V. Perricone M.D. Ltd. ("Perricone").

Batra has cross-moved seeking this Court to abstain or alternatively for a stay, citing *Colorado River Water Conservation Dist. v. United States,* 424 U.S. 800, 813, 96 S.Ct. 1236, 1244, 47 L.Ed.2d 483 (1976). For the reasons set forth below, a preliminary injunction will issue and the motion to abstain is denied.

Prior Proceedings

On March 13, 2006, Batra filed a complaint in California State Court seeking a declaratory judgment that the Non-compete Agreement was void under California Law. On March 15, 2006, Estee Lauder filed its complaint against Batra alleging: (1) breach of Batra's Non-compete agreement and (2) theft of trade secrets. On March 20, 2006, Batra cross-moved this Court by order to show cause for abstention and a stay.

Discovery was expedited. Hearings were conducted by way of deposition on March 22, March 23, and April 4, 2006. The motions of Estee Lauder and Batra were marked fully submitted on April 4, 2006.

Facts

For the purposes of this motion, the Court makes the following preliminary findings of fact, pursuant to Fed.R.Civ.P. 52(a) and 65, which are based on the affidavits submitted by the parties and the depositions conducted at the hearing.

I. The Parties

Plaintiff Estee Lauder is a corporation organized under the laws of the State of Delaware with its principal place of business located in New York, New York. Estee Lauder is engaged in the business of manufacturing and marketing skin care, makeup, fragrance, and hair care products.

Defendant Batra is an individual who resides in San Francisco, California, and did from 2004 until March 10, 2006, when he was employed as a senior executive for two of Estee Lauder's brands, Rodan and Fields ("R+F") and Darphin. On or about March 13, 2006, Batra began employment as the Worldwide General Manager of Perricone.

II. Estee Lauder's Business

Estee Lauder employs approximately 6,700 employees in New York and approximately 1,800 employees in California. Senior Management of Estee Lauder is located in New York, including the chief executive officer, chief operating officer, chief financial officer, head of operations, manufacturing, head of information systems, senior counsel, head of worldwide Human Resources, and group presidents. Of the 14 General Brand Managers, 11 are located in New York. The Darphin general manager is located in Paris, the R+F General Brand Manager (Batra) is located in San Francisco, and the Aveda General Brand Manager is located in Minneapolis.

In 2003, Estee Lauder acquired R+F, a dermatologist-founded skin care brand, and Darphin, a Paris-based pharmacy skin care and make-up company. Both the R+F and Darphin brands market and sell their products in the cosmetic dermatology market. R+F was founded by Stanford-trained dermatologists Katie Rodan, M.D. and Kathy Fields, M.D. R+F develops skin care products marketed to consumers seeking products and regimens created by expert dermatologists. The R+F skin care line offers products for specific skin problems, such as severe acne conditions and sensitive skin. Darphin is a Paris-based brand, originally sold in European pharmacy channels, that offers prestige skin care, make-up and personal care products created from plant extracts and botanical aromas. Darphin products are sold in more than 55 countries and territories. In North America, Darphin is primarily distributed through high-end retail establishments and specialty stores.

The R+F and Darphin brands report directly to Senior Management in New York.

III. Batra's Employment with Estee Lauder

Batra was hired as Global General Brand Manager of R+F as of January 5, 2004. Effective July 1, 2005, Batra also assumed the role as General Manager for Darphin, North America. In his role for R+F, Batra was the senior executive in charge of the brand and was responsible for overseeing all aspects of R+F's business, including, research and development, marketing and distribution, pricing, packaging development, corporate finance, regulatory affairs, internet development, and public relations. In his role for Darphin, Batra was responsible for marketing and distribution, pricing and overall accounts management strategies for the Darphin brands in North America.

Batra had worldwide responsibility for R+F. Similarly, he is assuming worldwide responsibility for Perricone. As brand manager of R+F, Batra was responsible for product development and for guiding new product entries into different market segments. This required him to participate in new product development meetings and to keep abreast of the technologies and key ingredients for the products developers were asked to create for R+F. In this capacity, Batra was responsible for preparing and implementing brand strategies for the R+F brand for fiscal years 2007 and 2008.

At the commencement of his employment, Batra signed an employment agreement with Estee Lauder, which contained confidentiality, non-solicitation, non-competition provisions. In return for signing the agreement (which all Estee Lauder executive employees are required to sign) Batra received a $100,000 signing bonus. In addition, Batra was provided with a compensation package of $300,000 per year, benefits, an automobile allowance, stock options, and bonus eligibility. On July 1, 2004, Batra's base salary was increased to $325,000. In July, 2005, in conjunction with his new responsibilities for Darphin, Estee Lauder increased Batra's base salary to $375,000.

The non-competition clause, contained in Paragraph 4 of the employment agreement that Batra signed in January 2004, provides as follows:

You recognize that the Company's business is very competitive and that to protect its Confidential Information the Company expects you not to compete with it for a period of time. You therefore agree that during your employment with the Company, and for a period of twelve (12) months after termination of you employment with the Company, regardless of the reason for the termination, you will not work for or otherwise actively participate in any business on behalf of any Competitor in which you could benefit the Competitor's business or harm the Company's business by using or disclosing Confidential Information. This restriction shall apply only in the geographic areas for which you had work-related responsibility during the last twelve (12) months of your employment by the Company and in any other geographic area in which you could benefit the Competitor's business through the use or disclosure of Confidential Information.

In addition, the agreement contained a non-solicitation provision, contained in Paragraph 5, pursuant to which Batra agreed that he would:

not, directly or indirectly, solicit, induce, recruit, or encourage any of the Company's employees to terminate their employment with the Company or to perform services for any other business.

Paragraph 7 of the agreement provides that:

During the period in which you are subject to the non-competition restrictions of paragraph 4, the Company will continue to pay you your last regular salary at the Company. If at any time during this period the Company gives you a written release from the restriction, the Company will no long be obligated to make the payments provided for in this Paragraph.

Batra's employment agreement with Estee Lauder also contains a confidentiality provision, which states:

You recognize that the Company's Confidential Information is extremely valuable to it and that disclosure or use of Confidential information outside the Company could irreparably damage the Company. You therefore agree that you will not use any Confidential Information for any purpose other than to benefit the Company. In furtherance of that commitment you will disclose Confidential Information to other persons within the Company only if they have a need to know the information in order to perform their job responsibilities for the Company and will not disclose Confidential Information to any person outside the Company.... You understand and agree that your confidentiality obligations under this paragraph will continue after termination of your employment with the Company, regardless of the reason for the termination, as long as the information is not generally known to the public.

Pursuant to the terms of the agreement, "Company" is defined as:

The Estee Lauder Companies Inc. or any entity in which 50 percent or more of the outstanding voting shares are owned directly or indirectly by The Estee Lauder Companies Inc.

The term "Competitor" is defined as:

[A]ny business that is engaged in, or is preparing to become engaged in, the cosmetics, skin care, hair care, toiletries or fragrance business or other business in which the Company is engaged or preparing to become engaged, or that otherwise competes with, or is preparing to compete with, the Company.

Pursuant to the agreement, "Confidential Information":

Means information concerning the Company that is disclosed to you or otherwise learned by your as a result of your employment by the Company that is not generally known by Competitors, including, but not limited to, such information concerning: research and development, trade secrets, sales, products, services, accounts, customers, purchasers of the Company's products, marketing, packaging, merchandising, distribution, manufacturing, finance, technology, intellectual property (patents, design patents, trademarks, trade dress, copyrights), strategies, business structures, operations or ventures or other business affairs or plans.

Finally, the Non-compete Agreement contained a choice of law provision, which states:

This agreement shall be governed by, and construed and interpreted in accordance with, the laws of the State of New York without regard to the conflict of law rules thereof.

IV. Batra's Possession of Trade Secrets

Batra admits that among his responsibilities as brand manager of R+F and as General Manager for Darphin, North America, he was in charge of developing strategies for the brands of these companies. He further admits that with respect to R+F products, he has a general idea of the plans for launch of new products, including the marketing and geographic plans and the channels of distribution for these products, over the next six to nine months. On January 18, 2006, a yearly brand strategy meeting was held in New York for the R+F brand. Present at the meeting was William Lauder, the chief executive officer of Estee Lauder; Dan Brestle, the chief operating officer of Estee Lauder; Rick Kunes; and Patrick Bousquet-Chavanne ("Bousquet-Chavanne"), Group President of Estee Lauder Companies, Inc. Via videolink, from San Francisco were also, Batra, Annie Jackson, and Suzie Henricks. For this meeting, Batra prepared a yearly brand strategy exercise which set forth a review of the future of the business and forward-looking plans concerning business development, investment, geographic expansion, and new product development. In addition, the brand strategy exercise presented confidential information regarding product launches for fiscal years 2006, 2007, 2008.

Documents introduced at the R+F brand strategy meeting, which were prepared by Batra during his employment with Estee Lauder, were submitted for consideration on this motion. Contained in these documents is confidential information regarding twelve new products that are presently in the pipeline. In addition the documents contained the confidential geographic plans for R+F over the next two to three years.

On January 18, 2006, a yearly brand strategy meeting was also held for the Darphin brand. Batra did not attend the meeting. However, he was given direct access to the plan following the meeting, which also contained confidential information regarding new marketing activities and new product development planned for the next three years. Additionally, Batra was privy to all of the information surrounding Darphin's upcoming marketing and product development strategies for Darphin. According to Bousquet-Chavanne, Batra has "the road map in terms of expenses and investments that [Estee Lauder is] planning to put behind [its] development for the Darphin brand . . . and the expected revenues from those investments." Batra was also responsible for preparing a plan of potential accounts the Darphin brand would seek to enter over the next twelve months.

V. Batra's Departure

In fall of 2006, Batra began discussing an opportunity at Perricone with Nick Perricone. Throughout the fall, Batra met with Perricone and individuals from an investment company called, TSG Consumer Products ("TSG"). At that time, TSG was interested in purchasing Perricone, and Batra was asked to give his opinion on how good the Perricone brand was, so that TSG could determine whether or not it would be a profitable investment. While Batra initially intended to leave Estee Lauder in November 2005, his discussions with TSG and Perricone continued into the winter of 2005 and 2006. Throughout this time, Batra routinely worked on Perricone matters during his day at Estee Lauder in breach of his duty of loyalty to Estee Lauder, preparing for upcoming meetings with TSG and Perricone and even drafting the press release for his new position with Perricone on an Estee Lauder computer. Additionally, during this time, Batra solicited advice and assistance on his work with Perricone from another R+F senior executive, the executive director of marketing, Annie Jackson ("Jackson"). There were several emails exchanged establishing that throughout this time, Batra regularly solicited Jackson to breach her duty of loyalty to Estee Lauder by assisting him on preparing for meetings with TSG and Perricone. Both Jackson and Batra completed at least some of this work for Perricone during time that should have been devoted to Estee Lauder projects, using their Estee Lauder computers and email. On one occasion, Batra admits that he invited and brought Jackson to such a meeting. At this meeting on February 7, 2006, Batra and Jackson worked to persuade TSG that Perricone was a good brand and a good acquisition. The evidence in these emails also establishes that even though he never made an explicit offer of employment, Batra was actively soliciting Jackson to leave her position with R+F to come to Perricone with him. *(See* Exhibit 11, containing an email from Batra to Jackson dated February 6, 2006 stating "I would drag you with me kicking and screaming even if you didn't want to come").

Following the February 7, 2006 meeting, Batra began creating a strategy for Perricone to begin to grow its business, which he drafted on his Estee Lauder computer. On or about March 7, 2006, Batra telephoned Bousquet-Chavanne and informed him that he was resigning from Estee Lauder to become the Worldwide General Manager of Perricone. During this telephone call, Bousquet-Chavanne reminded Batra of his obligations under the Non-compete Agreement. Batra acknowledged these obligations and responded that he did not believe that Estee Lauder would be able to enforce the Non-compete Agreement because he understood that California law does not recognize such agreements. During this telephone call, Bousquet-Chavanne encouraged Batra to provide a period of notice and to assist in a transition before leaving the company. Following further discussions, Batra agreed on March 10, 2006 to consider the Company's requests that he provide assistance for a transitional period and delay his departure date. He indicated that he would come to the office on Monday, March 13, 2006 at which time he would contact Bousquet-Chavanne to discuss the matter further. Later that day, Batra sent an email to Bousquet-Chavanne at 2:40 P.M. suggesting that he would attend a meeting the following Wednesday, March 15, 2006, despite having already discussed with TSG and Perricone that same day the possibility of filing a lawsuit in California in the near future. In order to ensure obtaining jurisdiction in California, Batra misled Bousquet-Chavanne into thinking that he would seriously consider staying on at Estee Lauder for a transitional period, even though he admits he was ninety-five percent certain he would not return there. Batra admitted that it was in his interest to persuade Estee Lauder that he was continuing to negotiate in good faith so that Estee Lauder would not sue him to enforce the Non-compete Agreement in New York before he had an opportunity to file his suit against Estee Lauder in California.

Contrary to his word, Batra did not come to the office on March 13, 2006. Rather, on Monday, March 13, 2006, Batra telephoned Bousquet-Chavanne and informed him that he was confirming his resignation, effective the prior Tuesday, March 7, 2006. On that same day, Batra and Perricone commenced a lawsuit in California state court seeking a declaratory judgment that the Non-compete Agreement is unenforceable under California law.

Batra began employment as President of Perricone on Tuesday, March 14, 2006. In the course of the proceedings, he agreed to refrain from taking up his Perricone position until the resolution of the instant motions.

VI. Perricone Competes Directly with R+F and Darphin

All R+F products are conceived in association with two doctors, Doctors Rodan and Fields. All R+F products are based on medicines which are delivered in the products in non-prescription strengths. Perricone products are also developed by a dermatologist, Dr. Perricone, and as with R+F, the name of the dermatologist appears on the packaging.

While employed by Estee Lauder, Batra prepared a direct competitive assessment of R+F's Project Instant, a pending product in full development, and Perricone's active tinted moisturizer, an analysis which reflects Batra's personal understanding while employed with Estee Lauder that R+F and Perricone are competitors. Exhibits 1, 2, and 3 demonstrate that R+F and Darphin products are in direct competition with Perricone products in California department stores. Batra admitted that at the Nordstrom department store in San Francisco, the R+F display is located directly adjacent to the Perricone display, a positioning that reflects their head-to-head competition in that store. Similarly, at the Bloomingdales in Century City, the R+F and Perricone displays also are located side-by-side, and in the Nordstrom Department Store on the west side of Los Angeles, the side-by-side positioning of R+F and Perricone products reflects that they are direct competitors. Exhibit 38 also indicates that Perricone is closely competitive with R+F in terms of price point. Both brands offer exclusive, clinical products that are sold for similar prices. While Darphin offers cosmetic, rather than clinical products, it too competes with Perricone in that its products are priced similarly.

Discussion

* * *

II. Plaintiff's Motion for a Preliminary Injunction is Granted

A. Preliminary Injunction Standard

A preliminary injunction is an "extraordinary and drastic remedy, one that should not be granted unless the movant, by a clear showing, carries the burden of persuasion." *Mazurek v. Armstrong,* 520 U.S. 968, 972, 117 S.Ct. 1865, 138 L.Ed.2d 162 (1997)(emphasis in original). In the ordinary case, a preliminary injunction may be granted only when the party seeking the injunction establishes that "1) absent injunctive relief, it will suffer irreparable harm, and 2) either a) that it is likely to succeed on the merits, or b) that there are sufficiently serious questions going to the merits to make them a fair ground for litigation, and that the balance of hardships tips decidedly in favor of the moving party." *No Spray Coalition, Inc. v. City of New York,* 252 F.3d 148, 150 (2d Cir.2001).

B. Choice of Law

As a threshold matter, the Court first must determine which state's law controls—New York's or California's. As a court is to apply the choice-of-law rules prevailing in the state in which the court sits, *see, Klaxon Co. v. Stentor Elec. Mfg. Co.,* 313 U.S. 487, 496, 61 S.Ct. 1020, 85 L.Ed. 1477 (1941), New York law governs the choice of law determination.

Although New York recognizes the "choice of law principle that parties to a contract have a right to choose the law to be applied to their contract, this freedom of choice on the part of the parties is not absolute." *S. Leo Harmonay, Inc. v. Binks Mfg. Co.,* 597 F.Supp. 1014, 1025 (S.D.N.Y.1984), *aff'd* 762 F.2d 990 (2d Cir.1985). To determine the appropriateness of the parties' choice of law, New York follows the "substantial relationship" approach, as stated in Restatement (Second) of Conflicts of Law § 187:

(2) The law of the state chosen by the parties to govern their contractual rights and duties will be applied . . . unless either

(a) the chosen state has no substantial relationship to the parties . . . or

(b) application of the law of the chosen state would be contrary to a fundamental policy of a state which has a materially greater interest than the chosen state . . .

Leo Harmonay, 597 F.Supp. at 1025.

Generally, "[u]nder New York law . . . a contract's designation of the law that is to govern disputes arising from the contract . . . is determinative if the state has sufficient contacts with the transaction." *Zerman v. Ball,* 735 F.2d 15, 20 (2d Cir.1984) (citations omitted). However, there is an exception to this rule when "application of the law of the chosen state would be contrary to a fundamental policy of a state which has a materially greater interest than the chosen state." *Leo Harmonay,* 597 F.Supp. at 1025. For this exception to apply, "the issue [must be] of such overriding concern to the public policy of another jurisdiction as to override the intent of the parties and the interest of [New York] in enforcing its own policies."

Marine Midland Bank, N.A. v. United Missouri Bank, N.A., 223 A.D.2d 119, 123–24, 643 N.Y.S.2d 528, 531 (1st Dep't 1996).

In other words, three conditions must be met in order to override the intent of the contracting parties. First, Batra must establish that in the absence of the choice of law provision, California law would apply. Second, he must demonstrate that the application of New York law would be contrary to a fundamental policy of California. Third, Batra must demonstrate that California has a materially greater interest than New York in the determination of this dispute.

Batra argues, in essence, that irrespective of the presence of the New York forum selection clause in the contract, California law should apply due to the presence of significant contacts in California and to California's strong public policy against the enforcement of non-compete agreements.

For the first element of the inquiry, New York courts employ the "substantial relationship" test. "The New York Court of Appeals has addressed the 'substantial relationship' approach and held that while the parties' choice of law is to be given heavy weight, the law of the state with the 'most significant contacts' is to be applied." *Agricultural Ins. Co., Inc. v. Ace Hardware Corp.*, 98 Civ. 8708, 2003 U.S. Dist. LEXIS 711, 2003 WL 164272, at *5 (S.D.N.Y. Jan.17, 2003).

In support of his argument, Batra cites *Prod. Resource Group L.L.C. v. Oberman*, No. 03 Civ. 5366(JGK), 2003 WL 22350939 (S.D.N.Y.2003), in which the Honorable John G. Koeltl found that in the absence of the choice of law provision, California law would apply, based upon the following:

The non-competition provision was included in a contract pursuant to which Oberman worked primarily in California. During his tenure, his base was in California, and he spent far more time in California than he did in New York on his few trips there. He was paid for most of his tenure by the California subsidiary of PRG. Both Oberman's work under his employment agreement . . . and the work he now seeks to do is centered in California.

Oberman, 2003 WL 22350939, at *10. According to Batra, the facts here are analogous to those presented in *Oberman*, and therefore California law should apply.

While there are similarities between the facts here and those presented in *Oberman*, there are significant contacts to New York present in this case that were not present in *Oberman*. First, although, as in *Oberman*, Batra was a resident of California and was hired by a New York based employer to work in California, the work Batra did was not entirely "centered" in California. Rather, Batra was responsible for R+F's business worldwide and for Darphin's business throughout North America. Furthermore, while there are California components to the employment relationship, many of the significant functions for both brands are located in New York, including Corporate Administration, Creative/Names/Copy, Finance, Product Development, Packaging Development, Regulatory, Legal, Operations, Manufacturing, Shipping, Forecasting, Information Services,

Human Resources, Press Relations, Customer Service, and the Internet Division, while Sales and Marketing are directed out of California. Batra retained responsibility for all or many of these functions as to both brands, and New York personnel performing these functions for R+F and Darphin worked under Batra's management. Additionally, unlike in *Oberman,* Estee Lauder's principal place of business, and not simply its headquarters, is located in New York, and Batra's paychecks were issued from New York.

The facts underlying this case are also distinguishable from those in *SG Cowen Securities Corp. v. Messih,* No. 00 Civ. 3228(HB), 2000 WL 633434 (S.D.N.Y. May 17, 2000), *aff'd,* 224 F.3d 79 (2d Cir.2000),[3] upon which Batra also relies. As in *Oberman,* the contacts in *Messih* were found to be weighted toward California, although the Plaintiff employer's headquarters were in New York (but not his principal place of business) and some contract negotiations occurred in New York. *Id.* at *4. In *Messih,* Messih was hired to serve as the Managing Director of Technology in the Corporate Finance division of plaintiff's San Francisco office. *Id.* As such, even from SG Cowen's perspective, the work Messih did for the company had little to no relationship with New York. Here, in contrast, Batra was not hired to run a California office of Estee Lauder. The fact that Batra literally carried out many of his duties from California does not overcome the fact that work itself was the management of a New York-based brand with predominantly New York-based employees. Accordingly, while this may be a close call, it is not the situation present in *Oberman* or *Messih.*

Based on the foregoing, while Batra's employment relationship does not overwhelmingly point to New York, the management and control of Estee Lauder is entirely in New York, and a significant portion of Batra's responsibilities were centered in New York. Therefore, the totality of the number of contacts in New York well exceeds those present in *Oberman* and *SG Cowen.*

With respect to whether the application of New York law is contrary to a fundamental policy of California, Section 16600 of the California Business and Professions Code provides that "every contract by which anyone is restrained from engaging in a lawful profession, trade, or business of any kind is to that extent void." Cal. Bus. & Prof. Code § 16600. California and New York courts have held that Section 16600 reflects a "strong public policy" of California.

---

3. It is worth noting that the holding in *Messih* did not address whether California's fundamental policy against the enforcement of restrictive covenants warranted the application of California law. Rather, the district court focused exclusively on which states' contacts predominated, holding that because California's did, California possessed a materially greater interest. See *Messih,* 2000 WL 633434, at *4. Additionally, in affirming the denial of the preliminary injunction in *Messih,* the Second Circuit did not address the district court's determination that California's law should apply, but rather noted only generally "the many hurdles" Cowen faced in demonstrating a likelihood of success. *Messih,* 224 F.3d at 84.

Indeed, "California courts have held that 'the interests of the employee in his own mobility and betterment are deemed paramount to the competitive business interests of the employers, where neither the employee nor his new employer has committed any illegal act accompanying the employment change.'" *Id.* (quoting *Metro Traffic Control, Inc. v. Shadow Traffic Network,* 22 Cal.App.4th 853, 860, 27 Cal.Rptr.2d 573 (1994)).

Because, pursuant to California's fundamental policy against the enforcement of restrictive covenants, non-compete agreements, such as the one at issue in this case, are declared null and void under California law, the enforcement of Batra's agreement by this Court would be contrary to a fundamental policy of California, notwithstanding Estee Lauder's contention that there is no conflict between California's policy and the application of New York law.[4] *See Oberman,* 2003 WL 22350939, at *10 (concluding that the "fundamental policy of a state [California] which has a materially greater interest than the chosen state" warranted the application of California law despite the contractual provision that New York law would govern). Although restrictive covenants are enforceable under California law where there has been a misappropriation of trade secrets, Estee Lauder has not demonstrated that to date there has been such a misappropriation. Absent such a showing, the Non-compete Agreement would not be enforceable under California law. However, in spite of the fact that the application of New York law would run contrary to the fundamental policy of California, it is concluded that California's interest in this dispute is not materially greater than that of New York and that therefore, New York law shall apply.

Because, as set forth above, the contacts point toward New York, it is concluded that California's interest is not materially greater than that of New York. Just as California has a strong interest in protecting those employed in California, so too

4. Estee Lauder contends that the application of New York law would not be contrary to a fundamental policy of California on the grounds that the policies underlying the unfair competition rules of New York and California do not run contrary to one another. In essence, Estee Lauder argues that it is the policy of both states that: (1) employees have a duty of loyalty to their employer; (2) an employer's trade secrets shall be safeguarded from unfair competition arising from misappropriation both during and after an employment relationship; and (3) employees should generally be free to pursue the occupation of their choosing. To the extent that the policies of New York and California do overlap, Estee Lauder's reliance on such similarities is misplaced. The second prong of the choice of law analysis asks not whether the policy of California conflicts with the policy of New York, but rather whether the application of New York law would run contrary to California's fundamental policy. Irrespective of whether New York's general policies overlap with those of California, the fact remains that the enforcement of the restrictive covenant at issue under New York law would run contrary to California's policy against such enforcement. Indeed, as Plaintiff notes, "under New York's policy, a slightly different balance is struck," (Pl. Mem. L. In Supp. Mot. For PI p. 8), allowing for the enforcement of restrictive covenants under certain circumstances where reasonable in time and geographic scope. Therefore, when the application of this policy balances toward the enforcement of a non-compete agreement, that application runs contrary to California's fundamental policy.

does New York have a strong interest in protecting companies doing business here in keeping with:

> New York's recognized interest in maintaining and fostering its undisputed status as the preeminent commercial and financial nerve center of the Nation and the world. That interest naturally embraces a very strong policy of assuring ready access to a forum for redress of injuries arising out of transactions spawned here. Indeed, access to a convenient forum which dispassionately administers a known, stable, and commercially sophisticated body of law may be considered as much an attraction to conducting business in New York as its unique financial and communications resources.

Marine Midland, 223 A.D.2d at 124, 643 N.Y.S.2d 528 (internal citations omitted).

Accordingly, based upon New York's policy of enforcing restrictive covenants that are reasonable in time and scope and given New York's interest in having a predictable body of law that companies can rely on when employing individuals who will have close contact with trade secrets and confidential information, it is concluded that California's interest is not "materially greater" than New York's.

C. Estee Lauder Has Demonstrated Irreparable Harm

"Perhaps the single most important prerequisite for the issuance of a preliminary injunction is a demonstration that if it is not granted the applicant is likely to suffer irreparable harm before a decision on the merits can be rendered." *Citibank, N.A. v. Citytrust*,756 F.2d 273, 275 (2d Cir.1985). Irreparable harm is that injury which is so serious that "a monetary award cannot be adequate compensation." *Id.* at 275; *see also Warner-Lambert Co. v. Northside Development Corp.*, 86 F.3d 3, 8 (2d Cir.1996) (irreparable harm requirement may be met by showing that harm is unquantifiable in monetary terms). In order to demonstrate irreparable injury the movant must show "an injury that is neither remote nor speculative, but actual and imminent and cannot be remedied by an award of monetary damages." *Earthweb, Inc. v. Schlack*, 2000 WL 1093320, at *2, 2000 U.S. App. LEXIS 11446, at *5–6 (2d Cir. May 18, 2000) (finding plaintiff's showing insufficient to warrant a preliminary injunction where they failed to demonstrate that defendant had removed proprietary documents or information or was about to violate his duties under the agreement).

Irreparable harm is presumed where a trade secret has been misappropriated because, as the Court of Appeals for the Second Circuit has explained, "[a] trade secret once lost is, of course, lost forever" and, therefore, such a loss "cannot be measured in money damages." *FMC Corp. v. Taiwan Tainan Giant Indus. Co.*, 730 F.2d 61, 63 (2d Cir.1984). Even where a trade secret has not yet been disclosed, irreparable harm may be found based upon a finding that trade secrets will inevitably be disclosed where, as here, "the movant competes directly with the prospective employer and the transient employee possesses highly confidential or technical knowledge concerning [ ] marketing strategies, or the like." *EarthWeb, Inc. v. Schlack*, 71 F. Supp.2d 299, 309 (S.D.N.Y.1999).

It is concluded that Estee Lauder has carried its burden of demonstrating irreparable injury for the following reasons. First, if Batra does misappropriate Estee Lauder's trade secrets, it would be "very difficult to calculate the monetary damages that would successfully redress the loss," *Ticor Title Insurance Co. v. Cohen,* 173 F.3d 63, 68–69 (2d Cir.1999), given the difficulty in ascertaining empirically how much of a competitive advantage such information gives Perricone and/or how much detriment it might cause to the future profitability of R+F and/or Darphin products. *See Shipley Co. v. Clark,* 728 F.Supp. 818, 827 (D.Mass.1990) ("the task of quantifying the consequences of violating a non-competition clause is a particularly difficult and elusive one"). Additionally, as in *Ticor,* the employment agreement between Batra and Estee Lauder "concedes that in the event of breach of the post-employment competition provision, [Estee Lauder] shall be entitled to injunctive relief, because it would cause irreparable injury." As in *Ticor* therefore, the agreement's language "might arguably be viewed as an admission by [Batra] that plaintiff will suffer irreparable harm were he to breach the contract's non-compete agreement." *Ticor,* 173 F.3d at 69.

Batra contends that Estee Lauder has not demonstrated irreparable injury, but rather simply has speculated about the possibility that Batra will use the alleged confidential business information. According to Batra, Estee Lauder cannot satisfy this requirement because: (1) Batra does not have any technical expertise; (2) Perricone and Batra do not care about Plaintiff's technology as Perricone and Estee Lauder are not competitors; and (3) Batra has eliminated any risk of misappropriation of trade secrets by stipulating that he will be completely divorced from new product development in his position at Perricone.

With respect to the first contention, Batra's lack of technical expertise says nothing about whether or not Batra possesses trade secrets and/or protected confidential information. Under New York law, trade secrets are defined as set forth in the Restatement of Torts § 757, comment b (1939), which states that:

> A trade secret may consist of any formula, pattern, device or compilation of information which is used in one's business, and which gives [the owner] the opportunity to obtain an advantage over competitors who do not know or use it.

Softel, Inc. v. Dragon Med. & Scientific Commc'ns, Inc., 118 F.3d 955, 968 (2d Cir.1997). New York courts consider several factors in determining whether information constitutes a trade secret, including: (1) the extent to which the information is known outside of the business; (2) the extent to which it is known by employees and others involved in the business; (3) the extent of measures taken by the business to guard the secrecy of information; (4) the value of the information to the business and its competitors; (5) the amount of effort or money expended by the business in developing the information; and (6) the ease or difficulty with which the information could be properly acquired or duplicated by others. *See North Atlantic Instruments, Inc. v. Haber,* 188 F.3d 38, 44 (2d Cir.1999).

In determining whether something has trade secret status, "[t]he most important consideration is whether the information was secret." Price lists, product samples, and "marketing plans" are all items that are not, as a matter of law, protected as trade secrets. *Gemmy Indus. Corp. v. Crisha Creations Ltd.,* No. 04 Civ.1074 (RWS), 2004 WL 1406075, at * 12 (S.D.N.Y. June 23, 2004). Similarly, an employee's "knowledge of the intricacies of [his former employer's] business operation" does not enjoy trade secret status. *Reed, Roberts Assocs., Inc. v. Strauman,* 40 N.Y.2d 303, 309, 386 N.Y.S.2d 677, 353 N.E.2d 590 (1976).

Under this standard, Estee Lauder has established that Batra possesses trade secrets. The fact that Batra was not the scientist behind the formulas and the development of new products bears not on whether or not Estee Lauder has carried its burden of demonstrating irreparable injury. *PepsiCo, Inc. v. Redmond,* 54 F.3d 1262, 1270 (7th Cir.1995) (noting that even though it is not the typical case, strategic information regarding price, distribution, and marketing nevertheless falls within the realm of trade secret protection). Even if, as he contends, Batra knew no more about the components or technologies of Estee Lauder products than "the average consumer who can read the product ingredient label," it is conceded that he was responsible for developing the R+F brand strategies for the 2007 and 2008 fiscal years and was intimately involved in developing the Darphin brand strategies for the same time period. Moreover, his deposition testimony, as laid out above, also indicates that Batra was knowledgeable more than just marketing plans. He was knowledgeable about confidential products currently under development and product innovations scheduled for the coming years. Additionally, Batra has confidential information about the stage of development of products in the pipeline, wholly apart from specific secrets concerning its process, which is entitled to protection. *See Eastman Kodak Co. v. Powers Film Products,* 189 A.D. 556, 179 N.Y.S. 325, 330 (holding employer entitled to protection against disclosure to its competitor of the stage of its product development).

Finally, Batra seeks employment with a direct competitor of Estee Lauder. As such, it is concluded that, as in *Monovis, Inc. v. Aquino,*905 F.Supp. 1205, 1234 (W.D.N.Y.1994), "even assuming the best of good faith, it is doubtful whether the defendant could completely divorce his knowledge of the trade secrets from any . . . work he might engage in."

As to Batra's second argument, it is concluded that an individual's assertion that he "really doesn't care" about his former employer's trade secrets is not sufficient to overcome a demonstration of irreparable harm. As evidenced by the record in this case, Batra no longer feels allegiance to his former employer. Prior to leaving the company, he spent company time negotiating the terms of his new employment agreement with Perricone and solicited help on Perricone matters from another senior executive of Estee Lauder without regard to his and her obligations under their employment agreements or to the duty of loyalty they both owed Estee Lauder. As such, Estee Lauder should not be required to rely on Batra's characterization of the usefulness of the information he obtained while employed there.

Additionally, it might be argued that even if Batra had not shown himself to be lacking credibility, the information he obtained while employed with Estee Lauder could not cause irreparable injury in his hands at Perricone if Perricone was not interested in Estee Lauder's information. In other words, Batra might be correct that if Perricone products did not compete with R+F and Darphin products, Estee Lauder would face much greater difficulty carrying its burden of demonstrating irreparable injury. However, because it is concluded that Perricone products do compete with those of R+F and Darphin, this argument is inapposite.

Finally, Batra's stipulation that he will be divorced completely from product development for a short time period at Perricone also is not sufficient to overcome Estee Lauder's showing of irreparable injury. As noted, Batra has not proven the most trustworthy in the fulfillment of his obligations owed Estee Lauder. *See PepsiCo*, 54 F.3d at 1270 (holding the risk of inevitable disclosure further supported by the former employee's "lack of forthrightness" and "out and out lies"). Moreover, as stated above, the trade secrets Batra possesses are not limited to product formulas. Therefore the harm that could befall Estee Lauder if Batra were to misappropriate its trade secrets is not limited to a potential replication of its products, but rather could manifest as competitive advantage from knowing the when and how of Estee Lauder's future product introductions.

Accordingly, it is concluded that Estee Lauder has demonstrated that the measure of the damage caused by the misappropriation of its trade secrets is unquantifiable and that, therefore, Estee Lauder will suffer irreparable injury absent an injunction.

D. The Non-compete Agreement Under New York Law

New York law subjects a non-compete covenant by an employee to "an overriding limitation of reasonableness." *Karpinski v. Ingrasci*, 28 N.Y.2d 45, 49, 268 N.E.2d 751, 320 N.Y.S.2d 1 (1971). Courts must weigh the need to protect the employer's legitimate business interests against the employee's concern regarding the possible loss of livelihood, a result strongly disfavored by public policy in New York. *See id.* A covenant that is reasonable in time and geographic scope shall be enforced to the extent necessary "(1) to prevent an employee's solicitation or disclosure of trade secrets, (2) to prevent an employee's release of confidential information regarding the employer's customers, or (3) in those cases where the employee's services to the employer are deemed special or unique." *Ticor*, 173 F.3d at 70 (citing *Purchasing Assocs. v. Weitz*, 13 N.Y.2d 267, 272–73, 246 N.Y.S.2d 600, 196 N.E.2d 245 (1963)).

Batra argues that even under New York law, the Non-compete Agreement is unenforceable. First, Batra argues that the non-compete is overbroad and seeks to achieve a purpose deemed improper under New York law. Additionally, Batra claims that the agreement is unenforceable because, according to Batra, Estee Lauder has failed to establish that it can succeed on a claim for misappropriation of trade secrets, which, according to him, is required for a New York court to enforce a non-compete agreement.

1. The Agreement Does Not Seek to Achieve an Improper Purpose

With respect to Batra's first argument, Batra contends specifically that the Non-compete Agreement is being used for an impermissible purpose under New York law in that it seeks to insulate Estee Lauder from competition in contravention of New York's policy regarding covenants not to compete.

As set forth above, covenants not to compete are subjected to an overriding question of reasonableness, which takes particular account of the interests of employees. As Batra points out, the New York Court of Appeals has stated:

[O]ur economy is premised on the competition engendered by the uninhibited flow of services, talent and ideas. Therefore, no restrictions should fetter an employee's right to apply to his own best advantage the skills and knowledge acquired by the overall experience of his previous employment.

Reed, Roberts Assocs., Inc. v. Strauman, 40 N.Y.2d 303, 307, 386 N.Y.S.2d 677, 680, 353 N.E.2d 590 (1976). However, the Court of Appeals also has emphasized the competing interests involved in the analysis of non-compete agreements, highlighting the importance of balancing the interests of the employee and the public with those of the employer:

[T]he courts must also recognize the legitimate interest an employer has in safeguarding that which has made his business successful and to protect himself against deliberate surreptitious commercial piracy. Thus restrictive covenants will be enforceable to the extent necessary to prevent the disclosure or use of trade secrets or confidential customer information.

According to Batra, Bousquet-Chavanne's testimony regarding the purpose underlying the use of restrictive covenants at Estee Lauder demonstrates that they are used principally for an anti-competitive purpose. During his direct testimony, Bousquet-Chavanne stated:

Q: And what does the noncompete protect against?

A: The noncompete actually is a key element in preventing that our human capital on one side, management talent be tempted to basically join the competition. We protect our management talent first and foremost . . .

Later, on cross-examination, the witness stated:

Q: How does it protect against management talent? Isn't it designed to keep people there?

A: It protects existing management talent in the company, yes.

Q: So it's designed to keep people where they are?

A: It's designed to basically keep the people inside the other companies in terms of their career development at Estee Lauder.

Q: And creating a barrier for them to move outside?

A: It creates a barrier for the competition to access our talent because they know we will enforce [the] noncompete clause.

* * *

Q: It is not intended to be a disincentive to leave?

A: The primary objective is to secure the longevity of our management resources.

Q: And to do that you make it harder for them to leave, right?

A: We make it harder for our competition to approach them.

Additionally, Batra contends that the overbreadth of the express terms of the covenant underscore its improper purpose. "Competitor" is defined by the noncompete agreement as any business that is engaged in, or is preparing to become engaged in, the cosmetics, skin care, hair care, toiletries, or fragrance business or other business in which [Estee Lauder] is engaged or is preparing to become engaged, or that otherwise competes with, or is preparing to compete with, the Company. As such, Batra argues that in prohibiting him from "work[ing] for or otherwise actively participat[ing] in any business on behalf of any Competitor," the agreement unreasonably bars him from working in any of the businesses engaged in by Estee Lauder—the world's largest cosmetic company in the prestige beauty industry.

Initially, Batra's argument with respect to the overbreadth of the terms of the noncompete agreement ignores the qualifying language that immediately follows the word "Competitor" in the above-quoted passage. The relevant passage states in full that Batra shall "not work for or otherwise actively participate in any business on behalf of any Competitor in which [he] could benefit the Competitor's business or harm the Company's business by using or disclosing Confidential Information." Thus, by its express terms, the covenant does not prohibit Batra from employment with all Competitors of Estee Lauder and all Estee Lauder products, but rather limits this prohibition to positions with other companies in which Batra could misuse the trade secrets and confidential information to which he became privy while employed with Estee Lauder. As such, by its very terms, the covenant would be unenforceable if enforcement was sought against Batra for leaving Estee Lauder for employment with a company that did not directly compete with R+F and Darphin—the Estee Lauder brands in which Batra possesses knowledge of trade secrets.

With respect to Bousquet-Chavanne's testimony regarding the purpose of the Non-compete Agreement, all covenants not to compete are motivated at least in part by a company's desire to protect management talent to the extent that they are legally entitled to do so. New York law strikes a balance by permitting companies to protect their management from being lured by competitors only to the extent necessary to prevent the misuse of trade secrets. *See Am. Broad. Cos.*, 52 N.Y.2d at 404, 438 N.Y.S.2d 482, 420 N.E.2d 363;*Lucente v. IBM*, 117 F.Supp.2d 336, 348 (S.D.N.Y.2000) ("Courts will enforce employment restrictions only to the extent necessary to protect the employer from unfair competition which stems from the employee's use or disclosure of trade secrets or confidential customer lists, or confidential customer information."). To hold otherwise would essentially invalidate all covenants not to compete—a result New York courts obviously have not endorsed, given their longstanding dedication to the reasonableness inquiry.

Accordingly, Batra's argument that the purpose of the Non-compete Agreement is pernicious to New York's policy regarding covenants not to compete is not credited.

2. Estee Lauder Need Not Establish a Misappropriation of Trade Secrets

Batra's argument with respect to Estee Lauder's failure to establish that Batra misappropriated trade secrets is two-fold. First, Batra argues that the information that Estee Lauder seeks to protect is not of trade secret status, and therefore not protectable. Second, Batra contends that Estee Lauder has failed to demonstrate that Batra has taken or used anything belonging to Estee Lauder.

For the reasons set forth above with respect to Estee Lauder's demonstration of irreparable injury, Batra's first argument is without merit. Estee Lauder has established that Batra possesses information that is of trade secret status and that there is a substantial risk of Batra disclosing this information.

As to Batra's contention that Estee Lauder has failed to demonstrate that he has misappropriated trade secrets, such a showing is not necessary to prevail on its claim. *See, e.g., PepsiCo,* 54 F.3d at 1268 (outlining inevitable disclosure doctrine). While, as stated, New York courts will enforce a non-compete agreement only to the extent necessary to protect an employer's trade secrets, this is not to say that in order to obtain such protection the employer must demonstrate that such misappropriation has already taken place. Rather, Estee Lauder simply need establish that there is a risk of inevitable disclosure, as set forth above. The misappropriation claim is a separate and distinct claim.

3. Reasonableness of the Scope of the Agreement

Courts assessing the reasonableness of the scope of a restrictive covenant are to "focus[ ] on the particular facts and circumstances given context to the agreement." *BDO Seidman v. Hirshberg,* 93 N.Y.2d 382, 390, 712 N.E.2d 1220, 690 N.Y.S.2d 854 (1999). As such, there are no per se lines demarcating what constitutes an unreasonable durational or geographic scope. Rather, reasonableness will be judged by the specific facts underlying the agreement and the nature of the employer's confidential information. *See Business Intelligence Services, Inc. v. Hudson,* 580 F.Supp. 1068, 1072 (S.D.N.Y.1984).

Courts need not employ an all or nothing approach to the enforcement of employee restrictive covenants. Indeed, New York courts have "expressly recognized and applied the judicial power to sever and grant partial enforcement for an overbroad employee restrictive covenant." *BDO Seidman,* 93 N.Y.2d at 394, 690 N.Y.S.2d 854, 712 N.E.2d 1220, (citing *Karpinski,* 28 N.Y.2d at 51–52, 320 N.Y.S.2d 1, 268 N.E.2d 751 (giving effect to portion of the covenant barring the practice of oral surgery, but declining to do so with respect to the portion of the covenant barring the practice of all dentistry)). Pursuant to this rule, partial enforcement may be justified so long as "the employer demonstrates an absence of overreaching, coercive use of dominant bargaining power, or other anti-competitive misconduct, but has in good faith sought to protect a legitimate business interest, consistent with reasonable standards of fair dealing." *Id.*

In determining whether a covenant not to compete is reasonable in time and geographic scope, enforcement will only be granted to the extent necessary to protect the employer's legitimate interests: "(1) to prevent an employee's solicitation or disclosure of trade secrets, (2) to prevent an employee's release of confidential information regarding the employer's customers, or (3) in those cases where the employee's services to the employer are deemed special or unique." *Ticor,* 173 F.3d at 70 (citing *Purchasing Assocs.,* 13 N.Y.2d at 272–73, 196 N.E.2d at 248, 246 N.Y.S.2d at 604).

Under New York law, the durational reasonableness of a non-compete agreement is judged by the length of time for which the employer's confidential information will be competitively valuable. *See, e.g., Business Intelligence Servs. Inc. v. Hudson,* 580 F.Supp. 1068, 1073 (S.D.N.Y.1984).

An additional factor courts will look to in evaluating the reasonableness of a restrictive covenant is whether an employee receives continued consideration for his loyalty and good will. *See Bradford v. New York Times Co.,* 501 F.2d 51, 58 (2d Cir.1974) (noting that "this factor cannot be overlooked in determining the reasonableness of the restraint presented"). The desire to avoid "impairing the employee's ability to earn a living," *see Am. Broad. Cos.,* 52 N.Y.2d at 404, 438 N.Y.S.2d 482, 420 N.E.2d 363, is largely mitigated where an individual continues to receive a salary in return for not competing. *See Ticor,* 173 F.3d at 71–72 ("The significance of the salary paid in *Maltby,* [166 Misc.2d at 486, 633 N.Y.S.2d 926,] was that it helped alleviate the policy concern that non-compete provisions prevent a person from earning a livelihood.").

Under the terms of the Non-compete Agreement, Batra is to be subjected to a worldwide geographic limitation and a durational limitation of twelve months. The reasonableness of each component of the scope of the agreement shall be judged in accordance with Estee Lauder's need to protect trade secrets.

It is concluded that the geographical limitation of the covenant is reasonable under the circumstances. While under some circumstances, such a widespread restriction would be patently unreasonable, on the facts presented, it is not so here, given the scope of Batra's responsibilities for R+F and Darphin and the international scope of Estee Lauder's business and the cosmetic industry in general. Such broad geographic limitations have been deemed reasonable where warranted by the nature and scope of the employer's business. *See, e.g., Business Intelligence Services,* 580 F. Supp. at 1072–73 (finding worldwide scope reasonable "given the international nature of [the employer's] business"). Given that Estee Lauder contracted to pay Batra his salary for the duration of the twelve months, the fact that the geographic scope is all-encompassing will not render it overbroad and therefore void. In other words, although, under the contract, Batra essentially is prohibited from working for a competitor of R+F or Darphin anywhere in the world, the concern that the breadth of such a prohibition would make it impossible for him to earn a living is assuaged by the fact that he will continue to earn his salary from Estee Lauder, as he contracted to do so.

With respect to the durational restriction imposed upon Batra by the Non-compete Agreement, it is concluded that twelve months is not warranted in order to adequately protect Estee Lauder's interests. To be sure, under some circumstances covenants not to compete of one year or longer may be deemed reasonable. *See, e.g., BDO Seidman*, 93 N.Y.2d at 382, 690 N.Y.S.2d 854, 712 N.E.2d 1220 (holding 18-month covenant reasonable). However, under the facts of this case, it is determined that the period of time set forth in the agreement and advanced here is greater than necessary to adequately protect Estee Lauder's trade secrets and to protect the interests of Batra.

While, as Estee Lauder points out, some of the trade secrets to which Batra was privy arguably have a durational life of as much as two to three years, the evidence presented with respect to Estee Lauder's general behavior surrounding the enforcement of restrictive covenants suggests that such a length of time is generally unnecessary, and it is deemed unnecessary here.

First, similar covenants not to compete have not been enforced against other members of Estee Lauder management for twelve full months. During his deposition, Bousquet-Chavanne testified that the first time he left Estee Lauder his non-compete agreement was cut-down from six months to three months. Similarly, when another Estee Lauder executive, Claudia Poccia, the Manager of the Stila brand, recently left her position, her non-compete agreement was reduced from six months to between four and five months. There has been no demonstration here that Batra—who held a position comparable to those held by Bousquet-Chavanne and Stila Manager when their non-compete agreements were reduced—possesses trade secrets that warrant a longer protection than those possessed by Bousquet-Chavanne and the Stila Manager.

More importantly, in Batra's case, the evidence suggests that, upon announcement of his departure, Batra himself was offered a reduction of his non-compete to four months by Estee Lauder.

Therefore, in accordance with the authority to grant partial enforcement, a five-month period of enforcement is deemed reasonable. A five-month period takes into account the four-month period proposed by Estee Lauder upon Batra's announcement of his departure, plus the transitional period they sought from Batra. Given Estee Lauder's general practice regarding Non-compete agreements, as outlined above, it is determined that a five-month period will adequately protect the trade secrets Estee Lauder has identified regarding upcoming products while minimizing Batra's loss of liberty, in keeping with New York's policy regarding restrictive covenants.

For the reasons set forth above, it is concluded that Estee Lauder has established a likelihood of success on the merits of its claim.

E. Sufficiently Serious Questions Going to the Merits and a Balance of Hardships Decidedly in Its Favor

In the alternative, the Court is satisfied that, at a minimum, Estee Lauder has demonstrated sufficiently serious questions going to the merits of their claims to make them a fair ground for litigation. Therefore, because Estee Lauder has demonstrated a balance of hardships tipping decidedly in its favor, a preliminary injunction is warranted in this case. *Brewer v. W. Irondequoit Cent. Sch. Dist.*,212 F.3d 738, 743–744 (2d Cir.2000).

Here the risk of Batra's loss of livelihood is entirely mitigated by the fact that Estee Lauder will continue to pay Batra his salary of $375,000 per year for the duration of the "sitting out" period. While he will not be permitted to engage in any employment of his choosing, he will receive due consideration for fulfillment of his agreement not to work for a competitor. Not only is Batra entitled to his full salary from Estee Lauder during the non-competition period, he is permitted to earn additional compensation from non-competitive work during the period. Additionally, the evidence demonstrates that restrictive covenants are common in the prestige cosmetics industry. As such, it is concluded that Batra's absence from the industry for a few months will not significantly impair his ability to earn a livelihood in the future and therefore will not cause Batra undue hardship.

In contrast, Estee Lauder has shown that in the absence of a preliminary injunction it is likely to suffer irreparable harm if Batra were to use and/or disclose its confidential information. Accordingly, the evidence demonstrates that the balance of hardships tips decidedly in Estee Lauder's favor.

The Non-solicitation and Confidentiality Agreements

There has been no dispute over the enforceability of the non-solicitation and confidentiality clauses of the Agreement under New York or California law. Therefore, it is concluded that those portions of the Agreement are also enforceable, and for the same reasons set forth above, Batra shall be preliminarily enjoined from violating them.

Conclusion

The motion for the preliminary injunction is granted in accordance with this opinion and the motion to abstain is denied. Submit an order granting preliminary injunctive relief on notice.

It is so ordered.

Notes

1. Courts evaluate many factors when assessing the enforceability of a noncompete agreement. Here, the defendant plotted his exit from his employer on company time using company resources and tried to induce one of his co-workers to leave. How do you think the defendant's unsympathetic conduct influenced the court's holding?

2. Courts generally disfavor noncompete agreements and there has been a recent push legislatively to ban or significantly restrict the use of such agreements. Do you see value in non-competition agreements or do you view them as an unreasonable restraint? What is the underlying policy argument for your opinion?

E. Wage and Hour Compliance

Wage and hour compliance is a significant issue in the fashion and retail industries because disputes frequently arise regarding employee overtime, job classification, and meal and rest breaks, especially in California, where there are a myriad of nuanced rules and regulations pertaining to this issue. Fashion retailers are a major target of wage and hour litigation, which can result in millions of dollars of exposure because these issues involve large groups of employees. Retail employers can reduce the risks and costs associated with such lawsuits by implementing compliant wage policies and procedures, training employees on compliance, and holding employees who violate the policies accountable through written discipline and/or termination.

1. Wage and Hour Case Studies

Luna v. Chanel, Inc.

2016 U.S. Dist. LEXIS 187653 (C.D. Cal. Apr. 20, 2016)

KLAUSNER, District Judge.

I. Introduction

On November 10, 2015, Christian Luna, Anthony Hernandez, and Javier Delgado (collectively "Plaintiffs") filed a first amended class action complaint in Los Angeles Superior Court alleging violations of the Federal Fair Labor Standards Act ("FLSA") and California wage and hour laws. The action was removed to this Court on December 10, 2015. Plaintiffs allege the following state law claims: (1) failure to pay overtime and rest periods; (2) failure to furnish and maintain accurate payroll records; (3) failure to pay final wages on a timely basis; (4) unlawful business practices; and (5) conversion. Plaintiffs also allege a claim for failure to pay overtime wages in violation of the FLSA.

Presently before the Court is Plaintiffs' Motion for Class Certification under both Federal Rule of Civil Procedure ("Rule") 23 and the FLSA. For the reasons set forth below, the Court **DENIES** Plaintiffs' Motion.

II. Statement of Facts

Plaintiffs are shipping department employees of Defendant's Beverly Hills boutique. Plaintiffs are responsible for a list of daily tasks including packing and unpacking merchandise, lifting, carrying, cleaning, tagging merchandise, data entry, and record keeping. Plaintiffs' schedule was 9am to 6pm, but Plaintiffs often were required to stay past 6pm. Defendant's Beverly Hills boutique records employees' time through a punch card which rounds time to the nearest 15-minute increment. Plaintiffs allege that this practice results in underpayment for overtime.

Plaintiffs "Daily Shipping Checklist" lists each daily task that shipping department employees must complete, as well as corresponding time allocations for that task. There are no rest breaks listed on the Checklist. Further, the task to "Inspect All the Cushions on the Terrace" does not include a time allocation. Plaintiffs allege they were consistently told by managers to work with a "sense of urgency," which was stressful because they were dealing with expensive inventory and mistakes were not tolerated. Plaintiffs allege this practice forced them to stay after scheduled hours and supervisors discouraged them from taking breaks since they could not complete the tasks on the Checklist within the time allocated.

Further, Plaintiffs allege that other employees would require the shipping employees to perform more work after they had already clocked out and directed them to not clock back in, resulting in unpaid overtime. Plaintiffs allege they saw no other shipping employees take rest breaks, yet observed managers making rest breaks available to temporary employees. In April 2015, Plaintiff Hernandez complained about the lack of rest breaks to Human Resources, which was centrally located in New York. As a result, Human Resources posted a "Daily Break & Lunch Schedule" in the shipping department. However, Plaintiffs allege that because no changes were made to the workflow and daily task requirements, employees were still not receiving breaks. This Schedule was taken down after two weeks and Plaintiffs allege they have not been offered a break since.

Plaintiffs seek to certify the following two classes against Defendant:

Collective FLSA Class:

> All current and former employees of CHANEL'S shipping department, nationwide, who were employed as non-exempt employees at any of Defendant's locations anywhere in the United States within three years prior to this action's filing date and continuing while this action is pending.

California Class:

> All current and former employees of CHANEL'S shipping department who were employed as non-exempt employees at any of CHANEL'S locations within the State of California, at any time from four years prior to the initiation of this action until the date of certification.

Plaintiffs' allegations for both the FLSA and California class are premised on two theories of liability: (1) Defendant's practice of rounding time resulted in unpaid overtime; and (2) Defendant's practice of requiring shipping department employees to work after clocking out resulted in unpaid overtime. Additionally, Plaintiffs' allegations for the California Class are also premised on one additional theory of liability: Defendant's practice of scheduling each minute of its employees' workday results in violations of California rest break laws.

Plaintiffs also allege several derivative claims flowing from the core overtime and rest break violations: (1) failure to furnish and maintain accurate payroll records due to unpaid overtime; (2) failure to pay all final wages on a timely basis; (3) unlawful business practices by failing to pay wages; (4) conversion by failing to pay overtime wages; and (5) Private Attorney General Act ("PAGA") claim seeking civil penalties for violations of labor laws. Each of these ancillary claims necessarily relies on the alleged overtime and rest break violations; therefore, Plaintiffs' Motion for Class Certification will rise or fall solely on the overtime and rest break allegations.

III. FLSA Collective Action

Section 216(b) of the FLSA provides in pertinent part that an action may be maintained against an employer by any employees on behalf of themselves and other employees who are similarly situated. 29 U.S.C. § 216(b). This provision establishes an opt-in scheme whereby potential plaintiffs must notify the court of their intention to be a party to the collective action in order to be bound by and benefit from it. If employees do not opt-in by filing written consent, they are not bound by the outcome of the collective action and may bring a subsequent private action. *E.E.O.C. v. Pan Am. World Airways, Inc.*, 897 F.2d 1499, 1508 n.11 (9th Cir. 1990).

As stated in Section 216(b), only opt-in plaintiffs "similarly situated" to the named plaintiff may join the collective action. Courts use a two-stage analysis to determine whether opt-in plaintiffs are similarly situated. *See Hipp v. Liberty Nat'l Life Ins. Co.*, 252 F.3d 1208, 1218–19 (11th Cir. 2001). At the initial stage, decisions to certify a collective action are based primarily on pleadings and affidavits, and courts apply a "fairly lenient standard" for determining whether the plaintiffs are similarly situated. *Anderson v. Cagle's, Inc.*, 488 F.3d 945, 953 (11th Cir. 2007). A plaintiff need only show that his position is similar, not identical, to the positions held by the putative class members. *Hipp*, 252 F.3d at 1217. If the court, at this stage, conditionally certifies the class, "putative class members are given notice and the opportunity to 'opt-in.'" *Id.* at 1218. At the second stage, which usually occurs after discovery and upon motion for decertification by defendants, courts make a factual determination of whether the plaintiffs are similarly situated. "The 'similarly situated' standard at the second stage is less 'lenient' than at the first, as is the plaintiffs' burden in meeting the standard." *Anderson*, 488 F.3d at 953 (quoting *Thiessen v. Gen. Elec. Capital Corp.*, 267 F.3d 1095, 1103 (10th Cir. 2001)). Plaintiffs here seek conditional certification of a collective FLSA class to allow them to notify potential class members for opt-in purposes. At this stage, the Court analyzes whether Plaintiffs are "similarly situated" to the putative class members under the more lenient standard.

A. Federal Overtime Pay Requirements

The FLSA requires employers to pay employees who work in excess of 40 hours per week overtime compensation of one and one-half time the employees' regular wage. 29 U.S.C. § 207(a)(1). Plaintiffs' collective action is premised on uncompensated overtime pay due to Defendant's rounding practices and requirements that shipping department employees work after clocking-out. Plaintiffs must establish that they, together with **Chanel** shipping employees nationwide, were victims of Defendant's practices depriving employees of overtime pay.

B. Rounding Practices Result in Unpaid Overtime

Rounding practices are lawful if "used in such a manner that it will not result, over a period of time, in failure to compensate the employees properly for all the time they have actually worked." 29 C.F.R. §785.48(b). If Defendant applies "a consistent rounding policy that, on average, favors neither overpayment nor underpayment," its policy is lawful. *Alonzo v. Maximus, Inc.*, 832 F. Supp. 2d 1122, 1126 (C.D. Cal. 2011). Plaintiffs' allege that Defendant's rounding practices resulted in underpayment of overtime wages, but fail to provide evidence of this beyond their own declarations. While admitting that a rounding policy exists, Defendant submits declarations of multiple shipping employees nationwide stating that Defendant's rounding policy either works in the employees' favor or, at least, does not work against them.

The Court finds that Plaintiffs have failed to demonstrate that they are "similarly situated" as other nationwide shipping employees because Defendant's declarations from employees maintaining the same position as named Plaintiffs show that these employees did not experience underpayment of overtime wages due to Defendant's rounding policy.

C. Working After Clocking-Out Resulting in Unpaid Overtime

Plaintiffs allege that Defendant maintains an unofficial practice of asking shipping department employees to complete additional tasks after they have already clocked out. Specifically, Plaintiffs contend that because the "time clock was located on the third floor and shipping employees leave for the day before other employees," shipping employees "were always stopped on the way out" to help with further tasks. On these occasions, when Plaintiffs asked if they should clock back in, their managers said no. In disputing this alleged company-wide practice, Defendant asserts in several declarations from shipping employees nationwide, that they never worked off the clock. Any mistakes in these employees' timecards was immediately corrected and employees received the requisite overtime wages. For example, Torres' declaration states that "[o]n one occasion, there was an issue with several employees' paychecks where we were not paid for all overtime hours worked. Kim O'Brien was in charge of payroll at the time, and I remember she announced during a meeting that there was an error and she said it would be fixed in our next paychecks. When I got my next paycheck, I saw that the issue was fixed and I was paid time and a half for all overtime hours I worked in the previous pay period." Beyond their own unique experience, Plaintiffs fail to show a common policy of failing to pay overtime wages due to employees' working off the clock.

D. Unrealistic Daily Checklists Resulting in Unpaid Overtime Wages

Plaintiffs argue that Defendant's practice of requiring them to complete a Daily Checklist of tasks results in unpaid overtime wages because Plaintiffs could not complete the required tasks within an 8-hour workday. The Daily Checklist shows a schedule of tasks starting at 9am and ending at 6pm. However, the Checklist also requires shipping employees to "Inspect All the Cushions on the Terrace" ("Terrace Inspection") without an allocated time period. Presumably, if employees do not complete the tasks in less time than allowed by the Checklist, these employees will have to work overtime to complete the Terrace Inspection. The Daily Checklist, however, is not evidence that Defendant failed to pay Plaintiffs overtime wages because even if Plaintiffs must work overtime to complete the Terrace Inspection, the Checklist does not show whether Plaintiffs were paid for that overtime.

Defendant submits several declarations of nationwide shipping department employees stating that Defendant always compensated these employees for any overtime hours worked. As stated above, Defendant further demonstrates that the HR department promptly corrected any mistakes in overtime compensation. For instance, a shipping department employee in the Costa Mesa, California boutique states: "When finishing a task would require working overtime, I tell management that I can stay to complete the task, but that it will require overtime. . . . If management asks me to stay, I ask them if I will receive overtime, and they confirm that I will . . . I check my paystubs carefully every pay period, and if I work overtime, I check to make sure that I was paid for the overtime worked. My paystubs always reflect any overtime I have worked."

Further, Defendant's declarations from shipping department employees show that each boutique differs in workflow management—not all boutiques use a Daily Checklist of tasks. For example, a shipping department employee in the Boston boutique discusses her daily schedule typically includes a morning meeting, then unpacking boxes as they arrive, delivering product to sales people, and preparing outgoing shipments in the afternoon. This employee further explains, "I manage completion of my daily work myself. I have never received a prescribed schedule of daily tasks and I am free [to] alter the order in which I complete tasks, depending on the needs of the boutique." These differing experiences would require the court to conduct individualized inquiries that would overshadow common questions.

Plaintiff provides insufficient evidence demonstrating that shipping department employees nationwide are similarly situated to Plaintiffs. Defendant, on the other hand, provides substantial evidence establishing that shipping department employees nationwide do not share Plaintiffs' experience in uncompensated overtime. Plaintiff fails to demonstrate that they are "similarly situated" as other nationwide shipping employees. As such, the Court **DENIES** Plaintiffs' Motion to Conditionally Certify a Collective Class under FLSA.

IV. Rule 23 Class Certification

For certification of a class action under Federal Rule of Civil Procedure 23, the plaintiff bears the burden of establishing each of the prerequisites set forth in Rule 23(a). *Hanon v. Dataproducts, Corp.*, 976 F.2d 497, 508 (9th Cir. 1992). Rule 23(a) requires that "(1) the class is so numerous that joinder of all members is impracticable, (2) there are questions of law or fact common to the class, (3) the claims or defenses of the representative parties are typical of the claims or defenses of the class, and (4) the representative parties will fairly and adequately protect the interests of the class." Fed. R. Civ. P. 23(a).

In addition to finding that the requirements of Rule 23(a) have been satisfied, the Court must also find that at least one of the following three conditions of Rule 23(b) is satisfied: (1) the prosecution of separate actions would create risk of (a) inconsistent or varying adjudications, or (b) individual adjudications dispositive of the interests of other members not a party to those adjudications; (2) the party opposing the class has acted or refused to act on grounds generally applicable to the class; or (3) the questions of law or fact common to the members of the class predominate over any questions affecting only individual members, and a class action is superior to other available methods for the fair and efficient adjudication of the controversy. Fed. R. Civ. P. 23(b).

A. California Rest Break Requirements

When considering Rule 23 class certification, a district court may look beyond the pleadings, even to issues overlapping with the merits of the underlying claims, in order to ensure that Rule 23 requirements are actually met and not simply presumed from the pleadings. *Wal-Mart Stores, Inc. v. Dukes*, 131 S. Ct. 2541, 2551–52 (2011). Therefore, the Court provides a brief overview of the substantive law at issue.

"[California] law obligates employers to afford their nonexempt employees meal periods and rest periods during the workday." *Brinker Rest. Corp. v. Superior Court*, 273 P.3d 513, 521 (Cal. 2012) (citing Cal. Lab. Code §§ 226.7, 512). The meal period requirements are codified at § 512(a) of the California Labor Code, requiring employers to provide a 30-minute meal period for employees who work more than five hours and a second 30-minute meal period for employees who work more than ten hours. The rest period requirements are embodied in a Wage Order issued by the Industrial Welfare Commission. IWC wage order No. 5-2001 (Cal. Code Regs., tit. 8, § 11050). The Wage Order requires employers to provide 10 minutes of rest time for every four hours worked or major fraction thereof unless the employee's entire workday consists of less than 3.5 hours. *Id.* In other words, "Employees are entitled to 10 minutes rest for shifts from three and one-half to six hours in length, 20 minutes for shifts of more than six hours up to 10 hours, 30 minutes for shifts of more than 10 hours up to 14 hours, and so on." *Brinker*, 273 P.3d at 529.

"The employer satisfies [its meal and rest break] obligation if it relieves its employees of all duty, relinquishes control over their activities and permits them a reasonable opportunity to take an uninterrupted 30-minute break, and does not impede or discourage them from doing so." *Id.* at 536–37. An employer cannot contravene an official meal or rest break policy by imposing an informal practice that impedes or discourages its employees from taking compliant breaks. *Ricaldai v. U.S. Investigations Servs., LLC*, 878 F. Supp. 2d 1038, 1042 (C.D. Cal. 2012) (collecting cases holding that meal period violations were present in instances when an employer pressured employees to skip meal periods).

B. California Overtime Requirements

California law requires employers to pay employees who work over 8 hours per day or 40 hours per week at the rate of one and one-half times the employee's regular pay rate. Cal. Lab. Code § 510(a). California law requires employees who work more than 12 hours in one day or more than 8 hours on any seventh day of a workweek to be compensated at twice their regular pay rate. *Id.*

C. Rule 23(a)

1. Numerosity

Rule 23(a)(1) requires that the class be so "numerous that joinder of all members is impracticable." Fed. R. Civ. P. 23(a)(1). Generally, a class with over forty members satisfies the numerosity prerequisite. *See Consol. Rail Corp. v. Town of Hyde Park*, 47 F.3d 473, 483 (2d Cir. 1995). "The Ninth Circuit has not offered a precise numerical standard; other District Courts have, however, enacted presumptions that the numerosity requirement is satisfied by a showing of 25–30 members." *Slaven v. BP Am., Inc.*, 190 F.R.D. 649, 654 (C.D. Cal. 2000).

Defendant does not dispute that Plaintiffs have satisfied the numerosity requirement by proposing a California Class of approximately 30 current and former employees. However, Defendant disputes a sub-class of California shipping employees who have been terminated and seek relief on Plaintiffs' claim for failure to timely pay wages upon termination. Defendant asserts this subclass consists of only 17 former California employees, which is insufficient to meet the numerosity requirement. *Thomas v. Baca*, 231 F.R.D. 397, 400 (C.D. Cal. 2005) (finding groups fewer than 21 individuals not so numerous that joinder is impracticable).

Plaintiffs cite competing authority that holds classes of fifteen or less are too small. *Gomez v. Rossi Concrete, Inc.*, 270 F.R.D. 579, 588 (S.D. Cal. 2010). Plaintiffs sub-class of former employees falls in between 15 and 21. The Court finds Plaintiffs adequately demonstrated requisite numerosity for Rule 23(a).

2. Adequacy

Rule 23(a)(4) requires that "the representative parties will fairly and adequately protect the interests of the class." Fed. R. Civ. P. 23(a)(4). The prerequisite of adequacy is satisfied if (1) the named representative appears able to prosecute the action vigorously through qualified counsel, and (2) the named representative does not have antagonistic or conflicting interests with the unnamed members of the class. *See Lerwill v. Inflight Motion Pictures, Inc.*, 582 F.2d 507, 512 (9th Cir. 1978). Defendant does not dispute that Plaintiffs' counsel is competent to undertake the litigation at hand. (Farzam Decl. ¶ 6–9, ECF No. 15–2.) Further, no conflicts exists between named Plaintiffs and putative class members. Thus, the Court finds Plaintiffs have sufficiently demonstrated adequacy under Rule 23.

3. Typicality

Rule 23(a)(3) requires that the claims of the representative plaintiff be typical of the claims of the class. Fed. R. Civ. P. 23(a)(3). "[R]epresentative claims are typical if they are reasonably coextensive with those of absent class members; they need not be substantially identical." *Hanlon v. Chrysler Corp.*, 150 F.3d 1011, 1020 (9th Cir. 1998). To the extent that typicality requires the Court to analyze whether putative class members are in the same occupational role, the Court finds this requirement satisfied because all members of the putative class are shipping department employees. Both Plaintiffs and Defendant agree that shipping department employees have the same general duties across all of Defendant's boutiques, such that one shipping employee can easily fill in at different locations.

However, to the extent that typicality requires the Court to analyze whether putative class members suffer the same variety of injury stemming from the same standardized policies and procedures, the Court does not find this requirement satisfied. *Armstrong v. Davis*, 275 F.3d 849, 869 (9th Cir. 2001). As discussed, Plaintiffs fail to demonstrate that they suffer the same injury or experience the same policies as the remainder of putative class members.

4. Commonality

Rule 23(a)(2) requires that there be "questions of law or fact common to the class." Fed. R. Civ. P. 23(a)(2). "To show commonality, Plaintiffs must demonstrate that there are questions of fact and law that are common to the class. The requirements of Rule 23(a)(2)have 'been construed permissively,' and '[a]ll questions of fact and law need not be common to satisfy the rule.'" *Ellis v. Costco Wholesale Corp.*, 657 F.3d 970, 981 (9th Cir. 2011) (citations omitted). Commonality exists, and certification is proper, where the legality of a challenged policy poses a "significant question of law" that is "apt to drive the resolution of the litigation." *Abdullah v. U.S. Sec. Assocs., Inc.*, 731 F.3d 952, 963 (9th Cir. 2013) cert. denied, 135 S. Ct. 53, 190 L. Ed. 2d 30 (2014).

a. Rounding time results in unpaid overtime

As stated in the Court's analysis regarding FLSA class certification, the Court finds no questions of fact and law that are common to the class. Defendant submits multiple declarations of shipping department employees demonstrating that Plaintiffs' claims regarding rounding are not shared by putative class members. (Guillen Decl. ¶ 13, Ex. 8; Hughes Decl. ¶ 10, Ex.9, ECF No. 19-2.) Most persuasively, Defendant submits evidence from an employee in the shipping department of the Beverly Hills boutique—the same boutique as Plaintiffs' employment—stating, "I have never found that [the rounding policy] works against me in terms of the hours I have worked. The rounding seems to even out reasonably or in my favor." (Guillen Decl. ¶ 13, Ex. 8, ECF No. 19-2.) Plaintiffs, however, submit only declarations regarding their own experience. The Court finds this evidence unpersuasive in establishing commonality.

b. Working after clocking out results in unpaid overtime

Similarly, the Court finds Plaintiffs submit insufficient evidence demonstrating commonality as to working after clocking out without compensation. Defendant submits a declaration from an employee at the Costa Mesa, California store that directly contradicts Plaintiffs' contention regarding clocking out without compensation. Guillen, a shipping employee at the Beverly Hills boutique, states, "From my experience there, the Beverly Hills boutique is much more busy in the shipping and receiving department, because it handles more inventory and is a large boutique." The Court finds Plaintiffs' claims unique to them, or at the very least, unique to the Beverly Hills boutique. Plaintiffs thus fail to establish the requisite commonality under Rule 23(a).

c. Denying rest breaks

Plaintiffs fail to sufficiently demonstrate commonality regarding their rest break claims. Defendant's declarations from both a Costa Mesa, California shipping employee and a shipping employee in Beverly Hills describe how they were allowed to take breaks. The Costa Mesa employee describes how he can "take a break at any time." The Beverly Hills employee, who has worked directly with named Plaintiffs in the same position, states, "I have been told repeatedly by Carlos Cruz that I am permitted to take two rest breaks in my normal, eight-hour shift . . . I am always encouraged to take my rest breaks . . . I do not feel pressured not to take breaks from anyone." Plaintiffs rely solely on their own declarations in demonstrating commonality. The Court does not find this evidence persuasive enough to demonstrate that there are "questions of fact and law that are common to the class." *Ellis v. Costco Wholesale Corp.*, 657 F.3d 970, 981 (9th Cir. 2011) (citations omitted)

Because the Court finds Plaintiffs fail to demonstrate requisite commonality pursuant to Rule 23(a), the Court forgoes the remainder of Rule 23 analysis and **DENIES** Plaintiffs' Motion for Class Certification.

VI. Conclusion

For the foregoing reasons, the Court **DENIES** Plaintiffs' Motion for Class Certification.

IT IS SO ORDERED.

Otsuka v. Polo Ralph Lauren Corp.

251 F.R.D. 439 (N.D. Cal. 2008)

ILLSTON, District Judge.

Plaintiffs have filed a motion for class certification. The motion is scheduled for hearing on July 11, 2008. Pursuant to Civil Local Rule 7-1(b), the Court finds this matter appropriate for resolution without oral argument, and hereby VACATES the hearing. Having considered the arguments of the parties and the papers submitted, and for good cause shown, the Court hereby GRANTS plaintiffs' motion to certify the class.

Background

The subject of this litigation is an employment dispute over unpaid wages brought by former retail sales employees against defendants Polo Ralph Lauren Corporation, Polo Retail, LLC, Polo Retail Corporation, and Fashions Outlet of America, who operate 28 full-price and outlet stores in the state of California. On May 30, 2006, plaintiffs Ann Otsuka, Janis Keefe, Corrine Phipps, and Justin Kiser filed a putative class action complaint in state court against defendants. Defendants removed the action to federal court on May 29, 2007, on grounds that this Court has either diversity jurisdiction or jurisdiction pursuant to the Class Action Fairness Act. The complaint was amended multiple times in order to add named plaintiff

Renee Davis, remove plaintiff Kiser, and make other adjustments, such that the operative complaint is now the Third Amended Complaint ("TAC"), which was filed by stipulation of the parties in March 2008.

Plaintiffs have brought suit on behalf of all former California employees of defendants who worked as sales associates or cashiers and were injured by defendants' violation of employment laws from May 30, 2002 to the present. The gravamen of the complaint is that defendants failed to provide rest breaks, failed to pay employees for off-the-clock time spent inside the stores, improperly classified all sales associates as commission salespeople who are exempt from premium overtime compensation, and improperly used an arrears program in which sales associates who did not meet minimum commission requirements were subject to reduced earnings on future commissions above the minimum requirements. Plaintiffs contend that defendants use a single employee handbook for all California stores, and that defendants' policies and practices are standardized throughout California in both retail and outlet stores. One of these practices, plaintiffs contend, is to discourage or prevent employees from taking required rest breaks. Another practice is to conduct loss-prevention inspections (i.e. bag checks for stolen merchandise) on all employees every time they leave the store, such as at the end of their shifts or to take lunch breaks. Plaintiffs allege that these inspections only occur after an employee has clocked out, and that employees often have to wait for 10–15 minutes, and sometimes longer, for a manager to show up at the back door to conduct the inspection. Plaintiffs also allege that defendants treated all salespeople at retail stores as exempt from overtime compensation, even though many such employees did not sell enough merchandise to be considered exempt commissioned employees, and failed to conduct the promised "reconciliations" to determine whether the employees actually were exempt. These allegations are supported in large part by deposition testimony of the named plaintiffs and by declarations filed by absent class members, though competing declarations contesting many of these allegations have been filed by current employees on behalf of defendants.

The complaint alleges the following causes of action on behalf of all members of the putative class: failure to pay wages, including overtime wages; breach of contract; failure to pay all wages due upon separation from employment; failure to provide rest breaks; failure to maintain accurate pay records; and unfair business practices. The complaint also alleges additional causes of action on behalf of two subclasses of plaintiffs. The first subclass consists of former sales associates who were misclassified as exempt from premium overtime compensation ("the misclassified subclass"), while the second subclass consists of former sales associates who were required to participate in the arrears program ("the arrears subclass"). The complaint alleges a cause of action for fraud for the misclassified subclass and a cause of action for violation of California Labor Code § 221 for the arrears subclass.

Plaintiff Otsuka worked as a sales associate at the Palo Alto retail store in 2004. She alleges that defendants denied her overtime compensation, required her to participate in the arrears program, required her to wait for bag inspections without compensation, and discouraged her from taking rest breaks. Plaintiff Phipps worked as a sales associate at the San Francisco retail store in 2004. She alleges that defendants denied her overtime compensation, required her to participate in the arrears program, and required her to wait for bag inspections without compensation. Plaintiff Keefe worked as a sales associate at the San Francisco retail store in 2004 and 2005. She alleges that defendants denied her overtime compensation, required her to participate in the arrears program, required her to wait for bag inspections without compensation, and discouraged her from taking rest breaks. Plaintiff Davis worked at the Cabazon factory outlet store in 2002, 2003, and 2004. She alleges that defendants did not pay all overtime compensation due to her, required her to participate in the arrears program, required her to wait for bag inspections without compensation, and discouraged her from taking rest breaks. All named plaintiffs except Otsuka now move for class certification.

Legal Standard

The decision whether to certify a class is committed to the discretion of the district court within the guidelines of Federal Rule of Civil Procedure 23. *See Cummings v. Connell,* 316 F.3d 886, 895 (9th Cir.2003). A court may certify a class if a plaintiff demonstrates that all of the prerequisites of Rule 23(a) have been met, and that at least one of the requirements of Rule 23(b) have been met. *See* Fed.R.Civ.P. 23; *see also Valentino v. Carter-Wallace, Inc.,* 97 F.3d 1227, 1234 (9th Cir.1996). A class may be certified only "if the trial court is satisfied, after a rigorous analysis, that the prerequisites of Rule 23(a) have been satisfied." *Gen. Tel. Co. of the S.W. v. Falcon,* 457 U.S. 147, 161, 102 S.Ct. 2364, 72 L.Ed.2d 740 (1982). The burden is on the plaintiff to establish that the Rule 23(a) and Rule 23(b) requirements have been met. *Zinser v. Accufix Research Inst., Inc.,* 253 F.3d 1180, 1186 (9th Cir.2001).

Rule 23(a) provides four prerequisites that must be satisfied for class certification: (1) the class must be so numerous that joinder of all members is impracticable; (2) questions of law or fact exist that are common to the class; (3) the claims or defenses of the representative parties are typical of the claims or defenses of the class; and (4) the representative parties will fairly and adequately protect the interests of the class. *See* Fed.R.Civ.P. 23(a). A plaintiff must also establish that one or more of the grounds for maintaining the suit are met under Rule 23(b), including: (1) that there is a risk of substantial prejudice from separate actions; (2) that declaratory or injunctive relief benefitting the class as a whole would be appropriate; or (3) that common questions of law or fact predominate and the class action is superior to other available methods of adjudication. *See* Fed.R.Civ.P. 23(b).

In determining the propriety of a class action, the question is not whether the plaintiff has stated a cause of action or will prevail on the merits, but rather whether the requirements of Rule 23 are met. *Eisen v. Carlisle & Jacquelin,* 417 U.S. 156, 178, 94 S.Ct. 2140, 40 L.Ed.2d 732 (1974) (citing *Miller v. Mackey Int'l, Inc.,* 452 F.2d 424, 427 (5th Cir.1971)). The Court is obliged to accept as true the substantive allegations made in the complaint. *See In re Coordinated Pretrial Proceedings in Petroleum*

Prods. Antitrust Litig., 691 F.2d 1335, 1342 (9th Cir.1982); *Blackie v. Barrack*, 524 F.2d 891, 901 (9th Cir.1975). However, it "need not blindly rely on conclusory allegations which parrot Rule 23 requirements [and] may ... consider the legal and factual issues presented by plaintiff's complaints." 2 Herbert Newberg & Alba Conte, *Newbergon Class Actions* § 7.26 (3d ed.1992); *see also Castano v. Am. Tobacco Co.*, 84 F.3d 734, 744 (5th Cir.1996).

Discussion

Plaintiffs move to certify a class of all former sales associates and cashiers who worked for defendants in California from May 20, 2002 through the conclusion of this action. Plaintiffs also move to certify the misclassified subclass as well as the arrears subclass. Defendants vigorously object to class certification, arguing that plaintiffs fail to meet almost every requirement of Rule 23 for the main class and the two subclasses. As discussed below, however, defendants' arguments primarily dispute the merits of plaintiffs' claims and raise questions of fact that will not be resolved at this juncture, and the Court finds that class certification is appropriate because plaintiffs have satisfied the requirements of Rule 23(a) and Rule 23(b)(3).

I. Rule 23(a)

As mentioned above, "Rule 23(a) establishes four prerequisites for class action litigation, which are: (1) numerosity, (2) commonality, (3) typicality, and (4) adequacy of representation." *Staton v. Boeing Co.*, 327 F.3d 938, 953 (9th Cir.2003). Plaintiffs have demonstrated that each is present here.

A. Numerosity

Plaintiffs argue that the proposed main class consists of an estimated 5,300 former cashiers and sales associates. Defendants concede that this number of plaintiffs meets the numerosity requirement, and the Court agrees. *See, e.g., Immigrant Assistance Project of the LA. County Fed. of Labor v. INS*, 306 F.3d 842, 869 (9th Cir.2002) (finding that district court did not abuse discretion in certifying class of approximately 11,000 and stating that "[c]ourts have certified classes with far fewer members"). Plaintiffs argue that the misclassified subclass consists of approximately 69 former sales associates and possibly as many as 294 people, depending on the test used to determine whether the sales associates were misclassified. Plaintiffs also argue that the arrears subclass consists of approximately 49 members. Defendants contend that these subclasses are insufficiently numerous and that joinder is not impracticable as a result of their size. The Court disagrees. The Ninth Circuit has held that as few as 39 members may be sufficiently numerous under the right circumstances, *Jordan v. Los Angeles County*, 669 F.2d 1311, 1319–20 (9th Cir.1982), *rev'd another ground*, 713 F.2d 503(9th Cir.1983), and the Court finds that the spread of the subclasses throughout California, the likely small size of the damages claimed by the subclasses, and the fact that the subclass members are also members of the larger class, all suggest that the subclasses, though small, meet the numerosity requirement of Rule 23(a).

B. Commonality

Under Rule 23(a)(2), there must be "questions of law or fact common to the class." In the Ninth Circuit, the commonality requirement "has been construed permissively," such that "[t]he existence of shared legal issues with divergent factual predicates is sufficient, as is a common core of salient facts coupled with disparate legal remedies within the class." *Hanlon v. Chrysler Corp.*, 150 F.3d 1011, 1019 (9th Cir.1998). Plaintiffs persuasively argue that many questions of law and fact are common to the class, such as whether: (1) defendants' policy of not compensating employees for time spent waiting for loss-prevention inspections violates California law or constitutes an unfair business practice; (2) time spent waiting for these inspections was "postliminary" or *de minimis,* and whether these federal standards would even apply to plaintiffs' California law claims; (3) defendants breached their contracts with class members by failing to compensate them for time spent awaiting loss prevention inspections; (4) defendants had a policy of not providing or discouraging rest breaks; (5) defendants violated California law by failing to pay employees one hour's wage when rest breaks were not provided; (6) defendants failed to maintain accurate pay records as a result of these alleged labor code violations; and (7) whether defendants' failure to maintain accurate records was knowing and intentional. As these questions suggest, plaintiffs have sufficiently demonstrated that the commonality requirement of Rule 23(a) has been met with respect to the main class.

As for the subclasses, plaintiffs argue that there are common questions of law and fact posed by the claims of the misclassified subclass, such as whether defendants misclassified sales associates, whether defendants committed fraud by promising sales associates that they would perform "reconciliations" to determine whether the associates were entitled to overtime compensation, and whether defendants' policy of treating all sales associates as exempt employees constituted an unfair business practice. Defendants dispute the merits of the claims raised by the misclassified subclass, but do not explain why plaintiffs have failed to demonstrate that these questions are common to every member of the misclassified subclass.

Plaintiffs also argue that the arrears subclass meets the commonality requirement because the claims brought by this subclass raise common questions, such as whether the arrears program violated California law and constituted a breach of the employment agreement set forth in defendants' employee handbooks. In response, defendants raise questions with regard to the merits of plaintiffs' arrears claims—questions the Court does not and need not reach today—and also argue that the breach of contract claim would turn on individual questions about what each subclass member was told about the arrears program. Even if defendants are correct that individual inquiries would need to be made with regard to whether the terms of the program were misrepresented to plaintiffs, this in no way detracts from the common questions presented by the subclass claims, such as whether the program on the whole violated California law and whether the terms of the program had to be presented in writing. For these reasons, the Court finds that the commonality requirement has been met with regard to the two subclasses.

C. Typicality

Rule 23(a)(3) examines the class representatives and asks whether "the claims or defenses of the representative parties are typical of the claims or defenses of the class." As the Ninth Circuit has explained, "[u]nder the rule's permissive standards, representative claims are 'typical' if they are reasonably co-extensive with those of absent class members; they need not be substantially identical." *Hanlon,* 150 F.3d at 1020; *see also Armstrong v. Davis,* 275 F.3d 849, 869 (9th Cir.2001). Plaintiffs argue that the claims of the class representatives are typical of the main class because Keefe, Phipps, and Davis all should have been compensated for time spent waiting for loss-prevention inspections and missed rest breaks. Defendants do not take issue with the typicality of the representatives with regard to the loss-prevention inspections, but do argue that the rest break claims of the named plaintiffs are not typical of the class because Phipps testified that she took rest breaks, Davis testified that she missed only 25% of her rest breaks, and Davis worked at an outlet store rather than a full-priced Polo store. The Court finds that although Phipps may be unable to assert rest break claims, the other representatives allege that they were forced or coerced to skip rest breaks as part of a culture—alleged to exist at both outlet stores and full-priced stores—that discouraged the taking of rest breaks, and thus they meet the test for typicality. Although absent class members may have missed more or fewer rest breaks than the named plaintiffs, all were subjected to the same alleged policies with regard to rest breaks, and any individual differences in the number of breaks missed is a question that can be addressed if and when the amount of damages is determined. Plaintiffs also argue that Phipps and Keefe are members of both subclasses and have claims that are typical of the subclasses. Defendants make no argument with regard to the arrears subclass, and the Court finds that Phipps' and Keefe's arrears-based claims are typical of the claims of the arrears subclass. As for the misclassified subclass, defendants argue that Phipps and Keefe do not have claims for unpaid overtime wages based on misclassification because defendants performed a reconciliation in 2007 in which the amount of overtime owed to Phipps and Keefe was determined and paid to them. The Court disagrees with defendants' contention for two reasons. First, to the extent Phipps and Keefe are successful on their other claims, the number of overtime hours they worked may increase. Second, even though they may have been compensated for some of their overtime hours, Phipps and Keefe may still assert claims that are typical of the absent subclass members, such as the claim that defendants committed fraud by failing to conduct annual reconciliations or the claim that defendants engaged in an unfair business practice by treating all sales associates as exempt. Thus, the claims of the class representatives who are members of the subclasses are "reasonably co-extensive with those of absent class members," *Hanlon,* 150 F.3d at 1020, and the Court finds that plaintiffs have satisfied the typicality requirement with regard to the misclassified subclass.

D. Adequacy of representation

Finally, under Rule 23(a)(4), plaintiffs must demonstrate that "the representative parties will fairly and adequately protect the interests of the class." When considering the adequacy of a class representative, courts generally consider only two questions "(1) [d]o the representative plaintiffs and their counsel have any conflicts of interest with other class members, and (2) will the representative plaintiffs and their counsel prosecute the action vigorously on behalf of the class?" *Staton,* 327 F.3d at 957. Defendants' only objection to the adequacy of the named plaintiffs and their counsel is that disagreements arose in the past between class counsel and named plaintiff Ann Otsuka. These disagreements were resolved, however, by the appointment of separate counsel for Otsuka. In addition, Otsuka is no longer involved in this case other than as an absent class member, as she has been out of touch and has not asked to be named a class representative. The Court has not been made aware of any other problems between counsel and the class representatives, and defendants do not argue that any conflicts of interest exist or that plaintiffs and their counsel will not prosecute this action vigorously. The Court therefore finds that Keefe, Phipps, and Davis will fairly and adequately protect the interests of the class and the subclasses.

II. Rule 23(b)

In addition to meeting the requirements of Rule 23(a), plaintiffs must also demonstrate, to the Court's satisfaction, that at least one of the conditions of Rule 23(b) are satisfied. Here, plaintiffs argue that they satisfy Rule 23(b)(3), which provides:

> the court finds that the questions of law or fact common to class members predominate over any questions affecting only individual members, and that a class action is superior to other available methods for fairly and efficiently adjudicating the controversy. The matters pertinent to the findings include: (A) the class members' interests in individually controlling the prosecution or defense of separate actions; (B) the extent and nature of any litigation concerning the controversy already begun by or against class members; (C) the desirability or undesirability of concentrating the litigation of the claims in the particular forum; and (D) the likely difficulties in managing a class action.

Fed.R.Civ.P. 23(b)(3). Defendants argue that common questions do not predominate over individual questions and that a class action is not a superior vehicle for bringing plaintiffs' claims. For the following reasons, the Court disagrees.

A. Predominance

Under Rule 23(b)(3), plaintiffs must show that common questions of law and fact "predominate over any questions affecting only individual members." This "'inquiry tests whether proposed classes are sufficiently cohesive to warrant adjudication by representation.'" *Hanlon,* 150 F.3d at 1022(quoting *Amchem Prods., Inc. v. Windsor,* 521 U.S. 591, 623, 117 S.Ct. 2231, 138 L.Ed.2d 689 (1997)). The predominance analysis goes beyond the commonality requirement of Rule 23(a)(2) because it assumes the existence of common questions of law or fact and probes the relationship between these common questions and questions that arise based on the individual differences between class members. *See id.* Plaintiffs argue that common questions of law and fact predominate over individual questions because all of plaintiffs' claims address policies and procedures that defendants implement across the board at each of their California stores. These common questions include whether defendants' failure to compensate employees for time spent waiting for loss-prevention inspections violates California law, whether defendants discouraged employees from taking rest breaks and unlawfully failed to compensate them when rest breaks were skipped, and whether, if the first two questions are answered in plaintiffs' favor, defendants violated other sections of the labor code by, for example, intentionally or unintentionally keeping inaccurate pay records. Defendants, meanwhile, contend that individual questions predominate, but defendants support this contention primarily by advancing arguments that either address the legal merits of plaintiffs' claims or contest plaintiffs' factual allegations. As to the rest break claims, defendants first suggest that California law does not require them to *ensure* that all employees take rest breaks, only that they *provide* rest breaks. This disputed question of California law, of course, is itself a common issue of overriding importance in this action and, in any case, plaintiffs do in fact allege that defendants failed to provide rest breaks because defendants had a policy or practice of preventing or discouraging rest breaks. Defendants also argue that their policy is to provide rest breaks and that the employees who did not take rest breaks voluntarily waived them. This, too, poses a common question of fact regarding whether defendants had such a policy. While this contention does, as defendants argue, pose individual questions about why particular employees may have failed to take rest breaks and whether certain stores may have encouraged breaks while other stores discouraged them, the Court finds that these individual questions are secondary to the larger questions raised about whether defendants had an overall policy with regard to rest breaks and whether they are liable for missed rest breaks regardless of the reasons they were missed.

As to plaintiffs' claim for off-the-clock wages, defendants argue that because, under federal law, time spent waiting for loss-prevention inspections is not compensable if it was *de minimis, see Lindow v. United States,* 738 F.2d 1057, 1062–63 (9th Cir.1984), common questions do not predominate because in order to show that any waiting time was not *de minimis,* plaintiffs necessarily will get bogged down in individual questions about how long each class member had to wait for bag inspections after clocking out. Here, again, defendants actually raise a significant question of law that is common to all class members: whether the de minimis rule, derived from federal law, applies to plaintiffs' claims, which arise under California law. In addition, if, as plaintiffs argue, the *de minimis* rule does not apply here, then the most significant questions will still be whether plaintiffs were made to wait for inspections without compensation and whether this off-the-clock time is compensable, questions that are common to all class members. On the other hand, if defendants are correct that the *de minimis* rule applies to off-the-clock claims brought under California law, then the question whether the time spent by plaintiffs was *de minimis* will still raise other common questions, such as the "difficulty of recording small amounts of time for payroll purposes" and the regularity with which sales associates and cashiers were made to wait for bag inspections. *See id.* Thus, while defendants are correct that the application of the *de minimis* rule might require inquiries into the individual experiences of class members, these individual questions will arise only after significant common questions of law and fact have been answered, and may not arise at all in the liability context. The Court therefore finds that, as to the main class, common questions predominate over individual questions. *See Hanlon,* 150 F.3d at 1022 ("When common questions present a significant aspect of the case and they can be resolved for all members of the class in a single adjudication, there is clear justification for handling the dispute on a representative rather than on an individual basis.").

As to the subclasses, defendants do not seriously contend that common questions of fact or law do not predominate over individual questions. As discussed above, there are multiple common questions, of primary importance, raised by the claims asserted by the misclassified and arrears subclasses, and the Court therefore finds that common questions predominate for the subclasses as well.

B. Superiority

Plaintiffs must also demonstrate that a class action is "superior to other available methods for fairly and efficiently adjudicating the controversy." Fed.R.Civ.P. 23(b)(3). "Where classwide litigation of common issues will reduce litigation costs and promote greater efficiency, a class action may be superior to other methods of litigation," and is certainly superior "if no realistic alternative exists." *Valentino,* 97 F.3d at 1234–35. Plaintiffs argue that a class action is a superior vehicle for bringing their claims because it will further the interests of judicial economy and will facilitate meaningful access to redress for the class members, many of whom might not otherwise attempt to litigate their relatively small wage and hour claims against defendants. Defendants argue in response that plaintiffs could easily bring small claims actions or file complaints with California's Department of Labor and Standards Enforcement, either of which would be less onerous alternatives to filing individual suits in state or federal court. While the Court agrees with defendants that the class members certainly could file such claims, the Court finds that it would be far more efficient and far less costly to litigate their claims in a class action. *See Wiegele v. Fedex Ground Package Sys., Inc.,* 2008 WL 410691, (S.D.Cal. Feb. 12, 2008) ("Here, it would be far more costly and time consuming for each individual putative class member to seek and compel discovery of Defendants' policies and procedures, take multiple depositions, retain experts, and litigate damages issues. For these reasons, Courts often certify class actions when employer wage and hour practices similarly impact a large number of workers."); *Wang v. Chinese Daily News, Inc.,* 231 F.R.D. 602, 614 (C.D.Cal. Jan. 20, 2005) (noting that "courts have not hesitated to certify class actions for wage and hour claims simply because California law provides for administrative relief."). The Court also agrees with plaintiffs that, left to bring their own claims, many plaintiffs may choose not to do so given the potentially small individual recoveries and the possibility that many class members may not be aware that defendants may owe them additional compensation. This potential loss of access to the courts also supports plaintiffs' argument that a class action is superior to other available methods of resolving plaintiffs' claims. *See Tierno v. Rite Aid Corp.*, 2006 WL 2535056, *12 (N.D.Cal. Aug. 31, 2006).

Looking to the other factors laid out in Rule 23(b)(3), the Court finds nothing to warrant a finding that resolution on a class-wide would be inferior to other methods. Defendants do not argue, and there is no indication, that class members seek to individually control their cases or that there would be an advantage to doing so. Defendants also do not argue that this particular forum is undesirable for any reason, or that it would be difficult to manage a class action in this case. Finally, while plaintiffs acknowledge that one former named plaintiff has filed an individual claim in state court, the Court does not find that this single action suggests that a class action is not the superior method for resolving plaintiffs' claims.

Conclusion

For the foregoing reasons and for good cause shown, the Court hereby GRANTS plaintiffs' motion for class certification, and certifies the following class:

All former sales associates and cashiers who were employed in defendants' retail and outlet stores in the state of California between May 30, 2002 and the conclusion of this action.

The Court also certifies the following subclasses:

1. All members of the class who were sales associates and were misclassified as exempt inside commissioned salespeople.

2. All members of the class who were sales associates from whom defendants took back earned wages through its arrears program.

IT IS SO ORDERED.

Notes

1. Compare the holdings in the *Chanel* and *Polo Ralph Lauren* cases above. Why was class certification granted in the *Polo Ralph Lauren* case but not in the *Chanel* case?

2. Given the significant risk and financial exposure to companies, how would you suggest that employers ensure wage and hour compliance in fast-paced retail environments? If you were employment counsel for a fashion company, what measures would you recommend to ensure compliance?

Chapter 11

Privacy

Miriam Farhi and Meredith Halama
With contributions from Katherine Joseph and Rebecca Kravitz

A. Introduction

This chapter presents an overview of privacy laws that most commonly affect businesses in the fashion and retail industries. The focus of this chapter is primarily on U.S. federal and state laws, but it also touches on some international data protection laws—most notably, the European Union's General Data Protection Regulation ("GDPR")[1]—given their extraterritorial reach and the significant impact these laws have on how U.S. companies do business.

In the United States, there is no single, comprehensive federal law that regulates the treatment of personal information. Rather, privacy is regulated on a sectoral basis, with protections based on industry (e.g., healthcare, finance, education), type of individual (e.g., children), type of information (e.g., biometric data), and particular uses of personal information (e.g., marketing). At the federal level, the Federal Trade Commission ("FTC") has broad authority, by way of the Federal Trade Commission Act of 1914 ("FTC Act"), to regulate unfair and deceptive trade practices and it has employed that authority liberally in the context of privacy and data security. The states further contribute to this patchwork, with a plethora of laws regulating data breach notifications, security obligations, obligations to post privacy notices, and laws governing certain types of personal information, such as biometric data, Social Security numbers ("SSNs"), and driver's license information, among others.

The European Union ("E.U."), by contrast, has a comprehensive privacy regime. Born of its view that privacy is a fundamental human right, the E.U. has long had comprehensive privacy laws governing the collection, use, and disclosure of personal data, the most recent iteration of which is the GDPR, which is discussed in more detail below.

B. What Is Personal Information?

Before discussing the intricacies of U.S. and international privacy law, it is important to understand what these laws are designed to protect. "Personal information,"

1. Council Regulation, General Data Protection Regulation 2016/679, 2016 O.J. (L 119) 1.

"personally identifiable information," and "personal data" are terms of art that are used throughout privacy legislation, with variations in how they are defined. Essentially, however, these terms refer to information that, directly or indirectly, refers to an identified or identifiable individual. Recent laws like the GDPR and the California Consumer Privacy Act ("CCPA")[2] have significantly expanded the concept of personal information to include information like geolocation data, IP addresses, web browsing behavior, attributes assigned to a customer profile, and other identifiers captured automatically from an individual's computer or mobile device, even when they are not linked to or do not directly identify an individual the way that, for example, names, email addresses, phone numbers, and Social Security numbers may.

C. What Are Fundamental Privacy Concepts?

While privacy laws and industry standards differ in their precise implementation, they tend to reflect basic principles, including notice or transparency, choice (particularly as to unexpected practices or practices that are inconsistent with the purpose for which the personal information was collected), use of personal information consistent with specified purposes, data minimization, data quality, security, and accountability. These basic principles are often articulated as what are known as the Fair Information Practice Principles or "FIPPs," described in the following table.

Fashion Law in Practice: FIPPs

The FIPPs are a widely accepted framework that has become the cornerstone of the U.S. approach to privacy and data protection. The FIPPs provide a framework of principles for balancing the need for privacy with other competing interests, and are used to evaluate systems, processes, and programs that impact individual privacy. Although articulated slightly differently in various publications, the following table sets forth the FIPPs as they are described by the Organization for Economic Cooperation and Development (OECD):

Fair Information Practice Principles

Principle	*Description*
Collection Limitation	There should be limits to the collection of personal data and any such data should be obtained by lawful and fair means and, where appropriate, with the knowledge or consent of the data subject.
Data Quality	Personal data should be relevant to the purposes for which they are to be used, and, to the extent necessary for those purposes, should be accurate, complete, and kept up-to-date.

2. Cal. Civ. Code § 1798.100 *et seq.*

Principle	*Description*
Purpose Specification	The purposes for which personal data are collected should be specified not later than at the time of data collection and the subsequent use limited to the fulfillment of those purposes or such others as are not incompatible with those purposes and as are specified on each occasion of change of purpose.
Use Limitation	Personal data should not be disclosed, made available, or otherwise used for purposes other than those specified in accordance with [the Purpose Specification Principle] except: (a) with the consent of the data subject; or (b) by the authority of law.
Security Safeguards	Personal data should be protected by reasonable security safeguards against such risks as loss or unauthorized access, destruction, use, modification, or disclosure of data.
Openness	There should be a general policy of openness about developments, practices, and policies with respect to personal data. Means should be readily available of establishing the existence and nature of personal data, and the main purposes of their use, as well as the identity and usual residence of the data controller.
Individual Participation	An individual should have the right: (a) To obtain from a data controller, or otherwise, confirmation of whether or not the data controller has data relating to him; (b) To have communicated to them, data relating to them i. within a reasonable time; ii. at a charge, if any, that is not excessive; iii. in a reasonable manner; and iv. in a form that is readily intelligible to them; (c) To be given reasons if a request made under subparagraphs (a) and (b) is denied, and be able to challenge such denial; and (d) To challenge data relating to them and, if the challenge is successful, to have the data erased, rectified, completed, or amended.
Accountability	A data controller should be accountable for complying with measures which give effect to the principles stated above.
Source: OECD (2013), The OECD Privacy Framework, http://www.oecd.org/sti/ieconomy/oecd_privacy_framework.pdf.	

D. U.S. Federal Privacy Laws

1. Section 5 of the FTC Act

Although the United States lacks a single comprehensive federal privacy law, consumer privacy is far from unregulated. To the contrary, the FTC has liberally and creatively used its general authority under Section 5 of the FTC Act to regulate companies' privacy and security practices.[3]

3. 15 U.S.C. § 45 (2012).

Section 5 of the FTC Act prohibits businesses from engaging in "unfair" or "deceptive" acts or practices. To bring an unfairness claim, the FTC must find: (1) that the act or practice is likely to cause substantial injury to consumers; (2) there is no reasonable way for consumers to avoid injury; and (3) the potential injury is not outweighed by countervailing benefits to competition.[4] In contrast, to bring a deception claim, there must be: (1) a misrepresentation, omission, or practice that is (2) material and (3) likely to deceive consumers acting reasonably under the circumstances.[5] Under Section 5, the FTC generally lacks fining authority but can seek injunctive relief and disgorgement of profits.

The FTC has used Section 5 aggressively in the privacy space, bringing claims against companies for alleged failures to protect consumer data or to live up to their privacy commitments in privacy policies and other consumer-facing notices. These cases most often result in a settlement decree between the FTC and the company, whereby the company promises it will not repeat the offending behavior, agrees to implement specific privacy controls, and submits to 20 years of FTC oversight and monitoring. Despite the lack of court involvement, this body of complaints and settlement decrees are highly influential and informally comprise the "common law" of privacy and data security in the United States.

FTC privacy enforcement can largely be categorized into several buckets of offending behavior, giving brands and retailers guideposts to avoid running afoul of Section 5. These buckets include: (A) misrepresenting or insufficiently disclosing how the company collects, uses, or shares personal information; (B) using or sharing personal information for a *new* purpose without obtaining consumer consent; (C) circumventing consumers' privacy settings; and (D) misrepresenting a company's data security standards or practices.

a. Misrepresenting or Insufficiently Disclosing How the Company Collects, Uses, or Shares Personal Information

In this line of cases, the FTC complaints allege a failure to adequately describe how companies collect, use, and/or share consumers' personal information. *In re Sears Holdings Management Corporation*,[6] for example, the FTC alleged that Sears collected information about individuals who visited www.sears.com and www.kmart.com using a tracking software, without providing clear and conspicuous notice to website visitors about the types of information that would actually be collected. Specifically, the FTC found that Sears did not adequately inform website visitors that the tracking software would collect information about their web browsing activities (on Sears' websites and also on third-party websites), online purchases, business transacted during secure sessions, completion of online application forms, online checking

4. Fed. Trade Comm'n, Policy Statement on Unfairness (Dec. 17, 1980).

5. Fed. Trade Comm'n, Policy Statement on Deception (Oct. 14, 1983).

6. Complaint, In the Matter of Sears Holdings Mgmt. Corp., No. 0823099, F.T.C. C-4264 (Sept. 9, 2009).

accounts, and some web-based emails and instant messages. The FTC alleged that Sears' failure to adequately disclose this type of information collection constituted a deceptive practice in violation of Section 5.

In re Sears Holding Management Corp.

No. C-4264 (F.T.C. Aug. 31, 2009)

Complaint

The Federal Trade Commission, having reason to believe that Sears Holdings Management Corporation, a corporation, has violated the provisions of the Federal Trade Commission Act, and it appearing to the Commission that this proceeding is in the public interest, alleges:

1. Respondent Sears Holdings Management Corporation ("respondent" or "SHMC") is a Delaware corporation with its principal office or place of business at 3333 Beverly Road, Hoffman Estates, Illinois 60179. SHMC, a subsidiary of Sears Holdings Corporation ("SHC") with shares owned by Sears, Roebuck and Co. and Kmart Management Corporation, handles marketing operations for the Sears Roebuck and Kmart retail stores, and operates the sears.com and kmart.com retail Internet websites.

* * *

3. From on or about April 2007 through on or about January 2008, SHMC disseminated or caused to be disseminated via the Internet a software application for consumers to download and install onto their computers (the "Application"). The Application was created, developed, and managed for respondent by a third party in connection with SHMC's "My SHC Community" market research program.

4. The Application, when installed, runs in the background at all times on consumers' computers and transmits tracked information, including nearly all of the Internet behavior that occurs on those computers, to servers maintained on behalf of respondent. Information collected and transmitted includes: web browsing, filling shopping baskets, transacting business during secure sessions, completing online application forms, checking online accounts, and, through select header information, use of web-based email and instant messaging services.

5. SHMC, during the relevant time period, presented fifteen out of every hundred visitors to the sears.com and kmart.com websites with a "My SHC Community" pop-up box that said:

> Ever wish you could talk directly to a retailer? Tell them about the products, services and offers that would really be right for you? If you're interested in becoming part of something new, something different, we'd like to invite you to become a member of My SHC Community. My SHC Community, sponsored by Sears Holdings Corporation, is a dynamic and highly interactive on-line community. It's a place where your voice is heard and your opinion matters, and what you want and need counts!

> The pop-up box made no mention of the Application. Likewise, the general "Privacy Policy" statement accessed via the hyperlink in the pop-up box did not mention the Application.

6. The pop-up box message further invited consumers to enter their email address to receive a follow-up email from SHMC with more information. Subsequently, invitation messages were emailed to those consumers who supplied their email address. These emails stated, in pertinent part:

> From shopping, current events, social networking, to entertainment and email, it seems that the Internet is playing a bigger and bigger role in our daily lives these days.
>
> If you're interested in becoming part of something new, something different, we'd like to invite you to join a new and exciting online community; My SHC Community, sponsored by Sears Holdings Corporation. *Membership is absolutely free!*
>
> My SHC Community is a dynamic and highly interactive online community. It's a place where your voice is heard and your opinion matters, and what you want and need counts! As a member of My SHC Community, you'll partner directly with the retail industry. You'll participate in exciting, engaging and on-going interactions—always on your terms and always by your choice. My SHC Community gives you the chance to help shape the future by sharing and receiving information about the products, services and offers that would really be right for you.
>
> To become a member of My SHC Community, we simply ask you to complete the registration process which includes providing us with your contact information as well as answering a series of profile questions that will help us get to know you better. You'll also be asked to take a few minutes to download software that is powered by (VoiceFive). This research software will confidentially track your online browsing. This will help us better understand you and your needs, enabling us to create more relevant future offerings for you, other community members, and eventually all shoppers. You can uninstall the software at any time through the Add/Remove program utility on your computer. During the registration process, you'll learn more about this application software and you'll always have the opportunity to ask any and every question you may have.
>
> Once you're a member of My SHC Community, you'll regularly interact with My SHC Community members as well as employees of Sears Holdings Corporation through special online engagements, surveys, chats and other fun and informative online techniques. We'll ask you to journal your shopping and purchasing behavior. Again, this will be when you want and how you want to record it—always on your terms and always by your choice. We'll also collect information on your internet usage. Community engagements are always fun and always voluntary!

The email invitation message then described what consumers would receive in exchange for becoming a member of the My SHC Community, including a $10 payment for joining the "online community," contingent upon the consumer retaining the Application on his or her computer for at least one month. Consumers who wished to proceed further would need to click a button, at the bottom, center portion of the invitation email, that said "Join Today!"

7. Consumers who clicked on the "Join Today!" button in the email invitation were directed to a landing page that restated many of the aforementioned representations about the potential interactions between members and the "community" and about the putative benefits of membership. The landing page did not mention the Application.

8. Consumers who clicked on the "Join Today" button in the landing page were directed to a registration page. To complete registration, consumers needed to enter information, including their name, address, age, and email address. Below the fields for entering information, the registration page presented a "Privacy Statement and User License Agreement" ("PSULA") in a "scroll box" that displayed ten lines of the multi-page document at a time. A description of the Application's specific functions begins on approximately the 75 line down in the scroll box:

> Computer hardware, software, and other configuration information: Our application may collect certain basic hardware, software, computer configuration and application usage information about the computer on which you install our application, including such data as the speed of the computer processor, its memory capacities and Internet connection speed. In addition, our application may report on devices connected to your computer, such as the type of printer or router you may be using.
>
> Internet usage information: Once you install our application, it monitors all of the Internet behavior that occurs on the computer on which you install the application, including both your normal web browsing and the activity that you undertake during secure sessions, such as filling a shopping basket, completing an application form or checking your online accounts, which may include personal financial or health information. We may use the information that we monitor, such as name and address, for the purpose of better understanding your household demographics; however we make commercially viable efforts to automatically filter confidential personally identifiable information such as UserID, password, credit card numbers, and account numbers. Inadvertently, we may collect such information about our panelists; and when this happens, we make commercially viable efforts to purge our database of such information.
>
> The software application also tracks the pace and style with which you enter information online (for example, whether you click on links, type in webpage names, or use shortcut keys), the usage of cookies, and statistics about your use of online applications (for example, it may observe that during a given period of use of a computer, the computer downloaded X number of bytes of data using a particular Internet enabled gaming application).

> Please note: Our application does not examine the text of your instant messages or e-mail messages. We may, however, review select e-mail header information from web-based e-mails as a way to verify your contact information and online usage information.

The PSULA went on to describe how the information the Application would collect was transmitted to respondent's servers, how it might be used, and how it was maintained. It also described how consumers could stop participating in the online community and remove the Application from their computers. Respondent stated in the PSULA that it reserved the right to continue to use information collected prior to a consumer's "resignation."

9. Below the scroll box on the registration page was a link that consumers could click to access a printable version of the PSULA, and a blank checkbox next to the statement: "I am the authorized user of this computer and I have read, agree to, and have obtained the agreement of all computer users to the terms and conditions of the Privacy Statement and User License Agreement." To continue with the registration process, consumers needed to check the box and click the "Next" button at the bottom of the registration page.

10. Consumers who completed the required information, checked the box, and clicked the "Next" button on the registration page, were directed to an installation page that explained the Application download and installation process. Consumers were required to click a "Next" button to begin the download, and then click an "Install" or "Yes" button in a "security warning" dialog box to install the Application. Nothing on the installation page provided information on the Application.

11. When installed, the Application functioned and transmitted information substantially as described in the PSULA. The Application, when installed, would run in the background at all times on consumers' computers. Although the Application would be listed (as "mySHC Community") in the "All Programs" menu and "Add/Remove" utilities of those computers, and the Application's executable file name ("srhc.exe") would be listed as a running process in Windows Task Manager, the Application would display to users of those computers no visible indication, such as a desktop or system tray icon, that it was running.

12. The Application transmitted, in real time, tracked information to servers maintained on behalf of respondent. The tracked information included not only information about websites consumers visited and links that they clicked, but also the text of secure pages, such as online banking statements, video rental transactions, library borrowing histories, online drug prescription records, and select header fields that could show the sender, recipient, subject, and size of web-based email messages.

13. Through the means described in paragraphs 3-12, respondent has represented, expressly or by implication, that the Application would track consumers' "online browsing." Respondent failed to disclose adequately that the software application, when installed, would: monitor nearly all of the Internet behavior that occurs on consumers' computers, including information exchanged between consumers

and websites other than those owned, operated, or affiliated with respondent, information provided in secure sessions when interacting with third-party websites, shopping carts, and online accounts, and headers of web-based email; track certain non-Internet related activities taking place on those computers; and transmit nearly all of the monitored information (excluding selected categories of filtered information) to respondent's remote computer servers. These facts would be material to consumers in deciding to install the software. Respondent's failure to disclose these facts, in light of the representations made, was, and is, a deceptive practice.

14. The acts and practices of respondent as alleged in this complaint constitute unfair or deceptive acts or practices in or affecting commerce in violation of Section 5(a) of the Federal Trade Commission Act.

THEREFORE, the Federal Trade Commission this thirty-first day of August, 2009, has issued this complaint against respondent.

Notes

1. After the FTC filed the complaint, Sears entered into a consent agreement where it agreed, among other things, to destroy previously collected information, and to "clearly and prominently disclose the types of data the software will monitor, record, or transmit" if it advertises or disseminates any tracking application in the future.[7]

2. In 2017, Sears filed a petition requesting that the FTC reopen and modify the consent agreement. The petition stated that, due to changing circumstances, the order should be modified to change the existing definition of "tracking application," which Sears argued unnecessarily restricts its ability to operate in the mobile app marketplace.[8] The FTC approved the petition, stating that in the context of mobile applications that engage in the types of information collection that consumers expect, the notice and consent requirements are burdensome and counterproductive for consumers and Sears.

3. When it approved Sears' petition, the FTC stated that some consumers would be confused by the prominent disclosures and consent they would have to give for Sears to meet the requirements imposed on them by the FTC. Specifically, the FTC thought that the requests for consent would make it seem that data collected by the Sears apps was unusual or was being used in the way that the consumer may not want or expect. Do you agree with the FTC's reasoning? Would you feel this way

---

7. Press Release, Fed. Trade Comm'n, Sears Settles FTC Charges Regarding Tracking Software (June 4, 2009), https://www.ftc.gov/news-events/press-releases/2009/06/sears-settles-ftc-charges-regarding-tracking-software.

8. Press Release, Fed. Trade Comm'n, FTC Approves Sears Holding Management Corporation Petition to Reopen and Modify Commission Order Concerning Tracking Software (February 28, 2018), https://ftc.gov/news-events/press-releases/2018/02/ftc-approves-sears-holdings-management-corporation-petition.

if you were using a mobile app that had prominent disclosures or consent requests related to the collection, use, and disclosure of your personal information?

b. Using or Sharing Personal Information for a New Purpose without Obtaining Consumer Consent

In this line of cases, the FTC has brought enforcement actions against companies that made implicit or explicit promises to consumers about how they treat the consumers' personal information, but then violate these promises by using or sharing the personal information for other, undisclosed purposes without obtaining prior consent. For instance, the FTC found online retailer Toysmart.com engaged in deceptive practices when it sought to sell its customer list notwithstanding its promises that the personal information it collected was "never shared with a third party" and instead was "used only to personalize your experience online."[9]

c. Circumventing Consumers' Privacy Settings

In this line of cases, the FTC complaints allege that companies failed to honor consumers' choices with respect to how their personal information is processed. In *In re Nomi Technologies, Inc.*,[10] for instance, the FTC brought an action against an in-store consumer tracking software company alleging that the company deceptively failed to provide consumers with meaningful choice regarding its tracking of consumers at client retail locations. According to the FTC complaint, Nomi used sensors or Wi-Fi access points in its clients' stores to detect MAC addresses of mobile devices and information about the devices and the dates and times the devices were observed. Nomi used the information it collected to provide its clients with aggregate analytics about consumer traffic patterns, such as the percentage of individuals passing by the store who do not enter, the length of consumer visits, the percentage of repeat customers, the number of consumers visiting other locations within a chain, and the type of mobile devices used by individuals visiting a location. Nomi's online privacy policy stated that consumers could opt out of such tracking on Nomi's website or at the retailer's location. The FTC charged that this representation was deceptive in violation of Section 5 of the FTC Act because, while consumers could opt out at the Nomi website, consumers were not in fact informed of the tracking in stores using Nomi's technology and thus could not know to opt out.

In re Nomi Technologies, Inc.

No. C-4538 (F.T.C. Aug. 28, 2015)

Complaint

The Federal Trade Commission, having reason to believe that Nomi Technologies, Inc., a corporation, has violated the Federal Trade Commission Act, and it appearing to the Commission that this proceeding is in the public interest, alleges:

---

9. Complaint, FTC v. Toysmart.com, LLC, No. 00-11341-RGS (D. Mass. July 21, 2000).
10. Complaint, In the Matter of Nomi Tech., Inc., No. 1323251, F.T.C. C-4538 (Sept. 3, 2015).

1. Respondent Nomi Technologies, Inc. ("Nomi" or "respondent") is a Delaware corporation with its principal office or place of business at 26 West 17th Street, 2nd Floor, New York, NY 10011.

2. The acts and practices of respondent as alleged in this complaint have been in or affecting commerce, as "commerce" is defined in Section 4 of the Federal Trade Commission Act.

Respondent's Business Practices

3. Nomi uses mobile device tracking technology to provide analytics services to brick and mortar retailers through its "Listen" service. Nomi has been collecting information from consumers' mobile devices to provide the Listen service since January 2013.

4. Nomi places sensors in its clients' retail locations that detect the media access control ("MAC") address broadcast by a mobile device when it searches for WiFi networks. A MAC address is a 12-digit identifier that is unique to a particular device. Alternatively, in some instances Nomi collects MAC addresses through its clients' existing WiFi access points.

5. In addition to the MAC address, Nomi also collects the following information about each mobile device that comes within range of its sensors or its clients' WiFi access points:

A. the mobile device's signal strength;

B. the mobile device's manufacturer (derived from the MAC address);

C. the location of the sensor or WiFi access point observing the mobile device; and

D. the date and time the mobile device is observed.

6. Nomi cryptographically hashes the MAC addresses it observes prior to storing them on its servers. Hashing obfuscates the MAC address, but the result is still a persistent unique identifier for that mobile device. Each time a MAC address is run through the same hash function, the resulting identifier will be the same. For example, if MAC address 1A:2B:3C:4D:5E:6F is run through Nomi's hash function on ten different occasions, the resulting identifier will be the same each time. As a result, while Nomi does not store the MAC address, it does store a persistent unique identifier for each mobile device. Nomi collected information about approximately nine million unique mobile devices between January 2013 and September 2013.

7. Nomi uses the information it collects to provide analytics reports to its clients about aggregate customer traffic patterns such as:

A. the percentage of consumers merely passing by the store versus entering the store;

B. the average duration of consumers' visits;

C. types of mobile devices used by consumers visiting a location;

D. the percentage of repeat customers within a given time period; and

E. the number of customers that have also visited another location within the client's chain.

8. Through October 22, 2013, Nomi's Listen service had approximately 45 clients. Some of these clients deployed the service in multiple locations within their chains.

9. Nomi has not published, or otherwise made available to consumers, a list of the retailers that use or used the Listen service.

10. Nomi does not require its clients to post disclosures or otherwise notify consumers that they use the Listen service. Through October 22, 2013, most, if not all, of Nomi's clients did not post any disclosure, or otherwise notify consumers, regarding their use of the Listen service.

11. Nomi provided, and continues to provide, an opt out on its website for consumers who do not want Nomi to store observations of their mobile device. Once a consumer has entered the MAC address of their device into Nomi's website opt out, Nomi adds it to a blacklist of MAC addresses for which information will not be stored. Nomi did not make an opt out available through any other means, including at any of its clients' retail locations.

12. From at least November 2012, until October 22, 2013, Nomi disseminated or caused to be disseminated privacy policies on its website, nomi.com or getnomi .com, which included the following statement:

Nomi pledges to.... Always allow consumers to opt out of Nomi's service on its website as well as at any retailer using Nomi's technology.

13. In order to opt out of the Listen service on Nomi's website, consumers were required to provide Nomi with all of their mobile devices' MAC addresses, without knowing whether they would ever shop at a retail location using the Listen service. Consumers who did not opt out on Nomi's website and instead wanted to make the opt out decision at retail locations were unable to do so, despite the explicit promise in Nomi's privacy policies. Consumers were not provided any means to opt out at retail locations and were unaware that the service was even being used.

Violations of the FTC Act

Count I

14. As described in Paragraph 12, Nomi represented, directly or indirectly, expressly or by implication, that consumers could opt out of Nomi's Listen service at retail locations using this service.

15. In fact, Nomi did not provide an opt-out mechanism at its clients' retail locations. Therefore, the representation set forth in Paragraph 14 is false or misleading.

Count II

16. As described in Paragraph 12, Nomi represented, directly or indirectly, expressly or by implication, that consumers would be given notice when a retail location was utilizing Nomi's Listen service.

17. In fact, neither Nomi nor its clients disclosed to consumers that Nomi's Listen service was being used at a retail location. Therefore, the representation set forth in Paragraph 16 is false or misleading.

18. The acts and practices of respondent as alleged in this complaint constitute unfair or deceptive acts or practices in or affecting commerce in violation of Section 5(a) of the Federal Trade Commission Act.

THEREFORE, the Federal Trade Commission this twenty-eighth day of August, 2015, has issued this complaint against respondent.

Notes

1. Nomi and the FTC subsequently agreed to a 20-year consent decree that prohibits Nomi from misrepresenting either: (1) "the options through which . . . consumers can exercise control over the collection, use, disclosure, or sharing of information collected from or about them or their computers or devices" or (2) the extent to which consumers will be provided notice about the collection, use, or sharing of consumer data.[11] Violations of the final consent order can be subject to fines of up to $16,000 per day or per violation.

2. Two FTC commissioners dissented from the FTC enforcement action and argued that the punishment was too severe for the deception that took place and that consumers were not materially harmed by the FTC's misstatement in their privacy policy. The commissioners noted that, had Nomi not made any representations about its privacy practices, it would not have been subject to an enforcement action, and thus it was punished for being a good actor. Do you agree?

3. Tracking shoppers' movements and behavior in brick-and-mortar stores is increasingly becoming common practice. What sort of notice do you think retailers should provide to shoppers before collecting this type of information?

d. Misrepresenting a Company's Data Security Standards or Practices

By far the most numerous of the FTC's consent decrees relate to companies that claimed in their privacy policy that they applied "reasonable" or similarly adequate security standards, but then suffered a breach that, in the FTC's eyes, reflected a lack of reasonable security. Although many such cases are brought against financial institutions and technology companies, retailers are not immune. For instance, the FTC found retailer Life Is Good liable for unfair and deceptive practices stemming out of a data breach that exposed customers' credit card numbers and other personal information. In its complaint, the FTC pointed to several common alleged security failings, including storing consumer information in clear, readable text, storing consumer information indefinitely, storing credit card security codes, not

11. Decision and Order, In the Matter of Nomi Tech., Inc., No. 1323251, F.T.C. C-4538 (Sept. 3, 2015)

adequately assessing the vulnerability of their web application and network to commonly known or reasonably foreseeable attacks and not implementing readily available defenses to such attacks, not using readily available security measures to monitor and control connections from the network to the internet, and failing to employ reasonable measures to detect unauthorized access to consumer information.[12]

Section 5 of the FTC Act is supplemented by a host of laws that apply to particular sectors or with respect to a particular type of data or individual. The federal laws that most commonly apply to retailers and brands are described throughout the remainder of this Chapter.

2. Marketing

There are several federal laws that regulate the ways brands can use personal information to market to consumers. For example, the Controlling the Assault of Non-Solicited Pornography and Marketing Act, more commonly known as the "CAN-SPAM Act,"[13] regulates email communications, while the Telephone Consumer Protection Act ("TCPA")[14] and the Telemarketing Sales Rule[15] regulate text messages, phone calls, and fax advertisements.

To ensure compliance with the CAN-SPAM Act, brands that send emails to consumers should first determine whether those communications are *commercial* or *transactional* emails, as those terms are defined under the CAN-SPAM Act. "Commercial email" is defined as "any electronic mail message the primary purpose of which is the commercial advertisement or promotion of a commercial product or service."[16] This includes, but is not limited to, emails to consumers promoting a new product or service and business-to-business emails promoting new services to business partners. Alternatively, "transactional emails" are messages intended to facilitate a commercial transaction that the recipient previously agreed to enter into with the sender, to provide safety and warranty information concerning a product purchased by the recipient, to provide account or employment/benefits information, or to deliver goods or services that the recipient is entitled to receive pursuant to a previous transaction with the sender.[17] Transactional emails may include, for example, an email responding to a customer question, confirming a customer's order, or notifying a customer of changes to their account.

---

12. Complaint, In the Matter of Life is Good, Inc., No. 0723046, F.T.C. C-4218 (April 18, 2008).
13. Controlling the Assault of Non-Solicited Pornography and Marketing Act, 15 U.S.C. § §7701-7713 (2003).
14. 47 U.S.C. § 227 (1991).
15. 16 C.F.R. § 310 (2016).
16. 15 U.S.C. § 7702(2)(A).
17. *See id.* § 7702(17)(A).

Under CAN-SPAM, *commercial emails* must include the following:[18]

- A "From" line that identifies the sender and is not misleading;
- A non-deceptive "Subject" line. The subject line should indicate that the message is commercial in nature. This requirement does not apply if the recipient has affirmatively and expressly agreed (e.g., by checking a box) to receive commercial emails from the sender;
- A notice that the recipient has the right to opt out of receiving future e-mail messages from the sender. The law does not specify where the notice must appear, but it must be clear and conspicuous. The recipient should not have to search the message to find it;
- An internet-based opt-out mechanism capable of receiving opt-out requests for at least 30 days after the transmission of the message. The sender must honor an opt-out request within 10 business days; and
- The sender's physical postal address.

CAN-SPAM requires *transactional emails* to clearly indicate who the message is "From" and "To" and not include any inaccurate or misleading routing information.

Noncompliance with CAN-SPAM is subject to stiff penalties that are adjusted from time to time, but currently stand at more than $40,000 per violation.

As mentioned above, marketing calls and text messages are regulated at the federal level, under the TCPA and under the Telemarketing Sales Rules.[19] Both laws can be used both against the company that actually makes the call or sends the text message, and against the company that caused the call or text to be made or sent (the initiator of the call), so companies must exercise caution even when they outsource these functions to call centers, text message aggregators, and other vendors.

The TCPA generally regulates the use of automatic telephone dialing systems ("ATDS"), artificial or prerecorded voice messages, text messages to cell phones, and unsolicited fax advertisements. Companies that engage in any of these practices must obtain prior express consent of the "called party" (the definition of which has been debated in the courts—in particular, whether it refers only to the phone line actually dialed or to the individual the company intended to reach, in the event that person's number had been reassigned to a different individual) prior to sending any text message or initiating a call using an autodialer or artificial or prerecorded voice.[20] The definition of autodialer is broad and encompasses any equipment that has the *potential* capacity to store or produce telephone numbers to be called, using a random or sequential number generator and to dial such numbers.[21] If a text message includes an advertisement or marketing material, or if a voice call employs a

---

18. Fed. Trade Comm'n, CAN-SPAM Act: A Compliance Guide for Business (Sept. 2009).
19. 47 U.S.C. § 227.
20. *See id.*
21. *See id.*

prerecorded or artificial voice and includes an advertisement or marketing material, the consent must be written.

The TCPA has been construed broadly in many respects, and both government agencies and courts have applied principles of vicarious liability, meaning those partnering with others who actually make the calls or send the text messages could still be subject to claims in some instances. The TCPA provides a private right of action for injunctive relief and provides for statutory damages of $500–$1,500 per call or text sent without prior express consent.

The Telemarketing Sales Rule generally requires companies to honor opt-out requests and maintain a list of such requests (referred to as an "internal Do Not Call list"), and to avoid making calls at certain times.[22]

SAMPLE NOTICE AND CONSENT FOR SENDING MARKETING TEXT MESSAGES

To help mitigate TCPA risk, messaging along the following lines should be provided in a clear and conspicuous manner at the point where a consumer provides his or her phone number:

"By clicking submit, you agree to receive recurring automated marketing text messages from [insert company name] at the telephone number you provide. Consent is not a condition of a purchase. See our Privacy Policy for details."

Note that additional disclosures will also need to be included within the text messages themselves, including instructions for opting out of receiving future messages (e.g., "text STOP to opt out").

3. The Children's Online Privacy Protection Act

The Children's Online Privacy Protection Act ("COPPA") protects children under 13 when they engage in online activities.[23] Unlike Section 5, COPPA is backed by steep civil penalties of more than $40,000 per violation and thus is a more attractive hook for regulators than Section 5. COPPA is enforced by the FTC and state attorneys general. It is also enforced by the Children's Advertising Review Unit ("CARU"), a self-regulatory group that governs children's advertising and has adopted the COPPA rules into its own code of conduct. COPPA does not provide for a private right of action, but nevertheless has been creatively invoked by plaintiffs' attorneys to bring class action lawsuits under various state law theories. Accordingly, brands should take great care when offering websites, mobile applications, and other online services that collect age information from consumers or are specifically intended for kids.

22. 16 C.F.R. § 310.

23. Children's Online Privacy and Protection Act of 1998, 15 U.S.C. §§ 6501–6506 (2000).

COPPA applies to "operators" of "online services" such as websites, mobile apps, games, and other connected services that collect personal information *from* children.[24] Importantly, COPPA does not regulate personal information collected from parents or other adults *about* children. For instance, when parents or brands post pictures of children, those images fall outside of COPPA. COPPA also does not regulate data collected entirely offline.

Under the FTC's Rules implementing COPPA, the law applies in three contexts:[25]

- *When a company has actual knowledge that it is collecting personal information from a user who is under 13.* This is true even if a company is not seeking to attract child users (but rather is intended for an adult or "general" audience). Companies that have actual knowledge that they are collecting personal information from a child under 13 and do not take steps to block the user or comply with COPPA may be held liable for violations.
- *When a company offers online services that are directed to children under 13.* The FTC considers a host of factors to determine if a site or service is "directed to children," including the subject matter of the site or service, its visual content, the use of animated characters or child-oriented activities and incentives, music or other audio content, age of models, presence of child celebrities or celebrities who appeal to children, language or other characteristics of the website or online service, and whether advertising promoting or appearing on the website or online service is directed to children. If a site or service is directed to children, it may be either "primarily child-directed," where children under 13 are the service's primary audience or "mixed audience," where children under 13 are one of the site or service's intended audiences, but not the primary audience. On primarily child-directed services, operators must treat all visitors as children and not collect, use, or disclose personal information other than in accordance with COPPA's mandates (described below). On mixed-audience services, the operator may "age gate" users by asking them to provide their ages, but must accept all users (unlike general audience services, which may block users under 13). For users who provide an age under 13, the operator must treat them in accordance with COPPA, and for those who provide an older age, the operator may treat them as outside of COPPA.
- *When a company is collecting personal information directly from users of a site or service that it knows to be directed to children.* This provision of the rule is primarily intended to pick up "third parties" such as ad networks or social plugins. Such companies are subject to COPPA's mandates, but only when they know that the site or service through which they are collecting personal information is directed to children.

---

24. *See id.* § 6502.
25. *See id.*

Under COPPA, "personal information" includes typical data points such as name, email address, phone number, and postal address, but also includes less obvious identifiers such as audio and visual files, including the child's likeness or voice.[26] In its 2013 update to COPPA , the FTC further expanded "personal information" to include persistent identifiers that can be used to identify users across non-affiliated websites or services, such as third-party cookies, IP addresses, and mobile device IDs.[27] However, the FTC's rule also carves out from COPPA's notice and choice requirements operators that collect only such persistent identifiers and no other personal information if they use such identifiers only for "support for internal operations" of their services such as analytics, bug reporting, ad delivery, and frequency capping, and do *not* use the identifiers for interest-based advertising or to build a profile on the user. As a result, many child-directed services simply avoid collecting identifying information from children and engineer the child-directed portions of their experiences to only allow persistent identifiers for limited purposes.

Companies that are subject to COPPA must comply with the following obligations: (1) post a privacy policy that explains their data practices with respect to children's data; (2) provide a "direct notice to parents" that explains what information has been collected from the child, the purpose(s) for which the information was collected, and how the parent can consent to these data practices (or the consequences if the parent decides not to consent); and (3) obtain "verifiable parental consent" using a form that is "reasonably designed" to ensure that the person providing consent is the parent.[28] COPPA provides several approved methods of obtaining this consent, all of which are onerous, including charging the parent's credit card or using an approved third-party service.[29] In contrast to the E.U., which in many instances permits parents to consent in a relatively streamlined manner such as having parents accept a privacy policy and terms of service on the child's behalf, COPPA's approved methods are rigorous and often require the collection of additional personal information from the parent. Operators are also required to secure children's personal information and to allow parents to access and delete it.

United States v. Iconix Brand Group[30]

No. 1:09-cv-08864 (S.D.N.Y. Oct. 20, 2009)

Complaint

Plaintiff, the United States of America, by its attorney Preet Bharara, the United States Attorney for the Southern District of New York, acting upon notification and authorization to the Attorney General by the Federal Trade Commission ("FTC" or "Commission"), alleges for its Complaint that:

---

26. *See id.* § 6501.

27. 16 C.F.R. § 312.2.

28. *See id.* § 312.3.

29. *See id.* § 312.5.

30. Complaint, United States v. Iconix Brand Group, Inc., No. 09 Civ. 8864 (S.D.N.Y. Oct. 20, 2009).

1. Plaintiff brings this action under Sections 1303(c) and 1306(d) of the Children's Online Privacy Protection Act of 1998 ("COPPA"), 15 U.S.C. §§6501-6506, 6502(c) and 6505(d), and Sections 5(a)(1), 5(m)(1)(A), 13(b), 16(a) and 19 of the Federal Trade Commission Act ("FTC Act"), 15 U.S.C. §§41-58, 45(a)(1), 45(m)(1)(A), 53(b), 56(a) and 57(b), to obtain monetary civil penalties, a permanent injunction, and other equitable relief for Defendant's violations of the Commission's Children's Online Privacy Protection Rule (the "Rule"), 16 C.F.R. Part 312, and Section 5 of the FTC Act.

* * *

5. Congress enacted the COPPA in 1998 to protect the safety and privacy of children online by prohibiting the unauthorized or unnecessary collection of children's personal information online by operators of Internet websites or online services. COPPA directed the Federal Trade Commission to promulgate a rule implementing COPPA. The Commission promulgated the Children's Online Privacy Protection Rule, 16 C.F.R. Part 312, on November 3, 1999 under Section 1303(b) of COPPA, 15 U.S.C. §6502(b), and Section 553 of the Administrative Procedure Act, 5 U.S.C. §553. The Rule went into effect on April 21, 2000.

6. The Rule applies to any operator of a commercial website or online service, or portion thereof, directed to children that collects, uses, and/or discloses personal information from children, and to any operator of a commercial website or online service that has actual knowledge that it collects, uses, and/or discloses personal information from children.

* * *

Defendant's Course of Conduct

12. Defendant Iconix is a brand management and licensing company that owns numerous retail apparel brands, as well as several bath and bedding brands. Certain Iconix apparel brands, including Mudd, Candie's, Bongo, and OP, hold popular appeal with children and teens.

13. Since at least 2006, Defendant has operated individual, brand-specific websites that advertise and promote each of its apparel brands. Numerous Iconix websites permit users to register for website activities, such as receiving periodic electronic brand updates, participating in sweepstakes contests, and engaging in interactive brand awareness campaigns. On certain websites, including MyMuddWorld.com, users may publicly post pictures and personal stories.

14. To enroll users to receive electronic brand updates, Defendant generally collects a user's full name, email address, zip code, and date of birth; additionally, for some brand-related communications, Defendant collects a user's gender, full mailing address, and the answers to certain brand-preference questions (e.g., favorite season, favorite look, and "#1 reason you buy an item").

15. The sweepstakes areas on Defendant's websites generally collect a user's full name, mailing address, email address, and date of birth in connection with registration. In certain instances, Defendant also collects a user's phone number.

16. In addition, Defendant's www.mymuddworld.com website enables users to publicly share personal stories online. The website features a "Share Your Story" page aimed at highlighting how "Mudd Girls Move the World!" Defendant encourages girls to "Tell Us How You Move the World" by uploading a digital photo along with a story of personal philanthropy. Girls who choose to share their stories also are required to submit a date of birth, name, email address, and home state. . . . Defendant does not edit these stories and posts them as written on the Mudd website.

17. Since 2006, approximately 1,000 children under age 13 have registered on Iconix's websites. Through its online registration processes, Defendant has had actual knowledge that it has collected, maintained, and/or disclosed personal information from underage children. Defendant Iconix is an "operator" as defined in the Rule.

Defendant's Information Collection, Use, and Disclosure Practices

18. Iconix's online privacy policy, applicable to each website at issue in this complaint, states that:

> IV. INFORMATION FROM PERSONS UNDER THE AGE OF 13 We do not seek to collect personally identifiable information from persons under the age of 13 without prior verifiable parental consent. If we become aware that we have inadvertently received such information online from a child under the age of 13, we will delete it from our records. If you are under the age of 13, please do not submit any personally identifiable information to us. If you are the parent or guardian of a person under the age of 13 who has provided personally identifiable information to us, please inform us by contacting us at info@iconixbrand.com and we will remove such information from our database. If you are concerned about your children's use of the Site, you may use web filtering technology to supervise or limit access to the Site.

Users who register on any one of the relevant Iconix websites enter a date of birth as a part of the registration process. Despite Defendant's representation that it will delete all personally identifiable information from children about which it has knowledge, Defendant takes no such steps. Indeed, children who enter dates of birth indicating that they are under 13 years old are able to register on Defendant's websites, and their personal information is collected and used by Defendant.

18. After collecting dates of birth from children indicating that they are under 13, Defendant engages children in brand-related marketing campaigns by sending them periodic newsletters and brand updates, sent directly to their email addresses, and enrolling them in sweepstakes contests. After collecting birth date information from children on the MyMuddWorld.com website, Defendant permits them to upload and publicly post images of themselves and unedited personal stories on the website. In connection with the posting of children's images and/or stories, Defendant also publicly posts certain items of their information, including the child's name, age, and state.

19. As stated in Paragraph 17 above, Defendant posts a notice of its information practices online. . . . This notice does not clearly, completely, or accurately disclose

all of Defendant's information collection, use, and disclosure practices for children, as required by the Rule, nor does it make other Rule-required disclosures, including listing the name, address, and telephone number of all operators collecting or maintaining personal information from children.

20. Defendant does not take the steps required by the Rule to provide parents with a direct notice of its information practices prior to collecting, using, or disclosing their children's personal information.

21. Defendant does not take the steps required by the Rule to obtain verifiable consent from parents prior to collecting, using, or disclosing their children's personal information.

22. In approximately 1,000 instances, Defendant collected, used, and/or disclosed personal information from children without first providing their parents with notice of its information practices, either on Defendant's websites or directly; and without obtaining verifiable consent from the parents prior to the collection, use, or disclosure.

Count I

Defendant Violated the Children's Online Privacy Protection Rule

23. Since at least 2006, Defendant has operated its brand-related websites, through which it collected, with actual knowledge, personal information from children.

24. In connection with the acts and practices described above, Defendant collected, used, and/or disclosed personal information from children in violation of the Rule, including:

a. Failing to provide sufficient notice on the Defendant's websites of what information it collects online from children, how it uses such information, its disclosure practices, and all other required content, in violation of Section 312.4(b) of the Rule, 16 C.F.R. § 312.4(b);

b. Failing to provide direct notice to parents of what information Defendant collects online from children, how it uses such information, its disclosure practices, and all other required content, in violation of Section 312.4(c) of the Rule, 16 C.F.R. § 312.4(c); and,

c. Failing to obtain verifiable parental consent before any collection, use, and/or disclosure of personal information from children, in violation of Section 312.5 of the Rule, 16 C.F.R. § 312.5(a)(1).

25. Pursuant to Section 18(d)(3) of the FTC Act, 15 U.S.C. § 57a(d)(3), a violation of the Rule constitutes an unfair or deceptive act or practice in or affecting commerce, in violation of Section 5(a)(1) of the FTC Act, 15 U.S.C. § 45(a)(1). See COPPA, 15 U.S.C. § 6503(c).

Count II

Defendant Engaged in Unfair or Deceptive Acts or Practices in Violation of the FTC Act

26. Section 5(a) of the FTC Act, 15 U.S.C. § 45(a), prohibits "unfair or deceptive acts or practices in or affecting commerce." Misrepresentations constitute deceptive acts or practices prohibited by Section 5(a) of the FTC Act.

27. Through the statements in the Iconix privacy policy referenced in Paragraph 17 above, Defendant has represented, expressly or by implication, that it would not seek to collect personal information from children without obtaining prior verifiable parental consent, and would delete any and all personal information collected from children about which Defendant became aware.

28. In truth and in fact, Defendant has knowingly collected personal information from children without obtaining prior verifiable parental consent, and has not deleted such personal information collected from children about which Defendant became aware. Therefore, the representation set forth in Paragraph 27 was false and misleading.

29. Defendant's false and misleading representation, as set forth in Paragraph 27 above, constitutes a deceptive act or practice in violation of Section 5(a) of the FTC Act, 15 U.S.C. § 45(a).

* * *

Prayer

WHEREFORE, plaintiff United States of America, pursuant to Sections 5(a)(1), 5(m)(1)(A), 13(b) and 19 of the FTC Act, 15 U.S.C. §§ 45(a)(1), 45(m)(1)(A), 53(b) and 57(b), and the Court's own equitable powers, demands judgment against the Defendant as follows:

(1) Judgment against Defendant and in favor of Plaintiff for each violation of the Rule alleged in this Complaint;

(2) An award to Plaintiff of monetary civil penalties from Defendant for each violation of the Rule alleged in this Complaint;

(3) Permanent enjoinder of Defendant from violating the Rule and Act; and

(4) Such other and further relief as the Court may deem just, proper, or necessary to redress injury to consumers resulting from Defendant's violations of the Rule and Act.

Notes

1. Iconix Brand Group, Inc. had to pay a $250,000 civil penalty for knowingly collecting, using, or disclosing personal information of children online without parental consent in violation of COPPA.

2. It is important that brands pay special attention when collecting age information or designing online experiences for kids. A promotion targeting children, such as to promote kids' clothes, may be considered an online experience for which children are the intended audience, even if the purpose of the promotion is to encourage *parents* to make purchases. Other online experiences that are covered by COPPA include network-connected games, social networks, and purchasing goods or services online. If the experience is designed for kids, COPPA applies. If collecting age information, companies must make sure to block users under 13 or to obtain parental consent in accordance with COPPA's mandates.

3. COPPA defines "personal information" more broadly than some state and federal privacy laws. What are some less obvious examples of information that would be considered "personal information" under COPPA?

4. What are some examples of methods retailers can use to obtain parental consent?

4. The Health Insurance Portability Accountability Act

The Health Insurance Portability Accountability Act ("HIPAA"), regulates the privacy of "protected health information" ("PHI") in the United States.[31] HIPAA generally imposes notice, consent, and use restrictions on such data. Despite some common misconceptions about the scope of HIPAA's coverage, however, HIPAA applies only to "covered entities" (e.g., doctors, insurance companies, and others in the medical field) as well as to their "business associates" (those who process PHI on behalf of covered entities). HIPAA does not apply to entities that collect and store health-related data outside of this scope, and thus typically has limited impact on brands unless they collect PHI (for example, a fashion eyewear company might collect prescription information, which is covered by HIPAA). Wearables that collect heart rate data or other data about the human body typically fall outside of HIPAA because they are offered by technology companies directly to consumers rather than by or through covered entities. Brands do, however, need to be mindful of HIPAA with respect to their employee data, where they provide self-insured medical plans. Even if health-related data is not covered by HIPAA, however, it still may be considered sensitive by regulators or entitled to special protections under state laws. Brands accordingly are well-served to take special care when collecting such data.

5. The Fair Credit Reporting Act

The Fair Credit Reporting Act ("FCRA") governs the use of consumer information for purposes of determining consumers' eligibility for credit, employment, and housing.[32] Companies that compile reports for making such decisions, or credit reporting agencies ("CRAs") are obligated to ensure that their reports are accurate, to provide mechanisms for consumers to request and dispute their reports, and to ensure that their reports are not used for marketing purposes. The FCRA also requires "users" of such reports to meet certain obligations, such as to inform consumers of the reasons for their denial of covered benefits and to inform consumers of the source of the information. Finally, the FCRA imposes restrictions on those who provide information to CRAs for use in their files. Retail

31. The Health Insurance Portability and Accountability Act of 1996 (HIPAA), Pub. L. No. 104-191, 110 Stat. 1938 (1996).

32. Fair Credit Reporting Act (FCRA), 15 U.S.C. § 1681 (1970).

brands can trigger application of the FCRA when they issue branded credit cards or report information to CRAs.

E. U.S. State Privacy Laws

In the void of a general omnibus federal privacy law, states have layered on piecemeal protections that apply to personal information. These laws include broad-based consumer privacy legislation, data breach notification laws, laws requiring companies to adopt specific security measures or to post privacy notices, obligations specific to the collection of data at point-of-sale terminals, and laws governing the collection of sensitive categories of personal information, such as biometric data, Social Security numbers, and driver's license numbers.

1. Comprehensive Consumer Privacy Laws

There has been a wave of consumer privacy laws introduced by state legislatures across the country over the last two years, starting with the CCPA, which was signed by Governor Jerry Brown in June 2018.[33] The CCPA takes effect in 2020 and is one of the most significant pieces of privacy legislation ever passed in the United States. The law applies to any for-profit entity that does business in California, collects personal information, and meets at least one of the following threshold criteria:[34]

- Earns annual gross revenue above $25 million;
- Annually buys, sells, or, for commercial purposes, receives or shares personal information of at least 50,000 California consumers, households or devices; or
- Derives at least 50 percent of its annual revenue from selling California consumers' personal information.

If a business is subject to the CCPA, its subsidiaries and affiliates may also be covered if they share common branding, including a shared name, service mark, or trademark.

The CCPA requires greater transparency in data practices and gives consumers more control over their personal information. Under the law, "personal information" means any "information that identifies, relates to, describes, is reasonably capable of being associated with, or could reasonably be linked, directly or indirectly, with a particular consumer or household."[35] It includes obvious identifiers, such as names, addresses and email addresses, but it also covers categories of information not typically considered to be personal information in the United States, such as web browsing information and inferences drawn from other information to create a consumer profile.

---

33. California Consumer Privacy Act (CCPA), Cal. Civ. Code §§ 1798.100–1798.198 (2018).
34. Cal. Civ. Code § 1798.140.
35. *See id.*

The CCPA also provides California consumers with specific rights, including:

- **The Right to Transparency.**[36] Several provisions of the CCPA address consumers' rights to know about a company's data collection practices, such as the categories of personal information collected, the sources from which personal information is collected, the business or commercial purpose of such collection and categories of third parties with whom personal information is shared. Additionally, consumers have a right to know whether and to whom their personal information was sold or disclosed for a business purpose. Some of this information must be provided through notices, such as in privacy policy disclosures, whereas other disclosures must be made in response to verifiable consumer requests.
- **The Right to Access.**[37] Consumers have a right to access information about the personal information a business collects about them, including a right to the specific pieces of personal information collected. Upon receipt of a verifiable consumer request, a company must provide the requesting consumer with access to the specific pieces of information collected about that consumer over the prior 12 months, sometimes in a portable format.
- **The Right to Stop Sales of Personal Information.**[38] In addition to requiring businesses to make disclosures about the sale of personal information, the CCPA gives consumers more control over this business activity. Like other aspects of the law, "sale" is defined broadly to include "renting, releasing, disclosing or otherwise communicating a consumer's personal information to a third party for monetary or other valuable consideration." Some data sharing is exempt from the definition of sale, including certain information sharing with service providers. Generally, businesses that sell personal information to other businesses or third parties must permit consumers to opt out of such sales. Note, however, that explicit opt-in consent to the sale of personal information is required if such information relates to consumers under the age of 16. Finally, companies that sell personal information must also include a clear link on their websites' homepage (or platform or download page for mobile apps) and in their privacy policies labeled "Do Not Sell My Personal Information" that enables consumers to exercise their opt-out rights.
- **The Right to Deletion.**[39] Consumers have the right to request deletion of their personal information. Upon receipt of a verifiable request, a company must delete personal information held about a consumer unless an exception applies, such as the need to retain the information to complete a transaction, comply with a legal obligation, exercise free speech, or enable internal uses that are aligned with consumer expectations, among others.

---

36. *See id.* §§ 1798.100; 1798.110.
37. § 1798.130.
38. § 1798.120.
39. § 1798.105.

- **The Right to Nondiscrimination.**[40] Consumers also enjoy a general right to equal service and price, meaning that companies generally cannot discriminate against those who have exercised their privacy rights, subject to some exceptions. The law specifically prohibits denying goods or services, charging different prices, or providing different levels or quality of products or services to consumers who exercise their rights under the law, although certain exceptions may apply. At the same time, the CCPA also permits businesses to offer financial incentives in exchange for the collection or sale of personal information.

To comply with the CCPA, brands and retailers need to implement processes and procedures to authenticate and respond to verifiable consumer requests. A business must offer at least two methods through which consumers can make requests to exercise their rights, including, at the time of this writing, a toll-free phone number, and if the business maintains a website, a web address.[41] In addition, companies must update disclosures in their privacy policies at least annually. Any employees or contractors that handle consumer inquiries related to the company's privacy practices must receive training so they are familiar with consumer rights available under the CCPA and how consumers can exercise them.[42] The CCPA also sets forth certain provisions businesses should include in their contracts with service providers.

The California attorney general has broad enforcement authority under the CCPA. The attorney general may initiate civil actions against companies that fail to cure violations under the CCPA, with penalties reaching $2,500 per violation or up to $7,500 per intentional violation. The CCPA also contains a limited private right of action for uncured breaches of unencrypted data that are reportable under California's breach notification law. If such breaches occur as a result of a company's failure to implement reasonable security standards, individuals may each seek to recover the greater of actual damages or statutory damages up to $750 per violation (or such damages may be sought in a class action).

Since the CCPA was enacted, other states have proposed comprehensive consumer privacy legislation, including Connecticut, Hawaii, Illinois, Maine, Maryland, Massachusetts, Nevada, New Mexico, New York, North Dakota, Rhode Island, Texas, and Washington. While most of these bills have not yet been enacted, it is anticipated that more states will follow California's lead in passing sweeping consumer privacy laws that have a significant impact on how companies can collect, use, and share personal information.

---

40. § 1798.125.

41. § 1798.130.

42. *See id.*

2. Breach Notification Laws

All 50 states and the District of Columbia have enacted legislation that requires private entities (and in some cases, state agencies) to notify individuals in the event of a data breach that involves such individuals' personal information. California was the first state to enact this type of legislation in 2002, and many states have used the California law as a model for their own breach notification laws.[43]

California's breach notification law applies to any person, business, or state agency that does business in California and owns or licenses computerized data that contains personal information. A "security breach" is defined as an unauthorized acquisition of computerized data that compromises the security, confidentiality, or integrity of personal information maintained by the business.[44] Note that under this law, the definition of personal information is more limited than under other federal and state laws and refers specifically to an individual's first name or first initial and last name in combination with any one or more of the following data elements, when either the name or the data elements are not encrypted:[45]

- Social Security number;
- Driver's license number or state identification card number;
- Account number, credit card number, or debit card number in combination with any required security code, access code, or password that would permit access to an individual's financial account;
- Medical information;
- Health insurance information;
- Information collected through the use or operation of an automated license plate recognition system; or
- a username or email address, in combination with a password or security question and answer that would permit access to an online account.

Personal information does not include publicly available information that is lawfully made available to the general public from federal, state, or local government records.

In the event a business suffers a security breach, the business is required to disclose the breach to any California resident whose unencrypted personal information was, or is reasonably believed to have been, acquired by an unauthorized person.[46] Businesses are also required to disclose breaches of encrypted personal information where the encryption key or security credential was, or is reasonably believed to

43. Cal. Civ. Code §§ 1798.29; 1798.80 *et seq.*
44. *See id.* § 1798.82.
45. *See id.*
46. *See id.*

have been, acquired by an unauthorized persona and the business has a reasonable belief that this could render the personal information readable or usable.[47]

Where more than 500 California residents are impacted in a breach, the business must send breach notifications to the affected individuals in addition to notifying the California attorney general.

Under California law, breach notifications must be made in the most expedient time possible and describe the following:[48]

- The date of the notice;
- The name and contact information of the reporting business;
- The type(s) of personal information subject to the breach;
- The date, estimated date, or date range during which the breach occurred, if it can be determined;
- Whether notification was delayed as a result of law enforcement investigation, if that can be determined;
- A general description of the breach incident, if that information is possible to determine at the time the notice is provided;
- The toll-free phone number and addresses of the major credit reporting agencies, if the breach exposed a Social Security number or a driver's license or state identification card number; and
- If the business providing the notification was the source of the breach, an offer to provide appropriate identity theft prevention and mitigation services at no cost for at least 12 months.

At the business's discretion, the notice may also include information about what the business has done to protect affected individuals and advice on steps that the individual can take to protect him- or herself. Note that the California law provides specific requirements for how the notice must be formatted, including specific title and section headings and font requirements.

California residents have a private right of action and can sue for up to $750 per violation (which can quickly become very expensive for companies in the event of a class action). The California Attorney General can also initiate civil actions against companies, with penalties of up to $7,500 per intentional violation.

Fashion Law in Practice: Breach Readiness

Data breaches can lead to serious losses for brands and retailers, both in terms of monetary losses and customer trust and reputational damage. According to the 2019 *Cost of a Data Breach Report* published by the Ponemon Institute and IBM

47. *See id.*
48. *See id.*

Security, the average cost of a data breach in the retail industry is $1.84 million, with lost business being the biggest contributor to data breach costs.[49] In order to mitigate the damage, it is important for brands and retailers to have a plan in place that enables them to respond rapidly to known or suspected security breaches. This plan, generally referred to as an incident response plan, should assign roles and responsibilities to specific individuals within the company (generally, the incident response team is comprised of personnel from IT Security, Legal, Risk Management, and Corporate Communications). The plan should also set forth the company's processes for detecting, assessing, and responding to breaches and include template notices that satisfy the requirements under state breach notification laws. Finally, the plan should address how the company will institutionalize its learnings post-breach, including instructions for preparing an incident report, briefing corporate leadership, and possibly revising policies, practices, trainings, and audit processes.

3. Data Security Requirements

At least 25 states have laws that impose data security requirements on companies that process personal information. Most of these laws require companies to implement and maintain "reasonable" security practices that are appropriate to the nature of the information in order to protect such information from unauthorized access, destruction, use, modification, or disclosure. A handful of states, including Colorado, Massachusetts, and New York, are more prescriptive, imposing specific security requirements on companies that process specific types of personal information. Many states have also enacted data disposal laws that require companies to destroy or dispose of personal information such that it becomes unreadable or indecipherable.

Brands and retailers that process payment card information are also required to abide by the Payment Card Industry Data Security Standard ("PCI DSS"), which applies to entities in the payment processing chain that store, process, or transmit "cardholder data." Minnesota, Nevada, and Washington have incorporated the PCI DSS requirements into state law and require adequate protection for unencrypted account information.

To illustrate the stakes for companies that fail to provide reasonable security, it is worthwhile to consider the complaint filed by the California attorney general against Target Corporation after it suffered a massive cyberattack that compromised the payment card information of more than 40 million consumers, approximately 7.75 million of whom were California residents. Similar complaints were filed in 46 other states and the District of Columbia, eventually resulting in a settlement agreement whereby Target was required to pay $18.5 million. The following is an excerpt from the California attorney general's complaint:

49. 2019 Cost of a Data Breach Report, https://www.ibm.com/security/data-breach.

California v. Target Corp.[50]

No. CGC-17-559105 (Cal. Super. Ct. May 23, 2017)

1. Plaintiff, the PEOPLE OF THE STATE OF CALIFORNIA, by Xavier Becerra, Attorney General of the State of California, ("Plaintiff" or "the People") brings this action against Defendant Target Corporation ("Target" or "Defendant") for violating the California Unfair Competition Law (Bus. & Prof. Code, § 17200 et seq.), and alleges the following on information and belief.

* * *

5. On December 19, 2013, Target publicly announced, and reported to the Office of the Attorney General for the State of California, that it had discovered unauthorized access to payment card information at Target's stores in the United States, including stores in California. Target reported that the payment card information of over forty (40) million consumers was affected, approximately 7.75 million of whom were California residents.

6. The theft of the payment card data affected consumers who shopped at Target stores in the United States from November 27, 2013, through December 18, 2013. This included consumers who initiated a purchase of goods, purchased goods or who returned goods.

7. Upon further investigation, Target learned that on or about November 12, 2013, an intruder (or intruders) gained access to Target's remote-access system and deployed memory-scraping (or RAM-scraping) malware to Target's point of sale systems. The malware was designed to capture, in real time, payment card data from the magnetic strip of credit and debit cards, which the attacker eventually exfiltrated out of Target's internal network.

8. Some consumers who shopped at Target stores in the United States from November 27, 2013, to December 18, 2013, reported fraudulent charges to their payment cards.

9. In addition, on January 10, 2014, Target publicly announced that consumer contact information had been stolen. The customer contact information included customer name, mailing address, phone number, and/or email address. Target reported that the customer contact information for up to seventy (70) million individuals was affected, approximately 8.33 million of whom were California residents.

10. Under California Civil Code section 1798.81.5, subdivision (b), "[a] business that owns or licenses personal information about a California resident shall implement and maintain reasonable security procedures and practices appropriate to the nature of the information, to protect the personal information from unauthorized access, destruction, use, modification, or disclosure."

* * *

50. Complaint, California v. Target Corp., No. CGC-17-559105 (Cal. Super. Ct. May 23, 2017).

11. Target failed to implement and maintain reasonable security procedures and practices appropriate to protect the personal information of California residents from unauthorized access, destruction, use, modification, or disclosure.

* * *

13. Target, in the course of conducting retail transactions, engaged in business acts or practices that were unlawful, unfair, or deceptive, or misleading, and therefore violated section 17200 of the California Unfair Competition Law (Bus. & Prof. Code, § 17200). In particular, Target unlawfully violated California Civil Code section 1798.81.5, subdivision (b), by failing to implement and maintain reasonable security procedures and practices appropriate to protect the personal information of California residents that Target owned and thus did not protect that personal information from unauthorized access, destruction, use, modification, or disclosure.

Notes

1. In a world of rapidly changing business practices and innovative new technologies and online experiences, how should the law address data security? Would it be most effective to have a prescriptive regime, where the government creates specific requirements for private companies (i.e., two-step authorization, guidance for firewalls, etc.)? Or should the government take an incentive approach, allowing companies to address security independently but imposing consequences for failure to secure consumer data?

2. All 50 states now require companies to notify consumers of a breach. However, each state imposes different requirements in terms of what constitutes a breach, the requirements for what needs to be included in a notice of a breach, timelines for providing such notices to consumers (and in some cases, regulators), and consequences for noncompliance with these laws. How does this affect a company's ability to comply with breach notification laws? What are some proactive measures companies should take to minimize their liability in the event of a breach? Should there be a national standard, or should this subject be left to the states?

4. Privacy Notice Requirements

Posting online privacy policies and making copies of these policies available in brick-and-mortar retail stores has become a widespread practice for brands and retailers. As discussed above, Section 5 of the FTC Act has been interpreted to require clear and conspicuous notice about a company's information collection, use, and disclosure practices—and this notice is generally provided in the form of a privacy policy. In addition to Section 5, a handful of states have laws that impose specific obligations related to privacy policies. For instance, Delaware requires companies that collect personal information through their commercial websites or online services (including mobile applications) to make a privacy policy conspicuously available and to ensure the policy does the following:

- Identifies the categories of personal information that the company collects about users of its website or online service and the categories of third-party persons with whom the company may share that personal information;
- If the company maintains a process for an individual to review and request changes to any of his or her personal information, provide a description of that process;
- Describe the process by which the company notifies users of material changes to the privacy policy;
- Identifies the effective date of the privacy policy;
- Discloses whether other parties may collect personal information about an individual's online activities over time and across different websites or online services; and
- Discloses how the company responds to web browser "do not track" signals or other mechanisms that provide individuals with the ability to exercise choice regarding the collection of personal information about their online activities over time and across third-party sites or online services, if the company engages in that collection.[51]

Nevada and California have similar requirements for privacy policies.[52] In fact, California has several laws, in addition to the CCPA (discussed above), that impose requirements for privacy policies on companies that collect personal information, including the California Online Privacy Protection Act (known as CalOPPA), and California's Shine the Light law.[53] In 2014, the California attorney general also released recommendations for developing meaningful privacy policies.[54] These recommendations underscore the need for privacy policies to use plain, straightforward language and avoid technical or legal jargon. Among other things, the California attorney general recommendations encourage companies to:

- Explain the scope of the privacy policy (e.g., does it cover just online practices or both online and offline practices?);
- Make the policy conspicuously available (e.g., by using a link on a company's website homepage containing the word "privacy" and using a font type that is larger than the surrounding text, contrasting color, or symbols that call attention to it);
- Use short sentences and active voice;
- Use titles and headers to identify key parts of the policy;

---

51. Del. Code Tit. 6 § 205C.

52. NRS § 603A.340.

53. The Online Privacy Protection Act of 2003, Cal. Bus. & Prof. Code §§ 22575–22579; Cal. Civ. Code § 1798.83.

54. California Department of Justice, Making your Privacy Practices Public (2014), https://oag.ca.gov/sites/all/files/agweb/pdfs/cybersecurity/making_your_privacy_practices_public.pdf.

- Describe *how* information is collected (e.g., via cookies or web beacons) and be reasonably specific in describing the kinds of information collected;
- Describe the choices an individual has regarding the collection, use, and sharing of his or her personal information and provide clear instructions about how individuals can exercise these choices;
- Provide a general description of the security measures the company uses to safeguard personal information; and
- Inform individuals how they can contact the company with questions or concerns.

The CCPA, discussed above, will require additional disclosures for privacy policies. Under the CCPA, companies must ensure their privacy policies and/or California-specific privacy notices inform California consumers of the following:

- The categories of personal information collected about consumers in the preceding 12 months, using the categories enumerated in the definition of "personal information" in the law.[55]
- The business or commercial purposes for collecting, using, and, if applicable, selling personal information.[56]
- The categories of sources from which personal information is collected.[57]
- The categories of third parties with whom the business shares personal information.[58]
- A list of categories of personal information disclosed about consumers for a business purpose in the preceding 12 months using categories stipulated in the definition of "personal information" (or a statement that no personal information has been disclosed for a business purpose).[59]
- For companies that do not sell personal information about California consumers, a statement that your business has not sold consumer personal information in the preceding 12 months.[60] If your company does sell personal information, see additional requirements below.
- The consumer's right to request deletion of the consumer's personal information.[61]

55. Cal. Civ. Code §§ 1798.100(b),1798.110(c)(1),1798.130(a)(5)(B).

56. §§ 1798.100(b),1798.110(c)(3).

57. § 1798.110(c)(2).

58. § 1798.110(c)(4). Note that the California attorney general has also issued proposed regulations governing CCPA compliance, which introduce additional privacy notice requirements. Cal. Code Regs. tit. 11, § 999.300 *et seq.* These regulations are expected to be finalized in early 2020.

59. §§ 1798.115(c)(2), 1798.130(a)(5)(C)(ii).

60. §§ 1798.115(c)(1), 1798.130(a)(5)(C)(i).

61. § 1798.105(b).

- The consumer's right to request disclosure about information collected about that individual consumer, including categories of information collected, categories of sources from which it was collected, categories shared for business or commercial purposes, and categories of third parties that receive that consumer's personal information.[62]
- The consumer's right to request access to specific pieces of personal information collected about that consumer.[63]
- The consumer's right to request individualized disclosure about categories of personal information sold or disclosed for a business purpose and categories of recipients.[64]
- The consumer's right not to be discriminated against by the company if privacy rights are exercised.[65]
- One or more designated methods for consumers to submit requests for information required to be disclosed under the CCPA.[66]

In addition, for businesses that "sell" personal information about California consumers, privacy policies and/or California-specific privacy notices must include:

- A list of categories of personal information sold in the preceding 12 months using categories stipulated in the definition of "personal information."[67]
- Description of sale opt-out rights for adults and opt-in rights for consumers under 16 years of age.[68]
- A link titled "Do Not Sell My Personal Information" that directs consumers to a webpage where they can exercise their opt-out right.[69]

Brands and retailers should review their privacy policies to ensure they accurately and comprehensively describe their information practices and address all mandatory disclosure requirements under applicable laws. They should also have a process in place to review their privacy policies at least annually to ensure they stay current and accurately reflect how the company treats personal information.

62. §§ 1798.110(a),1798.130(a)(5)(A).
63. §§ 1798.110(a)(5), 1798.130(a)(5)(A).
64. §§ 1798.115(a)(2)–(3), 1798.130(a)(5)(A).
65. §§ 1798.125(a), 1798.130(a)(5)(A).
66. §§ 1798.130(a)(1), 1798.130(a)(5)(A).
67. § 1798.115(c)(1), 1798.130(a)(5)(C)(i).
68. §§ 1798.120,1798.135(a)(2).
69. § 1798.135(a)(2).

5. Laws Regulating Information Collection at the Point of Sale

While many privacy laws contemplate the collection, use, and disclosure of personal information in an *online* context, there are several states that have passed laws that regulate the collection of personal information at the point of sale in brick-and-mortar stores. California was the first to adopt such a law, known as the Song-Beverly Credit Card Act,[70] which prohibits retailers from doing any of the following:

1. Requesting, or requiring as a condition to accepting the credit card as payment in full or in part for goods or services, the cardholder to write any personal identification information upon the credit card transaction form or otherwise;

2. Requesting, or requiring as a condition to accepting the credit card as payment in full or in part for the goods or services, the cardholder to provide personal identification information, which the person, firm, partnership, association, or corporation accepting the credit card writes, causes to be written, or otherwise records upon the credit card transaction form or otherwise; and

3. Utilizing, in any credit card transaction, a credit card form that contains preprinted spaces specifically designated for filling in any cardholder's personal identification information.

Violators of the Act are subject to civil penalties not to exceed $250 for the first violation and $1,000 for each subsequent violation.

Several other states, in addition to California, have enacted similar legislation, including Colorado, Delaware, the District of Columbia, Georgia, Kansas, Louisiana, Maryland, Massachusetts, Minnesota, Nevada, New Jersey, New York, Ohio, Oregon, Pennsylvania, Rhode Island, Texas, and Wisconsin. These laws have been invoked to allege that retailers have violated these state laws by requesting personal information, such as phone numbers, email addresses, or zip codes, at the checkout counter.

Harrold v. Levi Strauss & Co.

236 Cal. App. 4th 1259 (2015)

POLLAK, Acting P.J.

Plaintiff Stacie Harrold appeals from an order denying her motion to certify a class in her action against Levi Strauss & Co. and Levi's Only Stores, Inc. (collectively, Levi's), for requesting and recording e-mail addresses from customers paying for purchases with a credit card, allegedly in violation of the Song-Beverly Credit Card Act of 1971 (Civ. Code, § 1747 et seq.) (the Act), specifically section 1747.08.

---

70. Cal. Civ. Code § 1747.08.

The trial court determined that plaintiff's complaint fails to satisfy the requirements for certification of a class, based on its conclusion that section 1747.08 does not prohibit the collection of personal identification information once a credit card transaction has been concluded. The appeal turns on the correctness of this interpretation of the Act. Since we conclude the trial court correctly interpreted the statute, we shall affirm the order denying class certification.

Background

Plaintiff's first amended complaint alleges that "plaintiff entered into a credit card purchase transaction with defendants, which did not involve mail order, shipping or cash advances. However, as part of defendants' information capture policy, and in conjunction with the credit card sales transaction, plaintiff was asked for personal identification information, in the form of her email address, by defendants' employee attending to the transaction. [¶] ... Plaintiff provided the requested personal identification information, which was entered into the electronic sales register at the checkout counter adjacent to both defendants' employee and plaintiff." The amended complaint continued: "Defendants' conduct as alleged herein expressly violated California Civil Code section 1747.08. Civil Code section 1747.08(a)(2) provides, in relevant part, that: [N]o person, firm, partnership, association, or corporation that accepts credit cards for the transaction of business shall ... *request*, or require as a condition to accepting the credit card as payment in full or in part for goods or services, *the cardholder to provide personal identification information, which the person, firm, partnership, association, or corporation accepting the credit card writes, causes to be written, or otherwise records upon the credit card transaction form or otherwise.* (emphasis added)." For purposes of this appeal, Levi's has assumed, as shall we, that an e-mail address is "personal identification information" within the meaning of section 1747.08.

The amended complaint defines the purported class as "all persons from whom defendants requested and recorded personal identification information in conjunction with a credit card purchase transaction at a California retail store during [a defined time period]."

In support of her motion for certification of such a class plaintiff submitted her own declaration in which she stated: "On July 14, 2012, I visited the Levi's store in Napa, California. [¶] ... On that occasion, after selecting the items that I intended to purchase, I proceeded to the cashier's section of Levi's store to pay for the merchandise using a credit card. After I provided the items to the cashier at the register, the cashier informed me of the amount due. I then paid for the merchandise using my credit card. [¶] ... While I was standing at the cash register for my credit card purchase transaction, Levi's cashier requested my email address. Per the cashier's request, I provided the cashier with my email address." At her deposition, plaintiff testified she did not recall whether the request was made before or after she had signed for the purchase but that it was before the purchased merchandise was bagged and handed to her.

The papers submitted in support of and in opposition to the class certification motion indicate that Levi's conducts an e-mail marketing program and has a written policy concerning precisely when and how store clerks should request from customers their e-mail address for inclusion in the program. The documents articulating this policy have been filed under seal, so that we shall not here recite the particulars, but it is undisputed that under this policy the customer's e-mail address is not to be requested until after the credit card purchase transaction has been completed. Except to the extent that plaintiff's testimony may indicate a departure from this policy in the case of her purchase, no evidence was submitted indicating that the policy is not universally followed. Levi's submitted substantial evidence to the effect that employees are trained to adhere to this policy and that they "always wait[] until the receipt is printed, handed over to the customer and the merchandise is bagged before providing customers the opportunity to join the email program" and requesting their e-mail address. Except for plaintiff's testimony, the record contains no evidence of instances in which the policy has not been observed.

In denying class certification, the trial court held that section 1747.08 prohibits requests for personal identification information only "as a condition to accepting the credit card as payment" and that, therefore, such a request made after the credit card transaction has been completed does not violate the statute. Thus, class certification is not appropriate, the court ruled, because plaintiff failed to show that there is a numerous class of persons whose e-mail addresses have been obtained in violation of the terms of the statute. Moreover, since plaintiff has alleged that her e-mail address was requested before the transaction was completed, contrary to the policy that the evidence shows was applied to all other Levi's customers, her claim is not typical of the claims of other purported class members.

Discussion

Plaintiff contends that the trial court's ruling is based on an incorrect interpretation of section 1747.08. Plaintiff argues that "[r]egardless of when the cashier obtains a credit card customer's [personal identification information], whether it is prior to handing the customer the receipt and merchandise or a split second after, the retailer is still amassing unnecessary [personal identification information]. . . . [¶] Regardless of whether [Levi's] requested a credit card customer's [personal identification information] at the beginning, middle, or end of the transaction, it still violated section 1747.08. A violation of section 1747.08 occurs when a retailer requests and records [personal identification information] from a customer who pays by credit card."

"The Song-Beverly Credit Card Act of 1971 . . . [citation] is 'designed to promote consumer protection.' [Citation.] One of its provisions, section 1747.08, prohibits businesses from requesting that cardholders provide 'personal identification information' *during credit card transactions*, and then recording that information." (*Pineda v. Williams-Sonoma Stores, Inc.* (2011) 51 Cal.4th 524, 527 [120 Cal.Rptr.3d

531, 246 P.3d 612], italics added, citing Civ. Code, § 1747.08, subd. (a)(2).)[71] We agree with plaintiff that the prohibition applies at all times during and prior to the completion of a credit card transaction. However, there is no support for her contention that the prohibition continues beyond that point.

Plaintiff does not dispute that a credit card purchase may reasonably be considered to have been concluded when the customer receives a receipt for the purchase, following acceptance of the credit card, and the merchandise has been delivered to the customer. Levi's policy does not permit the sales clerk to ask the customer about joining its e-mail program or to request the customer's e-mail address prior to that point. The transaction having been concluded, such a request cannot reasonably be considered—by the customer or by anyone else—as a condition of acceptance of the credit card as a form of payment.

Plaintiff contends that the phrase "as a condition to accepting the credit card as payment in full or in part for goods or services" qualifies only the prohibition of "requiring" the submission of personal identification information as a condition to acceptance of the credit card for payment. She argues that this phrase does not qualify the prohibition of "requesting" such information from credit card customers. Plaintiff argues that this interpretation is required by the "last antecedent rule" of statutory interpretation under which by virtue of the comma following the word "request" in section 1747.08, subdivision (a)(2), the "as a condition" clause qualifies only the word "require." (*White v. County of Sacramento* (1982) 31 Cal.3d 676, 680 [183 Cal.Rptr. 520, 646 P.2d 191].) Under this reading, the statute imposes an absolute prohibition on requesting personal identification information from credit card customers. However, as White recognizes, there are two exceptions to this rule of statutory construction. First, the rule does not apply if the clause in question is equally applicable to the words before and after the comma. (Id. at pp. 680-681.) And secondly, the rule does not apply "'[w]here the sense of the entire act requires that a qualifying word or phrase apply to several preceding wo[r]ds.'" (Id. at p. 681; see the second case on which plaintiff relies, *Demchuk v. State Dept. of Health Services* (1991) 4 Cal.App.4th Supp. 1, 4 [6 Cal. Rptr.2d 635] [rule inapplicable if "the context or evident meaning of the statute requires a different construction . . ."].)

Both exceptions apply in the present case. As our Supreme Court explained in *Pineda v. Williams-Sonoma Stores, Inc.*, supra, 51 Cal.4th at page 535, "the 1990 version of former section 1747.8 [(now § 1747.08)] forbade businesses from 'requir[ing] the cardholder, as a condition to accepting the credit card, to provide personal

71. Section 1747.08, subdivision (a) provides, in pertinent part: "[N]o person, firm, partnership, association or corporation that accepts credit cards for the transaction of business shall. . . [¶] . . . [¶] (2) Request or require as a condition to accepting the credit card as payment in full or in part for goods or services, the cardholder to provide personal identification information, which the person, firm, partnership, association, or corporation accepting the credit card writes, causes to be written, or otherwise records upon the credit card transaction form or otherwise."

identification information. . . .' (Stats. 1990, ch. 999, § 1, p. 4191.) In 1991, the provision was broadened, forbidding businesses from '[r]equest[ing], or requir[ing] as a condition to accepting the credit card . . . , the cardholder to provide personal identification information. . . .' (Stats. 1991, ch. 1089, § 2, p. 5042, italics added.) 'The obvious purpose of the 1991 amendment was to prevent retailers from "requesting" personal identification information and then matching it with the consumer's credit card number.' [Citation.] '[T]he 1991 amendment prevents a retailer from making an end-run around the law by claiming the customer furnished personal identification data "voluntarily."'" Thus, the very purpose of adding "request" to the statute was to apply the prohibition against conditioning the acceptance of a customer's credit card to a request as well as to a requirement. The clause clearly was intended to apply to both a request and a requirement. As the Court of Appeal recognized in *Absher v. AutoZone, Inc.* (2008) 164 Cal.App.4th 332, 342 [78 Cal.Rptr.3d 817], citing legislative history to the 1991 amendment, 6 the Legislature's "stated purpose" of the amendment "was to clarify that merchants 'may neither require nor request, as a condition to accepting the credit card, the taking or recording of personal identification information from the cardholder.'" (*Absher*, at p. 342, italics added & underscore omitted.)

Moreover, while the statute is intended to protect consumer privacy and to prohibit merchants from obtaining personal identification information under the mistaken impression the information is required to process a credit card transaction, the Act is not intended to forbid merchants from obtaining such information voluntarily, if the customer understands that the information need not be disclosed in order to use a credit card. Neither the legislative history nor the cases that have interpreted the statute indicate that the Act prohibits merchants from requesting personal identification information if the request is not made under circumstances suggesting that a credit card will not be accepted as payment without such information. The statute "dovetails with policy by prohibiting the solicitation of information obtained under the false pretense that the transaction cannot or will not be completed without it." (*Florez v. Linens 'N Things, Inc.* (2003) 108 Cal.App.4th 447, 452 [133 Cal.Rptr.2d 465].)

"As evidenced by the 1991 amendment, section 1747.8 [(now § 1747.08)] is designed to prevent a 'request' for personal information, because a customer might perceive that request as a condition of credit card payment. In effect, the 1991 amendment prevents a retailer from making an end-run around the law by claiming the customer furnished personal identification data 'voluntarily.' In fact, the Enrolled Bill Report of the California Department of Consumer Affairs, Assembly Bill No. 1477 (1991-1992 Reg. Sess.), specifically addressed this problem, noting '[t]his bill would prohibit requesting or requiring that information.' As we read it, the legislative intent suggests the 1991 amendment simply clarified that a 'request' for personal identification information was prohibited if it immediately preceded the credit card transaction, even if the consumer's response was voluntary and made only for marketing purposes." (Id. at p. 453.) And more recently in

Apple Inc. v. Superior Court (2013) 56 Cal.4th 128, 139-140 [151 Cal.Rptr.3d 841, 292 P.3d 883], our Supreme Court observed that an analysis in a report of the Senate Committee on the Judiciary noted that "the 'problem' the bill was designed to address was retailers' practice of leading consumers 'to mistakenly believe that [personal identification information] is a necessary condition to complete the credit card transaction, when, in fact, it is not . . .'" and then using the information for the retailer's own business purposes.

Several courts, both state and federal, have recognized that the Act does not preclude merchants from operating e-mail marketing programs and requesting consumers to voluntarily provide their e-mail addresses or other identification information for use in such programs. In *Florez*, the Court of Appeal expressly noted "that nothing prevents a retailer from soliciting a consumer's address and telephone number for a store's mailing list, if that information is provided voluntarily." (*Florez v. Linens 'N Things, Inc.*, supra, 108 Cal.App.4th at p. 451.) In *Gass v. Best Buy Co., Inc.* (C.D.Cal. 2012) 279 F.R.D. 561, the district court embraced that view, noting that if the phrase "'as a condition to accepting the credit card'" does not apply to the word "request," "'then nothing ties a violation of the Act to a credit card transaction at all. . . . [¶] . . . [¶] Such a construction would mean that no business in California that accepts credit cards as payment can maintain a mailing list.'" (Id. at pp. 569-570, boldface omitted.) The district court rejected this interpretation of the statute. In denying an overly broad motion for class certification the court held that the statute is violated only if the request is made under circumstances in which the customer could perceive the request for personal identification information as a condition of completing a credit card transaction. Indeed, the court did not limit the circumstances under which the request may properly be made to requests following completion of the credit card transaction, but ruled that if "[a] business requests a customer's [personal identification information] during a credit card transaction, but does so in a manner such that no reasonable customer could perceive the request as a condition for the business accepting the credit card," the Act is not violated. (*Gass*, at pp. 570-571.) In *Gormley v. Nike, Inc.* (N.D.Cal., Jan. 28, 2013, No. C 11-893 SI) 2013 U.S.Dist. Lexis 11278, the retailer's policy, very similar to Levi's policy, provided that credit card customers were not to be asked for personal identification information "until after the credit card was authorized and the receipt was printing" (Id. at p. *5). The district court rejected the plaintiffs' contention that requests for personal identification information made in compliance with this policy violated the statute and that the Act prohibits any request for such information in conjunction with a credit card transaction. The court thus denied a motion for class certification on the ground that the named plaintiffs, who alleged that the policy had not been observed when their personal information was requested, were not typical of the purported class. The court held that the legality of the store's action depended on "whether a consumer would perceive the store's request . . . as a condition of the use of a credit card." (*Gormley*, at pp. *24-*25; *see, e.g., Rothman v. General Nutrition Corp.* (C.D.Cal., Nov. 17, 2011, No. CV 11-03617

SJO (RZx)) 2011 U.S.Dist. Lexis 134515, p. *16-*17 ["[I]f the personal information is requested as opposed to required, whether there has been a violation of the Act would depend upon whether the individual consumer reasonably believed that providing his personal information was a condition of consummating the credit card transaction."].)

Thus, consistent with all prior reported decisions, we conclude that the trial court correctly refused to certify a class in this action. In this case the merits of plaintiff's claim are "enmeshed with class action requirements." (*Linder v. Thrifty Oil Co.*, supra, 23 Cal.4th 429, 443.) Were plaintiff correct that Levi's violated the Act by requesting e-mail addresses from any customer using a credit card for payment, regardless of whether the credit card had already been approved and the transaction concluded, the requirements of a class action might well be satisfied. However, since the Act is violated only if the request is made under circumstances in which the customer could reasonably understand that the e-mail address was required to process the credit card transaction, and since such an understanding could not reasonably be conveyed by a request made after the transaction has been concluded, those requirements are not met. Plaintiff has made no showing that there are numerous, or indeed any, customers other than herself from whom Levi's has requested e-mail addresses in nonconformity with company policy—i.e., prior to the completion of a credit card transaction. Thus, plaintiff has failed to establish the necessary numerosity, the existence of an ascertainable class, or that her claim is typical of the purported class she seeks to represent. (*See, e.g.*, 23 Cal.4th at p. 435.)

Disposition

The order denying class certification is affirmed. Levi's motion for sanctions is denied.

Notes

1. In order to ensure compliance with retail point-of-sale laws, retailers should separate requests for personal information from credit card transactions to the extent possible. When requesting personal information from consumers at the point of sale, such as to enroll in a loyalty program or receive special offers from the company, they should separate that request from the credit card transaction so that it is clear that any personal information collection is not part of or required to complete the transaction. Consumers should receive the same ability to provide personal information whether they pay with cash, card, or app based payment method and should be invited to provide such information either before the transaction takes place or after it is complete. Can you think of ways retailers can separate data collection from credit card transactions? What about app based payment methods like Venmo and Apple Pay?

2. Retailers should also train sales associates not to pressure customers to provide their personal information. Sales associates should be trained to never suggest

that the personal information is necessary to process the consumer's purchase. In addition to mitigating risk under point of sale privacy laws, avoiding such pressure ensures a better customer experience. It is often helpful for companies to think of selling goods and services rather than trading in personal information.

6. Biometrics Laws

From wearables to smart mirrors and virtual fit technology, retailers and brands are increasingly collecting and using personal information to create a more personalized and engaging experience. The collection of biometric information, which is inherent in some of these technologies, introduces some interesting legal and compliance challenges.

Several states have enacted laws to regulate the collection, use, and disclosure of biometric data. Illinois was the first state to enact such a law in 2008, when it passed the Biometric Information Privacy Act ("BIPA").[72] Since then, Texas, Washington, and California have enacted their own biometric laws, but without private rights of action that have been popular in Illinois.[73]

These laws introduce a host of obligations for companies that collect or otherwise obtain biometric data. Examples of some of the requirements include: (1) providing written notice and obtaining informed consent prior to the collection of biometric data; (2) obtaining consent to disclose biometric data to third parties; (3) abiding by data retention requirements and providing a publicly available data retention/destruction policy; (4) adhering to limits on commercial use and disclosure; and (5) ensuring adequate security measures are in place to safeguard biometric data.

Unfortunately, the definition of what constitutes "biometric data" is not entirely consistent across these laws. In Illinois, Texas, and Washington, biometric data generally includes retina or iris scans, fingerprints, voiceprints, scans of hand or face geometry, and other unique biological patterns or characteristics used to identify a specific individual. California's definition, however, is much broader and includes gait patterns or rhythms and sleep, health, and exercise data that contain identifying information.

There have been a host of lawsuits under the Illinois law from plaintiffs claiming that companies collected biometric data without their consent. Given the sensitivity of this data and the ambiguity of laws governing it, brands should exercise caution when collecting data that relates to the human body and can be used to uniquely identify an individual. Risk mitigation steps include prominently posting notice of the use of any cameras and obtaining consent for use of technologies that identify individuals.

---

72. 740 ILCS 14/1.

73. Tex. Bus. & Com. Code § 503.001; RCW 19.375.010; Cal. Civ. Code § 1798.

F. General Data Protection Regulation (GDPR)

In contrast to U.S. law, E.U. privacy law protects all personal data, regardless of who collects it or how it is processed. The GDPR is an E.U. regulation that went into effect in May 2018 and was designed to harmonize data privacy laws across Europe.[74] The GDPR applies to organizations that are: (1) established in the E.U. and process personal data in the context of that establishment or (2) located outside of the E.U. but offer goods or services to, or monitor the behavior of, individuals in the E.U. The penalties for noncompliance with the GDPR are steep; fines can be as high as 20 million Euros or four percent of a company's worldwide annual revenue, whichever is greater. In addition, the GDPR authorizes lawsuits by affected individuals, or advocacy organizations acting on behalf of such individuals, and introduces direct liability for organizations found in violation of the regulation.

The GDPR significantly expands the rights of individuals and imposes corresponding obligations on companies that process personal data. "Process" is broadly defined under the GDPR to include essentially any handling of personal data, including collection, use, storage, disclosure, transmission, erasure, and destruction.[75] "Personal data" is also broadly defined to include any type of data that relates to an identified or identifiable person.[76] This includes traditional personal data (such as names and email addresses) and also location information, identification numbers, online identifiers, device identifiers, cookie IDs, IP addresses, and any other information specific to the physical, physiological, genetic, mental, economic, cultural, or social identity of an individual.

The GDPR imposes differing restrictions and obligations on "data controllers" and on "data processors." A "data controller" is an entity that determines the purposes, conditions, and means of the processing of personal data. In contrast, a "data processor" is the entity that processes personal data on behalf of, and at the direction of, the controller.[77]

Under the GDPR, companies are required to provide E.U. data subjects with greater visibility into and control over how their personal data is processed. The GDPR provides explicit requirements for the type of notice companies must provide to data subjects before processing their personal data. It also grants data subjects broad rights regarding the treatment of their personal data, including the right to be forgotten, the right to access and correct data, the right to data portability, the right to restrict certain processing, the right to object to automated decision making, the right to revoke consent for processing and the right to object to automated decision-making processes, including profiling.

---

74. Council Regulation, General Data Protection Regulation 2016/679, 2016 O.J. (L 119) 1.
75. Council Regulation, General Data Protection Regulation 2016/679, 2016 O.J. (L 119) 33.
76. *See id.*
77. *See id.*

Companies subject to the GDPR are also required to institutionalize privacy. Privacy by default requires companies to limit collection, processing, and storage of personal data. Privacy by design requires companies to implement appropriate technical and organizational measures when determining the means of processing data and when processing data. For example, whenever possible, companies are encouraged to implement pseudonymization by processing personal data in a manner such that it can no longer be attributed to a specific data subject. Additionally, the GDPR outlines standards regarding the security of data processing for both data controllers and data processors. Where a type of processing uses new technology or is likely to result in a high risk to data subjects, including profiling or large-scale processing of special categories of data, the data controller is required to carry out a privacy impact assessment. This assessment must be detailed and documented, and where the assessment indicates a "high risk," prior consultation with a supervisory authority is required.

The GDPR requires companies to keep clear and accurate records of their data processing activities and compliance efforts. Companies must document the flow of data within their organization and provide detailed information in the event of an audit. Companies may be required to designate a data protection officer to advise and monitor their compliance and to determine whether a data protection impact assessment is required.

The GDPR also imposes a high duty of care on data controllers in selecting service providers to process personal data on their behalf. Data processing contracts must be implemented and must include a range of specific information and obligations. Service providers have similar obligations to pass these contractual requirements down to any subprocessors.

The GDPR also introduced security breach notice requirements. In the event of a breach, companies must provide prompt, detailed notification to the supervisory authority unless the breach is unlikely to result in a high risk to the rights and freedoms of individuals and, if a breach is likely to result in a high risk to the rights and freedoms of individuals, to the affected data subjects as well.

The GDPR is extensive and contains various requirements for data processing in addition to those described above.

Fashion Law in Practice: GDPR Compliance

For retailers and brands that are subject to the GDPR, some of the key obligations that need to be addressed include:

1. Ensuring that personal data is processed lawfully, fairly, and in a transparent manner;
2. Ensuring that policies and procedures are in place to document their compliance with the GDPR;

3. Updating consumer-facing privacy policies, cookie policies, and other notices and consents;
4. Developing and implementing policies and procedures to respond to data subject requests, including requests to access, correct, erase, port, and restrict or object to the processing of personal information;
5. Implementing appropriate technical and organizational measures to safeguard personal data;
6. Maintaining detailed records of all data processing activities;
7. Providing timely notifications to affected customers, employees, and the relevant regulators in the event of a data breach;
8. Vetting all vendors that process personal data on their behalf and ensuring that data processing agreements with these vendors satisfy the contractual requirements set forth under the law;
9. Ensuring appropriate mechanisms are in place to lawfully transfer personal data outside of the E.U. (e.g., E.U.-U.S. Privacy Shield, model clauses, or binding corporate rules); and
10. Determining whether the company is required to appoint a data protection officer.

The GDPR is arguably the strongest data protection regime in the world and has inspired data protection laws in other jurisdictions—including but not limited to proposed and enacted privacy and security legislation in Brazil, Bahrain, Hong Kong, India, Switzerland, Singapore, and New Zealand, just to name a few examples. For brands doing business around the world, it will be important to take note of new data protection laws and assess how they compare to the obligations set forth under the GDPR.

G. Laws and Regulations Related to Targeted Advertising and Analytics

Display advertising refers to the practice of showing advertisements to internet users as they browse the web or use mobile applications. Such ads may be customized based on the content a user is viewing—for example, a luxury brand may choose to show ads on a website for high-end travel. Known as "contextual advertising," these ads typically do not depend on the collection or use of any data about the user and thus do not raise privacy concerns. Another form of display advertising, however, does depend on information about the user's browsing history or other information about the user and thus does raise privacy concerns. Typically, such ads work by setting bits of code known as "cookies" on consumers' browsers as they browse the web and recording information about the websites a user has visited. Ad networks and other advertising technology companies use cookies and similar technologies to show ads that are targeted to the browser users' presumed interests. For instance, a brand can partner with an advertising technology provider to record that a visitor to its website has looked at a particular pair of shoes, and then show an ad for those shoes when the user navigates to a news site (a practice often referred to as "retargeting").

This form of advertising, known broadly as "interest-based advertising," "behavioral advertising," "personalized advertising," or "targeted advertising," typically works without collecting the name or any other identifying information about the individual. Rather, users are identified and tracked via device identifiers such as unique values set in cookies, IP addresses, and identifiers assigned to users' mobile devices and collected through mobile apps, often referred to as pseudonymous identifiers because they do not identify a person but do identify a unique device and can, with additional data points, be linked to an individual. Nevertheless, this tracking raises privacy concerns because it depends on tracking users' behavior on the web and because it is typically invisible to users. Under the GDPR, the CCPA, and other privacy laws, moreover, IP addresses and other forms of device-identifying information are considered to be personal information, and thus are subject to general privacy obligations such as transparency, choice, and data minimization.

1. Regulation of Display Advertising in the United States

In the United States (in contrast to the E.U.), online advertising is largely unregulated, with no laws setting specific standards for notice or consent. Nevertheless, the FTC has used its authority to punish "unfair" and "deceptive" practices under Section 5 of the FTC Act (discussed above) liberally against companies engaged in online tracking, and has long reflected through its policy pronouncements a skepticism of online tracking and its implications for user privacy.

Fashion Law in Practice: FTC Enforcement Regarding Online Tracking

The FTC has also brought a host of enforcement actions against the technology companies that power online advertising. These enforcement actions can largely be categorized into several buckets of offending behavior, giving brands and retailers guideposts to avoid running afoul of norms governing online tracking. These buckets include:

1. **Providing Illusive Choice Mechanisms.** The FTC has brought several cases designed to send the message that whatever choice mechanism a company offers or describes, the failure of that choice mechanism to work as described is a deceptive practice. For instance, Chitika, Inc. concerned an ad network that offered the ability to opt out of targeted ads by setting an opt-out cookie on the user's browser. This opt out, however, lasted only 10 days. The FTC charged that Chitika, in offering consumers the ability to opt out, implicitly or explicitly represented that its opt out would last for a "reasonable" period of time, such that

its failure to provide an opt out that lasted for a reasonable period of time was deceptive.[78]

2. **Engaging in Comprehensive Tracking.** In this line of cases, the FTC reflected a suspicion of companies that track every move a user makes online. For instance, in a case brought against Sears (discussed in detail above), the FTC found that Sears engaged in a material omission when it tracked nearly every website a user visited and every action they took online via an application users could download in exchange for $10 and the opportunity to participate in a Sears user panel. Notably, the End User License Agreement (EULA) used for this program did disclose that once the application was installed it would monitor "all of the Internet behavior that occurs on the computer on which you install the application, including both your normal web browsing and the activity that you undertake during secure sessions, such as filling a shopping basket, completing an application form or checking your online accounts, which may include personal financial or health information." This disclosure, however, was buried deep within the agreement. From this, the FTC concluded that Sears failed to adequately disclose that the application would monitor nearly all internet behavior, a fact that would be material to consumers in deciding whether to install the application.
3. **Failure to Provide Meaningful Notice and Choice.** In policy pronouncements, the FTC has long made clear that notice should be provided to consumers where data is collected about them, and has backed that view up in several enforcement actions designed to ensure that consumer-facing companies have the information they need to give consumers meaningful notice and choice as to the tracking company's practices. For instance, in *In the Matter of Nomi Technologies, Inc.*, discussed above, the FTC brought an action against an in-store consumer tracking software company alleging that the company deceptively failed to provide consumers with meaningful choice regarding its tracking of consumers at client retail locations. A similar theme emerged in *InMobi*, where the FTC pointed not only to misrepresentations InMobi had made to consumers, but also to misrepresentations it had made to developers that integrated its software development kit (SDK) about how its location tracking worked.[79] As a result of these misrepresentations, the FTC reasoned, "[a]pplication developers could not provide accurate information to consumers regarding their applications' privacy practices" and consumers were deprived of the "ability to make informed decisions about their location privacy and to control the collection and use of their location information."
4. **Tracking Kids.** As discussed above, COPPA defines "personal information" to include cookies, device IDs, and other identifiers typically used in online tracking. The FTC has used its COPPA authority to go after both publishers of child-directed content and against tracking companies for showing kids targeted ads. For instance, in *Retro Dreamer* and *LAI Systems, LLC*, the FTC alleged that these developers of child-directed apps allowed interest-based ads to be served in their apps and allowed third-party advertising networks to collect personal

78. Complaint, Chitika, Inc., No. 1023087, F.T.C. C-4324 (June 17, 2011).
79. Complaint, U.S. v. InMobi Pte Ltd., No. 3:16-cv-3474 (N.D. Cal. June 22, 2016).

information in the form of persistent identifiers.[80] *InMobi* similarly faced COPPA allegations relating to its collection of personal information in the form of device identifiers and location information from applications whose developers had informed InMobi were directed to children. Most recently, the FTC brought an enforcement action against YouTube alleging that YouTube tracked users and showed interest-based ads on child-directed video content, resulting in a record $170 million fine to the FTC and New York Attorney General.

In addition to Section 5, display advertising that collects personal information from users online can trigger claims under other U.S. laws. For instance, the Video Privacy Protection Act, 18 U.S.C. § 2710, has been invoked to challenge sharing of device identifiers for advertising purposes when shared from video content.[81] The federal Electronic Communications Privacy Act and similar state wiretapping laws have also been invoked to bring claims against companies engaging in online advertising using novel or unexpected technologies, though to date such claims have been largely unsuccessful.

2. Regulation of Display Advertising in the E.U.

In the E.U., online advertising is regulated both under the GDPR, discussed above, and under a separate law known as the ePrivacy Directive (the "Directive").[82] The Directive regulates various forms of marketing, including email and phone-based marketing, and also the use of cookies and other technologies that rely on accessing user's "terminal equipment." The Directive generally requires the operators of websites where data will be collected to obtain consent before setting cookies unless the cookies are "strictly necessary" to provide the service. "Strictly necessary" is a high bar and typically limited to cookies used to make a service function (e.g., remember items in a shopper's cart, remember a website visitor's selected language, and facilitate quick and effective page loads). "Strictly necessary" does *not* include setting cookies for analytics purposes or for purposes of showing interest-based advertising.[83]

The "consent" required to set or access a user's terminal equipment (such as by setting or reading a cookie to power online advertising) is determined by reference to the GDPR definition of "consent." To meet this standard, consent must be "freely given, specific, informed and unambiguous" and provided by a "clear affirmative action, signifying agreement to processing of personal data." The European Data

---

80. Complaint, United States v. LAI Systems, LLC, No. 2:15-cv-9691 (C.D. Cal. Dec. 17, 2015); Complaint, United States v. Retro Dreamer, No. 5:15-cv-2569 (C.D. Cal. Dec. 17, 2015).

81. *See, e.g.*, Yershov v. Gannett Satellite Info. Network, Inc., 820 F.3d 482 (1st Cir. 2016); In re Nickelodeon Consumer Privacy Litig., 827 F.3d 262 (3d Cir. 2016); Eichenberger v. ESPN, Inc., 876 F.3d 979 (9th Cir. 2017).

82. Commission Directive 2002/58/EC.

83. It is worth noting that the ePrivacy Directive is undergoing review and will be replaced with the ePrivacy Regulation, which is likely to change which cookies require consent as well as what form that consent must take.

Protection Board, the European Commission's advisory body on data privacy, has stated that at least the following information is required for obtaining valid consent:

- The identity of each "data controller" (e.g., the entity providing the site and each company engaged in interest-based advertising or similar practices);
- The purpose of each of the processing operations for which consent is sought;
- What type of data will be collected and used;
- The existence of the right to withdraw consent; and
- Information about the use of the data for decisions based solely on automated processing, including profiling.

To meet these requirements, each website where data is collected for interest-based advertising or analytics purposes must surface a consent mechanism that obtains consent for the use of such cookies. At the time of writing, regulators across the E.U. are evaluating the precise form this consent should take for online advertising.

3. Self-Regulatory Rules Governing Online Advertising and Tracking

In the vacuum of specific rules governing online advertising and tracking, and in an effort to stave off legislation imposing specific requirements, industry self-regulatory groups have adopted rules governing the online advertising ecosystem. The Network Advertising Initiative's ("NAI") Code of Conduct is binding only on tracking companies that voluntarily agree to abide by NAI standards, but the Digital Advertising Alliance ("DAA") has adopted principles that it enforces (through the Council for Better Business Bureaus) on the entire online tracking ecosystem, including online tracking companies, publishers, and advertiser brands. These rules generally require that brands or other sites or online services that allow third parties (such as ad networks) to collect data for interest-based advertising on their properties disclose that collection, and that they provide a mechanism for individuals to opt out of the collection of information about their web browsing activity for advertising purposes, such as by linking to an industry opt-out page where participating member companies host an opt-out mechanism (typically either the NAI or DAA opt-out pages). Under these rules, brands themselves typically do not need to have an opt-out mechanism for these practices, but they do need to link to an opt-out mechanism provided by the third parties with which they partner.

The E.U. also has self-regulatory principles for interest-based advertising. These principles, which are based upon the Internet Advertising Bureau's OBA framework,[84] contain many of the same standards as U.S. interest-based advertising self-regulatory frameworks, but are largely defunct under the GDPR.

---

84. *See* Interactive Advertising Bureau, *IAB Europe Framework for Online Behavioural Advertising*, available at https://www.iabeurope.eu/policy/iab-europe-eu-framework-for-online-behavioural-advertising/.

Chapter 12

International Issues

Arthur Artinian and Catherine Adam
With contributions from Simon Casinader,
Serena Totino, Keisha Phippen, Jennifer Marsh,
Oliver Bates, and Niall Lavery

A. Initial Steps Before Going Beyond the United States of America

Although the initial focus of a fashion business will ordinarily be on its local market, with the increased globalization of supply chains and distribution networks, and the ability to scale internationally through digital channels and social media, it is likely that sooner, indeed very much sooner, rather than later, the business will likely become international. Although there are significant benefits from a global approach, there are a number of key legal issues that must be considered once the company starts doing business beyond the confines of one country. In particular, there are a number of legal risks that can arise and need to be mitigated, particularly with respect to intellectual property, contract law, consumer law, corporate citizenship, competition law, and potential counterfeits.

1. Trademarks—"First to File"

With respect to the protection of the trademark, a key issue outside the United States is countries such as China that operate a "first to file" trademark system (as opposed to a "first to use" trademark system). These countries create a significant risk of brand hijacking for companies looking to go offshore.

A "first to file" system means that the law does not recognize rights to a trademark unless it has been filed for registration at the local trademark office, regardless of how long the mark has been used prior in that country (or internationally). As a result, in countries like China there are sophisticated entities who seek to file trademarks before the legitimate brand owner has even thought about registering in the market. Such third-party registration can frustrate a brand's expansion into the lucrative markets and cause that brand headaches for years to come. In light of this it is prudent to consider immediately registering a foreign trademark as a Chinese trademark (irrespective of their plans to launch in the country) and to consider other first to file countries closely.[1]

Fashion Law in Practice: Case Study

It is not just start-up businesses that can be impacted by brand hijackers in first to file countries. In 2015, a Chinese Court found that multinational sports brand New Balance had infringed a Chinese trademark for 新百倫 pronounced "Xin Bai Lun." owned by a Chinese company. "Xin" means "New" in Chinese and "Bai Lun" is a phonetic translation of "Balance." The Chinese mark had been adopted by New Balance as its Chinese language brand. However, as the third-party Chinese company had registered the Xin Bai Lun mark first, under Chinese Law the Chinese company was seen as the true owner of the mark in China and New Balance was ordered to pay significant damages, publicly apologize and refrain from further use.

2. Disclosure of Designs

Another important issue that fashion businesses must consider is the risk of prior disclosure of a design invalidating design rights in other countries. For example, in the European Union ("E.U.")[2] it is vital that any E.U.-registered design application is filed within the 12 month priority period extending from any public disclosure of a design. If an international design right is invalidated (even as a result of actions before considering international expansion) it can severely hamper a business' ability to protect key IP rights in its products.

Fashion Law in Practice: Case Study

One brand to suffer invalidation of a design right due to international disclosure was Crocs. In 2016, the E.U. General Court found that where there is proof of prior disclosure anywhere in the world, the burden shifts to the rights holder to show that this could not reasonably have become known to the relevant circles in the European Union. As the facts before the General Court established that Crocs' well-known shoe design was disclosed on the rights holder's website, at a major nautical trade fair and through general sale in the United States, the Court found that Crocs was unable to establish that these could not reasonably have become known in the European Union more than 12 months prior to the filing. In particular, the website was accessible globally, the trade fair was a large, well-attended international event, and no evidence was presented to rebut the necessary presumption in relation to widespread sales in the United States.

1. Such as Argentina, Austria, Brazil, France, Germany, Greece, Japan, Russia, and the United Kingdom—to name but a few.

2. The countries in the European Union are: Austria, Belgium, Bulgaria, Croatia, Republic of Cyprus, Czech Republic, Denmark, Estonia, Finland, France, Germany, Greece, Hungary, Ireland, Italy, Latvia, Lithuania, Luxembourg, Malta, Netherlands, Poland, Portugal, Romania, Slovakia, Slovenia, Spain, and Sweden.

B. Protection of Intellectual Property Internationally

1. Trademark Protection

Trademarks, like most intellectual property rights, are jurisdiction-specific. As a result, any trademark will only be protected in the country/jurisdiction within which it is registered. As a result, there are a number of potential trademark-related risks with respect to expanding internationally.

a. Trademark Clearance Searches

Even if a business has a mature trademark portfolio in its home country, an important preliminary step will be to conduct international clearance searches (especially with respect to key branding elements like the brand name, logo, and any important taglines). Although businesses may not wish to incur the costs of filing trademark applications in many or all countries in which it plans to operate, trademark clearance searches across a wide range of countries will identify whether there are any high-level risks that trading (unregistered) will infringe third-party trademark rights. There can, however, be a number of challenges with trademark clearance searches, including:

1. **Costs**— The costs associated with global trademark clearance searches may make them prohibitively expensive for the business, even if the benefit to the business is evident. Ways in which the costs can be managed include limiting the countries to be searched to only key markets and/or focusing on "knock-out" searches that only identify red flag issues (and do not seek to address more complex legal arguments).
2. **Logos**— For logo marks the ability to search images on trademark registers internationally can be variable. Although some jurisdictions like the European Union and Australia have sophisticated image searching capabilities, a number of countries rely on key words for image searching (like the United States) or require complex searching methodologies (like Japan). Accordingly, the potential costs and difficulties of logo mark clearance searches will be greater than those for mere word marks.
3. **European Union and E.U. member states**—With the complex overlay of trademark rights that exist in the European Union (with E.U. trademarks covering all member states while each member state also maintains national trademark registers), there are a number of challenges in clearing the E.U. region. However, by focusing on key member states in the European Union that are of concern, it is possible to develop a searching methodology that provides the best expansion plan.

b. International Trademark Filings

Once the business has moved from "freedom to operate searches," it is likely that it will seek to file trademark applications for key brand elements in priority countries.

Filing in all countries around the world, much like with clearance searches, is likely to be prohibitively expensive. However, a comprehensive international trademark filing scheme can be developed that relies upon the following filing systems:

1. **Madrid Protocol**—International trademark applications filed through the Madrid Protocol filing scheme. The Madrid Protocol is a scheme administered by the World Intellectual Property Organization ("WIPO") that allows filings in multiple countries at the same time, and is streamlined through the local trademark offices. Not only does the Madrid Protocol filing scheme assist with cost management by removing the need for local legal representation (unless issues arise during prosecution), an international registration under the Madrid Protocol also makes future management of the portfolio more streamlined as renewals are handled centrally by WIPO. Members of the Madrid Protocol include the European Union, the United States, and a number of countries throughout Asia (such as China, Japan, and South Korea) and new members are added regularly, with Canada joining in June 2019;
2. **National trademarks**—National trademark applications filed directly by local representatives in circumstances where the country is not a member of the Madrid Protocol (such as the United Arab Emirates ("U.A.E.") and South Africa) or where for other strategy reasons it is advantageous to do so; and
3. **Convention priority**—Paris Convention priority, which allows international trademark applications (either national applications or under the Madrid Protocol trademark application) to be filed within six months of the first filing of the national application and retain the original filing date. As priority dates can be vital and there can be commercial advantages in spreading out the costs of an international trademark filing scheme, the convention priority period can be very valuable.

However, there are a number of potential legal challenges that might arise with an international trademark scheme, including:

1. **Local Law Differences**—In local trademark law (despite there being a general harmonization of processes), such as the subclass system operated by the Chinese National Intellectual Property Administration or countries where the term of protection is not the standard 10 years (such as Saudi Arabia where they are valid for nine years and eight months (10 Hijrah years) from the filing date);
2. **Terms**—The varying terms in which registered trademarks can be attacked for non-use (usually three or five years) and whether use needs to be established proactively (such as in the United States and Philippines) or whether it is reliant on a third party seeking the cancellation of the mark as a result of non-use (such as in the European Union);
3. **Expense**—The need in some countries for potentially expensive translation of documents or authentication or legalization of powers of attorney (such as with a number of Middle Eastern countries); and

4. **Translation**— Translation and transliteration issues with respect to the trademarks themselves (in order to take account of varying local languages and local cultural sensitivities).

c. Nontraditional Trademarks

In addition, recent years have seen an expansion of the international trademark offices around the world allowing parties to register nontraditional trademarks such as colors, shapes, sounds, smells, patterns, holograms, movements, three-dimensional signs, and combinations of the same. In particular, the Directive (E.U.) 2015/2436 of the European Parliament and of the Council of December 16, 2015, and Regulation (E.U.) 2017/1001 of the European Parliament and of the Council of June 14, 2017, on the European Union trademark led to members of the European Union largely adopting this broader definition of trademarks.

Fashion Law in Practice: Case Study

In the Louboutin case[3] on June 12, 2018, the Court of Justice of the European Union confirmed that Christian Louboutin's red outer sole can be a trademark. Of particular note from this decision is that:

a. A sign consisting of a color applied to the sole of a shoe does not consist exclusively of a "shape"; and

b. Nontraditional trademarks that are largely to be a combination of characteristics may face unique registrability concerns.

2. Design Protection

Intellectual property rights are often compared to a toolbox to have ready in case a company is called to defend rights against infringers, or the time has come to sell the business or obtain investments. Design protection can help provide evidence that the idea is innovative. The difficult part is protecting the new products from all possible angles in order to obtain a monopoly in the market for a certain period and make it difficult for other companies to imitate them.

Here is when design comes into play, as it can capture multiple features of a product. Under most non-U.S. legal systems, a design protects the appearance of a product, part of a product, or its ornamentation (including logos), as long as it is visible, new, and has individual character. The requirement of novelty is material in this context, as a design has to be different from what has already been made available to the public in order to be protected. In other words, disclosure is key.

a. Disclosure

In a digital world, the first question that comes to mind when considering disclosure is: *where* should (or should not) disclosure take place? The short answer

3. Louboutin Sas v. van Haren Schoenen BV (Case C-163/16).

is: worldwide. This rule has been recently tested by Crocs, which lost its design rights for its iconic clog sandals in the European Union due to the design having been shown in a U.S. boat show before the priority date.[4]

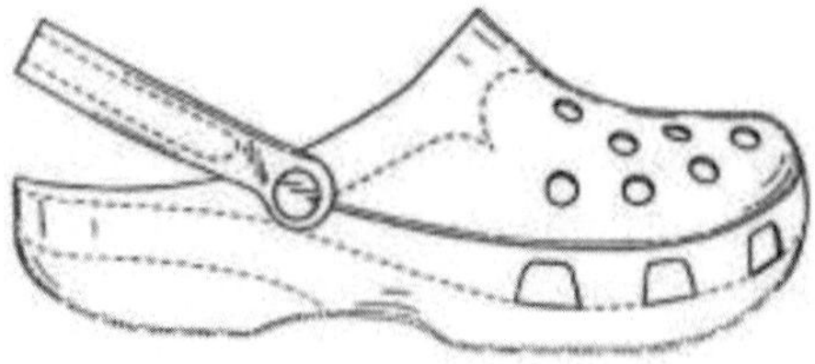

As with respect to trademarks in the United States, a priority date is the date when a design application is first filed anywhere in the world. In order for a design to be new in the market, no disclosure should have taken place more than 12 months before the date of filing (i.e., the priority date). This effectively provides a grace period that is a helpful tool for designers who have some time to test their products in the market before investing in a registration. If an application is filed after the 12-month grace period has passed, the design may be subject to invalidation.

b. Unregistered Design Protection in the European Union/United Kingdom

If this is the case, all is not lost. Designers can still claim unregistered rights in certain jurisdictions, such as the United Kingdom and the European Union. As the name suggests, unregistered rights arise automatically and generally last for a shorter period compared to registered rights (i.e., registered designs last for up to 25 years (depending on the jurisdiction within the E.U./U.K.), whereas unregistered designs have a duration of 10 or 15 years in the U.K. and three years in the E.U.). However, unregistered design rights only prevent commercial use of a design if copying can be proven and, with specific regard to the European Union, unregistered design rights only arise if disclosure takes place in the European Union. Therefore, if an infringer is able to prove that it was not aware of the existence of a prior design, no protection will be granted to unregistered designs.

Fashion Law in Practice: Case Study

One of the leading cases in the matter of unregistered designs is *Karen Millen Fashions Ltd. v. Dunnes Stores.* In this decision, the Court of Justice of the European Union ("CJEU") held that for an unregistered design to be valid in the European Union, individual character should have regard to a single earlier design, not to features of multiple prior designs, and that the rights holder will only have to indicate the elements of the design that give rise to individual character, not to provide evidence of individual character. As a result, it may be easier for designers to rely on unregistered rights in circumstances where the life of a design is expected to be short.

4. Gifi Diffusion v. EUIPO (Case T-424/16).

Nonetheless, rights holders should consider that design is one of the most cost-effective IP rights in many countries. For example, in the European Union, fees are fairly low and a registration certificate is normally issued by the European Union Intellectual Property Office ("EUIPO") in one to two days, as no substantial examination is conducted. However, despite their upfront benefits, designs are vulnerable to invalidation (i.e., when an examination is conducted in relation to all requirements, such as novelty, individual character, and a number of exclusions that do not fall within the scope of this brief introduction to design rights). In a nutshell, designs may be easy to obtain but difficult to enforce.

c. International Variations

As for all IP rights, there are a number of national peculiarities in design law, such as:

1. a limited number of countries recognize unregistered rights;
2. a grace period may not be available (this is the case in China) or may be shorter than 12 months (in Japan, the grace period is six months);
3. a substantive examination may be required and consequently it may take longer for a design to reach registration (like in the United States and Canada);
4. a formal examination may be requested by third parties (as provided by Australian law);
5. duration varies (e.g., 10 years in Canada, 15 years in Australia, 20 years in the United States); and
6. formalities may be required in certain jurisdictions (e.g., in the United States a declaration of inventorship is required).

d. Hague Convention

Technicalities at the global level may be difficult to handle and, for this reason, the international design system should be considered when applying for a design in multiple countries (i.e., the Hague Convention). An international design application can be filed with WIPO for up to 100 designs covering 88 countries. However, every country must be specifically designated, and different fees are due for each country (like in the Madrid system for international trademarks). Notable absences are China, most of South America, and the Middle East, as well as Australia. An international application allows the filing of a single application with a single office, simplifying formalities and language barriers. However, national law still applies as the design application will be forwarded by WIPO to the national IP offices that will follow their national practice.

In conclusion, when it comes to design law, pitfalls may not be avoided altogether, but setting an international strategy at the early stage may mitigate risks in the long term.

Fashion Law in Practice: International Design Strategy Checklist

√ Is the design new? Am I aware of prior art?

√ Do I have records of independent development (invalidation evidence)?

√ Where/when do I disclose the design? Is the European Union a key jurisdiction (novelty and grace period)?

√ Is it an iconic design or a one-season design (unregistered rights)?

√ In how many countries should I register the design (national versus international applications)?

√ Do I plan to register the design in Asia (grace period considerations)?

Fashion Law in Practice: Illustration

The fashion company X has designed a new iconic bag. In order to best protect its new product, X will prepare and keep a record of the design team's creative process, including dates of creations and prior art. Since X operates mainly in Asia, it decides to file in China before disclosing the design to the public. X presents its new iconic bag at the Milan fashion show, and in the next six months, X files a design application in Japan.

After 12 months from the disclosure in the European Union, X decides to file an international application with WIPO, designating key markets such as the United States, South Korea, Russia, and Singapore. However, since the bag did not sell well in the European Union, X decides to rely on unregistered rights in the European Union, as the bag will not be sold in the European Union for more than three years.

C. Ownership of Employment-Generated Intellectual Property

1. Not "At Will" Employment

"At will" employment is unique to the United States. Generally, countries around the world have very stringent rules relating to the protection, treatment, and termination of employees. Employment law is more formal and structured than it is in the United States and written contracts usually detail the conditions under which an employee's contract can be terminated. Employers are not permitted to terminate an employee's contract for any reason or without notice and there is often a requirement for notice and a need to show cause.

2. Employee- and Employer-Owned Intellectual Property

As a general rule, employers own intellectual property that is created by their employees during the course of the employees' employment. However, this is contingent on the execution of a written agreement (this could be by way of a provision in the contract of employment), whereby the employee specifically assigns to the employer any and all intellectual property created by the employee "during the course of employment." Ideally, such written agreement should be executed prior to the commencement of the employment relationship.

As the question of whether intellectual property was created "during the course of employment" is key, it is also important to clearly define the scope of the employee's engagement and the terms of their employment in their contract of employment to avoid any potential dispute concerning whether a work was created "during the course of employment" or not.

3. Independent Contractors and Agencies

As an independent contractor/agency is an independent party, unless otherwise agreed, as in the United States, all intellectual property created by the contractor/agency will be owned by them.

Therefore, it is important to ensure that an appropriate consultancy agreement is entered into with the contractor/agency. The agreement should include the terms of the engagement and a provision like the work-for-hire provision in the United States that expressly states that intellectual property in the deliverables and the services will transfer to the company immediately upon creation.

4. Importance of Written Assignments, Formalities

In many countries, assignments of intellectual property must be in writing to be enforceable. A written assignment also establishes a clear chain of transfer.

It is advisable to register an assignment of intellectual property rights with the appropriate authority. For example, an assignment of a U.K. registered trademark should be registered with the U.K. Intellectual Property Office using Form TM16 (application to record a change of ownership).

D. Anticounterfeiting

1. Customs Programs

One of the primary ways a brand owner can seek to fight counterfeiting (particularly by sophisticated entities) is to set up international customs programs with the customs agency in key countries. Although the process for arranging such programs may differ from country to country, as a general rule, registered trademarks, designs, and/or copyright works can be recorded with the authority—putting them on notice of the rights owned by the brand. As a part of the usual inspection of imported (and possibly exported goods), customs offices will inspect goods for those that may infringe the rights. The customs office then has the ability to seize any products that feature infringing trademarks, designs or copyright works and that are not genuine; there is usually a process by which the brand owner is notified and can take further action.

2. Legal Reforms

For many years, China was seen as the primary source of counterfeit goods; however, recent reforms have changed this. In particular, under China's new e-commerce Law that came in to force on January 1, 2019, e-commerce market operators are obliged to take necessary measures to deter alleged IP infringements so long as the IP owner provides *prima facie* evidence of the infringement.

In addition, the issue of Original Equipment Manufacturing ("OEM")[5] in China is of crucial importance to retailers with the prominence of brand hijacking in China. Even for businesses that do not trade in China, it is very likely that most businesses will source products from Chinese manufacturers. Fortunately for brand owners, Chinese Courts have recognized an OEM exemption where, if goods are manufactured in China exclusively for export, even if a third party owns a Chinese trademark for the brand, the use of the mark on the goods will not be infringing if the brand owner owns the trademark where the goods are to be exported to (and other conditions are met).

3. E-Commerce Anticounterfeiting Programs

Most large e-commerce retailers, including Amazon, eBay, and Ali Express operate their own brand protection systems, such as eBay's VeRO program and Ali Express's IP Protection Platform. These self-governed brand protection systems are usually a quick and efficient way of having listings promoting the sale of infringing products removed from sale (without the need to incur significant legal costs). If a brand owner can establish that legal rights owned by it are being infringed (such as by providing proof of a trademark registration featured in the listing), the e-commerce retailer will be prepared to remove the listing. However, due to the large number of potential online sales of counterfeit goods across many different platforms, the management of this process can be prohibitively expensive for rights owners. Accordingly, there are now third-party service providers that offer monitoring and removal services at competitive rates.

---

5. OEM is a form of outsourced-manufacturing. An OEM company is responsible for designing and building a product according to the requirements of other companies who will trade the products under their own branding.

E. Contracts

Unsurprisingly, contract structures and drafting styles tend to vary from jurisdiction to jurisdiction. Whereas a specific drafting style has developed in the United States (by custom and through the requirements of laws and regulations), the same is true for other countries, and much will often be influenced by the underlying legal system, especially common law versus civil law. Agreements in civil law jurisdictions will frequently make reference to provisions stipulated by their civil codes (e.g., the Bürgerliches Gesetzbuch in Germany and the Code Civil in France), while the same may not be true of common law jurisdictions—although, as noted below, terms can be implied in contracts governed by common law also.

Below are some key considerations relating to contracts outside of the United States.

1. Governing Law and Jurisdiction

When expanding beyond the United States, a company may wish to use existing template agreements already used in the United States and, as a general rule, this is not a bad starting point. What the business will need to consider is what governing law it wishes to use outside of the United States and expressly stipulate this in the agreement, as well as making any other changes necessary to comply with the chosen governing law. Effectively, the governing law clause enables the parties to agree to specify the system of law that will apply to the interpretation of an agreement and its effect if a dispute arises. It identifies the substantive law that will be applied when determining and interpreting the rights and obligations of the parties and any disputes that may arise. A governing law clause does not, however, indicate how disputes are to be resolved; for example, through the courts or arbitration, and this is why a jurisdiction clause typically supplements (or is included in) the governing law clause specifying which court or courts are to hear a dispute (or alternatively, whether arbitration or mediation applies).

Choice of governing law and jurisdiction can be influenced by a number of factors, such as the location of the parties, where the contract/services are going to be fulfilled/provided, a desire to select a more neutral and/or stable jurisdiction, procedure for litigation, cost of litigation, and the ability to enforce a judgment. A key point to take away is that contracts should contain governing law and jurisdiction clauses to establish certainty over which law will govern:

1. the contractual rights and obligations irrespective of the place where a dispute is determined (the governing law element)
2. the place where future disputes between the parties will be litigated (the jurisdiction element). This is particularly important in cross-border transactions where several legal systems may be relevant to the contract (e.g., location of the parties and location of performance).

In addition, contracts may give rise to noncontractual rights and obligations such as tortious claims like negligence and misrepresentation, unjust enrichment, and restitution. Although some jurisdictions automatically extend governing law and jurisdiction clauses to contractual and noncontractual obligations (e.g., Brazil, Russia, and Japan) this is not always the case and, consequently, governing law and jurisdiction clauses should always expressly extend to noncontractual obligations that arise out of or in connection with the agreement to ensure consistency.

In commercial contracts it will often be helpful to have arbitration as a dispute resolution mechanism rather than in the courts of a foreign country. Arbitration is often considered a more efficient, predictable, and manageable forum for dispute resolution. Importantly, it can also mean that disputes are resolved confidentially without reported decisions being made public.

2. Choice of Court and Enforcement of Judgments

As mentioned above, the clause that specifies where any litigation will be fought is known as a jurisdiction clause (also known as a choice of court agreement or forum selection clause). This is an important consideration not only for convenience and cost reasons, but also for prospects of success and, perhaps most significantly, for the ability to enforce any judgment obtained against the counterparty.

3. Location of Counterparty

Perhaps the most significant consideration is the location of the counterparty, or, rather, the location of the counterparty's assets. Very often it will be preferable to sue the counterparty in the jurisdiction in which it or its assets are located. If a forum that is different from the location of the counterparty is selected, the two primary considerations a business will have will be service of proceedings and enforcement of the judgment.

4. Service

Some jurisdictions have particular requirements for service where the party to be served is based outside the jurisdiction of the relevant court. In some cases an exclusive jurisdiction clause in favor of that jurisdiction will be sufficient to avoid lengthy and complex service procedure, but it depends on the countries involved. To get around this problem, it is advisable to insist that the counterparty maintain an agent for service within the jurisdiction of the relevant court, and that this is recorded in the contract in a process agent clause. Such clauses are frequently resisted because of the ongoing cost involved.

Where it is required to serve proceedings in a different country, this may be covered by an international treaty or convention that will require it to serve in a particular way. The United States, along with many other countries, is a signatory to the

1965 Hague Service Convention. Between parties based in some signatory nations, service is quick and straightforward; between others it is longer and more complex. When serving directly in another jurisdiction, it is always necessary to take local advice as service will need to comply with local procedural law.

5. Enforcing Judgments in Other Jurisdictions

It is important to consider the cross-border enforceability of any judgment the company obtains. Some countries have reciprocal enforcement treaties with others, meaning that it is straightforward to enforce judgments made in one country, in the other. Currently there is free movement of judgments between countries in the European Union. The United States does not currently have any reciprocal enforcement treaties with other countries in respect of court judgments. Enforcement of a U.S. judgment in the U.K., for instance, requires the issue of fresh proceedings as an action on the judgment.

6. Who Will Sue Whom?

Another consideration is whether it is more likely that the business, or the counterparty, will sue under the contract. It is not always possible to make a judgment as to which party to a dispute it is likely to be. If the business considers that it is more likely to be the defendant, it may wish to specify the home court as the court with jurisdiction for its own cost and convenience (and the increased cost and inconvenience of the counterparty).

7. Home Advantage

In some jurisdictions, there is a perceived "home advantage" for individuals from or companies incorporated in that jurisdiction. That is commonly believed to be the case in the United States, China, Italy, and Japan to name but a few, particularly if the dispute is likely to be tried before a jury. It is not the case in other jurisdictions, such as the United Kingdom.

8. Subject Matter of Dispute

It is important to consider the likely subject matter of a dispute. Some court systems are more effective at dealing with certain types of disputes. For example, the Business and Property Courts of England and Wales in London have a global reputation for dealing effectively with complex and high-value commercial disputes, and they have separate lists for different types of disputes with specialist judges.[6]

6. The lists for the different types of dispute include the: Business list, Intellectual Property List, Financial list, Insolvency list and Companies List among others.

There are other jurisdictions that also have strong reputations for certain types of disputes.

9. Remedies

Another consideration is the remedy sought by the plaintiff. While most jurisdictions are good options for money claims, some are more amenable than others to awarding specific performance of a contractual obligation. Similarly, if a company thinks that it may need to seek emergency interim relief, such as an injunction to do or stop doing something, it is important to ensure that that such interim relief is available from the courts of the jurisdiction such a company selects.

10. Costs

An additional consideration is who pays the costs of any dispute. All jurisdictions have different rules on cost recovery. In some jurisdictions, such as the U.K., the general rule is that the losing party pays the costs of the winning party. In others, such as the United States, generally speaking, the winning party does not recover its costs (although there are exceptions in some states). This is a factor to be considered in the risk analysis of selecting a particular venue.

11. Types of Jurisdiction Clause

Jurisdiction clauses can be exclusive, nonexclusive, hybrid, or carve-out. Exclusive clauses appoint a single court to resolve all disputes between the parties. Nonexclusive parties appoint a court but do not prohibit the issue of proceedings in a different court with jurisdiction by either party. Hybrid clauses (also known as one-sided, asymmetrical, or sole option clauses) require one party to issue proceedings in a particular jurisdiction, but permit the other to issue proceedings in any other court with jurisdiction. Therefore, a fashion business based in the United States may require any proceedings issued by the counterparty to be issued in a particular U.S. state, but permit proceedings issued against the counterparty to be issued elsewhere. This approach can enable a party to have the best of both worlds; however, these clauses are not enforceable in all jurisdictions and thus if such a clause is to be used, its enforceability in the jurisdictions relevant to the contract should be confirmed beforehand. Carve-out clauses can be used to carve-out from the agreement disputes in relation to a particular subject matter, for example IP disputes, so that they can be dealt with differently.

12. Terms

Once the governing law and jurisdiction of an agreement have been selected, the business must ensure that the contract terms it is seeking to be bound by are compliant with applicable law. If using an existing agreement drafted under a different governing law, it should be reviewed by local counsel and revised as necessary for compliance. In addition, the business should be mindful that many jurisdictions may imply terms into the agreement and it should make inquiries in that respect to have a full picture of what the business will be bound by.

13. Express and Implied Terms

A contract will consist of the express terms agreed between the parties (and expressed accordingly) and terms that are implied in the contract by the law applicable to the contract. An understanding of the terms that may be implied into a contract, how they interact with the contract's express terms, and when the implied terms may be excluded are important:

1. when drafting a contract, to assess and shape the parties' obligations.
2. when a dispute arises in connection with a contract and a party needs to assess whether a court will imply a term incorporating it into the contract.

14. Contracting Out/Excluding Terms

Once implied terms have been identified, the business may wish to expressly contract out of or limit these, such that the actual express contract provides the entire system governing the obligations. Unfortunately, in many instances it will not be possible to expressly exclude implied terms as they serve to provide minimum standards even in business-to-business contracts. Set out below are a few examples of different positions relating to implied terms:

1. Under the Council Directive 86/653/EEC of December 18, 1986, on the coordination of the laws of the Member States relating to self-employed commercial agents (broadly known as the "Commercial Agents Directive"), it is not possible for the parties to a commercial agency agreement to contract out of or reduce the compensation or indemnity payment requirements on termination of the agreement.
2. The Contracts (Rights of Third Parties) Act 1990 in the U.K. allows third parties (i.e., someone other than a signatory) to enforce terms of a contract in their own right (e.g., the purchaser of a building to be used as a retail shop may be given rights to enforce terms in the contracts between the seller and the professional consultants who designed the building). This implied term is something that can be contracted out of.
3. Although not strictly an implied term, it should be noted that in the U.K. the Unfair Contract Terms Act 1977 ("UCTA") legislates limitation clauses in business-to-business contracts and provides that the following types of liability can neither be excluded nor limited: (i) fraud (dishonesty) by a contracting party; (ii) injury or death caused by lack of reasonable care; and (iii) supplying goods without the right to do so. As a result, you will frequently

find express clauses in contracts governed by English law that specify liability in this instance is neither limited nor excluded; were a clause to attempt such exclusion or limitation it would be void.

F. E-Commerce and Consumer Law

E-commerce has opened the global market to even the smallest fashion brands. However, with these opportunities come the risks associated with the fact that they are accessible worldwide, which could give rise to the following legal risks and considerations.

1. Website Requirements (Non-Transactional)

A fashion retailer's website should contain provisions about access to/use of the retailer's website, information about the website owner, disclaimers for material published on the website or linked to/ from it, rules about how such materials may be used, and warnings about unacceptable user behavior (such as hacking, introducing viruses, and uploading illegal or defamatory content).

2. Distance Selling Requirements (Transactional Website)

Consumer protection regulations apply to all consumer sales made online.

In almost every country in the world there are consumer laws and regulations that apply to sales of goods or services to consumers without face-to-face contact. Typically, under these regimes, such as the *Consumer Contracts (Information, Cancellation and Additional Charges) Regulations 2013*, a customer must:

1. be given specified information before a sale is made;
2. confirm prior to acceptance certain information in a durable form (for example, in writing or email);
3. have a right to cancel their order;
4. have their contractual obligations fulfilled within a set period (e.g., 30 days) unless otherwise agreed; and
5. be given a full refund for a certain period after receiving their goods, if they change their mind (subject to some exceptions, including goods made to a customer's specification (but not standard upgrades or variations), perishable goods, and newspapers and magazines).

Furthermore, there are likely to be requirements that all goods must be as described, fit for purpose for which they were intended, and of satisfactory quality. If goods are found to be faulty, a retailer will likely be required to give a full refund up to a set period after the item was purchased. If goods prove faulty and they cannot be repaired or replaced, consumers are also entitled to receive a full refund in most cases.

Additionally, there are usually legal regimes in place that require a party advertising or selling (online or in person), to provide information such as:

1. its business name, geographical address, and contact details;
2. details of trade organizations or professional bodies it belongs to;
3. information on any authorization scheme (for example, for financial services);
4. its Value Added Tax ("VAT") or other official number; and
5. its prices, and whether it includes taxes and delivery costs.

Consumers in both European Union and non-European Union countries may be protected by their own mandatory consumer laws, which may apply irrespective of the choice of governing law in the contract.

3. Canceling "Online" Orders

In the European Union, consumers have the right to return purchases (for any reason) where the purchase was made online or through other types of distance selling, such as by phone, mail order, or from a door-to-door salesperson, within 14 days after the date of receiving the goods for a full refund.

This 14-day cooling-off period does not apply to all purchases (some of the exemptions include plane and train tickets, concert tickets, hotel bookings, car rental reservations and catering services for specific dates, goods made to order or clearly personalized (such as a tailor-made suit), and online digital content, if the consumer has already started downloading or streaming the content).

If goods are purchased in a shop, there is no E.U. legal right to return the goods (for exchange or refund) unless the item is faulty. However, many shops voluntarily allow customers to return or exchange goods during a certain period, provided that they have the receipt.

4. Localization for Sales into Overseas Countries

There are occasions when a brand wishes to target their products and services at multiple markets at once, which can bring an inherent challenge.

Localization is the process of adapting a product or service from one specific locale or market to meet the requirements of another specific locale or market. When localizing it is important to consider different cultural values.

For example: in 2013 and 2014, Coca Cola launched its "Share a Coke" campaign, in which the label of the bottles was replaced by a simple phrase: "Share a Coke with John." On each Coca Cola label, there was a different name, which connected with people directly. In Ireland, for example, Irish names were used on the bottles (such as Aoife and Oisín).

Similarly, in China, culturally it is not considered to be respectful to address a person by their first name and therefore, instead of names, Coca Cola used terms such as "close friend," and "classmate."

5. General Data Protection Regulation (GDPR)

A retailer must take the security and privacy of its consumers seriously. Privacy and data protection laws and regulations vary by jurisdiction.

The General Data Protection Regulation ("GDPR"), for example, sets strict rules for protecting the personal data of E.U. citizens. It gives individuals greater control over their data and sets out a number of additional safeguards that organizations need to follow when processing consumer data. It applies to all forms of data processing, including in the context of marketing, employment, information security, and customer service. The processing, transmitting, and storing of consumer data is central to a retail transaction, and therefore any organization selling to an E.U. citizen will need to take steps to ensure they are in compliance with the GDPR.

Please refer to Chapter 11 for more specific information about the GDPR.

G. Promoting and Marketing Your Brand

1. Regulation of Marketing

Marketing is regulated to protect consumers from misleading advertisements and to ensure that trading is fair.

There are differences between jurisdictions in respect of the regulation of marketing, but in the U.K., for example, there are regulations that restrict what advertisers can and cannot do and two advertising codes of practice to help retailers to advertise legally:

- *The Consumer Protection from Unfair Trading Regulations* prevent retailers from misleading or harassing consumers.
- *The CAP non-broadcast code* covers non-broadcast advertising (for example: print, online), sales promotion, and direct marketing (such as telesales and email). The *CAP broadcast code* covers issues that include taste, decency, and product placement, and describes how businesses should advertise.

Failure to comply with marketing regulations could result in:

1. Bad publicity, loss of reputation, and brand damage;
2. Referral to regulators and action taken by any such bodies, including censure, fines, legal action, and criminal prosecution;

3. Legal action by consumers or competitors;
4. Costly recall and reprinting of direct marketing material;
5. Product recalls; and
6. Disappointed consumers and loss of consumer confidence.

2. Localized Accounts and Operation on Social Media

Having a "one size fits all" social media strategy will not be sufficient and it is important to consider how different target audiences may use social media and what they use it for.

Successful brands adapt their social media strategy for their global markets and understand how to localize their social media content for their target market by carrying out market research and by gaining an understanding into their target market. For example:

- Facebook boasts a global usage penetration of 22.9 percent and India takes first place for the highest volume of Facebook users at 250 million users.
- Russians use a platform that looks and works similarly to Facebook called "VKontakte," which has more than 46.6 million monthly users.
- In China, there are 900 million users of WeChat. This network allows companies and celebrities to create accounts for promotional purposes.
- Research suggests that consumers are more likely to buy a product if it is marketed in their native language.

3. Regulation of Influencers

Influencers commonly make improper and unclear disclosures and/or fail to refer to the paid nature of a post.

The U.K.'s Competition and Markets Authority recently launched an investigation into improper disclosure of sponsored influencer content, in an attempt to regulate influencers. The U.K.'s advertising regulator, the Advertising Standards Authority, already has rules in place for paid influencer content.

In France, the advertising self-discipline organization, Autorité de Régulation Professionnelle de la Publicité ("ARPP"), has produced guidance on how influencers should conduct their digital advertising.

The Istituto dell'Autodisciplina Pubblicitaria ("IAP"), a non-profit Italian organization, has developed a self-regulatory framework to outline the "best practice" for influencer content. Although voluntary in nature, the IAP's framework is widely recognized as an authoritative source, including by the Italian Supreme Court.

In the United States, the Federal Trade Commission has established guidelines for influencer content paid for by brands.

The Audited Media Association of Australia has started working on better guidelines around influencer marketing campaigns.

Platforms like Instagram and YouTube have also offered their own solutions to the issue, by launching "paid tags," which are to be used in conjunction with sponsored posts.

Ultimately, an agreed-upon list of influencer regulations and rules that crosses borders and spans platforms would be the most useful means to limiting or preventing improper disclosures by influencers, but, for the time being, there are different rules in different countries and various solutions offered by a variety of platforms.

H. Corporate Citizenship

Be it as a result of legislation or consumer pressure, there has never before been such a big emphasis on the need for companies to be good "corporate citizens." In the face of global environmental concerns, sustainability pressures, growing desires and requirements for transparent and ethical supply chains, companies—and in many respects fashion companies in particular—need to be at the forefront of these issues. Many fashion houses are taking proactive stances when it comes to the materials they use in producing their clothing (e.g., banning furs and exotic leathers) but corporate citizenship goes beyond that and, when expanding internationally, a business must ensure it addresses the modern slavery and anti-bribery requirements that are increasingly being imposed on companies throughout the world.

1. Modern Slavery and Ethical Supply Chain Regulations

There is mounting pressure on companies to eradicate modern slavery and forced labor from their supply chains. Laws are being passed across the globe (e.g., Modern Slavery Act 2018 in Australia, "La loi relative au devoir de vigilance des sociétés mères et des entreprises donneuses d'ordre" adopted in France in 2017, and the Modern Slavery Act 2015 in the U.K.) and consumers and other stakeholders (investors, lenders, and governments alike) are also exercising sustained pressure. This, combined with the presence of many organizations that monitor and rate countries and companies on their supply chains, and the presence of modern slavery (e.g., Walk Free Foundation Global Slavery Index) means that, even when staying domestic, companies (and in particular fashion companies) must take steps to ensure their supply chains are free from modern slavery and that they comply with applicable modern slavery and ethical supply chain laws and regulations.

What should a business be thinking about when going international? When expanding the supply chain, due diligence will be required not only to ensure compliance with applicable laws, but also to ensure that internal governance standards are complied with and the client base is not inadvertently alienated by the inclusion of supply chain elements that do not align with their expectations of the brand.

In the same way that commercial and quality control considerations influence the choice of supply chain partners, so should concerns for modern slavery and other ethical elements. Vendors must agree in writing to comply with ethical policies—including those related to manufacturing, employment, discrimination, health and safety, and transparency; and the fashion company should have the right to audit and inspect factories and housing provided for workers (including interviewing both management and employees) and penalize vendors for lack of compliance.

Fashion Law in Practice: Case Study

U.K.—The Modern Slavery Act 2015 (the "Act")

On October 29, 2015, the Act came into force requiring companies that: (i) have a turnover or combined group turnover of £36m or more; and (ii) carry on business within the U.K. or are incorporated in the U.K., to publish a modern slavery statement annually, for the financial years ending on or after March 31, 2016.

The key purpose of the Act is to increase the transparency of companies' supply chains and structures to reduce human trafficking and slavery. The modern slavery statement is required to be approved by the company's board, signed by a director of the company and displayed on the company's homepage.

The Home Office has, in addition, published accompanying Guidance[7] (the "Guidance") which was most recently updated on October 22, 2018, providing information to companies on the content of the modern slavery statement and the processes for approving and publishing the statement. The Guidance confirms that it is up to companies how to present the information contained in the statement, as long as it is covers the appropriate points, provides appropriate links to relevant publications, documents, or policies for the company and is in simple language that is easily understood. Information that should be covered in the statement includes information about:

(a) the organization's structure, its business, and its supply chains;

(b) its policies in relation to slavery and human trafficking;

(c) its due diligence processes in relation to slavery and human trafficking in its business and supply chains;

(d) the parts of its business and supply chains where there is a risk of slavery and human trafficking taking place, and the steps it has taken to assess and manage that risk;

7. *Transparency in Supply Chains etc. A Practical Guide*. The Home Office.

(e) its effectiveness in ensuring that slavery and human trafficking is not taking place in its business or supply chains, measured against such performance indicators it considers appropriate; and

(f) the training about slavery and human trafficking available to its staff.

2. Anti-Bribery and Corruption Regulation

In 1977 the United States introduced the Foreign Corrupt Practices Act ("FCPA") and Europe followed suit with analogous legislation including the United Kingdom's 2010 Bribery Act and France's 2016 Sapin II Act. In China the 1980 Criminal Law of the People's Republic of China criminalized the offenses of bribery and corruption. The FCPA prohibits U.S. citizens and permanent residents, both public and private U.S. companies, and certain non-U.S. individuals and entities from bribing foreign government officials to obtain a business advantage. The Bribery Act criminalizes both the receipt and payment of bribes.

Like the FCPA, the Bribery Act and many other anti-bribery laws across Europe have extraterritorial application. It is important for companies to have policies and procedures in place to comply with the anti-bribery laws to which they are subject. It is likely that many U.S. companies will have anti-bribery policies and procedures in place prior to conducting business internationally in light of the FCPA and it is advisable to have these reviewed in light of the territories the company is seeking to do business in and/or with amending and/or supplementing them as necessary. Once relevant anti-bribery and corruption requirements are identified, depending on any unusual attributes a specific law might have (e.g., it may want to earmark any particularly onerous requirements to the specific legislating country), a practical way forward is likely to be applying a "highest common factor" approach, meaning that a unified policy and procedure is adopted to ensure compliance across a number of jurisdictions.

By way of example, when considering a unified approach, France, Germany, Italy, Spain, the Netherlands, and United Kingdom all have a similar definition for what constitutes a bribe (i.e., a benefit, of something of value that is given to someone to affect their behavior for the benefit of the offender or someone he represents) and broadly criminalize the bribery of public officials (or their acceptance of bribes) at home or abroad. Private sector bribery is, however, dealt with somewhat differently across those countries, with France and the U.K. (for example) not distinguishing between public and private sector bribes. Therefore, in this scenario, it may choose to adopt policies that require the counterparts to comply with requirements extending to the private sector or it may wish to have different policies to avoid imposing potentially unrealistic requirements on certain jurisdictions.

Noncompliance with anti-bribery and corruption laws is a criminal offense that may result in imprisonment, typically accompanied by (sometimes unlimited) fines. Other consequences may include infringing companies being banned from public contracting (Germany, Italy, Spain, and the U.K.), withdrawal of licenses

(Germany and Italy) and court supervision (France and Italy). It is therefore crucial that anti-bribery and corruption compliance and procedures are a key consideration in international expansion.

I. Distribution and Licensing

1. Introduction to Distribution in the European Economic Area

Once a fashion business has incorporated a company in the European Economic Area ("EEA"),[8] secured and registered its E.U. intellectual property rights, and established its manufacturing operations, the next step, and arguably the most crucial, is to consider how it is going to sell its products in the EEA market. Also known as a go-to-market strategy, any brand owner—including those in the fashion industry—must decide how to sell its products to consumers, taking into account a multitude of considerations including cost, complexity, the level of control over the sale of the products, brand protection, and the legal constraints and challenges posed by E.U. law and the inviolability of the E.U. single market.

There are three main ways in which a brand owner can market its products within the EEA. These options are not exclusive to one another and a combination of these models can be used. While there are different options and nuances within each method of distribution, in short, they are as follows:

1. **Direct to consumer**— a brand owner may choose to sell its products directly to consumers, either through its own brick-and-mortar stores or through its e-commerce offering. In choosing to sell the products itself, a brand owner will retain direct control over the way they are branded and their price in the market. However, this option requires the brand owner to have its own retail network, which is usually costly, opens the brand owner up to greater liability to consumers, and is generally administratively burdensome. There are various consumer law issues that arise when a brand owner sells its products directly, which are addressed in Chapter 9.

2. **Using agents**— where a brand owner does not have its own retail operations in certain jurisdictions (or indeed at all), the brand owner may elect to sell its products through a third-party agent. Under E.U. law, an agent would serve as an extension of the brand owner. This permits the brand owner to exercise the same level of control as option 1 above, but often with the administrative burden taken on by the agent in return for a fee. However, as with option 1, using an agent is often costly. The brand owner will also generally have the same liability as if it sold directly to consumers, assuming liability for the agent's actions. Difficulties can also arise when terminating an agency relationship. The use of agency as a method of distribution is addressed later in this chapter.

---

8. The EEA consists of the European Union, Iceland, Liechtenstein, Norway, and Switzerland.

3. **Distribution networks**—A brand owner may wish to use various independent, third-party wholesale distributors and retailers to place its products on the European market. While this method is often the cheapest and least arduous option for brand owners, it also provides them with the lowest level of control over how their products are commercialized. While there are various strategies that can be utilized to retain some influence, there are a number of legal pitfalls that a brand owner must be aware of in this context to ensure compliance with E.U. law and avoid substantial fines from the European Commission or national competition regulators. This is explored in greater detail below.

If a brand owner chooses to sell its products in the European Union through a network of wholesale distributors and resellers, there are a number of key E.U. legal principles that will apply. Article 101 of the Treaty on the Functioning of the European Union ("TFEU") governs agreements between undertakings, such as a brand owner and its distributors, and prohibits any agreements that may affect trade between E.U. Member States that have as their object or effect the prevention, restriction, or distortion of competition within the E.U. single market. Under Article 101 TFEU, there are three key prohibited practices that all brand owners, including those in the fashion industry, should avoid:

(i) dictating the price at which its products are to be sold by a distributor and/or reseller, also known as resale price maintenance ("RPM"),

(ii) dictating where a distributor and/or reseller may sell its products within the EEA and by what channel, or

(iii) dictating to whom a distributor and/or reseller may sell its products.

Brand owners that are found to be engaged in unlawful, anticompetitive conduct, such as that outlined above, can face fines of up to 10 percent of their group worldwide turnover from competition regulators and private damages actions. In addition, employees and/or directors of the brand owner may face criminal charges for their involvement in such conduct.

2. Resale Price Maintenance

Unlike in the United States, where brand owners can impose unilateral pricing policies that set the minimum price at which a reseller and/or distributor may sell its products, such practices in the European Union are generally considered straightforward breaches of E.U. competition law—i.e., a restriction of competition. While brand owners may set recommended resale prices as a guide for retailers as to what level to price the products, this should only be a recommendation. If a brand owner fixes or sets a minimum price at which a reseller must sell its product or acts in a way that has an equivalent effect, it will in all but the most exceptional circumstances have breached E.U. competition law and be subject to substantial fines from either the European Commission or national competition regulators. For example, in December 2018 the European Commission fined GUESS €40 million (reduced from €80 million for cooperating with the investigation) for, among other offenses, dictating the prices at which its products must be sold by retailers. Four electronics brand owners were also fined a total of €111 million for RPM practices.

3. Territorial Restrictions

Other than in the context of certain exclusive distribution arrangements (explored in greater detail below), imposing territorial restrictions on sales within the EEA by resellers and/or wholesale distributors is a prohibited practice under Article 101 TFEU. In other words, a brand owner cannot prevent a reseller based in one EEA state—for instance, Germany—selling to a consumer or another distributor situated in another EEA state—for instance, France. Territorial restrictions are deemed to be by object restriction of competition and a brand owner found to be imposing such restraints of trade will be subject to enforcement action from regulators and substantial fines. Following on from the example above, in the same case GUESS was also found to have unlawfully imposed territorial restrictions. However, while territorial restrictions within the EEA are generally prohibited, brand owners are permitted to prevent resellers from making sales across the EEA border—i.e., from outside the EEA or vice versa.

When Territorial Restrictions Are Permissible—The Safe Harbor of the Vertical Block Exemption Regulation and Exclusive Distribution Arrangements

While a brand owner restricting where a reseller and/or distributor can sell products within the EEA is generally prohibited, such restrictions can be permissible under the safe harbor of the Vertical Block Exemption Regulation ("VBER"),[9] E.U.-wide legislation that identifies certain vertical agreements (for example, between brand owner and its distributors) that are automatically considered lawful under E.U. law. In order to take advantage of the safe harbor of VBER, the brand owner and distributor must each have a market share of 30 percent or less.[10] If the brand owner's market share is more than 30 percent, such restrictions will not benefit from the safe harbor of VBER and will need to be individually assessed.

Where a brand owner's market share comes under this threshold and VBER applies, it may prevent its resellers and/or distributors from making active sales into a territory (for instance, a Member State or even an area within a Member State) that it has exclusively allocated to another reseller or distributor, or that it has exclusively reserved to itself. An important point to note is that a brand owner may only restrict active sales in these circumstances and not passive sales—i.e., a brand owner may prohibit a reseller from actively marketing and seeking sales in a territory exclusively allocated to another but may not prevent them from

9. Regulation 330/2010.
10. Article 3(1).

making unsolicited sales to a customer situated in that same territory. Any attempt to restrict passive, unsolicited sales from one territory to another within the EEA would constitute a hardcore restriction, and likely be considered unlawful, by object restriction of competition.

4. Online Sales Restrictions

The importance of online selling has been stressed by the European Commission in its Vertical Guidelines[11] and online sales bans have been the subject of investigations by a number of national regulators across the European Union. The French and German competition authorities have investigated and fined Pierre Fabre, Stihl, and Kerr-Optika[12] for imposing online sales bans that were found not to pursue legitimate aims. Online sales are considered as a form of passive selling and as such, any restriction is considered a hardcore restriction not benefiting from the safe harbor of VBER. There is therefore a significant risk in a brand owner imposing any controls on online selling by its resellers and/or distributors as it will be subject to a standard Article 101 assessment of whether such a practice prevents, restricts, or distorts competition within the European Union; an uncertain test, failing which involves substantial risks.

Notwithstanding the above, online marketplace bans and restrictions are in many circumstances permissible under E.U. law.[13] These can be utilized to protect the brand owner's brand from sales made by third parties via this channel.

5. Customer Restrictions

Once a brand owner has sold its products to its distributors and/or resellers, it cannot ordinarily control who they sell those products to. This would likely be considered as unlawful, anticompetitive conduct under Article 101 TFEU. However, in some circumstances, brand owners may create a closed network of distributors and/or resellers who may only sell the brand owner's products to other resellers and/or distributors within the network. Such a network, also known as a selective distribution system, grants a brand owner greater control over who can sell its products, how its brand is perceived in the market and the experience a customer has when purchasing the brand owner's goods.

---

11. European Commission Guidelines on Vertical Restraints, § 52.

12. Pierre Fabre (Decision No 08-D-25 of Conseil de la concurrence, case C-439/09 of Court of Justice of European Union), Stihl (Decision No 18-D-23 of the Autorité de la concurrence), and Kerr-Optika (case C-108/09 of Court of Justice of European Union).

13. As confirmed in the case of *Coty* (C230-16) and the Commission Policy Brief of April 2018 on the same.

6. Selective Distribution Systems

A selective distribution system permits a brand owner to select the distributors and/or resellers who are authorized to sell its products on the basis of criteria—i.e., authorized partners, which for example may relate to how the product is displayed, the level of customer service provided, and/or the distributor/reseller's delivery/returns policies. The brand owner can then restrict sales by its authorized partners to either (i) end-users, or (ii) another partner within the authorized partner network. A selective distribution system is the only way a brand owner can control to whom its distributors and/or resellers can sell in the EEA.

To ensure that a selective distribution is valid and lawful, the criteria outlined in the cases of *Metro* and *L'Oréal* need to be followed.[14] The criteria must be: (i) objective, (ii) qualitative in nature, usually relating to the nature of the product in question, (iii) determined uniformly, (iv) applied in a nondiscriminatory manner—i.e., applied in the same way for each reseller and/or distributor, and (v) proportionate—i.e., not go beyond what is necessary to achieve the objectives of the system (e.g., to protect the brand).

Ideally, any selective distribution system imposed should comply with the above to make sure it is legally defensible if challenged. However, where the brand owner's system benefits from the safe harbor of VBER, it has greater flexibility in the criteria it imposes and the manner in which it enforces them.

7. Franchises

Another option available to brand owners in the fashion industry is the franchising model. Under this model, the brand owner will typically grant licenses of certain intellectual property rights (such as trademarks and/or know-how) to be used in the distribution of the fashion products. For example, a brand owner may grant its franchisees the right to display and market the products under the name, logo, and/or images of the brand owner. This ensures consistent branding of the brand owner's image and that of its products. In return for the licence of the intellectual property, the brand owner will typically impose certain restrictions on the distribution of the products, often taking the form of a selective distribution system or an exclusive distribution arrangement. Brand owners will also commonly impose non-compete restrictions on its distributors as part of the franchise model, preventing their involvement in a business that competes with the brand owner.

8. Agency

As briefly outlined above, there are a number of benefits for a brand owner employing an agency model when distributing its products for sale in the EEA.

---

14. Also known as the *Metro Criteria* from the cases of *Metro* (Case 26/76) and *L'Oreal* (Case 31/80).

Through an agency model, a brand owner may carry out the three practices that are not permitted under a normal distribution model, namely to dictate to the agent the price at which it may sell the products, where it may sell the products, and to whom. In short, a brand owner can impose complete control over how an agent sells its products without needing to have its own presence in a particular jurisdiction.

While a brand owner is able to impose a great deal of control over how an agent sells its products, there are a number of limitations in choosing an agency model. First, the brand owner's control over the products ceases once the agent has sold them. In other words, a brand owner cannot control how the agent's customers choose to sell those products, unless it chooses to also employ a selective distribution system (see above). Second, under an agency relationship, the brand owner will generally assume liability for the agent's actions, including liability to all of their customers, which can prove to be a high-risk approach to the distribution of products for the brand owner. Third, and finally, across the EEA, the law on agency is agent-friendly, often requiring substantial compensation to be paid to an agent on the termination of the agency relationship. The choice of this model by the brand owner can therefore be a costly one.

9. Using a Combination of Distribution Models

If a brand owner wishes to, it is permitted under E.U. law to use a combination of the various distribution models that are outlined in this chapter. For instance, a brand owner can choose to sell its products directly to consumers out of its own brick-and-mortar shops and website, or through that of an agent, while also employing a selective distribution system for its third-party resellers. Alternatively, a brand owner may choose to operate a two-tier distribution system, with different models in place at the wholesale and retail levels. Brand owners can also operate different distribution systems in different EEA Member States, for example employing a franchising model in France but a selective distribution system in Spain and Portugal. However, brand owners should act with caution when mixing different distribution models and should always assess their EEA distribution system holistically, not only to ensure that it complies with E.U. law, but also to confirm that it is effective in achieving its commercial, operational, and reputational goals for the region.

Table of Cases

Index

W

Z